JUNOS Enterprise Routing

Other resources from O'Reilly

Related titles   Internet Core Protocols: ScreenOS Cookbook™
                                 The Definitive Guide   Security Power Tools

IPv6 Essentials   TCP/P Network

JUNOS Cookbook™   Administration

oreilly.com   *oreilly.com* is more than a complete catalog of O'Reilly books. You'll also find links to news, events, articles, weblogs, sample chapters, and code examples.

oreillynet.com is the essential portal for developers interested in open and emerging technologies, including new platforms, programming languages, and operating systems.

Conferences   O'Reilly brings diverse innovators together to nurture the ideas that spark revolutionary industries. We specialize in documenting the latest tools and systems, translating the innovator's knowledge into useful skills for those in the trenches. Visit *conferences.oreilly.com* for our upcoming events.

Safari Bookshelf (*safari.oreilly.com*) is the premier online reference library for programmers and IT professionals. Conduct searches across more than 1,000 books. Subscribers can zero in on answers to time-critical questions in a matter of seconds. Read the books on your Bookshelf from cover to cover or simply flip to the page you need. Try it today for free.

JUNOS Enterprise Routing

Doug Marschke and Harry Reynolds

O'REILLY®

Beijing · Cambridge · Farnham · Köln · Sebastopol · Taipei · Tokyo

JUNOS Enterprise Routing
by Doug Marschke and Harry Reynolds

Published by O'Reilly Media, Inc., 1005 Gravenstein Highway North, Sebastopol, CA 95472.

O'Reilly books may be purchased for educational, business, or sales promotional use. Online editions are also available for most titles (*safari.oreilly.com*). For more information, contact our corporate/institutional sales department: (800) 998-9938 or *corporate@oreilly.com*.

Editor: Mike Loukides	**Indexer:** Angela Howard
Developmental Editor: Patrick Ames	**Cover Designer:** Karen Montgomery
Production Editor: Sumita Mukherji	**Interior Designer:** David Futato
Copyeditor: Audrey Doyle	**Illustrator:** Jessamyn Read
Proofreader: Mary Brady	

Printing History:

March 2008:   First Edition.

ISBN: 978-0-596-51442-6
[M]   [10/09]

Table of Contents

Foreword

In 1998, Juniper Networks launched its first product, the M40 router, and in doing so sparked a period of innovation in IP routing that continues to accelerate. Although the M40 was designed to carry Internet traffic for Internet service providers (ISPs), the benefits of IP networking were becoming apparent to other companies as well, and a short time later Juniper began to build routers with the specific goals of the rapidly developing IP business network market in mind.

The book you're holding exists to help you understand and implement the most critical elements of business networking using Juniper Networks routers running the JUNOS operating system. JUNOS contains a set of powerful tools that allow intelligent policies to replace large amounts of basic configuration, which gives the engineer a brilliantly practical way to deploy services beyond simple routing. JUNOS represents the most valuable contribution to networking that Juniper has made: it's reliable, flexible, secure, and simple to use, and an increasing numbers of businesses are finding that these qualities are compelling enough to move to Juniper and away from legacy "first-generation" routers and their less capable operating systems.

Why Enterprise Routing?

Many books have been written about JUNOS, but this book is unique in that it will prepare you to use JUNOS in an enterprise-centric sense. *Enterprise* is a term that equipment manufacturers and others use to distinguish the internal networks of "normal" businesses from the typically larger ones run by service providers, phone companies, and other network providers. Although there are, of course, similarities, every type of business requires its own unique set of capabilities from its network infrastructure regardless of its size: financial institutions have different needs from those of retail chains, which themselves differ from governments and universities.

Enterprise business networks are not simply small service provider networks. Although some aspects of networking technology—such as faster interfaces and greater degrees of reliability—continue to be attributes of both environments, their design goals and operational techniques differ greatly. A service provider usually maintains a network for the benefit of *paying customers who produce revenue*, whereas the network of an enterprise such as a bank has traditionally been viewed as an *investment whose operational expense should be minimized*. This essential difference has meant that service providers have usually been seen as the custodians of network innovation, with enterprises reluctant to invest more than the bare minimum in their infrastructure because of the uncertainty of real return on their investment.

There are signs that this attitude is changing. Companies in virtually every industry have embraced the idea that more effective use of their IT infrastructure can make them more competitive and efficient. To that end, enterprise executives are increasingly interested in innovative ways to capitalize on their investments in data networks. This trend is most pronounced in data-intensive industries such as banking, finance, and insurance, but it extends into even less obvious areas such as manufacturing and transportation.

Service provider and enterprise networks continue to be different in terms of their customer base and their relationship to technology, but networking in general is becoming increasingly important to the competitiveness of all types of companies. Some of the most outstanding examples of the ways that networking can improve business fundamentals are those related to developments in IP routing, and many of those developments have recently come from Juniper Networks.

Why Is Routing So Important?

Routing is the hub around which all of IP connectivity revolves. At the simplest level, routing establishes basic internetwork communications, implements an addressing structure that uniquely identifies each device, and organizes individual devices into a hierarchical network structure. Traditionally, routers have also served as the media adapters that have connected remote offices to the headquarters via a WAN. The most recent trend, though, is to see routers as the integration platforms for a wide variety of network enhancements such as security, policy, and services that extend the capabilities of IP to support telephony, video, legacy service integration, and other applications over a converged network.

This means the router has become the primary control point in the increasingly complex network environment, holding responsibility for service quality and security, monitoring and efficiency, and other attributes that allow networks to add value. If you control the routers, you control the network. This is true in a static network, of course, but even more so in today's typical case of a rapidly evolving enterprise, where migration to fully IP-based services is underway. This book will show you how you can use Juniper routers to ease this migration and arrive at a more successful outcome with less work than other platforms would require. This is important because although the basics of routing remain somewhat the same, the more advanced aspects are under constant development, and the authors have done a great job of showing you how to address the continually changing enterprise network environment.

Juniper has long understood that constant change is a fact of today's networks, and has worked to bring new levels of performance, dependability, and scalability to routing platforms and the software that runs them. CIOs and IT departments realize that by deploying a more powerful, flexible tool at their networks' control points, they enable their networks to address new challenges more easily and economically, and that's the best way to support the competitiveness of their company.

How This Book Will Help You

I have known and worked with Doug and Harry for years, and have watched both of them add to their earlier careers in telecommunications with outstanding work for Juniper and SNT. Both have extensive experience in training and certification, and both are established authors of educational materials, course guides, and books that have helped thousands of networking engineers obtain knowledge to set them apart from the competitive field. Their students and readers have gone on to form an elite group.

This book will serve two purposes for you. First, it will allow you to quickly acquire the knowledge to succeed in implementing enterprise networks, no matter how advanced, with Juniper Networks routers. Second, it will help you to prove your knowledge by passing the Juniper Networks Certified Internet Expert (JNCIE-ER) examination, one of the most highly regarded certifications in the industry. Each chapter's tutorial trains you in the most essential elements of the subject, and the review questions at the end of each chapter allow you to confirm the knowledge you've acquired. Doug and Harry have extensive experience in both the practical and the pedagogical components of this mission, and this book is an excellent example of how theory and practice can come together in one comprehensive yet concise package.

Juniper Networks routers and the JUNOS operating system are changing the way IT departments are regarding their IP networks, allowing them to put greater trust in the capabilities of their routing infrastructures and thereby deliver much greater value to the bottom lines of their organizations. With this book, Doug and Harry have delivered the tools necessary for every network engineer to add valuable knowledge and skills to his professional portfolio, and to help his company reap the benefits of the enterprise IP revolution. All that's required is for you to accept the challenge!

—Matt Kolon
Hong Kong, January 2008

Credits

About the Authors

Doug Marschke is an engineering graduate from the University of Michigan currently working with various consulting firms, including Strategic Networks Training and Cubed Networks. He is JNCIE-ER #3-, JNCIE-M #41-, and JNCIS-FW-certified. He was heavily involved in the Juniper certification exams from the start, having contributed to test writing, and he is a coauthor of the current JNCIE Enterprise Exam. Doug currently spends his time working with both service providers and enterprises to optimize their IP networks for better performance, cost, and reliability. He also flies around the world sharing his knowledge in a variety of training classes and seminars with topics ranging from troubleshooting to design and certification preparation. If Doug is not on the road, you can find him at his bar in San Francisco, Underdogs Sports Bar, discussing a wide variety of topics.

Harry Reynolds has more than 25 years of experience in the networking industry, and for the past 15 years has focused on LANs and LAN interconnection. He is CCIE #4977- and JNCIE #3-certified, and holds various other industry and teaching certifications. Harry was a contributing author on the *Juniper Networks Complete Reference* (McGraw-Hill), and he wrote the JNCIE and the JNCIP *Juniper Networks Certification Study Guides* for Sybex Books. Prior to joining Juniper, Harry served time in the U.S. Navy as an avionics technician, worked for equipment manufacturer Micom Systems, and spent much time developing and presenting hands-on technical training curricula targeted to both enterprise and service provider needs. Harry has presented classes for organizations such as American Institute, American Research Group, Hill Associates, and Data Training Resources. He is currently employed by Juniper Networks, where he functions as a senior test engineer in the JUNOS software Core protocols group. Harry also functioned at Juniper as a consulting engineer on an aerospace routing contract, and as a senior education services engineer working on courseware and certification offerings.

About the Lead Technical Reviewers

Mario Puras is a Juniper Networks systems engineer supporting major enterprise and state government accounts in Florida. He has more than 10 years of experience in the networking industry, focusing on providing routing, switching, and security solutions for large enterprise and service providers. He is JNCIP #119-certified and holds a JNCIA-FW, JNCIA-WX, and various other industry certifications. Prior to joining Juniper Networks, Mario served in the U.S. Army and worked at Metrolink, Duro Communications, and Solunet Inc. He is married to his best friend of 12 years, Stacy.

Jack W. Parks has more than 15 years of experience in IT and has worked in almost every position known in the realm of IT. Most recently, he has focused on enterprise routing and switching, service provider routing, and MPLS and VPNs. Jack holds a BS in business information systems from John Brown University and has received several industry certifications, including CCI #11685, JNCIS-M, JNCIA-SSL, and JNCIA-FWV. After serving eight years in the U.S. Air Force, Jack transitioned into the corporate world working for service providers in the enterprise and ISP market spaces. Jack is currently a Juniper systems engineer based in Atlanta.

Preface

The world of enterprise routing with Juniper Networks devices is getting very exciting—new technologies, products, and network developments are making the enterprise network environment one of the most dynamic places to be. However, we, the authors, hope to focus that energy by providing you with a detailed and practical foundation that ensures effective use of JUNOS software in your day-to-day job.

Because we are also involved in the development and testing of certification exams, including those for enterprise routing, this book does double duty. It is both a field guide and a certification study guide. Readers who are interested in attaining a Juniper Networks certification level are wise to note that we discuss and cover topics that are relevant to the official exams (hint, hint), and the end of each chapter provides a listing of examination topics covered as well as a series of review questions that allow you to test your comprehension.

Regardless of one's certification plans, this one-of-a-kind book will not be obsolete just because you pass an exam. In fact, we wrote this material to serve as a field guide to be useful almost anytime you log on to a Juniper Networks router. The extensive use of tutorials, samples of actual command output, and detailed theoretical coverage go well beyond any certification exam, to provide you with something that can't be tested—getting things to work the right way, and on the first time. When plan A fails, the material also provides the steps needed to monitor network operation and quickly identify and resolve the root cause of malfunctions.

As trainers who deal with large numbers of both experienced and inexperienced users on a regular basis, we have seen it all. Within this guide, you will find the many pearls of our accumulated wisdom, any one of which can easily pay for this book many times over in increased network uptime and performance.

Some of our chapters tend to be on the longer side, simply because they are packed with detailed information regarding theory, configuration, and troubleshooting for each topic. Rather than create more chapters, "soft breaks" and summaries within the chapters are used to identify boundaries within the material that afford a convenient place to take a breather, or as we often provide in our training classes, a "biology break and stretch." Dog-ear the pages, write notes in the margins, augment the topology illustrations with something more akin to your network—just remember that this is a beastly JUNOS book: part exam, part training class, part knowledge base. It's meant to be used, abused, and put to work. Let's get going.

What Is Enterprise Routing?

After you've spent some time in the networking field, you tend to notice that there is rarely a single way to do things, and in many cases, a single precise definition for terms. After all, often a network engineer's best answer is "it depends." Such is the case with enterprise routing, so let's start off with a definition question: what is an enterprise network? Is it a large multinational network used by a manufacturing company; is it a government network supporting a state or a county; is it a regional network used by a parts distributor; or is it a network that supports your local dentist's office?

Of course, it's probably all of these, and many more. At a very high level, you can state that an enterprise network is one that is used to support activities as opposed to generating revenue, as in a service provider's network. Some might say that if someone pays you to access your network, you are providing a service to him and you're no longer an enterprise network. But that sweeping statement doesn't really apply if that someone is paying you to cover your costs to provide that service. So, as you can see, it depends.

Defining an enterprise network also manifests itself into how Juniper Networks defines its products within the enterprise world. On the one hand, Juniper designates certain hardware platforms as enterprise routers, but then many enterprise networks require density and throughput options from a platform listed as a service provider product. From the software side of things, the same issue arrives. Whereas a technology such as IPSec is used by all types of networks around the globe, is it used more by enterprise networks than by service provider networks? Some engineers would answer yes to that question, but then, you can't say that a service provider will never use IPSec.

From the perspective of hardware platforms, Juniper Networks has designated the following as enterprise products:

- J-series routers to include the J2300, J2320, J2350, J4350, and J6350
- M7i and M10i routers
- M120 routers

However, larger enterprise networks may find platforms such as the M320 and MX960/480 very useful for their environments. In fact, the reverse is also true in that a traditional service provider network may very well find an appropriate need and use for platforms designated as enterprise routers.

The good news in all this is that you have a well-thought-out operating system in JUNOS. The JUNOS software is a single train of features that operates across all of the various routing platforms. So, whether you run an enterprise network or a service provider network, and regardless of your actual hardware platform, there is a single version of software code to load. Although this single code train has lots of hidden benefits, such as stability, ease of expandability, lower total operational costs, and more, what it really means is the ability to have the same features available on all devices. So, from a learning perspective, we can talk about the software and its features without having to constantly caveat our discussion with "except for on this platform" or "only on these particular platforms." Although such exceptions do occur, and they result from hardware enhancements that are unique to a particular platform, these cases tend to be exceptions and are infrequent enough to remember.

Throughout this book, we will attempt to simplify the discussion by limiting ourselves to the J-series platforms and the M7i router as we discuss the various features and options available to configure. We also focus on those topics that the vast majority of enterprise networks care about and actually use. We will also define an enterprise network as one that uses an Internet connection as opposed to a network that provides connectivity to the Internet as its sole function.

Juniper Networks Technical Certification Program (JNTCP)

This book is an official study guide for the JNTCP Enterprise Routing tracks. Use it to prepare and study for the JNCIA-ER, JNCIS-ER, and JNCIE-ER certification exams. For the most current information on Juniper Networks' Enterprise Routing certification tracks, visit the JNTCP web site at *http://www.juniper.net/certification*.

How to Use This Book

Let's look at some specifics on how this book can help you. We'll talk about what we cover in the various chapters, how the book is laid out, and some resources to help you along the way. To start, let's discuss what you should know before you begin to read this book.

We are assuming a certain level of knowledge on the reader's part. This is important because we are assuming you to be conversant in the following topic areas:

OSI model
> The Open Systems Interconnection (OSI) model defines seven different layers of technology: Physical, Data Link, Network, Transport, Session, Presentation, and Application. This model allows network engineers and network vendors to easily discuss and apply technology to a specific OSI level. This segmentation lets engineers divide the overall problem of getting one application to talk to another

into discrete parts and more manageable sections. Each level has certain attributes that describe it and each level interacts with its neighboring levels in a very well-defined manner.

Switches

These devices operate at Layer 2 of the OSI model and use logical local addressing to move frames across a network. Devices in this category include Ethernet, Asynchronous Transfer Mode (ATM), and Frame Relay switches.

Routers

These devices operate at Layer 3 of the OSI model and connect IP subnets to each other. Routers move packets across a network in a hop-by-hop fashion.

Ethernet

These broadcast domains connect multiple hosts together on a common infrastructure. Hosts communicate with each other using Layer 2 media access control (MAC) addresses.

Point-to-point links

These network segments are often thought of as WAN links in that they do not contain any end users. Often, these links are used to connect routers together in disparate geographical areas. Possible encapsulations used on these links include ATM, Frame Relay, Point-to-Point Protocol (PPP), and High-Level Data Link Control (HDLC).

IP addressing and subnetting

Hosts using IP to communicate with each other use 32-bit addresses. Humans often use a dotted decimal format to represent this address. This address notation includes a network portion and a host portion, which is normally displayed as 192.168.1.1/24.

TCP and UDP

These Layer 4 protocols define methods for communicating between hosts. The Transmission Control Protocol (TCP) provides for connection-oriented communications, whereas the User Datagram Protocol (UDP) uses a connectionless paradigm. Other benefits of using TCP include flow control, windowing/buffering, and explicit acknowledgments.

ICMP

Network engineers use this protocol to troubleshoot and operate a network as it is the core protocol used by the ping and traceroute (on some platforms) programs. In addition, the Internet Control Message Protocol (ICMP) is used to signal error and other messages between hosts in an IP-based network.

JUNOS CLI

The command-line interface (CLI) used by Juniper Networks routers, which is the primary method for configuring, managing, and troubleshooting the router. JUNOS documentation covers the CLI in detail, and it is freely available on the Juniper Networks web site (*http://www.juniper.net*).

What's in This Book?

The ultimate purpose of this book is to be the single, most complete source for working knowledge related to Juniper Networks enterprise routing. Although you won't find much focus on actual packet formats and fields, topics for which there is already plentiful coverage on the Internet and in bookstores, you will find how to effectively deploy JUNOS technology in your network.

Here's a short summary of the chapters and what you'll find inside:

Chapter 1, *Introduction to JUNOS Enterprise Routing*
> This chapter provides an overview of the hardware and software architecture on Juniper enterprise routers, as well as an overview of the JUNOS CLI for both new and experienced users.

Chapter 2, *Interfaces*
> This chapter provides an overview of JUNOS interface organization. Then it dives into some of the most common interface types and configurations seen in networks today. Finally, it concludes with a troubleshooting section with real-life scenarios seen every day.

Chapter 3, *Protocol Independent Properties and Routing Policy*
> This chapter provides a condensed but comprehensive overview of JUNOS Protocol Independent Properties (PIPs), such as static and aggregate route, and of routing policy, which is used to control route advertisement, redistribution, and attribute manipulation.

Chapter 4, *Interior Gateway Protocols and Migration Strategies*
> This chapter provides a detailed review of Interior Gateway Protocol (IGP) operation, and then focuses on multivendor deployments of the Routing Information Protocol (RIP) and Open Shortest Path First (OSPF). The material also focuses on IGP migration strategies and includes an EIGRP-to-OSPF migration case study.

Chapter 5, *Border Gateway Protocol and Enterprise Routing Policy*
> After providing a detailed review of what the Border Gateway Protocol (BGP) is and how it can benefit an enterprise, this chapter provides a series of case studies that build in complexity, starting with a single homed network with no Internal BGP (IBGP) speaker and ending with a multihomed-to-multiple-providers scenario, to include a redundant IBGP route reflection design that avoids running IBGP on all internal routers. The policy treatment is focused on practical enterprise routing goals, and it details both inbound and outbound policy that includes autonomous system (AS) path regex matching and BGP attribute manipulation.

Chapter 6, *Access Security*

This chapter provides an overview of a large variety of security concepts and the tools available to deploy them. These tools include user authentication and authorization, remote access, firewall filters, policers, Unicast Reverse Path Forwarding, the Simple Network Management Protocol (SNMP), and syslog.

Chapter 7, *Introduction to JUNOS Services*

This chapter provides an overview of the Layer 2 and Layer 3 services that can be deployed on a Juniper Networks router. Layer 2 services include features such as link bundling and Generic Routing Encapsulation (GRE), whereas Layer 3 services include stateful firewalls, IPSec, and Network Address Translation (NAT). This chapter also lays the CLI foundation to discuss more scenarios in Chapter 8.

Chapter 8, *Advanced JUNOS Services*

This chapter dives into the complex scenarios of the features discussed in Chapter 7. It walks through various deployed NATs, IPSec virtual private networks (VPNs), IPSec over GRE, and all possible Layer 3 services combined.

Chapter 9, *Class of Service*

This chapter provides an overview of IP class of service (CoS) and includes a detailed primer on IP DiffServ. The material then details the similarities and differences in CoS handling between the J-series and M7i routers, which is a common source of confusion. A practical CoS case study serves as the foundation for CoS deployment and operational verification. The chapter also demonstrates the J-series-specific Virtual Channel CoS feature.

Chapter 10, *IP Multicast in the Enterprise*

Multicast tends to see little deployment and is a common area of confusion. This chapter details IP multicast concepts, provides an overview of multicast protocols, and then demonstrates several Physical Interface Module (PIM) sparse mode scenarios, to include PIM sparse mode with static, bootstrap, and Anycast-RP. Through all the examples, practical verification and fault isolation steps are provided.

Chapter 11, *JUNOS Software with Enhanced Services*

This hot-off-the-press chapter includes the first official coverage of the new JUNOS software with enhanced services release. This chapter gives you the heads-up needed to understand what JUNOS software with enhanced services offers, how to migrate from JUNOS to JUNOS software with enhanced services, and the various things you need to know before deploying JUNOS software with enhanced services.

In addition, you can also use this book to attain one of the Juniper Networks certification levels related to enterprise routing. To that end, each chapter in the book includes a set of review questions and exam topics that have been covered, all of it designed to get you thinking about what you've just read and digested. If you're not in the certification mode, the questions will provide a mechanism for critical thinking, potentially prompting you to locate other resources to further your knowledge.

Topology of This Book

Figure P-1 displays the topology of the book that appears beginning in Chapter 3. It consists of 11 J-series routers running version 8.0R1.9 and 2 Cisco routers running IOS Release 12.3(15b). The Cisco routers are primary employed in Chapter 4, where they are used for both RIP interoperability and as part of an EIGRP-to-OSPF migration exercise. The topology uses only Fast Ethernet and T1 interfaces; however, other interface types are examined in Chapter 2. You might recognize the hostnames of the routers—they all relate to a beverage that was created more than 7,000 years ago (with evidence to consumption) in Mesopotamia. The names are chosen due to the international appeal of the resultant product and for the resultant food value only, as beer is an excellent way to preserve the nutritional value of grain.

Conventions Used in This Book

The following typographical conventions are used in this book:

Italic

> Indicates new terms, URLs, email addresses, filenames, file extensions, pathnames, directories, and Unix utilities

`Constant width`

> Indicates commands, options, switches, variables, attributes, keys, functions, types, classes, namespaces, methods, modules, properties, parameters, values, objects, events, event handlers, XML tags, HTML tags, macros, the contents of files, and the output from commands

`Constant width bold`

> Shows commands and other text that should be typed literally by the user, as well as important lines of code

`Constant width italic`

> Shows text that should be replaced with user-supplied values

 This icon signifies a tip, suggestion, or general note.

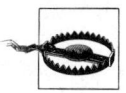 This icon indicates a warning or caution.

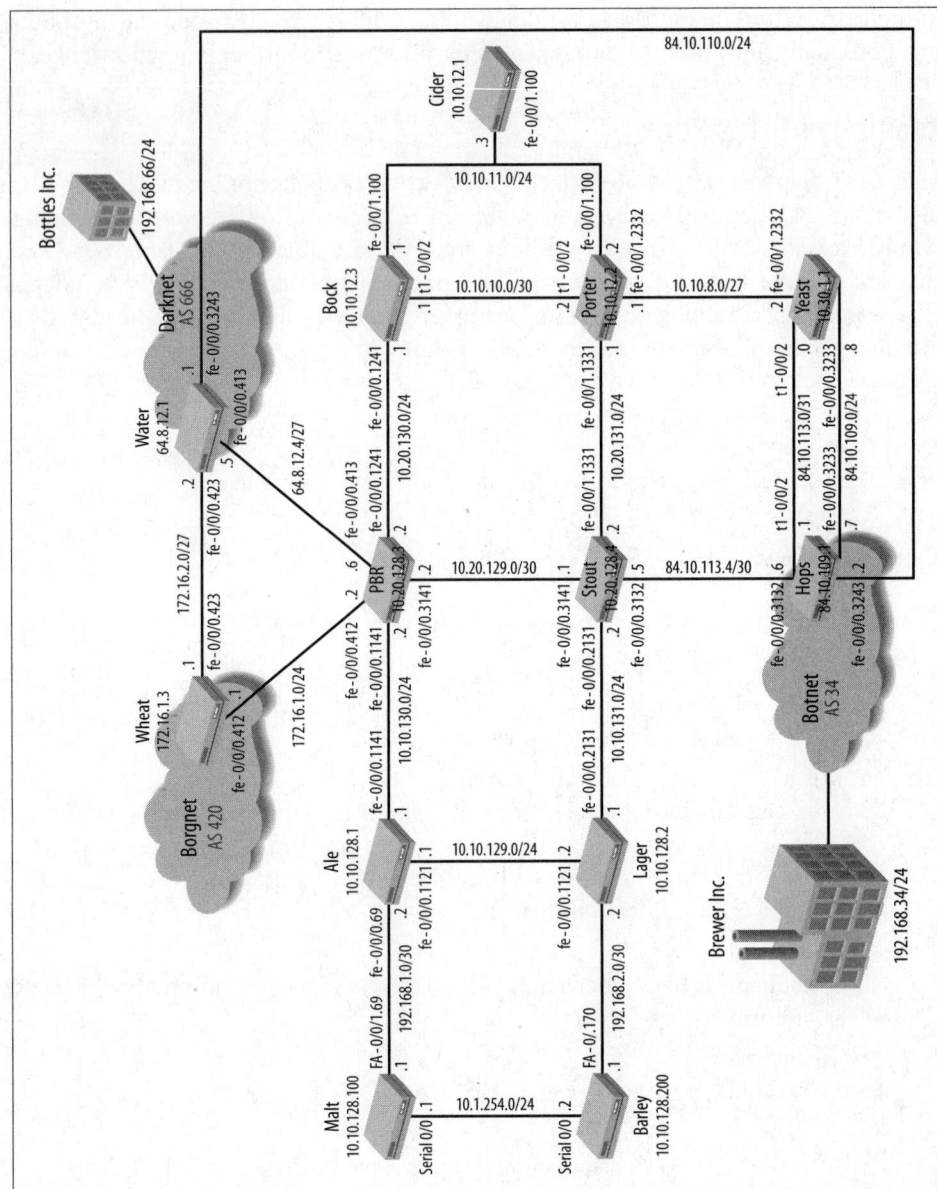

Figure P-1. This book's topology

Using Code Examples

This book is here to help you get your job done. In general, you may use the code in this book in your own configuration and documentation. You do not need to contact us for permission unless you're reproducing a significant portion of the material. For example, deploying a network based on actual configurations from this book does not require permission. Selling or distributing a CD-ROM of examples from this book does require permission. Answering a question by citing this book and quoting example code does not require permission. Incorporating a significant amount of sample configurations or operational output from this book into your product's documentation does require permission.

We appreciate, but do not require, attribution. An attribution usually includes the title, author, publisher, and ISBN. For example: "*JUNOS Enterprise Routing* by Doug Marschke and Harry Reynolds. Copyright 2008 Doug Marschke and Harry Reynolds, 978-0-596-51442-6."

If you feel your use of code examples falls outside fair use or the permission given here, feel free to contact us at *permissions@oreilly.com*.

Comments and Questions

Please address comments and questions concerning this book to the publisher:

> O'Reilly Media, Inc.
> 1005 Gravenstein Highway North
> Sebastopol, CA 95472
> 800-998-9938 (in the United States or Canada)
> 707-829-0515 (international or local)
> 707-829-0104 (fax)

We have a web page for this book, where we list errata, examples, and any additional information. You can access this page at:

> *http://www.oreilly.com/catalog/9780596514426*

or:

> *http://cubednetworks.com*

To comment or ask technical questions about this book, send email to:

> *bookquestions@oreilly.com*

For more information about our books, conferences, Resource Centers, and the O'Reilly Network, see our web site at:

> *http://www.oreilly.com*

Safari® Books Online

 When you see a Safari® Books Online icon on the cover of your favorite technology book, that means the book is available online through the O'Reilly Network Safari Bookshelf.

Safari offers a solution that's better than e-books. It's a virtual library that lets you easily search thousands of top tech books, cut and paste code samples, download chapters, and find quick answers when you need the most accurate, current information. Try it for free at *http://safari.oreilly.com*.

Acknowledgments

The authors would like to gratefully and enthusiastically acknowledge the work of many professionals who assisted us in the development of the material for this book. Although our names are printed on the book as authors, in reality no author works alone. The contributions of many people have made this book possible, and others have assisted us with their technical accuracy, typographical excellence, and editorial inspiration.

Many thanks are owed to the official technical editors of this material. Mario and Jack were extremely responsive to the demanding needs of our schedule. Your attention to detail and wealth of knowledge no doubt saved us many an embarrassing bit of errata. To this end, we also thank Colleen Gorman for her fine developmental editing, and Audrey Doyle for her thorough copyediting, that resulted in a much improved experience for you, the reader.

We would also like to acknowledge Juniper Networks in general, for the assistance provided on various fronts, and specifically *Monear Jalal*, *David Ranch*, and *Jerish Parapurath*, for their efforts in making Chapter 11 possible. We also extend thanks to *Jonathon Looney*, who volunteered to provide a technical review for the services chapters (Chapters 7, 8, and 11), for his detailed knowledge of JUNOS software with enhanced services, and for the inspiration he provided with regard to the BGP policy treatment. We would also like to thank *Chris Heffner*, who provided the routers used for this book via *http://www.certified-labs.com/*, with a price that could not be matched—free of charge.

Thanks also to *Matt Kolon*, for taking time from his busy schedule to evaluate the material, and for his inspirational Foreword.

And last but not least, special thanks to *Jason Rogan* and *Patrick Ames* for their assistance and behind-the-scenes activations that made this effort possible. They were the ones that really pushed the ideas of two wacky authors into a reality.

From Doug Marschke

I would like to acknowledge all my friends who helped me through this very time-consuming and, at times, stressful effort with many words of encouragement and well-timed stress relievers. I would like to thank Becca Morris in particular for her free time spent correcting my horrible grammar to avoid embarrassment before editorial submission. I would also like to thank my roommate, Catherine la O', for putting up with the man writing in the cave. Of course, I would be remiss if I did not thank my furry quadruped friend, Josh, who was by my side the entire time, offering a woof to any potential distracters.

From Harry Reynolds

I would like to acknowledge my wife, Anita, and two lovely daughters, Christina and Marissa, for once again understanding and accommodating my desire to engage in this project. Also, special thanks to my managers at Juniper Networks, Corinne Rattay and Sreedhevi Sankar, for their understanding and support. I really appreciate their willingness to accommodate the occasional glitch in my "day job" schedule that was needed to make this happen. Lastly, I'd like to thank Doug Marschke (whose name I can never spell, but shall never forget), for offering me the chance to participate in this project. I take great pride in seeing how far Doug has come in his professional career and fully expect to find myself working for him one day. You go, Doug!

## CHAPTER 1

Introduction to JUNOS Enterprise Routing

When the founding engineers of Juniper decided to create routers, they took the view of forwarding packets as quickly as possible (line rate) with services enabled, which spawned the marketing decree "Service without Compromise."

All Juniper Networks routers share the same common design philosophy, which is to have a clean separation of the control and forwarding planes. In the M-series, this separation is created in hardware, whereas the J-series maintains this divide in software. The forwarding plane is referred to as the Packet Forwarding Engine (PFE), and the control plane is called the Routing Engine (RE).

The RE's primary functions are to manage the PFE, control the router's software (JUNOS), manage the command-line interface (CLI), provide troubleshooting tools, and maintain the route tables and the master forwarding table. This forwarding table is passed down to the PFE and is used to forward any transit packet to the next hop destination. In this way, the RE never has to be directly involved in packet forwarding (i.e., process switching), which allows more resources for the actual control functions (see Figure 1-1). One example is the ability to issue "debug" commands without degrading the performance of the router!

 The route table in JUNOS software is defined as all routes learned from *all* protocols (Open Shortest Path First [OSPF], Border Gateway Protocol [BGP0, static, interfaces, etc.]). The forwarding table provides the "best" routes that will be used to forward packets based on protocol preference and metrics.

The PFE's sole purpose in life is to forward packets as fast as it can. In an M-series router, the PFE consists of several application-specific integrated circuits (ASICs) contained on various cards that are placed into the chassis. In the J-series, the PFE is a virtualized real-time thread with the ASIC functionality modeled with various APIs and sockets. Since the J-series' PFE is implemented in software, we will examine it in the software section, but let's take a brief look at the M-series now to better understand the PFE.

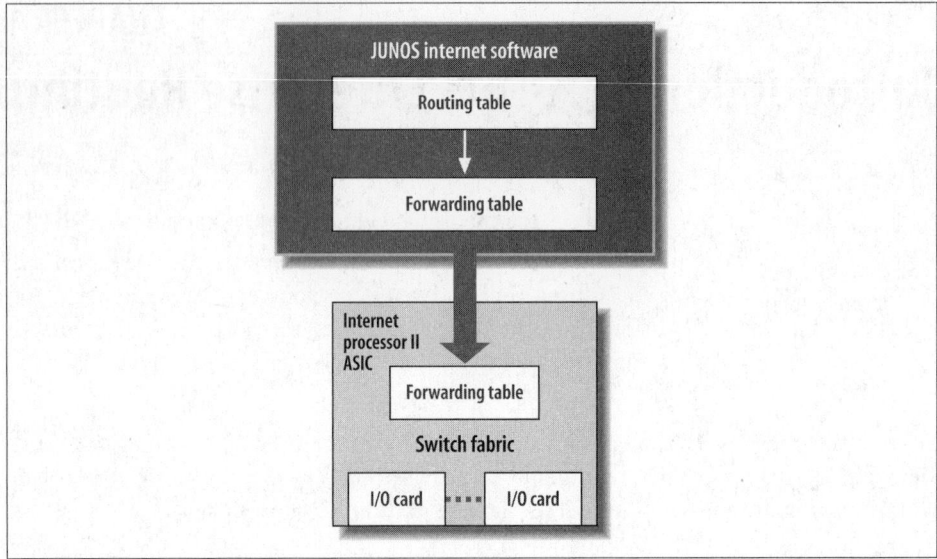

Figure 1-1. Juniper architecture design philosophy

In an M-series router, the PFE is not just one physical card in the router, but a series of cards, each containing a different ASIC. The fundamental building block of the PFE on any M-series router is the Physical Interface Card (PIC). The PIC is the card that the physical media such as Ethernet, Serial, or Asynchronous Transfer Mode (ATM) will plug into. This PIC contains an ASIC that will pull and place data on the wire as well as deal with the actual interface framing. The final piece of the PFE is the compact Forwarding Engine Board (cFEB), which contains several ASICs that deal with packet storage, forwarding, queuing, and filtering. An M7i contains just a single cFEB, whereas an M10i will contain both a primary and a backup cFEB.

 The M120 router contains six FEBs that are mapped to chassis slots and provide N+1 standby redundancy.

As previously mentioned, the PFE of a J-series router is *virtualized*. However, like any router in our networking universe, it must contain interfaces. The J2320, J2350, J4350, and J6350 enterprise routers have changeable cards similar to the PIC of an M-series router, called Physical Interface Modules (PIMs) or Enhanced Physical Interface Modules (EPIMs). The primary difference between a PIM and an EPIM is that EPIMs support higher-speed interfaces and must be installed in certain slots on the router.

 It may seem that the two modules, PIC and PIM, essentially do the same thing, but with different nomenclature. Although this is true, there is a method behind all the madness, as PIMs can be used only in J-series routers and PICs can be used only in M/T-series devices.

JUNOS Overview

JUNOS software is cool. It just is. The designers of JUNOS software put tremendous thought into making a stable, robust, and scalable operating system that would be a positive for the router. They were able to learn from previous vendors' mistakes, and created an OS that other companies will forever use as their model.

The core philosophy of JUNOS software was to create a modular *and* stable operating system. The modularization was created by the use of software daemons, and the stability was achieved by choosing a well-known, open source, and stable kernel of FreeBSD. This kernel is usually hidden to the user, but many features of FreeBSD have been ported to the command line of JUNOS. The kernel also maintains the forwarding table synchronization between the RE and the PFE.

Riding on top of the kernel are all the fully independent software processes for routing, CLI, interfaces, and so forth. Figure 1-2 shows a small subset of these processes; you can show a complete list in the router by issuing a show system processes command. These processes are fully independent, so a failure of one process will not affect the other. For example, Figure 1-2 shows the Simple Network Management Protocol (SNMP) process pulling information from the interface, chassis, and routing processes. If this SNMP process fails or contains a software bug, it affects only this process and not the others. This is a major shift from other routing vendors that operated monolithic code where one change in the interface code could affect just about anything without reason.

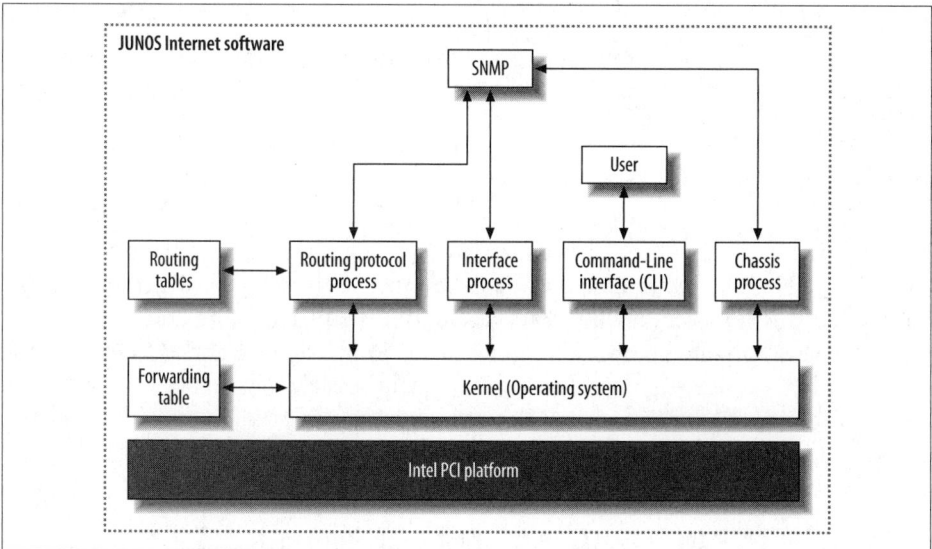

Figure 1-2. JUNOS software architecture

Every Juniper Networks router is created from the same code base, so all run JUNOS software. Since the J-series did not contain any ASICs for the PFE and certain interface drivers such as high-speed OC-192 links were deemed unnecessary, a new image had to be created for these devices. This is still JUNOS, however, with almost the same feature set as the ASIC-driven image.

 This means that there is a single image per version for all M/T-series routers regardless of model number, and a single image per version for all J-series routers. The days of creating and maintaining large spreadsheets or lists per router are now gone.

The major difference in the J-series image is the inclusion of a new software process called *fwdd* (forwarding devices daemon), which acts as the virtualized PFE. It is essentially a series of real-time threads operating over the kernel, as shown in Figure 1-3. Instead of an ASIC providing the functionality of the PFE, sockets and APIs will interface with the kernel, providing a deterministic performance.

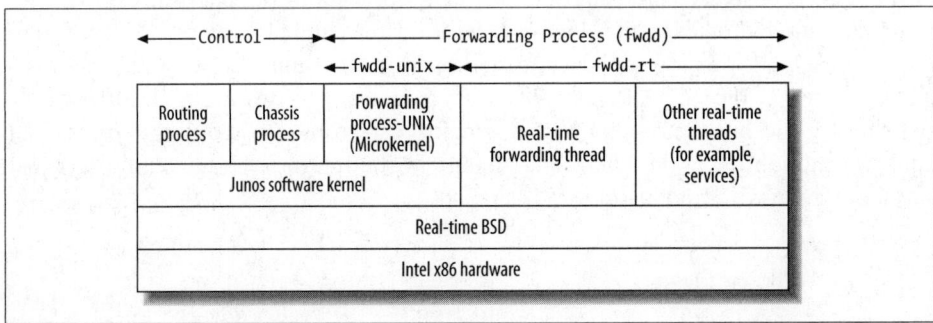

Figure 1-3. J-series software architecture

CLI Review

The tool that will most often be used to configure and troubleshoot the router is the CLI. The JUNOS software CLI is one of the most user-friendly and feature-rich in the industry. Most users spend years attempting to master other router vendors' CLIs, whereas JUNOS software can be mastered in just a few hours. Other configuration methods do exist, such as a web GUI called *Jweb* (see Figure 1-4), which is often used on the J-series routers. Note that the operation of Jweb is beyond the scope of this book, so all configuration examples will be shown via CLI commands instead.

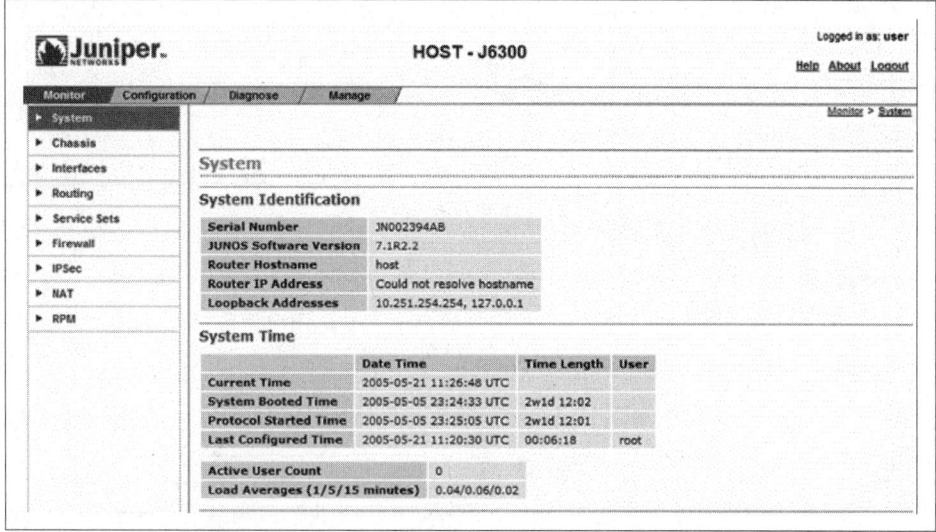

Figure 1-4. Jweb

General CLI Features

The CLI has two modes: operational and configuration. Operational mode is where you can troubleshoot and monitor the software, router, and network. Configuration mode is where the actual statements for interfaces, routing protocols, and others are placed.

Every command that can be run in operational mode can also be used in configuration mode with the additional keyword run. For example, if the command show route is issued in operational mode, it can be issued as run show route in configuration mode.

When a user first enters the router via Telnet, Secure Shell (SSH), or direct console access, the user will see a login prompt. After entering the correct username and password, the user will be placed directly into operational mode. Operational mode will be designated by the > (chevron) character at the router prompt of username@hostname. As shown here, user doug logs into a router called Hops:

```
Hops (ttyd0)

login: doug
Password:

--- JUNOS 8.0R1.9 built 2006-08-11 16:25:40 UTC
doug@Hops>
```

An exception to being automatically placed into operational mode occurs when you log in as user root. In this case, the user will actually be placed into the shell (designated by the percent sign) and will have to start the CLI process manually:

```
Hops (ttyd0)

login: root
Password:

--- JUNOS 8.0R2.8 built 2006-09-29 09:22:36 UTC
root@Hops% cli
root@Hops>
```

Most of the commands that you will run in operational mode are show commands, which allow you to gather information about the routing protocols, interfaces, router's software, and router's hardware. Ping, traceroute, telnet, and ssh can also be performed from this mode. Finally, some very JUNOS-specific commands, such as request, restart, and test, may be issued. Request commands perform system-wide functions such as rebooting, upgrading, and shutting down the router. Restart commands are similar to the Unix-style kill commands, which allow you to restart certain software processes. Test commands allow verifications for save configuration files, proactive testing of policies, and interface testing such as BERT (bit error rate testing) and FEAC (far-end alarm and control) loopbacks.

 You should use the restart command with great caution! Depending on the software process being restarted, the consequences could be severe. Restarting the SNMP process would probably get you a slap on the wrist, but restarting the routing process could be a reason to go into hiding on a remote island!

There are a few general JUNOS software CLI features worth mentioning, including command completion, EMACs-style keys, and pipe commands.

Command completion

The command completion feature will save you lots of time and energy, as it provides syntax checking as you type. Gone are the days when a command is typed on a line and, after pressing Enter, the command is either invalid or not supported on that version of software. Any error or ambiguity will be detected early, and the router will present a list of possible valid completions. Command completion is accomplished by using either the Space bar or the Tab key. Either one will complete a command for you, but the Tab key can also complete variables such as interface names, IP addresses, filter names, and filenames. For example, to view the configuration of a certain ATM interface, you would type the following:

```
doug@Hops> sh<space>ow conf<space>iguration int<space>erfaces
at<tab>-0/2/1 <enter>
```

Notice that the Space bar is used until a variable is reached and the interface name is used when the Tab key *must* be used (as the Space bar completes only commands and not variables).

 For the reader with experience using Cisco's IOS, command completion makes for an easy transition. First, forget about the word *IP*, as the IOS command show ip route simply becomes show route in JUNOS. Also, common IOS abbreviations such as sh int will still work in JUNOS if you type **doug@hops> sh<space>ow int<enter>**.

In the previous example, the syntax checker went word by word each time the Space bar or Tab key was pressed, and the minimum characters were typed to avoid ambiguity. What would happen if the syntax checker noticed an error or incomplete word? It would state this ambiguity and list the possible completions:

```
user@host> show ip<space>
                    ^
'ip' is ambiguous.
Possible completions:
  ipsec            Show IP Security information
  ipv6             Show IP version 6 information
```

EMACs

Another useful JUNOS feature set in the router itself is the use of EMACs-style keystrokes when in vt100 mode. This allows you to move the cursor around the command line or to edit the command line. Some useful EMACs keystrokes are:

Ctrl-b
Move the cursor back one character.

Ctrl-a
Move the cursor to the beginning of the command line.

Ctrl-e
Move the cursor to the end of the command line.

Ctrl-k
Delete all words from the cursor to the end of the line.

Ctrl-x
Delete or clear the entire line.

Ctrl-l
Redraw the current line.

Ctrl-p
Scroll backward through the previously typed commands. You also can use the Up arrow for this purpose.

Ctrl-n

Scroll forward through the previously typed commands. You also can use the Down arrow for this purpose.

Ctrl-r

Search the previous CLI history for a search string.

Pipe commands

The last important feature to call out in the JUNOS software CLI is the use of pipe commands to control the output of any command. For example, when a command such as show is issued, the data is placed into a buffer and is displayed when the Enter key is pressed. A pipe command allows the display buffer to be altered. Many pipe commands can be used on the router, but let's examine the most common applications and pipe commands:

count

Count the lines in the output:

```
doug@Hops> show interfaces terse | count
Count: 29 lines
```

display

Show additional data; for example, XML tags or set commands:

```
doug@Hops> show configuration | display set
set version 8.0R2.9
set system host-name Hops
set system backup-router 10.210.8.30
set system backup-router destination 0.0.0.0/0
set system ports console type vt100
set system root-authentication encrypted-password "$1$G/
pd5odz$eYJi89TZkRxDWitUBB3of0"
set system login class view-only permissions view
set system login user doug uid 2019
set system login user doug class super-user
set system login user doug authentication encrypted-password "$1$sr.a1nvE$K573iU.
bHSZkLiW9SMWwg."
set system login user lab uid 2021
set system login user lab class super-user
set system login user lab authentication encrypted-password "$1$/
z4qeiUp$ocnPhXAbz1xzDoTUKRhgm."
set system login user restricted uid 2022
set system login user restricted class view-only
set system login user restricted authentication encrypted-password "$1$tYpOu.
Hv$tpeTOxf.3pIrlsOZEPNlsO"
set system services ftp
set system services ssh
set system services telnet
set system syslog user * any emergency
set system syslog file messages any notice
set system syslog file messages authorization info
set system syslog file cli-commands interactive-commands any
```

```
        set system syslog file cli-commands archive size 1m
        set system syslog file cli-commands archive files 10
        set system syslog file config-changes change-log any
        set system compress-configuration-files
        set interfaces lo0 unit 0 family inet address 192.168.16.1/32
        set routing-options static route 0.0.0.0/0 next-hop 10.210.8.30
        set routing-options static route 0.0.0.0/0 retain
        set routing-options static route 0.0.0.0/0 no-readvertise
```

except

Omit lines from the output:

```
doug@Hops> show interfaces terse | except fe
Interface        Admin Link Proto  Local          Remote
at-0/2/0         up    up
at-0/2/0.100     up    up   inet   10.0.16.1/24
at-0/2/1         up    up
at-0/2/1.100     up    up   inet   10.0.15.2/24
dsc              up    up
fxp0             up    up
fxp0.0           up    up   inet   10.210.8.1/27
fxp1             up    up
fxp1.0           up    up   inet   10.0.0.4/8
                                   tnp    4

gre              up    up
ipip             up    up
lo0              up    up
lo0.0            up    up   inet   192.168.16.1   --> 0/0
lo0.16385        up    up   inet
lsi              up    up
mtun             up    up
pimd             up    up
pime             up    up
tap              up    up
```

find

Begin the output at the specified string:

```
Doug@Hops> show interfaces fe-0/0/2 extensive | find traffic
  Traffic statistics:
   Input  bytes  :          8574            0 bps
   Output bytes  :         11923            0 bps
   Input  packets:            88            0 pps
   Output packets:           127            0 pps
  Input errors:
    Errors: 0, Drops: 0, Framing errors: 0, Runts: 0, Policed
    discards: 0, L3 incompletes: 0, L2 channel errors: 0, L2 mismatch
    timeouts: 0, FIFO errors: 0, Resource errors: 0
  Output errors:
    Carrier transitions: 1, Errors: 0, Drops: 0, Collisions: 0, Aged
    packets: 0, FIFO errors: 0, HS link CRC errors: 0, MTU errors: 0,
    Resource errors: 0
  Active alarms  : None
  Active defects : None
```

hold

Retain the output in the buffer until cleared:

```
doug@Hops> show route | hold

inet.0: 10 destinations, 10 routes (10 active, 0 holddown, 0 hidden)
+ = Active Route, - = Last Active, * = Both

0.0.0.0/0          *[Static/5] 03:47:27
                    > to 10.210.8.30 via fxp0.0
10.0.15.0/24       *[Direct/0] 03:02:54
                    > via at-0/2/1.100
10.0.15.2/32       *[Local/0] 03:02:54
                    Local via at-0/2/1.100
10.0.16.0/24       *[Direct/0] 03:05:15
                    > via at-0/2/0.100
10.0.16.1/32       *[Local/0] 03:05:15
                    Local via at-0/2/0.100
10.0.21.0/24       *[Direct/0] 03:14:56
                    > via fe-0/0/2.0
10.0.21.1/32       *[Local/0] 03:14:56
                    Local via fe-0/0/2.0
10.210.8.0/27      *[Direct/0] 03:47:27
                    > via fxp0.0
10.210.8.1/32      *[Local/0] 03:47:27
                    Local via fxp0.0
192.168.16.1/32    *[Direct/0] 03:14:56
                    > via lo0.0


__juniper_private1__.inet.0: 2 destinations, 2 routes (2 active,
0 holddown, 0 hidden)
+ = Active Route, - = Last Active, * = Both

10.0.0.0/8         *[Direct/0] 08:39:21
                    > via fxp1.0
10.0.0.4/32        *[Local/0] 08:39:21
                    Local via fxp1.0


__juniper_private1__.inet6.0: 5 destinations, 5 routes (5 active,
0 holddown, 0 hidden)
+ = Active Route, - = Last Active, * = Both

fe80::/64          *[Direct/0] 08:39:21
                    > via fxp1.0
fe80::200:ff:fe00:4/128
                   *[Local/0] 08:39:21
                    Local via fxp1.0
fe80::2a0:a5ff:fe12:2775/128
                   *[Direct/0] 08:39:21
                    > via lo0.16385
fec0::/64          *[Direct/0] 08:39:21
                    > via fxp1.0
fec0::10:0:0:4/128 *[Local/0] 08:39:21
                    Local via fxp1.0
---(more 100%)---
```

match

Display only lines with the specified string:

```
doug@Hops> show log messages | match "jun  4"
Jun  4 09:04:13  HongKong login: LOGIN_PAM_AUTHENTICATION_ERROR: PAM
authentication error for user lab
Jun  4 09:04:13  HongKong login: LOGIN_FAILED: Login failed for user
lab from host
Jun  4 09:04:16  HongKong login: LOGIN_INFORMATION: User lab logged
in from host [unknown] on device ttyd0
Jun  4 09:07:04  HongKong sshd[3685]: Accepted publickey for root from
10.210.8.28 port 58349 ssh2
Jun  4 09:07:08  HongKong sshd[3690]: Accepted publickey for root from
10.210.8.28 port 62534 ssh2
Jun  4 10:50:45  HongKong mgd[3681]: UI_RESTART_EVENT: User 'lab'
restarting daemon 'Routing protocol daemon'
Jun  4 10:50:45  HongKong rpd[3083]: RPD_SIGNAL_TERMINATE: first
termination signal received
Jun  4 10:50:45  HongKong snmpd[3108]: SNMPD_CLOSE_SA_IPC:
ipc_free_local: closed IPC socket /var/run/rpd_s
```

no-more

Do not paginate the output:

```
doug@Hops> show system statistics arp | no-more
arp:
        3429 datagrams received
        32 ARP requests received
        243 ARP replys received
        17 resolution requests received
        0 unrestricted proxy requests
        0 received proxy requests
        0 proxy requests not proxied
        0 with bogus interface
        0 with incorrect length
        0 for non-IP protocol
        0 with unsupported op code
        0 with bad protocol address length
        0 with bad hardware address length
        0 with multicast source address
        0 with multicast target address
        0 with my own hardware address
        3 for an address not on the interface
        0 with a broadcast source address
        0 with source address duplicate to mine
        3151 which were not for me
        10 packets discarded waiting for resolution
        16 packets sent after waiting for resolution
        269 ARP requests sent
        32 ARP replys sent
        0 requests for memory denied
        0 requests dropped on entry
        0 requests dropped during retry
```

save

Save the output to a file to the user home directory:

```
doug@Hops> show interfaces | save interface_hops
Wrote 272 lines of output to 'interface_hops'
```

Multiple pipe commands are treated as a logical AND, meaning the output must match *both* of the commands listed. This could come in the form of different pipe commands in the command list or as the same pipe command listed multiple times. To count how many /27 masks are in your route table, issue this command:

```
doug@Hops> show route | match /27 | count
Count: 1 lines
```

In comparison, use the same pipe command on a single line to show all /32 routes that start with a 10.0 prefix:

```
doug@Hops> show route | match /32 | match 10.0
10.0.15.2/32      *[Local/0] 03:18:28
10.0.16.1/32      *[Local/0] 03:20:49
10.0.21.1/32      *[Local/0] 03:30:30
10.0.0.4/32       *[Local/0] 08:54:55
```

Pipe commands are not limited to a logical AND, however, as a logical OR operation can also be performed. Do this by wrapping the string in quotation marks and using the OR operator:

```
doug@Hops> show route | match "/32|10.0"
10.0.15.0/24      *[Direct/0] 03:22:46
10.0.15.2/32      *[Local/0] 03:22:46
10.0.16.0/24      *[Direct/0] 03:25:07
10.0.16.1/32      *[Local/0] 03:25:07
10.0.21.0/24      *[Direct/0] 03:34:48
10.0.21.1/32      *[Local/0] 03:34:48
10.210.8.1/32     *[Local/0] 04:07:19
192.168.16.1/32   *[Direct/0] 03:34:48
10.0.0.0/8        *[Direct/0] 08:59:13
10.0.0.4/32       *[Local/0] 08:59:13
fec0::10:0:0:4/128 *[Local/0] 08:59:13
```

Configuration Mode

To actually configure the router, enter configuration mode by typing the word **configure** in operational mode. The router prompt will change to the octothorpe (#) symbol:

```
doug@Hops> configure
Entering configuration mode

[edit]
doug@Hops#
```

By default, when entering configuration mode, multiple users can enter the router and make changes at the same time. To avoid any issues that may arise, you can use the `configure exclusive` or `configure private` command. The former command allows only a single user to configure the router, whereas the latter command allows multiple users to configure *different* pieces of the configuration. If you use `configure exclusive`, no other users can make changes to the configuration besides the single user that entered exclusively. Using private mode, each user will get a copy of the current configuration and only changes that they make will be applied. If two users attempt to make the same change, such as adding an IP address to the same interface, the change will be rejected and both users will exit configuration mode to resolve their conflict.

In configuration mode, you can add configuration by using a set command. For example, to enable the Telnet server application on the router, issue this command:

```
doug@Hops# set system services telnet
```

The CLI is actually composed of many directories and subdirectories, which will eventually contain the command that is input. You can think of this as you would a PC, where the hard drive is normally named *C:* and it is partitioned into directories such as Windows, program files, drivers, and so on. These directories may contain subdirectories, which will eventually contain files or applications.

```
C:\>dir/w
 Volume in drive C has no label.
 Volume Serial Number is 7806-197A

 Directory of C:\

AUTOEXEC.BAT                  [Backup]
bi-admin.dat                  Catalog.LiveSubscribe
[Config.Msi]                  CONFIG.SYS
[dell]                        [Dell962]
dlbx.log                      dlbxscan.log
[Documents and Settings]      [drivers]
DVDPATH.TXT                   [ERDNT]
[f403a5940e14ba07a40a99897c]  [HP LJ1160-LJ1320]
HuskyInstallerLog.txt         [i386]
INFCACHE.1                    [ipv0011]
[ipv0021]                     [My Downloads]
[nslabs]                      [Program Files]
[reg_backup]                  statusclient.log
tmuninst.ini                  ut.bat
ut9x.bat                      [WINDOWS]
[Xitami]                      YServer.txt
              14 File(s)     4,055,509 bytes
              18 Dir(s)  26,173,308,928 bytes free
```

In JUNOS software, the top level, or *C:*, is named edit, with multiple directories partitioned below it. You can view these directories by using the set ? command:

```
[edit]
doug@Hops# set ?
Possible completions:
> access             Network access configuration
> accounting-options Accounting data configuration
> applications       Define applications by protocol characteristics
+ apply-groups       Groups from which to inherit configuration data
> chassis            Chassis configuration
> class-of-service   Class-of-service configuration
> event-options      Event processing configuration
> firewall           Define a firewall configuration
> forwarding-options Configure options to control packet sampling
> groups             Configuration groups
> interfaces         Interface configuration
> policy-options     Routing policy option configuration
> protocols          Routing protocol configuration
> routing-instances  Routing instance configuration
> routing-options    Protocol-independent routing option configuration
> security           Security configuration
> services           Service PIC applications settings
> snmp               Simple Network Management Protocol configuration
> system             System parameters
```

So, when you issue the command set system services telnet, the system directory is accessed, followed by the subdirectory services and ending in the command telnet to enable the Telnet service. Figure 1-5 shows a partial directory tree to illustrate this process. Thankfully, you do not need to memorize the entire hierarchical tree structure, but it is important to understand the hierarchical structure and how it relates to configuration mode commands.

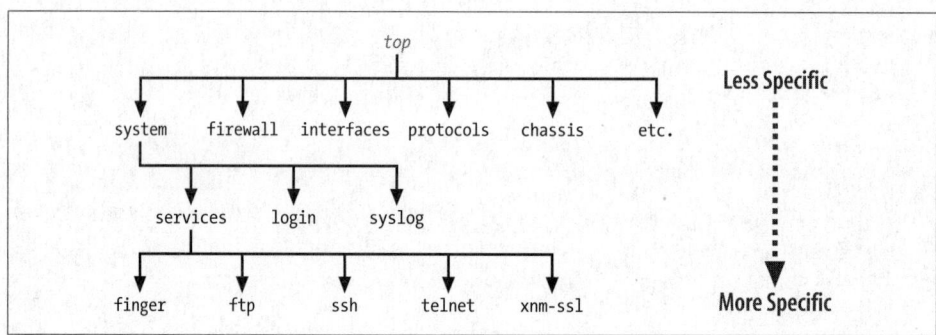

Figure 1-5. Subsection of JUNOS configuration tree

The opposite of the set command to remove configuration from the router is the delete command. Usually this command is used to remove a single line, but you also can use it to remove an entire hierarchy. In the simplest case, for example, to remove the Telnet service from the router, change the previous set command to a delete command:

```
doug@Hops# delete system services telnet
```

 Be careful when issuing a delete command without noting any specific command, as this could remove an entire directory and have less than desirable consequences.

You can issue configuration commands such as set and delete from the top root level or from inside a subdirectory. To navigate to a subdirectory, issue an edit command, which is essentially a change directory command. If the Telnet service needed to be enabled, you could use an alternative method of moving into the subdirectory system services and then issuing a short set command:

```
[edit]
doug@Hops# edit system services

[edit system services]
doug@Hops# set telnet
```

Using the edit command is not necessary, but it allows the user to issue shorter set commands when compared to the top level. Just like choosing a color for a new car, you can choose how you want to configure the router as long as the desired result is achieved. Once in a certain directory, there are multiple ways to navigate the directory tree using commands such as up, top, and even exit. The up command will move you up one level in the directory tree or multiple levels if a numerical value is given after the up command:

```
[edit system services]
doug@Hops# up

[edit system]
doug@Hops# edit services

[edit system services]
doug@Hops# up 2

[edit]
doug@Hops#
```

From any hierarchy, you can issue the top command to move you up to the root level of the configuration tree. It has the added functionality of allowing multiple configuration statements after issuing the command, such as top edit or top set:

```
[edit system services]
doug@Hops top

[edit]
doug@Hops# edit system services

[edit system services]
doug@Hops# top edit protocols ospf

[edit protocols ospf]
doug@Hops#
```

Another nice feature of configuration mode allows you to view the configuration that was just completed by issuing a show command. For instance, to view the configuration of the system services, issue this command:

```
[edit]
doug@Hops# show system services
ftp;
ssh;
telnet;
```

Or try yet another way to view the system services, by issuing the show command inside the subdirectory in question. A show command with no additional arguments shows the configuration from that hierarchy and below:

```
[edit]
doug@Hops# edit system services

[edit system services]
doug@Hops# show
ftp;
ssh;
telnet;
```

After issuing a plethora of set and delete commands, the keen user will notice that no changes have actually occurred in the router! To apply the changes, a special word—one that is often difficult to say in the real world—must be used: *commit*. To understand what is occurring when issuing the commit command, it's best to examine the different types of configurations that occur in the JUNOS router.

A Juniper Networks router has two configuration files that are always present: the *candidate configuration* and the *active configuration*. The active configuration is the current *running* configuration in the router, whereas the candidate configuration is the temporary text file that is being modified while in configuration mode. When the commit command is issued, the candidate configuration becomes the active configuration if no syntax errors are detected. In addition, the old active configuration is archived into a file called a rollback 1. So, if a mistake is made, you can easily recover the old active configuration by issuing a rollback 1. This causes the candidate configuration to be replaced by the *old* active configuration. A commit command must then be issued to activate this rollback file. JUNOS saves not only this last active configuration, but also the previous 49 configurations. Each time a commit is issued, the archived file shifts down the list of 49. The first commit creates a rollback 1, the second commit (the old active) becomes rollback 1, the old rollback 1 becomes rollback 2, and so on, down the line. Figure 1-6 illustrates this rollback process.

Another important rollback command that can be useful is a *rollback 0*, which copies the active configuration to the candidate configuration. As an example, imagine that user doug logs into a router and issues a command to change the hostname of the router to a less desirable name, but does not actually activate the change.

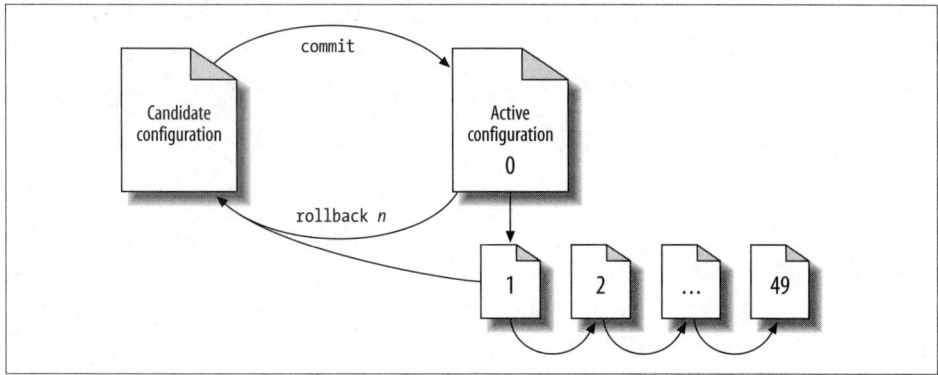

Figure 1-6. Configuration and rollback

```
doug@Hops> configure
Entering configuration mode

[edit]
doug@Hops# set system host-name yousmell

[edit]
doug@Hops# exit
The configuration has been changed but not committed
Exit with uncommitted changes? [yes,no] (yes) yes

Exiting configuration mode

doug@Hops> exit
```

A new user logs into the router, enters configuration mode, and observes that changes have occurred:

```
doug@Hops> configure
Entering configuration mode
The configuration has been changed but not committed

[edit]
lab@Hops#
```

It would seem at first glance that the new user is in between a rock and a hard place, but JUNOS has a very useful pipe command you can use—the compare command. This command allows *any* two files, including rollback files, active files, and candidate files, to be compared and the differences displayed. In this example, the candidate and active configurations will be compared:

```
[edit]
doug@Hops# show | compare
[edit system]
-   host-name Hops;
+   host-name yousmell;
```

It appears that user doug has been up to his old pranks again, attempting to change the hostname of the router. If a commit is issued, the hostname Hops will be removed and the hostname yousmell will be added. To wipe out these statements, a rollback 0 could be issued to stop doug and his mischievous ways:

```
doug@Hops# rollback 0
load complete

[edit]
lab@Hops# show | compare
```

One last key point of the two configuration types is that any operational mode command can be issued in configuration mode as long as the keyword run is issued before the command. For instance:

```
lab@Hops# ping
          ^
unknown command.

[edit]
dougHops# run ping 10.210.8.2
PING 10.210.8.2 (10.210.8.2): 56 data bytes
64 bytes from 10.210.8.2: icmp_seq=0 ttl=64 time=0.387 ms
64 bytes from 10.210.8.2: icmp_seq=1 ttl=64 time=0.296 ms
^C
--- 10.210.8.2 ping statistics ---
2 packets transmitted, 2 packets received, 0% packet loss
round-trip min/avg/max/stddev = 0.296/0.342/0.387/0.045 ms
```

Loading and Saving Configurations

To save the candidate configuration to the user's home directory, you must issue the save command while in configuration mode.

 To save an active configuration, issue a show configuration command and pipe to save.

It is important to realize which configuration directory you are located in when issuing the save command, as the command saves from the *current* hierarchy. To save the entire candidate configuration, issue the save command from the top of the directory tree:

```
[edit]
doug@Hops# save junos_is_cool
Wrote 413 lines of configuration to 'junos_is_cool'
```

Sometimes it is not desirable to save the entire configuration, so to save a portion, simply navigate into the desired directory to be saved. For instance, if every router in your network has the same system login information, you may want to save only that portion to load into other routers later:

```
[edit system login]
doug@Hops# save only_system_login
Wrote 31 lines of configuration to 'only_system_login'
```

It would be fantastic to eliminate the need to issue manual saves, so system archival allows for the automatic saving of configurations when issuing a commit or at a set time interval:

```
doug@Hops# set archival configuration ?
Possible completions:
+ apply-groups          Groups from which to inherit configuration data
+ apply-groups-except   Don't inherit configuration data from these groups
> archive-sites
  transfer-interval     Frequency at which file transfer happens (minutes)
  transfer-on-commit    Transfer after each commit
```

These files can be FTP'd or scp'd off to a server under the archivel-sites configuration. In the example that follows, every time a commit is issued, the configuration file is sent to an FTP server with user doug, password okemos123, and IP address 66.17.3.254, and then into the */config/junos* directory:

```
archival {
    configuration {
        transfer-on-commit;
        archive-sites {
            "ftp://doug:okemos123@66.17.3.254/config/junos";
        }
    }
```

The opposite of saving a configuration is loading a configuration, which you can accomplish by the load command. There are several variations of the load command:

```
doug@Hops# load ?
Possible completions:
 factory-default Override existing configuration with factory default
 merge           Merge contents with existing configuration
 override        Override existing configuration
 patch           Load patch file into configuration
 replace         Replace configuration data
 set             Execute set of commands on existing configuration
 update          Update existing configuration
```

Although each type of load command has its advantages, we will examine only the most common command variations here. One of the most common loads is the override command, which replaces the current candidate configuration with the specified file:

```
[edit]
doug@Hops# load override junos_is_cool
load complete
```

The merge switch will also be used often when just a small piece of configuration needs to be added to the candidate configuration. For instance, you can issue the following command to add the system login configuration saved previously:

```
[edit]
doug@Hops# load merge only_system_login
load complete
```

Since it is highly likely that more than one router will exist in a network, cutting and pasting configurations can give you a few more hours of free time in your life. There are several ways to cut and paste configurations into the router, including using variations of the load command, or copying set commands directly into the router. The oldest JUNOS software method is to use the load command with the terminal option, which opens a terminal buffer, allowing full or partial configurations to be pasted in:

```
doug@Hops# load merge terminal
[Type ^D at a new line to end input]
system {
services {
        ftp;
        ssh;
        telnet;
    }
}
load complete
```

Cutting and pasting using this method definitely takes some practice, as the proper number of levels and braces must always be present. The terminal command always assumes that the entire top-level hierarchy is known. If the upper-level directories are not included, errors will occur and the relative keyword could become very useful:

```
[edit]
doug@Hops# load merge terminal
[Type ^D at a new line to end input]
services {
    ftp;
  terminal:2:(7) syntax error: ftp
   [edit services]
     'ftp;'
       syntax error
 ssh;
     telnet;
}
[edit]
   'services'
     warning: statement has no contents; ignored
load complete (1 errors)
```

Since the pasting started at the services level and not at the system level, the pasting causes errors and does not complete. One solution is to navigate to the system directory and indicate that the configuration will be loaded relative to that directory:

```
[edit]
doug@Hops# edit system

[edit system]
doug@Hops# load merge terminal relative
[Type ^D at a new line to end input]
services {
    ftp;
    ssh;
    telnet;
}
load complete
```

Or perhaps a simpler method would be to load set commands directly into the router by simply pasting a carriage return after each set command or by using the load set command:

```
doug@Hops load set terminal
[Type ^D at a new line to end input]
set system services ftp
set system services ssh
set system services telnet
load complete
```

S.O.S., I Need Help!

If the router is causing you problems, simply ask it for help. You can accomplish this in a few ways. The first is with a question mark (?) to display possible command completions:

```
doug@Hops# set system login ?
Possible completions:
  announcement          System announcement message (displayed after
login)
+ apply-groups          Groups from which to inherit configuration
data
+ apply-groups-except   Don't inherit configuration data from these
groups
> class                 Login class
  message               System login message
> password
> user                  Username
```

The > character indicates a directory that contains subdirectories, + indicates a command that takes multiple arguments, and no symbol means the command takes a single argument or is in fact the end statement of a command.

The help command is a secret resource of which few are aware. This displays the same technical documentation that can also be located online. Sometimes a small piece of a command is remembered but not the full statement; help can aid in finding that full command by searching through the JUNOS software configuration tree for a particular string:

```
doug@Hops# help apropos host-name
set system host-name <host-name>
    Hostname for this router
set system static-host-mapping <host-name>
    Fully qualified name of system
set system services dhcp static-binding <mac-address> host-name
<host-name>
    Hostname for this client
set system syslog host
    Host to be notified
set interfaces <interface_name> services-options syslog host
<host-name>
    Name of host to notify
set accounting-options routing-engine-profile <profile-name> fields
host-name
    Hostname for this router
set services l2tp tunnel-group <name> syslog host <host-name>
    Name of host to notify
set services service-set <service-set-name> syslog host <host-name>
    Name of host to notify
```

If you encounter a command in the router that needs clarification, you can obtain
more information by issuing the help topic or help reference command. The former
will display general usage guidelines for that command:

```
doug@Hops# help topic ospf hello-interval
 Modifying the Hello Interval

   Routers send hello packets at a fixed interval on all interfaces,
   including virtual links, to establish and maintain neighbor
   relationships. This interval, which must be the same on all routers
   on a shared network, is advertised in the hello interval field in
   the hello packet. By default, the router sends hello packets every
   10 seconds.

   To modify how often the router sends hello packets out of an
   interface, include the hello-interval statement:
     hello-interval seconds;

   For a list of hierarchy levels at which you can configure this
   statement, see the statement summary section for this statement.

   On nonbroadcast networks, the router sends hello packets every 120
   seconds until active neighbors are detected by default. This
   interval is long enough to minimize the bandwidth required on slow
   WAN links. To modify this interval, include the poll-interval
   statement: poll-interval seconds;

   +-------------------------------------------------------------+
   |NOTE:  The poll-interval statement is valid for OSPFv2 only. |
   +-------------------------------------------------------------+

     For a list of hierarchy levels at which you can configure this
     statement, see the statement summary section for this statement.
```

```
        Once the router detects an active neighbor, the hello packet
        interval changes from the time specified in the poll-interval time
        statement to the specified in the hello-interval statement.
```

After you've learned what a certain command accomplishes and when you should use it, you can view the actual syntax and possible options using the help reference command. It's similar to the manual command seen on other operating systems:

```
[edit]
doug@Hops# help reference ospf hello-interval
hello-interval

    Syntax

hello-interval seconds;

    Hierarchy Level

[edit logical-routers logical-router-name protocols ospf area area-id
peer-interface
    interface-name],
[edit logical-routers logical-router-name protocols (ospf | ospf3) area
area-id
    interface interface-name],
[edit logical-routers logical-router-name protocols (ospf | ospf3) area
area-id virtual-link],
[edit logical-routers logical-router-name routing-instances
routing-instance-name
    protocols (ospf | ospf3) area area-id interface interface-name],
[edit logical-routers logical-router-name routing-instances
routing-instance-name
    protocols (ospf | ospf3) area area-id virtual-link],
[edit protocols ospf area area-id peer-interface interface-name],
[edit protocols (ospf | ospf3) area area-id interface interface-name],
[edit protocols (ospf | ospf3) area area-id virtual-link],
[edit routing-instances routing-instance-name protocols (ospf | ospf3)
area area-id
    interface interface-name],
[edit routing-instances routing-instance-name protocols (ospf | ospf3)
area area-id
    virtual-link]

    Release Information

Statement introduced before JUNOS Release 7.4.

    Description

Specify how often the router sends hello packets out the interface.
The hello interval must be the same for all routers on a shared
logical IP network.

    Options
```

```
seconds--Time between hello packets, in seconds.
Range: 1 through 255 seconds
Default: 10 seconds; 120 seconds (nonbroadcast networks)

    Usage Guidelines

See "Modifying the Hello Interval".

    Required Privilege Level

routing--To view this statement in the configuration.
routing-control--To add this statement to the configuration.

    See Also

dead-interval
```

Advanced CLI and Other Cool Stuff

Lots of other fantastic configuration options are available, but explaining them all
would require a separate book. The JUNOS documentation contains many time-
saving tips, and the *JUNOS Cookbook* by Aviva Garrett (O'Reilly) is a great resource
too. To whet your appetite, here are three JUNOS software CLI tips.

Most changes that you need to make on a router can be done at only certain times,
often referred as *maintenance windows*. Since these windows are often at the most
inconvenient times for those who have to use them, changes represented by commit
can actually be scheduled:

```
[edit]
doug@Hops# commit at 07:05
configuration check succeeds
commit at will be executed at 2007-06-10 07:05:00 UTC
Exiting configuration mode
```

When the commit has been scheduled, other users cannot change any piece of the
new locked configuration:

```
joe@Hops> configure
Entering configuration mode
Users currently editing the configuration:
  doug terminal d0 (pid 11035) on since 2007-06-05 05:04:51 UTC
      commit-at

[edit]
joe@Hops# set system host-name foo
error: configuration database locked by:
  doug terminal d0 (pid 11035) on since 2007-06-05 05:04:51 UTC
      commit at

[edit]
joe@Hops# commit
error: Another commit is pending
```

If the system needs to be unlocked before the specified time, a clear command can stop the timed action:

```
joe@Hops# run clear system commit
Pending commit cleared
```

You can take advantage of another fantastic shortcut when large common pieces of configuration need to be removed from the router. The router can search through the entire configuration looking for a string and delete every line that contains that string:

```
[edit]
jane@R1# wildcard delete interfaces fe-
  matched: fe-0/0/1
  matched: fe-2/0/0
  matched: fe-2/0/1
Delete 3 objects? [yes,no] (no) yes
```

Lastly, you can make common configuration changes in one large swoop with the replace command. Any string can replace any other string, with a string being anything from a character to any POSIX 1003.2 expression. For example, this command could be useful is when IPs referenced in filters, policies, and so on need to be updated to a new value:

```
[edit]
jane@R1# replace pattern 172.17.30.254 with 172.17.30.200
```

Conclusion

This chapter provided a quick definition of what enterprise routing is and how Juniper routers fit into this environment. Then we examined the router's hardware and software design, stressing the key components that will help make your life easier. Lastly, we reviewed the actual CLI and illustrated the important features. The CLI is one of the most flexible and user-friendly in the industry, allowing expert status to be achieved in record time. As your familiarity with the CLI increases, you will discover even more features. Now that we've established the groundwork, the rest of the book will dive into the specific configuration details.

Exam Topics

We examined the following Enterprise Exam Topics in this chapter:

- List the enterprise router product line.
- Describe transit and host processing.
- Identify the difference between packet flow on the M7i/M10i and on the J-series routers.
- Identify key differences between the M7i/M10i and J-series routers.

- Describe configuration management.
- Identify the features of the JUNOS CLI (CLI modes, prompts, auto-complete, EMACs shortcuts, help, and pipe).
- Identify the commands used in configuration mode (edit, set, delete, and commit).
- Identify options for manipulating "saved" configuration files. Include rollback options, load options, and rollback file locations.
- Describe the configuration hierarchy.
- Describe active, candidate, and rollback configurations.

Chapter Review Questions

1. Which of the following two Juniper Networks routers are classified as enterprise routers? (Choose two.)
   a. T640
   b. M7i
   c. J4350
   d. M320

2. Which hardware component controls debugging on the router?
   a. Packet Forwarding Engine
   b. Route Processor
   c. System Control Board
   d. Routing Engine

3. True or False: Since the J-series has only a single processor, there is no Packet Forwarding Engine.

4. Which JUNOS software daemon controls the CLI?
   a. clid
   b. rpd
   c. mgd
   d. inetd

5. Which command would be issued to reboot the router?
   a. request system reboot
   b. reload
   c. reboot
   d. restart router

6. Which pipe command can you use to find every occurrence of the word *error* in the syslog file messages?

    a. match

    b. find

    c. search

    d. hold

7. What is the default password to enter configuration mode on the router?

    a. juniper

    b. enable

    c. There is no password

    d. root

8. Which CLI command should be issued to navigate to the *[edit protocols ospf]* directory?

    a. cd protocols ospf

    b. edit protocols ospf

    c. cd /edit/protocols/ospf

    d. dir protocols ospf

9. Which CLI command must be issued to activate configuration changes in the router?

    a. apply

    b. copy

    c. save

    d. commit

10. What is the top level of the configuration tree called?

    a. *C:/*

    b. */var*

    c. *edit*

    d. *root*

11. Which CLI command should be issued to return to the previously activated configuration?

    a. rollback 1

    b. rollback 0

    c. rollback active

    d. rollback previous

12. Which command should be issued in the router to find out information about Layer 3 VPNs?

    a. `layer 3 vpn ?`

    b. `help topic layer3-vpns overview`

    c. `help reference layer3-vpn overview`

    d. `man layer3-vpn`

Chapter Review Answers

1. Answer: B, C. The T640 and M320 are valid Juniper Networks router models but are usually deployed in service provider networks.

2. Answer: D. The Routing Engine is the component in the router that controls all management functions, including commands that would be used to debug the router.

3. Answer: False. The J-series routers do contain a virtualized PFE with API and sockets replacing the ASICs that are found in the M-series routers.

4. Answer: C. The CLI is actually a process that runs off the kernel, called mgd. Of the other services listed, clid is invalid, rpd controls the routing process, and inetd manages network services.

5. Answer: A. Request commands are used to issue system-wide functions such as rebooting the router. The rest of the options are invalid CLI commands.

6. Answer: A. The pipe command `match` will find every occurrence of a string in the output of the command. The `find` command will locate the first occurrence of the string, `search` is an invalid option, and `hold` will hold text without exiting the `–More--` prompt.

7. Answer: C. There is no password to enter configuration mode. Users are allowed into configuration mode based on access privileges.

8. Answer: B. To change the directory in configuration mode, use the `edit` command.

9. Answer: D. To activate the changes in the router, issue a `commit` command. Of the remaining options, `copy` and `save` are valid CLI commands but are used for configuration management.

10. Answer: C. When at the top level of the configuration tree, the CLI banner will display the `[edit]` prompt.

11. Answer: A. The first archive is stored in `rollback 1`. `rollback 0` is used to copy the active configuration to the candidate configuration, and the other options are not valid rollback commands.

12. Answer: B. The help topic command displays general information about any topic referenced in the Juniper documentation. The actual output of the command is as follows:

```
lab@P1R1> help topic layer3-vpns overview
Layer 3 VPN Overview

    In JUNOS software, Layer 3 VPNs are based on RFC 2547bis. RFC
    2547bis defines a mechanism by which service providers can use
    their IP backbones to provide VPN services to their customers. A
    VPN is a set of sites that share common routing information and
    Layer 3 whose connectivity is controlled by a collection of
    policies. The sites that make up a Layer 3 VPN are connected over
    a provider's existing public Internet backbone.

    RFC 2547bis VPNs are also known as BGP/MPLS VPNs because BGP is
    used to distribute VPN routing information across the provider's
    backbone, and MPLS is used to forward VPN traffic across the VPN
    backbone to remote sites.

    Customer networks, because they are private, can use either public
    addresses or private addresses, as defined in RFC 1918, Address
    Allocation for Private Internets. When customer networks that use
    private addresses connect to the public Internet infrastructure,
    overlap with the same private addresses used by other network
    users the private addresses might MPLS/BGP VPNs solve this problem
    by adding a VPN identifier prefix to each address from a
    particular VPN site, thereby creating an address that is unique
    to the VPN and within the public Internet. In addition, each VPN has
    both within its own VPN-specific routing table that contains the
    routing information for that VPN only.
```

CHAPTER 2

Interfaces

This chapter describes the interface configurations for a Juniper Networks router. It starts with a description of the types of interfaces, the naming conventions, and the interface properties. It then identifies how to configure a large variety of interface media, such as T1 interfaces, Fast Ethernet, and Serial interfaces. Lastly, we will examine common interface problems, concentrating on the tools available to detect these issues.

Before you begin to design a network's routing topology, you should ensure that all the proper physical connections are in place and are operational. With such a large variance in interface types, this can often be a challenging task, so it is important to understand how an interface is organized within the JUNOS software.

Juniper Networks routers contain two major categories of interfaces: *permanent* and *transient*. Users cannot remove permanent interfaces, whereas they can move, change, and remove transient interfaces. Other technical differences exist that are evident when you examine the applications for each interface type.

The interface topics covered in this chapter include:

- Permanent interfaces
- Transient interfaces
- Interface properties
- Interface configuration examples
- Interface troubleshooting

Permanent Interfaces

A permanent interface is any interface that is always present on the router (it cannot be altered). These interfaces can be management interfaces such as Ethernet, software pseudointerfaces such as tunnel interfaces, or fixed-port LAN/WAN interfaces.

On an M/T-series router, two management interfaces exist:

fxp0

This is an Out of Band (OOB) management Ethernet interface. It is connected to the router's Routing Engine (RE) and can be used for Out of Band management access to the router. It can also be used to send management messages such as syslog or Simple Network Management Protocol (SNMP) traps. This interface is a *nontransit interface*, which means that traffic cannot enter this interface and exit via a LAN/WAN interface, nor can it enter a LAN/WAN interface and exit through the management interface.

 When running routing protocols, be very careful when using the fxp0 interface. If you don't configure the routing protocol correctly, you could have a route in your route table that points to the fxp0 interface and blackhole traffic, since this is a nontransit interface. To protect yourself from these types of situations, you should not run any routing protocols over this interface.

fxp1

This is an internal Fast Ethernet or Gigabit Ethernet (depending on the model of router) interface between the RE and the Packet Forwarding Engine (PFE). This interface is never configured but can be helpful when troubleshooting router issues. It is only in application-specific integrated circuit (ASIC) platforms (M/T-series) and not in the virtualized PFE J-series platforms.

Many software pseudointerfaces also exist that the router will create at startup. We will examine many of these interfaces in depth in Chapter 7. Here is a short list of these interfaces:

lo0

This is a loopback interface that ties to the router itself and not to any one physical interface. This is often assigned an address to provide a stable address for management traffic and routing protocols, which allows your router to adapt to network and physical interface failures. Also, when configured with firewall filters, this interface serves to protect the RE from attacks destined to the router.

sp

This service interface is used when configuring features such as Network Address Translation (NAT), IPSec, and stateful firewalls.

pd

This Physical Interface Module (PIM) de-encapsulation interface allows a multicast rendezvous point (RP) to process PIM register messages.

pe

This PIM encapsulation interface is used in multicast to create a unicast PIM register message to send to the RP.

ip

This is an IP-over-IP encapsulation interface to create IP-in-IP tunnels.

dsc

This is a discard interface, which can be used to silently discard packets. This is often used to create a choke point for denial of service (DoS) attacks.

tap

This is a virtual Ethernet interface historically used for monitoring on FreeBSD systems. This interface could be used to monitor discarded packets on a router but is no longer officially supported.

The last type of permanent interface is the fixed LAN/WAN ports found on J-series routers and M7i routers. We will examine these in depth in the next section.

Transient Interfaces

Transient interfaces are any interfaces that the user can remove, move, or replace. These include ports on M-series routers, Physical Interface Cards (PICs), and J-series PIMs. Examples of transient interfaces are Fast Ethernet, Asynchronous Transfer Mode (ATM), SONET, and T1/E1, as well as service PICs such as tunnels, multi-links, link services, Adaptive Services PICs (ASPs), and passive monitoring.

Interface Naming

All JUNOS interfaces follow the same naming convention—the interface name followed by three numbers that indicate the location of the actual interface. The general convention is illustrated by the interface sequence MM-F/P/T, where:

- MM = media type
- F = chassis slot number
- P = PIC slot number
- T = port number

Media type

The first part of the interface name is the interface media name (MM) indicating the type of interface. Common interface media names include:

ae

Aggregated Ethernet, a logical linkage of multiple Ethernet interfaces defined in the IEEE 802.3ad standard.

at

ATM, which sends fixed 53-byte cells over the transport media. This interface could also be used for ATM over digital subscriber line (DSL) connections.

br
> Physical Integrated Services Digital Network (ISDN) interface.

e1
> Standard digital communication standard over copper at a rate of 2.048 Mbps, used mostly in Europe.

e3
> Standard digital communication standard over copper at a rate of 34.368 Mbps, used mostly in Europe.

t1
> Basic physical layer standard used by the digital signal level 1 at a rate of 1.544 Mbps, used extensively in North America.

t3
> Basic physical layer standard used by the digital signal level 3 at a rate of 44.736 Mbps, used extensively in North America.

fe
> 100 Mbps standard initially created by Xerox in the 1970s for connecting multiple computers together; referred to as a LAN today.

ge
> Higher-speed Ethernet standard at 1 Gbps or 10 Gbps.

se
> Interface used for serial communications (one bit at a time). Serial interfaces include standards such as EIA 530, V.35, and X.21.

ct1
> T1 interface that is channelized by splitting the interface into 24 DSO channels.

Chassis slot number

The next part of the interface name is F, a chassis slot number represented by a Flexible PIC Concentrator (FPC) slot number on an M-series router or a PIM slot number on a J-series router. The M-series routers have two possible FPC alignments: horizontal slots or vertical slots. The larger M-series routers (M40e, M320) have vertically mounted FPCs with slot numbers starting at slot 0 and counting from left to right (see Figure 2-1). The smaller M-series routers (M7i, M10i) have horizontal slots starting at slot 0 and counting from top to bottom (see Figure 2-2).

 The M7i slot 1 is reserved for the Fixed Interface Card slots.

A J-series router does not contain any FPCs but does have PIM slots that are represented by the variable F. All fixed-port slots are always assigned slot 0, and PIM slots are assigned 1–6 numbering from top to bottom and left to right (see Figure 2-3).

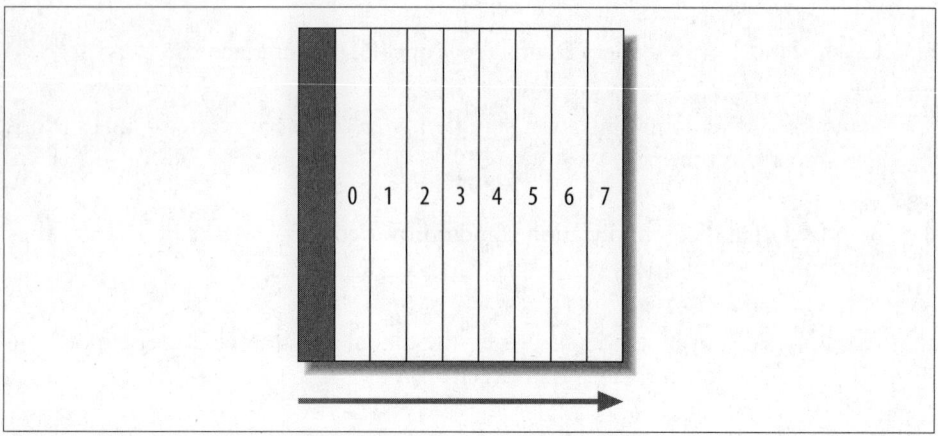

Figure 2-1. Vertical FPC slots (M40e and M320)

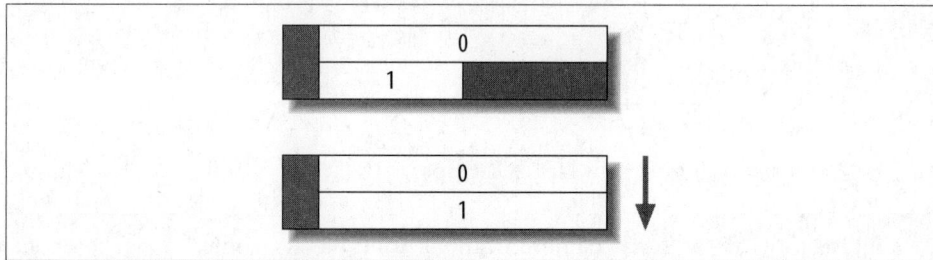

Figure 2-2. Horizontal FPC slots (M7i and M10i)

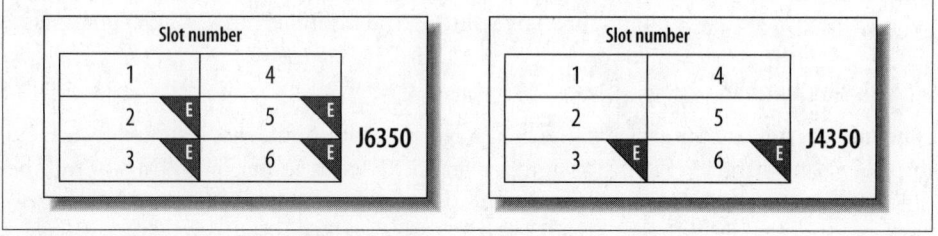

Figure 2-3. J6350 and J4350 PIM slot numbers

PIC slot number

The next part of the interface name is the PIC slot number, represented by the variable P. In M-series routers, four PICs can fit into a single FPC slot. The slot numbers begin at 0 and continue to the final slot, 3. In M-series routers, the direction of PIC slot numbering depends on whether the chassis slots are vertically or horizontally aligned. In a vertically aligned M-series router, the PIC slot number is counted from top to bottom, as shown in Figure 2-4.

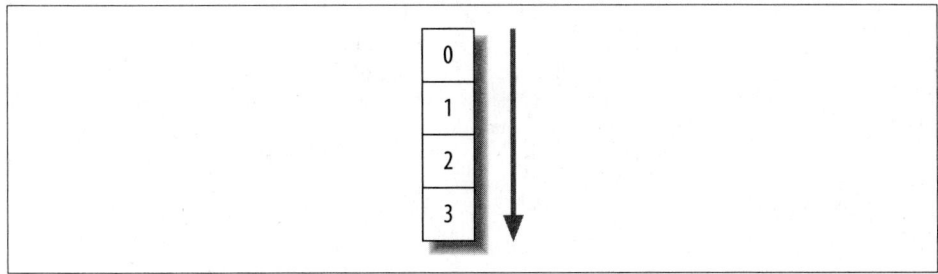

Figure 2-4. PIC slot numbers for M40e and M320

PIC slot numbering in horizontally aligned systems such as the M7i and M10i is a little less standard. In these systems, the PIC slot numbering goes from right to left, starting at 0 and ending at slot 3, as shown in Figure 2-5. The M7i's second FPC slot contains only two possible PIC slot numbers, and as shown in Figure 2-6, slot 2 is used for the built-in tunnel interface, or Adaptive Services Module (ASM), and slot 3 is used for the fixed Ethernet interfaces.

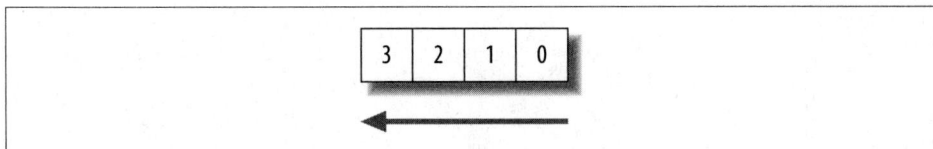

Figure 2-5. PIC slot numbers for M7i, M10i, and M20

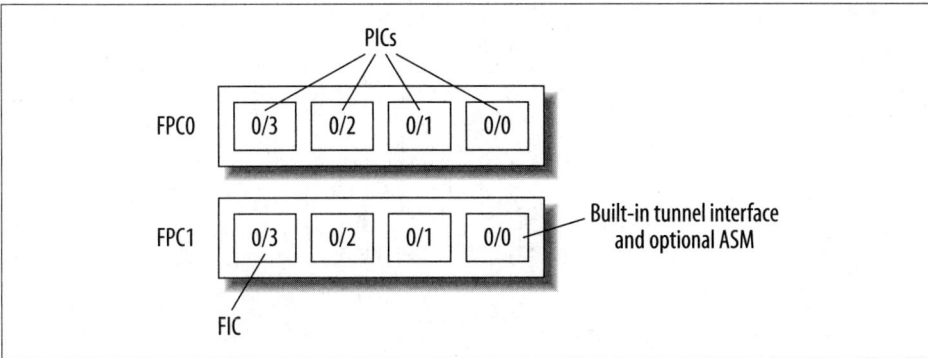

Figure 2-6. M7i PIC slot numbering

Life is much simpler in a J-series router that does not have any PIC slot numbers; thus, the interface naming (F) convention is always set to a value of 0.

It seems counterintuitive that PIC slot numbering is counted from right to left. The reason harkens back to the first routers (m40), which were vertically aligned FPC slots with PIC slot numbering from top to bottom. Next came the horizontally aligned FPC slot (m20), which was essentially a vertically aligned router turned on its side, which caused the PIC slot to shift to right to left.

Port number

The last part of the interface name is represented by the variable T, or the actual physical port number. M-series routers have port numbers with a variety of schemes depending on the PIC and the router model (horizontal versus vertical slots). For vertical FPC routers (m40e, M320), port numbers start from the top right and continue from the bottom to the top and then move right to left. For horizontal FPC routers (m20, m7i, m10i), port numbers start from the bottom right and then move right to left and from the bottom to the top. It's easier to see by examining Figures 2-7 through 2-10, which show this sequence in the different chassis types.

To avoid any confusion or spontaneous brain combustions, remember that the port number is always written on the PIC itself.

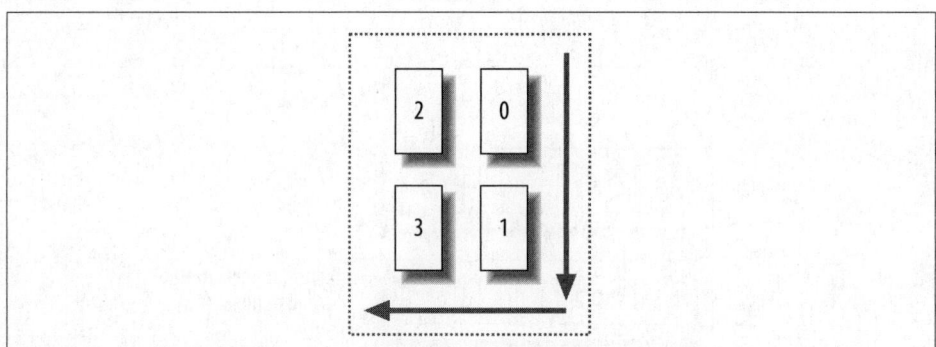

Figure 2-7. Port numbers on a vertical FPC chassis starting at the top right

The fixed Ethernet ports on the M7i follow the convention of Figure 2-10 and count from right to left, starting at port 0.

Port numbers are greatly simplified in a J-series router, as all ports are always numbered from left to right. This includes ports on a PIM (see Figure 2-11) as well any fixed ports on the chassis (see Figure 2-12).

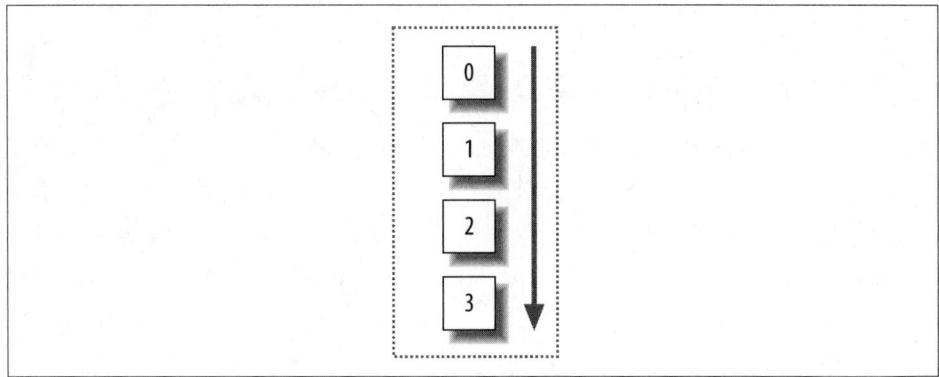

Figure 2-8. Port numbers on a vertical FPC chassis starting at the top

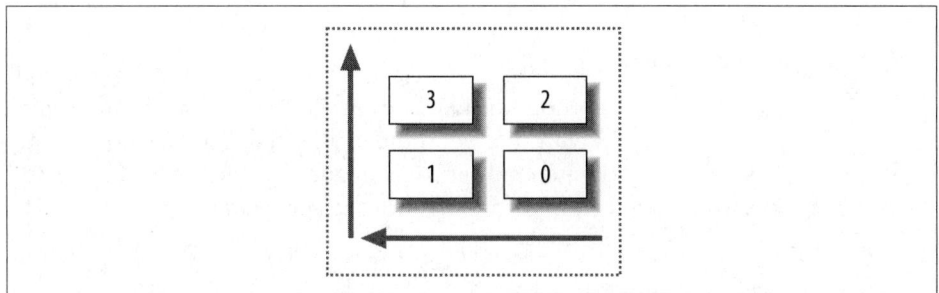

Figure 2-9. Port numbers on a horizontal FPC chassis starting at the bottom right

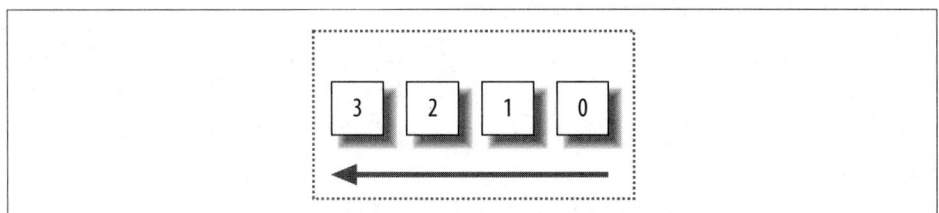

Figure 2-10. Port numbers on a horizontal FPC chassis starting on the right

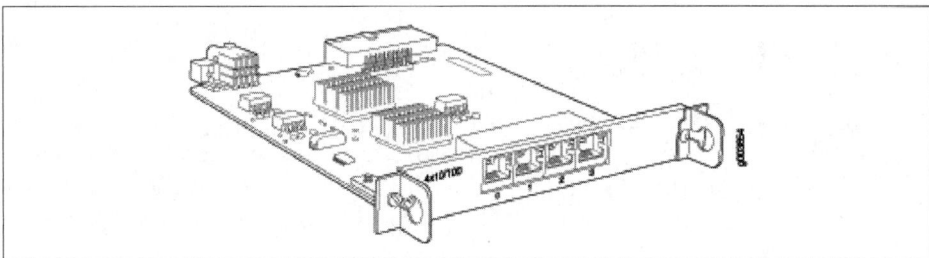

Figure 2-11. Four-port Fast Ethernet E-PIM

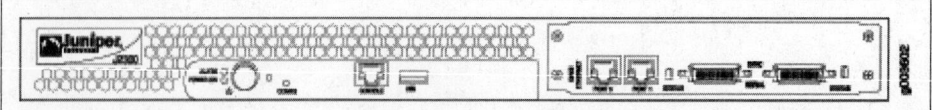

Figure 2-12. J2300 dual FE/serial ports with right-to-left numbering

Here are a few M-series example interfaces:

se-1/0/0
> Serial interface in FPC slot 1, PIC slot 0, and port 0

fe-0/2/1
> Fast Ethernet interface in FPC slot 0, PIC slot 2, and port 2

t1-1/0/1
> T1 interface in FPC slot 1, PIC slot 0, and port 1

Logical unit and channel numbers

Interfaces also have a logical portion of the name represented by either a unit number or a channel number. A *logical unit* is a numerical number that represents the subinterface properties of the router and can be configured in the range of 0–16,385. This is designated by a period (.) in the interface name. For example:

fe-0/0/0.0
> Unit 0 configured on the Fast Ethernet interface

e3-1/0/2.12
> Unit 12 configured on the e3 interface

The other logical division could be a channel number—for example, when breaking up a T1 interface into multiple DS0 channels (up to 24). Channel values are represented using a colon (:). For example:

ct-1/1/2:14
> Channel 14 on a channelized T1 interface

We will cover logical units in depth in "Logical Properties," later in this chapter.

Interface Properties

Each interface has two types of properties assigned to it: physical properties and logical properties. *Physical properties* are tied to the entire physical port, whereas *logical properties* affect only that logical portion of the interface represented by unit numbers or channel numbers.

Physical Properties

A physical property on an interface is any property that should be assigned to the entire physical port. Depending on the interface media, a large range of properties can be configured, but they can be divided into a few major categories:

Clocking
> This aligns the bits as they are transmitted out of the interface. The clocking can be learned either from an external source or from the router itself.

Encapsulation
> This is the Layer 2 encapsulation that is going to be used on the interface. Examples include Frame Relay, Point-to-Point Protocol (PPP), and Cisco High-Level Data Link Control (HDLC).

MTU
> This is the maximum transmission unit, which is the maximum size of the frame transmitted from the interface.

Keepalives
> These are mechanisms used to verify the operation of the interface. Most encapsulations have keepalives enabled by default, but you can disable them to aid in troubleshooting.

Layer 1/2 options
> These are various bit and byte settings for the interface media. For a T1 interface, this includes byte encodings, framing, frame check sequences (FCSs), and line buildouts. In comparison, a Fast Ethernet interface might have options such as flow control, loopbacks, and source address filters.

A physical property should always be configured before any logical identifier, such as a unit number. For example, the following is a serial interface with *no* logical properties configured but with physical properties of encapsulation cisco-HDLC and no-keepalives, and with clocking set to internal:

```
se-0/0/2 {
    no-keepalives;
    encapsulation cisco-hdlc;
    serial-options {
        clocking-mode internal;
    }
    unit 0;
}
```

Logical Properties

All router interfaces that will send and receive transit traffic require a logical unit to be configured. This logical unit creates a division of the physical interface into multiple parts. For instance, an Ethernet interface can be subdivided into multiple virtual LANs (VLANs), each requiring its own logical unit.

 Many router vendors refer to a logical unit as a *subinterface*; they do not require a subinterface on every physical interface, whereas a Juniper Networks router does.

Some interface types, such as point-to-point interfaces and non-VLAN-tagged Ethernet interfaces, still require a logical unit to be configured. This is a unique feature of JUNOS software and may take a little getting used to if you're coming from other router vendors' hardware. These interfaces require a unit number because any logical property that needs to be configured *must* be defined after the unit number definition. The most common types of logical properties include:

Protocol family
> Indicates which Layer 3 protocols can be sent and received on the interface. The router can have one protocol family per logical unit or multiple families per logical unit configured. The most common family configured is `family inet`, which enables the sending and receiving of all packets in the Transmission Control Protocol/Internet Protocol (TCP/IP) suite (e.g., TCP, User Datagram Protocol [UDP], Internet Control Message Protocol [ICMP], and IP). Other common families are inet6 (IPv6), Multiprotocol Label Switching (MPLS), and ISO (ISIS packets).

Protocol address
> The Layer 3 family address, such as a `family inet` IP address.

Virtual circuit address
> Circuit identifier used when dividing the physical interface into multiple logical interfaces. These could be the VLAN ID, Frame Relay data-link connection identifiers (DLCIs), or ATM virtual path/Virtual Channel Identifier (VP/VCIs).

The logical unit number when configuring VLAN, Frame Relay, or ATM can be any value from 0–16,385. The current best practice, however, is to keep the circuit address the same as the unit number for easier troubleshooting. So, if you have a VLAN ID of 40 configured on your interface, the logical interface should also be a unit of 40, although it's not required. If you are configuring a point-to-point circuit or non-VLAN-tagged Ethernet, the logical unit number *must* be zero. Think of this unit as a placeholder for all the logical properties that will need to be configured on that interface.

Here is an example of a T1 interface configuration with the default parameters (PPP encapsulation), `family inet` support, and an IP address of 66.32.3.2/30. Note that since this is a point-to-point circuit, the unit number must be configured as unit 0.

```
t1-0/0/2 {
    unit 0 {
        family inet {
            address 66.32.3.2/30;
        }
    }
}
```

Interface Configuration Examples

A walkthrough of configuration examples, starting with basic examples and then getting into a few more complex configurations, will help to put this into perspective. The order of the walkthrough uses the following configuration example:

Fast Ethernet interfaces
Fast Ethernet with VLAN tagging
T1 interface with Cisco HDLC
Serial interface with PPP
Serial interface with Frame Relay
DSL
ISDN
MLPPP

Initially, we will use a step-by-step approach to establish the configuration fundamentals. Then the walkthrough will move toward configuration results that build on the fundamentals and become advanced. Once you grasp the fundamentals, you should be able to follow the advanced configurations. At the end of this section, we will discuss the use of the Virtual Router Redundancy Protocol (VRRP).

Fast Ethernet Interface

First, let's build an interface on router Lager that connects directly to router Ale over the fe-2/0/1 interface.

Check the status of the fe-0/0/0 interface by issuing a show interfaces fe-0/0/0 terse command. JUNOS software interfaces are automatically "enabled" when the physical connection is wired.

```
root@Lager> show interfaces terse fe-0/0/0
Interface               Admin Link Proto    Local            Remote
fe-0/0/0                up    up
```

 If an interface needs to be administratively disabled, issue the set interfaces *<interface name>* disable command.

The interface appears to be physically up, so next, configure the interface to allow IP traffic to flow as well as add an IP address. Begin by entering configuration mode, dropping down to the hierarchy of the interface, and configuring the correct family and local IP address:

```
root@Lager> configure
Entering configuration mode
```

```
[edit]
root@Lager# edit interfaces fe-0/0/0

[edit interfaces fe-0/0/0]
root@Lager# set unit 0 family inet address 10.10.20.122/24
```

Since this is a non-VLAN-tagged Ethernet interface, unit 0 *must* be used when configuring the logical properties of family inet.

Also, note that JUNOS software requires a mask for every IP address in the classless interdomain routing (CIDR) "slash" notation. An absence of the mask can lead to the less desirable result of configuring a /32 subnet on your interface. (Look for other JUNOS software address issues in "Interface Troubleshooting," later in this chapter.)

Verify the configuration and activate the changes by issuing a commit and-quit command:

```
[edit interfaces fe-0/0/0]
root@Lager# show
unit 0 {
    family inet {
        address 10.10.20.122/24;
    }
}


[edit interfaces fe-0/0/0]
root@Lager# commit and-quit
commit complete
Exiting configuration mode
```

Verify the status of the interface. Note that the status now includes the logical portion as well as the physical portion of the interface:

```
root@Lager> show interfaces terse fe-0/0/0
Interface          Admin Link Proto    Local              Remote
fe-0/0/0           up    up
fe-0/0/0.0         up    up   inet     10.10.20.122/24
```

Lastly, test connectivity by issuing a ping command toward the other end of the link of Ale:

```
root@Lager> ping 10.10.20.121
PING 10.10.20.121 (10.10.20.121): 56 data bytes
64 bytes from 10.10.20.121: icmp_seq=0 ttl=64 time=7.758 ms
64 bytes from 10.10.20.121: icmp_seq=1 ttl=64 time=10.394 ms
^C
--- 10.10.20.121 ping statistics ---
2 packets transmitted, 2 packets received, 0% packet loss
round-trip min/avg/max/stddev = 7.758/9.076/10.394/1.318 ms
```

Notice the Ctrl-C sequence used to break out of the ping command. JUNOS software will send an endless number of pings unless a break is issued or a specific number of ping packets are specified with the count command:

```
root@Lager> ping 10.10.20.121 count 3
PING 10.10.20.121 (10.10.20.121): 56 data bytes
64 bytes from 10.10.20.121: icmp_seq=0 ttl=64 time=16.822 ms
64 bytes from 10.10.20.121: icmp_seq=1 ttl=64 time=20.382 ms
64 bytes from 10.10.20.121: icmp_seq=2 ttl=64 time=10.370 ms

--- 10.10.20.121 ping statistics ---
3 packets transmitted, 3 packets received, 0% packet loss
round-trip min/avg/max/stddev = 10.370/15.858/20.382/4.144 ms
```

Fast Ethernet with VLAN Tagging

Continuing with our example, let's add VLAN tagging between Lager and Porter, which is already configured with a VLAN ID of 100. The first step is to enable VLAN tagging on the physical interface of Lager:

```
root@Lager> configure
Entering configuration mode

[edit]
root@Lager# edit interfaces fe-2/0/1

[edit interfaces fe-2/0/1]
root@Lager# set vlan-tagging
```

Next, add a VLAN ID of 100 on logical unit 0:

```
[edit interfaces fe-2/0/1]
root@Lager# set unit 0 vlan-id 100

[edit interfaces fe-2/0/1]
root@Lager# show
vlan-tagging;
unit 0 {
    vlan-id 100;
    family inet {
        address 10.10.20.122/24;
    }
}
```

Juniper routers do not have a default VLAN, as every VLAN must be explicitly configured. Many switches use a default VLAN of 1, so make sure you explicitly configure a vlan-id of 1 on the router for connectivity.

Although this is a valid configuration on unit 0, the best practice is to always keep the same unit number as the VLAN tag, so let's change the unit number with the rename command:

```
[edit interfaces fe-2/0/1]
root@Lager# rename unit 0 to unit 100

[edit interfaces fe-2/0/1]
root@Lager# show
vlan-tagging;
unit 100 {
    vlan-id 100;
    family inet {
        address 10.10.20.122/24;
    }
}
```

Lastly, activate the changes, verify the interface status, and test connectivity:

```
[edit interfaces fe-2/0/1]
root@Lager# commit
commit complete

[edit interfaces fe-2/0/1]
root@Lager# run show interfaces terse fe-2/0/1
Interface               Admin Link Proto    Local           Remote
fe-2/0/1                up    up
fe-2/0/1.100            up    up   inet    10.10.20.122/24

[edit interfaces fe-2/0/1]
root@Lager# run ping 10.10.20.121 count 1
PING 10.10.20.121 (10.10.20.121): 56 data bytes
64 bytes from 10.10.20.121: icmp_seq=0 ttl=64 time=46.668 ms

--- 10.10.20.121 ping statistics ---
1 packets transmitted, 1 packets received, 0% packet loss
round-trip min/avg/max/stddev = 46.668/46.668/46.668/0.000 ms

[edit interfaces fe-2/0/1]
root@Lager# run show interfaces terse fe-2/0/1
Interface               Admin Link Proto    Local           Remote
fe-2/0/1                up    up
```

Notice the use of the command run to issue the operational mode command ping in configuration mode.

T1 Interface with Cisco HDLC Encapsulation

The T1 interface is the most popular basic physical layer protocol used by the Digital Signal level 1 (DS1) multiplexing method in North America. For point-to-point interfaces on Juniper Networks routers, the default Layer 2 encapsulation is PPP, which differs from many other vendors' default behavior. To quickly interoperate with those vendors, change the encapsulation to their default setting, which is usually Cisco HDLC. Since we already showed the step-by-step configuration in the previous configuration, we show here only the result of adding the correct encapsulation:

```
t1-0/0/2 {
    encapsulation cisco-hdlc;
    unit 0 {
        family inet {
            address 10.200.8.9/30;
        }
    }
}
```

An inquiring mind may wonder why the encapsulation has the word *cisco* in it. Is there a non-Cisco HDLC? As a matter of fact, there is! There is a standard HDLC protocol (ISO 13239), used in protocols such as X.25 and SDLC. The original specification did not have multiprotocol support, so Cisco decided to create its own version with this support with different header fields and definitions. Although this protocol is officially proprietary, the workings are open and have been implemented by many different router vendors.

Serial Interface with PPP

A serial interface can come in a variety of different physical forms, such as V.35, X.21, and EIA-530. The choice of physical media often depends on geographical location; V.35 is the most common choice in the United States and Europe, and X.21 is more common in Japan. Regardless of physical media, all serial interfaces have the same idea of defining a data circuit-terminating equipment (DCE) device and a data terminal equipment (DTE) device. The DTE device is the end unit that receives data encoding, clocking, and signal conversion from the DCE device. In modern communications, the DCE device often takes the form of a channel service unit/data service unit (CSU/DSU) or a modem; however, when connecting two routers in a back-to-back fashion, one of the routers takes the role of a DCE.

Router Ale and router Bock have a back-to-back serial connection using V.35 with the default encapsulation of PPP. Normally, a router will default to DTE mode, but in this case, Ale is automatically chosen as the DCE based on the detection of a DCE cable. You can observe this detection in the Local mode field of the show interfaces command:

```
root@ale# run show interfaces se-1/0/0 extensive | find "serial media"
  Serial media information:
    Line protocol: v.35
    Resync history:
      Sync loss count: 0
    Data signal:
      Rx Clock: OK
```

```
        Control signals:
          Local mode: DCE
          To DTE: CTS: up, DCD: up, DSR: up
          From DTE: DTR: up, RTS: up
        DCE loopback override: Off
        Clocking mode: internal
        Clock rate: 8.0 MHz
        Loopback: none
        Tx clock: non-invert
        Line encoding: nrz
```

Since one of the roles of the DCE is to provide clocking to the DTE, an internal
clocking mode needs to be configured on Ale. This allows Ale to generate a clocking
signal toward Bock using the internal clock with a default clock rate of 8 MHz:

```
[edit interfaces]
root@ale# show se-1/0/0
serial-options {
    clocking-mode internal;
}
unit 0 {
    family inet {
        address 172.16.1.1/30;
    }
}
```

Bock has no clocking mode configured and takes the default clock mode of loop-
timed, which takes the transmitted clock from Ale. Bock could also have been configured for DCE mode, which would have the same result in this case. Here is the Bock
configuration:

```
[edit interfaces se-1/0/1]
root@Bock# show
unit 0 {
    family inet {
        address 172.16.1.2/30;
    }
}
```

You can verify the local mode, clocking mode, and clock rate on Bock by using the
show interfaces command:

```
[edit interfaces se-1/0/1]
root@Bock#run show interfaces se-1/0/1 extensive | find "serial media"
  Serial media information:
    Line protocol: v.35
    Resync history:
      Sync loss count: 0
    Data signal:
      Rx Clock: OK
    Control signals:
      Local mode: DTE
      To DCE: DTR: up, RTS: up
      From DCE: CTS: up, DCD: up, DSR: up
```

```
Clocking mode: loop-timed
Clock rate: 8.0 MHz
Loopback: none
Tx clock: non-invert
Line encoding: nrz
```

 Clocking can often be a confusing topic for many users. For back-to-back router connections, Juniper made it simple by allowing multiple different clocking modes to be configured and still "do the right thing." The only combinations that will not work for back-to-back connections are the DCE in loop mode and the DTE in loop or DCE mode. However, when connecting to a CSU/DSU or a modem, proper care must be taken to configure the correct clock mode.

Serial Interface with Frame Relay

Frame Relay is a Layer 2 encapsulation that enables the connection of your LAN via a WAN connection to a Frame Relay node. Frame Relay creates a tunnel called a permanent virtual circuit (PVC) over a private or leased line to provide connectivity to other sites over the Internet service provider's (ISP's) infrastructure. With the emergence of DSL and IP-based networks, Frame Relay is not often seen anymore, except in rural areas as a cheaper, "always on" connection.

To establish a Frame Relay connection with the Frame Relay node, the proper encapsulation of `frame-relay` (RFC 1490) must be configured as well as the local circuit identifier for the PVC represented by the logical property of a `dlci` number:

```
se-1/0/0 {
    encapsulation frame-relay;
    unit 645 {
        description "to R3";
        dlci 645;
        family inet {
            address 172.17.24.130/30;
        }
    }
}
```

The router can also support back-to-back router connections by configuring one router to operate in DCE mode or by turning off keepalives on each router. If keepalives are disabled, the router will not wait for any local management messages to enable that interface. Also, turning keepalives off can help in troubleshooting by allowing for loopback testing, which we'll discuss later in this chapter.

 FRF.15 and FRF.16 are also supported standards that we will discuss in Chapter 7.

ADSL Using PPPoE over ATM

DSL is one of the more popular connection media for both companies and consumers due to the fact that the local service is provided via a normal phone line with a DSL modem. This connection terminates at the telco digital subscriber line access multiplexer (DSLAM), a device that concentrates multiple DSL connections together. Some J-series routers have support for ATM over asymmetrical digital subscriber line (ADSL)—Annex A for DSL over POTS or Annex B for DSL over ISDN—and symmetric high-speed digital subscriber line (SHDSL) configurations that allow them to act as the DSL modem at the customer site. The interfaces appear to be ATM connections but do not support native ATM, only the use of ATM over a DSL connection.

Router PBR has an ADSL Annex A PIM installed in slot 6 and will act as a client to the DSLAM. This connection is using Point-to-Point Protocol over Ethernet (PPPoE) over ATM for the DSL connection, which requires that two different interfaces be configured. The first interface that is configured is the physical ATM interface of at-6/0/0. To configure the interface, the ATM virtual path and virtual channel identities must be the same values that are provisioned at the DSLAM. The rest of the parameters can be learned from the DSLAM by setting an operating mode of auto. Since PBR will be using PPPoE, the encapsulation *must* be configured at *both* the physical and the logical layers:

```
[edit]
doug@PBR# show interfaces
at-6/0/0 {
    encapsulation ethernet-over-atm;
    atm-options {
        vpi 0;
    }
    dsl-options {
        operating-mode auto;
    }
    unit 0 {
        encapsulation ppp-over-ether-over-atm-llc;
        vci 0.39;
    }
}
```

The next interface that must be configured is the PPPoE internal router interface. This interface maps the physical interface where PPPoE will be running, sets the access server's name and underlying service to be requested, and sets an IP address. The IP address can be learned automatically from the access server by specifying the negotiate-address command, as seen in the configuration of PBR that follows, or by setting the IP address to be static:

```
pp0 {
    unit 0 {
        pppoe-options {
            underlying-interface at-6/0/0.0;
            access-concentrator mgmgrand;
```

```
            service-name "pppserv@mgmgrand";
            auto-reconnect 5;
        }
        family inet {
            negotiate-address
            }
        }
    }
}
```

Verify the correct operation of the PPPoE negotiation by issuing the show pppoe interfaces command:

```
[edit]
doug@PBR# run show pppoe interfaces
pp0.0 Index 68
  State: Session up, Session ID: 4,
  Service name: pppserv@mgmgrand, Configured AC name: mgmgrand,
  Session AC name: mgmgrand, AC MAC address: 00:05:85:ca:7a:a8,
  Session uptime: 00:22:43 ago,
  Auto-reconnect timeout: 5 seconds, Idle timeout: Never,
  Underlying interface: at-6/0/0.0 Index 66
```

ISDN

ISDN is a protocol designed to run over the circuit-switched telephone network. It allows digital transmission of both voice and video over your telephone circuit. With the advent of DSL, ISDN is starting to see less deployment, and today it is common mostly in rural areas or for backup links. When ISDN is configured on a Juniper Networks router, two interfaces must be configured: a physical interface (br) and a logical dialer interface (dl0). The physical interface will contain the dialing number information and switch type. In the following example, br-0/0/4 is configured to use a switch type of etsi, which indicates NET3 for Europe. Also, a dial pool of pool1 is mapped to the physical interface to tie the interface to a logical unit in the dialer interface.

```
Dialer filter:
-------------
[edit interfaces]
   br-0/0/4 {
       isdn-options {
           switch-type etsi;
       }
       dialer-options {
           pool pool1;
       }
   }
```

The logical dialer interface also needs to be configured. This interface contains the number that needs to be dialed, an IP address, and a pool to map the logical unit to the physical interface. In the following code snippet, the dl0 interface is mapped with pool1, which is also configured on the physical interface. The number 12345 is being dialed, and an IP address of 12.12.12.1 is configured. Also, this ISDN interface is set to establish the connection only when there is interesting traffic that will be defined in the dialer filter, called `dial_filter`:

```
dl0 {
    unit 0 {
        dialer-options {
            pool pool1;
            dial-string 12345;
        }
        family inet {
            filter {
                dialer dial_filter;
            }
            address 12.12.12.1/24;
        }
    }
}
```

This simple filter creates the connection when there are packets that are destined for the IP address of 12.12.12.2 by specifying the note action. All other destinations are ignored by term b because this term contains no from statement:

```
[edit]
    firewall {
        family inet {
            dialer-filter dial_filter {
                term a {
                    from {
                        destination-address {
                            12.12.12.2/32;
                        }
                    }
                    then note;
                }
                term b {
                    then ignore;
                }
            }
        }
    }
```

Recall that an ISDN interface could be used as a backup for other interfaces. To configure backup links, the dl0 interface will be mapped to the interface that requires the backup. In this case, fe-0/0/1 is being backed up by dl0.0:

```
[edit interfaces fe-0/0/1 unit 0]
    backup-options {
        interface dl0.0;
    }
```

The ISDN interface will be used if the fe-0/0/1 interface is down. Since Ethernet interfaces are often connected to switches, the interface could stay in the up state even if the entire path is not reachable.

 A protocol called *Bidirectional Forwarding Detection* (BFD) was developed to solve Ethernet path issues when the connection is via a hub or switch. BFD is essentially a fast hello protocol that is media-independent. For details on how BFD operates, see *http://www.ripe.net/ripe/ meetings/ripe-48/presentations/ripe48-eof-bfd.pdf*.

In this case, it is wise to configure a listing of IP networks that should be reachable when the primary interface is working. If there is no route to these networks, the ISDN interface will be used. In the following example, a single network of 13.13.13/24 is used to verify that the primary interface is working by listing that network in a watch list:

```
dl0 {
    unit 0 {
        dialer-options {
            pool pool1;
            dial-string 12345;
            watch-list {
                13.13.13.0/24;
            }
        }
        family inet {
            address 12.12.12.1/24;
        }
    }
}
```

An ISDN interface may dial and accept calls from other ISDN devices. To accept a call, an incoming map can be configured on the dl0 interface:

```
dl0 {
    unit 0 {
        dialer-options {
            pool pool1;
            incoming-map {
                caller 384030;
            }
        }
        family inet {
            address 12.12.12.1/24;
        }
    }
}
```

To verify whether the ISDN interface is working properly, issue the show isdn and show dialer commands. The show isdn status command verifies that the ISDN connection is up from Layer 1 to Layer 3, as well as the type of switch to which the call is connected:

```
doug@PBR> show isdn status
Interface: br-0/0/4
 Layer 1 status: active
 Layer 2 status:
  CES: 0, Q.921: up, TEI: 64
 Layer 3 status: 1 Active calls
  Switch Type        : NI1
  Interface Type     : USER
  T310               : 10 seconds
  Tei Option         : Power Up
```

The show dialer command will indicate each ISDN channel's individual status. In this case, only channel 2 is currently active:

```
doug@PBR> show dialer pools brief
Pool            Dialer interface      Subordinate interface
                Name    State         Name        Flags      Priority
1               dl0.0   Active        bc-0/0/4:1  Inactive   1
                                      bc-0/0/4:1  Inactive   1
                                      bc-0/0/4:2  Active     1
```

MLPPP

To incrementally increase the speed of individual PPP links without adding speed to the physical interfaces, the Multilink Point-to-Point Protocol (MLPPP) was created under RFC 1990. This is essentially a "software" bond of multiple physical PPP interfaces to form one larger logical link, called a *bundle*. JUNOS software allows for up to eight physical interfaces to be assigned to a bundle.

To support MLPPP on any Juniper Networks router, the router must support this special service. This support could be in the form of an additional hardware PIC on an M-series router, or it could inherit software support on a J-series router. We discuss services in detail in Chapters 7 and 8.

The first step is to configure the pseudolink service interface, which takes the form of ls-0/0/0 on a J-series router, or an ml, lsq, or ls interface on an M-series router depending on the PIC type (see Table 7-2 in Chapter 7 for a summary). This interface will take all the same characteristics of a normal PPP interface, such as an IP address, but will have a logical encapsulation of multilink-ppp. This is configured at the logical layer of the interface to allow multiple bundles and types of bundles on the same router by configuring multiple unit numbers. As shown here, the bundle is assigned to logical unit 0:

```
ls-0/0/0 {
    unit 0 {
        encapsulation multilink-ppp;
        family inet {
            address 172.8.17.30/30;
```

```
            }
        }
    }
```

Next, configure the physical interfaces to link the newly created link service interface. In the following example, interfaces se-1/0/0 and se-1/0/1 are linked to the logical bundle unit 0 on the ls-0/0/0 interface:

```
se-1/0/0 {
    unit 0 {
        family mlppp {
            bundle ls-0/0/0.0;
        }
    }
}
se-1/0/1 {
    unit 0 {
        family mlppp {
            bundle ls-0/0/0.0;
        }
    }
}
```

To verify the status, issue the show interfaces terse command. Notice that both the serial interfaces and the link service interfaces are tracked. The link service will be in the up state as long as one of the physical interfaces is also in the up state. You can modify this by configuring the minimum-links number command under the link service interface. This command sets the number of physical links that must be in the up state for the bundle to be labeled up.

```
root@Bock# run show interfaces terse | match "se|ls-"
ls-0/0/0            up    up
ls-0/0/0.0          up    up    inet    172.17.8.30/30
se-1/0/0            up    up
se-1/0/0.0          up    up    mlppp   ls-0/0/0.0
se-1/0/1            up    up
se-1/0/1.0          up    up    mlppp   ls-0/0/0.0
```

GRE

Generic Routing Encapsulation (GRE) is a tunneling protocol that enables the transport of a variety of Layer 3 protocols. The tunnel created by GRE was designed to be "stateless" with no monitoring of the tunnel endpoint. GRE tunnels are used for a variety of applications, including providing backup links, transporting non-IP protocols over an IP network, and connecting "islands" of IP networks.

To create a GRE tunnel on a Juniper Networks router, the router must be equipped with Layer 2 service capabilities, which are native in a J-series router or are available via a hardware PIC in an M-series router. When these services are enabled on a router, a pseudointerface called gr is created. The interface must be configured with the source IP address for the GRE packets, the destination of the tunnel, and the families of protocols that will be carried in the protocol. The GRE tunnel configured in the following case is carrying IP traffic and is using a source IP address of 10.20.1.38 and a destination of 172.66.13.1. An IP address for the gr-0/0/0 interface is not required but could be useful for management purposes.

```
gr-0/0/0 {
    unit 0 {
        tunnel {
            source 10.20.1.38;
            destination 172.66.13.1;
        }
        family inet
    }
}
```

 It is important not to mistake the internal gre interface with the gr interface on the router. The gre interface is used by the router internally and should not be configured to create GRE tunnels.

The final piece is mapping actual traffic for use by the GRE tunnel. This is accomplished in a variety of methods depending on the type of traffic entering the GRE tunnel. Common mapping examples for IP include creating a static route with a next-up of the gr interface or even running a routing protocol such as Open Shortest Path First (OSPF) over the interface!

VRRP

Anybody that is using a PC for Internet surfing, music downloads, or gaming uses IP as the network protocol. The PC will have an IP address assigned as well as a default gateway address to reach any destinations that are not on the local subnet. In the following code snippet, a PC is using an IP address of 10.70.129.36 with a mask of 255.255.255.0 and a default gateway of 10.70.129.1:

```
Microsoft Windows XP [Version 5.1.2600]
(C) Copyright 1985-2001 Microsoft Corp.

C:\Documents and Settings\Douglas Marschke>ipconfig

Ethernet adapter Local Area Connection 3:

        Connection-specific DNS Suffix  . : eu-af.regus.local
        IP Address. . . . . . . . . . . : 10.70.129.36
        Subnet Mask . . . . . . . . . . : 255.255.255.0
        Default Gateway . . . . . . . . : 10.70.129.1
```

This default gateway address is either statically defined by the user or learned via the Dynamic Host Configuration Protocol (DHCP) process. Regardless of the method, the default gateway will be used as the next hop address for the default route that will be created to reach remote destinations:

```
Microsoft Windows XP [Version 5.1.2600]
(C) Copyright 1985-2001 Microsoft Corp.

C:\Documents and Settings\Douglas Marschke>netstat -r

Route Table
===================================================================
Interface List
0x1 ........................ MS TCP Loopback interface
0x2 ...00 12 f0 ac 46 d5 ..... Intel(R) PRO/Wireless 2200BG Network
Connection - Packet Scheduler Miniport
0x3 ...00 12 3f 12 d7 59 ...... Broadcom NetXtreme 57xx Gigabit
Controller - Packet Scheduler Miniport
0x20005 ...00 ff e8 25 91 85 ..... Juniper Network Connect Virtual
Adapter
===================================================================
Active Routes:
Network Destination        Netmask          Gateway    Interface  Metric
          0.0.0.0          0.0.0.0   10.70.129.1 10.70.129.36      20
       10.70.129.0   255.255.255.0 10.70.129.36 10.70.129.36      20
      10.70.129.36 255.255.255.255     127.0.0.1    127.0.0.1      20
    10.255.255.255 255.255.255.255 10.70.129.36 10.70.129.36      20
         127.0.0.0       255.0.0.0     127.0.0.1    127.0.0.1       1
         224.0.0.0       240.0.0.0 10.70.129.36 10.70.129.36      20
   255.255.255.255 255.255.255.255 10.70.129.36 10.70.129.36       1
   255.255.255.255 255.255.255.255 10.70.129.36            2       1
   255.255.255.255 255.255.255.255 10.70.129.36        20005       1
Default Gateway:       10.70.129.1
===================================================================
Persistent Routes:
  None
```

If the default gateway was a single device and that device failed, a PC would not be able to reach destinations outside the local subnet. In a fault-tolerant network, it would be ideal to have a backup gateway device, without having to modify the configuration on the PC, as well as being able to load-share with multiple PCs on the LAN.

VRRP was created to eliminate single points of behavior that are inherent to static default routed networks. VRRP creates a logical grouping of multiple physical routers to a "virtual" router that will be used as the default gateway for end hosts. This allows the PC to always maintain the same gateway address even if the physical gateway has changed (see Figure 2-13). The routers that are part of the same VRRP logical group will share this "virtual" IP address as well as a "virtual" media access control (MAC) address. Essentially VRRP describes an election protocol to maintain ownership of this virtual IP (VIP) address and MAC address. One router in the VRRP group will be the master router, which controls this VIP address unless a failure occurs that results in a release of that ownership. This failure causes another router to claim ownership of the VIP by issuing a VRRP message and a gratuitous Address Resolution Protocol (ARP) to claim the virtual MAC address. Once a router becomes the master, it will periodically advertise VRRP messages to indicate its overall health and reachability.

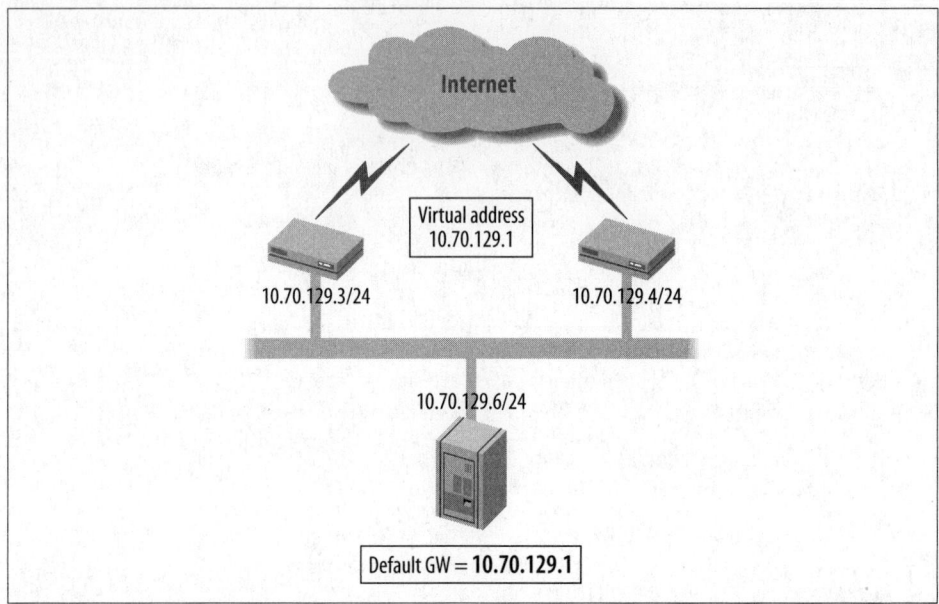

Figure 2-13. VRRP example

When configuring VRRP for the first time on a Juniper Networks router, it can seem like locating the configuration is similar to trying to find a needle in a haystack. The configuration will be within the logical property and will be configured after the family inet address. A VRRP group value (1–255) is assigned on every router that needs to be part of the virtual router. Also, a VIP address is assigned that the hosts will use as their gateway address. This could be an address owned by one of the routers in the group or an address taken out of the address block owned by the LAN. Lastly, a priority value can be configured to change the default value of 100, which is used to elect the master router of the VRRP group. The router with the highest priority value becomes the master for that group; if the priorities are equal, the tie breaker goes to the highest local LAN IP address.

```
lab@LAGER# show interfaces
fe-0/0/1 {
    vlan-tagging;
    speed 100m;
    link-mode full-duplex;
    unit 1115 {
        description LAGER-to-ALE;
        vlan-id 1115;
        family inet {
            address 10.40.1.2/24 {
                vrrp-group 1 {
```

```
                virtual-address 10.40.1.200;
                priority 200;


              }
            }
          }
      }
```

Verify the operation of VRRP with the show vrrp summary command. Router Lager is
the master for group 1 due to a higher priority.

```
[edit interfaces fe-0/0/1]
lab@LAGER# run show vrrp summary
Interface   Unit  Group  Type  Address        Int state   VR state
fe-0/0/1    1115  1      lcl   10.40.1.2      up          master
                         vip   10.40.1.200
```

 Priority values range from 0–255; however, only values 1–254 are con-
figurable. Priority 0 is reserved for the master router to issue an imme-
diate release of mastership. A priority of 255 is used if the VIP is an
actual interface IP that is owned by that router.

Another option that can be configured is the ability to track the interface priority settings. If an interface goes down, the advertised priority will be subtracted by a configured value. This could result in a new master router for the virtual router. This is
very useful to ensure upstream reachability. In the example on Lager, a T1 interface
is being tracked. If this interface goes down, 150 will be subtracted from the configured priority of 200.

```
lab@LAGER# show interfaces
fe-0/0/1 {
    vlan-tagging;
    speed 100m;
    link-mode full-duplex;
    unit 1115 {
        description LAGER-to-ALE;
        vlan-id 1115;
        family inet {
            address 10.40.1.2/24 {
                vrrp-group 1 {
                    virtual-address 10.40.1.200;
                    priority 200;
                    track {
                        interface t1-0/0/2.0 priority-cost 150;
                    }
                }
            }
        }
    }
}
```

You can force an interface failure by administratively disabling the T1 interface:

```
lab@LAGER# top set interfaces t1-0/0/2 disable

[edit interfaces fe-0/0/1]
lab@LAGER# commit
commit complete
```

The result of this failure is a mastership change, as Lager is now the backup router:

```
[edit interfaces fe-0/0/1]
lab@LAGER# run show vrrp summary
Interface  Unit Group Type Address      Int state  VR state
fe-0/0/1   1115 1     lcl  10.40.1.2    up         backup
                      vip  10.40.1.200
```

Notice in the show vrrp track command that Lager has a configured (cfg) priority value of 200, but a priority of 50 is currently being used because we've subtracted the cost of 150 from the downed T1 interface:

```
lab@LAGER# run show vrrp track
Track if       State Cost Interface      Group Cfg Run VR State
t1-0/0/2.0     down  150  fe-0/0/1.11151 200   50  backup
```

The default behavior of VRRP is to use *preemption*, which causes a router with a higher priority to become the master at any time. When Lager's T1 interface is reenabled, it will again become the master for the virtual router:

```
[edit]
lab@LAGER# rollback 1
load complete

[edit]
lab@LAGER# commit
commit complete

[edit]
lab@LAGER# run show vrrp track
Track if       State Cost Interface      Group Cfg Run VR State
t1-0/0/2.0     up    150  fe-0/0/1.11151 200   200 master
```

Since preemption could cause a temporary disruption in the network, a no-preempt command can also be configured.

Lastly, according to RFC 3768, "A VRRP router SHOULD not forward packets addressed to the VIP Address(es) it becomes Master for if it is not the owner." That means if we have an IP address that is not owned by any router and is simply an address from the subnet that was used as the VIP, operational issues may appear. The most common issue is not being able to ping the virtual address. In the case just examined, 10.40.1.200 was the VIP address chosen out of the 10.40.1/24 subnet, but it was not actually configured on either Lager or Ale. Juniper routers allow you to break this rule by configuring the accept-data command to allow the master router to respond to the VIP address. This will allow testing to occur toward the VIP; however, care must be taken to avoid unnecessary traffic on the LAN.

Interface Troubleshooting

Interfaces can have a variety of issues depending on the actual interface type, and listing all the possibilities would require a separate book! Instead, in this section, we will discuss a few common issues that illustrate the types of troubleshooting commands available on the router.

Address Configuration Issues

Since Juniper Networks routers allow multiple IP addresses to be configured on a single logical unit, configuration errors can occur if care is not taken. Lager has an IP address of 10.10.20.122 configured on its fast Ethernet interface with a subnet mask of /24. This was noticed to be a configuration error as the mask should have been configured for /27.

```
[edit interfaces fe-2/0/1]
root@Lager# show
vlan-tagging;
unit 100 {
    vlan-id 100;
    family inet {
        address 10.10.20.122/24;
    }
}
```

Here, the address of 10.10.20.122 is added with the correct subnet of /27:

```
[edit interfaces fe-2/0/1]
root@Lager# set unit 100 family inet address 10.10.20.122/27
```

When you view the resultant interface configuration the router appears to contain the duplicate IP addresses with varying subnet masks. This illustrates the fact that IP addresses are not overridden per logical unit, but simply are added to the logical unit.

```
[edit interfaces fe-2/0/1]
root@Lager# show
vlan-tagging;
unit 100 {
    vlan-id 100;
    family inet {
        address 10.10.20.122/24;
        address 10.10.20.122/27;
    }
}
```

To correct this, the old address with the /24 mask is removed by use of the delete command:

```
[edit interfaces fe-2/0/1]
root@Lager# delete unit 100 family inet address 10.10.20.122/24
```

Another solution with the same result is to use the rename command to change the subnet mask from /24 to /27:

```
[edit interfaces fe-2/0/1 unit 100]

root@Lager# rename address 10.10.20.122/24 to address 10.10.20.122/27
```

Since Juniper Networks routers allow placement of multiple addresses on a single logical interface, care must also be taken to allow for the router to choose the correct source IP address for outgoing packets on that interface. By default, the source IP address is chosen by using the primary and preferred addresses assigned to the interface. Each unit can have only one primary address, but each interface can have multiple preferred addresses. Simply put, a primary address is the address chosen to source local packets out of the interface destined for a remote network. As shown in the following output, 10.20.20.122 is the only address on the interface, and as such, it contains both a primary and a preferred flag:

```
root@Lager# run show interfaces fe-2/0/1.100
  Logical interface fe-2/0/1.100 (Index 67) (SNMP ifIndex 45)
   Flags: SNMP-Traps 0x4000 VLAN-Tag [0x8100.100] Encapsulation: ENET2
    Input packets : 2215
    Output packets: 23
    Protocol inet, MTU: 1500
      Flags: None
     Addresses, Flags: Is-Preferred Is-Primary
        Destination: 10.10.20.96/27, Local: 10.10.20.122,
        Broadcast: 10.10.20.127
```

Now configure two additional IP addresses, 6.6.6.6 and 6.6.6.4, on the interface and observe the results:

```
root@Lager# set address 6.6.6.4/24
root@Lager# set address 6.6.6.6/24
[edit interfaces fe-2/0/1 unit 100 family inet]
root@Lager# commit
commit complete

[edit interfaces fe-2/0/1 unit 100 family inet]
root@Lager# run show interfaces fe-2/0/1.100 | find protocol
    Protocol inet, MTU: 1500
      Flags: None
     Addresses, Flags: Is-Preferred Is-Primary
        Destination: 6.6.6/24, Local: 6.6.6.4, Broadcast: 6.6.6.255
     Addresses
        Destination: 6.6.6/24, Local: 6.6.6.6, Broadcast: 6.6.6.255
     Addresses, Flags: Is-Preferred
        Destination: 10.10.20.96/27, Local: 10.10.20.122,
        Broadcast: 10.10.20.127
```

The primary address has changed to 6.6.6.4, and now two addresses contain the preferred flag: addresses 6.6.6.6 and 10.10.20.122. The preferred address is used as the source IP address if you're trying to reach a network that is locally attached. In this case, if traffic is destined for 172.16.1.2, the source IP address of 6.6.6.4 is used, but if the destination address is 10.10.20.121, the source IP address of 10.10.20.122 will be used. JUNOS software by default will choose the primary and preferred addresses based on the lowest IP address that is configured. The primary address will be the lower IP address configured on the interface, and the preferred address will be the lowest IP address configured for each local subnet. In the earlier example, traffic destined to a host on the 6.6.6/24 subnet is sourced from 6.6.6.4. You can modify these defaults by configuring the appropriate flag (primary or preferred) to the address of choice:

```
[edit interfaces fe-2/0/1 unit 100 family inet]
root@Lager# set address 10.10.20.122/27 primary

[edit interfaces fe-2/0/1 unit 100 family inet]
root@Lager# commit
commit complete
```

The 10.10.20.122 address has now been configured for the primary address of the interface, as indicated by the show interfaces command:

```
[edit interfaces fe-2/0/1 unit 100 family inet]
root@Lager# run show interfaces fe-2/0/1.100 | find protocol
    Protocol inet, MTU: 1500
      Flags: None
      Addresses, Flags: Is-Preferred
        Destination: 6.6.6/24, Local: 6.6.6.4, Broadcast: 6.6.6.255
      Addresses
        Destination: 6.6.6/24, Local: 6.6.6.6, Broadcast: 6.6.6.255
      Addresses, Flags: Primary Is-Preferred Is-Primary
        Destination: 10.10.20.96/27, Local: 10.10.20.122,
        Broadcast: 10.10.20.127
[edit interfaces fe-2/0/1 unit 100 family inet]
root@Lager# set address 6.6.6.6/24 preferred
```

Encapsulation Mismatches

For two routers' interfaces to communicate properly, the same Layer 2 encapsulation must be configured on each device; depending on the type of encapsulation, this could be a difficult error to determine. A common interface medium where this could occur is Ethernet. The interface on router Lager is configured to send VLAN tagged frames on the 10.10.20/24 subnet; however, a ping to router Hangover in that segment fails:

```
[edit interfaces fe-2/0/1 unit 100]
root@Lager# run ping 10.10.20.121
PING 10.10.20.121 (10.10.20.121): 56 data bytes
^C
--- 10.10.20.121 ping statistics ---
3 packets transmitted, 0 packets received, 100% packet loss
```

Looking at the statistics on Lager's Ethernet interface, a number of Layer 2 channel errors are recorded:

```
root@Lager# run show interfaces fe-2/0/1 extensive
Physical interface: fe-2/0/1, Enabled, Physical link is Up
  Interface index: 142, SNMP ifIndex: 37, Generation: 143
  Link-level type: Ethernet, MTU: 1518, Speed: 100mbps, Loopback:
Disabled,
  Source filtering: Disabled, Flow control: Enabled
  Device flags   : Present Running
  Interface flags: SNMP-Traps Internal: 0x4000
  CoS queues     : 8 supported, 8 maximum usable queues
  Hold-times     : Up 0 ms, Down 0 ms
  Current address: 00:12:1e:76:1e:29, Hardware address:
00:12:1e:76:1e:29
  Last flapped   : 2007-04-05 22:01:18 UTC (1w0d 10:11 ago)
  Statistics last cleared: 2007-04-13 08:10:48 UTC (00:02:18 ago)
  Traffic statistics:
   Input  bytes  :                    0                    0 bps
   Output bytes  :                  230                    0 bps
   Input  packets:                    0                    0 pps
   Output packets:                    5                    0 pps
  Input errors:
   Errors: 0, Drops: 0, Framing errors: 0, Runts: 0, Policed discards:
   0, L3 incompletes: 0, L2 channel errors: 42, L2 mismatch timeouts:
   ,0 FIFO errors: 0, Resource errors: 0
  Output errors:
   Carrier transitions: 0, Errors: 0, Drops: 0, Collisions: 0, Aged
   packets: 0, FIFO errors: 0, HS link CRC errors: 0, MTU errors: 0,
   Resource errors: 0
  Egress queues: 8 supported, 8 in use
  .....
```

To see whether the Layer 2 channel errors are currently increasing or whether they are older counters that have not been cleared, the monitor interface fe-2/0/1 command is issued. The second column in the following code snippet shows the interface counter statistics, and the current delta column indicates real-time statistics recorded since issuing the monitor command. Layer 2 channel errors are currently increasing, as the current delta counter indicates:

```
Lager                            Seconds: 14        Time: 08:13:54
                                                    Delay: 0/0/50

Interface: fe-2/0/1, Enabled, Link is Up
Encapsulation: Ethernet, Speed: 100mbps
Traffic statistics:                                 Current delta
 Input bytes:               0 (0 bps)                   [0]
 Output bytes:            230 (0 bps)                   [0]
 Input packets:             0 (0 pps)                   [0]
 Output packets:            5 (0 pps)                   [0]
Error statistics:
 Input errors:              0                           [0]
 Input drops:               0                           [0]
 Input framing errors:      0                           [0]
```

```
Policed discards:              0                          [0]
L3 incompletes:                0                          [0]
L2 channel errors:           105                         [18]
L2 mismatch timeouts:          0    Carrier transit       [0]
```

An additional monitor command is now used to verify that the router is sending out the correct packets. The monitor traffic command is the router's tcpdump* utility that allows local router traffic to be observed on a particular interface. Since Ethernet requires the IP address to MAC address mapping before sending the FRAME, a series of ARP requests with an 802.1Q (VLAN) header are sent out to the interface with no response received. The layer2-header switch is used to obtain some Ethernet header information as the monitor command is usually Layer 3 and Layer 4 only:

```
[edit interfaces fe-2/0/1 unit 100]
root@Lager# run monitor traffic interface fe-2/0/1 layer2-headers
verbose output suppressed, use <detail> or <extensive> for full protocol decode
Listening on fe-2/0/1, capture size 96 bytes

08:18:09.764757 Out 0:12:1e:76:1e:29 > Broadcast, ethertype 802.1Q (0x8100), length
46: vlan 100, p 0, ethertype ARP, arp who-has 10.10.20.121 tell 10.10.20.122
08:18:10.564781 Out 0:12:1e:76:1e:29 > Broadcast, ethertype 802.1Q (0x8100), length
46: vlan 100, p 0, ethertype ARP, arp who-has 10.10.20.121 tell 10.10.20.122
08:18:12.214889 Out 0:12:1e:76:1e:29 > Broadcast, ethertype 802.1Q (0x8100), length
46: vlan 100, p 0, ethertype ARP, arp who-has 10.10.20.121 tell 10.10.20.122
08:18:12.814634 Out 0:12:1e:76:1e:29 > Broadcast, ethertype 802.1Q (0x8100), length
46: vlan 100, p 0, ethertype ARP, arp who-has 10.10.20.121 tell 10.10.20.122
08:18:13.414648 Out 0:12:1e:76:1e:29 > Broadcast, ethertype 802.1Q (0x8100), length
46: vlan 100, p 0, ethertype ARP, arp who-has 10.10.20.121 tell 10.10.20.122
08:18:14.314858 Out 0:12:1e:76:1e:29 > Broadcast, ethertype 802.1Q (0x8100), length
46: vlan 100, p 0, ethertype ARP, arp who-has 10.10.20.121 tell 10.10.20.122
^C
7 packets received by filter
0 packets dropped by kernel

[edit interfaces fe-2/0/1 unit 100]
root@Lager#
```

Router Hangover is then accessed and a ping command toward Lager is issued. The monitor traffic command is issued at Hangover with similar output, except for a single important difference. While router Lager is sending out the ARP packets with an 802.1Q header (0×8100), router Hangover appears to be sending a non-VLAN-tagged Ethernet frame (0×0806), which is the cause of the Layer 2 channel errors that were previously discovered:

```
doug@hangover> monitor traffic interface fe-2/0/0 layer2-headers
verbose output suppressed, use <detail> or <extensive> for full protocol decode
Listening on fe-2/0/0, capture size 96 bytes
```

---

* tcpdump is a common debugging tool that allows the user to intercept and display IP packets being transmitted or received over a network interface.

```
08:20:32.901733 Out 0:12:1e:75:fa:28 > Broadcast, ethertype ARP (0x0806), length 42:
arp who-has 10.10.20.122 tell 10.10.20.121
08:20:33.801530 Out 0:12:1e:75:fa:28 > Broadcast, ethertype ARP (0x0806), length 42:
arp who-has 10.10.20.122 tell 10.10.20.121
08:20:34.601659 Out 0:12:1e:75:fa:28 > Broadcast, ethertype ARP (0x0806), length 42:
arp who-has 10.10.20.122 tell 10.10.20.121
08:20:35.301622 Out 0:12:1e:75:fa:28 > Broadcast, ethertype ARP (0x0806), length 42:
arp who-has 10.10.20.122 tell 10.10.20.121
08:20:36.001475 Out 0:12:1e:75:fa:28 > Broadcast, ethertype ARP (0x0806), length 42:
arp who-has 10.10.20.122 tell 10.10.20.121
08:20:36.941611 Out 0:12:1e:75:fa:28 > Broadcast, ethertype ARP (0x0806), length 42:
arp who-has 10.10.20.122 tell 10.10.20.121
^C
7 packets received by filter
0 packets dropped by kernel
```

After correcting the configuration error on Hangover to allow for VLAN encapsulation with the correct VLAN ID, the ping succeeds and is verified:

```
root@Lager# run monitor traffic interface fe-2/0/1 layer2-headers
verbose output suppressed, use <detail> or <extensive> for full protocol decode
Listening on fe-2/0/1, capture size 96 bytes

08:20:55.076174  In 0:12:1e:75:fa:28 > Broadcast, ethertype 802.1Q (0x8100), length
60: vlan 100, p 0, ethertype ARP, arp who-has 10.10.20.122 tell 10.10.20.121
08:20:55.076308 Out 0:12:1e:76:1e:29 > 0:12:1e:75:fa:28, ethertype 802.1Q (0x8100),
length 46: vlan 100, p 0, ethertype ARP, arp reply 10.10.20.122 is-at 0:12:1e:76:1e:
29
08:20:55.096237  In PFE proto 2 (ipv4): 10.10.20.121 > 10.10.20.122: ICMP echo
request seq 0, length 64
08:20:55.096272 Out 0:12:1e:76:1e:29 > 0:12:1e:75:fa:28, ethertype 802.1Q (0x8100),
length 102: vlan 100, p 0, ethertype IPv4, 10.10.20.122 > 10.10.20.121: ICMP echo
reply seq 0, length 64
```

Path MTU Issues

When an IP packet is transiting a network, it is often fragmented so that it can transverse interfaces with varying sizes of MTUs. However, some applications do not allow this fragmentation, so you must ensure that the ingress MTU is not larger than a transit MTU for those applications. One simple tool you can use to test whether the proper MTU is assigned is the *packet internet groper* (ping) command. Connectivity to a remote system is confirmed on router Lager by issuing a ping command to an address of 172.17.20.2:

```
root@Lager> ping 172.17.20.2
PING 172.17.20.2 (172.17.20.2): 56 data bytes
64 bytes from 172.17.20.2: icmp_seq=0 ttl=62 time=7.133 ms
64 bytes from 172.17.20.2: icmp_seq=1 ttl=62 time=10.375 ms
^C
--- 172.17.20.2 ping statistics ---
2 packets transmitted, 2 packets received, 0% packet loss
round-trip min/avg/max/stddev = 7.133/8.754/10.375/1.621 ms
```

Issue the traceroute command to check the path these packets take to reach the destination. Router Lager appears to be located two IP systems away from the destination of 172.17.20.2:

```
root@Lager> traceroute 172.17.20.2
traceroute to 172.17.20.2 (172.17.20.2), 30 hops max, 40 byte packets
 1   10.10.20.121 (10.10.20.121)  18.572 ms  12.953 ms  35.782 ms
 2   172.17.20.2 (172.17.20.2)  9.804 ms  9.497 ms  10.003 ms
```

The application that is being tested requires an MTU of 1,508 bytes, so a ping of size 1,500 is sent with 8 bytes of overhead to the remote station:

```
root@Lager> ping 172.17.20.2 size 1500 count 3
PING 172.17.20.2 (172.17.20.2): 1500 data bytes
1508 bytes from 172.17.20.2: icmp_seq=0 ttl=63 time=11.591 ms
1508 bytes from 172.17.20.2: icmp_seq=1 ttl=63 time=10.580 ms
1508 bytes from 172.17.20.2: icmp_seq=2 ttl=63 time=20.939 ms

--- 172.17.20.2 ping statistics ---
3 packets transmitted, 3 packets received, 0% packet loss
round-trip min/avg/max/stddev = 10.580/14.370/20.939/4.663 ms
```

The ping succeeds, and at first glance, all appears well, but let's not count our chickens before they hatch! Some observation into the operation of the ping command is needed before giving the green light of approval. By default, the ping packet will be sent out with the do-not-fragment bit cleared in the IP header. This means that although the ping packet will exit the router with a size of 1,508 bytes, it could be fragmented along the way. So, now issue the ping command with the do-not-fragment flag set and observe the results:

```
root@Lager> ping 172.17.20.2 size 1500 count 3 do-not-fragment
PING 172.17.20.2 (172.17.20.2): 1200 data bytes
36 bytes from 10.10.20.121: frag needed and DF set (MTU 1119)
Vr HL TOS  Len   ID Flg  off TTL Pro  cks      Src       Dst
 4  5  00 04cc af90   2 0000   40  01 a809 10.10.20.122  172.17.20.2

36 bytes from 10.10.20.121: frag needed and DF set (MTU 1119)
Vr HL TOS  Len   ID Flg  off TTL Pro  cks      Src       Dst
 4  5  00 04cc af91   2 0000   40  01 a808 10.10.20.122  172.17.20.2

^C
--- 172.17.20.2 ping statistics ---
2 packets transmitted, 0 packets received, 100% packet loss
```

It appears that the intermediate station cannot handle a packet larger than 1,119 bytes on its outgoing interface toward the destination, as observed by the ICMP message that is returned. Luckily, we found this out before the application was deployed, so we were able to correct this problem!

 If the *outgoing* interface on an intermediate system did not contain the proper MTU size, an ICMP error message will be generated. If the *incoming* interface was configured with a smaller-than-needed MTU, the observation will be different. Since the packet is dropped at input, no ICMP MTU message will be received. Instead, oversize frame errors would increase on the intermediate system's input interface.

Looped Interfaces

Creating a physical loop on an interface has been a troubleshooting tool for many years. Since the physical path of a leased line frequently consists of multiple segments, often a problem can be localized by testing the circuit segment by segment. The idea is to create a loop at the endpoint of the circuit and send a series of tests toward that endpoint that can determine whether packets are lost or corrupted during transmission. Two types of loops are supported on most types of interfaces: a remote loop and a local loop. A *local loop* creates a loop toward the router, whereas a *remote loop* is a line loop that is created toward the downstream network device (see Figure 2-14).

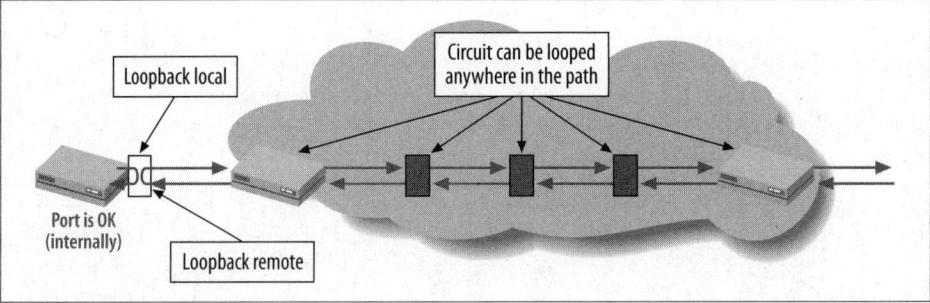

Figure 2-14. Loopback types

Often, the local LEC will go through a series of tests during the provisioning process to ensure that the circuit integrity includes loopback testing. The circuit may also be left in the looped state to avoid any local alarm generation. To see whether a loop is still in place, issue a ping toward the remote end of the circuit. If the remote end is looped (remote), the ping packets will continue until the Time to Live (TTL) expires, resulting in ICMP TTL expiration messages.

```
[edit]
doug@PBR# run ping 10.200.8.10
PING 10.200.8.10 (10.200.8.10): 56 data bytes
36 bytes from 10.200.8.9: Time to live exceeded
Vr HL TOS  Len   ID Flg  off TTL Pro  cks      Src        Dst
 4  5  00 0054 30e2   0 0000   01  01 6325 10.200.8.9  10.200.8.10
```

```
36 bytes from 10.200.8.9: Time to live exceeded
Vr HL TOS  Len   ID Flg  off TTL Pro  cks      Src      Dst
 4  5  00 0054 30e3   0 0000  01  01 6324 10.200.8.9  10.200.8.10

36 bytes from 10.200.8.9: Time to live exceeded
Vr HL TOS  Len   ID Flg  off TTL Pro  cks      Src      Dst
 4  5  00 0054 30e6   0 0000  01  01 6321 10.200.8.9  10.200.8.10

^C
--- 10.200.8.10 ping statistics ---
4 packets transmitted, 0 packets received, 100% packet loss
```

On the remote device, a loop will be indicated (remote or local) by examining the loopback flag in the show interfaces command:

```
dougl@closing_time# run show interfaces  t1-0/0/2
Physical interface: t1-0/0/2, Enabled, Physical link is Up
  Interface index: 139, SNMP ifIndex: 37
  Link-level type: Cisco-HDLC, MTU: 1504, Clocking: Internal, Speed: T1,
  Loopback: Remote, FCS: 16, Framing: ESF
  Device flags   : Present Running
  Interface flags: Point-To-Point SNMP-Traps 16384
  Link flags     : No-Keepalives
  CoS queues     : 8 supported
  Last flapped   : 2007-04-17 16:55:37 UTC (00:02:01 ago)
  Input rate     : 200 bps (0 pps)
  Output rate    : 224 bps (0 pps)
  DS1   alarms   : None
  DS1   defects  : None
```

Conclusion

An interface is the fundamental building block of any router with a large variety of possible interface types. Although JUNOS software allows for many different interface types, the general configuration process is consistent across each type. This also helps when it is time to troubleshoot the problem interface. The specifics of the media signals will vary, but the operational commands used are the same. Once a router has all its interfaces, operational routes to remote networks can be configured via routing protocols. We will examine these protocols in subsequent chapters.

Exam Topics

We examined the following Enterprise Exam Topics in this chapter:

- Identify valid options for interface names, logical units, and protocol families within the JUNOS software.
- Describe how to monitor interfaces in real time.
- Describe the information contained within the show interfaces extensive command.

- Describe the uses of network utilities such as ping and traceroute.
- Configure MLPPP.
- Configure IPv4 addressing.
- Implement Frame Relay.
- Create VLAN-tagged interfaces.
- Provide redundancy and high availability with VRRP.
- Link bundling and aggregated interfaces.
- Establish point-to-point or point-to-multipoint links with a variety of Layer 2 encapsulations.

Chapter Review Questions

1. On a J-series router interface, what are the possible values for the PIC slot number?

    a. 1

    b. 0

    c. Variable, depending on the physical location of the interface

    d. A range of 0–4

2. Which two interfaces are considered permanent interfaces on a Juniper Networks router? (Choose two.)

    a. lo0

    b. fe-0/1/0

    c. fxp3

    d. fxp0

    e. loopback0

3. On a point-to-point interface, which logical unit(s) can be assigned to an interface?

    a. None

    b. 4095

    c. 100

    d. 0

4. Which interface name indicates that it is a serial interface in a J-series router that is located in PIM slot 1 and port number 1?

    a. se-1/1

    b. se-1/0/1

    c. serial1/1

    d. se-0/1/1

5. Which JUNOS software command allows for real-time display of interface statistics?

    a. `monitor interface`

    b. `show interface statistics`

    c. `monitor traffic`

    d. `monitor statistics`

6. True or False: an interface must be administratively enabled before it is operationally in the up status.

7. What is the default Layer 2 encapsulation for a serial interface?

    a. SDLC

    b. HDLC

    c. X.121

    d. PPP

8. What is the maximum number of interfaces that can be added to an MLPPP bundle?

    a. 8

    b. 6

    c. 16

    d. 4

9. What is the default clocking mode on a serial interface?

    a. DCE

    b. Internal

    c. Loop

    d. DTE

10. Which CLI command would administratively disable the `fe-0/0/0` interface?

    a. `no shutdown`

    b. `set interface fe-0/0/0 disable`

    c. `deactivate interface fe-0/0/0`

    d. `disable interface fe-0/0/0`

11. True or False: all Juniper Networks routers contain an `fxp0` OoB management interface.

12. Which type of interface would be used to create a GRE tunnel?

    a. `gre`

    b. `tunnel.0`

    c. `gr`

    d. `ip.0`

Chapter Review Answers

1. Answer: B. J-series routers do not contain PICs, so this value in the interface name is always set to zero and is sometimes referred to as the virtual PIC value.

2. Answer: A, D. fe-0/1/0 is a transient interface, whereas fxp3 and loopback0 are invalid media types.

3. Answer: D. A point-to-point interface has only one valid logical unit number, which is unit 0.

4. Answer B. Every transient interface always takes the form of MM-F/P/T, with F indicating the PIM slot and T representing the port number.

5. Answer: A. The monitor statistics command in an invalid command, whereas monitor traffic displays local TCP/IP traffic and show interfaces does not display information dynamically.

6. Answer: False. Juniper interfaces are always administratively enabled when installed.

7. Answer: D. The default encapsulation is PPP on all point-to-point interfaces.

8. Answer: A. As of JUNOS software version 8.3, eight interfaces are allowed in a single bundle.

9. Answer: C. A serial interface always attempts to obtain its transmit timing from the line itself, using what is called *loop timing*. Other valid options that can be configured include internal and dce. DTE is not a configurable option.

10. Answer: B. The only other valid JUNOS software command listed in the answer choices is the deactivate command. This command comments out the configuration that the running system will ignore.

11. Answer: False. Only M/T series routers contain an fxp0 OoB management interface. J-series routers must be managed via console, auxiliary ports, or regular PFE interfaces.

12. Answer: C The software pseudointerface that is used to create GRE tunnels is the gr interface. The gre interface is used internally by the router and should not be configured. The ip.0 and tunnel.0 interfaces are not valid interface types.

## CHAPTER 3

Protocol Independent Properties and Routing Policy

This chapter is divided into two main sections. The first section details routing capabilities and features that are not specific to any particular routing protocol, hence the phrase *protocol independent*. Although termed *independent*, these features often interact with one or more routing protocols, and in some cases may be required for proper protocol operation! The second half of the chapter investigates JUNOS software routing policy. Routing policy provides a toolbox that facilitates the control of route distribution, including route filtering and route attribute manipulation.

In many cases, you combine the functions of Protocol Independent Properties (PIPs) and routing policy to achieve some goal. For example, a static route is defined using PIP, but this same static route can then be redistributed, perhaps with a modified attribute such as a route tag or Border Gateway Protocol (BGP) community, as a result of routing policy.

This chapter exposes the reader to PIP and routing policy in a manner that is analogous to a mechanic being introduced to each tool comprising a complete toolbox. To continue the analogy, the ways in which tools can be used, either alone or in combinations, are virtually limitless. For example, your hammer can be used as part of the repair of a hole in a boat's hull, or it can be used to make the hole, perhaps in an effort to scuttle the craft. Although the boat may have some opinion, it's safe to say that the tool—the hammer, in this case—is just happy to be used, with no real concern as to the nature of the task.

The routing and service examples covered in subsequent chapters of this book all make use of the PIP and policy tools to solve some requirement specific to the example being discussed in that chapter. Since practical PIP and policy-related applications are provided throughout the remainder of this book, the goal of this chapter is to expose the reader to the general capabilities and configuration of PIP and policy so that subsequent case study examples are fully understood.

The PIP topics include:

- Static, aggregated, and generated routes
- Global preference
- Martian routes
- Route tables and routing information base (RIB) groups
- Autonomous system (AS) number and router ID

Routing policy topics include:

- Policy overview, import and export policy
- Policy components (terms, match conditions, actions, policy chains)
- Route filters
- Advanced policy concepts

Protocol Independent Properties

PIPs are used for a variety of functions, such as static and aggregate routes, protocol preferences, route tables, router ID, and so forth. The range of PIPs is configured at the [edit routing-options] hierarchy.

Static, Aggregate, and Generated Routes

Although the use of static routing is sometimes considered bad form, especially during a routing-protocol-based practical examination, there are many practical applications for static routes, along with their aggregate/generated counterparts.

Static routing suffers from a general lack of dynamism (though Bidirectional Forwarding Detection [BFD] can mitigate this issue), which often leads to loss of connectivity during network outages due to the inability to reroute. Static routes can quickly become maintenance and administration burdens for networks that have frequent adds, moves, or changes. With that said, static routing is often used at the network edge to support attachment to stub networks, which, given their single point of entry/egress, are well suited to the simplicity of a static route.

Static routes are often used to promote stability through advertisement into a routing protocol, such as BGP, where a single route that is always up is used to represent the connectivity of numerous, more specific routes, which individually may come and go (flap) due to instability in the attached network's infrastructure. By suppressing the specifics in favor of a single static route, the world is shielded from the day-to-day flapping while overall connectivity is preserved.

Static, aggregate, and generated routes are similar in that all are defined statically, and all can have mask lengths that represent *super-nets* (aggregated network prefixes), or *subnets* (extending the network ID into the host field of a classful address to gain more networks, each with fewer hosts). As such, there is often confusion about the differences, and why all three types of static routing are needed. Table 3-1 summarizes how these route types differ.

Table 3-1. Static, aggregate, and generated route comparison

Route type	Next hop type	Comment
Static	Discard, reject, IP/interface next hop, label-switched path (LSP) next hop	Global preference of 5; can be used for forwarding. Supports qualified and indirect next hops. Activated by valid next hop.
Aggregate	Reject (default), discard	Global preference of 130; not used for forwarding, activated by contributing route. Default reject for matching traffic.
Generated	Preferred contributer (default) or discard	Default forwarding next hop based on prefered contributer.

Next hop types

Static and aggregate routes support various next hop types, some of which provide forwarding and others which do not. Understanding the differences between one next hop type and another is critical to achieving desired goals. Here are the specifics for each type of next hop:

Discard

A discard next hop results in the silent discard of matching traffic. *Silent* here refers to the fact that no Internet Control Message Protocol (ICMP) error message is generated back to the source of the packet. You normally choose a discard next hop when the goal is to advertise a single aggregate that represents a group of prefixes, with the expectation that any traffic attracted by the aggregate route will longest-match against one of the more specific routes, and therefore be forwarded according to the related next hop rather than the reject or discard next hop of the aggregate route itself.

The use of discard is best current practice when advertising an aggregate because the generation of ICMP error messages can consume system resources and may end up bombarding an innocent third party, as in the case of spoofed source addressing as part of a distributed denial of service (DDoS) attack.

Reject

A reject next hop results in the generation of an ICMP error message reporting an unreachable destination for matching traffic. This is the default next hop type of an aggregated route and for a generated route when it has no contributors.

Forwarding

A forwarding next hop is used to move traffic to a downstream node, and it is typically specified as the IP address of a directly connected device. Matching traffic is then forwarded to the specified next hop. On a multiaccess network such as a LAN, this involves the resolution of the IP address to a link layer address through the Address Resolution Protocol (ARP) or some form of static mapping.

When directing traffic over a point-to-point interface, the next hop can be specified as an interface name; however, LAN interface types require an IP address next hop due to their multipoint nature.

Forwarding next hop qualifiers. When defining a static route with a forwarding next hop, you can use qualifiers that influence how the next hop is resolved and handled. Specifically:

resolve
> The resolve keyword allows you to define an indirect next hop for a static route, which is to say an IP forwarding address that does not resolve to a directly connected interface route. For example, you could specify a static route that points to a downstream neighbor's loopback address. In this case, matching traffic will result in a recursive lookup against the specified (lo0) next hop to select a directly connected forwarding next hop. If a parallel connection exists, the failure of the currently used link results in a new recursive lookup and selection of the remaining link for packet forwarding.

qualified-next-hop
> The qualified-next-hop keyword allows you to define a single static route with a list of next hops that are individually qualified with a preference. In operation, the most preferred qualified next hop that is operational—that is, the next hop can be resolved and the interface that is operational is used. When that next hop is no longer usable, the next-best-qualified next hop is selected. That is to say, when the primary link is down, the router selects the next preferred next hop, which may point to a low-speed backup facility.

Static versus aggregate routes

Simply realizing that an aggregate/generated route supports a subset of the next hop options supported by a simple static route does not really explain the real operational mode differences between these route types. A static route is active whenever it has a viable next hop. This next hop can take the form of discard/reject, which effectively nails the route up.

Aggregates need contributing routes. In contrast, both aggregate and generated routes require at least one *contributing* route to become active. A contributing route is simply a more specific route that is learned through some other mechanism, such as static definition or dynamic learning through a protocol such as Open Shortest Path First (OSPF). A route is more specific, and is therefore able to contribute to an aggregate route (when it has a mask length longer than the associated aggregate) while sharing the same prefix as the aggregate (as indicated by the aggregate route's mask length). For example, the aggregate route 10.1/16 can be activated by route 10.1.1/24 because it has a longer (more specific) mask and shares the same 16 high-order prefix bits as the aggregate route. In contrast, the route 10.2.2/24 does not contribute to a 10.1/16 aggregate as it does not share the same aggregate prefix.

You can use routing policy to filter the set of routes that are allowed to contribute to an aggregate, which helps you control when the corresponding aggregate becomes active. Because only active routes are subject to routing policy, this in turn can influence when a given aggregate is advertised in a routing protocol. For example, you can filter all other contributes so as to advertise an aggregate for 10.1/16 into BGP based strictly on the absence or presence of a 10.1.1.0/30 route. By default, the preferred or primary contributing route is selected from the pool of viable candidates based on global preference. To break preference ties, the numerically smallest contributing route is preferred.

A given route can contribute only to a single aggregate route. However, an active aggregate route can recursively contribute to a less specific matching aggregate route. For example, an aggregate route to the destination 10.1.0.0/16 can contribute to an aggregate route to 10.0.0.0/8.

Aggregate versus generated routes

People often get confused about aggregate and generated routes—because both require contributors to become active and both are assigned the same routing preference of 130. The key difference between the two types of routes is that an aggregate route is *never* used for forwarding. Although it may attract plenty of traffic, the next hop of an aggregate route is either a discard or a reject—no ifs, ands, or buts. In contrast, a generated route installs the next hop associated with the preferred contributor, and therefore can be used to forward matching traffic. For this reason, a generated route is sometimes called a route of last resort. This is because in the general case, traffic typically matches a more specific route and is routed appropriately, just as in the case of an aggregate route—when the most specific (longest) match is against the generated route itself, it is forwarded to a gateway of last resort, as identified by the next hop associated with the currently preferred contributor route.

These operational differences are shown via the command-line interface (CLI) at Cider using a 10.10/16 aggregate versus a 10.10/16 generated route:

```
[edit routing-options]
lab@Cider# show aggregate
route 10.10.0.0/16;

[edit routing-options]
lab@Cider# run show route protocol aggregate detail

inet.0: 10 destinations, 10 routes (10 active, 0 holddown, 0 hidden)
10.10.0.0/16 (1 entry, 1 announced)
        *Aggregate Preference: 130
                Next hop type: Reject
                Next-hop reference count: 2
                State: <Active Int Ext>
                Age: 1:50
                Task: Aggregate
```

```
Announcement bits (1): 0-KRT
AS path: I (LocalAgg)
Flags:                    Depth: 0        Active
AS path list:
AS path: I Refcount: 2
Contributing Routes (2):
        10.10.11.0/24 proto Direct
        10.10.12.1/32 proto Direct
```

A 10.10/16 aggregate is activated by the presence of directly connected routes that contribute to the aggregate. Direct routes for multiaccess networks cannot contribute to an aggregate because a forwarding next hop can not be derived from the mere presence of the local interface, as is possible in the case of a point-to-point link, where the interface itself can be specified as a next hop.

To reiterate, a generated route remains hidden when only direct multiaccess routes are present to contribute:

```
[edit routing-options]
lab@Cider# show generate
route 10.10.0.0/16;

[edit routing-options]
lab@Cider# run show route protocol aggregate detail hidden

inet.0: 10 destinations, 10 routes (9 active, 0 holddown, 1 hidden)
10.10.0.0/16 (1 entry, 0 announced)
        Aggregate
                Next hop type: Reject
                Next-hop reference count: 1
                State: <Hidden Int Ext>
                Age: 3:10
                Task: Aggregate
                AS path: I
                        Flags: Generate Depth: 0        Inactive
```

This is because the next hop for a generated route is based on the forwarding next hop of the preferred contributor, and for a multiaccess type of network, this requires a static or learned route that identifies a next hop on one of the direct interface routes. In this example, a static route with a forwarding next hop pointing out Cider's fe-0/0/1.100 interface toward Bock is used to activate the generated route:

```
[edit routing-options]
lab@Cider# set static route 10.10.1/24 next-hop 10.10.11.1

[edit routing-options]
lab@Cider# commit
commit complete

[edit routing-options]
lab@Cider# run show route 10.10.1/24 detail

inet.0: 11 destinations, 11 routes (11 active, 0 holddown, 0 hidden)
```

```
10.10.1.0/24 (1 entry, 1 announced)
        *Static Preference: 5
                Next-hop reference count: 5
                Next hop: 10.10.11.1 via fe-0/0/1.100, selected
                State: <Active Int Ext>
                Age: 17
                Task: RT
                Announcement bits (2): 0-KRT 1-Aggregate
                AS path: I

[edit routing-options]
lab@Cider# run show route protocol aggregate detail

inet.0: 11 destinations, 11 routes (11 active, 0 holddown, 0 hidden)
10.10.0.0/16 (1 entry, 1 announced)
        *Aggregate Preference: 130
                Next-hop reference count: 5
                Next hop: 10.10.11.1 via fe-0/0/1.100, selected
                State: <Active Int Ext>
                Age: 11:34
                Task: Aggregate
                Announcement bits (1): 0-KRT
                AS path: I
                            Flags: Generate Depth: 0        Active
                Contributing Routes (1):
                        10.10.1.0/24 proto Static
```

Note that both the 10.10.1.0/24 static route and the resultant generated route share the same forwarding next hop. As the only viable contributing route, the 10.10.1.0/24 route is the preferred contributor in this example.

Route attributes and flags

When you define a static route, you can include various route attributes such as AS path, BGP community, route tag, metric, and so forth. These attributes may or may not come into play later when the route is redistributed into a specific routing protocol. For example, OSPF has no notion of a BGP community or AS path, and therefore these attributes are not injected into OSPF despite being attached to the route. The route attributes can be defined individually for each route or as part of a default template that is inherited by all related routes, unless specifically overwritten by a competing attribute.

You can also attach flags to a static route that controls various aspects of how the route is handled or operates. For example, the no-advertise flag prevents the associated route from being exported into routing protocols, even when the policy configuration otherwise selects that route for redistribution. You can display the list of available route attributes and flags with the CLI's ? feature:

```
lab@Cider# set static route 10/8 ?
Possible completions:
```

```
  active              Remove inactive route from forwarding table
+ apply-groups        Groups from which to inherit configuration data
+ apply-groups-except Don't inherit configuration data from these groups
> as-path             Autonomous system path
> bfd-liveness-detection  Bidirectional Forwarding Detection (BFD) options
> color               Color (preference) value
> color2              Color (preference) value 2
+ community           BGP community identifier
  discard             Drop packets to destination; send no ICMP unreachables
  install             Install route into forwarding table
> lsp-next-hop        LSP next hop
> metric              Metric value
> metric2             Metric value 2
> metric3             Metric value 3
> metric4             Metric value 4
+ next-hop            Next hop to destination
  next-table          Next hop to another table
  no-install          Don't install route into forwarding table
  no-readvertise      Don't mark route as eligible to be readvertised
  no-resolve          Don't allow resolution of indirectly connected next hops
  no-retain           Don't always keep route in forwarding table
  passive             Retain inactive route in forwarding table
> preference          Preference value
> preference2         Preference value 2
> qualified-next-hop  Next hop with qualifiers
  readvertise         Mark route as eligible to be readvertised
  receive             Install a receive route for the destination
  reject              Drop packets to destination; send ICMP unreachables
  resolve             Allow resolution of indirectly connected next hops
  retain              Always keep route in forwarding table
> tag                 Tag string
> tag2                Tag string 2
```

The reader is encouraged to consult JUNOS software documentation at *http://www.juniper.net/techpubs/software/junos/junos81/swconfig81-routing/html/routing-tables-config.html* for details on the various attributes and flags that can be attached to static or aggregated routes. The commonly used attributes are demonstrated either in this chapter or within the various scenarios demonstrated throughout this book. Figure 3-1 illustrates a typical application of a static route via a sample routing topology.

Global Route Preference

Routing information can be learned from multiple sources. In order to break ties among equally specific routes learned through multiple sources, each source is assigned a global preference. It can be said that the global preference determines the overall believability or "goodness" of a routing source. As such, routes that are learned through local administrative action—for example, static routes—are more believable than the same routes learned through a routing protocol such as OSPF. In Cisco IOS, this concept is called *administrative distance*. Table 3-2 shows the default protocol preferences for JUNOS software.

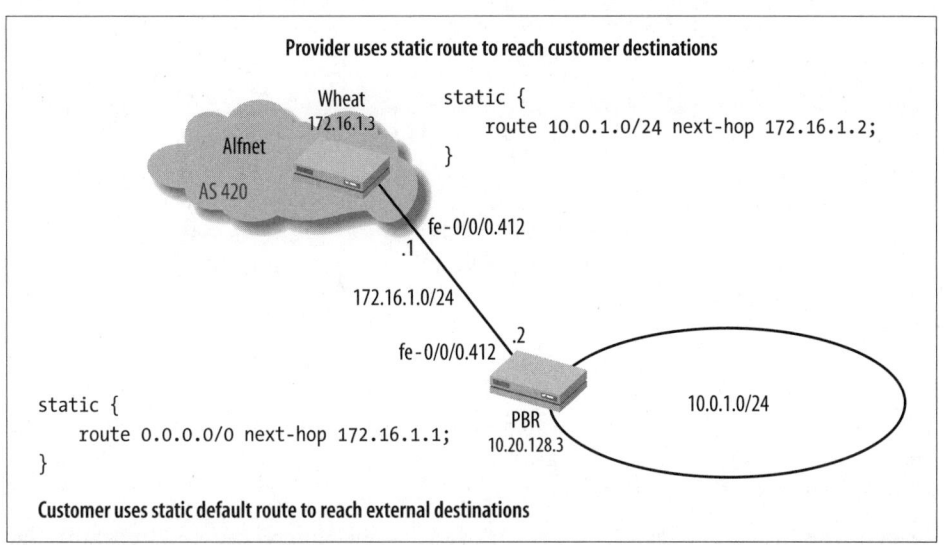

Provider uses static route to reach customer destinations

Wheat
172.16.1.3

Alfnet

AS 420

```
static {
    route 10.0.1.0/24 next-hop 172.16.1.2;
}
```

fe-0/0/0.412
.1

172.16.1.0/24

.2
fe-0/0/0.412

10.0.1.0/24

PBR
10.20.128.3

```
static {
    route 0.0.0.0/0 next-hop 172.16.1.1;
}
```

Customer uses static default route to reach external destinations

Figure 3-1. Static routing configuration

Table 3-2. Global protocol preference values

Source	Purpose	Default preference
Local	Local IP address of the interface	0
Directly connected network	Subnet corresponding to the directly connected interface	0
Static	Static routes	5
RSVP	Routes learned from the Resource Reservation Protocol used in Multi-protocol Label Switching (MPLS)	7
LDP	Routes learned from the Label Distribution Protocol used in MPLS	9
OSPF internal route	OSPF internal routes such as interfaces that are running OSPF	10
IS-IS Level 1 internal route	Intermediate System-to-Intermediate System Level 1 internal routes such as interfaces that are running ISIS	15
IS-IS Level 2 internal route	Intermediate System-to-Intermediate System Level 2 internal routes such as interfaces that are running ISIS	18
Redirects	Routes from ICMP redirect	30
Kernel	Routes learned via route socket from kernel	40
SNMP	Routes installed by Network Management System through the Simple Network Management Protocol	50
Router discovery	Routes installed by ICMP Router Discovery	55
RIP	Routes from Routing Information Protocol (IPv4)	100
RIPng	Routes from Routing Information Protocol (IPv6)	100
PIM	Routes from Protocol Independent Multicast	105
DVMRP	Routes from Distance Vector Multicast	110
Aggregate	Aggregate and generated routes	130

Table 3-2. Global protocol preference values (continued)

Source	Purpose	Default preference
OSPF AS external routes	Routes from Open Shortest Path First that have been redistributed into OSPF	150
IS-IS Level 1 external route	Routes from Intermediate System-to-Intermediate System Level 1 that have been redistributed into ISIS	160
IS-IS Level 2 external route	Routes from Intermediate System-to-Intermediate System Level 2 that have been redistributed into ISIS	165
BGP	Routes from Border Gateway Protocol	170

As with a route metric, numerically lower preference values are preferred. You can alter the default preference values when needed to accommodate some specific goal, such as route redistribution during an Interior Gateway Protocol (IGP) migration, which is demonstrated in Chapter 5.

Readers familiar with Cisco Systems may note a few differences between how the two vendors assign distance/preference. For example, Cisco has a separate distance for Internal BGP (IBGP) versus External BGP (EBGP) (200 versus 20), whereas Juniper uses the same value. In this case, there is no operational impact because in the route selection process JUNOS software prefers EBGP over IBGP, resulting in the same behavior for both vendors. One area where the vendors differ is in regard to IGP versus EBGP distance. Here, Cisco assigns an OSPF IGP distance of 110; since this is higher than the EBGP distance of 20, it results in the selection of an EBGP route over an equivalent OSPF route. In the same setup, a Juniper router chooses the OSPF route, owing to the preference values shown in Table 3-2.

Although you could alter JUNOS software preference to mimic IOS behavior, Juniper created a compatibility knob for this situation, called `advertise-inactive`. When applied to an EBGP peering session, this knob results in the advertisement of the best BGP route that happens to be inactive because of IGP preference. When using the `advertise-inactive` option, the JUNOS device continues to use the OSPF copy for forwarding, and the IOS device uses the EBGP copy to forward. However, from the perspective of an EBGP peer in a neighboring AS, both vendors appear to behave the same.

Floating static routes

A floating static route is nothing more than a static route that has a modified preference, causing it to be less preferred than a dynamically learned copy. The defaults cause a static route to always be preferred over a dynamic route. A floating static route is often used to provide backup in the event of a network or protocol malfunction. When all is operating normally, the static route remains idle because the dynamically learned routing is preferred. When routing protocol disruption results in the loss of a learned route, the previously inactive static route becomes active.

The following code sample creates a floating static route by assigning a modified preference that makes the route *less* preferred than an OSPF internal route, which has a default preference of 10:

```
[edit routing-options static route 0.0.0.0/0]
lab@PBR# show
next-hop 172.16.1.1;
preference 11;

[edit routing-options static route 0.0.0.0/0]
lab@PBR# run show route 200.0.0.0

inet.0: 12 destinations, 12 routes (12 active, 0 holddown, 0 hidden)
+ = Active Route, - = Last Active, * = Both

0.0.0.0/0          *[Static/11] 00:00:06
                    > to 172.16.1.1 via fe-0/0/0.412
```

Martian Routes

JUNOS software supports the concept of martian routes, which is a euphemistic way to describe a route that should not be present. Most network operators consider local use addressing, as defined in RFC 1918, "Address Allocation for Private Internets," as an example of martian routes, at least when received outside of the context of a virtual private network (VPN).

Routes contained in the martian table are excluded from route update processing, which prevents them from ever being installed into the route table. The martian mechanism provides a consolidated way to filter bogus routing information from all protocol sources without the use of explicit policy.

You can display martian entries with a show route martians command. In this example, only entries for the main inet.0 route table are displayed through the table keyword:

```
[edit routing-options]
lab@Bock# run show route martians table inet.0

inet.0:
                 0.0.0.0/0 exact -- allowed
                 0.0.0.0/8 orlonger -- disallowed
                 127.0.0.0/8 orlonger -- disallowed
                 128.0.0.0/16 orlonger -- disallowed
                 191.255.0.0/16 orlonger -- disallowed
                 192.0.0.0/24 orlonger -- disallowed
                 223.255.255.0/24 orlonger -- disallowed
                 240.0.0.0/4 orlonger -- disallowed
```

The default entries permit private use of RFC 1918 private addressing space while filtering prefixes that should never appear in a route update—for example, the 127.0.0.1 loopback address or the IANA reserved 192.0.0.0/24 network block. You can add entries to the table, which can later be removed using set and delete, respectively.

You cannot explicitly remove predefined martian entries, but you can add new entries that negate their effect. For example, rather than trying to delete the 0/0 exact allow entry, you negate its effect by *adding* a new entry with a competing action. For instance, the default martian table allows the default route, which in this example is being advertised via OSPF from Bock to Cider:

```
[edit]
lab@Cider# run show route protocol ospf

inet.0: 11 destinations, 11 routes (11 active, 0 holddown, 0 hidden)
+ = Active Route, - = Last Active, * = Both

0.0.0.0/0          *[OSPF/150] 00:00:07, metric 0, tag 0
                    > to 10.10.11.1 via fe-0/0/1.100
. . .
224.0.0.5/32       *[OSPF/10] 00:00:27, metric 1
                    MultiRecv
```

The martian table for the inet.0 route table is modified with a set 0/0 exact deny statement, which overrides the previous entry for the 0/0 exact route. Note that a deny action is the default for any entry in the martian table:

```
[edit routing-options martians]
lab@Cider# set 0/0 exact

[edit routing-options martians]
lab@Cider# show
0.0.0.0/0 exact;
```

After the change is committed, the results are confirmed:

```
[edit routing-options martians]
lab@Cider# run show route martians table inet.0

inet.0:
            0.0.0.0/0 exact -- disallowed
            0.0.0.0/8 orlonger -- disallowed
            127.0.0.0/8 orlonger -- disallowed
            128.0.0.0/16 orlonger -- disallowed
            191.255.0.0/16 orlonger -- disallowed
            192.0.0.0/24 orlonger -- disallowed
            223.255.255.0/24 orlonger -- disallowed
            240.0.0.0/4 orlonger -- disallowed

[edit routing-options martians]
lab@Cider# run show route protocol ospf | match 0.0.0.0
```

The lack of an OSPF-learned default route at Cider confirms the modified martian table results in ignoring routing information for the 0/0 route.

Routing Tables and RIB Groups

All JUNOS-based routers maintain a number of route tables that are used for specific purposes. In addition to the automatically created tables, you can create your own route tables, either indirectly through the use of virtual routers or Layer 2/Layer 3 VPNs and the related Virtual Route and Forwarding (VRF) tables, or directly through the use of RIB groups.

Generally speaking, each route table/RIB populates a designated portion of the forwarding table. This creates a single forwarding table that is partitioned based on a specific route table context. Packets are forwarded based on this route table context, which allows for distinct forwarding behavior on a per-route-table basis. It's a key component of any VPN type of service, where per-VRF (per VPN site) route tables are maintained along with a corresponding VPN-specific forwarding table context.

You can view the contents of a particular route table using the command show route table <table name>. The general naming convention for route tables takes the form of the protocol family such as inet (Internet) or inet6, iso (ISO), or mpls, followed by a period and a nonnegative integer. Routing instance table names are somewhat the exception here, taking the form of instance-name.inet.0, where the first part consists of a user-assigned symbolic name, followed by the protocol family and table ID, which is inet.0 in this example.

Default route tables

The default route tables created by JUNOS software include:

inet.0
> The inet.0 table is the default unicast route table for the IPv4 protocol. This is the main route table used to store unicast routes such as interface local/direct, static, or dynamically learned routes.

inet.1
> The inet.1 table serves as a multicast forwarding cache. This table constrains the various IPv4 (S,G) group entries that are dynamically created as a result of join state.

inet.2
> The inet.2 table houses unicast routes that are used for multicast reverse path forwarding (RPF) lookup, typically as learned through MP-BGP using SAFI 2. The IPv4 unicast routes stored in this table can be used by multicast protocols such as the Distance Vector Multicast Routing Protocol (DVMRP), which requires a specific RPF table. In contrast, PIM does not need an inet.2 because it can perform RPF checks against the inet.0 table. You can import routes from inet.0 into inet.2 using RIB groups, or install routes directly into inet.2 from a multicast routing protocol.

inet.3

The inet.3 table contains MPLS LSP information. This table contains the egress address of the MPLS LSP, along with the LSP name and outgoing interface, and is populated by both RSVP and LSP. The inet.3 table is used when the local router functions as the ingress to an LSP.

instance_name.inet.0

When you configure a VRF or VR routing instance, the resultant instance creates a route table based on the routing instance's name. For example, defining a Layer 3 VPN instance called ce1 results in the creation of a route table named ce1.inet.0. A routing instance differs from a logical router in that various routing instances share a single instance of the routing protocol daemon (rpd), whereas each LR gets its *own* instance of rpd, which in turn provides greater isolation. Note that LRs are not supported on J-series platforms with the 8.0 release used to write this book.

inet6.0

The inet6.0 table is used to house IPv6 unicast route tables.

bgp.l3vpn.0

The bgp.l3vpn.0 table contains routes learned from other Provider Edge (PE) routers in a Layer 3 VPN environment via BGP. Routes in this table are copied into a particular Layer 3 VRF when there is a matching route table.

bgp.l2vpn.0

The bgp.l2vpn.0 table contains routes learned from other PE routers in a Layer 2 VPN environment via BGP. The related Layer 2 routing information is copied into Layer 2 VRFs based on matching target communities.

mpls.0

The mpls.0 table houses the MPLS label-switching operations used when the local router is acting as a transit label-switching router (LSR) in support of LSPs.

iso.0

The iso.0 table houses IS-IS routes, which consist of a network entity title (NET) and a host ID. When using IS-IS in support of IP routing, you can expect to see only the local router's NET, which is typically assigned to the loopback interface, because in this context the IS-IS protocol is used to convey IP, not IS-IS routes.

juniper_private

JUNOS software needs to communicate internally with service Physical Interface Cards (PICs). The juniper_private tables are created as needed to facilitate these internal communications between the RE and service PIC hardware.

When you issue a show route command, all tables are listed chronologically starting with inet.0. Within each table, you will also see the total number of routes in the table and a listing further breaking down active routes and hidden routes. The following sample output from a show route command displays many of the tables described earlier, and it is taken from a router configured to support a BGP-signaled Layer 3 VPN using RSVP-based LSP transport. The router also has the inet6 and iso families enabled on its loopback interface.

The purpose of the following output display is simply to show a real-world example in which many of the default route tables are populated and used. The specific details of which routes are present or how a given entry in some particular table is actually used, are not the focus here, hence a related topology diagram is not needed for the purpose of simply observing the presence of multiple route tables. Subsequent chapters in this book expand on these specifics as needed in the context of enterprise routing:

```
user@L3_VPN_router> show route

inet.0: 23 destinations, 23 routes (22 active, 0 holddown, 1 hidden)
+ = Active Route, - = Last Active, * = Both

1.12.1.0/24          *[Direct/0] 00:33:41
                      > via ge-1/0/0.0
1.12.1.1/32          *[Local/0] 00:33:41
                        Local via ge-1/0/0.0
. . .
10.255.66.50/32      *[OSPF/10] 00:32:53, metric 1
                      > to 1.12.1.2 via ge-1/0/0.0
. . .
192.168.64.0/21      *[Direct/0] 5d 02:42:28
                      > via fxp0.0
192.168.66.47/32     *[Local/0] 5d 02:42:28
                        Local via fxp0.0
192.168.102.0/23     *[Static/5] 5d 02:42:28
                      > to 192.168.71.254 via fxp0.0
. . .
224.0.0.5/32         *[OSPF/10] 00:33:41, metric 1
                        MultiRecv

__juniper_private1__.inet.0: 2 destinations, 2 routes (2 active,
0 holddown, 0 hidden)
+ = Active Route, - = Last Active, * = Both

10.0.0.0/8           *[Direct/0] 5d 02:41:34
                      > via fxp1.0
10.0.0.4/32          *[Local/0] 5d 02:42:28
                        Local via fxp1.0

__juniper_private2__.inet.0: 1 destinations, 1 routes (0 active,
0 holddown, 1 hidden)

ce1.inet.0: 3 destinations, 3 routes (3 active, 0 holddown,
0 hidden)
+ = Active Route, - = Last Active, * = Both

1.1.1.0/24           *[Direct/0] 00:33:41
                      > via fe-1/2/0.0
```

```
1.1.1.2/32          *[Local/0] 00:33:41
                       Local via fe-1/2/0.0
10.255.66.52/32     *[BGP/170] 00:33:24, localpref 100
                       AS path: I
                     > to 1.1.1.1 via fe-1/2/0.0

iso.0: 1 destinations, 1 routes (1 active, 0 holddown, 0 hidden)
+ = Active Route, - = Last Active, * = Both

47.0005.80ff.f800.0000.0108.0001.0102.5506.6047/152
                    *[Direct/0] 5d 02:42:28
                     > via lo0.0

mpls.0: 3 destinations, 3 routes (3 active, 0 holddown, 0 hidden)
+ = Active Route, - = Last Active, * = Both

0                   *[MPLS/0] 00:33:41, metric 1
                       Receive
1                   *[MPLS/0] 00:33:41, metric 1
                       Receive
2                   *[MPLS/0] 00:33:41, metric 1
                       Receive

inet6.0: 2 destinations, 2 routes (2 active, 0 holddown, 0 hidden)
+ = Active Route, - = Last Active, * = Both

abcd::10:255:66:47/128
                    *[Direct/0] 5d 02:42:28
                     > via lo0.0
fe80::2a0:a5ff:fe12:47ed/128
                    *[Direct/0] 5d 02:42:28
                     > via lo0.0

__juniper_private1__.inet6.0: 4 destinations, 4 routes (4 active,
0 holddown, 0 hidden)
+ = Active Route, - = Last Active, * = Both

fe80::/64           *[Direct/0] 5d 02:41:34
                     > via fxp1.0
fe80::200:ff:fe00:4/128
                    *[Local/0] 5d 02:42:28
                       Local via fxp1.0
fec0::/64           *[Direct/0] 5d 02:41:34
                     > via fxp1.0
fec0::a:0:0:4/128   *[Local/0] 5d 02:42:28
                       Local via fxp1.0
```

User-defined RIBs and RIB groups

You can define additional route tables with the rib keyword. This capability is rarely used, but it is demonstrated here for completeness. In the following example, the user has configured a custom IPv4 RIB called inet.69, in which a single static route had been defined:

```
[edit routing-options]
lab@PBR# show
rib inet.69 {
    static {
        route 10.1.0.0/16 discard;
    }
}
```

The contents of the user-defined RIB are displayed with a show route table <table name> command:

```
[edit routing-options]
lab@PBR# run show route table inet.69

inet.69: 1 destinations, 1 routes (1 active, 0 holddown, 0 hidden)
+ = Active Route, - = Last Active, * = Both

10.1.0.0/16        *[Static/5] 00:15:53
                    Discard
```

You can group together multiple route tables (RIBs) to form a *route table group*. Within a group, a routing protocol can import routes into all the route tables in the group, and it can export routes from a single route table. Simply put, RIB groups provide a way to copy routing information from one route table to another. In operation, a RIB group consists of one primary and one or more secondary route tables—the first route table specified is the *primary* route table, and any additional route tables function as *secondary* route tables. The primary route table determines the address family of the route table group. To configure an IPv4 route table group, specify inet.0 as the primary route table. To configure an IPv6 route table group, specify inet6.0 as the primary route table.

Each RIB group must contain one or more route tables that JUNOS software uses as the source of any imported routes, as specified with the import-rib statement.

In the following example, a rib-group called my_interface_routes is configured to import interface route entries from inet.0 into inet.2. The my_interface_routes RIB group is defined under the interface-routes hierarchy, which specifies the protocol (direct) that is used to match against when copying the routes into inet.2:

```
[edit routing-options]
lab@PBR# show
interface-routes {
    rib-group inet my_interface_routes;
}
rib-groups {
    my_interface_routes {
        import-rib [ inet.0 inet.2 ];
    }
}
```

The result of the interface routes RIB group definition is confirmed with a display of the inet.2 table both before and after the changes are committed:

```
[edit routing-options rib-groups]
lab@PBR# run show route table inet.2

[edit routing-options rib-groups]
lab@PBR# commit
commit complete
```

After the commit, the inet.2 table is correctly populated with interface routes, as copied from the inet.0 table:

```
[edit routing-options rib-groups]
lab@PBR# run show route table inet.2

inet.2: 11 destinations, 11 routes (11 active, 0 holddown, 0 hidden)
+ = Active Route, - = Last Active, * = Both

10.10.130.0/24      *[Direct/0] 00:00:04
                     > via fe-0/0/0.1141
10.10.130.2/32      *[Local/0] 00:00:04
                       Local via fe-0/0/0.1141
10.20.128.3/32      *[Direct/0] 00:00:04
                     > via lo0.0
10.20.129.0/24      *[Direct/0] 00:00:04
                     > via fe-0/0/0.3141
10.20.129.2/32      *[Local/0] 00:00:04
                       Local via fe-0/0/0.3141
10.20.130.0/24      *[Direct/0] 00:00:04
                     > via fe-0/0/0.1241
. . .
```

If desired, you can use import policy to add additional control over which routes are copied between RIBs.

Router ID and Antonymous System Number

The last PIP-related configuration to be discussed is related to the router ID (RID) and BGP AS number.

Router ID

Many routing protocols require that the source of routing information be uniquely identified using the concept of a RID. A RID normally takes the form of an IPv4 address, and in most cases does not have to be reachable to correctly function as a RID. Stated differently, a router can receive a BGP or OSPF route update from a router identified as 1.1.1.1, and correctly process the related routing information, even though it may not have a route to 1.1.1.1. With that said, it is common to use a routable IP address as the RID because this can simplify operations by enabling pings or telnet to the RID.

You can specify only one RID, and the same value is used by all protocols that require a RID (OSPF, OSPFv3, and BGP). The current best practice is to base the

RID on the router's globally routable lo0 address. You explicitly configure a RID as follows:

```
[edit routing-options]
lab@PBR# set router-id 1.1.1.1

[edit routing-options]
lab@PBR# show
router-id 1.1.1.1;
```

When you explicitly configure a RID that is based on an address assigned to the router's lo0 interface, you will have to run an explicit IGP instance (typically passive) on that interface to advertise reachability to the RID, when desired. When a RID is not explicitly configured, the router obtains its RID from the primary address of the first interface that comes online. This is typically the loopback interface, when it has been assigned a nonmartian (non-127.0.0.1) address. Because changes in RID are disruptive to protocol operation, it's a good practice to manually configure a RID to ensure that changes to lo0 addressing do not cause unanticipated churn.

Historically, JUNOS software automatically advertised a stub route to the interface from which the RID is obtained. This meant that you did not need to run an IGP instance on the loopback interface to advertise reachability to the RID. Starting with JUNOS Release 8.5, this behavior has changed. Now, whether you use an explicit or an automatically generated RID that is lo0-based, you need to enable OSPF on the loopback interface to advertise reachability to the related loopback address, even when it is the source of an automatically selected RID.

Autonomous system number

An autonomous system (AS) number is required for BGP operation; you cannot commit a BGP-related configuration without also defining the local router's AS number. In this regard, it can be said that the AS number is not really protocol-independent, but for whatever reason it is configured under [routing-options], rather than under BGP itself.

Chapter 5 provides a detailed description of what an AS number is and how BGP uses it. The following is a sample AS number configuration:

```
lab@PBR# set autonomous-system ?
Possible completions:
  <as_number>        Autonomous system number (1..65535)
  loops              Maximum number of times this AS can be in an AS path
[edit routing-options]
lab@PBR# set autonomous-system 100

[edit routing-options]
lab@PBR# show
autonomous-system 100;
```

The loops option allows you to configure tolerance for occurrences of the local ASN in received route updates; normally such an occurrence indicates a BGP routing loop and results in the related route being discarded. There are certain corner-case scenarios, mostly related to VPNs and the support of EBGP on the PE-CE customer links, where you might need to alter the default value. Note that the default value of 1 indicates that a route with a single instance of the local ASN should be discarded. Therefore, to support reception of routes with a single instance of the local ASN, specify a loop value of 2.

Summary of Protocol-Independent Properties

This section discussed common PIPs that are typically used in enterprise networks. Topics included the creation of static, aggregate, and generated routes, along with their differences and associated various next hop options. Global preference, which is used to break ties between competing sources of routing information, was discussed, as was the configuration of a floating static route—which is simply a static route with an altered global preference that makes it less preferred than a route learned via a dynamic routing protocol. This section also described the use and purpose of the default JUNOS software route tables, and how RIBs and RIB groups are used to create and link route tables. We ended with a description of how the RID can be explicitly configured or automatically computed, in addition to how the local AS number is configured to support BGP operation.

The next section delves into JUNOS software routing policy, which provides you with complete control over route exchanges and attribute modification.

Routing Policy

This section details JUNOS software routing policy operation and configuration. The actual application of policy to solve some specific networking requirement is generally left to the protocol-specific coverage found in subsequent chapters. You configure policy-related options and statements at the [edit policy-options] hierarchy. Routing policy and firewall filters have a similar syntax in JUNOS software. The former deals with routes in the control plane, whereas the latter deals with packets in the data plane.

What Is a Routing Policy, and When Do I Need One?

Simply put, routing policy is used to:

- Control what routes are installed into the route table for possible selection as an active route
- Control what routes are exported from the route table, and into which protocols

• Alter attributes of routes, either at reception or at the time of advertisement to other peers

Given that routing policy is used to control the reception and transmission of routing information and to alter route attributes, it's safe to say that you need routing policy when the default policy does not meet your requirements.

The specifics of the various default policies are covered later, but to provide an example, consider that, by default, directly connected routes are not advertised into any routing protocol; in the case of RIP, not even when RIP is configured to run on those directly connected interfaces. If your goal is to get direct routes advertised into RIP, the default policy obviously does not meet your needs, and a custom policy must be written, and applied, to achieve your goal of redistributing direct routes into RIP.

Where and How Is Policy Applied?

You can apply policy in one of two places: either at import or at export. Generally speaking, use a command of the form set protocols *<protocol-name>* import to apply an import policy, or use set protocols *<protocol-name>* export to apply an export policy. Figure 3-2 illustrates this concept.

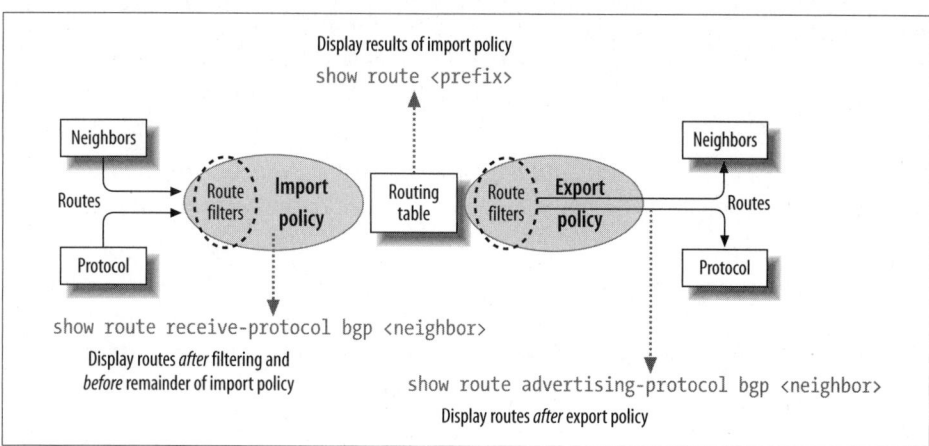

Figure 3-2. Policy application and monitoring points

Figure 3-2 shows routes being received through some protocol, and how import policy serves to filter and adjust route attributes before they are copied into the route table. In contrast, export policy comes into play when routes are being selected from the route table for inclusion in transmitted route updates. Once again, the export policy serves to filter and adjust route attributes to meet the specific needs of the networking environment.

It is worth noting that distance vector protocols such as BGP and RIP actually support the notion of received and transmitted routes. These protocols support the show route receiving-protocol <protocol-name> <neighbor-address> and show route advertising-protocol <protocol> <neighbor-address> commands, which are very useful when troubleshooting or analyzing policy operation. Figure 3-2 shows how the receiving-protocol form of the command is used to display routes *after* route filtering, but *before* attribute manipulation. In contrast, the advertising-protocol form of the command is executed after all export policy operations, including route filtering and attribute modification. Simply issue a show route <prefix> command to display a route as it exists in the route table, which will include any modified attributes resulting from import policy operations.

Applying policy to link state routing protocols

Link state (LS) protocols such as OSPF and IS-IS do not send and receive routes directly. Instead, they flood link-state advertisement (LSA) packets, which are used to build a topological database from which each router computes a route table. As such, LS protocols do not support much in the way of import policy. Support for OSPF import policies that prevent installation of external routes into the route table was only recently added; and supported in the 8.0 JUNOS software release; it's interesting to note that the current (8.5) documentation has not yet caught up, and still indicates that OSPF does not support application of import policy (for more information, see *http://www.juniper.net/techpubs/software/junos/junos85/swconfig85-policy/id-10148641.html#jN1272A*). Documentation PR 262917 was raised to get this corrected, by the way.

If you wish to filter LSAs, protocol-specific mechanisms are required to ensure that LS database consistency is maintained. Chapter 4 covers the concepts of OSPF stub areas and LSA filtering.

You can apply export policy to an LS protocol to effect route redistribution, but the external route is still flooded in an LSA rather than being sent outright; the result is that the show route receiving protocol and show route-advertising protocol commands are not effective when dealing with LS protocols.

When you apply policy to an LS protocol, you do so globally, which is to say the policy is not applied to particular interfaces or areas. In the case of OSPF, you apply export policy at the [edit protocol ospf] hierarchy:

```
[edit protocols ospf]
lab@PBR# show
export test_export; ## 'test_export' is not defined
```

The CLI warning provides a nice reminder that the related test_export policy does not yet exist. Because the presence (or absence) or a policy can have a dramatic effect on overall network operation, you will not be able to commit a configuration with this type of omission. You can define a policy that is never applied—but once applied, the policy must exist before you can commit the changes.

Applying policy to BGP and RIP

Both BGP and RIP support the application of import and export policy, and both support policy application at different hierarchies. Focusing on BGP for the moment, you can apply a policy at one of three different hierarchies—global, group, or neighbor. The following code snippet provides an example of this concept:

```
[edit protocols bgp]
lab@PBR# show
export global_export;
group internal {
    export internal_export;
    neighbor 1.1.1.1 {
        export neighbor_1.1.1.1_export;
    }
    neighbor 2.2.2.2;
}
group other {
    neighbor 3.3.3.3;
}
```

In this example, a policy named global_export is applied at the global level, another policy named internal_export is applied at the group level, and yet a third policy named neighbor_1.1.1.1_export is applied at the neighbor level.

A key point, and one that is often misunderstood and that can lead to problems, is that in such a configuration, *only* the most explicit policy is applied. A neighbor-level policy is more explicit than a group-level policy, which in turn is more explicit than a global policy. Hence, neighbor 1.1.1.1 is subjected only to the neighbor_1.1.1.1_export policy, whereas neighbor 2.2.2.2, lacking anything more specific, is subjected only to the internal_export policy. Meanwhile, neighbor 3.3.3.3 in group other has no group- or neighbor-level policy, so it uses the global_export policy.

So, what if you need to have neighbor 1.1.1.1 perform the function of all three policies? Simple—you could write and apply a new neighbor-level policy that encompasses the functions of the other three, or simply apply all three *existing* policies, as a chain, to neighbor 1.1.1.1. Note the use of brackets in the following command to open a set of values; if desired, each policy can be specified individually:

```
[edit protocols bgp group internal]
lab@PBR# set neighbor 1.1.1.1 export [global-export internal_export]

[edit protocols bgp]
lab@PBR# show group internal neighbor 1.1.1.1
export [ neighbor_1.1.1.1_export global_export internal_export];
```

As with access control lists (ACLs) or firewall filters, chained policy statements are evaluated in a specific left-to-right order and only up to the point when a route is either accepted or rejected. As a result, you must consider factors such as whether a policy makes use of a match-all deny term at its end, which is common for a standalone policy. However, when applied at the front of a policy chain, the match-all aspect of such a policy prevents route processing by any remaining policies. To help illustrate this point, consider two policies, one named *deny*, which denies all, and another named *accept*, which accepts all. Given the nature of the two policies, you will see a dramatic difference between these two policy chains, even though they are composed of the same parts:

```
export [accept deny];
export [deny accept];
```

Here, the first policy chain results in *all* routes being *accepted*, whereas the reverse application results in *all* routes being *denied*. You can use the CLI's insert feature to rearrange the order of applied policies, or simply delete and reapply the policies to get the order needed. Note that a newly applied policy always takes the leftmost place in a policy chain, where it becomes the first in line for route evaluation.

 We covered a few critical points here, so much so that they bear repeating in another form. The first point is that when multiple policies are applied at different CLI hierarchies for the same protocol, only the most specific application is evaluated, to the exclusion of other, less specific policy applications. Second, a given route is evaluated against a chain of policies starting with the leftmost policy, up until the route meets a terminating action of either accept or reject. This leads to ordering sensitivity of both terms within a policy, and for policies when they are chained together.

Although these points always seem to make sense when you are learning them, they are somehow easily forgotten during router configuration, when two policies that individually worked as expected suddenly break when they are combined, or when you mistakenly believe that a neighbor-level policy is combined with a global or group-level policy, only to find that your policy behavior is not as anticipated.

Policy Components

Generally speaking, a policy statement consists of one or more named terms, each consisting of two parts: a from statement that defines a set of match criteria, and a corresponding then statement that specifies the set of actions to be performed for matching traffic. It is possible to create a policy with a single term, in which case the term can be unnamed, such as in these two examples:

```
[edit policy-options]
lab@PBR# show
policy-statement explicit_term {
    term 1 {
        from protocol direct;
        then accept;
    }
```

```
    }
    policy-statement implict_term {
        from protocol direct;
        then accept;
    }
```

The two policy statements perform identical functions; both have a match criterion of direct, and both have an associated action of accept. The explicit term format is generally preferred, because new terms can be added without the need to redefine the existing term. Note that any new terms are added to the end of the policy statement, as shown here, where, oddly enough, a new term named new is added to the explict_term policy statement:

```
[edit policy-options]
lab@PBR# set policy-statement explicit_term term new from protocol direct

[edit policy-options]
lab@PBR# set policy-statement explicit_term term new then reject

[edit policy-options]
lab@PBR# show policy-statement explicit_term
term 1 {
    from protocol direct;
    then accept;
}
term new {
    from protocol direct;
    then reject;
}
```

As with policy chains, term ordering within a policy is significant. In the example, explicit_term policy, term 1, and term new are diametrically opposed, with one accepting and the other denying the same set of direct routes. Although making little practical sense, it does afford the opportunity to demonstrate term resequencing with the insert function:

```
[edit policy-options]
lab@PBR# edit policy-statement explicit_term

[edit policy-options policy-statement explicit_term]
lab@PBR# insert term new before term 1

[edit policy-options policy-statement explicit_term]
lab@PBR# show
term new {
    from protocol direct;
    then reject;
}
term 1 {
    from protocol direct;
    then accept;
}
```

There is no practical limit to the number of terms that can be specified in a single policy, or to how many policies can be chained together.

Logical OR and AND functions within terms

It's possible to define a term with multiple match criteria defined under a single `from` statement. For a match to occur, all of the `from` conditions must be met, which is a logical AND. However, for a specific match type, such as `protocol`, you can specify multiple values, in which case each protocol match condition functions as a logical OR. Consider this example:

```
[edit policy-options]
lab@PBR# show
policy-statement test {
    term 1 {
        from {
            protocol [ bgp rip ]; ##logical OR within brackets
            interface fe-0/0/0.0; ## logical AND with other match criteria
        }
        then next term;
    }
}
```

In this case, a match will occur when a route is learned over the `fe-0/0/0` interface *and* is learned from BGP *or* RIP.

Policy Match Criteria and Actions

JUNOS software policy provides a rich set of criteria you can match against, and an equally rich set of actions that can be performed as a result of a match. The various match and action functions are well documented, so the goal here is not to re-create the wheel by rehashing each option—as noted at the beginning of this chapter, the object is to acquaint you with a box of tools; later chapters will provide specific examples of those tools being used.

Policy match criteria

The list of available match criteria is long in the JUNOS software 8.0 release:

```
lab@PBR# set policy-statement test term 1 from ?
Possible completions:
  aggregate-contributor  Match more specifics of an aggregate
+ apply-groups           Groups from which to inherit configuration data
+ apply-groups-except    Don't inherit configuration data from these groups
  area                   OSPF area identifier
+ as-path                Name of AS path regular expression (BGP only)
+ as-path-group          Name of AS path group (BGP only)
  color                  Color (preference) value
  color2                 Color (preference) value 2
+ community              BGP community
> external               External route
```

```
    family
    instance           Routing protocol instance
  + interface          Interface name or address
    level              IS-IS level
    local-preference   Local preference associated with a route
    metric             Metric value
    metric2            Metric value 2
    metric3            Metric value 3
    metric4            Metric value 4
  > multicast-scope    Multicast scope to match
  + neighbor           Neighboring router
  + next-hop           Next-hop router
    origin             BGP origin attribute
  + policy             Name of policy to evaluate
    preference         Preference value
    preference2        Preference value 2
  > prefix-list        List of prefix-lists of routes to match
  > prefix-list-filter List of prefix-list-filters to match
  + protocol           Protocol from which route was learned
    rib                Routing table
  > route-filter       List of routes to match
    route-type         Route type
  > source-address-filter  List of source addresses to match
  + tag                Tag string
    tag2               Tag string 2
```

The key takeaway here is that you can match on things such as interface, protocol, route tag, AS path, communities, source address, metric, and so on. Route filtering based on prefix and mask length is performed with the route-filter keyword. There is significant power (and complexity) in router filtering, and it is covered in the section "Route Filters," later in this chapter.

Policy actions

When a match occurs, a wide range of actions are available:

```
[edit policy-options]
lab@PBR# set policy-statement test term 1 then ?
Possible completions:
    accept             Accept a route
  + apply-groups       Groups from which to inherit configuration data
  + apply-groups-except Don't inherit configuration data from these groups
  > as-path-expand     Prepend AS numbers prior to adding local-as (BGP only)
    as-path-prepend    Prepend AS numbers to an AS path (BGP only)
    class              Set class-of-service parameters
  > color              Color (preference) value
  > color2             Color (preference) value 2
  > community          BGP community properties associated with a route
    cos-next-hop-map   Set CoS-based next-hop map in forwarding table
    damping            Define BGP route flap damping parameters
    default-action     Set default policy action
  > external           External route
    forwarding-class   Set source or destination class in forwarding table
```

```
> install-nexthop      Choose the next hop to be used for forwarding
> load-balance         Type of load balancing in forwarding table
> local-preference     Local preference associated with a route
> metric               Metric value
> metric2              Metric value 2
> metric3              Metric value 3
> metric4              Metric value 4
  next                 Skip to next policy or term
> next-hop             Set the address of the next-hop router
  origin               BGP path origin
> preference           Preference value
> preference2          Preference value 2
  reject               Reject a route
> tag                  Tag string
> tag2                 Tag string 2
  trace                Log matches to a trace file
```

Actions include AS path prepending, changing route color (internal tie-breaker), evoking damping, altering local preference, specifying metric and community, altering a packet's forwarding class, adding a route tag, and so forth. Key actions include accept and reject, which are termination actions. The next keyword allows you to skip to the next term, or policy in the chain, and it is useful for shunting routes from one term or policy into another.

Route Filters

The ability to match on specific routes to accept or reject them or to modify some attribute is a critical aspect of virtually any networking scenario. The majority of JUNOS software routing policy strikes most users as intuitive and logical, given the easy-to-follow *if, then* construct of policy syntax.

The exception always seems to be route filtering, because to truly understand how this is performed in JUNOS software, you must first understand the binary radix tree nature of the route lookup table and how the binary tree is used in conjunction with route filters.

Binary trees

Binary trees have been used in computer science for several decades as a way to quickly locate a desired bit of information. In the case of route lookup, the goal is to quickly find the longest match for some prefix, with the corresponding next hop being the information that is sought. The Juniper Networks implementation of a binary tree is called the J-Tree, and it forms the basis of both route lookup and policy-based route filtering. Figure 3-3 shows the root of a binary tree, along with a few of its branches.

Figure 3-3 shows a binary to powers of a decimal chart, to help with understanding the structure of the J-Tree. For example, the binary sequence 0100 000 equates to a decimal 64, whereas 0110 0000 codes a decimal 96. In this example, bit 8, which has

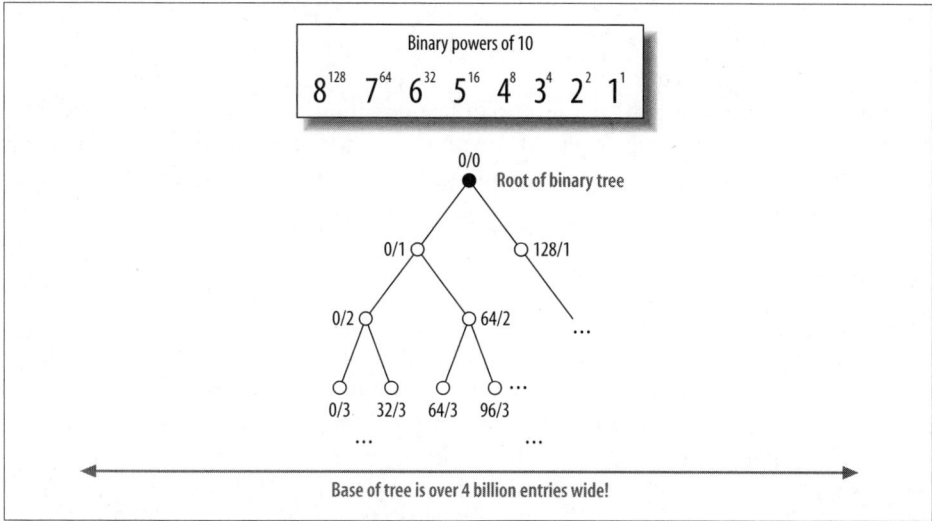

Figure 3-3. A binary tree

the decimal power of 128, represents the second set of nodes from the top of the tree. The top of the tree represents no bit, and the first pair of nodes down represents a test of the MSB, which is bit 8 in this example, as either 0 (0), or 1 (128).

The binary tree is based on nodes that test the state of a particular bit that makes up the 32-bit IP address or route prefix. The bit being tested is indicated by the related prefix (mask) length. For example, the top of the tree is testing no bits, as indicated by the /0 prefix length. All prefixes match when you do not bother to test any bits, so the top of the tree effectively represents a default route, which is to say when no other patterns match you are guaranteed to match the first node. Whether such a match, actually results in forwarding depends on whether a default route has been installed, but that is another story.

The tree branches to the left when a given bit is a 0, and it branches to the right for a 1. As a result, the first two nodes below the root represent the state of the most significant bit in the most significant byte, which is either a 0 or a 1. If it is a 0, you have a 0/1 match, which codes a decimal 0. If that bit is a 1, you have a 1/1 match, which codes a decimal 128. Each node then branches out, based on the test of the next bit, until you reach the bottom of the tree, which represents a test of all 32 bits (which is *sometimes* necessary when doing a route lookup or route filter that is based on a /32 prefix length).

In actual operation, the J-Tree is optimized and can quickly jump to a longest match when other portions of the tree are eliminated. It could be said that the act of finding a longest match against a binary tree is not so much finding what you seek as it is quickly eliminating all that cannot be what you want, and then simply looking at what is left. By way of example, a 32-bit IP address can take more than 4 billion combinations.

However, half of these (2 billion) will have a 0 in the high-order bit position, whereas the other half will have a 1. By simply testing the status of one bit, you have effectively eliminated one-half of the tree as not being possible to match. With each subsequent bit test eliminating one-half of the remaining possibilities, you quickly arrive at a node that either matches all 32 bits of the prefix, or does not match the prefix being evaluated, in which case you back up one node. That is the longest match for this prefix.

Route filters and match types

When you configure a route filter, you specify a starting prefix and initial prefix length, and then include a match type to indicate whether routes with prefixes longer than the initial value should be considered as matching. Put another way, a route filter is based on a match against the specified prefix bits, as based on the provided mask, in addition to the overall mask length of the prefix being evaluated. As such, it can be said that a Juniper route filter cares as much about the prefix *length* as it does the *prefix itself*.

Figure 3-4 illustrates the supported `route-filter` match types in the context of a J-Tree; it was said before, and is stated here again, that you cannot effectively use route filters if you do not first understand the operation of the J-Tree. This is especially true for the through match type, which 99.9% of the time is applied incorrectly, and therefore does *not* do what the operator wanted.

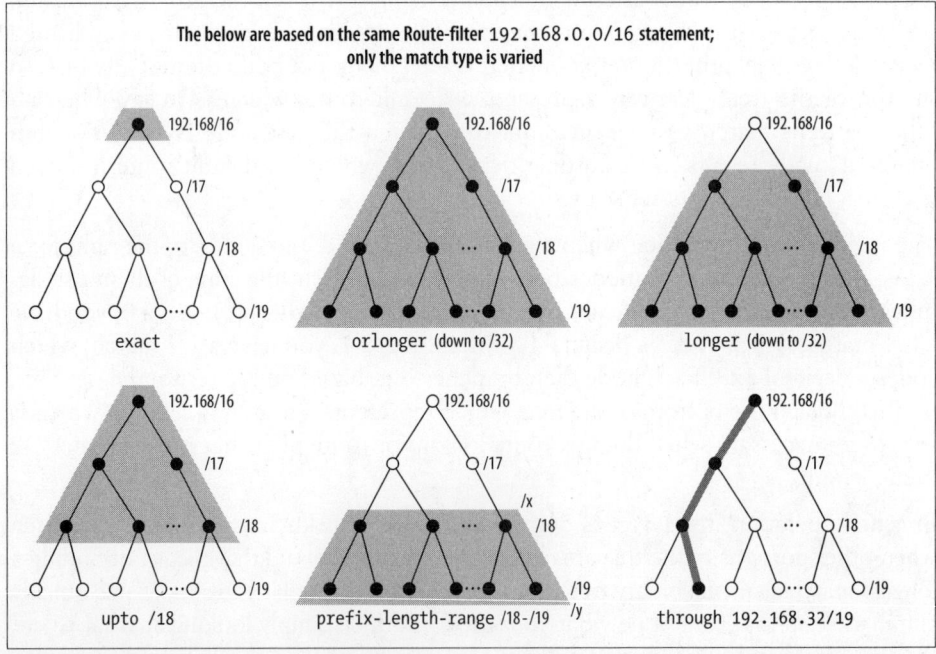

Figure 3-4. Route filter match types and the J-Tree

Figure 3-4 is based on a portion of the J-Tree that represents route 192.168/16. Entries below the starting node all share the same high-order 16 bits of 192.168, but differ from the root prefix in that they have longer mask lengths, as shown by the two nodes below the first, each of which is testing bit 17, therefore indicating a /17 mask length.

Each route filter match type is described against the corresponding portion of the figure:

exact

> The exact match type is just what it sounds like. To match with exact, both the initial prefix bits must match, and the prefix length must be equal to the value specified. If the prefix bits do not match, or if the prefix length is either shorter or longer, the exact match type does not match. Figure 3-4 shows that route filter 192.168.0.0/16 exact matches only on that node of the J-Tree, to the exclusion of all others.

or-longer

> The or-longer match type matches the specified prefix and initial mask length and matches on prefixes with longer mask lengths when they share the same high-order bits, as indicated by the specified prefix. In this example, the result is a match against 192.168.0.0/16 itself, as well as 192.168.0/17 and 192.168.128/18 and all longer mask lengths, up to /32.

longer

> The longer match type excludes the exact match and catches all routes with the same prefix bits, but only when their masks are longer than the prefix length specified. The difference between or-longer and longer is shown in Figure 3-4, where the latter excludes the exact match, which is prefix 192.168.0.0/16 in this case.

upto

> The upto match type matches against the initial prefix and mask length, as well as matching prefixes with masks that are longer than the initial value, upto the ending mask length value. In the example, the initial prefix of 192.168.0.0/16 matches, as well as all other 192.168 prefixes that have mask lengths upto the specified value, which is 18 in this example. Therefore, 192.168.192/18 will match, whereas 192.168.1/24 will not.

prefix-length-range

> The prefix-length-range match type matches against routes with the same prefix as specified in the initial mask length, but only when the associated mask falls between the starting and ending values. The result is that the exact match is excluded, whereas routes with the same high-order prefix bits, but masks that fall within the specified range, are accepted. This match type is especially useful when the goal is to filter the route based on mask length alone, which is a common policy within service provider networks, as many refuse to carry routes with

masks longer than 28 in an effort to keep route table size manageable. To prevent installation of any route with a mask length longer than /28, you can use a route-filter 0/0 prefix-length-range /28-/32 reject statement. Because the initial prefix length is 0, all prefix values match, making the decision to reject one that is based strictly on mask length.

 It's worth noting that route-filter syntax supports a short form of action linking, in which the related then action can be specified directly on the route-filter line. Functionally there is no difference between the short form and adding an explicit then action.

through

The through match type is generally misunderstood, and it rarely works the way folks think it should. This is not to say that it is broken, but it has led to this somewhat humorous rule of thumb: "When you are thinking of using through, think again." In most cases, when people use through, what they wanted is more of the upto or prefix-length-range type of match. The statement is intended to warn the user that in most cases, through is not what you really want, and that the decision to use it should be carefully thought, pardon the pun, through.

A through match type matches the initial prefix and mask length exactly, as well as the ending prefix and mask length, and matches on the *contiguous* set of nodes between the two points. The through match type was originally offered to meet a corner case, in which a customer was found to be using 32 exact matches, all based on some form of a default route. Although a true default is 0/0, the customer wanted to ensure that they did not install any 0.0.0.0 prefixes, regardless of mask length. So, rather than a 0.0 exact, 0/1 exact, 0/2 exact ... 0/32 exact, the through match type was created to allow the same effect with a single 0/0 through 0/32 statement. This matches the top of the tree, all the way down the left side to the very bottom, and all contiguous points in between.

In Figure 3-4, the through match type is specified as 192.168.0.0/16 through 192.168.32.0/19. The line shows the sequence of contiguous matches between the two points, which in this case includes 192.168.0.0/16, 192.168.0.0/17, 192.168.0.0/18, and 192.168.32.0/19. Now ask yourself (and be honest) is this what you expected a 192.168/16 through 192.168.32/19 to match?

Longest match wins, but may not.... As with routing in general, route filter processing is based on finding a longest match, and then performing the action associated with that match. There are cases where this may lead to unexpected behavior because users do not always take into account the consequences of different match types. Recall that the longest-match function is based on the high-order prefix bits, whereas the match type focuses more on mask length. Consider this route-filter example, and what will happen when route 200.0.67.0/24 is evaluated against it:

```
[edit policy-options policy-statement test_me]
user@host# show
from {
    route-filter 200.0.0.0/16 longer reject;
    route-filter 200.0.67.0/24 longer;
    route-filter 200.0.0.0/8 orlonger accept;
}
then {
    metric 10;
    accept;
}
```

The question is, will route 200.0.67.0/24 match this term, and if so, is it accepted, is it rejected, or does it have its metric set to 10 before being accepted? Think carefully, and consider how longest matching is performed, along with how the match type comes into play.

If you answered "The route does not match, and is neither accepted, nor rejected, and no metric modification is made," give yourself a well-deserved pat on the back. It's quite OK if you answered differently—this little tidbit alone may well justify the expenditure for this book (you did pay for this book, right?). The key here is that the longest match, as based on specified prefix, is against the second route-filter statement—here the first 24 bits of the prefix do in fact match 200.0.67/24, which is more exact than either 200/8 or 200.0/16. However, the longest match in this example has a match type of longer, meaning that only a route with a mask length of /25–/32 with the 24 high-order bits set to 200.0.67 is considered to match.

Because this route has a mask length that is equal to the value specified, it does not match. A given route is only evaluated against the longest match in a given term. This is to say that if the longest match ends up not really matching, as shown in this example, other route-filter statements within that same term are not evaluated. Instead, the route falls through to the next term or policy—or lacking any of those, to the default policy for the routing protocol in question.

Default Policies

The last hurdle in understanding JUNOS software policy is to be familiar with the default policy associated with each protocol used in your network. Understanding the default policy is important because it ultimately decides the fate of any route that is not matched against in your user-defined policy. Some operators rely on the default policy to do something, and others prefer to ensure that their policy is written to match on *all* possible routes, which means the default policy is negated because it never gets a chance to come into play.

OSPF (and IS-IS) default policy

The default import policy for LS protocols is to accept all routes learned through that protocol. Recent JUNOS software releases support explicit import policy, but only for OSPF, and then *only* to filter external routes from being installed into the route table. Such an import policy does not filter external route LSAs from the database, however.

The default LS export policy is to reject everything. LSA flooding is not affected by export policy, and it is used to convey routing in an indirect manner in an LS protocol. The result of this flooding is the advertisement of local interfaces that are enabled to run OSPF, as well as the readvertisement (flooding) of LSAs received from other routers.

RIP default policy

The default RIP import policy is to accept all received RIP routes that pass a sanity check. In contrast, the default export policy is to advertise no routes. None, zip, nada, zilch. Not even RIP learned routes are advertised with the default RIP export policy. Although it may be an odd choice of default behavior, the net effect is that for any practical RIP deployment, you will need to create and apply a custom export policy to readvertise RIP learned and direct routes for interfaces running RIP to other RIP speakers.

BGP default policy

The default BGP import policy is to accept all received BGP routes that pass a sanity check—for example, those routes that do not have an AS loop, as indicated by the AS path attribute.

The default BGP export policy is to readvertise all learned BGP routes to all BGP speakers, while obeying protocol-specific rules that prohibit one IBGP speaker from readvertising routes learned from another IBGP speaker, unless it is functioning as a route reflector.

Advanced Policy Concepts

Congratulations. You have made it to this point, and therefore you now possess an in-depth and practical understanding of routing policy. This section explores some advanced policy concepts, some of which are quite interesting but rarely used. The use of regular expressions (regexes) is treated as an advanced topic, but differs from the remaining topics because the use of AS path or community regex matching is somewhat common, especially in large networks such as those operated by service providers.

Testing policy results

Making a mistake in a route-filter statement can have a dramatic impact on network stability, security, and overall operation. For example, consider the operator that does not notice that, in the following policy example (appropriately called whoops), rather than adding the then accept to term 1, as intended, the accept action is mistakenly added as part of a final, *unnamed* term. Because this term has no from statement, it matches on *all* possible routes and routing sources!

```
[edit policy-options]
lab@Wheat# show policy-statement whoops
term 1 {
    from {
        route-filter 0.0.0.0/0 prefix-length-range /8-/24;
    }
}
then accept; ###this action is part of an unnamed match all term!
```

Applying a broken policy such as this in a production network that deals with multiple live BGP feeds could result in network meltdown when all routes, rather than the expected subset, are suddenly advertised within your network.

JUNOS software offers a test policy feature that is designed to avoid this type of problem. You use the test command to filter routes through the identified policy to determine which routes are accepted (those displayed) versus rejected.

The test policy command is primarily useful for route-filter testing. You cannot test route redistribution policies, because the default policy for a policy test is to *accept all* protocol sources. This means that a given route filter policy might match against static routes, but the same policy when applied to BGP may *not* result in the advertisement of the same static routes. This is because the default policy for BGP does not accept static routes, whereas the default for the test policy does. As an example, consider this policy:

```
[edit policy-options]
lab@Wheat# show policy-statement test_route_filter
term 1 {
    from {
        route-filter 0.0.0.0/2 orlonger;
    }
    then next policy;
}
term 2 {
    then reject;
}
```

With the test_route_filter policy shown, the test policy command will match on and accept static, direct, OSPF, BGP, and routes that match the route filter (routes in the range of 0–63), while the same policy applied to BGP results in the advertisement of only BGP routes that match the filter. Again, this is because the matching routes are not explicitly accepted by the test_route_filter policy in this example, and would therefore be subjected to the default policy for BGP.

A number of static routes that range from 0–192 have been added to router Wheat. The test_route_filter policy is run against these routes:

```
lab@Wheat> test policy test_route_filter 82.137.128.0/18

Policy test_route_filter: 0 prefix accepted, 1 prefix rejected
```

The result confirms that a prefix outside the range of 0–63 is rejected:

```
lab@Wheat> test policy test_route_filter 6.1.0.0/16

inet.0: 815 destinations, 1500 routes (815 active, 0 holddown, 0 hidden)
+ = Active Route, - = Last Active, * = Both

6.1.0.0/16          *[Static/5] 00:44:51
                     Discard

Policy test_route_filter: 1 prefix accepted, 0 prefix rejected
```

This result confirms that a prefix inside the range of 0–63 is accepted. To test against all possible routes, use 0/0:

```
lab@Wheat> test policy test_route_filter 0/0

inet.0: 815 destinations, 1500 routes (815 active, 0 holddown, 0 hidden)
+ = Active Route, - = Last Active, * = Both

6.1.0.0/16          *[Static/5] 00:45:05
                     Discard
6.2.0.0/22          *[Static/5] 00:45:05
                     Discard
. . .
10.0.0.0/8          *[BGP/170] 20:42:56, localpref 100
                      AS path: 1282 I
                     > to 172.16.1.2 via fe-0/0/0.412
                     [BGP/170] 20:42:44, localpref 80
                      AS path: 666 1282 I
                     > to 172.16.2.2 via fe-0/0/0.423
12.0.48.0/20        *[Static/5] 00:45:05
                     Discard
. . .
                     Discard
63.207.252.0/22     *[Static/5] 00:45:05
                     Discard

Policy test_route_filter: 58 prefix accepted, 759 prefix rejected
```

The output confirms that both static and BGP routes are matching the route-filter in the test_route_filter policy. Note again that the policy being tested does not have an explicit accept action, and instead uses the next policy for matching routes; the acceptance in this case is the result of the default accept-all policy for the test policy. It's worth stating again that the same policy applied to BGP will advertise only BGP routes that match the filter, unless you add an explicit accept action to the first term.

Community and AS path regex matching

Complete coverage of regex matching is outside the scope of this book. The reader should consult technical documentation for a full description of the supported matching operators (e.g., *http://www.juniper.net/techpubs/software/junos/junos85/ swconfig85-policy/id-10256235.html#id-10256235*, which describes AS path regex matching).

Here are some general things to be aware of when dealing with regex matching:

- Regex matching provides a powerful tool to filter routes based on virtually any conceivable pattern of AS path or community attributes.

- In JUNOS software, community regex matching is POSIX 1003.2-compliant. In contrast, AS path regex matching is not, because in an AS path regex, a dot, . (the wildcard character), represents an entire AS number, rather than an atom or specific digit in the AS number.

- You can test your regular expression syntax against routes *already* present in the route table using a show route community *<community-regex>* or show route aspath-regex *<as-path-regex>* command. Once you feel the expression syntax results in the matches you expect, you can write a policy that uses the same regex.

- To use a community of AS path regexes in a policy, you must first define the regex using a symbolic name, which is then referenced in the policy.

The following example demonstrates a basic AS path regex:

```
[edit policy-options]
lab@PBR# show
policy-statement as_path_filter {
    term 1 {
        from {
            protocol bgp;
            as-path sample_as_regex;
        }
        then reject;
    }
}
as-path sample_as_regex "^. 1234 . 1111$";
```

Note that the symbolic name sample_as_regex is defined outside of any particular policy statement. In this example, the specified regex will match when the associated route has an AS path consisting of exactly four entries. The AS path can begin with any AS number, as indicated by the . wildcard (a wildcard matches a complete AS number in JUNOS software). The second AS number has to be 1234 and can be followed by any other AS number, but the final AS number entry must be 1111 to match. The ^ and $ characters are anchors, which force the initial and final matches to be against the beginning and end of the line, respectively.

The as_path_filter policy statement makes use of the defined AS path regex by matching against it in term 1. Here the result of an AS path regex match is rejection.

Here is a community regex matching example:

```
[edit policy-options]
lab@PBR# show
policy-statement community_regex_test {
    term 1 {
        from community comm_regex;
        then accept;
    }
}
community comm_regex members "^(.*):(.*)1:(11.1)(.*):(.*)$";
```

In this example, the comm_regex expression is written to match on a sequence of three community strings, but only when the first is from any AS number and any community value, and the second is from AS 1 with a community value of 11x1, where the x represents any decimal value between 0 and 9. This example shows that for community regex matching, the . wildcard represents a single digit, rather than a complete AS number, as was the case with AS path regex matching. Lastly, a match occurs in this example only when the first two matches are followed by a third community value, and like the first, respectively). Note that because communities are acted upon as a single value, rather than as a sequence or set (as is the case with AS matching), you cannot easily match against a community list based on some specific count, as you can with an AS regex. As a result, in this example the beginning and end of line markers (^ and $, respectively), do not result in a match occurring when exactly three matching communities are present. In fact, in this case a string of 10 communities will match as long as any three consecutive values match the regex.

Additional details and examples of community regex matching are available at *http://www.juniper.net/techpubs/software/junos/junos85/swconfig85-policy/id-10223306.html#id-10223306.*

Policy subroutines (nesting)

Routes that match a given term in a policy can reference another policy as the associated action. The policy is called a policy *subroutine*, or a *nested policy*. This is a powerful capability that allows you to build modular policies that, rather than being applied as a policy chain, are called from within a master policy.

A common usage of a policy subroutine takes the form of a martian or bogon filter. Rather than applying the same martian filter as part of each policy chain, or rather than adding the complete martian filter logic to every policy you write, you could simply have a term in all your policies that calls the martian policy as a subroutine.

The key to effectively using policy subroutines lies in understanding the result code that is handed back from the calling policy by the called policy. Figure 3-5 illustrates policy subroutine behavior.

In Figure 3-5, things begin in the upper left, where a route is handed to the *master* or *calling policy* for evaluation. In this example, the first term in the calling policy has a match criterion specifying from policy <sub-routine-name>. This directive evokes the

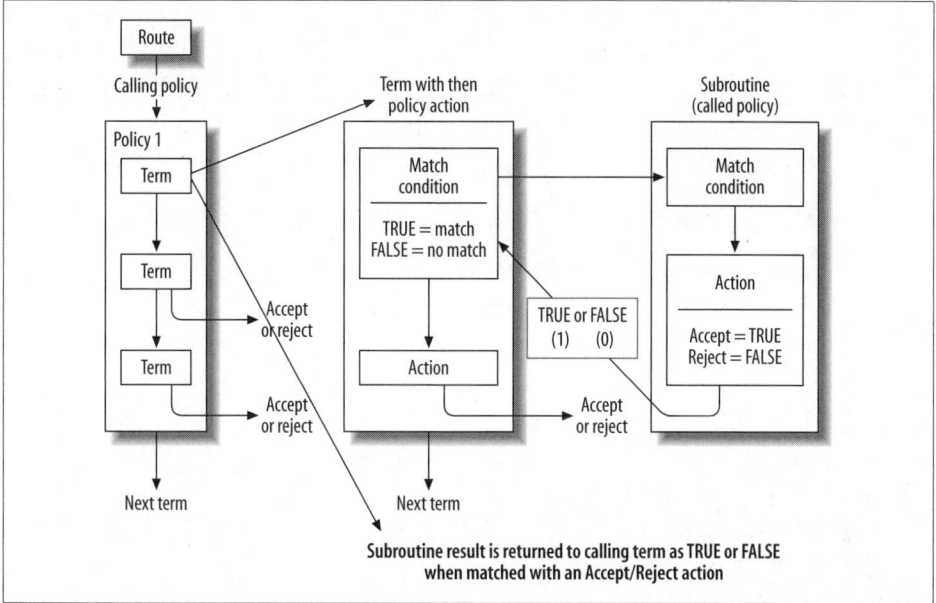

Figure 3-5. *Policy subroutines*

called policy for route evaluation; meanwhile, the main policy suspends its processing pending a result code that is handed back to the calling policy once the called policy completes its evaluation.

When the called policy/subroutine completes its evaluation, the result is either a 1 or a 0. Here, the former indicates an accept action by the called policy, and the latter represents a reject action. When the result code is handed back to the calling policy, a 1 is interpreted as a positive match, which results in the execution of the calling term's then action. A return of 0 indicates no match, and policy processing continues with the next term.

> For reliable operation, you must make sure that all policy subroutines match *all* routes with either an accept or a reject action.
>
> You will encounter inconsistent behavior with policy subroutines if the subroutine is not written to match against *all* possible routes. This is because when a route is not matched, the subroutine cannot perform an accept or a reject action, and therefore returns an empty value to the calling policy. The lack of a definitive result from the called policy often leads to unpredictable operation in the calling policy.

Boolean grouping

We covered the use of policy chains previously—a policy chain is a grouping of policies that are evaluated in sequence until an accept or reject action is encountered. JUNOS software also supports policy expressions, which provide Boolean grouping functionality. This is a fancy way to say you can logically AND, OR, or NOT a given policy. You can find details on policy expressions at *http://www.juniper.net/techpubs/software/junos/junos85/swconfig85-policy/id-10418934.html#id-10418934*.

By way of an example, consider the following policy:

```
[edit policy-options]
lab@PBR# show
policy-statement community_regex_test {
    term 1 {
        from community comm_regex;
        then accept;
    }
}
community comm_regex members "^(.*):(.*)1:(11.1)(.*):(.*)$";
```

As previously described, this policy matches on, and as a result, accepts routes with a particular community sequence. What do you feel will happen if a community_regex_test policy is applied as an import with a Boolean NOT?

```
[edit protocols bgp]
lab@PBR# set import (!community_regex_test)

[edit protocols bgp]
lab@PBR# show
import ( ! community_regex_test );
```

If you guessed that all routes that were formerly accepted will now be rejected, you are correct. The Boolean NOT inverts the results of policy evaluation, changing an accept (1) to a reject (0), and vice versa.

As a final example, consider this policy expression:

```
[edit protocols ospf]
lab@PBR# show
export ( policy1 && policy2 );
```

The use of the logical AND indicates that for a route to be exported into OSPF, it must be evaluated as true by *both* policy1 and policy2. Any route that is evaluated as false or rejected by either policy is not considered viable for export into OSPF.

Summary of Routing Policy

We just detailed JUNOS software routing policy. The policy framework provides a consistent and easy-to-fathom environment for all of your route-exchange and attribute-manipulation needs. Although route filters and the whole J-Tree thing can be a bit daunting when first encountered, the overall logic of a JUNOS policy is easy to follow, and the consistent way in which they are applied to routing protocols makes network administration that much easier. With Juniper policy rather than a collection of network statements, default-information-originate statements, distribute lists, route maps, and so on, you create and advertise a static route into OSPF, or BGP, or RIP, using the same approach and syntax.

Advanced features such as regex-based AS path and community matching, policy subroutines, and policy expressions ensure that you can never run out of creative and elegant ways to meet your network's policy goals.

This section also covered the commands and procedures used to monitor and debug the operation of your import and export policies.

Conclusion

JUNOS software PIPs and routing policy may not be very sexy by themselves, but together they form the foundation of virtually all sophisticated network configurations.

The PIP toolbox provides many useful tools that allow you to create static and aggregate routes, create and group route tables, and alter protocol preferences. Routing policy provides a powerful and consistent set of rules and syntax that supplies fine-grained control over the exchange of routes, along with modification of route attributes. Once you understand the basic concepts of import and export policy, you quickly come to appreciate the elegance of being able to perform similar tasks on different protocols, using the same policy framework, rather than a collection of mechanisms such as route maps, distribute lists, network statements, and so on, which may or may not work in a given protocol context.

When combined, PIP and policy yield a powerful mechanism that enables you to bend a network's operation to suit your will. The skills and concepts covered in this chapter are demonstrated throughout the remainder of this book, in various real-world and practical scenarios.

Exam Topics

We examined the following Enterprise Exam Topics in this chapter:

- PIPs:
  - Identify static, aggregate, and generated routes.
  - Describe the configuration of static routes.
  - Describe the purpose of the default JUNOS software route tables.
  - Describe global route preference and the concept of a floating static route.
- Routing policy:
  - Identify the two types of policy application.
  - Identify policy components (terms, match conditions, actions, and policy chains).
  - Identify points where routing policy may be applied.
  - Describe the processing of routing policies.
  - Evaluate the result of a given routing policy.

Chapter Review Questions

1. After defining an aggregate route for 0/0, you note that the M7i's system board CPU utilization increases. What might account for this?

    a. The default route is attracting traffic that is not specifically matched, leading to a reject action and corresponding ICMP error packet generation

    b. The default route is attracting traffic that is not specifically matched, leading to discard and ICMP error packet generation

    c. The default route is attracting traffic that matches more specific prefixes and is being forwarded, hence the increased CPU usage

    d. The default route is attracting traffic that matches more specific prefixes and is being dropped, hence the increased CPU usage

2. Which of the following defines a floating static route that backs up an OSPF externally learned route?

    a. Set static route 1.1.10/24, next hop t1-0/0/2

    b. Set static route 1.1.10/24, next hop t1-0/0/2, preference 11

    c. Set static route 1.1.10/24, next hop t1-0/0/2, preference 151

    d. Set static route 1.1.10/24, next hop t1-0/0/2, qualified next hop

    e. None of the above

3. You issue the command set routing-options autonomous-system loops 3. What does it do?

    a. Tolerates as many as three instances of the local AS number in transmitted route updates

    b. Tolerates as many as three instances of the local AS number in received route updates

    c. Tolerates as many as two instances of the local AS number in transmitted route updates

    d. Tolerates as many as two instances of the local AS number in received route updates

4. After defining a generated route for 10/8, you find that the route is inactive, despite having interfaces that are locally numbered from the 10.*x.x*.0/24 space. What could account for this?

    a. Your interfaces are all multipoint, and you have not learned any routes over any of them, so there is no forwarding next hop for the generated route

    b. Your interfaces are all point-to-point, and you have not learned any routes over any of them, so there is no forwarding next hop for the generated route

    c. You must define an explicit policy to list which routes are allowed to contribute

    d. Your interfaces are all multipoint, and you have learned routes over them, which makes the generated route unneeded

5. What command displays the route table for a Layer 3 VPN routing instance named l3_vpn?

    a. show route

    b. show route table l3_vpn

    c. show route table l3_vpn.inet.0

    d. All of the above

6. You have configured RIP between three routers connected in a serial chain, but no RIP routes are being learned. Which policy results in full RIP connectivity for all direct routes?

    a. A RIP import policy of the form:

```
term 1 {
    from protocol [ rip direct ];
    then accept;
}
```

    b. A RIP export policy of the form:

```
term 1 {
    from protocol [ rip direct ];
    then accept;
}
```

    c. A RIP import policy of the form:

```
term 1 {
    from protocol direct;
    then accept;
}
```

    d. A RIP export policy of the form:

```
term 1 {
    from protocol direct;
    then accept;
}
```

7. What happens when the static route 192.168.10/24 is evaluated by this policy?

```
[edit policy-options policy-statement test]
lab@PBR# show
term 1 {
    from {
        protocol bgp;
        route-filter 192.168.0.0/16 orlonger reject;
        route-filter 192.168.10.0/24 exact {
            metric 10;
            accept;
        }
    }
}
```

    a. Nothing, because no match occurs

    b. The route is longest-matched against the first route filter and rejected

c. The route is longest-matched against the second route filter and has its metric set to 10

d. Both b and c

8. What happens if the not policy matches a route with a reject action in the following policy expression?

```
[edit protocols ospf]
lab@PBR# show
export (( ! not ) && and );
```

a. The result is inverted to an accept, and the second policy is evaluated

b. The reject action in the not policy ensures that the AND condition cannot be met, so the second policy is never evaluated

c. Both policies are evaluated, and the logical result, which is false because of the reject in the not policy, is inverted, so the route is accepted

d. None of the above

9. What type of import policy can you apply to OSPF?

a. None; LS protocols do not support the notion of import policies because it breaks database consistency

b. You can apply policy to filter certain LSA types, such as AS externals to create a stub area

c. Import policy for OSPF can only be used to filter AS external LSAs from being flooded

d. Import policy for OSPF can be used to prevent installation of AS external routes into the route table, but has no effect on flooding

10. In the following configuration, which export policy is peer 1.1.1.1 subjected to?

```
[edit protocols bgp]
lab@PBR# show
import ( ! community_regex_test );
export globalize;
group internal {
    export keep_it_on_down_low;
    neighbor 1.1.1.1;
    neighbor 1.1.1.2 {
        export bad_peer_filter;
    }
}
```

a. The globalize policy

b. The keep_it_on_down_low policy

c. The bad_peer_filter policy

d. The globalize and keep_it_on_down_low policies

e. First the keep_it_on_down_low, and then the globalize policy

11. From where does a Juniper router obtain its RID?

    a. From explicit configuration at the [edit routing-options] hierarchy

    b. From the first nonmartian address found on the first interface that is found

    c. Both a and b

    d. Either a or b

12. You were provided a network diagram that told you to number your network from the 191.255.0.0/16 space. OSPF is enabled and adjacencies are up, but no routers are learning any routes. What can explain this?

    a. The default OSPF export policies advertise nothing, so you need to apply export policy

    b. The default OSPF import policy rejects all OSPF routes, so you need to apply import policy

    c. You need to modify the martian table with a 191.255.0.0/16 accept statement

    d. You need to enable OSPF on the lo0 interface to provide a route to the RID of each router in the network

Chapter Review Answers

1. Answer: A. The default next hop type for an aggregate route is reject, which when matched does result in the M7i's system board having to create an ICMP error. Even with rate-limiting safeguards, these messages consume system processing, but not forwarding resources.

2. Answer: C. A floating static needs to have a preference that is less preferred than the route it backs up. OSPF externals have a preference of 150, so you need a value that is higher; otherwise, the static route will take precedence over the OSPF route.

3. Answer: D. The loops argument to the autonomous-system statement affects received route updates only. Further, whatever value is specified, subtract one for the number of local AS instances that are permitted. The default setting of 1 will reject any route with 1 instance of the local AS number.

4. Answer: A. Point-to-point interfaces can contribute to a generated route because an explicit next hop is not required. LAN interfaces require some route—either static or learned—to activate an aggregate or generated route. Policy is used to exclude routes from contributing, not to include.

5. Answer: D. All of the commands listed will display the Layer 3 VPN instance route table. Some are simply more verbose or more direct by displaying only the table desired.

6. Answer: B. The default RIP import policy accepts RIP routes. To send direct routes, you need the direct protocol, and to readvertise RIP learned routes, you need the RIP protocol. The default RIP export policy is to reject all.

7. Answer: A. A static route can never match a from protocol BGP condition, so it does not match the term. There is a logical AND for distinct conditions such as route-filter and protocol when listed under the same statement.

8. Answer: A. The negative/reject result of the not policy is inverted, which becomes true, and this enables the evaluation of the second policy. When the first policy is false, a logical AND can never be satisfied, so without the ! function, the second policy would not be evaluated in this case.

9. Answer: D. You cannot use policy to control LSA flooding. Until recently, no import could be applied, and even now IS-IS does not support any import policy.

10. Answer: B. Only the most explicit policy is executed, which in this case is the group-level policy because neighbor 1.1.1 has no neighbor-level export policy.

11. Answer: D. There can be only one RID in effect at any time, and it is disruptive to change it. The router uses an explicit value when present; otherwise, it automatically derives one. There is no need to be able to route to the RID, at least not for proper protocol operation.

12. Answer: C. You really have to watch those pesky martians....

Interior Gateway Protocols and Migration Strategies

This chapter reviews key concepts and characteristics of Interior Gateway Protocols (IGPs) commonly deployed in enterprise networks. It starts with a brief description of the three most common enterprise IGPs and provides examples of IGP configuration and operational analysis in a JUNOS software environment. The chapter also discusses current best practices to minimize network disruption when migrating from one IGP to another, with configuration examples for Routing Information Protocol to Open Shortest Path First (RIP to OSPF) and Enhanced Interior Gateway Routing Protocol to OSPF (EIGRP to OSPF) migration. The topics discussed in this chapter include:

- IGP overview
- RIP deployment case study
- IGP migration
- RIP to OSPF migration case study
- EIGRP migration case study

From an IGP perspective, a Juniper Networks router supports RIP, the OSPF protocol, and the Intermediate System-to-Intermediate System (IS-IS) routing protocols. This chapter does not address IS-IS given that it is normally seen in service provider networks and rarely is found in the enterprise.

It should be noted that Juniper Networks routers do not support the Cisco Systems proprietary Interior Gateway Routing Protocol (IGRP), or the updated version known as EIGRP. Technical merits aside, licensing restrictions combined with the closed nature of these protocols prevent Juniper Networks from implementing either of these IGPs. Given that IGRP/EIGRP was commonly deployed in many small to medium-size enterprises, a large portion of this chapter focuses on migration strategies designed to ease such a transition between the two vendors.

IGP Overview

As its name would imply, the role of an IGP is to provide routing connectivity *within* or *interior* to a given routing domain (RD). An RD is defined as a set of routers under common administrative control that share a common routing protocol. An enterprise network, which can also be considered an autonomous system (AS), may consist of multiple RDs, which may result from the (historic) need for multiple routed protocols, scaling limitations, acquisitions and mergers, or even a simple lack of coordination among organizations making up the enterprise. *Route redistribution*, the act of exchanging routing information among distinct routing protocols, is often performed to tie these RDs together when connectivity is desired.

IGP functions to advertise and learn network prefixes (routes) from neighboring routers to build a route table that ultimately contains entries for all sources advertising reachability for a given prefix. A route selection algorithm is executed to select the best (i.e., the shortest) path between the local router and each destination, and the next hop associated with that path is pushed into the forwarding table to affect the forwarding of packets that longest-match against that route prefix. The IGP wants to provide full connectivity among the routers making up an RD. Generally speaking, IGPs function to promote, not limit, connectivity, which is why we do not see IGPs used between ASs—they lack the administrative controls needed to limit connectivity based on routing policy. This is also why inter-AS routing is normally accomplished using an Exterior Gateway Protocol (EGP), which today takes the form of Border Gateway Protocol (BGP) version 4. We discuss enterprise application of BGP in Chapter 5.

When network conditions change, perhaps due to equipment failure or management activity, the IGP both generates and receives updates and recalculates a new best route to the affected destinations. Here, the concept of a "best" route is normally tied to a route metric, which is the criterion used to determine the relative path of a given route. Generally speaking, a route metric is significant only to the routing protocol it's associated with, and it is meaningful only within a given RD. In some cases, a router may learn multiple paths to an identical destination from more than one routing protocol. Given that metric comparison between two different IGPs is meaningless, the selection of the best route between multiple routing sources is controlled by a route preference. The concept of route preference is explored in detail later in this chapter in "IGP Migration: Common Techniques and Concerns" and is also known as *administrative distance* (AD) on Cisco Systems routers.

In addition to advertising internal network reachability, IGPs are often used to advertise routing information that is external to that IGP's RD through a process known as *route redistribution*. Route redistribution is often used to exchange routing information between RDs to provide intra-AS connectivity. Route redistribution can be tricky because mistakes can easily lead to lack of connectivity (black holes) or, worse yet, routing loops. To ensure identical forwarding paths, you may also need to map the metrics used by each routing protocol to ensure that they are meaningful to the IGP into which they are redistributed. Route redistribution is performed via routing policy in JUNOS software. We introduce routing policy later in this chapter and cover it in detail in Chapter 3. On Cisco Systems platforms, redistribution is often performed through some combination of the `redistribute` command, through distribute lists, or through route maps and their associated IP access lists. Although there is a learning curve, it's often a delight for those familiar with the IOS way of performing redistribution when they realize that JUNOS software routing policy provides the same functionality with a consistent set of semantics/syntax, for all protocols, and all in one place!

The reader of this book is assumed to have an intermediate level understanding of the IP protocol and the general operation and characteristics of IGPs that support IP routing. This section provides a review of major characteristics, benefits, and drawbacks of the IGPs discussed in this chapter to prepare the reader for the configuration and migration examples that follow.

Routing Information Protocol

RIP is one of the oldest IP routing protocols still in production network use and is a true case of "if something works, why fix it?" The original specification for RIP (version 1) is defined in RFC 1058, originally published in June 1988! RIP version 2 (RIPv2) was originally defined in RFC 1388 (1993) and is currently specified in RFC 2453 (1998).

RIP is classified as a Distance Vector (DV) routing protocol because it advertises reachability information in the form of distance/vector pairs—which is to say that each route is represented as a cost (distance) to reach a given prefix (vector) tuple. DV routing protocols typically exchange entire route tables among their set of directly connected peers, on a periodic basis. This behavior, although direct and easy to understand, leads to many of the disadvantages associated with DV routing protocols. Specifically:

- Increased network bandwidth consumption stemming from the periodic exchange of potentially large route tables, even during periods of network stability. This can be a significant issue when routers connect over low-speed or usage-based network services.
- Slow network convergence, and as a result, a propensity to produce routing loops when reconverging around network failures. To alleviate (but not eliminate) the potential for routing loops, mechanisms such as split horizon, poisoned reverse, route hold downs, and triggered updates are generally implemented. These stability features come at the cost of prolonging convergence.

- DV protocols are normally associated with crude route metrics that often will not yield optimal forwarding between destinations. The typical metric (cost) for DV protocols is a simple hop count, which is a crude measure of actual path cost, to say the least. For example, most users realize far better performance when crossing several routers interconnected by Gigabit Ethernet links, as opposed to half as many routers connected over low-speed serial interfaces.

On the upside, DV protocols are relatively simple to implement, understand, configure, and troubleshoot, and they have been around *forever*, allowing many network engineers a chance to become proficient in their deployment. The memory and processing requirements for DV protocols are generally less than those of a link state (LS) routing protocol (more on that later).

To help illustrate what is meant by *slow to converge*, consider that the protocol's architects ultimately defined a *hop count* (the number of routers that need to be crossed to reach a destination) of 16 to be infinity! Given the original performance of initial implementations, the designers believed that networks over 16 hops in dimension would not be able to converge in a manner considered practical for use in production networks; and those were 1980s networks, for which demanding applications such as Voice over IP were but a distant gleam in an as yet grade-school-attending C-coder's eye. Setting infinity to a rather low value was needed because in some conditions, RIP can converge only by cycling through a series of route exchanges between neighbors, with each such iteration increasing the route's cost by one, until the condition is cleared by the metric reaching infinity and both ends finally agree that the route is not reachable. With the default 30-second update frequency, this condition is aptly named a *slow count to infinity*.

Stability and performance tweaks

Hold downs serve to increase stability, at the expense of rapid convergence, by preventing installation of a route with a reachable metric, after that same route was recently marked as unreachable (cost = 16) by the local router. This behavior helps to prevent loops by keeping the local router from installing route information for a route that was *originally* advertised by the local router, and which is now being *readvertised* by another neighbor. It's assumed that the slow count to infinity will complete before the hold down expires, after which the router will be able to install the route using the lowest advertised cost.

Split horizon prevents the advertisement of routing information back over the interface from which it was learned, and poisoned reverse alters this rule to allow readvertisement back out the learning interface, as long as the cost is explicitly set to infinity: a case of "I can reach this destination, NOT!" This helps to avoid loops by making it clear to any receiving routers that they should not use the advertising router as a next hop for the prefix in question. This behavior is designed to avoid the need for a slow count to infinity that might otherwise occur because the explicit indication that "I cannot reach destination X" is less likely to lead to misunderstandings when compared to the absence of information associated with split horizon. To prevent unnecessary bandwidth waste that stems from bothering to advertise a prefix that you cannot reach, most RIP implementations use split horizon, except when a route is marked as unreachable, at which point it is advertised with a poisoned metric for some number of update intervals (typically three).

Triggered updates allow a router to generate event-driven as well as ongoing periodic updates, serving to expedite the rate of convergence as changes propagate quickly. When combined with hold downs and split horizon, a RIP network can be said to receive bad news fast while good news travels slow.

RIP and RIPv2

Although the original RIP version still works and is currently supported on Juniper Networks routers, it's assumed that readers of this book will consider deploying only RIP version 2. Although the basic operation and configuration are the same, several important benefits are associated with RIPv2 and there are no real drawbacks (considering that virtually all modern routers support both versions and that RIPv2 messages can be made backward-compatible with v1 routers, albeit while losing the benefits of RIPv2 for those V1 nodes).

RIPv2's support of Variable Length Subnet Masking/classless interdomain routing (VLSM/CIDR), combined with its ability to authenticate routing exchanges, has resulted in a breath of new life for our old friend RIP (pun intended). Table 4-1 provides a summary comparison of the two RIP versions.

Table 4-1. Comparing characteristics and capabilities of RIP and RIPv2

Characteristic	RIP	RIPv2
Metric	Hop count (16 max)	Hop count (16 max)
Updates/hold down/route timeout	30/120/180 seconds	30/120/180 seconds
Max prefixes per message	25	25 (24 when authentication is used)
Authentication	None	Plain text or Message Digest 5 (MD5)
Broadcast/multicast	Broadcast to all nodes using all 1s, RIP-capable or not	Multicast only to RIPv2-capable routers using 224.0.0.9 (broadcast mode is configurable)
Support for VLSM/CIDR	No, only classful routing is supported (no netmask in updates)	Yes
Route tagging	No	Yes (useful for tracking a route's source; i.e., internal versus external)

Open Shortest Path First

The OSPF routing protocol currently enjoys widespread use in both enterprise and service provider networks. If OSPF can meet the needs of the world's largest network operators, it's safe to say that it should be more than sufficient for even the largest enterprise network. OSPF version 2 is defined in RFC 2328, but numerous other RFCs define enhanced capabilities for OSPF, such as support of not-so-stubby areas (NSSAs) in RFC 3101, Multiprotocol Label Switching (MPLS) Traffic Engineering Extensions (MPLS TE) in RFC 3630, and in RFC 3623, which defines graceful restart extensions that minimize data plane disruption when a neighboring OSPF router restarts. OSPF supports virtually all the features any enterprise could desire, including VLSM, authentication, switched circuit support (suppressed hellos), and MPLS TE extensions, among many more.

OSPF is classified as an LS routing protocol. This is because, unlike a DV protocol that exchanges its entire route table among directly connected neighbors, OSPF exchanges *only* information about the local router's links, and these updates are flooded to *all routers* in the same area. Flooding ensures that all the routers in the area receive the new update at virtually the same time. The result of this flooding is a link-state database (LSDB) that is replicated among all routers that belong to a given area. Database consistency is critical for proper operation and the assurance of loop-free forwarding topologies. OSPF meets this requirement through reliable link-state advertisement (LSA) exchanges that incorporate acknowledgment and retransmission procedures. Each router performs a Shortest Path First (SPF) calculation based on the Dijkstra algorithm, using itself as the root of the tree to compute a shortest-path graph containing nodes representing each router in the area, along with its associated links. The metrically shortest path to each destination is then computed, and that route is placed into the route table for consideration to become an active route by the path selection algorithm.

OSPF advertises and updates prefix information using LSA messages, which are sent only upon detection of a change in network reachability. LSAs are also reflooded periodically to prevent their being aged out by other routers. Typically, this occurs somewhere between 30 and 45 minutes, given the default 3,600-second LSA lifetime. In addition, rather than sending an entire route table or database, these LSAs carry only the essential set of information needed to describe the router's new LS. Upon sensing a change in their local LSDBs, other routers rerun the SPF and act accordingly.

OSPF dynamically discovers and maintains neighbors through generation of periodic hello packets. An adjacency is formed when two neighbors decide to synchronize their LSDBs to become routing peers. A router may choose to form an adjacency with only a subset of the neighbors that it discovers to help improve efficiency, as described in the subsequent section, "Neighbors and adjacencies."

It should be no wonder that OSPF has dramatically improved convergence characteristics when one considers its event-driven flooding of small updates to all routers in an area. This is especially true when contrasted to RIP's period exchange of the entire route table among directly connected neighbors, who then convey that information to their neighbors at the next scheduled periodic update.

The downside to all this increased performance is that CPU and memory load are increased in routers as compared to the same router running a DV protocol. This is because an LS router has to house *both* the LSDB and the resulting route table, and the router must compute these routes by executing an SPF algorithm each time the LSDB changes. Considering that router processing capability and memory tend to increase, while actual costs tend to decrease for the same unit of processing power, these drawbacks are a more-than-acceptable trade-off for the benefit of ongoing reduced network loading and rapid convergence. Another drawback to LS routing protocols is their relative complexity when compared to DV protocols, which can make their operation difficult to understand, which in turn can make fault isolation more difficult.

OSPF was designed to support Type of Service (ToS)-based routing, but this capability has not been deployed commercially. This means that a single route table is maintained, and that for each destination, a single path metric is computed. This metric is said to be *dimensionless* in that it serves only to indicate the relative goodness or badness of a path, with smaller numbers considered to be better. Exactly what is better cannot be determined from the OSPF metric, LSDB, or resulting route table. Whether the OSPF metric is set to reflect link speed (default), hop count, delay, reliability, or some combination thereof is a matter of administrative policy.

Neighbors and adjacencies

Previously, it was noted that OSPF dynamically discovers neighbors using a periodic exchange of hello packets. It should also be noted that OSPF contains sanity checks that prevent neighbor discovery (and therefore, adjacency formation) when parameters such as the hello time, area type, maximum transmission unit (MTU), or subnet mask are mismatched. The designers of the protocol felt it was much easier to troubleshoot a missing adjacency than the potential result of trying to operate with mismatched parameters, and having dealt with more than a few misconfigured OSPF networks, the protocol architects were absolutely right.

The designated router. To maximize efficiency, OSPF does not form an adjacency with every neighbor that is detected, because the maintenance of an adjacency requires compute cycles and because on multiaccess networks such as LANs, a full mesh of adjacencies is largely redundant. On multiaccess networks, an election algorithm is performed to first elect a designated router (DR), and then a backup designated router (BDR). The DR functions to represent the LAN itself and forms an adjacency with the BDR and all other compatible neighbors (DRother) on the LAN segment.

The DRother routers form two adjacencies across the LAN—one to the DR and one to the BDR. The neighbor state for DRother neighbors on a DRother router itself is expected to remain in the "two-way" state. This simply means that the various DRothers have detected each other as neighbors, but an adjacency has not been formed.

The DR is responsible for flooding LSAs that reflect the connectivity of the LAN. This means that loss of one neighbor on a 12-node LAN results in a single LSA that is flooded by the DR, as opposed to each remaining router flooding its own LSA. The reduced flooding results in reduced network bandwidth consumption and reduced OSPF processing overhead. If the DR fails, the BDR will take over and a new BDR is elected.

OSPF elects a DR and BDR based on a priority setting, with a lower value indicating a lesser chance at winning the election; a setting of 0 prevents the router from ever becoming the DR. In the event of a tie, the router with the highest router ID (RID) takes the prize. The OSPF DR Election algorithm is nondeterministic and nonrevertive, which means that adding a new router with a higher, more preferred priority does not result in the overthrow of the existing DR. In other words, router priority matters only during active DR/BDR election. This behavior minimizes the potential for network disruption/LSA flooding when new routers are added to the network. Thus, the only way to guarantee that a given router is the DR is to either disable DR capability in all other routers (set their priority to 0), or ensure that the desired router is powered on first and never reboots. Where possible, the most stable and powerful router should be made the DR/BDR, and a router should ideally be the DR for only one network segment.

OSPF router types

OSPF describes various router roles that govern their operation and impact the types of areas in which they are permitted. To become proficient with OSPF operation and network design, you must have a clear understanding of the differences between OSPF area types and between the LSAs permitted within each area:

Internal router
> Any router that has all its interfaces contained within a single area is an internal router. If attached to the backbone area, the router is also known as a backbone router.

Backbone router
> Any router with an attachment to area 0 (the backbone area) is considered a backbone router. This router may also be an internal or area border router depending on whether it has links to other, nonbackbone areas.

Area border router (ABR)
> A router with links in two or more areas is an ABR. The ABR is responsible for connecting OSPF areas to the backbone by conveying network summary information between the backbone and nonbackbone areas.

Antonymous system boundary router (ASBR)
    A router that injects external routing information into an OSPF domain is an ASBR.

Areas and LSAs

As previously noted, LS protocols flood LSAs to all routers in the same area in order to create a replicated LSDB from which a route table is derived through execution of an SPF algorithm. The interplay of these processes can lead to a downward-scaling spiral in large networks, especially when there are large numbers of unstable links.

As the number of routers and router links within an area grows, so too does the size of the resulting LSDB. In addition, more links means a greater likelihood of an interface or route flap, which leads to greater need for flooding of LSAs. The increased probability of LSDB churn leads to an increased frequency of the SPF calculations that must be performed each time the LSDB changes (barring any SPF hold downs for back-to-back LSA change events). These conditions combine to form the downward spiral of increased flooding, larger databases, more frequent SPF runs, and a larger processing burden per SPF run, due to the large size of the LSDB.

But don't fear: OSPF tackles this problem through the support of areas, which provides a hierarchy of LSDBs. As a result, LSA flooding is now constrained to each area, and no one router has to carry LS for the entire RD. Because each area is associated with its own LSDB, a multiarea OSPF network will, for the average router, result in a smaller LSDB. Each router must maintain an LSDB only for its attached areas, and no one router need attach to every area. This is a key point, because in theory it means OSPF has almost unlimited scaling potential, especially when compared to nonhierarchical protocols such as Cisco's EIGRP or RIP. In addition, with fewer routers and links, there is a reduced likelihood of having to flood updated LSAs, which in turn means a reduced number of SPF runs are needed—when an SPF run is needed, it is now executed against a smaller LSDB, which yields a win-win for all involved.

Routers that connect to multiple areas are called ABRs and maintain an LSDB for each area to which they attach. An ABR has a greater processing burden than an internal router, by virtue of maintaining multiple LSDBs, but the processing burden associated with two small LSDBs can still be considerably less than that associated with a single, large database, for reasons cited earlier. It is common to deploy your most powerful routers to serve the role of ABRs, because these machines will generally have to work harder than a purely internal router, given that they must maintain an LSDB per attached area, and have the greater chance of a resulting SPF calculation. However, the trade-off is being able to use smaller, less powerful routers within each area (internal routers), because of the reduced LSDB size that results from a hierarchical OSPF design.

Interestingly, OSPF is truly link-state *only within* a single area due to the scope of LSA flooding being confined to a single area. An ABR runs SPF for each attached area's LSDB and then summarizes its intraarea LS costs into other areas in DV-like fashion. This behavior is the reason OSPF requires a backbone area that is designated as area 0—generally speaking, each ABR generates and receives summaries *only* from the backbone, which exists to provide a loop-free environment over which these summaries can be exchanged. Put another way, the backbone serves to prevent loop formation that could result from the information that is hidden by ABRs when they summarize the contents of their nonbackbone area LSDBs into simple distance/vector pairs. A router receiving a summary advertisement uses SPF against that area's LSDB to compute the shortest path to the router that generated the summary advertisement, and then it simply adds the summary cost, as originally calculated by the advertising router, to obtain the total path cost.

Having said all this, it is not unheard of to see large, globally spanning OSPF networks consisting of hundreds of routers successfully deployed within a single OSPF area. There simply are no hard rules regarding the age-old question of "how many routers can I put into a single area," because too many variables exist. In addition to a simple router count, one must also consider factors such as link count, link stability, router processing power, the percentage of external versus internal LSAs, and the general robustness of the protocol's implementation. The significance of the latter should not be underestimated. A poorly implemented OSPF instance running on the world's fastest hardware will likely not perform very well, unless, of course, you consider the number of core files dumped and/or reboots per unit of time, which is a significant IGP benchmark. Seriously, it's bad enough when one network node keeps rolling over to play dead, but it's worse when instability in a single node rapidly ripples out to affect the operation of other routers, even those with well-behaved code.

OSPF area types. OSPF defines several different area types. To truly understand OSPF operation, you must have a clear understanding of the differences between OSPF area types, and between the LSAs permitted within each area:

Backbone
> To ensure loop-free connectivity, OSPF maintains a special area called the backbone area, which should always be designated as area 0. All other OSPF areas should connect themselves to the backbone for interarea connectivity; normally, interarea traffic transits the backbone.

Stub
> Stub areas do not carry AS external advertisements, with the goal being a reduction of LSDB size for internal routers within that stub area. Because routers in a stub area see only LSAs that advertise routing information from *within* the OSPF RD, a default route is normally injected to provide reachability to external destinations. Stub area routers use the metrically closest ABR when forwarding to AS external prefixes.

Totally stubby area

A totally stubby area is a stub area that *only* receives the default route from the backbone. Routers in the totally stubby area do not see OSPF internal routes from other OSPF areas. Their LSDBs represent their own area and the injected default route, which is now used to reach both AS external and interarea destinations.

NSSAs

As noted previously, an OSPF stub area does not carry external routes, which means you cannot redistribute routes into a stub area because redistributed routes are always treated as AS externals in OSPF. An NSSA bends this rule and allows a special form of external route within the NSSA. Although an NSSA can originate AS externals into OSPF, external routes from other areas are still not permitted within the NSSA. This is a case of having one's cake (small LSDB due to not being burdened by externals from other areas) while eating it too (being allowed to burden other routers with the external routes you choose to generate). The NSSA's ABRs can translate the special form of external route used in an NSSA for flooding over the rest of the OSPF domain.

Transit areas

Transit areas pass traffic from one adjacent area to the backbone or to another area if the backbone is more than two hops away from an area.

Primary LSA types. LSAs are the workhorse of OSPF in that they are used to flood information regarding network reachability and form the basis of the resulting LSDB. Table 4-2 describes the LSA types used by modern OSPF networks. It bears restating that a true understanding of OSPF requires knowledge of what type of routing information is carried in a given LSA, in addition to understanding each LSA's flooding scope. For example, an LSA with area scope is never seen outside the area from which it was generated, whereas an LSA with global scope is flooded throughout the entire OSPF RD, barring any area type restrictions; that is, AS externals are never permitted within a stub area. Figure 4-1 provides a graphical summary of the purpose and scope of the most common LSA types.

Table 4-2. Common OSPF LSA types

LSA type	Generated by/contents/purpose	Flooding scope
Type 1, router	Generated by all OSPF routers, the Type 1 LSA describes the status and cost of the router's links.	Area
Type 2, network	Generated by the DR on a LAN, the Type 2 LSA lists each router connected to the broadcast link, including the DR itself.	Area
Type 3, network summary	Generated by ABRs, Type 3 LSAs carry summary route information between OSPF areas. Typically, this information is exchanged between a nonbackbone area and the backbone area, or vice versa. Type 3 LSAs are not reflooded across area boundaries; instead, a receiving ABR generates its own Type 3 LSA summarizing its interarea routing information into any adjacent areas.	Area

Table 4-2. Common OSPF LSA types (continued)

LSA type	Generated by/contents/purpose	Flooding scope
Type 4, ASBR summary	Each ABR that forwards external route LSAs must also provide reachability information for the associated ASBR so that other routers know how to reach that ASBR when routing to the associated external destinations. The Type 4 LSA provides reachability information for the OSPF domain's ASBRs. As with Type 3 LSAs, each ABR generates its own Type 4 when flooding external LSAs into another area.	Area
Type 5, AS external LSA	Generated by ASBRs, the Type 5 LSA carries information for prefixes that are external to the OSPF RD.	Global, except for stub areas
Type 7, NSSA	Generated by ASBRs in an NSSA, the Type 7 LSA advertises prefixes that are external to the OSPF RD. Unlike the Type 5 LSA, Type 7 LSAs are not globally flooded. Instead, the NSSA's ABR translates Type 7 LSAs into Type 5 for flooding throughout the RD.	Area
Type 9, 10, and 11, opaque LSAs	Generated by enabled OSPF routers to carry arbitrary information without having to define new LSA types, the Type 9 LSA has link scope and is currently used to support graceful restart extensions, whereas the Type 10 LSA has area scope and is used for MPLS TE support.	Type 9, link; Type 10, area; Type 11, global scope

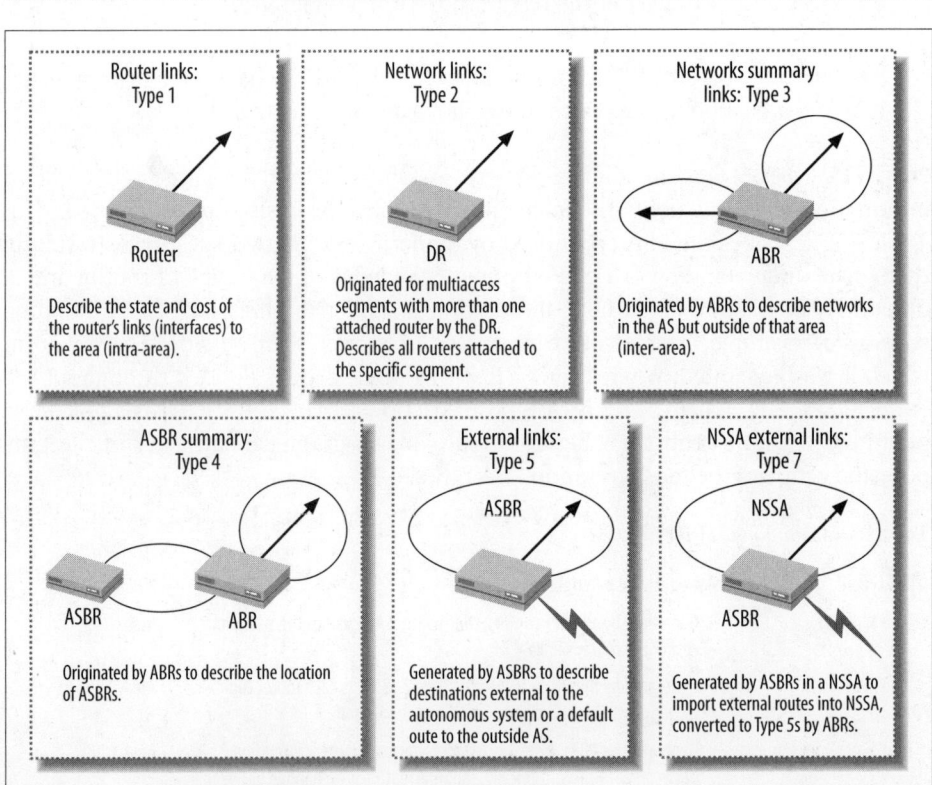

Figure 4-1. OSPF LSA types and scope

OSPF stability and performance tweaks

Breaking a large OSPF domain into multiple areas can have a significant impact on overall performance and convergence. In addition, most OSPF implementations support various timers to further tune and tweak the protocol's operation.

The Juniper Networks OSPF implementation is quite optimized and lacks many of the timers and hold downs that readers may be familiar with in IOS. It is not uncommon to see users new to Juniper asking for JUNOS software analogs and receiving the standard answer that "they do not exist because they are not needed." The development engineers at Juniper feel that artificially delaying transmission of an LSA—ostensibly to alleviate the processing burden associated with its receipt—does nothing except prolong network convergence.

Table 4-3 maps OSPF-related knobs from IOS to their JUNOS software equivalent, when available.

Table 4-3. IOS versus JUNOS software OSPF timers

IOS name	JUNOS software name	Comment
carrier-delay (0)	hold-time (0)	Delay notification of interface up/down events to damp interface transitions. Default is 0, but notification times can vary based on interrupt versus polled.
timers throttle spf (spf-start, spf-hold, spf-max-wait)	spf-delay (200)	Control the rate of SPF calculation. In JUNOS software, the value is used for as many as three back-to-back SPF runs, and then a 5-second hold down is imposed to ensure stability in the network.
timers throttle lsa all (lsa-start, lsa-hold, lsa-max ((0, 5000, 5000)))	N/A	By default, JUNOS software sends 3 back-to-back updates with a 50 msec delay, and then a five-second hold down.
timers lsa arrival	N/A	Controls the minimum interval for accepting a copy of the same LSA.
timers pacing flood (33 msec)	transmit-interval (30 msec)	Delay back-to-back LSA transmissions out the same interface.
ispf	N/A	Enable incremental SPF calculations; JUNOS software does not support ISPF but does perform partial route calculations when the ospf topology is stable and only routing information changes.

JUNOS software has added an additional optimization in the form of a periodic packet management process daemon (ppmd) that handles the generation and processing of OSPF (and other protocol) hello packets. The goal of ppmd is to permit scaling to large numbers of protocol peers by offloading the mundane processing tasks associated with periodic packet generation. The ppmd process can run directly in the PFE to offload RE cycles on application-specific integrated circuit (ASIC)-based systems such as the M7i.

In addition to the aforementioned timers, both vendors also support Bidirectional Forwarding Detection (BFD), which is a routing-protocol-agnostic mechanism to provide rapid detection of link failures, as opposed to waiting for an OSPF adjacency timeout. Note that interface hold time comes into play only when a physical layer fault is detected, as opposed to a link-level issue such as can occur when two routers are connected via a LAN switch, where the local interface status remains up even when a physical fault occurs on the remote link. As of this writing, IOS support for BFD is limited and varies by platform and software release; Cisco Systems recommends that you see the Cisco IOS software release notes for your software version to determine support and applicable restrictions.

Enhanced Interior Gateway Routing Protocol

The EIGRP is an updated version of Cisco Systems' proprietary IGRP. The original version of EIGRP had stability issues, prompting the release of EIGRP version 1, starting in IOS versions 10.3(11), 11.0(8), and 11.1(3). This chapter focuses strictly on EIGRP because it has largely displaced IGRP in modern enterprise networks.

EIGRP is sometimes said to be a "DV protocol that thinks it's an LS." EIGRP does in fact share some of the characteristics normally associated with LS routing, including rapid convergence and loop avoidance, but the lack of LSA flooding and the absence of the resulting LSDB expose EIGRP's true DV nature. This section highlights the major operational characteristics and capabilities of EIGRP. The goal is not an exhaustive treatment of EIGRP's operation or configuration—this subject has been covered in numerous other writings. Instead, the purpose here is to understand EIGRP to the degree necessary to effectively replace this proprietary legacy protocol with another IGP, while maintaining maximum network availability throughout the process.

The operational characteristics of EIGRP are as follows:

- It uses nonperiodic updates that are partial and bounded. This means that unlike typical DV protocol operation, EIGRP generates *only* triggered updates, that these updates report *only* affected prefixes, and that the updates are sent to a bounded set of neighbors.

- It uses a Diffusing Update Algorithm (DUAL) to guarantee a loop-free topology while providing rapid convergence. The specifics of DUAL operation are outside the scope of this book; suffice it to say that DUAL is the muscle behind EIGRP's rapid converge and loop guarantees.

- It uses a composite metric that, by default, factors delay and throughput. Also, it supports the factoring of dynamically varying reliability and loading, but users are cautioned not to use this capability. EIGRP uses the same metric formula as IGRP, but it multiplies the result by 256 for greater granularity.

- It supports VLSM/CIDR and automatic summarization at classful boundaries by default.
- It supports unequal cost load balancing using a *variance* knob.
- It supports neighbor discovery and maintenance using multicast.
- It automatically redistributes to IGRP when process numbers are the same.
- It features protocol-independent modules for common functionality (reliable transport of protocol messages).
- It features protocol-dependant modules for IP, IPX, and AppleTalk that provide multiprotocol routing via the construction of separate route tables using protocol-specific routing updates.

At first glance, the multiprotocol capabilities of EIGRP may seem enticing. After all, this functionality cannot be matched by today's *standardized* routing protocols. There was a time when many enterprise backbones were in fact running multiple network protocols, and the lure of a single, high-performance IGP instance that could handle the three most common network suites was hard to resist. However, there has been an unmistakable trend toward IP transport for virtually all Internet-working suites, including IBM's SNA/SAA. (We have a hard time recalling the last time we knew of an enterprise still deploying the native Netware or AppleTalk trans-port protocols.) In contrast, these proprietary-routed protocols are being phased out in favor of native IP transport, which serves to render EIGRP's multiprotocol fea-tures moot in this modern age of *IP* internetworking.

EIGRP can load-balance across paths that are not equal in cost, based on a variance setting, which determines how much larger a path metric can be as compared to the minimum path metric, while still being used for load balancing. This characteristic remains unique to IGRP/EIGRP given that neither RIP nor OSPF supports unequal cost load balancing.

EIGRP metrics

EIGRP uses a composite metric that lacks a direct corollary in standardized IGPs. EIGRP metrics tend to be large numbers. Although providing great granularity, these huge numbers represent a real issue for a protocol such as RIP, which sees any met-ric greater than 16 as infinity. It's quite unlikely that any enterprise would migrate from EIGRP to RIP anyway, given the relatively poor performance of RIP and the widespread availability of OSPF on modern networking devices, so such a transition scenario is not addressed in this chapter.

For reference, the formula used by EIGRP to calculate the metric is:

$$\text{Metric} = [K1 * Bw + K2 * Bw/(256 - Load) + K3 * Delay] * [K5/(Reliability + K4)]$$

Although the MTU is not used in the calculation of the metric, it is tracked across the path to identify the minimum path MTU. The K parameters are used to weigh each of the four components that factor into the composite metric—namely, bandwidth, load, delay, and reliability. The default values for the weighing result in only K1 and K3 being nonzero, which gives the default formula of Bw + Delay for the metric.

 Note that Cisco Systems does not recommend user adjustment of the metric weighting. So, in practical terms, EIGRP's metric is a 32-bit quantity that represents the path's cumulative delay (in tens of microseconds) and the path's minimum throughout in Kb/s, divided by 10^7 (scaled and inverted).

For EIGRP, the result is then multiplied by 256 to convert from IGRP's 24-bit metric to EIGRP's 32-bit metric. It should be obvious that one cannot perform a simple one-to-one mapping of legacy EIGRP metrics to OSPF, given that EIGRP supports a 32-bit metric and OSPF's is only 16-bit. This is not a significant shortcoming in practice, given that few enterprise networks are composed of enough paths to warrant 4 billion levels of metric granularity anyway!

Figure 4-2 shows an example network to help illustrate how EIGRP calculates a path metric.

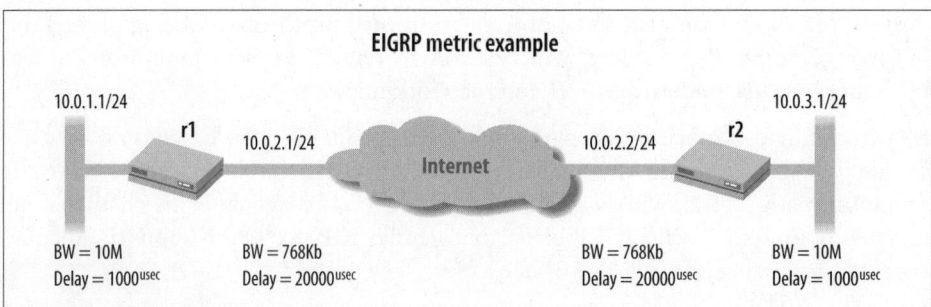

Figure 4-2. EIGRP metric example

Using the default composite metric weighting for the topology shown in Figure 4-2, router r1's metric to reach 10.0.3.0/24 is computed based on the minimum bandwidth and the sum of the path delay, using the formula:

Metric = 256 * (10^7/minBW Kbs) + (delay sum usec/10)

Plugging in the specifics for this example yields a path metric of 3,870,976 for the path to 10.0.3.0/24, from the perspective of r1:

Metric = 256 * (10^7/768) + (20,000 + 1,000 /10)
Metric = 256 * (13021) + (2100)
Metric = 256 * 15121
Metric = 3,870,976

By way of comparison, the same network running OSPF with JUNOS software defaults for OSPF reference bandwidth yields a path metric of only 137! A key point here is that although 137 is certainly much smaller than the 3,870,976 value computed by EIGRP, the range of OSPF metrics, from 1–65,534, should be more than sufficient to differentiate among the number of links/paths available in even the largest enterprise network.

Also, recall that the OSPF metric is said to be dimensionless, which is to say that a smaller value is always preferred over larger values, but the exact nature of *what* is smaller is not conveyed in the metric itself. By default, OSPF derives its metric from interface bandwidth using a scaling factor, but the scaling factor can be altered, and the metric can be administratively assigned to reflect any parameter chosen by the administrator. When all is said and done, as long as a consistent approach is adopted when assigning OSPF metrics, the right thing should just happen. By way of example, consider a case where OSPF metrics are assigned based on the economic costs of a usage-based network service. The resultant *shortest path* measures distance as a function of economic impact and will result in optimization based on the least expensive paths between any two points. Thus, OSPF has done its job by locating the *shortest* path, which in this example means the *least expensive* path, given that the administration considers distance to equate to money. We revisit the subject of EIGRP to OSPF metric conversions in "EIGRP-to-OSPF Migration Summary," later in this chapter.

EIGRP: A grand past and a dubious future

It's worth restating that, unlike open standards protocols such as RIP and OSPF, EIGRP is proprietary to Cisco Systems. As a result, only Cisco Systems products can speak EIGRP, both because of the closed nature of the specification and because of the licensing and patent issues that prevent others from implementing the protocol. Most enterprise customers (and service providers, for that matter) prefer not to be locked into any solution that is sourced from a single vendor, even one as large and dominant as Cisco Systems.

EIGRP's lack of hierarchical support significantly limits its use in large-scale networks due to scaling issues. EIGRP lacks the protocol extensions needed to build a traffic engineering database (TED), as used to support MPLS applications. Although MPLS is still somewhat rare in the enterprise, it currently enjoys significant momentum and is in widespread use within service provider networks across the globe. Considering that many of the requirements of service providers three or four years ago are the same requirements that we are seeing in the enterprise today, an enterprise would be wise to hedge its bets by adopting protocols that can support this important technology, should the need later arise.

Support is an important factor that must be considered when deploying any protocol. At one point, it was difficult to find off-the-shelf or open source protocol analysis for IGRP/EIGRP. Cisco could change the specification at any time, making obsolete any such tools that exist. At the time of this writing, the Wireshark analysis program (*http://www.wireshark.org/*) lists EIGRP support; however, it's difficult to confirm the decode accuracy without an open standard to reference against.

Given the drawbacks to a single-vendor closed solution, an enterprise should consider the use of open standard protocols. In the case of IGPs, you gain higher performance, vendor independence, and off-the-shelf support capabilities. EIGRP's multiprotocol capability aside, the largest IP networks on the planet (those of Internet service providers [ISPs]) generally run OSPF. Service provider networks are all about reliability, stability, rapid convergence at a large scale, and the ability to offer services that result in revenue generation—given these IGP requirements, the reader is left to ponder why service provider networks are never found to be running EIGRP within their networks.

IGP Summary

IGPs provide the indispensable service of maintaining internal connectivity throughout the myriad link and equipment failures possible in modern IP internetworks. IGP performance and stability in the face of large volumes of network change can provide a strategic edge by quickly routing around problems to maintain the highest degree of connectivity possible.

This section overviewed the RIP, OSPF, and EIGRP protocols to prepare the reader for the following deployment and IGP migration scenarios. Now is a good time to take a break before you head into the RIP deployment case study that follows.

RIP Deployment Scenario

OK, that's enough of an IGP overview. There's little doubt that the router-jockey readers of this book are chomping at the bit to start routing some packets! Let's demonstrate basic RIP configuration and operational mode commands that assist in troubleshooting a RIP operation in a JUNOS software environment.

Figure 4-3 depicts the topology for the Cisco Systems/IOS to Juniper Networks/ JUNOS software RIP integration scenario. It shows the existing Beer-Co RIP network, which currently consists of two Cisco Systems 2600 series routers running IOS version 12.3(15b) and interconnected by a serial link. Beer-Co is expanding its widget operation and plans to add two additional locations. Despite the existing infrastructure, the CIO has opted to become a multivendor shop, and a decision has been made to deploy two Juniper Networks J-series routers. The existing (and planned) IP addressing is shown and contains a mix of subnetted class A and class C addresses (just to keep things interesting). Each router's loopback address is also shown, along with a simulated customer network that is instantiated via a static route (labs commonly use a static route to represent a customer network for purposes of reducing equipment requirements). Note that the last digit of each router's loopback address is tied numerically to that router's simulated customer network to help ease requirements on the reader's memory.

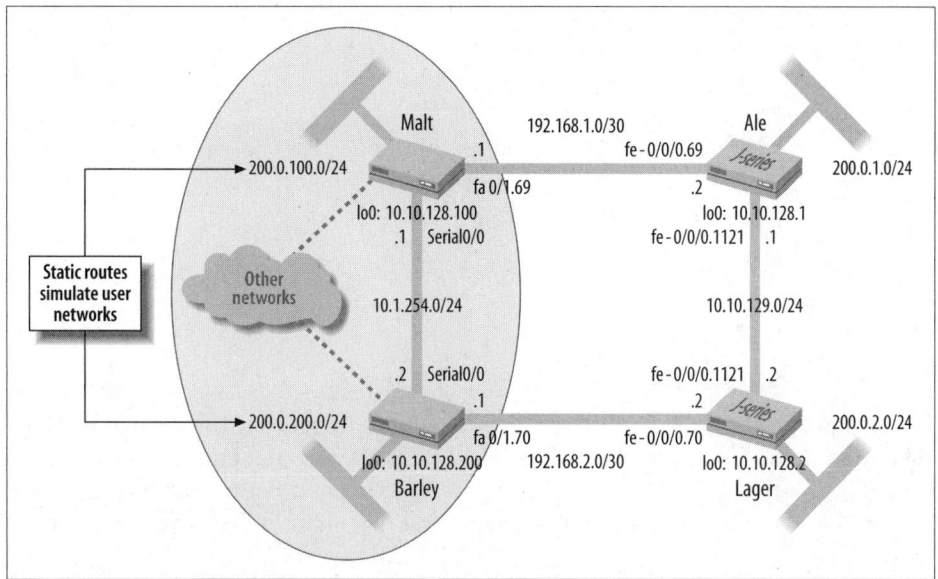

Figure 4-3. RIP topology

As a reminder, recall that in this lab, each router's Fast Ethernet interface is tied to a virtual LAN (VLAN) switch, and VLAN tags are used to establish links between communicating routers. The subinterface/logical unit of each interface match the associated VLAN tag value, which is also shown in the figure. You may assume that all router interface properties are correctly configured to permit communication with directly attached neighbors. The following code snippets show the Fast Ethernet interface configuration at Cisco router Malt and Juniper router Ale.

Malt's FastEthernet0/1 interface and subinterface configuration:

```
interface FastEthernet0/1
 no ip address
 duplex auto
 speed auto
!
interface FastEthernet0/1.69
 encapsulation dot1Q 69
 ip address 192.168.1.1 255.255.255.252
 ip rip authentication mode md5
 ip rip authentication key-chain test
 no snmp trap link-status
```

Ale's fe-0/0/0 interface and logical unit configuration:

```
[fe-0/0/0 {
    vlan-tagging;
```

```
    unit 69 {
        description Ale-to_Malt;
        vlan-id 69;
        family inet {
            address 192.168.1.2/30;
        }
    }
    unit 1121 {
        description Ale-to_Lager;
        vlan-id 1121;
        family inet {
            address 10.10.129.1/24;
        }
    }
}
```

Existing RIP Configuration

Before adding the new RIP routers, it makes sense to first inspect the related RIP configuration in the Cisco platform to get a feel for what RIP configuration tasks will be needed on the Juniper Networks boxes. The RIP-related configuration parts from router Malt are shown, along with some inline comment as to what each part is doing:

```
Malt#show run
Building configuration...
. . .
!
key chain test
 key 1
  key-string jncie
. . .
```

The key chain configuration is used to provide authentication to various routing protocols, ostensibly RIP, in this example. The named key chain has a single key that is numbered as 1 using a key value of jncie. Key chains provide the ability to rotate the current key, based on start and end times (which are not specified in this example). As of this writing, JUNOS software supports authentication key chains only for the Label Distribution Protocol (LDP), OSPF, and BGP. RIP supports a single password-MD5 key, which is good for us because that is just what's needed here:

```
interface FastEthernet0/1.69
 encapsulation dot1Q 69
 ip address 192.168.1.1 255.255.255.252
 ip rip authentication mode md5
 ip rip authentication key-chain test
 no snmp trap link-status
!
. . .
```

The two subinterface-level IP rip authentication statements configure RIP authentication for messages sent out, or received from, the related interface. The commands specify the associated key chain and authentication approach, which again is MD5 in this example:

```
router rip
 version 2
 redistribute connected
 redistribute static route-map TAGGING
 network 10.0.0.0
 network 192.168.1.0
 distribute-list 3 out static
 no auto-summary
 . . .
```

This portion of the configuration actually enables the RIP process. Things begin with the specification that RIP version 2 is to be run. Considering the VLSM in effect, this is a very good choice. The network statements, which are assumed to fall on classful boundaries, define the set of interfaces on which RIP should operate. Rather than listing interfaces directly by name, they are indirectly identified through the interface's IP address. Notice the two forms of route redistribution in effect. The redistribute connected and redistribute static statements, the latter with an associated route map, serve to redistribute connected and static routes, respectively. A distribution list could also have been used to control the routes advertised into RIP. The connected routes will catch the router's serial, Fast Ethernet, and loopback interface subnets. You will have to wait and see what static route redistribution is doing when you inspect the related route map.

The no-auto-summary statement disables the default (Cisco) behavior of automatically summarizing at classful network boundaries. When combined with RIP version 2, which conveys a network mask, VLSM/CIDR is supported.

```
ip route 0.0.0.0 0.0.0.0 Null0
ip route 200.0.100.0 255.255.255.0 Null0
!
access-list 3 permit 200.0.100.0
access-list 4 permit 0.0.0.0
!
```

 The whole classful addressing concept is totally alien to a Juniper Networks router, as the boxes were designed in an era well after the concept of class-based addressing had come and gone. To help illustrate this point, JUNOS software has no need for an ip classless statement as always seen in IOS, and consistently uses CIDR / notation for prefix lengths.

This portion of the configuration defines two static routes: the former is a default route and the latter is the simulated customer network associated with Malt. Both are pointed to null0 as a next hop, which means that any traffic that longest-matches either of these two routes will be discarded.

This may strike the reader as odd, so some additional explanation is warranted. The assumption is that the real customer network will be assigned a mask longer than the /24 used by the static route that currently represents it—for example, a /28. Therefore, packets actually sent to hosts within the customer network will longest-match against the customer network interface route (longest-match rules), and are thereby spared the ignominious treatment of a one-way trip to null0 land. If, on the other hand, the customer network interface is down, these packets are discarded as they now longest-match against the static route—meanwhile, the presence of the static route is preventing route churn in the rest of the network because it's always being advertised in RIP. This stability comes with the downside that, during a customer network interface outage, other routers in the RIP domain have a false belief that hosts on the customer network are still reachable, and the resultant traffic is forwarded over the enterprise network only to be discarded by the last hop. This technique is somewhat common in service provider networks, because control plane stability is generally more important than the network bandwidth that is wasted by forwarding packets across a network only to shunt them to null0.

In the RIP scenario, the two Cisco routers are attached to some other network cloud. Rather than run a routing protocol or define numerous static routes, the administrator relies on a default route to direct matching traffic into this cloud. The dotted lines on the drawing represent that this cloud is not part of the actual test bed.

Also, note the two related IP access control lists (ACLs), each matching on one of the two static routes. These ACLs are in turn referenced by the route map:

```
route-map TAGGING permit 10
 match ip address 3
 set metric 3
 !
route-map TAGGING permit 20
 match ip address 4
 set tag 100
 . . .
End
```

The TAGGING route map first matches against ACL 3 and sets the outgoing metric to 3 for matching prefixes (the simulated customer network route in this case). The default metric would be 1, so this action simulates a network that is two router hops farther away than it actually is. This might be done to cause another source of this route to be preferred (the lower hop count wins), or, perhaps, to limit the scope of stations that can reach this network (recall that in RIP, 16 means you cannot get there). Like it or not, this is an example of how route maps are used in IOS to alter route attributes, perhaps just to keep the scenario interesting.

The permit 20 statement evokes ACL 4, which matches the default route for purposes of setting a route tag. In this example, the tag happens to be based on the router's loopback address. It's common to tag routes that are redistributed for purposes of tracking down the source of the route when troubleshooting, or for use in policy matching based on tag values. This is especially important when performing mutual route redistribution, which is a process prone to routing loops when route filtering precautions are not exercised.

Baseline operation

A quick look at the state of the IP route table at router Malt is performed before any modifications are made. This will serve as the network baseline for future comparison:

```
Malt#show ip route
Codes: C - connected, S - static, R - RIP, M - mobile, B - BGP
       D - EIGRP, EX - EIGRP external, O - OSPF, IA - OSPF inter area
       N1 - OSPF NSSA external type 1, N2 - OSPF NSSA external type 2
       E1 - OSPF external type 1, E2 - OSPF external type 2
       i - IS-IS, su - IS-IS summary, L1 - IS-IS level-1, L2 - IS-IS
level-2
       ia - IS-IS inter area, * - candidate default, U - per-user s
tatic route
       o - ODR, P - periodic downloaded static route

Gateway of last resort is 0.0.0.0 to network 0.0.0.0

R    200.0.200.0/24 [120/3] via 10.1.254.2, 00:00:03, Serial0/0
S    200.0.100.0/24 is directly connected, Null0
     10.0.0.0/8 is variably subnetted, 4 subnets, 2 masks
C       10.10.128.100/32 is directly connected, Loopback0
R       10.10.128.200/32 [120/1] via 10.1.254.2, 00:00:03, Serial0/0
C       10.1.254.0/24 is directly connected, Serial0/0
C       10.1.254.2/32 is directly connected, Serial0/0
     192.168.1.0/30 is subnetted, 1 subnets
C       192.168.1.0 is directly connected, FastEthernet0/1.69
     192.168.2.0/30 is subnetted, 1 subnets
R       192.168.2.0 [120/1] via 10.1.254.2, 00:00:04, Serial0/0
S*   0.0.0.0/0 is directly connected, Null0
```

No real surprises here. Malt has several directly connected routes, in the form of its FA 0/1.69, loopback 0, and serial 0/0 interfaces. And the two locally defined static routes, 0.0.0.0 and 200.0.0.100, are both pointing to null0. Lo and behold, Malt has learned three routes via RIP: Barley's FA 0/1.70 route (192.168.2.0), its loopback interface route (10.10.128.200), and the simulated customer route (200.0.200.0). Note that the customer route received from Barley demonstrates the effects of the route map. This route's received hop count is 3 whereas the other two routes advertised by Barley were received with the default value of 1. The hop count/metric is displayed just after the administrative distance, which for RIP is 120. Here is a summary view of the RIP routes at Barley:

```
Barley#show ip route rip
R    200.0.100.0/24 [120/3] via 10.1.254.1, 00:00:14, Serial0/0
     10.0.0.0/8 is variably subnetted, 4 subnets, 2 masks
R       10.10.128.100/32 [120/1] via 10.1.254.1, 00:00:14, Serial0/0
     192.168.1.0/30 is subnetted, 1 subnets
R       192.168.1.0 [120/1] via 10.1.254.1, 00:00:14, Serial0/0
```

With `Barley` displaying the same type and number of routes, baseline operation is confirmed.

Summary of RIP Requirements

The operational aspects of the RIP network design, as determined through analysis of the legacy RIP configuration, are as follows:

- RIPv2 (without auto-summarization).
- Defaults are in place for update, hold down, and route timeout timers.
- MD5 authentication is in effect using key ID 1 with string `jncie`.
- Direct networks are being redistributed.
- The static route representing an attached customer network is redistributed with an artificially escalated hop count of 3.

Enter Juniper Networks

Based on the analysis of the IOS RIP configuration, we know what needs to be done at `Ale` and `Lager`. To help mitigate any operational impacts, it is decided to first bring up the RIP peerings between `Ale` and `Lager` before attaching them to the existing RIP backbone.

Configure static routes

The configuration begins with the definition of the static route that simulates an attached customer network. The configuration steps for `Ale` are:

```
lab@Ale> configure
Entering configuration mode

[edit]
lab@Ale# edit routing-options

[edit routing-options]
lab@Ale# set static route 200.0.1/24 discard

[edit routing-options]
lab@Ale# show
static {
    route 200.0.1.0/24 discard;
}
```

With the static route defined, the change is committed and the result confirmed (while still in configuration mode). In this example, traffic matching the static route is directed to a discard next hop, which means that no responses will be generated for matching traffic—a true black hole from which nothing will escape. Another option would be reject, which generates an Internet Control Message Protocol

(ICMP) error reporting that the destination is unreachable. This creates functionality similar to IOS's null0, in that matching traffic will generate host unreachable error messages. The reject option can assist in troubleshooting, but it consumes router resources in the form of message generation, which can be an issue during a large-scale denial of service (DoS) attack, making discard the preferred target for such a route:

```
[edit routing-options]
lab@Ale# commit
commit complete

[edit routing-options]
lab@Ale# run show route protocol static

inet.0: 6 destinations, 6 routes (6 active, 0 holddown, 0 hidden)
+ = Active Route, - = Last Active, * = Both

200.0.1.0/24        *[Static/5] 00:00:37
                     Discard
```

Configure RIP

The RIP configuration is now added to Ale. Start by moving to the RIP configuration hierarchy, where the general options are shown:

```
[edit routing-options]
lab@Ale# top edit protocols rip

[edit protocols rip]
lab@Ale# set ?
Possible completions:
+ apply-groups          Groups from which to inherit configuration data
+ apply-groups-except   Don't inherit configuration data from these groups
  authentication-key    Authentication key (password)
  authentication-type   Authentication type
  check-zero            Check reserved fields on incoming RIPv2 packets
> graceful-restart      RIP graceful restart options
> group                 Instance configuration
  holddown              Hold-down time (10..180 seconds)
+ import                Import policy
  message-size          Number of route entries per update message (25..255)
  metric-in             Metric value to add to incoming routes (1..15)
  no-check-zero         Don't check reserved fields on incoming RIPv2 packets
> receive               Configure RIP receive options
> rib-group             Routing table group for importing RIP routes
  route-timeout         Delay before routes time out (30..360 seconds)
> send                  Configure RIP send options
> traceoptions          Trace options for RIP
  update-interval       Interval between regular route updates (10..60 seconds)
[edit protocols rip]
lab@Ale# set
```

It should be apparent that many aspects of RIP are configurable within JUNOS software. Some options are global, such as the authentication key/type or import/export policy, which means they apply to all groups (unless negated by a more specific group setting, if available). Other parameters can be specified only at a subsequent hierarchy. For example, a neighbor can be defined only within a group. You can quickly explore the options available under send and receive using the command-line interface's (CLI's) ? help utility:

```
[edit protocols rip]
lab@Ale# set send ?
Possible completions:
  broadcast             Broadcast RIPv2 packets (RIPv1 compatible)
  multicast             Multicast RIPv2 packets
  none                  Do not send RIP updates
  version-1             Broadcast RIPv1 packets
[edit protocols rip]
lab@Ale# set receive ?
Possible completions:
  both                  Accept both RIPv1 and RIPv2 packets
  none                  Do not receive RIP packets
  version-1             Accept RIPv1 packets only
  version-2             Accept only RIPv2 packets
```

It's apparent from the display that the send and receive settings globally control the RIP version and whether multicast (default for v2) or broadcast packets are sent. It just so happens that these same settings can also be specified on a per-neighbor (interface) basis—recall that in JUNOS software, the more-specific group-level configuration hierarchy settings override the less-specific global values. Let's take a quick look at the options available under a group, which is where you can define neighbors (interfaces) that run RIP:

```
[edit protocols rip]
lab@Ale# set group rip ?
Possible completions:
  <[Enter]>             Execute this command
+ apply-groups          Groups from which to inherit configuration data
+ apply-groups-except   Don't inherit configuration data from these groups
> bfd-liveness-detection  Bidirectional Forwarding Detection options
+ export                Export policy
+ import                Import policy
  metric-out            Default metric of exported routes (1..15)
> neighbor              Neighbor configuration
  preference            Preference of routes learned by this group
  route-timeout         Delay before routes time out (30..360 seconds)
  update-interval       Interval between regular route updates (10..60 seconds)
|                       Pipe through a command
```

Configuration options found at the neighbor level include the import or export keyword, which is used to apply routing policy to receive or transmit route updates, respectively. Note that when applied at the neighbor level, any globally defined import or export policies are negated. The router runs *either* the global or the group policy, never both, and the router always chooses the most specific application—a neighbor level is more specific than a global level, of course. You may recall that policy is used to control route exchange and alter route attributes. The global preference for routes learned from a particular neighbor can also be configured here. Note that in JUNOS software, the concept of global preference is equivalent to that of IOS's administrative distance—this value is altered to make a source of routing information more (lower value) or less (higher value) preferred.

The terminology of groups and neighbors may seem a bit confusing at first, given the way RIP is configured in IOS. JUNOS software is optimized when routing peers with similar export policy are placed into the same group. As a result, even if you have only one peer, that neighbor needs to belong to a RIP group. Also, the term *neighbor* here actually means *interface*, given that RIP messages are not unicast to specific machines, but instead are broadcast or multicast to all RIP speakers on a given link. This means that specifying a single neighbor in the form of a multiaccess interface results in RIP communications with all RIP-capable routers on that LAN segment.

Ale's RIP configuration. Ale's RIP stanza is now configured in accordance with the RIP design guideline discovered when analyzing the legacy RIP configuration. Recall that the plan is to first establish RIP peerings between Ale and Lager before trying route exchanges to the Cisco routers (see Figure 4-3). Here is the resulting RIP stanza, along with the set commands used to create it courtesy of the display set function in the CLI:

```
[edit protocols rip]
lab@Ale# show
send multicast;
receive version-2;
authentication-type md5;
authentication-key "$9$cf3rK84oGiHm-VgJ"; ## SECRET-DATA
group rip {
    inactive: neighbor fe-0/0/0.69;
    neighbor fe-0/0/0.1121;
}
[edit protocols rip]
lab@Ale# show | display set
set protocols rip send multicast
set protocols rip receive version-2
set protocols rip authentication-type md5
set protocols rip authentication-key "$9$cf3rK84oGiHm-VgJ"
deactivate protocols rip group rip neighbor fe-0/0/0.69
set protocols rip group rip neighbor fe-0/0/0.1121
```

The global send multicast statement ensures that we will only speak to RIPv2 nodes, as RIPv1 routers will not see multicast updates. The receive version-2 ensures that we process only multicast updates, thereby configuring the router for RIPv2-only operation. The authentication settings specify a (now ciphered) text string of jncie and indicates that MD5-based authentication should be used.

 JUNOS software always encrypts passwords; IOS requires that the password encryption service be enabled for the same functionality.

Lastly, notice the two neighbor statements that identify what interfaces RIP should run on. Note that the link to Malt is currently deactivated (inactive), which means that portion of the configuration will be ignored. This will result in Ale running RIP only on the fe-0/0/0.1121 interface to Lager. Once RIP has been confirmed between Ale and Lager, this link will be activated to enable RIP exchanges with the Cisco routers.

The one part of Ale's configuration yet to be addressed is the redistribution into RIP of its connected and simulated customer static routes. Recall that in JUNOS software, control over what routes enter and leave the route table and the modification of attributes associated with these routes, is controlled by routing policy. Here is an example of the JUNOS route policy needed to match the Cisco router's redistribution of connected (direct) routes and the route map function that sets the metric on a redistributed static route:

```
[edit policy-options policy-statement rip_export]
lab@Ale# show
term 1 {
    from protocol direct;
    then accept;
}
term 2 {
    from {
        protocol static;
        route-filter 200.0.1.0/24 exact;
    }
    then {
        metric 3;
        accept;
    }
}
[edit policy-options policy-statement rip_export]
lab@Ale# show | display set
set policy-options policy-statement rip_export term 1 from protocol direct
set policy-options policy-statement rip_export term 1 then accept
set policy-options policy-statement rip_export term 2 from protocol static
set policy-options policy-statement rip_export term 2 from route-filter 200.0.1.0/24
exact
set policy-options policy-statement rip_export term 2 then metric 3
set policy-options policy-statement rip_export term 2 then accept
```

The newly created RIP policy is applied to the RIP group (alternatively, it could be applied globally in this example) as export, where it will control the exchange of routes that are advertised into RIP. The default RIP import policy, which is to accept RIP routes, is left unaltered.

```
[edit]
lab@Ale# set protocols rip group rip export rip_export

[edit]
lab@Ale# show protocols rip
send multicast;
receive version-2;
authentication-type md5;
authentication-key "$9$cf3rK84oGiHm-VgJ"; ## SECRET-DATA
group rip {
    export rip_export;
    inactive: neighbor fe-0/0/0.69;
    neighbor fe-0/0/0.1121;
}
```

You may assume that a compatible RIP policy configuration has been added to Lager and that the changes are committed.

Confirm RIP Operation: Ale and Lager

With the RIP and related static route/policy configuration in place at Ale and Lager, the operation of RIP can be confirmed. Start with the confirmation that RIPv2 is running, and that it is doing so on the expected interfaces:

```
lab@Ale> show rip neighbor
                      Source        Destination    Send    Receive   In
Neighbor      State   Address       Address        Mode    Mode      Met
--------      -----   -------       -----------    ----    -------   ---
fe-0/0/0.1121   Up    10.10.129.1   224.0.0.9      mcast   v2 only    1
```

The output of the show rip neighbor command confirms that Ale is set for v2 operation, and that RIP is running on its link to Lager. The Up status indicates that the interface is operational, but not that any particular neighbor has been detected. The In Met column displays the metric value that will be added to any route updates received over the associated interfaces; by default, each received update has its metric incremented by one before being placed into the route table.

The general RIP statistics confirm that updates are being sent and received, that no errors are occurring, and that in the case of Ale, three routes have been learned via RIP, indicating that RIP is operating correctly between Ale and Lager:

```
lab@Ale> show rip statistics
RIPv2 info: port 520; holddown 120s.
    rts learned  rts held down  rqsts dropped  resps dropped
            3              0              0              0

fe-0/0/0.1121:  3 routes learned; 3 routes advertised; timeout 180s;
update interval 30s
Counter                     Total   Last 5 min   Last minute
-------                     -----------  -----------  -----------
```

Updates Sent	25	11	2
Triggered Updates Sent	1	0	0
Responses Sent	0	0	0
Bad Messages	0	0	0
RIPv1 Updates Received	0	0	0
RIPv1 Bad Route Entries	0	0	0
RIPv1 Updates Ignored	0	0	0
RIPv2 Updates Received	17	11	2
RIPv2 Bad Route Entries	0	0	0
RIPv2 Updates Ignored	0	0	0
Authentication Failures	1	0	0
RIP Requests Received	1	0	0
RIP Requests Ignored	0	0	0

And now we confirm the presence of RIP routes in Ale's route table:

```
lab@Ale> show route protocol rip

inet.0: 10 destinations, 10 routes (10 active, 0 holddown, 0 hidden)
+ = Active Route, - = Last Active, * = Both

10.10.128.2/32     *[RIP/100] 00:09:54, metric 2, tag 0
                    > to 10.10.129.2 via fe-0/0/0.1121
192.168.2.0/30     *[RIP/100] 00:09:54, metric 2, tag 0
                    > to 10.10.129.2 via fe-0/0/0.1121
200.0.2.0/24       *[RIP/100] 00:09:54, metric 4, tag 0
                    > to 10.10.129.2 via fe-0/0/0.1121
224.0.0.9/32       *[RIP/100] 00:10:57, metric 1
                    MultiRecv
```

Ale's route table contains the expected RIP routes, considering that RIP is not yet enabled to Malt and Barley. Notice that Lager has advertised its directly connected loopback interface (10.10.128.2) route to Ale. Also of note is that the JUNOS software route table displays the local RIP cost, as opposed to the metric received in the route update. This differs a bit from IOS, which displays the received RIP metric rather than local cost (received + 1 by default). The 200.0.0.2/24 static route defined at Lager has been injected into RIP with a metric of 3 due to the action of its export policy—this route is installed in Ale's route table with a local cost of 3 + 1, or 4. You'll also see that the RIP global preference in JUNOS software is 100.

A later section details additional operational mode commands that assist in debugging RIP operation. But right now, all seems to be working as expected, so there is not much to debug. Of course, things might change when tying into the Cisco portion of the network.

Confirm RIP: Juniper Networks to Cisco Systems Integration

With RIP operation in the Juniper and Cisco domains confirmed, it's time to fire up RIP between the two vendors' boxes to see what happens. RIP is a simple protocol, so what could go wrong? Things start with the activation of the RIP neighbor (interface) linking Ale to Malt. Similar steps are performed at Lager for its RIP interface to Barley:

```
lab@Ale> configure
Entering configuration mode

[edit]
lab@Ale# activate protocols rip group rip neighbor fe-0/0/0.69

[edit]
lab@Ale# commit
commit complete
```

Confirm route exchange

After a few minutes, RIP updates should have propagated. Let's start with a quick look at RIP statistics at router Lager, as any problems will likely manifest in the form of an incrementing error counter:

```
[edit]
lab@Lager# run show rip statistics
RIPv2 info: port 520; holddown 120s.
    rts learned  rts held down  rqsts dropped  resps dropped
           10              0              0              0


fe-0/0/0.1121:  3 routes learned; 3 routes advertised; timeout 180s;
update interval 30s
Counter                      Total   Last 5 min  Last minute
-------                ----------- ----------- -----------
Updates Sent                    29          11            2
Triggered Updates Sent           1           0            0
Responses Sent                   0           0            0
Bad Messages                     0           0            0
RIPv1 Updates Received           0           0            0
RIPv1 Bad Route Entries          0           0            0
RIPv1 Updates Ignored            0           0            0
RIPv2 Updates Received          29          10            2
RIPv2 Bad Route Entries          0           0            0
RIPv2 Updates Ignored            0           0            0
Authentication Failures          0           0            0
RIP Requests Received            0           0            0
RIP Requests Ignored             0           0            0


fe-0/0/0.70:  7 routes learned; 3 routes advertised; timeout 180s;
update interval 30s
Counter                      Total   Last 5 min  Last minute
-------                ----------- ----------- -----------
Updates Sent                    29          11            2
Triggered Updates Sent           1           0            0
Responses Sent                   0           0            0
Bad Messages                     0           0            0
RIPv1 Updates Received           0           0            0
RIPv1 Bad Route Entries          0           0            0
RIPv1 Updates Ignored            0           0            0
RIPv2 Updates Received          31          11            2
RIPv2 Bad Route Entries          0           0            0
```

```
RIPv2 Updates Ignored              0           0           0
Authentication Failures            0           0           0
RIP Requests Received              0           0           0
RIP Requests Ignored               0           0           0
```

The RIP statistics indicate that all is normal. Lager is confirming that 10 routes have been learned via RIP, with three coming from its link to Ale and the balance learned from its link to Barley. Authentication is clearly working, given the learned routes and no indication of message discards or errors.

Next, confirm whether any RIP routes are present in the route table of Lager:

```
[edit]
lab@Lager# run show route protocol rip

inet.0: 18 destinations, 18 routes (18 active, 0 holddown, 0 hidden)
+ = Active Route, - = Last Active, * = Both

0.0.0.0/0          *[RIP/100] 00:16:35, metric 2, tag 200
                   > to 192.168.2.1 via fe-0/0/0.70
10.1.254.0/24      *[RIP/100] 00:16:35, metric 2, tag 0
                   > to 192.168.2.1 via fe-0/0/0.70
10.1.254.1/32      *[RIP/100] 00:16:35, metric 2, tag 0
                   > to 192.168.2.1 via fe-0/0/0.70
10.10.128.100/32   *[RIP/100] 00:16:35, metric 3, tag 0
                   > to 192.168.2.1 via fe-0/0/0.70
10.10.128.200/32   *[RIP/100] 00:16:35, metric 2, tag 0
                   > to 192.168.2.1 via fe-0/0/0.70
10.10.128.1/32     *[RIP/100] 00:16:29, metric 2, tag 0
                   > to 10.10.129.1 via fe-0/0/0.1121
192.168.1.0/30     *[RIP/100] 00:16:29, metric 2, tag 0
                   > to 10.10.129.1 via fe-0/0/0.1121
200.0.1.0/24       *[RIP/100] 00:16:29, metric 4, tag 0
                   > to 10.10.129.1 via fe-0/0/0.1121
200.0.100.0/24     *[RIP/100] 00:16:35, metric 5, tag 0
                   > to 192.168.2.1 via fe-0/0/0.70
200.0.200.0/24     *[RIP/100] 00:11:44, metric 4, tag 0
                   > to 192.168.2.1 via fe-0/0/0.70
224.0.0.9/32       *[RIP/100] 00:16:50, metric 1
                      MultiRecv
```

RIP routes are present. The routes learned through RIP include the serial link between Malt and Barley (10.1.254.0/24 and associated host routes), the two simulated customer networks (200.0.100/24 and 200.0.200/24), and the RIP peering network for the link between Malt and Ale (192.168.2.0/30). Also present are the /32 routes for Malt's and Barley's loopback 0 interfaces (10.10.128.100 and 10.10.128.200). The default route is present, and it's correctly pointing to neighbor Barley, given the metric should be less via this path than forwarding through Ale to reach the default advertised by Barley.

The RIP routes at Barley are examined next:

```
Barley#show ip route rip
R    200.0.1.0/24 [120/4] via 10.1.254.1, 00:00:27, Serial0/0
```

```
R     200.0.2.0/24 [120/3] via 192.168.2.2, 00:00:25, FastEthernet0/1.70
R     200.0.100.0/24 [120/3] via 10.1.254.1, 00:00:27, Serial0/0
      10.0.0.0/8 is variably subnetted, 7 subnets, 2 masks
R        10.10.128.100/32 [120/1] via 10.1.254.1, 00:00:27, Serial0/0
R        10.10.129.0/24 [120/1] via 192.168.2.2, 00:00:25, FastEthernet0/1.70
R        10.10.128.1/32 [120/2] via 10.1.254.1, 00:00:27, Serial0/0
R        10.10.128.2/32 [120/1] via 192.168.2.2, 00:00:25, FastEthernet0/1.70
      192.168.1.0/30 is subnetted, 1 subnets
R        192.168.1.0 [120/1] via 10.1.254.1, 00:00:27, Serial0/0
```

The display confirms that RIP exchanges are working between the Juniper Networks routers and the Cisco boxes; Barley has a RIP route for both of Ale's and Lager's simulated customer networks (200.0.1/24 and 200.0.2/24) as well as the link between Ale and Lager (10.10.129.0/24), in addition to the /32 loopback addresses assigned to Ale and Lager (10.10.128.1 and 10.10.128.2).

Confirm forwarding path

A traceroute is performed from Lager to the simulated network on Barley to validate the data plane and resulting forwarding paths (the no-resolve switch ensures that the local router does not waste time trying to perform reverse Domain Name System [DNS] lookups on the resulting IP addresses in the event that DNS is not configured in the lab):

```
[edit]
lab@Ale# run traceroute no-resolve 200.0.200.1
traceroute to 200.0.200.1 (200.0.200.1), 30 hops max, 40 byte packets
 1  192.168.1.1  9.498 ms  9.705 ms  10.127 ms
 2  10.1.254.2  19.700 ms  20.004 ms  20.073 ms
 3  10.1.254.2  19.772 ms !H *  20.392 ms !H
```

The traceroute results are as expected; router Ale crossed two routers to reach the simulated customer network, and as previously noted, the null0 action of the longest match resulted in ICMP host unreachable messages, as indicated by the !H in the return. The results seem to indicate that RIPv2 is working between JUNOS software and IOS. Congratulations!

RIP troubleshooting scenario. Actually, nothing in the realm of internetworking works the first time. In fact, the results of that traceroute should have gotten you thinking a bit. Given the RIP topology, Ale *should* have two equal cost paths to the simulated customer network attached to Barley. After all, it's two hops to reach Barley via Malt, but also two hops to reach Barley via Lager. Knowing that JUNOS software automatically performs load balancing over as many as 16 equal cost paths, you'd expect to see Ale with two equal cost routes for the 200.0.200/24 route. Unfortunately, previous displays confirm this is not the case. A similar condition exists at Lager with regard to the simulated customer route at Malt.

There are a few tools for troubleshooting this type of issue in JUNOS software. One approach is protocol tracing, used to show the RIP messages being sent and received, and the overall results of RIP message processing. Tracing is similar to the IOS *debug* feature. Given that RIP is a DV protocol, you can also avail yourself of the show route advertising-protocol and the show route receiving-protocol commands. As their names imply, these commands display what routes the local router is advertising out a given interface or what routes are being received (learned) from a particular neighbor. The process begins at router Lager:

```
[edit]
lab@Lager# run show route advertising-protocol rip ?
Possible completions:
<neighbor>         IP address of neighbor (local for RIP and RIPng)
```

The command syntax help string of ? is useful here because it reminds us that for the RIP form of this command, you must specify the *local interface address*; recall that RIP generates broadcast or multicast updates to all neighbors on the link, so unlike BGP, where a specific neighbor address is specified, it's the local IP address for RIP.

```
[edit]
lab@Lager# run show route advertising-protocol rip 10.10.129.2

inet.0: 18 destinations, 18 routes (18 active, 0 holddown, 0 hidden)
+ = Active Route, - = Last Active, * = Both

10.10.128.2/32      *[Direct/0] 02:31:29
                     > via lo0.0
192.168.2.0/30      *[Direct/0] 02:31:29
                     > via fe-0/0/0.70
200.0.2.0/24        *[Static/5] 02:32:10
                     Discard
```

The result leaves something to be desired—something such as a route advertisement for the 200.0.200/24 route, that is! The receiving-protocol form of the command is used to confirm that whatever is wrong is at least symmetrical:

```
lab@Lager# run show route receive-protocol rip ?
Possible completions:
<peer>              IP address of neighbor
```

Note that for the receiving-protocol command, RIP requires the specification of a *specific neighbor IP* address, which in turn is reachable via a RIP-enabled interface (a good way to look at this is to consider that transmitted updates are sent to all neighbors, but received updates come from a specific neighbor—a source IP address is never of the multicast/broadcast form):

```
[edit]
lab@Lager# run show route receive-protocol rip 10.10.129.1

inet.0: 18 destinations, 18 routes (18 active, 0 holddown, 0 hidden)
+ = Active Route, - = Last Active, * = Both

10.10.128.1/32      *[RIP/100] 01:01:13, metric 2, tag 0
                     > to 10.10.129.1 via fe-0/0/0.1121
```

```
   192.168.1.0/30      *[RIP/100] 01:01:13, metric 2, tag 0
                        > to 10.10.129.1 via fe-0/0/0.1121
   200.0.1.0/24        *[RIP/100] 01:01:13, metric 4, tag 0
                        > to 10.10.129.1 via fe-0/0/0.1121
```

The preceding output proves that, like Lager, Ale is not readvertising the 200.0.100/24 route learned from Malt. For added verification, we configure RIP tracing at Ale.

```
[edit protocols rip]
lab@Ale# set traceoptions file rip_trace

[edit protocols rip]
lab@Ale# set traceoptions flag ?
Possible completions:
  all                 Trace everything
  auth                Trace RIP authentication
  error               Trace RIP errors
  expiration          Trace RIP route expiration processing
  general             Trace general events
  holddown            Trace RIP hold-down processing
  normal              Trace normal events
  packets             Trace all RIP packets
  policy              Trace policy processing
  request             Trace RIP information packets
  route               Trace routing information
  state               Trace state transitions
  task                Trace routing protocol task processing
  timer               Trace routing protocol timer processing
  trigger             Trace RIP triggered updates
  update              Trace RIP update packets
[edit protocols rip]
lab@Ale# set traceoptions flag update detail

[edit protocols rip]
lab@Ale# commit
```

No one wants a tool he can't use when he needs it. JUNOS software protocol tracing is much like Cisco Systems' debug in that it's a great way to gain insight into the operation of a given protocol, especially when things are not working. The upside is that you can deploy tracing on a Juniper Networks router, in a production network, with little to no operational impact—that is, the manual does not warn against using tracing, which is the case for debug in IOS. With that said, it is a best practice to enable tracing only when needed and only at the level of detail needed, and then to remove the tracing configuration when the job is done.

Also note that the Juniper Networks architecture cleanly separates the control and forwarding planes, which means that you can monitor interface traffic (tcpdump) or trace protocol operation only when it is sourced from or destined to the local router's Routing Engine (RE). You cannot monitor or trace transit traffic unless a sampling configuration is used to sample/mirror such traffic out of a specific interface.

This example shows the RIP tracing options along with a sample RIP tracing configuration. Here, traffic matching the update flag is written to a file called *rip_trace*. Various other trace flags exist and are useful when dealing with specific issues, such as using the auth flag when you suspect an authentication problem. The *rip_trace* file is monitored in real time with the monitor start command:

```
[edit protocols rip]
lab@Ale# run monitor start rip_trace
. . .
Aug 15 02:00:30.039884 Update job: sending 20 msgs; nbr: fe-0/0/0.1121;
group: rip; msgp: 0x876a000.
Aug 15 02:00:30.039916  nbr fe-0/0/0.1121; msgp 0x876a000.
Aug 15 02:00:30.039985                0.84.1.20/0x46c25e20: tag 3, nh
0.0.0.0, met 0.
Aug 15 02:00:30.040011            10.10.128.1/0xffffffff: tag 0, nh
0.0.0.0, met 1.
Aug 15 02:00:30.040027            192.168.1.0/0xfffffffc: tag 0, nh
0.0.0.0, met 1.
Aug 15 02:00:30.040041             200.0.1.0/0xffffff00: tag 0, nh
0.0.0.0, met 3.
Aug 15 02:00:30.040053         sending msg 0x876a004, 4 rtes
(needs MD5)
Aug 15 02:00:30.040691 Update job done for nbr fe-0/0/0.1121
group: rip
Aug 15 02:00:32.560426 received response: sender 10.10.129.2,
command 2, version 2, mbz: 0; 5 routes.
Aug 15 02:00:32.560579     10.10.128.2/0xffffffff: tag 0, nh
0.0.0.0, met 1.
Aug 15 02:00:32.560645     192.168.2.0/0xfffffffc: tag 0, nh
0.0.0.0, met 1.
Aug 15 02:00:32.560694     200.0.2.0/0xffffff00: tag 0, nh
0.0.0.0, met 3.

*** monitor and syslog output disabled, press ESC-Q to enable ***
```

You can enter the Esc-q key sequence to suspend trace output to the screen while information is still being written to the trace field. Pressing Esq-q again resumes output to the screen. It's nice to be able to enable tracing and suspend it on demand so that you can read what has been painted to the screen, without having to type something such as "undebug IP rip," all while your screen is overflowing with debug data. Use the monitor stop command to stop tailing the logfile. The monitor list command shows any logfiles that are being monitored.

The RIP tracing information relating to neighbor fe-0/0/0.1121 confirms the results of the show route-advertising protocol command; namely that Lager is not readvertising routes that it learns via RIP to other RIP neighbors. Having seen what there is to be seen, RIP tracing is diligently removed:

```
[edit protocols rip]
lab@Ale# delete traceoptions
```

```
[edit protocols rip]
lab@Ale# commit
commit complete
```

The Problem

Think back to your knowledge of JUNOS software routing policy; you'll recall that
an export policy is the entity responsible for taking *active* routes from the route table
and placing them into outgoing protocol updates. Because the problem route is in
the route table, is active, and is confirmed as not being advertised to another RIP
neighbor, it would seem to be a classic case of broken export policy. But why is our
export broken?

In JUNOS software, all protocols have a default import and export policy. The
default import policy for RIP is to accept all (sane) RIP routes, as you might expect.
However, the default RIP export policy is to *advertise nothing*; not even routes
learned through RIP! Put another way, and for whatever reason, the configuration of
RIP in JUNOS software is not a simple matter of router rip combined with a few
network statements. You will almost always want the RIP router to propagate routes
learned via RIP; to do this you will need to add explicit export policy.

You already have a RIP export policy in effect to advertise the direct (connected) and
the simulated customer static routes. Therefore, a quick modification will put things
right again in RIP land:

```
[edit policy-options policy-statement rip_export]
lab@Ale# show
term 1 {
    from protocol direct;
    then accept;
}
term 2 {
    from {
        protocol static;
        route-filter 200.0.1.0/24 exact;
    }
    then {
        metric 3;
        accept;
    }
}

[edit policy-options policy-statement rip_export]
lab@Ale# set term 3 from protocol rip

[edit policy-options policy-statement rip_export]
lab@Ale# set term 3 then accept

[edit policy-options policy-statement rip_export]
lab@Ale# show
```

```
term 1 {
    from protocol direct;
    then accept;
}
term 2 {
    from {
        protocol static;
        route-filter 200.0.1.0/24 exact;
    }
    then {
        metric 3;
        accept;
    }
}
term 3 {
    from protocol rip;
    then accept;
}
```

A similar change is also made (and committed) to the export policy at Lager. After a few minutes, the results are confirmed:

```
[edit]
lab@Lager# run show route receive-protocol rip 10.10.129.1

inet.0: 19 destinations, 19 routes (19 active, 0 holddown, 0 hidden)
+ = Active Route, - = Last Active, * = Both

10.1.254.2/32       *[RIP/100] 00:01:22, metric 3, tag 0
                     > to 10.10.129.1 via fe-0/0/0.1121
10.10.128.100/32    *[RIP/100] 01:31:13, metric 3, tag 0
                        to 192.168.2.1 via fe-0/0/0.70
                     > to 10.10.129.1 via fe-0/0/0.1121
10.10.128.1/32      *[RIP/100] 01:31:07, metric 2, tag 0
                     > to 10.10.129.1 via fe-0/0/0.1121
192.168.1.0/30      *[RIP/100] 01:31:07, metric 2, tag 0
                     > to 10.10.129.1 via fe-0/0/0.1121
200.0.1.0/24        *[RIP/100] 01:31:07, metric 4, tag 0
                     > to 10.10.129.1 via fe-0/0/0.1121
200.0.100.0/24      *[RIP/100] 01:31:13, metric 5, tag 0
                     > to 192.168.2.1 via fe-0/0/0.70
                        to 10.10.129.1 via fe-0/0/0.1121


__juniper_private1__.inet.0: 2 destinations, 2 routes (2 active,
0 holddown, 0 hidden)
```

The show route-receiving protocol rip command at Lager confirms that Ale is now correctly readvertising RIP routes learned from Malt. You can also see the effects of the modified export policy in the show route-advertising protocol rip command issued at Lager:

```
[edit]
lab@Lager# run show route advertising-protocol rip 10.10.129.2

inet.0: 19 destinations, 19 routes (19 active, 0 holddown, 0 hidden)
+ = Active Route, - = Last Active, * = Both

0.0.0.0/0          *[RIP/100] 01:31:24, metric 2, tag 200
                    > to 192.168.2.1 via fe-0/0/0.70
10.1.254.0/24      *[RIP/100] 01:31:24, metric 2, tag 0
                    > to 192.168.2.1 via fe-0/0/0.70
10.1.254.1/32      *[RIP/100] 01:31:24, metric 2, tag 0
                    > to 192.168.2.1 via fe-0/0/0.70
10.10.128.200/32   *[RIP/100] 01:31:24, metric 2, tag 0
                    > to 192.168.2.1 via fe-0/0/0.70
10.10.128.2/32     *[Direct/0] 03:05:21
                    > via lo0.0
192.168.2.0/30     *[Direct/0] 03:05:21
                    > via fe-0/0/0.70
200.0.2.0/24       *[Static/5] 03:06:02
                       Discard
200.0.200.0/24     *[RIP/100] 01:26:33, metric 4, tag 0
                    > to 192.168.2.1 via fe-0/0/0.70
```

Lager's output confirms that it too is now readvertising RIP learned routes. As a final verification, the route table at Lager is inspected for the customer network associated with Malt:

```
[edit]
lab@Lager# run show route 200.0.100.0

inet.0: 19 destinations, 19 routes (19 active, 0 holddown, 0 hidden)
+ = Active Route, - = Last Active, * = Both

200.0.100.0/24     *[RIP/100] 01:33:57, metric 5, tag 0
                    > to 192.168.2.1 via fe-0/0/0.70
                      to 10.10.129.1 via fe-0/0/0.1121
```

The route's presence with two forwarding next hops confirms the earlier suspicion that there should be multiple equal cost paths for some RIP destinations in this lab topology. From Lager's there are now two equal cost paths to 200.0.100/24—one via Barley and the other through Ale.

RIP Deployment Summary

RIP really is a simple protocol, and configuring JUNOS software to interoperate with IOS for RIP was, for the most part, pretty straightforward. The most common problem you'll encounter with this scenario is unfamiliarity with the default RIP export policy, which is not intuitive, to say the least. This section demonstrated basic RIP configuration and operational mode commands that assist in troubleshooting RIP operation in a JUNOS software environment.

The next section addresses ways to migrate a network from one IGP to another, a concept called *IGP migration*. Once again, now is an opportune time to take a break before moving on.

IGP Migration

This section examines current best practices for IGP migration, referring to the exchange of a network's existing, or legacy, IGP with a different version of IGP. Generally, the overall goals are to minimize network disruption while also taking the opportunity to improve on the network's design and operation. The IGP plays a critical role in the operation of any IP network. Upgrading a legacy network's IGP can result in dramatic performance improvements and new service capabilities, and can align a company with an open standards-based solution, which in turn facilitates a best-of-breed decision among networking boxes.

IGP migration is an excellent time to clean house, so to speak, by reevaluating all aspects of the current network's design. Some factors to consider include:

- The potential for readdressing to better accommodate hierarchical design and route summarization
- The number and types of routers needed
- How those routers interconnect (WAN/LAN technologies may have evolved since the original network deployment)
- Ways to improve reliability

The need to maintain high network availability may preclude significant redesign. Usually a compromise must be reached between the need for availability versus potential optimizations, based on the specifics unique to each enterprise. In some cases, a new backbone is deployed in parallel (the integration model), which affords the luxury of complete redesign at the cost of additional gear.

IGP Migration: Common Techniques and Concerns

Before discussing specific migration approaches, it makes sense to examine some of the issues and considerations common to all approaches. General factors and concepts applying to IGP migrations include the following:

Global route preference

   IGP transitions often touch on the concept of *global route preference*, which is known as *administrative distance* in IOS. A route's global preference indicates the overall *goodness* of a source of routing information and is used to break ties when two or more protocols announce reachability to the same prefix. Recall that longest match always rules; therefore, a longest-matching RIP route will always be preferred over a less specific version (a shorter netmask) that is learned from a more preferred protocol. For example, a /24 OSPF internal route will lose to a /32 RIP route every day of the week despite its much lower, and therefore preferred, preference. Global preference breaks ties *only* when routes with the *same level of specificity* are learned by multiple routing protocols.

Route redistribution

Route redistribution is the act of exchanging route information among different routing protocols and is a common aspect of most IGP migration strategies. In many cases, you will not configure all routers for the new IGP at the same time and will maintain connectivity between IGP domains by redistributing routes between the new and legacy IGPs at select routers. Because this will typically be mutual, also known as bidirectional route redistribution, you must remain ever-vigilant or else fall victim to the effects of routing loops. Accurate policy is needed to ensure that routes originating within IGP A that are sent into IGP B are never redistributed back into IGP A, and vice versa.

Concurrent IGP operation

Many migration scenarios will require that a device be configured to run instances of both the old and the new IGPs at the same time. The first issue here is whether the device offers support for both protocols. For example, running EIGRP on a Juniper Networks router is simply not an option. Then there are matters of performance—can the device be expected to run two instances of an IGP and still operate reliably? There are numerous cases of IGP migration (ones that were planned to occur with little or no disruption, we might add) that instead melted down when a box started rebooting or peers start flapping, all because of insufficient memory or CPU power when tasked with running both IGPs concurrently. This is something that is often not considered when testing a migration scenario in a lab, where boxes may be running at far lower memory and CPU levels than they would in the production environment.

As a general rule, you can safely run both IGPs concurrently if an existing device's CPU load is less than 50% while its memory load is less than 60%. If the device's CPU or memory load is higher, you should consider a device upgrade or a migration approach that does not place both IGPs in service at the same time.

Network cleanup and design

IGP migration is an opportune time to rid your network of excess baggage and poor design characteristics that may have evolved in an ad hoc fashion over the years. Before migration, you should make sure your network documentation is accurate and that you have reduced as much clutter as possible by removing any unauthorized or unneeded addresses, networks, peers, protocols, and so forth. Careful thought should be leveled at the design of the new IGP. Will it be flat or hierarchical? Does the existing addressing model accommodate? How will metrics be mapped between the old and new IGPs? Where will you place ABRs and ASBRs, and which routers should function as the DRs on LAN segments?

IGP Migration Models

Several proven approaches to IGP transitions have been developed over the years, and most of these approaches share common elements to one degree or another. Each enterprise network is unique, and the specifics of your network design, your standards for acceptable levels of disruption, and your budget will come into play when deciding on a specific approach. The migration strategies are presented in an order representing easiest to most difficult. The more difficult strategies are often combined with a more extensive network redesign given the work already being performed.

The Overlay Model

The overlay model is generally considered the most straightforward IGP migration approach. The overlay is best suited to networks that have a similar *before and after* logical topology. For example, if the legacy network is a flat RIP network and the proposed design is a single area OSPF network, logically both networks are flat and IGP migration will be straightforward. Using an overlay approach to move from a flat to a hierarchical network can be rife with difficulties. For example, a flat network's addressing scheme may not accommodate a sound hierarchical design, and the placement of nodes may not accommodate the desired location or level of redundancy for things such as ABRs.

Figure 4-4 illustrates a network running both the legacy (RIP) and the new (OSPF) IGPs. Because Layer 2 switching is often used in the access and aggregation layers, the focus of most IGP migrations is centered on the core layer—the techniques demonstrated here are applicable for access and aggregation layer migrations as well. Note how both IGPs are configured at the same time, that the new IGP is initially set to be less preferred (both OSPF preference values are larger than RIP's default 100), and that each router sends updates for both IGPs in a ships-in-the-night fashion, meaning that neither IGP is aware of the other's operation.

The overlay model hinges on all devices having the ability to run both the old and the new IGPs concurrently, and it makes heavy use of route preference to keep the new IGP's routes from becoming active, and therefore installed in the forwarding table, until all aspects of the new IGP's operation are determined to be satisfactory. When ready to make the cutover, the route preference is altered to have the routers prefer the new IGP's routes. Ideally, this is all done in parallel, because having some devices use one IGP's routes while other routers use a different IGP's routes can lead to loops stemming from variances between each protocol's take on the best route. In many cases, the odds of which can be improved by the careful mapping of old to new metrics, the forwarding paths of both protocols will be identical and you can get away with an incremental, box-at-a-time shift in protocol preference. When the new IGP's operation is deemed stable, the old IGP is decommissioned by removing its configuration from each router (there is no need to perform this in parallel, as you

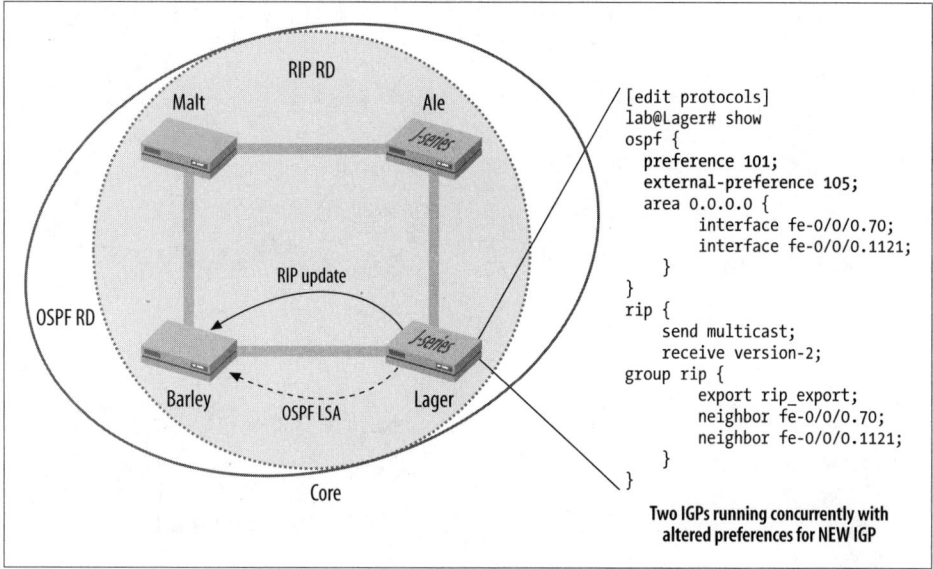

```
                                    [edit protocols]
                                    lab@Lager# show
                                    ospf {
                                        preference 101;
                                        external-preference 105;
                                        area 0.0.0.0 {
                                                interface fe-0/0/0.70;
                                                interface fe-0/0/0.1121;
                                        }
                                    }
                                    rip {
                                        send multicast;
                                        receive version-2;
                                    group rip {
                                            export rip_export;
                                            neighbor fe-0/0/0.70;
                                            neighbor fe-0/0/0.1121;
                                        }
                                    }

                                    Two IGPs running concurrently with
                                    altered preferences for NEW IGP
```

Figure 4-4. The overlay model

are now using the new IGP). It's a good idea to keep a copy of the old configuration around, and you should consider using the deactivate function of the JUNOS software CLI to comment out the old IGP's stanza, all the while knowing that you can safely bring it back at any time by activating that portion of the configuration.

The Redistribution Model

The redistribution model is often used when an overlay approach is not workable due to a migration from a flat to a hierarchical design or because some of the devices cannot run both IGPs concurrently. The latter condition may be due to lack of device support or because of performance limitations. Figure 4-5 illustrates a before-and-after view of a network that, given the shift to a hierarchical design, represents a good candidate for the route redistribution model.

The first phase of the migration from RIP to OSPF is shown in Figure 4-6. Here, backbone routers Ale and Lager are configured to run both RIP and OSPF concurrently, with the OSPF backbone being formed as a result. The arrow shows a RIP update sent by Malt and received by Ale, where it will be injected into the nascent backbone as a Type 5 AS external LSA. Though not shown, routes originating in the OSPF backbone undergo a similar process whereby they are injected into the RIP domain to maintain full connectivity. It is critical to stress that controls must be in place to ensure that routes are never redistributed back into the RD from where they originated, unless your goal is a network-wide test of the IP Time to Live (TTL) mechanism. A well-planned addressing approach always makes the filtering of route updates easier, as does a consistent approach to route tagging (where supported by the protocol). The use of route tags makes control over route redistribution much easier to configure and consequently far less prone to human error.

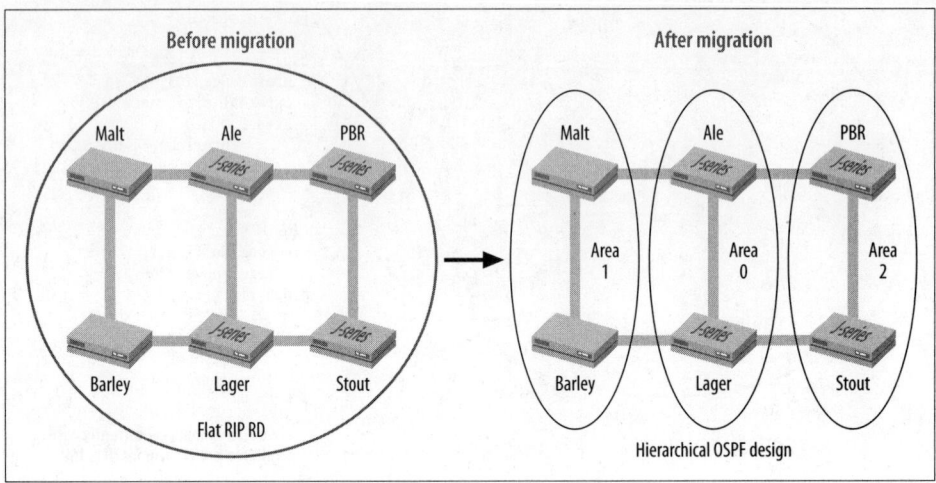

Figure 4-5. The redistribution model

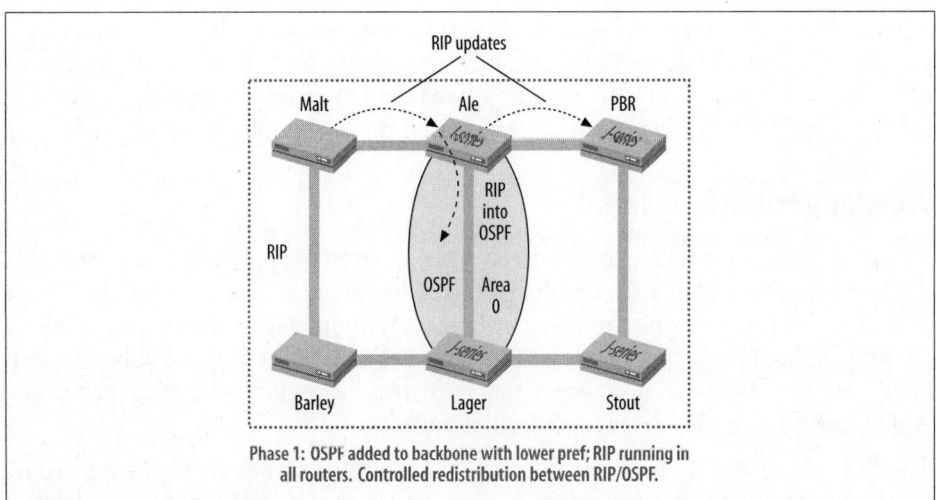

Figure 4-6. Route tagging in the redistribution model to control route exchange

Once again, the OSPF preference is altered to be *less preferred* than that of the original IGP, as was the case in the overlay model. The default global preference for JUNOS software is 100 for RIP and 10/150 for OSPF internal and AS external, respectively. Setting these preferences to 101/110 achieves the goal of ensuring that RIP is preferred. This step ensures that the backbone will always prefer routes in their native RIP form, thus avoiding routing loops and suboptimal routing. By way of example, consider that without this step, router Barley's 200.0.200/24 route might be initially learned by Lager as an OSPF route, via a RIP update that was generated by Malt and then redistributed into OSPF by Ale. By this time, Lager should have also received a RIP update for the same prefix direct from Barley. If the preferences are such that Lager prefers OSPF externals over RIP, we would have an extra hop as Lager forwards packets for 200.0.200/24 route over the OSPF backbone through Ale, rather than the direct shot via Barley.

 In this example, the default JUNOS software route preferences would have resulted in the desired behavior. When redistributed into OSPF, the RIP routes take the form of AS externals, which by default have a preference of 150, which makes them less preferred than RIP anyway. Nonetheless, it's recommended that you always explicitly set preferences. It's rarely a good idea to leave such things to chance in your network!

The next phase of the migration is depicted in Figure 4-7, where routers PBR and Stout have been converted to OSPF and placed into Area 2. The specific approach taken to make this change could have been that of an overlay, where the routers run RIP and OSPF concurrently, or as a hot cutover that removed the old and added the new IGP in one fell swoop. Such cutovers are made a little less stressful with the "nothing happens until you commit" nature of JUNOS software. IOS users would likely paste such changes in from a configuration file to try to minimize disruption. It ends with routers Barley and Malt remaining in the RIP domain along with the associated interfaces on Ale and Lager. The next phase of the migration is an iterative process that repeats the same procedure on Barley and Malt to create Area 1. The IGP migration is completed with removal of any RIP remnants from the configurations of Area 0 routers Ale and Lager.

The Integration Model

The integration model is also well suited to IGP migrations that transition from a flat to a hierarchical design, especially when a significant IP readdressing and/or network infrastructure upgrade is planned as part of the migration. In the integration model, a new backbone network is deployed and tied to the legacy backbone, where mutual route redistribution is performed. Portions of the legacy network are transitioned to the new backbone in a phased manner. This type of migration is not hitless, but its does afford a near green-field chance to redesign your IGP while confining down time to those segments that are actively being transitioned. Once all segments have been migrated to the new backbone, the legacy backbone is decommissioned. This process is shown in Figure 4-8, which begins with the legacy backbone and moves on to the buildout of a new backbone and the migration of one network segment. The process ends with the rightmost diagram showing all network segments transitioned to the new backbone and removal of the legacy backbone infrastructure.

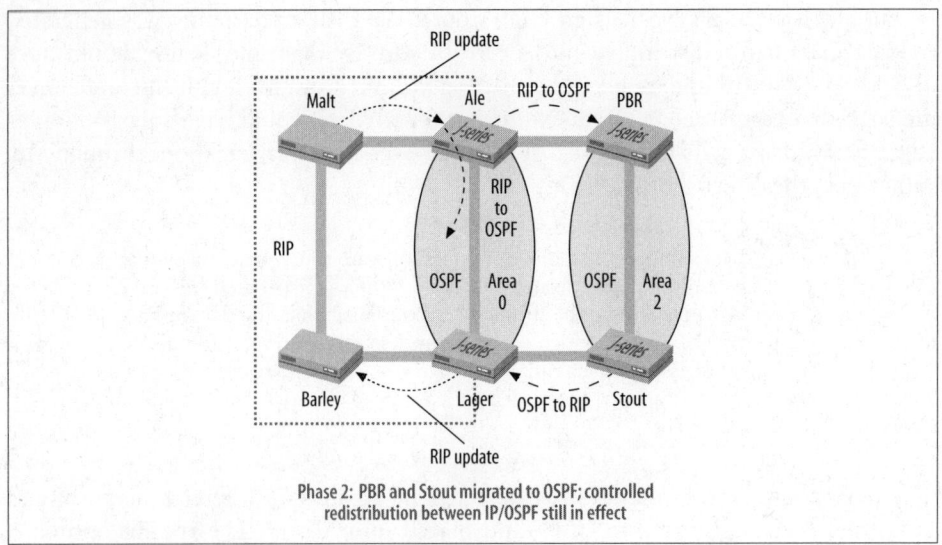

Figure 4-7. Route redistribution IGP migration: Phase 2

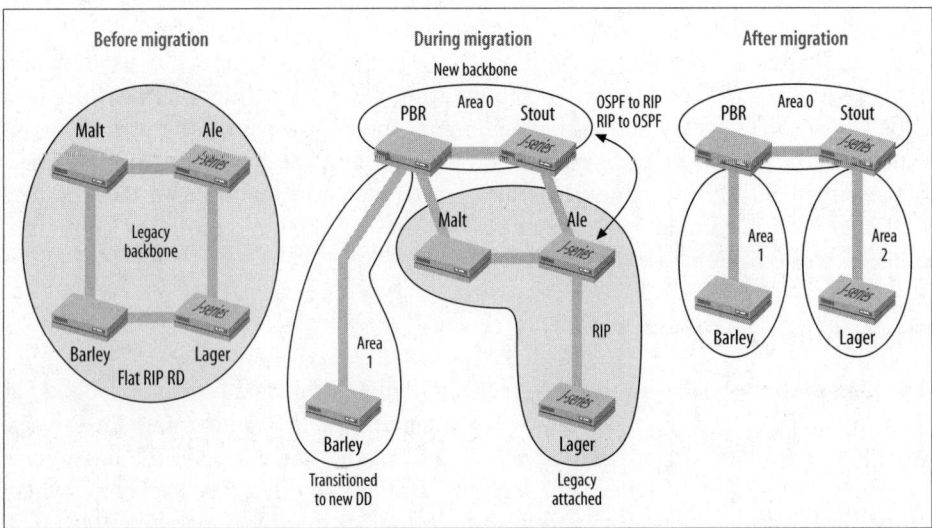

Figure 4-8. The integration model

You'll again find mutual route redistribution at play, and also this requires strict control to prevent routes from being sent back to their originating IGP. As each network segment is transitioned, you may be able to deploy an overlay approach or you might be forced into a hot cutover based on equipment capability and the level of network redesign (e.g., any renumbering that is also planned).

It goes without saying, but we will state it here anyway, that the integration model represents the largest degree of effort and capital expenditure. There is the cost of new equipment and new backbone buildout, and then the sustaining costs of both the legacy and new backbones as segments are transitioned. During these transitions, there may be significant renumbering and a need to deploy the new backbone protocol on routers as they become part of the new IGP.

IGP Migration Summary

Networks, like people, evolve and change over time. Many networks are still running yesterday's IGP and could benefit from a facelift in the interior routing department. Or maybe your network is running some proprietary routing protocol and you have decided that it is time to add another vendor to the network, for whatever reason. Either way, the techniques and concepts discussed here can help to minimize disruption and make the shift to a new IGP as pain-free as possible.

In the next section, you will put this theory into practice as you migrate a network from RIP to the OSPF protocol.

Overlay Migration Scenario: RIP to OSPF

Just when you are considering some well-deserved time off, given the success of the recently deployed RIPv2 internetwork, you receive notification from the new CIO that the Beer-Co network must migrate to OSPF as part of a modernization initiative. Beer-Co has conducted a design review and determined that a single OSPF area with the ability to expand to a hierarchal design in the near future is required.

Considering the migration methods described in the previous section and the current design criteria, you propose an overlay-based migration. The reasons for this recommendation include the following:

- Both the legacy and planned networks are flat.
- Both the legacy Cisco and new Juniper Networks gear support the legacy and new IGPs.
- It's the most direct migration strategy, and you are still smarting from tilting at RIP.

Figure 4-9 shows the before, during, and after networks. In the middle, both IGPs are running, but altered preferences ensure that RIP routes remain active, which provides you the chance to verify all aspects of OSPF *before* its routes become active. The key to the overlay model is altered protocol preferences, and the figure also shows the beginning, initial modification, and final preference values for RIP and OSPF internal/external routes.

The critical point occurs before OSPF is activated (especially in IOS, where changes take effect immediately as they are entered). Both the internal and external preferences are set so that RIP remains unperturbed until you are ready to retire it.

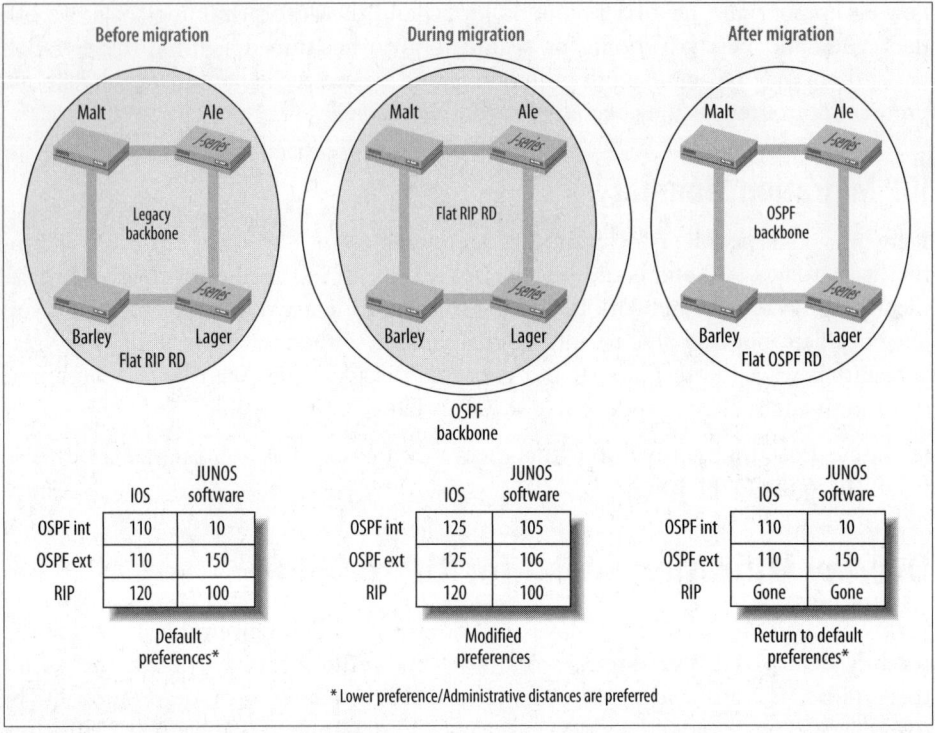

	Before migration			During migration			After migration	

Figure 4-9. RIP-to-OSPF overlay topology

Failing to ensure that OSPF external preference is set lower (is more preferred) than RIP leads to a Frankenstein-like forwarding model that has the simulated customer networks and redistributed loopback routes forwarding over OSPF paths while the internal routes continue to forward via RIP.

The Juniper boxes are configured first (recall that, until you commit, no change takes effect, so you have a safety net of rollback or commit confirmed in case you do not like the results). The OSPF stanza is displayed at Ale along with the associated set commands using the CLI's show | display set command. The authentication key value jncie is reused here. Also of note are the altered preference values for OSPF internal and external routes—that authentication is configured at the area level while the specifics are set on a per-interface basis:

```
[edit protocols ospf]
lab@Ale# show
preference 105;
external-preference 106;
export ospf_export; ## 'ospf_export' is not defined
area 0.0.0.0 {
    authentication-type md5;
    interface fe-0/0/0.69 {
        authentication {
```

```
                md5 1 key "$9$Yb4JD3nCuOI.PF/"; ## SECRET-DATA
            }
        }
        interface fe-0/0/0.1121 {
            authentication {
                md5 1 key "$9$WitXNbiHmTQn4ajq"; ## SECRET-DATA
            }
        }
    }
}

[edit protocols ospf]
lab@Ale# show | display set
set protocols ospf preference 105
set protocols ospf external-preference 106
set protocols ospf export ospf_export
set protocols ospf area 0.0.0.0 authentication-type md5
set protocols ospf area 0.0.0.0 interface fe-0/0/0.69 authentication
md5 1 key "$9$Yb4JD3nCuOI.PF/"
set protocols ospf area 0.0.0.0 interface fe-0/0/0.1121 authentication
md5 1 key "$9$WitXNbiHmTQn4ajq"
```

Like RIP, OSPF requires an export policy for route redistribution, and the CLI's copy
feature is evoked to save some effort:

```
[edit protocols ospf]
lab@Ale# top edit policy-options

[edit policy-options]
lab@Ale# copy policy-statement rip_export to policy-statement
ospf_export

[edit policy-options]
lab@Ale# edit policy-statement ospf_export

[edit policy-options policy-statement ospf_export]
lab@Ale# show
term 1 {
    from protocol direct;
    then accept;
}
term 2 {
    from {
        protocol static;
        route-filter 200.0.1.0/24 exact;
    }
    then {
        metric 3;
        accept;
    }
}
term 3 {
    from protocol rip;
    then accept;
}
```

Looking over the copy of the RIP policy, now in its renamed ospf_export form, it seems that the only term that is out of place is term 3 and the bit about matching RIP. You certainly do not want any RIP-to-OSPF redistribution in this example! We remove term 3 (committing the changes) and make similar changes to Lager:

```
[edit policy-options policy-statement ospf_export]
lab@Ale# delete term 3
```

After a few moments, the OSPF adjacency status is confirmed between Ale and Lager. Recall that Malt and Barley have not been configured with OSPF at this time:

```
[edit]
lab@Ale# run show ospf interface
Interface        State     Area      DR ID        BDR ID        Nbrs
fe-0/0/0.1121    DR        0.0.0.0   10.10.128.1  10.10.128.2   1
fe-0/0/0.69      DR        0.0.0.0   10.10.128.1  0.0.0.0       0
```

The output from the show ospf interface command confirms that OSPF is running on the desired interfaces and that local router Ale has won the DR election on both of its interfaces. Considering that Ale is alone (zero neighbors have been detected) on its fe-0/0/0.69 interface, its DR status on that segment should be no surprise. You can also verify the area 0 setting and that the only other router on the fe0-0/0/0.1121 link has delegated itself to be the backup DR. Remember that priority and RID factor only during an active election. Given the matched priority and Ale's lower RID (its lo0 address is lower than Lager's), this must be a case of Ale having been configured for OSPF first. The first non-0 priority router up always becomes the DR:

```
[edit]
lab@Ale# run show ospf neighbor
  Address         Interface       State     ID           Pri Dead
  10.10.129.2     fe-0/0/0.1121   Full      10.10.128.2  128  38
```

The show ospf neighbor command verifies that a full adjacency has been formed between Ale and Lager, which is a very good sign indeed:

```
[edit]
lab@Ale# run show route protocol ospf

inet.0: 19 destinations, 22 routes (19 active, 0 holddown, 0 hidden)
+ = Active Route, - = Last Active, * = Both

10.10.128.2/32      [OSPF/105] 00:01:03, metric 1
                    > to 10.10.129.2 via fe-0/0/0.1121
192.168.2.0/30      [OSPF/105] 00:01:03, metric 2
                    > to 10.10.129.2 via fe-0/0/0.1121
200.0.2.0/24        [OSPF/106] 00:01:03, metric 3, tag 0
                    > to 10.10.129.2 via fe-0/0/0.1121
224.0.0.5/32        *[OSPF/10] 00:07:52, metric 1
                    MultiRecv
```

Showing the routes learned via OSPF confirms several important points. One is simply that routes are being learned via OSPF (Lager's 10.10.126.2 loopback and the

192.168.2.0 link to Barley), and equally significant is that none of these learned OSPF route are currently active.

 Unlike IOS, which requires that you run OSPF on the loopback interface to advertise its associated route, JUNOS software automatically advertises a stub route to the *default* address used as the source of the RID, assuming that a RID has not been explicitly set under [routing-options]. Because the lo0 interface is the first to be activated, the lo0 interface's *primary* address is used as the RID. In contrast, for IOS it is common to either run a passive OSPF instance on the loopback interface or to redistribute the connected router into OSPF, as shown in the following example.

A final confirmation that our route preference changes are working comes when we display the route to Lager's customer network at Ale:

```
[edit]
lab@Ale# run show route 200.0.2.0

inet.0: 19 destinations, 22 routes (19 active, 0 holddown, 0 hidden)
+ = Active Route, - = Last Active, * = Both

200.0.2.0/24        *[RIP/100] 02:47:22, metric 4, tag 0
                     > to 10.10.129.2 via fe-0/0/0.1121
                     [OSPF/106] 00:09:29, metric 3, tag 0
                     > to 10.10.129.2 via fe-0/0/0.1121
```

Perfect! Ale has both OSPF and RIP copies of the customer route. The key thing here is that the original RIP version is, and has always been, active. Unlike RIP, the displayed OSPF route metric does not reflect Ale's interface costs to reach Lager. With the default scaling factor of 100,000,000, the cost for Ale's Fast Ethernet interface is 1 (you can confirm this with a show ospf interface detail command), so you might expect to see Ale display a cost of 4 for the 200.0.0.2/24 prefix. The reason for this situation is that the OSPF_export policy at Lager did not bother to specify a Type 1 external metric, so the default Type 2 metric is generated, and by OSPF standards this metric is never incremented by other routers. A sample of a policy modification that alters the metric type is provided, along with the results observed back at Ale. These changes are then rolled back to restore the initial behavior:

```
[edit policy-options policy-statement ospf_export]
lab@Lager# show
term 1 {
    from protocol direct;
    then accept;
}
term 2 {
    from {
        protocol static;
        route-filter 200.0.2.0/24 exact;
    }
```

```
           then {
               metric 3;
               external {
                   type 1;
               }
               accept;
           }
       }
       }
       [edit]
       lab@Ale# run show route 200.0.2.0

       inet.0: 19 destinations, 22 routes (19 active, 0 holddown, 0 hidden)
       + = Active Route, - = Last Active, * = Both

       200.0.2.0/24        *[RIP/100] 03:03:06, metric 4, tag 0
                            > to 10.10.129.2 via fe-0/0/0.1121
                            [OSPF/106] 00:02:35, metric 4, tag 0
                            > to 10.10.129.2 via fe-0/0/0.1121
```

With the OSPF overlay working on the Juniper Networks portion of the network, we
place the equivalent configuration into effect at the Cisco boxes. It is critical that the
modified OSPF preference (setting both the internal and external to a distance higher
than RIP's) be the first thing configured to help ensure that RIP is not impacted—in
IOS land, changes go into effect as soon as they are entered. By default, IOS assigns
the same administrative distance to OSPF internals and externals (and interarea, for
that matter), so we should adopt the same approach—as long as the distance for all
OSPF routes is less preferred than RIP, it will be OK. The commands entered on Malt
are shown. Similar commands are also entered on Barley.

```
Malt# configure terminal
Enter configuration commands, one per line.  End with CNTL/Z.
Malt(config)#router ospf 10
Malt(config-router)#distance 125
Malt(config-router)# area 0 authentication message-digest
Malt(config-router)# redistribute static route-map TAGGING
% Only classful networks will be redistributed
Malt(config-router)# network 10.0.0.0 0.255.255.255 area 0
Malt(config-router)# network 192.168.2.0 0.0.0.3 area 0
Malt(config-router)# default-information originate route-map FOO
Malt(config-router)#exit
Malt(config)#interface fastEthernet 0/1.69
Malt(config-subif)#ip ospf message-digest-key 1 md5 jncie
Malt(config-router)#exit
Malt(config)#interface serial 0/0
Malt(config-subif)#ip ospf message-digest-key 1 md5 jncie
Malt(config)#route-map FOO permit 20
Malt(config-route-map)# match ip address 4
Malt(config-route-map)# set tag 100
Malt(config-subif)#^Z
Malt#
*Mar  1 04:01:28.603: %SYS-5-CONFIG_I: Configured from console by
console
```

```
*Mar  1 04:01:30.495: %OSPF-5-ADJCHG: Process 10, Nbr 10.10.128.1 on FastEthernet0/1.
69 from LOADING to FULL, Loading Done
```

The resultant OSPF portion of the configuration is shown next, along with the new route map. Note the log message in the previous capture reporting an up adjacency on Malt's fa 0/1.69 interface. This is a good indication that we have compatible OSPF settings between the Cisco and Juniper routers.

```
router ospf 10
 log-adjacency-changes
 area 0 authentication message-digest
 redistribute static route-map TAGGING
 network 10.0.0.0 0.255.255.255 area 0
 network 192.168.2.0 0.0.0.3 area 0
 default-information originate route-map FOO
 distance 125
!
. . .
route-map FOO permit 20
 match ip address 4
 set tag 100
!
```

The configuration creates an OSPF instance identified as 10, enables MD5 authentication in area 0, redistributes and route-maps the same routes used in the RIP example, and enables OSPF area 0 in the serial 0/0 and fa 0/1.60 interfaces. Note that in the IOS implementation, OSPF will not redistribute a default static route. You must use the `default-information originate` command instead. Using the preexisting `TAGGING` route map did not work, so a new route map named `FOO` was created. It's things such as this that make you appreciate the consistent nature of JUNOS software routing policy.

In an approach that is similar to JUNOS software OSPF configuration, the specific MD5 key ID and key value are set under each interface. The difference is that for JUNOS software, this was done within the OSPF configuration proper, whereas for IOS, it is under the interface configuration. The OSPF authentication settings are also shown for one of Malt's interfaces:

```
interface FastEthernet0/1
 no ip address
 duplex auto
 speed auto
!
interface FastEthernet0/1.69
 encapsulation dot1Q 69
 ip address 192.168.1.1 255.255.255.252
 ip rip authentication mode md5
 ip rip authentication key-chain test
 ip ospf message-digest-key 1 md5 jncie
 no snmp trap link-status
!
```

After a few moments, the OSPF status is analyzed on Malt:

```
Malt#show ip ospf interface fastEthernet 0/1.69
FastEthernet0/1.69 is up, line protocol is up
  Internet Address 192.168.1.1/30, Area 0
  Process ID 10, Router ID 10.10.128.100, Network Type BROADCAST,
Cost: 1
  Transmit Delay is 1 sec, State BDR, Priority 1
  Designated Router (ID) 10.10.128.1, Interface address 192.168.1.2
  Backup Designated router (ID) 10.10.128.100, Interface address
192.168.1.1
  Timer intervals configured, Hello 10, Dead 40, Wait 40,
Retransmit 5
    oob-resync timeout 40
    Hello due in 00:00:05
  Index 3/3, flood queue length 0
  Next 0x0(0)/0x0(0)
  Last flood scan length is 1, maximum is 1
  Last flood scan time is 0 msec, maximum is 4 msec
  Neighbor Count is 1, Adjacent neighbor count is 1
    Adjacent with neighbor 10.10.128.1  (Designated Router)
  Suppress hello for 0 neighbor(s)
  Message digest authentication enabled
    Youngest key id is 1
```

The show ip ospf interface command for Malt's fa 0/1.69 verifies the presence of a neighbor with RID 10.10.128.1 (Ale's loopback address/RID) and confirms the authentication and timer settings that are in effect. As expected, Ale remains the DR because in OSPF, this DR election is not revertive.

```
Malt#show ip ospf neighbor
Neighbor ID     Pri  State     Dead Time  Address     Interface
10.10.128.1     128  FULL/DR   00:00:38   192.168.1.2 FastEthernet0/1.69
10.10.128.200   0    FULL/ -   00:00:36   10.1.254.2  Serial0/0
```

The show ip ospf neighbor command confirms the expected adjacencies to both Barley and Ale. We next display a simulated customer route to confirm that the RIP copy is still being used at the Cisco boxes:

```
Malt#show ip route 200.0.2.0
Routing entry for 200.0.2.0/24
  Known via "rip", distance 120, metric 4
  Redistributing via rip
  Last update from 10.1.254.2 on Serial0/0, 00:00:03 ago
  Routing Descriptor Blocks:
  * 10.1.254.2, from 10.1.254.2, 00:00:03 ago, via Serial0/0
      Route metric is 4, traffic share count is 1
    192.168.1.2, from 192.168.1.2, 00:00:14 ago, via FastEthernet0/1.69
      Route metric is 4, traffic share count is 1
```

The output confirms that the RIP version of the route is still active. Unfortunately, IOS displays *only* the active route, making it hard to confirm that OSPF shadow versions also exist. The LSDB is inspected to make this determination:

```
Malt#show ip ospf database external adv-router 10.10.128.2

              OSPF Router with ID (192.168.1.1) (Process ID 120)

              OSPF Router with ID (10.10.128.100) (Process ID 10)

                   Type-5 AS External Link States

  LS age: 97
  Options: (No TOS-capability, DC)
  LS Type: AS External Link
  Link State ID: 10.10.128.2 (External Network Number )
  Advertising Router: 10.10.128.2
  LS Seq Number: 80000006
  Checksum: 0x2858
  Length: 36
  Network Mask: /32
        Metric Type: 2 (Larger than any link state path)
        TOS: 0
        Metric: 0
        Forward Address: 0.0.0.0
        External Route Tag: 0

  Routing Bit Set on this LSA
  LS age: 397
  Options: (No TOS-capability, DC)
  LS Type: AS External Link
  Link State ID: 200.0.2.0 (External Network Number )
  Advertising Router: 10.10.128.2
  LS Seq Number: 80000006
  Checksum: 0x92B6
  Length: 36
  Network Mask: /24
        Metric Type: 2 (Larger than any link state path)
        TOS: 0
        Metric: 3
        Forward Address: 0.0.0.0
        External Route Tag: 0
```

The external (in fixed code) argument to the show ip ospf database command filters
the output such that only AS LSAs sent by Lager are shown. The adv-router argument specified Lager's OSPF RID to identify it from all other sources of AS external
LSAs in the OSPF RD. The output confirms that Lager's customer route (200.0.2/24)
is being advertised into OSPF.

RIP-to-OSPF Migration: Cutover to OSPF

With various aspects of OSPF operation confirmed, it's time to make the cut from
RIP to OSPF. This should be a nondisruptive process, but as with all IGP migration procedures, it's best to perform the cutover in a maintenance window as added insurance—the interplay of complex internetworking protocols is sometimes hard to predict.

The actual transition normally occurs in two phases. First, make the OSPF routes active, and then, after you confirm proper operation, remove all traces of the legacy protocol and reset the new protocol to its default preference values.

To achieve the first goal you could reconfigure the OSPF internal and external preferences to be more preferred than RIP, or you could alter RIP's preference to be less preferred than OSPF. Either way, if something blows up, you can roll back or simply remove the OSPF configuration, and return to RIP operation while determining what went wrong. Given that IOS is now set with a single preference for both OSPF and RIP, the amount of change is a wash. On the JUNOS devices, it will be easier to change the one RIP preference rather than both OSPF values. Therefore, the plan is to set the RIP administrative distance to 126 on the IOS devices, while setting the RIP preference to 107 on the JUNOS devices. In both cases, the change will make RIP a less-preferred protocol.

The changes are shown for the Juniper router Ale. Similar commands are also executed at Lager:

```
[edit protocols]
lab@Ale# set rip group rip preference 107
```

The RIP administrative distance is altered on both IOS boxes:

```
Malt#conf terminal
Enter configuration commands, one per line.  End with CNTL/Z.
Malt(config)#router rip
Malt(config-router)#distance 126
```

After a few moments, it's confirmed that the OSPF version of Lager's 200.0.2.0 route is now preferred at Barley:

```
Barley#show ip route 200.0.2.0
Routing entry for 200.0.2.0/24
  Known via "ospf 10", distance 125, metric 3, type extern 2, forward
metric 1
  Last update from 192.168.2.2 on FastEthernet0/1.70, 00:03:42 ago
  Routing Descriptor Blocks:
  * 192.168.2.2, from 10.10.128.2, 00:03:42 ago, via FastEthernet0/1.70
      Route metric is 3, traffic share count is 1
```

Back at the Juniper side of things, you should make a similar determination as to which set of routes is preferred. Note how routes learned through multiple sources are clearly shown in JUNOS software, and that the active versions of these routes are now OSPF-based:

```
lab@Ale# run show route

inet.0: 19 destinations, 26 routes (19 active, 0 holddown, 0 hidden)
+ = Active Route, - = Last Active, * = Both

0.0.0.0/0          *[OSPF/106] 00:00:25, metric 1, tag 200
                    > to 10.10.129.2 via fe-0/0/0.1121
```

```
                            [RIP/107] 06:14:07, metric 2, tag 100
                            > to 192.168.1.1 via fe-0/0/0.69
10.1.254.0/24               *[OSPF/105] 00:08:03, metric 66
                            > to 10.10.129.2 via fe-0/0/0.1121
                            [RIP/107] 06:14:07, metric 2, tag 0
                            > to 192.168.1.1 via fe-0/0/0.69
10.1.254.1/32               *[RIP/107] 04:14:22, metric 3, tag 0
                            > to 10.10.129.2 via fe-0/0/0.1121
10.1.254.2/32               *[RIP/107] 06:14:07, metric 2, tag 0
                            > to 192.168.1.1 via fe-0/0/0.69
10.10.128.100/32            *[OSPF/105] 00:08:03, metric 67
                            > to 10.10.129.2 via fe-0/0/0.1121
                            [RIP/107] 06:14:07, metric 2, tag 0
                            > to 192.168.1.1 via fe-0/0/0.69
10.10.128.200/32            *[OSPF/105] 00:08:03, metric 3
                            > to 10.10.129.2 via fe-0/0/0.1121
10.10.128.1/32              *[Direct/0] 3d 21:34:05
                            > via lo0.0
10.10.128.2/32              *[OSPF/105] 00:08:03, metric 1
                            > to 10.10.129.2 via fe-0/0/0.1121
                            [RIP/107] 05:45:43, metric 2, tag 0
                            > to 10.10.129.2 via fe-0/0/0.1121
10.10.129.0/24              *[Direct/0] 2d 22:32:39
                            > via fe-0/0/0.1121
10.10.129.1/32              *[Local/0] 3d 21:34:05
                            Local via fe-0/0/0.1121
192.168.1.0/30              *[Direct/0] 2d 22:32:39
                            > via fe-0/0/0.69
192.168.1.2/32              *[Local/0] 3d 06:03:32
                            Local via fe-0/0/0.69
192.168.2.0/30              *[OSPF/105] 00:08:03, metric 2
                            > to 10.10.129.2 via fe-0/0/0.1121
                            [RIP/107] 05:45:43, metric 2, tag 0
                            > to 10.10.129.2 via fe-0/0/0.1121
200.0.1.0/24                *[Static/5] 2d 07:10:57
                            Discard
200.0.2.0/24                *[OSPF/106] 00:08:03, metric 3, tag 0
                            > to 10.10.129.2 via fe-0/0/0.1121
                            [RIP/107] 05:45:43, metric 4, tag 0
                            > to 10.10.129.2 via fe-0/0/0.1121
200.0.100.0/24              *[OSPF/106] 00:08:03, metric 3, tag 0
                            > to 10.10.129.2 via fe-0/0/0.1121
                            [RIP/107] 06:14:07, metric 4, tag 0
                            > to 192.168.1.1 via fe-0/0/0.69
200.0.200.0/24              *[OSPF/106] 00:08:03, metric 3, tag 0
                            > to 10.10.129.2 via fe-0/0/0.1121
224.0.0.5/32                *[OSPF/10] 03:14:39, metric 1
                            MultiRecv
224.0.0.9/32                *[RIP/100] 00:08:03, metric 1
                            MultiRecv
```

The display shows the default route in its OSPF and RIP forms, both of which are tagged due to route-map actions. Here, A1e has installed the default generated by

Barley (tag 200), with the RIP version learned directly from Malt also listed (tag 100). The JUNOS software CLI's matching function is used to identify any remaining active RIP routes. The \ is used here to escape the * character, so it is not incorrectly expanded as a shell wildcard, rather than a specific match condition:

```
[edit protocols]
lab@Ale# run show route protocol rip | match \*
+ = Active Route, - = Last Active, * = Both
10.1.254.1/32      *[RIP/107] 04:16:48, metric 3, tag 0
10.1.254.2/32      *[RIP/107] 06:16:33, metric 2, tag 0
224.0.0.9/32       *[RIP/100] 00:10:29, metric 1
```

Besides the multicast route associated with RIPv2, only the /32 host routes from the Malt–Barley serial link are still active as a RIP route. This is not an issue, as the related subnet 10.1.254.0/24 is correctly advertised into OSPF (see the previous route display). These results confirm that it's safe to remove RIP from the internetwork. Things begin first at the Juniper Networks boxes:

```
[edit]
lab@Ale# delete protocols rip
```

And then the change occurs at the Cisco boxes:

```
Malt#conf terminal
Enter configuration commands, one per line.  End with CNTL/Z.
Malt(config)#no router rip
Malt(config)#^Z
Malt#
```

Though not shown, the related RIP policy and route maps can now be safely removed. After a few moments of waiting, no angry users surface, and OSPF routing is verified at Ale. Perhaps it's now time for that vacation….

```
[edit]
lab@Ale# run show route protocol rip

inet.0: 16 destinations, 16 routes (16 active, 0 holddown, 0 hidden)

__juniper_private1__.inet.0: 2 destinations, 2 routes (2 active,
0 holddown, 0 hidden)
```

No more RIP routes, as planned:

```
[edit]
lab@Ale# run show route 200.0.200.0

inet.0: 16 destinations, 16 routes (16 active, 0 holddown, 0 hidden)
+ = Active Route, - = Last Active, * = Both

200.0.200.0/24     *[OSPF/106] 00:16:20, metric 3, tag 0
                    > to 10.10.129.2 via fe-0/0/0.1121
```

The active route is still OSPF, and a traceroute confirms identical connectivity:

```
[edit]
lab@Ale# run traceroute 200.0.200.1 no-resolve
traceroute to 200.0.200.1 (200.0.200.1), 30 hops max, 40 byte
packets
  1  10.10.129.2  17.647 ms  14.877 ms  14.854 ms
  2  192.168.2.1  8.879 ms  10.982 ms  9.878 ms
  3  192.168.2.1  10.287 ms  !H *  10.282 ms  !H
```

Before You Go, Can You Set Up Area 1 Real Quick?

So, the CIO of Beer-Co is so impressed with the success of the RIP-to-OSPF migration that you have been asked to bring up an Area 1 attachment to router PBR. This is
to be a stub area, with a default route injected by the area's ABR so that PBR can
reach the various OSPF external destinations now present in the new network.
Figure 4-10 shows the new topology. You may assume that interface parameters are
correctly set.

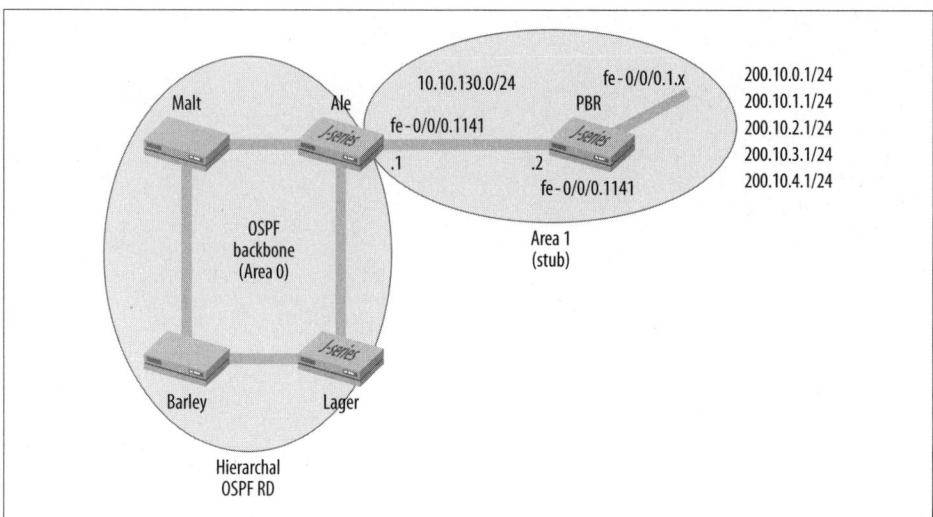

Figure 4-10. A hierarchical OSPF network

In Figure 4-10's example, PBR's fe-0/0/1 interface has been looped back (to ensure
that it's declared up, even if not connected), and five VLANs have been created, each
with an IP address in the form of 200.10.*x*.1/24. All five of these logical interfaces
have been placed into OSPF area 1, which has been set as a stub area. PBR's OSPF
and fe-0/0/1 configuration is as follows:

```
[edit]
lab@PBR# show interfaces fe-0/0/1
vlan-tagging;
fastether-options {
    loopback;
```

```
    }
    unit 1 {
        vlan-id 1;
        family inet {
            address 200.10.1.1/24;
        }
    }
    unit 2 {
        vlan-id 2;
        family inet {
            address 200.10.2.1/24;
        }
    }
    unit 3 {
        vlan-id 3;
        family inet {
            address 200.10.3.1/24;
        }
    }
    unit 4 {
        vlan-id 4;
        family inet {
            address 200.10.4.1/24;
        }
    }
    unit 5 {
        vlan-id 5;
        family inet {
            address 200.10.5.1/24;
        }
    }
}

[edit]
lab@PBR# show protocols ospf
area 0.0.0.1 {
    stub;
    interface fe-0/0/1.1;
    interface fe-0/0/1.2;
    interface fe-0/0/1.3;
    interface fe-0/0/1.4;
    interface fe-0/0/1.5;
    interface fe-0/0/0.1141;
}
```

Meanwhile, a compatible OSPF area 1 configuration has been added at Ale:

```
[edit protocols ospf area 0.0.0.1]
lab@Ale# show
stub default-metric 10;
interface fe-0/0/0.1141;
```

Note that to inject a default route into the stub, you must specify a default metric. After a few moments, OSPF operation is confirmed at PBR. The show ospf neighbor command confirms that the adjacency to Ale is established:

```
[edit protocols ospf]
lab@PBR# run show ospf neighbor
  Address          Interface      State      ID            Pri  Dead
  10.10.130.1      fe-0/0/0.1141  Full       10.10.128.1   128  39
```

The display of OSPF routes verifies the presence of the default route, injected by
ABR router Ale, and reveals an absence of AS externals, which are not permitted in a
stub network. *Only* LSA types 1, 2, and 3 are permitted in a stub area—the OSPF
route table at PBR contains only intraarea and interarea routes, thus confirming this
aspect of OSPF stub area operation:

```
[edit]
lab@PBR# run show ospf route
Prefix           Path    Route    NH    Metric  NextHop             Nexthop
                 Type    Type     Type          Interface           addr/label
10.10.128.1      Intra   Area BR  IP    1       fe-0/0/0.1141       10.10.130.1
0.0.0.0/0        Inter   Network  IP    11      fe-0/0/0.1141       10.10.130.1
10.10.128.1/32   Intra   Network  IP    1       fe-0/0/0.1141       10.10.130.1
10.10.128.2/32   Inter   Network  IP    2       fe-0/0/0.1141       10.10.130.1
10.10.129.0/24   Inter   Network  IP    2       fe-0/0/0.1141       10.10.130.1
10.10.130.0/24   Intra   Network  IP    1       fe-0/0/0.1141
10.10.131.0/24   Inter   Network  IP    3       fe-0/0/0.1141       10.10.130.1
192.168.1.0/30   Inter   Network  IP    2       fe-0/0/0.1141       10.10.130.1
192.168.2.0/30   Inter   Network  IP    3       fe-0/0/0.1141       10.10.130.1
200.10.1.0/24    Intra   Network  IP    1       fe-0/0/1.1
200.10.2.0/24    Intra   Network  IP    1       fe-0/0/1.2
200.10.3.0/24    Intra   Network  IP    1       fe-0/0/1.3
200.10.4.0/24    Intra   Network  IP    1       fe-0/0/1.4
200.10.5.0/24    Intra   Network  IP    1       fe-0/0/1.5
```

PBR relies on the ABR-generated default route to reach external destinations because
AS external LSAs are not advertised into stub areas:

```
[edit protocols ospf]
lab@PBR# run show route 200.0.200.1

inet.0: 21 destinations, 21 routes (21 active, 0 holddown, 0 hidden)
+ = Active Route, - = Last Active, * = Both

0.0.0.0/0          *[OSPF/10] 00:04:31, metric 11
                    > to 10.10.130.1 via fe-0/0/0.1141
```

You can add the no-summaries keyword to the area 1 configuration at the stub area's
ABR (Ale) to also filter Type 3 network summary LSAs, which also result in the use
of a default route for interarea destinations. With this change, a totally stubby area is
born:

```
[edit protocols ospf area 0.0.0.1]
lab@Ale# set stub no-summaries

[edit protocols ospf area 0.0.0.1]
lab@Ale# commit
```

The results are confirmed at PBR, whose LSDB just got much smaller:

```
[edit]
lab@PBR# run show ospf route
Prefix          Path   Route    NH    Metric NextHop        Nexthop
                Type   Type     Type         Interface      addr/label
10.10.128.1     Intra  Area BR  IP    1      fe-0/0/0.1141  10.10.130.1
0.0.0.0/0       Inter  Network  IP    11     fe-0/0/0.1141  10.10.130.1
10.10.128.1/32  Intra  Network  IP    1      fe-0/0/0.1141  10.10.130.1
10.10.130.0/24  Intra  Network  IP    1      fe-0/0/0.1141
200.10.1.0/24   Intra  Network  IP    1      fe-0/0/1.1
200.10.2.0/24   Intra  Network  IP    1      fe-0/0/1.2
200.10.3.0/24   Intra  Network  IP    1      fe-0/0/1.3
200.10.4.0/24   Intra  Network  IP    1      fe-0/0/1.4
200.10.5.0/24   Intra  Network  IP    1      fe-0/0/1.5

[edit protocols ospf]
lab@PBR# run show route 192.168.1.1

inet.0: 16 destinations, 16 routes (16 active, 0 holddown, 0 hidden)
+ = Active Route, - = Last Active, * = Both

0.0.0.0/0          *[OSPF/10] 00:01:41, metric 11
                    > to 10.10.130.1 via fe-0/0/0.1141
```

A final task: Aggregate network summaries into the backbone

Area 1 is now quite optimized, but it has been called to your attention that the five 200.10.x.1/24 networks owned by PBR are being flooded into the backbone as individual Type 3 network summary LSAs. This is normal for OSPF, but your CIO wants to run a tight ship and has asked that you generate a single summary LSA into area 0 in place of the current five. Before making changes, you confirm that the CIO has correctly described the network summary situation by displaying Type 3 LSAs generated by ABR Ale. Note that these summaries are in backbone area 0.

```
[edit]
lab@Lager#run show ospf database netsummary advertising-router
10.10.128.1

    OSPF link state database, Area 0.0.0.0
 Type      ID           Adv Rtr      Seq        Age  Opt  Cksum  Len
Summary   10.10.130.0  10.10.128.1  0x80000003 421  0x22 0xc449 28
Summary   10.20.128.3  10.10.128.1  0x80000002 421  0x22 0x46bd 28
Summary   200.10.1.0   10.10.128.1  0x80000002 421  0x22 0xb11f 28
Summary   200.10.2.0   10.10.128.1  0x80000002 421  0x22 0xa629 28
Summary   200.10.3.0   10.10.128.1  0x80000002 421  0x22 0x9b33 28
Summary   200.10.4.0   10.10.128.1  0x80000002 421  0x22 0x903d 28
Summary   200.10.5.0   10.10.128.1  0x80000002 421  0x22 0x8547 28
```

Taking note of Lager's current area 0 LSDB state, you make a change to the area 1 portion of Ale, which results in the summarization of matching network summary LSAs:

```
[edit protocols ospf area 0.0.0.1]
lab@Ale# set area-range 200.10/16

[edit protocols ospf area 0.0.0.1]
lab@Ale# show
stub default-metric 10 no-summaries;
area-range 200.10.0.0/16;
interface fe-0/0/0.1141;
```

The area-range statement replaces individual network summaries that fall within the configured range with a single network summary representing the entire range. Adding the restrict keyword as part of the area-range statement serves to block any network summaries that are equal in length to the area-range's mask. In other words, the area-range is normally a *longer* function with regard to prefix length, but adding the restrict keyword alters this match type to that of orlonger. The latter results in filtering of any summaries *equal* in length to the specified area-range prefix length.

Your work is confirmed with a look at the network summaries now advertised into area 0 by Ale:

```
[edit]
lab@Lager# show ospf database netsummary advertising-router
10.10.128.1
    OSPF link state database, Area 0.0.0.0
 Type      ID           Adv Rtr     Seq        Age  Opt  Cksum  Len
 Summary   10.10.130.0  10.10.128.1 0x8000000a   9  0x22 0xb650  28
 Summary   10.20.128.3  10.10.128.1 0x80000009   9  0x22 0x38c4  28
 Summary   200.10.0.0   10.10.128.1 0x80000001   9  0x22 0xbe14  28
```

As a final check, the connectivity from Cisco router Barley to one of the 200.10.*x*.1/ 24 networks on PBR is confirmed:

```
Barley#traceroute 200.10.1.1

Type escape sequence to abort.
Tracing the route to 200.10.1.1

  1 192.168.2.2 4 msec 4 msec 12 msec
  2 10.10.129.1 8 msec 4 msec 12 msec
  3 200.10.1.1 4 msec 8 msec 8 msec
```

Awesome! This result completes the RIP-to-OSPF migration. This example also touched on stub area and area-range summarization configuration.

RIP Migration with the Overlay Model Summary

This section demonstrated a typical RIP-to-OSPF IGP migration using the overlay model. This was demonstrated in a multivendor environment to help show that the principles and procedures are somewhat universal, albeit with slightly varied command syntax that serves only to confuse the innocent. The modification of global route preferences allowed a smooth, hitless transition. Once the new IGP was found to be operating as expected, a quick change of preference resulted in use of the new IGP's forwarding paths while retaining the legacy IGP's configuration (and legacy protocol neighbors/adjacency state), in the event that the change needs to be backed out quickly. The migration ends with the removal of all legacy IGP traces from the router configurations.

This section also showed the conversion of a flat OSPF network into a hierarchical design that included the function of stub networks, totally stubby networks, and area-range syntax to consolidate network summaries as they enter the backbone.

Now is a good time to take another break. The next section continues our discussion of IGP migration, but this time in the context of an EIGRP-to-OSPF scenario.

EIGRP-to-OSPF Migration

This section demonstrates a smooth migration from a legacy EIGRP network to a hierarchical OSPF IGP. You could take many approaches to facilitate such a migration. The best approach will depend on numerous factors, such as device support of old and new IGPs and whether new equipment is being added, and if so, whether it's added to replace or augment an existing network's infrastructure. Also of consideration is the legacy network's design with regard to addressing and hierarchy, in combination with the design goals for the new network's efficiency and scalability.

The tactic demonstrated here is of the route redistribution variety. But considering that Juniper Networks routers have never spoken EIGRP, a bit of the integration model has to be at work as well—after all, a new backbone is being built out. It is acknowledged that leveraging existing network infrastructure will be of prime concern for most enterprises, and therefore that a typical EIGRP-to-OSPF migration will center on the phased reconfiguration of existing IOS devices to begin running the new and stop running the old IGP. This chapter demonstrates a migration approach in which Juniper Networks routers are added to form a new OSPF backbone while *minimal* changes are made to the legacy infrastructure to accommodate communications between the EIGRP and OSPF domains.

The solution demonstrated accommodates graceful growth of the OSPF backbone while the legacy EIGRP backbone is phased out. The migration goals for this scenario are as follows:

- There should be a minimal impact to the existing IOS configurations and existing EIGRP backbone operation.
- The solution should accommodate a phasing out of the legacy backbone IGP (though not necessarily the current devices) toward an all-OSPF backbone.
- The solution should be as simple as possible and be workable for small-to-large-scale enterprise migrations.
- The design must minimize the impact of large numbers of AS external LSAs for low-end routers.

Mutual Route Redistribution

To make this scenario work, mutual route redistribution is needed between EIGRP and OSPF. As always, you must ensure that routes are redistributed only once, because loops will violate the "minimal impact to existing backbone" criterion. In addition, route preference adjustments may be needed to ensure optimal routing, depending on the default preferences for internal versus external EIGRP and OSPF between the two vendors.

 As much as you might prefer to have all this happen on the JUNOS software devices, the simple fact is that they cannot run EIGRP, while the Cisco boxes support both EIGRP and OSPF. This means the redistribution work will have to occur in IOS land. From the viewpoint of the Juniper routers, however, this is just another OSPF network, albeit one with a lot of tagged AS externals.

Figure 4-11 provides the topology and addressing specifics to assist the reader in tracking down which devices and IGPs own which routes.

Figure 4-12 provides the summary plan of action, as derived from the design criteria provided.

The overall plan is to *add* an OSPF process on the Cisco routers that redistributes connected, static, and EIGRP learned routes *after* adding a tag value to these routes. In this case, the tag chosen is based on the EIGRP domain's AS (process) number (it could be any unique value, however). In addition, the existing EIGRP configuration is modified to redistribute OSPF into EIGRP *after* tagging these routes in a similar fashion. In both cases, the *first* step in the respective route maps is to *deny* any routes that already have the EIGRP process tag value. It's critical that the deny action occur first, as the whole point of the route tags is to simplify the blocking of routes that originated in EIGRP from being redistributed back onto EIGRP from OSPF. Likewise, we need to block routes that originated in OSPF from being sent back into OSPF by EIGRP; the same tag value is also used for this filtering requirement.

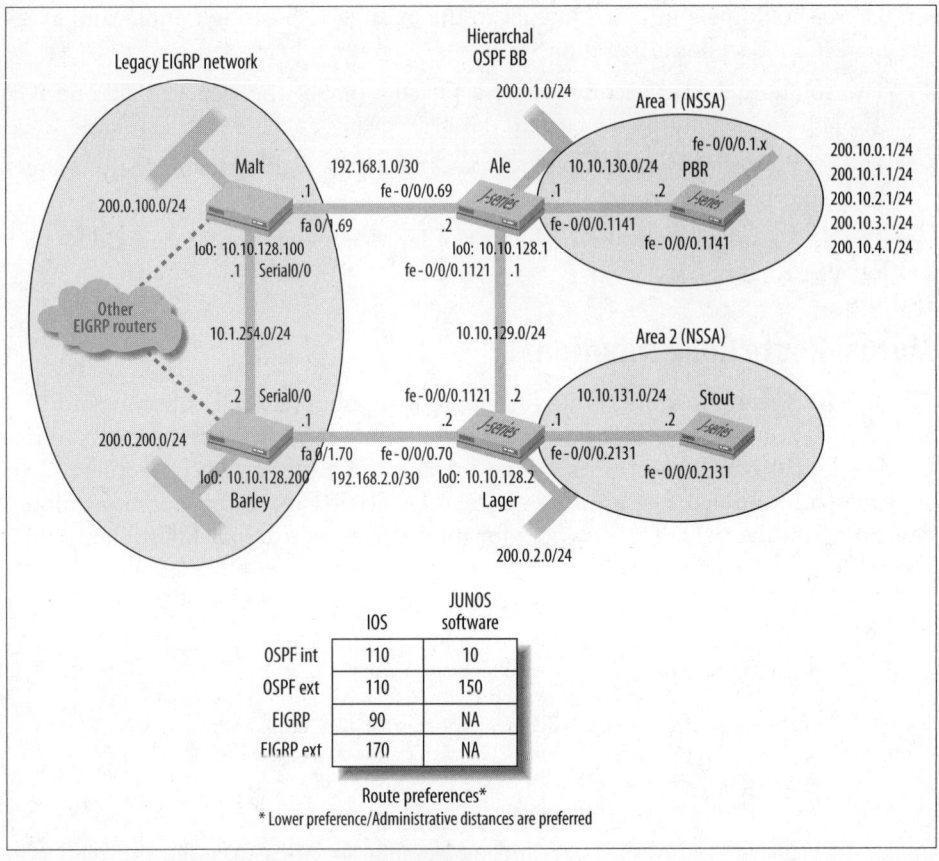

Figure 4-11. EIGRP-to-OSPF migration topology

Recall that redistribution of connected, static, or EIGRP routes into OSPF results in Type 5 AS external LSAs, which are in turn flooded over the entire OSPF domain (except stub areas). This is a significant point, because one of the design goals is to minimize the impact of large numbers of external LSAs on low-end routers. This is why the new, nonbackbone OSPF areas are configured as NSSA areas in this example. As with the stub area example, the default route injected by the ABRs provides connectivity to the external destinations—for example, EIGRP—and the NSSA capability accommodates future placement of an ASBR to originate AS external routes from these areas as needed.

The JUNOS software OSPF configuration

On the JUNOS software side, things are pretty straightforward, and the OSPF and related policy bits are shown for Ale.

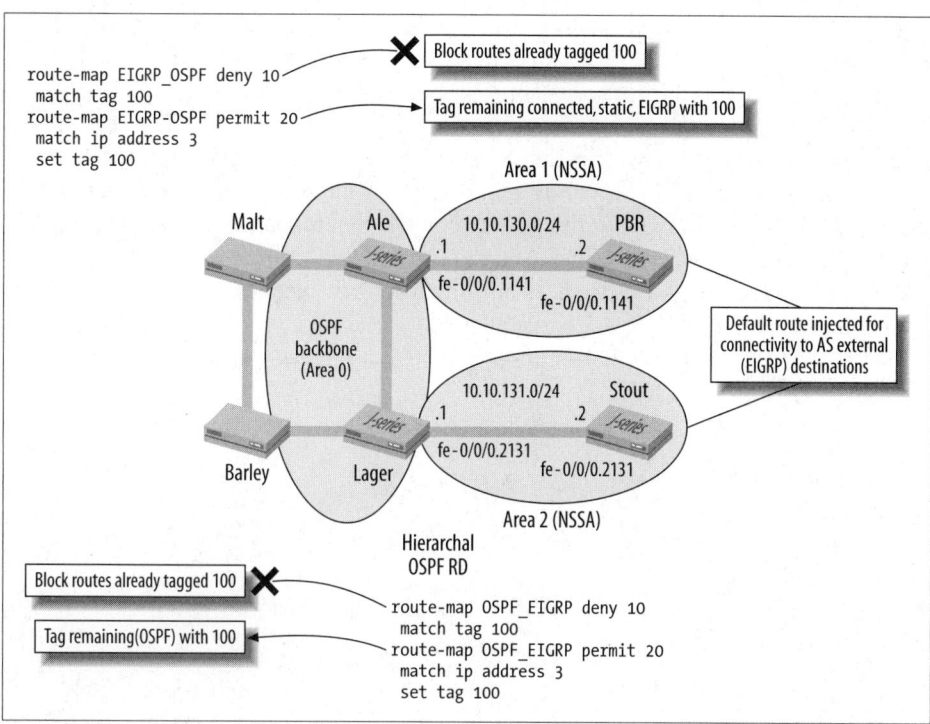

Figure 4-12. EIGRP-to-OSPF migration plan overview

```
[edit]
lab@Ale# show protocols ospf
export static;
area 0.0.0.0 {
    interface fe-0/0/0.69;
    interface fe-0/0/0.1121;
}
area 0.0.0.1 {
    nssa {
        default-lsa default-metric 10;
    }
    interface fe-0/0/0.1141;
}

[edit]
lab@Ale# show policy-options policy-statement static
term 1 {
    from {
        protocol static;
        route-filter 200.0.1.0/24 exact;
    }
    then accept;
}
```

The OSPF export policy redistributes the simulated customer static route into OSPF. No route tagging is being performed here, because if tag 100 were added, these routes would be filtered from redistribution into the EIGRP domain. Area 1 is configured as an NSSA, and a default route is configured (via the default-metric statement) for use by routers within the NSSA when routing AS external destinations. Recall that all the EIGRP routes will be become AS externals once they are injected into the OSPF domain, making the presence of the default route in stub areas critical for maintaining connectivity. The configuration of JUNOS software router Stout is shown for completeness, but there is not much to say, except that its area 2 is compatibly configured as an NSSA.

```
[edit]
lab@stout# show protocols ospf
area 0.0.0.2 {
    nssa;
    interface fe-0/0/0.2131;
}
```

The IOS configuration

The real work is being done on the IOS side because these devices are able to run both the old and the new IGPs.

Before adding the new OSPF process to any of the legacy Cisco routers, you must first verify that they have the capacity to run both IGPs without encountering performance issues. The current best practice is to confirm that CPU and memory use are less than 50% to 60%, respectively. If the router is already running short of resources, adding a new IGP and related redistribution may well push it over the limit. Older routers that are already having trouble keeping up should be replaced or upgraded before proceeding.

The show memory and show processes command output indicates that Beer-Co's IOS boxes are not heavily taxed, so we are free to proceed:

```
Malt#show mem stat
              Head Total(b)  Used(b)   Free(b) Lowest(b) Largest(b)
Processor 82B00CC0 18493864  6288376  12205488  12000052   11685420
      I/O  3C00000  4194304  2013112   2181192   2174960    2181148
Malt#show processes cpu sorted
CPU utilization for five seconds: 0%/0%; one minute: 0%;
five minutes: 0%
 PID Runtime(ms)  Invoked uSecs  5Sec   1Min   5Min TTY Process
   3       15492     3513  4409  0.31%  0.80%  0.26%  0 Exec
   1           0        2     0  0.00%  0.00%  0.00%  0 Chunk Manager
   2           4     2527     1  0.00%  0.00%  0.00%  0 Load Meter
   4         320     2958   108  0.00%  0.00%  0.00%  0 OSPF Hello
 . . . .
```

Having determined sufficient resource capacity, the migration proceeds; the modified portions of Cisco router Malt are shown here:

```
router eigrp 100
 redistribute connected
 redistribute static
 redistribute ospf 10 metric 10 100 255 1 1500 route-map OSPF_EIGRP
 network 10.0.0.0
 no auto-summary
 !
router ospf 10
 network 192.168.1.0 0.0.0.3 area 0
 redistribute eigrp 100 metric 4 route-map EIGRP_OSPF subnets
 redistribute static metric 3 route-map EIGRP_OSPF subnets
 redistribute connected tag 100 subnets metric 2
 !
access-list 3 permit any
 !
route-map OSPF_EIGRP deny 10
 match tag 100
 !
route-map OSPF_EIGRP permit 20
 match ip address 3
 set tag 100
 !
route-map EIGRP_OSPF deny 10
 match tag 100
 !
route-map EIGRP_OSPF permit 20
 match ip address 3
 set tag 100
```

The modified portions of the IOS configuration are highlighted to help to call out the delta. The EIGRP process was instructed to redistribute routes from the OSPF process identified as "10," setting the EIGRP bandwidth, delay, reliability, loading, and MTU values to 10, 100, 255, 1, and 1500, respectively. The redistribution is controlled by the logic in the route map named OSPF_EIGRP.

The entire OSPF process is new and was added to integrate with the new Juniper router-based backbone. Because connected routes could not be filtered through the existing EIGRP_OSPF route map, tagging for the connected routes is configured directly on the distribute line.

In contrast, both static and EIGRP routes are being redistributed through the control of the common EIGRP_OSPF route map. The subnet keyword inverts the default behavior of redistributing only classful networks. Lastly, you'll see that OSPF area 0 is configured to run on the link connecting Malt to Ale.

Both route maps make use of an initial deny term for any route with a tag value of 100. Remaining routes are then matched against the match-all IP access list 3, with the result being the addition of tag value 100. When combined, the operation of the two route maps serves to ensure that a route is never redistributed back into the IGP from where it originated, which should prevent loop formation.

You use JUNOS software routing policy to combine the various effects of IOS's distribute, distribute-list, ACL, and route-map functions. For example, here is a policy example that functions to reject and tag routes, much as the EIGRP_OSPF route map does, albeit for RIP and OSPF given the lack of EIGRP support. The RIP_to_OSPF policy is applied to the OSPF protocol as an export policy to redistribute only untagged RIP routes into OSPF, at which time a tag value of 100 is added:

```
[edit policy-options]
regress@plato# show policy-statement RIP_to_OSPF
term 1 {
    from tag 100;
    then reject;
}
term 2 {
    from protocol rip;
    then {
        tag 100;
        accept;
    }
}


[edit policy-options]
regress@plato# show policy-statement RIP_to_OSPF | display
set
set policy-options policy-statement RIP_to_OSPF term 1 from
tag 100
set policy-options policy-statement RIP_to_OSPF term 1 then
reject
set policy-options policy-statement RIP_to_OSPF term 2 from
protocol rip
set policy-options policy-statement RIP_to_OSPF term 2 then
tag 100
set policy-options policy-statement RIP_to_OSPF term 2 then
accept
```

To better understand how the tagging works, refer back to Figure 4-12 and then consider an EIGRP (or connected, or static) route *x* that originates in the EIGRP domain and is evaluated for redistribution into OSPF. According to the EIGRP_OSPF route map, the first action is to deny any route with the tag value 100. Because route *x* originates within EIGRP, it has no tag and therefore the route falls to the next term. Action 20 adds tag 100 to the route and sends it into OSPF. Route *x*, which is now an OSPF Type 5 LSA, is then flooded into the OSPF RD, where it arrives at Cisco router Barley. In most cases, Barley will already have a more preferred EIGRP route to this destination (recall that it originated in EIGRP to begin with), but if not, it will install the OSPF route to *x*, as learned from Malt's OSPF advertisement.

Now Barley's OSPF process considers OSPF route *x* for redistribution into EIGRP. Fortunately, the first term in its OSPF_EIGRP route map denies any routes with tag 100. This action serves to prevent route *x* from being sent back into its originating EIGRP IGP. Any routes that originate in the OSPF domain, regardless of whether they are internal or AS external, arrive at Barley with no tag. This permits the redistribution of these routes into the EIGRP process, after they have been tagged. This tag will in turn keep router Malt from sending the route back into the OSPF domain.

What about route preferences? Referring back to Figure 4-11, you can see the default preferences for the route sources used in this example. At first glance, it seems that we want both Malt and Barley to prefer all OSPF routes regardless of whether they are internal or external. This is to ensure that both Cisco routers forward directly into the OSPF cloud when routing to OSPF originated routes, rather than backhauling over the EIGRP backbone because they prefer a redistributed EIGRP version of the same route. This is fortunate here because the OSPF routes redistributed into EIGRP are considered EIGRP externals, and the default distance for these routes is 170, making them less preferred than the native OSPF copy with a default distance of 110.

The default settings mean that the EIGRP domain will always prefer a learned OSPF route over the same copy in the (redistributed) external EIGRP form. The JUNOS software boxes have only one IGP, so there is no need to alter any preference there, of course. Time will tell whether we need to revisit this thinking....

Confirm EIGRP/OSPF Mutual Route Redistribution

With all routers configured, confirm proper redistribution and forwarding. Begin at Cisco router Malt, where the IP route table is displayed:

```
Malt# show ip route
Codes: C - connected, S - static, R - RIP, M - mobile, B - BGP
       D - EIGRP, EX - EIGRP external, O - OSPF, IA - OSPF inter area
       N1 - OSPF NSSA external type 1, N2 - OSPF NSSA external type 2
       E1 - OSPF external type 1, E2 - OSPF external type 2
       i - IS-IS, su - IS-IS summary, L1 - IS-IS level-1, L2 - IS-IS level-2
       ia - IS-IS inter area, * - candidate default, U - per-user static route
       o - ODR, P - periodic downloaded static route

Gateway of last resort is not set

O E2 200.0.200.0/24 [110/3] via 192.168.1.2, 00:05:09, FastEthernet0/1.69
O IA 200.10.4.0/24 [110/3] via 192.168.1.2, 00:05:09, FastEthernet0/1.69
O IA 200.10.5.0/24 [110/3] via 192.168.1.2, 00:05:09, FastEthernet0/1.69
O E2 200.0.1.0/24 [110/0] via 192.168.1.2, 00:05:09, FastEthernet0/1.69
```

```
O IA 200.10.1.0/24 [110/3] via 192.168.1.2, 00:05:09, FastEthernet0/1.69
O E2 200.0.2.0/24 [110/0] via 192.168.1.2, 00:05:09, FastEthernet0/1.69
O IA 200.10.2.0/24 [110/3] via 192.168.1.2, 00:05:09, FastEthernet0/1.69
S      200.0.100.0/24 is directly connected, Null0
O IA 200.10.3.0/24 [110/3] via 192.168.1.2, 00:05:10, FastEthernet0/1.69
        10.0.0.0/8 is variably subnetted, 11 subnets, 2 masks
D          10.10.128.200/32 [90/2297856] via 10.1.254.2, 03:10:02, Serial0/0
O          10.10.129.0/24 [110/2] via 192.168.1.2, 00:05:10, FastEthernet0/1.69
O          10.10.128.1/32 [110/1] via 192.168.1.2, 00:05:10, FastEthernet0/1.69
O IA       10.10.130.0/24 [110/2] via 192.168.1.2, 00:05:14, FastEthernet0/1.69
O          10.10.128.2/32 [110/2] via 192.168.1.2, 00:05:14, FastEthernet0/1.69
O IA       10.10.131.0/24 [110/3] via 192.168.1.2, 00:05:14, FastEthernet0/1.69
O IA       10.20.128.4/32 [110/3] via 192.168.1.2, 00:05:14, FastEthernet0/1.69
O IA       10.20.128.3/32 [110/2] via 192.168.1.2, 00:05:14, FastEthernet0/1.69
C          10.10.128.100/32 is directly connected, Loopback0
C          10.1.254.0/24 is directly connected, Serial0/0
C          10.1.254.2/32 is directly connected, Serial0/0
        192.168.1.0/30 is subnetted, 1 subnets
C          192.168.1.0 is directly connected, FastEthernet0/1.69
        192.168.2.0/30 is subnetted, 1 subnets
O          192.168.2.0 [110/3] via 192.168.1.2, 00:05:14, FastEthernet0/1.69
```

From a quick look, it seems that all the routes are there: PBR's five 200.10.*x*/24 routes as network summaries (interarea), the simulated customer routes from Ale and Lager as AS externals, and their loopback/OSPF interface routes appearing as OSPF internals (intraarea). It certainly appears that these routes are preferred in their OSPF form, despite their being redistributed into EIGRP at Barley, which is desired behavior for optimal routing between the EIGRP and OSPF domains. Note how Barley's loopback 0 address (10.10.128.200) is displayed as an EIGRP learned internal route with a distance of 90.

To confirm that the OSPF routes are really being redistributed into EIGRP (IOS displays only the active route), the EIGRP topology table for one of PBR's 200.0.1.0/24 routes is shown here:

```
Malt# show ip eigrp topology 200.0.1.0
IP-EIGRP (AS 100): Topology entry for 200.0.1.0/24
   State is Passive, Query origin flag is 1, 1 Successor(s), FD is
256025600
   Routing Descriptor Blocks:
   192.168.1.2, from Redistributed, Send flag is 0x0
      Composite metric is (256025600/0), Route is External
      Vector metric:
        Minimum bandwidth is 10 Kbit
        Total delay is 1000 microseconds
        Reliability is 255/255
        Load is 1/255
        Minimum MTU is 1500
        Hop count is 0
      External data:
        Originating router is 10.10.28.100 (this system)
        AS number of route is 10
```

```
External protocol is OSPF, external metric is 0
Administrator tag is 100 (0x00000064)
```

The route's presence is confirmed in the EIGRP topology table, and the tag value of 100 proves that the OSPF_EIGRP route map is working.

Troubleshoot a preference issue

Overall, the output from the show ip route command at Malt is what you want to see. There is one problem, however, with respect to the simulated customer route owned by Barley: the display shows that Malt prefers the OSPF external version of the 200.0.200/24 route because the EIGRP external distance is higher (less preferred) than OSPF's (as noted previously, this is part of the migration plan). This occurs *only* for the simulated customer routes because EIGRP is set to run on the serial and loopback interfaces as a result of the network 10.0.0.0 statement. These routes are therefore considered *internal* to the EIGRP process and they have a distance of 90. In contrast, the simulated customer static route is *redistributed* into EIGRP, making it an EIGRP external. This situation results in an extra hop when Malt tries to reach Barley's customer network, and vice versa:

```
Malt#trace 200.0.200.1
Type escape sequence to abort.
Tracing the route to 200.0.200.1

  1 192.168.1.2 4 msec 8 msec 8 msec
  2 10.10.129.2 8 msec 8 msec 8 msec
  3 192.168.2.1 12 msec 8 msec 12 msec
  4 192.168.2.1 !H  !H  *
```

Rethinking the default preferences, it was correct to assert that *all* OSPF routes would be preferred over EIGRP externals, which for the majority of our routes is exactly what is desired. The redistributed statics are causing issues with this plan, however. Changing OSPF external preferences may fix the issue with the problematic static routes, but will then create problems for the other OSPF routes that are now doing what they should be doing.

Some possible solutions include running EIGRP passively on the related customer interface so that the route is advertised as an EIGRP internal. This solution requires an actual interface (or loopback instance), and these statics were used to reduce gear requirements in the first place. Still, no new gear is needed for an IOS loopback 1 interface. Or, you could define a static route, but this represents administrative work and may lead to a black hole if the legacy EIGRP backbone fails. Using a qualified/ recursive static should result in traffic falling back to the learned OSPF version should the static route's next hop become unreachable, but this would need to be tested to make sure of failover behavior. Yet another solution would be to simply tolerate the inefficient routing, given that connectivity is still provided and the condition should be transient as the EIGRP network is phased out. Being a purist, you opt to alter the IOS configurations to add a new loopback instance that will run EIGRP on behalf of the simulated customer network. Such changes are shown here:

```
!
interface Loopback1
 ip address 200.0.100.1 255.255.255.0
!
. . .
router eigrp 100
 redistribute connected
 redistribute static
 redistribute ospf 10 metric 10 100 255 1 1500 route-map OSPF_EIGRP
 network 10.0.0.0
 network 200.0.100.0
 passive-interface Loopback1
 no auto-summary
```

A new loopback instance has been defined to represent the simulated customer network that previously was represented by a static route. The static route has also been removed (not shown), and the EIGRP process is configured to run passively on the loopback 1 interface. The passive declaration ensures that CPU cycles are not wasted on the EIGRP neighbor discovery that is doomed to fail, given the lonely neighborhood that is loopback 1. And yes, loopback 0 should be set to be passive for the same reasons, but that is saved for another day. After similar changes are made at Barley, the active EIGRP routes are displayed and the previous traceroute is repeated:

```
Malt#showip route eigrp
D    200.0.200.0/24 [90/2297856] via 10.1.254.2, 00:11:42, Serial0/0
     10.0.0.0/8 is variably subnetted, 11 subnets, 2 masks
D       10.10.128.200/32 [90/2297856] via 10.1.254.2, 04:24:16,
Serial0/0
Malt#traceroute 200.0.200.1

Type escape sequence to abort.
Tracing the route to 200.0.200.1

 1 10.1.254.2 16 msec 12 msec *
```

Excellent, just what you wanted to see. Before moving on, traceroutes to a few other destinations in the OSPF domain are executed for added confirmation. Note that the simulated customer network routes at Ale and Lager are set to discard, so you should expect no reply from them:

```
Malt#trace 10.20.128.3

Type escape sequence to abort.
Tracing the route to 10.20.128.3

  1 192.168.1.2 4 msec 4 msec 12 msec
  2 10.20.128.3 4 msec 8 msec 8 msec
Malt#trace 200.10.5.1
```

```
Type escape sequence to abort.
Tracing the route to 200.10.5.1

  1 192.168.1.2 8 msec 8 msec 8 msec
  2 200.10.5.1 4 msec 20 msec 100 msec
```

The traceroutes to the loopback address and OSPF area 1 routes on PBR are successful and are observed to take a reasonable forwarding path. Similar results are
observed at Barley:

```
Barley# trace 200.10.2.1

Type escape sequence to abort.
Tracing the route to 200.10.2.1

  1 192.168.2.2 20 msec 4 msec 12 msec
  2 10.10.129.1 4 msec 28 msec 12 msec
  3 200.10.2.1 8 msec 8 msec 8 msec
```

Let's temporarily down the OSPF adjacency at Malt (traffic will reroute through
Barley) to confirm that Malt falls back to the EIGRP versions of the OSPF domain's
routes and actually begins to forward through Barley:

```
Malt(config)#interface fastEthernet 0/1
Malt(config-if)#sh
Malt(config-if)#^Z
. . .
```

After a few moments, the route table is again displayed at Malt:

```
Malt#show ip route
Codes: C - connected, S - static, R - RIP, M - mobile, B - BGP
       D - EIGRP, EX - EIGRP external, O - OSPF, IA - OSPF inter area
       N1 - OSPF NSSA external type 1, N2 - OSPF NSSA external type 2
       E1 - OSPF external type 1, E2 - OSPF external type 2
       i - IS-IS, su - IS-IS summary, L1 - IS-IS level-1, L2 - IS-IS level-2
       ia - IS-IS inter area, * - candidate default, U - per-user static route
       o - ODR, P - periodic downloaded static route

Gateway of last resort is not set

D    200.0.200.0/24 [90/2297856] via 10.1.254.2, 00:31:34, Serial0/0
D EX 200.10.4.0/24 [170/256537600] via 10.1.254.2, 00:00:36, Serial0/0
D EX 200.10.5.0/24 [170/256537600] via 10.1.254.2, 00:00:36, Serial0/0
D EX 200.0.1.0/24 [170/256537600] via 10.1.254.2, 00:00:36, Serial0/0
D EX 200.0.1.1.0/24 [170/256537600] via 10.1.254.2, 00:00:36, Serial0/0
D EX 200.0.2.0/24 [170/256537600] via 10.1.254.2, 00:00:36, Serial0/0
D EX 200.10.2.0/24 [170/256537600] via 10.1.254.2, 00:00:36, Serial0/0
C    200.0.100.0/24 is directly connected, Loopback1
D EX 200.10.3.0/24 [170/256537600] via 10.1.254.2, 00:00:37, Serial0/0
     10.0.0.0/8 is variably subnetted, 11 subnets, 2 masks
D       10.10.128.200/32 [90/2297856] via 10.1.254.2, 04:44:10, Serial0/0
D EX    10.10.129.0/24 [170/256537600] via 10.1.254.2, 00:00:37, Serial0/0
D EX    10.10.128.1/32 [170/256537600] via 10.1.254.2, 00:00:37, Serial0/0
D EX    10.10.130.0/24 [170/256537600] via 10.1.254.2, 00:00:39, Serial0/0
```

```
D EX    10.10.128.2/32 [170/256537600] via 10.1.254.2, 00:00:39, Serial0/0
D EX    10.10.131.0/24 [170/256537600] via 10.1.254.2, 00:00:39, Serial0/0
D EX    10.20.128.4/32 [170/256537600] via 10.1.254.2, 00:00:39, Serial0/0
D EX    10.20.128.3/32 [170/256537600] via 10.1.254.2, 00:00:39, Serial0/0
C       10.10.128.100/32 is directly connected, Loopback0
C       10.1.254.0/24 is directly connected, Serial0/0
C       10.1.254.2/32 is directly connected, Serial0/0
     192.168.1.0/30 is subnetted, 1 subnets
D EX    192.168.1.0 [170/256537600] via 10.1.254.2, 00:00:34, Serial0/0
     192.168.2.0/30 is subnetted, 1 subnets
D EX    192.168.2.0 [170/2172416] via 10.1.254.2, 00:00:40, Serial0/0
```

The display confirms that the EIGRP versions of the redistributed OSPF routes are now active. A traceroute confirms the expected forwarding path, given the down fa 0/0 interface at Malt:

```
Malt#traceroute 200.10.5.1
Type escape sequence to abort.
Tracing the route to 200.10.5.1

  1 10.1.254.2 12 msec 12 msec 12 msec
  2 192.168.2.2 20 msec 16 msec 20 msec
  3 10.10.129.1 116 msec 24 msec 20 msec
  4 200.10.5.1 48 msec 28 msec 36 msec
Malt#
```

Malt's fa 0/1 interface is returned to operation and the OSPF adjacency is allowed to reform. You should then inspect the route table to ensure that the network state has returned to the initial state. Issues with route redistribution/preference are often timing-dependent, and you may find that after a failure, the network does not return to the desired state. Here, expect to find that the OSPF versions of the routes are again preferred over the EIGRP version:

```
Malt#
*Mar  1 06:02:24.202: %OSPF-5-ADJCHG: Process 10, Nbr 10.10.128.1 on FastEthernet0/1.
69 from LOADING to FULL, Loading Done
Malt#
Malt#show ip route eigrp
D    200.0.200.0/24 [90/2297856] via 10.1.254.2, 00:36:14, Serial0/0
     10.0.0.0/8 is variably subnetted, 11 subnets, 2 masks
D       10.10.128.200/32 [90/2297856] via 10.1.254.2, 04:48:48, Serial0/0
Malt#
```

The display confirms that the native OSPF routes are again active, being they are preferred over redistributed EIGRP copies. This validates that the network is able to fail over, and then switch back to a steady state. Connectivity between the two RDs has already been demonstrated, so let's conclude our IGP migration verification with some selective captures in the OSPF domain, starting by examining the "large" external LSA database now on backbone routers:

```
[edit]
lab@Ale# run show ospf database extern
    OSPF AS SCOPE link state database
```

```
Type      ID              Adv Rtr          Seq        Age   Opt  Cksum   Len
Extern  10.1.254.0        10.10.28.100  0x8000000b    850  0x20  0xe0c4   36
Extern  10.1.254.0        10.10.28.200  0x8000000b    783  0x20  0x86ba   36
Extern  10.1.254.1        10.10.28.200  0x8000000b    783  0x20  0x7cc3   36
Extern  10.1.254.2        10.10.28.100  0x8000000b    850  0x20  0xccd6   36
Extern  10.10.128.100     10.10.28.100  0x80000009   1607  0x20  0xfbbc   36
Extern  10.10.128.100     10.10.28.100  0x80000009   1531  0x20  0xb59c   36
Extern  10.10.128.200     10.10.28.100  0x80000009   1607  0x20  0x242e   36
Extern  10.10.128.200     10.10.28.200  0x80000009   1531  0x20  0xb53a   36
Extern  *200.0.1.0         10.10.128.1  0x80000005   2101  0x22  0x87c7   36
Extern  200.0.2.0          10.10.128.2  0x80000005   2427  0x22  0x76d6   36
Extern  200.0.100.0       10.10.28.100  0x8000000d    592  0x20  0xdda2   36
Extern  200.0.100.0       10.10.28.200  0x80000002    526  0x20  0xad77   36
Extern  200.0.200.0       10.10.28.100  0x80000002    351  0x20  0xb76d   36
Extern  200.0.200.0       10.10.28.200  0x80000002    526  0x20  0x4979   36
```

Well, it seems that *large* truly is a subjective term. However, more than 10 Type 5 LSAs are in the backbone area's database, and considering the small scope of the EIGRP network in this lab example, it's safe to say that a large enterprise could easily generate hundreds if not thousands of these AS external LSAs.

```
[edit]
lab@Ale# run show ospf database extern detail | match tag
  Type 2, TOS 0x0, metric 2, fwd addr 0.0.0.0, tag 0.0.0.100
  Type 2, TOS 0x0, metric 2, fwd addr 0.0.0.0, tag 0.0.0.100
  Type 2, TOS 0x0, metric 2, fwd addr 0.0.0.0, tag 0.0.0.100
  Type 2, TOS 0x0, metric 2, fwd addr 0.0.0.0, tag 0.0.0.100
  Type 2, TOS 0x0, metric 2, fwd addr 0.0.0.0, tag 0.0.0.100
  Type 2, TOS 0x0, metric 4, fwd addr 0.0.0.0, tag 0.0.0.100
  Type 2, TOS 0x0, metric 4, fwd addr 0.0.0.0, tag 0.0.0.100
  Type 2, TOS 0x0, metric 2, fwd addr 0.0.0.0, tag 0.0.0.100
  Type 2, TOS 0x0, metric 0, fwd addr 0.0.0.0, tag 0.0.0.0
  Type 2, TOS 0x0, metric 0, fwd addr 0.0.0.0, tag 0.0.0.0
  Type 2, TOS 0x0, metric 2, fwd addr 0.0.0.0, tag 0.0.0.100
  Type 2, TOS 0x0, metric 4, fwd addr 0.0.0.0, tag 0.0.0.100
  Type 2, TOS 0x0, metric 4, fwd addr 0.0.0.0, tag 0.0.0.100
  Type 2, TOS 0x0, metric 2, fwd addr 0.0.0.0, tag 0.0.0.100
```

Next, the CLI's matching function, combined with the detail switch, allows confirmation that most of these externals originated in the EIGRP domain, given that the majority are sporting a tag with an EIGRP process number.

The new OSPF network was designed to be hierarchical to promote scaling. To take this a step further, let's also deploy NSSAs to reduce the processing demands on nonbackbone routers. Internal routers within a stub area do not see any AS external LSAs, which in this type of a migration can substantially reduce their load. Confirm this fact at router PBR:

```
[edit]
lab@PBR# run show ospf database

    OSPF link state database, Area 0.0.0.1
```

```
Type      ID            Adv Rtr       Seq        Age  Opt  Cksum   Len
Router    10.10.128.1   10.10.128.1   0x8000000c  273  0x20 0xac79  48
Router   *10.20.128.3   10.20.128.3   0x80000008  928  0x20 0x6124 108
Network  *10.10.130.2   10.20.128.3   0x80000007  928  0x20 0x7b49  32
Summary   10.10.128.2   10.10.128.1   0x80000008 2223  0x20 0xda30  28
Summary   10.10.129.0   10.10.128.1   0x80000008 2073  0x20 0xe328  28
Summary   10.10.131.0   10.10.128.1   0x80000008 1773  0x20 0xd731  28
Summary   10.20.128.4   10.10.128.1   0x80000007 1473  0x20 0x5aa4  28
Summary   192.168.1.0   10.10.128.1   0x8000000b  625  0x20 0x9a9c  28
Summary   192.168.2.0   10.10.128.1   0x80000006  573  0x20 0xa396  28
NSSA      0.0.0.0       10.10.128.1   0x80000008  423  0x20 0xa1ea  36
NSSA      200.0.1.0     10.10.128.1   0x80000005 2373  0x20 0x89c5  36
```

Note the absence of Type 4 and Type 5 LSAs, and the presence of the default route, which provides the internal stub area routers with a route to external destinations.

```
[edit]
lab@PBR# run show route 200.0.200.4

inet.0: 23 destinations, 23 routes (23 active, 0 holddown, 0 hidden)
+ = Active Route, - = Last Active, * = Both

0.0.0.0/0          *[OSPF/150] 04:26:43, metric 11, tag 0
                    > to 10.10.130.1 via fe-0/0/0.1141
```

This last display confirms the use of the default route for AS external destinations by the internal NSSA router PBR.

With initial connectivity confirmed, the EIGRP-to-OSPF migration can proceed through a phased movement of legacy EIGRP segments to the new OSPF backbone. Alternatively, the EIGRP domain can be shrunk back by increasing the scope of the OSPF domain and moving the EIGRP redistribution points until there is no EIGRP left.

EIGRP-to-OSPF Migration Summary

This section demonstrated how you can integrate a new OSPF backbone into an existing EIGRP infrastructure, while maintaining loop-free connectivity through careful use of route filtering. Filtering is needed to ensure that those routes are redistributed only once. The example used route tags to simplify filtering. Address-based filters can also work, especially if the two IGP domains have distinct numbering that can easily be summarized.

Mutual route redistribution is always a bit tricky, and careful thought should be leveled against any migration plan to try to head off potential issues stemming from protocol preferences or incomplete route filtering. In this example, the interaction of OSPF and EIGRP external preferences created a problem for static routes redistributed into EIGRP. Although connectivity was maintained and no loops were formed, the condition resulted in suboptimal forwarding for some destinations. The specifics of this example allowed the creation of a new loopback interface, which then ran a passive instance of EIGRP to stand in for the static route, yielding optimal connectivity for all destinations in the test bed.

Conclusion

The IGP is a critical component in any enterprise network. The IGP functions to provide optimal connectivity to interior destinations in the face of changing network conditions. To perform this function, the IGP must balance the opposing forces of rapid convergence against instability and routing loops. A well-designed and implemented IGP can easily spell the difference between a high-performing network and an ongoing litany of trouble tickets and support calls.

Historically, enterprise networks needed to support multiple routed protocols, and the dominance of Cisco Systems in these early years resulted in widespread deployment of its proprietary IGRP and EIGRP IGP solutions. Since that time, most enterprise networks have completed a migration to an all-IP routing infrastructure. Simply stated, the world seems to have settled on the mantra "IP over everything, and everything over IP." Although EIGRP does a good job at routing IP, its closed nature, coupled with its lack of routing hierarchy and MPLS TE support, cast serious concerns over its future high-performance enterprise networks.

Over the years, several tried and proven strategies have been developed to ease the pain and disruption that often accompany IGP migration. Whether an enterprise chooses to deploy JUNOS software or not, these migration techniques can get your legacy network weaned off of EIGRP and onto an open standard such as OSPF.

Juniper Networks routers support all standardized IGPs, and their implementation has been successfully battletested in the planet's largest service provider networks. The same OSPF code running in the multiterabit iron of the Juniper Networks flagship TX Matrix core router can also be found purring away in the smallest enterprise-targeted Juniper devices. Although historically designed for service provider networks, Juniper Networks continues to evolve its IGP implementation to meet the needs of both its service provider and enterprise customers.

Exam Topics

We covered the following Enterprise Exam Topics in this chapter:

- The role and function of an IGP
- Operational characteristics of RIP, RIPv2, OSPF, and IGRP/EIGRP
- RIP and OSPF configuration on Juniper Networks routers
- Operational analyses of RIP and OSPF on Juniper Networks routers
- The overlay, redistribution, and integrated IGP migration models

Chapter Review Questions

1. Which of the following defines *split horizon*?

    a. Sending routes out the interface they were learned from

    b. Sending routes out the interface they were learned from with infinite metric

    c. Holding a recently unreachable route in the table for a fixed time to allow other routers to be notified

    d. Not sending routes out the interface they were learned from

2. When you configure RIP on a Juniper Networks router, how do you specify what interfaces the protocol should operate on?

    a. You use a network statement with a network mask

    b. You use a network statement with a wildcard mask

    c. You specify interface names and logical units explicitly as part of RIP neighbor configuration

    d. You use routing policy

    e. None of the above

3. What command displays the RIP routes a Juniper Networks router is sending out to a given interface?

    a. This is not possible given the LS nature of RIP

    b. show route protocol rip

    c. show route advertising-protocol rip <neighbor>

    d. show route receiving-protocol rip <neighbor>

4. Which type of router generates a Type 2 LSA?

    a. Internal

    b. ABR

    c. ASBR

    d. DR

5. Which is true regarding a stub area with no-summaries?

    a. The area uses a default to reach interarea destinations

    b. The area imports external routes as Type 7 LSAs

    c. The area does not receive Type 3 summary LSAs from the backbone

    d. The area has no OSPF routers in it

6. When you add a new OSPF router to a LAN, what factor(s) determine whether it will become the DR?

    a. Its priority setting

    b. The RID

c. Whether any other routers are already operating on that LAN

d. All of the above

7. What determines which route will be active when a given prefix is learned by multiple routing protocols?

    a. The lowest metric

    b. The path with the fewest hops

    c. The protocol with the highest numerical preference is chosen

    d. The protocol with the lowest numerical preference is chosen

8. Which syntax at an ABR would suppress individual summaries for routes in the 10.0/16 block in area 1 while replacing them with a single summary?

    a. `[edit protocols ospf area 0.0.0.1]`

      `set area-range 10.0/16 restrict`

    b. `[edit protocols ospf area 0.0.0.0]`

      `set area-range 10.0/16`

    c. `[edit protocols ospf area 0.0.0.1]`

      `set area-range 10.0/16`

    d. This is not possible; LSAs cannot be filtered without breaking LS protocol operation

9. Which is true regarding the overlay migration model?

    a. You first set the legacy IGP to be less preferred than the new IGP

    b. You first set the new IGP to be less preferred than the legacy IGP

    c. Route redistribution is needed to maintain connectivity through the migration

    d. A new backbone is needed

10. What is the primary mechanism for loop prevention in the redistribution model?

    a. A common LSDB ensures a loop-free topology

    b. Strict controls that ensure routes are not redistributed back to their originating IGP

    c. Setting the new IGP to be more preferred than the legacy IGP

    d. A careful mapping of metrics between originating and receiving IGPs

11. What types of authentication are supported in JUNOS software for OSPF?

    a. Simple password

    b. MD5 checksum

    c. Hitless key chain of MD5 keys/checksums

    d. All of the above

12. Which configuration will inject a default route into stub area 1?

    a. area 0.0.0.1 {

        stub default-metric 10 no-summaries;

        area-range 10.0.0.0/16 restrict;

        }

    b. area 0.0.0.0 {

        stub default-metric 10;

        }

    c. area 0.0.0.1 {

        stub no-summaries;

        area-range 10.0.0.0/16 restrict;

        }

    d. area 0.0.0.1 {

        stub default-metric;

        area-range 10.0.0.0/16 restrict;

        }

Chapter Review Answers

1. Answer: D. Split horizon rules prevent a router from readvertising routing information back out the same interface it was learned from; poisoned reverse alters this behavior to permit such updates as long as they have an infinite metric.

2. Answer: C. You specify RIP-enabled interfaces by name and unit number, under the [edit protocols rip group <*name*> neighbor] hierarchy.

3. Answer: C. The show route advertising protocol <*protocol*> <neighbor> command is used to display the route the local router is sending out an interface to a neighbor for RIP/BGP, respectively. The receiving-protocol form of this command shows the routes being learned over an interface.

4. Answer: D. Only designated routers, which are elected only on multiaccess networks, generate Type 2 network summary LSAs. This LSA type is used to report the list of OSPF neighbors (including the DR itself) attached to the multiaccess segment.

5. Answer: C. A stub area with no-summaries does not receive summary LSAs from the backbone. They rely on an injected default route to reach interarea and AS external destinations.

6. Answer: D. All of the factors listed influence whether a given router can become the DR. Recall that DR election is not revertive. A router's ID and priority come into play only during an active DR election.

7. Answer: D. The protocol with the numerically lowest preference (or administrative distance) is considered more "reliable" and is chosen as the source of the active route.

8. Answer: C. Your goal is to filter from area 1 into area 0, so the `area-range` statement needs to be applied to area 1. The restrict keyword should not be used here as it will also filter on the summary, in effect converting from a match type of longer to one of orlonger. The goal is to permit the summary which makes answer A false.

9. Answer: B. To avoid disruption, the legacy protocol must operate until all aspects of the new IGP have been put in place and confirmed. The new IGP has to be less preferred than the original until you are ready to actually make the switchover.

10. Answer: B. You must diligently use filtering mechanisms to ensure that routes are never redistributed back into the IGP from where they originated, or else loops will likely form.

11. Answer: D. For OSPF, JUNOS software supports simple passwords, MD5, and a key chain of MD5 secrets. RIP does not support key chain authentication as of the JUNOS software 8.3 release.

12. Answer: A. JUNOS software will generate a default route only when a metric value is specified using the `default-metric` command.

CHAPTER 5

Border Gateway Protocol and Enterprise Routing Policy

This chapter reviews the Border Gateway Protocol (BGP) version 4 operation and key attributes to accommodate a detailed discussion of BGP enterprise applications. BGP is all about the *control* of routing information *between* autonomous systems (ASs). Emphasis is placed on the use of routing policy to facilitate load balancing and common enterprise applications of inbound and outbound routing requirements when customers are dual-homed to different service providers. The topics covered include:

- BGP overview and enterprise applications
- External BGP (EBGP) peering with asymmetric load balancing
- BGP policy for the enterprise
- BGP dual-homing scenario with route reflection and outbound policy
- Implementation of a dual-homed inbound policy by manipulating BGP attributes

Juniper Networks routers offer extensive feature support for BGP. In fact, the list of supported standards is too long to be valuable here. Consult the BGP overview in the JUNOS documentation to confirm the list of supported RFCs and drafts for your particular JUNOS software release.

What Is BGP?

BGP is an interdomain routing protocol, which means it operates between networks that are under different administrative control—making BGP an Exterior Gateway Protocol (EGP) that operates between ASs. An AS is defined as a group of IP networks operated by one or more network operators that has a single, clearly defined routing policy.

BGP is a path-vector routing protocol that relies on the uniqueness of AS path numbers for loop prevention. Rather than advertising a simple vector (prefix), as in the case of the Routing Information Protocol (RIP), BGP's reachability information is a prefix with associated attributes that describe the *path* to that prefix. The rich set of supported attributes in turn allows for an equally rich set of policy actions.

BGP is somewhat unique in that it uses a reliable Transmission Control Protocol (TCP)-based transport for its control and update messages. Reliable transport means there is no need for periodic route updates, which is really, really good, considering that a full BGP table typically comprises more than 220,000 routes! BGP does generate periodic keepalive traffic in the absence of route update activity to ensure that the underlying TCP transport is still functional.

BGP version 4 has been in use for more than two decades, with the current version (BGP 4) originally defined in RFC 1654 back in 1994. This RFC was obsoleted by RFC 1771, which in turn was obsoleted by the current specification, RFC 4271. The fact that BGP still enjoys a growing deployment base, with no replacement looming on the horizon, is a testament to the architects' forward-thinking design. BGP is based on the use of parameter type, parameter length, and parameter value tuples (sometimes called *tag length values*, or TLVs). It is these TLVs that provide the inherent extensibility without the need for significant protocol changes. You want IPv6 address family support? Simple; just define a new network layer reachability information (NLRI) attribute. You need route reflection? No problem; add some new attributes to communicate cluster and originator ID information. Meanwhile, the basic operation and protocol mechanisms remain unaltered and, in many cases, backward-compatible.

Inter-AS Routing

In several regards, you can think of BGP as the antithesis of an Interior Gateway Protocol (IGP). For example, an IGP functions *within* an AS and strives to *promote* connectivity, whereas a BGP operates *between* ASs and tends to *limit* connectivity. That last point may require a bit more clarification. An IGP normally actively seeks to discover routing peers (neighbor discovery). Once the neighbors are found, routes are exchanged and connectivity is promoted by virtue of always seeking the best path between endpoints. BGP, on the other hand, has to be explicitly told which neighbors to peer with, and then the use of administrative policy is used to filter and modify routing information to select the "best" route that meets the network operator's defined policy. The word *best* is quoted here because when routing between ASs, the concept of what constitutes a best path is cloudy at best. For example, a company may choose to filter large portions of BGP connectivity from best path consideration, based solely on a local policy that does not allow the use of a specific competitor's backbone. Exactly why such a policy is in place is not the question, although many good answers spring to mind, including potential concerns of corporate espionage. The point here is that with BGP, you are normally as concerned about restriction/ignoring routing information as you are about receiving it in the first place. The IGP is focused on getting you there, whereas BGP is more concerned with *how* you get there.

Figure 5-1 illustrates a simple interdomain routing scenario, where each AS is represented by a cloud. The cloud is, of course, the universal symbol for "don't ask, don't tell." This is to say that specifics of each AS are left to the administrators of that network and are generally not known outside of that scope. It might be possible for a transit network to deploy an avian-based transport technology, as per RFC 1149;* as long as they meet their service level agreements (SLAs), the details of how they manage to pull it off are typically not a matter of concern.

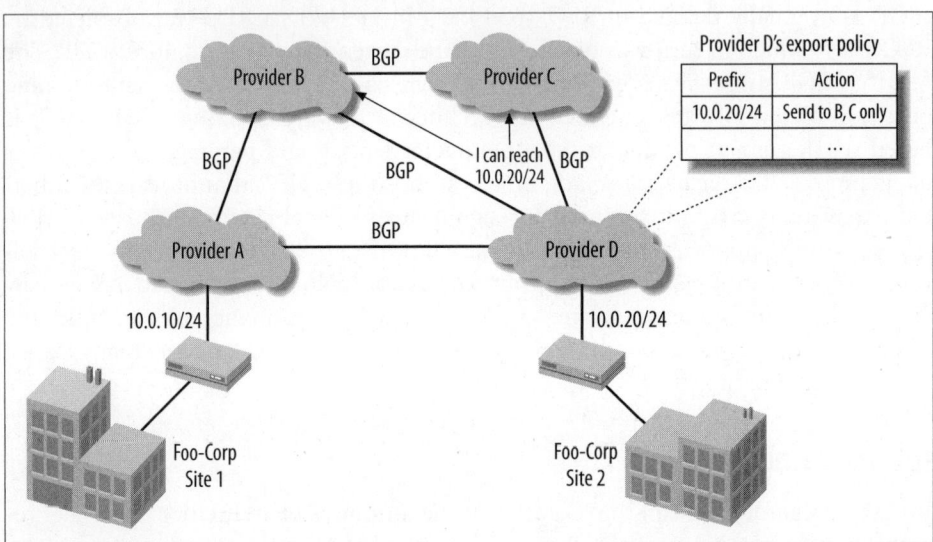

Figure 5-1. Interdomain routing with BGP

BGP operates on the links that tie these networks together, in effect serving as the *public face* of each network. The BGP speakers in each AS advertise network reachability to the ASs they are configured to peer with, under the confines of their specific export policy. In like fashion, each BGP speaker filters received information through its respective import policy before placing what remains into its route table for consideration for the active route selection process. Figure 5-1 shows that Provider D's policy prevents the advertisement of the 10.0.20/24 prefix from Site 2 to Provider A. Provider A will have to receive the Site 2 prefix from Provider B. As a result, the two customer sites will be forwarding over additional AS hops to reach each other. This point helps to demonstrate that for BGP, connectivity is as much a matter of politics as it is performance.

---

* RFC 1149 is one of the more notorious "less than serious" RFCs, as indicated by its April 1 publication date.

BGP Route Attributes

BGP advertises route reachability (NLRI), along with various attributes that describe the path to that prefix. The terms *NLRI*, *route*, and *prefix* are synonymous and are used interchangeably in this chapter. This section describes key BGP path attributes. Policy discussions later in this chapter require that you understand what these attributes do and how you work with them to achieve your routing goals.

All BGP route attributes fall into one of the following categories based on whether all BGP speakers are expected to understand the attribute and whether the attribute has local-AS or end-to-end scope:

Well-known mandatory
A well-known mandatory attribute must be supported by all BGP speakers and must be present in all BGP updates that contain an NLRI.

Well-known discretionary
A well-known discretionary attribute must be supported by all BGP speakers and may or may not be present in a given NLRI update.

Optional transitive
An optional transitive attribute is an optional attribute that may not be understood by all speakers and is expected to transit the local AS, even if it is not understood by the local speaker.

Optional nontransitive
An optional nontransitive attribute is an optional attribute that may not be understood by all speakers and does not transit the local AS—that is, it is not readvertised to another, remote AS.

Common BGP path attributes include:

Next hop
The next hop is a mandatory attribute that carries the IP address of a BGP speaker (or a third party when permitted) to identify where packets should be forwarded when using the associated route. The next hop is changed by default for EBGP and is unchanged for Internal BGP (IBGP); however, this default behavior can be altered with policy.

Local preference
Local preference is a well-known discretionary attribute used to influence BGP path selection with regard to the desired egress point for traffic from within an AS. Traffic flows toward the peer advertising the highest (most preferred) local preference. Local preference is present only in IBGP updates (nontransitive).

AS path
The mandatory attribute AS path lists the AS numbers that will be crossed when forwarding to the associated NLRI. The AS path attribute is used for loop prevention and influences path selection in accordance with the motto "the fewer

ASs in a path, the better." Each AS adds its AS number to the front of the current AS sequence when generating *EBGP* updates; the lack of updated AS path information in IBGP updates is why IBGP speakers are not permitted to readvertise routes learned from IBGP back to other IBGP speakers. By default, BGP discards any route advertisement that contains its local AS number in the AS path, because this indicates that the route has already passed through the local AS once; that is, a loop has formed.

Origin

The origin code is a well-known, mandatory attribute that identifies the original source of a route as being learned from an IGP, EGP, or unknown source. In route selection, a BGP speaker will prefer IGP to EGP, and EGP to unknown. Origin is present in all route updates and is subject to modification with policy (transitive).

Multiple exit discriminator

The multiple exit discriminator (MED) attribute is an optional, nontransitive attribute, which means that some BGP speakers may not understand or use MED. MED is added on updates sent over EBGP links, and is then advertised by IBGP within the receiving AS to influence its outbound routing. However, the MED attribute does not transit beyond the AS into which it was originally advertised—BGP speakers in upstream ASs either receive no MED or receive a new MED value created by that peering AS.

MED functions like a conventional routing metric in that speakers prefer the route with the lowest MED when all preceding decision points are equal. The MED advertised by the originating AS to an adjacent AS provides a clue to the adjacent AS regarding what links should be used for *egress* from the neighbor AS back toward the originating AS, and therefore what links are used as *ingress* to the local AS. Stated differently, the MED is used by the local AS to influence the routing decisions in an adjacent AS for traffic that is inbound to the local AS. When absent, JUNOS software assumes an MED value of 0, which is the most preferred setting. In contrast, the absence of a local preference is assumed to be a value of 100.

Community

The community attribute allows for the arbitrary grouping of routes that share one or more characteristics via the addition of a common community tag value. The community tags can be used for a variety of purposes, such as route filtering and attribute modification. For example, all routes learned from customers may be assigned the community value of 65000:100. When this community is seen on a route, the local policy will set a more preferred local preference. As another example, consider the well-known community, *no-export*. When attached to a route, this community tells the adjacent AS that the associated route should not be readvertised to any remote ASs.

BGP Path Selection

A BGP speaker that is presented with two or more updates, specifying the same prefix, performs a route selection process to select the best BGP path for that prefix. Once the best path is selected, the route is installed in the route table, where it may become active if the same prefix is not being learned by a protocol with a better global preference. The JUNOS software BGP path selection process consists of the following decision steps:

1. Can the BGP next hop be resolved?
2. Prefer the path with the highest local preference value.
3. Prefer the path with the shortest AS-path length.
4. Prefer the path with the lowest origin value.
5. Prefer the path with the lowest MED value.
6. Prefer the path learned using EBGP over paths learned using IBGP.
7. Prefer paths with the lowest IGP metric:
   a. Examine route tables inet.0 and inet.3 for the BGP next hop, and then install the physical next hop(s) for the route with the better preference.
   b. For preference ties, install the physical next hop(s) found in inet.3.
   c. For preference ties within the same route table, install the physical next hop(s) where the greater number of equal-cost paths exists.
8. Prefer paths with the shortest cluster length.
9. Prefer routes from the peer with the lowest router ID (RID), unless multipath is enabled:
   a. For external routes from different ASs, do not alter the active route based on the lowest RID to prevent MED oscillation.
10. Prefer routes from the peer with the lowest peer ID (BGP peering address), unless multipath is enabled.

Configuring the multipath option deactivates the last two decision points, which are normally used as tie breakers. When multipath is enabled, all paths that are equal up to step 9 are installed in the route table. Multipath supports EBGP and IBGP, but is normally associated with EBGP sessions because IBGP will often achieve its load-balancing functionality through the underlying IGP when equal cost paths to the IBGP speaker exist. Use multipath for IBGP when two or more IBGP speakers advertise the same prefix and you wish to install both speakers as viable next hops.

Figure 5-2 demonstrates the BGP path selection process at work.

Here, NLRI 10.0.20/24 is originated into BGP by AS 65000. Note that when advertised to ASs 65010 and 65069, this NLRI is associated with an AS path attribute that consists of a single AS and has an origin value of "I" indicating IGP learned.

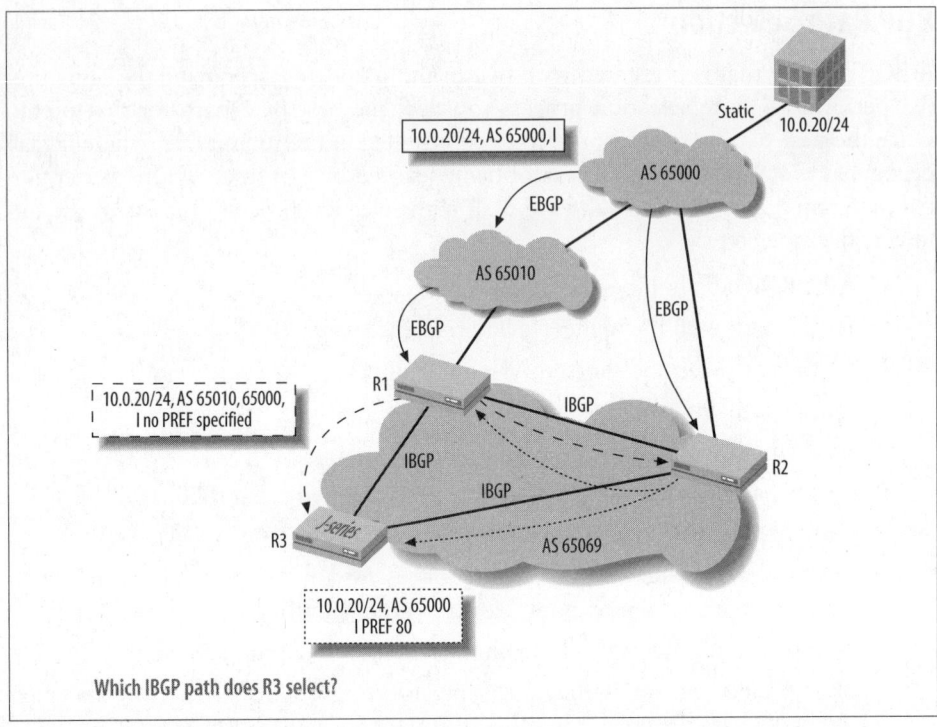

Figure 5-2. BGP path selection

This value could be a default value for redistribution of static routes into BGP or the result of policy setting. The NLRI is then readvertised into AS 65069 by AS 65010. Initially, routers R1 and R2 prefer their local copy of this path, so both R1 and R2 select it as active and advertise the NLRI to all IBGP peers, which means that R3 receives two updates for the same path. In this example policy, R2 causes the route to be sent into IBGP with a modified local preference value of 80. Also note that the route received from AS 65010 has an AS sequence that is one AS longer than the route sent to R2 directly from AS 65000.

Running through the path selection process steps listed previously, it's safe to assume that R3 will make a decision early in the process, preferring the copy of the route with a default local preference of 100. Had both local preference values been the same, the selection criterion would now become the shortest AS path length, resulting in R3 forwarding through R2. Note that R1 and R2 will also send their 10.0.20/24 updates to each other. This means that R2 prefers the path through R1, and therefore now sends another update to R1 and R3, withdrawing its earlier IBGP update for 10.0.20/24. The example also helps to demonstrate how local preference is used to influence the egress point in the local AS.

JUNOS software is designed to display all valid BGP paths, and even includes the reason why a given path was not selected. This greatly simplifies the network administrator's job when the goal is to make a currently inactive path the active path; policy can be applied to alter the criterion that leads to the original path being preferred. Here's the output from a show route detail command, to illustrate this point:

```
user@host> show route 10.0.20/24 detail
inet.0: 52 destinations, 94 routes (52 active, 0 holddown, 0 hidden)
10.0.20.0/24 (3 entries, 1 announced)
        *BGP    Preference: 170/-201
                Source: 192.168.32.1
                Next hop: 10.222.28.2 via fe-0/0/0.0, selected
                Protocol next hop: 192.168.32.1 Indirect next hop:
858b4e0 73
                State: <Active Int Ext>
                Local AS: 65069 Peer AS: 65069
                Age: 18:57      Metric2: 3
                Task: BGP_65432.192.168.32.1+1042
                AS path: 65000 65010 I
                Localpref: 100
                Router ID: 192.168.32.1
         BGP    Preference: 170/-101
                Source: 10.222.29.2
                Next hop: 10.222.29.2 via ge-0/1/0.0, selected
                State: <Ext>
                Inactive reason: Local Preference
                Local AS: 65069 Peer AS: 65069
                . . .
                Localpref: 80
```

From the sample output, it is quite clear that because of the local preference comparison, the path through 192.168.32.1 is preferred. Knowing that this BGP route was not chosen due to the local preference value makes it a relatively simple task to change the selection of the path through 192.168.32.1 by setting its preference to be higher than 100.

Internal and External BGP

We have already used the terms *Internal BGP* and *External BGP* (IBGP/EBGP) a few times leading up to this point. It's time to explore what this terminology signifies. For the most part, BGP operation is the same when operating internally to an AS versus externally to a remote AS, but Table 5-1 summarizes the key differences.

Table 5-1. IBGP and EBGP

Characteristic/attribute	IBGP	EBGP
Local AS added to AS path	No	Yes
Next hop overwritten	No	Yes

Table 5-1. IBGP and EBGP (continued)

Characteristic/attribute	IBGP	EBGP
New MED added	No; the MED received on an EBGP link can be advertised via IBGP within the local AS	Yes
Local preference	Yes	No
Peering address	Normally loopback, recursive lookup provided by IGP, Time to Live (TTL) = 64	Normally peers directly to interface address, no recursion or IGP needed, TTL = 1
Update received from EBGP, is sent to:	All IBGP peers	Other EBGP peers
Update received from IBGP, is sent to:	No IBGP peers	All EBGP peers

Although the differences may seem trivial, they can have a significant impact. For example, because IBGP updates do not alter the AS path attribute, loops become a concern, and this leads to the restriction that IBGP speakers cannot readvertise an IBGP update to other IBGP speakers, which leads to the requirement that IBGP speakers must be fully meshed.

The next hop-handling differences often lead to IBGP routes that are hidden because the receiver cannot resolve the associated BGP next hop. By default, the next hop identifies the EBGP speaker in the adjoining AS, and often the IGP will not carry this route, thereby leading to an unreachable next hop. An IBGP export policy that over-writes the BGP next hop, typically to the IBGP peering address, is normally used to resolve this issue (no pun intended).

The MED attribute is normally added only when a route is advertised over an EBGP peering, and its absence may be interpreted as the lowest or highest possible value, depending upon implementation—Juniper assumes the lowest value, which is 0. In contrast, local preference is present only in IBGP updates, and by standard is assumed to be 100 when absent. When received from an EBGP peer, the MED value can be advertised to other speakers within that AS using IBGP.

The peering differences are significant for several reasons. EBGP normally peers to a neighbor using an address on the directly connected link between the routers. As a result, no route recursion is needed to resolve the BGP peering address to a next hop forwarding address, given that they are one and the same. This means that an IGP, to include static routing, is normally *not* required to support EBGP peering. It also means that loss of the directly connected network/peering interface results in loss of the EBGP session. For security reasons, the TTL for EBGP sessions is set to 1 by default, which prevents attempts to peer from a remote link. This behavior is altered by configuring multihop on the EBGP session. Lastly, a local-address (referred to as *update-source* in IOS) is normally *not* used for an EBGP session, because by default, it is sourced from the same directly connected network interface that the two BGP routers are peering over; therefore, the source and destination addresses for the BGP session will be from the same, directly connected subnet.

IBGP, in contrast, is normally configured to peer between the loopback addresses of the routers. This provides resiliency from the failure of individual networks or interfaces. IBGP inherently supports multihop, which is good because IBGP neighbors can be located anywhere with the AS and often do not share a link. A recursive route lookup is needed to resolve the loopback peering address to an IP forwarding next hop, and thus this service is normally provided by the network's underlying IGP. When defining a BGP loopback peering session, you need to correctly match the source address used by the local peer to ensure that it matches the session definition at the remote peer. Recall that by default, the router will source traffic from its egress interface, which will not be the loopback interface, and this can make the incoming connection request appear to come from an undefined peer.

Scaling IBGP with Route Reflection

The previous sections touched on the fact that IBGP speakers should be fully meshed due to the restrictions that IBGP has on readvertising updates to other IBGP speakers. When BGP was first envisioned more than 20 years ago, conventional wisdom was that the global Internet would consist of only a few ASs, and that each AS would have a few BGP speakers, and that these speakers would be dealing with a few hundred routes. Recall also that the VP of IBM once announced a worldwide market for mainframes to be around 10 units! Maintaining a full IBGP mesh among a few routers is trivial, but doing so among hundreds of routers is nearly impossible.

Given the modern reality of transit provider networks needing to run IBGP on virtually every router in their AS, and that there may be hundreds of these routers, you can quickly conclude that maintaining a full mesh of IBGP sessions quickly becomes unmanageable. The formula to compute the number of sessions required for a full mesh is $v * (v - 1)/2$, where v is the number of BGP speakers. Using the formula, we see that for 10 IBGP speakers, a total of 45 IBGP sessions are needed ($10 * (9)/2 = 45$). Increase the number of speakers by a mere 50%—to 15—and the number of sessions required increases geometrically to 105! It's clear that the full-mesh model simply does not scale; soon routers would exhaust all their control plane resources just maintaining all their BGP sessions. A solution was needed, and route reflection, as currently defined in RFC 4456, provides a remarkably elegant solution to what could have been a significant protocol shortcoming. Figure 5-3 shows a small IBGP cloud before and after route reflection is added.

Note that in the first example, an IBGP session is missing, resulting in a less than full mesh, which in turn leads to holes in the BGP topology. In the second example, however, R2 has been configured to perform reflection, using but a single command to assign a cluster ID. The only change made to clients R1, R3, and R4 is the removal of their now unneeded IBGP sessions.

Route reflection adds two new attributes to IBGP updates to address concerns about BGP loops that would otherwise occur, given that IBGP updates do not modify the

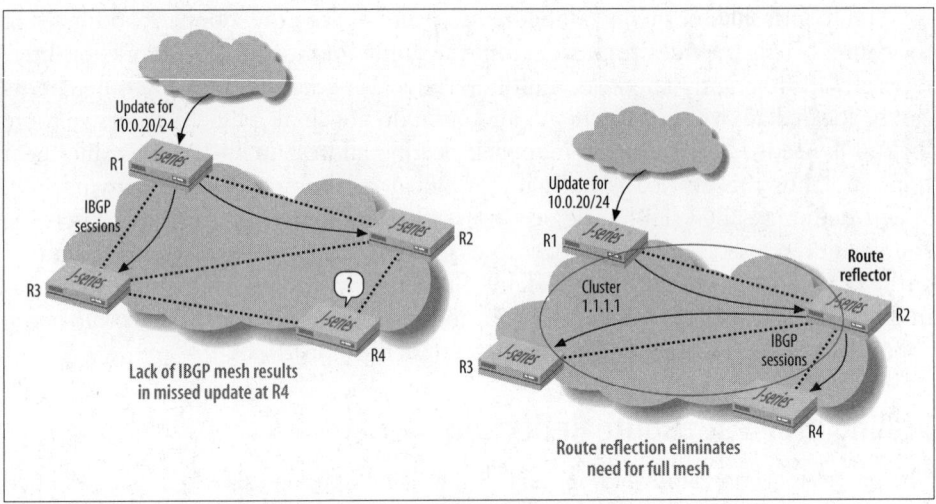

Figure 5-3. BGP route reflection

AS path. These attributes are added by the route reflector when it first touches a client's route. Configuration of reflection is performed only on the route reflector itself; no configuration changes are needed for a route reflector client, other than perhaps to decommission unneeded IBGP peering definitions to other clients in the same cluster.

The cluster list attribute identifies the route reflection clusters that the route has visited, whereas the originator ID attribute identifies the route's original source. These attributes are processed by route reflectors to prevent loops by ensuring that IBGP updates are echoed only once to each reflector client and nonreflector client. Simply put, a cluster's reflector will not readvertise an IBGP update into cluster ID n, when cluster ID n is already present in the cluster list attribute. The reflector also uses the originator ID attribute to ensure that updates are never sent back to the client that originated the route. Note that the route reflector first performs the best path selection process on all updates and reflects only the paths it chooses as best.

You typically want the forwarding topology to differ from the reflection topology, which is to say that packets can be forwarded directly between two BGP speakers, despite their learning each other's routes through a reflector. If the IGP's shortest path does not lead through the reflector, the packets should not flow through the reflector. Care must be taken with any next hop self-policy applied to a reflector to ensure that it does not rewrite the next hop on IBGP routes that it is reflecting—doing so will force extra hops on packets that now need to cross the reflector. A next hop self-policy is often applied to IBGP updates to rewrite the BGP next hop of EBGP learned routes with the peering address of the local speaker. This prevents problems with internal speakers not being able to resolve the next hop originally received in the EBGP update, which is set to the remote EBGP speaker's peering address and normally not altered in IBGP updates.

Route reflection and redundancy

Reflection can represent a single point of failure, making it common to add redundancy by deploying multiple reflectors. Normally, each reflector IBGP peers with each client in the cluster, and the two route reflectors are then joined via a nonclient IBGP session. There always seems to be endless debate in such designs as to whether each reflector should be assigned the same or a unique cluster ID. Figure 5-4 illustrates the two design alternatives.

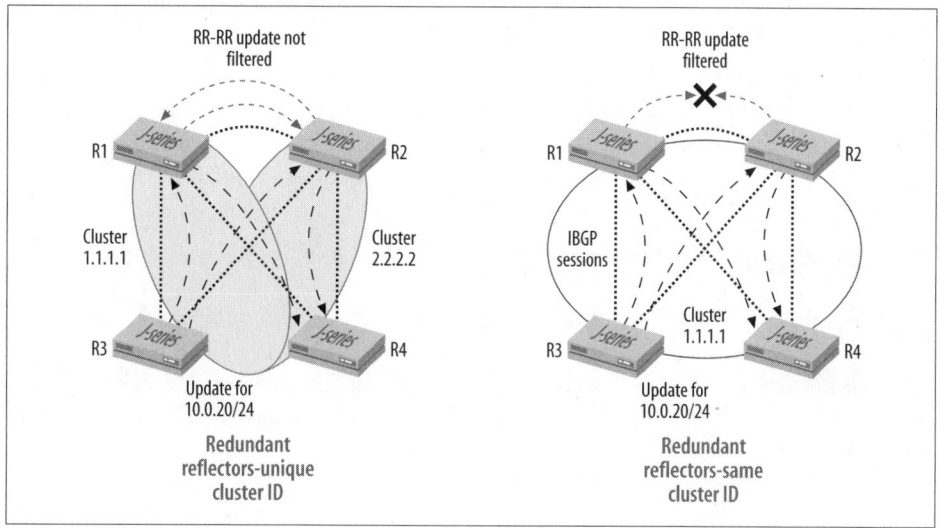

Figure 5-4. Route reflection redundancy

In most cases, a design using unique cluster IDs—which technically results in two route reflector clusters, each having one reflector—is considered the best approach for maintaining connectivity in the event of failures. This is because the reflectors do not see their own cluster ID in the updates they send each other via the route reflector–route reflector IBGP session, and therefore the reflectors will learn of both their intracluster and intercluster paths, resulting in a more complete BGP table at the reflectors. For example, if the R3–R1 IBGP session should fail, R1 is still able to reach R3 via the path learned from R2 in cluster 2.2.2.2. The dual-cluster approach does have the drawback of increased BGP route state at the reflectors, prompting some to prefer the shared cluster ID model.

We discussed the main drawback to the shared cluster ID approach earlier—namely, the potential for client-to-reflector session loss and the resultant lack of connectivity. However, if we assume loopback-based peering, there is actually little risk to the shared cluster model. This is because it's extremely unlikely that a client-to-reflector IBGP session will be lost while the client is still able to maintain connectivity to the rest of the network. You should use unique cluster IDs if you're using interface-based peering so as to provide tolerance for failure of individual interfaces.

Scaling IBGP: Confederations

A BGP confederation effectively divides a large AS into smaller, mini ASs known as a *member ASs*. Within each member AS, you normally find a full IBGP mesh, but route reflectors can also be deployed as part of a confederation solution. It's normal to see member ASs assigned AS numbers from the private numbering space because member AS numbers are not seen external to the AS confederation anyway. Because the number of routers within each sub-AS is relatively small, maintaining a full IBGP mesh is manageable. To the outside world, all these confederation shenanigans are hidden, and the entire AS confederation is represented by a single AS number.

Confederation use is rare in enterprise networks, and we will not explore the subject here other than to mention that Juniper routers offer full support for BGP confederations. For more information on BGP confederations, consult JUNOS software documentation or RFC 3065, "Autonomous System Confederations for BGP."

BGP and the Enterprise

The preceding section provided a targeted review of BGP's operational characteristics and scaling approaches. BGP is normally associated with Internet service provider (ISP) networks that offer transit services for Internet traffic. This section focuses on how BGP can be applied to meet the routing needs of enterprise networks.

When Should an Enterprise Run BGP?

BGP is a sophisticated routing protocol that can help to optimize an enterprise's routing, but that doesn't mean all enterprise networks will see a benefit from its deployment. An enterprise decision to run BGP normally hinges on the benefits that can be gained by making intelligent outgoing routing decisions and by using BGP attributes in an attempt to influence how upstream networks route toward your network to help control which links are used for ingress traffic. The common factor to both of these scenarios is a network with at least two external connections—such a network is considered to be *dual-homed*. Enterprise networks with a single attachment to a service provider will normally not benefit by running BGP and should simply use a static default route. When dual-attached to the same provider, two static defaults can be used to achieve some measure of outbound load balancing.

A word about AS numbers

Although likely obvious by now, we must state that to run BGP you must first have an AS number. Like IP addresses, there are both public and private AS number pools. Public AS numbers are assigned by a Regional Internet Registry—for example, ARIN for the Americas, Caribbean, and sub-Saharan Africa, APNIC for Asia Pacific, or RIPE for Europe, the Middle East, and Northern Africa.

Historically, the ASN space was limited by the use of a 2-byte value, which permitted a maximum of 65,535 ASs. Support of 4-byte coding for ASNs, which can provide more than 4 billion unique ASNs, is defined in draft-ietf-idr-as4 and is supported in JUNOS software.

An enterprise should expect to justify its need to the Regional Internet Registry when applying for a public ASN. Requirements vary, but normally you qualify for a public ASN only when your network is multihomed and has a single, clearly defined routing policy that is different from its providers' routing policies. This brings up a key point about BGP, policy, and dual homing. When you are attached to a single upstream provider, from the perspective of the rest of the world your policy must, by definition, match that of your provider. This is because only one external view of that enterprise's routes is being made available, and this view is based on your provider's policy. BGP can still be used when connected to a single upstream provider, but in these cases, you will often configure the routers with an ASN from the private AS space. The provider will then strip the private ASN and replace it with its ASN when announcing these routes to other networks. The private ASN space, which is technically allocated to the IANA itself, ranges from 64,512–65,534, inclusive. These numbers are often used to number subconfederations within a confederated AS.

ASN Portability

An organization may obtain its ASN directly from a regional numbering authority or as part of its service agreement with a local provider, which in this case functions as a Local Internet Registry (LIR) by delegating ASNs (and address blocks) from its assigned pool. In most cases, ASNs obtained from an LIR will not be portable if you later decide to move to a new provider. This situation is similar to nonportable IP address blocks, which stay with the provider should you choose to obtain service elsewhere. Although AS renumbering is certainly less work than IP renumbering, both can be disruptive and time-consuming—careful thought should be given to the potential need for ASN portability when planning your BGP deployment.

Dual-homed: Single versus multiple providers

Being dual-homed is a great way to improve performance and reliability. But do all dual-homed environments warrant use of BGP? In most cases, this is a function of whether the enterprise is dual-homed to the same or to different upstream providers. Figure 5-5 shows the two types of dual-homing arrangements. Note that both models support multiple attachments to the same ISP, whether for reasons of redundancy or added capacity. In fact, the simplest form of the dual-homed single-provider/dual-provider model is to use a single router with dual links. Relying on a single device for all external connectivity suffers obvious reliability concerns, and it is assumed rare for all but the smallest of enterprise networks.

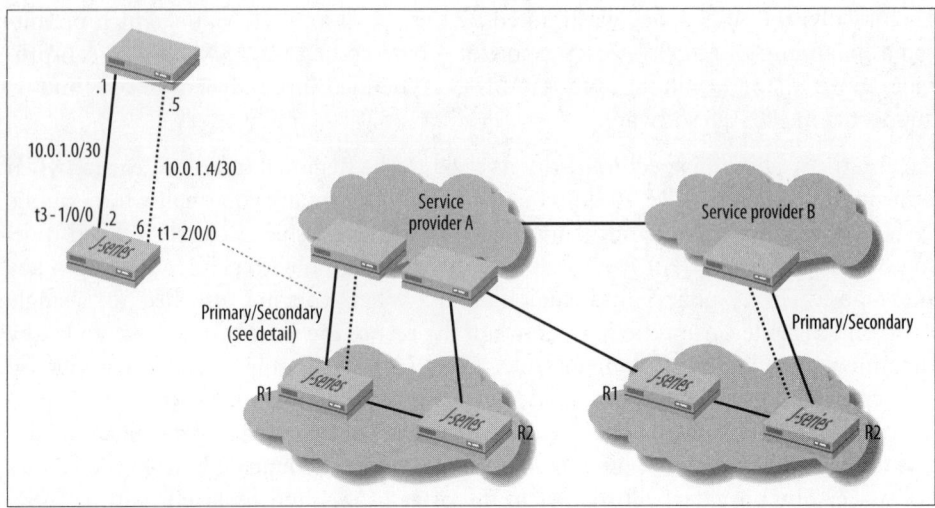

Figure 5-5. BGP dual homing

Running BGP is normally overkill when you are dual-homed to the same provider, especially when the parallel connections are in close geographic proximity. This is because you are pretty much at the mercy of your provider's policy, and BGP cannot do much to alter the way traffic enters or exits your network—your global view of the Internet must match that of your provider because it is the only view you receive. An enterprise with this type of connectivity is often well served with a simple static default route. Load balancing can occur in one of two ways. For a single router with dual attachments, the load balancing occurs at that router, using the underlying IGP (static) to map prefixes or flows to one of the two links. This router is in turn configured to advertise a default route into the IGP to attract nonlocal traffic. When dual routers are used, each with a single provider uplink, it's common to see each router generate and advertise a default route into the IGP, while they in turn each have a static default pointing toward that router's provider uplink.

Asymmetric Link Speed Support

The use of asymmetric link speeds for redundant attachment to the same provider is common in both models. When running BGP, the bandwidth community can be used to provide unequal cost load balancing proportionate to the link speed. In contrast, static routing over asymmetric links is typically done by directing all traffic over the high-speed link until it becomes unavailable, at which point the traffic is switched to the lower-speed secondary. In JUNOS software, this is accomplished with a static route along with a *qualified next hop*. A qualified next hop is a list of next hops with varying preferences/metrics that are used in order of their preference, based on the ability to resolve the associated next hop. The following code snippet shows how a dual-homed customer could configure all traffic to egress on a high-speed T3 link, unless the T3 interface/next hop becomes unavailable, at which point the traffic will switch to the qualified next hop with the next most preferred (next lowest) preference:

```
[edit routing-options static]
ruser@router# show
route 0.0.0.0/0 {
    qualified-next-hop 10.0.1.1 {
        preference 20;
        interface t3-1/0/0.0;
    }
    qualified-next-hop 10.0.1.5 {
        preference 30;
        interface t1-2/0/0.0;
    }
}
```

Which Routers Should Run IBGP?

Great! You've made it this far, which shows that you still feel your network either justifies use of BGP, or simply needs a puppy. From this point forward, this chapter assumes a network that is dual-homed to multiple providers, as is your desire for fine-grained control over how traffic enters and exits your network. Having reached this determination, the next logical question is, "Where should I configure BGP?" Knowing where to run EBGP is pretty straightforward; you must configure EBGP on the routers that peer to other ASs. The real question is where do you have to run IBGP, and this is a very, very good question indeed.

First, consider that most service provider networks run *both* an IGP and an IBGP on *all* of their core routers.[*]

Service providers need to run BGP on all their routers to ensure that the Internet core remains a default free routing zone, and because no service provider in its right mind would (intentionally) try to redistribute a full BGP table into its IGP. For the first point, any transit network that does not carry full Internet routing, and therefore relies on some type of default route, will be prone to loops. If the network is not running BGP on all transit routers, and there is no default route, the implication is that the IGP is in fact carrying a full Internet route table. Even the best implemented IGPs are not intended to carry hundreds of thousands of external routes, making such a design implausible given the sheer size of Internet route tables.

---

[*] The notable exception here is the "BGP free core," typically based on Multiprotocol Label Switching (MPLS) to avoid the need for full routing state in the core.

It's interesting to note that JUNOS software does not have the concept of IGP–BGP synchronization, making a no synchronization configuration statement unnecessary. In IOS, the BGP process expects the IGP to have a copy of each route before that route can be advertised by BGP, unless, of course, you have turned off synchronization. This is why disabling synchronization is the first step in almost any IOS configuration. Consider this one less command to get BGP up and running on a Juniper!

By running BGP on all its routers, a service provider does not rely on a default route, and it can mercifully spare its IGP an ignoble meltdown. By running both protocols, the IGP is left to do what it does best: providing connectivity between the loopback interfaces used for IBGP peering, while BGP routes keep the transit traffic from looping about and also provide needed administrative policy controls.

No Transit Services

Service provider networks are richly interconnected to the outside world, and they are optimized for making money by transporting traffic that neither originates on nor terminates in their networks. This is, after all, what makes them *transit* service providers. In contrast, an enterprise network is concerned with the transport of its own traffic, albeit sometimes needing to venture offsite to obtain required information. By not providing transit services, an enterprise can avoid running IBGP on every router. When possible, the network should be designed so that the BGP speakers are geographically localized, thus minimizing the portions of the network that need to run BGP. Figure 5-6 provides a sample topology to illustrate this concept.

The figure shows a network topology that runs BGP for its own connectivity, not for providing transit/connectivity services to other networks. The BGP speakers have been positioned near the network's edge and in geographic proximity, in an effort to constrain the scope of routers that need to run BGP. Routers R1 through R3 are BGP-enabled and speak EBGP to their attached service providers and IBGP among themselves. BGP is needed between these routers because Internet-destined traffic originating within the enterprise can arrive at any of these, and the consistent BGP tables ensure that traffic egresses the network according to local policy, even if some additional hops across the backbone are needed to reach the desired egress point.

A default route is generated by two of the IBGP speakers and is injected into the IGP to provide the non-BGP-speaking routers with external connectivity. The use of a generated route, as opposed to a simple static route, allows the withdrawal of an advertised default when the BGP speaker has problems with its EBGP session—the generated route is made active by the presence of learned EBGP routes. Internal routers simply select the remaining default route that is metrically closest to maintain their external connectivity.

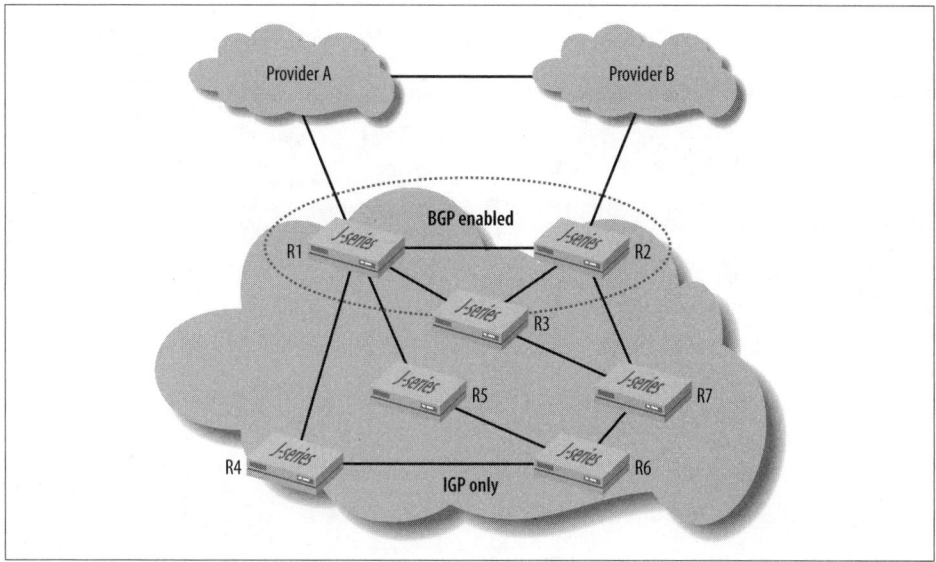

Figure 5-6. Which routers need to run IBGP?

The Impact of Accepting Specifics Versus a Default from Your Provider

The need to run IBGP on routers that do not speak EBGP is normally a function of whether the enterprise's import policy accepts only a default route or is configured to accept specific routes. In the latter case, you will need to run BGP on any routers that are used to interconnect your EBGP/IBGP-speaking nodes to prevent routing loops. Figure 5-7 provides an example of how inconstant routing knowledge can lead to a routing loop. The inconsistency arises from forwarding state that is known to the BGP speakers only while other routers rely on a default route. If all routers accepted only a default or the same set of specifics, this condition would not arise.

In this example, routers R1 and R2 are running EBGP with import policies that accept specific routes. Both routers IBGP-peer to each other. All other routers are running an IGP only. Things begin at step 1 in Figure 5-7, where both R1 and R2 generate a default route that is injected into Open Shortest Path First (OSPF). Step 2 shows Provider B advertising the 10.0.1/24 prefix, which is accepted by R2, given its import policy that accepts specifics and rejects the default route. R2 advertises this route to R1 over the IBGP session at step 3. R1 installs this route as active in this example because the same route learned from ISP A will have a longer AS path length.

Things begin to go wrong at step 4 in Figure 5-7, when R4 decides to avail itself of the default route to forward a packet to destination 10.0.1.1. In this example, R4 sends the packet to R3, but sending it directly to R1 would not change things in the

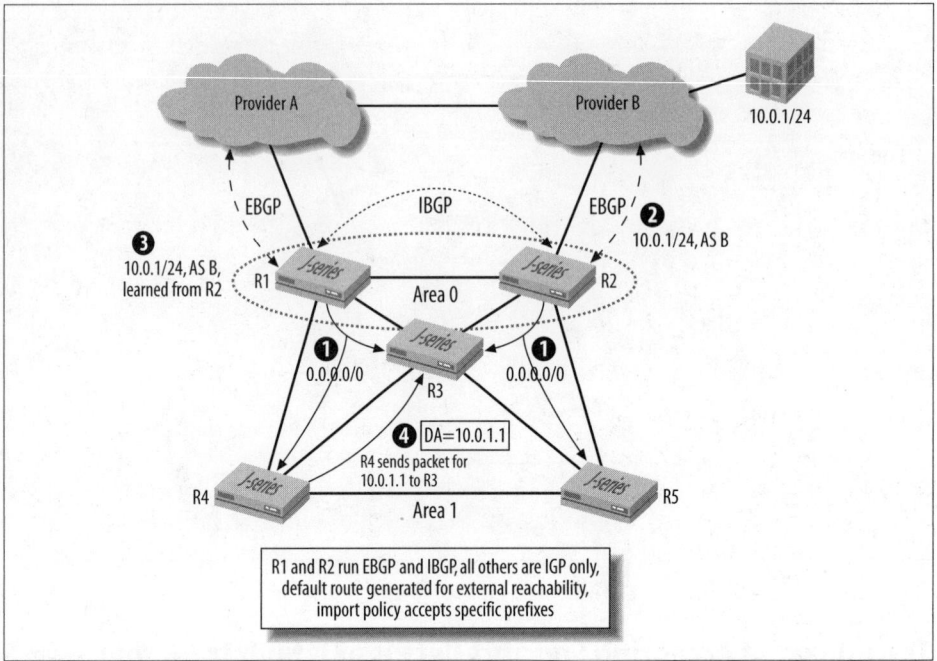

Figure 5-7. Routing loop from lack of BGP routing knowledge

long run. Recall that R3 is not running BGP and is therefore relying on the default route to reach this destination, as did R4. If R3 decides to forward to the default it learned from R2, everything is alright. But there is a 50% chance that it will decide to forward to the default route it learns from R1. As a BGP speaker, R1 has specific routing information for this prefix, which it learned over its IBGP session to R2. R1's routing decision determines that the packet should be forwarded toward the protocol next hop advertised by R2, that is, R2's loopback address. The result of R1's recursive route lookup on R2's loopback address may be the decision to forward the packet over the R1–R2 link or over the set of R1–R2–R3 links, as determined by IGP metrics. If R1 forwards the packet back to R3, a loop is formed, given that R3 has already handled this packet and decided to send it to R1.

Two solutions present themselves:

Enable IBGP on R3
> If you enable IBGP on R3, and then fully mesh the IBGP speakers, R3 would have never used the default route to forward this packet and would have sent it directly to R2 for dispatch into AS B.

Reject specifics
> If the import policy at R1 and R2 is altered to accept only a default, this route could be redistributed into the IGP. The EBGP learned version of the default route will remain active at both R1 and R2, even if the BGP speakers readvertise

the default route to each other, owing to the route selection step that prefers EBGP learned over IBGP learned routes. Now, when a packet addressed to 10.0.1.1 arrives at R1, it longest-matches against the default route learned from Provider A and is not sent back to either R2 or R3, so no loops form.

Although the second solution prevents a routing loop, sending to ISP A is probably not the optimal way for this enterprise to reach prefix 10.0.1.0/24. This helps to illustrate why accepting specific routes, and then running IBGP among the routers that can be used to transit between EBGP speakers, is generally the optimal way for an enterprise to deploy BGP.

Summary of Enterprise BGP Requirements

To summarize, an enterprise should consider running EBGP when it is multihomed, to take advantage of the optimal routing and routing controls provided by BGP. The enterprise should run IBGP on any router that runs EBGP, and it must carefully consider what other routers should be IBGP-enabled. Recall that IBGP requires a full mesh or the use of route reflection/confederations for proper operation. Because BGP is not redistributed into your IGP, failing to run IBGP on all routers will result in those routers not having a complete view of BGP reachability. Normally, a generated default route is injected into the IGP to accommodate external routing for the non-BGP speakers. Remember that BGP will need to be enabled on routers that are expected to provide transit service *between* your EBGP speakers when the enterprise policy is to accept specific routes from your service providers to prevent against routing loops. Rejecting specifics and accepting only a default route lessens this requirement, as described earlier.

This section gave a comprehensive review of BGP and its key capabilities and operational characteristics. We also discussed how BGP can benefit an enterprise by helping to make optimized outbound routing decisions, and when all goes to plan, to also help influence your peer's outbound decisions to effect better control of how traffic arrives at your network's boundaries.

You may consider taking a brief break before diving into the next section. Some of the hands-on scenarios are a bit lengthy because of the numerous inclusions of actual router output, which are added to ensure that the reader is able to follow the details of the case study.

BGP Deployment: Asymmetric Load Balancing

Having made it through the protocol overview and enterprise application section, it is now time to apply your knowledge of BGP and JUNOS software to the first of three practical BGP deployment scenarios.

The first scenario begins when the CIO at Beer-Co seizes upon the organization's newfound appreciation for all things BGP by applying for a public ASN and detailing a BGP deployment plan that ultimately involves dual-homing to multiple providers. BGP deployment will occur in a phased approach, and you have been selected to head up phase 1: establishment of the initial BGP peering and related policy to Botnet in AS 34.

The deployment goals for initial BGP peering with Botnet are as follows:

- Establish EBGP interface-based peering to Botnet/AS 34.
- Use import policy to reject all but the default route that originates within Botnet/AS 34.
- Use export policy to advertise a single aggregate route that represents Beer-Co's internal prefixes.
- Use a static route to direct traffic to the backup link *only* in the event of BGP session disruption, and to ensure that traffic switches back to the primary upon service restoration.
- Redistribute a default route to provide external reachability for internal Beer-Co routers.

Figure 5-8 details the current Beer-Co internal topology and the newly activated access links to Botnet.

Figure 5-8 shows that Botnet is attached to other service providers, and to a particular customer, Brewer Inc., which has been assigned a 192.168.34.0/24 address block. The numbers enclosed within parentheses represent the range of route prefixes that Botnet is expected to advertise. In this example, these routes are instantiated as locally defined static routes, complete with associated AS numbers and origin code. This technique helps to simulate the learning, and subsequent readvertisement, of BGP routes between Botnet and its BGP peers. The customer route shown for provider Brewer, which is 192.168.34.0/24 in this case, is set to a reject next hop so that reachability can be confirmed, even when the customer site does not exist. Note that you expect to receive an Internet Control Message Protocol (ICMP) destination unreachable message due to the reject-style next hop, but this error message serves to validate reachability for our purposes.

Note also that Beer-Co has redundant links to Botnet. The huge disparity in link speed (100 Mbps versus 1.5 Mbps) drives the decision to use the faster link as a primary with the second link used only in the event of problems on the primary interface or a related BGP peering session. Care must be taken to ensure that the static route used to direct traffic over the secondary link is *less preferred* than any BGP routes learned from AS 34, which is not the default behavior given that a static route is more preferred than any dynamically learned one. A mistake here could easily mean paying for a 100 Mbps pipe while throughput is limited to a paltry 1.544 Mbps!

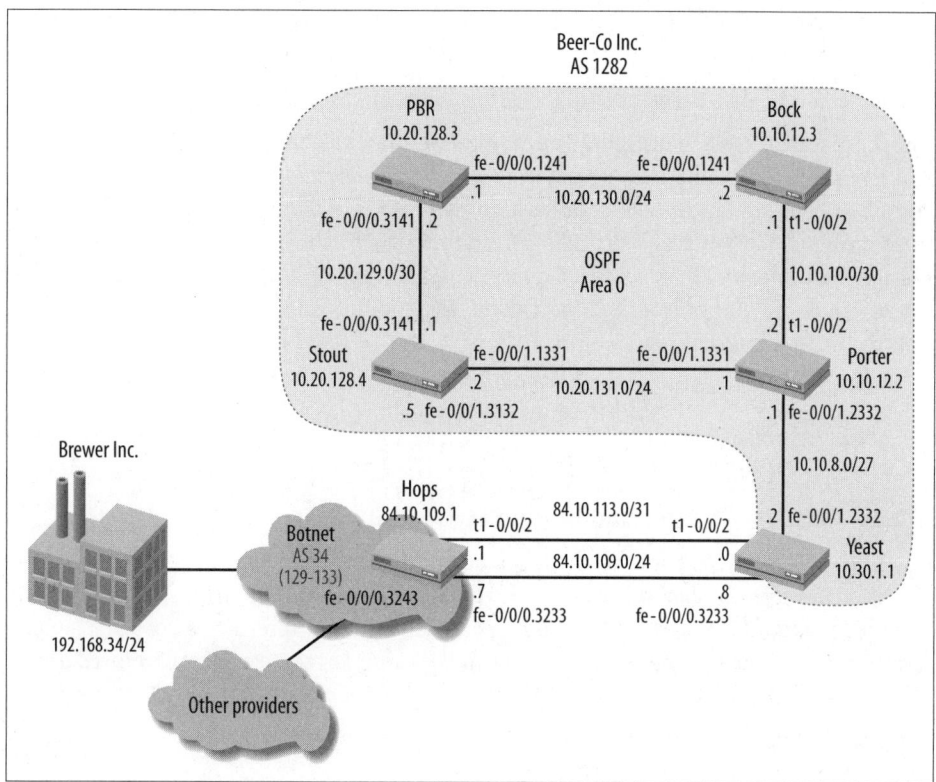

Beer-Co Inc.
AS 1282

PBR
10.20.128.3

fe-0/0/0.1241   fe-0/0/0.1241
.1   10.20.130.0/24   .2

Bock
10.10.12.3

fe-0/0/0.3141 .2

10.20.129.0/30

OSPF
Area 0

.1 t1-0/0/2

10.10.10.0/30

fe-0/0/0.3141 .1

Stout
10.20.128.4

fe-0/0/1.1331   fe-0/0/1.1331
.2   10.20.131.0/24   .1

.2 t1-0/0/2

Porter
10.10.12.2

.5 fe-0/0/1.3132

.1 fe-0/0/1.2332

10.10.8.0/27

Brewer Inc.

Hops
84.10.109.1

84.10.113.0/31

.2 fe-0/0/1.2332

Botnet
AS 34
(129-133)

t1-0/0/2
.1
84.10.109.0/24

t1-0/0/2
.0

Yeast
10.30.1.1

fe-0/0/0.3243
.7
fe-0/0/0.3233

.8
fe-0/0/0.3233

192.168.34/24

Other providers

Figure 5-8. Beer-Co to Botnet peering

Validate Baseline Operation

Configuration gets underway at router Yeast with the definition of a generated static route. Recall that a generated route differs from an aggregated route in that the former has a forwarding next hop determined by the most preferred contributing route. In contrast, an aggregate route can only point to a discard or reject next hop. The generated route is redistributed into OSPF to provide connectivity to Internet destinations for Beer-Co's internal routers.

The OSPF configuration for area 0 is preexisting, and all routers have a similar configuration—the OSPF stanza at Porter is displayed, along with its adjacency status:

```
lab@Porter> show configuration protocols ospf
area 0.0.0.0 {
    interface fe-0/0/1.1331;
    interface fe-0/0/1.2332;
    interface t1-0/0/2.0;
}
lab@Porter> show ospf neighbor
```

```
Address         Interface       State   ID              Pri  Dead
10.20.131.2     fe-0/0/1.1331   Full    10.20.128.4     128  33
10.10.8.2       fe-0/0/1.2332   Full    10.30.1.1       128  36
10.10.10.1      t1-0/0/2.0      Full    10.10.12.3      128  32
```

The single-area OSPF configuration at Porter matches the topology in Figure 5-8, and the router has all three expected OSPF adjacencies; one each to routers Stout, Yeast, and Bock. The routes being learned by OSPF are displayed and piped through the command-line interface's (CLI's) match function to show only those routes with a /32 network mask. These routes represent the loopback addresses assigned to each router (they are the only /32 IP addresses assigned), and therefore provide a quick sanity check of internal reachability.

```
lab@Porter> show route protocol ospf | match /32
10.10.12.3/32       *[OSPF/10] 00:05:54, metric 3
10.20.128.3/32      *[OSPF/10] 00:05:54, metric 2
10.20.128.4/32      *[OSPF/10] 00:23:46, metric 1
10.30.1.1/32        *[OSPF/10] 00:22:18, metric 1
224.0.0.5/32        *[OSPF/10] 01:03:03, metric 1
```

The output confirms a route to the loopback addresses of Stout, Yeast, PBR, and Bock. The metric values associated with each route seem reasonable in this topology. The default scaling factor of 100 Mbps assigns a Fast Ethernet interface a cost of 1, which results in avoidance of the T1 link between Bock and Porter. Porter therefore sees an OSPF cost of 3 to reach the loopback interface of Bock via Stout and PBR. Next, the route to Brewer Inc. is displayed:

```
lab@Porter> show route 192.168.34.0

lab@Porter>
```

The output confirms that Porter cannot route to the 192.168.34/24 route associated with Brewer Inc., which also confirms the lack of a default route in area 0. As a final verification step, reachability is confirmed to the EBGP peering addresses on both the primary and secondary links between Botnet and Yeast:

```
lab@Yeast> ping 84.10.113.1 count 1
PING 84.10.113.1 (84.10.113.1): 56 data bytes
64 bytes from 84.10.113.1: icmp_seq=0 ttl=64 time=26.887 ms

--- 84.10.113.1 ping statistics ---
1 packets transmitted, 1 packets received, 0% packet loss
round-trip min/avg/max/stddev = 26.887/26.887/26.887/0.000 ms

lab@Yeast> ping 84.10.109.7 count 1
PING 84.10.109.7 (84.10.109.7): 56 data bytes
64 bytes from 84.10.109.7: icmp_seq=0 ttl=64 time=12.255 ms

--- 84.10.109.7 ping statistics ---
1 packets transmitted, 1 packets received, 0% packet loss
round-trip min/avg/max/stddev = 12.255/12.255/12.255/0.000 ms
```

Configure Generated Route

A generated default route that uses policy to constrain the set of contributing routes to the direct route associated with the backup peering link to Botnet. The premise here is that in normal operation, Yeast will have two default routes: one learned through BGP that points to the primary Botnet peering, and a second, generated default route pointing to the secondary peering. Route preference adjustments are made to ensure that the BGP route will be preferred when available. Loss of the BGP session results in the generated static route becoming active. Either way, an OSPF export policy redistributes the default route, be it learned or generated, into OSPF. The default route is withdrawn only in the event that Yeast loses its BGP session at the same time as its t1-0/0/2 interface goes down, in which case the decision to forego guaranteed diverse routing for the primary and secondary circuits may come into question.

The configuration starts with the static route and, at this stage, is quite straightforward. By beginning with the generated default, you have a chance to test failover to secondary link behavior before the primary link is brought up. It's always a good idea to periodically confirm operation of backup links during a maintenance window, rather than waiting until your primary fails. The generated route portion of Yeast's configuration is displayed:

```
[edit]
lab@Yeast# show routing-options generate
route 0.0.0.0/0 policy gen_default;

[edit]
lab@Yeast# show policy-options policy-statement gen_default
term 1 {
    from {
        protocol direct;
        route-filter 84.10.113.0/31 exact;
    }
    then accept;
}
term 2 {
    then reject;
}
```

The configuration results in the generation of a 0/0 route that, when matched, will forward over the next hop assigned to the preferred contributing route. Here, the set of possible contributors is constrained by the policy named gen_default, which matches only on the 84.10.113.0/31 route assigned to the t1-0/0/2 interface. The policy's second term guarantees that no other route can contribute by rejecting all remaining routes and sources. Operation of the generated route is verified:

```
[edit]
lab@Yeast# run show route protocol aggregate detail
```

```
inet.0: 17 destinations, 17 routes (17 active, 0 holddown, 0 hidden)
0.0.0.0/0 (1 entry, 1 announced)
        *Aggregate Preference: 130
                Next-hop reference count: 2
                Next hop: via t1-0/0/2.0, selected
                State: <Active Int Ext>
                Age: 10:07
                Task: Aggregate
                Announcement bits (1): 0-KRT
                AS path: I
                                Flags: Generate Depth: 0      Active
        Contributing Routes (1):
                84.10.113.0/31 proto Direct
```

The highlighted portions of the output confirm that all is working to plan with the generated route. A default route is present, it is currently active (there is no BGP learned version yet), and traffic matching this route will be directed out the t1-0/0/2 interface. Further, the expected number of contributing routes, 1, is shown, and that route matches the direct route for the secondary peering. Note that the route is considered to be of the type aggregate, and that the preference for this route is 130. Thinking ahead, you'll recall that this route ultimately needs to be less preferred than any BGP learned version, and that the default preference for BGP is 170. The generated route's preference is set to be just higher than BGP's, so it will be less preferred when a BGP learned version becomes available.

```
[edit]
lab@Yeast# set routing-options generate route 0.0.0.0/0 preference 175
```

The T1 interface is briefly brought down, and the show route command is repeated to validate that the generated route's fate tracks that of the t1-0/0/2 interface.

```
[edit]
lab@Yeast# set interfaces t1-0/0/2 disable

[edit]
lab@Yeast# commit
commit complete

[edit]
lab@Yeast# run show route protocol aggregate detail

inet.0: 16 destinations, 16 routes (15 active, 0 holddown, 1 hidden)
```

The command output does not display any active aggregate routes. The highlight calls out that one route, of an as-yet-unknown type, is hidden, however. To display a hidden route, add the hidden switch. Here, the display confirms that the hidden route is, in fact, the generated default—the route is now hidden because of a lack of contributors:

```
[edit]
lab@Yeast# run show route protocol aggregate detail hidden
```

```
inet.0: 16 destinations, 16 routes (15 active, 0 holddown, 1 hidden)
0.0.0.0/0 (1 entry, 0 announced)
        Aggregate
            Next hop type: Reject
            Next-hop reference count: 3
            State: <Hidden Int Ext>
            Age: 1:19:04
            Task: Aggregate
            AS path: I
                         Flags: Generate Depth: 0        Inactive
```

The change is rolled back and committed (not shown) at Yeast to ensure that the t1-0/0/2 interface is no longer disabled. Next, a policy is written to redistribute a default route from any protocol source. The ospf_default policy is applied to the OSPF protocol as export:

```
[edit]
lab@Yeast# show policy-options policy-statement ospf_default
term 1 {
    from {
        route-filter 0.0.0.0/0 exact;
    }
    then accept;
}

[edit]
lab@Yeast# show protocols ospf export
export ospf_default;
```

The ospf_default policy is written to be protocol-agnostic, because the goal is to have an active default route stemming from *either* BGP or the aggregate protocol sources. If you prefer a tight ship, you could always add a logical OR match condition for the two protocols, aggregate and bgp. After committing the changes, an OSPF learned default route is confirmed in area 0 at router PBR:

```
lab@PBR> show route 192.168.34.0

inet.0: 20 destinations, 20 routes (20 active, 0 holddown, 0 hidden)
+ = Active Route, - = Last Active, * = Both

0.0.0.0/0          *[OSPF/150] 00:03:04, metric 0, tag 0
                    > to 10.20.129.1 via fe-0/0/0.3141
```

Great! As planned, the longest match for the 192.168.34/24 route to Brewer Inc. at PBR is now the OSPF learned default route. A traceroute verifies connectivity to Botnet customers from within Beer-Co. The traceroute has an auspicious beginning, but it soon degrades to timeouts:

```
lab@PBR> traceroute 192.168.34.1 no-resolve
traceroute to 192.168.34.1 (192.168.34.1), 30 hops max, 40 byte
packets
 1  10.20.129.1  14.345 ms  9.916 ms  8.099 ms
 2  10.20.131.1  11.864 ms  30.002 ms  20.016 ms
```

```
3   10.10.8.2  9.901 ms  29.991 ms  9.984 ms
4   * * *
5   *^C
lab@PBR>
```

The traceroute result shows the expected routing path through Beer-Co's intranet—
from PBR to Stout, and then to Porter—and it makes it as far as the 10.10.8.2 address
assigned to Yeast's fe-0/0/1.2332 interface. This makes it seem like there's a problem on the Porter–Yeast link, except that previous observations showed that the
OSPF adjacency was stable. To narrow down the issue, a ping is generated from
Yeast, but this time it is sourced from the router's loopback interface. This is an
important point because it will reveal any potential routing issues that may impact
Botnet's ability to route back into Beer-Co's 10/8 address block.

```
lab@Yeast> ping 84.10.113.1 count 1
PING 84.10.113.1 (84.10.113.1): 56 data bytes
64 bytes from 84.10.113.1: icmp_seq=0 ttl=64 time=16.750 ms

--- 84.10.113.1 ping statistics ---
1 packets transmitted, 1 packets received, 0% packet loss
round-trip min/avg/max/stddev = 16.750/16.750/16.750/0.000 ms

lab@Yeast> ping 84.10.113.1 count 1 source 10.30.1.1
PING 84.10.113.1 (84.10.113.1): 56 data bytes

--- 84.10.113.1 ping statistics ---
1 packets transmitted, 0 packets received, 100% packet loss
```

Eureka! The default ping, as sourced from the shared direct connection, succeeds,
whereas the loopback sourced ping fails. This demonstrates a routing problem
within Botnet. It is not uncommon to encounter difficulties such as this. After a few
phone calls, you are assured that everything is (now) in order with the newly
installed static route back to your network; it seems that confusion stemmed from
Botnet's misunderstanding that BGP would be used to advertise an aggregate for
your network, and it shall—once it's up and running, that is. The traceroute is
repeated, and its successful completion indicates that you are ready to move on to
BGP configuration.

```
lab@PBR> traceroute 192.168.34.1 no-resolve
traceroute to 192.168.34.1 (192.168.34.1), 30 hops max, 40 byte
packets
1   10.20.129.1  14.807 ms  9.827 ms  9.949 ms
2   10.20.131.1  19.967 ms  40.010 ms  13.579 ms
3   10.10.8.2  16.439 ms  10.131 ms  9.777 ms
4   84.10.113.1  39.727 ms !N  40.154 ms !N  17.789 ms !N
```

Recall that in this lab, you expect an ICMP unreachable error message for the final
hop because a static route pointing to a reject next hop is used within Botnet to simulate the Brewer Inc. network.

Configure Initial BGP Peering

With the backup link and its associated static routing/generated route confirmed, you'll move on to the task of configuring BGP. In addition to the BGP session, you also need to create an aggregate route representing Beer-Co's internal reachability, along with the export policy needed to advertise it into EBGP. The aggregate route is critical because it enables remote ASs to route toward Beer-Co. An import policy that rejects all but a Botnet-originated default route is also needed. In most cases, you will want to write and apply policy before the BGP session is actually activated to guard against unwanted side effects that stem from receiving or advertising undesired routes, or worse yet, before hitting a platform scaling limit that leads to an unpredictable operation.

 We must emphasize that enterprise routing platforms are not always capable of handling a full BGP table, especially when the same platform is also taxed with value-added services such as stateful firewalls, Network Address Translation (NAT), virtual private network (VPN) tunnels, and so on. Exceeding platform scaling limits can result in control plane instability and possible forwarding plane impact. Care should be exercised to factor the effects of route table size, the number of routing peers, the impact of enabled services, and internal resource consumption for managing interfaces (IFDs/IFLs) and Address Resolution Protocol (ARP) tables before adding a new protocol or service to any production router. When in doubt, simulation testing should be performed. When simulation is not possible, you should closely monitor device operation and resource usage as new peers and services are activated to prevent operational problems caused by resource exhaustion.

As of this writing, Juniper Networks recommends that J-series routers expected to handle a full BGP route table, in conjunction with services being enabled, have 1 GB of memory. The J2300 platform serving the role of Yeast in this network is equipped with only 256 MB of DRAM. However, the limited set of BGP routes known to exist in this lab, combined with the absence of enabled services and lack of need for scaling in other dimensions such as support of large numbers of interfaces or ARP entries, affords the liberty of adding the import policy *after* the EBGP session is established. This method is adopted here to help demonstrate the effects of import policy using a before-and-after approach.

We've already stated this, but we will say it one more time. It is highly recommended that you write and apply *both* your export and import policies *before* you attempt to establish any EBGP peerings. Failing to do this could result in router meltdown due to excessive BGP table size or the potential for unwanted routing exchange/forwarding behavior. The JUNOS software candidate configuration and commit functionality makes it easy to build and apply a policy before any of the changes take effect at commit time.

The BGP configuration begins at Yeast with configuration of the local router's ASN. The ASN is configured under the [edit routing-options] hierarchy, rather than within the BGP stanza, where you may expect to find it when you are familiar with the IOS way of configuring BGP:

```
[edit]
lab@Yeast# edit routing-options

[edit routing-options]
lab@Yeast# set autonomous-system 1282
```

You next define a BGP group to house the 84.10.109.7 neighbor associated with the Botnet peering. At a minimum, you must create the group, declare the group type as internal or external, specify the peer, and in the case of an external group, specify the ASN associated with the peer. The resulting BGP stanza is displayed along with the set commands that created it:

```
[edit protocols bgp]
lab@Yeast# show
group as_34 {
    type external;
    peer-as 34;
    neighbor 84.10.109.7;
}

[edit protocols bgp]
lab@Yeast# show | display set
set protocols bgp group as_34 type external
set protocols bgp group as_34 peer-as 34
set protocols bgp group as_34 neighbor 84.10.109.7
```

To better evaluate the impact of adding EBGP to Yeast, the current memory and CPU usage is examined before the changes are committed:

```
[edit protocols bgp]
lab@Yeast# run show task memory summary
Memory InUse: 3101 kB [2%] Max: 3383 kB [2%]

[edit protocols bgp]
lab@Yeast# run show chassis routing-engine
Routing Engine status:
  Temperature             56 degrees C / 132 degrees F
  CPU temperature         56 degrees C / 132 degrees F
  DRAM                    256 MB
  Memory utilization      88 percent
  CPU utilization:
    User                  0 percent
    Real-time threads     10 percent
    Kernel                4 percent
    Idle                  86 percent
  Model                   RE-J.1
  Serial ID               AA06500394
  Start time              2007-08-07 07:04:45 UTC
```

```
Uptime                   21 days, 17 hours, 52 minutes, 44 seconds
Load averages:           1 minute   5 minute  15 minute
                           0.27       0.15      0.09
```

The output from the show task memory command displays memory usage from the perspective of rpd, the routing daemon. In this case, it's rather low, indicating that rpd is having an easy time. The show chassis routing-engine command output shows that the Routing Engine's (RE's) CPE is largely idle. J-series platforms preallocate a chunk of physical memory to the real-time forwarding thread, which accounts for the seemingly high memory usage of 88% on an otherwise idle box.

With the pre-BGP resource snapshot in place, the new BGP configuration is committed at Yeast. After a few moments, BGP session status is determined with a show bgp summary command:

```
[edit protocols bgp]
lab@Yeast# commit and-quit
commit complete
Exiting configuration mode

lab@Yeast> show bgp summary
Groups: 1 Peers: 1 Down peers: 1
Table  Tot Paths  Act Paths Suppressed  History Damp State    Pending
inet.0         0          0          0        0      0            0
Peer        AS     InPkt     OutPkt     OutQ   Flaps Last Up/Dwn State|#Active/
Received/Damped...
84.10.109.7       34         0          0        0      0   11 Active
```

The command output shows that Yeast is actively trying to establish its BGP session to peer 84.10.109.7. This is a good sign, but it's not as good as an established session. A status of *idle*, for example, indicates that the router cannot even begin to initiate a session, likely because of no route to the peering address. BGP will retry its connection every 30 seconds or so, making patience a virtue here. About a minute later, the status is again displayed:

```
lab@Yeast> show bgp summary
Groups: 1 Peers: 1 Down peers: 0
Table  Tot Paths  Act Paths Suppressed  History Damp State    Pending
inet.0       434        434          0        0      0            0
Peer        AS     InPkt     OutPkt     OutQ   Flaps Last Up/Dwn State|#Active/
Received/Damped...
84.10.109.7       34       285          7        0      0   2:25
801/801/0        0/0/0
```

The output confirms BGP session establishment—the highlighted display indicates that a total of 801 routes have been learned from the 84.10.109.7 peering, and that all of the received routes have been selected as active. It also notes the total number of routes learned from this peer and the number of routes currently damped, respectively. In this example, Botnet has advertised a total of 831 routes, all of which are currently active at Yeast.

As of this writing, a full BGP feed is approximately 230,000 routes. Obviously, the BGP table used in this lab is a bit smaller. The goal here is to have enough routes to simulate a real BGP experience, without the hassle of obtaining a live feed.

You can view details for the peering session with a show bgp neighbor command. The display includes any negotiated options, session hold time, supported NLRI queued messages, and so on:

```
lab@Yeast> show bgp neighbor
Peer: 84.10.109.7+179 AS 34    Local: 84.10.109.8+2333 AS 1282
  Type: External     State: Established     Flags: <ImportEval Sync>
  Last State: OpenConfirm    Last Event: RecvKeepAlive
  Last Error: None
  Options: <Preference PeerAS Refresh>
  Holdtime: 90 Preference: 170
  Number of flaps: 0
  Peer ID: 84.10.109.1    Local ID: 10.30.1.1     Active Holdtime: 90
  Keepalive Interval: 30        Peer index: 0
  Local Interface: fe-0/0/0.3233
  NLRI advertised by peer: inet-unicast
  NLRI for this session: inet-unicast
  Peer supports Refresh capability (2)
  Table inet.0 Bit: 10000
    RIB State: BGP restart is complete
    Send state: in sync
    Active prefixes:              801
    Received prefixes:            801
    Suppressed due to damping:    0
    Advertised prefixes:          0
  Last traffic (seconds): Received 8     Sent 8     Checked 8
  Input messages:  Total 296    Updates 280   Refreshes 0   Octets 15175
  Output messages: Total 18     Updates 0     Refreshes 0   Octets 368
  Output Queue[0]: 0
```

Here the output shows that the EBGP session to Botnet is in the established state, that it supports IPv4 unicast NLRI, that the session has negotiated the BGP refresh option, and that the hold time is 90 seconds, which leads to a 30-second keepalive timer. The refresh option allows a BGP speaker to request that its peer resend previously advertised routing information. This is useful when a change in import policy may result in acceptance of a route that was previously denied. Without refresh, the BGP session would have to be bounced to force the peer to resend routes. Recall that BGP uses TCP transport, so there is, in theory, no reason for a BGP speaker to ever readvertise routing information that it has already sent.

The receipt of valid BGP routing is confirmed by displaying BGP routes in the route table:

```
lab@Yeast> show route protocol bgp detail

inet.0: 818 destinations, 819 routes (818 active, 0 holddown, 0 hidden)
0.0.0.0/0 (2 entries, 1 announced)
        *BGP     Preference: 170/-101
                 Next-hop reference count: 1602
                 Source: 84.10.109.7
                 Next hop: 84.10.109.7 via fe-0/0/0.3233, selected
                 State: <Active Ext>
                 Local AS:  1282 Peer AS:    34
                 Age: 2:26:23
                 Task: BGP_34.84.10.109.7+179
                 Announcement bits (2): 0-KRT 3-OSPFv2
                 AS path: 34 I
                 Localpref: 100
                 Router ID: 84.10.109.1

6.1.0.0/16 (1 entry, 1 announced)
        *BGP     Preference: 170/-101
                 Next-hop reference count: 1602
                 Source: 84.10.109.7
                 Next hop: 84.10.109.7 via fe-0/0/0.3233, selected
                 State: <Active Ext>
                 Local AS:  1282 Peer AS:    34
                 Age: 9:04
                 Task: BGP_34.84.10.109.7+179
                 Announcement bits (1): 0-KRT
                 AS path: 34 666 420 11537 668 1455 I
                 Localpref: 100
                 Router ID: 84.10.109.1
    . . .
```

The display confirms many active BGP routes at Yeast. The highlights call out key route attributes such as the AS path, the origin of the route, the forwarding next hop, and local/remote ASNs. This example shows that a default route is advertised, and the AS path, by virtue of the single entry for 34, confirms that this route originates within AS 34. In contrast, the route to 6.1/16 indicates an origin in AS 1455, and subsequent transversal of ASs 668, 11537, 420, 666, and 34 (Botnet), before arriving at Beer-Co. Note that these routes have an *assumed* local preference of 100 as per BGP standards. A local preference value attribute is not attached to any of these routes because this attribute is not supported on EBGP links.

The announcement bits for the 0/0 BGP route indicate that it is being redistributed into OSPF. Because only active routes are subject to export policy, this implies that the BGP version of the default route must be preferred over the generated one. This is easily confirmed:

```
lab@Yeast> show route 0.0.0.0/0

inet.0: 818 destinations, 801 routes (818 active, 0 holddown, 0 hidden)
+ = Active Route, - = Last Active, * = Both
```

```
0.0.0.0/0              *[BGP/170] 00:26:28, localpref 100
                         AS path: 34 I
                       > to 84.10.109.7 via fe-0/0/0.3233
                       [Aggregate/175] 16:56:59
                       > via t1-0/0/2.0
```

The display shows that the BGP default is active with a preference of 170, and the highlights show that traffic matching this default route will be forwarded over the high-speed BGP peering link. Should the BGP session malfunction, Yeast will lose the BGP version of the default and fall back to the generated copy, which in turn forwards traffic over the secondary T1 link.

To confirm what routes are being received, or sent, to a specific BGP peer, use the show route-advertising protocol or show route receive-protocol command:

```
lab@Yeast> show route receive-protocol bgp 84.10.109.7

inet.0: 818 destinations, 801 routes (818 active, 0 holddown, 0 hidden)
  Prefix            Nexthop        MED   Lclpref  AS path
* 0.0.0.0/0         84.10.109.7                   34 I
* 129.1.0.0/16      84.10.109.7                   34 11537 3112 3112 I
* 129.2.0.0/16      84.10.109.7                   34 11537 10886 27 I
* 129.7.0.0/16      84.10.109.7                   34 11537 4557 7276 I
* 129.7.0.0/17      84.10.109.7                   34 11537 4557 7276 I
* 129.7.128.0/19    84.10.109.7                   34 11537 4557 7276 I
* 129.7.160.0/19    84.10.109.7                   34 11537 4557 7276 I
* 129.7.192.0/19    84.10.109.7                   34 11537 4557 7276 I
* 129.7.224.0/19    84.10.109.7                   34 11537 4557 7276 I
* 129.8.0.0/16      84.10.109.7                   34 11537 2153 2152
11422 2150 I
---(more)---[abort]

lab@Yeast> show route advertising-protocol bgp 84.10.109.7

lab@Yeast>
```

The show route receive-protocol bgp 84.10.109.7 command confirms the receipt of prefixes from neighbor 84.10.109.7. You can add the detail or extensive switch to see additional information. In contrast, the show route advertising-protocol bgp 84.10.109.7 command confirms that no routing information is being sent back to Botnet. This is expected, given that recent JUNOS software releases no longer echo received BGP routes back to their source, and because the default BGP export policy is to advertise active BGP routes. Here, all the active BGP routes were learned from neighbor 84.10.109.7; hence, there is nothing for Yeast to advertise back.

Readers familiar with the IOS display format for BGP routes may appreciate the terse switch:

```
lab@Yeast> show route protocol bgp terse

inet.0: 818 destinations, 801 routes (818 active, 0 holddown, 0 hidden)
```

```
+ = Active Route, - = Last Active, * = Both

A Destination      P Prf Metric 1  Metric 2  Next hop      AS path
* 0.0.0.0/0        B 170    100            >84.10.109.7   34 I
* 129.1.0.0/16     B 170    100            >84.10.109.7   34 11537 3112 3112 I
* 129.2.0.0/16     B 170    100            >84.10.109.7   34 11537 10886 27 I
* 129.7.0.0/16     B 170    100            >84.10.109.7   34 11537 4557 7276 I
* 129.7.0.0/17     B 170    100            >84.10.109.7   34 11537 4557 7276 I
* 129.7.128.0/19   B 170    100            >84.10.109.7   34 11537 4557 7276 I
* 129.7.160.0/19   B 170    100            >84.10.109.7   34 11537 4557 7276 I
* 129.7.192.0/19   B 170    100            >84.10.109.7   34 11537 4557 7276 I
* 129.7.224.0/19   B 170    100            >84.10.109.7   34 11537 4557 7276 I
* 129.8.0.0/16     B 170    100            >84.10.109.7   34 11537 2153 2152 11422
2150 I
* 129.10.0.0/16    B 170    100            >84.10.109.7   34 11537 10578 156 I
* 129.11.0.0/16    B 170    100            >84.10.109.7   34 11537 20965 786 I
. . .
```

In the preceding display, the local preference is shown under the Metric 1 column.
Before moving on, you gauge the effects of running BGP by again analyzing resource
utilization at Yeast:

```
lab@Yeast> show task memory summary
Memory InUse: 3289 kB [2%] Max: 3383 kB [2%]

lab@Yeast> show chassis routing-engine
Routing Engine status:
    Temperature            56 degrees C / 132 degrees F
    CPU temperature        55 degrees C / 131 degrees F
    DRAM                   256 MB
    Memory utilization     89 percent
    CPU utilization:
      User                 0 percent
      Real-time threads    10 percent
      Kernel               1 percent
      Idle                 89 percent
    Model                  RE-J.1
    Serial ID              AA06500394
    Start time             2007-08-07 07:04:45 UTC
    Uptime                 21 days, 18 hours, 44 minutes, 58 seconds
    Load averages:         1 minute   5 minute  15 minute
                             0.01       0.04       0.04
```

The output confirms very little change to resource consumption. However, we must
stress that you are dealing with a very small number of peers (1) and a very limited
set of routes (800 or so), and that these routes are stable, resulting in very little
ongoing BGP process churn.

Configure Initial BGP Policy

The initial BGP peering session is confirmed operational. To complete this task, you now create and apply both BGP import and export policy. The former is to reject all received BGP routes except a default route that originates in AS 34. The latter needs to advertise a single 10/8 aggregate to represent the internal connectivity of Beer-Co. An import policy is created and displayed at Yeast:

```
[edit]
lab@Yeast# show policy-options policy-statement as_34_import
term 1 {
    from {
        protocol bgp;
        as-path 34_originate;
        route-filter 0.0.0.0/0 exact;
    }
    then accept;
}
term 2 {
    from protocol bgp;
    then reject;
}

[edit]
lab@Yeast# show policy-options as-path 34_originate
"^34$";

[edit]
lab@Yeast# show protocols bgp group as_34 import
import as_34_import;
```

The as_34_import policy matches on a specific route (0/0) and route source (BGP), and forces the associated AS path to match the AS regular expressions defined in 34_originate. The AS path regular expression functions to guarantee that only a default route that originates in AS 34 will be accepted—all routes originating within AS 34 will have an AS path list that starts and ends with 34; the associated regex uses the ^ and $, respectively, to force AS 34 to be the first and last AS number in the list. The as_34_import policy is applied to the as_34 BGP group at import, and the results are confirmed.

```
[edit]
lab@Yeast: run show route protocol bgp
inet.0: 818 destinations, 819 routes (18 active, 0 holddown, 800 hidden)
+ = Active Route, - = Last Active, * = Both

0.0.0.0/0          *[BGP/170] 02:34:36, localpref 100
                      AS path: 34 I
                    > to 84.10.109.7 via fe-0/0/0.3233
```

The output confirms that only the default route is accepted and installed into the route table, resulting in some 800 routes being hidden.

 Generally speaking, the output of the show route receive-protocol command displays routing information as received, before import policy is applied. The exception to this rule is route filtering, which occurs *before* the show route receive-protocol command output is compiled. This means that if your import policy is set to remove a given community, you can expect to see the community (that is to be removed) in the show route receive-protocol output, but not when the route is installed into the route table, because your import policy will have taken effect and will have removed the specified community. In contrast, if your import policy uses route-filter syntax to reject routes, these routes will not be observed in either the route table or the output of a show route receive-protocol command. This condition is demonstrated here, where only the 0/0 default that is accepted by import policy route filtering is displayed:

```
lab@Yeast> show route receive-protocol bgp 84.10.109.7

inet.0: 818 destinations, 819 routes (18 active, 0 holddown,
800 hidden)
  Prefix                    Nexthop              MED
  Lclpref     AS path
* 0.0.0.0/0                 84.10.109.7                34 I
```

Add the hidden keyword to display received routes that are hidden, perhaps due to route filtering actions.

Your export policy requires that you define a 10/8 aggregate, and then advertise this aggregate into BGP. At this time, it's assumed that Botnet is routing back into your AS using its static route that points to the slow-speed T1 interface, making this a critical step for proper operation. In theory, it has configured its network to prefer a BGP learned version of the 10/8 route, which results in use of the high-speed link for inbound traffic once you advertise the route through BGP. Here are the aggregate route definition and BGP export policy:

```
[edit]
lab@Yeast# show routing-options aggregate
route 10.0.0.0/8;

[edit]
lab@Yeast# show policy-options policy-statement as_34_export
term 1 {
    from {
        protocol aggregate;
        route-filter 10.0.0.0/8 exact;
    }
    then accept;
}

[edit]
```

```
lab@Yeast# show protocols bgp group as_34 export
export as_34_export;
```

After committing the change, the aggregate route is confirmed active and advertised to Botnet via EBGP:

```
lab@Yeast> show route protocol aggregate

inet.0: 801 destinations, 451 routes (18 active, 0 holddown, 432 hidden)
+ = Active Route, - = Last Active, * = Both

0.0.0.0/0          [Aggregate/175] 17:57:54
                   > via t1-0/0/2.0
10.0.0.0/8         *[Aggregate/130] 00:00:13
                      Reject

lab@Yeast> show route advertising-protocol bgp 84.10.109.7

inet.0: 801 destinations, 451 routes (18 active, 0 holddown, 432 hidden)
  Prefix            Nexthop         MED    Lclpref   AS path
* 10.0.0.0/8        Self                             I
```

The 10/8 aggregate route is active, which is good given that only active routes can be redistributed through policy. Note that unlike the generated route, the aggregate route has a nonforwarding next hop, which happens to be the default reject-style next hop in this case. Traffic routed into Beer-Co should normally match a more specific route (OSPF or direct) and be forwarded toward that destination. If not, the traffic is shunted to reject, and an ICMP error message is generated reporting an unreachable destination. The show route advertising-protocol command confirms that a single route, the 10/8 aggregate, is advertised to Botnet.

For final verification, the previous traceroute is repeated at PBR:

```
lab@PBR> traceroute 192.168.34.1 no-resolve
traceroute to 192.168.34.1 (192.168.34.1), 30 hops max, 40 byte packets
 1  10.20.129.1  53.267 ms  13.506 ms  10.634 ms
 2  10.20.131.1  9.955 ms  9.985 ms  9.996 ms
 3  10.10.8.2  9.977 ms  10.042 ms  10.034 ms
 4  84.10.109.7  15.349 ms !N  24.503 ms !N  19.968 ms !N
```

The traceroute again succeeds, but this time the final hop is 84.10.109.7; this confirms that the high-speed primary interface is now used to forward traffic into AS 34. This completes the initial BGP peering scenario.

Use BGP for Asymmetric Load Balancing

While congratulating you on the fine work, the CIO of Beer-Co respectfully suggests that you find a way to use the secondary link also. After all, 1.544 Mbps is nothing to sneeze at, and paying for a backup circuit that will never see any use except during a primary outage can be painful.

...ct solution to this problem is to bring up a second EBGP session to ...ply enable BGP multipath. The multipath option removes the tie-...he active route decision process, thereby allowing otherwise equal-...learned from multiple sources to be installed into the forwarding ...ple next hops are installed in the forwarding table, a specific for-...s selected by the default JUNOS software per-prefix load-balancing ...cess hashes against a packet's source and destination addresses to ...p the prefix paring onto one of the available next hops. Per-...s best when the hash function is presented with a large number ...ght occur on an Internet peering exchange, and it serves to pre-...among pairs of communicating nodes.

...will normally want to alter the default behavior to evoke a ...ing algorithm. *Per-packet* is quoted here because its use is a ...n the historic behavior of the original Internet Processor ...niper Networks routers support per-prefix (default) and ...e latter involves hashing against various L3 and L4 head-...e source address, destination address, transport proto-...pplication ports. The effect is that now individual *flows* ...op, resulting in a more even distribution across avail-...routing between fewer source and destination pairs. ...g, packets comprising a communication stream ...resequenced, but packets within individual flows

W...   per-packet load balancing, the extreme asymme-
try...   s a technical challenge. Either way, the prefixes/
flow...   will exhibit degraded performance when compare...   E access link, and worse yet, with heavy traffic
loads,...   ing is likely to result in total saturation of the
T1 lin...   from packet loss.

Fortuna...   ation supports the notion of a bandwidth
commun...   codes the bandwidth of a given next hop,
and wher...   load-balancing algorithm will distribute
flows acro...   ional to their relative bandwidths. Put
another wa...   d a 1 Mbps next hop, on average nine flows
will map to t...   xt hop for every one that uses the low speed.

As of this writing, use of BGP bandwidth community is supported only with per-packet load balancing.

The current configuration task is divided onto two parts:

- Configure a second EBGP peering session, enable multipath, and define an import policy to tag routes with a bandwidth community that reflects link speed.
- Enable per-packet (really per-flow) load balancing for optimal distribution of traffic.

You start with the definition of the second EBGP peering session at Yeast. Though not shown here, the generated default route is removed from the configuration because it is no longer needed. Recall that you now expect two default routes, both learned from BGP, with proportionate load balancing when both routes are active:

```
[edit]
lab@Yeast# show protocols bgp
group as_34 {
    type external;
    import as_34_import;
    export as_34_export;
    peer-as 34;
    neighbor 84.10.109.7;
    neighbor 84.10.113.1;
}
```

The new session shares the same group-level import and export policy, which results in accepting only a default route and the advertisement of only the 10/8 aggregate. After a minute or so, you confirm successful establishment of the second Botnet peering session:

```
[edit]
lab@Yeast# run show bgp summary
Groups: 1 Peers: 2 Down peers: 0
Table  Tot Paths  Act Paths Suppressed    History Damp State  Pending
inet.0     1602          1         0          0         0         0
Peer          AS    InPkt OutPkt OutQ   Flaps Last Up/Dwn State|#Active/
Received/Damped...
84.10.109.7   34      824    329    0       0   2:42:55 1/801/0
0/0/0
84.10.113.1   34      462      3    0       0        6 0/801/0
0/0/0
```

The display confirms establishment of the second peering session. Of special interest is the fact that 801 routes have been learned over each session, and only one of these routes is active, for only one of the sessions. Recall that the goal here is to receive an active default route from each peering. For additional details, we display the default route:

```
[edit]
lab@Yeast# run show route protocol bgp detail

inet.0: 818 destinations, 1619 routes (18 active, 0 holddown, 1600
hidden)
0.0.0.0/0 (2 entries, 1 announced)
```

```
*BGP     Preference: 170/-101
         Next-hop reference count: 802
         Source: 84.10.109.7
         Next hop: 84.10.109.7 via fe-0/0/0.3233, selected
         State: <Active Ext>
         Local AS:  1282 Peer AS:    34
         Age: 2:46:39
         Task: BGP_34.84.10.109.7+179
         Announcement bits (2): 0-KRT 3-OSPFv2
         AS path: 34 I
         Localpref: 100
         Router ID: 84.10.109.1
BGP      Preference: 170/-101
         Next-hop reference count: 801
         Source: 84.10.113.1
         Next hop: 84.10.113.1 via t1-0/0/2.0, selected
         State: <NotBest Ext>
         Inactive reason: Update source
         Local AS:  1282 Peer AS:    34
         Age: 3:50
         Task: BGP_34.84.10.113.1+179
         AS path: 34 I
         Localpref: 100
         Router ID: 84.10.109.1
```

The display shows that each BGP peer is advertising the 0/0 route, and it confirms that only one version of the route is active. This active route is learned through peer 84.10.109.7, and as such the route shows a single forwarding next hop of fe-0/0/0.3233. There is no hope of any load balancing until both of the next hops for both BGP routes are installed into the forwarding table. The problem here is called out by the update source inactive reason. According to documentation, this indicates that a route was not selected due to characteristics associated with the source, which means either the RID or the BGP peering address. These last two steps in the active route selection process exist to break ties, which is exactly what has happened here. Because both peering sessions terminate on the same router (Hops), the RID is the same, and therefore the route learned from the numerically lowest peering address is selected. To disable the tie-breaking rules and allow use of multiple otherwise equal-cost BGP routes, you must enable multipath:

```
[edit]
lab@Yeast# set protocols bgp group as_34 multipath

[edit]
lab@Yeast# commit
commit complete
```

The change is confirmed by the presence of both the 84.10.109.7 *and* 84.10.113.1 BGP next hops in the show route display:

```
[edit]
lab@Yeast# run show route protocol bgp detail
inet.0: 818 destinations, 1619 routes (18 active, 0 holddown, 1600
```

```
hidden) 0.0.0.0/0 (2 entries, 1 announced)
    *BGP    Preference: 170/-101
            Next-hop reference count: 1
            Source: 84.10.109.7
            Next hop: 84.10.109.7 via fe-0/0/0.3233, selected
            Next hop: 84.10.113.1 via t1-0/0/2.0
            State: <Active Ext>
            Local AS:  1282 Peer AS:    34
            Age: 2:54:43
            Task: BGP_34.84.10.109.7+179
            Announcement bits (2): 0-KRT 3-OSPFv2
            AS path: 34 I
            Localpref: 100
            Router ID: 84.10.109.1
     BGP    Preference: 170/-101
            Next-hop reference count: 801
            Source: 84.10.113.1
            Next hop: 84.10.113.1 via t1-0/0/2.0, selected
            State: <NotBest Ext>
            Inactive reason: Update source
            Local AS:  1282 Peer AS:    34
            Age: 11:54
            Task: BGP_34.84.10.113.1+179
            AS path: 34 I
            Localpref: 100
            Router ID: 84.10.109.1
```

The display still shows that only one route is active, but without the tie-breakers in effect, the next hops associated with both routes have been installed for use, thereby enabling load balancing. Your next goal is to adjust the as_34_import policy to tag routes with a bandwidth community, based on the peering from where they are learned. You start by defining the two extended bandwidth communities. The format of this community is bandwidth:asn:bandwidth_value, where the bandwidth is entered in bytes per second. The actual values entered are not as important as having the correct ratio because it is the ratio that actually determines the percentage of flows/prefixes mapped to each next hop:

```
[edit policy-options]
lab@Yeast# show community bw_slow
members bandwidth:1287:193000;

[edit policy-options]
lab@Yeast# show community bw_fast
members bandwidth:1287:12500000;
```

The bw_slow and bw_fast communities are set to reflect the byte-per-second rates of a T1 and Fast Ethernet interface, respectively. The ratio of the two is approximately .01544, meaning that for every 100 prefixes/flows, you expect to see 1.5 of them mapped to the T1. In the Juniper implementation, the flow count is rounded up, giving us an expected spread of 2 flows mapped to the T1 for every 98 mapped to the

---

Fast Ethernet. The existing as_34_import policy is rewritten, and the modified policy is displayed:

```
[edit]
lab@Yeast# show policy-options policy-statement as_34_import
term slow_peer {
    from {
        protocol bgp;
        neighbor 84.10.113.1;
        as-path 34_originate;
        route-filter 0.0.0.0/0 exact;
    }
    then {
        community add bw_slow;
        accept;
    }
}
term fast_peer {
    from {
        protocol bgp;
        neighbor 84.10.109.7;
        as-path 34_originate;
        route-filter 0.0.0.0/0 exact;
    }
    then {
        community add bw_fast;
        accept;
    }
}
term reject-all {
    then reject;
}
```

The new as_34_import policy makes use of a from neighbor match condition to tag the matching route with the identified bandwidth community. In theory, this can also be done as part of an export policy within Botnet, but this puts reliance on the administration of the remote AS, which may involve delays and the potential for billing and mistakes. Expected operation is verified by once again displaying details about the active BGP route:

```
[edit policy-options]
lab@Yeast# run show route protocol bgp detail

inet.0: 818 destinations, 1619 routes (18 active, 0 holddown, 1600
hidden) 0.0.0.0/0 (2 entries, 1 announced)
        *BGP    Preference: 170/-101
                Next-hop reference count: 1
                Source: 84.10.109.7
                Next hop: 84.10.109.7 via fe-0/0/0.3233 balance 98%
                Next hop: 84.10.113.1 via t1-0/0/2.0 balance 2%, selected
                State: <Active Ext>
                Local AS: 1282 Peer AS:     34
                Age: 3:48:08
```

```
                 Task: BGP_34.84.10.109.7+179
                 Announcement bits (2): 0-KRT 3-OSPFv2
                 AS path: 34 I
                 Communities: bandwidth:1287:12500000
                 Localpref: 100
                 Router ID: 84.10.109.1
           BGP   Preference: 170/-101
                 Next-hop reference count: 801
                 Source: 84.10.113.1
                 Next hop: 84.10.113.1 via t1-0/0/2.0, selected
                 State: <NotBest Ext>
                 Inactive reason: Update source
                 Local AS:  1282 Peer AS:     34
                 Age: 1:05:19
                 Task: BGP_34.84.10.113.1+179
                 AS path: 34 I
                 Communities: bandwidth:1287:193000
                 Localpref: 100
                 Router ID: 84.10.109.1
```

The highlights in the show route output confirm that balancing now occurs in proportion to link speed, as required. To complete this task, a per-packet load-balancing policy must be placed into effect at Yeast. A policy named lb_per_packet is created, and it is applied to the main routing instance's forwarding table:

```
[edit]
lab@Yeast# show policy-options policy-statement lb_per_packet
then {
    load-balance per-packet;
    accept;
}

[edit]
lab@Yeast# show routing-options forwarding-table
export lb_per_packet;
```

The lb_per_packet policy matches on all possible routes and effectively converts the system from per-prefix to per-flow load balancing. The effect of your work is confirmed back on router PBR, where traceroutes are performed. The test traffic is sourced from various IP addresses owned by PBR in an attempt to trigger the per-flow hashing function to use both next hops. Note that by enabling per-flow load balancing, fewer bits are made available for hashing against the source address/destination address pair. The result is that without a wide degree of source address/destination address variance, there is a good chance that all test traffic will hash to the same next hop. To accurately test Juniper per-prefix or per-flow load balancing, a large number of flows should be generated, preferably from a traffic source. Put another way, as the number of flows/prefixes increases, so too does the likelihood of observing ideal balancing among the set of available next hops. Bearing this in mind, the bw_slow community is temporarily set to equal bw_fast so that we can expect a 50/50 load-balancing split.

This will increase the chances of observing load balancing at play with the limited number of flows available in the lab setup.

```
lab@PBR> traceroute 192.168.34.1 no-resolve source 10.20.129.2
traceroute to 192.168.34.1 (192.168.34.1) from 10.20.129.2, 30 hops
max, 40 byte packets
 1  10.20.129.1  14.553 ms   9.782 ms   8.084 ms
 2  10.20.131.1  21.914 ms   9.935 ms   9.988 ms
 3  10.10.8.2    10.081 ms  19.865 ms  10.002 ms
 4  84.10.113.1  15.697 ms !N  14.286 ms !N  18.954 ms !N
```

The final hop of the traceroute to Brewer Inc.'s 192.168.34.1 route is the 84.10.113.1 address associated with the low-speed Botnet peering link. In this example, test traffic is explicitly sourced from the 10.20.129.2 address on the PBR–Stout link, which happens to be the same IP address that the packet would normally take. Next, a different flow is created by generating an ICMP echo packet from the same source address, but to a different host address (.100), on the 192.168.34.0/24 subnet. The goal here is to try and trigger a different flow hashing result by altering some of the bits used in the flow hashing algorithm. Here, we change both the protocol (ICMP versus UDP), and some of the bits in the addresses's host ID.

```
lab@PBR> ping 192.168.34.100 rapid count 1 source 10.20.129.2
PING 192.168.34.100 (192.168.34.100): 56 data bytes
36 bytes from 84.10.109.7: Destination Net Unreachable
Vr HL TOS  Len   ID Flg  off TTL Pro  cks      Src        Dst
 4  5  00 0054 5e00   0 0000  3d  01 b186 10.20.129.2  192.168.34.100
.
--- 192.168.34.100 ping statistics ---
1 packets transmitted, 0 packets received, 100% packet loss
```

The destination unreachable error message generated by 84.10.109.7 proves that the ICMP test packet was forwarded over the high-speed Botnet peering link. Satisfied that per-flow load balancing is working, you restore the bw_slow community to its previous value and take a well-deserved break.

```
[edit]
lab@Yeast# rollback 1
load complete

[edit]
lab@Yeast# show | compare
[edit policy-options community bw_slow]
-    members bandwidth:1287:12500000;
+    members bandwidth:1287:193000;

[edit]
lab@Yeast# commit
commit complete
```

Initial BGP Peering Summary

This section showed you an example of how to configure and verify basic EBGP peering using JUNOS software. We also showed the use of routing policy to filter received routes and to control the routes that you advertise, along with the redistribution of a BGP-learned default route into your IGP to provide external reachability for non-BGP speakers within your AS. You also saw how to use a static route with an altered global preference (a concept known as a *floating static route* in IOS speak) to back up a BGP peering, and how the BGP bandwidth community is used to provide asymmetric load balancing based on link speed.

The next section explores typical enterprise applications of BGP routing policy, which in turn prepares you for the increasingly complicated BGP deployment scenarios that follow later in this chapter. Now is a good time to take a break, perhaps to think back over the points covered in this section or just to clear your mind for the outbound and inbound policy discussions in the next section.

Enterprise Routing Policy

You have now been exposed to various applications of JUNOS software routing policy, here and in earlier chapters. We discussed the operational theory of routing policy in detail in Chapter 3. In summary, import routing policy is responsible for placing routes into the route table, possibly with modified attributes, and export policy is responsible for placing copies of routes into outgoing routing protocol updates, again possibly with modified attributes. The complexity of an organization's policy is typically tied directly to the degree of its interconnectivity requirements. An enterprise that is single-homed needs very little policy; in most cases, such an attachment does not even warrant use of BGP!

This section focuses on applying JUNOS software routing policy to meet the needs of an enterprise that is dual-homed to different providers.

Inbound and Outbound Routing Policies

In a majority of cases, a dual-homed enterprise network will have distinctly different inbound and outbound policies. Your inbound policy is intended to control how traffic enters your AS from other networks, whereas your outbound policy dictates how traffic leaves your AS to enter other networks. You use specific instances of export and import policy to facilitate your organization's inbound and outbound policy goals.

Achieving your inbound policy goals can be difficult, or even impossible, given that you do not have direct control over the outbound policies of the networks that you peer with. In the end, each network operator has complete control of its local outbound policy, so at best your inbound policy can influence its policy decisions only within the limits that are permitted by that network's outbound policy. In some cases, achieving your inbound policy goals may require selecting ISPs that are willing to work with your needs—this is a political, not a technical, issue. In contrast, you have complete control over your outbound policy. Simply put, it's your network, and you can configure it to do whatever you want in this regard.

As with most network design considerations, each network must carefully weigh its policy desires against the potential costs, measured in increased administrative/support burdens, potential economic impacts, performance considerations, equipment capabilities, and so on. The network then must decide on a set of policies that best balance all of the factors involved.

Common Policy Design Criteria

Although the specifics always vary, many common elements drive most policy decisions:

Topology-driven

A topology-driven policy is based on the physical connectivity of your network and is typically concerned with locating the lowest-cost (lowest-metric) path for traffic. In many cases, a topology-driven policy will use IGP metrics to locate the best egress point, and in turn will send the IGP metric as the MED in EBGP updates. Recall that MED is like a true metric, in that lower values are preferred. If your peer honors MEDs in their decision process, this should result in traffic entering your AS at the point that is metrically closest to the actual destination. You can set the MED in BGP policy using the `metric` keyword. Support for automatically tracking the IGP metric is also provided.

The topology-driven model is the easiest to implement because in most cases, you leave all attributes unmodified and simply rely on the route selection algorithm to select the best route, which will normally be the shortest path (the fewest number of ASs, best origin, lowest MED, and lowest IGP metric).

Primary/secondary

A primary/secondary policy is based on the preferential use of a primary access link. Motivations for a primary/secondary model tend to be performance-driven, but can also factor economic, reliability, or security concerns. The last factor, security, is often overlooked. Knowing that all your traffic leaves and enters on the same set of links greatly simplifies deployment of stateful firewalls and NAT devices. This is because state instantiated by the transmission of traffic is readily available to match against the return traffic. Sending traffic out of one device, and having the response handled at a different access point by a different device, makes stateful services quite complex.

In a *strict* primary/secondary model, no traffic should use the secondary links unless the primary link becomes unavailable. In contrast, in a *loose* model, some traffic, perhaps based on topology considerations, is allowed to use the secondary, even when the primary is operating. Your design should also factor the desire to revert back to a primary after service is restored. A revertive design switches back to the primary, but this behavior can cause issues when chronic problems plague the primary link. This is because ongoing disruption occurs each time traffic is redirected to and from the bouncing primary circuit. Here, a nonrevertive policy that promotes stability over other factors such as cost, or raw bandwidth, would be preferred.

Using equal capacity links in conjunction with a strict primary/secondary model provides the highest degree of redundancy because either link can handle the offered load with equal performance. With the loose variation, usable bandwidth can be the sum of both link capacities; therefore, the failure of either link reduces overall capacity and may impact performance. This is also true of a strict model that uses asymmetric link speeds to save on bandwidth costs.

Load-sharing
A load-sharing policy attempts to maximize use of all available resources by spreading traffic over the set of available access points. This is typically performed on a per-prefix basis, where some set of routes is mapped to one link while another set is mapped to a different link. In a failure scenario, traffic from affected links is switched to the next most preferred operational link.

A word on outbound/inbound versus export/import policy

Before moving on, it's worth noting that there is somewhat of a reverse relationship between your inbound/outbound policy and the type of JUNOS software routing policy that is applied to your EBGP session. For example, you will normally use *export* policy when you wish to instantiate an *inbound* policy to control how other networks route traffic into your AS. Likewise, you normally use *import* policy to adjust attributes in received routes that in turn affect your *outbound* policy—for example, setting local preference on routes as they are received from an EBGP peer.

If that were not confusing enough, you will likely find that in many cases, you can achieve the same effect using either an import or an export policy. For example, local preference can be set at reception from an EBGP peer using an import policy or when sending the route to other IBGP speakers using an export policy. In fact, you may use an import to set an attribute to some local value, and then use an export to send a modified value to other peers. Wherever possible, you should take a consistent approach to help minimize support burdens and overall network complexity.

Know your ISP's policy

Because your BGP speakers are expected to interact with those under the control of your ISP, it pays to be familiar with your ISP's general policies. For example, many

ISPs set route attributes within their network, based on the receipt of certain communities attached by their customers. As another example, consider that there is no point in advertising a prefix with a /32 network mask if your ISP's policy is not to accept any routes with a prefix length longer than /28.

Most providers use local preference to prefer routes from their customers over those learned from their peers, filter route updates based on prefix lengths, and filter updates received from their customers to ensure that they are not acting as transit peers. Providers often post their policies on public web sites where the information can be used to comparison-shop when seeking service.

Enterprise Policy Summary

This section broke down the seemingly daunting task of BGP and policy into the categories of inbound and outbound policies, which helps to make things more manageable. In most cases, an enterprise will need to be dual-homed to take full advantage of the power of BGP and JUNOS software routing policy. Remembering that you use *export* policy to affect your *inbound* routing goals, and use *import* policy for your *outbound* goals, helps to eliminate a lot of potential confusion.

By default, BGP settles on a topology-based model, but in many cases you will want to alter this behavior based on your organization's needs and desires. You have direct control over your own network's output routing, making that part of the equation straightforward. Effectively establishing a desired inbound policy means you have managed to influence the outbound action of routers in a remote network, which are not under your direct control. That is the mark of a true BGP policy guru.

In the next section, you will begin to apply complex enterprise routing policies, right after you multihome the network by adding a new EBGP peering and deploy a route-reflected IBGP topology within Beer-Co.

Multihome Beer-Co

Beer-Co's initial BGP peering with Botnet in AS 34 is operating successfully, and it's time to bring up a second EBGP session to Borgnet in AS 420. When multihomed to dual providers, the true benefit of BGP and its policy controls can be fully realized. Figure 5-9 provides the new BGP peering topology and illustrates how Borgnet connects to service provider Darknet in AS 666, which is also peered with Botnet. It seems that things could get quite interesting here.

The figure shows key details of each AS. These include the EBGP peering router's name, its loopback address, and the set of routes that originate within that AS and the customer routes associated with that network. The figure calls out three particular customer prefixes within Borgnet, Darknet, and Botnet, which are assigned to customers Cap-co Inc., Bottles Inc., and Brewer Inc., respectively. The 192.168.*xx*/24 prefixes

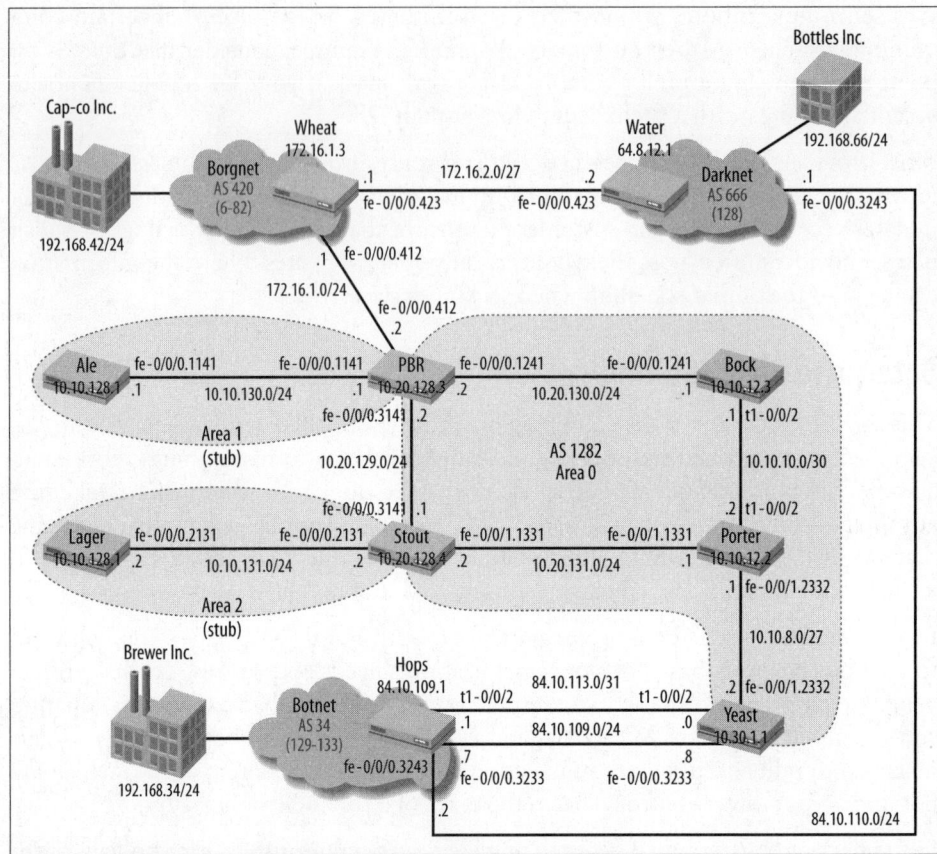

Figure 5-9. Beer-Co goes multihomed with a connection to Borgnet

associated with these extranet partners demonstrate the effects of inbound and outbound policy actions in the following sections.

In this scenario, Beer-Co's IGP consists of an area 0 backbone with two stub areas. Area border routers (ABRs) PBR and Stout originate an OSPF default route into their respective stub areas.

The design goals for the new BGP peering arrangement are as follows:

* Deploy new import policy at routers Yeast and PBR to accept only routes that originate in the peering AS, including a default route generated by both providers.

* Establish the new EBGP peering session between PBR and Wheat and advertise a 10/8 aggregate.

* Configure loopback-based IBGP peering on a minimal set of routers as needed for loop-free transport within Beer-Co.

* Use route reflection to reduce the total number of IBGP sessions and ensure no single point of failure.

- Establish an outbound policy that prefers each peer's customer routes, with all other destinations using the Borgnet link as a revertive primary.

The result of the initial BGP multihoming task is a (default) topology-driven inbound policy and a hybrid outbound policy that combines elements of the topology-driven and primary models. Route filtering and route reflection are used to minimize BGP processing demand on routers with limited memory.

To help put these requirements into a functional perspective, the expected behavior is summarized as follows:

- EBGP speakers accept only peer customer routes (customer routes).
- When sending to customer routes, forward directly to the AS that owns that route when the related peering session is operational.
- When sending to other BGP destinations, all BGP speakers use the default route associated with the primary peering to Borgnet.
- Routers in stub areas use a default to reach the closest ABR, at which point BGP forwarding takes effect.
- The failure of any access link should not sever communications; upon restoration, traffic should again adhere to the loose primary outbound policy.

Implement Beer-Co's Outbound Policy

Configuration begins by creating the import policy at PBR that accepts only those routes that originate within Borgnet. The intention is to protect the relatively small access router from the potentially harmful effects associated with the receipt of a full BGP route table from Wheat. Similar policy actions will also be performed at Yeast. The effect is a topology-driven outbound routing model for the routes owned by each peering AS, and the use of the metrically closest default route for destinations that originate outside of these ASs; for example, the 128/8 and 192.168.66/24 routes that are originated by the nonadjacent AS Darknet.

This type of BGP import policy normally uses an AS path regular expression because it greatly simplifies the matching criteria against the numerous route prefixes that could originate within a given AS. In this example, the routes owned by Borgnet are shown as being in the range of 6–82, making a route filter feasible. However, you also need to consider its internal/direct routes, in this case the 172.16.1.3 loopback address of Wheat. When really tight control is needed, you can always combine the effects of route filters and AS path regular expressions. The import policy created for PBR uses an AS path regular expression to only accept routes with one or more instances of ASN 420. The regular expression is written in this manner to accommodate the potential of AS path prepending within Borgnet. This way, even if there are 10 instances of ASN 420 in the prefix, the route is still considered to have originated within that specific AS. PBR's import policy is displayed:

```
[edit policy-options]
lab@PBR# show
policy-statement as_420_import {
    term 1 {
        from {
            protocol bgp;
            as-path as_420_originate;
        }
        then accept;
    }
    term 2 {
        then reject;
    }
}
as-path as_420_originate "^420+$";
```

The first term of the as_420_import policy accepts routes from BGP with an AS path matching the named expression as_420_originate. The second term defeats the default BGP import policy, which is to accept all (sane) BGP routes. The AS path regular expression uses the ^ and $ anchors to force a match against the start and end of the AS path attribute, respectively. The + multiplier indicates that the proceeding pattern (420) must appear at least once, but can appear multiple times. The combined effect is a match against any AS path attribute that begins and ends with the value 420, which may contain zero or more repetitions of that same value. The as_34_import policy at Yeast is modified to accept all BGP routes originating in AS 34:

```
[edit]
lab@Yeast# show policy-options policy-statement as_34_import
term slow_peer {
    from {
        protocol bgp;
        neighbor 84.10.113.1;
        as-path 34_originate;
        route-filter 0.0.0.0/0 exact;
    }
    then {
        community add bw_slow;
        accept;
    }
}
term fast_peer {
    from {
        protocol bgp;
        neighbor 84.10.109.7;
        as-path 34_originate;
        route-filter 0.0.0.0/0 exact;
    }
    then {
        community add bw_fast;
        accept;
    }
}
```

```
    term reject-all {
        then reject;
    }
```

The highlights call out sections of the exiting policy that are *removed* to meet the new route filtering criterion. Now, rather than accepting only a default route, Yeast accepts all routes that originate in AS 34.

EBGP Peering to AS 420

With the import policy defined, you need a BGP stanza with which to apply it. The EBGP peering definition at PBR is pretty straightforward:

```
[edit]
lab@PBR# show protocols bgp
group as_420 {
    type external;
    import as_420_import;
    neighbor 172.16.1.1 {
        peer-as 420;
    }
}
```

The newly created as_420_import policy has been applied as import. The commit failure offers a friendly reminder that, for BGP to operate, a local ASN is required. This is quickly remedied:

```
[edit]
lab@PBR# commit
[edit protocols]
  'bgp'
    Error in neighbor 172.16.1.1 of group as_420:
must define local autonomous system when enabling BGP
error: configuration check-out failed

[edit]
lab@PBR# set routing-options autonomous-system 1282

[edit]
lab@PBR# commit
commit complete
```

BGP session status is verified with a show bgp summary command:

```
[edit]
lab@PBR# run show bgp summary
Groups: 1 Peers: 1 Down peers: 0
Table    Tot Paths  Act Paths Suppressed  History Damp State  Pending
inet.0        806        123          0        0         0          0
Peer        AS    InPkt    OutPkt    OutQ    Flaps Last Up/Dwn State|#Active/
Received/Damped...
172.16.1.1   420    356       257       0        0     2:06:57
123/806/00/0/0
```

The EBGP session to Borgnet is established, as confirmed by the x/x/x field that summarizes active routes, received routes, and damped routes, respectively. This display also begins to validate the as_420_import policy, in that only 123 of the 806 routes received are active. The presence of hidden routes, ostensibly due to filtering, is confirmed:

```
[edit]
lab@PBR# run show route hidden detail

inet.0: 825 destinations, 826 routes (143 active, 0 holddown, 682 hidden)
64.8.12.1/32 (1 entry, 0 announced)
         BGP                  /-101
                 Next-hop reference count: 929
                 Source: 172.16.1.1
                 Next hop: 172.16.1.1 via fe-0/0/0.412, selected
                 State: <Hidden Ext>
                 Local AS:  1282 Peer AS:   420
                 Age: 2:19:43
                 Task: BGP_420.172.16.1.1+1530
                 AS path: 420 666 I
                 Localpref: 100
                 Router ID: 172.16.1.3

128.3.0.0/16 (1 entry, 0 announced)
         BGP                  /-101
                 Next-hop reference count: 929
                 Source: 172.16.1.1
                 Next hop: 17^C[abort]
---(more)---
. . .
```

The summary portion of the show route hidden detail command confirms both a large number of hidden routes (682) and that the hidden route displayed has an AS path that *does not* indicate origin in AS 420. This shows that the route is hidden due to your AS path-based import filtering. The CLI's AS path regular expression filter is used for final confirmation:

```
[edit]
lab@PBR# run show route aspath-regex ^420+$ | match path
                    AS path: 420 I
                    AS path: 420 I
                    AS path: 420 I
                    AS path: 420 I
                    AS path: 420 I
   . . .
[edit]
lab@PBR# run show route aspath-regex ^420+$ | match path | count
Count: 124 lines
```

The regex-filtered show route display verifies that all matching routes have an AS path consisting of only AS 420. The CLI's count function is then used to confirm that PBR has received a total of 124 routes from Borgnet that pass the as_420_import policy.

One of these should be a default route that is used to reach BGP destinations that do not originate in either AS 34 or AS 420:

```
[edit]
lab@PBR# run show route

inet.0: 825 destinations, 826 routes (143 active, 0 holddown, 682 hidden)
+ = Active Route, - = Last Active, * = Both

0.0.0.0/0          *[OSPF/150] 02:24:20, metric 0, tag 0
                    > to 10.20.130.1 via fe-0/0/0.1241
                    [BGP/170] 00:28:13, localpref 100
                      AS path: 420 I
                    > to 172.16.1.1 via fe-0/0/0.412
```

The show route display at PBR confirms the receipt of a BGP default route but shows a potential problem as well; PBR also receives the default route redistributed into OSPF by Yeast, and it prefers the OSPF version due to global preference (known as administrative distance in IOS land).

The goal of your hybrid topological/primary outbound routing policy is to have routers forward to peer customer routes using a topology model that hands traffic directly to the AS that owns those routes, while a default route is used to reach filtered BGP destinations over the primary Borgnet peering. To meet the requirements, this default route should always direct traffic over the Borgnet link when it is operational. Therefore, in normal operation, all routers must prefer the default route advertised by PBR over any copy advertised by Yeast.

In the current setup, a BGP learned default route from AS 34 is being redistributed into OSPF at router Yeast. Recall that this was necessary because up until now, Yeast was the only BGP speaker in Beer-Co. Given that you are now, or soon will be, deploying IBGP among a set of Beer-Co's internal routers, the need to redistribute the default into OSPF can be revisited. The stub area routers already rely on an OSPF default generated by each area's ABR, so this discussion centers on what is done for routers PBR, Bock, Stout, Porter, and Yeast. Figure 5-10 details the plan of action for IBGP deployment on Beer-Co's backbone.

Figure 5-10 shows that all OSPF area 0 routers will be configured to run IBGP. Recall from an earlier discussion that deciding which routers need to run IBGP is a function of whether your import policy accepts only a default, and whether intermediate routers are in the forwarding path between EBGP speakers. Also recall that an EBGP speaker should always be enabled for IBGP unless there is only one BGP speaker in your network. Because your EBGP speakers are accepting only specific prefixes, IBGP should be enabled on any router that can forward traffic between the speakers. In this example, that means Stout, Bock, and Porter must support IBGP. Because the backbone routers will run BGP, they can learn the default route through BGP; this means that redistribution of the BGP default into OSPF is no longer necessary. With this understanding, the ospf_default export policy is removed at Yeast.

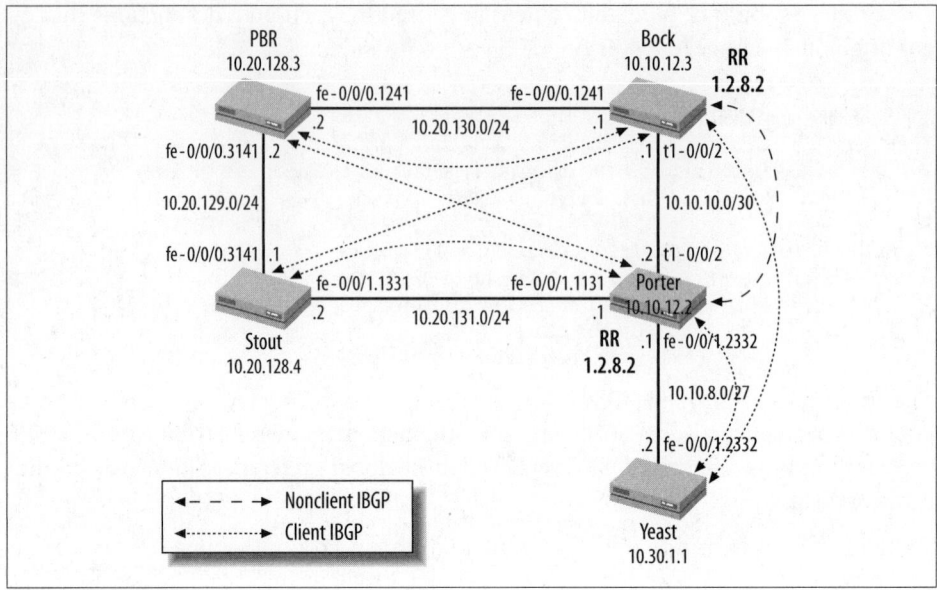

Figure 5-10. Beer-Co IBGP deployment details

```
[edit]
lab@Yeast# delete policy-options policy-statement ospf_default

[edit]
lab@Yeast# delete protocols ospf export
```

The effect of this change is confirmed at PBR, where now only the BGP version of the default route is present and is therefore made active:

```
[edit]
lab@PBR# run show route

inet.0: 827 destinations, 827 routes (145 active, 0 holddown, 682 hidden)
+ = Active Route, - = Last Active, * = Both

0.0.0.0/0          *[BGP/170] 17:26:08, localpref 100
                     AS path: 420 I
                   > to 172.16.1.1 via fe-0/0/0.412
```

Export Beer-Co Aggregate to Borgnet

The requirements state that PBR should advertise a single 10/8 aggregate to its EBGP peers representing Beer-Co's internal connectivity. The same approach used at Yeast is brought to bear here. Specifically, an aggregate route is defined and policy is created to export it to Wheat in AS 420:

```
[edit]
lab@PBR# show routing-options aggregate
route 10.0.0.0/8;
```

```
lab@PBR# show policy-options policy-statement as_420_export
term 1 {
    from {
        protocol aggregate;
        route-filter 10.0.0.0/8 exact;
    }
    then accept;
}

[edit]
lab@PBR# show protocols bgp group as_420 export
export as_420_export;
```

Validation of the as_420_export policy is straightforward:

```
[edit]
lab@PBR# run show route advertising-protocol bgp 172.16.1.1

inet.0: 827 destinations, 827 routes (145 active, 0 holddown, 682 hidden)
  Prefix                Nexthop              MED   Lclpref   AS path
* 10.0.0.0/8            Self                               I
```

Although not shown, a similar state of EBGP learned and advertised routes is also confirmed to exist at router Yeast, except that is has learned the 129–133 and 192.168.34/24 customer routes from AS 34. This completes the EBGP peering and initial import policy phases of the BGP multihoming scenario. It is time to add IBGP to the network.

Monitor system load

Before adding EBGP to Yeast, system resources were analyzed using the show chassis routing-engine and show task memory commands. Now that EBGP has been added, it is a good idea to reexamine resource usage. If the router is having a hard time maintaining its current EBGP load for whatever reason, obviously the addition of IBGP sessions will not help matters. The hidden set task accounting command is used to get a better feel for how much burden BGP itself is adding to the router.

 Hidden commands are hidden because Juniper Networks support engineers feel inappropriate use can cause operational problems. As a general rule, you should never issue hidden commands on a production network router unless a support engineer has instructed you to do so.

This command displays the resource consumption of the various components of the routing daemon (rpd) and is hidden because it requires the router's resources to run, which could make a bad situation worse. Because there is no reason to believe that any of Beer-Co's routers are actually running short on resources, task accounting is enabled (note that there is no CLI auto-completion, hence the term *hidden*). After a few moments, the results are displayed, and task accounting is turned back off. Task accounting should be enabled only when needed, and then only long enough to get the information desired. Also note that set task accounting on is an operational mode command:

```
lab@PBR> set task accounting on
Task accounting enabled.

lab@PBR>
```

After a few moments, the results are displayed:

```
lab@PBR> show task accounting
Task accounting is enabled.

Task                   Started User Time System Time Longest Run
Scheduler                  425      0.004       0.007       0.000
LMP Client                  75      0.001       0.002       0.000
Memory                       6      0.000       0.000       0.000
OSPFv2 I/O./var/run/ppmd_   120      0.001       0.002       0.000
BGP RT Background           32      0.000       0.000       0.000
OSPFv2                     100      0.000       0.001       0.000
BFD I/O./var/run/bfdd_con   29      0.000       0.000       0.000
BGP_420.172.16.1.1+1530     38      0.000       0.001       0.000
KRT                         12      0.000       0.000       0.000
Redirect                     2      0.000       0.000       0.000
MGMT_Listen./var/run/rpd_    2      0.000       0.000       0.000
SNMP Subagent./var/run/sn    3      0.000       0.000       0.000
```

The output indicates that the EBGP peering at PBR is not consuming appreciable system resources. Note that instability and resulting route flaps (repeated route withdrawals and readvertisement) could change this situation. BGP route damping is used to buffer the effects of flapping routes when needed. In operation, once an unstable prefix is damped, subsequent updates/withdrawals are ignored for a specified period to preserve the local router's control plane resources.

Task accounting is again disabled to prevent unnecessary resource usage:

```
lab@PBR> set task accounting off
Task accounting disabled.
```

IBGP Peering Within AS 1282

Referring back to Figure 5-10 and the scenario's design requirements, it's obvious that you need to configure IBGP on the backbone routers. Route reflection is used to minimize the total number of IBGP sessions required. Dual route reflectors are deployed for redundancy, in this case using the same cluster ID. The use of loopback-based IBGP peering means that the potential for session disruption to one reflector, but not the other, is virtually nonexistent, making the lack of cluster 1.2.8.2 updates over the route reflector–route reflector IBGP session a nonissue. Using the same cluster ID on both reflectors reduces the BGP routing information base (RIB) size on the reflectors because they filter updates received from each other that contain the

shared cluster ID. Note that the two route reflectors peer to each other as noncli-
ents. The same cluster ID value is configured on both reflectors. In this example, the
cluster ID is based on Beer-Co's ASN 1282.

Configuration of route reflection begins with creation of the route reflector–route
reflector IBGP peering session on Porter:

```
[edit]
lab@Porter# set routing-options autonomous-system 1282

[edit]
lab@Porter# edit protocols bgp group 1282_rr

[edit protocols bgp group 1282_rr]
lab@Porter# set type internal neighbor 10.10.12.3

[edit protocols bgp group 1282_rr]
lab@Porter# set local-address 10.20.12.2

[edit protocols bgp group 1282_rr]
lab@Porter# top show routing-options
autonomous-system 1282;

[edit protocols bgp group 1282_rr]
lab@Porter# show
type internal;
local-address 10.20.12.2;
neighbor 10.10.12.3;
```

With definition of the local system's ASN under the routing-options stanza complete, you create a BGP group called 1282_rr; this group is designated as an internal
group, making the configuration of a peer-as unnecessary. The highlights show how
a loopback-based peering session is defined through specification of the neighbor's
loopback address in conjunction with a local-address statement representing the
local loopback address. The use of the local-address statement is crucial for proper
loopback peering. Omitting the local-address, which is known as update-source in
IOS, results in a session that is sourced from whatever interface the session is routed
over. Because the remote router is configured to peer with a loopback address, the
incoming session, which is now sourced from a physical interface's IP, appears
unexpected, and peering is refused. Generally speaking, you can omit the local-
address from one end, as both ends try to form a connection by default, but best
practices for loopback peering call for both ends to be configured symmetrically.

A similar configuration is added to Bock:

```
[edit protocols bgp group 1282_rr]
lab@Bock# show
type internal;
local-address 10.10.12.3;
neighbor 10.10.12.2;
```

After a minute or two, the reflector-to-reflector IBGP session status is verified:

```
[edit]
lab@Porter# run show bgp summary
Groups: 1 Peers: 1 Down peers: 1
Table   Tot Paths Act Paths Suppressed History Damp State  Pending
inet.0          0         0          0       0         0        0
Peer         AS    InPkt    OutPkt    OutQ   Flaps Last Up/Dwn State|#Active/
Received/Damped...
10.10.12.3  1282        0        0       0         4:35 Idle
```

Things do not look good at Porter. The Idle state implies that the BGP session cannot even be routed, let alone established. A glance at Bock shows an Active state, meaning that the router is at least able to route its TCP session toward its peer and is therefore actively trying to establish a TCP connection:

```
[edit protocols bgp group 1282_rr]
lab@Bock# run show bgp summary
Groups: 1 Peers: 1 Down peers: 1
Table   Tot Paths Act Paths Suppressed History Damp State  Pending
inet.0          0         0          0       0         0        0
Peer         AS    InPkt    OutPkt    OutQ   Flaps Last Up/Dwn State|#Active/
Received/Damped...
10.10.12.2  1282        0        8       0         2:33 Active
```

Troubleshoot an IBGP peering problem

Attention is focused at Porter because its BGP session status is the lesser/worse of the two. Because loopback-based peering requires an IGP to resolve the forwarding next hop used to reach the session's target loopback address, it's reasonable to begin fault isolation with the IGP infrastructure. The first step is to confirm whether Porter has a route to Bock's loopback address:

```
[edit]
lab@Porter# run show route 10.10.12.3

inet.0: 20 destinations, 21 routes (20 active, 0 holddown, 0 hidden)
+ = Active Route, - = Last Active, * = Both

10.10.12.3/32     *[OSPF/10] 02:24:59, metric 3
                  > to 10.20.131.2 via fe-0/0/1.1331
```

The output confirms that Porter has an OSPF learned route to Bock's loopback address. A traceroute is performed *between* the IBGP peering addresses. This is achieved by sourcing the traceroute from Porter's loopback address, as highlighted:

```
[edit]
lab@Porter# run traceroute 10.10.12.3 source 10.10.12.2
traceroute to 10.10.12.3 (10.10.12.3) from 10.10.12.2, 30 hops max,
40 byte packets
 1  10.20.131.2 (10.20.131.2)  12.790 ms  14.714 ms   5.128 ms
 2  10.20.129.2 (10.20.129.2)  24.976 ms   9.342 ms   9.845 ms
 3  10.10.12.3 (10.10.12.3)  10.103 ms  27.564 ms  31.800 ms
```

The traceroute succeeds, and in so doing vindicates the IGP as the source of the IBGP peering problem. From a loopback-based IBGP perspective, all that is required of the IGP is a route between loopback addresses, and clearly that part is working here. The next step is to add BGP protocol tracing to see whether that sheds any light. Tracing is added to Porter, and the trace file is monitored in real time using the monitor start command:

```
[edit protocols bgp]
lab@Porter# show traceoptions
file bgp_trace;
flag open detail;

[edit protocols bgp]
lab@Porter# commit
commit complete

[edit protocols bgp]
lab@Porter# run monitor start bgp_trace
```

BGP trace output is observed after a minute or so; use the clear bgp neighbor <peer address> command to help expedite activity when you are impatient:

```
*** bgp_trace ***
Sep  1 01:49:02.088247
Sep  1 01:49:02.088247 BGP RECV 10.10.12.3+1601 -> 10.10.12.2+179
Sep  1 01:49:02.088335 BGP RECV message type 1 (Open) length 45
Sep  1 01:49:02.088423 BGP RECV version 4 as 1282 holdtime 90 id
10.10.12.3 parmlen 16
Sep  1 01:49:02.088447 BGP RECV MP capability AFI=1, SAFI=1
Sep  1 01:49:02.088460 BGP RECV Refresh capability, code=128
Sep  1 01:49:02.088469 BGP RECV Refresh capability, code=2
Sep  1 01:49:02.088508
Sep  1 01:49:02.088508 BGP SEND 10.10.12.2+179 -> 10.10.12.3+1601
Sep  1 01:49:02.088537 BGP SEND message type 1 (Open) length 29
Sep  1 01:49:02.088552 BGP SEND version 4 as 1282 holdtime 90 id
10.10.12.2 parmlen 0
Sep  1 01:49:02.088566
Sep  1 01:49:02.088566 BGP SEND 10.10.12.2+179 -> 10.10.12.3+1601
Sep  1 01:49:02.088583 BGP SEND message type 3 (Notification) length 21
Sep  1 01:49:02.088689 BGP SEND Notification code 2 (Open Message
Error) subcode 5 (authentication failure)
Sep  1 01:49:02.089581 bgp_pp_recv: NOTIFICATION sent to 10.10.12.3+1601
proto): code 2 (Opelist
monitor start "bgp_trace" (Last changed Sep  1 01:49:02)
(Message Error) subcode 5 (authentication failure), Reason: no group
for 10.10.12.3+1601 (proto) from AS 1282 found (peer idled), dropping
him
```

The highlights call out key aspects of the trace. Things begin when Porter receives a BGP session open from Bock. Note that this session is correctly sourced between the loopback addresses associated with routers Bock and Porter. Porter responds with a notification message that reports an authentication failure. In the BGP context, this type of message means that an unknown peer has tried to establish a peering session. BGP normally communicates only with explicitly configured peers (unless you add the allow *<prefix>* keyword). The last highlight is telling—the local system reports that this peer does not belong to any configured groups. The lack of Porter-initiated BGP session requests is expected here; recall that its connection is in the idle state, which means that it cannot begin to form a session, so there would be nothing to trace.

The IBGP configuration is examined with extra scrutiny, because you are sure that Porter has peer 10.10.12.3 configured in the 1282_rr group:

```
[edit protocols bgp]
lab@Porter#
*** monitor and syslog output disabled, press ESC-Q to enable ***

[edit protocols bgp]
lab@Porter# show
traceoptions {
    file bgp_trace;
    flag open detail;
}
group 1282_rr {
    type internal;
    local-address 10.20.12.2;
    neighbor 10.10.12.3;
}
```

The IBGP configuration problem at Porter jumps out and slaps you in the head, emitting a d'oh-like sound that echoes between your ears. The local-address statement incorrectly specifies a nonexistent address. This accounts for the local state of idle because the router cannot create a packet with a spoofed address! This effectively puts the 1282_rr group into an idle state, which in turn leads to the authentication failure for the session initiated by Bock. The tracing configuration is removed, the mistake is corrected, and session status is confirmed to be operational a short time later:

```
[edit protocols bgp]
lab@Porter# delete traceoptions

[edit protocols bgp]
lab@Porter# set group 1282_rr local-address 10.10.12.2

[edit protocols bgp]
lab@Porter# run show bgp summary
Groups: 1 Peers: 1 Down peers: 0
Table      Tot Paths  Act Paths Suppressed    History Damp State    Pending
inet.0           0          0          0          0       0          0
Peer             AS     InPkt     OutPkt      OutQ   Flaps Last Up/Dwn State|#Active/
Received/Damped...
10.10.12.3 1282            5          6         0       0        1:52 0/0/0
0/0/0
```

Configure route reflection

The configuration for cluster 1.2.8.2 is now added to each reflector. Here is Bock's 1282_clients group:

```
[edit protocols bgp group 1282_clients]
lab@Bock# show
type internal;
local-address 10.10.12.3;
##
## Warning: requires 'bgp-reflection' license
##
cluster 1.2.8.2;
neighbor 10.20.128.3;
neighbor 10.20.128.4;
neighbor 10.30.1.1
```

The 1282_rr_clients group is similar to the previously created 1282_rr group, except for the inclusion of a cluster ID, which makes the local router a route reflector for all peers in that group. All three client loopback addresses are configured, making them clients for cluster 1.2.8.2. The nag warning in the display reminds you that, for the J-series, BGP route reflection is considered to be a value-added service that requires separate licensing. The J-series soft license model means you can expect the feature to work properly, even when unlicensed, but you can also expect a lack of Juniper Networks support and ongoing nags at each commit. You normally obtain feature licenses from the distributor that sold you the router. You make a note to get a license, and for now move on with configuration. A similar configuration is added to Porter.

> A note on next-hop self and route reflectors is in order here. It is common to have an IBGP export policy on EBGP speakers that sets the advertised next hop to the IBGP speaker's peering address to eliminate issues with other routes not being able to resolve the EBGP next hop originally advertised by the remote AS. Applying such a policy for routes that are reflected among clients can easily result in suboptimal forwarding, as traffic will be forced to transit the reflector. In most cases, you want the reflection topology to be independent of the forwarding topology, and leaving the next hop unchanged on reflected routes achieves this goal.

IBGP configuration at routers PBR, Stout, and Yeast is similar. Each router gets an IBGP group that defines loopback peering to each reflector. The use of redundant route refection doubles the total number of IBGP sessions needed for this network, bringing the total to 13. This is still far fewer than the 20 sessions needed to form a full mesh among five routers if reflection were not used. Here is the configuration of client Stout:

```
[edit protocols bgp group 1282_clients]
lab@stout# top show routing-options
```

```
autonomous-system 1282;

[edit protocols bgp group 1282_clients]
lab@stout# show
type internal;
local-address 10.20.128.4;
neighbor 10.10.12.3;
neighbor 10.10.12.2;
```

After the new 1282_clients peer group is added to client routers PBR, Stout, and
Yeast, IBGP session status is confirmed at client Stout:

```
[edit protocols bgp group 1282_clients]
lab@stout# run show bgp summary
Groups: 1 Peers: 2 Down peers: 0
Table    Tot Paths  Act Paths Suppressed  History Damp State    Pending
inet.0         0          0          0          0         0          0
Peer          AS      InPkt    OutPkt  OutQ   Flaps Last Up/Dwn State|#Active/
Received/Damped...
10.10.12.2  1282   13  14        0        0     6:19 0/0/0    0/0/0
10.10.12.3  1282   20  22        0        0     9:57 0/0/0    0/0/0

[edit protocols bgp group 1282_clients]
lab@stout# run show route protocol bgp

inet.0: 20 destinations, 20 routes (20 active, 0 holddown, 0 hidden)
```

The output is a bit of a mixed bag of results. On the one hand, both IBGP sessions
are established to the reflectors; on the other hand, no routes are being learned over
either session. Oddly, a show route advertising-protocol bgp command at PBR confirms that it is readvertising its EBGP learned routes to reflector Bock:

```
[edit protocols bgp group 1282_clients]
lab@PBR# run show route advertising-protocol bgp 10.10.12.2

inet.0: 827 destinations, 827 routes (145 active, 0 holddown, 682 hidden)
  Prefix           Nexthop           MED    Lclpref    AS path
* 0.0.0.0/0        172.16.1.1               100        420 I
* 6.1.0.0/16       172.16.1.1               100        420 I
* 6.2.0.0/22       172.16.1.1               100        420 I
. . . .
```

If PBR is advertising routes to the reflector, why are these routes not being reflected to
the cluster's clients?

Troubleshoot BGP next hop reachability

Attention shifts to the reflectors, given that the missing routes were last observed
being sent to them, while nothing is seen coming back from them. The show route
receive-protocol bgp command output on reflector Bock implies that *no* routes are
being received, which is not possible, given that PBR's output shows it advertised
routes to Bock, and the underlying TCP transport guarantees delivery!

```
[edit protocols bgp group 1282_clients]
lab@Bock# run show route receive-protocol bgp 10.20.128.3
```

```
inet.0: 825 destinations, 950 routes (19 active, 0 holddown, 930 hidden)
```

The presence of hidden routes is noted, so you investigate by adding the hidden switch:

```
[edit protocols bgp group 1282_clients]
lab@Bock# run show route receive-protocol bgp 10.20.128.3 hidden
```

```
inet.0: 825 destinations, 950 routes (19 active, 0 holddown, 930 hidden)
  Prefix              Nexthop              MED    Lclpref    AS path
  0.0.0.0/0           172.16.1.1                  100        420 I
  6.1.0.0/16          172.16.1.1                  100        420 I
. . .
```

The output confirms that the BGP routes advertised by PBR are in fact hidden at Bock. This explains the lack of reflection to other clients, because active routes only are subject to advertisement. The extensive switch is added to get as much detail as possible, but the output does not contain any additional information:

```
[edit protocols bgp group 1282_clients]
lab@Bock# ...protocol bgp 10.20.128.3 hidden extensive
```

```
inet.0: 825 destinations, 950 routes (19 active, 0 holddown, 930 hidden)
  0.0.0.0/0 (2 entries, 0 announced)
     Nexthop: 172.16.1.1
     Localpref: 100
     AS path: 420 I
. . .
```

The limited set of information displayed does include the route's associated BGP next hop, which here represents the address assigned to Wheat for use on its EBGP peering to PBR. Recalling that the BGP route selection process begins with a decision as to whether the next hop is reachable, you display the route to 172.16.1.1 at Bock:

```
[edit protocols bgp group 1282_clients]
lab@Bock# run show route 172.16.1.1
```

The output, or more correctly the lack thereof, confirms that the issue is one of BGP next hop reachability. The show route resolution unresolved detail command is used to confirm this fact:

```
[edit protocols bgp group 1282_clients]
lab@Bock# run show route resolution unresolved detail
Tree Index 1
133.3.0.0/16
        Protocol Nexthop: 84.10.109.7
        Indirect nexthop: 0 -
132.252.0.0/16
        Protocol Nexthop: 84.10.109.7
        Indirect nexthop: 0 -
. . . .
```

The display confirms that route reflector Bock is unable to resolve the EBGP next hop attached to the routes it learns from Yeast. There are several common solutions to this classic problem. Recall that by default, the BGP next hop is updated only on EBGP links. You could alter this behavior with a `next-hop self` policy on the EBGP speakers, which is then applied as an IBGP *export* policy to update the next hop of each route as it is readvertised to other IBGP speakers.

 Never apply a `next-hop self` policy as import for an EBGP session because the resulting routes appear to be looped and are hidden.

Another way to fix the unreachable next hop is to advertise the EBGP peering subnet into your IGP. You should do this by running a passive IGP instance on your EBGP peering links. The passive mode guarantees that an adjacency cannot form to the remote AS, which could be very, very bad (IGPs lack policy controls for inter-domain routing, and combining two large IGPs into a single, larger one may push routers beyond their limits).

An IBGP export to affect `next-hop self` behavior solves the problem. The changes made to PBR's configuration are also placed into effect at Yeast:

```
[edit]
lab@PBR# show policy-options policy-statement next_hop_self
term 1 {
    from protocol bgp;
    then {
        next-hop self;
    }
}

[edit]
lab@PBR# show protocols bgp group 1282_clients export
export next_hop_self;
```

The BGP summary display back at Stout confirms that route reflection is working:

```
[edit protocols bgp group 1282_clients]
lab@stout# run show bgp summary
Groups: 1 Peers: 2 Down peers: 0
Table      Tot Paths  Act Paths Suppressed  History Damp State  Pending
inet.0         1612        806          0        0        0          0
Peer             AS   InPkt    OutPkt    OutQ   Flaps Last Up/Dwn State|#Active/
Received/Damped...
10.10.12.2     1282     163        84       0       0     41:18 806/806/0
0/0/0
10.10.12.3     1282     259        92       0       0     44:56 0/806/0
0/0/0
```

The highlights show that Stout is receiving the same number of BGP routes from both reflectors, which is expected. Recall that BGP tie-breaking rules prefer routes learned from the router with the lowest RID, which is Porter in this case. You could enable multipath for IBGP to install both copies of the routes into the forwarding table. However, in this example, it does not buy anything, given that both copies point to the same forwarding next hop address. We will rely on the IGP to perform load balancing if there are multiple equal cost paths. Details for the customer route to Brewer Inc. are displayed to confirm various attributes for the route, including why the copy learned from Porter is preferred:

```
[edit protocols bgp group 1282_clients]
lab@stout# run show route 192.168.34.0 detail

inet.0: 826 destinations, 1632 routes (826 active, 0 holddown, 0 hidden)
192.168.34.0/24 (2 entries, 1 announced)
        *BGP    Preference: 170/-121
                Next-hop reference count: 2732
                Source: 10.10.12.2
                Next hop: 10.20.131.1 via fe-0/0/1.1331, selected
                Protocol next hop: 10.30.1.1
                Indirect next hop: 8791128 262144
                State: <Active Int Ext>
                Local AS:  1282 Peer AS:  1282
                Age: 30         Metric2: 2
                Task: BGP_1282.10.10.12.2+179
                Announcement bits (2): 0-KRT 4-Resolve tree 1
                AS path: 34 I (Originator) Cluster list:  1.2.8.2
                AS path:  Originator ID: 10.30.1.1
                Communities: bandwidth:1287:12500000
                Localpref: 120
                Router ID: 10.10.12.2
         BGP    Preference: 170/-121
                Next-hop reference count: 2732
                Source: 10.10.12.3
                Next hop: 10.20.131.1 via fe-0/0/1.1331, selected
                Protocol next hop: 10.30.1.1
                Indirect next hop: 8791128 262144
                State: <NotBest Int Ext>
                Inactive reason: Router ID
                Local AS:  1282 Peer AS:  1282
                Age: 4:29       Metric2: 2
                Task: BGP_1282.10.10.12.3+179
                AS path: 34 I (Originator) Cluster list:  1.2.8.2
                AS path:  Originator ID: 10.30.1.1
                Communities: bandwidth:1287:12500000
                Localpref: 120
                Router ID: 10.10.12.3
```

Confirm Outbound Policy Operation

The EBGP and IBGP peering is established within your network, and route reflection is confirmed operational. The verification of your output policy is performed at IBGP speaker Stout. Recall that Ale and Lager use the OSPF default to forward packets to their respective ABRs, which in turn now have BGP routing state and are expected to make the correct outbound forwarding decision.

Things start with traceroutes to customer networks in peering ASs Borgnet and Botnet:

```
lab@stout> traceroute 192.168.42.1
traceroute to 192.168.42.1 (192.168.42.1), 30 hops max, 40 byte packets
 1  10.20.129.2 (10.20.129.2)  6.360 ms  59.843 ms  15.233 ms
 2  172.16.1.1 (172.16.1.1)  10.191 ms !N  8.985 ms !N  10.114 ms !N

lab@stout> traceroute 192.168.34.1
traceroute to 192.168.34.1 (192.168.34.1), 30 hops max, 40 byte packets
 1  10.20.131.1 (10.20.131.1)  40.976 ms  34.719 ms  2.141 ms
 2  10.10.8.2 (10.10.8.2)  10.009 ms  18.695 ms  8.191 ms
 3  84.10.109.7 (84.10.109.7)  32.183 ms !N  19.530 ms !N  19.790 ms !N
```

The results match the topological aspects of Beer-Co's outbound policy—Stout is using the specific routes it has learned from the EBGP peering routers to forward directly to the peer AS that owns the customer route. The point being stressed here is that this aspect of outbound policy is a side effect of the route filtering performed at the EBGP-speaking routers. Yeast, for example, filters the copy of Cap-Co's 192.168.42/24 route when it is readvertised from Botnet because that route did not originate within AS 34. This means that although there are two copies of customer route 192.168.42/24, both copies identify the *same* BGP next hop, which is PBR in this example. There are two copies of this route because of the redundant route reflector design. Refer back to the previous show route display for full details. The following (filtered) display calls out that both copies of the 192.168.42/24 route point to the same BGP egress point, despite being learned from two different reflectors:

```
lab@stout> show route 192.168.42.0 detail | match next
                Next-hop reference count: 496
                Next hop: 10.20.129.2 via fe-0/0/0.3141, selected
                Protocol next hop: 10.20.128.3
                Indirect next hop: 8791000 262142
                Next-hop reference count: 496
                Next hop: 10.20.129.2 via fe-0/0/0.3141, selected
                Protocol next hop: 10.20.128.3
                Indirect next hop: 8791000 262142
```

Things are not so perfect when it comes to destinations that are filtered by both EBGP speakers—for example, the 192.168.66/24 Bottle Inc. route. Because the BGP speakers are relying on a learned default route, which has equal specificity for all such filtered destinations, special steps are required to meet the stated outbound policy to avoid a tie-breaker situation between the otherwise equal-cost versions of the default route. Recall that in this example, all IBGP speakers should prefer the default route learned through PBR and use the one learned from Yeast only when the PBR session is disrupted.

The route to Bottle Inc. is shown at Stout:

```
lab@stout> show route 192.168.66.0 detail

inet.0: 577 destinations, 1134 routes (577 active, 0 holddown, 0 hidden)
0.0.0.0/0 (2 entries, 1 announced)
        *BGP    Preference: 170/-101
                Next-hop reference count: 499
                Source: 10.10.12.3
                Next hop: 10.20.129.2 via fe-0/0/0.3141, selected
                Protocol next hop: 10.20.128.3
                Indirect next hop: 8791000 262142
                State: <Active Int Ext>
                Local AS:  1282 Peer AS:  1282
                Age: 1:15       Metric2: 1
                Task: BGP_1282.10.10.12.3+179
                Announcement bits (2): 0-KRT 4-Resolve tree 1
                AS path: 420 I (Originator) Cluster list:  1.2.8.2
                AS path:  Originator ID: 10.20.128.3
                Localpref: 100
                Router ID: 10.10.12.3
         BGP    Preference: 170/-101
                Next-hop reference count: 1729
                Source: 10.10.12.2
                Next hop: 10.20.131.1 via fe-0/0/1.1331, selected
                Protocol next hop: 10.30.1.1
                Indirect next hop: 8791128 262144
                State: <Int Ext>
                Inactive reason: IGP metric
                Local AS:  1282 Peer AS:  1282
                Age: 1:15       Metric2: 2
                Task: BGP_1282.10.10.12.2+179
                AS path: 34 I (Originator) Cluster list:  1.2.8.2
                AS path:  Originator ID: 10.30.1.1
                Communities: bandwidth:1287:12500000
                Localpref: 100
                Router ID: 10.10.12.2
```

The output confirms that Stout relies on a BGP learned default to reach destinations in nonadjacent ASs. The highlights show that Stout has learned of two copies of the default, one reflected by Bock that originates at PBR and the other via Porter, which originated at Yeast. In this example, the failure to adjust BGP attributes has left route selection to the default algorithm, which here selects the lowest metric IGP path, given that all other factors up to that decision step are the same. Your goal is to ensure that all IBGP speakers prefer the default advertised by PBR—this is not the case, so additional policy action is needed to meet the design requirements. The most direct way to alter which BGP routes are preferred by IBGP speakers is to adjust local preference:

```
lab@PBR# show protocols bgp group 1282_clients export
export [ next_hop_self prefer_Borgnet_transit ];

[edit]
lab@PBR# show policy-options policy-statement prefer_Borgnet_transit
term 1 {
    from {
        protocol bgp;
        route-filter 0.0.0.0/0 exact;
    }
    then {
        local-preference 110;
    }
}
```

After committing the change, the result is confirmed back at Stout:

```
lab@stout> show route 192.168.66.0

inet.0: 577 destinations, 1134 routes (577 active, 0 holddown, 0 hidden)
+ = Active Route, - = Last Active, * = Both

0.0.0.0/0          *[BGP/170] 00:02:47, localpref 110, from 10.10.12.2
                      AS path: 420 I
                    > to 10.20.129.2 via fe-0/0/0.3141
                    [BGP/170] 00:02:47, localpref 110, from 10.10.12.3
                      AS path: 420 I
                    > to 10.20.129.2 via fe-0/0/0.3141
```

Why Only Two Copies of the Default?

You may be wondering why a router such as Stout is not receiving four copies of the BGP default route. Given that it receives two copies of the 192.168.42/24 route that is advertised *only* by PBR, you might expect twice as many copies for a route that is sent by *both* PBR and Yeast. The answer lies in the active route selection process performed by the reflectors. Each reflector readvertises only routes that are locally active. Because each reflector learns of route 192.168.42/24 from a single source (PBR), each reflector installs the route as active and both reflect it to their clients. In contrast, the default route is learned by each reflector from both PBR and Yeast, and each reflector chooses the copy it considers best, reflecting only that copy to its clients.

As a result, if the current network were to lose one of its EBGP speakers, there would *still* be two copies of the default route at each client. The difference is that now both copies will be the same route, as advertised by the remaining EBGP speaker. The same result occurs if the local preference of one default route is altered, causing it to be preferred by both reflectors.

There are still two copies of the default route, one learned from each reflector, but now both copies identify PBR as the protocol next hop. Therefore, using either

---

version results in a forwarding path that directs traffic to nonadjacent ASs over the Borgnet peering. Both reflectors now prefer the route advertised by PBR because of its higher preference value. A traceroute is performed to confirm a normal forwarding path, and then the EBGP session at PBR is cleared to confirm fallback to Botnet:

```
lab@stout> traceroute 192.168.66.1
traceroute to 192.168.66.1 (192.168.66.1), 30 hops max, 40 byte packets
 1  10.20.129.2 (10.20.129.2)  9.087 ms  8.966 ms  29.973 ms
 2  172.16.1.1 (172.16.1.1)  9.289 ms  9.886 ms  9.868 ms
 3  172.16.2.2 (172.16.2.2)  30.022 ms !N  15.394 ms !N  23.853 ms !N
```

The EBGP session is clear at PBR:

```
[edit]
lab@PBR# run clear bgp neighbor 172.16.1.1
Cleared 1 connections
```

And now the traceroute takes the secondary path via Botnet:

```
lab@stout> traceroute 192.168.66.1
traceroute to 192.168.66.1 (192.168.66.1), 30 hops max, 40 byte packets
 1  10.20.131.1 (10.20.131.1)  39.481 ms  18.973 ms  20.043 ms
 2  10.10.8.2 (10.10.8.2)  159.897 ms  199.206 ms  10.097 ms
 3  84.10.109.7 (84.10.109.7)  39.908 ms  19.261 ms  13.438 ms
 4  84.10.110.1 (84.10.110.1)  16.441 ms !N  44.843 ms !N  34.459 ms !N
```

After a few minutes, PBR's EBGP session should be reestablished, making its default once again preferred, causing transit traffic to switch back (revertive behavior) to the Borgnet peering:

```
lab@stout> traceroute 192.168.66.1
traceroute to 192.168.66.1 (192.168.66.1), 30 hops max, 40 byte packets
 1  10.20.129.2 (10.20.129.2)  9.980 ms  8.803 ms  9.848 ms
 2  172.16.1.1 (172.16.1.1)  20.031 ms  29.300 ms  19.929 ms
 3  172.16.2.2 (172.16.2.2)  9.851 ms !N  9.394 ms !N  29.928 ms !N
```

The final verification is performed at stub router Lager, which has no BGP routes and uses the stub area default to reach its ABR:

```
lab@Lager> show route protocol bgp

inet.0: 19 destinations, 19 routes (19 active, 0 holddown, 0 hidden)
```

No BGP routes are present because Lager is not running BGP:

```
lab@Lager> show route 192.168.66.0

inet.0: 19 destinations, 19 routes (19 active, 0 holddown, 0 hidden)
+ = Active Route, - = Last Active, * = Both

0.0.0.0/0          *[OSPF/10] 05:19:25, metric 11
                    > to 10.10.131.2 via fe-0/0/0.2131

lab@Lager> show route 192.168.34.0

inet.0: 19 destinations, 19 routes (19 active, 0 holddown, 0 hidden)
+ = Active Route, - = Last Active, * = Both
```

```
0.0.0.0/0          *[OSPF/10] 05:19:30, metric 11
                    > to 10.10.131.2 via fe-0/0/0.2131
```

Lager uses the OSPF default to reach all AS external destinations:

```
lab@Lager> traceroute 192.168.34.1
traceroute to 192.168.34.1 (192.168.34.1), 30 hops max, 40 byte packets
 1  10.10.131.2 (10.10.131.2)  10.507 ms  10.555 ms  9.706 ms
 2  10.20.131.1 (10.20.131.1)  17.896 ms  21.192 ms  20.007 ms
 3  10.10.8.2 (10.10.8.2)  39.897 ms  19.354 ms  20.043 ms
 4  84.10.109.7 (84.10.109.7)  19.780 ms !N  19.619 ms !N  19.887 ms !N

lab@Lager> traceroute 192.168.42.1
traceroute to 192.168.42.1 (192.168.42.1), 30 hops max, 40 byte packets
 1  10.10.131.2 (10.10.131.2)  8.841 ms  8.663 ms  9.940 ms
 2  10.20.129.2 (10.20.129.2)  19.825 ms  9.554 ms  9.726 ms
 3  172.16.1.1 (172.16.1.1)  9.979 ms !N  9.345 ms !N  10.121 ms !N

lab@Lager> traceroute 192.168.66.1
traceroute to 192.168.66.1 (192.168.66.1), 30 hops max, 40 byte packets
 1  10.10.131.2 (10.10.131.2)  8.731 ms  8.681 ms  10.097 ms
 2  10.20.129.2 (10.20.129.2)  19.732 ms  9.801 ms  9.650 ms
 3  172.16.1.1 (172.16.1.1)  9.872 ms  9.606 ms  9.856 ms
 4  172.16.2.2 (172.16.2.2)  39.847 ms !N  19.351 ms !N  29.992 ms !N
```

Lager forwards all external traffic to its ABR. The ABR (PBR in this case) then uses its BGP knowledge to make an optimal forwarding decision that adheres to Beer-Co's outbound routing policy. This completes the multihomed outbound routing policy scenario.

Dual-Homing and Outbound Policy Summary

In this section, you added a second EBGP peering and deployed IBGP on the necessary subset of routers within the Beer-Co network. A redundant route reflection topology was used to minimize the number of IBGP peerings while eliminating single points of failure.

With multihoming in place, you implemented an outbound policy that was a hybrid of the topology driven and strict primary/secondary models. This was achieved via an import policy that accepted only a subset of the routes advertised by your external BGP peers. This filtering allows an optimal routing decision for the specific routes that are accepted, while significantly reducing hardware requirements associated with handling full BGP feeds. The use of local preference ensured that a specific BGP learned default route is used for all other destinations, which in turn provided the strict primary/secondary (with revertive behavior) aspect of the sample outbound policy.

The next section builds upon this foundation by delving into the mechanics of implementing a typical inbound policy by manipulating BGP path attributes through the use of BGP export policy.

Inbound Policy

Referring back to Figure 5-9, it strikes you that the Beer-Co network has come a long way in recent weeks. The network has migrated from being single-homed to one provider to being multihomed to multiple providers, and you have successfully implemented a hybrid outbound policy based on a topology-driven model for peers and a primary/secondary model for transit. With these aspects of BGP operation in check, attention is focused on your company's inbound policy goals.

The use of stateful firewalls and NAT at the EBGP egress points greatly benefits from symmetric routing. By this, we mean that if a packet is routed to Destination X out of router PBR, ideally the response traffic will return along the same path to ingress back on router PBR. The symmetric routing paths tend to produce symmetric performance, which can be reason enough when asymmetric peering links are present, but the real goal here is to ensure that response traffic correctly matches against the dynamic state created when the outbound request was processed by the border router's stateful firewall.

The design goals for inbound policy indicate they should mirror your outbound policy—namely, that peers should route directly into your AS while transit traffic should arrive via the peering with Borgnet when available. In the previous section, local preference made steering traffic toward the desired EBGP speaker/egress point a straightforward matter. But as previously stated it's generally quite easy to control how traffic flows within your *own* network. The real art and finesse of BGP policy comes to bear when the goal is to influence traffic flow in a remote network that is not under your direct control. The Beer-Co inbound policy should provide the following behavior:

- Topological policy for peers, which should route directly into Beer-Co when the peering session is up
- Revertive primary/secondary traffic for nonadjacent ASs, which should ingress at PBR when that peering session is up

Table 5-2 summarizes the BGP attributes that can impact the policy/routing actions of a remote network. As a rule, attributes that are evaluated sooner in the path selection process are more likely to have an impact than those that are evaluated later. For example, altering local preference, which is evaluated at step 2 of 10, is likely to have some impact, whereas changing origin code, which is evaluated at step 4 of 10, is less likely to change a peer's forwarding behavior. The table uses parentheses to identify at which step of the 10-step decision process a given attribute is evaluated. Refer back to "BGP Path Selection" for details on these steps.

Table 5-2. BGP attributes that influence speakers in other networks

Attribute	Mechanism	Scope/caveat
AS path	AS path prepending impacts AS path selection criteria (step 3 of 10).	Global, in that once added, ASNs cannot be removed from the AS path list.
Origin	Altering origin impacts path selection criteria (step 4 of 10).	Global, but can be overwritten by intervening networks.
MED	Altering MED impacts MED selection criteria (step 5 of 10).	Adjacent AS only; MEDs are nontransitive. Generally, useful only for influencing link selection when all links terminate at the same adjacent AS.
Communities	Tagged routes are treated to some pre-agreed action, such as altered local preference.	Generally adjacent AS only. Many network operators strip all community tags upon ingress to their network, and again at egress.

It warrants restating that in all cases, the receiving ASs' policy can thwart even the most skilled attempts at controlling their outbound routing. For example, they can set a higher local preference, which means that AS path length is never even considered, which in turn negates any AS path prepending action you may perform in the hope of altering their path selection. This is why a detailed understanding of each peer AS's policies, and a good working relationship with their administrators, is always beneficial.

The most difficult aspect of the desired inbound policy is the need to influence the routing actions of Darknet, which does not peer directly with your AS. The goal is to make Darknet prefer the 10/8 aggregate it learns through Borgnet such that it uses the advertisement learned from Botnet only when the former is unavailable.

Using MED is out of the question here because the MED, being nontransitive, does not transit the networks you peer with. Also, PBR has a single attachment to Borgnet, so there is no use for MED there. MED could be used on the Yeast/Botnet peering to help steer ingress traffic over the high-speed link, but this is not the current focus. Communities are likely not an option because you are not a Darknet customer, and it's quite likely that they do not take action on communities attached to noncustomer routes; besides, communities may be stripped when the routes are exchanged between Borgnet and Darknet.

Before settling on a solution, it's noted that both of Beer-Co's BGP peers have a published policy regarding the use of customer routes with specific community tags. This policy results in a modified local preference setting within that peer's network. Table 5-3 provides the community-to-local preference mappings.

Table 5-3. Peer AS community-to-local preference mappings

Community value	Modified local preference
ASN:110	110
ASN:100	100

Table 5-3. Peer AS community-to-local preference mappings (continued)

Community value	Modified local preference
ASN:90	90
ASN:80	80

After careful consideration, it appears that the main problem in achieving the desired inbound behavior lies with the route selection algorithm in nonadjacent AS Darknet. Because you do not peer directly with this AS, the use of MED, and likely communities, is out. This narrows your choice to AS path prepending as the primary mechanism for influencing path selection within AS 666.

Figure 5-11 shows the state of affairs with regard to path selection for the 10/8 prefix in router Darknet.

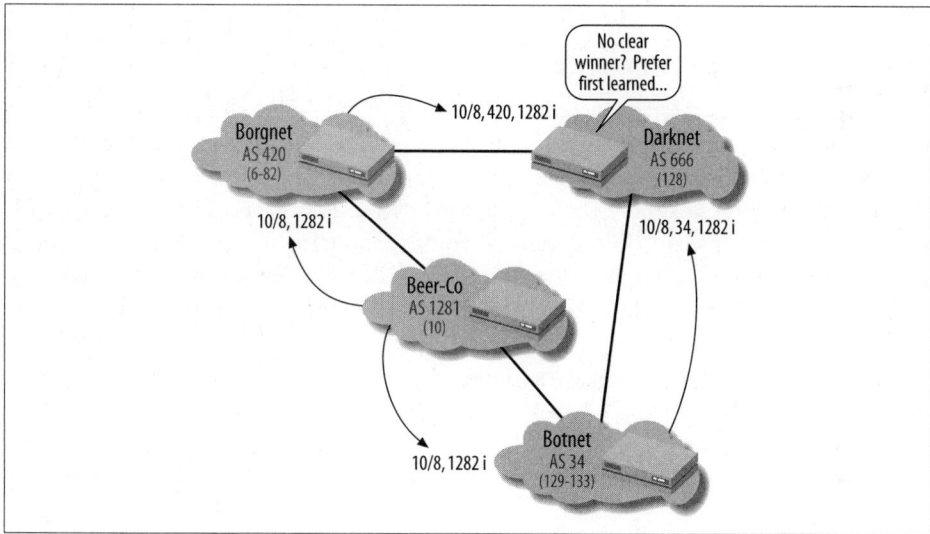

Figure 5-11. 10/8 route selection in Darknet

The figure shows that Darknet receives BGP updates for Beer-Co's 10/8 aggregate from both AS 420 and AS 34. Because all attributes are equal in this example, including the AS path length, the active path selected at Water is determined by which advertisement is learned first. To demonstrate, the 10/8 route is displayed at Water:

```
[edit]
lab@Water# run show route 10/8 detail

inet.0: 812 destinations, 1324 routes (812 active, 0 holddown, 0 hidden)
10.0.0.0/8 (2 entries, 1 announced)
        *BGP    Preference: 170/-101
                Next-hop reference count: 946
                Source: 84.10.110.2
                Next hop: 84.10.110.2 via fe-0/0/0.3243, selected
```

```
                State: <Active Ext>
                Local AS:    666 Peer AS:    34
                Age: 41:35
                Task: BGP_34.84.10.110.2+4664
                Announcement bits (2): 0-KRT 1-BGP RT Background
                AS path: 34 1282 I Aggregator: 1282 10.30.1.1
                Localpref: 100
                Router ID: 84.10.109.1
       BGP      Preference: 170/-101
                Next-hop reference count: 682
                Source: 172.16.2.1
                Next hop: 172.16.2.1 via fe-0/0/0.423, selected
                State: <Ext>
                Inactive reason: Active preferred
                Local AS:    666 Peer AS:    420
                Age: 39:41
                Task: BGP_420.172.16.2.1+179
                AS path: 420 1282 I Aggregator: 1282 10.20.128.3
                Localpref: 100
                Router ID: 172.16.1.3
```

The output shows that Water installed the path through AS 34 as the active path, and that the desired primary path is currently not preferred, simply because it was not learned first. Recall that for an EBGP learned route, step 9 of the active route selection process, which normally prefers the lower RID, is not performed due to MED oscillation issues. Instead, EBGP learned routes eliminate steps 9 and 10 to simply prefer the route that is learned first. Because this condition is timing-dependent, if something happens to the 10/8 advertisement from Botnet, the situation is reversed:

```
[edit]
lab@hops# run clear bgp neighbor 84.10.110.1
Cleared 1 connections
```

After waiting for the Botnet/Darknet EBGP peering to reform, the path to 10/8 is again displayed at Water:

```
[edit]
lab@Water# run show route 10/8

inet.0: 812 destinations, 1370 routes (812 active, 0 holddown, 0 hidden)
+ = Active Route, - = Last Active, * = Both

10.0.0.0/8        *[BGP/170] 00:43:43, localpref 100
                    AS path: 420 1282 I
                  > to 172.16.2.1 via fe-0/0/0.423
                   [BGP/170] 00:00:29, localpref 100
                    AS path: 34 1282 I
                  > to 84.10.110.2 via fe-0/0/0.3243
```

The display confirms that the tie-breaking action of prefer first-learned is not going to reliably produce the desired inbound policy; nor would relying on the RID/peering address tiebreakers for that matter. This looks like a classic example of how AS path prepending can help to steer path selection by remote networks—in this case, one that you do not even peer with. If the export policy at Yeast is altered to add an extra instance of the local AS number, the AS path length selection criterion should result in the path through AS 420 always being preferred by Darknet routers when available.

AS Path Prepend to Influence Nonadjacent AS Path Selection

Previous analysis of the policy showed that increasing the AS path length for the 10/8 prefix that Darknet learns from Botnet should result in the desired behavior of non-adjacent ASs routing to your network using Botnet as the primary transit AS.

The existing as_34_export policy is displayed at Yeast:

```
[edit]
lab@Yeast# show policy-options policy-statement as_34_export
term 1 {
    from {
        protocol aggregate;
        route-filter 10.0.0.0/8 exact;
    }
    then accept;
}
```

The as_34_export policy is modified to add *two* extra instances of ASN 1282 to the 10/8 update—based on Figure 5-11, it appears that only one instance is required, but extra padding should help to ensure that Darknet prefers the path through Borgnet and provides an additional safety margin to accommodate the potential for topology changes between Borgnet and Darknet. Such a routing change might result in transit through additional ASs and a corresponding increase in the AS path length over the preferred path.

```
[edit policy-options policy-statement as_34_export]
lab@Yeast# show
term 1 {
    from {
        protocol aggregate;
        route-filter 10.0.0.0/8 exact;
    }
    then {
        as-path-prepend "1282 1282";
        accept;
    }
}
```

The effects are examined from the perspective of router Water in the Darknet AS:

```
[edit]
lab@Water# run show route 10/8 detail

inet.0: 812 destinations, 1370 routes (812 active, 0 holddown, 0 hidden)
```

```
10.0.0.0/8 (2 entries, 1 announced)
        *BGP    Preference: 170/-101
                Next-hop reference count: 684
                Source: 172.16.2.1
                Next hop: 172.16.2.1 via fe-0/0/0.423, selected
                State: <Active Ext>
                Local AS:    666 Peer AS:    420
                Age: 53:05
                Task: BGP_420.172.16.2.1+179
                Announcement bits (2): 0-KRT 1-BGP RT Background
                AS path: 420 1282 I Aggregator: 1282 10.20.128.3
                Localpref: 100
                Router ID: 172.16.1.3
        BGP     Preference: 170/-101
                Next-hop reference count: 990
                Source: 84.10.110.2
                Next hop: 84.10.110.2 via fe-0/0/0.3243, selected
                State: <Ext>
                Inactive reason: AS path
                Local AS:    666 Peer AS:      34
                Age: 59
                Task: BGP_34.84.10.110.2+4730
                AS path: 34 1282 1282 I Aggregator: 1282 10.30.1.1
                Localpref: 100
                Router ID: 84.10.109.1
```

The output confirms that chance has been removed from the path selection process for the 10/8 prefix at Water. The longer AS path in the 10/8 prefix learned from the Botnet AS ensures that AS 666 always prefers to route through Borgnet to reach Beer-Co, unless that path is withdrawn (due to problems with the PBR–Wheat peering), at which point it falls back to the Botnet path.

To the casual observer, Beer-Co has met its inbound policy goals, all with a single-line addition to an existing export policy to affect AS path prepending. BGP policy is not really that hard, it would seem. Before heading out the door, you decide to confirm failover behavior. This begins by deactivating the secondary EBGP session to confirm that all traffic arrives at the Borgnet peering:

```
[edit]
lab@Yeast# deactivate protocols bgp group as_34

[edit]
lab@Yeast# commit
```

Traceroutes are now performed from routers *within* the adjacent and nonadjacent ASs. In most cases, you will need to inspect each AS's routing view, perhaps through a looking glass service, to confirm their forwarding paths.

All routers in the test network advertise their loopbacks (or an encompassing aggregate route) into BGP. All traceroutes are conducted between loopback addresses because full connectivity is expected among the prefixes used for loopback addressing.

What Is a Looking Glass?

A looking glass is basically a publicly accessible route server that allows you to view Internet routing, from the perspective of that particular route server. You use a looking glass to see the effects of that network's import policy and active route selection process, by displaying which BGP paths it has installed as active. You can also gauge the relative stability of a prefix, from the view of that looking glass, by examining how long a route has been known. The following example makes use of an AT&T looking glass, as listed at *http://www.nanog.org/lookingglass.html*, to display its view of the route to Juniper Networks:

```
-------------- route-server.ip.att.net ---------------

User Access Verification

Username: rviews
route-server>sho ip rou juniper.net
Routing entry for 207.17.136.0/22, supernet
  Known via "bgp 65000", distance 20, metric 0
  Tag 7018, type external
  Last update from 12.123.1.236 2w3d ago
  Routing Descriptor Blocks:
  * 12.123.1.236, from 12.123.1.236, 2w3d ago
      Route metric is 0, traffic share count is 1
      AS Hops 3
      Route tag 7018

route-server>sho ip bgp 207.17.136.0/22
BGP routing table entry for 207.17.136.0/22, version 181930
Paths: (18 available, best #13, table Default-IP-Routing-Table)
  Not advertised to any peer
  7018 2914 14203, (received & used)
    12.123.29.249 from 12.123.29.249 (12.123.29.249)
      Origin IGP, localpref 100, valid, external
      Community: 7018:5000 7018:33051
  . . .
```

The output suggests that AT&T has learned this route from 18 different speakers, that the prefix is stable (given that the last update was more than two weeks ago), and that the AS path to reach this prefix from within AT&T is 7018 (AT&T WorldNet), 2914 (Verio), and finally, 14203 (Juniper Networks itself).

```
[edit]
lab@Wheat# run traceroute 10.10.12.2 source 172.16.1.3
traceroute to 10.10.12.2 (10.10.12.2), 30 hops max, 40 byte packets
 1  172.16.1.2 (172.16.1.2)  17.316 ms  10.118 ms  21.751 ms
 2  10.20.129.1 (10.20.129.1)  12.798 ms  9.507 ms  9.711 ms
 3  10.10.12.2 (10.10.12.2)  16.981 ms  22.462 ms  19.689 ms
```

The traceroute to Porter's loopback address succeeds from within AS 420:

```
[edit]
lab@Water# run traceroute 10.10.12.2 source 64.8.12.1
traceroute to 10.10.12.2 (10.10.12.2), 30 hops max, 40 byte packets
 1  172.16.2.1 (172.16.2.1)  106.100 ms  17.772 ms  10.472 ms
 2  172.16.1.2 (172.16.1.2)  9.423 ms  9.373 ms  9.842 ms
 3  10.20.129.1 (10.20.129.1)  20.042 ms  39.411 ms  19.786 ms
 4  10.10.12.2 (10.10.12.2)  10.109 ms  9.390 ms  94.337 ms
```

The traceroute to Porter's loopback address succeeds from within AS 66:

```
[edit]
lab@hops# run traceroute 10.10.12.2 source 84.10.109.1
traceroute to 10.10.12.2 (10.10.12.2) from 84.10.109.1, 30 hops max, 40 byte packets
 1  84.10.110.1  45.013 ms  125.144 ms  25.062 ms
 2  172.16.2.1  8.442 ms  19.978 ms  9.940 ms
 3  172.16.1.2  30.019 ms  9.885 ms  9.849 ms
 4  10.20.129.1  16.135 ms  10.130 ms  13.433 ms
 5  10.10.12.2  15.628 ms  24.492 ms  16.888 ms
```

And finally, the traceroute to Porter's loopback address succeeds from within AS 34. So far so good, so the EBGP peering session to AS 34 is reactivated. After waiting for the EBGP session to Botnet to re-form, the traceroutes are repeated:

```
[edit]
lab@Wheat# run traceroute 10.10.12.2 source 172.16.1.3
traceroute to 10.10.12.2 (10.10.12.2), 30 hops max, 40 byte packets
 1  172.16.1.2 (172.16.1.2)  9.914 ms  8.950 ms  9.571 ms
 2  10.20.129.1 (10.20.129.1)  19.977 ms  19.534 ms  19.824 ms
 3  10.10.12.2 (10.10.12.2)  9.886 ms  9.498 ms  9.848 ms


lab@Water> traceroute 10.10.12.2 source 64.8.12.1
traceroute to 10.10.12.2 (10.10.12.2), 30 hops max, 40 byte packets
 1  172.16.2.1 (172.16.2.1)  19.317 ms  12.022 ms  16.594 ms
 2  172.16.1.2 (172.16.1.2)  9.889 ms  9.364 ms  10.281 ms
 3  10.20.129.1 (10.20.129.1)  19.596 ms  19.528 ms  7.891 ms
 4  10.10.12.2 (10.10.12.2)  21.967 ms  49.523 ms  9.720 ms
```

The results from Borgnet and Darknet are as before, and both are as expected. Things are not ideal from the perspective for Botnet, however:

```
[edit]
lab@hops# run traceroute 10.10.12.2 source 84.10.109.1
traceroute to 10.10.12.2 (10.10.12.2) from 84.10.109.1, 30 hops max, 40 byte packets
 1  84.10.110.1 (84.10.110.1)  8.589 ms  8.666 ms  10.118 ms
 2  172.16.2.1 (172.16.2.1)  29.935 ms  19.230 ms  20.005 ms
 3  172.16.1.2 (172.16.1.2)  20.021 ms  19.588 ms  19.710 ms
 4  10.20.129.1 (10.20.129.1)  9.916 ms  9.298 ms  10.128 ms
 5  10.10.12.2 (10.10.12.2)  21.422 ms  17.796 ms  14.098 ms
```

The traceroute from Botnet clearly shows that the traffic is failing to arrive at the peering exchange for that AS, resulting in extra AS hops as the traffic is directed over the primary path. This is a violation of the desired inbound policy. Displaying the route to 10/8 at Botnet confirms the problem and sheds lights on its cause:

```
[edit]
lab@hops# run show route 10/8 detail

inet.0: 817 destinations, 1069 routes (817 active, 0 holddown, 0 hidden)
10.0.0.0/8 (3 entries, 1 announced)
        *BGP    Preference: 170/-101
                Next-hop reference count: 750
                Source: 84.10.110.1
                Next hop: 84.10.110.1 via fe-0/0/0.3243, selected
                State: <Active Ext>
                Local AS:    34 Peer AS:    666
                Age: 43:41
                Task: BGP_666.84.10.110.1+179
                Announcement bits (2): 0-KRT 2-BGP RT Background
                AS path: 666 420 1282 I Aggregator: 1282 10.20.128.3
                Localpref: 100
                Router ID: 64.8.12.1
         BGP    Preference: 170/-101
                Next-hop reference count: 126
                Source: 84.10.109.8
                Next hop: 84.10.109.8 via fe-0/0/0.3233, selected
                State: <Ext>
                Inactive reason: Active preferred
                Local AS:    34 Peer AS:  1282
                Age: 4:36
                Task: BGP_1282.84.10.109.8+2957
                AS path: 1282 1282 1282 I Aggregator: 1282 10.30.1.1
                Localpref: 100
                Router ID: 10.30.1.1
         BGP    Preference: 170/-101
                Next-hop reference count: 126
                Source: 84.10.113.0
                Next hop: 84.10.113.0 via t1-0/0/2.0, selected
                State: <NotBest Ext>
                Inactive reason: Not Best in its group
                Local AS:    34 Peer AS:  1282
                Age: 4:32
                Task: BGP_1282.84.10.113.0+3127
                AS path: 1282 1282 1282 I Aggregator: 1282 10.30.1.1
                Localpref: 100
                Router ID: 10.30.1.1
```

IP internetworks are complicated systems, and with any such systems, making a change in one place can have unexpected consequences somewhere else. Before you added AS path prepending, both peer ASs had no problems preferring Beer-Co's 10/8 aggregate as learned directly from Beer-Co. This was because an AS path length of 1 is very hard to beat. The use of AS path prepending, in an attempt to make Darknet prefer the path through the Borgnet AS, has inadvertently altered the path selection in peer AS 34.

Even worse is that this situation results in path selection that is tied to the order in which routes are learned. Timing-related route selection issues are difficult to troubleshoot because administrative actions on one front—say, attribute modification—may trigger a change in the order that routes are learned. This can easily lead to an incorrect belief that policy changes are behind the altered path selection, when in reality things may change back at the next outage. Fortunately, there is a straightforward solution to this problem: community tags.

Use Communities to Influence Peer AS

Referring back to Table 5-3, notice that you can affect the local preference value within your peer ASs by attaching a specific community to your route updates. Because local preference is evaluated before AS path length, altering the local preference of the 10/8 route within AS 34 should be just the ticket. This change ensures that AS 34 always prefers the 10/8 learned directly from the Beer-Co peering regardless of the related AS path length.

Your changes begin with the definition of named communities. In this example, you need to set the 10/8 local preference to a value higher than 100, which is the default. Here, multiple communities are defined, but only the 110 community definition is required and used:

```
[edit]
lab@Yeast# show policy-options
. . .
community 100 members 1282:100;
community 110 members 1282:110;
community 70 members 1282:70;
community 80 members 1282:80;
community 90 members 1282:90;
community bw_fast members bandwidth:1287:12500000;
community bw_slow members bandwidth:1287:193000;
as-path 34_originate "^34$";
as-path 34_trans "^34.+$";
```

The existing as_34_export policy is altered to add the appropriate community, which is 110 in this example:

```
[edit policy-options policy-statement as_34_export]
lab@Yeast# show
term 1 {
    from {
        protocol aggregate;
        route-filter 10.0.0.0/8 exact;
    }
    then {
        community add 110;
        as-path-prepend "1282 1282";
        accept;
    }
}
```

The results are confirmed at router Hops in AS 34:

```
[edit]
lab@hops# run show route 10/8 detail

inet.0: 817 destinations, 1069 routes (817 active, 0 holddown, 0 hidden)
10.0.0.0/8 (3 entries, 1 announced)
        *BGP    Preference: 170/-111
                Next-hop reference count: 2
                Source: 84.10.109.8
                Next hop: 84.10.109.8 via fe-0/0/0.3233
                Next hop: 84.10.113.0 via t1-0/0/2.0, selected
                State: <Active Ext>
                Local AS:    34 Peer AS:  1282
                Age: 12
                Task: BGP_1282.84.10.109.8+2957
                Announcement bits (2): 0-KRT 2-BGP RT Background
                AS path: 1282 1282 1282 I Aggregator: 1282 10.30.1.1
                Communities: 1282:110
                Localpref: 110
                Router ID: 10.30.1.1
         BGP    Preference: 170/-111
                Next-hop reference count: 126
                Source: 84.10.113.0
                Next hop: 84.10.113.0 via t1-0/0/2.0, selected
                State: <NotBest Ext>
                Inactive reason: Update source
                Local AS:    34 Peer AS:  1282
                Age: 12
                Task: BGP_1282.84.10.113.0+3127
                AS path: 1282 1282 1282 I Aggregator: 1282 10.30.1.1
                Communities: 1282:110
                Localpref: 110
                Router ID: 10.30.1.1
         BGP    Preference: 170/-101
                Next-hop reference count: 749
                Source: 84.10.110.1
                Next hop: 84.10.110.1 via fe-0/0/0.3243, selected
                State: <Ext>
                Inactive reason: Local Preference
                Local AS:    34 Peer AS:   666
                Age: 1:11:39
                Task: BGP_666.84.10.110.1+179
                AS path: 666 420 1282 I Aggregator: 1282 10.20.128.3
                Localpref: 100
                Router ID: 64.8.12.1
```

Excellent! AS 34 now prefers the route learned directly from Beer-Co, and it still has a valid alternate path in the event of BGP session disruption to Beer-Co. The primary peering link is now deactivated to verify failover to the secondary and reversion back to the primary upon restoration:

```
[edit]
lab@PBR# deactivate protocols bgp group as_420
```

Traceroutes are now performed from adjacent and nonadjacent ASs:

```
[edit]
lab@Wheat# run traceroute 10.10.12.2 source 172.16.1.3
traceroute to 10.10.12.2 (10.10.12.2) from 172.16.1.3, 30 hops max, 40 byte packets
 1  172.16.2.2 (172.16.2.2)  8.411 ms  8.980 ms  9.840 ms
 2  84.10.110.2 (84.10.110.2)  20.057 ms  29.367 ms  9.886 ms
 3  84.10.113.0 (84.10.113.0)  19.999 ms  39.343 ms  20.021 ms
 4  10.10.12.2 (10.10.12.2)  13.796 ms  15.536 ms  19.873 ms


lab@Water> traceroute 10.10.12.2 source 64.8.12.1
traceroute to 10.10.12.2 (10.10.12.2) from 64.8.12.1, 30 hops max, 40 byte packets
 1  84.10.110.2 (84.10.110.2)  30.620 ms  21.427 ms  19.623 ms
 2  84.10.113.0 (84.10.113.0)  30.052 ms  16.285 ms  12.970 ms
 3  10.10.12.2 (10.10.12.2)  20.066 ms  35.912 ms  13.312 ms


[edit]
lab@hops# run traceroute 10.10.12.2 source 84.10.109.1
traceroute to 10.10.12.2 (10.10.12.2) from 84.10.109.1, 30 hops max, 40 byte packets
 1  84.10.113.0 (84.10.113.0)  8.924 ms  28.830 ms  9.856 ms
 2  10.10.12.2 (10.10.12.2)  9.846 ms  9.697 ms  9.795 ms
```

The results prove continued connectivity for both adjacent and nonadjacent ASs, with all traffic now arriving at the only functional peering exchange. The desired failover behavior is working. The Borgnet peering session is now reactivated to test the revertive behavior:

```
[edit]
lab@PBR# rollback 1
load complete
```

After session establishment, traceroutes are again performed to verify revertive primary behavior. Recall that the goal is to have peers route directly into AS 1282 while nonadjacent ASs route toward the Borgnet peering to ingress at PBR:

```
[edit]
lab@Wheat# run traceroute 10.10.12.2 source 172.16.1.3
traceroute to 10.10.12.2 (10.10.12.2) from 172.16.1.3, 30 hops max, 40 byte packets
 1  172.16.1.2 (172.16.1.2)  19.252 ms  12.858 ms  16.050 ms
 2  10.20.129.1 (10.20.129.1)  9.900 ms  9.498 ms  9.686 ms
 3  10.10.12.2 (10.10.12.2)  19.985 ms  19.611 ms  19.615 ms


lab@Water> traceroute 10.10.12.2 source 64.8.12.1
traceroute to 10.10.12.2 (10.10.12.2) from 64.8.12.1, 30 hops max, 40 byte packets
 1  172.16.2.1 (172.16.2.1)  9.220 ms  8.755 ms  29.928 ms
 2  172.16.1.2 (172.16.1.2)  9.844 ms  9.609 ms  9.873 ms
 3  10.20.129.1 (10.20.129.1)  29.962 ms  19.311 ms  20.003 ms
 4  10.10.12.2 (10.10.12.2)  9.862 ms  29.366 ms  29.967 ms


[edit]
lab@hops# run traceroute 10.10.12.2 source 84.10.109.1
traceroute to 10.10.12.2 (10.10.12.2) from 84.10.109.1, 30 hops max, 40 byte packets
 1  84.10.113.0 (84.10.113.0)  9.691 ms  8.756 ms  9.864 ms
 2  10.10.12.2 (10.10.12.2)  19.969 ms  29.445 ms  9.859 ms
```

The results confirm desired inbound policy behavior, thereby concluding the EBGP multihomed enterprise routing scenario. For completeness, the complete protocols and policy stanzas for EBGP routers PBR and Yeast, reflector Porter, and client Stout are shown.

Here is router PBR's configuration:

```
[edit]
lab@PBR# show policy-options | no-more
policy-statement as_420_export {
    term 1 {
        from {
            protocol aggregate;
            route-filter 10.0.0.0/8 exact;
        }
        then accept;
    }
}
policy-statement as_420_import {
    term 1 {
        from {
            protocol bgp;
            as-path as_420_originate;
        }
        then accept;
    }
    term 2 {
        then reject;
    }
}
policy-statement next_hop_self {
    term 1 {
        from protocol bgp;
        then {
            next-hop self;
        }
    }
}
policy-statement prefer_Borgnet_transit {
    term 1 {
        from {
            protocol bgp;
            route-filter 0.0.0.0/0 exact;
        }
        then {
            local-preference 110;
        }
    }
}
as-path as_420_originate "^420+$";

[edit]
lab@PBR# show protocols
```

```
bgp {
    group as_420 {
        type external;
        import as_420_import;
        export as_420_export;
        neighbor 172.16.1.1 {
            peer-as 420;
        }
    }
    group 1282_clients {
        type internal;
        local-address 10.20.128.3;
        export [ next_hop_self prefer_Borgnet_transit ];
        neighbor 10.10.12.3;
        neighbor 10.10.12.2;
    }
}
ospf {
    area 0.0.0.0 {
        interface fe-0/0/0.3141;
        interface fe-0/0/0.1241;
    }
    area 0.0.0.1 {
        stub default-metric 10;
        interface fe-0/0/0.1141;
    }
}
```

Here is router Yeast's configuration:

```
[edit]
lab@Yeast# show policy-options | no-more
policy-statement as_34_export {
    term 1 {
        from {
            protocol aggregate;
            route-filter 10.0.0.0/8 exact;
        }
        then {
            community add 110;
            as-path-prepend "1282 1282";
            accept;
        }
    }
}
policy-statement as_34_import {
    term slow_peer {
        from {
            protocol bgp;
            neighbor 84.10.113.1;
        }
        then {
            community add bw_slow;
        }
    }
}
```

```
        term fast_peer {
            from {
                protocol bgp;
                neighbor 84.10.109.7;
            }
            then {
                community add bw_fast;
            }
        }
    }
    policy-statement as_34_originate {
        term 1 {
            from {
                protocol bgp;
                as-path 34_originate;
            }
            then accept;
        }
        term 2 {
            then reject;
        }
    }
    policy-statement lb_per_packet {
        then {
            load-balance per-packet;
            accept;
        }
    }
    policy-statement next_hop_self {
        term 1 {
            from protocol bgp;
            then {
                next-hop self;
            }
        }
    }
    community 100 members 1282:100;
    community 110 members 1282:110;
    community 70 members 1282:70;
    community 80 members 1282:80;
    community 90 members 1282:90;
    community bw_fast members bandwidth:1287:12500000;
    community bw_slow members bandwidth:1287:193000;
    as-path 34_originate "^34$";
    as-path 34_trans "^34.+$";

[edit]
lab@Yeast# show protocols | no-more
bgp {
    group as_34 {
        type external;
        import [ as_34_import as_34_originate ];
        export as_34_export;
        peer-as 34;
```

```
                multipath;
                neighbor 84.10.109.7;
                neighbor 84.10.113.1;
            }
            group 1282_clients {
                type internal;
                local-address 10.30.1.1;
                export next_hop_self;
                neighbor 10.10.12.3;
                neighbor 10.10.12.2;
            }
        }
        ospf {
            area 0.0.0.0 {
                interface fe-0/0/1.2332;
            }
        }
    }
```

Here is route reflector Porter's configuration:

```
    [edit]
    lab@Porter# show policy-options

    [edit]
    lab@Porter# show protocols | no-more
    bgp {
        group 1282_rr {
            type internal;
            local-address 10.10.12.2;
            neighbor 10.10.12.3;
        }
        group 1282_clients {
            type internal;
            local-address 10.10.12.2;
            ##
            ## Warning: requires 'bgp-reflection' license
            ##
            cluster 1.2.8.2;
            neighbor 10.20.128.4;
            neighbor 10.20.128.3;
            neighbor 10.30.1.1;
        }
    }
    ospf {
        area 0.0.0.0 {
            interface fe-0/0/1.1331;
            interface fe-0/0/1.2332;
            interface t1-0/0/2.0;
        }
    }
```

Here is client Stout's configuration:

```
    [edit]
    lab@stout# show policy-options
```

```
[edit]
lab@stout# show protocols | no-more
bgp {
    group 1282_clients {
        type internal;
        local-address 10.20.128.4;
        neighbor 10.10.12.3;
        neighbor 10.10.12.2;
    }
}
ospf {
    area 0.0.0.0 {
        interface fe-0/0/0.3141;
        interface fe-0/0/1.1331;
    }
    area 0.0.0.2 {
        stub default-metric 10;
        interface fe-0/0/0.2131;
    }
}
```

BGP Inbound Policy Summary

This section demonstrated ways in which a dual-homed enterprise can manipulate BGP path attributes to achieve a desired inbound policy goal. The example demonstrated the need for both AS path manipulation and the use of BGP communities, which worked together to influence the routing decisions of both adjacent and nonadjacent ASs.

Conclusion

BGP can have a dramatic impact on the operation of an enterprise network when the network is multihomed, and even more so when it is multihomed to multiple providers. BGP itself is not a very complex protocol, but the myriad ways in which its attributes are acted upon, and the cascading effects of advertising only what the local speaker considers the best route, often lead to an unanticipated result. To the uninitiated, this often leads to confusion and what might seem to be unpredictable behavior. JUNOS software provides a complete set of diagnostic tools, from the CLI's operational mode displays to the extensive protocol tracing, which makes most BGP problems easy to diagnose. For example, the way the software displays *why* a given BGP path was not selected makes changing the results for that BGP decision step a straightforward matter, that is, whatever attribute caused the route to lose should be modified.

EBGP and IBGP are similar, but they have key differences in the way they are typically configured and in how they operate. This chapter detailed those differences and demonstrated typical EBGP physical peering and IBGP loopback-based peering.

Because IBGP does not rewrite the next hop, you will often need a next hop self-policy or some other method of advertising the external EBGP peering address into your IGP.

Bringing up BGP peerings is really just the start of the process. BGP is all about policy and administrative control over route exchanges, and therefore forwarding paths. Outbound policy controls how your network chooses to reach destinations and is relatively easy to implement as you control all aspects of your own network's operation. Inbound policy is far trickier, because here you are attempting to impact decisions made in remote ASs, over which you have no direct control. A detailed understanding of the BGP attributes that reach into, and beyond, other networks increases the probability that remote networks will bend to your will, resulting in ingress traffic patterns that optimize those factors that matter most within your organization.

The large size of BGP tables means that careful consideration should be leveled as to which routers need to run the protocol and on the import policy that determines which prefixes are accepted. The careful application of policy can easily reduce a BGP table from more than 230,000 routes to a more manageable set that can be distributed among lower-end routers. A partial table can be used to make intelligent routing decisions that optimize network resources and performance. When a full BGP table is not feasible, some form of a default route is used to balance the remaining prefixes or to direct the network traffic to a primary egress point as local policy dictates.

Route reflection is often used to reduce the burden of maintaining a full IBGP mess among a network's IBGP speakers, and when combined with route filtering, it allows the deployment of BGP on even the smallest of enterprise routers.

Exam Topics

We examined the following Enterprise Exam Topics in this chapter:

- Explain the use of BGP.
- Differentiate between IBGP and EBGP sessions.
- Policies to control route advertisement.
- Miscellaneous BGP configuration options.
- Load-balancing BGP routes.
- ISP multihoming scenarios.
- Configure an IBGP route reflection topology.
- Configure EBGP sessions.
- Identify BGP attributes that can be modified using policies.
- Implement a BGP policy for routing traffic over multiple ISP connections.

Chapter Review Questions

1. What BGP attribute guards against loops?

   a. MED

   b. Barring an IBGP speaker from resending IBGP updates

   c. Cluster ID

   d. AS path

2. What BGP attribute is most likely to influence egress from your AS?

   a. AS path

   b. Local preference

   c. MED

   d. Cluster length

   e. None of the above

3. What BGP attribute is mostly likely to influence a remote AS that you do not peer with?

   a. This is not possible given the local scope of BGP

   b. AS path

   c. MED

   d. Local preference

4. Which of the following correctly describes how IBGP differs from EBGP?

   a. IBGP peers to the interface address while EBGP peers to loopbacks

   b. IBGP updates do not alter the next hop attribute

   c. EBGP updates do not alter the next hop

   d. EBGP requires a full mesh

5. When export policy is specified at the global, group, and neighbor levels, which policy is executed?

   a. Only the least specific, which is global export

   b. Only the most specific, which is neighbor-level export

   c. All three are chained, and the global, group, and neighbor policies are executed

   d. None of the above; export can be defined only at the group level

6. When you issue a `show bgp summary` command, what is indicated by the Active state?

   a. The router is actively trying to form the BGP session; you should wait

   b. The session is established and active; you are done

c. The router is unable to even route the session; you should suspect a routing problem

d. At least one route has been received and made active

7. What command displays the routes you are receiving from a BGP peer?

    a. `show route advertising-protocol bgp`

    b. `show route receive-protocol bgp`

    c. `show route protocol bgp`

    d. `show ip route bgp`

8. Which type of JUNOS software policy is normally applied at an EBGP speaker to achieve an organization's *outbound* policy?

    a. Export policy

    b. Import policy

    c. Inbound policy

    d. Outbound policy

9. When implementing loopback-based peering, what is the purpose of the `local-address` statement?

    a. It ensures that the router sources the connection from its loopback address

    b. It ensures that the router sources the connection from the interface closest to the session target

    c. It eliminates the need for recursive route lookup in EBGP peering

    d. It eliminates the need for recursive route lookup in IBGP peering

10. Which of the following is/are true regarding route reflection on a J-series router?

    a. A license is required for support, not operation

    b. A single command is needed on the reflector

    c. New attributes are needed to prevent route looping

    d. Reflectors can hide parts of the topology because they reflect only their choice of best route

    e. All of the above

11. When configuring BGP in JUNOS software, where is the local router's AS defined?

    a. At the [`edit protocols bgp`] hierarchy

    b. At the [`edit routing-options`] hierarchy

    c. At the [`edit protocols bgp group`] hierarchy

    d. At the [`edit protocols bgp group <group name> neighbor`] hierarchy

12. In the following display, why is the route learned from 84.10.109.8 not active?

```
inet.0: 817 destinations, 1069 routes (817 active, 0 holddown, 0 hidden)
10.0.0.0/8 (3 entries, 1 announced)
```

```
*BGP      Preference: 170/-101
          Next-hop reference count: 750
          Source: 84.10.110.1
          Next hop: 84.10.110.1 via fe-0/0/0.3243, selected
          State: <Active Ext>
          Local AS:    34 Peer AS:   666
          Age: 43:41
          Task: BGP_666.84.10.110.1+179
          Announcement bits (2): 0-KRT 2-BGP RT Background
          AS path: 666 420 1282 I Aggregator: 1282 10.20.128.3
          Localpref: 100
          Router ID: 64.8.12.1
 BGP      Preference: 170/-101
          Next-hop reference count: 126
          Source: 84.10.109.8
          Next hop: 84.10.109.8 via fe-0/0/0.3233, selected
          State: <Ext>
          Inactive reason: Active preferred
          Local AS:    34 Peer AS:   1282
          Age: 4:36
          Task: BGP_1282.84.10.109.8+2957
          AS path: 1282 1282 1282 I Aggregator: 1282 10.30.1.1
          Localpref: 100
          Router ID: 10.30.1.1
 BGP      Preference: 170/-101
          Next-hop reference count: 126
          Source: 84.10.113.0
          Next hop: 84.10.113.0 via t1-0/0/2.0, selected
          State: <NotBest Ext>
          Inactive reason: Not Best in its group
          Local AS:    34 Peer AS:   1282
          Age: 4:32
          Task: BGP_1282.84.10.113.0+3127
          AS path: 1282 1282 1282 I Aggregator: 1282 10.30.1.1
          Localpref: 100
          Router ID: 10.30.1.1
```

a. When all else is equal, an EBGP speaker prefers the first route learned

b. When all else is equal, an IBGP speaker prefers the first route learned

c. When all else is equal, the router prefers the route with best preference

d. The AS path is shorter

Chapter Review Answers

1. Answer: D. The AS path attribute records each AS that a route update has passed through, and is updated on EBGP links. A BGP speaker discards received updates that contain the local ASN in the AS path.

2. Answer: B. The local preference attribute is evaluated early in the BGP decision process, before AS path, MED, origin, and so on.

3. Answer: B. The AS path attribute has global significance; once a value has been added, no other speaker can remove that ASN from the list because this would break BGP's loop prevention. The AS path is considered early in the selection process, and so has a good chance of impacting forwarding decisions in remote ASs. MED does not transit the peer AS, local preference is not supported on EBGP links, and communities can be stripped.

4. Answer: B. The next hop is unchanged on IBGP updates, but it is rewritten on EBGP links. EBGP does not require a full mesh, because the AS path is updated on EBGP links.

5. Answer: B. JUNOS software applies only the most specific policy applications, and a neighbor level is more specific than a group level, which is more specific than a global level. If you need a particular neighbor to execute what you consider a global, group, and neighbor policy, all three must be changed at the neighbor level.

6. Answer: A. The Idle state indicates an inability to route the session, and an established session is displayed with an x/x/x, for active, received, and damped routes, respectively.

7. Answer: B. The show route protocol bgp command shows all routes learned via BGP, not those from a given neighbor.

8. Answer: B. By filtering and setting attributes in received routes, you most directly impact how your network in turn sends to external destinations. Export policy is normally used to influence peers in the remote AS to affect your inbound policy goals.

9. Answer: A. Loopback-based peering requires that the router source the connection from its loopback interface to match the definition at the remote peer. A recursive route lookup is always required for a loopback-based peering because the remote router's loopback address can never be direct, and therefore must be resolved to a direct forwarding next hop via an IGP, to include a static route.

10. Answer: E. All of the options listed are true.

11. Answer: B. The local router's autonomous number is configured under routing options. The peer AS number is configured at the group or neighbor level for EBGP groups.

12. Answer: A. The RID and peering address tie breakers are replaced by first-learned for EBGP learned routes only. In this example, all three routes have the same local preference, global preference, and AS path length.

Access Security

This chapter discusses the techniques of securing the router via different types of access security. *Access security* is a broad term that includes the creation of users with various authorization levels or allowing access to particular services or networks. Also included in *access security* is verifying that the router has not been compromised and is performing as you expected. The topics covered include:

- Security concepts
- Securing access to the router
- Firewall filters and policers
- Spoof prevention
- Router monitoring

Security Concepts

Everybody wants to have a secure network, but providing that security is often a very complex and difficult process due to the multiple levels that need to be examined. For example, it does not do much good if you provide very detailed filters and access privileges on a router, when the physical access is an unlocked door in a wiring closet at a remote location. Security must not be an afterthought; it must be designed literally from the ground up, from physical access to the network to filters that allow only certain types of traffic. When implementing security at any layer, design toward the security concepts that are displayed in Figure 6-1: integrity, availability, and confidentiality. These concepts will help to build the network's circle of trust.

The first concept of security design is to ensure the *integrity* of the data. In other words, the data should not be altered in any way without purpose. This includes data that could be modified by unauthorized personnel, but does not exclude data manipulation by authorized personnel. Many network breaches are sourced from an "insider," someone who either works or did work for the company. This could be a disgruntled employee who decides to wreak havoc on the network because he never

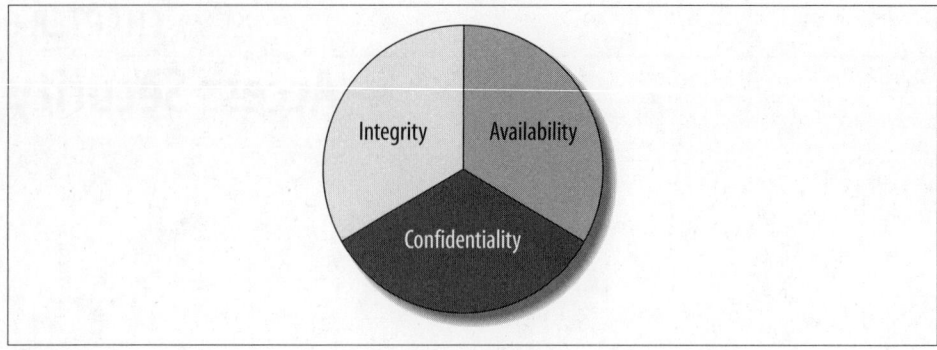

Figure 6-1. Security circle of trust

received his new office stapler! Also, data integrity implies that the data is consistent across internal and external access—that is, a user should not have the experience of making changes to a device from home only to discover that those changes were never propagated to the network.

The next concept is *availability*, which is *access* to reliable and consistent data. You can divide availability into two parts: data that needs to be accessible and the network elements to reach that system. This requires elements such as system redundancy, along with Out-of-Band (OoB) network access to routers and switches. For example, a router that is under a denial of service (DoS) attack may prevent remote access from one location to fail; however, is there another way to reach the router to thwart the attack? Design your network with the correct security tools; and most important, and often overlooked, make sure the tools actually work before disaster strikes. In other words, what good does it do to have protection in place if you cannot log in to the system to implement your tools or monitor and troubleshoot the devices? In recent years, horrible events such as terrorist attacks, earthquakes, and tsunamis have reopened many people's eyes to the importance of availability and redundancy.

Lastly is the *confidentiality* of the data; this means ensuring that unauthorized disclosure has not been unintentionally or intentionally given. In the modern age of thumb drives, BlackBerry devices, Treos, and PCs, the ability to access information has never been greater, and so are the security vulnerabilities. How many times have users left themselves logged in to a cybercafé somewhere? It takes just a few seconds for an evil network engineer lurking in the shadows to notice the open PC, log in to a router session that has been left open, delete the configuration, and walk away, ecstatic.

Are you getting scared yet? We hope so. A security expert without any fear is a very naïve one! Security must take a multiphase and dynamic approach; you will make mistakes, but the objective is to learn from those mistakes, use the tools available to you, and make the necessary corrections so that you avoid those mistakes later.

Always remember: security is a process and not an event! As Homer said, "Even a fool may be wise after the event." As we examine each topic in the remaining chapters, remember to think of the security circle of trust and where each feature fits and enables your security to be a circle without holes.

Summary of Security Concepts

Most people find the security concepts presented here to be somewhat common sense. The issue is that humans are inherently lazy, and security by its very definition tends to get in the way of our need to access information. The need for connectivity often overshadows the need to secure those communications, until the damage is done and it is too late to plug the holes. Always keep these security principles in mind when designing a new network or hardening an existing one.

The next section details ways to secure access to the router itself, which is a critical aspect of an overall security plan.

Securing Access to the Router

The goal of this chapter is to secure the network in Figure 6-2, which consists of three routers—Ale, PBR, and Bock—that are running Open Shortest Path First (OSPF) as the Interior Gateway Protocol (IGP). PBR connects to multiple Internet service providers (ISPs) via the Border Gateway Protocol (BGP). Various types of traffic are sent and received from the two ISPs, including web browsing, email, and a variety of remote accounting and engineering applications. The first step will be to secure access to Ale, PBR, and Bock so that only authorized users have access to each router.

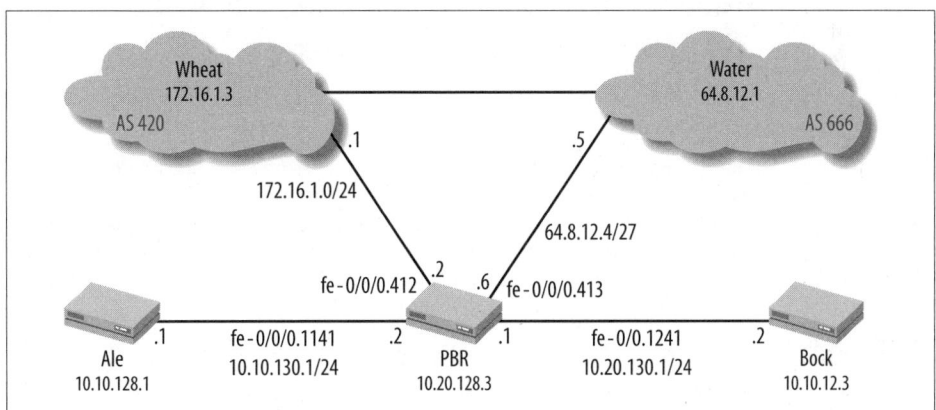

Figure 6-2. Network topology

User Authentication

There are two types of users on a Juniper Networks router—a nonroot user and a root user, both of which must be secured. Recall that user root is the only user who is predefined by default, accessible only via the console port without any default password. You must set a root password before the router will allow you to commit the configuration. To set up a root password, issue to the user the root-authentication keyword under the [edit system] level:

```
lab@Bock# set system root-authentication ?
Possible completions:
  + apply-groups          Groups from which to inherit configuration
                          data
  + apply-groups-except   Don't inherit configuration data from these
                          groups
    encrypted-password    Encrypted password string
    load-key-file         File (URL) containing one or more ssh keys
    plain-text-password   Prompt for plain text password (autoencrypted)
  > ssh-dsa               Secure shell (ssh) DSA public key string
  > ssh-rsa               Secure shell (ssh) RSA public key string
```

 Remember that user root is very powerful. When logged in as root, you are placed directly into the kernel in the form of a BSD shell! As a result, root can log in only via the console port, by default. You can enable Secure Shell (SSH) by using the set system services ssh root-login allow command.

The password can either be a plain-text password that will be encrypted automatically in the configuration, an SSH key, or an encrypted string for copying and pasting to other routers. In this case, a password of Bia&abi55a is supplied:

```
lab@Bock# set system root-authentication plain-text-password
New password:
Retype new password:
```

 When issuing a plain text password, JUNOS has some default requirements for password length and content. The password must be between six and 128 characters and must contain one change of case or special character. You can modify these defaults under [edit system password].

Once the password is set on Bock, it automatically becomes encrypted:

```
lab@Bock# show system root-authentication
encrypted-password "$1$ioLTVCdC$2jViYwTCG.kET399/uF/yO";
## SECRET-DATA
```

The encrypted string is now copied to other routers (PBR and Ale) without needing knowledge of the actual password:

```
lab@PBR# load merge terminal relative
[Type ^D at a new line to end input]
encrypted-password "$1$ioLTVCdC$2jViYwTCG.kET399/uF/yO";
## SECRET-DATA
load complete

[edit system root-authentication]
lab@PBR# show
encrypted-password "$1$ioLTVCdC$2jViYwTCG.kET399/uF/yO";
## SECRET-DATA
```

Next, nonroot users are configured. These users can be defined with local user pass-words and permissions, or an external server such as RADIUS or TACACS could be used. In either case, three items need to be configured for the user:

- Username
- Permissions
- Password

A user or user template must always be configured on the router, but the permissions and password could be configured on an external server. To illustrate the possible options, this scenario has the following six requirements:

1. Define two local users, doug and harry, and provide them with maximum access.

2. A group will be created for the NOC group consisting of 15 engineers. Each NOC engineer will have his own username, but will share the same permissions of read-only commands and maintenance commands for troubleshooting.

3. A group will be created for the design engineer group, consisting of three engineers. This group will have full access to all command-line interface (CLI) commands, except for the restart and request commands.

4. All users will be authenticated using a RADIUS server with a shared secret of "brianbosworth."

5. Authorization is defined on the local router.

6. If the RADIUS server is down, only harry and doug may log in to the router.

> One user that is not explored in this case study is the remote user. This is a user that could be created for use on the router if the authenticated user does not exist on the local router or if the authenticated user's record in the authentication server specifies a local user. You can think of this as a default fallback account.

Each user defined must be associated with a login class, which assigns the permissions for a user. The login class can be one of the four default classes listed in Table 6-1, or a custom-defined class.

Table 6-1. Predefined JUNOS user classes

Class	Permissions
superuser or super-user	All
read-only	View
operator	Clear, Network, Reset, Trace, View
unauthorized	None

Users harry and doug require maximum access, so it makes sense to use a predefined JUNOS software class called super-user. Here we show the step-by-step process for harry only, as user doug has identical steps:

```
lab@Ale# set system login user harry class super-user authentication
plain-text-password
New password:
Retype new password:

[edit]
lab@Ale# show system login
user harry {
    class super-user;
    authentication {
        encrypted-password "$1$oOspqmHP$jlxUulOcAgPq3j88/7WQP/";
        ## SECRET-DATA
    }
}
```

For brevity and sanity, the configuration examples show one router, but the reader should assume that the configuration is copied to all routers in the network.

Next, a group of 15 NOC engineers are defined. Since configuring 15 local users will be a pain to manage and tiresome to type, we will use a *user template*. A user template allows multiple users defined on the RADIUS server with unique passwords to be grouped to a single local Juniper user. Since a predefined class will not satisfy the authorization level for the NOC engineers of read-only and maintenance commands, we will define a custom class:

```
[edit system login]
lab@Ale# set class ops permissions [view maintenance trace]
```

Refer to the access-privilege technical documentation to see each command that is allowed for every permission setting.

Next, we assign the user ops the new class, also called ops:

```
[edit system login]
lab@Ale# set user ops class ops

[edit system login]
lab@Ale# show class ops
permissions [ trace view maintenance ];
lab@Ale# show user ops
uid 2000;
class ops;
```

The RADIUS server will then have 15 users defined that all map to the same Juniper-local user of ops. For example, the configuration for 2 of the 15 users using a RADIUS server would be similar to the following:

```
bruiser   Auth-Type = Local, Password = "iamaDog"
          Service-Type = Login-User,
          Juniper-Local-User-Name = "ops"

josh      Auth-Type = Local, Password = "plumper1"
          Service-Type = Login-User,
          Juniper-Local-User-Name = "ops"
```

The design engineer group requirement will also use a template but will make use of special allow and deny commands that we can also define in a class. If the permission bits that are set are too broad, we can deny individual commands within the permission settings. (And vice versa; if we need an additional command or set of commands that go beyond the permission setting, we can allow them.) These allow and deny statements could be a single command or a group of commands using regular expressions. They are also separated in allow or deny operational mode commands or configuration mode:

```
[edit system login]
lab@Ale# set class design ?
Possible completions:
  allow-commands        Regular expression for commands to allow explicitly
  allow-configuration   Regular expression for configure to allow explicitly
+ apply-groups          Groups from which to inherit configuration data
+ apply-groups-except   Don't inherit configuration data from these groups
  deny-commands         Regular expression for commands to deny explicitly
  deny-configuration    Regular expression for configure to deny explicitly
  idle-timeout          Maximum idle time before logout (minutes)
  login-alarms          Display system alarms when logging in
  login-tip             Display tip when logging in
+ permissions           Set of permitted operation categories
```

The design engineer's class will have the permission bits set to all, and all commands that start with *r* (request and restart) will be disallowed:

```
[edit system login]
lab@Ale# set class design permissions all
```

```
[edit system login]
lab@Ale# set class design deny-commands "^r.*$"

lab@Ale# set user design class design
```

 Regular expressions are beyond the scope of the book, but here is a list
of common operators:

- . (any character)
- * (zero or more characters)
- ^ (start of string to which the regex is applied)
- $ (end of string to which the regex is applied)
- ? (zero or one character)

As mentioned, we can define users locally on the router or on an external server such
as RADIUS or TACACS. In this chapter's case study, we specified a RADIUS server
earlier, in requirement 4. The RADIUS server's IP address and secret password are
configured:

```
[edit system]
design@Ale# set radius-server 10.20.130.5 secret brianbosworth
```

For the system to use the RADIUS server, we must configure the authentication-
order statement. This indicates which order of authentication method should be
used, with the default being the local router database only. In this section of our case
study, we must decide between the following configuration choices:

1. authentication-order [radius password]

2. authentication-order [radius]

In either configuration, the local database will be consulted if the RADIUS server is
down, so the difference between the two options is evident when the RADIUS server
returns a reject. This reject could be caused by a mistyped password or a username
that is not defined in the RADIUS server. In option 1, the RADIUS server returns the
reject and the local database will be consulted. Option 2 consults the local database
only if the RADIUS server is unresponsive; processing stops if the server returns a
reject message. The requirements state that the RADIUS server should always be
used when available (as specified in option 1). If the RADIUS server is not available,
users doug and harry will be allowed to log in using the local database since they are
the only users with locally defined passwords on the router. These users are also
defined on the RADIUS server:

```
doug    Auth-Type = Local, Password = "superbowlshuffle5"
        Service-Type = Login-User
```

Here is a complete system login configuration that meets all six of the criteria specified earlier:

```
[edit system]
design@Ale# show
host-name Ale;
authentication-order radius password;
ports {
    console type vt100;
}
root-authentication {
    encrypted-password "$1$85xXcov4$fLHtgMlqxRSg24zO8Kbe81"; ##
    SECRET-DATA
}
radius-server {
    10.20.130.5 secret "$9$KdgW87db24aUcydsg4Dj69AORSWLN24ZNd.5TFAt";
    ## SECRET-DATA
}
login {
    class design {
        permissions all;
        deny-commands "^r.*$";
    }
    class ops {
        permissions [ trace view maintenance ];
    }
    user design {
        uid 2004;
        class design;
    }

    user harry {
        uid 2001;
        class super-user;
        authentication {
            encrypted-password "$1$oOspqmHP$jlxUulOcAgPq3j88/7WQP/";
            ## SECRET-DATA
        }
    }
    user doug {
        uid 2003;
        class superuser;
        authentication {
            encrypted-password "$1$ocs3AXkS$JdlQW7z4ZIJblfFZD.fqH/";
            ## SECRET-DATA
        }
    }
    user ops {
        uid 2000;
        class ops;
    }
}
services {
    ftp;
    ssh;
    telnet;
```

```
    }
    syslog {
        user * {
            any emergency;
        }
        file messages {
            any notice;
            authorization info;
        }
        file config-changes {
            change-log any;
        }
    }
}
```

Lastly, to verify that the user has the correct permissions, log in to the router and
issue a show cli authorization command:

```
design@Ale> show cli authorization
Current user: 'design     ' class 'design'
Permissions:
    admin      -- Can view user accounts
    admin-control-- Can modify user accounts
    clear      -- Can clear learned network information
    configure  -- Can enter configuration mode
    control    -- Can modify any configuration
    edit       -- Can edit full files
    field      -- Special for field (debug) support
    floppy     -- Can read and write from the floppy
    interface  -- Can view interface configuration
    interface-control-- Can modify interface configuration
    network    -- Can access the network
    reset      -- Can reset/restart interfaces and daemons
    routing    -- Can view routing configuration
    routing-control-- Can modify routing configuration
    shell      -- Can start a local shell
    snmp       -- Can view SNMP configuration
    snmp-control-- Can modify SNMP configuration
    system     -- Can view system configuration
    system-control-- Can modify system configuration
    trace      -- Can view trace file settings
    trace-control-- Can modify trace file settings
    view       -- Can view current values and statistics
    maintenance -- Can become the super-user
    firewall   -- Can view firewall configuration
    firewall-control-- Can modify firewall configuration
    secret     -- Can view secret configuration
    secret-control-- Can modify secret configuration
    rollback   -- Can rollback to previous configurations
    security   -- Can view security configuration
    security-control-- Can modify security configuration
    access     -- Can view access configuration
    access-control-- Can modify access configuration
```

```
    view-configuration-- Can view all configuration (not including
    secrets)
Individual command authorization:
    Allow regular expression: none
    Deny regular expression: ^r.*$
    Allow configuration regular expression: none
    Deny configuration regular expression: none
```

Remote Access

After the users are configured on the router, we must decide what kind of remote access will be provided to the router, as all methods are disabled by default. Here are the possible options:

Dynamic Host Configuration Protocol (DHCP)

> Provides dynamic IP assignment from a pool of addresses to clients attached to the interface on a J-series router only. This option is most often used for the auto-installation feature.

Finger

> A protocol to get information about a user logged in to the router. This protocol is no longer used on a large scale and should never be enabled on the router:

```
% finger lab@10.20.128.3
[10.20.128.3]
Login: lab                          Name:
Directory: /var/home/lab            Shell: /usr/sbin/cli
On since Mon Sep 24 00:31 (UTC) on ttyd0, idle 0:01
No Mail.
No Plan.
%
```

FTP

> Provides file transfer services. Although FTP is a widely used protocol, it transfers files in plain text, which can lead to security issues. When possible, you should use secure copy (SCP).

Rlogin

> The Remote login protocol, which allows remote login to the CLI. This Unix utility has several security flaws and was used only in private environments. This utility is enabled by a hidden command on the router and should never be enabled on the router.

 A *hidden command* is a command that does not show up when you use ? in the CLI and does not autocomplete with the Space bar. One of the most famous hidden commands in JUNOS software is show version and haiku. Try it yourself if you want to read some really bad poetry!

SSH

Allows for two devices to communicate over an encrypted tunnel. This ensures not only availability, but also data integrity and confidentiality. When SSH is enabled, this automatically enables SCP.

Telnet

A common protocol to remotely manage a system developed in 1969. Telnet transits all data in clear text, so you should use SSH when possible.

Web management

Enables the use of the jweb web GUI on the router for management and configuration. These can be either encrypted or unencrypted Hypertext Transfer Protocol (HTTP) connections.

JUNOScript server

Enables the router to receive commands from a JUNOScript server via clear text or Secure Sockets Layer (SSL) connections.

Netconf

The Network Configuration protocol, which is defined in RFC 4741 and uses XML for configuration and messages. Netconf is the Internet Engineering Task Force (IETF) standard created as a replacement for the Simple Network Management Protocol (SNMP) and is based on JUNOScript.

The most secure methods of remote access on the router will be SSH and transferring files using SCP. To enable any service, simply set it under the [edit system services] directory:

```
[edit system services]
lab@Ale# set ?
Possible completions:
+ apply-groups          Groups from which to inherit configuration
                        data
+ apply-groups-except   Don't inherit configuration data from these
                        groups
> dhcp                  Configure DHCP server
> finger                Allow finger requests from remote systems
> ftp                   Allow FTP file transfers
> netconf               Allow NETCONF connections
> service-deployment    Configuration for Service Deployment (SDXD)
                        management application
> ssh                   Allow ssh access
> telnet                Allow telnet login
> web-management        Web management configuration
> xnm-clear-text        Allow clear text-based JUNOScript connections
> xnm-ssl               Allow SSL-based JUNOScript connections
```

Each service will have a variety of options, such as setting a maximum number of connections, rate-limiting the inbound connections, and choosing a certain protocol version.

XML Tags

JUNOScript is a tool you can use to configure and manage the router. Every JUNOS output and configuration contains XML tags that can be referenced by a JUNOScript client. Here is an example of a configuration and an operational command that displays the XML tags for each field:

```
lab@PBR> show system users | display xml
<rpc-reply xmlns:junos="http://xml.juniper.net/junos/8.0R2/junos">
    <system-users-information xmlns="http://xml.juniper.net/junos/
    8.0R2/junos">
        <uptime-information>
            <date-time junos:seconds="1190796857">8:54AM</date-time>
            <up-time junos:seconds="207372">2 days,  9:36</up-time>
            <active-user-count junos:format="1 user">1</active-user-
            count>
            <load-average-1>0.06</load-average-1>
            <load-average-5>0.02</load-average-5>
            <load-average-15>0.00</load-average-15>
            <user-table>
                <user-entry>
                    <user>lab</user>
                    <tty>d0</tty>
                    <from>-</from>
                    <login-time junos:seconds="1190593874">Mon12AM</login-time>
                    <idle-time junos:seconds="0">-</idle-time>
                    <command>-cli (cli)</command>
                </user-entry>
            </user-table>
        </uptime-information>
    </system-users-information>
    <cli>
        <banner></banner>
    </cli>
</rpc-reply>

lab@PBR> show configuration routing-options | display xml
<rpc-reply xmlns:junos="http://xml.juniper.net/junos/8.0R2/junos">
    <configuration>
        <routing-options>
            <static>
            <route>
                    <name>10.10.128.1/32</name>
                    <next-hop>10.10.111.1</next-hop>
            </route>
            </static>
        </routing-options>
    </configuration>
    <cli>
        <banner></banner>
    </cli>
```

```
lab@Ale# set system services ssh ?
Possible completions:
  <[Enter]>              Execute this command
+ apply-groups           Groups from which to inherit configuration data
+ apply-groups-except    Don't inherit configuration data from these groups
  connection-limit       Maximum number of allowed connections (1..250)
+ protocol-version       Specify ssh protocol versions supported
  rate-limit             Maximum number of connections per minute
                         (1..250)
  root-login             Configure root access via ssh
  |                      Pipe through a command
```

In this case, SSH is enabled on the router using the default parameters of 150 connection attempts and 75 active sessions per minute:

```
[edit]
lab@Ale# set system services ssh
```

Bock then initiates a session to Ale. The first connection will need to establish the RSA fingerprint for authentication:

```
lab@Bock> ssh 10.10.128.1
The authenticity of host '10.10.128.1 (10.10.128.1)' can't be
established.
RSA key fingerprint is 5d:f5:51:91:51:0e:ff:54:0c:f4:0a:07:51:3b:70:3a.
Are you sure you want to continue connecting (yes/no)? yes
Warning: Permanently added '10.10.128.1' (RSA) to the list of known
hosts.
lab@10.10.128.1's password:
--- JUNOS 8.0R2.8 built 2006-09-29 09:22:36 UTC
lab@Ale> exit

Connection to 10.10.128.1 closed.
```

However, once Ale is added to the list of known hosts, future sessions do not require reverification:

```
lab@Bock> ssh 10.10.128.1
lab@10.10.128.1's password:
--- JUNOS 8.0R2.8 built 2006-09-29 09:22:36 UTC
lab@Ale>
```

When SSH is enabled on the router, it also automatically enables SCP to initiate secure file exchanges. You can upload or download files using variations of the file copy command. In this case, PBR transfers a file called *test* to Ale. PBR must add Ale into its good hosts file:

```
lab@PBR> file copy test lab@10.10.128.1:test.txt
The authenticity of host '10.10.128.1 (10.10.128.1)' can't be
established.
RSA key fingerprint is 5d:f5:51:91:51:0e:ff:54:0c:f4:0a:07:51:3b:70:3a.
Are you sure you want to continue connecting (yes/no)? yes
Warning: Permanently added '10.10.128.1' (RSA) to the list of
known hosts.
```

```
lab@10.10.128.1's password:
test                               100% 9480      9.3KB/s   00:00
```

After Ale is learned as a host, future transfers will pass the authentication check because both Ale and PBR know each other as trusted hosts:

```
lab@PBR> file copy test2 lab@10.10.128.1:test2.txt
lab@10.10.128.1's password:
test                               100% 9480      9.3KB/s   00:00
```

Summary of Access Security

Routers are the very fabric of any IP-based network, making it critical that access be limited to only those users that are authorized to access the system, and only for those tasks they are authorized to perform. JUNOS software provides a variety of tools, ranging from local and remote authentication and authorization to secure access and file transfer protocols, which make it easy to secure the router from unauthorized access and many forms of DoS attacks.

The next section details packet-based (stateless) firewall filtering and policing capabilities, which are another critical aspect of a total security solution.

Firewall Filters

To protect the router, you can deploy packet filters to allow only certain traffic into the router's control plane (Routing Engine [RE]). These filters have different names on each router OS, but they still operate in the same stateless manner. On a Cisco device, these filters are called *access lists*, and on a Juniper router, they are called *firewall filters*. These filters look similar to the policy we discussed in Chapter 3; however, filters operate on the actual data-forwarding plane. Table 6-2 provides a comparison of the two features.

Table 6-2. Firewall filters versus routing policies

Feature	Firewall filter	Routing policy
Operates in…	Forwarding plane	Control plane
Match keyword	from	from
Action keyword	then	then
Match attributes	Packet fields	Route attributes
Default action	Discard	Depends on default policy
Applied to…	Interfaces	Routing protocols/tables
Named terms required	Yes	No
Chains allowed	Yes	Yes
Absence of from statement	Match all	Match all

Firewall filter syntax takes a human-friendly, intuitive form:

```
firewall {
    family inet {
        filter filter-1 {
            term term-1 {
                from {
                    protocol tcp;
                    destination-port telnet;
                }
                then {
                    accept;
                }
            }
        }
    }
}
```

This filter matches on Telnet traffic and accepts the packets. As observed, the syntax is very similar to a routing policy with the match conditions in the `from` term and the actions specified in a `then` term.

Filter Processing

Similar to a policy, a filter is made up of multiple terms, and each term is examined in the order listed. If there is a match in a term and there is a terminating action, no other term is examined (see Figure 6-3). Terminating actions are:

accept
: Allows the packet through the filter

discard
: Silently discards the packet

reject
: Discards the packet with an Internet Control Message Protocol (ICMP) error message (the default is administratively prohibited)

Action modifier
: Any action modifier, such as `log`, `count`, `syslog`, and so on

 The presence of an action modifier such as count without an explicit accept, discard, or reject will result in a default action of accept. If the desired action is to discard or reject the packet, it must be explicitly configured.

If the packet does not match any terms in the filter it is discarded.

You also can apply multiple filters to the interface, and in this case it operates in the same fashion down the filter list until there is a terminating action. If no match occurred in the filter list, the packet is discarded (see Figure 6-4).

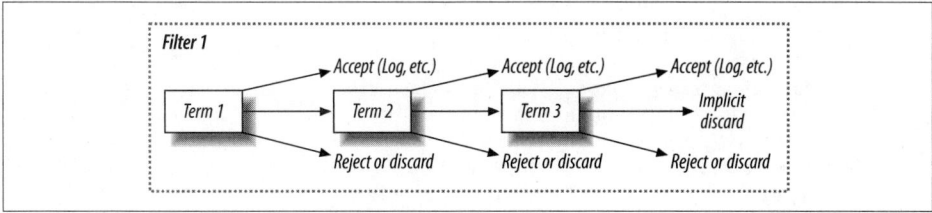

Figure 6-3. Filter processing

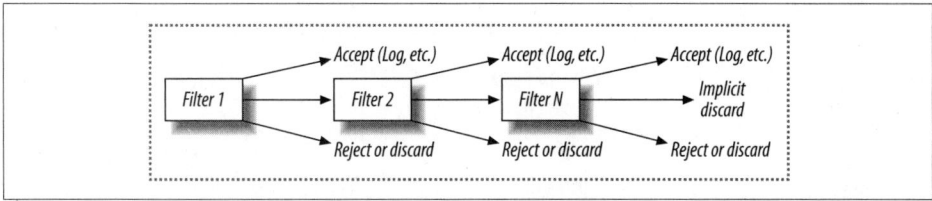

Figure 6-4. Filter chaining

Filter Match Conditions

When examining the possible match conditions, the general rule of thumb is that if it is a field in the IP, Transmission Control Protocol (TCP), User Datagram Protocol (UDP), or ICMP header, it is probably a potential match:

```
lab@PBR# set firewall family inet filter foo term 1 from ?
Possible completions:
> address              Match IP source or destination address
+ apply-groups         Groups from which to inherit configuration
                       data
+ apply-groups-except  Don't inherit configuration data from these
                       groups
> destination-address  Match IP destination address
+ destination-port     Match TCP/UDP destination port
+ destination-port-except  Do not match TCP/UDP destination port
  destination-prefix-list  Match IP destination prefixes in named
                           list
+ dscp                 Match Differentiated Services (DiffServ) code
                       point
+ dscp-except          Do not match Differentiated Services (DiffServ)
                       code point
+ esp-spi              Match IPSec ESP SPI value
+ esp-spi-except       Do not match IPSec ESP SPI value
  first-fragment       Match if packet is the first fragment
+ forwarding-class     Match forwarding class
+ forwarding-class-except  Do not match forwarding class
  fragment-flags       Match fragment flags
+ fragment-offset      Match fragment offset
+ fragment-offset-except  Do not match fragment offset
+ icmp-code            Match ICMP message code
+ icmp-code-except     Do not match ICMP message code
+ icmp-type            Match ICMP message type
```

```
+ icmp-type-except       Do not match ICMP message type
> interface              Match interface name
+ interface-group        Match interface group
+ interface-group-except Do not match interface group
> interface-set          Match interface in set
+ ip-options             Match IP options
+ ip-options-except      Do not match IP options
  is-fragment            Match if packet is a fragment
+ packet-length          Match packet length
+ packet-length-except   Do not match packet length
+ port                   Match TCP/UDP source or destination port
+ port-except            Do not match TCP/UDP source or destination
                         port
+ precedence             Match IP precedence value
+ precedence-except      Do not match IP precedence value
> prefix-list            Match IP source or destination prefixes in
                         named list
+ protocol               Match IP protocol type
+ protocol-except        Do not match IP protocol type
> source-address         Match IP source address
+ source-port            Match TCP/UDP source port
+ source-port-except     Do not match TCP/UDP source port
> source-prefix-list     Match IP source prefixes in named list
  tcp-established        Match packet of an established TCP connection
  tcp-flags              Match TCP flags
  tcp-initial            Match initial packet of a TCP connection
+ ttl                    Match IP ttl type
+ ttl-except             Do not match IP ttl type
```

The match conditions fall into three general categories: numeric, address, and bit field matches (see Table 6-3).

Table 6-3. General match conditions

Numeric matches	Address matches	Bit fields
Protocol fields	Source address	IP options
Port numbers	Destination address	TCP flags
Class of service (CoS) fields	Source-prefix lists	IP fragmentation
ICMP type codes	Destination-prefix lists	Time to Live (TTL)

A term can have zero or many match conditions specified. The absence of a from statement creates a match all condition, whereas multiple match conditions are treated as a logical AND or OR depending on common versus uncommon match conditions. A common match is treated as a logical OR, which the router will group together in square brackets. The filter example matches on TCP or UDP packets:

```
filter example {
    term common {
        from {
            protocol [ tcp udp ];
        }
```

```
        }
    }
```

An uncommon match is treated as a logical AND. You can combine these logical ANDs and ORs in the same term with limitless possibilities. Adding to the example, the following filter matches on TCP or UDP packets and port 123:

```
filter example {
    term common {
        from {
            protocol [ tcp udp ];
            port 123;
        }
    }
}
```

Also, numeric matches such as port or protocol values can either take the numeric match or the more user-friendly keywords. For example, the first term and second term of the filter called same are equivalent, but the second term is written in a more efficient and user-friendly method:

```
firewall {
    filter same {
        term numbers {
            from {
                protocol 6;
                port 23;
            }
            then accept;
        }
        term user-friendly {
            from {
                protocol tcp;
                port telnet;
            }
            then accept;
        }
    }
}
```

 Bit field matching such as IP options and TCP flags also support numeric values or more user-friendly terms. In these cases, the numeric support must be written in hex format, so a TCP flag match for SYN packets could be written with the keyword syn or the value 0x2. No reason to break out the hex converter—make life easy and use the keywords!

Can your mother read this?

When writing a filter, always try to adhere to the KISS (Keep It Short and Simple) method. An individual security element may not be that difficult, but when combined with other security functions as a whole, it can contribute to a large web of complexity.

In other words, try to create a filter that the average network engineer can understand without compromising any security. A great start to reach this goal is to use the alpha names for protocol, port numbers, and bit fields instead of the actual numerical values. Additionally, JUNOS has even more to offer using text synonyms to map common bit mappings. These allow the casual reader to quickly understand a filter at a glance and avoid panicked and hysterical research to find what service maps to a numerical value (see Table 6-4).

Table 6-4. Text synonyms

Text synonym	Match equivalent	Common use
first-fragment	Offset = 0, MF = 1.	Match on the first fragment of a packet for counting and logging.
is-fragment	Offset does not equal zero.	Protect from fragmented DoS attacks.
tcp-established	ACK or RST.	Allow only established TCP sessions over an interface. This option does not implicitly check that the protocol is TCP. Use the TCP match condition.
tcp-initial	SYN and not ACK.	Allow sessions to be initiated either inbound or outbound.

Filter Actions

Besides the terminating actions that we already discussed (accept, discard, and reject), other action modifiers are commonly used. These include:

count <counter name>
> Counts the total number of packets and bytes that match a term. You can view counters with the show firewall command.

log
> Records the packet header information and stores the information in memory on the router, which limits the size to approximately 400 entries and clears upon a router reboot. To view the log, issue a show firewall log command.

syslog
> Records the packet header information and stores the log into a file or sends it to a syslog server. The syslog facility of the firewall will allow any local file to be created for this information.

policer
> Rate-limits traffic based on bandwidth and burst size limits (discussed later in this chapter).

forwarding-class
> Sends packets to a forwarding class, which maps to a queue.

sample
> Creates cflowd export records.

`next term`

Allows packets to match a term and then move on to the next term listed. Since the presence of any action modifier implies an accept, this action allows packets to pass through to the next term. This is often deployed when all packets need to be counted before being rejected farther in the chain.

Applying a Filter

The final step after writing the filter is to actually apply it to the interface. You can apply filters to either transit or nontransit traffic. To apply a filter to transit traffic, apply the filter to any Packet Forwarding Engine (PFE) interface as either an input or an output filter or as part of a list of filters. Filters are applied on a logical unit basis:

```
lab@hops# set interfaces fe-0/0/0 unit 0 family inet filter ?
Possible completions:
+ apply-groups          Groups from which to inherit configuration data
+ apply-groups-except   Don't inherit configuration data from these groups
  group                 Group to which interface belongs
  input                 Name of filter applied to received packets
+ input-list            List of filter modules applied to received packets
  output                Name of filter applied to transmitted packets
+ output-list           List of filter modules applied to transmitted packets
```

 You can apply a single filter with the input or output command, or a list with input-list or output-list, so why the option for both? Historically in JUNOS, only a single filter could be applied per direction per unit, but in later code the concept of a list was created. It is recommended that even if just a single filter is being applied to an interface, to use the list command. This adds flexibility in adding more filters to the chain at a later time.

To protect traffic to the router itself (local traffic), you can apply a filter of filter-list to the loopback interface (see Figure 6-5). Local traffic is any packet that is destined to the router itself, such as routing protocols, ICMP, SSH, and other management protocols.

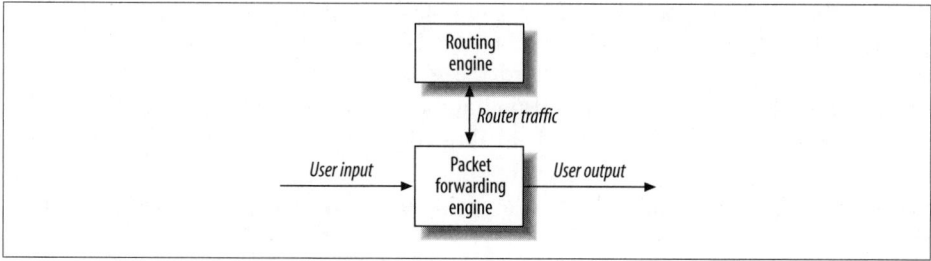

Figure 6-5. Transit versus loopback filters

Case Study: Transit Filters

It is common to see a filter applied to the router's connection to the Internet. Before sitting down to begin typing away on the router, always write down the goals of the filter. In this case study, all outbound traffic from the network to the Internet is allowed while some traffic from the Internet will be filtered. The goals here are as follows:

- TCP connections are only allowed to be initiated outbound to the Internet, except to access a local web server.
- No fragmented ICMP or UDP packets should be allowed.
- TCP fragments are allowed.
- UDP packets should be allowed inbound for traceroutes and return traffic for outbound UDP connections.
- Ping and traceroute are allowed outbound.
- Traceroute is allowed inbound.

First create a prefix list for the internal subnets, which in this case are as follows:

```
10.10.128/22
10.20.128/22
10.10.12/22
[edit]
lab@PBR# set policy-options prefix-list internal-subnets 10.10.128/22

[edit]
lab@PBR# set policy-options prefix-list internal-subnets 10.20.128/22

[edit]
lab@PBR# set policy-options prefix-list internal-subnets 10.20.12/22

lab@PBR# show policy-options prefix-list internal-subnets
10.10.128.0/22;
10.10.12.0/22;
10.20.128.0/22;
```

Now the filter called `internet-in` will be examined with each term explained to match on the five goals stated at the beginning of this case study. First, we define our first term to allow established TCP sessions inbound, which are destined for internal subnets in the first term. The keyword `tcp-established` allows only packets with a TCP flag of `ack` or `rst`. As a result of the implicit deny, all at the end of the filter list, this term will also accomplish task 1, in allowing only outbound TCP sessions. Also, the `fragment-offset` keyword allows for unfragmented packets or first packet fragments to be received as only the first fragmented packet has the headers needed for the check:

```
lab@PBR# show firewall family inet
filter internet-in {
    term allow-established-tcp-sessions {
```

```
    from {
        destination-prefix-list {
            internal-subnets;
        }
        fragment-offset 0;
        tcp-established;
        protocol tcp;
    }
    then accept;
}
```

Next, TCP connections are allowed to the web server at 10.20.12.9 using port numbers https (443) and 8080. Port 80 connections are not allowed toward this web server to add an additional layer of security:

```
term allow-webserver-connections {
    from {
        destination-address {
            10.20.12.9/32;
        }
        protocol tcp;
        destination-port [  https 8080 ];
    }
    then accept;
}
```

UDP and ICMP fragments are denied as these types of packets are normally used in popular DoS attacks. The fragment-offset command is matching on all ICMP and UDP fragments, including the first packet. If is-fragment and first-fragment were used, two terms would have been required:

```
term deny-udp-icmp-frags {
    from {
        fragment-offset 0-8191;
        protocol [ icmp udp ];
    }
    then {
        discard;
    }
}
```

TCP fragments are allowed, however. Recall that the is-fragment keyword matches on all fragments except the first fragment, which was matched in the first term of the filter:

```
term allow-tcp-frags {
    from {
        is-fragment;
        protocol tcp;
    }
    then {
        accept;
    }
}
```

Next, incoming UDP packets are allowed to internal subnets that are not fragments. This is to allow return traffic for outbound UDP sessions as well as inbound traceroute packets that use UDP inbound:

```
term allow-udp {
    from {
        destination-prefix-list {
            internal-subnets;
        }
        protocol udp;
    }
    then accept;
}
```

Lastly, ping and traceroute are allowed outbound. Since this is an input filter, the return traffic is actually being allowed in for both ping (echo replies) and traceroute (time exceed messages). Additionally, unreachable messages are allowed in for any possible outbound error responses:

```
term allow-some-icmp-outbound {
    from {
        destination-prefix-list {
            internal-subnets;
        }
        protocol icmp;
        icmp-type [ echo-reply time-exceeded unreachable ];
    }
    then accept;
}
}
```

The filter is applied to both WAN interfaces on router PBR as the input list of one to allow for filter additions at a later date:

```
lab@PBR# show interfaces
fe-0/0/0 {
    vlan-tagging;
    unit 412 {
        description PBR-to-Wheat;
        vlan-id 412;
        family inet {
            rpf-check;
            filter {
                input-list internet-in;
            }
            address 172.16.1.2/24;
        }
    }
    unit 413 {
        description PBR-to-Water;
        vlan-id 413;
        family inet {
            rpf-check fail-filter match-spoofs;
            filter {
```

```
                    input-list internet-in;              }
            address 64.8.12.6/27;
```

Case Study: Loopback Filters

Next, traffic destined to the router itself needs to be secured. The goals of this case study are to allow:

- OSPF traffic
- BGP traffic from configured peers only
- SSH from internal subnets
- Virtual Router Redundancy Protocol (VRRP) packets
- Ping and traceroute
- Domain Name System (DNS) replies
- SNMP and Network Time Protocol (NTP)

First, define a prefix list for the internal subnets in your network:

```
lab@PBR# show policy-options
prefix-list internal-subnets {
    10.10.128.0/22;
    10.10.12.0/22;
    10.20.128.0/22;
}
```

Since BGP traffic should be from configured peers only, the apply-path command is used to avoid any IP change issues or neighbor additions that may happen in the future. The apply-path allows configuration elements to be matched when the prefix-list is applied by using regular expressions. In this case, this will create a list of BGP peers for every BGP group configured due to the match all * regular expression:

```
prefix-list bgp-configured-peers {
    apply-path "protocols bgp group <*> neighbor <*>";
}
```

The filter protect-router is created with the first term allowing SSH traffic to *and* from the router due to the port command, which matches on either the source or destination port:

```
filter protect-router {
    term allow-ssh {
        from {
            source-prefix-list {
                internal-subnets;
            }
            protocol tcp;
            port ssh;
        }
        then accept;
    }
```

Create a term to allow for OSPF packets:

```
term allow-ospf {
    from {
        protocol ospf;
    }
    then accept;
}
```

Then take advantage of the prefix list that was previously created to allow only the configured BGP peer's traffic:

```
term allow-bgp {
    from {
        source-prefix-list {
            bgp-configured-peers;
        }
        protocol tcp;
        port bgp;
    }
    then accept;
}
```

Allow VRRP traffic:

```
term allow-vrrp {
    from {
        protocol vrrp;
    }
    then accept;
}
```

Don't forget about DNS replies. Since these are stateless, filter the return traffic so that DNS resolution is allowed in:

```
term dns-replies {
    from {
        protocol udp;
        source-port 53;
    }
    then accept;
}
```

SNMP is allowed:

```
term snmp {
    from {
        protocol udp;
        port [ snmp snmptrap ];
    }
    then accept;
}
```

Also allowed are UDP packets with a TTL of 1 for traceroute to operate:

```
term traceroute {
    from {
```

```
                    protocol udp;
                    ttl 1;
                }
            then accept;
        }
```

Allow pings, traceroutes, and error messages:

```
        term allow-icmp {
            from {
                protocol icmp;
                icmp-type [ echo-request echo-reply time-exceeded
                unreachable ];
            }
            then accept;
        }
```

NTP is also allowed:

```
        term allow-ntp {
            from {
                prefix-list {
                    internal-subnets;
                }
                protocol udp;
                port ntp;
            }
            then accept;
        }
```

Lastly, there is a term that denies all other traffic (which is the default) but allows this traffic to be counted as well as logged to a syslog file:

```
        term match-denied {
            then {
                count bad-packets;
                syslog;
                discard;
            }
        }
    }
}
```

The filter is then applied to the loopback interface as an input filter. Even though it is just a single filter, it is added as a list for future expansion:

```
    lab@PBR# set interface lo0.0 family inet filter input-list
    protect-router
```

This is a good point to dust off the commit confirmed to make sure the filter does not break the current network or, worse yet, lock you out of the router:

```
    [edit]
    lab@PBR# commit confirmed
    commit confirmed will be automatically rolled back in 10 minutes unless
    confirmed
    commit complete
```

```
# commit confirmed will be rolled back in 10 minutes
[edit]
lab@PBR# commit
commit complete
```

Policers

To rate-limit traffic entering an interface, you can deploy a *policer*. The policers that are implemented in the Juniper router are token-based and use the IP packet to limit based on bandwidth and bursts. The bandwidth is measured as the average number of bits in over a one-second interval (see Figure 6-6). The burst size is the number of bytes that can exceed the bandwidth constraints.

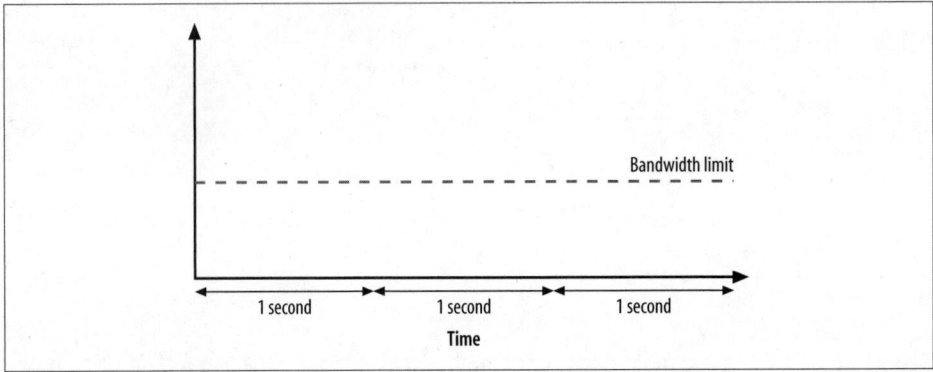

Figure 6-6. Bandwidth limit

The burst size is what implements the policer's "token"-based behavior. The burst size will set the initial and maximum sizes of a bucket in bytes (tokens) that would be accessed each time data needs to be sent. As a packet is sent, the bucket bytes (tokens) are removed from the bucket. If there are not enough tokens to send the packet, the packet will be policed. The bucket is then replenished at the bandwidth rate.

In Figure 6-7, a packet that bursts above the bandwidth limit is nonetheless sent, as there are enough tokens in the bucket. After the packet is sent, the tokens are decreased based on the packet size.

Then, some time later, another packet needs to be sent that is also above the bandwidth limit. Since there are no longer enough tokens left in the bucket, the packet is policed (see Figure 6-8).

As time goes by, the bucket will replenish at a rate equal to the bandwidth limit. When a new packet arrives, it can be sent, as tokens are now available in the bucket. This process continues over a one-second interval, and the result is a rate equal to the bandwidth limit (see Figure 6-9).

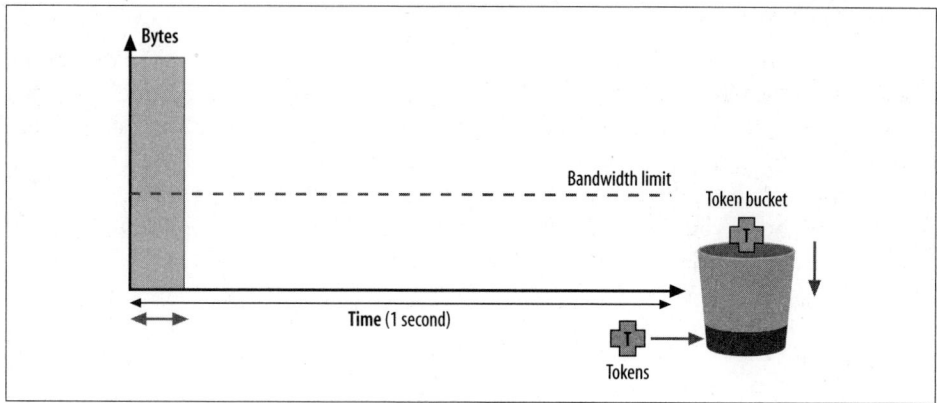

Figure 6-7. Initial burst

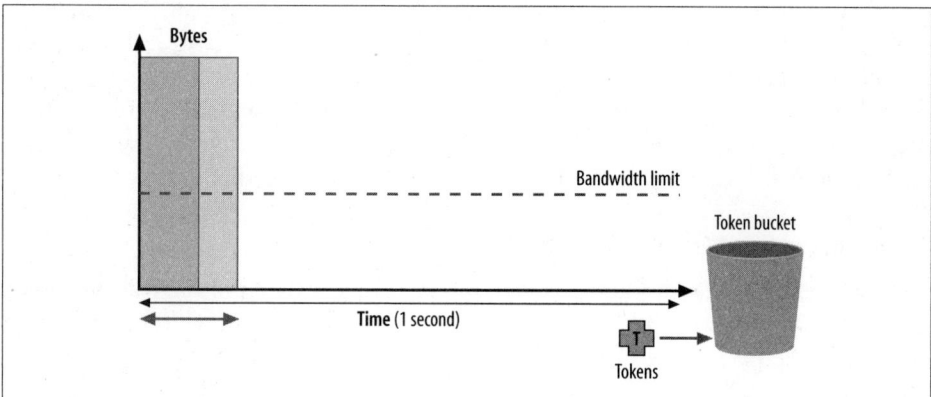

Figure 6-8. Empty token bucket

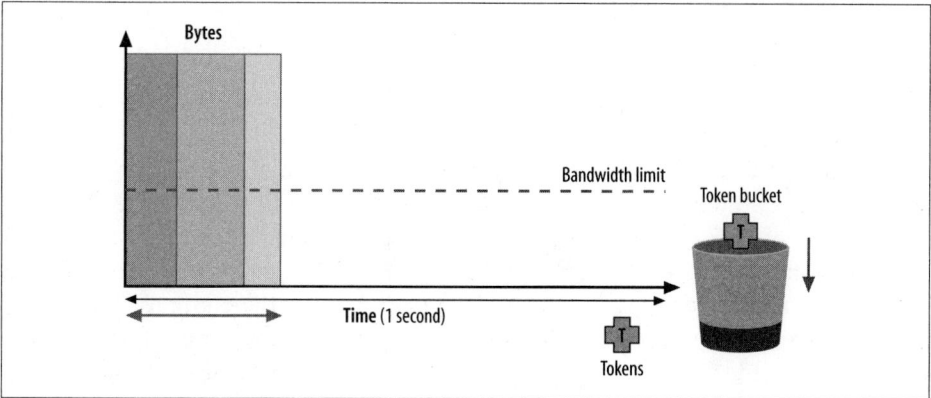

Figure 6-9. Token bucket replenishing

Burst-size limit mystery

The setting of the burst size has always seemed to be a mystery for many operators. Set this value too low, and potentially all packets will be policed. Set the value too high, and no packets will be policed. The rule of thumb is that the burst size should never be lower than 10 times the maximum transmission unit (MTU). The recommended value is to set the amount of traffic that can be sent over the interface in five milliseconds. So, if your interface is a Fast Ethernet interface, the minimum is 15,000 bytes (10 * 1,500), and the recommended value would be 62,500 bytes (12,500 bytes/ ms * 5).

Policer actions

Once the policer limits have been configured, you must choose the action taken if a packet exceeds the policer. Two types of policing are available: *soft* policing and *hard* policing. Hard policing specifies that the packet will be dropped if it exceeds the policer's traffic profile. Soft policing simply marks the packet or reclassifies the packet, which could change the probability of the packet being dropped at the egress interface during times of congestion. Soft policing is implemented by either setting the packet loss priority (PLP) setting on the packet or by placing the packet into a different forwarding class. We will examine these concepts further in Chapter 9.

Configuring and applying policers

Policers are configured under the [edit firewall] level. The policer will be named and then the burst size will be applied in bytes/second, the bandwidth limit in bits/ second, or the percentage of interface bandwidth set along with the policer action. For example:

```
policer simple {
    if-exceeding {
        bandwidth-limit 50m;
        burst-size-limit 15k;
    }
    then discard;
}
```

Once you have configured the policer, you must apply it to an interface. You can do this in one of two ways: either by applying the policer directly underneath the interface or by referencing the policer name in the firewall filter. If you apply the policer directly to the interface, no match conditions can be used. If you reference the policer in a filter, specific types of traffic can be policed as the entire toolkit of filter actions is allowed. You can apply both an interface policer and a policer in a filter at the same time. In this case, a kind of hierarchical policing is used as interface policers are evaluated before input filters and after output filters. Figure 6-10 shows policer processing.

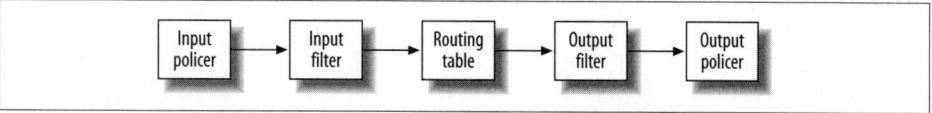

Figure 6-10. Policer processing

Since you can apply the same filter to multiple interfaces, you can apply the same policer to multiple interfaces. In this case, the aggregate bandwidth of all the interfaces is examined before any policing parameters. To avoid this behavior and create a separate instance for each interface, include the interface-specific command in the filter. This will create unique policers and counters for each interface to which the filter is applied.

Policer example

In this section, we will examine a very simple two-level policer that:

- Limits virtual LAN (VLAN) 1241 to 1 MB with a burst size of 5,000 bytes
- Limits FTP to 10% of the bandwidth and ICMP to 500,000 bits per second

First, the policers are defined under the firewall level:

```
lab@Bock# show firewall
policer total-int {
    if-exceeding {
        bandwidth-limit 1m;
        burst-size-limit 5k;
    }
    then discard;
}
policer limit-ftp {
    if-exceeding {
        bandwidth-percent 10;
        burst-size-limit 500k;
    }
    then discard;
}
policer police-icmp {
    if-exceeding {
        bandwidth-limit 500k;
        burst-size-limit 500k;
    }
    then discard;
}
```

Then a filter is created to match on FTP and ICMP traffic to limit each application to certain thresholds. The interface-specific keyword is used to create a unique instance if the filter if applied to multiple interfaces. This is required if a policer is referenced that uses bandwidth percentage such as the limit-ftp policer:

```
firewall {
    family inet {
        filter police-traffic {
            interface-specific;
            term police-ftp {
                from {
                    protocol tcp;
                    port [ ftp ftp-data ];
                }
                then policer limit-ftp;
            }
            term police-icmp {
                from {
                    protocol icmp;
                }
                then policer police-icmp;
            }
            term catch-all {
                then accept;
            }
        }
    }
}
```

Apply the filter and policer to the interface:

```
lab@Bock# show interfaces fe-0/0/0
vlan-tagging;
unit 1241 {
    description Bock-to-PBR;
    vlan-id 1241;
    family inet {
        filter {
            input-list police-traffic;
        }
        policer {
            input total-int;
        }
        address 10.20.130.1/24;
    }
}
```

To verify whether the policer is applied, issue a show interfaces policers command:

```
lab@Bock> show interfaces policers
Interface       Admin Link Proto Input Policer      Output Policer
fe-0/0/0        up    up
fe-0/0/0.1241   up    up   inet  total-int-fe-0/0/0.1241-inet-i
gr-0/0/0        up    up
ip-0/0/0        up    up
ls-0/0/0        up    up
lt-0/0/0        up    up
mt-0/0/0        up    up
pd-0/0/0        up    up
pe-0/0/0        up    up
```

```
sp-0/0/0          up    up
sp-0/0/0.16383    up    up    inet
fe-0/0/1          up    up
fe-0/0/1.100      up    up    inet
t1-0/0/2          up    up
t1-0/0/2.0        up    down  inet
t1-0/0/3          up    up
dsc               up    up
gre               up    up
ipip              up    up
loo               up    up
loo.0             up    up    inet
loo.16385         up    up    inet
lsi               up    up
mtun              up    up
pimd              up    up
pime              up    up
pp0               up    up
tap               up    up
```

To examine whether packets are exceeding the traffic parameters, view the policer counters. For interface policers, you can see packet counts with the show policer command:

```
lab@Bock> show policer total-int-fe-0/0/0.1241-inet-i
Policers:
Name                                          Packets
total-int-fe-0/0/0.1241-inet-i                      5
```

Policers that are referenced in a firewall filter automatically get counters created for them based on the policer name, interface applied, and direction. You can view these in the same command as normal counters for filters, with the show firewall command:

```
lab@Bock> show firewall
Filter: fe-0/0/0.1241-i
Policers:
Name                                          Packets
police-icmp-police-icmp-fe-0/0/0.1241-i             0
limit-ftp-police-ftp-fe-0/0/0.1241-i               0
Filter: __default_bpdu_filter__
Filter: police-traffic
Policers:
Name                                          Packets
police-icmp-police-icmp                             0
limit-ftp-police-ftp                                0
```

A difficulty is determining how much traffic the policer is allowing to ascertain if the exceeding parameters are too large or too small. You can do this using the policer counters, interface statistics, and a little math. First, determine the byte-per-packet size the policer sees by dividing the bytes by the number of packets as seen by the policer counter. Then, multiply the egress rate in packets per second by the per-packet size and 8 bits to get the bytes per second.

For example, say the policer counter claimed 1,406,950 bytes and 18,494 packets exceeded the policer. This would calculate to an average per-packet size of 76 bytes (1,406,950/18,494). Then, via the show interfaces command, the interface rate would be determined to be 203 packets per second (pps). So, 203 pps multiplied by 76 bytes divided by a packet time of 8 bits per second will provide a bytes-per-second rate of 123,424, which should be close to the configured bandwidth rate.

Summary of Firewall Filters and Policers

Stateless firewall filters offer the advantage of high-speed processing, which allows you to maintain local control plane and transit security at near-wire-rate speeds. The easy-to-read and intuitive nature of JUNOS filter and policer syntax makes it easy to create, deploy, monitor, and modify filters.

You may also consider the use of stateful firewall filtering, which provides for enhanced packet and application layer processing, using the techniques covered in Chapters 7, 8, and 11. The flexibility of JUNOS software allows you to choose which solution is best for a specific set of needs and, when desired, to use both types of filtering for an optimal security and performance solution.

The next section details ways in which JUNOS can help to prevent the use of bogus source addressing, which is a common occurrence in a distributed DoS (DDoS) attack.

Spoof Prevention (uRPF)

Many distributed DoS attacks take advantage of address "spoofing" by randomly selecting an address in the source field of IP packets. In some attacks, this source address is deterministic to the target network under attack. In other words, this address will be taken out of the network's address block to create attacks on other internal machines generating ICMP error messages or other traffic back to the spoofed addresses. You can protect yourself from these types of attacks by applying ingress filtering at the edge of your network, which denies incoming packets with addresses out of the network's address block. This filtering has traditionally been solved with an inbound packet filter.

Referring back to the topology in Figure 6-2, note that three internal address blocks are assigned to PBR, Ale, and Bock's network:

        10.10.128/22
        10.20.128/22
        10.10.12/22

So, a simple filter would deny any addresses from those address blocks coming from the WAN connection off PBR:

```
[edit firewall]
lab@PBR# show
family inet {
    filter spoof-prevention {
        term my-addresses {
            from {
                source-address {
                    10.10.128.0/22;
                    10.20.128.0/22;
                    10.10.12.0/22;
                }
            }
            then {
                count spoofs;
                log;
                discard;
            }
        }
        term allow-rest {
            then count no-spoof;
        }
    }
}
```

Apply the firewall filter as an input filter on fe-0/0/0.412 and fe-0/0/0.413:

```
lab@PBR# show interfaces fe-0/0/0
vlan-tagging;
unit 412 {
    description PBR-to-Wheat;
    vlan-id 412;
    family inet {
        filter {
            input-list spoof-prevention;
        }
        address 172.16.1.2/24;
    }
}
unit 413 {
    description PBR-to-Water;
    vlan-id 413;
    family inet {
        filter {
            input-list spoof-prevention;
        }
        address 64.8.12.6/27;
    }
}
```

After applying the filter, we can see that spoofed addresses are being properly denied over PBR's fe-0/00.413 interface, as shown in the firewall log:

```
lab@PBR> show firewall log
Log :
```

```
Time      Filter    Action Interface      Protocol Src Addr       Dest Addr
01:39:18  pfe       D      fe-0/0/0.413   ICMP     10.10.12.3     10.20.128.3
01:39:17  pfe       D      fe-0/0/0.413   ICMP     10.10.12.3     10.20.128.3
01:39:16  pfe       D      fe-0/0/0.413   ICMP     10.10.12.3     10.20.128.3
01:39:15  pfe       D      fe-0/0/0.413   ICMP     10.10.12.3     10.20.128.3
01:39:14  pfe       D      fe-0/0/0.413   ICMP     10.10.12.3     10.20.128.3
01:39:13  pfe       D      fe-0/0/0.413   ICMP     10.10.12.3     10.20.128.3
01:39:12  pfe       D      fe-0/0/0.413   ICMP     10.10.12.3     10.20.128.3
01:39:11  pfe       D      fe-0/0/0.413   ICMP     10.10.12.3     10.20.128.3
01:39:10  pfe       D      fe-0/0/0.413   ICMP     10.10.12.3     10.20.128.3
01:39:09  pfe       D      fe-0/0/0.413   ICMP     10.10.12.3     10.20.128.3
```

The problem with ingress firewall filters is that you must update them manually when an address block or network changes. A more dynamic method that has been developed to prevent spoofing is called *unicast Reverse Path Forwarding* (uRPF). RPF is a mechanism that is used in multicast networks to avoid looping based on the source IP address (the reverse path), not the destination IP address. In essence, the source IP address is compared against the route table to see whether it was learned over that interface. If the packet was received via the incoming interface on which it was learned, it is accepted; if not, the packet will be dropped.

This concept has now been extended to Unicast packets for spoof prevention to create dynamic filters based on the route table. The mechanism will remain the same, in that the source IP address will need to be "verified" for incoming packets. Unicast RPF can operate on one of two modes:

Strict
    The incoming packet must be received on the interface that would be used to forward traffic to the source IP address. Strict mode is the default.

Loose
    The incoming packet's source address must be in the route table.

Strict mode provides a reliable, simple, fast, and cheap filter at the edge of any network. The configuration to enable strict mode is quite simple; just add the `rpf-check` command under the proper interface:

```
lab@PBR# show interfaces fe-0/0/0
vlan-tagging;
unit 412 {
    description PBR-to-Wheat;
    vlan-id 412;
    family inet {
        rpf-check;
        address 172.16.1.2/24;
    }
}
unit 413 {
    description PBR-to-Water;
    vlan-id 413;
    family inet {
        rpf-check;
        address 64.8.12.6/27;
```

```
            }
        }
```

Verify that uRPF is enabled by looking for the uRPF flag in the interface:

```
[edit]
lab@PBR# run show interfaces fe-0/0/0.413 | match uRPF
    Flags: uRPF
```

The packets that fail the RPF check are automatically counted on the interface:

```
[edit]
lab@PBR# run show interfaces fe-0/0/0.413 extensive | match RPF
    Flags: uRPF
    RPF Failures: Packets: 8, Bytes: 672
```

Strict mode is the preferred solution when possible, but it does run into some problems under certain scenarios. In particular, it assumes symmetrical traffic flows. In the case of a BGP multihoming environment or redundant IGP paths, this may not always be the case.

 Remember that the default load balancing for a Juniper router is to choose a single next hop to install in the forwarding table per destination.

PBR is multihomed to two ISPs (see Figure 6-11) and receives the same set of routes from each; however, only the route received from autonomous system (AS) 666 is active.

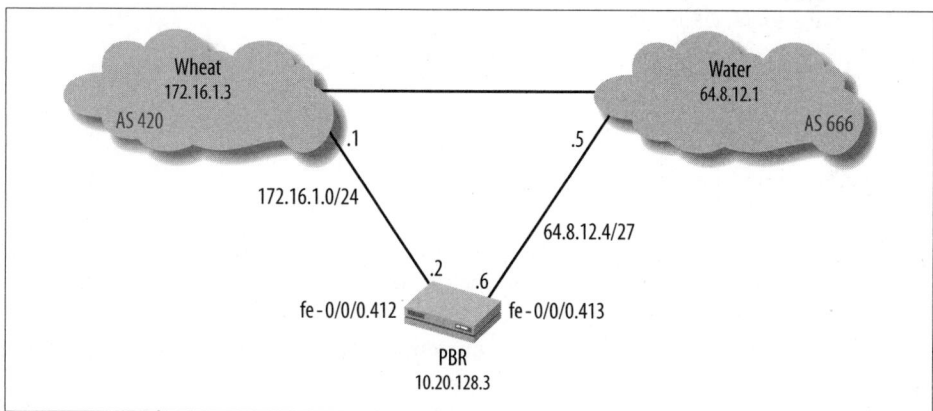

Figure 6-11. Multihoming

```
lab@PBR# run show bgp summary
Groups: 2 Peers: 2 Down peers: 0
Table          Tot Paths  Act Paths Suppressed    History Damp State    Pending
inet.0              497        249          0          0         0          0
Peer             AS      InPkt     OutPkt     OutQ   Flaps Last Up/Dwn
State|#Active/Received/Damped...
```

```
64.8.12.5          666      1239     1114      0     0    9:15:56 248/248/0
0/0/0
172.16.1.1         420      1354     1238      0     0    9:15:26 0/248/0
0/0/0
```

This means that any traffic received from AS 420 that is an inactive route will fail the
RPF check. An example is the 128.3/16 address block:

```
[edit]
lab@PBR# run show route 128.3.3.4

inet.0: 264 destinations, 513 routes (264 active, 0 holddown, 1 hidden)
+ = Active Route, - = Last Active, * = Both

128.3.0.0/16       *[BGP/170] 09:20:20, localpref 100
                      AS path: 666 11537 293 16 I
                   > to 64.8.12.5 via fe-0/0/0.413
                    [BGP/170] 09:19:50, localpref 100
                      AS path: 420 666 11537 293 16 I
                   > to 172.16.1.1 via fe-0/0/0.412
```

Since JUNOS performs uRPF against active paths only, in order to allow for multihoming or asymmetric traffic flows you can configure a feature called *feasible paths*.
This knob allows every possible path in the route table to be considered, including
active and inactive paths. You enable this global command for the entire router
under the [edit routing-options] stanza:

```
lab@PBR# show routing-options
aggregate {
    route 10.10.128.0/22;
    route 10.20.128.0/22;
    route 10.10.12.3/32;
}
autonomous-system 1282;
forwarding-table {
    unicast-reverse-path feasible-paths;
}
```

Loose RPF provides less security, as it verifies only that the route is in the route table
and does not check which interface it points to. This is more of a route presence
check than an actual verification of the reverse path. The only benefit would be for
route martians, or packets that are not currently being routed. One such example
could be a private RFC 1918 address if only publicly routable addresses are used in
the network. Since loose mode sacrifices directionality, it is not a recommended
approach to spoof prevention and has limited scope.

 Another problem with loose mode occurs when a default route is
present in the table. In this case, every packet would pass the check
and thus uRPF checks would be negated. Strict mode with a default
route will still verify that the packet entered on the interface to which
the default route points.

To enable loose mode on an interface, specify the loose command after turning on uRPF:

```
lab@PBR# set interfaces fe-0/0/0.412 family inet rpf-check mode loose
```

Other filters could still be applied to the interface when uRPF mode is enabled; in this case, the input filter is examined first, and the uRPF checks process only the traffic that passes this filter. Due to this processing, it is hard to perform a log action for packets that failed the RPF filter. In this instance, you can configure a *fail* filter. A fail filter is performed after the RPF check and on all traffic that has failed the RPF check (see Figure 6-12).

Figure 6-12. Firewall filter and uRPF relationship

You can use a fail filter to:

- Allow traffic that would normally fail an RPF check, such as DHCP on a LAN interface
- Allow traffic that would normally fail an RPF check to be accepted and counted
- Allow failed traffic to be processed by a filter modifier such as counting or logging

An example of the first filter could be DHCP requests that would always fail an RPF check:

```
filter rpf-dhcp {
        term dhcp {
            from {
                source-address {
                    0.0.0.0/32;
                }
                destination-address {
                    255.255.255.255/32;
                }
            }
            then accept;
        }
    }
}
```

If traffic that fails the RPF check should be further examined, you also can use a fail filter. The following filter would be able to log all packets that are failing the RPF check:

```
filter match-spoofs {
    term 1 {
```

```
        then {
            log;
            discard;
        }
    }
}
```

Apply the fail filter to the interface:

```
[edit interfaced fe-0/0/0]
lab@PBR# show
unit 413 {
    description PBR-to-Water;
    vlan-id 413;
    family inet {
        rpf-check fail-filter match-spoofs;
        address 64.8.12.6/27;
    }
}
```

View the packets that are failing uRPF by examining the firewall log:

```
lab@PBR# run show firewall log
Log :
Time      Filter  Action Interface      Protocol Src Addr     Dest Addr
02:23:59  pfe     D      fe-0/0/0.413   ICMP     10.10.12.3   10.20.128.3
02:23:58  pfe     D      fe-0/0/0.413   ICMP     10.10.12.3   10.20.128.3
02:23:57  pfe     D      fe-0/0/0.413   ICMP     10.10.12.3   10.20.128.3
02:23:56  pfe     D      fe-0/0/0.413   ICMP     10.10.12.3   10.20.128.3
02:23:55  pfe     D      fe-0/0/0.413   ICMP     10.10.12.3   10.20.128.3
02:23:54  pfe     D      fe-0/0/0.413   ICMP     10.10.12.3   10.20.128.3
02:23:53  pfe     D      fe-0/0/0.413   ICMP     10.10.12.3   10.20.128.3
02:23:52  pfe     D      fe-0/0/0.413   ICMP     10.10.12.3   10.20.128.3
```

Summary of Spoof Prevention

Current best practices suggest that all source addresses should be validated as close to the ingress point of traffic as is possible. Historically, the added processing led to poor forwarding performance due to a lack of processing resources. This often resulted in a total lack of address enforcement, and the resulting ease in which DDoS attacks can be successfully launched.

The unique design of JUNOS software allows you to enable spoof prevention features while still maintaining a high level of forwarding performance.

The next section details ways that JUNOS can help monitor the router to actively and proactively determine the presence of attacks.

Monitoring the Router

Once the access configuration is in place, you should monitor the router for health and analysis. The two primary methods of remote monitoring are via SNMP and syslog (system logging). SNMP is a way to gather statistics and other event information off the router, whereas syslog is used to gather various log messages off the router. To validate these types of messages, you should use proper time and date stamping, which is often implemented by using NTP.

Syslog

Syslog was originally developed as a method to send information for the sendmail application in BSD, but it was so useful that it was extended to other applications and operating systems. Essentially, syslog is a standard way to send log messages across an IP network.

Syslog describes the actual transport mechanism used to send these messages and is often used to describe the actual application that is sending them. Originally, it was an "industry" standard and was not attached to an informational RFC until 2001, with RFC 3164, "The BSD Syslog Protocol."

Syslog messages are sent over UDP with a destination port of 514. The IP transport mechanism is defined and not the actual syslog content. It is left to the discretion of the application or system coder to create an informative message to the receiver. The message always contains a message severity level and a facility level. The *facility level* can be defined as the type of message that is being sent, and the *severity level* indicates the message's importance. Table 6-5 defines the severity levels.

Table 6-5. Syslog severity levels

Numerical code	Severity
0	Emergency: system is unusable
1	Alert: action must be taken immediately
2	Critical: critical conditions
3	Error: error conditions
4	Warning: warning conditions
5	Notice: normal but significant condition
6	Informational: informational messages
7	Debug: debug-level messages

Table 6-6 lists the facility levels that are available in JUNOS.

Table 6-6. Syslog facility levels

Facility	Description
Any	All facilities (all messages)
Authorization	Authentication and authorization attempts
Change-Log	Changes to the configuration
Conflict-Log	Specified configuration is invalid on the routing platform type
Daemon	Actions performed or errors encountered by system processes
DFC	Events related to dynamic flow capture
Firewall	Packet filtering actions performed by a firewall filter
FTP	Actions performed or errors encountered by the FTP process
Interactive commands	Commands executed by the user interface
Kernel	Actions performed or errors encountered by the JUNOS kernel
PFE	Actions performed or errors encountered by the Packet Forwarding Engine
User	Actions performed or errors encountered by user-space processes

The default system log is called "messages"; you can view it with the show log
messages command:

```
lab@PBR> show log messages
Nov 20 06:00:00 PBR newsyslog[2858]: logfile turned over due to size>128K
Nov 21 09:47:59  PBR login: LOGIN_PAM_AUTHENTICATION_ERROR: PAM authentication error
for user lab
Nov 21 09:47:59  PBR login: LOGIN_FAILED: Login failed for user lab from host
Nov 21 09:48:03  PBR login: LOGIN_INFORMATION: User lab logged in from host [unknown]
on device ttyd0
Nov 21 09:48:06  PBR mgd[2978]: UI_DBASE_LOGIN_EVENT: User 'lab' entering
configuration mode
Nov 21 09:54:36  PBR mgd[2978]: UI_DBASE_LOGOUT_EVENT: User 'lab' exiting
configuration mode
Nov 21 09:54:55  PBR mgd[2978]: UI_REBOOT_EVENT: System rebooted by 'lab'
Nov 21 09:55:09  PBR /kernel: KERNEL_MEMORY_CRITICAL: System low on free memory,
notifying init (#1).
Nov 21 09:55:09  PBR rpd[2800]: Received low-memory signal: no job active, 34 free
pages
Nov 21 09:55:09  PBR rpd[2800]: Processing low memory signal
Nov 21 09:55:49  PBR shutdown: reboot by lab:
Nov 21 09:55:49  PBR init: watchdog (PID 2768) terminate signal sent
Nov 21 09:55:49  PBR init: chassis-control (PID 2770) terminate signal sent
Nov 21 09:55:49  PBR init: alarm-control (PID 2771) terminate signal sent
Nov 21 09:55:49  PBR craftd[2772]: craftd_user_conn_shutdown: socket 8, errno = 0
Nov 21 09:55:49  PBR init: craft-control (PID 2772) terminate signal sent
Nov 21 09:55:49  PBR snmpd[2811]: SNMPD_CLOSE_SA_IPC: ipc_free_local: closed IPC
socket /var/run/craft
Nov 21 09:55:49  PBR init: management (PID 2773) terminate signal sent
Nov 21 09:55:49  PBR init: inet-process (PID 2775) terminate signal sent
```

```
Nov 21 09:55:49  PBR init: syslogd (PID 2682) terminate signal sent
Nov 21 09:55:49  PBR init: ecc-error-logging (PID 2779) terminate signal sent
Nov 21 09:55:49  PBR init: forwarding (PID 2780) terminate signal sent
Nov 21 09:55:49  PBR init: usb-control (PID 2781) terminate signal sent
Nov 21 09:55:49  PBR init: mib-process (PID 2799) terminate signal sent
Nov 21 09:55:49  PBR snmpd[2811]: SNMPD_CLOSE_SA_IPC: ipc_free_local: closed IPC
socket /var/run/mib2d
Nov 21 09:55:49  PBR init: routing (PID 2800) terminate signal sent
Nov 21 09:55:49  PBR rpd[2800]: RPD_SIGNAL_TERMINATE: first termination signal
received
Nov 21 09:55:49  PBR init: l2-learning (PID 2801) terminate signal sent
Nov 21 09:55:49  PBR init: vrrp (PID 2802) terminate signal sent
Nov 21 09:55:49  PBR snmpd[2811]: SNMPD_CLOSE_SA_IPC: ipc_free_local: closed IPC
socket /var/run/vrrpd
Nov 21 09:55:49  PBR rpd[2800]: RPD_OSPF_NBRDOWN: OSPF neighbor 10.20.130.1 (fe-0/0/
0.1241) state changed from Full to Down due to KillNbr (event reason: interface went
down)
Nov 21 09:55:49  PBR init: sampling (PID 2803) terminate signal sent
Nov 21 09:55:49  PBR init: class-of-service (PID 2804) terminate signal se
```

Many of the syslog messages will have headers specified in uppercase letters that you
can input into the help command specifying which facility the message was logged
on, the severity level, a description, and a recommended action. Looking at the log
entry for November 21, one such header is noted as RPD_OSPF_NBRDOWN:

```
Nov 21 09:55:49  PBR rpd[2800]: RPD_OSPF_NBRDOWN: OSPF neighbor 10.20.130.1 (fe-0/0/
0.1241) state changed from Full to Down due to KillNbr (event reason: interface went
down)
```

You can examine this message using the help syslog command, which indicates that
an OSPF neighbor went down due to an event:

```
lab@PBR> help syslog RPD_OSPF_NBRDOWN
Name:         RPD_OSPF_NBRDOWN
Message:      OSPF neighbor <neighbor> (<interface>) state changed from
              <old-state> to <new-state> due to <event> (event reason:
              <event-reason>)
Help:         OSPF neighbor adjacency was terminated
Description:  An OSPF adjacency with the indicated neighboring router was
              terminated. The local router no longer exchanges routing
              information with, or directs traffic to, the neighboring router.
Type:         Event: This message reports an event, not an error
Severity:     notice
```

You can create custom logs by specifying a filename, facility, message facility, and
location to send the message. The message can either be stored in a local file, sent to
a syslog server, sent to the console, or sent to a user or group of users when logged in
to the router.

The factory default configuration enables three system logs: two logs that are sent to
a file, and one log that is sent to any user that is logged in. Although the default system log receives all information as specified with the any keyword, you can create
other files for easier log parsing:

```
syslog {
    user * {
        any emergency;
    }
    file messages {
        any any;
        authorization info;
    }
    file interactive-commands {
        interactive-commands any;
    }
}
```

Case study: Syslog

To avoid having to specify every syslog option available, let's examine a realistic example with specific goals. The goals are as follows:

- Increase the default size of the *messages* file to 1 MB and the number of archives to 15.

- Send all messages to a syslog server with a domain name of *syslog.underdogssf.com*.

- Ensure that all messages sent to the syslog server are in the same format as the Cisco routers in your network.

- Create a syslog file to log all firewall filter log information.

Each syslog file that is created on a Juniper Networks router is stored in the file directory *var/log* and is given a size of 128 KB on a J-series router and 1 MB on an M-series router. When the file is full, the file is cleared, an archive is created of the old data, and the file is written to again. For example, once 128 KB of data is written into the *messages* file, that file will be cleared and the information will be moved into a *message.0* file. When the *messages* file is filled up again, the old data is archived into *messages.0* and the old *messages.0* now becomes *messages.1*. This will continue for 10 archives until the data is written. In the case study, you should increase the default number of archives to 15 and the file size to 1 MB. You can do this with the following archive configuration:

```
[edit system syslog]
lab@PBR# set file messages archive files 15 size 1M

[edit system syslog]
lab@PBR# show file messages
any notice;
authorization info;
archive size 1m files 15;
```

Next, syslog messages need to be sent to a syslog server:

```
[edit system syslog]
lab@PBR# set host syslog.underdogssf.com any any
```

The default JUNOS message does not send the priority (facility value and severity) of the syslog message, which could cause issues when trying to parse the output at the receiver. Cisco routers by default do send this priority field; to ensure that both vendors send the same message format, configure the explicit-priority keyword:

```
[edit system syslog]
lab@PBR# set host syslog.underdogssf.com explicit-priority
```

Lastly, a new syslog file is created to log firewall entries:

```
[edit system syslog]
lab@PBR# set file fw-log firewall info
```

Here is the complete stanza:

```
[edit system syslog]
lab@PBR# show
user * {
    any emergency;
}
host syslog.underdogssf.com {
    any any;
    explicit-priority;
}
file messages {
    any notice;
    authorization info;
    archive size 1m files 15;
}
file interactive-commands {
    interactive-commands any;

}
file fw-log {
    firewall info;
}
```

SNMP

SNMP is a standard protocol used for a network management station to receive information for the router (or agent; see Figure 6-13). The manager can poll the router for router health information such as memory utilization, link status, or firewall filter statistics in the form of a GET command. The router can also send event information to the network manager without polling, in a process called a *TRAP*.

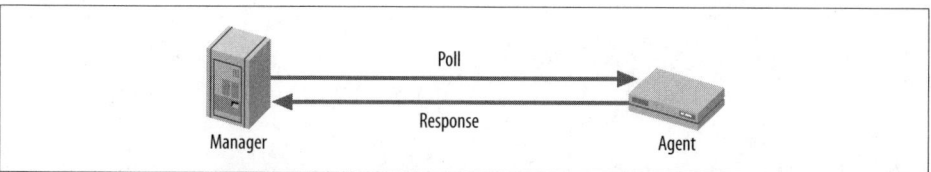

Figure 6-13. SNMP concept

The data structure that is used to carry information is called a Management Information Base (MIB). An MIB has a structure in the format of a tree that defines groups of objects into related sets. These MIBs are identified by an Object Identifier (OID), which names the object. The leaf of the OID contains the actual managed objects. MIBs are defined into two categories: standard and enterprise-specific. Standard MIBs are defined by the IETF in various RFCs, whereas enterprise-specific MIBs are defined by the vendor and must be compiled into the management station. Here is an example of MIB data taken from a network manager:

```
SNMPv2-MIB::sysDescr.O = STRING: M120 - Okemos, MI
SNMPv2-MIB::sysObjectID.O = OID: JUNIPER-MIB::jnxProductNameM120
SNMPv2-MIB::sysUpTime.O = Timeticks: (80461526) 9 days, 7:30:15.26
SNMPv2-MIB::sysContact.O = STRING: Doug Marschke - x8675309
SNMPv2-MIB::sysName.O = STRING: PBR-3
SNMPv2-MIB::sysLocation.O = STRING: Okemis, MI USA - Rack 4
SNMPv2-MIB::sysServices.O = INTEGER: 4
```

To configure SNMP on a Juniper router, you must specify a community string on the router. This acts as a password to verify incoming SNMP information on the management station:

```
[edit snmp]
lab@PBR# set community sample

[edit snmp]
lab@PBR# show
community sample;
```

 Juniper Networks routers support SNMP v1, SNMP v2, and SNMP v3.

With this basic configuration, SNMP GETs can be received on any interface from any management statement. It is recommended that access is restricted to particular interfaces and clients:

```
lab@PBR# show
interface fe-0/0/0.1141;
community sample {
    clients {
        10.10.12.4/32;
        0.0.0.0/0 restrict;
    }
}
```

Also, the router may want to initiate some information in the form of TRAPs. TRAPs are sent to a specified list of targets and are defined by categories. Possible categories include:

Authentication
> User login authentication failures

Chassis
> Chassis and environmental notifications

Configuration
> Notification of configuration changes

Link
> Link status changes

Remote operations
> Remote operation notifications

Rmon-alarm
> Events for RMON alarms

Routing
> Routing protocol information such as neighbor status changes

Services
> Events for additional JUNOS services such as Network Address Translation (NAT) and stateful firewall

Sonet-alarm
> A variety of SONET alarms such as loss of light, BER defects, and so on

Start-up
> Warm and cold boots

VRRP events
> VRRP events such as mastership changes

In the following example, a TRAP group called health is added to the SNMP configuration that sends chassis and link TRAPs to station 10.10.12.4:

```
lab@PBR# show
interface fe-0/0/0.1141;
community sample {
    clients {
        10.10.12.4/32;
        0.0.0.0/0 restrict;
    }
}
trap-group health {
    categories {
        chassis;
        link;
    }
    targets {
        10.10.12.4;
    }
}
```

 By default, both SNMP v1 and v2 TRAPs are sent. You can overwrite this by specifying a version under the TRAP group.

It may also be useful to walk down the MIB tree to verify information in the MIB and for troubleshooting purposes. To perform an SNMP walk on the router, issue the show snmp mib *<object>* command. In this case, the system MIB is examined on the router:

```
lab@PBR> show snmp mib walk system
sysDescr.0    = Juniper Networks, Inc. j6300 internet router, kernel JUNOS 8.0R2.8
#0: 2006-09-29 09 Build date: 2006-09-29 08:22:29 UTC Copyright (c) 1996-2006 Juniper
Networks, Inc.
sysObjectID.0 = jnxProductNameJ6300
sysUpTime.0   = 50415199
sysContact.0
sysName.0     = PBR
sysLocation.0
sysServices.0 = 4
```

NTP

When examining logs, it is essential to ensure that the proper date and time are recorded for each event. You can set the time and date manually on each router using the set date command:

```
lab@PBR> set date ?
Possible completions:
  <time>  New date and time (YYYYMMDDhhmm.ss)
  ntp     Set system date and time using Network Time Protocol servers
```

However, since many devices are likely to be managed at once, each with slightly different clock speeds and drift, it is virtually impossible to keep all the clocks on every device synchronized. NTP was developed for the purpose of clock synchronization. NTP works in one of three modes:

Client
A client has a one-way synchronization with a server.

Symmetric active
There is equal peer synchronization with each other's local clock.

Broadcast
The server sends periodic broadcast messages on shared media, and clients listen to these messages for synchronization.

NTP uses a concept of *clock strata* to define the distance from the clock reference and the accuracy. A stratum 0 clock is the reference clock (such as an atomic clock), and each level of peering relationship decreases in accuracy and stratum level (see Figure 6-14).

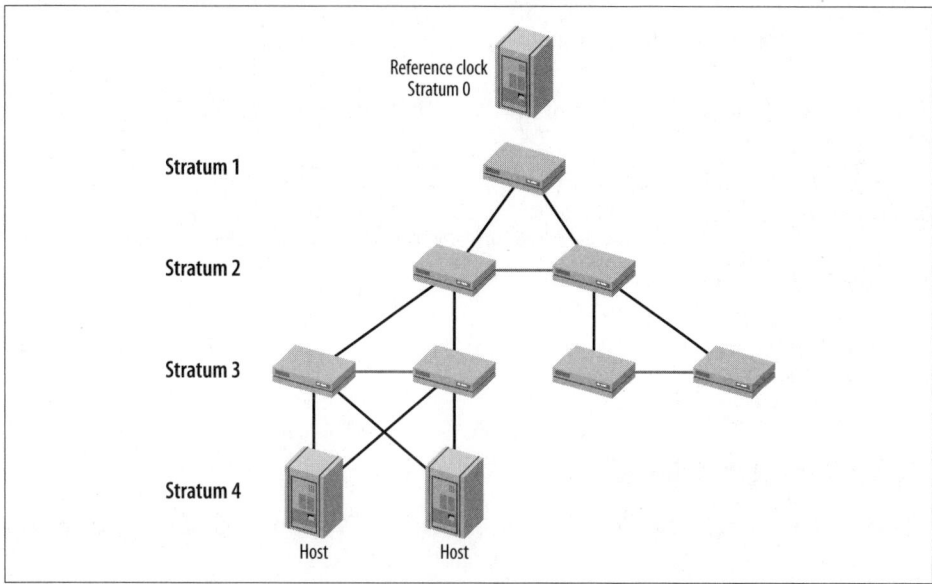

Figure 6-14. NTP stratum levels

All NTP configurations are set under [edit system ntp]. In the following configuration, Bock is configured in client mode with a server of 10.20.130.5. Also, a boot server is configured to allow the initial clock setting to be set at boot time:

```
lab@Bock> show configuration system ntp
boot-server 10.20.130.5;
server 10.20.130.5;
```

If a router is configured for NTP and the clocks are more than 128 seconds apart, the synchronization process will fail. In the past, to recover from that scenario, the operator either rebooted the device with the boot server configuration or set the date manually within 128 seconds. JUNOS software now allows you to synchronize the device by simply issuing the set date ntp command and avoiding a reboot:

```
lab@Bock> set date ntp 10.20.130.5
10 Feb 13:50:21 ntpdate[794]: step time server 10.20.130.5 offset 0.000163 sec
```

To verify that NTP has worked correctly, issue the show ntp associations command and look for the * next to the remote IP:

```
lab@Bock> show ntp associations
     remote      refid  st t when poll reach  delay  offset  jitter
==================================================================
*10.20.130.5  LOCAL(0)  11 u   10 . 64   17  0.491  12.991  10.140
```

Check the correct time:

```
lab@Bock> show system uptime
Current time: 2007-11-22 03:53:35 UTC
System booted: 2007-11-20 04:58:58 UTC (1d 22:54 ago)
```

```
Protocols started: 2007-11-20 04:59:24 UTC (1d 22:54 ago)
Last configured: 2007-11-22 03:40:02 UTC (00:13:33 ago) by lab
 3:53AM  up 1 day, 22:55, 1 user, load averages: 0.19, 0.10, 0.03
```

You also can change the time zone in the router by issuing a set system time-zone command:

```
lab@Bock# set system time-zone ?
Possible completions:
  <time-zone>            Time zone name or POSIX-compliant time zone string
  Africa/Abidjan
  Africa/Accra
  Africa/Addis_Ababa
  Africa/Algiers
  Africa/Asmera
---(more 5%)---[abort]
```

Is NTP REALLY Working?

The show ntp associations command is often a source of mass confusion and terror for operators, as there is no distinct "broken field." The synchronization process will be indicated by interpreting the delay and offset fields, as well as by noting the presence or absence of a * character.

Here is an example of an association that has failed. Notice the space in front of the 10.20.130.5 as well as the zeros is the delay and offset fields. This is an indication that no messages have been sent at all!

```
lab@Bock> show ntp associations
    remote      refid  st t when poll reach   delay   offset  jitter
==============================================================================
 10.20.130.5 0.0.0.0      0 u  12   64    0   0.000   0.000 4000.00
```

In comparison, here is another association that failed; however, notice that there are values in the delay and offset fields. These indicate that NTP messages have been exchanged but synchronization has not been achieved, as no * has been displayed next to the remote peer. The large offset is usually an indication that the clocks are too far apart (above the 128-second threshold):

```
lab@Bock> show ntp associations
    remote      refid  st t when poll reach   delay   offset  jitter
==============================================================================
 10.20.130.5 LOCAL(0)    11 u  25   64   37  0.492  2542804 4000.00
```

After issuing a set date ntp command, the clocks synchronize without having to reboot the router. Note the more sane offset value and the presence of the illustrious star next to the remote peer address:

```
lab@Bock> show ntp associations
    remote      refid  st t when poll reach   delay   offset  jitter
==============================================================================
*10.20.130.5 LOCAL(0)    11 u  10   64   17  0.491   12.991  10.140

3:53AM  up 1 day, 22:55, 1 user, load averages: 0.19, 0.10, 0.03
```

Since NTP uses a step process to synchronize the clocks after issuing the set date ntp command, the association could still appear to be broken. This is normal for NTP, so just sit back, enjoy a drink, and after three to five minutes, everything should be working as normal.

Summary of Router Monitoring

Many types of attacks and network abuse leave telltale signs, if the operator only takes the time to look for them. The Unix underpinnings of JUNOS software offer full syslogging capabilities, which when synchronized to other routers via the NTP protocols can provide invaluable forensics when problems are being investigated. Using SNMP to remotely monitor network operations to include the receipt of asynchronous TRAPs reporting anomalous conditions provides an excellent way to adopt a more proactive stance toward securing your network.

Conclusion

When the router is deployed in the network, you must secure it properly to protect your network, investments, and hard work. The first step is to configure the proper users with access privileges. Depending on the number of users, the local router or an external server database may be used to hold this information, or an external server.

Once the users are in place, you need to deploy packet filters to protect the router. These filters may be very elaborate or quite simple depending on your security policies. Also, you may need to rate-limit some applications in your network using policers.

It also does not do much good to have a secure router if you can't gather router health and other statistical information from it. Therefore, you also should deploy standard protocols such as SNMP, syslog, and NTP to achieve these management goals.

Exam Topics

We examined the following Enterprise Exam Topics in this chapter:

- List the various user authentication methods.
- Describe the uses of login classes.
- Describe authentication order.
- Describe system logging.
- Identify the configuration of a stateless packet filter.
- Secure the router by applying packet filters to protect the Routing Engine.
- Evaluate the result of a given stateless packet filter.

- Configure SNMP.
- Customize class templates with varying permissions and commands.
- Configure and operate the Network Time Protocol.

Chapter Review Questions

1. What is the default password on the router?

    a. Juniper

    b. Cisco

    c. There is no password

    d. Enable

2. Which predefined login class allows the user to have access rights to any login command?

    a. Privileged

    b. Super-user

    c. Privileged exec

    d. Power-user

3. What is the default action at the end of a firewall filter chain?

    a. Discard

    b. Reject

    c. Accept

    d. Do nothing

4. Which interface would you apply to a filter to protect the router's local traffic?

    a. `fxp1`

    b. `fxp0`

    c. `manage`

    d. `lo0`

5. Which command is used to view all firewall filter counters, including counters automatically created in policers?

    a. `show counters`

    b. `show policer`

    c. `show interfaces filters counters`

    d. `show firewall`

6. Which two features can you use to protect your network against spoofed IP addresses? (Choose two.)

    a. Firewall filters

    b. Spoof routes

c. Unicast reverse path forwarding

d. Secondary addresses

7. Which three parameters are specified in a policer? (Choose three.)

   a. Bandwidth limit

   b. Policer action

   c. Bucket level

   d. Burst size

   e. Leak rate

8. Choose two possible reasons for using a fail filter using uRPF. (Choose two.)

   a. Allow packets to pass through RPF

   b. Log packets that fail RPF

   c. Implement NAT

   d. Send traffic through a tunnel

9. Which syslog facility logs all CLI commands?

   a. `cli-commands`

   b. `accounting`

   c. `change-log`

   d. `interactive-commands`

10. In which directory are all logfiles stored?

    a. */var/home/user*

    b. */log*

    c. */var/home/log*

    d. */var/log*

    e. */syslog*

11. Which feature of SNMP v2 acts as a password to authenticate SNMP messages?

    a. MIBs

    b. Communities

    c. OID

    d. TRAPs

12. Which command allows NTP synchronization without a router reboot?

    a. `set system ntp`

    b. `request system time update`

    c. `set date ntp`

    d. `set ntp boot-server`

Chapter Review Answers

1. Answer: C. There is no default password on a Juniper router in the factory default configuration. A single user, root, will be configured with no password.

2. Answer: B. The class of superuser allows users to issue any command that they desire on the router. The other options listed are not supported classes.

3. Answer: A. At the end of a filter chain, if a packet has not matched any other term, it will be discarded. Special care must always be taken when writing a filter to allow traffic that would otherwise be denied by the final implicit discard at the end of the filter.

4. Answer D. If a filter is applied to the loopback interface, any traffic local to the router can be protected, including routing protocol, ICMP, and FTP traffic.

5. Answer: D. You can use the show firewall command to view counters defined in any firewall filter. Also, any policer that is referenced in a filter will have a counter automatically created and viewed by this command. The show policer command will only show the counter for policers applied directly to the interface.

6. Answer: A, C. Both firewall filters and Unicast RPF will help to avoid packets with spoofed IP addresses. Unicast RPF could provide for more dynamic and automatic filtering.

7. Answer: A, B, D. Policers must specify bandwidth and burst size limit. Also, once a packet hits one of the limits, an action to either hard- or soft-police must be specified.

8. Answer: A, B. A fail filter matches on packets that fail the RPF check. You could use this to accept packets such as DHCP, which would always fail an RPF check, or to count or log packets that have passed an RPF check.

9. Answer: D. The facility interactive-commands will log any commands that were typed via any user interface method, including the CLI.

10. Answer: D. This is the directory for all syslog and trace-options files.

11. Answer: B. A community will act as a password for SNMP messages. This community value is sent in clear text on the wire, which could easily be captured. The next version of SNMP corrects this issue.

12. Answer: C. If the NTP server is reachable, set date ntp will restart the NTP update process without having to reboot the router, thus eliminating the need for a boot-server configuration statement.

Introduction to JUNOS Services

Once the routing aspect of a network has been deployed, you'll want additional services to be added to fit your network requirements. In the past, a separate device would have performed these types of services, but in modern networking these tasks have been moved to the router itself. *Service* is a broad term that can include tasks that are performed at Layer 2 (such as link bonding) or at Layer 3 (such as Network Address Translation [NAT]). We will examine all of these services in this chapter, as well as provide additional detail regarding more specific services throughout the book.

Because many of these services require intensive packet processing on the router, you may have to install additional hardware to avoid any degradation in packet forwarding and throughput. Although this may seem to be a slight nuisance at first, it does solve the problem of increased services causing decreased throughput, as is observed in most other router implementations.

The service topics covered in this chapter include:

- JUNOS services
- Layer 2 services
- Layer 3 services
- Layer 3 service command-line interface (CLI) configuration
- Additional service options

The information covered in this chapter, and in Chapter 8, is based on services that are implemented via ASP on the M7i, or on the J-series through its emulation of ASP functionality. Starting with Release 8.5, Juniper Networks has made available its JUNOS software with enhanced services. The reader should be aware that the primary difference between JUNOS and JUNOS software with enhanced services relates to services. In the JUNOS software with enhanced services release, these services are based on ScreenOS functionality. Along with the improved services comes new configuration syntax.

Readers who are not deploying JUNOS software with enhanced services, or who will deploy both JUNOS software and JUNOS software with enhanced services, will need to know the ASP-based service configuration, as covered here and in Chapter 8. Readers who plan to deploy only JUNOS software with enhanced services should focus on the material covered in Chapter 11. Note that at this writing the Juniper Networks Certified Internet Expert (JNCIE-ER) examination is not based on JUNOS software with enhanced services, so readers interested in passing the JNCIE-ER examination will need to be familiar with ASP-based service definitions.

JUNOS Services

A JUNOS software service consists of a variety of Layer 2 and Layer 3 services, including:

- Multilink Point-to-Point Protocol (MLPPP)
- Multilink Frame Relay (MLFR)
- Compressed Real-Time Transport Protocol (CRTP)
- Multiclass MLPPP
- Stateful firewall
- NAT
- Intrusion detection service (IDS)
- IPSec
- Layer 2 Tunneling Protocol (L2TP)
- Active monitoring (cflowd)
- Tunnel services (Generic Routing Encapsulation [GRE], IP-IP, Physical Interface Module [PIM] register encapsulation)
- Data link switching (DLSw)

In an M-series router, enabling these services will require an additional piece of hardware: a Physical Interface Card (PIC) for packet processing. A J-series router supports most of the features in the preceding list and performs the packet processing within the software, so no additional hardware is necessary. Depending on the type of service required and the size of the service, different PICs can be used. The current offerings include:

Link Services PIC
    Provides simultaneous support for three separate capabilities: enhanced multilink bundling, tunneling, and link fragmentation and interleaving (LFI)

Encryption Services PIC
    Provides IPSec encryption for IPSec tunnels

Monitoring Services PIC
> Provides J-Flow accounting at high speeds and across millions of flows, using standards-based cflowd v5 and v8 records

Tunnel Services PIC
> Provides tunnel services such as GRE, IP-IP, IPv6 in IPv4, and multicast tunnels

Adaptive Services PIC (ASP)
> Supports all services at Layer 2 and Layer 3

Multiservices PIC
> Offers all the same services as ASP with a higher capacity and throughput

Adaptive Services Module (ASM)
> Internal module for the M7i only which supports all services at a reduced rate, as well as one of the PICs that supports L2TP LTP Network Server (LNS) functionality

---

Which PIC to Use?

Deciding which PIC to use is a delicate balance of feature set versus price. For example, if all you require are IPSec tunnels (which can be provided on an Encryption Services PIC[a]), you may not need to use the more expensive Multiservices PIC. However, you should also consider your need for future services. So, if you require NAT, you would have to use a new PIC (an ASP, or a Multiservices PIC); since the Multiservices PIC will do both NAT and IPSec, ideally this should be your first choice.

---

[a] The Encryption Services PIC has a completely different configuration from a Monitoring Services PIC, ASM, or ASP, and is beyond the scope of this book.

The most common implementation of services will be to use a J-series, an ASM in an M7i, or a Monitoring Services PIC in other M-series routers. Table 7-1 lists the performance and scaling values for these deployments.

Table 7-1. Service scaling number

Feature	Multiservices Type 1	ASP	ASM	J-series
Throughput	920 Mbps	800 Mbps	256 Mbps	Varies
Service sets	2,000	2,000	500	10
Flows	1.6 million	1 million	400,000	8,000–64,000
MLPPP links	2,048	2,044	2,044	128
MLPPP bundles	1,023	255	255	16
IPSec throughput	950 Mbps	640 Mbps	200 Mbps	Varies
IPSec tunnels	5,000	2,048	512	256

In addition to scaling differences in the various PICs and platforms, there are some minor configuration differences when referencing the interface names for Layer 2 service, as shown in Table 7-2.

Table 7-2. Service interface naming

Service interface	ASM	ASP	Multiservice	Multilink service	J-series
Layer 2	lsq	lsq	lsq	ml	ls
Layer 3	sp	sp	sp	None	sp

 Most of the configuration captures used in this chapter are from a J-series router, so the ls interface will be used. If you are using an M-series router, you still have to substitute the interface name, but the rest of the configuration will be the same.

Layer 2 Services

Layer 2 services are essentially the services that are enabled on a physical interface such as LFI (FRF.12), MLFR (FRF.15), user-to-network interface (UNI) NNI (FRF.16), MLPPP, and multiclass MLPPP.

Multilink PPP

MLPPP (RFC 1490) allows the router to combine multiple links together into one large logical bundle (as shown in Figure 7-1). This was originally created to bond multiple Integrated Services Digital Network (ISDN) bearer signals together, but it is now used for any two systems with multiple links between them. Multilink is negotiated during the initial Link Control Protocol (LCP) option negotiation. When configuring MLPPP on a Juniper router, you can combine into one bundle any eight PPP links of the *same* type on the chassis. To configure MLPPP, first create a logical bundle link (lsq-*x/x/x* on an ASP or ls-*x/x/x* on a J-series).

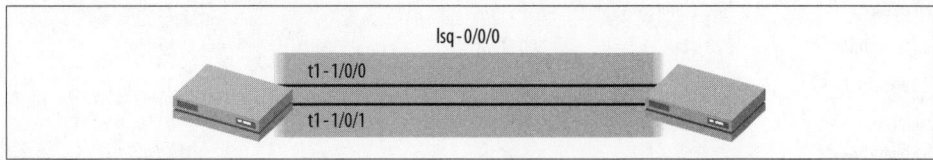

Figure 7-1. MLPPP bundle

```
lsq-0/0/0 {
    unit 0 {
        encapsulation multilink-ppp;
        family inet {
            address 166.8.67.30/30;
```

```
            }
         }
      }
```

Next, configure the physical interfaces to link the newly created link service interface. In the following example, interfaces t1-1/0/0 and t1-1/0/1 are linked to the logical bundle unit 0 on the lsq-0/0/0 interface:

```
t1-1/0/0 {
    unit 0 {
        family mlppp {
            bundle lsq-0/0/0.0;
        }
    }
}
t1-0/0/1 {
    unit 0 {
        family mlppp {
            bundle lsq-0/0/0.0;
        }
    }
}
```

When there are multiple links in your bundle, packets above the minimum maximum transmission unit/maximum received reconstructed unit (MTU/MRRU) size of all links in the bundle will be fragmented on a packet-by-packet basis across all the physical links. MRRU is similar to an interface MTU except that it applies only to multilink bundles. To avoid out-of-order issues, a sequence number is added to each packet. The receiving end will then reassemble the fragments into the full packet size. The advantage of this approach is that the high-bandwidth flows are able to use the full capacity of all the egress links. The disadvantage of this per-packet approach is that smaller packets may have to "wait" for larger packets to be transmitted.

For example, imagine you have low delay-sensitive data packets traversing with a size of 1,250 bytes and high delay-sensitive voice traffic with a size of 64 bytes. If the data packet arrives first on a link and the voice packet arrives second, the voice packet will have to wait until the data packet is done before it can be sent. On low-speed interfaces with a high serialization delay, this could greatly affect the high delay-sensitive traffic. To solve this problem, you can configure LFI.

The first step is to fragment the larger-size packets to allow the router to balance the fragments across multiple links, thus reducing the time it takes to transmit the packet:

```
root@P1R1# set interfaces ls-0/0/0 unit 0 fragment-threshold ?
Possible completions:
  <fragment-threshold> Fragmentation threshold in 64-byte steps (bytes)
[edit]
root@P1R1# set interfaces ls-0/0/0 unit 0 fragment-threshold  128
```

Now that the larger packets are fragmented, we want to place the nonfragmented packets on the link with the fragmented packets. Otherwise, the voice traffic will have to wait for *all* fragments to transmit before being sent. To turn on this behavior, configure the `interleave-fragments` command underneath the bundle configuration:

```
root@P1R1# set interfaces ls-0/0/0 unit 0 interleave-fragments
```

It is also recommended when LFI is turned on that the member links turn on traffic shaping to reduce jitter. Configure the shaping rate to be equal to the combined physical interface bandwidth for the constituent links. To apply shaping rates to interfaces, you must enable per-unit scheduling in the interfaces.

Since each egress link may not have the same delay, the packets that are not fragmented and are part of the same traffic flow may arrive out of order at the far end. To avoid this scenario (which will increase delay and jitter), each flow should take the same egress link.

By default, the JUNOS software chooses a single link for each unfragmented Transmission Control Protocol/User Datagram Protocol (TCP/UDP) flow over MLPPP links using a hash algorithm, based on the source and destination addresses, source and destination port numbers, and protocol field. This default behavior ensures that flows stay on the correct link and arrive in the correct order at the far end.

The final issue to think about is to enable the voice traffic to have a higher priority and thus be transmitted before the data traffic. Although we will discuss class of service (CoS) in a later chapter, we will provide a high-level discussion here.

To ensure that voice traffic is transmitted first, place it into a higher-priority queue. For CRTP traffic, this mapping occurs automatically, whereas for other traffic, it will have to be configured. Note that the J-series and M-series differ on this mapping. In a J-series router, high-priority traffic, including CRTP, should *only* be mapped to queue 2 on an MLPPP link. When the router maps traffic to constituent links, traffic from queue 2 of the bundle interface will be mapped to queue 2 on the constituent links, whereas traffic from all other queues on the bundle interface will be mapped to a default queue of 0 (as shown in Figure 7-2). Traffic that is placed into other queues on the bundle interface and that is mapped into queue 0 on a constituent link will be serviced according to the relative priority. In other words, if traffic on the bundle interface is placed into queue 1 with a medium-high priority and into queue 4 with a medium-low priority, queue 1 will be scheduled first and will be placed into the constituent link's queue 0 first. In an M-series router using multiclass MLPPP, other queues besides queue 0 and queue 2 could be utilized.

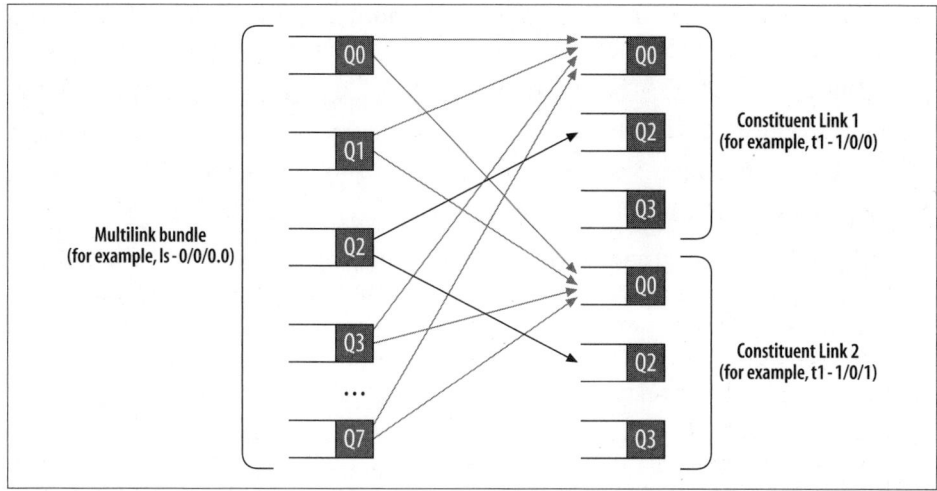

Figure 7-2. J-series queuing and LFI

Multiclass MLPPP

Sometimes when using LFI, fragments from different classes cannot be interleaved. This means that all fragments from a single packet must be sent before any fragments from another packet can be sent. Using LFI, nonfragmented packets can be interleaved with fragmented packets to reduce the latency of the nonfragmented packets. The nonfragmented packets can also be placed into a different queue to be transmitted first, which basically enables two classes of packets: *fragmented* and *nonfragmented*. This model extends to scenarios in which the delay-sensitive traffic comprises the nonfragmented packets, but fails if there is high-priority fragmented traffic that must take precedence over the nonfragmented traffic. In this case, it would make sense to be able to assign a higher priority for some fragmented traffic over nonfragmented traffic by placing some fragmented traffic into a higher-priority queue. This mapping of fragments to different queues is referred to as Multiclass Multilink PPP (MCML).

 MCML is supported only on PICs with link services intelligent queuing (LSQ) interface support—that is, ASPs, ASMs, and Multiservices PICs. It is not supported on a J-series router.

Also, when using classic LFI on MLPPP, packets that are nonfragmented will be balanced across a link on a per-flow basis. This can lead to the *hot link* scenario where a single flow will always take the same link and will not fully utilize the full-bundle bandwidth. MCML can help with this problem by allowing packets that are not fragmented to be load-balanced across multiple links.

Lastly, MCML can be used if you simply need more than two CoSs for either fragmented or nonfragmented packets. In general, MCML needs to be deployed if any of these criteria has to be met:

- Some fragmented traffic needs to be transmitted before nonfragmented traffic.
- Nonfragmented traffic needs to be balanced across multiple links.
- More than two queues (0 and 2) are required.

To configure MCML, you should configure a fragmentation map where a fragmentation threshold is configured and a multilink class is assigned the forwarding class. The other option is to disable fragmentation on a per-forwarding class basis using the no-fragmentation command. If the no-fragmnetation command is used, the fragment-threshold and multilink-class statements cannot be configured:

```
[edit class-of-service fragmentation-maps sample forwarding-class
expedited-forwarding]
lab@PBR# set ?
Possible completions:
+ apply-groups          Groups from which to inherit configuration
data
+ apply-groups-except  Don't inherit configuration data from these
groups
  fragment-threshold   Fragmentation threshold (64..9192 bytes)
  multilink-class      Multilink-Class assigned to this FC (0..7)
  no-fragmentation     Don't allow fragmentation
```

Lastly, the fragmentation map must be tied to the bundle interface under the class-of-service stanza:

```
class-of-service {
    interfaces {
        lsq-0/3/0 {
            unit 1 {
                fragmentation-map sample;
            }
        }
    }
}
```

CRTP

On lower-speed interfaces, serialization and queuing delay can be a factor for delays of sensitive traffic. *Serialization delay* is the time it takes to move the packet out the network interface, and it depends on the clock rate and the size of the packet. For instance, for a 512-byte packet on a T1, the serialization delay would be:

(512 * 8)bits/1,544,000 bits/sec = 2.65 ms

Queuing delay is the time it takes for the packet to be buffered in the router when other packets are being transmitted. This delay is variable but is related to the serialization delay, as each packet has to wait for the previous packet to be sent before it can be transmitted. So, if the buffer is three packets deep, the delay to transmit the 512-byte packet is not 2.65 ms, but perhaps 8 ms to 19 ms.

The most common type of delay for sensitive traffic is voice traffic, which is often transported using the Real-Time Transport Protocol (RTP). RTP is simply a standard packet format to transport voice or video over an IP network, usually using UDP ports in the range of 384–32,767. It produces a header of 40 bytes—12 bytes for RTP, 8 bytes for UDP, and 20 bytes for IP.

One quick way to reduce serialization and, potentially, queuing delay is to reduce the packet size. When using RTP, you can compress the entire IP/UDP/RTP header to a 2- or 4-byte header. As explained earlier in this chapter, this is referred to as Compressed RTP (CRTP) and is standardized in RFC 2508.

Juniper Networks routers can compress RTP traffic in MLPPP bundles. J-series routers can also compress RTP traffic on standard PPP interfaces.

> All CRTP voice traffic is automatically placed into queue 2 on a J-series router.

To enable CRTP on any interface, configure the compression parameters on the link services interface. The router maps which traffic to compress by either matching on a range of UDP port numbers or matching on the queue on which the packet was placed. You can configure both conditions, and the router treats the match as a logical OR. In the following example, a standard PPP interface is using CRTP with a port range of 384–32,767:

```
ls-0/0/0 {
    unit 0 {
        compression {
            rtp {
                port minimum 384 maximum 32767;
            }
        }
        family inet {
            address 10.10.10.1/30;
        }
    }
}
```

You can then map the physical interface to the link services compression interface:

```
t1-0/0/2 {
    description Bock-to-porter;
    unit 0 {
        compression-device ls-0/0/0.0;
    }
}
```

 If you are using CRTP with MLPPP, simply add the compression con-figuration to the existing bundle.

To verify that CRTP is working, use the show services crtp command:

```
lab@Bock# run show services crtp ?
Possible completions:
  <[Enter]>          Execute this command
  extensive          Show CRTP extensive output
  flows              Show CRTP flow table entries
  interface          Name of link services interface
  |                  Pipe through a command
```

Use the show services crtp extensive command to verify correct configuration as well as track statistics for packets exiting the interface:

```
[edit]
lab@Bock# run show services crtp extensive
Interface: ls-0/0/0.0
  Port minimum: 384, Port maximum: 32767
  Maximum UDP compressed sessions: 256
  CRTP maximum period: 256, CRTP maximum time: 5
  Compression ratio: 0, Decompression ratio: 0, Discards: 0
  CRTP stats                    Receive       Transmit
  Sessions                            0              0
  IP bytes                            0              0
  Compressed bytes                    0              0
  CRTP packets                        0              0
  CUDP/CNTCP packets                  0              0
  Full header packets                 0              0
  Context state packets               0              0
  IP packets                          0              0
  Compressed packets                  0              0
```

Multilink Frame Relay

Similar to bonding multiple PPP sessions together, a router can also bond multiple Frame Relay circuits together. These will have the same fragmentation and interleaving characteristics as previously discussed with MLPPP. One bonding standard is FRF.15, which allows the router to bind multiple Frame Relay data-link connection identifiers (DLCIs) together into a single logical interface, as shown in Figure 7-3. The DLCIs could be on the same physical interface or on multiple physical interfaces, but the aggregate bandwidth cannot be greater than a DS3. The advantage of FRF.15 is that the provider does not have any knowledge that link bonding has occurred, but the disadvantage is that the each MLFR bundle can communicate with only a single endpoint.

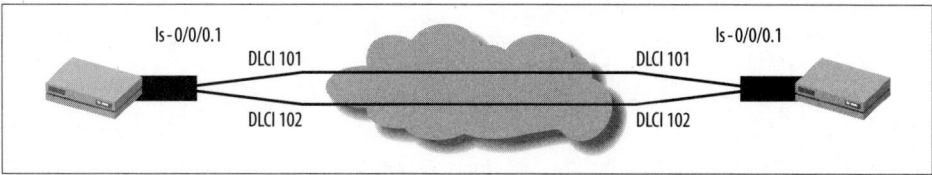

Figure 7-3. FRF.15

> FRF.15 on J-series routers is supported only on T1/E1 interfaces, as of
> JUNOS 8.0R2.

To configure FRF.15, first create a logical unit with the bundle IP address on the link
services interface and specify the desire for FRF.15 with encapsulation `multilink-frame-relay-end-to-end`:

```
ls-0/0/0 {
    unit 1 {
        encapsulation multilink-frame-relay-end-to-end;
        family inet {
            address 84.10.113.1/31;
        }
    }
}
```

Then bond the local DLCIs' values together to the newly created bundle interface. In
this case, the DLCIs were on the same physical interface but could have also been on
different physical interfaces:

```
[edit interfaces t1-0/0/2]
lab@Yeast# show
description Yeast-to-hops2;
encapsulation frame-relay;
unit 101 {
    dlci 101;
    family mlfr-end-to-end {
        bundle ls-0/0/0.1;
    }
}
unit 102 {
    dlci 102;
    family mlfr-end-to-end {
        bundle ls-0/0/0.1;
    }
}
```

Verify that the links are bonded by viewing the bundle interface:

```
lab@hops# run show interfaces ls-0/0/0.1
    Logical interface ls-0/0/0.1 (Index 70) (SNMP ifIndex 37)
        Flags: Point-To-Point SNMP-Traps 0x4000 Encapsulation: Multilink-FR
        Bandwidth: 3072kbps
```

```
Statistics          Frames        fps          Bytes         bps
Bundle:
  Fragments:
    Input :           71           0            5030           0
    Output:            3           0             264           0
  Packets:
    Input :           71           0            4604           0
    Output:            3           0             270           0
Link:
  t1-0/0/2.101
    Input :           36           0            2540           0
    Output:            2           0             176           0
  t1-0/0/2.102
    Input :           35           0            2490           0
    Output:            1           0              88           0
Protocol inet, MTU: 1500
  Flags: None
  Addresses, Flags: Is-Preferred Is-Primary
    Destination: 84.10.113.0/31, Local: 84.10.113.1
```

Another type of Frame Relay bonding is called FRF.16, which allows the router to take multiple physical connections from the provider and tie them into a single logical connection, as shown in Figure 7-4. Once this connection is bonded together, one or more DLCIs could be configured over this single logical connection. This allows for incremental and increased bandwidth Frame Relay connections, while also allowing the provider to combine each bundle into multiple high-speed bundles in the network. The advantage over FRF.15 is that a different endpoint in each bundle is supported, but the disadvantage is that the provider is no longer transparent to bundling.

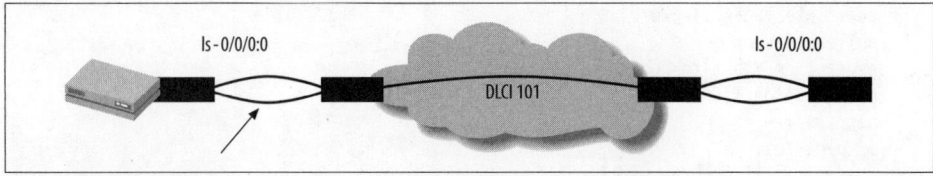

Figure 7-4. FRF.16

To configure FRF.16 on a Juniper router, the link services interface is configured and *channelized*. A channel is designated, but the colon (:) represents the FRF.16 logical bundle. You can configure a single DLCI or multiple DLCIs to different endpoints in this bundle.

First, to create a channelized bundle interface, set the mlfr-unu-nni-bundles statement under [edit chassis]. Channels start counting at zero, so the following configuration will create an ls-/0/0/0:0:

```
chassis {
    fpc 0 {
        pic 0 {
```

```
        mlfr-uni-nni-bundles 1;
    }
}
```

Here is a bundle specified as channel 1 with one DLCI specified:

```
ls-0/0/0:0{
    encapsulation multilink-frame-relay-uni-nni;
    unit 0 {
        dlci 101;
        family inet {
            address 101.88.77.1/30;
        }
    }
}
```

A last point to understand in MLFR is that the physical interfaces, such as those with two Juniper T1s, will need to be bonded together to the logical bundle ls-0/0/0:0 interface:

```
t1-0/0/2 {
    encapsulation multilink-frame-relay-uni-nni;
    unit 0 {
        family mlfr-uni-nni {
            bundle ls-0/0/0:0
        }
    }
}

t1-0/1/2 {
    encapsulation multilink-frame-relay-uni-nni;
    unit 0 {
        family mlfr-uni-nni {
            bundle ls-0/0/0:0
        }
    }
}
```

GRE

We already examined the configuration for a basic GRE tunnel in Chapter 2:

```
gr-0/0/0 {
    unit 0 {
        tunnel {
            source 10.20.1.38;
            destination 172.66.13.1;
        }
        family inet
    }
}
```

Although various PICs will allow a GRE tunnel to be created on an M-series router, using an ASP, a Multiservices PIC, or a J-series router can enable a few additional features, namely key numbers (ASP, Monitoring Services only), fragmentation, and tunnel MTU.

 Although GRE tunnels are supported on an M-series router using an ASP in Layer 2 or Layer 3 mode, fragmentation and GRE keys are supported only in Layer 3 mode.

The first feature is taken from RFC 2890 and is called "Key and Sequence Number Extensions to GRE." This RFC adds two more optional fields that can be carried in the GRE header: a *key field* and a *sequence number field.* The key field is inserted by the sender and is matched at the receiver to identify fields. If the key fields do not match, the packet is dropped. Currently, only the ASP and Monitoring Services PIC support this feature, and only one key is allowed per source and destination pair. To enable this feature, manually configure a key value under the logical unit:

```
lab@Cider set interfaces gr-0/0/0 unit 0 tunnel key 123
```

A concern when configuring any type of tunnel is making sure the maximum payload is no larger than the MTU across the entire path. By default, the gr interface has an unlimited physical MTU and a protocol MTU that is equivalent to the MTU of the next hop interface toward the tunnel destination. So, when an IP packet arrives at the ingress router, the GRE header is added, with the do-not-fragment bit set, and the IP packet is sent to the egress router. If a transit router had a smaller MTU than the ingress router, the packet would be dropped.

 In JUNOS 8.0R2.8, path MTU is enabled by default. You can disable it for GRE tunnels.

A few tools in the router can solve this issue. For example, use path MTU discovery to determine the MTUs that are along the path. In the current JUNOS release, path discovery is enabled by default. The following example shows that the maximum IP protocol MTU can be 726:

```
[edit]
lab@Water# run show interfaces gr-0/0/0.0 extensive | match mtu
   Type: GRE, Link-level type: GRE, MTU: Unlimited, Speed: 800mbps
      Protocol inet, MTU: 726, Generation: 141, Route table: 0
```

A problem can arise when traffic is coming into the router with an MTU that is too large and the do-not-fragment bit is set. If you must send traffic with the do-not-fragment bit over the tunnel, you can override the sender's wishes by having the router clear the do-not-fragment bit. In the following example, router Wheat is trying to send traffic over the GRE tunnel that is too large, and Water is sending an Internet Control Message Protocol (ICMP) error message indicating that the packet is being dropped:

```
[edit]
root@Wheat# run ping 5.5.5.5 size 700 do-not-fragment
PING 5.5.5.5 (5.5.5.5): 700 data bytes
36 bytes from 1.1.1.2: frag needed and DF set (MTU 726)
Vr HL TOS  Len   ID Flg  off TTL Pro  cks      Src      Dst
 4  5  00 02d8 3274   2 0000  40  01 f9a5 1.1.1.1  5.5.5.5

36 bytes from 1.1.1.2: frag needed and DF set (MTU 726)
Vr HL TOS  Len   ID Flg  off TTL Pro  cks      Src      Dst
 4  5  00 02d8 3275   2 0000  40^C
--- 5.5.5.5 ping statistics ---
2 packets transmitted, 0 packets received, 100% packet loss
```

On a J-series router or with the ASP, ASM, or Monitoring Services PIC, you can enable a `clear-dont-fragment` command, which allows for ingress fragmentation as well as clearing the do-not-fragment bit on all packets that transmit the tunnel. Note, however, that although the original packets have the do-not-fragment bit cleared, the GRE packets still have the DF bit set. This command is set on Water:

```
[edit]
lab@Water# set interfaces gr-0/0/0 unit 0 clear-dont-fragment-bit

[edit]
lab@Water# commit
[edit interfaces gr-0/0/0]
  'unit 0'
    gr-0/0/0.0: Must configure INET family MTU
error: configuration check-out failed
```

To use this command, you must also set the MTU value so that the ingress router knows which size packets to begin fragmenting. This MTU value should be the smallest value along the entire path of the GRE tunnel.

```
lab@Water# set interfaces gr-0/0/0 unit 0 family inet mtu 726
```

Verify correct operation by reissuing the ping command from router Wheat:

```
[edit]
root@Wheat# run ping 5.5.5.5 size 1400 do-not-fragment
PING 5.5.5.5 (5.5.5.5): 700 data bytes
1408 bytes from 5.5.5.5: icmp_seq=0 ttl=63 time=18.449 ms
1408 bytes from 5.5.5.5: icmp_seq=1 ttl=63 time=120.600 ms
1408 bytes from 5.5.5.5: icmp_seq=2 ttl=63 time=30.325 ms
^C
```

Layer 2 Services Summary

This section examined many of the services that you can enable, such as multilink bonding compression and GRE features. The rest of the chapter examines the Layer 3 services that you can also deploy in your network. You may consider taking a brief break before diving into the next section, as it moves a layer up in the protocol stack—because this one layer is Layer 3, the network layer, it will be a large jump!

Layer 3 Services

The JUNOS software services are not limited to just Layer 2 services, but can also include Layer 3 services. These services include stateful firewall, NAT, IDS, and IPSec tunnels. We will give an overview of these services here and will provide a detailed discussion of them in Chapter 8.

 On the ASP or Multiservices-100 PIC, you must choose to enable *either* Layer 2 *or* Layer 3 services; the ASM on the M7i and the J-series router support *both* Layer 2 and Layer 3 concurrently.

Stateful Firewall

Usually when certain traffic needs to be blocked on a router, a simple stateless packet filter is applied to an interface. On a Juniper router, these are called *firewall filters* (other vendors call these *access lists*). Regardless of the name, all stateless filters function in the same manner—they look at a packet and operate on a series of match rules. If the packet matches a rule, it can be either accepted or discarded.

The important point about a packet filter is that it works on a packet-by-packet basis and does not associate a packet with a traffic flow or stream. In other words, it does not maintain any connection state. This type of filter will work in many situations when applications are using well-known port numbers or TCP applications, where the initiator is always in the same direction. Stateless packet filters become more difficult when the application uses random port numbers—TCP initiators are not always the same—or when UDP input and output flows need to be associated with each other. For example, if a Domain Name System (DNS) server was located outside your network, you could easily write a packet filter that allows outbound access to UDP port 53, but you would need to write a rule for the inbound packet as well. The source port would be port 53, but the destination port could be any port from 1024–65534, depending on which random port the host chose. Allowing this large of a UDP port opens up a large hole in your network.

A stateful firewall will track *flows* of traffic for a given application such as DNS, which will provide for much stronger security. This means that if a packet hits the firewall rule and is accepted based on the match conditions, the system will calculate the return packet, so no reverse rule will have to be created. A flow is usually defined by parameters such as source and destination addresses, source and destination port numbers, and protocol values. A bidirectional flow between the source and destination devices is often called a *session* or a *conversation*. Once a session or conversation is created, it is stored in memory, so the firewall rules do not need to process any additional packets that are part of that flow. These conversations will be stored until a period of inactivity occurs, which is 30 seconds by default for most protocols. You can modify this globally under the service interface:

```
lab@hops# set interfaces sp-0/0/0 services-options inactivity-timeout ?
Possible completions:
  <inactivity-timeout>  Inactivity timeout period for established sessions
```

A flow is removed from the table under the following conditions:

- If a TCP RESET or FIN packet is received. The flow is marked for deletion and is removed in approximately five seconds.

- If the TCP flow appears to be idle (no traffic). In this case, the router implements a TCP tickle by sending an ACK message with the last seen sequence number, minus one numeral, to the end host. This verifies whether the ports are open. If no response is received, the flow is marked for deletion in approximately five seconds.

- If the forward flow of the UDP conversation reaches the inactivity timeout period. Since the reverse flow will be created based on the forward flow, this flow will not be tracked for inactivity.

The stateful firewall will also add a layer of protection by checking to make sure there are no strange protocol anomalies that could indicate a denial of service (DoS) attack. Some examples of protocol anomalies that are checked include the following:

- The Time to Live (TTL) in the IP packet equals 0.
- The source IP address equals the destination IP address.
- An IP fragment is missed.
- The TCP or UDP port is set to 0.
- TCP flags are set to an invalid combination.
- A SYN packet is received without a SYN-ACK response.
- The first flow packet is not a SYN packet.
- ICMP unreachable errors occur for SYN or UDP packets.

This is a small list of the possible anomalies; please consult the Juniper Technical Documentation for a more complete list.

Application Layer Gateways

Most of the time, the stateful firewall will easily be able to predict the packets that will be required for the return flow of a conversation by simply reversing the source and destination port numbers, addresses, and so forth. However, some applications, such as FTP, H.323, RTSP used by RealAudio, and SIP, are more difficult to predict because the application may initiate separate connections for data and control flows or may generate new protocol flows based on an open connection. In this case, special care must be taken to analyze the packets and allow the new connections to be established. Each application may have a unique set of parameters that must be examined, which are implemented as Application Later Gateways (ALGs).

The classic example of why an ALG is needed is when you look at an application such as an active outgoing FTP, which uses both a control and a data channel. First, the TCP three-way handshake is established between the client (84.10.113.0) and the server (84.10.113.1) using a destination port of 20:

```
02:21:00.500569  In IP 84.10.113.0.4290 > 84.10.113.1.20: Syn
02:21:00.500627 Out IP 84.10.113.1.20 > 84.10.113.0.4290: Syn Ack
02:21:00.510683  In IP 84.10.113.0.4290 > 84.10.113.1.20: .   Ack
```

Then the server initiates a new connection for the data transfer using a new source port of 21 and a destination port that the client gives to the server in the initial connection using a PORT command (56958, in this case):

```
02:26:28.024058 Out IP 84.10.113.1.21 > 84.10.113.0.56958: Syn
02:26:28.032298  In IP 84.10.113.0.56958 > 84.10.113.1.21: Syn Ack
02:26:28.032362 Out IP 84.10.113.1.21 > 84.10.113.0.56958: . Ack
```

So, the problem with the active mode FTP application and standard firewall rules is that the connections are initiated by both the server and the client, and the connection initiated by the server to the client is using an unpredictable port number.

The ALG solves this problem by looking deep into the packets during the initial connection phase for the PORT command, indicating which port number the client will be expecting from the server during the data phase and allowing the firewall to create a predictable pinhole for the server-to-client connection.

If passive FTP is used, all connections are initiated from the client to the server, but the ALG must still monitor the PORT command from the server to open the data connection.

Another example in which ALG is needed is when you're using H.323, the umbrella specification for a family of protocols for transporting voice and video over data networks. H.323 involves protocols that open control and data channels similar to our FTP example. In a common setup and data flow, these steps occur:

1. First, an H.225 connection is created for call signaling, the media (audio and video), the stream packetization, the media stream synchronization, and the control message formats.

2. During the H.225 connection, information is exchanged to also establish an H.245 connection.

3. An H.245 connection is established to convey control information for the media flow, such as encryption and flow control as well as port information for RTP/RTCP flows.

4. RTP/RTCP data traffic flows begin.

The ALG that is used for H.323 is more complex than in the FTP example, but the general idea of watching one conversation to open more flows is the same. The ALG watches the H.225 connection for information to open the H.245 connection and then watches this connection to open the media connections.

Since these ALGs can be very complex, most of them are already created in the Juniper Networks router for you, although you can create custom ALGs. You can view all the Juniper-defined ALGs by issuing the show groups junos-defaults applications command from configuration mode. All default system applications will begin with the junos keyword.

Network Address Translation

NAT is simply the changing of the IP address (source, destination, or both) of the packet as it traverses the router. These translations are stored in a table to allow for traffic flows from the source to the destination systems. Additionally, port numbers could also be translated (often referred to as Network Address Port Translation [NAPT] or Port Address Translation [PAT]). Traditionally, NAT was used to hide private addresses behind a public network or to try to conserve address space by mapping multiple port numbers to a single IP address. When NAT is configured, you must answer the following questions:

- Which IP address is going to be translated: the source IP (source-NAT), the destination IP (destination-NAT), or both (bidirectional NAT)?
- Does port translation need to occur?
- Does the mapping need to be the same (static) or can a pool of addresses and ports be used (dynamic)?

Next, you must examine the type of NAT that must be configured. The NAT types available on a Juniper router include the following:

Static source NAT
    Maps a pool of private IP addresses to a pool of public addresses on a one-to-one basis. This means traffic from a private address, such as 192.168.2.1, will always be mapped to the same public address, such as 207.12.18.2.

Dynamic source NAT
    Maps a pool of private IP addresses to a pool of public addresses. This mapping is dynamic, so 192.168.2.1 could be translated to the configured public address pool.

Source NAT with port translation
    Maps a pool of private IP addresses to a single address or pool of public addresses, while also translating the port numbers. This allows for one-to-many NAT, when many private IP addresses are translated to a single public address.

Destination NAT
    Behaves the same as source NAT, except it operates on the incoming flow of the destination address. Destination NAT will translate an incoming public address

to one or many private addresses. One use of this is to allow the Internet to use a public address to contact a server on the internal network that is configured with a private IP address.

Bidirectional NAT
A combination of a source NAT and destination NAT in which Host A can initiate a session with Host B and Host B can also initiate a session with Host A. This is common when an email server is onsite.

Twice NAT
Defined in RFC 2663 and similar to bidirectional NAT. The major difference is that in twice NAT, the source and destination addresses are translated within the same flow, whereas bidirectional NAT would use different flows.

You can configure NAT on a Juniper Networks router as a standalone service or combine it with another service, such as stateful firewall.

Intrusion Detection Services

Intrusion detection monitors traffic flows and looks for hostile patterns. If such a pattern exists, the event can be logged. Intrusion detection and prevention (IDP) takes this one step further by stopping an attack once a hostile pattern is recognized. The Juniper Networks router is limited in its IDP implementation, as it does not match on any higher-layer signature attacks. Essentially, the IDP implantation can aid in protecting your network from attacks such as the following:

Port scanning
When a hostile machine probes the network for open ports to attack.

SYN flood attacks
When a high number of SYN packets are received in an attempt to flood the network.

IP fragmentation attacks
Protects against packets with the `more fragments` flag set, such as attacks like Teardrop and Boink. Teardrop attacks exploit the reassembly of fragmented IP packets by offsetting the options in the IP header. When the sum of the offset and size of one fragmented packet differ from that of the next fragmented packet, the packets overlap, and the server attempting to reassemble the packet can crash.

ICMP floods
When ICMP echo requests overload its victim with so many requests that all its resources respond until it can no longer process valid network traffic.

When any of these attacks occur, events are logged and are sent to a collector for analysis, or in the case of flood attacks, are rate-limited. You also can prevent SYN floods by configuring SYN cookie protection that will cause the router to operate as a *SYN proxy*. We will discuss this further in Chapter 8.

IPSec VPN

When securing data over a public network, often a tunnel is configured between the two networks. A tunnel simply encapsulates your data into another packet or frame to transport it across the public network. For instance, you can create a tunnel to connect Remote Office A to Corporate Office B over the public Internet, as shown in Figure 7-5, to create a virtual private network (VPN).

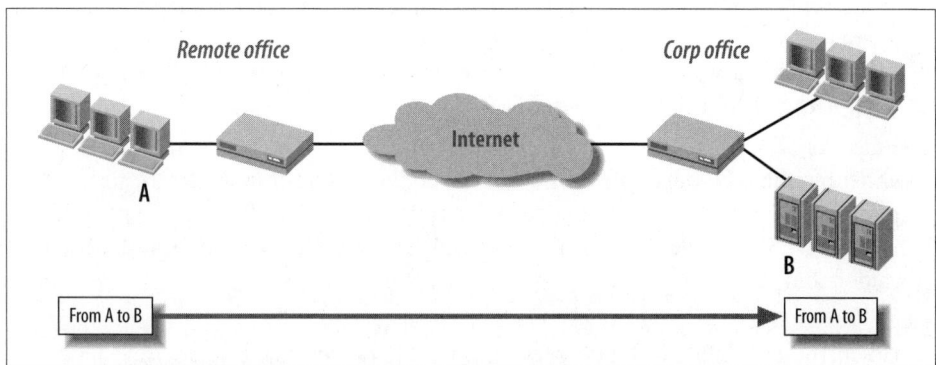

Figure 7-5. Connecting a remote office to the corporate office

 The purpose of this book is not to teach IPSec theory; a number of books do that well, such as *IPSec: The New Security Standard for the Internet, Intranets, and Virtual Private Networks* (Prentice Hall).

You can use many tunneling protocols for this connection, but one of the most widely deployed protocols for transporting IP traffic is IPSec. IPSec can provide the following security functions:

Source authentication
> Ensures that the data is from the expected sender. This is accomplished by the ingress router of the IPSec tunnel, creating a one-way hash value of certain parameters of the packet as well as a password (preshared key) that is known by both endpoints. It will insert this hash value into the packet so that when the receiving endpoint examines the packet, it can compare this value with the hash that will be locally computed. If they are the same, the authentication passes; if they are different, the authentication fails. Common algorithms to accomplish this are Message Digest 5 (MD5) and the Secure Hash Algorithm (SHA-1).

 A *hash function* is a predictable mathematical calculation that takes some variable-size input and produces a fixed-size string called a *hash*. A key attribute of a hash is that it is one-way operation—so, the hash value can be created based on the input but the input cannot be recreated based on the hash value. Hash functions are used in both authentication and data integrity.

Data integrity

Ensures that the data was not altered during packet transmission. A hash value is computed and is placed into the packet based on packet fields. The receiving router will compute a hash based on the same fields of the packet and then compare the computed hash value with the received hash value. If they are not equivalent, the data was altered and the packet will be dropped. The hash algorithm that is used is normally MD5 or SHA-1.

Confidentiality

Ensures that the data cannot be read over the public infrastructure. IPSec provides confidentiality by encrypting the traffic using the Data Encryption Standard (DES), Triple DES (3DES), or Advanced Encryption Standard (AES) algorithm.

Replay protection

Even though data can be encrypted, a hostile device can intercept a packet, recreate it, and send a flood of that packet to the endpoint to try to create a DoS attack. To protect against this, sequence numbers are verified to avoid packet duplication.

When an IPSec tunnel is made, the tunnel endpoints create a security association (SA) with each VPN. An SA is a list of the protocols, algorithms, and protected networks upon which both endpoints have agreed. These SAs can be created manually on each side, or dynamically with the use of the Internet Key Exchange (IKE) protocol. IKE consists of two phases: Phase 1 establishes the protocols and shared secrets needed to create a secure channel; and Phase 2 uses this secure channel to exchange the protocols, algorithms, and other parameters that will be used for the data exchange, thus creating the SAs. When Phase 2 has completed, data can flow securely between the two endpoints, as shown in Figure 7-6.

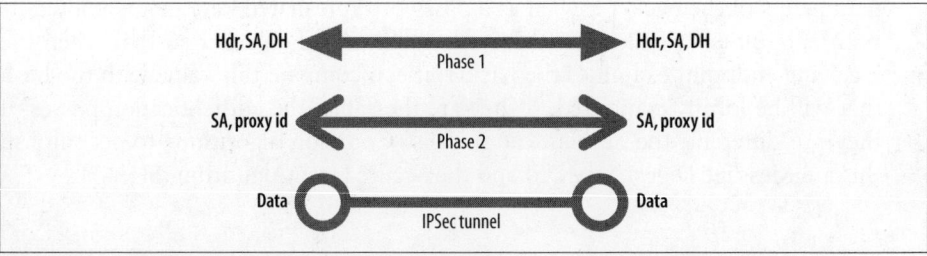

Figure 7-6. IPSec VPN dynamic tunnel establishment

Layer 3 Services Summary

This section examined many Layer 3 services, including NAT, stateful firewall, IDP, and IPSec-based VPNs. In the next section, we will put this theory into practice as we configure and operationally verify various network layer services.

Layer 3 Services Configuration

The first step when configuring Layer 3 services on your router is to enable the hardware for those services. If the ASP or Multiservices PIC is used, you must specify the layer of service as either Layer 2 or Layer 3:

```
lab@sake# set chassis fpc 1 pic 2 adaptive-services service-package ?
Possible completions:
  layer-2              Layer 2 service package
  layer-3              Layer 3 service package
[edit]


lab@sake# show chassis hardware
Hardware inventory:
Item          Version Part number Serial number Description
Chassis                           A1609         M7i
Midplane      REV 04  710-008761  CR6773        M7i Midplane
Power Supply 1 Rev 06 740-008537  6039089       AC Power Supply
Routing Engine REV 01 740-011202  1000618737    RE-850
CFEB          REV 08  750-010464  CR5380        Internet Processor II
FPC 0                                           E-FPC
  PIC 0       REV 11  750-002992  CT2202        4x F/E, 100 BASE-TX
  PIC 2       REV 08  750-005724  CR1650        2x OC-3 ATM-II IQ, MM
FPC 1                                           E-FPC
  PIC 2       REV 07  750-009487  CP5197        ASP - Integrated
  PIC 3       REV 10  750-009098  CR4858        2x F/E, 100 BASE-TX
```

The ASM and J-series routers do not contain this limitation and can support *both* types of services concurrently. The main building block when configuring JUNOS software services is called a *service set*, which is a list of service interfaces, service types, and service rules applied to either an interface or a routing next hop. A service set can contain one type of Layer 3 service or a grouping of services such as NAT, IDS, and stateful firewall. If an IPSec VPN is required, you must place it in its own unique service set.

To match which packet will be processed by each service set, you must write a set of rules with a match condition and an action. These rules have a similar format to JUNOS software policies and stateless firewall filter rules, containing a from statement for the match portion and a then statement for the action. But a major difference is that service rules are always processed in a stateful manner, so the match clauses do not need to account for return traffic. The match clauses will have a variety of options depending on the service configured, and the actions will define which service to apply. You also can combine the rules for each service to form a rule set, as shown in Figure 7-7.

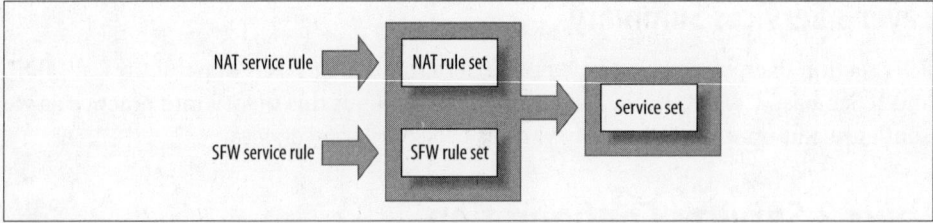

Figure 7-7. CLI rule, rule set, and service set relationship

When you create your service set, you'll need to decide whether it should be applied as an interface or a next hop. An interface-style service set is applied directly to the interface affecting traffic as it leaves and enters the interface.

 An interface-style service set tracks session on a per-service-set basis. This means that the same service set could be applied to multiple physical interfaces to design around asymmetrical traffic flows.

A next hop-style service set makes use of two logical service interfaces, called the *inside* and *outside* interfaces. Traffic is mapped to these interfaces as a result of a routing next hop lookup. The traffic can enter or exit *either* the inside or the outside interface depending on the configuration, which depends primarily on the routing configuration and stateful-firewall rules.

Both types of service styles use the service interface, named sp-, in the definition of the service set. This interface is the software interface that the router will send traffic to if a Layer 3 service is required. The interface-style service set requires a single logical unit to be configured with IPv4 support enabled:

```
lab@Porter# set interfaces sp-0/0/0 unit 0 family inet

lab@Porter# show interfaces
sp-0/0/0 {
    unit 0 {
        family inet;
```

 When configuring the sp- interface, the system generally reserves unit 0 for service logging and other communication from the service PIC; however, you can use it for an interface-style service set not used in a virtual router. Next hop service sets cannot use unit 0.

The next hop service set requires the service interface to be logically divided into an inside and outside interface:

```
[edit]
lab@Porter# set interfaces sp-0/0/0 unit 1 service-domain inside family inet
```

```
[edit]
lab@Porter# set interfaces sp-0/0/0 unit 2 service-domain outside family inet

[edit]
lab@Porter# show interfaces sp-0/0/0
unit 0 {
    family inet;
}
unit 1 {
    family inet;
    service-domain inside;
}
unit 2 {
    family inet;
    service-domain outside;
}
```

After creating the service interfaces, you'll need to create the service rules and the service sets. When creating the service rules, one item you must configure is a direction of either *input* or *output*, as shown in Figure 7-8. The direction that is recorded for a packet must match for the service rule to match. This direction is straightforward for an interface-style service set, as input is for incoming traffic to the physical interface, and output is for traffic leaving the physical interface.

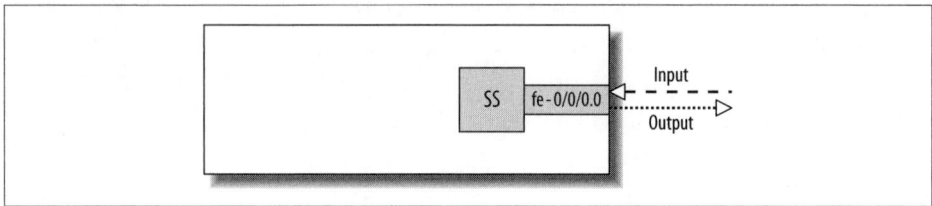

Figure 7-8. Directions for interface-style service sets

But when you look at a next hop-style service set, the direction is a bit more complex because now the next hop could point to two possible logical interfaces. If the next hop points to the inside interface, the direction is *input*, and if the next hop points to the outside interface, the direction is *output*. The direction for next hop-style service sets is often misconfigured, which causes traffic to be serviced incorrectly. Figure 7-9 shows the proper directions that you should use when creating service rules.

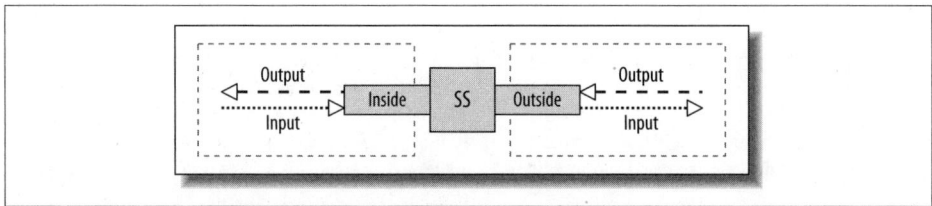

Figure 7-9. Directions for next hop-style service sets

When configuring service rules for next hop-style service sets, you should consider traffic flow from the perspective of the inside interface. Traffic that the router routes to the inside interface is considered input traffic on the inside interface and is considered input traffic by the router when it evaluates service rules. Traffic that the router receives on the outside interface, processes, and then transmits out the inside interface is considered output traffic on the outside interface and is considered output traffic by the router when it evaluates service rules. In general, it may be much less confusing to point traffic to the inside interface when possible, as the directions seem to be as expected, while the outside interface appears to be opposite from what is expected. Although traffic mapping to an inside interface may make more sense in the human mind, the router makes no logical distinction, so mapping to either the inside or the outside configuration will work.

Since next hop-style service sets are a little more complex, it seems as though interface-style service sets would be preferred. Each service set, however, has its own advantages and disadvantages, as detailed in Table 7-3.

For instance, an interface-style service set has the following limitations:

- It cannot support multicast traffic matched through the service set (including IPSec tunnels).
- It cannot have overlapping address spaces (such as RFC 1918) that need to be NATed.
- It cannot run routing protocols over the service sets, such as IPSec tunnels.
- Locally generated traffic will not match the rules.

So, to solve any of those four general limitations, you *must* use a next hop service set.

Interface-style service sets do have their place, though; they are much easier to configure for simple tasks, and they are easier to apply to multiple interfaces. If the same service needs to be applied to multiple interfaces with separate route tables for individual customers, a next hop service set would require multiple service sets, whereas an interface-style service set might require only a single service set. Also, an interface-style service set allows for the use of an external interface address for certain NAT circumstances that a next hop service set cannot accomplish. Therefore, you should choose a service set based on which features need to be supported. Table 7-3 can assist you as a general guideline for choosing your service style.

Table 7-3. Summary of service-style feature support

Service style	General configuration complexity	Multicast support	Routing protocols over IPSec	Overlapping NAT addresses	PAT with external interface in the NAT pool	Treat IPSec tunnels as a link	Number of security zones supported
Interface	Easy	No	No	No	Yes	No	One

Table 7-3. Summary of service-style feature support (continued)

Service style	General configuration complexity	Multicast support	Routing protocols over IPSec	Overlapping NAT addresses	PAT with external interface in the NAT pool	Treat IPSec tunnels as a link	Number of security zones supported
Next hop	Hard	Yes	Yes	Yes	No	Yes	Many

You will have to apply the service set for it to take effect. You can apply it directly to the interface unit (interface style) or reference the service interface (next hop).

First, here is an example of a service set applied directly to interface t1-0/0/2:

```
lab@Porter# show interfaces t1-0/0/2
description Porter-to-Bock;
unit 0 {
    family inet {
        service {
            input {
                service-set test-rule;
            }
            output {
                service-set test-rule;
            }
        }
        address 10.10.10.2/30;
    }
}
```

The service set test-rule is applied to the interface at the logical unit level and is applied for family inet (IPv4) traffic. The strange piece of this configuration is the fact that the service set must be applied as *both* an input and an output service, and it *must* be the same service set. This means direction is never inferred when applying a service set to an interface. Recall that the direction of a rule is decided in the service rule and not in the direction in which the service set is applied to the interface!

 Applying the service set to both the input and the output of an interface has no real purpose in the current implementation; it was created as part of the original specification outline. There was a thought that asymmetrical traffic with different service sets would be supported, but it was decided later not to implement that function in JUNOS software.

If a next hop service type is used, simply configure the router to forward packets to either the inside or the outside service interface. This is usually done by creating a static route that points to the service interface, which in turn creates another route table to point traffic to the service interface or runs a routing protocol over the service interface. This example sends all 5.5.0/19 traffic to the sp-0/0/0.1 (inside) interface:

```
[edit]
lab@Porter# show routing-options
static {
    route 5.5.0.0/19 next-hop sp-0/0/0.1;
}
```

This verifies that the route is active:

```
[edit]
lab@Porter# run show route protocol static

inet.0: 10 destinations, 10 routes (10 active, 0 holddown, 0 hidden)
+ = Active Route, - = Last Active, * = Both

5.5.0.0/19          *[Static/5] 00:00:08
                     > via sp-0/0/0.1
```

Simple Interface-Style Service Set

We will discuss Layer 3 services in more detail in the next chapter, but here let's examine a simple example of a stateful-firewall rule to illustrate how the CLI pieces fit together using the topology shown in Figure 7-10. A stateful firewall is going to be applied on Porter's t1-0/0/2 interface for traffic from Bock to Yeast's loopback address of 10.30.1.1.

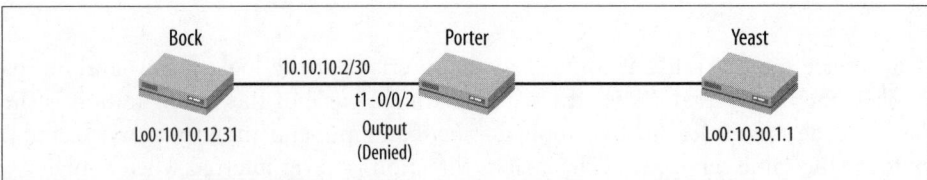

Figure 7-10. Topology for a simple interface-style stateful firewall

This firewall will allow traffic to be initiated from the Bock loopback to Yeast's loopback, but not initiated from Yeast to Bock. To configure, first create a logical unit on the sp- interface with IPv4 support on Porter:

```
lab@Porter#  show interfaces
sp-0/0/0 {
    unit 0 {
        family inet;
    }
}
```

Then configure a stateful rule to allow traffic from Bock to Yeast's loopback address. Since this is going to be applied on Porter's t1-0/0/2 interface for traffic received from Bock, the direction should be input:

```
[edit services]
lab@Porter# show
```

```
stateful-firewall {
    rule simple-rule {
        match-direction input;
        term 1 {
            from {
                destination-address {
                    10.30.1.1/32;
                }
            }
            then {
                accept;
            }
        }
    }
}
```

Now create an interface-style service set and apply the rule and service interface:

```
[edit services]
lab@Porter# show service-set test-rule
stateful-firewall-rules simple-rule;
interface-service {
    service-interface sp-0/0/0.0;
}
```

Apply the service set to the t1-0/0/2 interface as both an input and an output:

```
[edit services]
lab@Porter# top show interfaces t1-0/0/2
description Porter-to-Bock;
unit 0 {
    family inet {
        service {
            input {
                service-set test-rule;
            }
            output {
                service-set test-rule;
            }
        }
        address 10.10.10.2/30;
    }
}
```

The last step is to test the stateful firewall on Porter, so a ping is issued from Bock to Yeast to test connectivity; this example shows that it succeeds:

```
[edit]
lab@Bock# run ping 10.30.1.1 count 100 rapid size 700
PING 10.30.1.1 (10.30.1.1): 700 data bytes
!!!!!!!!!!!!!!!!!!!!!!!!!!!!!!!!!!!!!!!!!!!!!!!!!!!!!!!!!!!!!!!!!!!!!!!!!!!!!!!!!!!!!!!!
!!!!!!!!!!!!!!!!
--- 10.30.1.1 ping statistics ---
100 packets transmitted, 100 packets received, 0% packet loss
round-trip min/avg/max/stddev = 17.787/23.982/125.399/14.994 ms
```

To verify that the packets are traversing the stateful firewall, several show services state-firewall commands are issued. The first command is show services stateful-firewall flows, which displays the active flows that are transiting the system. In this case, the ping from Bock to Yeast is observed with 100 packets (Frm count) sent in both directions:

```
[edit services]
lab@Porter# run show services stateful-firewall flows
Interface: sp-0/0/0, Service set: test-rule
Flow                                     State   Dir   Frm count
ICMP    10.30.1.1:8471  -> 10.10.10.1   Watch   O     100
ICMP    10.10.10.1:8471 ->  10.30.1.1   Watch   I     100
```

When there is a related flow from input to output and output to input, it is called a *conversation*, and you can view it with the show services stateful-firewall conversations command. A flow must exist in each direction to be stored as a conversation that is *not* traffic-dependent, as the router will always create the return flow after the initial communication is initiated. Once again, the test ping traffic is observed:

```
[edit services]
lab@Porter# run show services stateful-firewall conversations
Interface: sp-0/0/0, Service set: test-rule

Conversation: ALG protocol: icmp
  Number of initiators: 1, Number of responders: 1
Flow                                     State   Dir   Frm count
ICMP    10.10.10.1:8471  ->  10.30.1.1   Watch   I     100
ICMP    10.30.1.1:8471   -> 10.10.10.1   Watch   O     100
```

 Every flow is given a state of either Forward, Drop, or Watch. A Forward flow forwards without looking at the payload, a Drop discards, and a Watch looks at the payload of the packet to determine whether the packet should be forwarded. If a flow is part of an ALG, it will always remain in the Watch state, but if it is part of a predicted flow, it may transition to the Forward state.

A final, useful command, show services stateful-firewall statistics, is used to view the statistics for a given service set rule. Notice in the following example that 200 packets have been accepted: 100 for the ICMP echo, and 100 for the ICMP reply, created when we issued the ping command on Bock:

```
[edit services]
lab@Porter# run show services stateful-firewall statistics
Interface   Service set    Accept   Discard   Reject   Errors
sp-0/0/0    test-rule      200      0         0        0
```

Lastly, verify that the stateful firewall is blocking traffic initiated from Yeast to Bock by pinging the loopback of Bock and sourcing from Yeast's loopback address:

```
lab@Yeast# run ping 10.10.12.3 source 10.30.1.1 rapid count 100
PING 10.10.12.3 (10.10.12.3): 56 data bytes
```

```
.......................................................................
..............
--- 10.10.12.3 ping statistics ---
100 packets transmitted, 0 packets received, 100% packet loss
```

All packets are being lost, and you can verify this on Porter by looking at the flow and the drop states, as well as by viewing the stateful-firewall statistics and noting that the Discard counter is increasing:

```
[edit services]
lab@Porter# run show services stateful-firewall flows
Interface: sp-0/0/0, Service set: test-rule
Flow                                      State    Dir      Frm count
ICMP      10.30.1.1:36119 ->  10.10.12.3  Drop     0               3

[edit services]
lab@Porter# run show services stateful-firewall statistics
Interface   Service set    Accept   Discard   Reject    Errors
sp-0/0/0    test-rule         200       100        0         0
```

Service Filters and Post-Service Filters

You can configure some additional configuration options on the interface where the service set is applied. For instance, you can apply multiple service sets to a single logical interface:

```
t1-0/0/2 {
    description Porter-to-Bock;
    unit 0 {
        family inet {
            service {
                input {
                    service-set new-service-set;
                    service-set test-rule;
                }
                output {
                    service-set new-service-set
                    service-set test-rule;
                }
            }
            address 10.10.10.2/30;
        }
    }
}
```

However, if multiple service sets are applied to a single logical interface, traffic must be mapped to one service set or another. You can accomplish this with service filters, as indicated when trying to issue a commit with the preceding configuration:

```
lab@Porter# commit
[edit interfaces t1-0/0/2 unit 0 family inet service input]
  'service-set new-service-set'
     Service will never be used without service filter on previous service-set
```

```
[edit]
  'interfaces'
    error parsing interfaces object
error: configuration check-out failed
```

A service filter is configured under the [edit firewall] level and has very similar match conditions as a standard JUNOS firewall filter. A major difference is that it must be configured under [edit firewall family inet].

In this example, the goal will be to have traffic destined for 10.30.1.1 serviced by set new-service-set, and all other traffic serviced by test-rule.

The service filter choose-service-set matches on all packets except for those with a destination IP of 10.30.1.1. So, any packet besides 10.30.1.1 will be serviced, and a packet with the destination address 10.30.1.1 will be skipped:

```
family inet {
    service-filter choose-service-set {
        term 1 {
            from {
                destination-address {
                    0.0.0.0/0;
                    10.30.1.1/32 except;
                }
            }
            then service;
        }
    }
}
```

 Remember that the default behavior within a service filter is then skip. If no service filter is applied, the default behavior is then service.

The router processes the service sets in the order of the list under the family inet service hierarchy. In our example, test-rule is examined followed by and then new-service-set. Therefore, traffic with any destination IP address other than 10.30.1.1 will be serviced by the test-rule service set, and traffic destined for 10.30.1.1 will be processed by new-service-set, since it is the service set listed next in the unit's [family inet service input] stanza. All seems well, and the service filter is applied to the logical interface:

```
t1-0/0/2 {
    description Porter-to-Bock;
    unit 0 {
        family inet {
            service {
                input {
                    service-set test-rule service-filter choose-service-set;
                    service-set new-service-set;
                }
                output {
```

```
        service-set test-rule;
        service-set new-service-set;
```

After issuing a commit, however, the router reports an error:

```
[edit interfaces t1-0/0/2]
lab@Porter# commit
[edit interfaces t1-0/0/2 unit 0 family inet service output]
  'service-set new-service-set'
    Service will never be used without service filter on previous service-set
[edit interfaces t1-0/0/2 unit 0 family inet]
  'service'
    Both input and output services must be configured
[edit]
  'interfaces'
    error parsing interfaces object
error: configuration check-out failed
```

You will also need to look at traffic in the return direction; otherwise, it will be serviced only by the first service set in the output list. So, a second service filter will skip the traffic from 10.30.1.1 and will service all other traffic:

```
service-filter rest-of-traffic {
    term 1 {
        from {
            source-address {
                10.30.1.1/32;
            }
        }
        then skip;
    }
    term 2 {
        then service;
    }
}
```

Finally, the service filter is applied to the service sets under the logical interface. This configuration will cause all packets with the destination address 10.30.1.1 to be serviced by the new-service-set service set, and all other traffic to be serviced by the test-rule service set:

```
t1-0/0/2 {
    description Porter-to-Bock;
    unit 0 {
        family inet {
            service {
                input {
                    service-set test-rule service-filter choose-service-set;
                    service-set new-service-set;
                }
                output {
                    service-set test-rule service-filter rest-of-traffic;
                    service-set new-service-set;                }
            }
```

```
                address 10.10.10.2/30;
            }
        }
    }
```

Pings are issued to verify that the proper flows are serviced by the correct service set:

```
lab@Porter# run show services stateful-firewall flows
Interface: sp-0/0/0, Service set: new-service-set
Flow                                    State  Dir  Frm count
ICMP       10.20.131.2:27176 ->    10.30.1.1  Watch  I        13
ICMP        10.30.1.1:27176 ->  10.20.131.2  Watch  O        13


Interface: sp-0/0/0, Service set: test-rule
Flow                                    State  Dir  Frm count
ICMP       10.20.131.2:27432 ->    10.10.8.2  Watch  I         6
ICMP        10.10.8.2:27432 ->  10.20.131.2  Watch  O         6
```

You also can use a service filter to exclude traffic from being serviced through all service sets applied to an interface. Simply use the skip action to exclude certain traffic:

```
lab@Porter# set firewall family inet service-filter example term 1 then ?
Possible completions:
+ apply-groups        Groups from which to inherit configuration data
+ apply-groups-except Don't inherit configuration data from these groups
  count               Count the packet in the named counter
  log                 Log the packet
  port-mirror         Port-mirror the packet
  sample              Sample the packet
  service             Forward packets to service processing
  skip                Skip service processing
```

You can apply one last type of filter to a service set: post-service-filter. This is a stateless packet filter that is evaluated after the service set has processed the packet. This type of filter is available only on input, and it applies only to non-IPSec-VPN packets. Lastly, and most importantly, it will apply only to packets that have been processed by the service set, and it is applied after they have been processed (so, if addresses have been changed by NAT rules, you would match on the post-NAT addresses).

In the following code snippet, a post-service filter called test is applied to the t1-0/0/2.0 interface:

```
t1-0/0/2 {
    description Porter-to-Bock;
    unit 0 {
        family inet {
            service {
                input {
                    service-set test-rule service-filter choose-service-set;
                    service-set new-service-set;
                    post-service-filter test;

                }
```

```
                    output {
                        service-set test-rule service-filter rest-of-traffic;
                        service-set new-service-set;                  }
                }
                address 10.10.10.2/30;
            }
        }
    }
```

Simple Next Hop-Style Service Set

In this section, we will again create a stateful firewall, but this time using a next hop-style service set. The topology is slightly different, as shown in Figure 7-11, because PBR would like to limit all Telnet traffic coming from Water with a source IP subnet of 64.8.12.0/27 and destined for the loopback of router Bock.

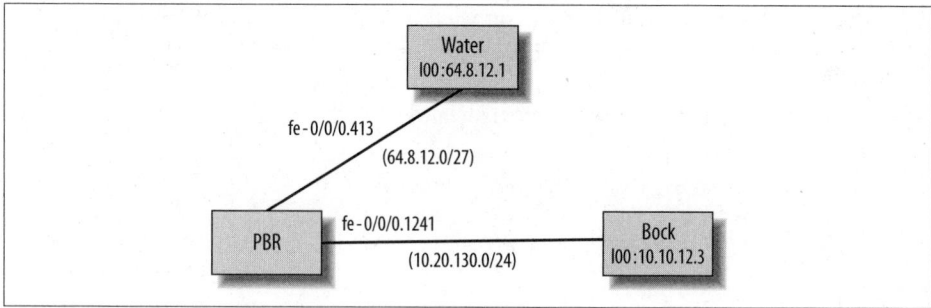

Figure 7-11. Simple next hop service set topology

First, create an inside and outside interface on the service interface using any unit except for unit 0:

```
lab@PBR# show interfaces sp-0/0/0
unit 1 {
    family inet;
    service-domain inside;
}
unit 2 {
    family inet;
    service-domain outside;
}
```

Then create the stateful-firewall rule to allow the Telnet traffic through PBR using an application of junos-telnet, since this is the only traffic currently allowed in. The match direction in this case is specified at input, as traffic is going to be directed into the inside interface.

```
stateful-firewall {
    rule restricted-telnet {
        match-direction input;
        term 1 {
```

```
        from {
            source-address {
                64.8.12.0/27;
            }
            destination-address {
                10.10.12.3/32;
            }
            applications junos-telnet;
        }
        then {
            accept;
        }
    }
  }
}
```

 This rule is very restrictive to illustrate an example. All routing proto-
cols, ICMP traffic, and so on would also be blocked by this stateful
firewall, so in everyday practice, the rule would be more complex.

Next, create the service set and link the rule and service interfaces together:

```
service-set telnet-set {
    stateful-firewall-rules restricted-telnet;
    next-hop-service {
        inside-service-interface sp-0/0/0.1;
        outside-service-interface sp-0/0/0.2;
    }
}
```

The last piece is to map the traffic to the service set. You can do this in a variety of
ways, but in this case we will create a static route that maps the 10.10.12.3 traffic to
the service interface:

```
lab@PBR# set routing-options static route 10.10.12.3 next-hop sp-0/0/0.1
```

After applying the configuration, however, a telnet from Water fails:

```
lab@Water> telnet 10.10.12.3
Trying 10.10.12.3...
^C
```

Examining the flow, it appears that traffic is matching the rule and is traversing the
router in the input direction, but no return traffic is being counted despite the creation of the correct return flow:

```
lab@PBR# run show services stateful-firewall flows
Interface: sp-0/0/0, Service set: telnet-set
Flow                                    State    Dir  Frm count
TCP    64.8.12.5:3827 -> 10.10.12.3:23  Forward  I       8
TCP    10.10.12.3:23  -> 64.8.12.5:3827 Forward  O       0

lab@PBR# run show services stateful-firewall conversations
Conversation: ALG protocol: tcp
```

```
   Number of initiators: 1, Number of responders: 1
Flow                                           State    Dir  Frm count
TCP     64.8.12.5:3827  -> 10.10.12.3:23       Forward  I        8
TCP     10.10.12.3:23   -> 64.8.12.5:3827      Forward  O        0
```

Examine the stateful-firewall statistics and identify whether any errors are incrementing. In this case, it appears that they are:

```
[edit]
lab@PBR# run show services stateful-firewall statistics
Interface   Service set   Accept   Discard   Reject   Errors
sp-0/0/0    telnet-set      48        6         0        59
```

When examined further, these errors seem to be SYN errors—multiple SYN packets are being seen from the same flows:

```
lab@PBR# runs show services statful-firewall statistics extensive | find "TCP Errors"
   TCP errors:
     TCP header length inconsistencies: 0
     Source or destination port number is zero: 0
     Illegal sequence number and flags combinations: 0
     SYN attack (multiple SYN messages seen for the same flow): 132
     First packet not a SYN message: 13
     TCP port scan (TCP handshake, RST seen from server for SYN): 0
     Bad SYN cookie response: 0
   UDP errors:
```

Lastly, examine the log (we will discuss logs later in the section "Logging and Tracing") to ensure that the rule created is indeed matching and correct. The first two log entries indicate that there is no issue with the stateful-firewall rule, but the next entries indicate a SYN attack:

```
Aug 10 02:57:01  (FPC Slot 0, PIC Slot 0) {telnet-set}[FWNAT]: ASP_SFW_RULE_ACCEPT:
proto 6 (TCP) application: any, fe-0/0/0.413:64.8.12.5:2250 -> 10.10.12.3:23, Match
SFW accept rule-set: , rule: restricted-telnet, term: 1
Aug 10 02:57:01  (FPC Slot 0, PIC Slot 0) {telnet-set}[FWNAT]: ASP_SFW_CREATE_ACCEPT_
FLOW: proto 6 (TCP) application: any, fe-0/0/0.413:64.8.12.5:2250 -> 10.10.12.3:23,
creating forward or watch flow
Aug 10 02:57:01  (FPC Slot 0, PIC Slot 0) {telnet-set}[FWNAT]: ASP_IDS_TCP_SYN_
ATTACK: proto 6 (TCP), sp-0/0/0.2:64.8.12.5:2250 -> 10.10.12.3:23, TCP SYN flood
attack
Aug 10 02:57:01  (FPC Slot 0, PIC Slot 0) {telnet-set}[FWNAT]: ASP_IDS_TCP_SYN_
ATTACK: proto 6 (TCP), sp-0/0/0.2:64.8.12.5:2250 -> 10.10.12.3:23, TCP SYN flood
attack
Aug 10 02:57:01  (FPC Slot 0, PIC Slot 0) {telnet-set}[FWNAT]: ASP_IDS_TCP_SYN_
ATTACK: proto 6 (TCP), sp-0/0/0.2:64.8.12.5:2250 -> 10.10.12.3:23, TCP SYN flood
attack
Aug 10 02:57:01  (FPC Slot 0, PIC Slot 0) {telnet-set}[FWNAT]: ASP_IDS_TCP_SYN_
ATTACK: proto 6 (TCP), sp-0/0/0.2:64.8.12.5:2250 -> 10.10.12.3:23, TCP SYN flood
attack
Aug 10 02:57:01  (FPC Slot 0, PIC Slot 0) {telnet-set}[FWNAT]: ASP_IDS_TCP_SYN_
ATTACK: proto 6 (TCP), sp-0/0/0.2:64.8.12.5:2250 -> 10.10.12.3:23, TCP SYN flood
attack
```

```
Aug 10 02:57:01  (FPC Slot 0, PIC Slot 0) {telnet-set}[FWNAT]: ASP_IDS_TCP_SYN_
ATTACK: proto 6 (TCP), sp-0/0/0.2:64.8.12.5:2250 -> 10.10.12.3:23, TCP SYN flood
attack
Aug 10 02:57:01  (FPC Slot 0, PIC Slot 0) {telnet-set}[FWNAT]: ASP_IDS_TCP_SYN_
ATTACK: proto 6 (TCP), sp-0/0/0.2:64.8.12.5:2250 -> 1
```

The stateful firewall believes there is a SYN attack because of the two-service interface concept of a next hop service set. Recall that traffic is sent from one service
interface to another. In this case, traffic is arriving into PBR's physical interface fe-0/
0/0.413, and a route table lookup is performed:

```
lab@PBR> show route 10.10.12.3

inet.0: 18 destinations, 18 routes (18 active, 0 holddown, 0 hidden)
+ = Active Route, - = Last Active, * = Both

10.10.12.3/32      *[Static/5] 00:24:47
                    > via sp-0/0/0.1
```

This route points to the inside interface, so traffic is sent to be serviced. The problem is that after traffic is serviced, it exits the outside interface and performs another
route lookup. This route lookup points back to the inside interface, and a service
loop is created, as shown in Figure 7-12.

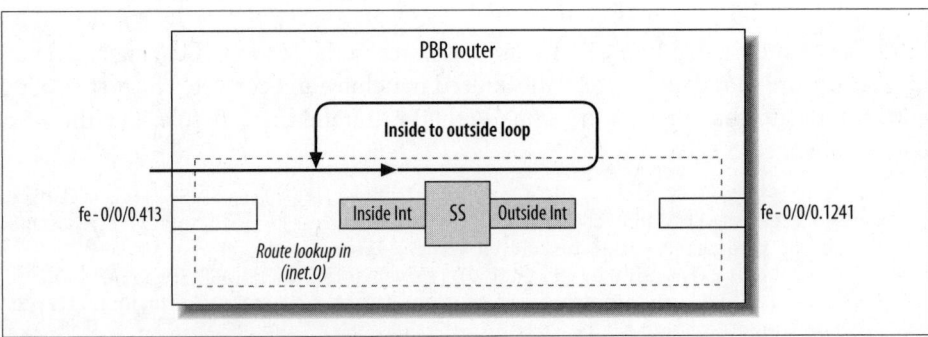

Figure 7-12. Next hop service set loop with single route table

You could also see this loop by viewing the service interface with a show interfaces
sp-0/0/0.1 command and noticing the ttl-exceeded flag. This flag indicates that it is
OK to receive a packet with an expired TTL, which the router would normally not
do. Although this does not actually indicate a loop, since there is no internal TTL
method, it should throw a red flag. Remember that no loop actually occurred
because the router determined the loop was a SYN attack and dropped the packets:

```
Logical interface sp-0/0/0.1 (Index 64) (SNMP ifIndex 41)
    Flags: Point-To-Point SNMP-Traps Encapsulation: Adaptive-Services
    Input packets : 7
    Output packets: 0
    Protocol inet, MTU: 9192
      Flags: Receive-options, Receive-TTL-Exceeded
```

There are multiple ways to fix the loop, but typically each method will try to achieve the same goal: when the packets are serviced and the second lookup is performed, the packet must point to a different route in a different route table. One way to create a new route table is to create a virtual router (VR). With a VR, it is easy in JUNOS to create a different route table and a forwarding table and then add routes in those tables. In a VR, you can specify interfaces, create static routes, and even run routing protocols in their own instances. So, any packet that arrives on an interface that is configured in the VR will perform a route lookup in the VR's route table. In this way, traffic can be easily mapped to a new table without the need for filters or policies. Let's create a VR to allow for the two lookups in two tables with the inside interface in the main instance and the outside interface in the newly created VR, as shown in Figure 7-13.

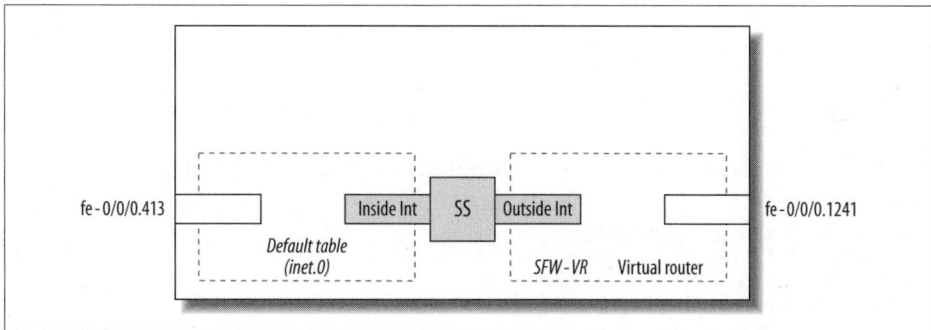

Figure 7-13. VR setup

First, create a VR by naming the routing instance and specifying the instance type:

```
lab@PBR# set routing-instances SFW-VR instance-type virtual-router
```

Next, add the interfaces that should be linked to the VR. One interface will be the outgoing interface on PBR toward Bock, and the other interface will be the outside service interface. Adding the outside service interface allows the VR's table to be used for the second lookup:

```
lab@PBR# set routing-instances SFW-VR interface sp-0/0/0.2

[edit]
lab@PBR# set routing-instances SFW-VR interface fe-0/0/0.1241
```

Lastly, you need to configure routing for the return flow to succeed. When traffic is received on interface fe-0/0/0.1241, it should be directed to the outside interface, serviced, and sent out the inside interface. Finally, a route table lookup should be performed in the main inet.0 table. You can accomplish this just like you did before by creating a static route, but this time pointing it to the outside interface:

```
lab@PBR# set routing-instances SFW-VR routing options static route
0.0.0.0/0 next-hop sp-0/0/0.2
```

Here is the entire routing instance, with Open Shortest Path First (OSPF) also configured between PBR and Bock for internal connectivity:

```
lab@PBR# show routing-instances
SFW-VR {
    instance-type virtual-router;
    interface sp-0/0/0.2;
    interface fe-0/0/0.1241;
    routing-options {
        static {
            route 0.0.0.0/0 next-hop sp-0/0/0.2;
        }
    }
    protocols {
        ospf {
            area 0.0.0.0 {
                interface fe-0/0/0.1241;
            }
        }
    }
}
```

A route table is automatically created with the form *<routing-instance-name>*.inet.0. Notice the static route that was configured and the direct route that represents the links on the fe-0/0/0.1241 interface:

```
[edit]
lab@PBR# run show route table SFW-VR

SFW-VR.inet.0: 7 destinations, 7 routes (7 active, 0 holddown, 0
hidden) + = Active Route, - = Last Active, * = Both

0.0.0.0/0          *[Static/5] 03:27:05
                    > via sp-0/0/0.2
10.10.10.0/30      *[OSPF/10] 03:24:23, metric 66
                    > to 10.20.130.1 via fe-0/0/0.1241
10.10.12.2/32      *[OSPF/10] 03:24:23, metric 66
                    > to 10.20.130.1 via fe-0/0/0.1241
10.10.12.3/32      *[OSPF/10] 03:24:23, metric 1
                    > to 10.20.130.1 via fe-0/0/0.1241
10.20.130.0/24     *[Direct/0] 03:27:05
                    > via fe-0/0/0.1241
10.20.130.2/32     *[Local/0] 03:27:05
                    Local via fe-0/0/0.1241
224.0.0.5/32       *[OSPF/10] 03:24:43, metric 1
                    MultiRecv
```

After committing the changes on PBR, the telnet now succeeds on Water:

```
lab@Water> telnet 10.10.12.3
Trying 10.10.12.3...
Connected to 10.10.12.3.
Escape character is '^]'.
```

```
Bock (ttyp1)

login:
```

The conversation is now complete, as shown in the session table on PBR:

```
lab@PBR# run show services stateful-firewall conversations
Interface: sp-0/0/0, Service set: telnet-set

Conversation: ALG protocol: tcp
  Number of initiators: 1, Number of responders: 1
Flow                                      State    Dir   Frm count
TCP    64.8.12.5:1874   ->  10.10.12.3:23    Forward  I        9
TCP    10.10.12.3:23    ->  64.8.12.5:1874   Forward  O        7
```

Logging and Tracing

Since you can configure system logging and tracing in a variety of places in the configuration file, it can be confusing which statement is actually doing the logging. The rule in JUNOS software is that the more specific configuration will always override the more global configuration. The levels of logging possible, in order of global to specific, are as follows:

Interface logging
```
lab@PBR# set sp-0/0/0 services-options syslog host 1.1.1.1 services ?
Possible completions:
  <[Enter]>        Execute this command
  alert            Conditions that should be corrected immediately
  any              All levels
  critical         Critical conditions
  emergency        Panic conditions
  error            Error conditions
  info             Informational messages
  none             No messages
  notice           Conditions that should be handled specially
  warning          Warning messages
  |                Pipe through a command
```

Service set logging
```
lab@PBR# set services service-set telnet-set syslog host 1.1.1.1 services ?
Possible completions:
  <[Enter]>        Execute this command
  alert            Conditions that should be corrected immediately
  any              All levels
  critical         Critical conditions
  emergency        Panic conditions
  error            Error conditions
  info             Informational messages
  none             No messages
  notice           Conditions that should be handled specially
  warning          Warning messages
  |                Pipe through a command
```

Feature rule (stateful firewall, IPSec, etc.) logging
```
set stateful-firewall rule restricted-telnet term 1 then syslog
```

So, if logging was enabled at the service interface level and three service sets were configured, all three service sets would inherit the service-level logging settings. If a single service set also enabled logging, those settings would override the service-level logging for that service set. The remaining service sets would inherit the service interface logging settings.

There are also different types of logging: standard syslog and traceoptions. Syslog will send a system log message to a syslog server or the local router, and traceoptions will only send information to the local router. When you are viewing services, traceoptions usually gives you a view of the actual software operations on the Routing Engine (RE) and not the service PIC itself.

You can send syslog information to a remote syslog server by indicating a host, or send it to the local router by specifying the keyword `local`:

```
sp-0/0/0 {
    services-options {
        syslog {
            host local {
                services any;
            }
        }
    }
}
```

If you specify that the syslog messages should be sent to the local router, you can send the messages to the default system log of *messages* or to another designated file. Also, for those messages to actually appear, you will have to configure the router to accept messages for the `local2` facility. To place these syslog entries in the *messages* file, you can use this configuration:

```
[edit]
lab@PBR# set system syslog file messages local2 any
```

An example of the types of syslog messages is messages that show which rules have been matched and created. Here, router PBR is monitoring the *messages* file in real time, and you can see that a stateful-firewall rule was matched and a flow was created based on that match:

```
[edit]
lab@PBR# run monitor start messages

*** messages ***
Aug 10 06:45:50  (FPC Slot 0, PIC Slot 0) {telnet-set}[FWNAT]: ASP_SFW
_RULE_ACCEPT: proto 6 (TCP) application: any, fe-0/0/0.413:64.8.12.5:
10.10.12.3:23, Match SFW accept rule-set: , rule: restricted-telnet,
term: 1
Aug 10 06:45:50  (FPC Slot 0, PIC Slot 0) {telnet-set}[FWNAT]: ASP_SFW_CREATE_ACCEPT_
FLOW: proto 6 (TCP) application: any, fe-0/0/0.413:64.8.12.5:3225 -> 10.10.12.3:23,
creating forward or watch
flow
```

If you need to examine the service's software operation, you can configure traceoptions at the PIC level. If no file is specified, the information will be placed into a file called *spd*:

```
lab@PBR# set services adaptive-services-pics traceoptions flag ?
Possible completions:
  all                 Trace everything
  configuration       Trace configuration events
  kernel-object       Trace kernel object management
  routing-protocol    Trace routing protocol events
  routing-socket      Trace routing socket events
  snmp                Trace SNMP operations
```

Here is an example of the types of messages you would see in *spd*. In this code snippet, software sockets have been created and resources have been assigned when services were configured:

```
lab@PBR# run show log spd
Aug 10 07:13:27 spd process starting, pid 12555
Aug 10 07:13:27 rpd session connected
Aug 10 07:13:27 registered async opaque handler for traps
Aug 10 07:13:27 Added sp-0/0/0 snmpindex 21 fpc_slot 0 pic_slot 0 to database
Aug 10 07:13:27 Loading initial state from kernel...
Aug 10 07:13:27 Processed ASP_CFG_GLOBAL_OPTIONS config object
Aug 10 07:13:27 Adding blob to set: id = 1, type = 16, size = 92, pic = sp-0/0/0 (0)
Aug 10 07:13:27 Blob id = 1, type = 16, size = 92 is new, adding
Aug 10 07:13:27 Imported config object (type 16, id 1)
Aug 10 07:13:27 Adding blob to set: id = 1, type = 16, size = 92, pic = sp-0/0/0 (0)
Aug 10 07:13:27 State initialization from kernel complete
Aug 10 07:13:27 ------ Finished with RTSOCK initialization ------
Aug 10 07:13:28 get_pic_index sp-0/0/0.1 pic index 0
Aug 10 07:13:28 get_pic_index sp-0/0/0.1 pic index 0
Aug 10 07:13:28 Adding blob to set: id = 2, type = 12, size = 912, pic = sp-0/0/0 (0)
Aug 10 07:13:28 get_pic_index sp-0/0/0 pic index 0
Aug 10 07:13:28 Adding blob to set: id = 1, type = 16, size = 92, pic = sp-0/0/0 (0)
Aug 10 07:13:28 Blob id = 1 is not changed, skipping
Aug 10 07:13:28 Blob id = 2, type = 12, size = 912 is new, adding
Aug 10 07:13:28 Added service set telnet-set (id 2, pic sp-0/0/0 (0))
Aug 10 07:13:28 Adding blob to set: id = 2, type = 12, size = 912, pic = sp-0/0/0 (0)
Aug 10 07:13:28 rpd session established
```

Layer 3 Services Configuration Summary

This section described the various Layer 3 service offerings as well as the CLI configuration steps that were needed. We also discussed the option of interface-style or next hop-style service sets. In addition, we covered some basic examples to illustrate the CLI options. We will cover more complex examples in the next chapter.

Now is a good time to take a break, perhaps to think about the points we covered in this section. The next section will examine some additional features that are less common but could be deployed in your own network.

Additional Service Options

You can enable many other services that are not as common but could play a large role in your network. We will briefly discuss these services here, but you should consult the router or PIC documentation at *http://www.juniper.net/techpubs* for more detailed configuration information.

Layer 2 Tunneling Protocol (L2TP)

L2TP is a tunneling protocol that tunnels PPP packets across a network, acting like a Layer 2 data link tunneling protocol. L2TP headers and payload are actually sent in a UDP datagram, so maybe people claim it to be a Layer 5 or Layer 4.5 protocol. Each endpoint of the tunnel has its own designation, one being an LNS and the other an LT2P Access Concentrator (LAC). A Juniper Networks router can act as an LNS.

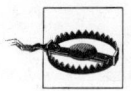 Only M7i, M10i, and M120 routers support LT2P.

Real-Time Performance Monitoring (RPM)

RPM is a feature for tracking and monitoring your network by sending network *probes* to other devices. These probes could be ICMP, UDP, or TCP,[*] depending on the configuration. You can use these probes to measure packet round-trip times, jitter, delay, and packet (probe) loss. You also can use RPM to verify the path toward Border Gateway Protocol (BGP) neighbors.

 RPM does not require an ASP or Multiservices PIC, unless you are configuring RPM timestamping, which was released in JUNOS 8.1 for the sender and in JUNOS 8.3 for the responder.

You can configure probes with a variety of parameters, such as the type or contents of the probe. Also, you can set thresholds to trigger syslog messages and Simple Network Management Protocol (SNMP) TRAPs. In the following example, router PBR has a probe to send an ICMP ping to Porter at 10.10.12.2. Seven probes should be sent every three seconds:

```
[edit services rpm]
lab@PBR# show
probe foo {
    test Porter {
        probe-type icmp-ping;
```

---

[*] UDP and TCP probes require a Juniper server.

```
            target address 10.10.12.2;
            probe-count 7;
            probe-interval 3;
        }
    }
```

To verify that probes are being sent and data is being received, you can examine SNMP Management Information Bases (MIBs) or use the local router sending the probes by issuing show services rpm commands. The first command, history-results, should show the time at which the probes are sent and the round-trip length of the probe:

```
lab@PBR# run show services rpm history-results
    Owner, Test          Probe received            Round trip time
    foo, Porter          Wed Aug  8 07:02:54 2007        46097 usec
    foo, Porter          Wed Aug  8 07:07:41 2007        33662 usec
    foo, Porter          Wed Aug  8 07:07:44 2007        20133 usec
    foo, Porter          Wed Aug  8 07:07:47 2007        20112 usec
    foo, Porter          Wed Aug  8 07:07:50 2007        20112 usec
    foo, Porter          Wed Aug  8 07:07:53 2007        20104 usec
    foo, Porter          Wed Aug  8 07:07:56 2007        20092 usec
    foo, Porter          Wed Aug  8 07:07:59 2007        20104 usec
```

Verify the actual probe results by issuing a show services rpm probe-results command:

```
[edit services rpm]
lab@PBR# run show services rpm probe-results
    Owner: foo, Test: Porter
    Target address: 10.10.12.2, Probe type: icmp-ping, Test size: 7 probes
    Probe results:
      Response received, Wed Aug  8 07:07:59 2007
      Rtt: 20104 usec
    Results over current test:
      Probes sent: 7, Probes received: 7, Loss percentage: 0
      Measurement: Round trip time
        Minimum: 20092 usec, Maximum: 33662 usec, Average: 22046 usec,
        Jitter: 13570 usec, Stddev: 4742 usec
    Results over last test:
      Probes sent: 7, Probes received: 7, Loss percentage: 0
      Test completed on Wed Aug  8 07:07:59 2007
      Measurement: Round trip time
        Minimum: 20092 usec, Maximum: 33662 usec, Average: 22046 usec,
        Jitter: 13570 usec, Stddev: 4742 usec
    Results over all tests:
      Probes sent: 7, Probes received: 7, Loss percentage: 0
      Measurement: Round trip time
        Minimum: 20092 usec, Maximum: 33662 usec, Average: 22046 usec,
        Jitter: 13570 usec, Stddev: 4742 usec
```

You also can examine the paths to configured BGP peers by sending probes to configured peers. Once RPM is configured, probes will be sent to neighbors configured for BGP automatically. In this example, router PBR has one BGP neighbor to router

Porter. The probes will be ICMP pings with five probes sent at an interval of one second. They will be 255 bytes with ICMP data of hex 0123456789. The test will run every 60 seconds:

```
[edit services rpm]
lab@PBR# show
bgp {
    probe-type icmp-ping;
    probe-count 5;
    probe-interval 1;
    test-interval 60;
    history-size 10;
    data-size 255;
    data-fill 0123456789;
}
```

As previously mentioned, you can retrieve the results via show services rpm commands or via SNMP in MIBs such as the following:

- pingResultsTable
- jnxPingResultsTable
- jnxPingProbeHistoryTable
- pingProbeHistoryTable

The following, final example details the show services rpm probe-results for PBR's BGP peer:

```
[edit services rpm]
lab@PBR# run show services rpm probe-results
    Owner: Rpm-Bgp-Owner, Test: Rpm-Bgp-Test-0
    Target address: 10.10.12.2, Source address: 10.20.128.3,
    Probe type: icmp-ping, Test size: 5 probes
    Probe results:
      Response received, Wed Aug  8 07:20:37 2007
      Rtt: 20135 usec
    Results over current test:
      Probes sent: 5, Probes received: 5, Loss percentage: 0
      Measurement: Round trip time
        Minimum: 20102 usec, Maximum: 69744 usec, Average: 30049 usec,
        Jitter: 49642 usec, Stddev: 19847 usec
    Results over last test:
      Probes sent: 5, Probes received: 5, Loss percentage: 0
      Test completed on Wed Aug  8 07:20:37 2007
      Measurement: Round trip time
        Minimum: 20102 usec, Maximum: 69744 usec, Average: 30049 usec,
        Jitter: 49642 usec, Stddev: 19847 usec
    Results over all tests:
      Probes sent: 10, Probes received: 10, Loss percentage: 0
      Measurement: Round trip time
        Minimum: 20102 usec, Maximum: 69744 usec, Average: 25119 usec,
        Jitter: 49642 usec, Stddev: 14875 usec
```

Data Link Switching (DLSw)

DLSw is a protocol that offers IP routing support for unroutable, legacy protocols such as System Network Architecture (SNA) and NETBUI/NetBIOS. Once configured, the routers set up connections with their local end systems, as well as with other peer routers, and the traffic flow from one end system to another is transparent, meaning the presence of the routed IP network is not known to the end stations. When DLSw is configured, TCP sessions are established between peer routers and capabilities are negotiated. Then a circuit is established between the end system and the router.

 DLSw is supported only on J-series routers.

For example, in the SNA example shown in Figure 7-14, the sequence would be as follows:

1. An SNA device sends out an explorer frame looking for Mainframe 1.
2. The router receives this frame and sends a canureach frame to its peer DLSw routers.
3. The remote routers forward the canureach message to their attached Mainframes.
4. Mainframe 1 sends an icanreach response to its local router, which in turn forwards the frame toward the DLSw peers.
5. After the frames have been exchanged, a circuit is established between the SNA devices and the local routers, as well as between the peer routers.

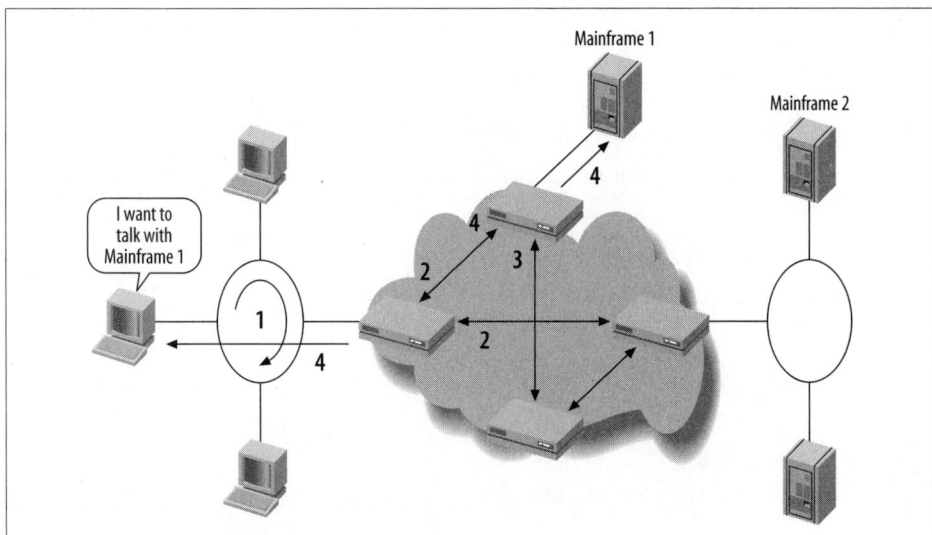

Figure 7-14. DLSw example flow

Flow Monitoring

Juniper Networks routers give you the ability to take monitored traffic flows and export this data in cflowd format or direct the flows in their native format to different packet analyzers. You can also encrypt the flows when sending them.

One common type of monitoring that you can perform is called *active monitoring*, whereby the router takes the inbound traffic, extracts the flow into a cflowd format, and sends the cflowd record of the matched traffic to a flow collector device, as shown in Figure 7-15. The original packet is usually forwarded toward the destination, but other options do exist, including *discard accounting*, whereby the cflowd record is sent to the flow collector and the original packet is discarded, or *port mirroring*, whereby the entire packet is copied and sent to an additional interface and the original packet is forwarded on to its intended destination.

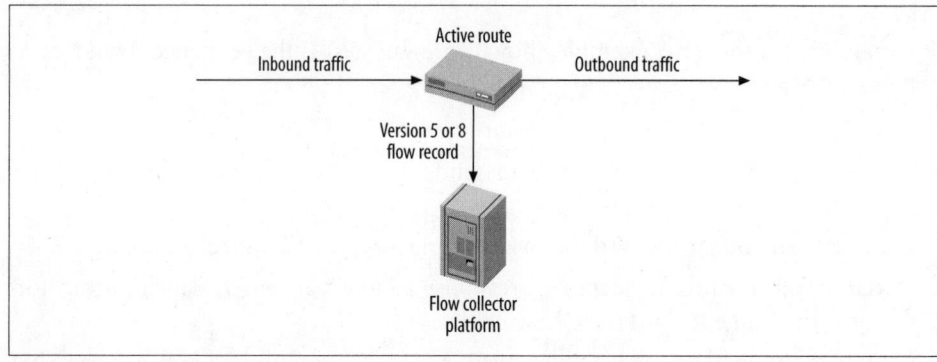

Figure 7-15. Active flow monitoring

There are some restrictions on how many actions can be performed on a network flow in the router:

- Sampling (cflowd) to a collector *or* port mirroring at one time
- Forwarding the original packet *or* discard accounting at one time

And only certain combinations of configurations are allowed on the *same* set of traffic:

- Port mirroring and forwarding
- Port mirroring and discard accounting
- Sampling and forwarding
- Sampling and discard accounting

Sampling (cflowd) and port mirroring can be performed at the same time only if they are on different sets of traffic.

Tunnel Services

We have already discussed a variety of different tunnels, and even more can be configured. You can use these tunnels for external connections or for connections with the same router. Any tunnel that is created will get an internal interface created for it. These interfaces are as follows:

ip

> For configuring an IP-IP tunnel that encapsulates one IP packet inside another. This type of tunnel is often seen in mobile environments where the endpoint address changes, and is migrated to different networks. This could also be useful in tunneling IPv6 packets over an IPv4 network.

lt

> Creates internal tunnel connections between different logical routers or VRs in the same chassis. In a J-series router, you also can use this interface to implement CoS on DLSw and RPM.

mt

> Used to create multicast tunnels. These tunnels are automatically created when running multicast in a Layer 3 BGP/Multiprotocol Label Switching (MPLS) VPN.

pd

> Used to de-encapsulate PIM register messages sent from a designated router to a rendezvous point (RP) in a multicast network.

pe

> Used to encapsulate PIM register messages sent from a designated router to an RP in a multicast network.

vt

> Used to loop a packet through the Packet Forwarding Engine (PFE) as an additional instance. This is normally used in a VPN environment to concurrently perform both an MPLS lookup and an IP lookup. This is supported only on M/T-series routers and not on J-series routers.

Conclusion

JUNOS software offers a vast number of both Layer 2 and Layer 3 services that you can run on your network. Not all of these services will likely be running on your network at the same time, but often you'll use them for the features and security they offer. This chapter examined the basic building blocks of those services, and how to deploy them on a single-service feature basis. The next chapter examines more complex scenarios with multiple services running concurrently.

Exam Topics

We examined the following Enterprise Exam Topics in this chapter:

- Configure MLPPP.
- Configure Layer 2 services to optimize voice traffic.
- Configure and apply an interface-style service set.
- Configure a next hop-style service set.
- Identify the match direction given a network diagram.
- Understand and implement various types of service sets.
- Describe the differences between stateful firewalls and stateless packet filters.
- Describe NAT and PAT.
- Describe the functions of ALGs.
- Configure a stateful firewall via the CLI.
- Monitor a stateful firewall.
- Explain the uses of IPSec VPNs.
- Intrusion detection and prevention (IDP).
- Virtual routers to segment secure services.

Chapter Review Questions

1. Which type of service allows for multiple physical interfaces running Frame Relay to be bonded together into a single logical bundle?

    a. MLPPP

    b. FRF.15

    c. FRF.12

    d. FRF.16

2. Which type of service set would you choose if you wanted to service multicast traffic?

    a. Interface-style

    b. Next hop-style

3. True or False: All Layer 2 services will always use the ls- interface.

4. Which CLI command displays a session for a stateful firewall?

    a. show services stateful-firewall conversations

    b. show services stateful-firewall packets

    c. show services stateful-firewall session

    d. show services stateful-firewall flows bidirectional

---

5. Which feature of an IPSec VPN allows for confidentiality of data?

    a. IKE

    b. MD5 hashes

    c. AES encryption

    d. Sequence numbers

6. What type of load balancing is used across MLPPP links for fragmented traffic?

    a. Per packet

    b. Per flow

    c. Per fragment

    d. Per port

7. If fragmentation is turned on for MLPPP, what type of load balancing would occur for unfragmented packets?

    a. Per packet

    b. Per flow

    c. Per fragment

    d. Per port

8. Which feature will help to lower latency of voice traffic on a point-to-point link?

    a. CHAP

    b. Codecs

    c. RTP

    d. CRTP

9. If traffic was arriving on the outside interface of a service set, for which direction would the rule be configured?

    a. input

    b. output

    c. bi-directional

    d. no-direction

10. Which feature would allow traffic to be skipped in a service set?

    a. Post-service filter

    b. Firewall filter

    c. Service filter

    d. Service skipping

11. Which type of service PIC can be integrated on an M7i?

    a. ASM

    b. ASP

c. Monitoring Services

d. Hardware acceleration

12. How is traffic chosen to be compressed when configuring CRTP? (Choose two.)

a. IP address

b. Port numbers

c. Packet size

d. Queue

Chapter Review Answers

1. Answer: D. FRF.16 allows bonding of physical interfaces together, whereas FRF.15 bonds multiple DLCIs together.

2. Answer: B. The only way to service multicast traffic is to use a next hop service set. Interface-style service sets ignore multicast traffic.

3. Answer: False. Some PICs will use an lsq interface, and others will use an ls interface. lsq allows for more CoS features than ls.

4. Answer: A. In JUNOS software, a session is referred to as a conversation, which is a flow in each direction.

5. Answer: C. To achieve data confidentiality, you should encrypt the traffic. One algorithm you can use to encrypt traffic is AES.

6. Answer: C. When MLPPP is enabled, packets will be sent down each link on a per-fragment basis. Since each packet fragment will have an MLPPP header with a sequence number, order will be maintained by the end device.

7. Answer: B. If fragmentation does not occur on an MLPPP link, the packets are balanced over a flow (source IP, destination IP, protocol, etc.). Since nonfragmented packets will not contain an MLPPP header, per flow is the only way to maintain packet order.

8. Answer: D. Compressed RTP decreases the header size to a few bytes, which reduces serialization and queuing delay.

9. Answer: B. Traffic arriving on the outside service interface will be in the output direction. Traffic arriving on the inside service interface will be in the input direction.

10. Answer: C. You can apply a service filter to an interface with an action of skip to allow traffic to pass any service rules.

11. Answer: A. You can integrate ASM into an M7i router only. For other M-series routers, you must install a physical PIC into a slot.

12. Answer: B, D. Traffic can be classified for RTP compressed based on port numbers or based on which queue a packet was placed into. If both match conditions are configured, a packet will be compressed if either condition is met.

Advanced JUNOS Services

We discussed the framework for JUNOS services in Chapter 7. This chapter will dive into more advanced scenarios and configurations. Often, you will need to use many Layer 3 services simultaneously, such as Network Address Translation (NAT), stateful firewall, and IPSec virtual private networks (VPNs), so you must plan properly to create transparent service additions.

The topics we will cover in this chapter include:

- Route tables and next hop service sets
- IPSec VPNs
- NAT
- Combined Layer 3 services
- Packet flow

This chapter assumes that the reader grasps the concepts discussed in the preceding chapter; specifically, the types of service sets and command-line interface (CLI) configurations. If these concepts are unfamiliar, please review the preceding chapter.

Route Tables and Next Hop Service Sets

When using a next hop service set, remember that the packet must go through the "two-legged table" of the inside and outside interfaces. Regardless of which interface the packet enters, two route table lookups will always be performed. To avoid a routing loop, the pre- and post-service lookups must return different next hop values. You can accomplish this in a few ways:

- Implement virtual routers (VRs)
- Use filter-based forwarding (FBF)
- Perform destination NAT to change the destination address

VRs are the most preferred method, followed by FBF and destination NAT. VRs and FBF solve the double next hop issue by using multiple route tables, whereas destination NAT attempts to use a single route table.

With destination NAT, the forward direction can be fairly cut and dried, as Figure 8-1 demonstrates; simply perform a lookup on the original destination address, which causes the packet to be serviced, and then change the destination address and perform a second lookup on the new destination address to be used for forwarding. Issues arise in the reverse direction, where the destination address would normally stay the same. In this case, you would have to use a method such as FBF to solve this problem.

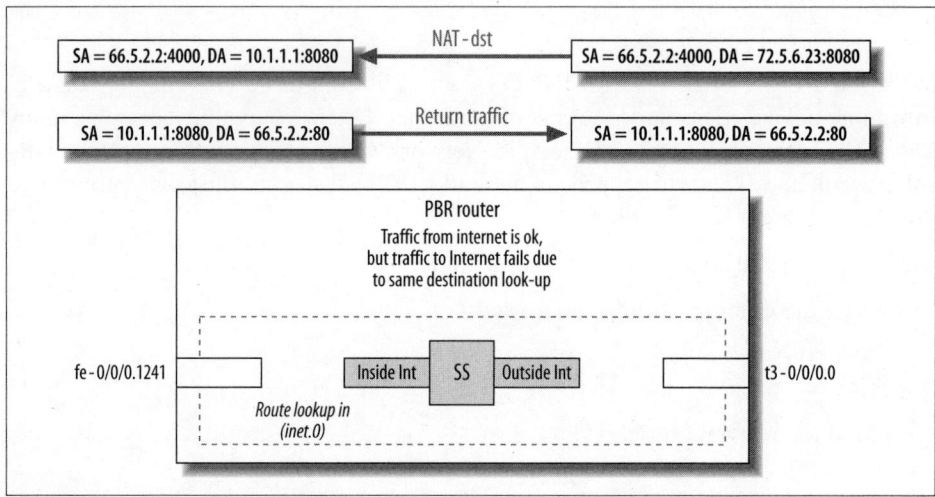

Figure 8-1. Destination NAT

FBF uses JUNOS software packet filters to redirect traffic to a new route table. These filters are applied to a physical interface to match traffic that should be serviced. This traffic is then sent to a new route table containing a route, which causes the traffic to be serviced (see Figure 8-2). The problem with FBF is that the configuration can be complex and not as scalable or secure as VRs.

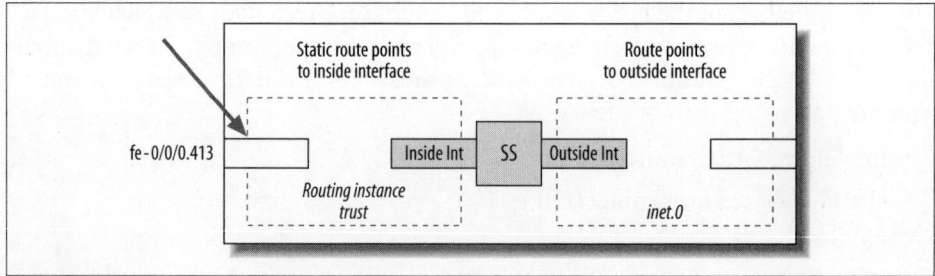

Figure 8-2. FBF

The first step when using FBF is to create a *routing instance*. A routing instance is simply a way to create a new route table. The properties of the route table will depend on the instance type (forwarding, nonforwarding, Virtual Route and Forwarding [VRF], VR, etc.). Instance types include:

Forwarding
Used for FBF applications when a route table and forwarding table are required.

l2vpn
Used to create Kompella-based Border Gateway Protocol/Multiprotocol Label Switching (BGP/MPLS) VPNs.

Nonforwarding
Used when a separation of routing information is required. Sometimes it is used to monitor certain prefixes by an NMS system.

VR
Used to create a local VPN, with local interfaces and protocols.

VRF
Used to create Layer 3 BGP/MPLS VPNs.

The instance is named, which creates the name of the route table with the format `<instance name>.inet.0`. In this case, we create a forwarding instance of type `forwarding`, which creates a route and a forwarding table for the instance:

```
lab@PBR# set routing-instances example instance-type forwarding
```

Next, create the filter to match which traffic should be serviced and sent to the new table. In this case, external traffic destined for 128.3.3/24 will be sent to the instance example. It is vital not to forget about the default behavior of a filter, which is to deny all traffic at the end of processing. This could cause major problems on the interface for internal transit traffic, so make sure you always have additional terms that allow this traffic. The `filter match-outbound term 2` allows all other traffic through the interface for route lookups in the default route table, `inet.0`:

```
lab@PBR# show firewall
family inet {
    filter match-outbound {
        term 1 {
            from {
                destination-address {
                    128.3.3.0/24;
                }
            }
            then routing-instance example;
        }
        term 2 {
            then accept;
        }
    }
}
```

Apply the filter to the interface where incoming traffic needs to be matched, such as a LAN interface:

```
lab@PBR# show interfaces fe-0/0/0 unit 1241
description PBR_to_Bock;
vlan-id 1241;
family inet {
    filter {
        input-list match-outbound;
    }
    address 10.20.130.2/24;
}
```

So far, we've covered the easy part, but now things get a bit trickier as we enable routing. When traffic enters the new example.inet.0 table, it should be sent to an sp- service interface to be serviced. To do this, you should add static routes to the routing instance. This could be in the form of a series of static routes or a default, as needed:

```
[edit routing-instances example]
lab@PBR# show
instance-type forwarding;
routing-options {
  static {
    route 0.0.0.0/0 next-hop sp-0/0/0.1;
  }
}
```

If only the required configuration would end there—but it continues. For any static route to be active in a route table, the next hop value must be reachable in that route table. Since the route points to the service interface sp-0/0/0.1, we must ensure that the interface is in the example.inet.0 route table. To accomplish this, we must copy the route from the inet.0 table to the example.inet.0 table, which is implemented in a concept called *rib-groups*.

 Over the years, many network engineers have struggled with the rib-group concept. Rib-groups are often difficult to understand. They are even harder to explain even if you think you actually understand the concept. In current JUNOS code, there are many ways to avoid the use of rib-groups, such as using VRs, which is one of the reasons FBF is not the preferred approach.

The first rule for a rib-group is the local logical grouping definition that defines which tables will be able to share routes. These definitions are spelled out in the [edit routing-options] stanza. The rib-group will be named, as it will need to be referenced later. In this case study, we define a rib-group called test to share the sp-0/0/0.1 interface in inet.0 and example.inet.0. Here is the result:

```
[edit routing-options]
lab@PBR# show
rib-groups {
  test {
    import-rib [ inet.0 example.inet.0 ];
  }
}
```

After the rib-group is defined, we must configure which information is actually placed into the rib-group. In other words, we must decide whether Open Shortest Path First (OSPF), BGP, static routes, interface routes, and so on are going to be shared. To have the sp- interface shared, we need to apply interface routes to the test rib-group:

```
[edit routing-options]
lab@PBR# set interface-routes rib-group inet test
```

The issue that arises with this command is that *all* interface routes in inet.0 will be placed into example.inet.0 when only the sp- interface is required. To allow only that interface to be copied from inet.0, we must configure a policy and apply it to the rib-group. The policy should send the sp-0/0/0.1 interface to the correct table and deny all other routes from being moved:

```
    }
    policy-statement inside-interface {
        term service {
            from interface sp-0/0/0.1;
            to rib example.inet.0;
            then accept;
        }
        term reject {
            then reject;
        }
    }
```

Once we apply the policy to the rib-groups, the route table will contain one default route that points to the service interface. Here is the final result after the policy is applied:

```
[edit routing-options]
lab@PBR# show
interface-routes {
  rib-group inet test;
}
rib-groups {
  test {
      import-policy inside-interface;
      import-rib [ inet.0 example.inet.0 ];
  }
}
```

Using rib-groups and FBF usually results in a maximum use of brain-cell capacity. To reduce the number of brain cells being used and reserve them to concentrate on other things, try the preferred method for next hop service sets: VRs. VRs provide the cleanest, easiest, most scalable, and more secure solution. By using VRs, you can align with the *security zone* concept, in which interfaces are placed within certain logical zones (we will outline this zone concept in more detail in Chapter 11). In the case of a router, a zone is actually a new route table, so when a packet hits an interface in a zone (VR), a table lookup is performed in that VR. The most basic case would be two VRs—a trust VR for LAN interfaces and an untrust VR for WAN interfaces (see Figure 8-3).

 Every router always contains one default VR called the *default VR*. In JUNOS software, this is represented by the route table inet.0. When creating two VRs, you can either create two new "trust" or "untrust" VRs or use the default VR as one of the VRs.

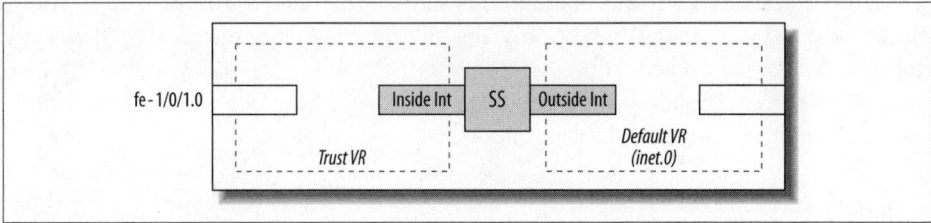

Figure 8-3. The VR concept

The VR concept can extend to as many VRs as needed. For example, some external servers may have special services applied to them that don't fall into a trust or untrust category. This third category is often referred to as the *demilitarized zone* (DMZ). Figure 8-4 illustrates the three-category setup.

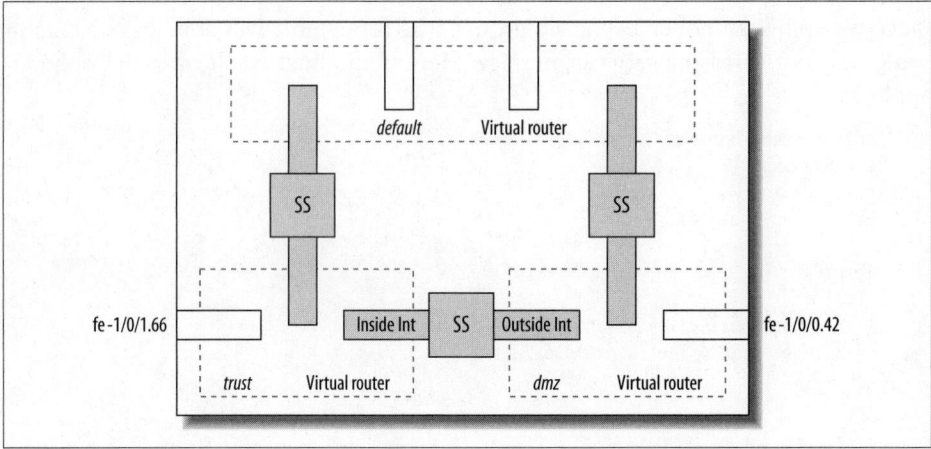

Figure 8-4. Three-zone VRs

A large advantage of a VR is the fact that rib-groups and firewall filters are avoided since interfaces are now tied to the routing instance and are placed in the instance's route table. As a result, traffic arriving over the applied interface automatically has a route lookup performed in the instance's route table. VRs also allow routing protocols to be configured to automatically populate the route table. This actually creates a new process or instance of that protocol, so the standard show commands must be followed by the instance switch. More to the point, if a VR called trust was config-ured with OSPF, a show ospf neighbor instance trust would be issued in order to view the OSPF neighbors. As in Figure 8-3, a VR trust is going to be configured with LAN interface fe-1/0/1 and inside service interfaces of sp-0/0/0.1 and lo0.1:

```
routing-instances {
    trust {
        instance-type virtual router
        interface sp-0/0/0.1;
        interface fe-1/0/1.0;
        interface lo0.1;

}
```

 The lo0.1 interface is created for routing protocol use in a VR. When a new logical interface is configured on the loopback interface, it must be applied to a routing instance to avoid commit failures.

Next, routing is configured to send traffic to the service interface for servicing (the stateful firewall, NAT, intrusion detection service [IDS], etc.). Similar to FBF, a static default route is used with a next hop value of the service interface. Also, OSPF is enabled on the LAN Fast Ethernet interface. Here is the result of the entire VR configuration:

```
routing-instances {
    trust {
        instance-type virtual router
        interface sp-0/0/0.1;
        interface fe-1/0/1.0;
        interface lo0.1;
        routing-options {
            static {
                route 0.0.0.0/0 next-hop sp-0/0/0.1;
            }
        }
        protocols {
            ospf {
                area 0.0.0.0 {
                    interface fe-1/0/1.0;
                }
            }
        }
    }
}
```

 The FBF and Virtual Router example shows traffic in only one direc-tion. Additional routes for return traffic may need to be created to the outside interface depending on the type of service.

Compared to FBF, the VR configuration should let you sleep much easier at night due to its simplicity. The next hop service set examples that follow utilize the preferred VR solution.

Summary of Route Tables and Next Hop-Style Service Sets

When using the flexible next hop-style service set, you must consider multiple route table lookups. Due to the multiple lookup requirement, a unique result must be present in each lookup iteration. You can accomplish this by using destination NAT, FBF, or VRs. The recommended method, and the foundation for the remaining chapters, is to use VRs.

In the next section, we will look at one of the common services used in enterprise networks today: IPSec VPNs.

IPSec VPNs

IPSec VPNs, as discussed in Chapter 7, tunnel IP traffic across an IP network to provide security features such as data privacy and integrity. When building an IPSec tunnel, you must decide on a few parameters:

- Protocol (Encapsulating Security Payload [ESP], authentication header [AH], or Bundle)
- Encryption algorithm (Advanced Encryption Standard [AES], Data Encryption Standard [DES], Triple DES [3DES], or none)
- Authentication algorithm (Message Digest 5 [MD5], Secure Hash Algorithm [SHA-1])
- Perfect forward secrecy (on/off)
- Anti-replay (on/off)

Together, these parameters form a *proposal*. The proposal must be equivalent on each side of the tunnel for the tunnel to become established. These proposals can be statically configured or dynamically negotiated using the Internet Key Exchange (IKE) protocol. Static proposals are rarely used, as they are cumbersome to manage, prone to error, and difficult to change on the fly. IKE uses a method of key exchanges to exchange parameters in a secure manner over two phases. Phase 1 establishes the parameters needed to exchange information to form a secure IPSec tunnel. Phase 2 establishes the actual security parameters for that IPSec tunnel. When viewing commands on the router, Phase 1 is seen as an IKE security association, and Phase 2 is seen as an IPSec security association.

Since multiple tunnels can be established between two peers, there has to be some way to identify which packets belong to each tunnel. To do this, a database is created with entries called security associations (SAs) for each tunnel. An SA identifies each tunnel by the following parameters:

- Destination IP address
- Security protocol and parameters (protocol, encryption, and authentication)
- Security Parameter Index (SPI)
- Secret keys

 IPSec theory is beyond the scope of this book; we focus instead on network implementation and design. Please consult O'Reilly dedicated IPSec books for more information on the specifics of ESP, AH, encryption, and IKE.

Minimum IPSec Tunnel Configuration

When configuring an IPSec tunnel, as with all Layer 3 services, you will need a service set. These service sets contain the rules for matching traffic that should transit the IPSec tunnel. The rules can include policies that link the various proposals that the tunnel will use (see Figure 8-5). There can be separate policies and proposals for the Phase 1 (IKE) and Phase 2 (IPSec) SAs.

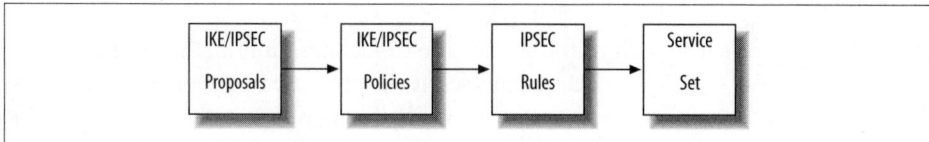

Figure 8-5. IPSec rule, policy, and proposal relationships

PBR is going to form an IPSec tunnel with the extranet Cans for traffic to a 128.3.3/24 address block to secure traffic (see Figure 8-6). The remote endpoint of the tunnel is 128.3.3.4 and the local address on PBR is 172.16.1.2. PBR is learning the 123.3.3/24 subnet via BGP with Wheat.

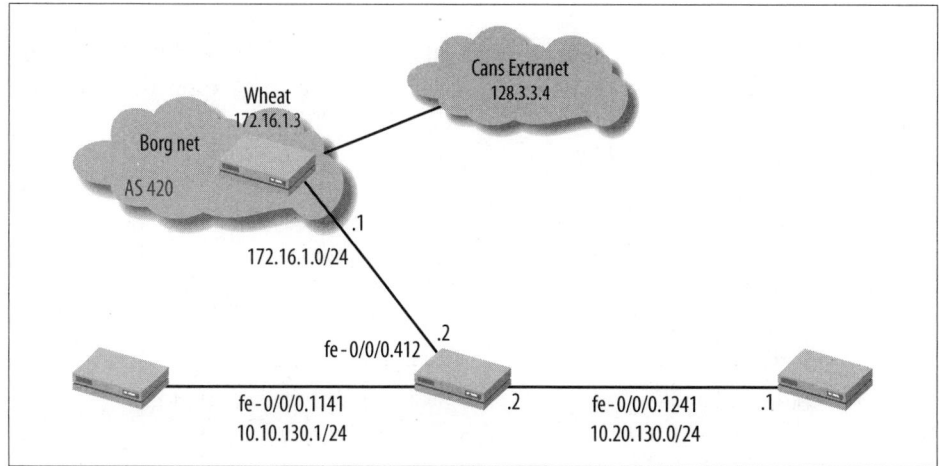

Figure 8-6. Sample topology

The tunnel will be set up with the default parameters shown in Table 8-1.

Table 8-1. Default parameters for tunnel

	IKE	IPSec
Mode	Main	N/A
Protocol	N/A	ESP
Encryption	3DES-CBC (cipher block chaining)	3DES-CBC
Authentication	SHA-1	Hashed Message Authentication Code (HMAC)-SHA-1-96
Lifetime	3,600 seconds	28,800 seconds
Additional options	N/A	Antireplay, no Perfect Forward Secrecy (PFS) protocol

Interface-style service set

First we will implement the tunnel as an interface-style service set and then as a next hop service set. Begin by creating the service interface to use for the interface-style service set:

```
[edit interfaces]
lab@PBR# set sp-0/0/0 unit 0 family inet
```

Now create the rule to match traffic sent to the tunnel and, minimally, an IKE policy to be applied. An IKE policy referencing either a preshared key or a certificate is required, and IPSec policies are optional. With this configuration, the tunnel will inherit the default parameters listed in Table 8-1:

```
[edit services ipsec-vpn]

ike {
        policy min-policy {
            pre-shared-key ascii-text "$9$BSJ1RSdVYJUH8XGDHkPfIEh";
## SECRET-DATA
        }
    }
```

Create the IPSec VPN rule to match on the required traffic and send it through the tunnel toward the endpoint. The IKE policy will also need to be applied, along with a direction in which to *encrypt* traffic:

```
lab@PBRt# show services
ipsec-vpn {
    rule secure-extranet {
        term 1 {
            from {
                destination-address {
                    128.3.3.0/24;
                }
            }
            then {
                remote-gateway 128.3.3.4;
                dynamic {
```

```
        ike-policy min-policy;
        }
    }
}
    match-direction output;
}
    }
```

 The router automatically created bidirectional SAs, so when specify-
ing traffic to be secured in the outbound direction, the router automat-
ically secures the inbound direction. This means that when specifying
an interface-style service set, the output direction is generally used,
whereas a next hop-style service set will use the input direction.

Next, we need to create the service set that maps the IPSec rule and the service interface. Additionally, we need to configure the local gateway for the IPSec tunnel. This
will be the address used to source all IPSec packets as well as the address to which
the remote tunnels will connect. You can have only a single gateway address in a service set, but you can configure multiple remote gateways in the IPSec rules.

```
[edit services]
lab@PBR# show service-set basic-vpn
interface-service {
    service-interface sp-0/0/0.0;
}
ipsec-vpn-options {
    local-gateway 172.16.1.2;
}
ipsec-vpn-rules secure-extranet;
```

Apply the service set to the tunnel's outbound interface:

```
lab@PBR# top show interfaces fe-0/0/0 unit 412
description PBR-to-Wheat;
vlan-id 412;
family inet {
    service {
        input {
            service-set basic-vpn;
        }
        output {
            service-set basic-vpn;
        }
    }
    address 172.16.1.2/24;
```

After committing the configuration, you can view the tunnel status with the show
service ipsec command. In this case, the tunnel appears to be down, as no Phase 2
SAs appear:

```
lab@PBR# run show services ipsec-vpn ipsec security-associations
Service set: basic-vpn
```

```
Rule: secure-extranet, Term: 1, Tunnel index: 1
Local gateway: 172.16.1.2, Remote gateway: 128.3.3.4
Tunnel MTU: 1500

--- No IPSec SA information available ---
```

Issuing a ping to the remote gateway address of 128.3.3.4 on PBR indicates the problem:

```
lab@PBR# ping 128.3.3.4
PING 128.3.3.4 (128.3.3.4): 56 data bytes
ping: sendto: No route to host
ping: sendto: No route to host
ping: sendto: No route to host
ping: sendto: No route to host
^C
--- 128.3.3.4 ping statistics ---
4 packets transmitted, 0 packets received, 100% packet loss
n
```

Recall that the 128.3.3/24 network was learned via BGP. When viewing the BGP neighbor status toward Wheat, the session appears to be down, as seen by the connect state:

```
lab@PBR# run show bgp summary
Groups: 1 Peers: 1 Down peers: 1
Table    Tot Paths  Act Paths Suppressed  History Damp State  Pending
inet.0          0          0          0        0        0         0
Peer            AS     InPkt    OutPkt    OutQ   Flaps Last Up/Dwn State|#Active/
Received/Damped...
172.16.1.1     420       198       184       0       7        6:30 Connect
```

The BGP session is down because the service set is applied to the session's interface. Remember that once a service set is applied to an interface, any traffic that does not match the term is serviced by default. To avoid this problem, you should apply a service filter to skip the procession of BGP traffic. The default action of a service filter is skip, so make sure other traffic is serviced accordingly:

```
[edit firewall]
lab@PBR# show
family inet {
    service-filter allow-bgp {
        term 1 {
            from {
                protocol tcp;
                port bgp;
            }
            then skip;
        }
    }
        term 2 {
            then service;
        }

}
```

Apply the service filter to the interface in both directions:

```
lab@PBR# top show interfaces fe-0/0/0 unit 412
description PBR-to-Wheat;
vlan-id 412;
family inet {
    service {
        input {
            service-set basic-vpn service-filter allow-bgp;
        }
        output {
            service-set basic-vpn service-filter allow-bgp;
        }
    }
    address 172.16.1.2/24;
```

After the service filter has been applied, the BGP session and the IPSec tunnel will become established. Verify the tunnel using the show services ipsec command. First, verify Phase 1, ensuring that the state is matured:

```
[edit firewall family inet service-filter allow-bgp]
lab@PBR# run show services ipsec-vpn ike security-associations
Remote Address   State         Initiator cookie   Responder cookie
Exchange type
128.3.3.4        Matured       773036d8a2d22e7b   ef23082150245a03
Main
```

Often, an operator will view the IKE SA, and when nothing appears, the operator will assume that the IPSec tunnel is down. This is not always the case, as IKE associations appear only on an "as needed" basis. So, if the IPSec SA has been established, the IKE SA may time out. Using default parameters, the lifetime of an IKE SA is 3,600 seconds and the lifetime of IPSec is 28,800 seconds, which means that a stable network may not have an active IKE SA for up to 7 hours! Make sure that if any changes occur that could prevent two-way IKE communication between the remote peers, the IPSec SA is cleared to force a renegotiation of the IKE SA. Otherwise, a filter-blocking IKE message may not been seen for several hours before the IPSec SA reaches its lifetime.

Now verify that Phase 2 has an inbound and outbound SA for bidirectional traffic flows:

```
[edit firewall family inet service-filter allow-bgp]
lab@PBR# run show services ipsec-vpn ipsec security-associations
Service set: basic-vpn

  Rule: secure-extranet, Term: 1, Tunnel index: 1
  Local gateway: 172.16.1.2, Remote gateway: 128.3.3.4
  Tunnel MTU: 1500
    Direction  SPI         AUX-SPI   Mode     Type      Protocol
    inbound    2579118494  0         tunnel   dynamic   ESP
    outbound   247425684   0         tunnel   dynamic   ESP
```

 By default, the establishment of an IPSec tunnel is data-driven. This means that the tunnel is not established until a packet matches a rule that requires the tunnel. If you want to change this behavior, use the establish-tunnels immediately command.

When IPSec is deployed on the router, the router must know how to direct traffic to the service Physical Interface Card (PIC) or service module to authenticate, de-encrypt, and de-encapsulate the packet. The router accomplishes this by creating forwarding table entries based on the source IP address, destination IP address, and protocol tuple. These entries will be seen as /72s in the forwarding table with a next hop of service:

```
[edit firewall family inet service-filter allow-bgp]
lab@PBR# run show route forwarding-table | find /72
172.16.1.2.128.3.3.4.50/72
                        user     0              service   324     3
172.16.1.2.128.3.3.4.51/72
                        user  0              service   324   3
   172.16.1.3/32        user  0 172.16.1.1    ucst   332   5 fe-0/0/0.412
   172.16.1.255/32      dest  0 172.16.1.255  bcst   320   1 fe-0/0/0.412
   224.0.0.0/4          perm  1              mdsc   13    1
   224.0.0.1/32         perm  0 224.0.0.1    mcst   9     3
   224.0.0.5/32         user  1 224.0.0.5    mcst   9     3
   255.255.255.255/32 perm  0              bcst   10    1

Routing table: __juniper_private1__.inet
Internet:
Destination        Type RtRef Next hop     Type Index NhRef Netif
default            perm  0              rjct   62    1
10.0.0.1/32        intf  1 10.0.0.1     locl   321   2
10.0.0.16/32       intf  0 10.0.0.16    locl   322   1
224.0.0.0/4        perm  0              mdsc   61    1
224.0.0.1/32       perm  0 224.0.0.1    mcst   57    1
255.255.255.255/32 perm  0              bcst   58    1
```

The consequence of these entries, if you are using an interface-style service set, is that traffic received on any interface, regardless of where the service set is applied, will be serviced.

Next hop-style service set

The same IPSec VPN is now implemented using a next hop-style service set. As with every next hop-style service set, you must configure the two "legs" of the inside and outside service sets:

```
sp-0/0/0 {
    unit 0 {
        family inet;
    }
    unit 1 {
```

```
            family inet;
            service-domain inside;
        }
        unit 2 {
            family inet;
            service-domain outside;
        }
    }
}
```

Then you need to create the IPSec rules. These rules will look the same as they did in the previous example using interface-style service sets, with one notable exception: *rule direction*. Since traffic is going to be mapped to the inside interface for encryption, a match-direction of input should be used:

```
ipsec-vpn {
    rule secure-extranet {
        term 1 {
            from {
                destination-address {
                    128.3.3.0/24;
                }
            }
            then {
                remote-gateway 128.3.3.4;
                dynamic {
                    ike-policy min-policy;
                }
            }
        }
        match-direction input;
    }
```

Now traffic is mapped to the inside service interface to be encrypted in the IPSec tunnel. You can accomplish this mapping in a variety of ways; the simplest is with a static route:

```
lan@PBR set routing-options static route 128.3.3/24 next-hop sp-0/0/0.1
```

After committing the configuration and sending traffic from Bock to the extranet 128.3.3/24 subnet, the IKE and IPSec SAs are created:

```
[edit]
lab@PBR# run show services ipsec-vpn ike security-associations
Remote AddressState   Initiator cookie Responder cookie Exchange type
128.3.3.4       Matured 833d31c69f915b75 4326d4b9c69e624f Main


lab@PBR# run show services ipsec-vpn ipsec security-associations
Service set: basic-vpn

  Rule: secure-extranet, Term: 1, Tunnel index: 1
  Local gateway: 172.16.1.2, Remote gateway: 128.3.3.4
  IPSec inside interface: sp-0/0/0.1, Tunnel MTU: 1500
    Direction SPI       AUX-SPI      Mode      Type      Protocol
```

```
inbound    612210302   0        tunnel   dynamic  ESP
outbound   1652494959  0        tunnel   dynamic  ESP
```

Also verify that the traffic from Bock to the extranet is actually being encrypted *and* decrypted by viewing the IPSec statistics:

```
lab@PBR# run show services stateful-firewall ipsec-vpn ipsec statistics
PIC: sp-0/0/0, Service set: basic-vpn

ESP Statistics:
  Encrypted bytes:            4400
  Decrypted bytes:            5336
  Encrypted packets:            50
  Decrypted packets:            63
AH Statistics:
  Input bytes:                   0
  Output bytes:                  0
  Input packets:                 0
  Output packets:                0
Errors:
  AH authentication failures: 0, Replay errors: 0
  ESP authentication failures: 0, ESP decryption failures: 0
  Bad headers: 0, Bad trailers: 0
```

The interface-style service set requires a service filter to allow the external BGP session to be established; however, these filters do not exist in next hop-style service sets, nor are they required. Simply ensure that only traffic that should be serviced is mapped to the service interface.

Besides the usual show command to troubleshoot IPSec tunnels, you also can configure IKE traceoptions via set services ipsec-vpn traceoptions flag ike. These messages are automatically placed into a file called *kmd*.

Unique Proposals

You can create a variety of different proposals for both the IKE and IPSec negotiations. You can change these values from the default values based on security constraints and objectives, or simply for interoperability with other vendors. Recall from the beginning of the chapter that we mentioned the link between proposals and policies: proposals link to policies, which link to IPSec rules. When viewing the default parameters, the keen observer will notice that not all of the strongest authentication, encryption, and keys are being used. There are two reasons for this: interoperability and memory usage. It makes sense to create default parameters that most vendors and systems can support. Also, as the algorithms become more complex and the keys larger, the memory and CPU required also increase. This creates a very delicate balance between desired algorithms and performance. We must examine the memory usage when creating an IPSec tunnel with very minimal traffic flow:

```
[edit services ipsec-vpn]
lab@PBR# run show services service-sets memory-usage
Interface    Service Set                          Bytes Used
sp-0/0/0     basic-vpn                                  4310

[edit services ipsec-vpn]
lab@PBR# run show services service-sets summary
             Service sets                   CPU
Interface  configured     Bytes used Policy bytes used  utilization
sp-0/0/0             1 4392 ( 0.03 %)   1764 ( 0.00 %)      0.00 %
```

Now create unique IKE and IPSec policies and see how they affect memory usage.
The IKE proposal is going to use the strongest values and the largest keys possible:

```
[edit services ipsec-vpn
lab@PBR# show ike
proposal unique-ike {
    authentication-method pre-shared-keys;
    dh-group group2;
    authentication-algorithm sha-256;
    encryption-algorithm aes-256-cbc;
}
```

Then the proposal is linked to the policy, and a preshared key is configured:

```
[edit services]
lab@PBR show ike | find policy
    policy unique-ike-policy {
        proposals unique-ike;
        pre-shared-key ascii-text "$9$Tz9peK8N-wO17VbsJZz36ApBEclKWLREVw"; ## SECRET-
DATA
    }
}
```

An IPSec proposal is also created with the strongest algorithms possible:

```
[edit services]
lab@PBR# show | find ipsec
ipsec {
    proposal unique-ipsec {
        authentication-algorithm hmac-sha1-96;
        encryption-algorithm aes-256-cbc;
    }
```

Then the proposals are linked to an IPSec policy. This policy also enables PFS:

```
    policy unique-ipsec-policy {
        perfect-forward-secrecy {
            keys group2;
        }
        proposals unique-ipsec;
    }
}
```

 PFS is a method that creates new keys that are not mathematically related to each other. This creates an additional level of security in case a security key is compromised.

Apply the new policies to an IPSec rule in the action statement:

```
lab@PBR# show rule secure-extranet
term 1 {
    from {
        destination-address {
            128.3.3.0/24;
        }
    }
    then {
        remote-gateway 128.3.3.4;
        dynamic {
            ike-policy unique-ike-policy;
            ipsec-policy unique-ipsec-policy;
        }
    }
}
match-direction input;
```

Once the tunnel is up, you can view the parameters when using the detailed or extensive switch on the SA commands:

```
[edit services ipsec-vpn]
lab@PBR# run show services ipsec-vpn ike security-associations detail
IKE peer 128.3.3.4
  Role: Initiator, State: Matured
  Initiator cookie: 38d4aa648ce7b6b5, Responder cookie: e39275d71141441d
  Exchange type: Main, Authentication method: Pre-shared-keys
  Local: 172.16.1.2:500, Remote: 128.3.3.4:500
  Lifetime: Expires in 3587 seconds
  Algorithms:
   Authentication        : sha256
   Encryption            : aes-cbc (256 bits)
   Pseudo random function: hmac-sha256
  Traffic statistics:
   Input  bytes  :                   772
   Output bytes  :                   872
   Input  packets:                     4
   Output packets:                     5
  Flags: Caller notification sent
  IPSec security associations: 1 created, 0 deleted
  Phase 2 negotiations in progress: 1

    Negotiation type: Quick mode, Role: Initiator, Message ID: 533813962
    Local: 172.16.1.2:500, Remote: 128.3.3.4:500
    Local identity: ipv4_subnet(any:0,0.0.0.0/0)
    Remote identity: ipv4_subnet(any:0,[0..7]=128.3.3.0/24)
    Flags: Caller notification sent, Waiting for done
```

```
[edit services ipsec-vpn]
lab@PBR# run sh services ipsec-vpn ipsec security-associations
 extensive Service set: basic-vpn

  Rule: secure-extranet, Term: 1, Tunnel index: 1
  Local gateway: 172.16.1.2, Remote gateway: 128.3.3.4
  IPSec inside interface: sp-0/0/0.1, Tunnel MTU: 1500
  Local identity: ipv4_subnet(any:0,0.0.0.0/0)
  Remote identity: ipv4_subnet(any:0,[0..7]=128.3.3.0/24)

    Direction: inbound, SPI: 1138084291, AUX-SPI: 0
    Mode: tunnel, Type: dynamic, State: Installed
    Protocol: ESP, Authentication: hmac-sha1-96, Encryption: aes-cbc (256 bits)
    Soft lifetime: Expires in 28640 seconds
    Hard lifetime: Expires in 28775 seconds
    Anti-replay service: Enabled, Replay window size: 64

    Direction: outbound, SPI: 795324419, AUX-SPI: 0
    Mode: tunnel, Type: dynamic, State: Installed
    Protocol: ESP, Authentication: hmac-sha1-96, Encryption: aes-cbc (256 bits)
    Soft lifetime: Expires in 28640 seconds
    Hard lifetime: Expires in 28775 seconds
    Anti-replay service: Enabled, Replay window size: 64
```

How much additional processing was actually used? Viewing the memory usage after the more labor-intensive proposals were created shows a 4% increase from the default case. Adding a higher volume of traffic again increases these values:

```
lab@PBR# run show services service-sets memory-usage
Interface    Service Set                           Bytes Used
sp-0/0/0     basic-vpn                                 4454

[edit services ipsec-vpn]
lab@PBR# run show services service-sets summary
          Service sets                          CPU
Interface  configured      Bytes used Policy bytes used utilization
sp-0/0/0            1 4536 ( 0.03 %)    1764 ( 0.00 %)     0.00 %
```

Backup Tunnels

One application of an IPSec tunnel is for redundancy, if physical redundancy does not exist. You can establish a tunnel over another private network or over a public network, such as the Internet. In the case study shown in Figure 8-7, PBR, which is the WAN router for Internet connectivity, there is a single link to Stout. If that link fails, an IPSec tunnel will be used between PBR and Stout. This tunnel will actually be established over the path from the Water Internet service provider (ISP) to Hops.

First, you must configure the tunnel endpoints. They could be physical or loopback interfaces. For the purposes of this example, the tunnel from PBR to Stout is going to be established from PBR's WAN interface to Water (64.7.12.6) to Stout's loopback interface (10.20.128.4). PBR's physical interface was chosen for optimal path redundancy (i.e., to avoid the tunnel establishment via ISP Wheat). A simple IPSec VPN is

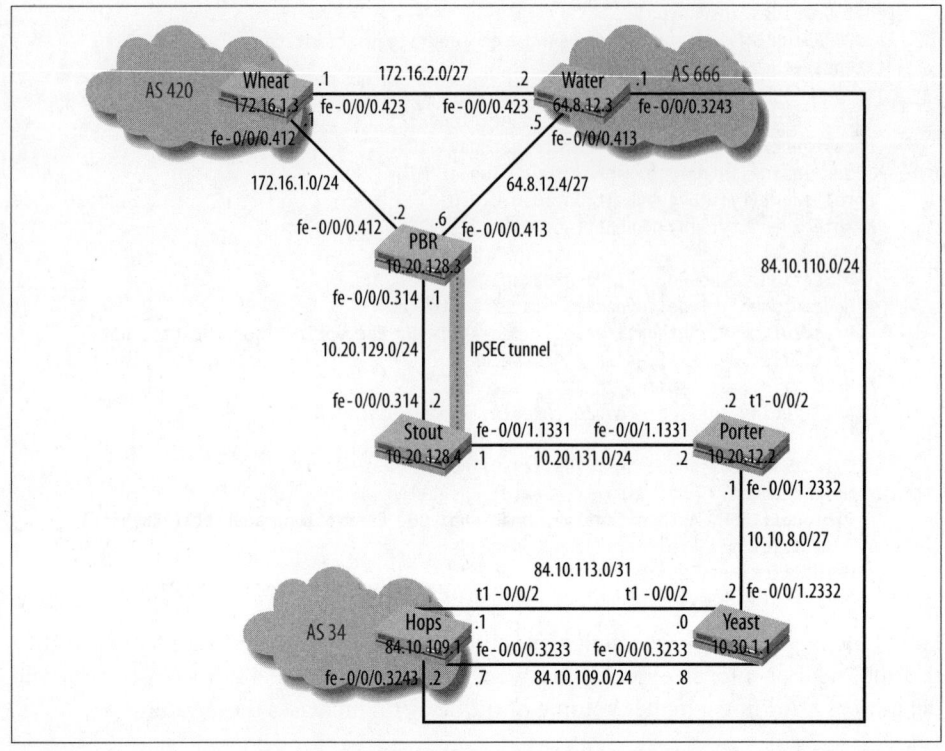

Figure 8-7. Backup tunnel

created using JUNOS default parameters on Stout. You must use a next hop-style
service set since OSPF will be running over the IPSec tunnel:

```
lab@stout> show configuration services
service-set Basic-ipsec {
    next-hop-service {
        inside-service-interface sp-0/0/0.2;
        outside-service-interface sp-0/0/0.1;
    }
    ipsec-vpn-options {
        local-gateway 10.20.128.4;
    }
    ipsec-vpn-rules simple-rule;
}
ipsec-vpn {
    rule simple-rule {
        term 1 {
            from {
                source-address {
                    0.0.0.0/0;
                }
                destination-address {
                    0.0.0.0/0;
                }
```

```
                }
            then {
                remote-gateway 64.8.12.6;
                dynamic {
                    ike-policy basic-ike;
                }
            }
        }
        match-direction input;
    }
    ike {
        policy basic-ike {
            pre-shared-key ascii-text "$9$iqPQ/CuEclFnclKMN-Hqm";
## SECRET-DATA
        }
    }
    establish-tunnels immediately;
}


}
lab@stout> show configuration interfaces sp-0/0/0
unit 1 {
    family inet;
    service-domain outside;
}
unit 2 {
    family inet;
    service-domain inside;
}
```

The configuration is mirrored on router PBR with only the local gateway and remote gateway address-swapping. Notice two differences from previous examples. One is the open IPSec rule set of any address configured, as well as the establish-tunnels immediately keyword. These are used to speed up the failover process and avoid having to wait for the IPSec tunnel establishment.

```
lab@PBR# show services
service-set Basic-ipsec {
    next-hop-service {
        inside-service-interface sp-0/0/0.2;
        outside-service-interface sp-0/0/0.1;
    }
    ipsec-vpn-options {
        local-gateway 64.8.12.6;
    }
    ipsec-vpn-rules simple-rule;
}
ipsec-vpn {
    rule simple-rule {
        term 1 {
            from {
                source-address {
                    0.0.0.0/0;
```

```
                }
                destination-address {
                    0.0.0.0/0;
                }
            }
            then {
                remote-gateway 10.20.128.4;
                dynamic {
                    ike-policy basic-ike;
                }
            }
        }
        match-direction input;
    }
    ike {
        policy basic-ike {
            pre-shared-key ascii-text "$9$iqPQ/CuEclFnclKMN-Hqm";
## SECRET-DATA
        }
    }
    establish-tunnels immediately;
```

Also configure OSPF over the inside interface on Stout and PBR, in order to run OSPF over the IPSec tunnel:

```
[edit]
lab@stout# set protocols ospf area 0 interface sp-0/0/0.2

[edit]
lab@stout# commit
commit complete
```

Verify that OSPF is running over the tunnel. The tunnel is treated as a standard point-to-point interface in OSPF:

```
lab@stout# run show ospf neighbor
  Address          Interface       State  ID            Pri  Dead
  10.20.129.2      fe-0/0/0.3141   Full   10.20.128.3   128  38
  10.20.131.1      fe-0/0/1.1331   Full   10.10.12.2    128  31
  10.20.128.3      sp-0/0/0.2      Full   10.20.128.3   128  32
```

Since the tunnel should be treated as a backup and not as an equal cost, increase the metric in the sp-0/0/0.2 interface to 1,000 on both Stout and PBR:

```
[edit]
lab@stout# set protocols ospf area 0 interface sp-0/0/0.2 metric 1000
```

Routing and verification for IPSec tunnels

Before you can test the IPSec tunnel, the proper routing has to be in place. First, the loopback address of Stout on PBR must point over ISP Water to be used during a failover. Also, you must create an aggregate route for the internal network and advertise it via BGP. Lastly, generate a default into OSPF if the link to Water is up.

```
[edit]
lab@PBR# show routing-options
static {
    route 10.20.128.4/32 next-hop 64.8.12.5;
}
aggregate {
    route 10.0.0.0/8;
}
generate {
    route 0.0.0.0/0 policy isp-routers;
}
autonomous-system 1282
```

 Setting routes to the loopback of Bock may seem strange, so as an alternative you could configure an additional loopback address (nonprimary) for tunnel establishment and failover.

For completeness, the policy for the default generated route, the policy to export the generated route into OSPF, and the policy to advertise the internal autonomous system (AS) 1282 address block (10/8) are shown:

```
lab@PBR# show policy-options
policy-statement default-ospf {
    term 1 {
        from {
            protocol aggregate;
            route-filter 0.0.0.0/0 exact accept;
        }
    }
}
policy-statement isp-routers {
    term 1 {
        from {
            protocol bgp;
            neighbor 64.8.12.5;
        }
        then accept;
    }
    term 2 {
        then reject;
    }
}
policy-statement send-agg {
    from {
        route-filter 10.0.0.0/8 exact accept;
    }
    then accept;
}
```

Verify that the internal subnet is being advertised to Water via BGP:

```
[edit]
lab@PBR# run show route advertising-protocol bgp 64.8.12.5
```

```
inet.0: 701 destinations, 1389 routes (701 active, 0 holddown, 0
hidden)
   Prefix                 Nexthop     MED   Lclpref   AS path
 * 10.0.0.0/8             Self                         I
```

When the physical Ethernet interface is up, all the OSPF routes point to the fe-0/0/
0.3141 interface since the IPSec tunnel is eliminated in the Shortest Path First (SPF)
calculation.

```
lab#PBR> show route protocol ospf
inet.0: 701 destinations, 1389 routes (701 active, 0 holddown, 0
hidden)
+ = Active Route, - = Last Active, * = Both

10.10.8.0/27         *[OSPF/10] 00:12:32, metric 3
                      > to 10.20.129.1 via fe-0/0/0.3141
10.10.12.2/32        *[OSPF/10] 00:12:32, metric 2
                      > to 10.20.129.1 via fe-0/0/0.3141
10.10.128.1/32       *[OSPF/10] 01:59:30, metric 1
                      > to 10.10.130.1 via fe-0/0/0.1141
10.20.128.4/32        [OSPF/10] 00:12:32, metric 1
                      > to 10.20.129.1 via fe-0/0/0.3141
10.20.131.0/24       *[OSPF/10] 00:12:32, metric 2
                      > to 10.20.129.1 via fe-0/0/0.3141
10.30.1.1/32         *[OSPF/10] 00:12:32, metric 3
                      > to 10.20.129.1 via fe-0/0/0.3141
64.8.12.6/32          [OSPF/150] 00:12:32, metric 0, tag 0
                      > to 10.20.129.1 via fe-0/0/0.3141
224.0.0.5/32         *[OSPF/10] 23:30:31, metric 1
                        MultiRecv

__juniper_private1__.inet.0: 2 destinations, 2 routes (2 active, 0
holddown, 0 hidden)
```

As shown in Figure 8-7, router Yeast is connected to an ISP called Hops. Yeast is not
running BGP, and instead relies on static routes due to its single-homed nature. To
reach the WAN interface of PBR (64.8.12.6), you need to configure a static route
pointing each T1 link toward the ISP:

```
lab@Yeast# show
static {
    route 64.8.12.6/32 next-hop [ 84.10.113.1 84.10.109.7 ];
}
autonomous-system 1282;
```

The problem is that if traffic is sourced from PBR's WAN IP address of 64.8.12.6, it
resolves over the default route redistributed in OSPF by PBR:

```
lab@stout# run show route 64.8.12.6

inet.0: 18 destinations, 18 routes (18 active, 0 holddown, 0 hidden)
+ = Active Route, - = Last Active, * = Both

0.0.0.0/0            *[OSPF/150] 00:21:45, metric 0, tag 0
                      > to 10.20.129.2 via fe-0/0/0.3141
```

This is OK when the physical link between PBR and Stout is up, but if the link goes down, Stout has no way to send traffic back to PBR for tunnel establishment. There are multiple ways to solve this issue, but we decided to redistribute the static route on Yeast into OSPF (policy send-static) instead of creating a static route on Stout and Porter. We did this to try to avoid a blackhole issue and have some dynamism by sending the 64.8.12.6 when a link from Yeast to Hops is in the "up" state.

```
lab@Yeast# top show protocols ospf
export send-static;
area 0.0.0.0 {
    interface fe-0/0/1.2332;
[edit]
```

After this change, Stout has a specific /32 route pointing toward Porter:

```
[edit]
lab@stout# run show route 64.8.12.6

inet.0: 18 destinations, 18 routes (18 active, 0 holddown, 0 hidden)
+ = Active Route, - = Last Active, * = Both

64.8.12.6/32        *[OSPF/150] 00:26:58, metric 0, tag 0
                    > to 10.20.131.1 via fe-0/0/1.1331
```

Finally, verify that the correct routing is in place by sending some traceroutes from PBR. First verify that PBR can reach Stout's loopback via ISP routing:

```
[edit]
lab@PBR# run traceroute 10.20.128.4
traceroute to 10.20.128.4 (10.20.128.4), 30 hops max, 40 byte packets
 1  64.8.12.5 (64.8.12.5)  14.087 ms  9.459 ms  8.301 ms
 2  84.10.110.2 (84.10.110.2)  41.429 ms  29.842 ms  30.051 ms
 3  84.10.113.0 (84.10.113.0)  9.856 ms  9.521 ms  10.061 ms
 4  10.10.8.1 (10.10.8.1)  9.863 ms  12.269 ms  18.228 ms
 5  10.20.128.4 (10.20.128.4)  39.245 ms  99.785 ms  130.072 ms
```

Ensure that the traffic to other internal networks—in this case, Porter's loopback—takes the correct and shortest path through the internal network:

```
[edit]
lab@PBR# run traceroute 10.10.12.2
traceroute to 10.10.12.2 (10.10.12.2), 30 hops max, 40 byte packets
 1  10.20.129.1 (10.20.129.1)  14.160 ms  17.784 ms  11.653 ms
 2  10.10.12.2 (10.10.12.2)  29.985 ms  29.766 ms  9.955 ms
```

In summary, you must meet these criteria for failover to work properly:

- PBR must have a route to Stout's loopback over the ISP networks.
- PBR must advertise its internal network subnet to the ISP.
- Yeast must have a route to PBR's WAN address.
- Stout must have a route to PBR's WAN address not pointing directly to PBR.
- A default route must be generated by PBR as it is the preferred exit point for all Internet traffic.

Physical interface goes down!

Here is the big moment: interface failure on PBR and Stout. Was all the hard work and design worth it or was it a fruitless effort? First, verify that OSPF is still enabled over the IPSec tunnel:

```
[edit]
lab@PBR# run show ospf neighbor
  Address          Interface      State     ID            Pri Dead
  10.10.130.1      fe-0/0/0.1141  Full      10.10.128.1   128  31
  10.20.128.4      sp-0/0/0.2     Full      10.20.128.4   128  36

[edit]
lab@PBR#
```

Next, verify that Stout has Internet connectivity by issuing a show route command on Water's link address to PBR. Notice that Stout is learning a default route over the IPSec tunnel. All appears good so far!

```
[edit]
lab@stout# run show route 64.8.12.5

inet.0: 16 destinations, 16 routes (16 active, 0 holddown, 0 hidden)
+ = Active Route, - = Last Active, * = Both

0.0.0.0/0          *[OSPF/150] 00:04:49, metric 0, tag 0
                    > via sp-0/0/0.2
```

Test internal connectivity from PBR by seeing whether Porter's loopback address is reached via the tunnel:

```
[edit]
lab@PBR> ping 10.0.12.2
PING 10.0.15.2 (10.0.15.2): 56 data bytes
64 bytes from 10.0.12.2: icmp_seq=0 ttl=64 time=0.221 ms
64 bytes from 10.0.12.2: icmp_seq=1 ttl=64 time=0.165 ms
^C
--- 10.0.15.2 ping statistics ---
2 packets transmitted, 2 packets received, 0% packet loss
round-trip min/avg/max/stddev = 0.165/0.193/0.221/0.028 ms
```

Lastly, verify that encrypted traffic is being sent and received over the IPSec tunnel:

```
lab@PBR# run show services ipsec-vpn ipsec statistics

PIC: sp-0/0/0, Service set: Basic-ipsec

ESP Statistics:
  Encrypted bytes:        144400
  Decrypted bytes:        127520
  Encrypted packets:        1850
  Decrypted packets:        1621
AH Statistics:
  Input bytes:                 0
  Output bytes:                0
```

```
    Input packets:               0
    Output packets:              0
  Errors:
    AH authentication failures: 0, Replay errors: 0
    ESP authentication failures: 0, ESP decryption failures: 0
    Bad headers: 0, Bad trailers: 0
```

Pat yourself on the back; the failover worked to perfection! Time to grab a beer (PBR me ASAP) and celebrate!

Dynamic IPSec Tunnels

So far, every IPSec tunnel used in this chapter has had static IP addresses on each side. What happens if the router is receiving requests from systems that have dynamic IPs? One such example would be a remote site with a cable modem receiving an address from the ISP via the Dynamic Host Configuration Protocol (DHCP). In this case, you could configure dynamic IPSec endpoints on the router with the static IP address (local router). The amazing thing about these dynamic tunnels is that there seems to be a magic man behind the curtain: the local router will automatically create the proper IPSec rules and static routes based on the incoming proxy information from the remote peer. The process is as follows:

1. The remote site (dynamic IP) initiates a connection with the local site (static IP).

2. The local router checks the incoming connection against the default proposals (see Table 8-2) or a list of custom proposals for Phase 1 on the connection process.

3. Phase 2 begins, and the local router verifies that the proxy ID (protected networks) of the remote system matches the allowed list. The default (0.0.0.0/0) matches any proxy ID sent.

4. After Phase 2 is completed, the kmd router process creates dynamic rules for encrypting traffic based on the received proxy ID. These rules are created for inside service interfaces so that they will always have a match direction of input.

5. Reverse Route Insertion (RRI) is performed. These are static routes for the remote protected networks and are automatically created to point to the inside interface. These routes are created only if the proxy ID is nondefault (0.0.0.0/0).

Table 8-2. Default IKE and IPSec proposals

Statement	Values
IKE	
Authentication method	Preshared keys
DH Group	Group 1 or Group 2
Authentication algorithm	SHA-1, SHA-256, MD5
Encryption algorithm	3DES-CBC, DES-CBC, AES-128, AES-192, AES-256
Lifetime	3,600 seconds

Table 8-2. Default IKE and IPSec proposals (continued)

Statement	Values
IPSec	
Protocol	ESP, AH, or Bundle
Authentication algorithm	HMAC-SHA-1-96, HMAC-MD5-96
Encryption algorithm	3DES-CBC, DES-CBC, AES-128, AES-192, AES-256
Lifetime	8 hours

To allow connection from dynamic peers, you need to configure an access profile and reference it in a service set. In the profile-specific client address, ranges are allowed, as are particular proxy IDs, proposals, and authentication using either pre-shared keys or RSA certificates. You also must configure the interface identifier, which will be used to map the remote router to a logical service interface. In the following example, PBR is configured to allow connections from any client (the * wildcard) using a preshared key for authentication and a proxy ID of 10/8 for local networks and 77.7.7/24 for remote networks. Since no proposals are specified, the default values are used. Lastly, an interface ID name of `single-interface-id` is tied to the profile.

```
[edit]
lab@PBR# show access
profile dynamic-peer {
    client * {
        ike {
            allowed-proxy-pair local 10.0.0.0/8 remote 77.7.7.0/24;
            pre-shared-key ascii-text "$9$Tz9peK8N-wO17VbsJZz36ApBEclKWLREVw"; ##
SECRET-DATA
            interface-id single-interface-id;
        }
    }
}
```

As with any other next hop service set, you will need to configure an inside and outside interface; however, an additional inside interface will also be used for the remote peer. This is the interface that the router will tie to each remote client. This logical interface could either be shared by multiple tunnels or dedicated per tunnel. In this case, unit 3 is defined for use with dynamic peers with the profile matching `single-interface-id`. This logical interface can be used by only a single tunnel due to the dedicated knob:

```
[edit]
lab@PBR# show interfaces sp-0/0/0
unit 0 {
    family inet;
}
unit 1 {
    family inet;
    service-domain inside;
```

```
    }
    unit 2 {
        family inet;
        service-domain outside;
    }
    unit 3 {
        dial-options {
            IPSec-interface-id single-interface-id;
            dedicated;
        }
        family inet;
        service-domain inside;
    }
```

Lastly, a next hop-style service set is created that references an inside and outside interface, a local gateway, and the access profile. Note that no rules are applied to the service set since they are dynamically created after Phase 2 of IPSec is completed:

```
[edit]
lab@PBR# show services
service-set basic-vpn {
    next-hop-service {
        inside-service-interface sp-0/0/0.1;
        outside-service-interface sp-0/0/0.2;
    }
    ipsec-vpn-options {
        local-gateway 172.16.1.2;
        ike-access-profile dynamic-peer;
    }
}
```

A remote connection is initiated to PBR with the correct proposals and preshared key:

```
lab@PBR# run show services ipsec-vpn ike security-associations
detail
IKE peer 128.3.3.4
  Role: Responder, State: Matured
  Initiator cookie: 5f5d01b859c5500c, Responder cookie:
cbf493d41825e544
  Exchange type: Main, Authentication method: Pre-shared-keys
  Local: 172.16.1.2:500, Remote: 128.3.3.4:500
  Lifetime: Expires in 3130 seconds
  Algorithms:
   Authentication        : sha256
   Encryption            : aes-cbc (256 bits)
   Pseudo random function: hmac-sha256
  Traffic statistics:
   Input  bytes  :                 1312
   Output bytes  :                 1320
   Input  packets:                    7
   Output packets:                    7
  Flags: Caller notification sent
  IPSec security associations: 2 created, 0 deleted
  Phase 2 negotiations in progress: 0
```

After Phase 2, the proxy ID is verified, which is protecting the PBR local network of 10/8 and a remote network of 77.7.7/24. The _junos_ rule was automatically created for logical interface sp-0/0/0.3:

```
lab@PBR# show service ipsec-vpn ipsec security-associations extensive
Service set: basic-vpn

  Rule: _junos_, Term: tunnel1, Tunnel index: 1
  Local gateway: 172.16.1.2, Remote gateway: 128.3.3.4
  IPSec inside interface: sp-0/0/0.3, Tunnel MTU: 1500
  Local identity: ipv4_subnet(any:0,[0..7]=10.0.0.0/8)
  Remote identity: ipv4_subnet(any:0,[0..7]=77.7.7.0/24)

    Direction: inbound, SPI: 3948527911, AUX-SPI: 0
    Mode: tunnel, Type: dynamic, State: Installed
    Protocol: ESP, Authentication: hmac-sha1-96, Encryption: aes-cbc
(256 bits)
    Soft lifetime: Expires in 28411 seconds
    Hard lifetime: Expires in 28501 seconds
    Anti-replay service: Enabled, Replay window size: 64

    Direction: outbound, SPI: 1740456130, AUX-SPI: 0
    Mode: tunnel, Type: dynamic, State: Installed
    Protocol: ESP, Authentication: hmac-sha1-96, Encryption: aes-cbc
(256 bits)
    Soft lifetime: Expires in 28411 seconds
    Hard lifetime: Expires in 28501 seconds
    Anti-replay service: Enabled, Replay window size: 64
```

Also, reverse routes are automatically created to the remote networks using the logical interface to the next hop with the dialer applied. These static routes will have a preference of 1 to avoid any contention with other routes on the system:

```
inet.0: 32 destinations, 37 routes (31 active, 0 holddown, 3 hidden)
+ = Active Route, - = Last Active, * = Both

77.7.7.0/24        *[Static/1] 00:05:44
                    > via sp-0/0/0.3

__juniper_private1__.inet.0: 2 destinations, 2 routes (2 active, 0
holddown, 0 hidden)
```

IPSec over GRE

Sometimes the names for network features seem to be created out of thin air, with no rhyme or reason. This is the case with an IPSec over GRE tunnel. The name does not accurately describe the feature, as it actually is a Generic Routing Encapsulation (GRE) tunnel that is secured with IPSec. A better name would be GRE over IPSec, but as we all know, network engineering can't be that logical. The most common usage of IPSec over GRE tunnels is to interoperate with older Cisco IOS codes that do not support routing over IPSec tunnels. In these cases, routing is configured over

GRE and then IPSec is added. In JUNOS, routing over IPSec tunnels is accomplished by using next hop-style service sets. However, when implementing IPSec over GRE, you can use either service set type, with one exception. If the GRE endpoints are the same as the IPSec tunnel endpoints, you should use interface-style service sets.

 You could use a next hop-style service set if the tunnel endpoints are the same and FBF was used to map the GRE packets to the IPSec tunnel, but this adds an additional level of complexity that you should avoid if possible.

As in Figure 8-6, an IPSec over GRE tunnel will be configured between PBR and the Cans extranet. First, an unnumbered GRE interface is created from PBR to Cans:

```
lab@PBR# show interfaces gr-0/0/0
unit 0 {
    tunnel {
        source 172.16.1.2;
        destination 128.3.3.4;
    }
    family inet;
}
```

 To aid in troubleshooting, you could add an IP address to the GRE tunnel, but it is not necessary.

Traffic to the extranet is mapped via a static route that points to the gr-0/0/0.0 interface:

```
[edit]
lab@PBR# show routing-options static route 128.3.3.0/24
next-hop gr-0/0/0.0;
```

Next, you need to configure unique proposals that map to Cisco defaults (for more information on custom proposals, see "Unique Proposals," earlier in this chapter):

```
ipsec {
    proposal cisco-interop {
        protocol esp;
        authentication-algorithm hmac-md5-96;
        encryption-algorithm des-cbc;
    }
    policy ipsecgre {
        perfect-forward-secrecy {
            keys group1;
        }
        proposals cisco-interop;
    }
}
```

```
        ike {
            proposal cisco-interop-ike {
                authentication-method pre-shared-keys;
                dh-group group1;
                authentication-algorithm md5;
                encryption-algorithm des-cbc;
            }
            policy main_ike {
                proposals cisco-interop-ike;
                pre-shared-key ascii-text "$9$JhUi.QF/OBEP5BEcyW8ZUjHP5z
36AuO"; ## SECRET-DATA
            }
        }
    }
```

Then, you need to create the rule to map the GRE packets to the IPSec tunnel. You
can do this by matching on the source IP address and destination IP address of the
GRE tunnel, as well as by mapping the Cisco interoperable proposals to the IPSec
tunnels:

```
lab@PBR# show services | find ipsec-vpn
ipsec-vpn {
    rule map-gre {
        term 1 {
            from {
                source-address {
                    172.16.1.2/32;
                }
                destination-address {
                    128.3.3.4/32;
                }
            }
            then {
                remote-gateway 128.3.3.4;
                dynamic {
                    ike-policy main_ike;
                    ipsec-policy ipsecgre;
                }
            }
        }
        match-direction output;
    }
```

A service set is then created and applied to the interface between PBR and Wheat:

```
lab@PBR# show services
service-set ipsec-gre {
    interface-service {
        service-interface sp-0/0/0.0;
    }
    ipsec-vpn-options {
        local-gateway 172.16.1.2;
    }
    ipsec-vpn-rules map-gre;
}
```

```
lab@PBR# show interfaces
fe-0/0/0 {
    vlan-tagging;
    unit 412 {
        description PBR-to-Wheat;
        vlan-id 412;
        family inet {
            service {
                input {
                    service-set ipsec-gre                }
                output {
                    service-set ipsec-gre
                }
            }
            address 172.16.1.2/24;
        }
    }
}
```

Two additional pieces of configuration should probably be added: IKE traceoptions and automatic tunnel establishment. IKE traceoptions will be used to help troubleshoot if the IPSec tunnel does not come up, and automatic tunnel establishment will be used to avoid lost packets that could result when GRE packets are sent before the IPSec tunnel is fully established:

```
[edit]
lab@PBR# set services ipsec-vpn establish-tunnels immediately

[edit]
lab@PBR# set services ipsec-vpn traceoptions flag ike traceoptions {
```

After the configuration is committed, the tunnel is established:

```
[edit]
lab@PBR# run show services ipsec-vpn ipsec security-associations
Service set: ipsec-gre

  Rule: map-gre, Term: 1, Tunnel index: 1
  Local gateway: 172.16.1.2, Remote gateway: 128.3.3.4
  Tunnel MTU: 1500
    Direction SPI         AUX-SPI    Mode      Type     Protocol
    inbound   4232427354  0          tunnel    dynamic  ESP
    outbound  83055442    0          tunnel    dynamic  ESP
```

However, traffic does not flow across the tunnel, and the BGP session to Wheat is down. The solution to this problem screams service filter!

```
[edit]
lab@PBR# run show bgp summary
Groups: 1 Peers: 1 Down peers: 1
Table    Tot Paths  Act Paths Suppressed  History Damp State  Pending
inet.0           0          0          0        0         0          0
Peer            AS    InPkt    OutPkt    OutQ   Flaps Last
Up/Dwn State|#Active/Received/Damped...
172.16.1.1   420   11892    10737       0       4       11:53 Active
```

It is obvious that we need to build a service filter to skip the BGP traffic from being serviced, while also ensuring that the GRE traffic gets sent down the IPSec tunnel. What might not be so obvious is that we need a service filter in *both* directions, because when GRE packets are encapsulated inside the system and the packets are circulated, the input interface becomes the next hop outgoing interface, as shown here and later in Figure 8-14 (we will examine this in detail in "The Life of a Packet," later in this chapter):

```
lab@PBR> show configuration firewall
family inet {
    service-filter match-vpn-input {
        term service {
            from {
                source-address {
                    128.3.3.4/32;
                }
                destination-address {
                    172.16.1.2/32;
                }
            }
            then service;
        }
        term skip {
            then skip;
        }
    }
    service-filter match-vpn-output {
        term service {
            from {
                source-address {
                    172.16.1.2/32;
                }
                destination-address {
                    128.3.3.4/32;
                }
            }
            then service;
        }
        term skip {
            then skip;
        }
    }
}
```

Apply the service filters to the WAN interface on PBR:

```
lab@PBR> show configuration interfaces fe-0/0/0 unit 412
description PBR-to-Wheat;
vlan-id 412;
family inet {
    service {
        input {
            service-set ipsec-gre service-filter match-vpn-input;
```

```
        }
        output {
            service-set ipsec-gre service-filter match-vpn-output;
        }
    }
    address 172.16.1.2/24;
```

Generate some test traffic to the extranet on the internal router Bock:

```
lab@Bock> ping 128.3.3.3 rapid count 100
PING 128.3.3.3 (128.3.3.3): 56 data bytes
!!!!!!!!!!!!!!!!!!!!!!!!!!!!!!!!!!!!!!!!!!!!!!!!!!!!!!!!!!!!!!!!!!!!!!!!
!!!!!!!!!!!!!!!!!!!!!!!!!!!!!!!!!!
--- 128.3.3.3 ping statistics ---
100 packets transmitted, 100 packets received, 0% packet loss
round-trip min/avg/max/stddev = 9.666/18.435/40.117/9.181 ms
```

Verify that the packets are both encrypted and decrypted to and from the Cans extranet:

```
lab@PBR# run show services ipsec-vpn ipsec statistics

PIC: sp-0/0/0, Service set: ipsec-gre

ESP Statistics:
  Encrypted bytes:            11200
  Decrypted bytes:            11200
  Encrypted packets:            100
  Decrypted packets:            100
AH Statistics:
  Input bytes:                    0
  Output bytes:                   0
  Input packets:                  0
  Output packets:                 0
Errors:
  AH authentication failures: 0, Replay errors: 0
  ESP authentication failures: 0, ESP decryption failures: 0
  Bad headers: 0, Bad trailers: 0
```

For reference purposes only, here is an example of what the configuration may look like on the Cisco side in the extranet:

```
crypto isakmp policy 1
 hash md5
 authentication pre-share
crypto isakmp key test address 172.16.1.2
crypto isakmp keepalive 10 2 periodic

!
!
crypto ipsec transform-set esp_des_set esp-des esp-md5-hmac
!
!
crypto map gre-to-ipsec 1 ipsec-isakmp
 set peer 172.16.1.2
 set transform-set esp_des_set
 set pfs group1
```

```
  match address 110


  access-list 110 permit ip host 128.3.3.4 host 172.16.1.2

  interface tunnel1
   tunnel mode gre ip
   tunnel destination 172.16.1.2
   tunnel source 128.3.3.4

  interface fast0
   crypto map gre-to-ipsec
```

Summary of IPSec VPNs

IPSec VPNs provide a secure method for protecting data over a private or public network. These could be VPNs with default proposals or VPNs with very specific authentication and encryption methods. Also, you can use these VPNs for a variety of applications, including securing access to an extranet, providing remote office connectivity, or providing a backup link for your internal network. Some of these VPNs may have dynamic endpoints or require GRE tunnels for interoperability with other vendors. You can accomplish all of this using JUNOS software and services.

The next section details another service that is offered: NAT.

NAT

NAT is simply a way to change the source or destination IP address of a packet due to public address exhaustion or a security mechanism to protect internal hosts. The internal hosts can be mapped to their own individual public addresses, or a pool of addresses could be used. Also, many addresses could be mapped to a single address utilizing different Transmission Control Protocol/User Datagram Protocol (TCP/UDP) port numbers for the flow, referred to as Port Address Translation (PAT). The most common NAT scenarios are listed here (and shown in Figure 8-8):

Destination NAT without port mapping
> The incoming public address is mapped to a private address. This is usually used to hide an internal server's address from the outside world.

Destination NAT with port mapping
> The incoming destination address and port are mapped to a private address. This allows for many services to be tied to the same destination address differentiated by port numbers. This is normally used when only a single external address is given that must map to multiple private connections.

NAT source without port translation
> The outgoing private source IP address is mapped to a public IP address. This is used when inside hosts want to reach external networks and the host information wants to remain hidden.

NAT source with port translation

> The outgoing private IP address is mapped to a public IP and the port number is also changed. This is used when multiple sources are mapped to a few public IP addresses.

Twice NAT

> This is used when both the source IP and the destination IP need to be changed. This could be a mail server that needs both inbound and outbound connections.

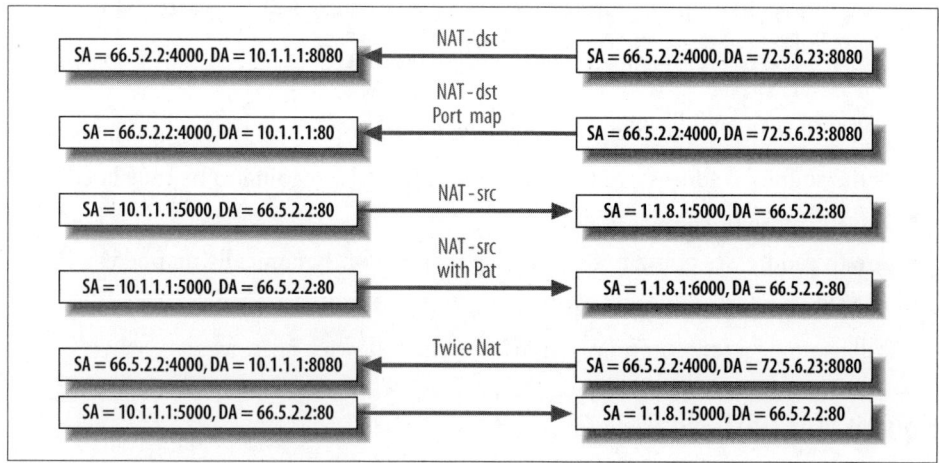

Figure 8-8. Common NAT deployments

The translated address can be either specified in the NAT rule or created as a pool of addresses. If PAT is required, you must use a pool. You can reuse a pool in multiple NAT rules. In the pool, you can specify a single address, a prefix, or a range of addresses. You also can enable port translation in the pool to select a range of port values or have the system automatically choose a value.

```
lab@PBR# set services nat pool example ?
Possible completions:
> address              Address or address prefix for NAT
> address-range        Range of addresses for NAT
+ apply-groups         Groups from which to inherit configuration
data
+ apply-groups-except  Don't inherit configuration data from these
groups
> port                 Specify ports for NAT
[edit]
```

The pool is then applied as a source or destination pool in the NAT rule.

 You also can configure an *overload pool* if the primary pool becomes exhausted.

In addition, you can apply a prefix without using a pool of addresses:

```
[edit]
lab@PBR# set services nat rule example term 1 then translated ?
Possible completions:
+ apply-groups         Groups from which to inherit configuration data
+ apply-groups-except  Don't inherit configuration data from these groups
  destination-pool     NAT pool for destination translation
  destination-prefix   NAT prefix for destination translation
  overload-pool        NAT pool to be used when source pool is overloaded
  overload-prefix      NAT prefix to be used when source pool is overloaded
  source-pool          NAT pool for source translation
  source-prefix        NAT prefix for source translation
> translation-type     Type of translation to perform
```

When deciding how to configure NAT, several questions drive the correct solutions:

- Is the source IP address and/or destination IP address going to be translated?
- Is port translation going to occur?
- Are the addresses going to be statically mapped or dynamically mapped?
- Should an address pool be used?

We will examine a few common scenarios in the following sections.

Source NAT with No PAT

A simple source NAT for all private addresses to an external address pool of 55.55.5/27 is implemented on PBR using the preferred solution of a next hop service set, as shown in Figure 8-9.

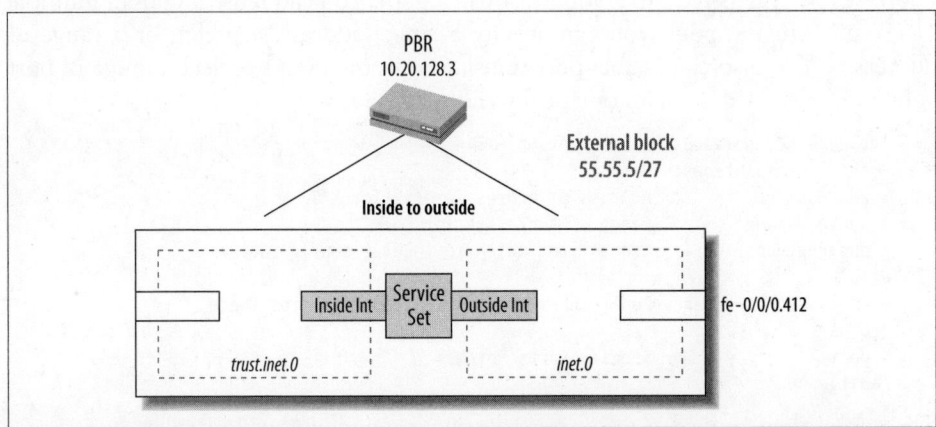

Figure 8-9. Source NAT example

First, an address pool called ext-block is created without port translation. An address block is not necessary but is used for future scalability:

```
lab@PBR# show services
nat {
```

```
    pool ext-block {
        address 55.55.5.0/27;
    }
```

Then a rule is created to translate all source addresses using this address block. This must be a dynamic translation since there is no matching source subnet:

```
rule basic-source {
    match-direction input;
    term 1 {
        then {
            translated {
                source-pool ext-block;
                translation-type source dynamic;
            }
        }
    }
}
```

A next hop service set is created to map the NAT rule:

```
service-set Trust-Untrust {
    nat-rules basic-source;
    next-hop-service {
        inside-service-interface sp-0/0/0.1;
        outside-service-interface sp-0/0/0.2;
    }
}
```

The external address block must be reachable by the outside world. Since PBR already has a hazy BGP relationship with AS 420, this address block is sent via BGP:

```
[edit]
lab@PBR# show protocols bgp
export [ send-agg send-ext-block ];
group as_420 {
    type external;
    neighbor 172.16.1.1 {
        peer-as 420;
    }
}
lab@PBR# run show bgp summary
Groups: 1 Peers: 1 Down peers: 0
Table    Tot Paths  Act Paths Suppressed History Damp State  Pending
inet.0         7          5         0       0        0       0
Peer        AS      InPkt    OutPkt    OutQ    Flaps Last Up/Dwn State|#Active/
Received/Damped...
172.16.1.1       420      7852      7077      0       2   2d
7:07:42 5/7/0 0/0/0

  ^
unknown command.
lab@PBR# run show route advertising-protocol bgp 172.16.1.1 55/8
```

```
inet.0: 21 destinations, 26 routes (20 active, 0 holddown, 5 hidden)
  Prefix              Nexthop      MED    Lclpref   AS path
* 55.55.5.0/27        Self                          I
```

Next, we create a VR to represent the internal trust (internal) portion of the network. The LAN interface of PBR is added, as well as the inside service interface. Also, the OSPF configuration is moved over the VR. This includes a policy called send-default (not shown) that sends a default route into OSPF for Internet connectivity. Also, a loopback is added for use in OSPF. Lastly, a default route is created to send all noninternal traffic to the inside service interface:

```
[edit]
lab@PBR# show routing-instances
trust {
    instance-type virtual-router;
    interface fe-0/0/0.1241;
    interface sp-0/0/0.1;
    interface lo0.0;
    routing-options {
        static {
            route 0.0.0.0/0 next-hop sp-0/0/0.1;
        }
    }
    protocols {
        ospf {
            export send-default;
            area 0.0.0.0 {
                interface fe-0/0/0.1241;
                interface lo0.1;
            }
        }
    }
}
```

For completeness, the policies on PBR are shown here. Please refer to Chapter 3 for a policy discussion.

```
[edit]
lab@PBR# show policy-options
prefix-list internal-subnets {
    10.10.12.0/22;
    10.10.128.0/22;
    10.20.128.0/22;
}
policy-statement send-agg {
    from protocol aggregate;
    then accept;
}
policy-statement send-default {
    from {
        route-filter 0.0.0.0/0 exact accept;
    }
}
policy-statement send-ext-block {
```

```
    from {
        route-filter 55.55.5.0/27 exact accept;
    }
}
```

Verify that all the static routes are active on the router in both the routing instance trust and the main route table. The 55.55.5/27 static route in the main instance was automatically created due to the NAT rule with a very low preference of 1, which points to the outside interface for return NAT traffic. The default route was manually created during the VR configuration:

```
lab@PBR# run show route protocol static

inet.0: 21 destinations, 26 routes (20 active, 0 holddown, 5 hidden)
+ = Active Route, - = Last Active, * = Both

55.55.5.0/27       *[Static/1] 00:14:38
                   > via sp-0/0/0.2


__juniper_private1__.inet.0: 2 destinations, 2 routes (2 active, 0 holddown, 0 hidden)

trust.inet.0: 16 destinations, 16 routes (16 active, 0 holddown, 0 hidden)
+ = Active Route, - = Last Active, * = Both

0.0.0.0/0          *[Static/5] 00:19:31
                   > via sp-0/0/0.1
```

Also, verify that all the internal routes are received via OSPF in the VR's route table, trust.inet.0:

```
[edit]
lab@PBR# run show route table trust

trust.inet.0: 16 destinations, 16 routes (16 active, 0 holddown, 0 hidden)
+ = Active Route, - = Last Active, * = Both

0.0.0.0/0          *[Static/5] 00:19:59
                   > via sp-0/0/0.1
10.10.8.0/27       *[OSPF/10] 00:13:32, metric 67
                   > to 10.20.130.1 via fe-0/0/0.1241
10.10.10.0/30      *[OSPF/10] 00:19:50, metric 66
                   > to 10.20.130.1 via fe-0/0/0.1241
10.10.11.0/24      *[OSPF/10] 00:19:50, metric 2
                   > to 10.20.130.1 via fe-0/0/0.1241
10.10.12.1/32      *[OSPF/10] 00:13:32, metric 2
                   > to 10.20.130.1 via fe-0/0/0.1241
10.10.12.2/32      *[OSPF/10] 00:13:32, metric 66
                   > to 10.20.130.1 via fe-0/0/0.1241
10.10.12.3/32      *[OSPF/10] 00:19:50, metric 1
                   > to 10.20.130.1 via fe-0/0/0.1241
10.20.128.4/32     *[OSPF/10] 00:13:32, metric 67
                   > to 10.20.130.1 via fe-0/0/0.1241
10.20.128.128/32   *[Direct/0] 00:19:59
                   > via lo0.1
```

```
10.20.129.0/24      *[OSPF/10] 00:13:32, metric 68
                     > to 10.20.130.1 via fe-0/0/0.1241
10.20.130.0/24      *[Direct/0] 00:19:59
                     > via fe-0/0/0.1241
10.20.130.2/32      *[Local/0] 00:19:59
                      Local via fe-0/0/0.1241
10.20.131.0/24      *[OSPF/10] 00:13:32, metric 67
                     > to 10.20.130.1 via fe-0/0/0.1241
10.30.1.1/32        *[OSPF/10] 00:13:32, metric 67
                     > to 10.20.130.1 via fe-0/0/0.1241
64.8.12.6/32        *[OSPF/150] 00:13:32, metric 0, tag 0
                     > to 10.20.130.1 via fe-0/0/0.1241
224.0.0.5/32        *[OSPF/10] 00:20:00, metric 1
                      MultiRecv
```

Now verify that the OSPF network is running correctly in the VR. Don't forget the instance switch!

```
[edit]
lab@PBR# run show ospf database instance trust

    OSPF link state database, Area 0.0.0.0
 Type      ID            Adv Rtr         Seq      Age  Opt Cksum  Len
 Router  10.10.12.1     10.10.12.1     0x8000016d 817  0x22 0x30df  48
 Router  10.10.12.2     10.10.12.2     0x8000022a 817  0x22 0x7889  84
 Router  10.10.12.3     10.10.12.3     0x8000017b 739  0x22 0x3575  84
 Router  10.20.128.4    10.20.128.4    0x800004fc 818  0x22 0xa79b  60
 Router *10.20.128.128  10.20.128.128  0x8000000c 160  0x22 0x5f14  48
 Router  10.30.1.1      10.30.1.1      0x80000227 818  0x22 0x4ef0  48
 Network 10.10.8.1      10.10.12.2     0x800000a1 817  0x22 0x45e7  32
 Network 10.10.11.1     10.10.12.3     0x80000003 816  0x22 0xbef1  32
 Network *10.20.130.2   10.20.128.128  0x80000004   9  0x22 0x1320  32
 Network 10.20.131.2    10.20.128.4    0x8000020b 818  0x22 0xf32f  32
    OSPF AS SCOPE link state database
 Type      ID            Adv Rtr         Seq      Age  Opt Cksum  Len
 Extern *0.0.0.0        10.20.128.128  0x80000001 562  0x22 0x7f14  36
 Extern  64.8.12.6      10.30.1.1      0x8000009b 818  0x22 0xf84   36
```

Traffic is sent to the Internet and verified by looking at the show services stateful-firewall flows output. When a NAT service set is applied, a stateful firewall that accepts all traffic is actually also applied. Notice that the source is being translated from 10.20.120.1 to 55.55.5.1 with no port translation, and the return flow is automatically created. Also, the state is watch because an ICMP Application Later Gateway (ALG) is being used:

```
[edit]
lab@PBR# run show services stateful-firewall flows
Interface: sp-0/0/0, Service set: Trust-Untrust
Flow                                    State     Dir      Frm count
ICMP        128.3.3.27:62239 ->         55.55.5.1     Watch    0    188
   NAT dest         55.55.5.1:62239    ->     10.20.130.1:0
ICMP        10.20.130.1:62239 ->        128.3.3.27    Watch    I    196
   NAT source      10.20.130.1:62239   ->      55.55.5.1:62239
```

You also can view the ALG by looking at the output of the conversations command, which is JUNOS terminology for the transit and receive flow:

```
lab@PBR# run show services stateful-firewall conversations extensive
Interface: sp-0/0/0, Service set: Trust-Untrust

Conversation: ALG protocol: icmp
  Number of initiators: 1, Number of responders: 1
Flow                               State     Dir       Frm count
ICMP        10.20.130.1:62239 ->      128.3.3.27      Watch   I   211
  NAT source      10.20.130.1:62239   ->        55.55.5.1:62239
  Byte count: 17724
  Flow role: Master, Timeout: 30, Protocol detail: echo request
ICMP        128.3.3.27:62239 ->       55.55.5.1      Watch    O   203
  NAT dest        55.55.5.1:62239    ->      10.20.130.1:0
  Byte count: 17052
  Flow role: Responder, Timeout: 30, Protocol detail: echo reply
```

The NAT pool is also examined, and although a /27 is configured in the pool, only 30 addresses have been allocated, excluding the 55.55.5.0 and 55.55.5.31 addresses:

```
lab@PBR# run show services nat pool
Interface: sp-0/0/0, Service set: Trust-Untrust
NAT pool        Type      Address               Port       Ports used
ext-block       dynamic         55.55.5.1-55.55.5.30
```

Source NAT with PAT

Now we will add port translation; refer back to "Source NAT with No PAT" to see the VR, rules, service setup, and so on. To enable PAT, simply add the port command in the address pool definition:

```
[edit]
lab@PBR# set services nat pool ext-block port automatic
```

After the change is committed, it still appears that the flows are not performing any port translation:

```
[edit]
lab@PBR# run show services stateful-firewall flows
Interface: sp-0/0/0, Service set: Trust-Untrust
Flow                               State     Dir       Frm count
ICMP        128.3.3.27:62239 ->       55.55.5.1      Watch    O   188
  NAT dest        55.55.5.1:62239    ->      10.20.130.1:0
ICMP        10.20.130.1:62239 ->      128.3.3.27      Watch   I   196
  NAT source      10.20.130.1:62239   ->        55.55.5.1:62239
```

You can verify this by looking at the NAT pool and seeing that no ports have been assigned:

```
lab@PBR# run show services nat pool
Interface: sp-0/0/0, Service set: Trust-Untrust
NAT pool        Type      Address               Port       Ports used
ext-block       dynamic         55.55.5.1-55.55.5.30
```

The port translation is not occurring because the change was done on the fly and the session had not timed out. To create a new session in the flow table, you must first clear the flows:

```
lab@PBR# run clear services stateful-firewall flows
Interface   Service set                           Conv removed
sp-0/0/0    Trust-Untrust                              1
```

Now the port number is being changed from 62239 to 1024, as expected:

```
[edit services nat pool ext-block]
lab@PBR# run show services stateful-firewall flows
Interface: sp-0/0/0, Service set: Trust-Untrust
Flow                               State   Dir      Frm count
ICMP        128.3.3.27:1024  ->        55.55.5.1      Watch    0   8
    NAT dest        55.55.5.1:1024    ->    10.20.130.1:62239
ICMP        10.20.130.1:62239 ->       128.3.3.27     Watch    I   8
    NAT source     10.20.130.1:62239   ->        55.55.5.1:1024
```

You can verify this by viewing the port range allowed (512–65535), and by the fact that a single port is shown to be in use out of the pool:

```
[edit services nat pool ext-block]
lab@PBR# run show services nat pool
Interface: sp-0/0/0, Service set: Trust-Untrust
NAT pool        Type    Address               Port       Ports used
ext-block       dynamic     55.55.5.1-55.55.5.30 512-65535    1
```

Destination NAT

Another common application is to change the incoming public IP address to a private IP address inside the network. Often, this is done to open a particular service from the WAN interface, frequently referred to as a *pinhole* for its hopefully diminutive access. In this case study, a custom application called *slingbox* is running over TCP and is using a port range of 4000–4050. This will be coming into public IP address 55.55.5.27 and will be mapped to internal address 10.10.12.3. Destination NAT must always be of type static, so the incoming public address range must map to the outgoing private address range.

Since a unique application must be used for this pinhole, first you must define an application that will later be referenced in the NAT rule. This application is called custom-app:

```
lab@PBR# show | find applications
applications {
    application custom-app {
        protocol tcp;
        destination-port 4000-4050;
    }
}
```

Create the NAT rule by referencing the incoming public destination address 55.55.5.27 and the custom-app, and by translating this address to 10.10.12.3. Use a destination-prefix instead of a destination-pool as this is a single address mapping. Since this is a destination NAT that is added to the previously created next hop service set, specify a direction of output because traffic will be received and directed to the outside interface by the already created 55.55.5/27 static route:

```
[edit services nat]
lab@PBR# show | find rule

        rule pin-hole {
            match-direction output;
            term 1 {
                from {
                    destination-address {
                        55.55.5.27/32;
                    }
                    applications custom-app;
                }
                then {
                    translated {
                        destination-prefix 10.10.12.3/32;
                        translation-type destination static;
                    }
                }
            }
        }
    }
```

Then add the rule to the previously created service set:

```
        service-set Trust-Untrust {
            nat-rules basic-source;
            nat-rules pin-hole;
            next-hop-service {
                inside-service-interface sp-0/0/0.1;
                outside-service-interface sp-0/0/0.2;
            }
        }
    }
```

 Remember that you can combine multiple rules into a rule set if desired.

Traffic is incoming to PBR's WAN interface and the destination NAT is verified. This flow happens to have an incoming port number of 4020, which does fall into the custom application range:

```
lab@PBR# run show services stateful-firewall conversations
Interface: sp-0/0/0, Service set: Trust-Untrust
```

```
Conversation: ALG protocol: tcp
  Number of initiators: 1, Number of responders: 1
Flow                                  State   Dir     Frm count
TCP        172.16.1.1:4216  ->    55.55.5.27:4020  Forward  0   1
    NAT dest       55.55.5.27:4020    ->      10.10.12.3:4020
TCP        10.10.12.3:4020  ->   172.16.1.1:4216  Forward  I   1
    NAT source     10.10.12.3:4020    ->      55.55.5.27:4020
```

NAT and the stateful firewall

By default, when NAT rules are exclusively applied in a service set, a stateful firewall is implicitly applied. This default stateful firewall matches on all traffic with an action of accept and is created in *both* directions. If a stateful-firewall rule is created later and applied to the service set, the default stateful-firewall rules are removed. This means that to allow for NAT traffic, you may need to create new stateful-firewall rules if a stateful-firewall rule is later applied to the service set. In a simple example, a stateful-firewall rule is created to allow all JUNOS ALGs and other traffic outbound from the internal network to the Internet:

```
stateful-firewall {
    rule allow-outbound {
        match-direction input;
        term 1 {
            from {
                application-sets junos-algs-outbound;
            }
            then {
                accept;
            }
        }
        term 2 {
            then {
                accept;
            }
        }
    }
}
```

Apply this stateful-firewall rule to the service set that already contains the NAT rules:

```
service-set Trust-Untrust {
    stateful-firewall-rules allow-outbound;
    nat-rules basic-source;
    nat-rules pin-hole;
    next-hop-service {
        inside-service-interface sp-0/0/0.1;
        outside-service-interface sp-0/0/0.2;
    }
}
```

Verify the source NAT and that all works as expected since the stateful firewall is allowing all outbound flows:

```
[edit]
lab@PBR# run show services stateful-firewall conversations
Interface: sp-0/0/0, Service set: Trust-Untrust

Conversation: ALG protocol: icmp
  Number of initiators: 1, Number of responders: 1
Flow                                State    Dir      Frm count
ICMP       10.20.130.1:11552 ->     128.3.3.27      Watch   I  31
   NAT source    10.20.130.1:11552    ->       55.55.5.1:1024
ICMP       128.3.3.27:1024  ->      55.55.5.1       Watch   O  31
   NAT dest       55.55.5.1:1024     ->       10.20.130.1:11552
```

Note that when test traffic is sent from ISP router Wheat to PBR for incoming destination NAT, the traffic is dropped by the newly applied stateful firewall that allows only outbound flows to be initiated, not inbound flows:

```
lab@Wheat> telnet 55.55.5.27 port 4020
Trying 55.55.5.27...

lab@PBR# run show services stateful-firewall flows
Interface: sp-0/0/0, Service set: Trust-Untrust
Flow                                State    Dir      Frm count
TCP       172.16.1.1:3469  ->      55.55.5.27:4020  Drop    0   0
```

So, to allow incoming NAT processing to occur in the output interface, the packet must be allowed through the stateful firewall. The incoming service flow when multiple service rules are applied is:

Stateful firewall → NAT

You cannot set this order at this point, which means that the stateful firewall must match on the static NAT address:

```
[edit servisce stateful-firewall]
lab@PBR# show | find rule allow-pin-hole

rule allow-pin-hole {
    match-direction output;
    term 1 {
        from {
            destination-address {
                55.55.5.27/32;
            }
        }
        then {
            accept;
        }
    }
}
```

Apply the new rule to the service set:

```
lab@PBR# show services service-set Trust-Untrust
stateful-firewall-rules allow-outbound;
stateful-firewall-rules allow-pin-hole;
```

```
    nat-rules basic-source;
    nat-rules pin-hole;
    next-hop-service {
        inside-service-interface sp-0/0/0.1;
        outside-service-interface sp-0/0/0.2;
    }
```

Now destination NAT works as expected, and TV can sling around the world with our special application:

```
lab@PBR# run show services stateful-firewall flows
Interface: sp-0/0/0, Service set: Trust-Untrust
Flow                                State   Dir      Frm count
TCP         10.10.12.3:4020  ->     172.16.1.1:1059  Forward  I   1
    NAT source     10.10.12.3:4020     ->       55.55.5.27:4020
TCP         172.16.1.1:1059  ->     =55.55.5.27:4020  Forward  O   1
    NAT dest       55.55.5.27:4020     ->       10.10.12.3:4020
```

[edit]

 Since multiple stateful-firewall rules are applied, this may be another place where a rule set could be helpful:

```
service-set Trust-Untrust {
    stateful-firewall-rule-sets in-out;
    nat-rules basic-source;
    nat-rules pin-hole;
    next-hop-service {
        inside-service-interface sp-0/0/0.1;
        outside-service-interface sp-0/0/0.2;
    }
}
rule-set in-out {
    rule allow-outbound;
    rule allow-pin-hole;
}
```

Twice NAT

Lastly, you can configure twice NAT on the router, which involves changing the source IP address for outbound flows and the destination address for inbound flows (see Figure 8-10). This is really no different from the scenarios we've already discussed, except that you must configure a source and a destination address, as well as a source prefix or pool and a destination prefix or pool. In the example that follows, traffic that matches 10.58.254.24 or 10.58.254.35 will be source-NAT'd using a static pool called src-pool.

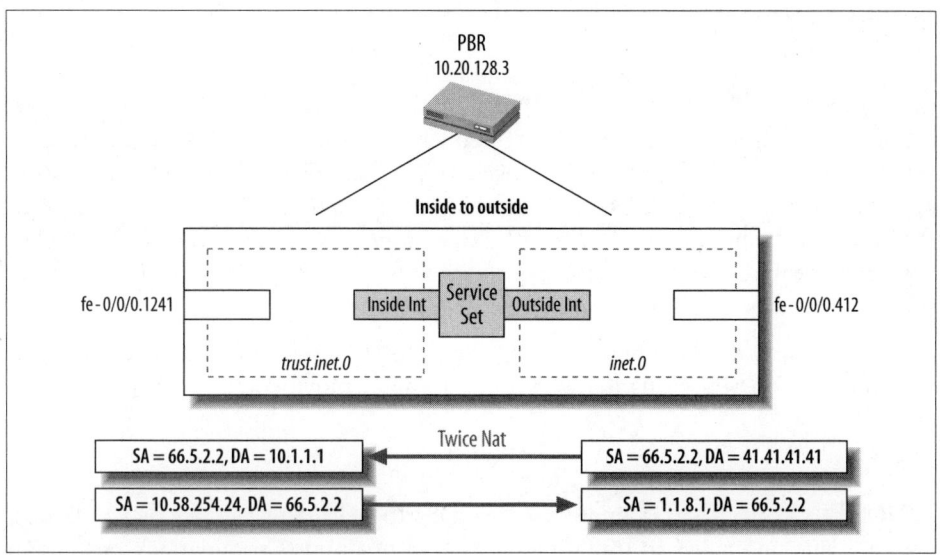

Figure 8-10. Twice NAT example

Traffic destined for 41.41.41.41/32 will be destination-NAT'd using a NAT pool called dst_pool:

```
[edit services nat]]
lab@Bock# show
rule twice-nat {
    match-direction input;
    term my-term1 {
        from {
            destination-address {
                41.41.41.41/32;
            }
            source-address-range {
                low 10.58.254.34 high 10.58.254.35;
            }
        }
        then {
            translated {
                source-pool src-pool;
                destination-pool dst_pool;
                translation-type source static destination static;
            }
        }
    }
}
```

 At the time of this writing, you cannot configure ALGs when twice NAT is configured.

Summary of NAT

NAT has become a common language and requirement for networks in every facet of the world due to the exhaustion of IPv4 addresses as well as a way to protect internal resources. Various types of NAT are defined, including source IP translation, destination IP translation, and port translation. Which method you choose should depend on a variety of factors, such as the number of public IPs that are assigned to the network, the number of incoming Internet connections allowed, and the level of invisibility required. In fact, you can combine many of these concepts into a newer standard called twice NAT.

The next section explains how to configure multiple services at the same time, and the configuration processing that will occur during deployment.

IDS

JUNOS services support a limited set of IDSs to help detect attacks such as port scanning and anomalies in traffic patterns. It also supports some attack prevention by limiting the number of flows, sessions, and rates. In addition, it protects against SYN attacks by implementing a SYN cookie mechanism. Since the intrusion detection and prevention (IDP) service does not support higher-layer application signatures, we must examine another solution.

The IDP solution is really more of a monitoring tool than an actual prevention tool. So, how does Juniper make the IDP claim? One response is that protection against a SYN attack can be configured. To prevent a SYN attack, the router will operate as a type of SYN "proxy" and will utilize cookie values. Essentially, when this feature is turned on, the router will respond to the initial SYN packet with a SYN-ACK packet that contains a unique cookie value in the sequence number field. If the initiator responds with the same cookie in the sequence field, the TCP flow is accepted; if the responder does not respond or if it responds with the wrong cookie, the flow is dropped. To kick off this defense, we must configure a SYN cookie threshold.

To enable the SYN cookie defense, an IDS rule action must contain a threshold that indicates when the feature should be enabled and an MSS value to avoid having the router manage segmented fragments when acting as a SYN proxy:

```
[edit]
lab@PBR# set services ids rule simple-ids term 1 then syn-cookie ?
Possible completions:
+ apply-groups          Groups from which to inherit configuration data
+ apply-groups-except   Don't inherit configuration data from these
groups
  mss                   MSS value for TCP delayed binding (128..8192)
  threshold             Threshold above which SYN cookies are enabled
[edit]
```

You would then apply this rule to a service set as you would any other service previously discussed.

 Since IDP and stateful firewalls are processed in parallel, you should configure a stateful-firewall rule alongside the IDS rule. If you forget a rule, the default stateful firewall of allow all will be used.

Along with SYN cookie protection, the IDS is used to detect attacks and gather information to create rules to stop these attacks. When looking at the possible IDS rule actions for detection of attacks, you can:

- Set up thresholds to monitor certain sources, destinations, or source and destination pairs
- Force "good" entries to the IDS table for tracking purposes
- Log packets when they hit a certain threshold:

```
lab@PBR# set services ids rule all term 1 then ?
Possible completions:
> aggregation          Define aggregation parameters
+ apply-groups         Groups from which to inherit configuration data
+ apply-groups-except  Don't inherit configuration data from these groups
  force-entry          Force entries in IDS tables for matching traffic
  ignore-entry         Ignore IDS events for matching traffic
> logging              Define system logging parameters
> session-limit        Define IDS session limit parameters
> syn-cookie           Define SYN cookie parameters
```

For example, here is a rule that logs packets as soon as an event happens (threshold 1), enables SYN cookie protection at five SYN packets per second, and forces all entries to be recorded:

```
[edit]
lab@PBR# show services
ids {
    rule all {
        match-direction input;
        term 1 {
            then {
                force-entry;
                logging {
                    threshold 1;
                    syslog;
                }
                syn-cookie {
                    threshold 5;
                    mss 1500;
                }
            }
        }
    }
}
```

```
service-set Trust-Untrust {
    ids-rules all;
    next-hop-service {
        inside-service-interface sp-0/0/0.1;
        outside-service-interface sp-0/0/0.2;
    }
}
```

The IDS tables can then be matched by source, destination, or pair:

```
[edit]
lab@PBR# run show services ids ?
Possible completions:
  destination-table    Show attack destination address table
  pair-table           Show attack source and destination address pair table
  source-table         Show attack source address table
```

Here is some output (not from this example) that shows some of the different types of anomalies that can be tracked:

```
user@underdogs> show services ids destination-table extensive
Interface: sp-1/3/0, Service set: null-sfw
Sorting order: Packets
Source address       Dest address    Time     Flags       Application

any                -> 10.58.255.146   35m52s SYN cookie
  Bytes:   34.0 m, Packets:  798.0 k, Flows:  266.0 k, Anomalies: 2251.0 k
    Anomalies                         Count   Rate(eps) Elapsed
    First packet of TCP session not SYN 160.0 k       0       14s
    TCP source or destination port zero 634.0 k   154.6    3m37s
    UDP source or destination port zero 633.0 k   170.0    3m37s
    ICMP header length check failed      2875      0.9    3m37s
    IP fragment assembly timeout       820.0 k     12.8    3m18s
    UDP header length check failed        385      0.5    3m53s
    TCP header length check failed        383      0.5    3m53s

Total IDS table entries:
87
Total failed IDS table entry insertions
0
Total number of
```

Combining Services

When combining multiple services, the general path must be remembered in the forward and reverse directions (see Figure 8-11). This is especially true when NAT is deployed to determine whether the pre- or post-NAT address should be used to match a rule. In the forward path from a LAN interface to a WAN interface, IDS and stateful firewall are performed first, then NAT, and finally IPSec. This means that the stateful firewall must match on a pre-NAT address whereas the IPSec tunnel would match on the post-NAT address.

In the return path, the IPSec packet will be processed first, then NAT, and finally the stateful firewall. This still allows IPSec to match a public address and the stateful firewall to match on a private address.

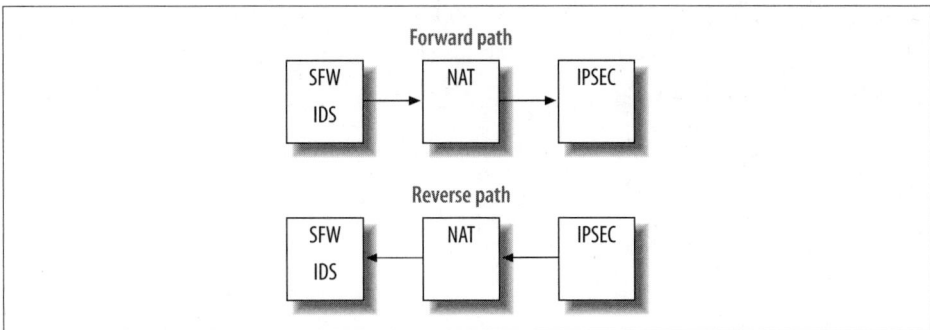

Figure 8-11. Service path

Everything becomes much more complicated when IPSec over GRE is implemented in the router with other services turned on. This is because JUNOS treats GRE packets in a very peculiar fashion after GRE encapsulation. After a packet is encapsulated in a GRE packet, it is marked with an input interface as the next hop outgoing interface. This causes GRE packets to be blocked if any input filters or input services are allowed that do not allow for this service.

In Figure 8-12, an IP packet comes into the fe-1/0/0.42 interface and a route lookup is performed that directs the packet into a GRE tunnel, which has an egress interface of se-1/0/0. After the GRE encapsulation, the input interface changes to the output interface. So, at the final stage, any stateful-firewall processing or stateless filters are going to see the packet coming into interface se-1/0/0 and out of interface se-1/0/0, which is unexpected!

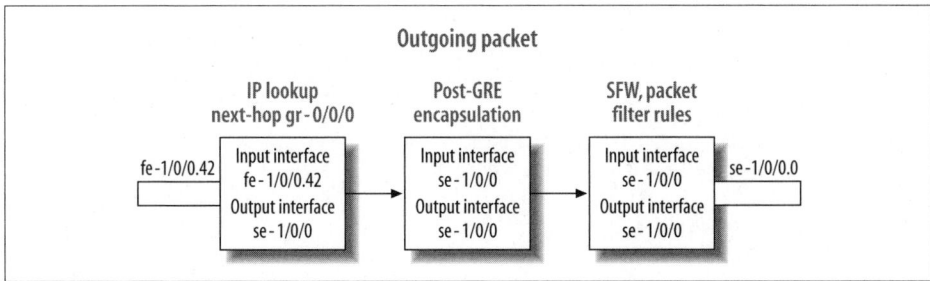

Figure 8-12. GRE processing with services

Stateful Firewall, NAT, and IPSec over GRE Together

To illustrate the uniqueness of GRE encapsulation, we will again examine the IPSec over GRE tunnel. This is the same tunnel we configured in "IPSec over GRE," earlier in this chapter. Just to recap, here is the complete IPSec over GRE configuration rule set that is applied as an interface-style service set:

```
service-set ipsec-gre {
    interface-service {
        service-interface sp-0/0/0.0;
    }
    ipsec-vpn-options {
        local-gateway 172.16.1.2;
    }
    ipsec-vpn-rules map-gre;
}
ipsec-vpn {
    rule map-gre {
        term 1 {
            from {
                source-address {
                    172.16.1.2/32;
                }
                destination-address {
                    128.3.3.4/32;
                }
            }
            then {
                remote-gateway 128.3.3.4;
                dynamic {
                    ike-policy main_ike;
                    ipsec-policy ipsecgre;
                }
            }
        }
        match-direction output;
    }
    ipsec {
        proposal cisco-interop {
            protocol esp;
            authentication-algorithm hmac-md5-96;
            encryption-algorithm des-cbc;
        }
        policy ipsecgre {
            perfect-forward-secrecy {
                keys group1;
            }
            proposals cisco-interop;
        }
    }
    ike {
        proposal cisco-interop-ike {
            authentication-method pre-shared-keys;
```

```
        dh-group group1;
        authentication-algorithm md5;
        encryption-algorithm des-cbc;
    }
    policy main_ike {
        proposals cisco-interop-ike;
        pre-shared-key ascii-text "$9$JhUi.QF/OBEP5BEcyW8ZUjHP5z
36AuO"; ## SECRET-DATA
    }
}
traceoptions {
    flag ike;
}
establish-tunnels immediately;
}
```

Stateful-firewall and NAT rules are to be configured from the LAN side of router PBR
to the WAN side of the router for all internally sourced traffic. Since IPSec requires
its own service set, a new service set called trust-untrust will be created that references the same service interface and a single NAT and stateful-firewall rule:

```
[edit services]

service-set trust-untrust {
    stateful-firewall-rules allow-outbound;
    nat-rules basic-source;
    interface-service {
        service-interface sp-0/0/0.0;
    }
}
```

A stateful-firewall rule is created to match on traffic that is sourced from the internal
network. Notice that only ALGs are allowed from the internal subnet, whereas the
second term contains no condition. The second term does not contain this condition
in order to allow some management traffic and BGP traffic to flow between the
172.16.1/24 network between PBR and Wheat (see Figure 8-6):

```
stateful-firewall {
    rule allow-outbound {
        match-direction output;
        term alg {
            from {
                source-address {
                    10.0.0.0/8;
                }
                application-sets junos-algs-outbound;
            }
            then {
                accept;
            }
        }
        term other {
            then {
```

```
                    accept;
                }
            }
        }
    }
```

Also, a source NAT rule is applied for all internal traffic using port translation:

```
nat {
    pool ext-block {
        address 55.55.5.0/27;
        port automatic;
    }
    rule basic-source {
        match-direction output;
        term 1 {
            from {
                source-address {
                    10.0.0.0/8;
                }
            }
            then {
                translated {
                    source-pool ext-block;
                    translation-type source dynamic;
                }
            }
        }
    }
}
```

The new service set is applied to the WAN interface on PBR. Take a look at the previous example to view the service filters match-vpn-input and match-vpn-output:

```
[edit interfaces fe-0/0/0 unit 412]
lab@PBR# show
description PBR-to-Wheat;
vlan-id 412;
family inet {
    service {
        input {
            service-set ipsec-gre service-filter match-vpn-input;
            service-set trust-untrust;
        }
        output {
            service-set ipsec-gre service-filter match-vpn-output;
            service-set trust-untrust;
        }
    }
    address 172.16.1.2/24;
```

After the configuration is committed, observe the flows through the stateful firewall. GRE packets are being dropped that were destined to 128.3.3.4. Notice that the direction is input, since after GRE encapsulation, the packet appears to be coming into the outgoing WAN interface. Because the stateful-firewall rules are now written to allow incoming GRE packets, the packets are dropped:

```
[edit services stateful-firewall rule allow-outbound]

lab@PBR# run show services stateful-firewall flows
Interface: sp-0/0/0, Service set: trust-untrust
Flow                                            State    Dir  Frm count
TCP    172.16.1.1:179    ->  172.16.1.2:2439   Forward  I        11
TCP    172.16.1.2:2439   ->  172.16.1.1:179    Forward  O        12
GRE    172.16.1.2:0      ->  128.3.3.4:0       Drop     I         0
```

Since the packets are being dropped by the stateful firewall, they are not even reaching the IPSec tunnel. You can see this by observing the 0 packet counts on the IPSec statistics:

```
[edit services service-set trust-untrust]
lab@PBR# run show services ipsec-vpn ipsec statistics

PIC: sp-0/0/0, Service set: ipsec-gre

ESP Statistics:
  Encrypted bytes:           0
  Decrypted bytes:           0
  Encrypted packets:         0
  Decrypted packets:         0
AH Statistics:
  Input bytes:               0
  Output bytes:              0
  Input packets:             0
  Output packets:            0
Errors:
  AH authentication failures: 0, Replay errors: 0
  ESP authentication failures: 0, ESP decryption failures: 0
  Bad headers: 0, Bad trailers: 0
```

We must now create a service filter to allow the GRE packets to bypass the stateful firewall and be encapsulated into the IPSec packet. This service filter must match on the source and destination IP addresses of the tunnel, as seen from the discard flows. Don't forget to service all other packets besides the GRE packets:

```
[edit firewall]
lab@PBR# show | find allow-gre
    service-filter allow-gre {
        term gre {
            from {
                source-address {
                    172.16.1.2/32;
                }
                destination-address {
                    128.3.3.4/32;
                }
            }
            then skip;
```

```
            }
        term all {
            then service;
        }
    }
}
```

Apply the service filter as an input service filter for the stateful firewall containing the service set:

```
[edit interfaces fe-0/0/0 unit 412]
lab@PBR# set family inet input service-set trust-untrust service-
filter allow-gre

[edit interfaces fe-0/0/0 unit 412]
lab@PBR# show
description PBR-to-Wheat;
vlan-id 412;
family inet {
    service {
        input {
            service-set ipsec-gre service-filter match-vpn-input;
            service-set trust-untrust service-filter allow-gre;
        }
        output {
            service-set ipsec-gre service-filter match-vpn-output;
            service-set trust-untrust;
        }
    }
    address 172.16.1.2/24;
}
```

After the filter has been applied, the service filter packets are encrypted and decrypted in the IPSec tunnel:

```
lab@PBR> show services ipsec-vpn ipsec statistics

PIC: sp-0/0/0, Service set: ipsec-gre

ESP Statistics:
  Encrypted bytes:            51408
  Decrypted bytes:            51408
  Encrypted packets:            459
  Decrypted packets:            459
AH Statistics:
  Input bytes:                    0
  Output bytes:                   0
  Input packets:                  0
  Output packets:                 0
Errors:
  AH authentication failures: 0, Replay errors: 0
  ESP authentication failures: 0, ESP decryption failures: 0
  Bad headers: 0, Bad trailers: 0
```

In addition, other internal flows are source-NAT'd as expected:

```
lab@PBR> show services stateful-firewall conversations
Interface: sp-0/0/0, Service set: trust-untrust

Conversation: ALG protocol: icmp
  Number of initiators: 1, Number of responders: 1
Flow                                  State    Dir      Frm count
IC  10.20.130.1:30242 -> 77.7.7.7     Watch    O              3
    NAT source      10.20.130.1:30242   ->       55.55.5.1:1033
ICMP 77.7.7.7:1033  ->      55.55.5.1   Watch   I              3
    NAT dest         55.55.5.1:1033     ->    10.20.130.1:30242

Conversation: ALG protocol: tcp
  Number of initiators: 1, Number of responders: 1
Flow                                  State   Dir  Frm count
TCP    172.16.1.2:1075  -> 172.16.1.1:179   Forward 0        77
TCP    172.16.1.1:179   -> 172.16.1.2:1075  Forward I        76
```

The Life of a Packet

When you've decided which services you need in your network, implementing them can seem like a daunting task. Which configuration do you apply first? Which addresses do you apply to a given service when applying a rule? How about if you have a class of service (CoS) applied? Where do packet filters fit into the packet flow?

Figures 8-13 and 8-14 should help you sort through this mystery and decide where configuration processes occur. These diagrams are not meant to represent every possible scenario, but rather to give you a general feel for the complex processing that could be involved. The exact processing will depend on whether a next hop- or an interface-style service set is applied (for more on CoS concepts, refer to Chapter 9).

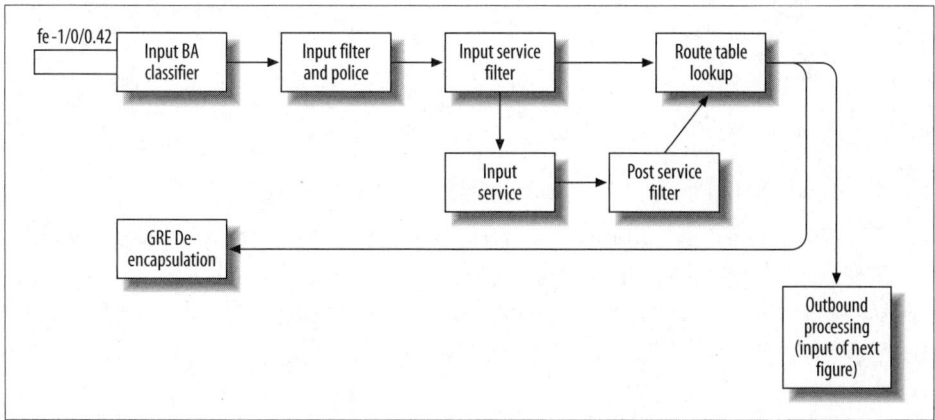

Figure 8-13. Incoming packet processing

The steps outlined in Figure 8-13 are as follows:

1. The packet enters the incoming interface.
2. The packet is classified by a behavior aggregate (BA) classifier.
3. The packet is processed by an input filter and policer (and may be reclassified).
4. The packet enters a service filter, and it is either serviced or skipped; if it is skipped, jump to step 7.
5. The input service is performed.
6. A post-service filter is applied.
7. The route lookup occurs.
8. If the result of the route lookup is a GRE packet, go to step 9; if not, send on for output processing.
9. De-encapsulate the GRE packet and go back to step 1.

After the packet is done with the input processing, it moves toward output processing (see Figure 8-14).

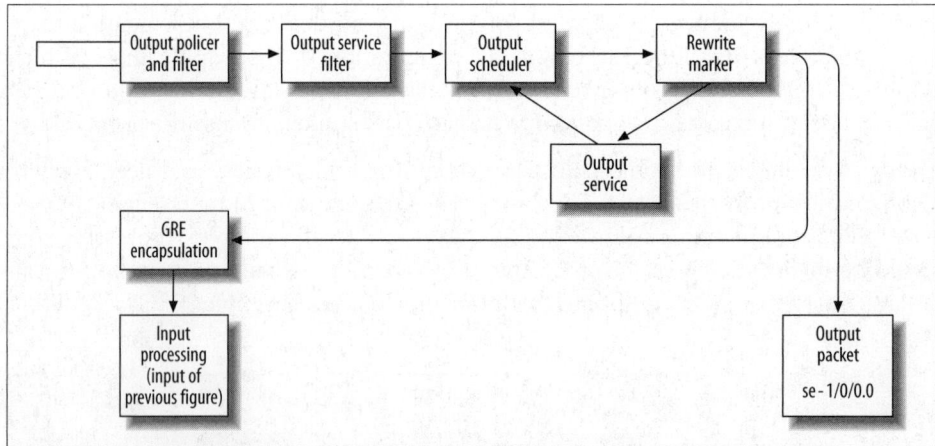

Figure 8-14. Outbound packet processing

The steps outlined in Figure 8-14 are as follows:

1. The packet is received from input processing and enters the output policer or filter.
2. The packet then goes through an output service filter to determine whether the packet will be marked for service. If the packet matches the service filter, the output interface is set to the service interface; if there is no match, the output interface is the outgoing physical interface.
3. The packet is sent to an output scheduler.
4. A write of the Type of Service (ToS) byte could occur. If the output interface is a service interface, go back to step 3; otherwise, go to step 5.

5. If the packet needs to be GRE-encapsulated, go to step 6; otherwise, go to step 7.

6. GRE encapsulation occurs, and the packet is sent back to the input processing stage where it is sent to step 1 of Figure 8-13 (input filters); after the GRE encapsulation, the input interface is the next hop outgoing interface of the GRE tunnel.

7. The packet is sent out the physical output interface.

Considerations Regarding Order of Operations

The packet processing order just discussed can be practically applied when designing the branch office connectivity for your network (see Figure 8-15). If connectivity is provided via IPSec VPNs and CoS is applied, where should the packet be classified? If an IPSec packet enters a router, the packet can be classified by setting the CoS value in the outer IP header using a BA classifier. However, after the packet is de-encapsulated, it enters the input filtering stage and is not sent through another BA classifier. That means that if packet classification is required on the de-encapsulated packet, you must use a multifield classifier (a firewall filter).

In comparison, if remote connectivity is provided by GRE tunnels, similar to IPSec tunnels, the incoming GRE packet could be classified using a BA classifier. The difference, however, is that once the GRE packet is de-encapsulated, it sends the inner packet through another BA classifier. This means you should apply the same classifier to the incoming interface and the gr- interface to avoid reclassification. Also, don't forget that when a GRE packet is encapsulated, it is reprocessed through all input filters and services on the output interface.

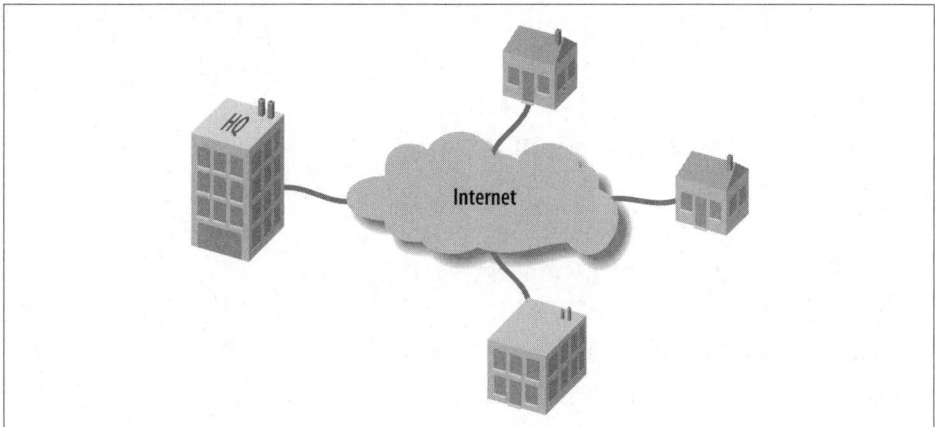

Figure 8-15. Branch office connectivity

The possible scenarios could fill an entire book, so be sure to consult Figures 8-13 and 8-14 for application to your network.

Conclusion

IP networks have changed drastically since they were first deployed 25 years ago, when addresses were plentiful and simple filters sufficed. In today's modern data networks, the concepts of yesteryear won't float for long. Packet filters will always have their place, but without tracking state, they will always have limitations; thus, the need for stateful firewalls. With IPv4 exhaustion coming to fruition, NAT has taken a front seat in network design and is now almost a requirement.

You can deploy these services individually or as a combined security design. When combining these services, be sure to verify each step along the way to avoid a broken configuration that is a bear to troubleshoot.

Although configuration may seem a bit daunting at first, the power and scalability of JUNOS are evident in the services code. For additional service examples to accompany this chapter, please consult *http://www.cubednetworks.com*.

Exam Topics

We examined the following Enterprise Exam Topics in this chapter:

- Configure and apply an interface-style service set.
- Configure a next hop-style service set.
- Identify the match direction given a network diagram.
- Understand and implement various types of service sets.
- Describe NAT and PAT.
- Configure a stateful firewall via the CLI.
- Monitor a stateful firewall.
- Configure NAT and PAT via the CLI.
- Monitor NAT and PAT via the CLI.
- Explain IPSec VPN processing on M-series and J-series routers.
- Configure an IPSec VPN via the CLI.
- Configure a route-based GRE tunnel (over IPSec) via the CLI.
- Monitor IPSec VPNs.
- IPSec tunnels as backup links.
- Routing over an IPSec or GRE tunnel.

Chapter Review Questions

1. Why are VRs the preferred implementation choice when deploying next hop-style service sets? (Choose two.)

   a. Added security benefits

   b. More features can be implemented

   c. Simplicity in configuration

   d. Automatic rules

2. Which match direction should be specified when creating an IPSec tunnel?

   a. De-encapsulation direction

   b. Both directions

   c. Encapsulation direction

   d. No direction

3. True or False: A single proposal can be applied to an IPSec tunnel.

4. Which type of service set would allow for OSPF routing over an IPSec tunnel?

   a. Next hop

   b. Interface

   c. Virtual router

   d. Route set

5. After an IP packet is encapsulated by a GRE header, what is the incoming interface of the packet set to?

   a. service interface

   b. gre interface

   c. outgoing interface

   d. loopback interface

6. Which type of NAT would be used to hide all local PCs' addresses as they connect to the Internet?

   a. Destination

   b. Half-Cone

   c. Twice NAT

   d. Source NAT

7. The following source NAT rule is applied to a next hop service set but doesn't seem to be working:

```
rule basic-source {
        match-direction output;
        term 1 {
```

```
                then {
                    translated {
                        source-pool ext-block;
                        translation-type source dynamic;
                    }
                }
            }
        }
    }
```

What is the possible issue?

    a. Missing a from statement

    b. Can't use dynamic translation for source NAT

    c. The match direction is incorrect

    d. Missing the accept action

8. True or False: IPSec VPNs must have their own service set.

9. If packets need to be skipped in an interface-style service set, what should be configured?

    a. A service rule allowing traffic to be skipped

    b. A post-service filter allowing traffic to be skipped

    c. A service filter allowing traffic to be skipped

    d. A firewall filter allowing traffic to be skipped

10. Which NAT type is *not* supported on a Juniper router?

    a. Dynamic source

    b. Static source

    c. Dynamic destination

    d. Static destination

11. What are the advantages of using a NAT pool? (Choose two.)

    a. Can reuse pool in other rules

    b. Can implement discontinuous addresses

    c. Doesn't have to reference in a rule

    d. Can enable port translation

12. Why might there not be an active IKE SA for a configured and operational VPN?

    a. SA is no longer needed

    b. VPN has yet to time out

    c. IKE SA was never established

    d. GRE tunnel was used instead

Chapter Review Answers

1. Answer: A, C. VRs add a security benefit over other solutions since the interfaces and route tables are separated from the main table. Also, VRs avoid the complexity of rib-groups that plague other solutions.

2. Answer: C. The direction that encapsulates the packet into the IPSec tunnel should be used. In an interface-style service set, this is normally set to output whereas a next hop service set usually uses input.

3. Answer: False. You can apply multiple proposals to the IPSec tunnel; only one proposal has to match on each side for tunnel establishment.

4. Answer: A. You must use a next hop-style service set to support routing protocols.

5. Answer: C. Strangely enough, after a packet gets GRE encapsulation, the incoming interface is set to the next hop outgoing interface. This causes the GRE packet to be subject to input filters and services on the outgoing interface.

6. Answer: D. If a PC wants to be hidden from the outside world, you should deploy source NAT. This changes the "private" source IP to one or more "public" IP addresses.

7. Answer: C. One of the most common configuration errors when making service rules is not specifying the correct direction, especially when using next hop-style service sets, and match directions often seem backward when compared to interface-style service sets. Remember that traffic mapped to the inside interface is input traffic and traffic mapped to the outside interface is output traffic.

8. Answer: True. At the time of this writing, IPSec VPNs are always a unique service set, and no other service rules can be combined in the set. If you need to implement other services on top of IPSec, they must have their own unique service set.

9. Answer: C. Service filters allow for some traffic to be skipped through a service set. They also allow certain services to be selected.

10. Answer: C. At the time of this writing, dynamic destination NAT is not supported. All destination NAT must be statically mapped to the same IP address.

11. Answer: A, D. NAT pools provide greater scalability, as they can be reused in multiple terms and in multiple rules. Also, a pool is required if port translation needs to be enabled.

12. Answer: A. The IKE SA is needed only during the initial tunnel establishment to negotiate the IPSec tunnel parameters. After the IPSec tunnel is established, the IKE SA will time out and will reestablish only on an as-needed basis.

CHAPTER 9
Class of Service

This chapter details M7i and J-series class of service (CoS) capabilities while also demonstrating typical CoS configuration and verification steps under JUNOS software. A detailed comparison between the ASIC-based M7i and the software-based J-series platform is provided to clarify their operational differences, which is a common source of confusion given that they have so many similarities. The topics covered include:

- What IP CoS is and why it is needed
- IP differentiated services primer
- M7i and J-series CoS capabilities
- DiffServ-based CoS deployment and verification
- J-series virtual channels

Juniper Networks routers offer extensive support for IP CoS. As of this writing, the list of supported standards includes:

- RFC 2474, "Definition of the Differentiated Services Field in the IPv4 and IPv6 Headers"
- RFC 2597, "Assured Forwarding PHB Group"
- RFC 2598, "An Expedited Forwarding PHB"
- RFC 2698, "A Two Rate Three Color Marker"

What Is IP CoS, and Why Do I Need It?

Simply put, CoS provides a mechanism by which certain packets are afforded preferred treatment in an effort to provide the associated application with a level of performance required for proper operation. Although the preceding sentence seems simple enough, it implies support for several capabilities that must work together within each node—and in a *consistent* manner network-wide—for an IP CoS deployment to be successful.

Why IP Networks Need CoS

IP networks are based on the principal of statistical multiplexing (stat MUX), which is a resource-sharing technique that allocates resources on an as-needed basis. A stat MUX provides efficiency gains by playing the odds that a given application or user will not be active at its peak rate 100% of the time. By allocating bandwidth resources only when needed, a large number of bursty applications can be supported over a network with an aggregate capacity that is significantly less than the potential aggregate rate of its user base.

To make all this work, some degree of buffering is needed to accommodate the occasional synchronized bursts. Because no network has infinite buffers, flow control (typically supported by a virtual circuit [VC] technology) or simple discard in the case of datagram operation (connectionless) is needed during chronic periods of congestion. Throwing more buffers at the problem only changes the symptom from one of discard to one of delay and delay variance, which is known as *jitter*. Although non-real-time applications such as an order-entry system can tolerate loss and lengthy/variable delays, the user will generally have a degraded experience and productivity can suffer. More demanding real-time applications such as Voice over IP rapidly become unusable when loss and delay/jitter are not kept within relatively stringent bounds.

IP networks are based on statistical multiplexing, and there is an increasing trend to converge all communications, be it data, voice, video, real-time simulation, and so on over a single IP infrastructure to maximize return on investment and economy of scale. Put differently, a single network is far less expensive to deploy and maintain, and much to the chagrin of Integrated Services Digital Network (ISDN) and Asynchronous Transfer Mode (ATM), that single network technology is shaping up to be IP. Saving money always looks good on paper, but these gains quickly disappear if the result is unproductive, angered workers who can no longer perform their jobs due to intermittent application performance.

Historically, network technologies were circuit-based and were designed to support toll-quality voice. Although there is little to find sexy in "toll-quality voice," these telephone network architects did not realize what they were dealing with: what would become the panacea of IP network quality of service (QoS)—namely, a service that provides (once connected) minimal and *fixed* delays, freedom from congestion, guaranteed bandwidth, in-sequence delivery, and low loss. Legacy circuit-switched networks are not without their drawbacks, and all indications are that the future of voice, data, and video transport will be packet- rather than circuit-based.

Overbuilding an IP network with excess bandwidth is a viable way to ensure that all applications work properly, even during periods of peak usage or network outages. The fact that costs associated with bandwidth are constantly dropping, and new ways are always being found to drive existing fiber to increasingly higher rates allows the "overbuild it and they will be happy" network design philosophy to pass the giggle test, which is to say that there are cases where adding bandwidth is more expedient, and potentially less costly, than deploying an IP CoS solution. This is especially true if existing IP infrastructure requires hardware upgrades to support CoS, which is often the case with legacy gear that may already be struggling in the basic IP routing role and that simply does not have the capability or resources to provide additional CoS processing.

When simply throwing bandwidth at the problem is not seen as feasible, due to either economic impact or equipment limitations, deploying IP CoS is the key to successfully converging services and applications onto an IP-based infrastructure.

Although there are CoS processing variances across the product line, all current Juniper Networks routing platforms provide IP CoS capabilities that you can deploy in a production network without negatively impacting basic IP packet forwarding performance.

Circuit-switching inefficiencies

Although legacy circuit-switched networks offered some mighty fine CoS, circuit-switched technologies are inefficient or poorly suited as a convergent technology in numerous areas. The root cause of this inefficiency is the lack of statistical multiplexing in circuit-switched networks, which prevents the sharing of resources during naturally occurring idle periods in communication streams. The issues with circuit switching and network efficiency are outlined in the following list, and they hold true whether using an analog or newer digital (ISDN) type of circuit switch:

Blocking during congestion
> Establishment of new circuits is blocked when the network reaches capacity through a call admission control (CAC) function (fast busy). This behavior helps to preserve the CoS of existing users, but lack of priority/preemption capabilities means that routine calls can lock out new users, even when their communication needs are high priority.

Dedicated resources
> Allocating guaranteed bandwidth in fixed chunks (64 Kbps DSO) is inefficient, even for voice, given that most communication is bursty—the simple fact that voice communication is inherently bursty, that it is half-duplex, and that speech waveforms are predictable and consist of idle periods is behind most speech compression algorithms.

Fixed bandwidth allocation
> The fixed allocation of bandwidth can be too coarse, given that it is based on multiples of a 3 KHz voice band coded into a 64 Kbps channel with standard Pulse Code Modulation (PCM). For some applications, this is too much bandwidth, and for others, it is not enough. Bonding multiple voice channels together

to form a higher-speed link is possible, but you are still forced to deal with complete channels—one channel may not be enough and two might be too much.

Poor survivability

In most cases, the failure of any link or node along a circuit-switched connection's path results in the loss of that connection. The user normally has to reestablish his connection to resume communications, which can take time. Furthermore, due to blocking, perhaps due to diminished capacity after equipment failure, the call may not succeed.

To date, most IP networks are not CoS-enabled. This is simply because the historic application of IP as an internetworking protocol for LAN and WAN interconnection simply did not warrant the added complexity, both in equipment design and in the network-wide configuration needed for a working CoS solution. In fact, with some early (non-Juniper) router architectures, enabling CoS services consumed so many resources that forwarding performance was actually *better* with CoS disabled.

In other cases, when some level of performance was actually required, engineers simply overbuilt the network from a capacity and bandwidth perspective. When all is said and done, the simple truth is that all of the world's most sophisticated CoS processing does no good for a packet that encounters a router with relatively empty queues anyway; CoS matters only when link utilization begins to exceed 80%; otherwise, packets are dispatched virtually as soon as they arrive, as there is no appreciable queue fill in such conditions. Put differently, enabling CoS on an underutilized network is akin to buying a low-emissions vehicle just so that you can use a carpool lane, and then finding your commute hours occur at 2:00 a.m. when the roadways are empty anyway.

Even though bandwidth prices continue to trend downward while the raw forwarding rates of routers continue to rise, there are practical limits to the "overbuild and they will be happy" philosophy of network design. In addition, the increasing trend toward the use of IP as a mission-critical infrastructure supporting many, if not all, of an enterprise's data, voice, and automation/manufacturing needs makes the prioritization of critical traffic a prudent decision. In the most basic sense, consider the outbreak of a fire that significantly reduces your network's capacity. With the "overbuild it" safeguard now up in smoke (pun intended), you reach for the last unmelted IP phone handset to summon emergency help. This is not the time that you should have to ask yourself whether you feel lucky; with IP CoS, you *know* that your critical voice signaling and related media packets will be the first to be routed, assuming, of course, that any routing is still possible.

The use of IP-based statistical multiplexing combined with a sound CoS deployment provides the best of all worlds—the efficiency gains of statistical multiplexing and easily extended IP-based signaling protocols that provide CAC (RFC 2205 RSVP) and/or preemption and priority (draft-ietf-tsvwg-mlpp-that-works), combined with the ability to support virtually all known application types over a single, future-proof network infrastructure.*

CoS Terms and Concepts

This section defines common IP network CoS terms and operational concepts in the context of JUNOS software, and the terminology used in the Internet QoS working group's survey titled "Network QoS Needs of Advanced Internet Applications." The reader is encouraged to consult this document for a detailed description of application-specific characteristics and typical CoS needs; the focus here is strictly on those QoS parameters and concepts associated with IP layer network operation and packet handling.

It should also be noted that the actual measurement of IP performance, including the effects of CoS, is defined in RFC 2544, "Benchmarking Methodology for Network Interconnect Devices."

This section explores the following terms and concepts:

- Network QoS parameters
- Classification
- Packet marking
- Forwarding classes, queues, and schedulers
- Congestion management
- Policing and shaping
- Typical CoS processing stages in a Juniper router

Network QoS parameters

In common vernacular, the terms *CoS* and *QoS* are used interchangeably. To help keep things clear, this chapter reserves the term *QoS* for individual network parameters such as delay or loss probability, and uses *CoS* to describe the combined effect of applying specific QoS parameters to a packet stream, which should result in a service differentiation among the supported traffic classes in your network.

By way of analogy, consider commercial aviation and the typical coach versus first-class traveling experience. First, if there were no differences between these service classes, the airline would have a hard time charging so much more for a first-class seat.

---

* Although the future of IP may well rest with IPv6, version 4 has shown a remarkable degree of resiliency and has quietly supported the world's internetworking needs while rival after rival has come and gone, leaving only obsolete certifications in their wake. There are numerous migration strategies to move from IPv4 to IPv6, and the CoS models are the same, which allows direct application of this material to an IPv6 infrastructure when needed.

It can be said that the service associated with these classes of travel is in turn a function of various QoS parameters, such as the maximum time to get a drink after being seated (delay), the likelihood of having your luggage make it to your destination (loss), and being treated to proper flatware and real food, as opposed to the experience of using a plastic spork (a combined spoon/fork) to choke down a bag lunch. The combined effects of these airline-based QoS parameters yield a particular CoS, and each such service class is differentiated so as to leave little ambiguity as to which class one happens to be traveling in at any given time.

To get maximum benefit of network QoS, the user's application should be QoS-aware so that it can request the appropriate resources during CAC (when supported) and correctly mark its traffic to ensure that it maps to the desired service class or classes.

The primary network QoS parameters are defined as follows:

Bandwidth
> Bandwidth is a measure of each link's information-carrying capacity. It is limited by the lesser of the bandwidth supported by each link crossed between two endpoints.

Delay
> Delay is a measure of the time taken to move a packet from one point to another. End-to-end delay is a cumulative function of serialization delays, propagation delays, and any queuing delays (buffering) that the packet may experience.

Delay variation (jitter)
> Delay variation, often called jitter, is a measure of the variance in transfer delays between packets that make up a stream. Jitter is significant to real-time applications because the receiver must dimension its jitter buffer based on maximum jitter, which adds delays for all packets and causes eventual loss when jitter values exceed buffer capacity.

Loss
> Loss measures the percentage of packets not delivered. Loss can stem from transmission errors or discard stemming from congestion in packet-based networks.

Loss pattern
> The loss pattern defines the nature of a loss event as either bursty (short duration) or chronic, which is sometimes called a *dribble error*.

Classification

Classification is the act of associating received packets with a defined forwarding class, which in turn maps to a queue. Classification is a critical aspect of IP CoS, given that the underlying principle of CoS is to enforce different forwarding behavior on one packet versus another, based on the associated set of QoS parameters defined for each forwarding class. Errors in classification result in incorrect handling of the associated packet stream, which may negate CoS benefits by treating all traffic the same or by causing congestion in one or more forwarding classes, which in turn leads to loss and delay-related problems for that forwarding class. Figure 9-1 shows how incoming packets are subjected to a classifier function that in turn maps each packet to a defined forwarding class.

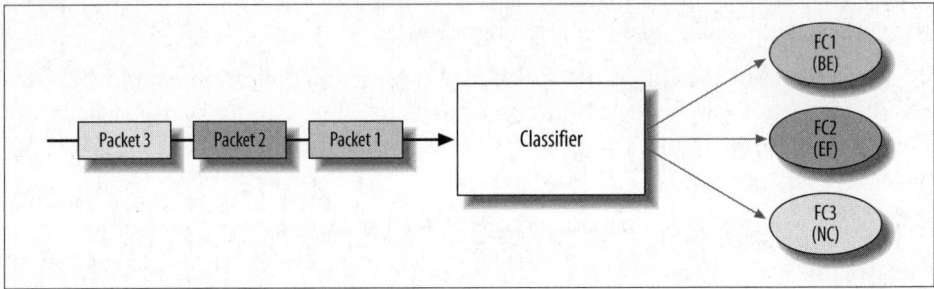

Figure 9-1. Classification

At egress, the forwarding class is used to link the packet to the correct output queue/ scheduler profile. Classification can be a resource drain on a router, because it adds processing steps to each received packet. Modern IP routers support two types of classification to help mitigate resource consumption concerns:

Multifield classification

> Multifield classifiers are the most flexible and therefore the most computation-ally burdensome type of classifier. As the name suggests, a multifield classifier is based on matches against multiple fields with the IP packet, including source and destination addresses, protocol type, ports, and so on.

Behavior aggregate (BA)

> A BA classifier uses a fixed field in the packet header to make classification deci-sions. This is highly efficient because of the fixed position, length, and meaning of the bits used in the BA classification field. Classifications based on IP precedence or Differentiated Services code points (DSCPs) are examples of BA classification.

Normally you deploy multifield classifiers at the network's edges, as close to the traf-fic source as possible—that is, in the access layer. Once correctly classified, the pack-ets are typically remarked to permit the more efficient BA type of classification in the aggregation and core layers. Juniper routers use firewall filters to perform multifield classification and support various types of BA classifiers, as detailed in "BA classifica-tion capabilities," later in this chapter. The highly efficient manner in which JUNOS software firewall filters are compiled and optimized allows large-scale use of multi-field classification without incurring a significant reduction in forwarding capacity. With that said, you should use BA type classification wherever possible to keep things streamlined.

Loss priority. Many CoS models expect that loss will be lower in some classes than in others, or that loss will be lower for traffic within a class when it conforms to the class's associated rate limit, versus a higher loss probability for nonconformant traffic. Technologies such as ATM and Frame Relay achieve this functionality with the cell loss priority (CLP) and discard-eligible (DE) bits, respectively.

The IP packet header does not have a mechanism for signaling a packet's loss priority. As a result, the loss priority status for an IP packet is an internal flag that is set based on classification or policing actions. Once a packet is flagged at ingress as having a low or high loss priority, other nodes are expected to make the same determination—policing is done at the edge, and the resultant loss status should not be altered once set. This is normally accomplished by rewriting the BA field. Downstream nodes then use the altered BA value during classification to determine that packet's loss priority.

Packet marking/rewriting

Once mapped to a forwarding class, a packet can be subjected to one or more rewrite rules. Rewrite rules are used to mark the packet to facilitate BA classification in downstream nodes. Figure 9-2 shows packet marking in action.

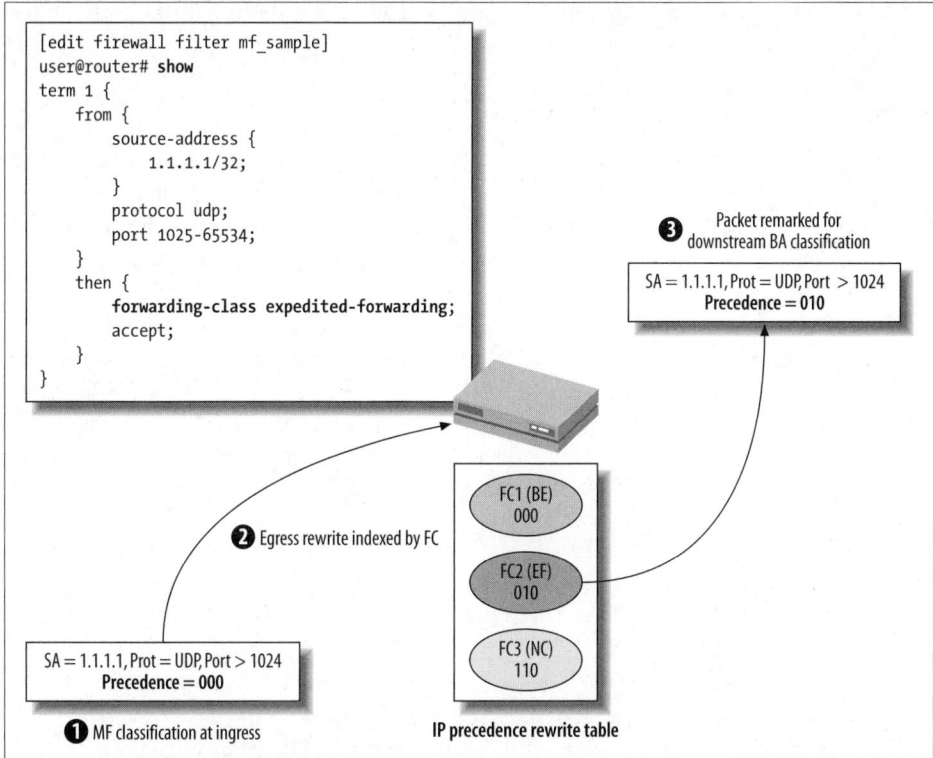

```
[edit firewall filter mf_sample]
user@router# show
term 1 {
    from {
        source-address {
            1.1.1.1/32;
        }
        protocol udp;
        port 1025-65534;
    }
    then {
        forwarding-class expedited-forwarding;
        accept;
    }
}
```

❸ Packet remarked for downstream BA classification

SA = 1.1.1.1, Prot = UDP, Port > 1024
Precedence = 010

❷ Egress rewrite indexed by FC

FC1 (BE)
000

FC2 (EF)
010

FC3 (NC)
110

SA = 1.1.1.1, Prot = UDP, Port > 1024
Precedence = 000

❶ MF classification at ingress

IP precedence rewrite table

Figure 9-2. Packet marking

Step 1 of Figure 9-2 shows an incoming packet with a default IP precedence field that is subjected to a multifield classifier. In this example, the packet matches against the source address, protocol, and port range criteria associated with the Expedited Forwarding (EF) class, which results in a mapping to forwarding class 2. At egress, the packet is subjected to an IP precedence rewrite rule that is indexed according to each packet's assigned forwarding class and drop priority. In this example, packets belonging to forwarding class 2 (EF) have their IP precedence field rewritten to a binary 010—the altered IP precedence field can now be used for BA-based classification in downstream nodes (steps 2 and 3, respectively). Though not shown, the packet's local packet loss priority (PLP) can also be factored into a rewrite pattern that enabled downstream nodes, which typically do not perfom policing actions, to make the same discard priority determination.

Generally speaking, you cannot rely upon user applications to correctly mark the BA fields of their traffic streams; doing so can easily lead to service abuse by savvy users who know how to alter their operating system's protocol stack to alter the default marking of their packets. The current best practice is to perform multifield classification and re-marking to the appropriate forwarding class at the networked edges to ensure that BA tags used in the core meet your organization's acceptable use CoS policy. If desired, you can rewrite the BA field to a default value at network egress, perhaps to meet the receiving application's expectations or simply to hide the markings used for classification in the core.

Forwarding classes, queues, and schedulers

It's been established that packet classification results in the mapping of each packet to a forwarding class. So, what is a forwarding class? In Juniper parlance, a forwarding class essentially maps to a queue. Typically, there is a one-to-one mapping of forwarding class to queue number, but a many-to-one mapping is also possible. For example, the default CoS configuration defines only two forwarding classes—Best Effort (BE) and Network Control (NC)—and the default IP precedence classifier maps the eight possible precedence values into these two forwarding classes (queues) in a 6:1 and 2:1 ratio, respectively. Forwarding classes are referenced by symbolic names, which you can redefine if desired. Table 9-1 shows the default mappings.

Table 9-1. Default forwarding class names and queue mappings

Forwarding class	Symbolic name	Queue number
0	Best-effort	0
1	Expedited-forwarding	1
2	Assured-forwarding	2
3	Network-control	3

In IP DiffServ terminology, a forwarding class maps to a *DS behavior aggregate*, or in the newer terminology, an *ordered aggregate*. The term *ordered* here refers to the fact that packets classified as part of the same micro flow should not be resequenced, and therefore the associated BA is expected to preserve sequencing. These terms describe the externally visible behavior of a DiffServ-compliant node for a given BA, which is a stream of packets with the same DSCP marking crossing a link in a particular direction. Stating this differently, and in English, a forwarding class is a stream of packets that, as a result of classification, are placed into the same egress queue and are therefore serviced by a common set of dequeuing parameters, resulting in consistent, and therefore predictable, handling of packets within that node.

Schedulers. Packets placed into an egress queue are serviced by a scheduler. The scheduler algorithm determines how often a queue is serviced, and in which order, based on an associated priority and transmit rate percentage. Packet scheduling combined with rate limiting and policing are an important aspect of IP CoS because together they provide the necessary isolation between forwarding classes. This isolation ensures that one misbehaving or nonconformant forwarding class does not degrade the service of other (compliant) forwarding classes.

The scheduler essentially controls how packets are dequeued for transmission, and it is therefore a critical component of the JUNOS software CoS model. Figure 9-3 illustrates the high-level operation of a scheduler.

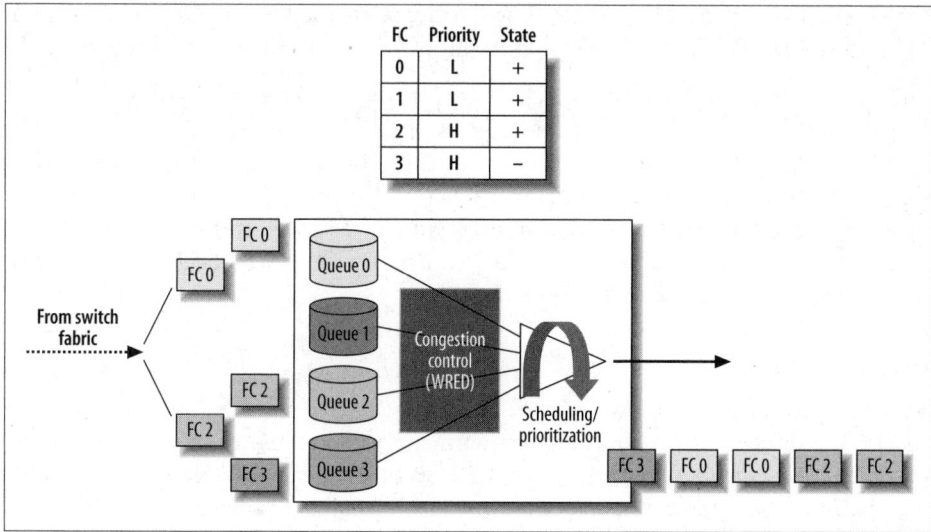

Figure 9-3. Scheduler operation

Figure 9-3 shows how packet notifications arriving from the switch fabric are placed into notification queues, based on their ingress classification. Recall that in the Juniper architecture, the packets themselves are placed into shared memory once, and only a notification that points to the packet's shared memory address is actually queued on the egress Flexible PIC Concentrator/Physical Interface Card (FPC/PIC).

The scheduler selects the next packet to dequeue based on a function on transmission credit and associated priority.

The basic algorithm (for M-series routers) is to service all high-priority queues with positive credit before moving on to service low-priority queues with positive credit. When no queues with positive credit remain, the scheduler divides any remaining bandwidth among those nonempty queues, typically using a simple round-robin algorithm (this can vary by platform, as detailed in "Scheduling and queuing" later in this chapter). The net result is that all queues are guaranteed to receive at least their configured transmission rate, and high-priority queues will exhibit less delay because the associated queue is serviced before low-priority queues as long as it remains within its configured transmit rate.

Figure 9-3 shows the scheduler state for each forwarding class as either positive (+) or negative (–) and also indicates the associated priority setting. In this example, queue 3 is set to high priority, but it is currently in negative credit—this means the queue has sent more traffic than its configured transmit percentage and must now wait to accumulate credit to go positive again. Queue 1 has no packets pending, so it is skipped—a work-conserving scheduler does not service empty queues. The result is that the high-priority queue (#2) with positive credit is serviced first, which results in the dequeuing of its two packets. Because there are no remaining high-priority queues with positive credit and pending notifications, the low-priority queues can be serviced, and queue 0, having pending traffic and positive credit, is serviced next.

Queue 0 is emptied after its two packets are serviced, leaving only queue 3 with traffic pending. Unless this queue is rate-limited, it will be serviced, despite its negative credit status, as long as no positive credit queues become active. However, servicing a queue with negative credit results in an increase in the queue's negative credit, up to some maximum value, which, while allowing a queue to send more than its configured transmit weight, ensures that other queues will be the first to be serviced as soon as they have a notification pending.

Congestion management

Statistically multiplexed networks are subject to congestion. This can be chronic as a function of design or transient due to equipment or circuit failures or because of synchronized bursts from users. In any of these events, a method is needed to deal with congestion gracefully, and in a manner that is fair to all users. Because datagram networks do not support flow control, discard is the only mechanism a router has to prevent total buffer meltdown during a congestion event.

Modern IP routers implement some form of Active Queue Management (AQM), which is intended to optimize discard actions to obtain maximum benefit and to ensure fairness. AQM for IP networks is defined in RFC 2309, "Recommendations on Queue Management and Congestion Avoidance in the Internet."

Put simply, when a queue is filling faster than it can be emptied, a router has two choices as to where to drop. It can wait until the queue can hold no more, and then simply drop all packets as they arrive (which is called *tail dropping*). Or it can detect incipient congestion and *proactively* begin to drop packets based on a probability function that is in turn tied to average queue depth. The latter technique is known as random early detection (RED) and has many advantages over simple tail dropping.

Tail dropping can allow hyperactive applications to lock out less busy users, and it tends to result in queues operating at near capacity. A queue is really useful only when it is able to absorb packet burst, and any queue, no matter how large, that is near its fill capacity becomes useless for absorbing burst (it's already full), and therefore serves only to add delay. RED acts before the queue is full, and works on the principle that Transmission Control Protocol (TCP) sources assume that lost segments stem from congestion, and lower their window advertisements as a result. This ultimately results in less traffic from the related TCP source.

RED seeks to maintain an average queue fill by taking more aggressive drop actions as the queue fill increases. Using the queue's average fill level allows tolerance for receiving packet burst, because discards are probable only when the *average* queue level rises above configured thresholds. RED begins to perform tail drops once the queue reaches 100% full, in which case no new notifications can be queued and they are dropped upon receipt. The random nature of RED discards avoids the potential of queue lockout of certain users, as can occur with simple tail drops. In fact, because RED makes a discard decision upon receipt of each packet, the busiest users experience the most RED-induced drops, which is more than fair.

Figure 9-4 shows a sample RED configuration block and a graphical depiction of the resultant profile.

Weighted RED. Weighted RED (WRED) is simply a RED algorithm that maintains different drop probability profiles based upon traffic type. In the Juniper implementation, you can index one of as many as four RED profiles, based on traffic type of TCP versus User Datagram Protocol (UDP) with a loss priority of high or low. The result is a weighting of RED drop actions, based on traffic type.

Policing and shaping

Packet-based networks are capable of interconnecting devices and links that operate at variable speeds. Packet buffers are critical when supporting mixed-link speeds because they provide an elastic coupling between the high- and low-speed links. As noted previously, a packet buffer is most useful when it operates at a low fill level. Any packet network that constantly operates near buffer capacity should be redesigned, because a full buffer has lost its ability to provide additional buffering and leads only to increased delays.

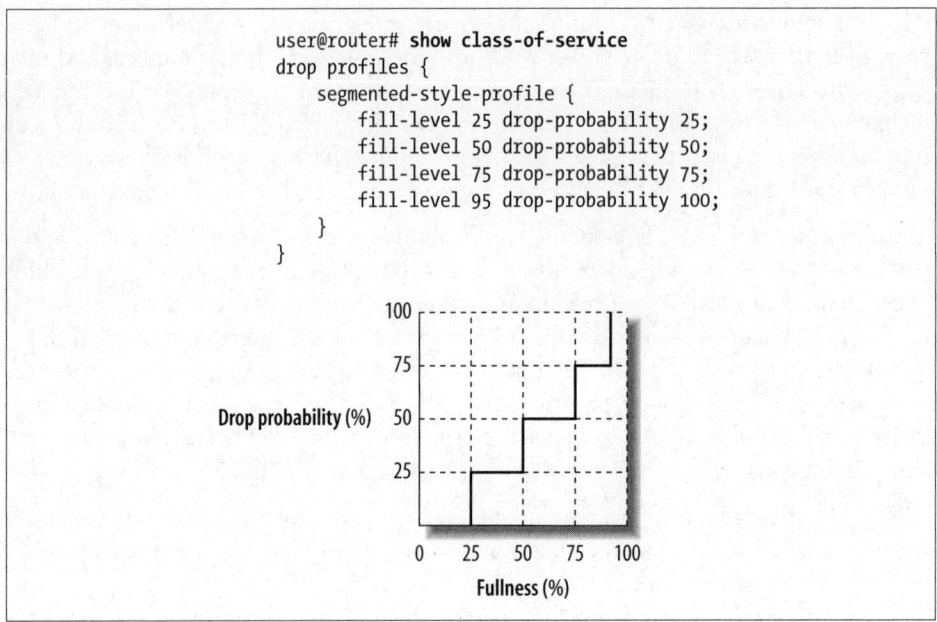

```
user@router# show class-of-service
drop profiles {
    segmented-style-profile {
        fill-level 25 drop-probability 25;
        fill-level 50 drop-probability 50;
        fill-level 75 drop-probability 75;
        fill-level 95 drop-probability 100;
    }
}
```

Figure 9-4. RED configuration and profile

The inherent support of mismatched device and link speeds, combined with the many-to-one nature of datagram networks, can result in a chronic condition in which more traffic arrives at a device than can be transmitted downstream. If left unchecked, this condition can lead to indiscriminate tail dropping—WRED tends to have little effect on UDP-based applications, so cannot be relied on to prevent congestion.

To resolve this type of problem, a mechanism is needed to limit, or *cap*, the amount of traffic that a device is able to send. Such a mechanism is called *policing* or *rate limiting*, and serves to limit the overall amount of traffic that can be sent over a given unit of time by placing limits on maximum packet rate and burst size.

Isolation is needed to preserve CoS. Isolation between forwarding classes is a critical aspect of IP CoS. Class-based isolation is provided by the scheduler via its priority and transmit weight settings. However, isolation between classes is not sufficient to ensure fair service for users that share the same class. Although policing can be used on a forwarding class basis, it's commonly used at the individual device, or even at a micro-flow level, to limit the amount of traffic that is accepted into the network. Policing provides the necessary isolation between users or applications in the same forwarding class to prevent one user from dominating the resources associated with that class.

Policing versus shaping. Users are often confused about the differences between policing and shaping. Figure 9-5 shows the operational differences.

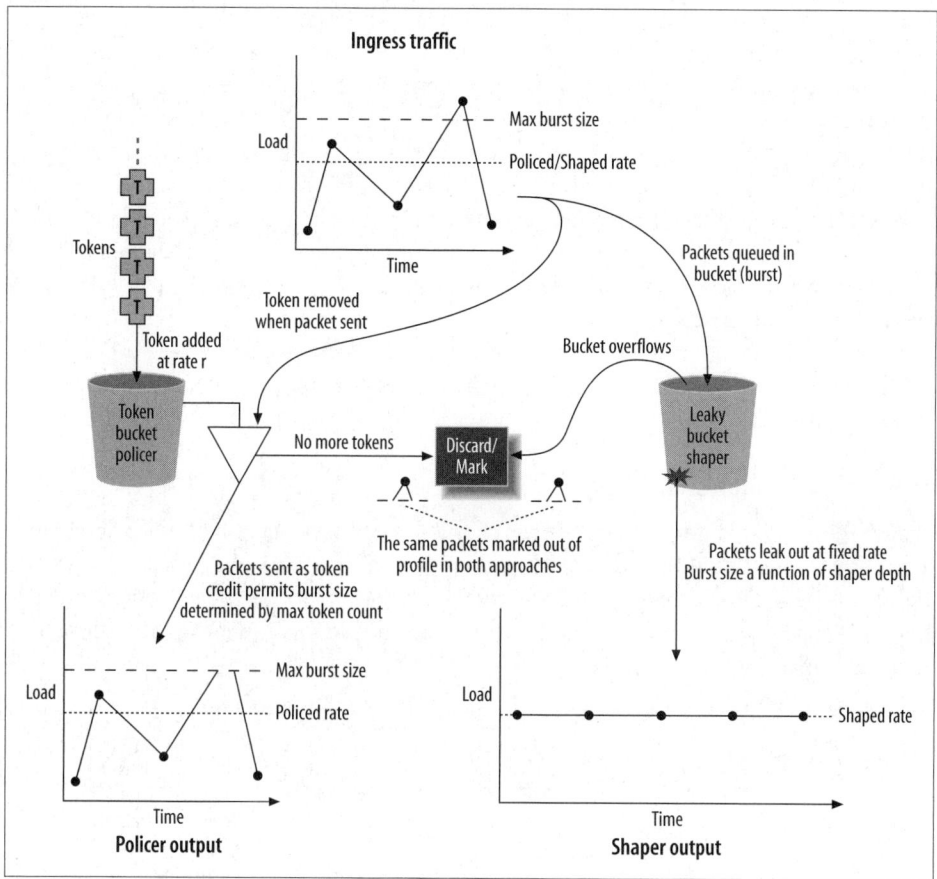

Figure 9-5. Policing versus shaping

The lefthand side of Figure 9-5 shows a typical token-rate-based policer. The size of the token bucket limits the total number of tokens that can accumulate, which in turn limits the maximum burst size. The rate at which new tokens are added limits the average transmission rate. Policers do not smooth traffic bursts, and they either mark or discard traffic that exceeds the configured burst size or average rate of token accumulation. A policer does not buffer the actual user traffic, and therefore does not add appreciable delays.

On the righthand side of the figure, the same input traffic is subjected to a leaky bucket-based shaper. The shaper buffers the actual user data (not tokens, as in the case of a policer), and the related output is spread over time to eliminate bursts—the shaper smoothes the peaks and valleys by buffering traffic and letting it leak out at a specified rate. The upside to shaping is that packet-buffering requirements are reduced in downstream nodes, given the lack of bursting. The downside is the need for buffering within the shaper, which adds delay and cost.

Generally speaking, on a macro level there is no difference in the amount of traffic transmitted (or marked/discarded) by a policer versus a shaper when they are configured with compatible parameters. At increasingly smaller time scales, the difference is manifest by the absence, or presence, of clumped packets (bursts) that instantaneously exceed the configured average rate. As long as downstream devices are not operating near buffer capacity, policing is generally preferred to shaping, given that it is less complex and less costly (buffers are not free), and does not induce any additional buffering delays. Stated differently, you perform shaping at an upstream device to *condition* traffic only when needed to meet the requirements of an attached device with limited buffering capabilities. If the downstream device is not buffer/capacity-challenged, it's far more efficient to quickly move traffic from point A to point B by sending bursts rather than artificially delaying each subsequent packet to eliminate clumping (bursts).

Summary of CoS processing steps

Figure 9-6 provides a big-picture view of the CoS processing stages associated with Juniper M- and J-series routers. Although useful in its own right, due to its detailed depiction of JUNOS CoS capabilities, the intent here is to tie the various terms and concepts discussed in this section into a single example to show how the various CoS process stages work together.

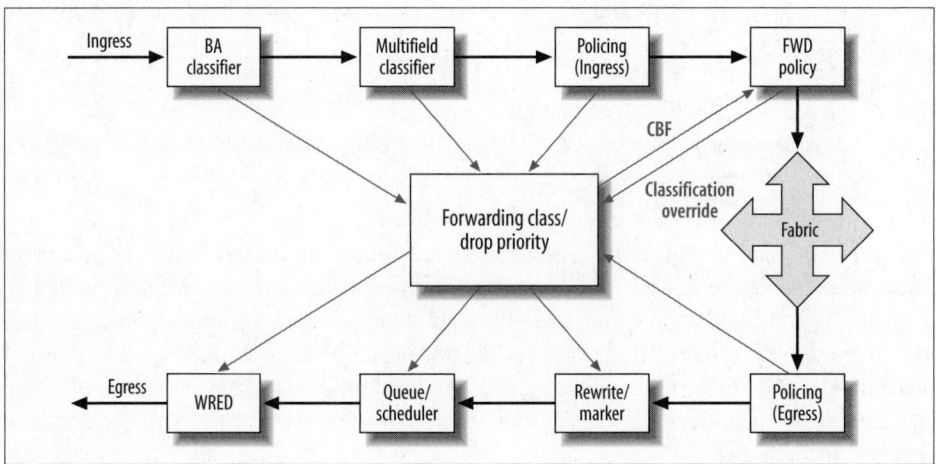

Figure 9-6. Big-picture CoS walkthrough

The discussion begins with a packet arriving at the ingress interface. The operation and general capabilities of each CoS stage encountered as a packet travels from ingress to egress are described as follows:

Ingress CoS processing

 BA classification

  Packets arriving at the router are first subjected to the BA classification stage. This stage sets the forwarding class and packet loss priority (PLP) using any of the supported BA classifier types, including IP precedence, Diff-Serv DSCP, IEEE 802.1P, and so on.

 Multifield classification

  The next processing stage is multifield classification. Here a firewall filter can be defined to match against numerous packet fields, incoming inter-faces, and so on, in order to set the forwarding class or PLP or to override the values set during previous BA classification.

 Ingress policing

  When desired, a firewall or interface-level policer can be applied to limit matching traffic, by discard, by reclassification, or by marking excess traffic with a loss priority of high. This means that in the event of congestion, a RED profile can be used to more aggressively drop PLP high traffic.

 Forwarding policy

  The last ingress processing stage is forwarding policy. This policy can alter the existing forwarding class or PLP setting, and it can be used to select a forwarding next hop based on a forwarding class, a feature called *Class-Based Forwarding* (CBF).

Egress CoS processing

 Egress policing

  After encountering the switching fabric, a packet begins its journey toward the selected egress interface. The first egress CoS processing state is output policing, which is again based on either a firewall or an interface-level policer. Once again, excess traffic can be discarded or marked with a loss priority for later discard in the event of congestion.

 Rewrite marker

  The rewrite marker stage allows you to alter one, or in some cases multiple packet fields, as the packet is transmitted to downstream nodes. Normally, you rewrite packet fields to accommodate downstream BA-based classification. Rewrite markers are indexed by protocol family and by forwarding class—for example, writing a 001 pattern into the precedence field of all family inet packets that are classified as BE.

 Queuing and scheduling

  The queuing stage involves placing packet notifications into the corresponding forwarding class queue, where they are serviced by a scheduler that factors priority and configured weight to determine when a packet should be dequeued from a given queue.

RED/congestion control

> The final CoS processing stage involves a WRED drop decision, based on protocol, loss priority, and average queue fill level. Recall that RED tends to operate at the head of the queue, and a RED decision is made against each packet selected for transmission by the scheduler stage.

At this stage, it should be clear that Juniper Networks enterprise routers offer a rich set of IP CoS capabilities that provide numerous points where a packet can be touched for CoS actions or manipulations. In most cases, a single router would not be configured to use all of these capabilities at the same time, but the Juniper design means that all CoS features can be deployed with minimal impact to the control and forwarding planes. As a point of fact, the default out-of-the-box configuration includes IP CoS, albeit in a relatively simplified manner. Details regarding the default CoS configuration are provided in "JUNOS Software CoS Defaults," later in this chapter.

A scalable CoS design strives to distribute the load—for example, by placing the relatively computationally intensive multifield classification function at the edges of the access layer only. Once classified, packets can be re-marked to accommodate streamlined BA-based classification in the core and distribution layers, where packet rates tend to be higher and more cycles need to be dedicated to forwarding traffic, rather than on complex classification tasks.

Figure 9-7 illustrates the CoS divide and conquer approach. It shows the CoS-enabled subset of the Beer-Co network, which has been divided into access and distribution/core layers. Generally speaking, CoS functionality is most complex at the edges of your network. This is because the network's edge has to deal with individual devices/micro-flows, whereas the core acts on traffic aggregates. Core devices are normally not burdened with CPU-intensive operations such as multifield classification, thus allowing these devices to focus their actions on actual packet forwarding. By policing at the network's edge, you throttle each user/application at ingress, making additional policing within the distribution and core layers unnecessary. Policing aggregate stream rates in the core is possible, but it has the serious drawback of allowing one or more hyperactive users to dominate the resources of that forwarding class. By performing rate limiting and related discard at the edges, as traffic initially ingresses the network, you can fairly limit all users to their assigned rate; when combined with a properly dimensioned core, additional policing actions are unnecessary.

The core CoS functionality of classification and resulting queuing/congestion control is performed by all nodes in the network to provide the consistent node-by-node, and therefore end-to-end, packet-handling behavior needed for a successful IP CoS deployment.

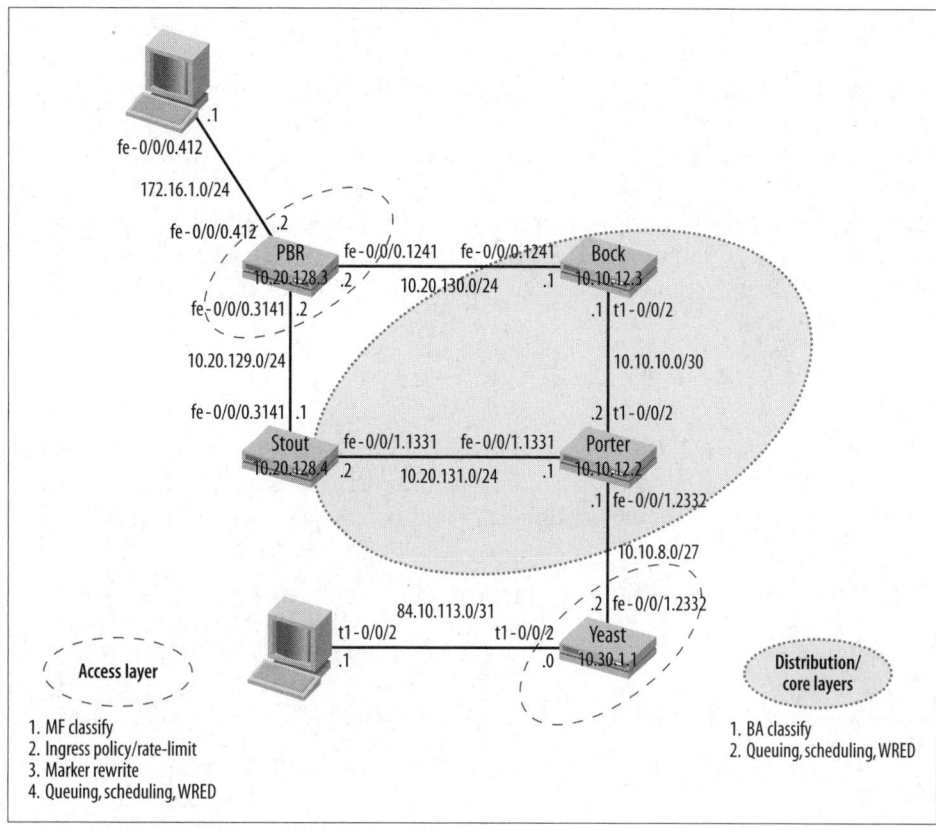

Figure 9-7. The CoS divide and conquer approach

IP CoS Summary

This section described IP CoS and why it's becoming increasingly important with the trends toward IP convergence. We defined basic network CoS/QoS terminology, and we walked through the typical CoS processing stages of a modern IP router.

Although likely not too earth shattering, there was a fair bit of information to digest here. You might consider taking a brief break before diving into the next section, which provides a primer on IP Differentiated Services (DiffServ).

IP Differentiated Services

Over the years, there have been several false starts to a standardized IP CoS solution. This section summarizes the history of IP CoS, and it provides a primer on the current solution known as IP Differentiated Services (DiffServ).

The original use of IP networks was to support robust communications in the face of battlefield conditions, an application to which datagram (connectionless) operation is well suited. This discussion is tempered with the knowledge that the concept of integrating services over IP internetworks was not considered by the protocol's architects, and wide-scale adoption of IP CoS has yet to occur. However, recent advancements in router platforms have enabled the high-bandwidth forwarding rates required to make IP-based convergence a commercial reality. With high-capacity forwarding in place, the final piece of the IP CoS puzzle is the intelligent handling of packets to effectively prioritize certain packets during times of reduced capacity or link congestion.

IP ToS

RFC 791 is the original RFC specification of the Internet Protocol (IP) and was published in 1981. The RFC defined an 8-bit field in the IP header as a Type of Service (ToS) field. Figure 9-8 shows the IP header and details the structure of the ToS field itself.

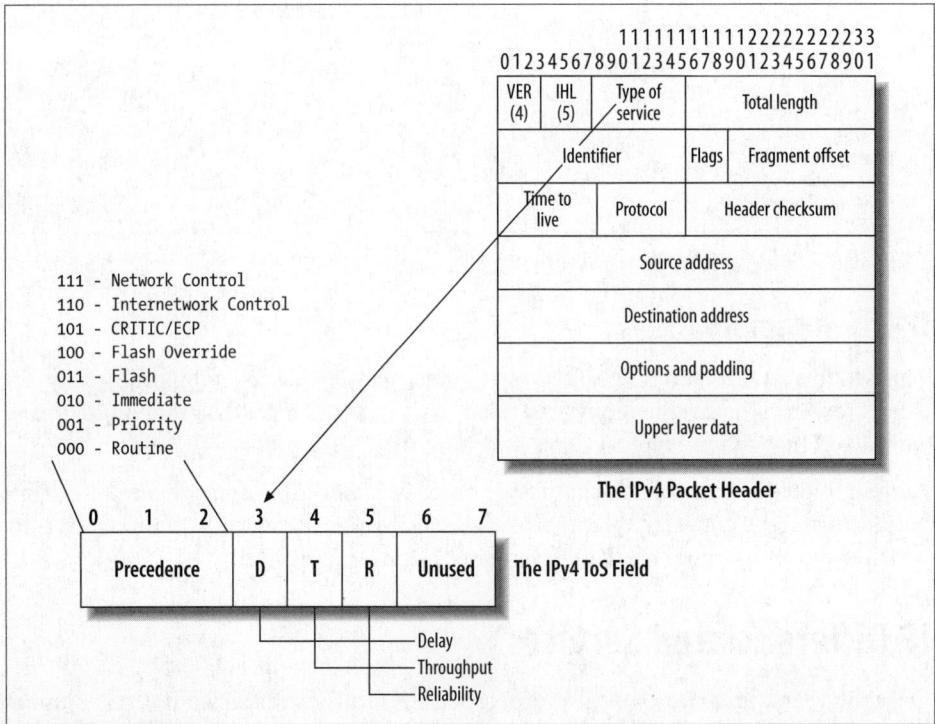

Figure 9-8. The IP ToS byte

The original IP ToS field is structured into a 3-bit precedence field, a 3-bit ToS indication field, and two reserved bits. The ToS bits were intended to provide a clue to the router as to which type of link metric (e.g., delay, throughput, or reliability) should be considered when handling the packet. This capability presumes a ToS-capable routing protocol, one that builds a routing information base (RIB) based on specific link metrics. Such a protocol has never seen use in commercial networks (Open Shortest Path First [OSPF] has this capability, but it never saw actual deployment).

Lack of ToS-capable Interior Gateway Protocols (IGPs) meant that the ToS bits have gone historically unused by routers. Many applications set these bits; for example, Telnet often sets the D bit to indicate low delay, but routers generally take no specific action upon any ToS combinations.

With bits 6 and 7 reserved, this left only the precedence field, which at 3 bits in length is able to code eight possible precedence levels (2^3). IP precedence is supposed to influence packet loss—generally speaking, each increase from the default value, which is 0, was expected to result in a reduced probability for discard. Unlike the ToS bits, IP precedence processing has been supported in routers for some time, but usually in a rather coarse, binary manner that results in two discard probabilities—a low probability for precedence values 6 and 7, which are associated with NC, and a higher probability for all other levels. In the Juniper implementation, the default behavior results in a maximum of four drop probabilities, two for non-NC classes and two for the NC class, based on a WRED profile set to act differently on high- versus low-loss probability traffic.

Most routing protocol stacks do in fact set the precedence bits of their control packets, as shown in the following monitor traffic sample, which explains how JUNOS software transmits an OSPF packet:

```
[edit]
lab@Bock# run monitor traffic interface fe-0/0/1.100 detail
Listening on fe-0/0/1.100, capture size 96 bytes
. . .
02:12:44.430326 Out IP (tos 0xc0, ttl  1, id 3867, offset 0, flags
[none], proto: OSPF (89), length: 68) 10.10.11.3 > 224.0.0.5: OSPFv2,=
Hello, length: 48
        Router-ID: 10.10.12.1, Backbone Area, Authentication Type:
none (0)
        Options: [External] [|ospf]
```

The hexadecimal value shown for the ToS field (*0xc0*) breaks down to a binary 1100 0000, which in turn codes IP precedence level 6 with the D, T, and R ToS bits cleared (not set). The default Juniper behavior is to classify based on IP precedence, such that NC messages are placed into queue 3, which is the default queue for the NC class, as shown here:

```
lab@PBR> show class-of-service classifiers type precedence name ipprec-compatibility
| match network-control
   110              network-control           low
   111              network-control           high
```

A breakdown of IP precedence to binary, along with the decimal equivalent, is provided. This can be useful when testing CoS using utilities such as ping or traceroute, because when you include the tos switch, the resultant values are specified in *decimal*, not binary or hexadecimal. Note that only IP ToS bits are supported with the CLI tos switch—you cannot specify a DSCP value. Table 9-2 provides a complete breakdown of IP precedence to binary and the resultant decimal equivalents.

Table 9-2. IP ToS to binary and decimal equivalents

Precedence	Binary	Powers of 10	Decimal
Precedence 7	1110 00xx	128+64+32+0+0+0+x+x	224
Precedence 6	1100 00xx	128+64+0+0+0+0+x+x	192
Precedence 5	1010 00xx	128+0+32+0+0+0+x+x	160
Precedence 4	1000 00xx	128+0+0+0+0+0+x+x	128
Precedence 3	0110 00xx	0+64+32+0+0+0+x+x	96
Precedence 2	0100 00xx	0+64+0+0+0+0+x+x	64
Precedence 1	0010 00xx	0+0+32+0+0+0+x+x	32
Precedence 0	0000 00xx	0+0+0+0+0+0+x+x	0

Enter IP Integrated Services

Recognizing an increasing need for functional IP CoS, the Internet Engineering Task Force (IETF) began work on an Integrated Services (IS, or IntServ) model that was first published in 1994 in RFC 1633, "Integrated Services in the Internet Architecture: An Overview." The authors felt that simple packet classification and scheduling was not enough to guarantee real-time services over the Internet, and specifically felt that some form of admission control and resultant resource reservation was needed. Figure 9-9 shows the IntServ concept.

The added functionality needed to support IntServ is shown in the upper-right portion of the router's control plane in Figure 9-9—specifically, the addition of the CAC and the reservation control entities, along with the related resource reservation database and related hooks into the router's management plane.

Put simply, the IntServ plan was to include the Resource Reservation Protocol (RSVP), as defined in RFC 2205, to routers and hosts, adding what amounts to a *call establishment* phase (for non-BE traffic). Here, the user specifically requests resources from the network, while also characterizing the nature of the related traffic with parameters such as average and peak rates, maximum transmission unit (MTU), and so on.

Each network node then either accepts or rejects the reservation request based on its local CAC function, which is run against that node's current resource availability, as shown at the bottom of the figure. When all nodes along the path accept the reservation, soft state is established for the duration of the reservation and is used to create

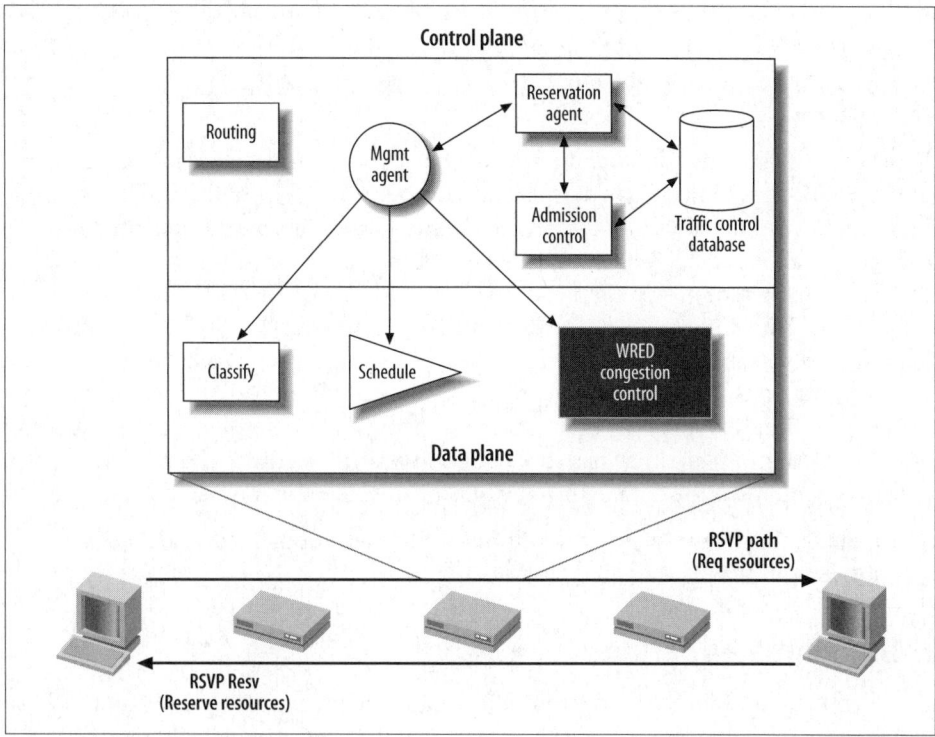

Figure 9-9. IP Integrated Services

the data plane state needed to support the new reservations. Specifically, a classifier is instantiated to match traffic belonging to that reservation using the details contained in the RSVP filter spec object. The reservation is torn down when it is no longer needed. This results in removal of the related data plane state and the freeing of allocated resources to accommodate the next reservation request. When a node is encountered that cannot meet the reservation's requirements, the session fails with the appropriate reason given—in theory, the user application will either keep trying, give up, or reduce its resource request to improve its chances of success.

Although all this sounds great, many practical issues resulted in little to no real deployment of IntServ. Ironically, the RSVP signaling protocol has seen significant commercial success as a Multiprotocol Label Switching (MPLS) signaling protocol within service provider networks, rather than in its original QoS signaling role.

The biggest nail in the IntServ coffin was the need to establish and maintain control plane state for every non-BE flow in the network. Even today the development of a large-scale, flow-based router remains a daunting task, at least at the scale needed for a modern Internet core router. Perhaps when the plan was IP at the edge supported by an ATM circuit-switched core, such a model could fly, but IntServ simply cannot scale to today's Internet needs. It is noted that RFC 3175, "Aggregation of RSVP for

IPv4 and IPv6 Reservations," offers a scalable model in which individual RSVP micro-flows can be aggregated into fewer, larger flows. Although promising, as of this writing, neither Juniper nor Cisco offers support for Aggregated RSVP in its shipping products.

IntServ results in network blocking when the network approaches capacity, meaning that no new reservations can be placed. Although not a problem for those users lucky enough to already hold a reservation, the total absence of (integrated) service for the remaining users was seen by many as a serious violation of the historical Internet paradigm of providing the same level of (degraded) service to all users in the same class. With IntServ, users at the *same* service level can be locked out by existing reservations, and the real rub is that this is true even when those existing reservations are not transporting traffic due to bursty sources. Many still have a hostile view toward the idea of blocking users in the control plane (putting aside the scaling issues of a control plane that has to interact on an end-user micro-flow basis), when at that very moment the data plane may well be idle, leading to wasted resources.

The commercial failure of IntServ prompted the development of a data-plane-only solution known as Differentiated Services.

IP Differentiated Services

IP Differentiated Services (DiffServ) was originally defined in RFCs 2474 and 2475 in 1998. Since that time, several RFCs have updated the original definition of the DSCP. RFC 3168 added explicit congestion notification (ECN) support, and RFC 3260 clarified the terminology to support MPLS traffic engineering, but the essence of the original DiffServ architecture remains.

DiffServ is scalable because it is a data-plane-only solution; there is no signaling component to DiffServ. DiffServ redefines the original IP ToS byte to support a 6-bit field, which, as noted previously, is called the DiffServ code point (DSCP). This provides for up to 64 levels of BA classification. Figure 9-10 shows the DiffServ definition of the IP ToS field. Related RFCs define the current set of per-hop behaviors (PHBs), which are described later, and essentially define the externally visible handling characteristics associated with a given forwarding class, or BA in DiffServ terminology.

Figure 9-10 also shows a table of the recommended DSCP mappings, most of which have yet to be defined. The Class Selector (CS) code points are designed to mimic the functionality of IP precedence, and they provide backward compatibility for non-DiffServ-aware routers, assuming any still exist. All of the CS code points have zeros where the original ToS definition placed the Delay, Throughput, and Reliability (DTR) flags. The 6-bit DSCP field leaves the original two least-significant bits (LSBs) of the original IP ToS field untouched, where they can be used for ECN signaling as per RFC 3168, "The Addition of Explicit Congestion Notification (ECN) to IP."

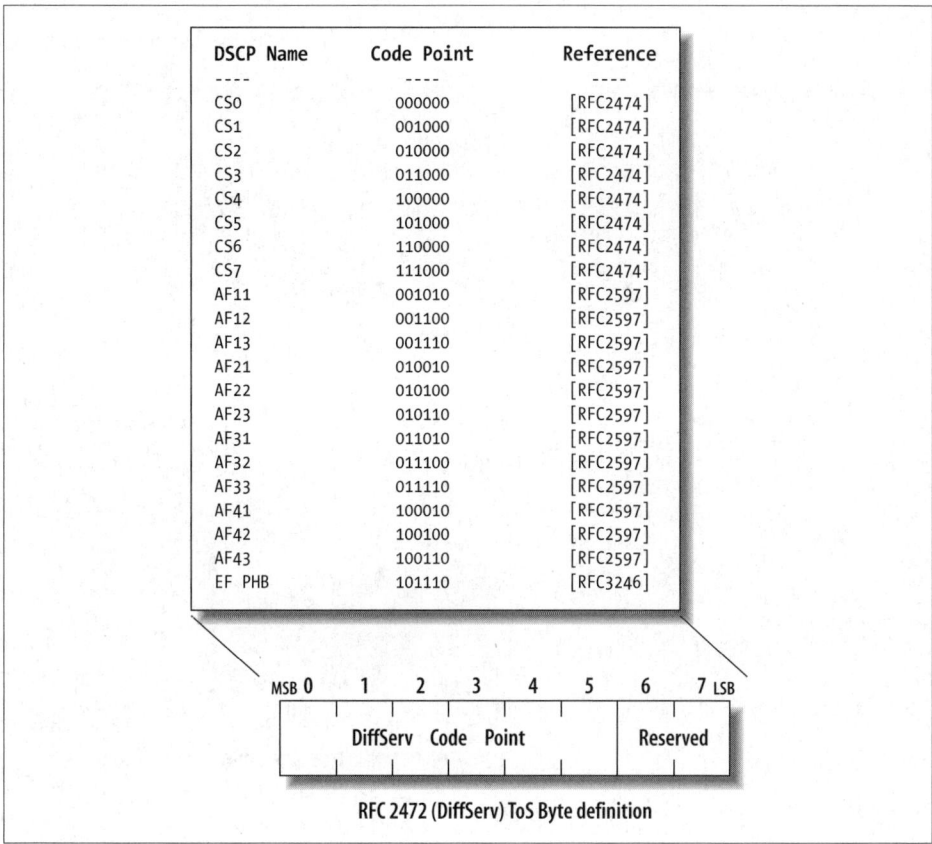

```
DSCP Name        Code Point        Reference
----             ----              ----
CS0              000000            [RFC2474]
CS1              001000            [RFC2474]
CS2              010000            [RFC2474]
CS3              011000            [RFC2474]
CS4              100000            [RFC2474]
CS5              101000            [RFC2474]
CS6              110000            [RFC2474]
CS7              111000            [RFC2474]
AF11             001010            [RFC2597]
AF12             001100            [RFC2597]
AF13             001110            [RFC2597]
AF21             010010            [RFC2597]
AF22             010100            [RFC2597]
AF23             010110            [RFC2597]
AF31             011010            [RFC2597]
AF32             011100            [RFC2597]
AF33             011110            [RFC2597]
AF41             100010            [RFC2597]
AF42             100100            [RFC2597]
AF43             100110            [RFC2597]
EF PHB           101110            [RFC3246]
```

MSB 0   1   2   3   4   5   6   7 LSB

DiffServ   Code   Point   Reserved

RFC 2472 (DiffServ) ToS Byte definition

Figure 9-10. The DiffServ code point

DiffServ Terminology

This section defines key DiffServ terms and operational concepts. Refer to Figure 9-11 to match the terms to their functional location in a DiffServ network.

BA
> This is a classification based on DSCP packets with a common DSCP belonging to the same BA.

DiffServ field
> This is the original IPv4 ToS byte. DSCPs occupy the six most significant bits of the DS field.

PHB
> This is the externally visible forwarding treatment associated with a given BA. Within a DiffServ domain, the set of PHBs should be consistent across all nodes, resulting in a consistent end-to-end handling of traffic.

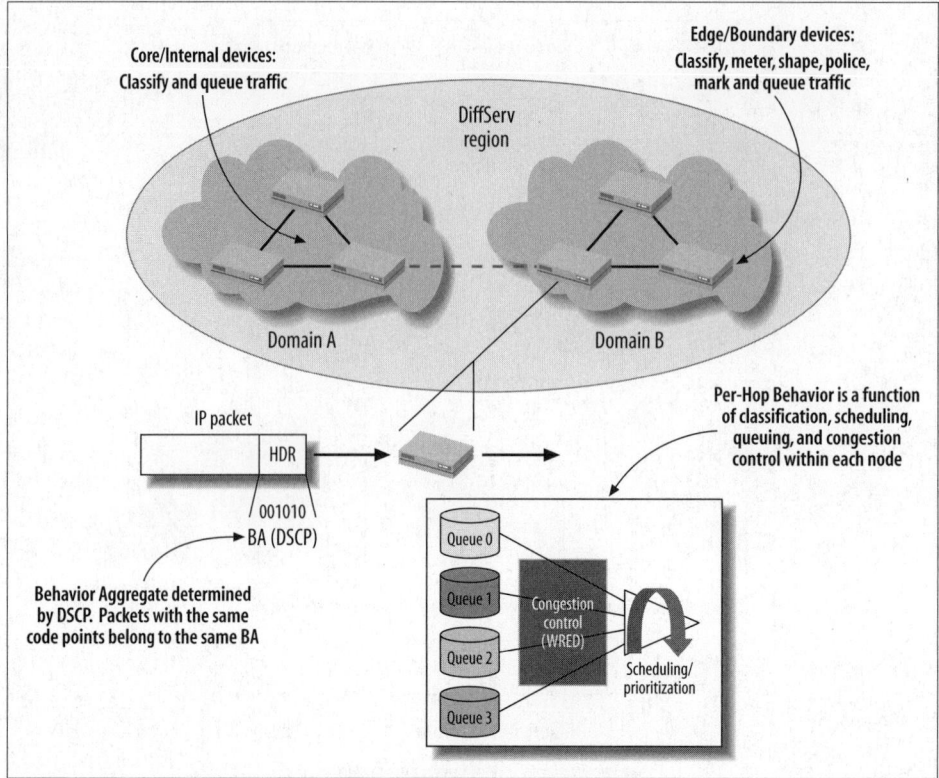

Figure 9-11. DiffServ terminology and concepts

PHB group

> This is a set of one or more PHBs that can only be meaningfully specified and implemented simultaneously, due to a common constraint applying to all PHBs in the set, such as a queue servicing or queue management policy. Currently, the only standardized group behavior relates to the Assured Forwarding (AF) PHB.

DiffServ domain

> This is a contiguous collection of nodes under a common policy with a common set of PHBs:
>
> • Edge/boundary devices classify, meter, shape, police, mark, and queue traffic.
> • Core devices classify and queue traffic.

DiffServ region

> This is a contiguous set of interconnected DiffServ domains.

DiffServ PHBs

Currently, four PHBs are standardized within DiffServ: the default PHB and the CS, EF, and AF groups:

The default PHB

The default PHB must be present in each DiffServ-compliant node, and it defines a BE delivery service. Any packets that are not explicitly classified into one of the other PHBs are considered to belong to the default group. Although the default group should not be starved, BE is generally serviced only after all other active PHBs have been given their share of bandwidth.

The CS PHB

The CS PHB is designed to subsume the historic drop behavior associated with the original IP precedence field definition. The PHB behavior set for the CS PHB is left somewhat vague, in keeping with the fact that IP precedence was used only to control drop probability and not to provide any delay, delay jitter, or minimum through guarantees. To be compliant, a DiffServ node supporting the CS PHB must demonstrate at least two different forwarding behaviors, and a packet with a CS value of 000xxx should be dropped in preference of a packet with a CS code point of 111xxx. Put simply, there are no throughput or delay guarantees in the CS PHB, and at a minimum, a node is expected to favor CS code points mapping to IP precedence 6 and 7 over all other CS values from a drop perspective.

The EF PHB

The EF PHB is associated with a low-latency, low-jitter, low-loss, end-to-end service. This type of service is suitable for circuit emulation, or the support of voice, video, or other real-time services. EF support is not mandated, but when offered, the EF PHB requires two independent functions: that each node is configured with a minimum departure rate that is independent of the activity levels of other PHBs within that node; and that the EF BA be conditioned through policing or shaping to ensure that the EF arrival rate at any node is always less than that node's configured minimum departure rate. The first behavior is defined within the EF PHB itself, and the second is a function of general traffic conditioning.

The AF PHB

The AF PHB is a family of PHBs, called a *PHB group*, which is used to classify packets into various drop precedence levels. The drop precedence assigned to a packet determines the relative importance of a packet within the AF class and generally also indicates whether that packet was within, or above, some guaranteed rate. Packets within the associated AF PHB group's minimum rate have the lowest drop probability and are expected to be delivered, whereas packets above the minimum rate have an increasing probability of loss.

The AF PHB can be used to implement a multitiered model consisting of three classes—bronze, silver, and gold—and is associated with loss-sensitive, nonreal-time applications. A minimal AF PHB implementation is required to recognize all three drop priorities within each supported AF group, but it has to offer only a minimum two-drop precedence within each AF group.

Recommended/default DHCPs. Each administrator of a DiffServ region is free to choose the specific DSCPs that map to supported PHBs. It's critical that any such mapping be consistent across all nodes in the DiffServ domain/region. Packet re-marking can be used to map between two regions that are part of the same domain, but this process is prone to error. The various IETF documents describing DiffServ PHBs provide recommended DSCP mappings, which were shown in Figure 9-10.

DiffServ Summary

This section provided a brief history of IP CoS, from the original ToS definition to the not-quite-successful IntServ model on up to the current approach known as IP Differentiated Services. The data-plane-centric approach defined in DiffServ provides a scalable solution that is known to work.

DiffServ is based on the principle of isolation between forwarding classes (BAs) and a consistent classification and resultant per-hop behavior across the routers in a Diff-Serv domain, such that predictable end-to-end CoS can be provided.

The next section provides a detailed description of M7i and J-series CoS capabilities and their differences. There is a lot to cover, so perhaps another break is in order before you dive back in.

M7i and J-Series CoS Capabilities

With a thorough grounding of IP CoS concepts and terminology now under your belt, it's time to get down to the particular CoS capabilities of Juniper's enterprise routing products, specifically the M7i and J-series service routers.

Although both the M7i and the J-series run pretty much the same JUNOS software, the ASIC-based HW design of the M7i versus the software-based J-series does lead to some operational differences and capabilities. Fortunately, the vast majority of CoS functionality is shared between the two platforms, and this section is structured accordingly—the common capabilities are covered first, followed by details regarding any specific exceptions or differences.

The discussion of CoS capabilities and default settings is presented in the context of the CoS packet processing steps available for transit traffic. This is done to provide structure and to reinforce your understanding of CoS processing stages within a Juniper router. You should refer back to Figure 9-6 as each CoS processing stage is discussed.

You configure CoS at the [edit class-of-service] hierarchy, which has quite a few options under it. The primary CoS configuration options are displayed:

```
[edit]
lab@Bock# edit class-of-service
```

```
[edit class-of-service]
lab@Bock# set ?
Possible completions:
> adaptive-shapers      Define the list of trigger types and associated rates
+ apply-groups          Groups from which to inherit configuration data
+ apply-groups-except   Don't inherit configuration data from these groups
> classifiers           Classify incoming packets based on code point value
> code-point-aliases    Mapping of code point aliases to bit strings
> drop-profiles         Random Early Drop (RED) data point map
> forwarding-classes    One or more mappings of forwarding class to queue number
> forwarding-policy     Class-of-service forwarding policy
> fragmentation-maps    Mapping of forwarding class to fragmentation options
> interfaces            Apply class-of-service options to interfaces
> loss-priority-maps    Map loss priority of incoming packets based on code point
value
> rewrite-rules         Write code point value of outgoing packets
> scheduler-maps        Mapping of forwarding classes to packet schedulers
> schedulers            Packet schedulers
> traceoptions          Trace options for class-of-service process
> virtual-channel-groups  Define list of virtual channel groups
> virtual-channels      Define the list of virtual channels
```

Input Processing

Input processing stages include BA classification, multifield classification, policing, and forwarding policy actions. Each is discussed separately.

BA classification capabilities

The BA classification stage supports classification based on the following Layer 3 and Layer 2 fields:

- DSCP (Layer 3, 64 levels in updated ToS byte)
- IP precedence (Layer 3, eight levels in ToS byte)
- MPLS EXP (Layer 2, four levels via experimental [EXP] bits in MPLS tag)
- IEEE 802.1p (Layer 2, eight priority levels in 802.1Q virtual LAN [VLAN] tag)

If you apply an IEEE 802.1p to a logical interface, you cannot apply any other classifier types to other logical interfaces on the same PIC port unless you are configuring an intelligent queuing (IQ)/IQ2 PIC (J-series routers emulate IQ/IQ2 PIC functionality). Some combinations of BA classifiers simply make no sense and are mutually exclusive; for example, you cannot apply both an IP precedence and a DSCP classifier to the same logical interface at the same time. You configure a BA classifier at the [edit class-of-service classifiers] hierarchy:

```
[edit class-of-service classifiers]
lab@Bock# set ?
Possible completions:
+ apply-groups          Groups from which to inherit configuration data
+ apply-groups-except   Don't inherit configuration data from these groups
```

```
> dscp               Differentiated Services code point classifier
> dscp-ipv6          Differentiated Services code point classifier IPv6
> exp                MPLS EXP classifier
> ieee-802.1         IEEE-802.1 classifier
> inet-precedence    IPv4 precedence classifier
```

The following example shows a user-defined IP precedence type classifier named test, with a defined code point that maps to the BE forwarding class with a low-loss priority:

```
[edit class-of-service classifiers inet-precedence test]
lab@Bock# show
forwarding-class best-effort {
    loss-priority low code-points 000;
}
```

When desired, you can populate a classifier table with default values, which is useful when your goal is to modify only some code points. The best practice is to always have complete classification tables, even when all possible code point values are not expected. Even though unmatched code points map to the BE class by default, explicitly stating this with a complete code point mapping can reduce confusion down the road.

```
[edit class-of-service classifiers inet-precedence test]
lab@Bock# set import ?
Possible completions:
  <import>            Include this classifier in this definition
  default             Default classifier for this code point type
  test
[edit class-of-service classifiers inet-precedence test]
lab@Bock# set import default

[edit class-of-service classifiers inet-precedence ]
lab@Bock# show
import default;
forwarding-class best-effort {
    loss-priority low code-points 000;
```

The BA classifier is placed into service when you apply it to one or more logical interfaces:

```
[edit class-of-service interfaces]
lab@Bock# set fe-0/0/0 unit 0 classifiers inet-precedence test

[edit class-of-service interfaces]
lab@Bock# show
fe-0/0/0 {
    unit 0 {
        classifiers {
            inet-precedence test;
        }
    }
}
```

 Note that a BA classifier is applied to an interface at the [edit class-of-service interfaces <interface-name> unit <unit-number>] hierarchy, whereas multifield classifiers are applied to an interface at the [edit interfaces <interface-name> unit <unit-number>] hierarchy. Keep this distinction in mind to avoid confusion down the road.

Multifield classification

In the Juniper architecture, multifield classification is implemented via firewall filters, using a variety of Layer 2 or Layer 3 match criteria. We discuss general firewall filter configuration and capabilities in Chapter 6.

Suffice it to say that you use a filter to perform multifield classification by associating a set of match criteria to a then forwarding-class action. To activate multifield classification, the filter is applied as an input filter on an ingress interface. Because BA classification is always performed first, you can always apply a multifield classifier in combination with any BA classifier. In case of conflict, the forwarding class associated with the BA match is overwritten by the multifield classifier's choice of forwarding class.

This example shows a simple multifield classifier that classifies a specific UDP protocol and port combination to the BE class with high-loss priority, while all other traffic is classified as BE with the default low-loss priority:

```
[edit firewall filter mf_class]
lab@Bock# show
term udp_port_5555 {
    from {
        protocol udp;
        port 5555;
    }
    then {
        loss-priority high;
        forwarding-class best-effort;
        accept;
    }
}
term default {
    then {
        loss-priority low;
        forwarding-class best-effort;
        accept;
    }
}
```

Policing

Policers are generally considered to be part of the JUNOS software firewall architecture, in that you normally link to a policer as a result of a multifield classification match. Juniper also supports policers that are applied directly to protocol families, on a per-logical-interface basis. From a CoS perspective, interface-level policers are really useful only when you classify based on the incoming interface—that is, all traffic received on interface *<name>* is forwarding class *x*, which is a somewhat corner case, given that most interfaces are assumed to carry a mix of forwarding classes.

Ingress policing is a key component of the traffic conditioning that is needed in the DiffServ model to ensure independence between forwarding classes and the associated PHBs, and between users in the same class. You should deploy policing on the network's edges, as close to the traffic sources as possible. The goal is to limit the aggregate rate of all non-BE traffic to constrain it to a value less than the aggregate rate of the transmission resources associated with all non-BE classes. This ensures that the non-BE PHBs can be met locally and by subsequent core nodes, which generally are not burdened by any CoS-related policing.

Where possible, you should police on a per-class basis for *each* user—JUNOS software features such as highly scalable firewall filters, combined with ease-of-use features such as per-prefix counting and policing, generally make such a fine-grained level of policing practical. This policing ensures that a few dominant users are not able to monopolize all the resources of a given forwarding class by providing per-user isolation within the same class.

Traffic that exceeds the policer's profile can be discarded, reclassified into a different class, or marked for increased discard probability by altering the internal PLP. The latter approach provides a minimum level of service with the potential for increased delivery during periods of low network utilization. In contrast, immediate discard caps the user at ingress, which helps to prevent network congestion from occurring in the first place.

Here is an example of a firewall filter that both classifies and polices on a per-forwarding class basis:

```
[edit firewall]
lab@Bock# show
policer EF_policer {
    if-exceeding {
        bandwidth-limit 128k;
        burst-size-limit 2k;
    }
    then discard;
}
filter mf_class_and_police {
    interface-specific;
    term EF_classify {
        from {
            protocol udp;
            port 6000-6100;
        }
        then {
```

```
                policer EF_policer;
                forwarding-class expedited-forwarding;
            }
        }
        term other {
            then forwarding-class best-effort;
        }
    }
```

In this example, UDP packets with a matching port range (either source or destination ports) are directed to a policer named EF_policer. Traffic within the policer profile is handed back to the calling term, where it's classified as EF and accepted. In this case, any excess traffic is summarily dropped. The final term in the filter classifies all remaining traffic as BE, which is not policed in this example.

It may seem odd that the EF class is policed—with a rather Draconian discard action, no less—while the BE class, which appears to be less important, is left to run unchecked. The reason for this seemingly backward policer application is due to the related scheduling priority, which for the EF class is often strict, or strict-high, and can lead to the starvation of lower-priority forwarding classes when there is an abundance of this traffic. Ingress policing with associated discard ensures an aggregate limit on the EF class, which prevents this problem. Ironically, it's relatively safe to accept all the BE traffic users care to generate, because BE is generally assigned a low priority (other classes cannot be starved) and a low transmit percentage (so that it does not significantly impact other classes), thus excess BE is sent only when one or more of the other forwarding classes are not using their full bandwidth allocation anyway.

The addition of the interface-specific statement allows the same filter to be applied to multiple interfaces, with each such application resulting in instantiation of a unique policer instance. The end result is that each interface to which this filter is applied will be limited to a maximum average EF rate of 128 Kbps. The aggregate EF class rate becomes a simple function of policer rate multiplied by the number of interfaces to which the filter is applied. Note that omitting the interface-specific statement and applying the same filter to multiple interfaces results in a shared policer, which in this example would cap the aggregate EF class rate to 128 Kbps.

CoS policy

CoS policy is used in one of two ways: to provide CBF or to perform classification override. CBF allows you to specify one or more next hops based on a packet CoS classification. CBF is not demonstrated in this chapter, but a good configuration example is provided in the user manual, located at *http://www.juniper.net/techpubs/ software/junos/junos80/swconfig80-cos/html/cos-based-forwarding4.html#1171479*.

Classification override does just what its name implies. This capability can be useful when performing CoS-related testing, or it can mitigate negative impacts that can result from an upstream device that is suspected of generating improperly marked traffic. The configuration example performs an override of any previous classification including overriding any loss-priority setting, and it resets all matching traffic to the BE class:

```
[edit]
lab@Bock# show policy-options
policy-statement AF_override {
    term 1 {
        from interface fe-0/0/0.0;
        then class reset_to_be;
    }
    term 2 {
        then accept;
    }
}
```

The AF_override policy is used to identify what traffic is subjected to classification override; in this example, all traffic received over interface fe-0/0/0 is marked as belonging to a CoS-related policy class named reset_to_be:

```
[edit]
lab@Bock# show class-of-service
forwarding-policy {
    class reset_to_be {
        classification-override {
            forwarding-class best-effort;
        }
    }
}
[edit]
lab@Bock# show routing-options forwarding-table
export AF_override;
```

A forwarding-policy is created at the [edit class-of-service] hierarchy that identifies the policy class that is subject to classification override. In this example, packets marked as belonging to the reset_to_be policy class have their initial classification, whatever that might be, reset to the BE class. The forwarding policy must be applied at the [edit routing-options forwarding-table export] hierarchy to take effect. Such a policy configuration might temporarily work around issues with an upstream device that incorrectly marks all traffic as EF, resulting in EF class congestion and violation of the related service level agreements (SLAs). The group managing the upstream device will quickly find the motivation needed to correct the configuration error when its users begin to complain about poor performance stemming from suddenly getting nothing but BE treatment.

Output Processing

Output CoS processing stages include egress policing, rewrite marking, queuing/scheduling, and active queue management through RED-based congestion control.

Egress policing

Policers are, well, policers, and there is really nothing unique about an output policer versus an input one, other than the simple fact that the policing action now occurs after the route lookup, rather than before. To an external observer, there is no difference between the use of input versus output policers. Consider an input policer, unless you must police based on the result of route lookup—that is, based on the forwarding next hop.

Rewrite marking

The rewrite marking stage is a critical component of a scalable CoS design because it's one-half of the BA classification story. For scalability, multifield classification should be used only at the network's access layer, where the function can be distributed among the largest set of routers with the smallest average packet forwarding requirements. Packet rates near the core typically dictate the more efficient BA type classification; Juniper routers are capable of wire-rate BA classification in all scenarios, whereas heavy use of firewall filters can degrade forwarding performance.

You should think of your input BA classifiers as a mirror image of the corresponding rewrite marker. This is to say that for each entry in a given BA table, there should be a corresponding entry in the associated rewrite marker table, and that entry is normally set to the same value—this ensures that the node downstream makes the same classification decision as did the local node. The consistent classification at each node between endpoints is a critical component of the DiffServ model, which presumes a consistent PHB among all nodes in a DS region. Figure 9-12 shows the interaction between multifield classification, marker rewrite, and resultant BA classification.

The sequence numbers in Figure 9-12 take you from initial ingress processing (where a multifield classification is used at step 1), on to step 2 (where the ingress node uses a DSCP rewrite table to write a specific DSCP pattern, based on its ingress classification). In this example, we assume EF with low PLP, so the packet's DSCP field is written to binary 101110. At step 3, the downstream node (which is in the distribution or core layer) performs *only* DSCP-based BA classification. Note that Bock's DSCP classifier entry for the EF class with low PLP matches the same value as that used in PBR's DSCP rewrite table. The result, shown in steps 4–7, is a consistent classification, and therefore there is a resulting consistency in the PHB across each node in the path.

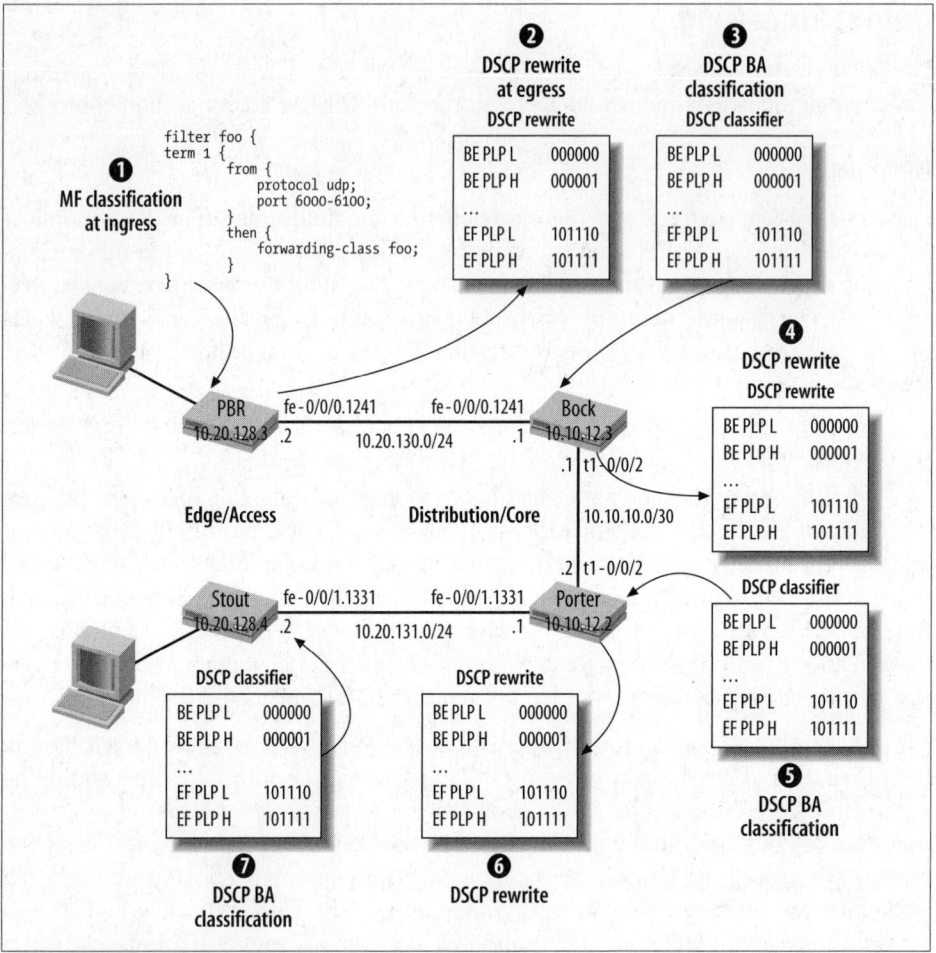

Figure 9-12. Multifield at the edge, BA in the core

The configuration example shown creates an IP precedence rewrite marker table that matches the example provided in the section "BA classification capabilities," earlier in this chapter.

```
[edit class-of-service rewrite-rules inet-precedence test]
lab@Bock# show
import default;
forwarding-class best-effort {
    loss-priority low code-point 000;
}
```

As in the case of BA classifiers, a rewrite table can be fully populated by importing any entries not explicitly defined by the user from the default set associated with that classifier type.

Scheduling and queuing

The scheduling stage determines when a given queue is serviced, in which order, and how much traffic can be drained at each servicing. Schedulers and queues are closely linked in the Juniper architecture. When you configure a scheduler, you can also control certain queue parameters such as maximum queue depth, and you also link that queue to one or more WRED profiles. You typically alter a queue's default size, which is based on the associated transmit weight, to control delay—larger buffer sizes favor less loss at the cost of increased latency.

Scheduling discipline. Both the M7i and J-series platforms implement a modified deficit round-robin (MDRR) scheduler. Because different transmit weights can be assigned to each queue, the algorithm is technically a modified weighted deficit round-robin (MWDRR) approach.

Scheduling is one area where the M-series and J-series implementation significantly differs. The M-series scheduling behavior is described here, along with general scheduling capabilities and concepts. "Differences Between J-Series and M7i CoS," later in this chapter, specifically calls out where the two platforms differ in scheduling behavior.

MDRR extends the basic deficit round-robin (DRR) mechanism by adding support for a priority queue that exhibits minimal delay. The deficit part of the algorithm's name stems from the allowance of a small amount of negative credit in an attempt to keep queues empty. The resultant negative balance from one servicing interval is carried over to the next quantum's credit allocation, keeping the average dequeuing rate near the configured transmit value.

An MDRR scheduler is defined by four variables:

Buffer size
> This is the delay buffer for the queue that allows it to accommodate traffic bursts. You can configure a buffer size as a percentage of the output interface's total buffer capacity or as a temporal value from 1–200,000 microseconds, which simply represents buffer size as a function of delay, rather than bytes.

The quantum
> The quantum is the number of credits added to a queue every unit of time and is a function of the queue's transmit weighting. In Juniper's implementation, a quantum is added 5,000 times per second (or once every 200 microseconds). The queue's transmit rate specifies the amount of bandwidth allocated to the queue and can be set based on bits per second or as a percentage of egress interface bandwidth. By default, a queue can be serviced when in negative credit, as long as no other queues have traffic pending. When desired, you can rate-limit a queue to its configured transmit rate with inclusion of the exact keyword.

Priority

The priority can be low, high, or strict-high, and it determines the sequence in which queues are serviced. The scheduler services high-priority queues with positive credit before it addresses any low-priority queues.

A strict-high priority queue is a special case of high priority, where the effective transmit weight is set to equal egress interface capacity. This means that a strict-high queue can never go negative, and therefore is serviced before any low-priority queue anytime it has traffic waiting. The result is a type of low-latency queuing (LLQ). Care should be used when a queue is set to strict-high to ensure that the queue does not starve low-priority traffic; a strict-high queue does not support shaping via the exact keyword. Normally, though, ingress policing/rate limiting is used to control the aggregate rate of traffic that can be placed into the strict-high queue. When you have two or more queues set to high priority (two high, or one high and one strict-high), the MDRR scheduler simply round-robins between them until they both go negative, or until the queue is empty in the case of strict-high, at which time the low-priority queues can be serviced.

Deficit counter

MDRR uses the deficit counter to determine whether a queue has enough credits to transmit a packet. It is initialized to the queue's quantum, which is a function of its transmit rate, and it is the number of credits that are added to the queue every quantum.

The Juniper implementation of MDRR scheduling on the M-series supports a basic deficit weighted round-robin (DWRR) scheduling discipline, or a combination of strict-priority queuing (SPQ) and DWRR scheduling when a high-priority queue is configured.

Scheduler configuration. You configure the scheduling and queuing stage by first defining a scheduler for each forwarding class used in your network. Schedulers are defined at the [edit class-of-service schedulers] hierarchy, and they indicate a forwarding class's priority, transmit weight, and buffer size.

```
[edit class-of-service]
lab@Bock# show schedulers
be_sched {
    transmit-rate percent 30;
    priority low;
    drop-profile-map loss-priority high protocol any drop-profile be_high_drop;
    drop-profile-map loss-priority low protocol any drop-profile be_low_drop;
}
ef_sched {
    buffer-size temporal 50k;
    transmit-rate percent 60 exact;
    priority high;
    drop-profile-map loss-priority high protocol any drop-profile ef_high_drop;
    drop-profile-map loss-priority low protocol any drop-profile ef_low_drop;
}
```

```
nc_sched {
    transmit-rate percent 10;
    priority low;
    drop-profile-map loss-priority high protocol any drop-profile nc_high_drop;
    drop-profile-map loss-priority low protocol any drop-profile nc_low_drop;
}
```

This example supports three forwarding classes—BE, EF, and NC—and each forwarding class's scheduler block is associated with a priority and a transmit rate. Priority support varies by platform and takes the form of strict-high, high, and low, with the J-series also supporting medium-high and medium-low priorities.

 The differences in scheduler priorities and behavior between M-series and J-series routers are discussed in "Differences Between J-Series and M7i CoS," later in this chapter. For example, although both platforms support a strict-priority scheduler setting, the effect is platform-dependent and significantly different.

The transmit rate can be entered as a percentage of interface bandwidth or as an absolute value. You can rate-limit (sometimes called *shape*) a queue with the exact keyword, which prevents a queue from getting any unused bandwidth, effectively capping the queue at its configured rate.

In this example, the EF scheduler is set to high priority and is rate-limited to 60% of the interface speed, even when all other schedulers are idle, through the addition of the exact keyword. Using exact is a common method of providing the necessary forwarding class isolation when a high-priority queue is defined, because it caps the total amount of EF that can leave each interface to which the scheduler is applied. Rate-limiting helps to ensure that the aggregate rate of EF traffic arriving at downstream nodes is not excessive, whereas ingress policing should limit the arriving EF to an aggregate rate that is less than the EF scheduler's transmit rate to ensure that the local node meets the associated PHB.

With the configuration shown, each of the three forwarding classes are guaranteed to get at least their configured transmit percentage. The EF class is limited to no more than 60%, while during idle periods both the BE and NC classes can use 100% of egress bandwidth. When it has traffic pending, the high-priority EF queue is serviced as soon as possible—that is, as soon as the BE or NC packet currently being serviced has been completely dequeued.

Assuming a somewhat worst-case T1 link speed (1.544 Mbps) and a default MTU of 1,504 bytes, the longest time the EF queue should have to wait to be serviced is only about 7.7 milliseconds (1/1.544e6 * (1504 * 8)). With higher speeds (or smaller packets), the servicing delay becomes increasingly smaller. Given that the typical rule of thumb for the one-way delay budget of a Voice over IP application is 150 milliseconds, this PHB can accommodate numerous hops before voice quality begins to suffer.

Delay Buffer Size

Notifications for packets pending transmission are stored in a delay bandwidth buffer that is sized according to the interface's speed and the platform's maximum delay buffer time. Both the M7i and J-series routers support at least 100,000 microseconds (or 100 milliseconds) of delay buffer time.

 When using low-speed interfaces, such as DSOs within a channelized T1/E1, you may want to enable IQ/IQ2 PIC large buffer support. With the q-pic-large-buffer knob in conjunction with supported IQ/IQ2 PIC hardware on the M7i, or with the channelized E1/T1 Physical Interface Modules (PIMs) for the J-series, you can increase delay buffer time to as much as 4 million microseconds (four seconds). The larger delay buffer can be useful on slow-speed interfaces due to the resultant increase in serialization delay, which is a function of link speed and MTU.

In this example, the delay buffer size for the BE and NC classes is left at the default remainder setting. This means that each is allocated a percentage of the 100-millisecond delay buffer based on its configured transmit weighting, and is allowed to grow into any unallocated buffer space, such as can occur when the sum of configured weights does not add up to 100%.

The formula to compute the actual delay buffer size is:

interface speed (bps) * delay buffer size (microseconds) = delay buffer size (bytes)

If we assume a J-series platform with a 100 Mbps Fast Ethernet interface in this example, the total scheduler delay buffer size is $100^6 * 100^{-3} = 1.25$ MB. By default, the BE and NC classes are assigned 30% and 10% of the scheduler's delay buffer, respectively.

In contrast, the EF queue has its buffer set to permit no more than 50,000 microseconds (50 milliseconds). When using a temporal setting, the maximum delay buffer size is computed by multiplying the interface speed by the configured temporal value.

Because the EF class has been assigned 60% of the transmit bandwidth, the default behavior would allocate 60% (60,000 microseconds) of delay buffer; by reducing the size of the delay buffer, as shown in the case of the EF class, you keep the higher transmit percentage while forcing a smaller buffer size. Setting a delay buffer that is smaller than the default results in a trade-off between the resultant increased probabilities of congestion-related loss versus a reduction in maximum delay and delay variance (jitter).

The scheduler block for each forwarding class also references WRED drop profiles, which provide active queue management to control congestion. Generally, you will have a different WRED profile for each forwarding class—for example, one aggressive profile that begins to drop at a lower fill, with a greater drop probability for the BE class, and another that waits until a higher queue fill before less-aggressive drops begin for the NC class. We will discuss drop profiles in "Congestion control," later in this chapter.

Scheduler Maps

Once you have defined your schedulers, you must link them to one or more egress interfaces using a scheduler-map. Scheduler maps are defined at the [edit class-of-service scheduler-maps] hierarchy.

```
[edit class-of-service]
lab@Bock# show scheduler-maps
three_FC_sched {
    forwarding-class best-effort scheduler be_sched;
    forwarding-class expedited-forwarding scheduler ef_sched;
    forwarding-class network-control scheduler nc_sched;
}
```

Applying a scheduler-map to an interface places the related set of schedulers and drop profiles into effect:

```
[edit class-of-service]
lab@Bock# show interfaces
fe-0/0/0 {
    scheduler-map three_FC_sched;
}
```

Defining scheduler blocks that are based on a transmit percentage rather than an absolute value, such as in this example, makes it possible to apply the same scheduler-map to all interfaces without worrying whether the sum of the transmit rates exceeds interface capacity, which results in a committed, but effectively ignored, CoS configuration that can be a real pleasure to debug. An example of this condition is shown for Bock, whose T1 interface cannot handle the 100 Mbps required when the rate is substituted for the same numeric value, but in Mbps!

```
lab@Bock# show class-of-service schedulers ef_sched
transmit-rate 35m exact;
buffer-size temporal 30k;
priority high;

[edit]
lab@Bock# run monitor list
monitor start "messages" (Last changed Oct 29 05:21:00)

[edit]
lab@Bock# commit
Oct 30 05:39:11  Bock mgd[2982]: UI_COMMIT: User 'lab' performed commit: no comment
Oct 30 05:39:15  Bock /kernel: RT_COS: COS IPC op 5 (SCHED POLICY DEF) failed, err 5
(Invalid)
Oct 30 05:39:15  Bock /kernel: RT_COS: COS IPC op 5 (SCHED POLICY DEF) failed, err 5
(Invalid)
```

```
Oct 30 05:39:15  Bock fwdd[2791]: COSMAN: queue 0 got tx_rate = 50000 kbps which is
too high for t1-0/0/2
Oct 30 05:39:15  Bock fwdd[2791]: COSMAN: policy update failed
Oct 30 05:39:15  Bock fwdd[2791]: COSMAN: queue 0 got tx_rate = 50000 kbps which is
too high for t1-0/0/2
Oct 30 05:39:15  Bock fwdd[2791]: COSMAN: policy update failed
. . .
```

A word on per-unit scheduling

By default, when you apply a scheduler to an interface, it takes effect at the port, or interface device (`ifd`) level. This is fine when the port in question is configured with a single logical interface (`ifl`), such as would be the case when running Cisco High-Level Data Link Control (HDLC) or the Point-to-Point Protocol (PPP). However, when the interface is partitioned into multiple logical units—for example, as the result of adding VLAN tagging—you need to apply a per-unit scheduler. A per-unit scheduler provides fine-grained queuing by creating a set of queues and an associated scheduler for each logical interface. M-series platforms require special IQ/IQ2 PIC hardware to support per-unit scheduling whereas the J-series achieves this via software, with no specific hardware needs.

You configure per-unit scheduling by adding the `per-unit-scheduler` statement at the interface level. Because some hardware combinations do not support fine-grained queuing, you should monitor the *messages* log when committing a per-unit scheduling configuration to make sure the configuration is compatible with installed hardware.

```
[edit interfaces fe-0/0/0]
lab@Bock# show
per-unit-scheduler;
vlan-tagging;
unit 0 {
    vlan-id 1241;
    family inet {
        address 10.20.130.1/30;
    }
}
```

Congestion control

The final CoS processing stage in the output direction is the WRED congestion control function. We described the reasoning behind active queue management previously—we'll reiterate that the general goal is to avoid the indiscriminate tail drops that occur when a queue reaches capacity, by sensing a queue that is beginning to fill and then randomly discarding packets from the head of the queue. The chance of actual discard rises from the first fill level and discard probability point until it reaches 100% at 100% fill. Configuring a discard profile with a fill/discard probability of 100/100 effectively disables RED on that queue. This is the default setting.

Configure WRED drop profiles

You configure a WRED drop profile at the [edit class-of-service drop-profiles] hierarchy. RED drop profiles are placed into effect on an egress interface via application of a scheduler-map. Recall that, as shown earlier, the scheduler-map references a set of schedulers, and each scheduler definition links to one or more drop profiles. It is an indirect process, to be sure, but it quickly begins to make sense once you have seen it in action.

Here are some examples of drop profiles, as referenced in the preceding scheduler-map example:

```
[edit class-of-service drop-profiles]
lab@Bock# show
be_high_drop {
    fill-level 40 drop-probability 0;
    fill-level 50 drop-probability 10;
    fill-level 70 drop-probability 20;
}
be_low_drop {
    fill-level 70 drop-probability 0;
    fill-level 80 drop-probability 10;
}
ef_high_drop {
    fill-level 80 drop-probability 0;
    fill-level 85 drop-probability 10;
}
ef_low_drop {
    fill-level 90 drop-probability 0;
    fill-level 95 drop-probability 30;
}
nc_high_drop {
    fill-level 40 drop-probability 0;
    fill-level 50 drop-probability 10;
    fill-level 70 drop-probability 20;
}
nc_low_drop {
    fill-level 70 drop-probability 0;
    fill-level 80 drop-probability 10;
}
```

In this example, the drop profiles for the BE and NC classes are configured the same, so technically a single-drop profile could be shared between these two classes. It's a best practice to have per-class profiles because ongoing CoS tuning may determine that a particular class will perform better with a slightly tweaked RED threshold setting.

Both the BE and NC queues begin to drop 10% of high-loss priority packets once the respective queues average a 50% fill level. You can specify as many as 64 discrete points between the 0% and 100% loss points, or use the interpolate option to have all 64 points automatically calculated around any user-supplied thresholds. In this example, only three points are specified. At 50% fill, 10% of PLP 1 BE and NC traffic is dropped; when the queue fill crosses 70%, the next discard threshold is activated and 20% of the packets are discarded. The 20% discard rate is maintained during an average queue fill of 70% to 99%. At 100% fill, tail drop begins, as the queue can no longer hold incoming notifications. The weighted aspect of the RED algorithm is shown with the configuration of a less-aggressive drop profile for BE/NC traffic with a low-loss priority.

A similar approach is taken for the EF class, except it uses a less aggressive profile for both loss priorities, with discards starting at 80% and 90% fill for high- and low-loss priorities, respectively. Some CoS deployments disable RED (100/100) for real-time classes such as EF because these sources are normally UDP-based and do not react to loss in the same way that TCP-based applications do. M-series platforms support WRED profiles based on TCP versus UDP, in addition to loss priority, which allows you to adopt a less aggressive RED profile for those application types that do not react to RED drop anyway. J-series platforms support WRED indexing based on loss priority only, but the J-series supports four drop priorities, so you can still index up to four RE profiles per queue. The examples shown are from a J-series, which forces the protocol to any.

Here's the be_high drop profile:

```
[edit]
lab@Bock# run show class-of-service drop-profile be_high_drop
Drop profile: be_high_drop, Type: discrete, Index: 27549
  Fill level    Drop probability
         40                   0
         50                  10
         70                  20
```

To provide contrast, the be_high profile is altered to use interpolate, which fills in all 64 points between 0% and 100% loss, as constrained by any user-specified fill/drop probability points:

```
edit]
lab@Bock# show class-of-service drop-profiles be_high_drop
interpolate {
    fill-level [ 40 50 70 ];
    drop-probability [ 0 10 20 ];
}
[edit]
lab@Bock# run show class-of-service drop-profile be_high_drop
Drop profile: be_high_drop, Type: interpolated, Index: 27549
  Fill level    Drop probability
          0                   0
          1                   0
          2                   0
          4                   0
          5                   0
          . . .
```

38	0
40	0
42	2
44	4
45	5
46	6
48	8
49	9
51	10
52	11
54	12
. . .	
78	41
80	46
82	52
84	57
85	60
. . .	
99	97
100	100

Differences Between J-Series and M7i CoS

The preceding section detailed the general CoS capabilities of the M7i and J-series routers, which for the most part are supported across all JUNOS-based routing platforms. This section calls out areas where the CoS capabilities differ. With so many similarities, the differences are easy to lose track of, but no matter how similar, they can have a pronounced operational impact if you do not understand and design for them.

Table 9-3 summarizes the differences between M7i and J-series CoS behavior.

Table 9-3. M7i versus J-series CoS behavior and capabilities

M7i	J-series
Per-unit scheduling only with IQ/IQ2 PIC hardware.	Per-unit scheduling on all interfaces.
DWRR scheduling to provide at least configured weight. Leftover bandwidth shared using priority-based round-robin. No scheduler-based shaping.	Strict priority scheduling with DWRR among queues of the same priority. Leftover bandwidth shared according to priority, and within a priority according to transmit weight. Supports scheduler-based shapers.
Two scheduling priorities: high and low. No support for LLQ.	Five scheduling priorities: strict-high, high, medium-high, medium-low, and low. LLQ support via strict-high (in 8.1).
Hierarchical shaping and shared schedulers with supported IQ/IQ2 PICs.	No hierarchical shaping. Shared scheduler via virtual channel construct.
No support for virtual channel CoS construct or adaptive shaping.	Supports scheduling into virtual channel, group to share a scheduler among a set of data-link connection identifier (DLCI)-based logical interfaces. Adaptive shaping based on forward explicit congestion notification (FECN).

Table 9-3. M7i versus J-series CoS behavior and capabilities (continued)

M7i	J-series
WRED based on TCP, UDP, and PLP. Head-drop-based, acts on packets as they are dequeued.	WRED based on PLP only—no TCP versus UDP indexes. Tail-drop-based, acts on packets as they are enqueued.
Sixteen WRED drop profiles per Enhanced FPC (E-FPC), two with original FPC.	Thirty-two WRED drop profiles per PIM.
Supports four queues.	Supports eight queues on all interfaces.
PLP based on classification/policer action only, no mapping of DE to PLP.	PLP based on classification, policer action, or in response to Frame Relay DE mapping.
Two loss priorities: high and low.	Four loss priorities: high, medium-high, medium-low, and low.
Maximum number of rewrite markers is not specified.	A total of 64 rewrite markers can be defined per PIM.

Table 9-3 makes it clear that there are quite a few operational differences between the ASIC-based M7i and the software-based J-series product line. We will examine the functional differences in detail in the following sections.

Per-unit scheduling

M-series platforms do not support per-unit scheduling unless the platform is equipped with an IQ-style PIC, in which case the actual queuing is moved from the chassis level onto to the PIC itself when you enable per-unit scheduling.

J-series platforms support fine-grained, per-unit scheduling on all interfaces through emulation of the on-PIC queuing capabilities of a Q-PIC.

In addition to logical unit-based queuing, per-unit scheduling also enables use of the shaping-rate command at the logical unit level to shape output traffic on all interfaces.

Weight- versus priority-based scheduling

One of the most pronounced differences between the M-series and J-series CoS functionality is the way in which the MDRR algorithm is implemented. The differences are so pronounced that you will typically find that an existing M-series scheduler configuration cannot be copied over and applied to a J-series, at least not if you expect similar CoS behavior!

The M-series weight-based scheduler. On M-series routers, the MDRR scheduler is based on guaranteed transmit weight with any leftover (unused) bandwidth divided on a prioritized, round-robin basis, which empties high-priority queues in negative credit before moving on to low-priority queues with negative credit. Figure 9-13 illustrates the operational characteristics of the M-series scheduler implementation.

Figure 9-13 shows a scheduler configuration supporting two priorities and three forwarding classes/queues. The scheduler first services all high-priority queues with positive credit, and then moves on to service low-priority queues with positive credit.

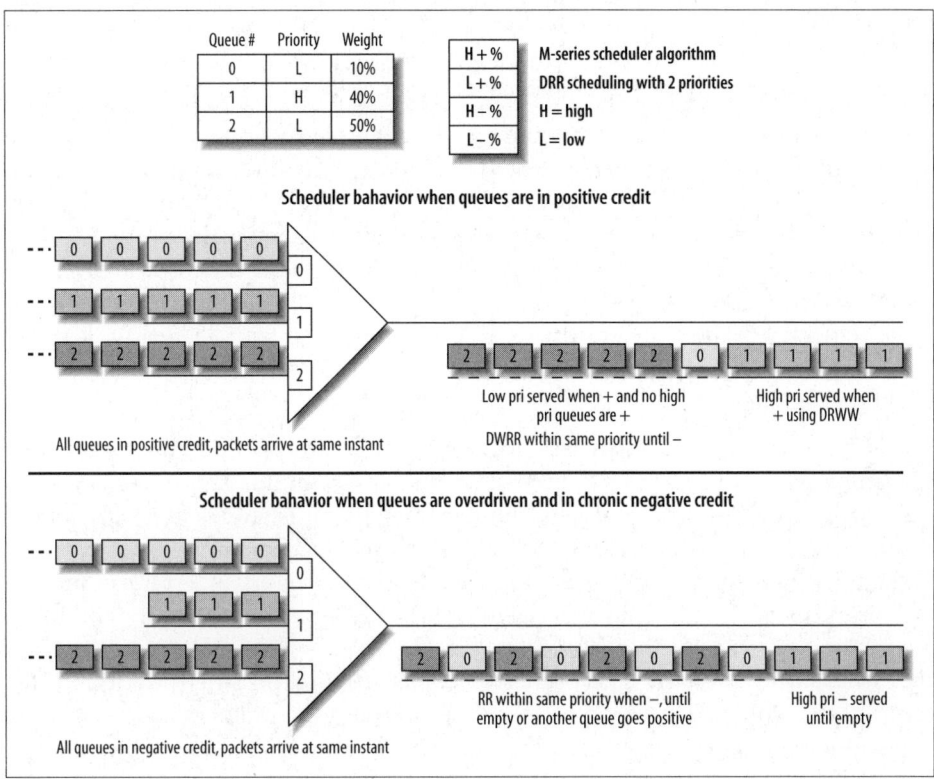

Figure 9-13. The M-series scheduler

Once all queues have been given at least their assigned weights, the queues go negative and the scheduler begins to allocate unused bandwidth. Because the dispatch of unused bandwidth is affected by numerous factors, including the number of priorities, number of queues, and average packet size, it is safe to say that the M-series algorithm for the allocation of unused bandwidth among negative credit queues is, practically speaking, nondeterministic. This does not mean the process is random, just that it is extremely difficult to predict how much extra bandwidth a given queue will end up getting.

The top half of the figure shows the scheduler's DWRR operation when queues are in positive credit. The scheduler services the high-priority queue until its transmit weight is satisfied, resulting in four forwarding class 2 packets, or 40% utilization in this example. Once the priority queue is in negative credit, the scheduler moves on to the low-priority level, which has two queues in this example. The scheduler services both of the low-priority queues according to their weight, resulting in one FC0 and five FC2 packets being transmitted.

The lower half of Figure 9-13 continues the example by showing M-series scheduler behavior among queues with negative credit. The leftover bandwidth is not allocated according to configured weight, but rather using a priority-based round-robin approach that empties one packet per queue, first emptying all high-priority queues and then moving on to round-robin between negative low-priority queues.

This approach can lead to some unexpected results, especially when queues are chronically overdriven and therefore tend to remain in negative credit, and when the average packet size differs within each queue. The lack of granularity in the per-packet round-robin handling of negative queues tends to favor the queue with the larger packet size. This can be most pronounced when that queue is also given the lowest weight, because it will be able to send the same number of packets as other negative queues at the same priority level. When combined with a larger packet size, such a queue winds up getting a larger percentage of the leftover bandwidth than you might first assume.

The M7i supports two priority levels: high and low. On the M-series, the strict-high priority is the same as high priority—the strict-high setting simply provides that queue with a 100% transmit weight, thus ensuring that it is always in positive credit and able to send. You cannot rate-limit a strict-high queue with the exact keyword because it always gets 100% of the interface transmit weight, and you can include only one strict-high queue in a given scheduler-map.

The J-series priority scheduler. The J-series scheduler is based on strict priority. In this context, the word *strict* means that each priority level at value n is considered a higher priority than level $n - 1$, and that the scheduler always services higher-priority queues before lower-priority queues, even if the higher-priority queue is negative while the lower-priority queue is in positive credit. This is a critical point, so it's restated differently, a few times:

- On the J-series, WRR/configured weight is honored only for queues at the same priority level.
- On the J-series, a high-priority queue can starve all other priorities unless it is rate-limited. The same goes for medium-high and medium, medium-low and low, and so on down the priority chain.

On a J-series, the strict-high setting is an actual priority level, making it, pardon the pun, *higher* than high. The strict-high setting is specifically offered to back up the LLQ feature, which is an 8.1 feature specific to the J-series.

A J-series strict-high queue cannot be rate-limited with the exact keyword. Instead, a policer is used to mark traffic above a configured limit as excess. Excess LLQ traffic is permitted only when all other queues have been emptied, meaning there is no interface congestion. The result is a queue that is always serviced as soon as possible, whenever it has traffic pending (the highest of all priorities, and only one strict-high queue is permitted per scheduler map), with a guarantee of at least the configured rate, while still permitting excess LLQ traffic when no other queues are congested.

If these differences were not enough to confuse the innocent, the J-series scheduler differs from the M-series by honoring configured weight when servicing negative credit queues at the same priority. As a side effect, you can configure shaping within a J-series scheduler. This shaping-rate can be less than the default 100%, but more than the configured transmit rate, which shapes the queue's output to the specified value while allowing limited used of unused bandwidth, as determined by the differences between the transmit and shaping rates.

Figure 9-14 shows the J-series scheduler behavior.

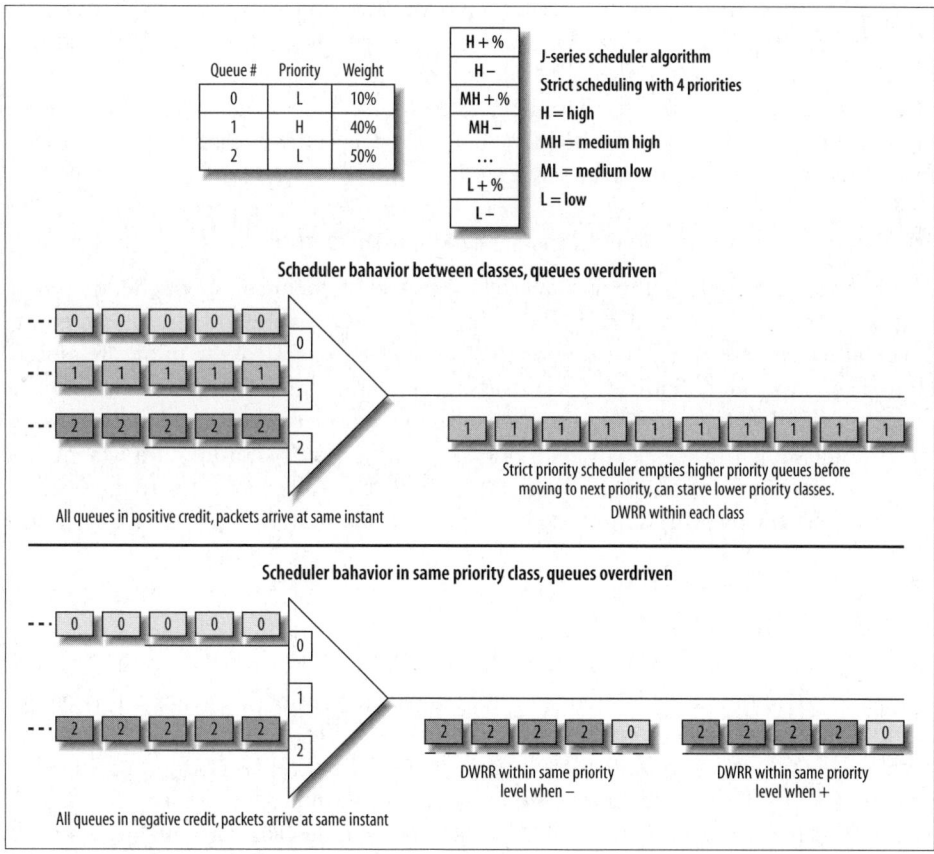

Figure 9-14. The J-series scheduler

The upper portion of Figure 9-14 shows the priority-based scheduling behavior, which results in the complete emptying of all queues at priority n before it moves to the next set of queues at priority $n - 1$. On the J-series, the configured transmit rate is significant only between classes at the *same* priority level. In this case, the higher-priority traffic associated with queue 1 is shown starving the two lower-priority queues.

To resolve this issue, you need to either rate-limit the high-priority traffic or assign all queues to the same priority level.

The lower half of Figure 9-14 shows how the J-series scheduler honors weight among negative credit queues at the same priority. Since no additional priority packets are pending in this example, the scheduler continues to serve the low-priority queues according to their weight, rather than using a simple round-robin scheme, as is the case with the M-series.

Although it's likely obvious, we are nonetheless explicitly stating here that, because of the differences in scheduler behavior, you cannot simply copy an existing M-series CoS configuration over to a J-series and just expect it to work the same way. Successful translation between the two scheduler models requires a complete understanding of the operational differences. The upcoming lab scenario provides an example of both an M-series and J-series scheduler that meet the same requirements, and therefore provide similar operational behavior.

Scheduler-based shaping to limit excess bandwidth usage

M-series routers do not support the shaping-rate statement under a scheduler. The only way to cap a forwarding class's usage of excess bandwidth is to use exact, which allows no excess bandwidth, or to use a policer to control the total rate of traffic in that class, which indirectly controls how much extra bandwidth it will use. In contrast, the J-series scheduler supports shaping above the configured transmit weight but below the line rate, which provides a guarantee of a minimum weight and a cap on some amount of excess bandwidth. By default, all schedulers are allowed to use all excess bandwidth, up to the line rate, unless limited by shaping-rate (J-series) or exact.

Scheduler priority levels

The M7i supports two scheduler priority levels: high and low. The strict-high setting on the M-series is no different from high, from a priority perspective. If you configure both a strict-high and a high priority queue, the scheduler serves each in round-robin manner until one or both go negative. The strict-high setting here simply prevents that queue from ever going negative by internally setting its transmit rate to 100%. As of this writing, the options for medium-high and medium-low are hidden in the M7i command-line interface (CLI), but you can configure and commit such a setting without any warnings. Note that even though the CLI displays the associated scheduler as having medium priority, in reality there are only two priority levels, with low and medium-low treated the same, as are medium-high, high, and strict-high.

In contrast, the J-series supports five distinct priority levels, with strict-high being an actual priority, not just an assumption of 100% transmit rate, as is the case with the M-series. On the J-series, you can define strict-high, high, medium-high, medium-low, and low priority values.

Hierarchical shaping and shared scheduling

M-series platforms with supported IQ-PICs (GE IQ2 PICs) can support both hierarchical shaping and shared scheduling resources. A hierarchical shaper is normally associated with the support of oversubscription and involves applying a shaper via the `input-shaping-map` statement at both the port and logical interface levels. The result is the ability to limit the input port rate to a value less than the port speed, and at the same time shape the individual logical interfaces based on transmit weights that are oversubscribed with respect to the (shaped) port speed.

A shared scheduler (or shaper) is a set of scheduling resources that is shared among multiple logical interfaces. This feature is designed to scale the platform by supporting large numbers of subscribers, on a per-VLAN basis, with a limited set of resources.

J-series platforms do not emulate IQ2 functionality, and therefore do not offer hierarchical shaping and scheduling in the same way as the M-series with an IQ2. Instead, the J-series use a virtual channel construct, which provides a close approximation of a shared scheduler or shaper. We describe J-series virtual channels in the next section.

J-series virtual channels

J-series routers support the notion of a virtual channel, which in the context of CoS is not a logical connection such as an ATM permanent virtual circuit (PVC), but instead a grouping of logical channels that share a common scheduler. We provide a virtual channel configuration example in the section "Virtual Channels," later in this chapter, so a detailed discussion is held until that time. For now, it is sufficient to say that virtual channels are designed to accommodate Frame Relay hub and spoke topologies by allowing a central site with a high-speed attachment the ability to schedule traffic into each DLCI based on some maximum rate, which is typically matched to the remote site's access rate.

RED behavioral differences

The M7i WRED implementation is head-of-line-based, which is to say that a RED decision is made at the time of packet servicing. This approach has the advantage of notifying senders of congestion sooner, but comes at the cost of allocating queue resources for a packet that is ultimately doomed. The M-series platform supports RED profiles that are indexed via protocol (TCP versus UDP) and loss status, for a total of four possible WRED profiles per queue.

The M7i can support up to 16 WRED profiles per enhanced (current) FPC.

The J-series WRED algorithm operates at the tail of the queue, as the notifications arrive rather than as the scheduler visits the next notification at the head of each queue. From a practical perspective, there is little operational impact to the different WRED approaches—we mention them here largely for the sake of completeness. As of this writing, J-series platforms support only a packet-loss-priority-based WRED index, supporting as many as four WRED profiles per queue. The trade-off in simplicity comes at the cost of not allowing a more aggressive drop profile for TCP-based traffic, which is sometimes desired as this type of traffic reacts best to implicit congestion notification, is normally not real-time-based, and has retransmission to recover from the loss, so no one is the wiser.

The J-series supports up to 32 WRED profiles per PIM.

Number of queues/forwarding classes

The M7i supports a maximum of four queues per logical interface. Note that on the M320 and T-series platforms, you can configure up to eight queues with certain IQ-type PICs.

J-series routers support eight queues on all interfaces. This obviously accommodates a finer-grained queuing model, but given the strict priority scheduler you will sometimes want to allocate additional queues to hold overflow traffic from other queues at various priority levels. These overflow queues are typically set to the same (low) priority level, and packets that wind up in one of these overflow queues are serviced according to the queue's assigned weight, but only when all higher-priority queues are empty.

PLP and adaptive shaping

M-series platforms support two PLPs: high and low. You can set the PLP using a policer, a multifield classifier, or a BA classifier. Adaptive shaping based on Frame Relay congestion notification is not supported, nor is setting the local PLP based on received DE bit status.

J-series routers support four PLP levels: high, medium-high, medium-low, and low. PLP can be set using a policer, a filter action, or a BA classifier as in the case of the M-series. J-series boxes can also map received Frame Relay DE indication into a loss priority using a `loss-priority-maps` statement. The following example shows a custom `frame-relay-de` map that happens to match the default, which is to say that received frames with DE = 1 are classified as having high PLP:

```
[edit class-of-service]
lab@PBR# show loss-priority-maps
frame-relay-de map_de_to_plp {
    loss-priority high code-points 1;
    loss-priority low code-points 0;
}
```

You can also apply a BA classifier to further classify traffic. The BA classifier occurs after any loss priority map and can overwrite the PLP, but only to a *higher*-loss priority value. The priority map supports only the high- and low-loss priorities, whereas the subsequent BA classifier stage supports all four priorities.

Adaptive shaping. Adaptive shaping is a J-series-specific feature that allows the use of two output shapers, based on the current congestion state of a Frame Relay network. Figure 9-15 shows the adaptive shaping feature in action.

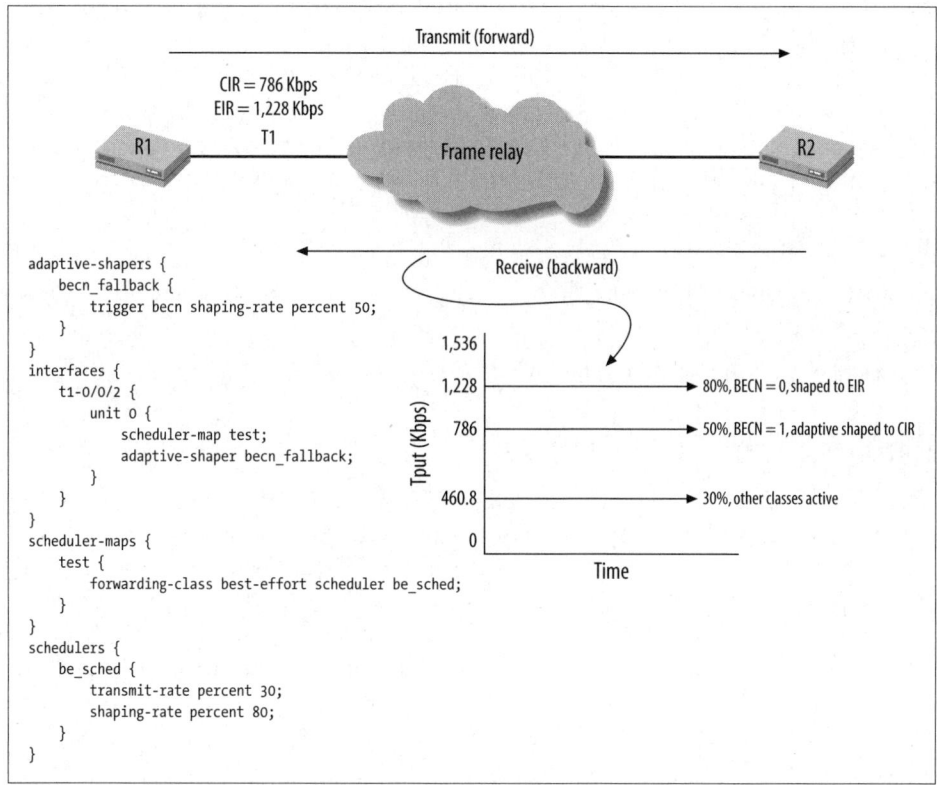

Figure 9-15. Adaptive shaping in response to network congestion

Figure 9-15 shows a pair of routers connected via Frame Relay. R1 is attached via a T1 interface and has a committed information rate (CIR) of 50% of T1 capacity, or 778 Kbps. The Frame service offers an extended burst through the excess information rate (EIR). EIR is not guaranteed, especially when the network experiences congestion, which is indicated in the forward direction by the receipt of frames with a set FECN bit, and in the backward direction with a set backward explicit congestion notification (BECN) bit.

The shaper for the BE class is set to 30% of the interface bandwidth. It is guaranteed only 30% of capacity, which equates to the 460.8 Kbps of throughput in this case. When other classes are not active, the BE class can burst to its shaped rate of 80%. The shaped rate matches the EIR parameter, which is good, because traffic in excess of the EIR can be discarded upon ingress by the network—the shaping configuration prevents immediate discard by limiting how much unused bandwidth the BE class can use. The maximum (EIR) rate is shown in the top throughput line and represents 80% of a T1's usable throughput.

An adaptive shaper is also configured and applied to the T1 interface. The adaptive shaper takes effect when the last frame received (assuming there is transmit traffic from R2 to R1) has a set BECN bit. When activated, the adaptive shaper enforces the CIR to prevent congestion-related discards within the network. When a frame is received with a cleared BECN bit, the adaptive shaper is removed and R1 is again able to send at the EIR, assuming that no other classes are active.

Number of rewrite markers

M-series platforms with E-FPCs do not have a known limit on the number of rewrite marker tables that can be defined.

J-series platforms are limited to 64 rewrite markers per PIM.

JUNOS Software CoS Defaults

JUNOS software comes with a set of default CoS settings that are designed to ensure that both transit and control plane traffic is properly classified and forwarded. The default CoS setting supports two forwarding classes (BE and NC) and implements an IP precedence-style BA classifier that maps network control into queue 3 while all other traffic is placed into queue 0 as BE. A scheduler is placed into effect on all interfaces that allocates 95% of the bandwidth to queue 0 and the remaining 5% to queue 3. Both of the queues are low priority, which guarantees no starvation in either platform.

A default WRED profile with a single loss point is placed into effect. The 100% drop at 100% fill setting effectively disables WRED.

No IP packet rewrite is performed with a default CoS configuration. Packets are sent with the same markers as when they were received.

Four forwarding classes, but only two queues

The default CoS configuration defines four forwarding classes: BE, EF, AF, and NC, which are mapped to queues 0, 1, 2, and 3, respectively. However, as noted earlier, there is no default IP classification that will result in any traffic being mapped to either the AF or the EF class. This is good, because as also noted earlier, no scheduling resources are allocated to queue 1 or 2 in a default CoS configuration. It's worth noting that the default MPLS EXP classifier table is capable of directing traffic into all four queues, but MPLS is not being deployed in this lab. Some very interesting and difficult-to-solve problems occur if you begin to classify AF or EF traffic without first defining and applying schedulers for those classes. Doing so typically results in intermittent communications (some small trickle credit is given to 0% queues to prevent total starvation) for the AF/EF classes; this intermittency is tied to the loading levels of the BE and NC queues, given that when there is no BE or NC traffic, more AF/EF can be sent, despite the 0% default weighting.

BA and rewrite marker templates

JUNOS creates a complete set of BA classifier and rewrite marker tables for each supported protocol family and type, but most of these tables are not used in a default CoS configuration. For example, there is both a default IP precedence (two actually) and a default DSCP classifier and rewrite table. You can view default and custom tables with the show class-of-service classifier or show class-of-service rewrite-rule command.

The default values in the various BA classifier and rewrite tables are chosen to represent the most common/standardized usage. In many cases, you will be able to simply apply the default tables. Because you cannot alter the default tables, it is suggested that you always create custom tables, even if they end up containing the same values as the default table. This does not involve much work, given that you can copy the contents of the default tables into a customer table, and in the future, you will be able to alter the customer tables as requirements change.

In a default configuration, input BA classification is performed by the ipprec-compatibility table and IP rewrite is in effect, meaning the ToS marking of packets at egress match those at ingress. The only rewrite table in effect in a default configuration is for MPLS using the exp-default table.

M-Series and J-Series CoS Summary

This section detailed the many common CoS capabilities of the M7i and J-series platforms, and it highlighted the few areas where their operation or capabilities differ. For example, the J-series has built-in per-unit scheduling capabilities, for which the M-series platforms require special IQ PICs. Also, the J-series scheduler is priority-based, which can be a common source of confusion for technicians who are familiar with the M-series scheduler behavior. Despite these differences, the use of a common code base and CLI, combined with relatively consistent CoS handling, means that the same set of commands are used to configure and monitor CoS operation.

The next section applies the knowledge gained thus far in a practical CoS deployment and verification scenario. Despite the fact that the lab sections are such fun, you should consider taking another break to think about the material covered to this point and to review any areas with which you are not comfortable.

DiffServ CoS Deployment and Verification

It was a long time getting here, but you have arrived, and you are now ready to rush headlong into a JUNOS software-based CoS configuration and verification lab. Figure 9-16 provides the network topology for the IP DiffServ CoS deployment scenario.

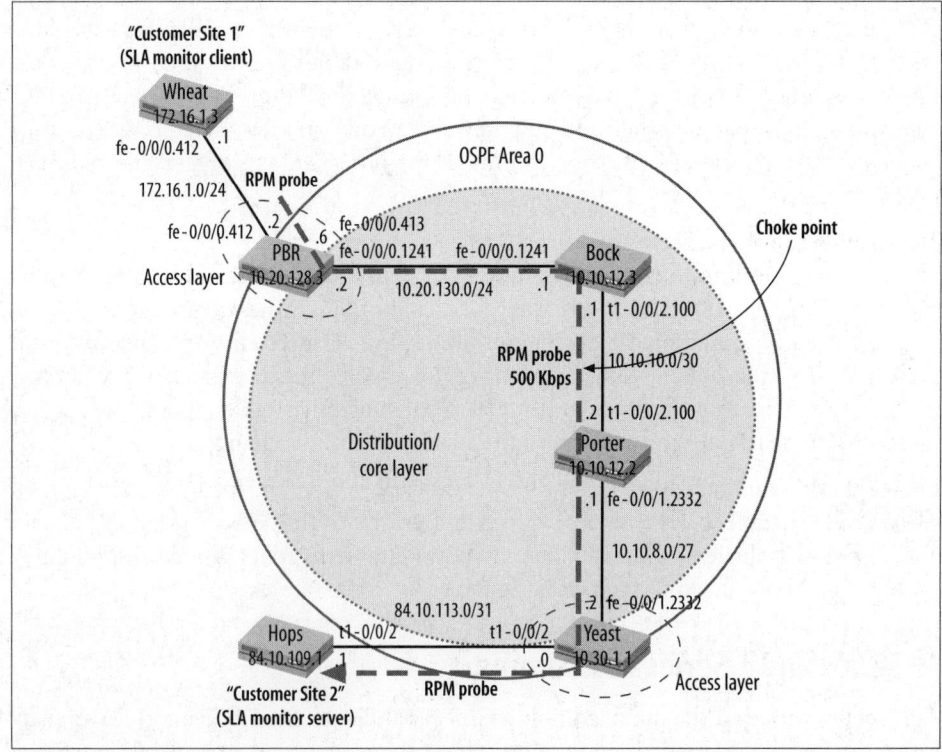

Figure 9-16. DiffServ CoS deployment topology

There are a few things to note in Figure 9-16. The test topology is somewhat simplified, and the test bed lacks the external test equipment needed to accurately measure and verify data plane performance. The first issue is not really a problem, because a workable CoS configuration is somewhat repetitive, basically involving the need to put the same configuration bits, consistently, in lots of places. As such, any network with a clearly marked edge and distribution/core devices services as a workable model with which to demonstrate CoS configuration and operational verification.

The subset of routers selected for the CoS topology was chosen in large part because of the (relatively) low-speed T1 interface interconnecting Bock and Porter. We noted previously that CoS matters only when link utilization begins to approach 80%. Obviously, with a given offered load, a slower link will exhibit higher utilization than a faster one—considering the lack of external traffic generators, it will be hard enough to congest a T1 link, let alone a 100 Mbps Fast Ethernet. In fact, to help stack the odds against a successful CoS demonstration, the T1 link between Bock and Porter is shaped to 500 Kbps. Although considerably less than the full T1 rate of 1536 Kbps, the shaped rate still qualifies as a broadband connection, which maintains a fair degree of realism.

Why Not Test CoS with Control-Plane-Generated Traffic?

The only true way to measure the impact of any CoS configuration is through data plane stimulation using a *reputable* external traffic generator. We stress the term *reputable* here because any device that is used to diagnose problems that might relate to a few extra milliseconds of queuing delay has to be spot-on accurate and believable; otherwise, you are likely to find that folks blame unexpected results on the test methodology and tools rather than on the router's CoS performance. Software-based traffic generators exist, and they are certainly better than trying to generate test traffic from a router's control plane, but a real router tester, one that is hardware-based, can easily cost tens of thousands of dollars.

The Juniper Networks architecture separates the control and data planes, and various rate-limiting and prioritization functions within the PFE and routing engine conspire against any attempt to generate either large volumes of traffic or test traffic with a high degree of time-based accuracy. To expand, internal RE-based rate limits control how much traffic the RE can generate using rapid or flood pings. The PFE also has a rate limit as to how many such Internet Control Message Protocol (ICMP) echo request packets it will even try to pass up to the host RE. If that were not enough, handling ICMP messages is considered a low priority within JUNOS software. Given the choice of replying to a ping or processing a Border Gateway Protocol (BGP) route update, a Juniper router always chooses the latter. This is not to say that the router will not reply to the ping; quite the opposite—it most certainly will reply, but only when it's good and ready. Although exceedingly reasonable, this behavior results in significant variance in ping response, even in a network that is largely idle in the control plane and is transporting very little data.

Putting issues with time-based inaccuracies aside for the moment, the JUNOS software control plane simply does not generate enough traffic to congest most modern network links. With no congestion, there is no way to consistently demonstrate any benefit to a CoS configuration.

Consider the output taken between PBR and Bock, when the *only* traffic in the network is periodic OSPF hellos and the ICMP test traffic itself:

```
[edit]
lab@PBR# run traceroute 10.10.12.3
traceroute to 10.10.12.3 (10.10.12.3), 30 hops max, 40 byte packets
 1  10.10.12.3 (10.10.12.3)  24.981 ms  6.937 ms  32.217 ms
```

The traceroute confirms that the direct 100 Mbps link is used between PBR and Bock, yet notice the large variance in ping response times, which is normal and expected given the Juniper design:

```
[edit]
lab@PBR# run ping 10.10.12.3 count 20
PING 10.10.12.3 (10.10.12.3): 56 data bytes
64 bytes from 10.10.12.3: icmp_seq=0 ttl=64 time=26.263 ms
64 bytes from 10.10.12.3: icmp_seq=1 ttl=64 time=10.116 ms
64 bytes from 10.10.12.3: icmp_seq=2 ttl=64 time=20.121 ms
64 bytes from 10.10.12.3: icmp_seq=3 ttl=64 time=10.126 ms
64 bytes from 10.10.12.3: icmp_seq=4 ttl=64 time=10.130 ms
64 bytes from 10.10.12.3: icmp_seq=5 ttl=64 time=44.755 ms
. . .
64 bytes from 10.10.12.3: icmp_seq=15 ttl=64 time=69.799 ms
64 bytes from 10.10.12.3: icmp_seq=16 ttl=64 time=10.124 ms
64 bytes from 10.10.12.3: icmp_seq=17 ttl=64 time=10.129 ms
64 bytes from 10.10.12.3: icmp_seq=18 ttl=64 time=10.162 ms
64 bytes from 10.10.12.3: icmp_seq=19 ttl=64 time=9.868 ms

--- 10.10.12.3 ping statistics ---
20 packets transmitted, 20 packets received, 0% packet loss
round-trip min/avg/max/stddev = 9.868/16.122/69.799/14.835 ms
```

The highlighted entries show the degree of response time variance considered par for the course in the Juniper design. Clearly, trying to validate CoS using rapid pings is simply not workable in JUNOS software, because you will not be able to generate enough traffic to reliably congest most links. Also, the test results will be all over the map, whether or not your CoS configuration is working, simply because the endpoints generating the test traffic treat it as a low-priority process, thereby breaking the CoS chain at its first link.

Cannot control classification of locally generated traffic

Generally speaking, unless you are running JUNOS software Release 9.0 or later, you have virtually no control over what egress queue locally generated traffic is placed into. The basic issue here is that when the RE injects traffic into the PFE, it bypasses ingress multifield and BA classification and simply does what it feels is best.

For example, a BGP transmission is normally placed into the BE queue (0), unless it is a retransmission, in which case it goes into the NC queue (3). As another example, you can generate a ping with any arbitrary ToS pattern, but this ping will be locally classified as BE and placed into queue 0. Downstream nodes can be expected to correctly recognize the packet's ToS field, because they see the traffic as transit.

The inability to apply your transit CoS actions to locally generated traffic is yet another reason why you cannot test a local nodes PHB with traffic sourced or received by that same node.

Enter resource performance monitoring

Juniper routers support an SLA monitoring feature that uses Real-Time Performance Monitoring (RPM) probes to measure performance, and if desired, to generate Simple Network Management Protocol (SNMP) alarms when performance falls below a configurable threshold. In the initial implementation, the RPM daemon ran as a user process in the RE—unfortunately, this resulted in inaccuracies when the RE CPU happened to be busy doing something else. Starting with Release 8.3, J-series routers can move the timestamp function into the real-time thread for significantly improved accuracy. Similar hardware timestamping functionality on the M-series requires use of the M7i's built-in services interface or an Adaptive Services PIC (ASP) on the M10i. The use of hardware timestamps does not cause the actual generation or processing of the RPM probes to be any more accurate, as the RE will still schedule the processing as it sees fit, but when the RE does get around to looking at the probe, the timestamp, already added at the hardware layer, allows for accurate performance measurements.

Although not nearly as definitive as a *real* traffic generator, the RPM service automatically tracks loss and summarizes one-way and round-trip delays, including jitter measurements, which beats the heck out of using pings and a pad of paper. Also, because the RPM service is instantiated on a pair of routers that are *external* to the CoS test bed, maximum accuracy can be expected. By *external*, we mean that Wheat and Hops simulate attached CE devices and are not taxed with any packet forwarding (other than the locally generated RP probes themselves) or any other processing task that could lead to large variances in RPM test probe results—these routers are not running *any* other services, are not running any routing protocols, and are not involved in the FTP transfer used to produce congestion. In this lab topology, Wheat and Hops function strictly as SLA monitoring devices—which is actually a realistic scenario, as some service providers deploy J-series routers in just such a capacity.

Configure DiffServ-Based CoS

Refer back to Figure 9-16 for the topology details of the IP DiffServ CoS scenario. You can assume that the network infrastructure is already configured with the interface addressing and single-area OSPF topology shown. A passive OSPF instance is enabled on the customer-facing interfaces at PBR and Yeast in order to provide reachability between their respective interface addresses. Your goal is to enable CoS in accordance with these criteria:

1. Perform the following multifield classification:
   - Classify ICMP timestamp messages received over customer-facing interfaces as EF to support RPM-based SLA monitoring for the EF class.
   - Classify Telnet traffic received over customer-facing interfaces as bronze (BR).
   - Classify OSPF in the core as NC.
   - Classify all other traffic as BE.
2. Perform DSCP-based BA classification at all other nodes, supporting the following forwarding classes and queue assignments:
   - BE, mapped to queue 0
   - EF, mapped to queue 1
   - BR, mapped to queue 2
   - NC, mapped to queue 3
3. Shape traffic on the Frame Relay link to 500 Kbps, in accordance with a 0 CIR service terminating in a 500 Kbps switch port.
4. Define and apply the following scheduler policy:
   - Provide BE at least 50% and allow use of excess bandwidth. Configure a PLP = 0 RED profile with 5% drop probability at 50%, and 20% drop probability at 80%, and a PLP = 1 RED profile with 20% drop probability at 50%, and 70% drop probability at 80%.
   - Limit BR to 10%; accept up to 1 Mbps/200 KB burst of BR from customers. Excess traffic must be treated as BE with high PLP by all nodes.
   - Provide EF at least 35% and ensure that it's serviced quickly to support low-latency applications. Traffic must not experience more than 30 milliseconds of buffering per hop.
   - Provide NC with at least 5% and ensure that it cannot be starved. The NC class must be able to use excess bandwidth.

At first glance, the long list of CoS requirements may seem daunting, but when tackled in small parts, the overall task becomes much easier to manage. CoS-related configurations tend to have a lot of common elements, which allows you to save time by configuring one node and then using that configuration as a template to bootstrap the configuration of the remaining routers.

Because the default CoS configuration offers scheduling support for the BE and NC classes only, it's a good idea to get as much of the CoS infrastructure up and running before you apply any classification that could result in traffic being mapped into queues other than 0 and 3. This avoids potential disruption resulting from traffic being assigned to a queue with no scheduling resources assigned.

This scenario calls for the use of DSCP classification. Previous sections detailed how the original IP precedence functionality is subsumed by the CS code point grouping. The default DSCP rewrite and classifier tables support the CS DSCPs. This means you can use the default IP precedence classifier at the network's edges while the rest of CoS is configured, including the DSCP BA classification and rewrite in the distribution and core layers. Stated differently, the goal is to enable CoS for all four forwarding classes, while maintaining the pre-CoS classification of only two forwarding classes in an attempt to minimize disruptions stemming from a network with partial CoS configuration. When all nodes are CoS-aware, MF classification is activated at the edge to enable use of all four forwarding classes.

Multifield classification and policing (task 1)

The first set of CoS functions to be configured are the multifield classifiers used at the edges to perform initial classification actions on the traffic received from customers. This is accomplished with firewall filters, which also provide a hook into the policing needed for the EF class in this example. Because the customer devices do not run any routing protocol, there is no need to support NC classification at ingress. If NC support is needed, it's a good idea to define explicit multifield classifier support, because the results of ingress BA classification can be overwritten by a multifield classifier, which could lead to NC being placed into the BE queue.

A multifield classifier and associated policer meeting the requirements of this example are configured at PBR:

```
lab@PBR# show
policer police_bronze {
    if-exceeding {
        bandwidth-limit 1m;
        burst-size-limit 200k;
    }
    then {
        loss-priority high;
        forwarding-class best-effort;
    }
}
filter mf_classify {
    term classify_ef {
        from {
            protocol icmp;
            icmp-type [ timestamp timestamp-reply ];
        }
        then {
            count ef_in;
            forwarding-class expedited-forwarding;
            accept;
        }
    }
    term classify_bronze {
        from {
```

```
                protocol tcp;
                port telnet;
            }
            then {
                policer police_bronze;
                count bronze_in;
                forwarding-class bronze;
            }
        }
        term else_be {
            then {
                forwarding-class best-effort;
                accept;
            }
        }
    }
}
```

The classify_ef term matches on ICMP timestamp-related messages, which are then classified as EF. This term supports the ICMP-based RPM probe request that is generated at Wheat, along with the probe replies generated at Hops. The classify_bronze term performs a similar function for matching Telnet traffic, except it also evokes a policer to limit traffic in this class. The associated bronze_policer is set with a traffic profile in accordance with the provided criteria for rate and burst size. Conforming traffic is handed back to the calling classify_bronze term, where it is classified as BR, while out-of-profile traffic is classified as BE with a high-loss priority. Both the EF- and BR-related terms evoke a counter action that can be used later when confirming that CoS handling and classification are working as expected. The final term matches on everything else for classification into the BE bin.

Although not shown, the same multifield classifier and policer configuration is also added to Yeast. Also, for reasons cited earlier, the multifield classifier is not yet placed into effect given that resources have not yet been defined for the EF or BR class.

BA classification and rewriting (task 2)

With multifield classification ready to be placed into effect, you move on to create the DSCP-based BA tables used by distribution and core layer devices for efficient packet classification. This example creates custom tables that are then populated with the defaults. This ensures full table population, which is a good housekeeping practice, given the required behavior of dispatching unmatched traffic into the BE queue. Note that unlike the default IP precedence classifier (which is actually in effect by default), the default DSCP tables support four forwarding classes: BE, AF, EF, and NC. This example replaces the AF class with a custom-defined class called bronze (BR). Once you define a forwarding class called BR and map it to queue 2, the classification and rewrite tables automatically associate any code point mapping to that queue as belonging to the BR class.

The default DSCP table entries do not support a high- and low-loss priority for BE traffic. To convey an ingress setting of PLP to other nodes, as required in this case study, you need to define an entry for BE traffic with high-loss priority. It is customary to use the least significant bit of a given BA field to denote loss priority, which is the approach taken here, such that the binary pattern 000000 is interpreted as BE with a low-loss priority, and binary 000001 indicates BE with a high-loss priority. Note how each entry in a BA classification should have a matching entry in the related rewrite table for consistent handling in downstream nodes.

The custom forwarding class definition and BA classification/rewrite configuration is shown at Bock:

```
[edit class-of-service]
lab@Bock# show forwarding-classes
queue 2 bronze;

[edit class-of-service]
lab@PBR# show classifiers
dscp dscp_classify {
    import default;
    forwarding-class best-effort {
        loss-priority high code-points 000001;
    }
}

[edit class-of-service]
lab@PBR# show rewrite-rules
dscp dscp_rewrite {
    import default;
    forwarding-class best-effort {
        loss-priority high code-point 000001;
    }
}
```

The forwarding-classes statement is used to define a new forwarding class alias called bronze, and to bind that alias to a queue number. In this case, only one non-default forwarding class alias is needed, and it is correctly mapped to queue 2; in a default configuration, this queue number is associated with the AF alias.

The user-defined DSCP BA classifier and rewrite tables are assigned names that denote their function and are initially populated with the code point defaults. A single modified entry is added to support the conveyance of loss priority for the BE class to downstream nodes.

The custom forwarding class definition and DSCP classification/rewrite tables are placed into effect on all noncustomer-facing interfaces at all nodes. There is no harm in applying these tables to the customer-facing interfaces; but there isn't much gain either. The multifield classification that will be used at the edge makes any BA classifier superfluous, given that the mf_classify filter is written to classify *all* traffic that is received and overrides the results of any BA classification anyway. A rewrite marker at the customer edge is generally used only when you wish to reset packet markings to some agreed upon default, or to help obfuscate the markings that are significant in the core, which could be used as ammunition in a CoS-centered denial of service (DoS) attack. In this example, packets are handed to the egress customer device, with whatever marking they were received with on the core-facing interface.

Here is the application of the user-defined DSCP classifier and rewrite tables, again at Bock:

```
[edit class-of-service]
lab@Bock# show interfaces
fe-0/0/0 {
    unit 1241 {
        classifiers {
            dscp dscp_classify;
        }
        rewrite-rules {
            dscp dscp_rewrite;
        }
    }
}
t1-0/0/2 {
    unit 0 {
        classifiers {
            dscp dscp_classify;
        }
        rewrite-rules {
            dscp dscp_rewrite;
        }
    }
}
```

At this stage, the custom forwarding class definition and DSCP BA configuration is replicated to all nodes. The DSCP classifier and rewrite tables are then applied on all interfaces in the CoS topology, with the exception of the customer-facing interfaces, which do not use a BA classifier or rewrite table.

Completing the aforementioned steps at all routers has accomplished a large portion of the needed CoS configuration. To recap, you now have a multifield classifier with policing on the network's edges (not yet activated, however), you have defined a custom forwarding class call bronze, and you created and applied custom DSCP classifiers and rewrite rules to support loss priority for the BE class on all noncustomer-facing interfaces.

The DSCP tables currently use default values for any entry not explicitly specified by the user because the import default statement is included. The default code points inherently support the IP precedence-based classification that is still in effect at the network's edges. The use of the default IP precedence classifier, combined with the inherent compatibility of IP precedence via the CS DSCPs, results in all traffic being classified into either the BE or the NC class at ingress, just as it was before you began the CoS configuration. Importantly, the ingress classification is maintained end to end even though downstream devices classify based on DSCP. It's noted again that the default scheduler configuration, which is still in effect, allocates resources only to the BE and NC classes, meaning that actions to this point should have had no operational effect on the network. It could be said that for the average core node, the only changes are a newly defined but still unused forwarding class and the use of DSCP rather than default IP precedence ingress classification. However, the compatibility between the precedence and DSCP tables means that the packets are classified into BE or NC with both the original and modified configurations.

CoS shaping (task 3)

Shaping, which reduces the maximum speed of an interface to some lesser value, is useful for a variety of reasons. You can rate-limit an interface using a policer, but this is problematic from a CoS perspective because the CoS components do not see the policed rate, but rather the rate of the interface itself. As a result, policing a 100 Mbps interface to 1 Mbps, and then configuring a scheduler with a 10% transmit rate, leads the scheduler to allocate 10% of 100 Mbps, not the policed rate of 1 Mbps. Shaping performed at the [edit class-of-service] hierarchy works around this issue, but is supported on only M-series routers when using IQ/IQ2 PICs. J-series routers support shaping on all interfaces because of their built-in support for per-unit scheduling.

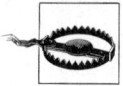 It is fortunate that we used shaping in this example. During testing, it was determined that a bug affecting buffer allocation (PR 236548) for IXP-based T1/E1 interfaces resulted in minimal benefit to CoS over the T1 interface, just where it was needed the most. The presence of the shaping statement corrects the buffer allocation issue, even when set to 95% of the line rate, and is a reasonable workaround for users on affected code. In addition to fixing bugs, Juniper is constantly enhancing the CoS capabilities of the J-series platform. Where possible, users should upgrade to 8.5 or later to get maximum CoS performance.

In this example, Bock and Porter are interconnected via a Frame Relay service provisioned with a 0 CIR, which terminates in a 500 Kbps port. Traffic sent in excess of the port speed results in immediate discard, so the T1 interfaces at Bock and Porter are shaped to a 500 Kbps rate. Later, when you apply a scheduler to these interfaces, the scheduler will allocate resources based on the *shaped* rate of 500 Kbps rather than the 1.536 Mbps physical rate. What follows are the Frame Relay interface configuration and related CoS shaping settings for Bock:

```
[edit]
lab@Bock# show interfaces t1-0/0/2
description Bock-to-porter;
per-unit-scheduler;
dce;
encapsulation frame-relay;
unit 100 {
```

```
    dlci 100;
    family inet {
        address 10.10.10.1/30;
    }
}

[edit]
lab@Bock# show class-of-service interfaces t1-0/0/2
unit 100 {
    shaping-rate 500k;
    classifiers {
        dscp dscp_classify;
    }
    rewrite-rules {
        dscp dscp_rewrite;
    }
}
```

The code highlights show the per-unit-scheduler statement, which is specified at the interface device level to back up the shaping-rate configuration at the [edit class-of-service interfaces interface-name unit unit-number] hierarchy. Also highlighted is the related Frame Relay configuration; in this case, Bock is set to a data circuit-terminating equipment (DCE) device to enable use of ANSI Annex D link integrity (keepalive) and PVC status polling from (default) data terminal equipment (DTE) Porter.

With shaping in place, the only CoS functionality yet to be configured is the scheduler definition and application to CoS-enabled interfaces.

Scheduler definition and application (task 4)

Up until this stage, the CoS configuration examples and steps shown are the same whether you are dealing with an M7i (equipped with IQ PICs) or a J-series platform. The differences in scheduler behavior between these platforms demand careful consideration—you will generally need different scheduler configurations for a J-series versus an M-series to produce similar scheduling effects.

The scheduling requirements of this scenario were decided upon in equal parts because they are typical, and because they help to demonstrate the differences in scheduling behavior. Table 9-4 summarizes the scheduling requirements.

Table 9-4. Summary of scheduling behavior for the DiffServ scenario

Class	Guaranteed rate	Priority; AQM; buffer	Excess bandwidth
BE	50%	Low; WRED based on PLP; N/A	Yes
BR	10%	Low; N/A; N/A	No/Yes, ingress policing sets excess as BE with PLP = 1
EF	35%	High; N/A; 30 msec	No
NC	5%	High; N/A; N/A	Yes

M-series scheduler definition. Table 9-4 shows that two priority levels are required to help expedite EF and NC traffic over BR and BE, and also details each queue's settings with regard to transmit weight, AQM (WRED)-enabled, buffer size restriction, and ability to use leftover bandwidth above its configured weight.

The following output shows an M-series scheduler definition that meets all of the specified requirements:

```
[edit class-of-service]
lab@M-Series# show schedulers
be_sched {
    transmit-rate percent 50;
    priority low;
}
ef_sched {
    transmit-rate percent 35 exact;
    priority high;
    buffer-size temporal 30k;
}
nc_sched {
    transmit-rate percent 5;
    priority high;
}
bronze_sched {
    transmit-rate percent 10 exact;
    priority low;
}
```

The EF class does not require use of excess bandwidth and is rate-limited through the use of the exact keyword. This limits EF traffic to its configured weight, which helps to ensure that the class is not oversubscribed in downstream nodes. Because both the EF and NC classes are set to high priority, you can guarantee that neither can starve the other. By not specifying strict-high, you also ensure that no starvation among low-priority queues should the nonpoliced NC class become overactive. This is because the M-series scheduler round-robins between high-priority queues until their transmit weight has been satisfied, and then moves on to service low-priority queues with positive credit.

The EF scheduler has its buffer depth manually set to 30 milliseconds of delay bandwidth (30,000 microseconds). This queue's relative high transmit weight combined with its high priority means it should maintain a low fill level anyway. The reduced buffer size and rate limiting leads to drops in the EF queue during periods of excessive EF traffic, even when all other classes are idle. In most cases, trying to accept overflow EF traffic—for example, by reclassifying the excess into another class or by configuring ever-larger buffer depths—results in more harm than good. This is because although you may reduce the overall number of EF drops, the resultant increase in delay and delay variance is often more disruptive to a real-time application than the outright loss such actions aimed to prevent. Worse yet, troubleshooting this type of problem is difficult when compared to the relatively straightforward task of correlating service complaints to excessive EF queue drops.

You cannot use the exact keyword for NC scheduling due to the requirement that it be able to use any excess bandwidth. Without some form of policing/rate limiting, it is possible that excess NC traffic could capitalize on all unused bandwidth, preventing both the BE and BR classes from being able to send traffic above their configured weights. Although it's easy enough to police NC traffic, this is seen as unnecessary here because:

- There is no requirement that the BE and BR classes must actually get excess bandwidth, just that they should be able to use it when it's available. Because M-series scheduling is not strict-priority-based, you need to worry about having high-priority queues affecting a low-priority queue's ability to get at least its configured weight.

- You are not accepting any NC traffic from customer/end devices, which means the only source of NC traffic is within the network, and you trust your network not to launch an NC-based DoS attack. The only source of NC in this network is OSPF, which unlike a full BGP table feed, does not generate appreciable volumes of NC. This is especially true for a small- to medium-scale network that is mostly stable.

The BR scheduler is also shaped to its transmit rate via the exact keyword; recall that ingress policing classifies excess BR as BE, so the BR class gets its excess bandwidth indirectly via the BE class.

J-series scheduler definition. Here is an example of a J-series scheduler that closely approximates the M-series example just described:

```
be_sched {
    transmit-rate percent 50;
    priority low;
}
ef_sched {
    transmit-rate percent 35 exact;
    priority high;
    buffer-size temporal 30k;
}
nc_sched {
    transmit-rate percent 5;
    shaping-rate percent 20;
    priority high;
}
bronze_sched {
    transmit-rate percent 10 exact;
    priority medium-high;
}
```

Because of the strict priority nature of a J-series scheduler, your first concern should be how to ensure that higher-priority classes do not prevent lower-priority classes from at least getting their configured weight. This is accomplished in a number of ways.

First the EF and NC classes are set to the same priority, which is the highest priority configured. This ensures that the EF and NC classes cannot be starved, and that they cannot starve each other. The EF class is again capped to its configured weight using exact. In this example, the NC class is *shaped*, rather than rate-limited, allowing it to use up to 20% of interface bandwidth.

Although not able to send at line rate, technically this meets the requirement given because the NC class is able to use excess bandwidth beyond its configured weight. This behavior differs from the M-series scheduler example, where the NC class could use up to 100% of available bandwidth when no other classes are active, but again, the behavior still meets all criteria specified.

Second, the shaped rate of 20% for the NC class, combined with the maximum 35% rate for the EF class, accounts for only 55% of transmit bandwidth. This leaves a guarantee that at least 45% of the bandwidth remains for use by the BE and BR classes. The BR class is serviced after the high-priority queues have reached their limits, but before the BE class due to its higher priority setting. Because the BR class is limited to a maximum of 10%, you can guarantee that the BE class will get at least 35% of interface bandwidth, using the following formula:

BE avail% = 100 − (EF max + NC max + BR max)
BE avail% = 100 − (35 + 20 + 10)
BE avail% = 100 − 65

The net result of all this interaction is that the BE class is *actually* guaranteed to get 35% of transmit bandwidth, despite its configured 50% weight. However, this reduction in BE capacity occurs *only* during periods of excessive NC activity, an event that should be both rare and transient. Besides, any negative impacts of the design are relegated to the BE class where folks are used to being treated poorly, so who will complain?

 This book is written to the 8.0 code base. Starting with Release 8.1, J-series platforms offer support for an LLQ feature that offers a fifth priority level called strict-high. You can define only one strict-high queue (well, technically, only the first one defined is actually considered strict-high). The exact command does not apply because a strict-high scheduler is automatically given 100% transmit. To prevent starvation when using the strict-high priority, you must define a policer (or as many as two) that limits how much traffic is guaranteed, that is dropped only when the egress interface is congested, or that is dropped regardless of egress congestion.

Refer to the JUNOS software documentation for Release 8.1 and later for additional details on the LLQ feature.

An Alternative J-Series Scheduler Approach

Although not demonstrated here, you can more closely approximate M-series sched-uler behavior by defining additional forwarding classes that are used to support over-flow traffic from higher-priority classes, and that are serviced only when no other *real* class has traffic pending. This approach is quite workable on the J-series, given the support of eight queues/forwarding classes.

Here is an example of the alternative scheduler approach:

```
be_sched {
    transmit-rate percent 49;
    priority low;
}
ef_sched {
    transmit-rate percent 35 exact;
    priority high;
    buffer-size temporal 30k;
}
nc_sched {
    transmit-rate percent 5 exact;
    priority high;
}
bronze_sched {
    transmit-rate percent 10 exact;
    priority medium-high;
}

nc_overflow_sched {
    transmit-rate percent 1;
    priority low;
}
```

Note that the scheduler now supports five classes. The new forwarding class is defined as nc_overflow, and the related scheduler is assigned a low priority, as well as a minimal transmit rate designed to minimize impact on the BE class. The NC sched-uler is now configured with an exact transmit rate of 5%. The support of excess NC is now backed up by a policer (not shown) that limits NC to 5% of the interface speed, which for Fast Ethernet would be 5 Mbps.

> To configure a policer that is based on a percentage of interface band-width, you must add the interface-specific keyword to the firewall filter that calls the policer.

Traffic exceeding the policer profile is classified as nc_overflow. Because the nc-overflow and BE classes are assigned the same priority, you ensure that excessive amounts of BE traffic cannot starve the NC overflow queue. This is a matter of choice here, as the requirements do not mandate that the NC class *always* be able to send more than its weight, just that it be able to when excess bandwidth is available.

With the alternative configuration, the NC class gets a guaranteed 5% as NC, and an additional 1% BE transmit rate, and can burst up to 100% when no other classes are active (95% of which will be treated as BE). At the same time, the BE class is now guaranteed to get at least 49% when all other classes are active and can burst to line rate when they are not. This configuration meets all requirements, and offers the additional benefit of allowing the NC scheduler to operate at 100% when other classes are idle.

Define RED Profiles

To complete the definition of the BE scheduler, you must define two drop profiles— one for PLP 0 and another for PLP 1 traffic—and link them to the be_sched scheduler. The drop profiles are shown, and the BE scheduler is updated to incorporate them. The same WRED configuration applies to both M- and J-series routers because the requirements do not expect drop behavior that is tied to TCP versus UDP, which is not supported on the J-series anyway. This is an example of WRED because two drop profiles are defined; in this case, the weighting is toward the internal loss-priority status of each packet in the BE queue.

```
[edit class-of-service]
lab@PBR# show drop-profiles
be_low_plp {
    fill-level 50 drop-probability 5;
    fill-level 80 drop-probability 50;
}
be_high_plp {
    fill-level 50 drop-probability 50;
    fill-level 80 drop-probability 70;
}

[edit class-of-service]
lab@PBR# show schedulers be_sched
transmit-rate percent 50;
priority low;
drop-profile-map loss-priority low protocol any drop-profile be_low_plp;
drop-profile-map loss-priority high protocol any drop-profile be_high_plp;
```

The remaining forwarding classes use the default RED profile, which effectively disables RED given that the only drop point specified is 100% drop at 100% fill.

Scheduler application

The J-series version of the scheduler definition is used in this example, in keeping with the J-series makeup of the enterprise routing lab. You apply a scheduler to an interface through a scheduler-map statement. Here is a working scheduler map and its application to all CoS-enabled interfaces, shown at node PBR:

```
[edit class-of-service]
lab@PBR# show scheduler-maps
```

```
er_cos_scheduler {
    forwarding-class best-effort scheduler be_sched;
    forwarding-class expedited-forwarding scheduler ef_sched;
    forwarding-class network-control scheduler nc_sched;
    forwarding-class bronze scheduler bronze_sched;
}

[edit class-of-service]
lab@PBR# show interfaces
fe-0/0/0 {
    unit 412 {
        scheduler-map er_cos_scheduler;
    }
    unit 1241 {
        scheduler-map er_cos_scheduler;
        classifiers {
            dscp dscp_classify;
        }
        rewrite-rules {
            dscp dscp_rewrite;
        }
    }
}
```

The scheduler-map links each defined forwarding class to a scheduling policy. When
applied to an interface, a scheduler is instantiated according to the combined policy
of the statements in the scheduler-map. Note that in this example the use of VLAN
tagging warrants the need for per-unit scheduling, which enables scheduling at the
logical interface—that is, at the VLAN level. By default, a per-unit scheduler assumes
the full physical interface bandwidth, unless it is shaped to a lesser value. The scheduler map shown will fail to commit unless per-unit-scheduling is also set at the
[edit interfaces interface-name] hierarchy, as shown:

```
[edit]
lab@PBR# show interfaces fe-0/0/0
per-unit-scheduler;
vlan-tagging;
unit 412 {
    description PBR-to-Wheat;
    vlan-id 412;
    family inet {
        address 172.16.1.2/24;
    }
}
unit 1241 {
    description PBR-to-Bock;
    vlan-id 1241;
    family inet {
        address 10.20.130.2/24;
    }
}
```

Activate multifield classification

Now that all forwarding classes have been defined with scheduling resources and you have a consistent BA classification scheme deployed throughout the network, it is safe to activate the previously defined multifield classification filter at edge nodes PBR and Yeast. The filter and related policer were defined in a previous step; all that is left now is to apply the filter in the input direction on all customer-facing interfaces:

```
[edit]
lab@PBR# show interfaces fe-0/0/0 unit 412
description PBR-to-Bock;
vlan-id 412;
family inet {
    filter {
        input mf_classify;
    }
    address 172.16.1.2/24;
}
```

The complete configuration

The various parts of the CoS configuration have been shown and discussed individually. Here is the complete CoS configuration at ingress node PBR, to give you a better perspective of the big picture:

```
[edit]
lab@PBR# show class-of-service | no-more
classifiers {
    dscp dscp_classify {
        import default;
    }
}
drop-profiles {
    be_low_plp {
        fill-level 50 drop-probability 5;
        fill-level 80 drop-probability 50;
    }
    be_high_plp {
        fill-level 50 drop-probability 50;
        fill-level 80 drop-probability 70;
    }
}
forwarding-classes {
    queue 2 bronze;
}
interfaces {
    fe-0/0/0 {
        unit 412 {
            scheduler-map er_cos_scheduler;
        }
        unit 1241 {
            scheduler-map er_cos_scheduler;
            classifiers {
                dscp dscp_classify;
```

```
                }
                rewrite-rules {
                    dscp dscp_rewrite;
                }
            }
        }
    }
    rewrite-rules {
        dscp dscp_rewrite {
            import default;
        }
    }
    scheduler-maps {
        er_cos_scheduler {
            forwarding-class best-effort scheduler be_sched;
            forwarding-class expedited-forwarding scheduler ef_sched;
            forwarding-class network-control scheduler nc_sched;
            forwarding-class bronze scheduler bronze_sched;
        }
    }
    schedulers {
        be_sched {
            transmit-rate percent 50;
            priority low;
            drop-profile-map loss-priority low protocol any drop-profile be_low_plp;
            drop-profile-map loss-priority high protocol any drop-profile be_high_plp;
        }
        ef_sched {
            transmit-rate percent 35 exact;
            buffer-size temporal 30k;
            priority high;
        }
        nc_sched {
            transmit-rate percent 5;
            shaping-rate percent 20;
            priority high;
        }
        bronze_sched {
            transmit-rate percent 10 exact;
            priority medium-high;
        }
    }

[edit]
lab@PBR# show interfaces fe-0/0/0
per-unit-scheduler;
vlan-tagging;
unit 412 {
    description PBR-to-Wheat;
    vlan-id 412;
    family inet {
        filter {
            input mf_classify;
        }
```

```
            address 172.16.1.2/24;
        }
    }
    unit 1241 {
        description PBR-to-Bock;
        vlan-id 1241;
        family inet {
            address 10.20.130.2/24;
        }
    }

[edit]
lab@PBR# show firewall
policer police_bronze {
    if-exceeding {
        bandwidth-limit 1m;
        burst-size-limit 200k;
    }
    then {
        loss-priority high;
        forwarding-class best-effort;
    }
}
filter mf_classify {
    term classify_ef {
        from {
            protocol icmp;
            icmp-type [ timestamp timestamp-reply ];
        }
        then {
            count ef_in;
            forwarding-class expedited-forwarding;
            accept;
        }
    }
    term classify_bronze {
        from {
            protocol tcp;
            port telnet;
        }
        then {
            policer police_bronze;
            count bronze_in;
            forwarding-class bronze;
        }
    }
    term else_be {
        then {
            forwarding-class best-effort;
            accept;
        }
    }
}
```

Most of the CoS configuration is common to all nodes, with the exception of interface names and the presence of multifield versus BA classification at customer-facing interfaces. Recall that T1 interface shaping is also in effect at nodes Bock and Porter. The t1-0/0/2 CoS configuration is displayed to show the shaping configuration, and the interface is set for DSCP-based BA classification and DSCP rewrite:

```
[edit]
lab@Bock# show class-of-service interfaces t1-0/0/2
unit 100 {
    scheduler-map er_cos_scheduler;
    shaping-rate 500k;
    classifiers {
        dscp dscp_classify;
    }
    rewrite-rules {
        dscp dscp_rewrite;
    }
}
```

Verify DiffServ-Based CoS

With the routers configured, it's time to verify that all this CoS mumbo jumbo actually amounts to a hill of beans, and better yet, happy end users.

Whenever you feel that a CoS-related configuration is not doing what you expected, it is a good idea to monitor the system's messages and cosd logfiles while you perform a commit. Some misconfigurations, or a configuration that requires some bit of missing hardware to function correctly, often pass the commit check while generating a log message, indicating that some aspect of the configuration is being ignored and for what reason.

A number of operational mode commands display CoS configuration, and more important, operational status. Most you can access with the show class-of-service command:

```
lab@PBR> show class-of-service ?
Possible completions:
  <[Enter]>          Execute this command
  adaptive-shaper    Show trigger types and associated rate for adaptive shaper
  classifier         Show mapping of code point to forwarding class/loss priority
  code-point-aliases Show mapping of symbolic name to code point bit pattern
  drop-profile       Show interpolated data points of named drop profile
  forwarding-class   Show mapping of forwarding class names to queue numbers
  forwarding-table   Show forwarding table information
  fragmentation-map  Show mapping of forwarding classes to fragmentation options
  interface          Show mapping of CoS objects to interfaces
  loss-priority-map  Show mapping of code point to loss priority
  rewrite-rule       Show mapping of forwarding class/loss priority to code point
  scheduler-map      Show mapping of forwarding classes to schedulers
```

```
        traffic-control-profile  Show traffic control profiles
        virtual-channel          Show virtual channel names
     virtual-channel-group  Show virtual channel group information
```

To save space, we will call upon the various commands when actually needed to verify CoS in the test network; we will cover the virtual channel and adaptive shaper-related commands in the next section.

You will also find that general firewall and the show interface queue commands come in particularly handy when checking CoS behavior—the former because firewall filters are used for multifield classification and to help debug CoS through match and count operations, and the latter because the resultant per-queue packet and drop counts provide critical information needed to verify classification-general queuing behavior. To display the queue statistics with show interface queue, you need an M-series platform equipped with an E-FPC, or any J-series platform.

Also note that you have the relative luxury of a test bed that, aside from OSPF, is completely quiescent unless stimulated in some way by user traffic, which is under your control. This makes it quite easy to confirm packet classification and general queuing behavior and to test the overall effects of CoS. This luxury is rarely afforded on a production network, and it is why it is always a good idea to stage a new CoS rollout in a proof-of-concept test bed where it is easy to validate and debug the results.

Confirm general CoS configuration

Things start at edge node PBR, where confirmation of the required forwarding classes is performed:

```
lab@PBR> show class-of-service forwarding-class
Forwarding class                    ID                Queue
  best-effort                        0                    0
  expedited-forwarding               1                    1
  bronze                             2                    2
  network-control                    3                    3
```

All four forwarding classes are present, including the custom bronze class. Good. You next verify CoS-related interface parameters for the core-facing Fast Ethernet interface at PBR with the show class-of-service interface command:

```
lab@PBR> show class-of-service interface fe-0/0/0.1241
  Logical interface: fe-0/0/0.1241, Index: 70
    Object            Name              Type        Index
    Scheduler-map     er_cos_scheduler  Output      21207
    Rewrite           dscp_rewrite      dscp        26780
    Classifier        dscp_classify     dscp        25819
```

The output confirms that the er_cos_scheduler map is in effect, and shows that the custom dscp_classify classifier and dscp_rewrite rewrite tables have been applied. The index numbers are used internally when referencing the various tables or scheduler map instances. The makeup of the er_cos_scheduler is now confirmed:

```
lab@PBR> show class-of-service scheduler-map er_cos_scheduler
Scheduler map: er_cos_scheduler, Index: 21207

  Scheduler: be_sched, Forwarding class: best-effort, Index: 54989
    Transmit rate: 50 percent, Rate Limit: none, Buffer size: remainder,
    Priority: low
    Drop profiles:
      Loss priority    Protocol    Index    Name
      Low              any         45889    be_low_plp
      Medium low       any             1    <default-drop-profile>
      Medium high      any             1    <default-drop-profile>
      High             any         14464    be_high_plp

  Scheduler: ef_sched, Forwarding class: expedited-forwarding, Index: 5877
    Transmit rate: 35 percent, Rate Limit: exact, Buffer size: 30000 us,
    Priority: high
    Drop profiles:
      Loss priority    Protocol    Index    Name
      Low              any             1    <default-drop-profile>
      Medium low       any             1    <default-drop-profile>
      Medium high      any             1    <default-drop-profile>
      High             any             1    <default-drop-profile>

  Scheduler: bronze_sched, Forwarding class: bronze, Index: 26824
    Transmit rate: 10 percent, Rate Limit: exact, Buffer size: remainder,
    Priority: medium-high
    Drop profiles:
      Loss priority    Protocol    Index    Name
      Low              any             1    <default-drop-profile>
      Medium low       any             1    <default-drop-profile>
      Medium high      any             1    <default-drop-profile>
      High             any             1    <default-drop-profile>

  Scheduler: nc_sched, Forwarding class: network-control, Index: 22188
    Transmit rate: 5 percent, Rate Limit: none, Buffer size: remainder,
    Priority: high, Shaping rate: 20 percent,
    Drop profiles:
      Loss priority    Protocol    Index    Name
      Low              any             1    <default-drop-profile>
      Medium low       any             1    <default-drop-profile>
      Medium high      any             1    <default-drop-profile>
      High             any             1    <default-drop-profile>
```

The output of the show class-of-service scheduler-map command contains a lot of gold. The various highlights call out key differences in the scheduler behavior for each forwarding class. For example, the BE class is associated with the two RED drop profiles that are indexed against packet loss priority. All other forwarding classes link to the default RED profile. The EF scheduler's high priority is called out, as is the time-based constraint on its buffer size.

The BR scheduler is called out for its `medium-high` priority, and its rate-limiting through use of exact. Excess traffic in this BR class is reclassified as high-loss BE, affording this class an indirect way of getting unused bandwidth. The NC scheduler has a 20% shaping rate, which caps that queue at 20% of the transmit bandwidth, even when all other forwarding classes are idle.

It's critical to note that in this example, the only mechanism that prevents higher-priority schedulers from starving lower-priority schedulers is the rate limiting achieved through use of either the exact or the `shaping-rate` keyword. As an alternative, you could also use a firewall-based policer to provide the isolation needed between traffic classes for a successful DiffServ deployment.

The RED profiles associated with the BE class are displayed:

```
ab@PBR> show class-of-service drop-profile
Drop profile: <default-drop-profile>, Type: discrete, Index: 1
  Fill level     Drop probability
       100                  100
Drop profile: be_high_plp, Type: discrete, Index: 14464
  Fill level     Drop probability
        50                   50
        80                   70
Drop profile: be_low_plp, Type: discrete, Index: 45889
  Fill level     Drop probability
        50                    5
        80                   50
```

The output confirms the 100%/100% setting for the default drop profile, and the two custom RED profiles reflect the required drop points, which differ for high versus low-loss priority BE traffic. You now confirm the DSCP BA and rewrite tables. For brevity's sake, we show only a portion of the classification table:

```
lab@PBR> show class-of-service classifier type dscp name dscp_classify
Classifier: dscp_classify, Code point type: dscp, Index: 25819
  Code point        Forwarding class               Loss priority
  000000            best-effort                     low
  000001            best-effort                     high
  000010            best-effort                     low
  000011            best-effort                     low
  . . .
```

The highlighted code calls out the custom portion of the table, which defines a high-loss priority BE class code point. With the basic components of CoS configuration confirmed, it's time to move on to confirm data plane behavior.

Confirm classification and queuing

Displayed here for reference is the RPM-related configuration for the SLA monitoring client Wheat. We will display and analyze the actual RPM probe status later in this section.

Verifying Control and Data Plane Consistency

Most of the operational-mode CoS commands shown in this chapter have a forwarding table counterpart. Generally speaking, the output of control plane versus data plane forwarding table-related commands should agree. In some cases, a configuration may be rejected, and as a result the changes are not pushed into the forwarding table. When troubleshooting a CoS problem, it's always a good idea to look for CoS-related log messages when you commit, and to confirm that the forwarding table state matches the configuration and related control plane displays. The following code sample taken from PBR shows that the forwarding table's view of the DSCP rewrite function does in fact match the configuration:

```
[edit]
lab@PBR# run show class-of-service forwarding-table rewrite-rule
Rewrite table index: 26780, # entries: 4, Table type: DSCP
FC#  Low bits  State    High bits  State    Medium    State    Medium     State
                                            Low bits           High bits

0    000000    Enabled  000001     Enabled
1    101110    Enabled  101110     Enabled
2    001010    Enabled  001100     Enabled
3    110000    Enabled  111000     Enabled
```

The output confirms that packets placed into queue 0, the BE queue, will have their DSCP rewritten to binary 000000 when classified as low loss, or 000001 when classified as high loss. The default DSCP classifier supports loss priority for the AF (now called bronze) and NC classes. User customization was required for BE loss priority support. The default settings for queue 1 (EF) result in the same marker regardless of PLP status.

```
[edit]
lab@Wheat# show services
rpm {
    probe test_cos {
        test icmp_timestamp_cos {
            probe-type icmp-ping-timestamp;
            target address 84.10.109.7;
            probe-count 2;
            probe-interval 1;
            test-interval 1;
            history-size 15;
            data-size 574;
            hardware-timestamp;
        }
    }
    probe-limit 100;
}
```

The RPM configuration defines a test called icmp_timestamp_cos that is owned by the test_cos entity. The target address specifies Hops's fe-0/0/0.3233 interface address.

Various other parameters are specified to control probe frequency, test count, and test repetition rate. In this case, we expect to see one probe generated each second, with two such probes constituting a test group and a new test beginning one second later. The service is configured to retain 15 history samples, which given these settings, represents approximately 15 seconds' worth of performance data.

The SLA probe routers are loaded with an 8.3 release to support timestamping within the real-time forwarding thread, which is enabled with the `hardware-timestamp` keyword. This significantly decouples general control plane activity from the processing of the probe message timestamps, thereby offering significantly improved accuracy.

No specific configuration is needed at the probe server because ICMP messages are replied to by default; the use of a TCP or UDP test probe requires a server configuration to ensure that a matching process is created to listen for incoming probe requests.

Multifield classification. CoS is configured in the test network in a symmetric, bidirectional manner. Still, it sometimes helps to think in a simplex manner when verifying CoS. Once proper behavior is verified in the Wheat-to-Hops direction, you simply perform the same steps, but now in the opposite direction to obtain full confirmation of CoS operation.

You begin confirmation of multifield classification at PBR because Wheat is the source of EF test probes. To ensure a clean slate, you clear all firewall and interface counters at PBR, and the interface counters at all other nodes; here are the commands issued on PBR:

```
lab@PBR> clear firewall all
```

```
lab@PBR> clear interfaces statistics all
```

After a few moments, you display the firewall counters associated with the `mf_classify` filter:

```
lab@PBR> show firewall filter mf_classify
Filter: mf_classify
Counters:
Name                                    Bytes        Packets
ef_in                                   56488             92
bronze_in                                   0              0
Policers:
Name                                  Packets
police_bronze-classify_bronze               0
```

The firewall counter and related policer output is a good indication that PBR is correctly classifying EF traffic. The presence of ICMP test probes is registering as EF traffic, and the lack of a Telnet session keeps the bronze class at zero. The police_bronze policer, which is called from the classify_bronze term, has a 0 count, indicating that no out-of-profile BR traffic has been reclassified as BE. Given that there is currently no traffic in the BR class, this too is in keeping with expectations.

To test the BR classification, a Telnet session is opened and subsequently closed, between Wheat and Hops:

```
lab@Wheat# run telnet 84.10.109.7
Trying 84.10.109.7...
Connected to 84.10.109.7.
Escape character is '^]'.

hops (ttyp0)

login: lab
Password:

--- JUNOS 8.3R3.2 built 2007-10-13 04:50:17 UTC
lab@hops> exit

Connection closed by foreign host.

[edit]
```

Correct multifield classification for the BR class is confirmed by redisplaying the counters associated with the multifield classifier:

```
lab@PBR> show firewall | match bronze
bronze_in                                 1986              35
police_bronze-classify_bronze                0
```

The bronze_in counter correctly reflects the generated Telnet traffic, which confirms multifield classification for BR traffic.

BA classification. There is no firewall counter for the BE class in this example. To verify correct BE classification, and for that matter general BA classification among all nodes in the forwarding path between Wheat and Hops, you examine egress queue statistics using the show interfaces queue command. In this example, the command is run on the customer-facing interface of egress node Yeast. Observing the expected queue statistics here goes a long way toward confirming that network-wide BA classification is working correctly.

 The 8.0R1 release used to develop this material was affected by a bug that incorrectly lumps the queue statistics for all locally generated network control traffic (OSPF) into a single logical interface for each physical interface device. Transit network control traffic (e.g., Internal BGP [IBGP]) is not affected. As a result of this issue, no NC count is observed on the core-facing interface at PBR, because the NC count was erroneously tallied against the customer-facing fe-0/0/0.412 interface, which is running a passive OSPF instance and should therefore reflect a 0 count for NC. PR 258580 is tracking this issue.

Before looking at the queue stats, we stimulate the BE class with some regular (not timestamp related) pings from Wheat to Hops. Recall that except for the background OSPF, this network is otherwise completely idle, which makes it easier to correlate test traffic to queuing statistics:

```
[edit]
lab@Wheat# run ping 84.10.109.7 rapid count 10
PING 84.10.109.7 (84.10.109.7): 56 data bytes
!!!!!!!!!!
--- 84.10.109.7 ping statistics ---
10 packets transmitted, 10 packets received, 0% packet loss
round-trip min/avg/max/stddev = 9.972/20.469/32.392/7.602 ms
```

Here are the egress queuing statistics for the customer-facing interface at router Yeast:

```
lab@Yeast# run show interfaces queue fe-0/0/0.3233
  Logical interface fe-0/0/0.3233 (Index 69) (SNMP ifIndex 41)
Forwarding classes: 8 supported, 8 in use
Egress queues: 8 supported, 8 in use
Burst size: 0
Queue: 0, Forwarding classes: best-effort
  Queued:
    Packets               :              10          0 pps
    Bytes                 :            1020          0 bps
  Transmitted:
    Packets               :              10          0 pps
    Bytes                 :            1020          0 bps
    Tail-dropped packets  :               0          0 pps
    RED-dropped packets   :               0          0 pps
     Low                  :               0          0 pps
     Medium-low           :               0          0 pps
     Medium-high          :               0          0 pps
     High                 :               0          0 pps
    RED-dropped bytes     :               0          0 bps
     Low                  :               0          0 bps
     Medium-low           :               0          0 bps
     Medium-high          :               0          0 bps
     High                 :               0          0 bps
Queue: 1, Forwarding classes: expedited-forwarding
  Queued:
    Packets               :             130          0 pps
    Bytes                 :           82160       5000 bps
  Transmitted:
    Packets               :             130          0 pps
    Bytes                 :           82160       5000 bps
    Tail-dropped packets  :               0          0 pps
    RED-dropped packets   :               0          0 pps
     Low                  :               0          0 pps
     Medium-low           :               0          0 pps
     Medium-high          :               0          0 pps
     High                 :               0          0 pps
    RED-dropped bytes     :               0          0 bps
     Low                  :               0          0 bps
```

```
      Medium-low            :                0              0 bps
      Medium-high           :                0              0 bps
      High                  :                0              0 bps
  Queue: 2, Forwarding classes: bronze
    Queued:
      Packets               :               36              0 pps
      Bytes                 :             2686              0 bps
    Transmitted:
      Packets               :               36              0 pps
      Bytes                 :             2686              0 bps
      Tail-dropped packets  :                0              0 pps
      RED-dropped packets   :                0              0 pps
       Low                  :                0              0 pps
       Medium-low           :                0              0 pps
       Medium-high          :                0              0 pps
       High                 :                0              0 pps
      RED-dropped bytes     :                0              0 bps
       Low                  :                0              0 bps
       Medium-low           :                0              0 bps
       Medium-high          :                0              0 bps
       High                 :                0              0 bps
  Queue: 3, Forwarding classes: network-control
    Queued:
      Packets               :                0              0 pps
      Bytes                 :                0              0 bps
    Transmitted:
      Packets               :                0              0 pps
      Bytes                 :                0              0 bps
      Tail-dropped packets  :                0              0 pps
      RED-dropped packets   :                0              0 pps
       Low                  :                0              0 pps
       Medium-low           :                0              0 pps
       Medium-high          :                0              0 pps
       High                 :                0              0 pps
      RED-dropped bytes     :                0              0 bps
       Low                  :                0              0 bps
       Medium-low           :                0              0 bps
       Medium-high          :                0              0 bps
       High                 :                0              0 bps
```

The display is long, but mostly repetitive in that the same information is repeated for each defined forwarding class. The command output displays the number of bytes/packets queued and transmitted—any differences in these counts indicate some type of drop. Tail and RED-induced drops are each counted, allowing you to determine the nature of any drops that happen to occur.

The sample output shows that no drops have occurred, and reflects that the 10 ordinary ICMP packets (nontimestamp-related) were classified as BE, that ongoing traffic is being tallied as EF (the RPM probes), and that 36 BR packets have been classified (the Telnet session). The NC queue is shown at zero, which is expected given that OSPF is not actively sending hellos on the Hops-facing interface. These results show that initial multifield classification at the edge is correctly conveyed among all nodes in the path via BA classification.

Confirm that all this CoS stuff actually does something

To this point the various operational mode commands have returned expected results, which imply that CoS is correctly configured and is up and doing its thing. But how can you really prove the benefit, especially when lacking external packet generation equipment?

The use of highly accurate RPM timestamp probes, combined with the relatively low-speed link (the 500 Kbps [shaped] between Bock and Porter), should allow a repeatable demonstration of IP CoS benefits.

No CoS benchmark

You begin by obtaining a no CoS network baseline. Later, when CoS is reenabled, the before and after results allow you to accurately gauge what effects CoS has in the current test bed. You remove CoS by stripping down the class-of-service stanza at Bock and Porter to leave only the 500 Kbps shaping rate. Remember, a CoS chain is only as strong as the weakest link, so removing CoS-aware packet handling at the 500 Kbps choke point should fatally weaken the entire chain. This actually provides an interesting demonstration of how a consistent PHB in *all nodes* is critical to overall CoS success—a single misconfigured router can ruin CoS performance on an end-to-end basis.

The modified CoS configuration is displayed at Bock:

```
[edit]
lab@Bock# show class-of-service
interfaces {
    t1-0/0/2 {
        unit 100 {
            shaping-rate 500k;
        }
    }
}
```

Meanwhile, back at Wheat, connectivity is confirmed and the RPM service is temporarily deactivated to ensure that a fresh history is created:

```
[edit]
lab@Wheat# run ping 84.10.109.7 rapid count 10
PING 84.10.109.7 (84.10.109.7): 56 data bytes
!!!!!!!!!!!
--- 84.10.109.7 ping statistics ---
10 packets transmitted, 10 packets received, 0% packet loss
round-trip min/avg/max/stddev = 9.884/22.581/39.944/9.170 ms

[edit]
lab@Wheat# deactivate services

[edit]
lab@Wheat# commit
```

An FTP transfer is started between Porter and Bock. Once the transfer begins, the RPM service is activated at Wheat:

```
[edit]
lab@Porter# run ftp 10.10.12.3
Connected to 10.10.12.3.
220 Bock FTP server (Version 6.00LS) ready.
Name (10.10.12.3:lab): lab
331 Password required for lab.
Password:
230 User lab logged in.
Remote system type is UNIX.
Using binary mode to transfer files.
ftp> mget ju*
mget junos-jseries-8.0R2.8-domestic.tgz? y
200 PORT command successful.
150 Opening BINARY mode data connection for 'junos-jseries-8.0R2.8-domestic.tgz'
(38563456 bytes).
0%   44888        14:19 ETA
```

With the transfer underway, the RPM service is reactivated:

```
[edit]
lab@Wheat# activate services

[edit]
lab@Wheat# commit
```

The probes are allowed to run for 15–30 seconds to get some statistical accuracy. The RPM history is displayed at Wheat:

```
[edit]
lab@Wheat# run show services rpm history-results
  Owner, Test                 Probe received          Round trip time
  test_cos, icmp_timestamp_cos Mon Oct 29 00:58:53 2007   266417 usec
  test_cos, icmp_timestamp_cos Mon Oct 29 00:58:54 2007   265010 usec
  test_cos, icmp_timestamp_cos Mon Oct 29 00:58:55 2007   237000 usec
  . . .
  test_cos, icmp_timestamp_cos Mon Oct 29 00:59:08 2007   268167 usec
  test_cos, icmp_timestamp_cos Mon Oct 29 00:59:09 2007   171237 usec
```

The display confirms some pretty long round-trip times, some as long as 265 milliseconds. Given that the one-way target delay for Voice over IP is only 150 milliseconds, it's safe to say there is no joy for IP telephony users in the current network.

You can display details about each probe, along with an average for all completed tests, using the show services rpm probe-results command:

```
[edit]
lab@Wheat# run show services rpm probe-results
    Owner: test_cos, Test: icmp_timestamp_cos
    Target address: 84.10.109.7, Probe type: icmp-ping-timestamp,
    Test size: 2 probes
    Probe results:
```

```
           Response received, Mon Oct 29 00:59:17 2007,
           Client and server hardware timestamps
           Rtt: 300236 usec, Round trip jitter: 283526 usec,
           Round trip interarrival jitter: 95059 usec
       Results over current test:
           Probes sent: 1, Probes received: 0, Loss percentage: 100
       . . .
       Results over all tests:
           Probes sent: 53, Probes received: 49, Loss percentage: 7
           Measurement: Round trip time
               Samples: 49, Minimum: 16710 usec, Maximum: 300236 usec,
               Average: 199529 usec, Peak to peak: 283526 usec, Stddev: 81768 usec
           Measurement: Positive round trip jitter
               Samples: 25, Minimum: 421 usec, Maximum: 283526 usec,
               Average: 82333 usec, Peak to peak: 283105 usec, Stddev: 75539 usec
           Measurement: Negative round trip jitter
               Samples: 23, Minimum: 1407 usec, Maximum: 280411 usec,
               Average: 88507 usec, Peak to peak: 279004 usec, Stddev: 71908 usec
```

The highlights call out that some probes are being lost, and that the average round-trip delay is more than 199 milliseconds. Note that average one-way jitter is rather large at some 82 milliseconds.

The CoS benchmark

OK, drum roll please…. A lot of work has led up to this point, and now it is time for the CoS rubber to meet the road, as it were. You restore the CoS configuration at Bock and Porter, and again deactivate the RPM service at Wheat to reset for a new test.

A new FTP session is started between Porter and Bock:

```
[edit]
lab@Porter# run ftp 10.10.12.3
Connected to 10.10.12.3.
220 Bock FTP server (Version 6.00LS) ready.
. . .
mget junos-jseries-8.0R2.8-domestic.tgz? y
200 PORT command successful.
150 Opening BINARY mode data connection for 'junos-jseries-8.0R2.8-domestic.tgz'
(38563456 bytes).
  0%  31856        40:12 ETA
```

With the new FTP session underway, the RPM service is again activated at Wheat:

```
[edit]
lab@Wheat# activate services

[edit]
lab@Wheat# commit
```

As before, we again wait 30 seconds or so to allow some RPM statistics to accumulate. After a long 30 seconds, the results are displayed:

```
[edit]
lab@Wheat# run show services rpm history-results
  Owner, Test                     Probe received              Round trip time
  test_cos, icmp_timestamp_cos Mon Oct 29 01:08:52 2007     17236 usec
  test_cos, icmp_timestamp_cos Mon Oct 29 01:08:53 2007     20896 usec
  . . .
  test_cos, icmp_timestamp_cos Mon Oct 29 01:09:06 2007     17769 usec
  test_cos, icmp_timestamp_cos Mon Oct 29 01:09:07 2007     18294 usec
  test_cos, icmp_timestamp_cos Mon Oct 29 01:09:08 2007     19068 usec
```

Well, the history results are far, far better than observed in the no-CoS benchmark. The round-trip delays now average only 18 milliseconds, as opposed to the 200+ result observed with no CoS. Once again, probe details are displayed:

```
[edit]
lab@Wheat# run show services rpm probe-results
    Owner: test_cos, Test: icmp_timestamp_cos
    Target address: 84.10.109.7, Probe type: icmp-ping-timestamp,
    Test size: 2 probes
    Probe results:
      Response received, Mon Oct 29 01:09:12 2007,
      Client and server hardware timestamps
      Rtt: 24557 usec, Round trip jitter: -13326 usec,
      Round trip interarrival jitter: 8125 usec
    Results over current test:
      Probes sent: 2, Probes received: 2, Loss percentage: 0
      Measurement: Round trip time
        Samples: 2, Minimum: 24557 usec, Maximum: 37883 usec,
        Average: 31220 usec, Peak to peak: 13326 usec, Stddev: 6663 usec
    . . .
    Results over all tests:
      Probes sent: 58, Probes received: 58, Loss percentage: 0
      Measurement: Round trip time
        Samples: 58, Minimum: 16455 usec, Maximum: 44654 usec,
        Average: 22455 usec, Peak to peak: 28199 usec, Stddev: 7167 usec
      Measurement: Positive round trip jitter
        Samples: 28, Minimum: 506 usec, Maximum: 26628 usec, Average: 8293 usec,
        Peak to peak: 26122 usec, Stddev: 8134 usec
      Measurement: Negative round trip jitter
        Samples: 29, Minimum: 7 usec, Maximum: 25318 usec, Average: 7781 usec,
        Peak to peak: 25311 usec, Stddev: 6889 usec
```

The probe details confirm that CoS has made a dramatic impact on network performance, at least when congestion is present and you are a member of the EF class! The average round-trip time is 22 milliseconds and the average one-way jitter is now only 8 milliseconds. A quick look at Bock's T1 interface stats confirms that all drops are confined to the BE class, and that the drops stem from the low-loss priority RED profile:

```
lab@Bock# run show interfaces queue t1-0/0/2.100
  Logical interface t1-0/0/2.100 (Index 69) (SNMP ifIndex 39)
Forwarding classes: 8 supported, 8 in use
```

```
Egress queues: 8 supported, 8 in use
Burst size: 0
Queue: 0, Forwarding classes: best-effort
  Queued:
    Packets            :        32519          0 pps
    Bytes              :     48570458          0 bps
  Transmitted:
    Packets            :        30047          0 pps
    Bytes              :     44852756          0 bps
    Tail-dropped packets :          0          0 pps
    RED-dropped packets  :       2472          0 pps
    Low                :         2472          0 pps
    Medium-low         :            0          0 pps
    Medium-high        :            0          0 pps
    High               :            0          0 pps
```

Note that the total queued versus transmitted packet counters for the BE class differ by the same number as displayed under RED drops. This confirms that RED is kicking in when the BE queue begins to fill. The lack of tail drops implies that the TCP-based FTP source correctly sensed the loss as an indication of congestion, and began to slow down the rate of traffic by reducing the window size.

Comparing pre- and post-CoS results leaves little doubt that JUNOS software CoS works. The only question that remains is "Why are you still here, reading this, when you should be adding CoS to your network, *now*?"

DiffServ Deployment Summary

This section demonstrated how Juniper Networks routers are configured to provide end-to-end CoS based on the DiffServ model. This involves the use of multifield classification at the network's edges, and custom BA classification in the core to convey loss priority for the BE class.

The scenario also demonstrated three different approaches to scheduling, two of which were based on the use of the M-series or J-series platform, and the third simply an alternative J-series approach that made use of an extra queue for handling overflow traffic.

We demonstrated the use of shaping, policing, and rate limiting to preserve class isolation, as well as the operational mode commands that allow you to confirm proper CoS behavior and operation. We proved that the JUNOS software CoS solution works through the use of external LSA monitoring probes that show a clear benefit to the CoS configuration when link congestion occurred.

The next section details specific J-series CoS capabilities that are designed to enhance interworking with Frame Relay. You should make sure you are comfortable with the configuration and confirmation examples used in this section before proceeding.

Displaying J-Series Tail Drops

Currently, the CoS statistics obtained via the CLI show interfaces queue command on a J-series router tally *both* RED and tail drops under the RED-dropped packets counter, which results in a constant 0 value for tail drops. This issue was tracked under PR 230928 and has been fixed, starting with the 8.2R4 release. The only way to view tail drops in previous code releases is to connect to the fwdd daemon to issue the show outq statistics command. The output displays the cumulative tail drops for all enabled interfaces:

```
[edit]
lab@Bock# run start shell
% su
Password:
root@Bock% vty fwdd

BSD platform (Pentium processor, 84MB memory, 8192KB flash)

FWDD(Bock vty)# show outq statistics

Number of packets queued in outq queues:      70412
Number of txdone callbacks:                    176652
Red drops:                 0

    Tail drops:                  0

Error counters:
        Invalid vctable base in packet enqueue:      0
        Bad result buffers:         0
        Queue not ready:            0
        Empty queue schedule:       0
        Transmit errors:               0
        Result stats increment errors:     0
        Invalid outq ifl index errors:     0
        Invalid txdone callbacks:          0
        Invalid requests for vctable base:      1

Ifl             Pkts In     Bytes In      Pkts Tx     Bytes Tx
---             -------     --------      -------     --------
fe-0/0/0.1241    79672      45260412       79672      45260412
t1-0/0/2.100     96980      45119122       96980      45119122
t1-0/0/2.100         0             0           0             0
```

J-Series Adaptive Shapers and Virtual Channels

This section focuses on J-series-specific CoS capabilities that are designed to work with Frame Relay. The virtual channel and adaptive shaping features help to optimize Frame Relay-based transport. Note that currently you cannot combine the functionality of an adaptive shaper with that of a virtual channel.

Configure Adaptive Shaping

Recall that Bock and Porter are connected via a 0 CIR Frame Relay service terminating in a 500 Kbps port. With the newly added DiffServ-based CoS infrastructure now in place, the idea of a 0 CIR service has been revisited. The result is a decision to pay extra for a guaranteed CIR of 256 Kbps, with the ability to burst to port speed via an EIR of 244 Kbps (CIR + EIR = port speed).

Simply configuring a scheduler or shaper that allows the router to send at maximum speed, all the time, is problematic because during network congestion only the CIR traffic is guaranteed for delivery. Ideally, you want to send at the EIR rate *only* when the network is not congested, and then fall back to the CIR when congestion is detected, in an effort to ensure that congestion-induced discards do not negate your CoS SLAs. This capability is exactly what adaptive shaping on J-series routers provides.

The configurations at Bock and Porter are updated to support adaptive shaping. The modified configuration at Bock is shown:

```
[edit class-of-service]
lab@Bock# show adaptive-shapers
becn_shaper {
    trigger becn shaping-rate 256k;
}

[edit class-of-service]
lab@Bock# show interfaces t1-0/0/2
unit 100 {
    scheduler-map er_cos_scheduler;
    adaptive-shaper becn_shaper;
    shaping-rate 500k;
    classifiers {
        dscp dscp_classify;
    }
    rewrite-rules {
        dscp dscp_rewrite;
    }
}
```

The changes to the configuration are highlighted, and they show the definition of an adaptive shaper called becn_shaper. The adaptive shaper is set to trigger on receipt of a set BECN bit, at which point the scheduler begins to shape to 256 Kbps. This rate matches the service's CIR, which prevents discards and the resulting impact to your CoS SLA. When the last frame received has a cleared BECN, the interface begins to schedule back into the 500 Kbps rate.

Here, use the show class-of-service interface and show class-of-service adaptive-shaper commands to verify adaptive shaping:

```
[edit class-of-service]
lab@Bock# run show class-of-service adaptive-shaper
Adaptive shaper: becn_shaper, Index: 44416
  Trigger type    Shaping rate
        BECN          256000 bps

[edit class-of-service]
lab@Bock# run show class-of-service interface t1-0/0/2.100
  Logical interface: t1-0/0/2.100, Index: 69
    Shaping rate: 500000
    Object              Name              Type      Index
    Scheduler-map       er_cos_scheduler  Output    21207
    Adaptive-shaper     becn_shaper                 44416
    Rewrite             dscp_rewrite      dscp      26780
    Classifier          dscp_classify     dscp      25819
```

The displays confirm that the adaptive shaper is correctly programmed and placed into effect on Bock's Frame Relay interface.

Virtual Channels

Virtual channels are used to ensure that a central site with a high bandwidth connection does not overrun remote sites that access the network at slower rates. Figure 9-17 illustrates a typical hub and spoke Frame Relay topology. The headquarters site has a significantly higher access rate when compared to the branch office spokes.

The key point of Figure 9-17 is that the central site terminates at a T1 switch port in the service provider's network, while the remote sites are terminated at significantly lower speeds. In a Frame Relay service, the absolute limit on data transfer rate is the logical port speed, which can be lower than the transmission link's physical bit rate; for example, Site 1 is using a Fractional T1 (FT1) circuit to access the provider, but pays for only 128 Kbps of port speed and can use only 128 Kbps of the T1's capacity. Regardless of CIR rate or the state of network congestion, Site 1 and Site 2 are physically limited to the reception of no more that 128/256 Kbps of traffic, respectively.

The problem, if not already obvious, is that the central site can easily burst to full T1 rates, and if these bursts are of any appreciable duration, there will be massive loss due to buffer overflow in the network. This causes TCP-based sources to sense

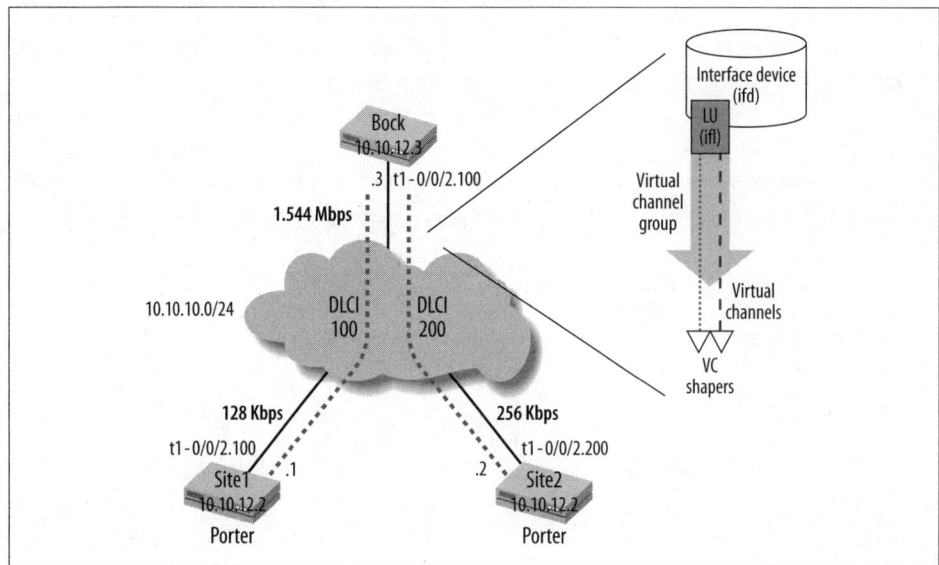

Figure 9-17. J-series virtual channels

congestion and throttle back. If not corrected, this can lead to an ongoing boom/bust cycle as the sources ramp up, sense loss, and then ramp back down, resulting in diminished throughput and higher latency due to buffering within the network. This is more than a simple issue of not knowing each virtual channel's CIR, as the topology shown in Figure 9-17 may well be based on a 0 CIR service. The issue is simply one of mismatched port speed over a network that does offer extensive buffering.

A virtual channel group is a collection of virtual channels that are applied to a logical interface. Each virtual channel within the group has its own queues and scheduler-map, and each can be shaped to a rate that is less than the physical interface speed. In some cases, you may choose to shape a virtual channel based on CIR, but in most cases the shaping rate is set to the lesser of the two port speeds. When not shaped, each virtual channel can burst to full interface speed, and when multiple unshaped virtual channels are active, they each get a round-robin fair share of the total physical interface bandwidth. There is no priority scheduling between virtual channels.

Firewall filters are used to direct traffic to the correct virtual channel based on some match condition—for example, the destination address. Unmatched traffic is sent to a default virtual channel. This requires that one virtual channel be designated as the default within each virtual channel group.

Configure virtual channels

The lack of logical router support for the J-series in the 8.0R1 code used in this lab, combined with the lack of Frame Relay switching, results in the need to use Porter twice—once as Site 1 using DLCI 100 and again as Site 2 with DLCI 200. This is why Figure 9-17 shows the same lo0 address for both Sites 1 and 2. Because there is no virtual channel configuration at remote sites, this example focuses on Bock, the central site router. In this example, we do not bother with a virtual router (VR) instance for the second connection from Porter to Bock; instead, a new logical unit is added to the t1-0/0/2 interface with a unique host ID, and the original IP address is reassigned under unit 100 to match the addressing shown in Figure 9-17:

```
[edit]
lab@Porter# show interfaces t1-0/0/2
description Porter-to-Bock;
per-unit-scheduler;
encapsulation frame-relay;
unit 100 {
    dlci 100;
    family inet {
        address 10.10.10.1/24;
    }
}
unit 200 {
    dlci 200;
    family inet {
        address 10.10.10.2/24;
    }
}
```

The addressing results in a duplicate subnet shared between units 100 and 200, but this is not a problem here:

```
[edit]
lab@Porter# run show ospf neighbor
  Address         Interface        State    ID           Pri  Dead
  10.10.8.2       fe-0/0/1.2332    Full     10.30.1.1    128  31
  10.10.10.1      t1-0/0/2.100     Full     10.10.12.3   128  31
  10.10.10.1      t1-0/0/2.200     Full     10.10.12.3   128  30

[edit]
lab@Porter# run show route 10.10.10/24

inet.0: 14 destinations, 16 routes (14 active, 0 holddown, 0 hidden)
+ = Active Route, - = Last Active, * = Both

10.10.10.0/24      *[Direct/0] 00:01:46
                    > via t1-0/0/2.200
                    [Direct/0] 00:01:46
                    > via t1-0/0/2.100
                    [OSPF/10] 00:01:45, metric 65
                    > via t1-0/0/2.100
10.10.10.1/32      *[OSPF/10] 00:01:45, metric 65
                    > via t1-0/0/2.200
                      via t1-0/0/2.100
10.10.10.2/32      *[Local/0] 00:01:46
                      Local via t1-0/0/2.100
```

```
10.10.10.3/32        *[Local/0] 00:01:46
                        Local via t1-0/0/2.200
```

The result is OSPF adjacencies over both the 100 and 200 logical units and two equal cost routes to Bock's IP address. Things are more interesting at Bock, where a multipoint Frame Relay interface is defined to create the logical connectivity shown in Figure 9-17:

```
[edit]
lab@Bock# show interfaces t1-0/0/2
description Bock-to-porter;
per-unit-scheduler;
dce;
encapsulation frame-relay;
unit 100 {
    multipoint;
    family inet {
        address 10.10.10.3/24 {
            multipoint-destination 10.10.10.1 dlci 100;
            multipoint-destination 10.10.10.2 dlci 200;
        }
    }
}
```

The modified configuration maps two locally defined DLCIs on the same logical interface to each associated IP address; DLCI 100 leads to Site 1's 10.10.10.1 address and DLCI 200 maps to the address of Site 2 and the 10.10.10.2 address. Per-unit scheduling must be enabled on the physical interface to support scheduling into each virtual channel.

At first glance, the show route command at Bock indicates that all traffic for the 10.10.10/ 24 subnet will use the same link, as indicated by the absence of logical unit 200:

```
[edit]
lab@Bock# run show route 10.10.10.2

inet.0: 12 destinations, 13 routes (12 active, 0 holddown, 0 hidden)
+ = Active Route, - = Last Active, * = Both

10.10.10.0/24        *[Direct/0] 00:13:24
                        > via t1-0/0/2.100
                        [OSPF/10] 00:13:12, metric 130
                        > to 10.10.10.2 via t1-0/0/2.100
```

The route to 10.10.10.2 seems to indicate that Bock plans to use the wrong DLCI, given that DLCI 200 maps to Site 2, not Site 3. The forwarding table, however, correctly reflects the correct IP-to-DLCI mapping as configured under the multipoint Frame Relay interface:

```
[edit]
lab@Bock# run show route forwarding-table destination 10.10.10.1
Routing table: inet
Internet:
```

```
Destination       Type RtRef Next hop      Type Index NhRef Netif
10.10.10.1/32     dest    0 dlci: 100      ucst  334     5 t1-0/0/2.100

[edit]
lab@Bock# run show route forwarding-table destination 10.10.10.2
Routing table: inet
Internet:
Destination       Type RtRef Next hop      Type Index NhRef Netif
10.10.10.2/32     dest    0 dlci: 200      ucst  336     1 t1-0/0/2.100
```

With the Frame Relay aspects confirmed, you move on to the virtual channel configuration:

```
[edit class-of-service]
lab@Bock# show virtual-channels
site1_default;
site2;
```

Two virtual channels are defined, one for each remote site. Here, Site 1 is set as the default virtual channel. Traffic that is routed out the logical interface to which the virtual channel group is applied will default to the virtual channel for Site 1, unless directed via a firewall filter to Site 2. The virtual channel group configuration is displayed:

```
[edit class-of-service]
lab@Bock# show virtual-channel-groups
er_vc_group {
    site1_default {
        scheduler-map er_cos_scheduler;
        shaping-rate 128k;
        default;
    }
    site2 {
        scheduler-map er_cos_scheduler;
        shaping-rate 256k;
    }
}
```

A virtual channel group configuration links multiple virtual channel definitions together for application to a logical interface. Here, the er_vc_group configuration links the site1 and site2 definitions, much like a scheduler-map links multiple scheduler policies. When applied to a logical interface, eight queues are created for each virtual channel associated with the group, and a scheduler-map is used to control scheduling into each set of per-virtual-channel queues. This example shapes each virtual channel to the remote site's port speed, but if desired, some virtual channels can be left unshaped to allow bursting up to physical interface speed.

The virtual channel group is applied to an interface, at the logical unit level. You will not be able to commit the configuration unless you remove any adaptive shaping, shaping, or scheduler-map configuration on the same logical unit:

```
[edit class-of-service]
lab@Bock# show interfaces t1-0/0/2
```

```
    unit 100 {
        virtual-channel-group er_vc_group;
        classifiers {
            dscp dscp_classify;
        }
        rewrite-rules {
            dscp dscp_rewrite;
        }
    }
}
```

The final step in the virtual channel configuration is the definition of the filter that directs traffic to the correct virtual channel, where it is in turn shaped according to the remote site's port speed. Recall that one virtual channel in each group must be designated the default virtual channel, which means it's used when no explicit virtual channel mapping is found. A working virtual channel mapping filter is shown at Bock:

```
[edit]
lab@Bock# show firewall
filter er_vc_select {
    term select_site2 {
        from {
            destination-address {
                10.10.10.2/32;
            }
        }
        then {
            virtual-channel site2;
            accept;
        }
    }
    term default_to_site1 {
        then {
            virtual-channel site1_default;
            accept;
        }
    }
}
```

The er_vc_select filter matches on packets addressed to Site 2 and directs them to the scheduler/shaper associated with the site2 virtual channel. Any traffic not matched by the select_site2 term is matched by the default_to_site1 term, which results in a mapping to the default virtual channel. The er_vc_select filter is placed into service in the output direction:

```
[edit]
lab@Bock# show interfaces t1-0/0/2 unit 100 family inet filter
output er_vc_select;
```

To confirm that your virtual channel configuration is active on a given interface, use the show class-of-service interface command:

```
[edit]
lab@Bock# run show class-of-service interface t1-0/0/2.100
```

```
Logical interface: t1-0/0/2.100, Index: 70
  Object                   Name            Type     Index
  Virtual-channel-group    er_vc_group              55210
  Rewrite                  dscp_rewrite    dscp     26780
  Classifier               dscp_classify   dscp     25819
```

The show class-of-service virtual-channel-group command confirms the details of er_vc_group:

```
[edit]
lab@Bock# run show class-of-service virtual-channel-group
Virtual channel group: er_vc_group, Index: 55210
        Virtual channel: site1_default
                Scheduler map: er_cos_scheduler
                Shaping rate : 128000 bps
        Virtual channel: site2
                Scheduler map: er_cos_scheduler
                Shaping rate : 256000 bps
```

Currently, you cannot obtain per-virtual-channel queuing statistics from the CLI. The output of the show interfaces queue t1-0/0/2.100 command displays the aggregate packet counts for all virtual channels in effect on the interface.

J-Series Adaptive Shaping and Virtual Channel Summary

This section demonstrated the configuration and operational analysis of the J-series-specific adaptive shaper and virtual channel features. The former allows dynamic switching between two shapers, one based on the service's CIR and another on the EIR, based on the congestion state of the network, as signaled by received BECN bits. By sending at or below the CIR during periods of network congestion, you avoid loss, and when the congestion clears, you are able to send at the EIR rate with a high probability of delivery, given the lack of congestion.

The virtual channel feature is designed to allow a central site route with a high-speed attachment to shape into individual virtual channels, with each such virtual channel dimensioned according to the remote site's port speed (or CIR). The goal of this feature is to prevent buffer overrun and loss that can occur when a site with a high-speed access rate sends to a remote site that is attached at a much slower speed.

Conclusion

IP CoS is an enabling factor for many value-added services, or a cost-effective convergence onto a single network infrastructure. Even though bandwidth may be relatively cheap and links always seem to get faster, you can still deploy CoS to ensure that you get the most of whatever bandwidth your network has to work with. All Juniper Networks routers support a robust and practical set of CoS capabilities that, given the general design of Juniper products, can be enabled in any production network without concerns of performance degradation or unpredictable behavior.

The future is IP-based, and more and more services are being adapted to IP transport each day. By deploying an effective CoS solution early, you gain a competitive advantage, now and in the future, because you will find you can confidently roll out new and ever-more-demanding applications, knowing that your network will make the most of its resources to deliver the goods that matter most.

Exam Topics

We examined the following Enterprise Exam Topics in this chapter:

- Describe the uses of CoS.
- Explain CoS processing on M-series and J-series routers.
- Identify the ways traffic can be classified.
- Explain the purpose of BAs.
- Explain the use of policers.
- Describe how traffic is mapped to queues.
- Configure the mapping of forwarding classes to queues.
- Explain the role of a scheduler and how M-series versus J-series behavior differs.
- Configure a scheduler to service queues based on a CoS design.
- Monitor a CoS implementation.
- Configure BA and multifield classification.
- Congestion management and avoidance.
- Code point rewriting.
- Rate-limiting with shaping, policing, or both.
- J-series adaptive shapers and virtual channels.

Chapter Review Questions

1. Which IP CoS approach requires signaling to reserve resources?
    a. IP ToS
    b. IntServ
    c. DiffServ
    d. ATM
2. In the DiffServ architecture, what is a BA?
    a. A sequence of packets with a shared marking, crossing a given link
    b. The collective behavior of all nodes in the domain
    c. The act of aggregating multiple reservations into a single, larger one, for scalability
    d. None of the above

3. With regard to J-series versus M-series CoS capabilities, which is true?

   a. The M-series can support only four queues; the J-series supports eight

   b. The M-series does not support per-unit scheduling

   c. The J-series WRED cannot be protocol-based, whereas the M-series WRED can be

   d. The M-series offers LLQ support, whereas the J-series does not

4. How do you convey packet loss priority to a downstream node?

   a. By implementing the same multifield classifiers as used originally at the ingress

   b. This is not possible because the IP header does not support a loss-priority flag

   c. You must reclassify all packets with high loss priority into a forwarding class reserved for that purpose

   d. Use a BA rewrite table with a matching BA classifier

5. What is the actual scheduling priority when used on an M7i?

   ```
   lab@PBR# show schedulers
   . . .
   bronze_sched {
       transmit-rate 10m exact;
       priority medium-high;
   }
   ```

   a. Low

   b. High

   c. Strict-high

   d. This will not commit because the M7i supports only two priority levels

6. Which of the following is true?

   a. On the J-series, strict-high and high are the same priority

   b. On the M-series, strict-high is a separate priority

   c. You must use the exact option with a strict-high queue to prevent starvation

   d. Policing should be used when strict-high is set, especially on the J-series

7. What is the purpose of the shaping-rate statement in the following code snippet?

   ```
   test_sched {
       transmit-rate percent 5;
       shaping-rate percent 20;
       priority high;
   }
   ```

   a. It ensures that this queue cannot starve other queues of their configured weight

b. It limits how much traffic this queue can send, even when all other queues are idle

c. It shapes the traffic allowed by the transmit rate so that at least 20% of the packets are not clumped

d. This is used in adaptive shaping, in order to set the maximum transmit rate when the network is not congested

8. When committing a CoS configuration, you notice the following log message. What does it mean?

```
Nov  3 00:25:25  PBR /kernel: RT_COS: COS IPC op 5 (SCHED POLICY DEF) failed, err
5 (Invalid)
Nov  3 00:25:25  PBR fwdd[2780]: COSMAN_FWDD: Wrr underflow, for fe-0/0/0
Nov  3 00:25:25  PBR fwdd[2780]: COSMAN: policy update failed
```

a. There is a problem in the configuration and the default settings are in effect

b. There is a problem in the configuration, causing it to fail commit

c. There is a problem in the configuration; the software adapts the configuration to meet the underlying capability

d. The error indicates that the sum of the assigned weights in the scheduler-map did not equal 100%

9. Consider the CoS configuration at PBR in the DiffServ scenario, as shown in Figure 9-16, and select the best option:

a. Each logical interface on fe-0/0/0 can send up to 100 Mbps

b. When both logical interfaces are active, each gets only 50 Mbps

c. Both A and B

d. None of the above

10. Refer to the output provided and select the best answer:

```
[edit class-of-service drop-profiles test]
lab@PBR# show
fill-level 50 drop-probability 0;
fill-level 70 drop-probability 10;
fill-level 80 drop-probability 20;
fill-level 90 drop-probability 30;
```

a. Between 70% and 80% fill, there is 10% drop probability

b. Between 75% and 80% fill, there is 15% drop probability

c. Between 70% and 80% fill, there is 10% drop probability for PLP = 1

d. Between 70% and 80% fill, there is 10% drop probability for PLP = 0

11. Which of the following is true?

a. BA overrides multifield classification

b. Multifield overrides BA classification

c. You cannot combine BA and multifield classification; a packet is classified only once

d. You should perform BA and multifield classification on all nodes for consistency

12. How can the PLP status be set?

 a. With multifield classification

 b. With BA classification

 c. With a policer

 d. Using policy

 e. All of the above

Chapter Review Answers

1. Answer: B. Only the Integrated Services (IntServ) model made use of control plane signaling for resource allocation.

2. Answer: A. In the DiffServ model, a BA is a collection of packets with a shared code point. It is expected that each node will have the same PHB for a given BA, and therefore end-to-end performance can be modeled.

3. Answer: C. J-series WRED has four drop priority levels, but no TCP/UDP index. The M-series can support eight queues and per-unit scheduling with IQ PICs. Only the J-series offers true LLQ.

4. Answer D. Although you could use multifield classification everywhere, this approach does not scale. Use a BA classifier and associated rewrite to convey PLP status between nodes.

5. Answer: B. The M7i has two hardware priority levels, and medium-high, high, and strict-high all map to the same value, which is high.

6. Answer: D. Because strict-high is given 100% of transmit weight, it should be used with a policer to ensure that other classes are not starved, especially on the J-series, where strict-high is an actual priority. You cannot use exact with a strict-high queue, but on the J-series you can use the shaping rate to cap total usage. However, a policer is preferred, as this allows excess bandwidth only when other queues are empty.

7. Answer: B. Supported on the J-series only, the shaping-rate limits the total amount of bandwidth available to the queue, regardless of activity in other queues. This in itself does not prevent starvation of lesser-priority queues, but it can help.

8. Answer: A. Many CoS configuration errors allow a commit, but they generate a log warning indicating that the configured values can be programmed. This means the default values are in effect.

9. Answer: C. Unless you shape at the logical interface level, each IFL can send up to line rate, and when multiple IFLs are active, they share available bandwidth. This is another benefit to using schedulers based on transmit percentage, rather than absolute values. The latter would result in one IFL getting 100 Mbps while the other receives a default scheduler configuration with 95%/5% assigned to queue 0 and 3, respectively.

10. Answer: A. The profile defines a 10% drop probability for fill levels between 70% and 80%. You cannot tell from the drop profile itself whether it affects PLP 0 or 1 (or UDP versus TCP), because the function of WRED against some criteria is performed via a `scheduler-map`, which was not shown.

11. Answer: B. Multifield overrides BA classification and generally is used only at network edges.

12. Answer: E. All of the methods listed can impact the PLP status of a given packet.

CHAPTER 10

IP Multicast in the Enterprise

This chapter explores typical enterprise deployment scenarios for IPv4 multicast. Focus is placed on the design and configuration of a scalable, fault-tolerant, multicast infrastructure using JUNOS software. Operational analysis and fault isolation are also demonstrated. The topics covered include:

- Multicast terminology and concepts
- Multicast protocols: group management and routing
- Protocol Independent Multicast (PIM) sparse mode using static rendezvous points (RPs)
- PIM sparse mode with bootstrap-based RP election
- PIM and Multicast Source Discovery Protocol (MSDP)-based Anycast-RP

Juniper Networks routers offer extensive support for IPv4 multicast. Consult the multicast overview in the JUNOS software documentation to confirm the list of supported RFC and drafts for your software release.

What Is Multicast?

Multicast defines the concept of a one-to-many communications stream. To a casual observer, multicast is similar to broadcast in that a single copy of a packet can be received by multiple nodes—however, multicast is not dependent on an underlying multiaccess medium. It can operate network-wide (unlike broadcast traffic that is not forwarded by routers), and is associated with protocols that attempt to automatically tune the network to eliminate unnecessary transport and delivery of multicast traffic.

Routers use multicast routing protocols to control the forwarding of multicast traffic to prevent loops and avoid inefficiencies associated with having multiple copies of a given packet transmitted over the same link multiple times. Multicast group membership protocols are used by hosts to express interest in one or more multicast groups—multicast traffic is not forwarded over an interface with attached hosts unless at least one host has explicitly requested the receipt of multicast traffic.

When all goes to plan, the presence of multicast traffic is noted only by those nodes that have expressed interest in that particular stream, which is in marked contrast to a link-level broadcast that forces reception of the packet by all nodes on that link. In summary, broadcast is one-to-all with a link-level scope, whereas multicast is one-to-many, network-wide, but only when there is express interest in receiving multicast.

The sources and destinations of multicast content are generally hosts, not routers. The role of a multicast router entails locating multicast sources, replicating packets for transmission over multiple interfaces, preventing routing loops, and connecting interested destinations with the proper source, all while keeping the flow of unwanted packets to a minimum.

Multicast Applications

There are numerous applications for IP multicast. In many cases, a given application is capable of operating in either unicast or multicast mode, depending on user settings and overall scaling needs. Network applications that can function with unicast but are better suited for multicast include collaborative groupware, teleconferencing, and distributed applications such as multiplayer gaming or virtual reality. Any IP network concerned with reducing network resource consumption for one-to-many or many-to-many applications, to include multimedia streams with multiple receivers such as IP-TV, benefits from multicast.

Multicast-enabled networks and applications provide significant scaling benefits. When unicast is employed by an Internet radio or news ticker service, for example, each recipient requires a *separate* traffic session. The processing load at the server and network bandwidth consumed increase linearly as each new receiver attaches to the server. This is extremely inefficient, whether dealing with the global scale of the Internet or a modest enterprise-scale network.

In a broadcast model, the source needs to generate only a single stream using a broadcast destination address. Ignoring for the moment that the link-level scope of broadcast makes this model unusable in a routed network, a broadcast model is extremely inefficient because it consumes maximum bandwidth and places the burden of packet rejection on each host.

Multicast provides the most efficient and effective solution for most one-to-many or many-to-many applications, with none of the drawbacks and all of the advantages of the unicast or broadcast model. With multicast, a single multicast packet stream finds its way to every interested receiver, and replication is performed in a distributed manner within each router as needed, allowing large-scale deployment because no one device is forced to replicate or handle all traffic associated with the application. With IP multicast, a sending host generates a single IP packet stream, whether there is one receiver or 1 million receivers, and links that connect to subnets consisting of entirely uninterested receivers carry no multicast traffic at all.

Locating content

Once you have enabled multicast in your network, the first question becomes "What new services and applications can I enable with it, and how will users know?" In other words, for maximum benefit, there needs to be a TV Guide-like function available to the end user. The *Session Directory tool* (known as SDR) is an end-user application that uses multicast protocols to locate and list available sessions in the network. Figure 10-1 shows the user interface for the SDR application.

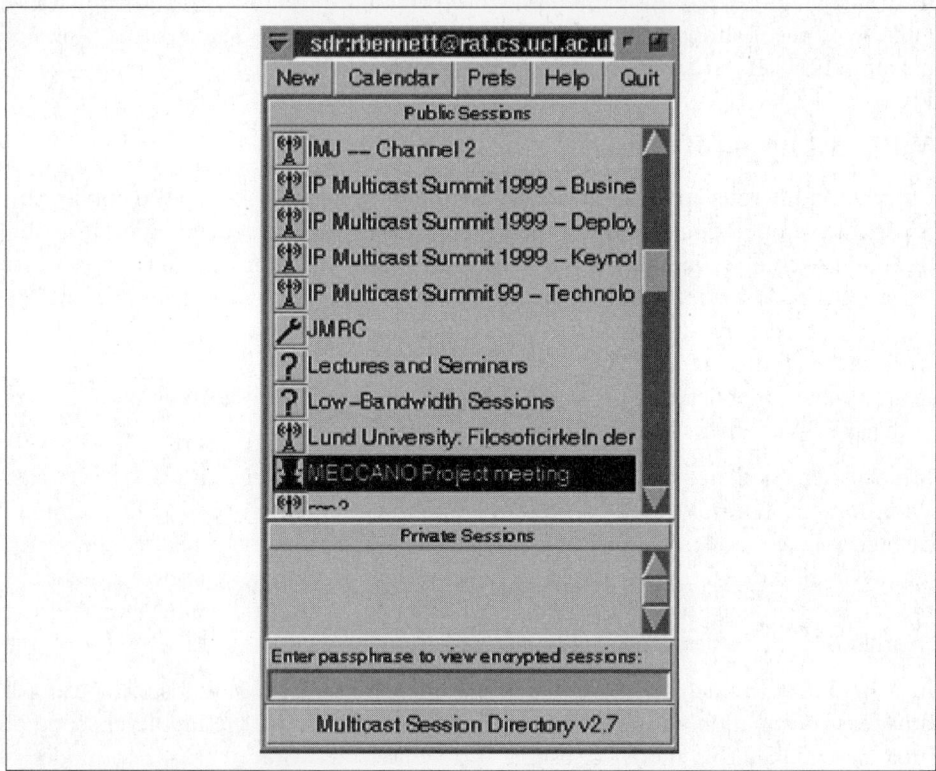

Figure 10-1. The Session Directory tool

The transport protocol used by the Session Directory tool is the Session Announcement Protocol (SAP). SAP messages are transmitted to the well-known multicast group address of 224.2.127.254, and they contain descriptions of currently available sessions formatted using the Session Description Protocol (SDP). You can download the SDR application and get additional information at *http://www-mice.cs.ucl.ac.uk/multimedia/software/sdr/*.

Multicast Terminology and Concepts

To the uninitiated, multicast can seem to be a jumble of confusing terms and concepts. It helps to keep in mind that multicast is largely state-driven, which is to say that things may or may not happen, based on the presence or absence or some other event. For example, a join message is generated when a router wishes to receive multicast traffic for a given group. As a result of this join, a multicast distribution tree is instantiated, or modified, which adds the interface on which the join was received in the outgoing interface list (OIL) for that group. After some period of time, lack of continued join activity results in this state timing out, the removal of the interface from the OIL, and the cessation of multicast forwarding for that group over that interface. This "now you see it, now you don't" aspect of multicast often leads to confusion, at least when compared to the more or less steady-state nature of unicast routing protocols. In Open Shortest Path First (OSPF), the absence or presence of a route is not a function of an actual desire or need to use the route. In contrast, a multicast "route" is actually a dynamic entry that is based on the presence of an active sender and, to some degree, the presence of at least one interested receiver.

Routing turned upside down

If the dynamic state of multicast is not reason enough for confusion, consider that multicast forwarding is actually a type of reverse routing. Unicast routing is based on longest-matching against the packet's destination address, with the overall goal being the forwarding of a packet toward its destination. In contrast, multicast forwarding is performed based on the *source* address, with the goal being the forwarding of the packet *away* from the source, as opposed to toward any particular destination. This behavior is known as reverse path forwarding (RPF) and is detailed in a later section.

Multicast terms

The reader should be familiar with the following terms and concepts before delving any further into multicast. Refer to Figure 10-2 to see how the terms relate to an IP multicast network.

Figure 10-2 looks complicated, so let's tackle each part individually:

Multicast sources
> The multicast sources for groups 1 and 2 are shown at the top of Figure 10-2. A multicast source is the entity that generates a stream of packets addressed to one or more multicast groups. The set of addresses from 224.0.0.0–239.255.255.255 (224/4) are reserved for IP multicast use. Any device that sends one or more packets to a destination address in this range is a multicast sender. No multicast-specific routing or group management protocol is required by a multicast sender; in fact, the sender does not even need to be able to receive multicast traffic. The sender is the root of a shortest-path tree (SPT).

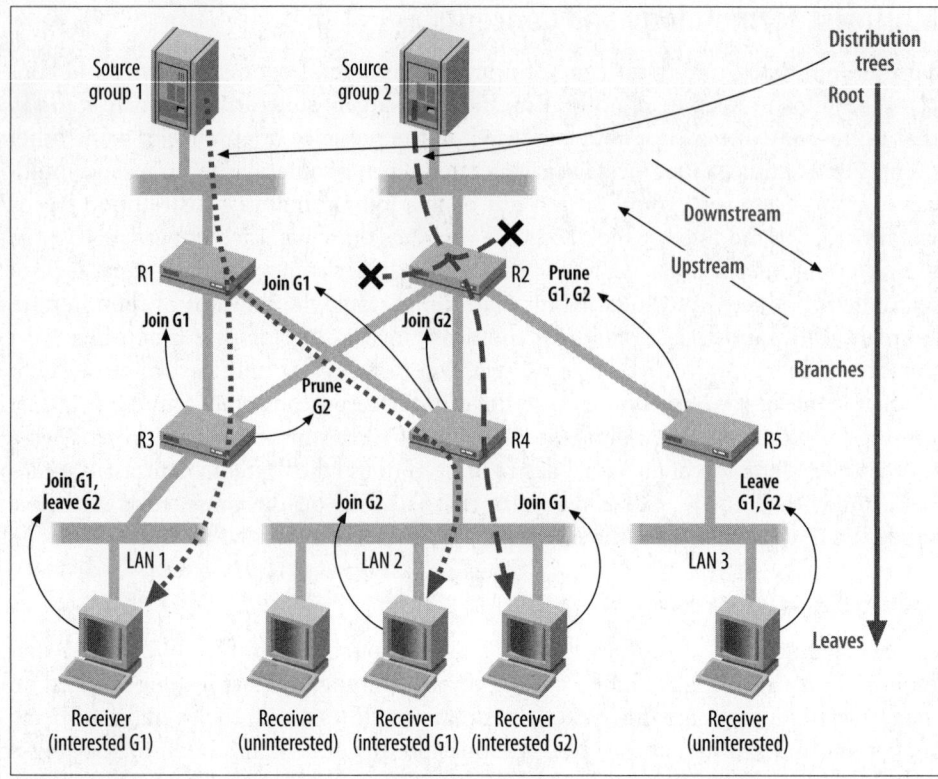

Figure 10-2. Multicast terms

Multicast receivers

> Several multicast receivers are shown at the bottom of Figure 10-2. The receivers form the leaves of a multicast distribution tree. Multicast receivers run the Internet Group Management Protocol (IGMP), to inform attached routers what multicast groups they are interested in. A node becomes a leaf on the distribution tree when it joins a given group. A branch is pruned from the multicast tree when no interested hosts remain; that is, when all of its leaves have fallen off. This condition is shown for LAN 3, where the sole receiver has indicated a desire to leave both multicast groups. Note how the group management protocol's leaves become a multicast routing protocol prune message, assuming that the first hop router has no other interested receivers (leaves) for the related branch.

Multicast protocols

> Multicast protocols control the flow of multicast traffic between sources and receivers. For now, it's sufficient to note that receivers use a group management protocol to inform their routers which groups they are interested in; receivers are not aware of the actual multicast topology. Routers run a group management protocol to communicate with attached receivers, and a multicast routing protocol when communicating with other multicast-aware routers. A multicast

routing protocol such as PIM is significantly more complex than the group management protocols used by receivers, and it is responsible for ensuring loop-free forwarding and management of the distribution tree based on the absence or presence of interested receivers.

Upstream/downstream

Many operations in multicast are directionally oriented. The multicast tree is rooted at each source and terminates at the various leaves. Traffic flows downstream, along the distribution tree, from the source to each receiver. In contrast, control messages that establish a prune/join state are sent upstream, in the direction of the receiver to the source. Figure 10-2 shows the multicast traffic from groups 1 and 2 flowing downstream toward interested receivers while the related control messages flow upstream.

Distribution trees, branches, and leaves (oh, my)

A distribution tree is the interconnection of nodes that lie between a sender and interested receivers. Figure 10-2 shows two senders, and each is associated with its own distribution tree. The tree is rooted at the sender in an SPT, or at the RP in a shared tree. The example in the figure consists of two SPTs. Traffic flows downstream on the tree while control messages flow upstream to influence multicast flow. Between the root and each leaf lies one or more branches. A router must replicate packets to each branch that leads to a leaf, noting, however, that the same effort is required whether there is one or 1,000 leaves on that branch. A leaf is a multicast receiver with interest in a given group. A branch is pruned from the tree when it has no remaining leaves. The figure shows R3 and R5 pruning branches from the tree in response to the receipt of leave messages that indicate no remaining leaves.

Dense and sparse modes

There are two primary strategies when it comes to forming the initial distribution tree. There is the *flood first, prune later* philosophy known as dense mode, and there is the *prune first and flood only when asked for* method known as sparse mode. Stated differently, dense mode is like a push model that assumes that all receivers want all multicast, and sparse mode functions in a client pull manner, where it is assumed that most receivers do not want any multicast. In both methods, the distribution tree is ultimately pruned of any leafless branches, but in the former, the expiration of state results in resumed dense mode flooding, whereas in the latter, an expiration of join state results in a return to the default pruned mode. Generally speaking, older multicast routing protocols such as the Distance Vector Multicast Routing Protocol (DVMRP) support only dense mode, whereas newer protocols such as PIM support both modes. In some cases, the same protocol can operate in a *sparse-dense* mode, whereby certain groups are handled in dense fashion while others are treated as sparse. Dense mode operation is best suited for use over LANs because its flood-first nature tends to consume more bandwidth. On the upside, dense mode does not require the complexities of an RP. Recall that in dense mode, any active source results in flooding down all branches, which are then pruned if not needed; this means that routers have no problems learning about active sources and groups. In contrast, sparse mode operation creates somewhat of a chicken-before-the-egg problem, in that a router must send an explicit join before it can receive traffic for a given group, but before it can send the join it has to know which groups and sources are active! This problem is resolved with the introduction of a shared tree and an RP, which we will detail in a subsequent section.

Additional multicast building blocks

This section discusses IP multicast concepts that are independent of any specific multicast routing protocol or mode of operation. Understanding these concepts prepares the reader for the upcoming IP multicast configuration and operational mode analysis examples.

Multicast addressing. Multicast uses the Class D IP address range, from 224.0.0.0–239.255.255.255. In modern vernacular, the concept of classful addresses has lost favor, so addresses in this range are commonly referred to as simply *multicast addresses*. A multicast address can be used only as the destination address of an IP packet—the source address must always be of the unicast form. A multicast address normally has a /32 prefix length, although other prefix lengths are allowed. Recall that a multicast address represents a logical grouping of devices rather than a physical collection of devices. Multicast addresses can still be described in terms of prefix length using traditional notation. For example, the entire multicast address range can be written as 224/8. The base address 224.0.0.0 is reserved and cannot be assigned to any group, addresses in the 224.0.0.1–224.0.0.255 range are reserved for local wire use, and the 239.0.0.0–239.255.255.255 range is reserved for administratively scoped addresses.

Internet numbering authorities normally do not allocate multicast addresses to their customers. This is because multicast addresses are concerned more with content than with a given physical device. Receivers do not require a multicast address, but they need to know the multicast address associated with the multicast content they are interested in. Multicast sources need an assigned multicast address only to produce the content, not to identify their place in the network. Every source, receiver, and numbered router interface still needs an ordinary, unicast IP address.

Many applications have been assigned a range of multicast addresses, either by the Internet Engineering Task Force (IETF) or by the applications' developers. Although statically assigned multicast addressing is certainly possible, in most cases you can simply use the application's defaults. Table 10-1 shows some application-to-multicast address mappings, as defined by the Internet Assigned Numbers Authority (IANA) at *http://www.iana.org/assignments/multicast-addresses*.

Table 10-1. IANA application-to-multicast address mappings (select examples)

Address	Application
224.2.0.0–224.2.127.253	Multimedia conference calls
224.4.0.0–224.4.0.254	London Stock Exchange
224.0.1.141	Dynamic Host Configuration Protocol (DHCP) servers
224.0.1.39	cisco-rp-announce

Mapping IP Multicast to Link Layer Multicast

On multiaccess networks such as LANs, using the broadcast address to forward IP multicast results in disruption to all nodes on that LAN segment, whether they are interested in multicast or not. Using a unicast address negates the one-to-many efficiency benefit of multicast. The solution is to map a Layer 3 IP multicast address, which is 32 bits in length, into a corresponding 48-bit media access control (MAC) layer multicast address. Figure 10-3 shows a sample of this mapping.

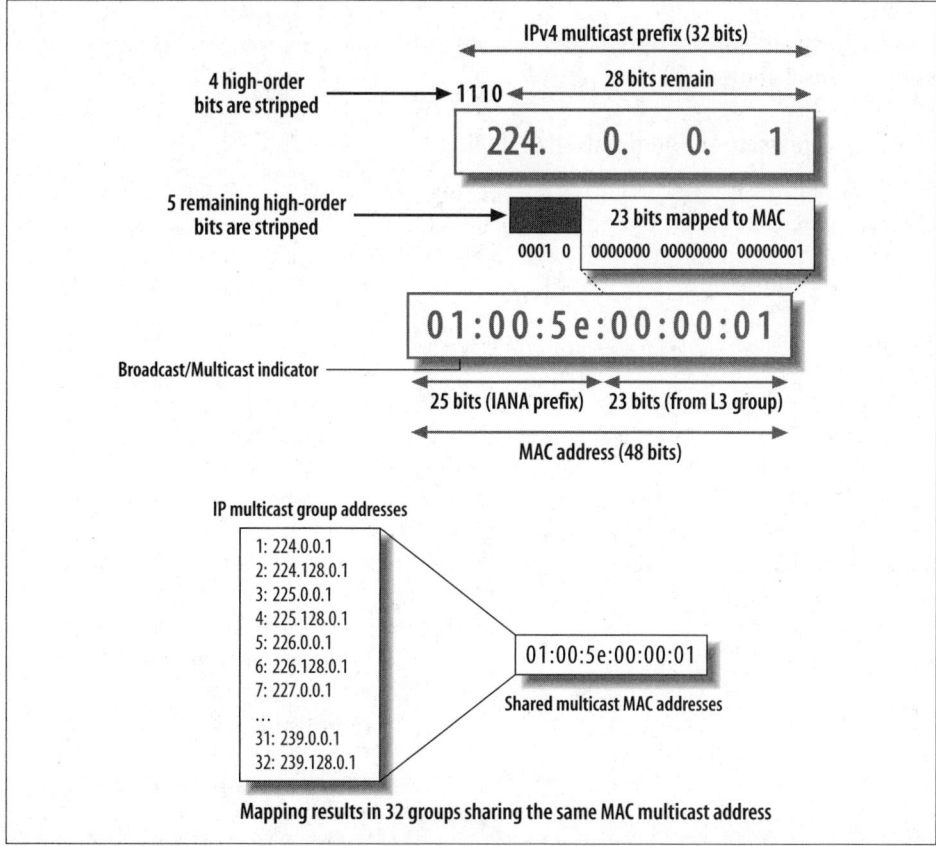

Figure 10-3. Layer 3 to Layer 2 multicast mapping

Given the different address lengths, a direct 1:1 mapping between Layer 2 and Layer 3 addresses is not possible. One-half of the IANA-owned block of Ethernet MAC addresses, the first 24 bits starting with 0x 01:00:5E, are reserved for multicast, yielding the usable range of 0100.5e00.0000–0100.5e7f.ffff inclusive. This allocation results in a 24-bit field, but because the first bit is always set to 0, only 23 bits remain to be populated with the IP multicast address. The mapping process strips the 4-bit class D identifier as well as the 5 high-order bits from the group ID, which leaves 23 bits remaining to be mapped into the multicast MAC address. Because 5 high-order bits are stripped from the group ID, there is a resulting loss of granularity in the Layer 3 to Layer 2 address mapping resulting in $32(2^5)$ different group addresses mapping to the same multicast MAC address, as shown at the bottom of Figure 10-3.

In a Layer 2 network, the sharing of a MAC address among as many as 32 IP multicast groups results in a loss of efficiency, because traffic sent to one multicast group will be received by all hosts using the same shared MAC layer multicast address, even though they do not subscribe to that particular group. Wherever possible, you should be careful when selecting IP multicast addresses to ensure that they map to a unique MAC layer multicast address; otherwise, host systems will have to expend cycles receiving, and then discarding, multicast traffic for groups that have no local applications listening.

Multicast addressing and administrative scoping

Multicast addresses are categorized according to their scope. Scoping is designed to limit the extent to which a multicast packet can travel. Scoping is used for both performance and administrative reasons. Table 10-2 details currently defined IPv4 multicast address scopes.

Table 10-2. IPv4 multicast address scopes

Address	Scope	Comment
224.0.0.0/24	Link local	Confined to a single link, often used for unicast routing protocols; allows same multicast address on each link
239.0.0.0–239.255.255.255	Administratively scoped	Further subdivided into site-local (239.255.0.0/16) and organizational (239.192.0.0/14) scopes
224.0.1.0–238.255.255.255	Global	Addresses with global scope, of which several static assignments exist: • 224.1.0.0–224.1.255.255: shared tree multicast groups • 224.2.0.0–224.2.127.253: multimedia conference calls • 224.2.127.254: SAPv1 announcements • 224.2.127.255: SAPv0 announcements • 224.2.128.0–224.2.255.255: SAP dynamic assignments • 224.252.0.0–224.255.255.255: DIS transient groups • 232.0.0.0–232.255.255.255: VMTP transient groups

Modern IP networks use address-based scoping rather than IP Time to Live (TTL)-based scoping. This is because TTL-based techniques are prone to problems in terms of being able to accurately predict TTL values network-wide, especially in the face of changes in forwarding topology during failover scenarios. Addresses in the link-local scope cannot be forwarded beyond the boundaries of a single link. These addresses tend to be used by unicast routing protocols such as Routing Information Protocol version 2 (RIPv2) and OSPF. The administratively scoped address range is broken into site-local and organizational boundaries. An enterprise might consist of a single site, the exact definition of which is left to the administrators of the routing domain, or it may consist of multiple sites. Generally, the organizational scope is defined as the extent of a routing domain. Administrators configure site or global scoping on the appropriate interfaces to block related traffic from leaving that interface. Figure 10-4 illustrates a scoping example.

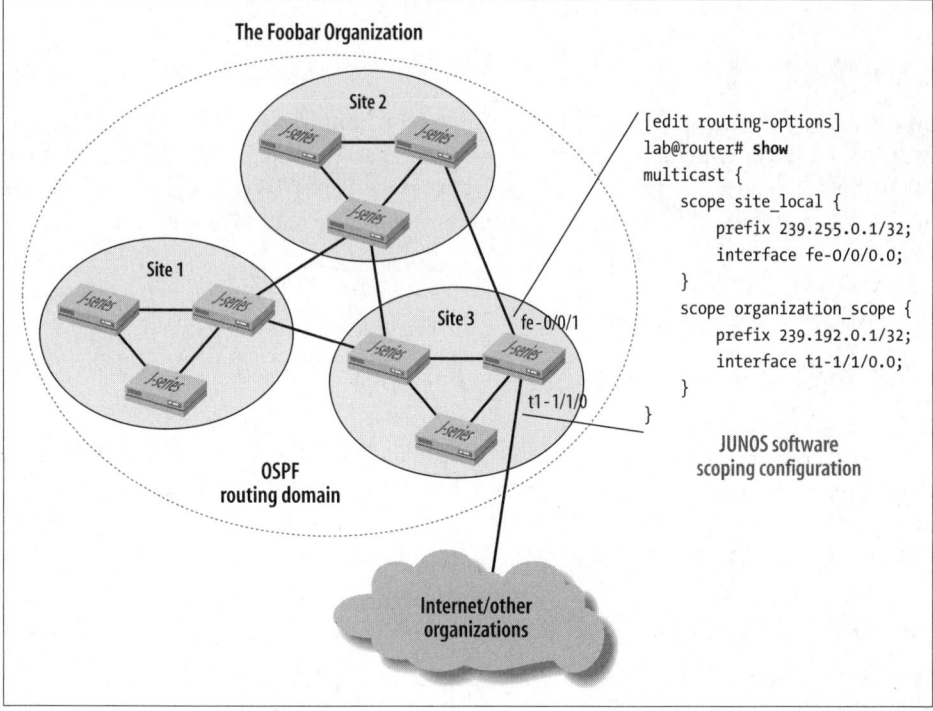

Figure 10-4. Multicast scoping

The approach shown in Figure 10-4 is address-based, but JUNOS software also supports scoping based on a scope-policy. Unlike address scoping, which is applied per interface, a scope-policy applies to all interfaces, and you cannot use it in conjunction with interface-level scoping. You confirm address scoping using the show multicast scope command. The remaining IP multicast address space is considered to have a global scope. Some addresses within the global range are statically assigned by the IANA, as shown in Table 10-2.

It is common to see scoping used to block the multicast addresses associated with the auto-RP discovery mechanism (224.0.1.39 and 224.0.1.40) at administrative boundaries to prevent the use of the local domain's RP by routers outside of local administrative control.

> You cannot use scoping to block RP discovery via the bootstrap proto-col because the bootstrap mechanism operates hop by hop and uses the 224.0.0.13 ALL-PIM-Routers multicast address, which, if scoped, would break other aspects of PIM operation. Normally, bootstrap messages are "scoped" by configuring interdomain interfaces to run PIMv1, which does not support bootstrap, or through definition of bootstrap import/export policy that blocks reception or transmission of bootstrap router (BSR) messages, respectively.

Interface lists

Multicast routers maintain state to determine which multicast packets should be for-warded, and over which interfaces copies of a packet should be sent. Part of this state is in the form of incoming and outgoing interface lists (IILs/OILs) for each active multicast source in the network. Maintaining accurate interface lists is critical for loop avoidance.

> Loops in any IP network are a bad thing. A multicast loop can be par-ticularly nasty given the replication action of routers, which serves to provide an amplification effect for any looping packets.

The interface that lies on the shortest path *back* to the source is the upstream (incoming) interface, and packets are never allowed to be forwarded *toward* the mul-ticast source. All remaining interfaces could become a downstream (outgoing) inter-face, depending upon join state.

A router with multicast forwarding state for a particular multicast group is "switched on" for that group's content. Interfaces on the router's outgoing interface list send copies of the group's packets received on the IIL for that group. Figure 10-5 shows this condition.

The router state that controls multicast forwarding is referred to as (S,G) or (*,G). In (S,G), the S refers to the unicast IP address of the source for the multicast traffic, and the G refers to the particular multicast group IP address for which S is the source. All multicast packets sent from this source have S as the source address and G as the destination address. The asterisk (*) in the (*,G) notation is a wildcard indicating that the state applies to any multicast source sending to group G. So, if two sources are originating content for multicast group 224.1.1.2, a router could use (*, 224.1.1.2) to

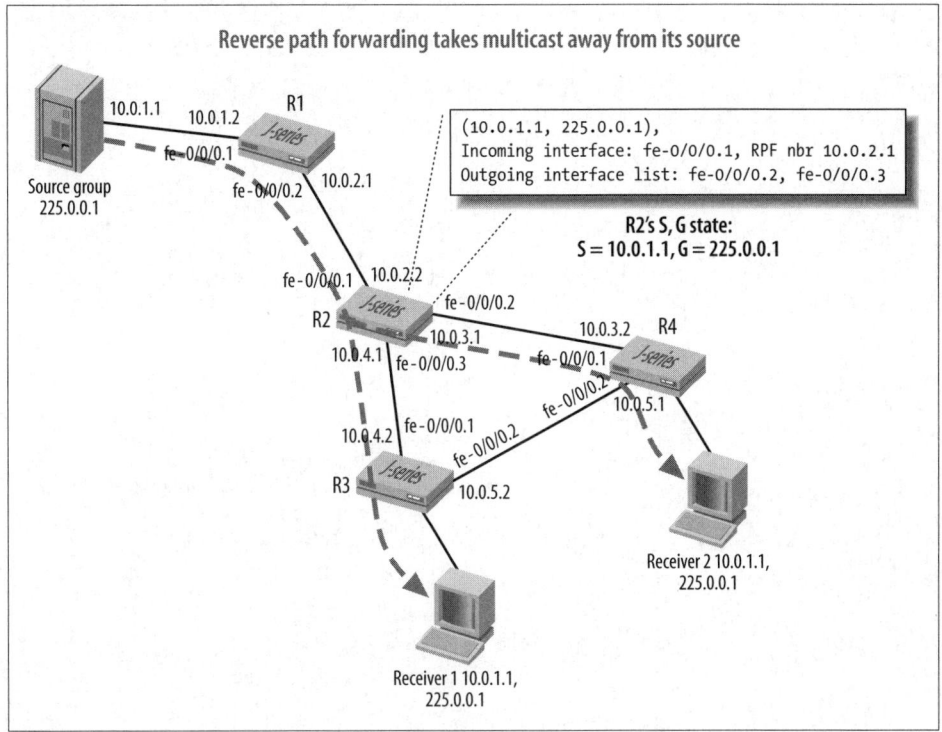

Figure 10-5. Interface lists

represent the state of a router forwarding traffic from both sources to members of that group, as is done in the case of a shared tree.

An incoming and outgoing interface list is maintained for each active source to group tuple. When you consider that group membership is itself often dynamic, and that this volatility leads to a need for ongoing maintenance of the related interface list, it becomes clear that a router handling large numbers of multicast groups can consume significant control plane resources maintaining multicast forwarding state. All Juniper Networks router architectures are well suited to hardware/real-time thread-based multicast replication and can forward multicast at the same (near-line-rate) performance level as unicast. A typical control plane scaling guideline for a router with 1 GB of memory is no more than 120,000 PIM entries [sum of (*,G) and (S,G)], 1,000 PIM neighbors, and 1,000 dynamic IGMP groups per interface.

Reverse path forwarding

Conventional routing is based on a longest match against the destination address of a packet. The unicast route table is maintained by unicast routing protocols such as the Routing Information Protocol (RIP) and OSPF, and it is used when forwarding unicast packets toward their destinations. As noted previously, multicast is like routing turned upside down, in that now the router actually forwards packets *away* from the source, based on the source rather than the destination address. A multicast router's forwarding state is thus organized based on a *reverse path* paradigm. As noted earlier, this process is known as reverse path forwarding (RPF) and is shown in Figure 10-6.

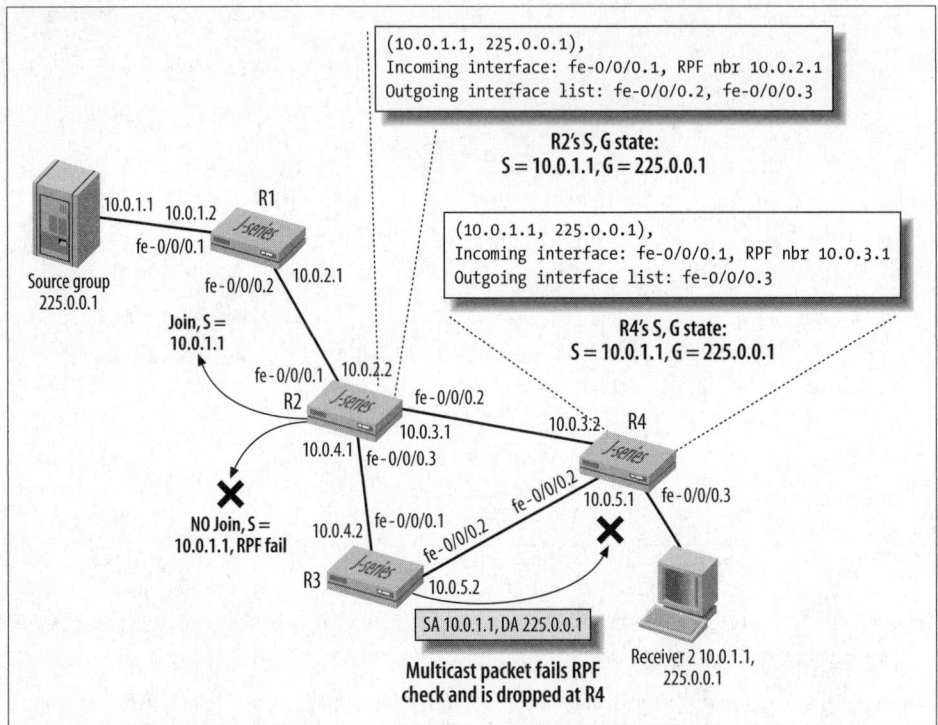

Figure 10-6. The multicast RPF check

An RPF check simply makes sure that a packet arrives on the same interface that would be used for egress by the local router when routing *back* to that multicast source using the Interior Gateway Protocol's (IGP's) shortest path—in effect, a multicast packet is routed twice, once based on the source address and, if that passes, again based on the group address, this time against the OIL for that group. It's important to note that RPF checks occur both in the control plane when processing joins, and in the data plane when deciding whether a packet should be forwarded. Multicast packets that fail the RPF check are dropped because the incoming interface is not on the shortest path back to the source. Figure 10-6 shows how router R4 drops a multicast packet from source 10.0.1.1 when it is received on an interface that would not be used when routing a unicast packet to address 10.0.1.1. The figure also shows that routers generate joins over the RPF interface back to the source.

In some cases, the multicast routing protocol maintains its own RPF table, which is used specifically for the purpose of forwarding multicast. DVMRP is an example of such a protocol. PIM, on the other hand, makes use of the existing unicast route table to perform its RPF checks. This capability is why PIM is considered to be *protocol-independent*; it can use any route source for its RPF checks, including static, IGP, and even Border Gateway Protocol (BGP) routes. JUNOS software supports extensions to unicast routing protocols to accommodate the building of a separate RPF table. Examples include the Multiprotocol Border Gateway Protocol (MBGP) and multi-topology routing in Intermediate System-to-Intermediate System (IS-IS), or M-IS-IS.

Using the main unicast route table for RPF checks provides simplicity; using a dedicated route table for RPF checks allows a network administrator to set up separate paths and routing policies for unicast and multicast traffic. This allows the multicast network to function more independently of the unicast network.

Distribution trees

Previous discussions have indicated that multicast traffic is distributed via a tree that is rooted at the source and branches as needed to pick up all interested leaves. Several different types of distribution trees exist, and in many cases multiple tree types are used (over time) for the same multicast stream.

SPT. SPT is a distribution tree that is rooted at the source. This is sometimes called a *source tree*. An SPT is formed by sending the appropriate join messages over the RPF path to the desired source. Figure 10-7 shows this process.

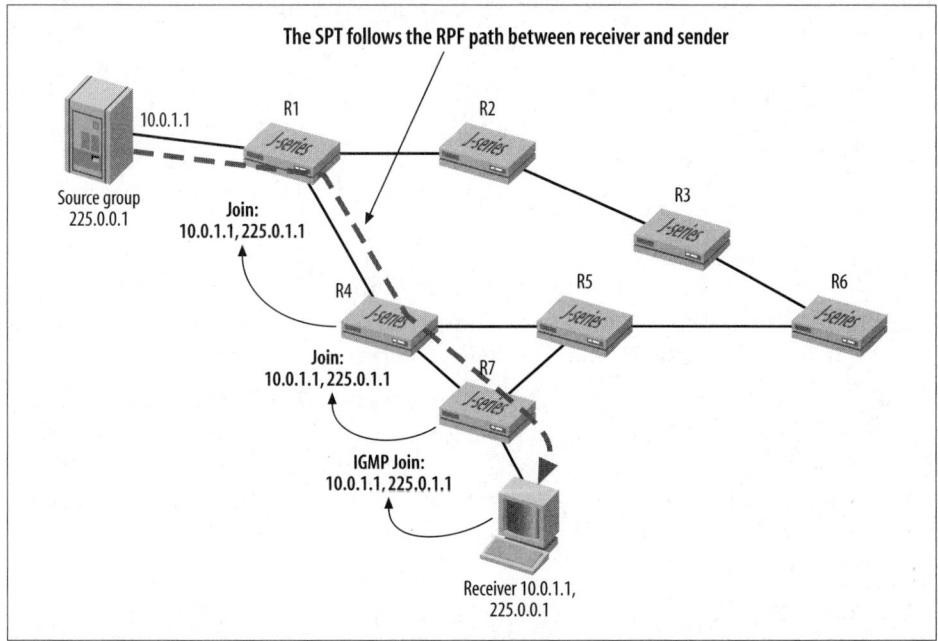

Figure 10-7. An SPT

Things begin when the receiver sends an IGMP join for source 10.0.1.1 and group 225.0.0.1. R7, the first hop (and, in this case, designated) router, generates the appropriate join message out the RPF interface for that source. This is referred to as an (S,G) join, because in this case both S and G are known. Router R4 receives the (S,G) join, which triggers the addition of the receiving interface to its OIL for the 10.0.1.1, 225.0.0.1 tuple. R4 now performs its own RPF check on the source address, and as a result R4 sends its (S,G) join message out its RPF interface for 10.0.1.1, causing reception of the (S,G) join at R1. The process stops when the join message reaches the router directly connected to the source or when it reaches a router that already has multicast forwarding state for this (S,G) tuple. The key point is that RPF handling of (S,G) join messages results in an SPT.

Shared trees and RPs. A shared multicast tree is rooted at an intermediate router, rather than at a specific source. The use of a shared tree can offer the benefit of less overall state, in that a single (*,G) entry can now represent state for numerous sources that may be sending to this group. In the most common multicast protocol in use today, PIM, the shared tree is short-lived and used only to make initial contact between senders and receivers, however. Once this initial contact is made, an SPT is established and the shared tree is no longer used for that (S,G) tuple. In PIM, the root of the shared tree is the RP, which functions to support sparse mode operation. Recall that in sparse mode, multicast is forwarded only as a result of an explicit join for the related group. Without prior knowledge of which senders are active for what groups, a router cannot generate an (S,G) join toward the source, because the source is not yet known.

 Source-specific multicast (SSM) describes a condition in which the receiver has preexisting knowledge of what source it wishes to join. This allows the generation of an SPT without the need for an RP. The use of receiver joins that do not specify a particular source is known as Any Source Multicast (ASM).

In a sparse mode Any Source Multicast (ASM) operation, the router generates an (*,G) join toward the RP, which results in joining a tree that is shared among all senders associated with that group. Figure 10-8 shows this process.

In the example in Figure 10-8, the receiver generates an IGMP join for group 225.0.0.1 that does not specify a particular source; hence, the *any* in the term Any Source Multicast and the use of a wildcard metacharacter to represent the resulting state (*,G). The last hop router, which functions as a designated router, performs an RPF check for the RP that handles this group, and the join is sent toward the RP rather than toward any particular source.

Figure 10-8 calls out how the source generates native multicast to the first hop router, R1 (which also functions as a designated router), which in turn encapsulates

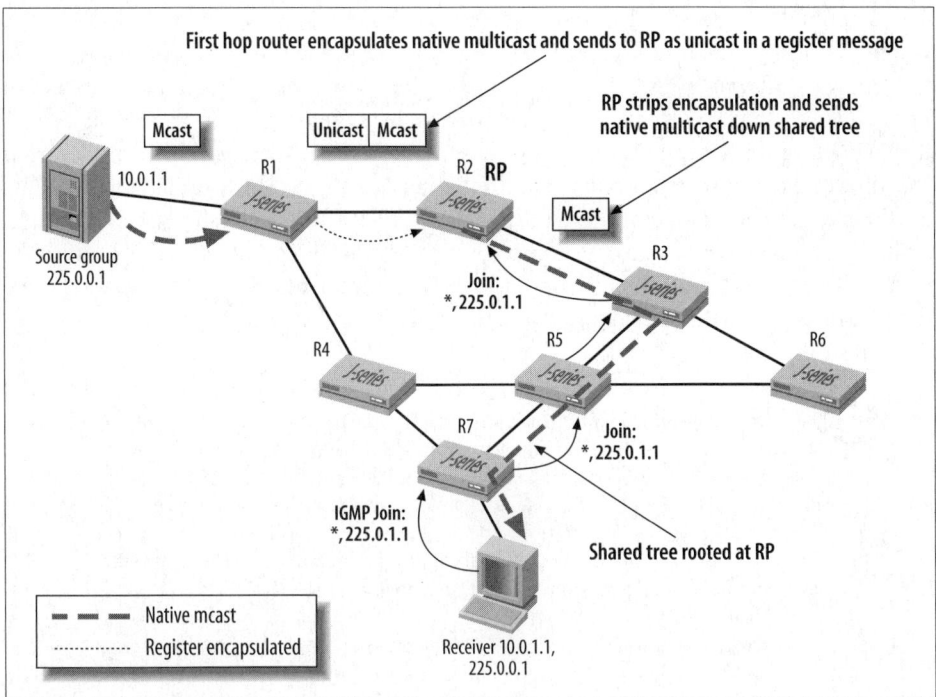

First hop router encapsulates native multicast and sends to RP as unicast in a register message

RP strips encapsulation and sends native multicast down shared tree

Mcast

Unicast | Mcast

R1

R2 **RP**

10.0.1.1

Mcast

Source group
225.0.0.1

R3

Join:
*, 225.0.1.1

R4

R5

R6

R7

Join:
*, 225.0.1.1

IGMP Join:
*, 225.0.1.1

Shared tree rooted at RP

- - - - Native mcast
.... Register encapsulated

Receiver 10.0.1.1,
225.0.0.1

Figure 10-8. An RP tree

the traffic into a unicast datagram addressed to the RP. Upon receipt, the RP strips the register message encapsulation and sends the now native multicast down the shared tree associated with that group.

The purpose of register encapsulation is to eliminate the need for multicast-enabled routers between sources and the RP. The downside is that the first hop routers (those attached directly to multicast sources) and the RP require tunneling hardware/ software support. On M-series platforms, this normally requires the presence of a Tunnel Services PIC—note that the M7i has a built-in Tunnel Services PIC whereas the M10i does not. J-series platforms perform multicast register message encapsulation in software, using the internal services interface, making additional hardware unnecessary.

Switching from a shared tree to an SPT. In PIM sparse mode operation, the shared RP tree (RPT) is used only for discovery of active sources. The receipt of traffic on the RPT initiates a switchover to an SPT by the last hop router (the router attached to the receiver), for each active source that is discovered. Once the SPT is formed, the last hop router begins to receive native multicast directly from the source, so an (S,G) prune is sent up the shared tree, toward the RP, to prevent reception of traffic over both the SPT and the RPT for that source. In some PIM implementations, a user-configurable threshold can be set to control when the switch to an SPT is instigated.

This capability is designed to prevent cutover to an SPT for short-lived sessions, where the traffic may no longer even be present by the time the SPT is established. In the JUNOS software PIM implementation, you can alter the default behavior of immediately switching to an SPT in favor of *never* switching to an SPT. You can do this with the spt-threshold infinity statement, in conjunction with a policy that specifies one or more (S,G) pairs that are subject to the modified behavior. The last hop router will never attempt to switch from the RPT to an SPT for matching (S,G) traffic. This behavior is desired for applications that send very low levels of multicast traffic, where the default behavior could result in undesired oscillation between SPT establishment, a timeout, and a resultant switch back to the RPT.

 PIM sparse mode operation requires tunnel services hardware (or software emulation) to perform the register encapsulation and decapsulation functions. J-series platforms can use the internal services interface for this functionality, as can the M7i with its built-in ASM hardware. The M10i requires the installation of tunnel services hardware to support register encapsulation. If your router lacks tunnel services, you can still commit a PIM sparse mode configuration, but things will simply not work if that router is the first hop attached to a source or when it functions as a (remote) RP, as both of these roles require processing of register messages. A Tunnel Services PIC is not required for dense or SSM modes of operation. You can also eliminate the need for register encapsulation and related tunnel PICs with the corner-case scenario of always having the first hop router also function as the RP.

Multicast Terminology Summary

This section defined the key terms and concepts associated with IP multicast. The next section explores multicast routing and group management protocols.

Multicast Protocols

This section describes the operation of group management and multicast routing protocols. We will focus on PIM sparse mode because it's the predominate form of multicast routing protocol in modern IP multicast networks. Simply stated, group management protocols are run by hosts to inform local routers of a host's interest, or lack thereof, in a particular multicast group. Multicast routing protocols are run only on routers and are concerned with RPF checks and the establishment and maintenance of (*,G) and (S,G) forwarding state.

Group Management Protocols

IGMP performs multicast group management and is run on hosts and on routers that attach to host segments. IGMP versions 1, 2, and 3 are currently defined in RFCs 1112, 2236, and 3376, respectively. The basic mechanics of IGMP operation center on hosts generating report messages to inform attached routers what groups the host is interested in, and to inform routers generating query messages to determine whether any active listeners still remain for a particular group.

There are three versions of IGMP—Juniper routers default to version 2, but you can configure them for version 1 or version 3 as needed. Although the various versions of IGMP are backward-compatible, this compatibility is achieved at the cost of having to drop back to the lowest common denominator. For example, if one host is running IGMPv1, any router attached to the LAN running IGMPv2 drops back to IGMPv1 operation, effectively eliminating the advantages of IGMPv2. Where possible, you should ensure that all multicast receivers run the highest version of IGMP that is supported and configured on the routers serving that network segment.

Table 10-3 identifies the key differences among IGMP versions.

Table 10-3. ICMP version comparison

Version	Characteristics	Comment
IGMPv1	Periodic generation of queries to the all-routers multicast address (224.0.0.1); hosts reply with list of interested groups; querier function performed by routing protocol	Join and leave latency stemming from periodic (60-second) nature of queries
IGMPv2	Lowest IP becomes querier for LAN; group-specific query and leave-group message	Routing protocol no longer performs the querier function; improved join/leave latency
IGMPv3	Support for group-source report messages	Supports SSM by allowing receivers to specify (S,G) tuples

Figure 10-9 details key aspects of IGMPv2 report and query behavior.

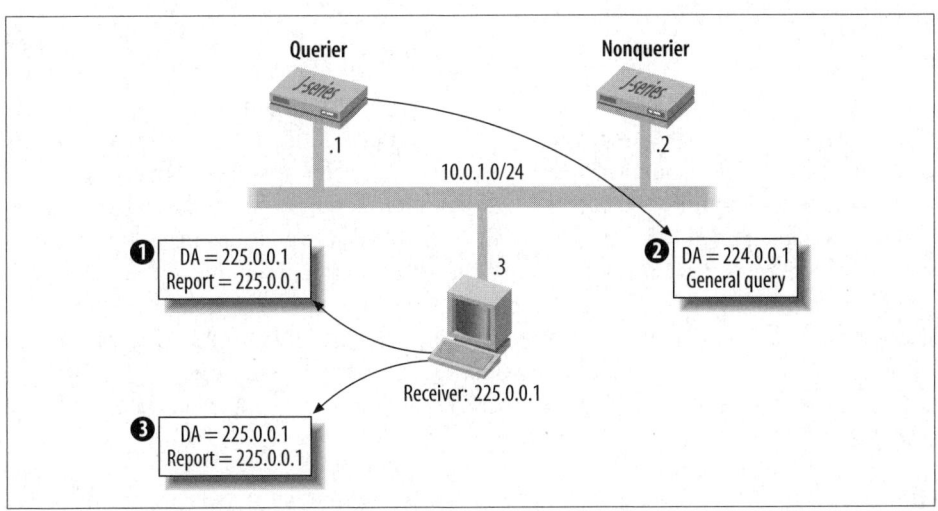

Figure 10-9. IGMPv2 operation

Things begin in Figure 10-9 when the receiver generates an IGMPv2 report, expressing interest in becoming a member of the 225.0.0.1 group. Note that the report is sent to the multicast address equating to the group being joined. Both multicast routers see this report. The router with the lowest IP address is elected the querier and periodically generates general queries to update its knowledge of host-to-group bindings on this LAN, as shown in step 2. All multicast-capable hosts receive the general query, and after a randomized delay, one of the interested hosts will reaffirm the group binding by generating a corresponding report message, which is shown in step 3. Other interested hosts suppress their reports upon seeing a matching report sent by any other node on the segment—the same level of multicast replication and forwarding is needed, be there one or 1,000 interested hosts on a given segment—therefore, only one report is needed to keep the group binding active.

Figure 10-10 goes on to show an IGMPv2 leave process.

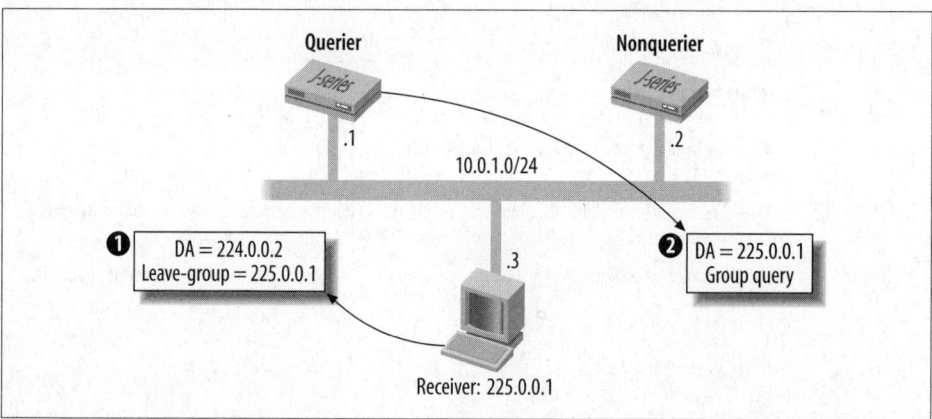

Figure 10-10. IGMPv2 leave process

Later on, the receiving host no longer desires content from group 225.0.0.1. It generates an IGMPv2 group-leave message, which is addressed to 224.0.0.2, the all-routers multicast address. The querier router now generates a group-specific query, which is addressed to the multicast address of the related group, in order to determine whether any interested listeners remain. If so, one will be the first to generate a group report, which keeps the binding active. Otherwise, after a small delay, the group join state is removed from the associated interface. The support of group leaves and general queries can greatly reduce join and leave latency. For example, in IGMPv1, the routing protocol must generate three queries before removing join state—with the default 60-second timer, this equates to 180 seconds of continued multicast delivery after the last interested host has left the group.

IGMPv3

IGMPv3 adds the concept of a source-specific join, which in turn enables SSM. The new capability allows a host to filter multicast content by group, as well as by source. With IGMPv1 or IGMPv2, a host simply has no way to express interest in a particular source, and therefore has to receive traffic from all active senders to that group. Because a source-specific join explicitly identifies the desired source, an SPT can be instantiated without the services of an RP. Figure 10-11 shows IGMPv3 SSM operation.

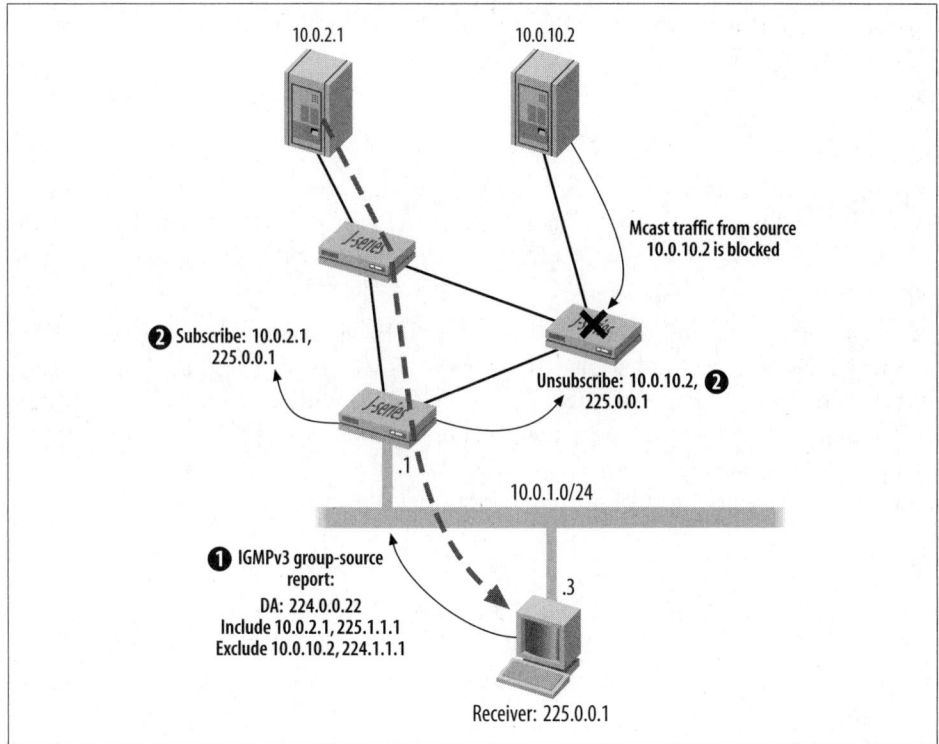

Figure 10-11. IGMPv3 SSM operation

In Figure 10-11, our trusty receiver (which is now IGMPv3-enabled) is told by its multicast application to *subscribe* to the multicast *channel* identified by the tuple 10.0.2.1,225.0.0.1. At the same time, the application instructs the machine to unsubscribe from the 10.0.10.2.225.0.0.1 channel. SSM uses the term *channel* in a manner analogous to the word *group* in ASM. Similarly, the terms *subscribe* and *unsubscribe* describe what in ASM is called *join* and *leave*. Note that the same protocol fields and values are used; the modified terminology simply helps to disambiguate which mode is being discussed, and more correctly describes ASM operation. Subscribing to an (S,G) is somewhat like tuning into a specific media channel when compared to IGMPv2's behavior of drawing traffic from all sources in the group.

Note that IGMPv3 group report messages are sent to all IGMPv3-capable multicast routers with a multicast address of 224.0.0.22, rather than to the multicast address of the group specified in the group address of the report message itself, as is done in versions 1 and 2.

The result, shown at step 1, is the receiver generating an IGMPv3 report that specifically lists the sources (and groups) for which content is desired. The same message can also be used to remove any previously subscribed-to sources. The LAN's designated router translates the IGMP report into the appropriate PIM join and prune messages, which in this context are referred to as subscribe and unsubscribe, respectively.

PIM

Several multicast routing protocols are still in use, but by far the most widely deployed is PIM. PIM was designed to avoid the dense-mode scaling issues of DVMRP and the potential performance problems of Core-Based Tree (CBT) at the same time. PIM supports dense mode, sparse mode, and sparse-dense modes of operation, and it has been in production use for several years.

PIM is a rapidly evolving Internet specification. PIM has seen two major revisions to its protocol operation (and packet structure)—PIM version 1 and PIM version 2—three major RFCs (RFC 4601 obsoleted RFC 2362, which in turn obsoleted RFC 2117), and numerous drafts describing major components of PIM. Work continues on PIM in a number of areas, such as bidirectional trees, and the rapid pace of development generates numerous PIM-related Internet drafts.

PIM versions

PIMv1 and PIMv2 can coexist on the same router, but not on the same interface. The main difference between PIMv1 and PIMv2 is the packet format. PIMv1 messages use IGMP packets, whereas PIMv2 has its own IP protocol number (103) and packet structure. All routers connecting to a shared IP subnet must use the same PIM version. Because the difference between PIMv1 and PIMv2 simply involves the message format, not the semantics or message processing rules, a router can easily support a mix of PIMv1- and PIMv2-enabled interfaces.

In this chapter, we are focusing on PIMv2 operating in sparse mode because this represents the most common usage of PIM in modern IP internetworks.

PIM components

The components needed to run PIM vary depending on operational mode. PIM dense mode requires only multicast sources and receivers and a series of interconnected PIM dense mode routers to allow receivers to obtain multicast content.

PIM sparse mode is more complicated because it requires the services of an RP in the network core. The RP is the root of a shared tree and is the point where upstream join messages from interested receivers meet downstream traffic from multicast sources. If there is only one RP in a routing domain, the RP and adjacent links might become congested and form a single point of failure for all multicast traffic. As a result, it is common to see multiple RPs deployed within a multicast network, for both performance and reliability reasons.

You can view PIM SSM as a subset of a special case of PIM sparse mode, and it requires no specialized equipment other than that used for PIM sparse mode (and IGMP version 3). When a host sends an IGMPv3 join for (S,G) the receiving designated router initiates creation of the SPT by sending an (S,G) join to its RPF neighbor for that source.

RP discovery. Having one or more routers configured as RPs is one thing, but how do the various sources and receivers come to learn which routers are acting as RPs, and for which multicast groups? You can take several approaches to propagate knowledge of the routing domain's RPs to client routers. They include:

Static

The simplest RP discovery mechanism is a static definition of the RP's address and group ranges on each client. This approach does not require any dynamic discovery protocols, but it is prone to reliability issues in the event that the statically defined RP fails, unless Anycast-RP is being used. PIM versions 1 and 2 support static RP assignments.

Auto-RP

The auto-RP mechanism is a nonstandard approach (developed by Cisco Systems) for the dissemination of RP information. Despite the lack of standards, auto-RP is supported in JUNOS software. The main drawback to auto-RP, aside from its nonstandard status, is the need for dense-mode handling of the two group addresses associated with auto-RP itself. This requirement forces sparse-dense mode operation on the network. The two auto-RP groups are 224.0.1.39 (announce), which is used to learn which routers in the network are possible candidate RPs, and 224.0.1.40 (discovery), which allows PIM routers to learn about the active group-to-RP mapping information. In operation, one or more routers are configured to perform the mapping function, which takes as input the set of candidate RPs learned in discovery messages and generates as output the chosen RP-to-group mappings that all routers should use. Auto-RP does support failover to backup RPs, but auto-RP does not support the ability to load-balance among multiple RPs for the same group range. Auto-RP is supported in PIM versions 1 and 2.

Bootstrap

The BSR mechanism is the standardized way to dynamically communicate a domain's RP to group address bindings. Unlike auto-RP, BSR does not require any dense-mode flooding. This is because bootstrap messages are propagated hop by hop rather than flooded via multicast, which thereby eliminates the cart-before-the-horse issues of auto-RP needing a working dense-mode multicast infrastructure before an RP can be communicated. The bootstrap mechanism is supported in PIM version 2 only. You can configure multiple candidate BSRs for redundancy—it is common to have the same routers configured as candidate RPs to be set as candidate BSRs also.

Once the BSR is elected (the router with the highest BSR priority), each candidate RP advertises its configured group ranges. The BSR processes the received advertisements, based in part on factors such as local policy, group range specificity, configured RP priority, and so on. The resulting RP set is communicated to all PIM routers, at which point each router is required to run its own hash to determine the RP for a given group. It is important to note that the hash algorithm ensures that all routers select the same RP-to-group mappings from the information in the domain's RP set, and when multiple candidate RPs are present, the algorithm automatically load-balances between those RPs. Stated differently, if two RPs both announce the default 224/4 range, bootstrap operation results in each RP handling one-half of the active groups. The failure of one RP results in all groups being shifted to the remaining RP—however, at no one time can multiple RPs be active for the same group when using bootstrap.

Anycast-RP

PIM supports the notion of Anycast-RPs, which bypasses the restriction of having one active RP per multicast group. With Anycast-RP, you can deploy multiple RPs for the same group range. Anycast-RP provides redundancy and load balancing, but unlike bootstrap, Anycast-RP can balance traffic from sources within the *same* group. With Anycast-RP, the various RPs share a common unicast IP address, such that clients simply choose the metrically closest route to the shared RP address. In the event of RP failure, the IGP simply reroutes to the next best path to the shared IP address, thus preserving connectivity. For proper operation, is it critical that each Anycast-RP be aware of active sources using other Anycast-RPs. This RP-to-RP communication can be performed using MSDP, as defined in RFC 3446, or using the newer, PIM-only approach defined in RFC 4610. Both methods are supported in JUNOS software.

PIM modes

PIM can operate in dense, sparse, sparse-dense, or SSM mode. Although in this chapter we are emphasizing PIM sparse mode in support of ASM, for completeness we will expand on the various modes here.

Dense mode. PIM dense mode is useful for multicast LAN applications, the main environment for all dense mode protocols. PIM dense mode uses the same flood first, prune later approach associated with DVMRP. The main difference between

DVMRP and PIM dense mode is that PIM provides protocol independence and can use the route table populated by any underlying unicast routing protocol to perform RPF checks. PIM dense mode supports the ASM model.

Sparse mode. PIM sparse mode is the most common way to deploy PIM. Sparse mode operation is considerably more complex than dense mode, but sparse mode offers the benefit of bandwidth conservation, which often more than justifies the added complexity. The various configuration examples shown in this chapter are based on PIM sparse mode. The key aspect of sparse mode operation is the need for an RP to serve as a liaison between active senders and any receivers that wish to obtain their content.

A PIM sparse mode router joins the RP-based shared tree upon receipt of an IGMP join from attached receivers. This is known as an (*,G) join because it matches any source sending to that group. If any sources are active for that group, their packets are sent down the shared tree until they reach the last hop router (the router directly attached to the receiver) and are delivered to the receiver(s) on that network segment. Receipt of traffic over the shared tree allows the last hop router to learn the address of active sources, at which point it initiates an SPT by sending an (S,G) over the RPF path toward each source. Once the SPT is established, the last hop router prunes that source from the shared tree by sending an (S,G) prune. This transitional aspect of PIM sparse mode from shared to source-based tree is one of the major attractions of PIM. This feature prevents overloading the RP or surrounding core links, which was the Achilles' heel of the CBT approach—which has yet to see commercial deployment.

PIM sparse mode supports the ASM and SSM models.

Source-specific multicast. The original multicast RFCs specify both many-to-many and one-to-many models. These modes are now known as ASM because ASM supports one or many sources for a multicast group's traffic. However, ASM operation requires that receivers be able to determine the locations of *all* sources for a particular multicast group, no matter where the sources might be located in the network. In ASM, *source discovery* is a critical and complex function within the network.

ASM makes sense in a highly dynamic environment where sources often come and go, as, for example, in a videoconferencing service. However, several promising multicast applications, such as IP-based television, are being brought to commercial realization quickly and efficiently through an assumption that there is a longer-lived single source for some particular content. PIM SSM is simpler than PIM sparse mode because only the one-to-many model is supported. PIM SSM therefore forms a subset of PIM sparse mode. It builds only SPTs, and an RP is no longer necessary, given that the user specifies the source address as part of his IGMPv3 report message.

PIM SSM can coexist with ASM by confining the SSM model to a subset of the IP multicast group address range. The IANA has reserved the address range 232.0.0.0–232.255.255.255 for SSM operation. JUNOS software allows SSM configuration for the entire range of IP multicast addresses (224.0.0.0–239.255.255.255). When a custom SSM range is defined, legacy IP multicast applications cannot receive any traffic for groups in that SSM range, unless the application is modified to support SSM (S,G) channel subscription.

PIM messages

PIM uses a variety of message types to do its job. The reader is encouraged to consult the appropriate RFC for an exhaustive description of each field found in the various PIM messages. Our purpose here is to describe *how* these PIM messages operate to establish SSM operation:

Join/prune
> PIM state is established and withdrawn using join/prune messages. An individual message may contain both join and prune information, join information (a join message) only, or prune information (a prune message) only. A single join/prune message can list multiple senders/groups to join or prune.

Register
> Routers connected to a multicast source encapsulate the multicast data stream into unicast packets that are addressed to the RP that serves that group range. A PIM register message contains an encapsulated multicast packet, which can be sent to the RP without the need for multicast transport between the sender and the RP. Once received by the RP, the register encapsulation is stripped and the RP forwards native multicast packets down the shared RPT.

Register stop
> The RP may wish to stop receiving the encapsulated multicast traffic from the first hop router, and the register-stop message is used to accomplish this goal. An RP may wish to stop receiving register-encapsulated messages for several reasons:
>
> - The RP has no join state for the group address of the traffic (there are no interested listeners on the RPT).
> - The RP may have received a prune message from the network for a group being forwarded along the RPT, perhaps as the result of SPT establishment leaving no interested receivers.
> - The RP itself might be receiving the multicast traffic natively from the network along an SPT.

The designated router

PIM defines specific functions for the first and last hop routers, which are known as designated routers. The designated router sends register and join/prune messages on behalf of directly connected senders and receivers, respectively. The designated router may or may not be the same router as the IGMP querier.

On multiaccess networks, a designated router is elected to ensure that packets and PIM control state are not duplicated. In operation, PIM neighbors on a shared LAN periodically send PIM Hello messages to each other. The sender with the highest IP address becomes the designated router for that LAN segment.

PIM assert. PIM supports an assert mechanism that prevents ongoing packet duplication, which can occur when there are parallel paths to a source or the RP. Figure 10-12 shows the PIM assert process in action.

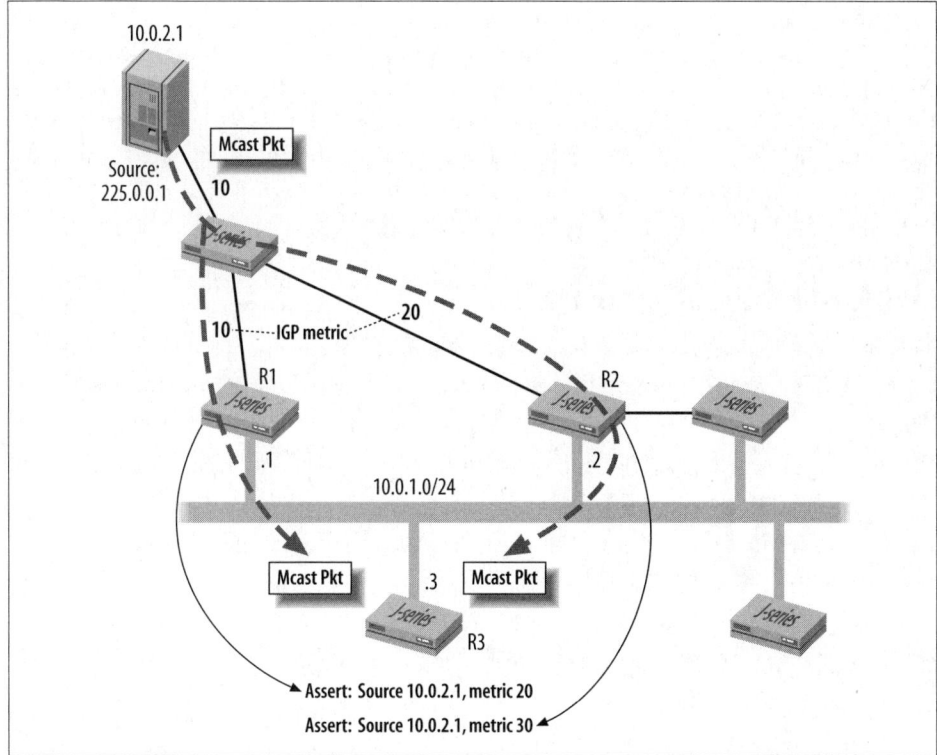

Figure 10-12. The PIM assert process

The figure shows three routers, R1–R3, connected to a shared LAN, along with an RP and a source for group 225.0.0.1. The figure also shows the IGP metrics to reach the source, as seen by routers R1 and R2. In this example, both R1 and R2 have added the multicast source to their OIL for their LAN attached interface. As a result, a packet sent from the source is replicated and forwarded by both R1 and R2, resulting in an extra copy of the packet on the LAN segment. To prevent ongoing occurrences, the PIM assert process is started, by which the upstream PIM routers assert their right to be the designated forwarder by sending assert messages to the 224.0.0.13 (ALL-PIM-ROUTERS) group multicast address. Each router places its IGP preference and corresponding metric to the source in its assert message. The router with the best preference, or lowest metric, wins (metrics are compared only in the event of a preference tie). In the event of a tie, the router with the highest IP address wins. Figure 10-12 also shows that R1 has a better metric and therefore becomes the forwarder for the LAN segment. Meanwhile, downstream router R3 has eavesdropped on the assert battle and takes note of the victor because this is the router to which R3 will subsequently send joins for that source.

PIM asserts are also needed for (*,G) entries. This is because the RPT and SPT for a given group may transit a shared media link such as a LAN. In these cases, the assert mechanism determines which of the two trees will carry the packet on the shared links, again to avoid unneeded packet duplication. According to the specifications, an SPT is always preferred over an RPT. When there are multiple paths to the RP through the LAN, the designated router may lose the (*,G) assert process to another router on the LAN. As a result, that router ceases to be the designated router for local receivers on that LAN, and the victor becomes the last hop router and is therefore responsible for sending (*,G) join messages to the RP.

Multicast Protocol Summary

This section detailed the function of group management protocols, which allow routers to determine which interfaces have attached listeners, and allow multicast routing protocols that provide for RPF checking and manage join and prune states.

We also discussed the use of shared and source-specific trees, as well as the role of the RP in supporting ASM and SSM.

In the next section, we will put multicast theory to the test with a PIM sparse mode deployment scenario using a static RP.

PIM Sparse Mode: Static RP

At this stage, you should have an extensive grounding in IP multicast theory in general, and in PIM sparse mode operation in particular. This knowledge is soon to bear fruit as you configure and validate the operation of PIM sparse mode using a statically defined RP with Juniper Networks' routers.

The initial PIM sparse mode deployment goals are as follows:

- Configure router PBR as an RP for the entire multicast address range.
- Configure all other routers to use PBR as the domain's RP without using BSR or auto-RP.
- Configure Cider to function as a multicast receiver for group 225.1.1.1.

- Use Ale as a multicast source to generate traffic to group 225.1.1.1.
- Verify RPT join and subsequent traffic-driven switches to SPT.

Figure 10-13 details the portion of Beer-Co's network that is to be enabled for multicast support. The figure also highlights key aspects of the IGP routing infrastructure now in place.

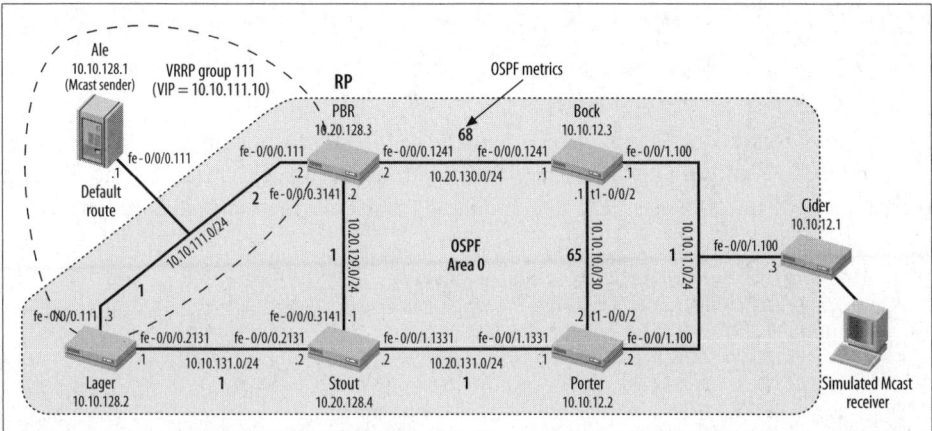

Figure 10-13. Beer-Co's multicast topology

Details to note in Figure 10-13 include the following:

- The default OSPF bandwidth scaling factor is in effect with the exception of PBR's end of the PBR–Lager link (asymmetric) and the PBR–Bock link. The metric for these links has been altered in an effort to favor the Lager–Stout–Porter path for communications between Ale and Cider.

- Router Ale is configured to emulate a host sending to a multicast group. Ale uses a default route pointing to the virtual IP (VIP) address associated with the PBR–Lager Virtual Router Redundancy Protocol (VRRP) group. No routing or multicast protocols are enabled at Ale.

- Cider is used to simulate a PIM-enabled router with a directly attached multicast receiver.

Validate the Baseline IGP Forwarding Path

Before starting any multicast configuration, a quick confirmation of IGP connectivity and the resulting forwarding paths through the network is performed. The use of a default route is confirmed at Ale, as is the use of the Lager, Stout, and Porter forwarding paths for communications between Ale and Cider:

```
[edit]
lab@Ale# run show route 10.10.12.1
```

```
inet.0: 4 destinations, 4 routes (4 active, 0 holddown, 0 hidden)
+ = Active Route, - = Last Active, * = Both

   0.0.0.0/0          *[Static/5] 00:00:04
                        > to 10.10.111.10 via fe-0/0/0.111
[edit]
lab@Ale# run traceroute 10.10.12.1 no-resolve
traceroute to 10.10.12.1 (10.10.12.1), 30 hops max, 40 byte packets
 1  10.10.111.3  11.837 ms   9.735 ms   10.115 ms
 2  10.10.131.2  19.716 ms  20.203 ms   9.681 ms
 3  10.20.131.1  10.109 ms  10.395 ms   9.298 ms
 4  10.10.12.1   20.214 ms   9.747 ms  19.893 ms
```

Symmetrical forwarding in the return path from Cider to Ale is also confirmed, as is
the use of OSPF routing at Cider; recall that unlike Ale, which is running no routing
protocols, Cider simulates a PIM/OSPF-enabled router with an attached receiver:

```
[edit]
lab@Cider# run traceroute 10.10.128.1 no-resolve
traceroute to 10.10.128.1 (10.10.128.1), 30 hops max, 40 byte packets
 1  10.10.11.2   9.945 ms   9.711 ms   9.856 ms
 2  10.20.131.2  20.054 ms  39.955 ms  19.863 ms
 3  10.10.131.1  19.854 ms  18.125 ms  31.839 ms
 4  10.10.128.1  19.792 ms  19.949 ms  20.214 ms

[edit]
lab@Cider# run show route 10.10.128.1

inet.0: 19 destinations, 19 routes (19 active, 0 holddown, 0 hidden)
+ = Active Route, - = Last Active, * = Both

10.10.128.1/32     *[OSPF/150] 00:20:10, metric 0, tag 0
                     > to 10.10.11.2 via fe-0/0/1.100
```

The OSPF route to the loopback address of Ale is seen as an OSPF external by router
Cider. This is because a static route representing Ale's lo0 address is redistributed
into OSPF at routers PBR and Lager, which is necessary here given that Ale does not
participate in OSPF routing. The 111 VRRP group shared by PBR and Lager is configured to make Lager the VRRP master when its fe-0/0/0.111 interface is operational
via the preempt keyword and a priority of 100—the accept-data option is added to
permit diagnostic ping testing to the VIP. According to the VRRP RFC, the VIP is
allowed to respond only to Address Resolution Protocol (ARP) requests, meaning
that unlike Cisco's HSRP, by default you cannot ping the VIP associated with a
VRRP group.

Lager's static route, related redistribution policy, and VRRP configuration are shown.
PBR has a similar configuration, except that its VRRP priority is set to 50.

```
[edit]
lab@Lager# show routing-options
static {
    route 10.10.128.1/32 next-hop 10.10.111.1;
```

```
    }

[edit]
lab@Lager# show policy-options
policy-statement Ale_lo0 {
    term 1 {
        from {
            protocol static;
            route-filter 10.10.128.1/32 exact;
        }
        then accept;
    }
}

[edit]
lab@Lager# show interfaces fe-0/0/0 unit 111
description Lager_PBR_Ale;
vlan-id 111;
family inet {
    address 10.10.111.3/24 {
        vrrp-group 69 {
            virtual-address 10.10.111.10;
            priority 100;
            preempt;
            accept-data;
        }
    }
}
```

Configure PIM Sparse Mode with Static RP

With the underlying IGP's operation confirmed, you move on to PIM configuration
on the routers making up the multicast test bed. In the JUNOS software implementation, enabling PIM on an interface automatically enables IGMPv2, making explicit
configuration of IGMP unnecessary unless you need to modify default settings.
IGMP is not required on links that connect only routers—hosts use IGMP to inform
routers of their group membership. Leaving IGMP enabled on these links does not
lead to appreciable resource consumption and ensures that things will work as
expected if hosts are added at a later time.

PIM configuration begins at router PBR because it's been designated as the RP in the
initial multicast topology; without an RP, PIM sparse mode cannot begin to operate.
PIM is configured at the [edit protocols pim] hierarchy. The configuration options
for PIM are displayed:

```
[edit protocols pim]
lab@PBR# set ?
Possible completions:
+ apply-groups          Groups from which to inherit configuration data
+ apply-groups-except   Don't inherit configuration data from these groups
  assert-timeout        Set assert timeout (5..210)
```

```
> dense-groups        Dense mode groups for sparse-dense mode
  disable             Disable PIM
> graceful-restart    Configure graceful restart attributes
+ import              PIM sparse import join policy
> interface           PIM interface options
> mdt                 Configure multicast data tunnel parameters
> rib-group           Routing table group
> rp                  Router's rendezvous point properties
> spt-threshold       Set shortest-path-tree threshold policy
> traceoptions        Trace options for PIM
  vpn-group-address   Group address for the VPN in provider space
```

The `assert-timeout` setting determines how often the forwarding router reasserts its right to do so, based on its belief that it has the lowest SPF RPF cost for a given source or RP; the router always generates an assert message when a multicast packet is *received* on an interface that is in the *outgoing* interface list for a given group. Internal rate-limiting of these event-driven assert messages (as with all control plane messaging in JUNOS software) ensures that the network and local processing resources are not overrun in the event of a packet loop or broken multicast forwarding state in an adjacent node.

The `dense-groups` configuration identifies any groups that are flooded in dense mode over interfaces set for sparse-dense mode operation. This setting is used when you operate in sparse mode but you still want dense mode flooding on a group-by-group basis, and is typically used to support auto-RP's need for dense mode flooding of its announce (224.0.1.39) and discovery (224.0.1.40) messages.

The `graceful-restart` settings control the graceful restart duration and can be used to specifically disable graceful restart for PIM when graceful restart is globally enabled under the [edit routing-options] stanza. The `import` keyword links to one or more policies that allow filtering of join messages, which prevents the resulting (*,G) or (S,G) state, therefore blocking the extent of multicast traffic distribution by preventing installation of related forwarding state in the control plane. In contrast, multicast scoping operates in the *data* plane to provide a similar effect. Generally speaking, the use of scoping is preferred over join filtering because the former scales better, and it prevents the transport of multicast traffic that could result from the use of dense mode flooding or a packet generation tool.

The `spt-threshold` determines whether the local router attempts a switch to an SPT after the first packet (default), or never when set to infinity. The use of multicast distribution tree (MDT) tunnels and routing information base (RIB) groups is beyond the scope of this book. Suffice it to say that MDT tunnels are used to support PIM sparse mode in a Layer 3 virtual private network (VPN) environment, and that use of RIB groups allows a PIM multicast forwarding topology that is independent of the unicast RPF table.

The interface keyword allows specification of which interfaces should run PIM, along with interface-level parameters such as PIM version, hello time, and so on. The options available at the [edit protocols pim interface *interface-name*] hierarchy are:

```
[edit protocols pim]
lab@PBR# set interface fe-0/0/0.111 ?
Possible completions:
  <[Enter]>             Execute this command
+ apply-groups          Groups from which to inherit configuration data
+ apply-groups-except   Don't inherit configuration data from these groups
  disable               Disable PIM on this interface
  hello-interval        Hello interval (0..255 seconds)
  mode                  Mode of interface
  priority              Hello option DR priority (0..4294967295)
  version               Force PIM version (1..2)
```

Most interface-level options are self-explanatory. The priority setting specified under an interface controls the router's likelihood of being elected the PIM designated router on that network segment; the default setting is 1, making the router least likely to be the designated router. The mode keyword determines whether the associated PIM interface operates in sparse, dense, or sparse-dense mode. When an interface is in sparse-dense mode, the list of groups specified with the dense-groups keyword is flooded in dense mode, and all other groups are handled as sparse.

You configure a router to be an RP, or to learn about other RPs using either the static, bootstrap, auto-RP or Anycast-RP mechanism under the [edit protocol pim rp] hierarchy. The configuration options available at this hierarchy are:

```
[edit protocols pim]
lab@PBR# set rp ?
Possible completions:
+ apply-groups          Groups from which to inherit configuration data
+ apply-groups-except   Don't inherit configuration data from these groups
> Auto-RP               Set Auto-RP mode (IPv4 only)
> bootstrap             Bootstrap properties
+ bootstrap-export      Bootstrap export policy (IPv4 only)
+ bootstrap-import      Bootstrap import policy (IPv4 only)
  bootstrap-priority    Eligibility to be the bootstrap router (IPv4 only)
+ dr-register-policy    DR policy applied to outgoing register messages
> embedded-rp           Set embedded-RP mode (IPv6 only)
> local                 Router's local RP properties
+ rp-register-policy    RP policy applied to incoming register messages
> static                Configure static PIM RPs
```

As you would expect, the properties that control auto-RP-based RP election are configured under the Auto-RP hierarchy. Auto-RP is not demonstrated here because it has lost favor to BSR-based election for reasons that were cited previously. Several bootstrap-related configuration keywords are used in bootstrap-based RP election—we will skip these knobs for now because we will explore them in a subsequent BSR configuration example.

The `dr-register-policy` and `rp-register-policy` keywords link to policy statements that filter register messages sent by the designated router or filter register messages received by the RP, respectively. This feature allows you to control the number of sources that a given RP can know about, and that might be used for performance or security-related reasons. The `embedded-rp` hierarchy controls the number of embedded RPs, as well as groups that can contain an embedded RP address. Embedded RP is used for interdomain IPv6 multicast and is beyond the scope of this book. Note, however, that IPv4 interdomain multicast is normally associated with MSDP.

Static definition of an RP is performed with the `static` keyword. A statically configured RP eliminates the need for dynamic RP election, but this simplicity can come at the cost of reduced reliability because routers may continue to use an RP that has ceased functioning. However, the use of a statically defined RP, in conjunction with Anycast-RP, alleviates many of these concerns, and we discuss it in detail in "PIM Sparse Mode with Anycast-RP Summary," later in this chapter.

Configure PIM on the RP

Local RP characteristics are defined under the [edit protocols pim local] hierarchy, and are used when the local router functions as an RP. Because PBR is the PIM domain's RP in this example, your configuration begins at PBR with the specification of its local RP properties. The command-line interface's (CLI's) ? function displays the configuration mode set options available at the [edit protocols pim rp local] hierarchy:

```
[edit protocols pim rp local]
lab@PBR# lab@PBR# set ?
Possible completions:
  address               Local RP address (IPv4 only)
+ apply-groups          Groups from which to inherit configuration data
+ apply-groups-except   Don't inherit configuration data from these groups
  disable               Disable this RP (IPv4 only)
> family                Local RP address family
> group-ranges          Group address range for which this router can be an RP (IPv4
only)
  hold-time             How long neighbor considers this router to be up, in seconds
(IPv4 only)
  priority              Router's priority for becoming an RP (IPv4 only) (0..255)
```

Use the `address` keyword to define the local RP address for IPv4 operation. Normally, this will be a globally routable address (i.e., a non-127.*x.x.x* address) assigned to the router's lo0 interface for maximum reliability, given that the virtual nature of a loopback interface tends to make it the last to fail. The `family` keyword is used to configure an IPv6-based RP under the `inet6` family. You may wish to divide the multicast address space among multiple RPs using the `group-ranges` keyword to help spread processing load or to improve overall robustness by eliminating a potential single point of failure for all multicast groups in the domain.

The configured hold-time value is included in candidate RP messages (sent to a domain's bootstrap router when using BSR), and determines how long the BSR includes that RP in the candidate RP set before the entry needs to be refreshed by receipt of a new candidate RP advertisement for that same RP. The priority value is used in the hash function that chooses a particular RP for a given group range from the set of candidate RPs. A numerically smaller priority value is preferred—the range is from 0–255, with 1 being the default. Note that a setting of 0 indicates that the BSR can override the received RP-to-group mappings in the candidate RP set that it advertises.

Because you are configuring a static RP environment, only the address keyword is of concern in the current configuration. "Configure PIM Sparse Mode with Bootstrap RP," later in this chapter, demonstrates BSR-based RP election. PBR is configured to use its globally routable loopback address as the domain's RP:

```
[edit protocols pim rp local]
lab@PBR# set address 10.20.128.3
```

The interfaces that should run PIM are configured next; there is no need or benefit to running PIM on the lo0 interface, so transit interfaces only are enabled for PIM. The completed PIM stanza at PBR is displayed:

```
[edit protocols pim]
lab@PBR# show
rp {
    local {
        address 10.20.128.3;
    }
}
interface fe-0/0/0.3141;
interface fe-0/0/0.1241;
interface fe-0/0/0.111;
```

After committing the changes to the local RP, status is confirmed:

```
lab@PBR# run show pim rps
Instance: PIM.master
Address family INET
RP address        Type         Holdtime Timeout Groups Group prefixes
10.20.128.3       static              0  None         0 224.0.0.0/4
```

The output of the show pim rps command shows that PBR is functioning as a statically defined RP for the entire multicast address 224/4 group range. You next verify that PIM is enabled on all transit interfaces used in the multicast test bed with a show pim interfaces command:

```
[edit protocols pim]
lab@PBR# run show pim interfaces
Instance: PIM.master
```

```
Name                  Stat Mode      IP V State Count DR address
fe-0/0/0.111          Up   Sparse    4  2 DR        0 10.10.111.2
fe-0/0/0.1241         Up   Sparse    4  2 DR        0 10.20.130.2
fe-0/0/0.3141         Up   Sparse    4  2 DR        0 10.20.129.2
pd-0/0/0.32769        Up   Sparse    4  2 P2P       0
```

The command output confirms that PIM is now running on all three of PBR's network interfaces used in the multicast test bed, and that sparse is the default mode of operation. Because PBR is the first, and so far the only, PIM-enabled router, it has won the designated router election on all of its multiaccess interfaces; a designated router is not required on point-to-point interfaces. The 0 count value indicates that no PIM neighbors have been detected, which is expected until other routers are enabled for PIM. The show pim neighbors command returns an empty list at this time (not shown).

The highlighted code in the output calls out that the router has automatically instantiated a PIM decapsulation (pd) interface using the J-series built-in services interface functionality. Recall that in sparse mode, the first hop router encapsulates multicast into a unicast register message (using a PIM encapsulate [pe] interface), which is then decapsulated back to native multicast at the RP for distribution down the shared tree. No explicit configuration is needed for these pd and pe interfaces; they are created automatically when PIM sparse mode is configured and the required tunnel support is present. On some platforms, such as the M10i, you must order and install tunnel hardware to support PIM sparse mode register message encapsulation.

As noted previously, in JUNOS software, enabling PIM automatically enables IGMP on that interface. The output of the show igmp interface command confirms that this is the case:

```
lab@PBR# run show igmp interface
Interface: fe-0/0/0.111
    Querier: 10.10.111.2
    State:         Up Timeout:    None Version:  2 Groups:      5
Interface: fe-0/0/0.1241
    Querier: 10.20.130.1
    State:         Up Timeout:    156 Version:   2 Groups:      0
Interface: fe-0/0/0.3141
    Querier: 10.20.129.1
    State:         Up Timeout:    154 Version:   2 Groups:      0

Configured Parameters:
IGMP Query Interval: 125.0
IGMP Query Response Interval: 10.0
IGMP Last Member Query Interval: 1.0
IGMP Robustness Count: 2

Derived Parameters:
IGMP Membership Timeout: 260.0
IGMP Other Querier Present Timeout: 255.
```

Configure PIM on remaining routers

With the domain's RP up and running, you move on to add PIM to the remaining routers. Aside from specifying PIM-enabled interfaces, you must also specify the domain's RP explicitly, given that this is a static RP scenario. The PIM configuration added to Stout is shown. All remaining routers have a similar PIM configuration.

```
[edit protocols pim]
lab@stout# show
rp {
    static {
        address 10.20.128.3;
    }
}
interface fe-0/0/0.2131;
interface fe-0/0/0.3141;
interface fe-0/0/1.1331;
```

The key to this PIM sparse mode configuration is the static definition of the domain's RP, which in this example is PBR's lo0 address. When desired, you can further define a static RP's group range and PIM version:

```
[edit protocols pim]
lab@stout# set rp static address 10.20.128.3 ?
Possible completions:
  <[Enter]>              Execute this command
+ apply-groups           Groups from which to inherit configuration data
+ apply-groups-except    Don't inherit configuration data from these groups
> group-ranges           Group address range of RP
  version                PIM version of RP (1..2)
```

In this example, the default version 2 and 224/4 group range are desired, so no further changes are needed. After the changes are committed, you confirm the presence of PIM neighbors at router Stout:

```
[edit protocols pim]
lab@stout# run show pim interfaces
Instance: PIM.master
```

Name	Stat	Mode	IP	V	State	Count	DR address
fe-0/0/0.2131	Up	Sparse	4	2	DR	1	10.10.131.2
fe-0/0/0.3141	Up	Sparse	4	2	NotDR	1	10.20.129.2
fe-0/0/1.1331	Up	Sparse	4	2	DR	1	10.20.131.2
pe-0/0/0.32769	Up	Sparse	4	2	P2P	0	

The display shows that Stout has detected one PIM neighbor on all but its pe encapsulation interface, which is expected given this setup. The output also shows that the local router is the designated router for two of its three network interfaces. To display neighbor information, issue a show pim neighbors command:

```
lab@stout# run show pim neighbors
Instance: PIM.master
```

```
Interface             IP V Mode        Option      Uptime Neighbor addr
fe-0/0/0.2131          4 2              HPLG        00:18:12 10.10.131.1
fe-0/0/0.3141          4 2              HPLG        00:18:12 10.20.129.2
fe-0/0/1.1331          4 2              HPLG        00:18:12 10.20.131.1
```

The display shows the IP address of each detected PIM neighbor, the associated interface, and the supported IP/PIM version. The Mode column is expected to be empty when configured for PIMv2 because v2 supports dense, sparse, and sparse-dense modes. The Option column displays a coded list of each neighbor's supported PIM options. The codes are interpreted as follows:

B   Bidirectional-capable

H   Hello option hold time

G   Generation identifier

P   Hello option designated router priority

L   Hello option LAN prune delay

Add the detail switch to view the specific timers and parameters associated with each neighbor:

```
[edit protocols pim]
lab@stout# run show pim neighbors detail
Instance: PIM.master
Interface: fe-0/0/0.2131

    Address: 10.10.131.1,        IPv4, PIM v2
        Hello Option Holdtime: 105 seconds 95 remaining
        Hello Option DR Priority: 1
        Hello Option Generation ID: 532624463
        Hello Option LAN Prune Delay: delay 500 ms override 2000 ms

    Address: 10.10.131.2,        IPv4, PIM v2, Mode: Sparse
        Hello Option Holdtime: 65535 seconds
        Hello Option DR Priority: 1
        Hello Option Generation ID: 756451044
        Hello Option LAN Prune Delay: delay 500 ms override 2000 ms
```

The PIM neighbor state is as expected at Stout. RP information is displayed with the show pim rps command:

```
[edit protocols pim]
lab@stout# run show pim rps
Instance: PIM.master
Address family INET
RP address           Type      Holdtime Timeout Groups Group prefixes
10.20.128.3          static           0   None       0 224.0.0.0/4

Address family INET6
```

The output displays the loopback address associated with router PBR, which is functioning as the Beer-Co domain's RP. Further, the display confirms that the RP was learned via static configuration (hence, no timeout), and that currently no multicast groups are mapped to this RP, as indicated by the 0 in the Groups column. Given that there are no active groups (or sources, for that matter) in the current network, the lack of any group-to-RP mappings is expected at this time. As further confirmation, PIM join state is displayed at Stout:

```
[edit protocols pim]
lab@stout# run show pim join
Instance: PIM.master Family: INET

Instance: PIM.master Family: INET6
```

The join list is empty, which indicates that no SPT or RPT joins have been instigated by the local router. This display confirms that no groups are currently mapped to the domain's RP. The lack of join state means there should be no multicast forwarding state, which is easily verified with a show multicast route command:

```
[edit protocols pim]
lab@stout# run show multicast route
Family: INET

Family: INET6
```

As expected, there are no active multicast routes, which is in keeping with no RPT or SPT join state. At this stage, the PIM network is awaiting an active source and an interested receiver.

Verify RPF

Before you activate any senders or multicast receivers, the RPF state of the current network is analyzed. Recall that multicast forwarding and control plane operations tend to center on the RPF function. An RPF check is, in essence, nothing more than a route lookup on a packet source, and then verification that the packet arrives on the same interface that would be used when routing packets addressed to that source.

Referring back to Figure 10-13, it is restated that IGP metrics are altered to prefer the lower forwarding path consisting of routers Lager, Stout, and Porter. The network's RPF state should reflect the IGP's preferred forwarding path, which is confirmed with a show multicast rpf command issued at router Bock for the prefix associated with the domain's RP:

```
[edit]
lab@Bock# run show multicast rpf 10.20.128.3
Multicast RPF table: inet.0 , 21 entries

10.20.128.3/32
    Protocol: OSPF
    Interface: fe-0/0/1.100
    Neighbor: 10.10.11.2
```

The output shows that Bock expects to receive packets sent from the 10.20.128.3 loopback address of PBR, via its fe-0/0/1.100 interface. Based on this RPF state, any packets from source 10.20.128.3 received on *any other* interface fail the RPF check, resulting in discard. The OSPF route to 10.20.128.3 is displayed at Bock to confirm that the shortest path route from Bock to PBR's loopback does in fact egress on its fe-0/0/1.100 interface.

```
[edit]
lab@Bock# run show route 10.20.128.3

inet.0: 21 destinations, 22 routes (21 active, 0 holddown, 0 hidden)
+ = Active Route, - = Last Active, * = Both

10.20.128.3/32      *[OSPF/10] 01:18:05, metric 4
                    > to 10.10.11.2 via fe-0/0/1.100
```

Configure the simulated receiver

The test bed used to develop this book did not have external multicast senders or receivers. Although unfortunate from an overall reality perspective, the upside is that their absence forces the use of JUNOS software to simulate their functionality, and these little-known techniques often prove useful when troubleshooting multicast issues because they allow you to isolate potential problems with attached hosts and their multicast applications/protocol stack.

A Word on Multicast Client Options

Multicast is a somewhat dry subject, and it is always nice to use some media content, such as a multiplayer game or cool streaming DVD video, to validate multicast operation and performance. If your test bed contains multicast-capable hosts, we suggest that you investigate programs such as VideoLAN, which supports streaming video over unicast or multicast, on a variety of platforms to include Windows and various flavors of Unix. For more information, see the VideoLAN development web site at *http://www.videolan.org*.

Unix platforms can use the *mgen/mrec utilities*, which respectively stand for multi-generator and dynamic-receiver. These utilities are available for download at *http://downloads.pf.itd.nrl.navy.mil/mgen/mgen3/*. The command line used to evoke drec to function as a receiver for group 225.1.1.1 in this scenario is similar to the example shown, but local interface names will vary:

```
%./drec -b 225.1.1.1 -n 1 -p 5000 -i em1 -S NOW /dev/null
DREC: Version 3.1a3
DREC: Loading event queue ...
DREC: Listening for packets ...
     (Hit <CTRL-C> to stop)
```

As for the command-line switches, the -b value specifies the base group address to join, and the -n value determines how many groups, starting at the base, are to be joined. The -p value specifies a User Datagram Protocol (UDP) port (5000 is the default), and the -i switch indicates the local interface that should be joined. The -S value determines test start time; test duration can also be specified. Once drec is launched, you would expect to see a join for the associated group, and would then fire up mgen with compatible settings to generate multicast traffic to that group. The command example uses the -t switch to set the desired TTL and the -r switch to set a rate of 10 packets per second:

```
%./ mgen -b 225.0.0.1:5000 -n 1 -i em1 -p 5000 -t 32 -r 10

MGEN: Version 3.1a3
MGEN: Loading event queue ...
MGEN: Seeding random number generator ...
MGEN: Beginning packet generation ...
       (Hit <CTRL-C> to stop)
```

A number of multicast test utilities are available for Windows platforms, but generally speaking, these tend to be somewhat crude when compared to the myriad options supported on Unix systems. The WSend and WListen utilities are popular options, and an Internet search will likely reveal several download locations; there no longer appears to be an official source for these applications. Figure 10-14 shows how the WListen utility is configured to support the role of the multicast receiver for group 225.1.1.1 in this lab.

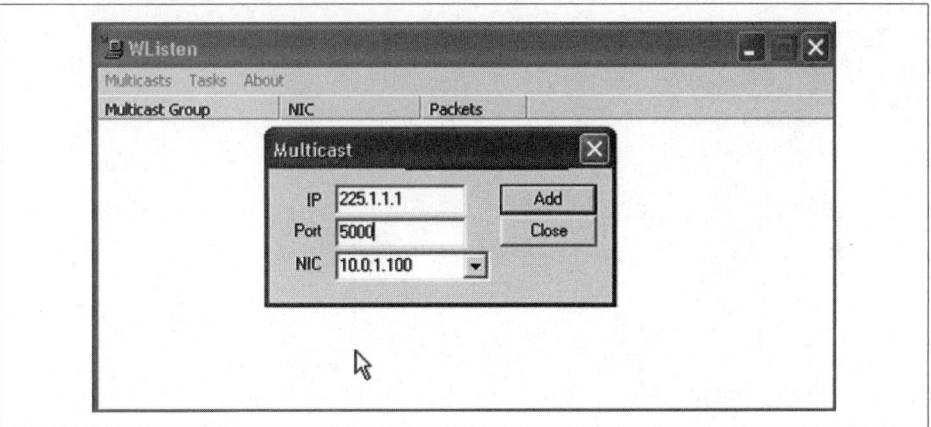

Figure 10-14. Configuration of the Windows-based WListen utility

Static IGMP membership. The simplest way to simulate an attached multicast receiver in JUNOS software is to configure a static IGMP join. The problem with a simple static join is that the local router does not join the group, and as such it does not receive any test traffic, which means that without an actual external receiver on the associated interface, there can be no hope of replies to generated multicast test traffic. With no such external receiver in this lab, the only way to confirm multicast forwarding is to monitor interface traffic stats on the receiver interface while trying to correlate the received packet count to the generated multicast test traffic. In a quiescent lab setup, this may be workable, but in any type of production network, there will likely be enough background traffic to make accurate matching of transmitted traffic to received multicast packets all but impossible. The syntax for a static IGMP join is shown, but this approach is not used because a different technique is planned for simulating a multicast receiver at router Cider:

```
[edit]
lab@Cider# show protocols igmp
interface fe-0/0/0.0 {
    static {
        group 225.1.1.1;
    }
}
```

Before moving on, it's noted that the lack of multicast hosts means there will be no IGMP activity to monitor in the lab. With the static join in place, you can view IGMP group status to familiarize yourself with the display. Things begin with the clearing of any IGMP membership to ensure that no stale state is displayed:

```
[edit]
lab@Cider# run clear igmp membership
Clearing Group Membership Info for fe-0/0/1.100
Clearing Group Membership Info for fe-0/0/0.0

[edit]
lab@Cider# run show igmp group
Interface: fe-0/0/0.0
    Group: 225.1.1.1
        Source: 0.0.0.0
        Last reported by: Local
        Timeout:      0 Type: Static
Interface: local
    Group: 224.0.0.2
        Source: 0.0.0.0
        Last reported by: Local
        Timeout:      0 Type: Dynamic
    Group: 224.0.0.5
        Source: 0.0.0.0
        Last reported by: Local
        Timeout:      0 Type: Dynamic
    Group: 224.0.0.6
        Source: 0.0.0.0
        Last reported by: Local
        Timeout:      0 Type: Dynamic
    Group: 224.0.0.22
        Source: 0.0.0.0
        Last reported by: Local
        Timeout:      0 Type: Dynamic
```

 As noted previously, multicast forwarding is all about dynamic state, and this state can seem to persist for an annoyingly long period of time if it's not cleared out manually. When testing any multicast environment, it is wise to let things cook for at least five minutes in all operational modes to ensure that things are really working the way you expect. Although bogus multicast state will generally not cause any negative impact to the router or network, it can affect communications for several minutes if left to age out using its own means.

The output of the show igmp membership command confirms the statically configured membership on interface fe-0/0/0 for the 225.1.1.1 group. The lack of a specific source address shows that this is an (*,G), or shared tree join. When IGMPv3 is enabled, you can specify a source address when configuring static membership to generate (S,G) state and a resulting SPT. Dynamic entries are associated with a timeout value indicating when the entry will age out if it is not refreshed as a result of a host membership report for that group. The local entries represent multicast addresses associated with local processes that need to listen to multicast traffic. The 225.0.0.5 and 225.0.0.6 addresses represent all OSPF routers and all OSPF designated router groups, 225.0.0.1 is the all hosts group, 225.0.0.2 is the all routers group, and 225.0.0.22 is the multicast group associated with IGMP reports.

Create a listening multicast process

Many multicast applications operate in a simplex fashion, meaning that a reply is not technically needed for the application to work. However, in this lab the goal is to use Internet Control Message Protocol (ICMP) echo packets sent to a multicast group address, with success being determined by the receipt of a unicast reply, because this is the most expedient way to confirm that multicast test traffic is successfully forwarded all the way to the multicast receiver.

 You can disable response generation to multicast-targeted pings by including the no-multicast-echo statement at the [edit system] hierarchy level, in JUNOS software releases 8.1 and later. This does not alter behavior for unicast-targeted pings.

The trick to making a Juniper router initiate a PIM join, while also creating a process that listens to the associated group in contrast to a static IGMP join, is to enable the SAP process on the group in question. SAP always operates on the well-known group address 224.2.127.254, using port 9875, but you can configure SAP to operate on other groups (and ports) as well. This is the approach we're taking for the test bed's 225.1.1.1 group.

 Active multicast sources transmit SDP messages infrequently, often on the order of minutes. This long delay between messages can cause problems in a PIM sparse mode network. The receipt of the SAP message by the RP causes it to examine its current join state for the 224.2.127.254 multicast group. If no state is enabled, the SAP message is not forwarded into the network. The end result is that the SDP message delay makes it extremely hard to get the SDP messages from the multicast source to the interested clients when operating in sparse mode. To reduce this delay, you can configure a SAP process on each router directly attached to receivers. This causes the router to generate a PIM join for the SAP group address of 224.2.127.254. The router refreshes this join state such that the RP maintains a constant forwarding tree for the SAP group. This allows the infrequent SDP messages to be forwarded to the interested clients and to populate the Session Directory tool. Frankly, it's hard to imagine something this good still being legal.

Before altering the configuration at Cider, a show pim join command is issued to confirm that no join state currently exists:

```
lab@Cider# run show pim join
Instance: PIM.master Family: INET

Instance: PIM.master Family: INET6
```

Cider's configuration is altered to instantiate a SAP process that will listen on 225.1.1.1, port 5000:

```
lab@Cider# show sap
listen 225.1.1.1 port 5000;
```

After the change is committed, PIM join state is again displayed. This time the extensive switch is added to view all possible details:

```
[edit protocols]
lab@Cider# run show pim join extensive
Instance: PIM.master Family: INET

Group: 224.2.127.254
    Source: *
    RP: 10.20.128.3
    Flags: sparse,rptree,wildcard
    Upstream interface: fe-0/0/1.100
    Upstream neighbor: 10.10.11.2
    Upstream state: Join to RP
    Downstream neighbors:
        Interface: Local

Group: 225.1.1.1
    Source: *
    RP: 10.20.128.3
    Flags: sparse,rptree,wildcard
    Upstream interface: fe-0/0/1.100
```

```
    Upstream neighbor: 10.10.11.2
    Upstream state: Join to RP
    Downstream neighbors:
        Interface: Local
```

The output indicates that the newly created SAP process has issued an RPT (shared tree, or [*,G]) join for both the well-known and user-configured SAP groups. The upstream (incoming) interface is the RPF interface leading toward the domain's RP, and the downstream (outgoing) interface list is empty because this join is the result of a local process rather than a received PIM join or IGMP membership report. The presence of a listening UDP process on both SAP-associated ports is now verified. Here the command makes use of CLI matching and logical OR functionality to make quick work of the task:

```
[edit protocols]
lab@Cider# run show system connections | match "(5000|9875)"
udp4      0      0  *.5000                *.*
udp4      0      0  *.9875                *.*
```

The output confirms the two expected UDP-based listening processes on the well-known and user-specified SAP ports. The lack of data activity on the 225.1.1.1 group results in no cached forwarding state, as evidenced by the lack of a multicast route for the 225.1.1.1 group at transit node Porter:

```
[edit]
lab@Porter# run show multicast route
Family: INET

Family: INET6
```

Before generating traffic, the network's RPT join state is again analyzed. Recall that PIM joins are sent using RPF toward the source, and that for an (*,G) join, that source is the RP. Given the metric adjustments in effect in the multicast topology, the RPF path from Cider to PBR (the RP) should consist of the path Porter, Stout, PBR. The presumed forwarding path is first confirmed:

```
[edit protocols]
lab@Cider# run traceroute 10.20.128.3
traceroute to 10.20.128.3 (10.20.128.3), 30 hops max, 40 byte packets
 1  10.10.11.2 (10.10.11.2)  9.235 ms   8.720 ms   9.706 ms
 2  10.20.131.2 (10.20.131.2)  10.190 ms  9.147 ms   7.321 ms
 3  10.20.128.3 (10.20.128.3)  12.943 ms  38.945 ms  9.847 ms
```

The traceroute results show that the unicast forwarding path from Cider to PBR's loopback address is as anticipated—therefore, an RPT join initiated at Cider should take this same path. Shared tree join state is displayed at Porter:

```
[edit]
lab@Porter# run show pim join 225.1.1.1
Instance: PIM.master Family: INET

Group: 225.1.1.1
    Source: *
```

```
RP: 10.20.128.3
Flags: sparse,rptree,wildcard
Upstream interface: fe-0/0/1.1331
```

The RPT join state at Porter is as expected, in that the upstream interface is pointing toward Stout. The join state for 225.1.1.1 is displayed at Stout:

```
[edit]
lab@stout# run show pim join 225.1.1.1
Instance: PIM.master Family: INET

Group: 225.1.1.1
    Source: *
    RP: 10.20.128.3
    Flags: sparse,rptree,wildcard
    Upstream interface: fe-0/0/0.3141
```

As expected, RPF forwarding of the shared tree join at Stout results in an upstream interface of fe-0/0/0.3141, which is the metrically closest way for Stout to reach PBR's 10.20.128.3 address.

The current state of the network correctly represents PIM sparse mode state for a receiver interested in a group with no active senders. In the next section, we will generate multicast traffic and examine the impact on network state.

Generate multicast traffic

With the receiver join state and resulting PIM sparse mode RP-rooted shared tree verified, it is time to shake things up by actually generating some multicast traffic! In this example, a Juniper router is used to simulate a multicast source with the ping command, in conjunction with the bypass-routing, ttl, and interface switches. The bypass-routing switch is needed to avoid the fact that the inet.1 table does not have multicast forwarding state for the 225.0.0.1 group; remember, Ale is a router, not a host. Because there is no routing entry to rely on, you must identify the egress interface for the test traffic using the interface switch. By default, locally generated multicast ping traffic uses a TTL of 1, which is done to limit the scope of the traffic to the local link. This is because in a real-world scenario, *numerous* receivers could be listening to the related group, and this in turn can result in significant packet replication and a resulting avalanche of replies. The test bed has only one receiver for the test traffic, making this a nonissue. A TTL value of at least 5 is recommended to ensure that the test traffic can make it all the way from Ale to Cider.

 A TTL value of 4 results in the test traffic being handed to Cider with a TTL of 1. Although adequate for unicast, in some cases multicast TTL may be decremented upon receipt, which can lead to intermittent replies for packets received with a TTL = 1. By setting the TTL higher than strictly necessary, you guarantee that you will not encounter this issue.

We have spent a lot of effort leading to this point, and several things are about to happen in rapid succession once the sender is fired up; specifically:

- The first hop router, Lager, encapsulates the native multicast into a unicast packet sent to 10.20.128.3, the domain's RP.

- The RP decapsulates the traffic based on join state for the associated group, and then sends the native multicast down the shared tree. Given the current join state, the traffic should be sent from the RP to Stout and Porter, and then to receiver Cider.

- The presence of multicast traffic results in the creation of a multicast route in transit routers. This route is placed into the inet.1 table, and you can think of it as a data-driven forwarding plane reaction to the control plane's join state. Note that without the control plane join, the data plane cannot establish these dynamic multicast forwarding states.

- Upon receipt of traffic from source 10.10.111.1 over the shared tree, router Cider initiates an SPT join toward the source. Once the SPT is established, multicast from 10.10.111.1 is transported directly over the SPT. To prevent duplicated packets, the first router in the data path that is on *both* the SPT and RPT (Stout in this case) sends an (S,G) prune toward the RP to prevent receipt of packets over both the SPT and the RPT.

- When there are no interested receivers on the RPT, the RP sends a register stop message to the source.

- Once the source is no longer active, the SPT state will eventually age out, resulting in a return to the RPT for group 225.1.1.1.

To help catch some of this behavior, PIM register message tracing is added to Lager:

```
[edit protocols pim]
lab@Lager# show traceoptions
file pim;
flag register detail;
```

Multicast pings are now initiated at Lager:

```
[edit]
lab@Ale# run ping ttl 5 225.1.1.1 interface fe-0/0/0.111 bypass-routing
PING 225.1.1.1 (225.1.1.1): 56 data bytes
64 bytes from 10.10.11.3: icmp_seq=0 ttl=61 time=16.776 ms
64 bytes from 10.10.11.3: icmp_seq=1 ttl=61 time=20.144 ms
. . .
```

The output confirms that responses are being received from 10.10.11.3, the address of Cider's fe-0/0/1.100 interface. The presence of replies is a most auspicious beginning, to be sure. Meanwhile, back at Lager, the following trace output is observed:

```
Sep 27 00:55:10.983201 PIM SENT 10.10.128.2 -> 10.20.128.3 V2 Register Flags:
0x40000000 Border: 0 Null: 1 Source 10.10.111.1 Group 225.1.1.1 sum 0x43f1 len 28
Sep 27 00:55:10.993582 PIM fe-0/0/0.2131 RECV 10.20.128.3 -> 10.10.128.2 V2
RegisterStop Source 10.10.111.1 Group 225.1.1.1 sum 0x80d1 len 18
```

The trace confirms that, as predicted, the first hop router sent a register message to the RP for source 10.10.111.1 and group 225.1.1.1, and the RP later generated a register stop for this (S,G) pair, thus indicating that no more listeners are present on the shared tree. This is a good indication that the SPT cutover was successful. Next, the resulting (S,G) join state is examined at Cider:

```
[edit protocols]
lab@Cider# run show pim join 225.1.1.1 extensive
Instance: PIM.master Family: INET

Group: 225.1.1.1
    Source: *
    RP: 10.20.128.3
    Flags: sparse,rptree,wildcard
    Upstream interface: fe-0/0/1.100
    Upstream neighbor: 10.10.11.2
    Upstream state: Join to RP
    Downstream neighbors:
        Interface: Local

Group: 225.1.1.1
    Source: 10.10.111.1
    Flags: sparse,spt
    Upstream interface: fe-0/0/1.100
    Upstream neighbor: 10.10.11.2
    Upstream state: Join to Source
    Keepalive timeout: 355
    Downstream neighbors:
        Interface: Local
```

Cider's display confirms that SPT join state is now also present for the 225.1.1.1 group. Cider remains on the RPT via its (*,G) join in case any other sender becomes active for the 225.1.1.1 group—this is an ASM example, after all. The join state at Stout also shows an SPT and RPT, but the RPT has been pruned for this (S,G) pair, given the presence of an SPT between the sender and receiver:

```
[edit]
lab@stout# run show pim join 225.1.1.1 extensive
Instance: PIM.master Family: INET

Group: 225.1.1.1
    Source: *
    RP: 10.20.128.3
    Flags: sparse,rptree,wildcard
    Upstream interface: fe-0/0/0.3141
    Upstream neighbor: 10.20.129.2
    Upstream state: Join to RP
    Downstream neighbors:
        Interface: fe-0/0/1.1331
            10.20.131.1 State: Join Flags: SRW Timeout: 179

Group: 225.1.1.1
    Source: 10.10.111.1
```

```
Flags: sparse,spt
Upstream interface: fe-0/0/0.2131
Upstream neighbor: 10.10.131.1
Upstream state: Join to Source, Prune to RP
Keepalive timeout: 303
Downstream neighbors:
    Interface: fe-0/0/1.1331
        10.20.131.1 State: Join Flags: S Timeout: 179
```

The join state at Stout is as expected. It too remains on the shared tree for group 225.1.1.1, in case any additional sources become active, and it too has generated an SPT join directly toward the source, as a result of receiving an (S,G) join on its downstream interface, as sent by Porter. The highlights call out the topology difference between the shared and source trees, with the shared tree at Stout pointing toward the RP while the source tree points toward the source. Stout has pruned source 10.10.111.1 from the shared tree, a state that is reflected at the RP:

```
[edit]
lab@PBR# run show pim join 225.1.1.1 extensive
Instance: PIM.master Family: INET

Group: 225.1.1.1
    Source: *
    RP: 10.20.128.3
    Flags: sparse,rptree,wildcard
    Upstream interface: Local
    Upstream neighbor: Local
    Upstream state: Local RP
    Downstream neighbors:
        Interface: fe-0/0/0.3141
            10.20.129.1 State: Join Flags: SRW Timeout: 156

Group: 225.1.1.1
    Source: 10.10.111.1
    Flags: sparse,spt
    Upstream interface: fe-0/0/0.111
    Upstream neighbor: Direct
    Upstream state: Local Source, Local RP
    Keepalive timeout: 337
    Downstream neighbors:
        Interface: fe-0/0/0.3141 (pruned)
            10.20.129.1 State: Prune Flags: SR Timeout: 156
```

With the PIM sparse mode control plane looking good, you examine the data plane state as it relates to the (S,G) flow currently active in the network:

```
[edit]
lab@stout# run show multicast route detail
Family: INET

Group: 225.1.1.1
    Source: 10.10.111.1/32
    Upstream interface: fe-0/0/0.2131
```

```
Downstream interface list:
    fe-0/0/1.1331
Session description: MALLOC
Statistics: 0 kBps, 1 pps, 1966 packets
Next-hop ID: 348
Upstream protocol: PIM
```

The highlights call out the expected upstream and downstream (incoming/outgoing) interfaces. Including the detail switch displays current traffic stats for each forwarding cache entry. When a well-known group address is detected, the session description reflects the associated application. In this case, no application is associated with 225.0.0.1, so the display simply indicates that the session belongs to the multicast allocation address space (MALLOC). The next hop ID field is used to tie this route into a forwarding table entry in the Packet Forwarding Engine (PFE). You can display the multicast forwarding table to confirm that this next hop ID is associated with the 10.10.111.1, 225.1.1.1 tuple:

```
[edit]
lab@stout# run show route forwarding-table multicast destination
225.1.1.1
Routing table: inet
Internet:
Destination        Type RtRef Next hop     Type Index NhRef Netif
225.1.1.1.10.10.111.1/64
                   user    0                mcrt   348    1
```

To actually display what the forwarding table does with the next hop index of 348, you have to access the PFE directly. The following commands are performed for illustrative purposes, and they use unsupported shell commands. Remember: you should use hidden and shell commands only under direct guidance of JTAC.

```
[edit]
lab@stout# run start shell
% su
Password:
root@stout% vty 1

BSD platform (Pentium processor, 84MB memory, 8192KB flash)
```

A shell is started and the user becomes root, because only the root user has access to the vty command used to attach to the forwarding devices daemon (fwdd) process. You connect to the software-based PFE, which on a J-series router is called fwdd, by connecting to tnp address 1. Once connected to the PFE, information is displayed for the next hop value of 348:

```
FWDD(stout vty)# show nhdb id 348
Nexthop Info:
  ID   Type    Interface      Next Hop Addr Protocol  Encap      MTU
  ---- ------- -------------- -------------- --------  --------- ----
  348 MultiRT -              -               IPv4      -          0
            fe-0/0/1.1331                    IPv4      Ethernet
```

The PFE output confirms that currently, a single outgoing interface is associated with next hop ID 348. A multicast route entry can have numerous next hop interfaces when the topology requires such replication. You now exit out of the vty connection and the shell to return to the CLI:

```
FWDD(stout vty)# exit

root@stout% exit
% exit

[edit]
lab@stout#
```

Multicast routes in a forwarding state are placed into the inet.1 route table. Unlike a learned route, information in inet.1 is a cache entry that is driven by the actual flow of traffic—the entry ages out a short while after traffic cessation.

```
[edit]
lab@stout# run show route table inet.1 detail

inet.1: 1 destinations, 1 routes (1 active, 0 holddown, 0 hidden)
225.1.1.1.10.10.111.1/64 (1 entry, 1 announced)
        *PIM    Preference: 105
                Next hop type: Multicast (IPv4)
                Next-hop reference count: 2
                State: <Active Int>
                Age: 39:25
                Task: PIM.master
                Announcement bits (1): 0-KRT
                AS path: I
```

The show multicast usage command is also handy when you want to determine the number and relative activity level of the various sources in your network:

```
[edit]
lab@stout# run show multicast usage
Group           Sources Packets         Bytes
225.1.1.1       1       2516            211344


Prefix          /len Groups Packets     Bytes
10.10.111.1     /32  1      2516        211344
```

Note that multicast usage information is displayed both by group and by (S,G) pairing. Multicast traffic generation is stopped at Ale:

```
64 bytes from 10.10.11.3: icmp_seq=7227 ttl=61 time=10.564 ms
^C
--- 225.1.1.1 ping statistics ---
7228 packets transmitted, 7228 packets received, 0% packet loss
round-trip min/avg/max/stddev = 8.079/21.507/201.323/10.705 ms
```

The lack of data plane activity results in aging out of the forwarding state. Because the receiver is still interested in group 225.1.1.1, the control plane join state is refreshed and remains:

```
[edit]
lab@stout# run show multicast route extensive source-prefix 10.10.111.1
Family: INET
Group: 225.1.1.1
    Source: 10.10.111.1/32
    Upstream interface: fe-0/0/0.2131
    Downstream interface list:
        fe-0/0/1.1331
    Session description: MALLOC
    Statistics: 0 kBps, 0 pps, 7306 packets
    Next-hop ID: 348
    Upstream protocol: PIM
    Route state: Active
    Forwarding state: Forwarding
    Cache lifetime/timeout: 171 seconds
    Wrong incoming interface notifications: 1

[edit]
lab@stout# run show pim join extensive 225.1.1.1
Instance: PIM.master Family: INET

Group: 225.1.1.1
    Source: *
    RP: 10.20.128.3
    Flags: sparse,rptree,wildcard
    Upstream interface: fe-0/0/0.3141
    Upstream neighbor: 10.20.129.2
    Upstream state: Join to RP
    Downstream neighbors:
        Interface: fe-0/0/1.1331
            10.20.131.1 State: Join Flags: SRW Timeout: 178

Group: 225.1.1.1
    Source: 10.10.111.1
    Flags: sparse,spt
    Upstream interface: fe-0/0/0.2131
    Upstream neighbor: 10.10.131.1
    Upstream state: Join to Source, Prune to RP
    Keepalive timeout: 169
    Downstream neighbors:
        Interface: fe-0/0/1.1331
            10.20.131.1 State: Join Flags: S Timeout: 178
```

After a few minutes, the (S,G) forwarding state is flushed from the network:

```
[edit]
lab@stout# run show multicast route extensive source-prefix
10.10.111.1
Family: INET
```

This result confirms expected PIM sparse mode control and data plane state and delivery of the multicast test traffic to the receiver by the returned echo replies. These results complete the PIM sparse mode with static RP configuration scenario.

PIM Sparse Mode with Static RP Summary

This section demonstrated the configuration and operational verification of a PIM-based IP multicast network that used a statically defined RP. In the next section, we will build on this experience by adding dynamic RP electing using the bootstrap protocol.

Configure PIM Sparse Mode with Bootstrap RP

In this section, we will convert the existing multicast topology from a statically defined RP to a bootstrap learned RP. As part of this conversion, the network is being redesigned to add a second RP for redundancy. The configuration objectives are as follows:

- Remove the static RP definition from all routers.
- Configure Stout as a second RP for the 224/4 group range.
- Use bootstrap-based RP election, and make sure that PBR is the BSR when operational.
- Ensure that there is no single point of RP/BSR failure in the network.

The new redundancy requirements make it clear that the network will need two RPs and two candidate BSRs. Further, the bootstrap priority will need to be higher (more preferred) at PBR to ensure that it is the BSR when operational. Figure 10-15 shows the updated topology.

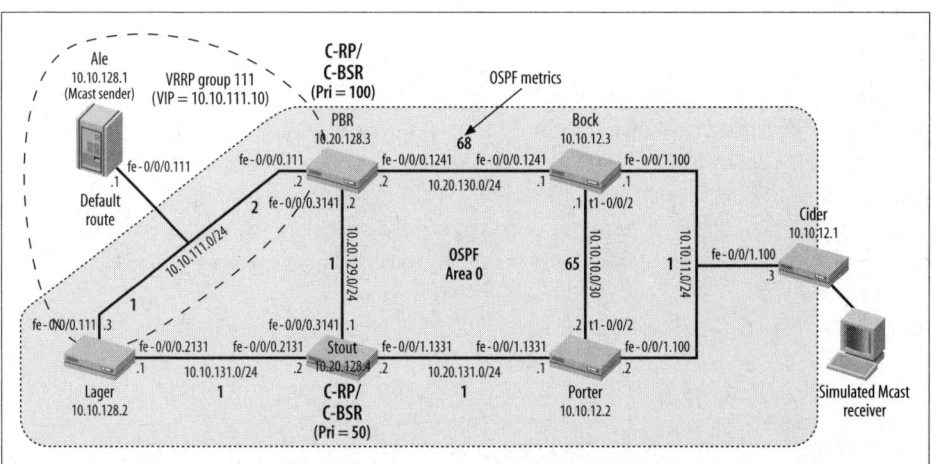

Figure 10-15. Bootstrap RP election

The figure shows that both PBR and Stout are configured to function as candidate RPs and candidate BSRs (C-RP and C-BSR). Although not technically necessary, currently it is a best practice to make the C-RP and C-BSR functionality collocated, given that the loss of either function kills PIM sparse mode operation and negates any benefits associated with distributing C-BSR and C-RP functionality among different nodes. The higher BSR priority setting at PBR results in its election as the domain's BSR when operational; otherwise, Stout steps in to take over.

When both RPs are operational, the BSR advertises a candidate RP set that lists *both* of the domain's RPs. Each PIM router hashes against this set to choose which of the two RPs to use for a specific group range. The hashing function ensures that all routers choose the same candidate RP for the same groups, and that a consecutive set of four groups always map to the same RP. The latter functionality is designed to accommodate applications that use consecutive groups for various elements that make up a single session—for example, an audio channel and the corresponding video stream—by helping to ensure similar latency among the session's component streams.

The static RP definition is removed from routers Lager, Stout, Bock, Porter, and Cider (not shown), and attention is focused on the need to configure candidate BSR functionality at PBR. The configuration is rather straightforward—all that is required is a single statement to enable BSR and assign a priority:

```
[edit protocols pim]
lab@PBR# show
rp {
    bootstrap-priority 100;
    local {
        address 10.20.128.3;
    }
}
interface fe-0/0/0.3141;
interface fe-0/0/0.1241;
interface fe-0/0/0.111;
```

The priority setting of 100 makes PBR a candidate BSR—note that a value of 0 does not disable BSR functionality, but such a setting does make it less likely that candidate PBR will become the BSR. Once a lower priority is set in the soon-to-be-configured Stout, you ensure that PBR is the domain's BSR when operational. In this example, the bootstrap statement is configured directly at the [edit protocols pim rp] hierarchy. The same set of options is available on a per-family basis using the family keyword:

```
[edit protocols pim]
lab@PBR# set rp bootstrap family inet ?
Possible completions:
+ apply-groups          Groups from which to inherit configuration data
+ apply-groups-except   Don't inherit configuration data from these groups
+ export                Bootstrap export policy
```

```
+ import               Bootstrap import policy
  priority             Eligibility to be the bootstrap router (0..255)
```

The import and export keywords link to one or more policy statements that filter bootstrap messages from being received or transmitted, respectively. Normally, you use such policy at the edges of a PIM domain to prevent routers in a remote domain from using the domain's local BSR, and vice versa.

After committing the change, BSR election begins and PBR starts a countdown timer intended to reduce thrashing by allowing time for any C-BSR messages to propagate through the domain before a decision is made as to which C-BSR should win to become the BSR. Use the show pim bootstrap command to display information about the domain's candidate BSRs:

```
[edit protocols pim]
lab@PBR# commit
commit complete

[edit protocols pim]
lab@PBR# run show pim bootstrap
Instance: PIM.master

BSR             Pri Local address      Pri State       Timeout
None              0 10.20.128.3        100 Candidate        54
None              0 (null)               0 InEligible        0
```

PBR is the only router now configured to be a C-BSR, and therefore it easily wins the election to become the domain's BSR:

```
[edit protocols pim]
lab@PBR# run show pim bootstrap
Instance: PIM.master

BSR             Pri Local address      Pri State       Timeout
10.20.128.3     100 10.20.128.3        100 Elected         37
None              0 (null)               0 InEligible        0
```

In the display, each router shows a null entry, as well as an entry for its loopback address and local C-BSR priority. C-BSR information that is learned is displayed on the lefthand side. The output from PBR makes it clear that the local router is also the BSR, and that it has a priority of 100.

 For proper BSR operation, a candidate BSR must have a routable address assigned to its lo0 interface. This is true even when a different address, perhaps one assigned to a physical interface, is configured as the BSR address. This requirement stems from an implementation decision that forces C-BSR messages to be sourced from the local router's lo0 address—C-BSR messages cannot be sent if no lo0 address is configured or if the only address configured is a 127.x.x.x loopback. You can commit such a configuration, and the result is not particularly easy to troubleshoot given that the symptom is simply a lack of generated C-BSR messages.

A few moments later, proper bootstrap operation is confirmed when all other routers have chosen the same C-BSR, as shown for Cider:

```
[edit]
lab@Cider# run show pim bootstrap
Instance: PIM.master

BSR              Pri Local address       Pri State      Timeout
10.20.128.3      100 10.10.12.1            0 InEligible      112
None               0 (null)               0 InEligible        0
```

The show pim bootstrap display at Cider confirms that it has received the C-BSR message that originated at PBR and was propagated via hop-by-hop multicast to all BSR-enabled routers. The presence of a single C-BSR with priority 100 is confirmed, as is election of PBR as the BSR:

```
[edit]
lab@Cider# run show pim rps
Instance: PIM.master
Address family INET
RP address       Type        Holdtime Timeout Groups Group prefixes
10.20.128.3      bootstrap        150     125      2 224.0.0.0/4

Address family INET6
```

The show pim rps display further confirms that an RP has been learned for the 224/4 range via the bootstrap protocol. With things working properly at the first C-BSR/C-RP, it's time to bring up the domain's backup C-BSR/C-RP. The configuration of Stout is modified and displayed:

```
[edit protocols pim]
lab@stout# show | compare
[edit protocols pim rp]
+  bootstrap-priority 50;
+  local {
+      address 10.20.128.4;
+  }
-  static {
-      address 10.20.128.3;
-  }
```

After waiting a minute or two for things to settle down, verification starts at Stout. The expectation is that Stout confirms PBR as the elected BSR while also listing itself as a viable contender:

```
BSR              Pri Local address       Pri State      Timeout
10.20.128.3      100 10.20.128.4          50 Candidate      123
None               0 (null)               0 InEligible        0
```

The output confirms those expectations and shows that BSR is operating as desired between the domain's two candidate BSRs. RP set information is displayed next:

```
[edit protocols pim]
lab@stout# run show pim rps
Instance: PIM.master
```

```
Address family INET
RP address       Type          Holdtime Timeout Groups Group prefixes
10.20.128.3      bootstrap          150     137     1 224.0.0.0/4
10.20.128.4      bootstrap          150     137     1 224.0.0.0/4
10.20.128.4      static               0    None     1 224.0.0.0/4
```

The show pim rps command output lists both of the domain's RPs as having been learned via bootstrap; the local RP definition at Stout is also listed as learned statically. Back at the last hop router, Cider, the state of RPs is also as expected:

```
 edit]
lab@Cider# run show pim rps
Instance: PIM.master
Address family INET
RP address       Type          Holdtime Timeout Groups Group prefixes
10.20.128.3      bootstrap          150     101     1 224.0.0.0/4
10.20.128.4      bootstrap          150     101     1 224.0.0.0/4
```

Awesome! And some folks think this multicast stuff is hard to understand. PIM join state is displayed at Cider. The display illustrates the bootstrap RP hashing function, in that the two joins associated with the listening SAP process hashed to a different RP:

```
[edit]
lab@Cider# run show pim join
Instance: PIM.master Family: INET

Group: 224.2.127.254
    Source: *
    RP: 10.20.128.3
    Flags: sparse,rptree,wildcard
    Upstream interface: fe-0/0/1.100

Group: 225.1.1.1
    Source: *
    RP: 10.20.128.4
    Flags: sparse,rptree,wildcard
    Upstream interface: fe-0/0/1.100
```

Once again, connectivity is verified at the sender:

```
[edit]
lab@Ale# run ping ttl 5 225.1.1.1 interface fe-0/0/0.111 bypass-routing
PING 225.1.1.1 (225.1.1.1): 56 data bytes
64 bytes from 10.10.11.3: icmp_seq=0 ttl=61 time=87.388 ms
. . .
```

So is the data-driven switch to an SPT at the last hop router:

```
[edit]
lab@Cider# run show pim join 225.1.1.1 detail
Instance: PIM.master Family: INET

Group: 225.1.1.1
    Source: *
    RP: 10.20.128.4
```

```
        Flags: sparse,rptree,wildcard
        Upstream interface: fe-0/0/1.100

    Group: 225.1.1.1
        Source: 10.10.111.1
        Flags: sparse,spt
        Upstream interface: fe-0/0/1.100
```

Before calling it quits, redundancy is verified by deactivating the RP and BSR functionality at PBR. The confirmed option is added to the commit to evoke automatic restoration of the previous (and currently active) configuration to save some keystrokes:

```
[edit protocols pim]
lab@PBR# deactivate rp

[edit protocols pim]
lab@PBR# show
inactive: rp {
    bootstrap-priority 100;
    local {
        address 10.20.128.3;
    }
}
interface fe-0/0/0.3141;
interface fe-0/0/0.1241;
interface fe-0/0/0.111;

[edit protocols pim]
lab@PBR# commit confirmed 3
commit confirmed will be automatically rolled back in 3 minutes
  unless confirmed
commit complete

# commit confirmed will be rolled back in 3 minutes
[edit protocols pim]
```

Failover behavior is confirmed back at Cider:

```
[edit]
lab@Cider# run show pim bootstrap
Instance: PIM.master

BSR             Pri Local address       Pri State      Timeout
10.20.128.4      50  10.10.12.1           0 InEligible     103
None              0  (null)               0 InEligible       0
```

The display confirms the removal of PBR as a candidate RP and the election of the remaining C-BSR (Stout), which is now the best choice. The join state takes a little while to catch up, but after a short while all joins are pointing to the remaining RP:

```
[edit]
lab@Cider# run show pim join
Instance: PIM.master Family: INET

Group: 224.2.127.254
    Source: *
```

```
RP: 10.20.128.4
Flags: sparse,rptree,wildcard
Upstream interface: fe-0/0/1.100

Group: 225.1.1.1
    Source: *
    RP: 10.20.128.4
    Flags: sparse,rptree,wildcard
    Upstream interface: fe-0/0/1.100

Group: 225.1.1.1
    Source: 10.10.111.1
    Flags: sparse,spt
    Upstream interface: fe-0/0/1.100
```

Once the automatic rollback occurs at PBR, things return to the expected state, which completes verification of the PIM sparse mode with bootstrap protocol scenario:

```
[edit]
lab@Cider# run show pim bootstrap
Instance: PIM.master

BSR            Pri Local address        Pri State      Timeout
10.20.128.3    100 10.10.12.1             0 InEligible     88
None             0 (null)                 0 InEligible      0
```

Troubleshoot a Bootstrap Problem

The Beer-Co topology has been altered to interface to another routing domain, as shown in Figure 10-16.

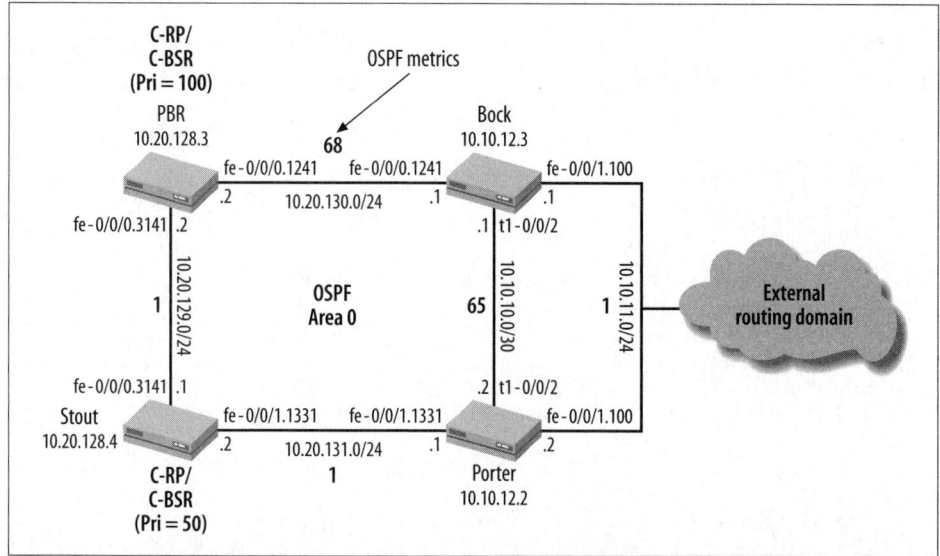

Figure 10-16. PIM BSR troubleshooting topology

Figure 10-16 details how PIMv1 has been configured on the now *external* interfaces at Bock and Porter to prevent the leaking of bootstrap protocol messages to and from the other routing domain. Recall that PIMv1 does not support bootstrap, making this a common approach to scoping BSR messages. The problem is that Bock does not display any learned BSRs, and therefore there is no bootstrap learned RP at Bock:

```
[edit]
lab@Bock# show protocols pim
interface fe-0/0/0.1241;
interface fe-0/0/1.100 {
    version 1;
}
interface t1-0/0/2.0;

[edit]
lab@Bock# run show pim bootstrap
Instance: PIM.master

BSR              Pri Local address    Pri State        Timeout
None               0 10.10.12.3         0 InEligible        0
None               0 (null)             0 InEligible        0
[edit]
lab@Bock# run show pim rps
Instance: PIM.master
```

All other routers display the expected BSR and RP set information. Bock was working properly prior to the shift to PIMv1, and connectivity over all of its interfaces has been verified with successful pings to direct neighbors.

Lacking any better suggestions, PIM bootstrap tracing is added to the configuration, and after a short while trace output is observed:

```
[edit protocols pim]
lab@Bock# show traceoptions
file pim;
flag bootstrap detail;

[edit protocols pim]
lab@Bock# run monitor start pim

*** pim ***
Sep 28 02:27:19.848100 PIM fe-0/0/0.1241 RECV 10.20.130.2 ->
224.0.0.13 V2 Bootstrap sum 0x6ab2 len 46
Sep 28 02:27:19.848182    tag 52078 masklen 30 priority 100 bootstrap
router 10.20.128.3
Sep 28 02:27:19.848208       group 224.0.0.0 count 2 fragcount 2
Sep 28 02:27:19.848230          rp address 10.20.128.3 holdtime 150
priority 1
Sep 28 02:27:19.848247          rp address 10.20.128.4 holdtime 150
priority 1
Sep 28 02:27:19.857917 PIM t1-0/0/2.0 RECV 10.10.10.2 -> 224.0.0.13
V2 Bootstrap sum 0x0cba len 46
Sep 28 02:27:19.858018    tag 10599 masklen 30 priority 100 bootstrap
router 10.20.128.3
```

```
Sep 28 02:27:19.858042        group 224.0.0.0 count 2 fragcount 2
Sep 28 02:27:19.858060          rp address 10.20.128.3 holdtime 150
priority 1
Sep 28 02:27:19.858073          rp address 10.20.128.4 holdtime 150
priority 1
```

The trace output is at once good and bad; good because it shows that valid boot-strap messages are being received on both of Bock's PIMv2-enabled interfaces, and bad because no obvious error or reason is displayed as to why the messages do not result in election of a BSR at Bock. Given that things worked until the shift to PIMv1 on fe-0/0/1.100, you decide to temporarily deactivate the fe-0/0/1 interface:

```
[edit]
lab@Bock# deactivate interfaces fe-0/0/1

[edit]
lab@Bock# commit
commit complete

[edit]
lab@Bock# run show pim bootstrap
Instance: PIM.master

BSR              Pri Local address      Pri State     Timeout
10.20.128.3      100 10.10.12.3           0 InEligible    100
None               0 (null)               0 InEligible      0
```

Quite interesting; the output confirms proper BSR election as long as the PIMv1 inter-face is deactivated—which makes little sense given that PIMv1 does not even support the BSR protocol! The change is rolled back to reactivate the fe-0/0/1.100 interface.

Strange; very strange indeed—recalling that RPF checks are critical to multicast oper-ation, you display the RPF route to 10.20.128.3 from Bock:

```
[edit]
lab@Bock# run show multicast rpf 10.20.128.3
Multicast RPF table: inet.0 , 21 entries

10.20.128.3/32
    Protocol: OSPF
    Interface: fe-0/0/1.100
    Neighbor: 10.10.11.2
```

The display shows that Bock considers 10.10.11.2 as the RFP neighbor for the 10.20. 128.3 route, which is reachable over the 10.10.11.0/24 subnet. Interestingly, this is also the interface that was set to PIMv1, and this explains the problem: PIM control mes-sages generally have to be received on the RPF interface to their source; otherwise, they are ignored. For the specific behavior discussed here, Section 3.6.3 of RFC 2362 states:

> When a router receives a Bootstrap message sent to 'ALL-PIM-ROUTERS' group, it performs the following:
>
> 1 If the message was not sent by the RPF neighbor towards the BSR address, the mes-sage is dropped.

The problem now becomes clear—given the OSPF metrics in effect, Bock expects to receive BSR messages on its fe-0.0/1/100 interface and is dropping BSR messages received on those interfaces that are not on the RPF path back to the BSR. Several solutions present themselves:

- Alter IGP metrics so that Bock no longer sees its fe-0/0/1.100 interface as the RPF interface back to the BSR—that is, either increase the 10.10.11.0 subnet metric or reduce the 10.20.130.0 or 10.10.10.0 subnet metric.

- Reconfigure the network to move BSR functionality to a node whose RPF check does not point to Bock's fe-0/0/1.100 interface. This option is not really viable in the sample topology unless a new router is added.

- Add a new link, or add PIM to a previously nonmulticast-enabled link, in order to affect a new RPF topology, again with the intent of removing fe-0/0/1.100 from the RPF check back to PBR.

Policy-based filtering of bootstrap messages is not considered here because in this scenario, it relies on the administration of the remote autonomous system (AS) to apply import policy to filter bootstrap messages exchanged over the shared LAN between Bock and Porter; egress filtering at Bock and Porter does not work because this filters all bootstrap messages from the LAN—currently Bock needs to receive the bootstrap messages from Porter over the shared LAN.

Extra points for creativity?

The solution demonstrated here is based on the "add another link" option discussed earlier, except the new link is instantiated as a Generic Routing Encapsulation (GRE) tunnel, meaning no new equipment or facilities are needed! No routing protocol operates over the tunnel—Bock uses two /32 static routes to direct traffic destined to the lo0 address of PBR and Stout over the GRE tunnel. This ensures that the only traffic subjected to the tunnel is that associated with the loopback addresses of PBR and Stout. All other traffic continues to follow the IGP's shortest path, thereby causing minimal impact to existing traffic patterns. If all this were not enough, the tunnel is instantiated between the loopback address of Bock and PBR and is routed between these addresses according to the IGP's shortest path. This means the GRE tunnel and associated static routing are not affected by the failures of individual links or interfaces, and that no policy/static routes are needed to advertise reachability to the tunnel endpoints given that the lo0s of Bock and Porter are already carried in OSPF. Because the static routes are preferred over any OSPF learned route (due to preference), the problems of receiving BSR messages on the wrong RPF interface are forever eliminated once PIM is enabled over the GRE tunnel.

The changes to Bock's configuration are shown. The changes at Porter are limited to GRE interface definition and enabling PIM on the resulting GRE interface. No static routes are needed at Porter because the 10.20.128.3 and 10.20.128.4 OSPF routes at Porter already lie on the RPF path back to PBR and Stout, respectively.

```
[edit]
lab@Bock# show interfaces gr-0/0/0
unit 0 {
    tunnel {
        source 10.10.12.3;
        destination 10.10.12.2;
    }
    family inet;
}

[edit]
lab@Bock# show routing-options
static {
    route 10.20.128.3/32 next-hop gr-0/0/0.0;
    route 10.20.128.4/32 next-hop gr-0/0/0.0;
}

[edit]
lab@Bock# show protocols pim
traceoptions {
    file pim;
    flag bootstrap detail;
}
interface fe-0/0/0.1241;
interface fe-0/0/1.100 {
    version 1;
}
interface t1-0/0/2.0;
interface gr-0/0/0.0;
```

Note that an unnumbered GRE tunnel is defined, which eliminates the need to advertise reachability to the tunnel endpoints; local tunnel traffic is based on the lo0 addresses of Bock and Porter, which are already advertised by OSPF. Verification begins by examining Bock's route to the lo0 addresses of PBR and Stout:

```
[edit]
lab@Bock# run show route 10.20.128/29

inet.0: 21 destinations, 24 routes (21 active, 0 holddown, 0 hidden)
+ = Active Route, - = Last Active, * = Both

10.20.128.3/32      *[Static/5] 00:04:39
                     > via gr-0/0/0.0
                     [OSPF/10] 00:16:27, metric 3
                     > to 10.10.11.2 via fe-0/0/1.100
10.20.128.4/32      *[Static/5] 00:04:39
                     > via gr-0/0/0.0
                     [OSPF/10] 00:16:27, metric 2
                     > to 10.10.11.2 via fe-0/0/1.100
[edit]
lab@Bock# run show multicast rpf 10.20.128/29
```

```
Multicast RPF table: inet.0 , 21 entries

10.20.128.3/32
    Protocol: Static
    Interface: gr-0/0/0.0
    Neighbor: (null)

10.20.128.4/32
    Protocol: Static
    Interface: gr-0/0/0.0
    Neighbor: (null)
```

The command output confirms the presence of active static routes at Bock and that the RPF interface to these loO addresses now points to the GRE tunnel. Note that there is no RPF neighbor (listed as null) because the tunnel is unnumbered in this example.

PIMv2 is confirmed operational on the new GRE interface, and a PIM neighbor has been detected:

```
[edit]
lab@Bock# run show pim interfaces
Instance: PIM.master

Name              Stat Mode      IP V State Count DR address
fe-0/0/0.1241     Up   Sparse    4  2 NotDR  1 10.20.130.2
fe-0/0/1.100      Up   Sparse    4  1 NotDR  2 10.10.11.3
gr-0/0/0.0        Up   Sparse    4  2 P2P    1
pe-0/0/0.32769    Up   Sparse    4  2 P2P    0
pe-0/0/0.32770    Up   Sparse    4  2 P2P    0
t1-0/0/2.0        Up   Sparse    4  2 P2P    1
```

The RPF issue with received bootstrap messages is resolved, thus allowing Bock to learn the domain's C-BSRs. With knowledge of the domain's BSR, Bock goes on to learn the domains RPs:

```
[edit]
lab@Bock# run show pim bootstrap
Instance: PIM.master

BSR           Pri Local address       Pri State       Timeout
10.20.128.3   100 10.10.12.3            0 InEligible   125
None            0 (null)                0 InEligible     0

[edit]
lab@Bock# run show pim rps
Instance: PIM.master
Address family INET
RP address      Type        Holdtime Timeout Groups Group prefixes
10.20.128.3     bootstrap        150     139      1 224.0.0.0/4
10.20.128.4     bootstrap        150     139      1 224.0.0.0/4
```

IGP connectivity is confirmed from Bock to the loopback address of PBR:

```
[edit]
lab@Bock# run traceroute 10.20.128.3
traceroute to 10.20.128.3 (10.20.128.3), 30 hops max, 40 byte packets
 1  10.10.12.2 (10.10.12.2)  105.258 ms  71.311 ms  11.741 ms
 2  10.20.131.2 (10.20.131.2)  9.808 ms  9.401 ms  9.677 ms
 3  10.20.128.3 (10.20.128.3)  10.100 ms  29.484 ms  9.734 ms
```

And the use of PIMv1 on the 10.10.11/24 subnet prevents learning of the BSR at
router Cider. This completes the PIM bootstrap troubleshooting exercise.

```
lab@Cider# run show pim bootstrap
Instance: PIM.master

BSR          Pri Local address      Pri State      Timeout
None           0 10.10.12.1           0 InEligible      26
None           0 (null)               0 InEligible       0
```

PIM Sparse Mode with Bootstrap RP Summary

In this section, you configured the bootstrap protocol to dynamically communicate
RP to group mappings. The bootstrap protocol allows all routers to select the same
RP for a given group, thereby spreading the multicast load among the set of RPs,
with the hashing function determining which groups are handled by which RP. This
section also showed how RPF checks can cause control plane messages to be
ignored, and it provided a creative solution using a GRE tunnel that required no
additional hardware.

In the next section, you will deploy Anycast-RP to support dynamic RP election and
load balancing with this same multicast group.

PIM-Based Anycast-RP

The final multicast configuration exercise in this chapter involves deployment of
Anycast-RP, with emphasis on a PIM-only solution. An alternative configuration
using MSDP is also provided.

With both auto-RP and BSR, only one RP is permitted to be active for any given
group at any one time. Anycast-RP relaxes this restriction and allows multiple RPs to
be active for the same group at the same time. Anycast-RP requires a mechanism by
which the multiple RPs share information about active sources. This inter-RP communication has historically been performed by MSDP, but JUNOS software also supports the PIM-only Anycast-RP solution, as specified in RFC 4610. The PIM-based
solution is attractive because it eliminates all need for MSDP within an organization,
allowing MSDP deployment as needed, and then only for its original purpose of
interdomain multicast support.

Because of the common RP address that is shared among all the RPs, receivers simply send their joins to the metrically closest Anycast-RP, and they are unaware of the
presence of multiple RPs.

The configuration objectives are as follows:

- Stout and Bock remain RPs, but both must now use 10.255.255.1 for RP functionality.

- Do not use BSR or auto-RP.

- Ensure no single points of failure.

The requirement that no dynamic RP discovery mechanisms be used may strike you as a bit odd, especially in light of the need for network resiliency to single points of failure. Recall that with Anycast-RP, all of the RPs for a given group range use the same RP address. Therefore, as long as at least one Anycast-RP remains operational, the statically defined RP address in non-RP routers continues to provide the needed connectivity. In an Anycast-RP environment, the use of a dynamic protocol to propagate knowledge of the single RP address is a bit overkill, but certainly not illegal.

Figure 10-17 provides a high-level walkthrough of an Anycast-RP operation.

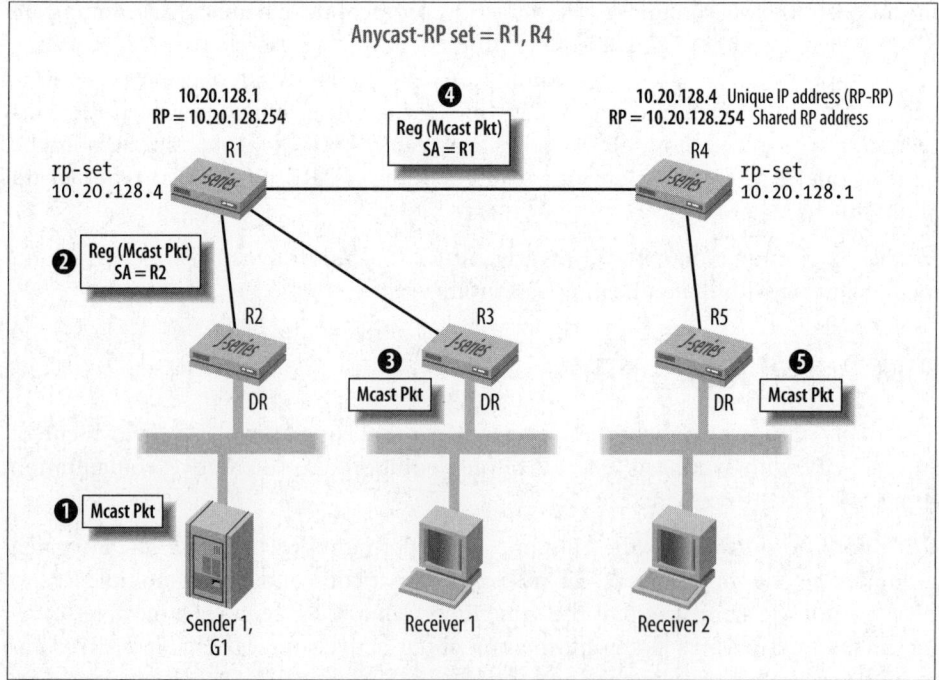

Figure 10-17. PIM Anycast-RP operation

To start, note how the domain's RPs are said to belong to an Anycast-RP set. Each RP within this set must have a unique, routable loopback address that is used for RP-RP (and other) communications, as well as a shared RP address that, in effect, represents all RPs in the set. Further, each RP in the set must have an explicit list of all other RPs, using their unique, not shared, IP address. Figure 10-17 shows how R1 and R4 have a configuration that identifies each other by their unique lo0 IP address.

Step 1 shows Sender 1 (S1) generating native multicast to group G1. The designated router for S1 encapsulates the multicast into a register message and sends it to the Anycast-RP address at step 2. Because all RPs in the set use the same RP address, the register message is routed by the IGP to the metrically closest RP, which is R1 in this example. Note that the register message received by R1 is sourced by R2. Step 3 shows R1 sending the now native multicast (register encapsulation has been stripped) down its shared tree toward Receiver 1. At step 4, R1 creates its *own* register message with a copy of the original multicast packet, which is sent to *all* RPs in the Anycast-RP set, which in this case means that R4 receives a register message with R1 as a source. R4 behaves as any other designated router by stripping the register encapsulation and sending the native multicast down its shared tree, thus allowing R2 to obtain a copy.

Configure Anycast-RP

Figure 10-18 shows the Anycast-RP topology. It details how the domain's two RPs, PBR and Stout, share an Anycast-RP address of 10.255.255.1, in addition to maintaining their unique loopback addresses. Configuration begins with removal of any existing RP and BSR functionality at PBR and Stout (the commit is not shown):

```
[edit]
lab@PBR# delete protocols pim rp
```

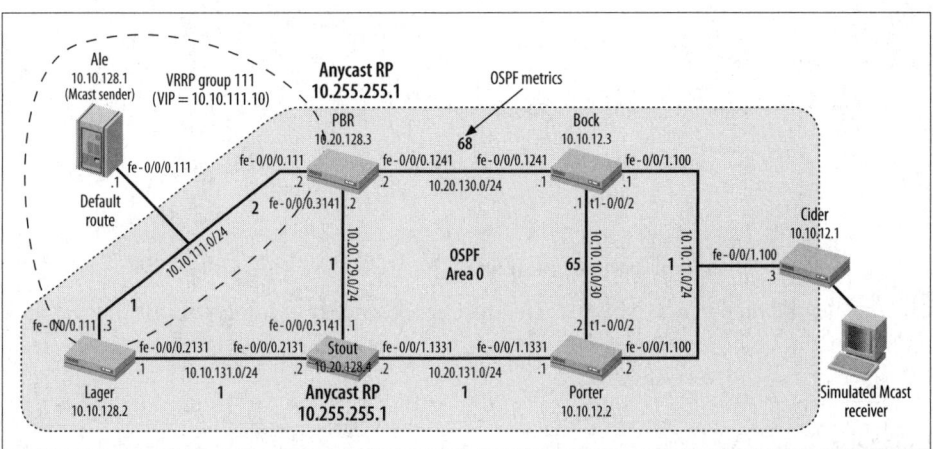

Figure 10-18. The Anycast-RP topology

This action leaves the domain with no RPs—recall that RP information was being disseminated via bootstrap, and the previous command removed all C-RP and C-BSR functionality from the domain.

Configure static RP on non-RP routers

The non-RP routers are a snap to configure; a single statement is needed to statically define the Anycast-RP address at all routers. The configuration of Lager is shown and is similar to all other non-RP nodes:

```
[edit]
lab@Lager# show protocols pim
rp {
    static {
        address 10.255.255.1;
    }
}
interface fe-0/0/0.2131;
interface fe-0/0/0.111;
```

After committing the changes, static RP operation is confirmed at Cider:

```
[edit]
lab@Cider# run show pim rps
Instance: PIM.master
Address family INET
RP address       Type         Holdtime Timeout Groups Group prefixes
10.255.255.1     static              0 None         2 224.0.0.0/4
. . .

[edit]
lab@Cider# run show pim join
Instance: PIM.master Family: INET

Group: 224.2.127.254
    Source: *
    RP: 10.255.255.1
    Flags: sparse,rptree,wildcard
    Upstream interface: unknown (no route)

Group: 225.1.1.1
    Source: *
    RP: 10.255.255.1
    Flags: sparse,rptree,wildcard
    Upstream interface: unknown (no route)
```

The output shows that the Anycast-RP address is correctly configured, but there is currently no route to the Anycast-RP address, which is expected given that the Anycast-RPs have not yet been configured.

Configure the Anycast-RPs

Configuration of the Anycast-RP begins with the addition of the shared Anycast-RP address to the lo0 interface. The existing (unique) address is flagged as primary to ensure no disruption to the IGP/BGP control plane through continued use of the unique lo0 address for non-PIM-related functions, such as OSPF/BGP router ID (RID) selection. Recall that when not explicitly set under routing-options, the RID is obtained from the primary address on the system's default interface, which is the lowest non-127.0.0.x address assigned to the lo0 interface.

```
[edit interfaces lo0 unit 0 family inet]
lab@PBR# set address 10.20.128.3/32 primary

[edit interfaces lo0 unit 0 family inet]
lab@PBR# set address 10.255.255.1
```

 By default, the numerically lowest local IP address is considered the interface's primary address, and the lo0 interface is the default interface when a non-127.0.0.x address is configured. The specifics of this example happened to use a numerically higher address for the Anycast-RP function, making declaration of the existing lo0 address as primary technically unnecessary. However, making a mistake here can lead to the difficult problem of troubleshooting missing routes due to duplicate RIDs, making the extra configuration step insurance that is well worth having.

The modified lo0 configuration is shown:

```
[edit interfaces lo0 unit 0 family inet]
lab@PBR# show
address 10.20.128.3/32 {
    primary;
}
address 10.255.255.1/32;
```

Similar changes are also made to Stout's lo0 configuration. PIM-based Anycast-RP is configured at the [edit protocols pim rp local family inet] hierarchy. The updated configuration and related set commands are shown for PBR:

```
[edit protocols pim rp local family inet]
lab@PBR# show
address 10.255.255.1;
anycast-pim {
    rp-set {
        address 10.20.128.4;
    }
}

[edit protocols pim rp local family inet]
lab@PBR# show | display set
set protocols pim rp local family inet address 10.255.255.1
set protocols pim rp local family inet anycast-pim rp-set address
10.20.128.4
```

Once again, a similar configuration is added and committed at Stout, whose configuration correctly specifies PBR's unique lo0 address under its rp-set stanza.

Verify the Anycast-RPs

After a few minutes, PIM join state is examined at Cider:

```
[edit]
lab@Cider# run show pim join 225.1.1.1
Instance: PIM.master Family: INET

Group: 225.1.1.1
    Source: *
    RP: 10.255.255.1
    Flags: sparse,rptree,wildcard
    Upstream interface: unknown (no route)
```

The display indicates that Cider still does not know how to route to the Anycast-RP address. This is quickly confirmed with a show route command:

```
[edit]
lab@Cider# run show route 10.255.255.1
```

Going back to one of the Anycast-RPs, the problem is quickly uncovered:

```
[edit]
lab@PBR# run show ospf interface
Interface        State    Area      DR ID        BDR ID       Nbrs
fe-0/0/0.111     BDR      0.0.0.0   10.10.128.2  10.20.128.3  1
fe-0/0/0.1241    BDR      0.0.0.0   10.10.12.3   10.20.128.3  1
fe-0/0/0.3141    BDR      0.0.0.0   10.20.128.4  10.20.128.3  1
```

OSPF is not running on the lo0 interface, which prevents the newly added 10.255.255.1 Anycast-RP address from being advertised into OSPF. Recall that the JUNOS software default is to advertise a stub route to the interface from which the router obtains its RID. The router uses the primary address on the default interface—which is normally the lo0 interface by default—as the RID; this is why the 10.20.128.3 lo0 address at PBR has been advertised into OSPF despite OSPF not being enabled on that interface previously.

 They automatically advertise the source of the RID behavior changed in release 8.5 due to PR 229200. In affected releases, you should run a passive OSPF instance on the router's lo0 to ensure the route is advertised into OSPF, which is needed for proper PIM functioning.

A passive OSPF instance is configured to run on the lo0 interface of both Anycast-RPs to get both of the assigned lo0 addresses advertised into OSPF:

```
[edit]
lab@PBR# set protocols ospf area 0 interface lo0 passive
```

The OSPF database confirms that PBR is now advertising the 10.255.255.1 address:

```
[edit]
lab@PBR# show ospf database advertising-router 10.20.128.3 router
detail
```

```
        OSPF link state database, Area 0.0.0.0
  Type       ID           Adv Rtr        Seq    Age  Opt  Cksum  Len
Router  *10.20.128.3  10.20.128.3   0x800000b4  41  0x22  0xff76  84
  bits 0x2, link count 5
  id 10.10.111.3, data 10.10.111.2, Type Transit (2)
  TOS count 0, TOS 0 metric 2
  id 10.20.130.1, data 10.20.130.2, Type Transit (2)
  TOS count 0, TOS 0 metric 68
  id 10.20.129.1, data 10.20.129.2, Type Transit (2)
  TOS count 0, TOS 0 metric 1
  id 10.20.128.3, data 255.255.255.255, Type Stub (3)
  TOS count 0, TOS 0 metric 0
  id 10.255.255.1, data 255.255.255.255, Type Stub (3)
TOS count 0, TOS 0 metric 0
```

The change allows Cider to route toward the Anycast-RP address, which in turn permits it to join the shared tree for 225.1.1.1:

```
[edit]
lab@Cider# run show pim join
Instance: PIM.master Family: INET

Group: 224.2.127.254
    Source: *
    RP: 10.255.255.1
    Flags: sparse,rptree,wildcard
    Upstream interface: fe-0/0/1.100

Group: 225.1.1.1
    Source: *
    RP: 10.255.255.1
    Flags: sparse,rptree,wildcard
    Upstream interface: fe-0/0/1.100
```

The current route to the Anycast-RP is displayed at Cider:

```
[edit]
lab@Cider# run show route 10.255.255.1

inet.0: 20 destinations, 20 routes (20 active, 0 holddown, 0 hidden)
+ = Active Route, - = Last Active, * = Both

10.255.255.1/32    *[OSPF/10] 00:03:53, metric 2
                    > to 10.10.11.2 via fe-0/0/1.100

[edit]
lab@Cider# run traceroute 10.255.255.1
traceroute to 10.255.255.1 (10.255.255.1), 30 hops max, 40 byte packets
 1  10.10.11.2 (10.10.11.2)  79.285 ms  98.810 ms  99.739 ms
 2  10.255.255.1 (10.255.255.1)  10.293 ms  9.213 ms  29.762 ms
```

The output shows that Stout is the RP currently used by Cider. Failover to metrically closest Anycast-RP is tested by increasing the path metric on the Porter–Stout link to 300:

```
lab@Porter# set protocols ospf area 0 interface fe-0/0/1.1331 metric 300
```

And the change is verified back at Cider, which still thinks it is using the same RP, but in reality, its join now goes to PBR via Bock:

```
[edit]
lab@Cider# run show pim join 225.1.1.1
Instance: PIM.master Family: INET

Group: 225.1.1.1
    Source: *
    RP: 10.255.255.1
    Flags: sparse,rptree,wildcard
    Upstream interface: fe-0/0/1.100

[edit]
lab@Cider# run show route 10.255.255.1

inet.0: 20 destinations, 20 routes (20 active, 0 holddown, 0 hidden)
+ = Active Route, - = Last Active, * = Both

10.255.255.1/32    *[OSPF/10] 00:19:02, metric 69
                    > to 10.10.11.1 via fe-0/0/1.100

[edit]
lab@Cider# run traceroute 10.255.255.1
traceroute to 10.255.255.1 (10.255.255.1), 30 hops max, 40 byte packets
 1  10.10.11.1 (10.10.11.1)  19.018 ms  12.334 ms  16.235 ms
 2  10.255.255.1 (10.255.255.1)  9.630 ms  29.665 ms  10.108 ms
```

The final PIM configuration is shown for Anycast-RP node Stout:

```
[edit]
lab@stout# show protocols pim
rp {
    local {
        family inet {
            address 10.255.255.1;
            anycast-pim {
                rp-set {
                    address 10.20.128.3;
                }
            }
        }
    }
}
interface fe-0/0/0.2131;
interface fe-0/0/0.3141;
interface fe-0/0/1.1331;
```

The asymmetric metrics (which is hard to say) in effect cause first hop router Lager to send its register message to PBR, while receiver Cider sends its join toward Stout. When PBR receives the register message from Lager, it generates a copy, sourced from its unique lo0 address, and sends it to Anycast-RP set member Stout. This allows

Stout to delivery a copy of the multicast packet to Cider over the shared tree, which in turn generates an (S,G) join to establish an SPT. Register message tracing is added to Lager and Stout to illustrate Anycast-RP interaction:

```
[edit]
lab@Lager# run traceroute 10.255.255.1
traceroute to 10.255.255.1 (10.255.255.1), 30 hops max, 40 byte
packets
 1  10.255.255.1 (10.255.255.1)  29.511 ms  38.646 ms  10.129 ms
```

The traceroute confirms that Lager sees PBR as the metrically closest RP. The multicast source is started, and register tracing is observed at Lager. Note that the register is sourced from Lager and sent to the shared Anycast-RP address:

```
[edit]
Sep 29 06:08:13.825061 PIM SENT 10.10.128.2 -> 10.255.255.1 V2
Register Flags: 0x40000000 Border: 0 Null: 1 Source 10.10.111.1
Group 225.1.1.1 sum 0x43f1 len 28
```

The register stop back from the Anycast-RP indicates that an SPT has been established or that no more interested receivers are left on the shared tree:

```
lab@Lager# Sep 29 06:06:13.774885 PIM fe-0/0/0.2131 RECV 10.255.255.1
-> 10.10.128.2 V2 RegisterStop Source 10.10.111.1 Group 225.1.1.1 sum
0x80d1 len 18
```

The register message trace output is observed at Stout:

```
[edit]
lab@stout# Sep 29 06:45:28.549924 PIM fe-0/0/0.3141 RECV 10.20.128.3
-> 10.20.128.4 V2 Register Flags: 0x00000000 Border: 0 Null: 0 Source
 10.10.111.1 Group 225.1.1.1 sum 0xdeff len 92

Sep 29 06:45:28.553631 PIM SENT 10.20.128.4 -> 10.20.128.3 V2
RegisterStop Source 10.10.111.1 Group 225.1.1.1 sum 0x80d1 len 18
```

Stout's trace shows that it receives a register from PBR—note how the register message is sent from/to the unique loo addresses of PBR and Stout, respectively. This mechanism differentiates registers received from first hop routers, which are sent to the Anycast-RP address, from those received from other RPs. The former are echoed to all other RPs in the RP set, whereas the latter are absorbed and acted upon locally. Lastly, the show pim source command is executed at Stout to confirm the learning of active group 225.1.1.1 via an Anycast-RP source, as indicated by the 10.255.255.1 address:

```
[edit]
lab@stout# run show pim source detail
Instance: PIM.master Family: INET

Source 10.10.111.1
    Prefix 10.10.111.0/24
    Upstream interface fe-0/0/0.2131
```

```
       Upstream neighbor 10.10.131.1
       Active groups:225.1.1.1

   Source 10.255.255.1
       Prefix 10.255.255.1/32
       Upstream interface Local
       Upstream neighbor Local
       Active groups:225.1.1.1
           224.2.127.254
```

What about MSDP?

Anycast-RP using native PIM is somewhat new, and you may find that some of the routers in your network do not support this method. In this case, you will need to deploy Anycast-RP using MSDP peering between all the RPs in the domain. MSDP conveys information about active sources between the domain's RPs. A working MSDP configuration for the current Anycast-RP topology is added to PBR and Stout. The configuration of MSDP is similar to that of PIM-based Anycast-RP, and it involves listing the unique neighbor addresses of all Anycast-RPs in the domain. The shared and unique IP addresses assigned to the lo0 interface are reused from the previous PIM-based Anycast-RP example. The modified configuration at PBR is as follows:

```
[edit]
lab@PBR# show protocols pim
rp {
    local {
        address 10.255.255.1;
    }
}
interface fe-0/0/0.3141;
interface fe-0/0/0.1241;
interface fe-0/0/0.111;
[edit]
lab@PBR# show protocols msdp
peer 10.20.128.4 {
    local-address 10.20.128.3;
}
```

The local-address statement ensures that the remote MSDP peer recognizes the connection as coming from one of its defined peers. As with loopback-based BGP peering, one end's local-address should match the other end's peer definition. You can use a similar statement with PIM-based anycast, but we omitted it because by default, PIM messages are sourced from the primary address on the lo0 interface.

After starting up the multicast source, the MSDP session state and listing of learned sources is displayed at Stout:

```
[edit]
lab@stout# run show msdp
```

```
Peer address  Local address State    Last up/down Peer-Group SA Count
10.20.128.3   10.20.128.4   Established 00:07:56              1/1

[edit]
lab@stout# run show msdp source-active
Group address   Source address  Peer address    Originator    Flags
225.1.1.1       10.10.111.1     10.20.128.3     10.20.128.3   Accept
```

These results complete the PIM sparse mode Anycast-RP configuration and verification example.

PIM Sparse Mode with Anycast-RP Summary

This section demonstrated a PIM-based solution to Anycast-RP and showed a working example that is based on MSDP. Because Anycast-RP has inherent fault tolerance, it's common to use a static RP definition on client routers to avoid the complexities of a dynamic RP election protocol such as the bootstrap or auto-RP protocol.

Conclusion

IP multicast offers the best of all worlds when supporting one-to-many or many-to-many applications. Using a unicast model for these applications quickly stresses processing power at the source due to replication load, and maximum network bandwidth is consumed. Using broadcast is expensive for all hosts and is confined to a single segment or bridging domain. Only IP multicast offers a scalable, standardized way to handle multipoint streams in a manner that distributes replication load and conserves network bandwidth when branches have no interested listeners. Many network operators are unfamiliar with IP multicast, which limits its widespread use. Multicast should be looked at anytime a network is designed or redesigned as a potentially powerful optimization tool that can also enable the rollout of emerging virtual simulation or multiplayer applications.

PIM sparse mode has become the predominant multicast routing protocol given its support of dense, sparse, and sparse-dense modes of operation and the variety of mechanisms that can be used to dynamically distribute RP information in a fault-tolerant manner. This chapter demonstrated typical PIM sparse mode deployment scenarios using static and bootstrap-based RP dissemination, and it showed PIM- and MSDP-based examples of Anycast-RP. JUNOS software supports a wide range of IP multicast standards and makes multicast configuration and verification relatively straightforward.

Exam Topics

We examined the following Enterprise Exam Topics in this chapter:

- Distance Vector Multicast Routing Protocol (DVMRP)
- Protocol Independent Multicast dense mode (PIM-DM)
- Protocol Independent Multicast sparse mode (PIM-SM)
- Bootstrap, auto-RP, anycast
- Source-specific multicast (SSM)

Chapter Review Questions

1. Which RP dissemination mechanism supports load balancing within the same group?

   a. Auto-RP

   b. Anycast-RP

   c. Bootstrap

   d. Static

2. Which RP dissemination mechanism supports load balancing on a group-by-group basis?

   a. Auto-RP

   b. Anycast-RP

   c. Bootstrap

   d. Static

3. Which methods can you use to scope bootstrap messages?

   a. This is not possible given the hop-by-hop forwarding using the All PIM Routers address

   b. By configuring bootstrap import or export policy

   c. By configuring RP register policy

   d. By configuring PIMv2 on external interfaces

4. Which correctly describes sparse-dense mode operation?

   a. Flooding all traffic until a prune is received, then switching to sparse mode

   b. Operating in sparse mode until a join is received, then switching to dense mode

   c. Operating in sparse mode, with the exception of specific groups that are treated as dense

   d. Sparse-dense mode is needed to support Anycast-RP

5. Which correctly describes PIM register policy?

    a. It allows you to filter register messages to control RP usage

    b. It controls which C-RPs can register with the BSR for inclusion in the RP set

    c. It supports Anycast-RP by allowing inter-RP communication regarding active sources

    d. It controls when the last hop router decides to join an SPT

6. Which correctly describes the default JUNOS software PIM sparse mode behavior?

    a. The first hop routers initiates an SPT join as soon as the first packet is sent

    b. The last hop router initiates an SPT join as soon as the first packet is received

    c. The first hop router initiates an RPT join before the source becomes active

    d. The last hop router initiates an RPT join as soon as traffic is received over the SPT

7. What command displays dynamic multicast forwarding state in the data plane?

    a. `show pim route`

    b. `show multicast route`

    c. `show muticast rpf`

    d. `show route table inet.2`

8. Which of the following best describes an RPF check?

    a. It discards packets that are received on an interface that is not used when routing back to that source

    b. It never sends a multicast packet out the interface used to reach the source

    c. It sends an SPT join out the interface used when routing to that source

    d. All of the above

9. Which is true regarding Anycast-RP?

    a. A shared 127.0.0.1 address is added to the lo0 interface

    b. The Anycast-RPs must communicate with each other using the Anycast-RP address

    c. Anycast-RP messages are flooded using sparse-dense mode

    d. The Anycast-RPs must communicate with each other using their unique lo0 addresses

10. Refer to the output provided and select the best answer:

```
lab@Porter> show multicast route
Family: INET

Group: 225.1.1.1
    Source: 10.10.111.1/32
    Upstream interface: fe-0/0/1.1331
```

```
       Downstream interface list:
           fe-0/0/1.100
```

a. This is an (S,G) entry on the RPT

b. This is an (*,G) entry on the RPT

c. This entry is pruned because only one interface exists in the outgoing list

d. This entry exists in the control plane as a result of an (*,G) join

e. This entry exists in the data plane as a result of multicast traffic

11. Which of the following is true?

a. IGMPv1 supports group leaves

b. IGMPv3 supports group leaves and SSM joins

c. IGMPv2 relied on the routing protocol to perform the querier function

d. IGMP must be explicitly configured to run on PIM-enabled interfaces

12. The querier router sends a query for group 225.1.1.1. What address is the query sent to?

a. The All PIM Routers multicast address

b. The All Hosts multicast address

c. The unicast address of the host that sent the membership

d. The address associated with the group being queried

Chapter Review Answers

1. Answer: B. Only Anycast-RP allows multiple RPs to be active at the same time for the same group.

2. Answer: C. The BSR mechanism automatically balances, on a group-range basis, among a set of C-RPs using a distributed hash function.

3. Answer: B. PIM bootstrap policy can be used to filter BSR messages being sent or received. Using PIMv1 also blocks BSR, as it is not supported in that version.

4. Answer C. Sparse-dense operation defaults to sparse mode, except for groups explicitly designated as dense.

5. Answer: A. PIM register policy allows filtering of registers at the first hop, or at the RP, which controls the number of sessions on the RP.

6. Answer B. The last hop router is in charge of making the switch from RPT to SPT, and in JUNOS software this occurs upon receipt of the first packet.

7. Answer: B. The show multicast route command displays dynamic data plane state that results from multicast traffic. Join-related commands show control plane state.

8. Answer: D. All of the operations described are based on an RPF check.

9. Answer: D. Anycast-RP requires a shared, and unique, lo0 address; the unique address is used for RP-RP communication.

10. Answer: E. This is a multicast route, in the data plane, which is created when allowed by join state and when data activity occurs. This is an (S,G) entry, and therefore it is not on the RPT.

11. Answer: B. IGMPv3 supports v2's group leave as well as SSM.

12. Answer: D. A group query is sent to the multicast address of the group itself.

CHAPTER 11

JUNOS Software with Enhanced Services

The release of JUNOS software with enhanced services represents a significant step forward in solving the needs of enterprise networks. This chapter is not intended to provide complete coverage of the new capabilities associated with JUNOS software with enhanced services. The goal is to prepare the reader for what is coming by providing a high-level overview of what JUNOS software with enhanced services is, detailed information on how to migrate from JUNOS to JUNOS software with enhanced services, and a before-and-after case study showing an Adaptive Services PIC (ASP)-based service set that is migrated to the new enhanced services format, along with the steps needed to validate their operation.

The JUNOS software with enhanced services topics include:

- An overview of JUNOS software with enhanced services
- Migrating from JUNOS to JUNOS software with enhanced services
- An enhanced services case study

JUNOS Software with Enhanced Services Overview

Starting with Release 8.5, you have the option of deploying JUNOS software with enhanced services on supported platforms to take advantage of significant security and service enhancements. It's important to note that even when running JUNOS software with enhanced services, JUNOS is JUNOS, and therefore, the majority of the platform concepts, command-line interface (CLI) commands, operational troubleshooting, and so on remain as covered throughout this book. This is especially true of routing protocol configuration and operational verification, which remains as before and is "classic" JUNOS all the way.

This is *not* a security-focused book, and therefore, comprehensive coverage of the JUNOS enhanced security and services feature set is not possible. This chapter covers migration of a production router from JUNOS to JUNOS software with enhanced services, and gets you familiar with what is different in the new set of enhanced services. It is expected that JUNOS software with enhanced services will continue to evolve, resulting in ongoing updates and additions to the enhanced services portfolio.

For the reader of this book, the changes related to JUNOS software with enhanced services impact those services that were handled by the J-series—for example, stateful firewalls, Network Address Translation (NAT), and IPSec virtual private networks (VPNs). With JUNOS software with enhanced services, these features are no longer ASP-based; instead, they are now based on capabilities born out of ScreenOS security solutions. Aside from the changes to security and services, as far as both configuration and general capabilities, the rest of the JUNOS configuration and operation remains unchanged. The coverage of ASP-based service sets continues to hold true for users of M- and T-series platforms, which do not support JUNOS software with enhanced services.

Supported Platforms

As of this writing, you can load JUNOS software with enhanced services on the following hardware platforms, most of which support digital signal level 3 (DS3) or T3, T1, Gigabit Ethernet, Fast Ethernet, E3, E1, serial, Asynchronous Transfer Mode over asymmetrical digital subscriber line (ATM over ADSL), ATM over symmetric high-speed digital subscriber line (ATM over SHDSL), channelized T1/E1/Integrated Services Digital Network (ISDN) Primary Rate Interface (PRI), and ISDN Basic Rate Interface (BRI) interfaces:

- J2320 and J2350 (DS3 and E3 interfaces are not supported)
- J4350
- J6350
- SSG320m and SSG350m (requires conversion kit)
- SSG520m and SSG550m (requires conversion kit)

In the future, additional platforms may offer JUNOS software with enhanced services support, so be sure to check the Juniper Networks web site for the latest platform support.

Users who purchased NetScreen Secure Security gateway (SSGm) 300 or 500 series devices can convert the machine to a J-series enhanced services router with the appropriate conversion kit. The conversion kit provides a new compact flash with JUNOS software with enhanced services and instructions on how to convert. You can also convert from a supported J-series router running JUNOS software with enhanced services to the equivalent Juniper SSGm firewall running ScreenOS, as shown in Table 11-1, using a similar process, but that is beyond the scope of our discussion.

Table 11-1 shows the mapping between SSGm and J-series router platforms.

Table 11-1. J-series to SSGm platform mapping

J-series model	SSGm model
J6350	SSG550m
J4350	SSG520m
J2350	SSG350m
J2320	SSG320m

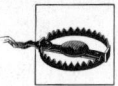 Once you perform a conversion, you must update your support contract with the new device information in order to ensure uninterrupted access to technical acceptance and customer support. Instructions for this procedure are provided in the conversion kits or JUNOS software with enhanced services conversion guides.

Packet Versus Flow-Based Processing

Historically, Juniper Networks routers use a packet-based forwarding model, in which each packet is individually processed and routed. In contrast, the Juniper SSG security devices are based on a flow model. Handling traffic as flows offers significant benefits for stateful services. In the flow model, the initial packets of a communication are typically processed in software and are subjected to various levels of packet security inspections and validity checks, in addition to a *single* route lookup. Once the packet is deemed permissible, a corresponding session state is installed into the forwarding plane to facilitate expedited forwarding for subsequent packets belonging to the same flow. In effect, the first packets are deeply scrutinized before being routed, and the remaining packets are switched according to the session table.

A *flow* is a unidirectional sequence of packets, when combined, for a sequential set of application data for the process that generated the flow. The matching flow in the return direction is grouped to form a session, which is therefore composed of two unidirectional flows.

Security zones

To understand and appreciate JUNOS software with enhanced services operation and capabilities, you must first be familiar with the concept of security zones. The Juniper ScreenOS Integrated Security Gateway (ISG) and Secure Services Gateway (SSG) appliances are based on the concept of zones. Figure 11-1 illustrates the concept of trust and untrust zones.

In a default configuration, there is a trust zone and an untrust zone. A *security zone* is a collection of one or more network segments that regulate inbound and outbound traffic via policies; policies are optional for traffic that originates and terminates in the same zone (intrazone). The result is that devices attached to interfaces belonging

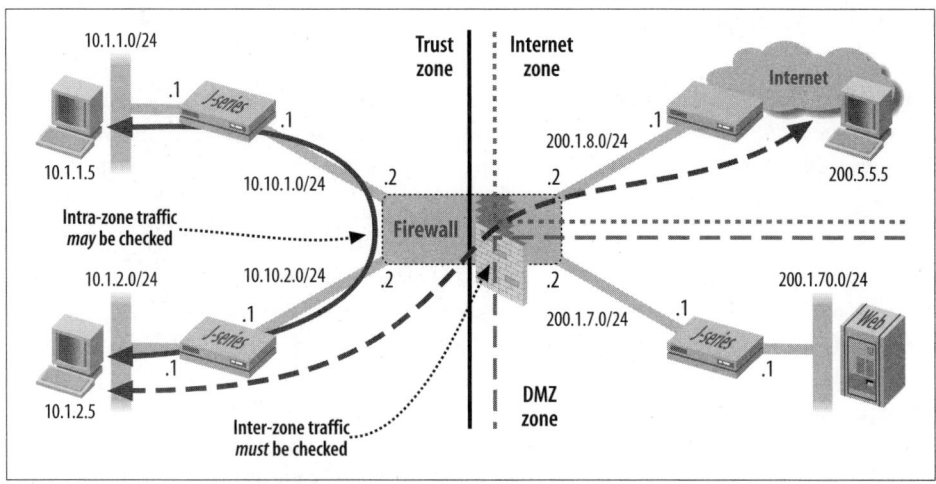

Figure 11-1. Zones and the tree of trust

to the same zone are able to communicate freely, whereas explicit policy is needed to permit communication between zones, and additional checks are leveled against traffic flowing between the trust and untrust zones.

Figure 11-1 shows a network composed of three zones and illustrates how intrazone traffic is permitted by default among all interfaces grouped into the trust zone, whereas interzone traffic must be explicitly allowed by a policy and may be subjected to deep packet inspection and other types of security services. In contrast, intrazone blocking is enabled by default for interfaces that share the same untrust zone, requiring a policy to permit communication among devices attached to different segments belonging to the same untrust zone. By grouping interfaces into zones and then managing interzone policies, you easily restrict and control interzone communications. The zone concept is also used to optimize firewall matching, as only rules that apply to the source and destination zones need to be checked.

Do I Need a Router or a Security Device?

In the past, users were expected to make some tough decisions when building out a new or existing network. Specifically, they often had to choose a device based on what was more important: world-class routing or world-class services. When both were equally important, a two-box, best-of-breed solution was often proposed. In this model, you had services/security devices that were deployed in parallel with a router infrastructure. In a divide-and-conquer model such as this, each device was left to do what it did best, with the combined effect being the best of both worlds.

Although the two-box solution was workable, and in fact is often the recommended solution today, such a design suffers from several drawbacks: two boxes are more expensive than one; there is a greater chance of failure due to more components; and generally, each new box added to the network increases overall operational costs.

Best-of-breed routing and security services

The release of JUNOS software with enhanced services holds the very real promise of eliminating the need for a two-box solution. By combining the power and proven performance of JUNOS software and its routing protocols with enhanced security and services from the best-in-class ScreenOS, users are able to get the best of both worlds, all in a single box.

The service updates in the initial release of JUNOS software with enhanced services primarily impact the security arena, and therefore, the changes in security-related services are the focus of this chapter. As noted previously, later updates may add nonsecurity-related services to the JUNOS software with enhanced services portfolio.

Architecture Changes

JUNOS software with enhanced services represents some significant changes in control plane capabilities through the introduction of new service daemons, and in packet forwarding behavior with the addition of flow-based processing. This section provides a high-level overview of the changes associated with the JUNOS software with enhanced services release.

Adding flow-based forwarding

One of the primary changes in JUNOS software with enhanced services is the addition of flow-based processing. This is along with to existing packet-based processing capabilities such as stateless firewall filters. The changes in JUNOS software with enhanced services result in a combination of packet- and flow-based treatment, as shown in Figure 11-2.

Figure 11-2 shows how the original packet-based forwarding process known as fwdd has been replaced with a flow-based process called flowd, which denotes the change from a packet- to a flow-based model. At the top of Figure 11-2, you can see that with JUNOS software, a packet can be directed into service processing as a result of an input or output filter or as a result of route lookup. In this model, forwarding is the prime concern and services were "tacked on to packets" as needed. The JUNOS software with enhanced services data plane is more service- and security-focused. All flows are inspected and passed through policy to determine whether they are allowed, at which point a single route lookup is performed. The differences can be summarized as a "route first, services maybe" philosophy in JUNOS versus a "services first, route if permitted" behavior in JUNOS software with enhanced services.

Packets are processed as flows after per-packet ingress handling and before per-packet egress handling. A *flow* is a stream of related packets that meet the same matching criteria and share the same characteristics. JUNOS software with enhanced services treats packets belonging to the same flow in the same manner. Specifically,

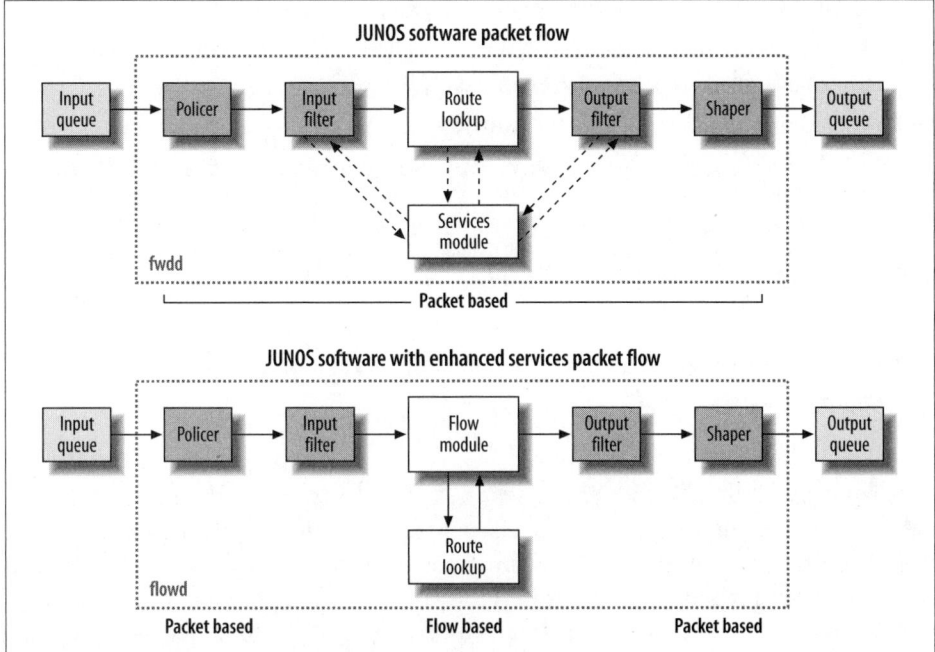

Figure 11-2. Combined packet- and flow-based processing

configuration settings that determine the fate of a packet—such as the security policy that applies to it, whether the packet is sent through an IPSec tunnel, or whether NAT is applied—are assessed for the first packet of a flow. The resultant set of actions and services is applied to the rest of the packets in the flow. The following criteria are used to determine whether a packet matches an existing flow:

- Source address
- Destination address
- Source port
- Destination port
- Protocol
- Session token

The *session token* is an internal index number that is set based on the packet's ingress zone. Packets that match an existing flow are treated according to the established flow state. Packets that do not match are treated as the first packets in a new flow and are used to create matching flow state for the related flow.

Flows and sessions. The stateful handling of flows requires the creation of a session. A session is created based on the characteristics of the first packet in a flow. Sessions are used for:

- Storing security measures to be applied to the packets of the flow
- Caching information about the state of the flow—that is, logging and counting data for a flow is cached in its session
- Allocating required resources for features such as NAT and IPSec tunnels
- Providing a framework for features such as Application Layer Gateways (ALGs) and firewall features

The combined effects of flow and session state bring together the following features and events that affect a packet as it undergoes flow-based processing:

- Flow-based forwarding
- Session management, including session aging and changes in routes, policy, and interfaces
- Management of VPNs, ALGs, and authentication
- Management of policies, NAT, zones, and screens

Each session resulting from a flow is associated with a timeout value. For example, the default timeout for the Transmission Control Protocol (TCP) is 30 minutes; the default timeout for the User Datagram Protocol (UDP) is 1 minute. When a flow is terminated, it is marked as invalid, and its timeout is reduced to 10 seconds. You can change the idle timeout value; it is designed to ensure that system resources are not tied up indefinitely on an otherwise defunct flow.

JUNOS software with enhanced services packet walk

In this section, we will follow a packet as it traverses the JUNOS software with enhanced services data plane, where it encounters a mix of packet- and flow-based handling steps. Figure 11-3 shows where the numbered events tie into the packet-handling steps described in the following text.

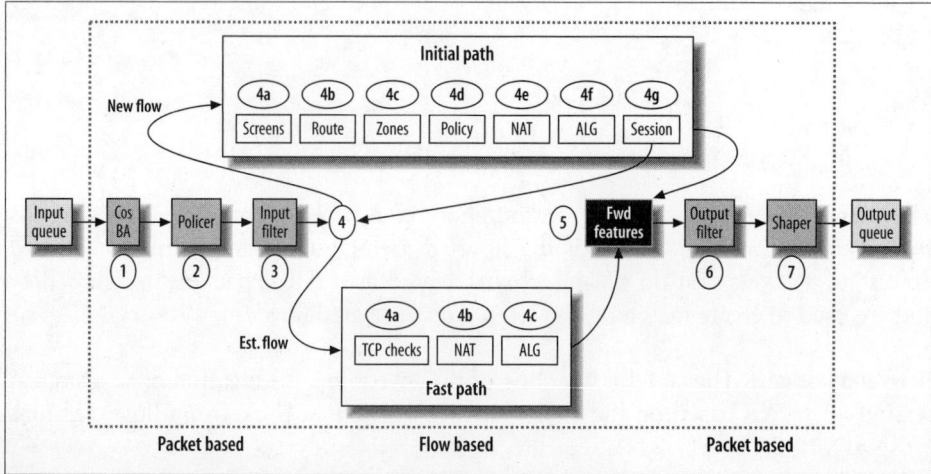

Figure 11-3. JUNOS software with enhanced services packet walk

The steps shown for the initial path represent the full set of checks and service instantiations that you can perform against the initial packets of a communications flow. In contrast, the fast path represents the streamlined steps executed for previously processed (and accepted) flows. The two-stage approach provides the ability to deeply inspect initial packets, which is computationally expensive but needed for true security, while at the same time offering high throughput by switching permitted flows based on established flow state. It should be noted that not all packets need to be touched at all possible processing points. For example, NAT is optional, and when not configured, NAT processing is not evoked. The packet processing steps are as follows:

1. Pull the packet from the queue, perform class of service (CoS) behavior aggregate (BA) classification, and note the ingress interface's zone for later policy lookup.
2. Ingress the policer/shaper.
3. Ingress the firewall filter; evoke the policer of multifield CoS classification.
4. Perform a lookup session; if no match, follow the initial path:
   a. Conduct a firewall screen check. When enabled, screen checks log or filter out packets with anomalous characteristics such as an attach signature.
   b. Perform a route lookup to determine the egress interface.
   c. Locate the destination (outgoing) zone, based on the route lookup result.
   d. Look up and execute policy based on incoming and outgoing zones; results include permit, deny, and reject.
   e. Allocate the NAT address based on the destination, source, or destination/source NAT policy directive.
   f. Set up ALGs as needed to support identified applications when NAT is active.
   g. Install a session tuple for fast path processing of related packets.

   If a session is matched, follow the fast path:
   a. Perform TCP checks to look for connection anomalies and match responses.
   b. Conduct NAT translation when evoked by policy.
   c. Perform ALG processing as needed by NAT.
5. Whether initial or fast path, perform forwarding services on the packet.
6. Perform egress firewall filtering, which can evoke a policer action.
7. Perform egress shaping or interface level policing; schedule and transmit the packet.

JUNOS Software with Enhanced Services Summary

The release of JUNOS software with enhanced services is a significant milestone in JUNOS software evolution. Looking back at Figure 11-3, you can appreciate the combined one-two punch of JUNOS software with enhanced services. You can now have the best of all worlds: the familiar JUNOS software CLI, its proven modular design that separates the control and data planes, the two-stage commit process, commit and operational scripts, and world-class routing protocol implementations. On top of this, you also get significant security and service features and enhancements. In the initial release, these enhancements are largely security-based and are derived from features available in ScreenOS. Later JUNOS software with enhanced services releases may contain additional, nonsecurity-focused features; given the modular design, just about anything is possible.

The combined packet- and flow-based processing means that packet-based features relating to firewall filters, policers, and shapers, packet classification, queuing, and CoS continue to operate as before. Likewise, ASP-based platforms such as the M10i and M7i will continue to use the service configurations and modes described in Chapters 6 and 7, which cover the introduction to services and advanced services, respectively.

For users initially deploying JUNOS software with enhanced services, the reverse stance on denying versus accepting packet flows by default may take a bit of getting used to. The choice of router versus secure operating contexts helps to mitigate this issue and allows you to deploy JUNOS software with enhanced services so that it operates like a traditional router or as an integrated firewall router, as required by the needs of your network.

Migrating from JUNOS to JUNOS Software with Enhanced Services

This section details the steps you need to follow to migrate a J-series router running JUNOS to run JUNOS software with enhanced services remotely, without losing network connectivity. Much of this information is summarized from the "JUNOS Enhanced Services Migration Guide," available at *http://www.juniper.net/techpubs/ software/junos-es/junos-es85/junos-es-migration/junos-es-migration.pdf*. Users are encouraged to consult the documentation for particulars about their hardware before performing any migrations.

Not having enough free compact flash space available to perform an upgrade is common, especially on routers that have large logs, trace files, or old software packages lying about in users' home directories. The migration guide provides detailed instructions on how to free up compact flash space to enhance the chances of being able to upgrade to JUNOS software with enhanced services on systems with 256 MB compact flash chips. The instructions have you delete various temporary and unneeded files using combinations of CLI and root shell mode commands, some of which are demonstrated on the following pages.

Understanding JUNOS Software with Enhanced Services Operational Modes

A J-series Services Router running JUNOS software with enhanced services can operate as either a stateful firewall or a router, depending on whether it is in the secure or router context:

Secure context

This mode allows a Services Router to act as a stateful firewall with only management access. To allow traffic to pass through a Services Router, you must explicitly configure a security policy for that purpose. In secure context, a Services Router forwards packets only if a security policy permits it; this is true even for traffic within the same zone (intrazone). The default intrazone block behavior in JUNOS software with enhanced services differs from that of ScreenOS, where intrazone blocking is disabled within the trust zone.

A J-series Services Router loaded with JUNOS software with enhanced services is shipped from the factory in a secure context.

Router context

This mode allows a Services Router to act as a router in which all management and transit traffic is allowed. In router context, an accept-all security policy is placed into effect and all interfaces are placed into the trust zone. To deny specific traffic, you must configure a security policy to do so.

Switching between secure and router contexts

Switching between secure and router contexts is not a binary function; that is, there is no single configuration statement that switches modes. Instead, the two modes are associated with a restrictive versus a permissive security policy that is configured at the [edit security] hierarchy. Switching between contexts does not affect the rest of the router's configuration; for example, its IP addressing and Border Gateway Protocol (BGP) session definitions remain unchanged. However, in a secure context, all communications, both between and within a given zone, must be permitted by policy. The accept-all policy associated with router context ensures that this condition is met to allow free communication among all interfaces listed in the common zone.

You can switch from router to secure context by loading the factory default configuration with a load factory-default command. The following settings are defined in the factory default secure context configuration:

- The built-in Gigabit Ethernet interface, ge-/0/0/0, is bound to a preconfigured zone called *trust*. All other interfaces are bound to a preconfigured zone named *untrust*.

- The ge-0/0/0 interface is configured to allow management access with Secure Shell (SSH) and Hypertext Transfer Protocol (HTTP) services enabled. The following host-inbound services are configured for the ge-0/0/0 interface in the trust zone:
  — HTTP
  — HTTPS
  — SSH
  — Dynamic Host Configuration Protocol (DHCP)

- TCP reset is enabled in the trust zone, and the default policy for the trust zone allows transmission of traffic from the trust zone to the untrust zone.

- All traffic within the trust zone is allowed.

- A screen is applied to a zone to protect against attacks launched from within the zone. The following screens are enabled for the untrust zone:
  — Internet Control Message Protocol (ICMP) Ping of Death
  — IP source route options
  — IP Teardrop
  — TCP Land attack
  — TCP SYN flood

- The default policy for the untrust zone is to deny all traffic.

The following commands load the factory default settings for JUNOS software with enhanced services Release 8.5, which places the router into a secure context. There is no root password in the default configuration, so you must assign one using the set system root-authentication command before you can commit.

```
[edit]
regress@propane# load factory-default
warning: activating factory configuration

[edit]
regress@propane# show | no-more
## Last changed: 2007-11-28 15:44:55 PST
system {
    autoinstallation {
        delete-upon-commit; ## Deletes [system autoinstallation] upon change/commit
        traceoptions {
            level verbose;
            flag {
                all;
            }
        }
```

```
        }
        services {
            ssh;
            web-management {
                http {
                    interface ge-0/0/0.0;
                }
            }
        }
        syslog {
            user * {
                any emergency;
            }
            file messages {
                any any;
                authorization info;
            }
            file interactive-commands {
                interactive-commands any;
            }
        }
        ## Warning: missing mandatory statement(s): 'root-authentication'
    }
    interfaces {
        ge-0/0/0 {
            unit 0;
        }
    }
    security {
        screen {
            ids-option untrust-screen {
                icmp {
                    ping-death;
                }
                ip {
                    source-route-option;
                    tear-drop;
                }
                tcp {
                    syn-flood {
                        alarm-threshold 1024;
                        attack-threshold 200;
                        source-threshold 1024;
                        destination-threshold 2048;
                        queue-size 2000;
                        timeout 20;
                    }
                    land;
                }
            }
        }
        zones {
            security-zone trust {
                tcp-rst;
```

```
            interfaces {
                ge-0/0/0.0 {
                    host-inbound-traffic {
                        system-services {
                            http;
                            https;
                            ssh;
                            telnet;
                            dhcp;
                        }
                    }
                }
            }
        }
        security-zone untrust {
            screen untrust-screen;
        }
    }
    policies {
        from-zone trust to-zone trust {
            policy default-permit {
                match {
                    source-address any;
                    destination-address any;
                    application any;
                }
                then {
                    permit;
                }
            }
        }
        from-zone trust to-zone untrust {
            policy default-permit {
                match {
                    source-address any;
                    destination-address any;
                    application any;
                }
                then {
                    permit;
                }
            }
        }
        from-zone untrust to-zone trust {
            policy default-deny {
                match {
                    source-address any;
                    destination-address any;
                    application any;
                }
                then {
                    deny;
                }
            }
```

```
        }
      }
    }
```

Note the presence of the from-zone trust to-zone trust policy that is required to permit open communication among all interfaces belonging to the trust zone. Recall that intrazone blocking is enabled in JUNOS software with enhanced services!

You can switch from secure to router context by loading the *jsr-series-routermode-factory.conf* file, which is stored in */etc/config*. The following configuration settings are defined for router context:

- A trust zone is created and all interfaces are placed into this zone.
- Flow security checks are disabled (no SYN or TCP Seq number checking).
- All host-bound services (ping, Telnet, etc.) and protocols are enabled.
- IPv6 traffic is forwarded.
- Screen options are disabled in the trust zone.
- ALG processing is not performed.

The following steps load the default router context and display the results. As with the default secure context, a root password must be assigned before you can commit:

```
[edit]
regress@propane# load override terminal /etc/config/jsr-series-routermode-factory.
conf
load complete

[edit]
regress@propane# show | no-more
## Last changed: 2007-11-28 15:54:14 PST
system {
    services {
        ssh;
        telnet;
        web-management {
            http {
                interface ge-0/0/0.0;
            }
        }
    }
    syslog {
        file messages {
            any any;
        }
    }
    ## Warning: missing mandatory statement(s): 'root-authentication'
}
interfaces {
    ge-0/0/0 {
        unit 0 {
            family inet {
```

```
                    address 192.168.1.1/24;
                }
            }
        }
    }
    security {
        zones {
            security-zone trust {
                tcp-rst;
                host-inbound-traffic {
                    system-services {
                        any-service;
                    }
                    protocols {
                        all;
                    }
                }
                interfaces {
                    all;
                }
            }
        }
        policies {
            default-policy {
                permit-all;
            }
        }
        alg {
            dns disable;
            ftp disable;
            h323 disable;
            mgcp disable;
            real disable;
            rsh disable;
            rtsp disable;
            sccp disable;
            sip disable;
            sql disable;
            talk disable;
            tftp disable;
            pptp disable;
        }
        forwarding-options {
            family {
                inet {
                    mode flow-based;
                }
                inet6 {
                    mode packet-based;
                }
                mpls {
                    mode packet-based;
                }
```

```
        }
    }
    flow {
        allow-dns-reply;
        tcp-session {
            no-syn-check;
            no-syn-check-in-tunnel;
            no-sequence-check;
        }
    }
}
```

Migration Steps

To migrate to JUNOS software with enhanced services, the J-series Services Router must already be running JUNOS software Release 8.3 or later, and it must have a compact flash card with at least 256 MB of storage. To use the Juniper Networks migration tools, you need a web support account, which you can obtain by completing the registration form for your product at the Juniper Networks web site.

Overall, migrating from JUNOS software to JUNOS software with enhanced services is similar to upgrading JUNOS software, except that you must first convert your JUNOS configuration file to a JUNOS software with enhanced services configuration file, and then place it in a location where it is used at the next boot. You then download the JUNOS software with enhanced services package, install the image on the router, and reboot the router so that the software and configuration take effect.

 You must migrate the original configuration file and correctly copy it to */var/config before* you load JUNOS software with enhanced services, or you will lose network connectivity after JUNOS software with enhanced services loads. Console access is unaffected.

The minimum steps needed to migrate from the J-series running JUNOS to the J-series running JUNOS software with enhanced services are as follows:

1. Obtain a copy of the current JUNOS configuration file.

2. Migrate the JUNOS configuration to a JUNOS software with enhanced services configuration, and confirm its accuracy.

3. Copy the migrated JUNOS software with enhanced services configuration file for use when the new software is loaded.

4. Download and install the JUNOS software with enhanced services package from Juniper Networks' support site. You need a support account to obtain software packages. JUNOS software with enhanced services packages have *jsr* in the name; for example, *junos-jsr-8.5R1.1-domestic.tgz*.

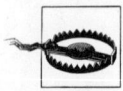

It's important that you follow the specific sequence of tasks outlined here. If you install JUNOS software with enhanced services code on the router *before* uploading a migrated configuration file, you will lose IP-based remote management access and must use the console port for access to the router.

You will need root access to perform the steps detailed in the migration example. Shell and root account access is needed to copy the migrated configuration to a location where it will load after JUNOS software with enhanced services is installed, and to make space available on the compact flash for the upgrade as needed. Also, the router being migrated needs network connectivity to facilitate copying JUNOS software with enhanced services onto the router for installation.

Before performing the migration, it's a good idea to back up your current software and configuration environment by backing up your primary boot device and configuration onto a secondary storage device (such as a USB storage drive) using the request system snapshot command. This way, you can easily recover the previous environment if something goes wrong with the migration, as might happen in the event of a power failure, which can corrupt the process, leaving the primary flash in an unusable state.

During a successful migration, the software package completely reinstalls the system base software and the JUNOS software components. The process tries to retain configuration files, logfiles, SSH keys, and similar information from the previous version, but you should move any files you cannot stand to lose to a remote storage device for safekeeping.

Migration example

The following steps demonstrate a JUNOS to JUNOS software with enhanced services migration. The router used in the demonstration is not part of the earlier topology, because as J2300s, they do not support JUNOS software with enhanced services. To help tie things back to this example in the book, the migration router is loaded with the CoS configuration used at PBR from Chapter 9. The only change made to the configuration file was to replace interface fe-0/0/0 with ge-0/0/2 in order to accommodate the new router's interface hardware. The new PBR supports JUNOS software with enhanced services migration because as a J4350, it's a supported platform, it has a 256 MB flash, and it is running JUNOS software Release 8.5 (a minimum of Release 8.3 is needed). Here are the relevant details of this router's hardware configuration:

```
[edit]
lab@PBR# run show chassis hardware detail
Hardware inventory:
```

```
Item              Version  Part number  Serial number Description
Chassis                                 JN1093EBXXXX  J4350
Midplane          REV 01   710-014594   NJ7284
System IO         REV 01   710-016210   NH9941        JX350 System IO
Crypto Module                                         Crypto Acceleration
Routing Engine    REV 05   710-015273   HY8015        RE-J4350-2540
  ad0     244 MB  256MB CRR             2466J7C50A62760004 Compact Flash
FPC 0                                                 FPC
  PIC 0                                               4x GE Base PIC
Power Supply 0

[edit]
lab@PBR# run show version
Hostname: PBR
Model: j4350
JUNOS Software Release [8.5R1.8]
```

Step 1: Copy the current configuration file

You can copy (and back up) the current JUNOS software configuration using a variety of approaches. The file should be stored off of the router that is being migrated for safekeeping, and to allow it to be run through the migration tool as described later.

Options here include saving the configuration and then transferring the file using FTP or SCP, or using the copy and paste function of a terminal emulator program. If you are particularly nerdy, you can follow the steps outlined in the migration guide, which give you access to a root shell to deal with the *juniper.conf.gz* configuration file directly. Note that this is a compressed file (*gunzip*), and you have to decompress it before you can work with its contents. The command gunzip juniper.conf.gz accomplishes this task and results in a *juniper.conf* text file.

The specific approach you take really does not matter, as long as you obtain the *entire* configuration file. In this example, the user saves the complete configuration to a local file, and then displays the configuration for copying into a terminal buffer. You also could use a single show configuration command to copy into a terminal buffer, but the file save operation makes it easy to FTP a copy of the configuration to a new location. Once in the terminal buffer, the contents are pasted into a text editor and saved as plain text (not shown). When you save the file, make sure the text editor preserves Unix-style line breaks and does not wrap text.

It's critical that you issue the save command at the *root* of the configuration hierarchy to avoid missing any parts of the configuration, as shown:

```
[edit]
lab@PBR# run file show old_junos_config | no-more
version 8.5R1.8;
system {
    host-name PBR;
    ports {
        console type vt100;
```

```
      }
      root-authentication {
          encrypted-password "$1$snnzRpPx$3Qj3oNJ9VjdCY95kRrM/T/"; ## SECRET-DATA
      }
      login {
          user lab {
              uid 2003;
    . . .
```

At this point, it's also a good idea to perform a system snapshot command with a supported USB media stick in the secondary flash slot. This way, if something should go wrong in the upgrade process, you can reboot from the secondary media with a request system reboot media usb command; if the router is not able to boot from primary flash, it automatically tries the USB device. Once booted from USB, you then perform another snapshot, this time to copy from the USB to the primary compact flash to restore the original environment.

Step 2: Migrate the existing configuration to a JUNOS software with enhanced services configuration

Juniper Networks has made a migration tool available to automate the configuration changes involved in migration from JUNOS to JUNOS software with enhanced services. To use the tool, you need a support account, which you also need in order to download JUNOS software with enhanced services. You can access the migration tool via a supported web browser at *http://migration-tools.juniper.net*.

JUNOS configurations without stateful-firewall, services nat, or services ipsec-vpn configuration statements are converted into router context so that an explicit security policy is not required to forward packets.

In contrast, JUNOS configurations that do contain these service types are converted to a secure context mode, along with the security policies needed for communication.

As with any conversion tool, it is the user's responsibility to pay attention to any warning or error messages, which may indicate an incomplete conversion or the presence of an unsupported feature. Most of the changes in JUNOS software with enhanced services relate to services, so configurations with autonomous system (AS) Physical Interface Card (PIC)-based security or NAT-related services require more adaptation.

The migration support tool is web-based, and it supports file upload or the simple pasting of your original configuration into the web page. Cut and paste tends to be better for smaller configurations or when you wish to perform migration on only a portion of a configuration. Figure 11-4 provides an example of the JUNOS software with enhanced services migration tool's user interface.

The settings shown in Figure 11-4 confirm that all warnings and errors are enabled, which is suggested to ensure that you are alerted to any possible issue with the conversion process. After uploading or pasting the configuration, simply click the

---

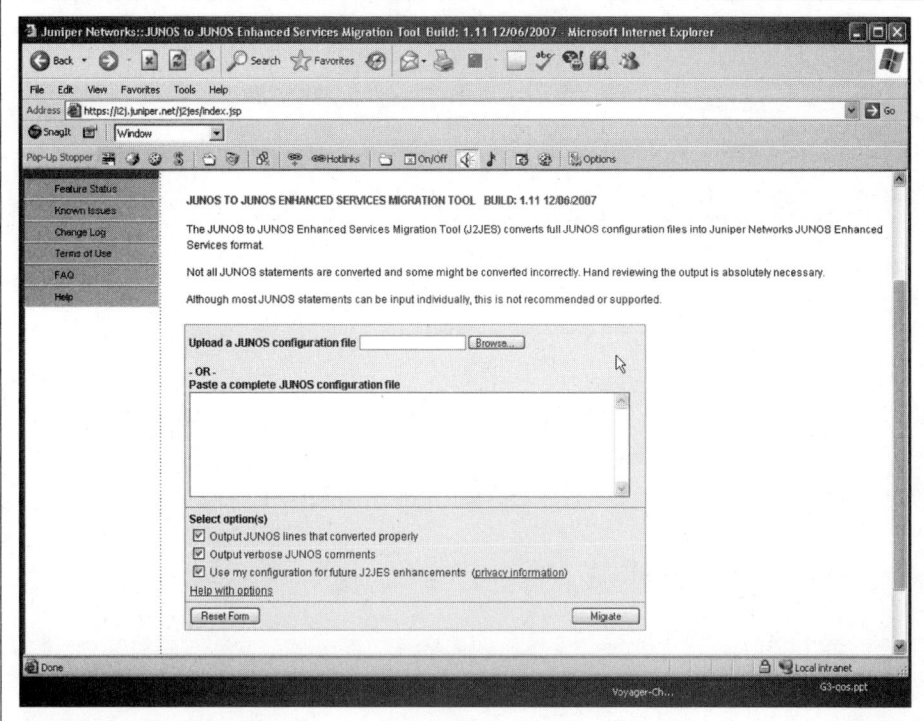

Figure 11-4. The JUNOS software with enhanced services migration tool

Migrate button to convert the configuration. Figure 11-5 shows the result with the sample CoS configuration from PBR.

The key thing to note in Figure 11-5 is that no informational, error, or warning messages were generated. This pretty much confirms that all went well with the conversion, but it's *still* suggested that you closely inspect the results before loading the configuration onto the router. You can either copy the migrated configuration back into a terminal buffer or use the download option to save a local copy of the file. Given the small size of the file, this example makes use of copying the results into the terminal buffer (again, not shown).

Step 3: Copy the migrated configuration for use when JUNOS software with enhanced services loads

To accomplish this step, you will require root shell access. You need this so that you can copy the migrated configuration file to a location where it will become active when the router later reboots with the new JUNOS software with enhanced services code. This process is required because the changes added to maintain existing network connectivity *after* the conversion to JUNOS software with enhanced services are *not compatible* with the JUNOS software now running on the router. Therefore,

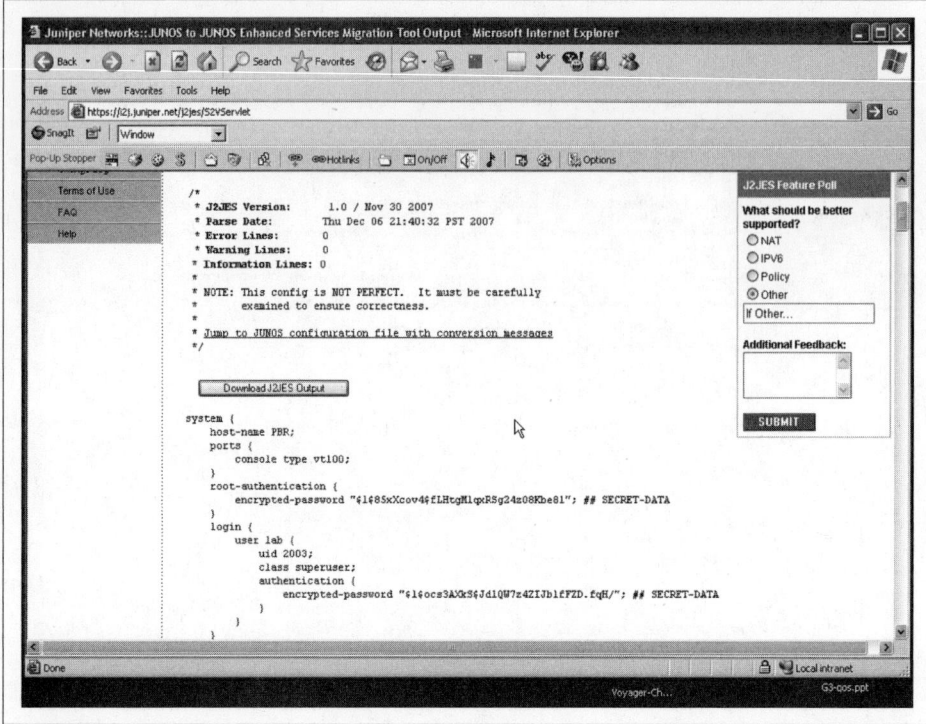

Figure 11-5. Viewing migration results

simply trying to paste the configuration using a load override terminal command results in load errors and the resulting loss of the JUNOS software with enhanced services-specific parts of the configuration that were added by the migration tool— and committing such a configuration will result in loss of network connectivity, requiring console access to recover.

To begin, you must get a copy of the migrated configuration file onto the router. Restating what we discussed earlier, you cannot use the load merge or override function at this time, because of the JUNOS software with enhanced services-specific components of the migrated configuration file. The router needs to have network connectivity so that JUNOS software with enhanced services can later be copied and installed, which means you can use file transfer protocols to accomplish this task. You can also access a shell to evoke the vi editor, paste the terminal buffer contents in insert mode, and then save the file. Because vi can be a bit frustrating to folks who are not familiar with its use, this process is demonstrated:

```
[edit]
lab@PBR# run start shell
% vi es_migrated_conf
```

You should now have a vi editor window open, which appears as shown:

```
~
~
~
~
~
~
~
~
~
~
~
~
~
~
~
~
~
~
~
~
~
~
~
~
~
~
es_migrated_conf: new file: line 1
```

You now press Esc-i to switch to insert mode—nothing obvious will happen, but you may hear a keyboard beep when you press the Esc key. You can now perform a paste operation from your terminal emulation program to paste the migrated configuration file into the vi editor:

```
system {
    host-name PBR;
    ports {
        console type vt100;
    }
    root-authentication {
        encrypted-password "$1$85xXcov4$fLHtgMlqxRSg24zO8Kbe81"; ## SECRET-DATA
    }
    login {
        user lab {
            uid 2003;
            class superuser;
            authentication {
                encrypted-password "$1$ocs3AXkS$JdlQW7z4ZIJblfFZD.fqH/"; ## SECR

  . . .
```

Once the paste is complete, you exit the vi editor while saving changes by pressing Esc-Z-Z—vi is case-sensitive, and those are uppercase Zs. You should see a line such as the following confirming the size of the file written to the media:

```
es_migrated_conf: new file: 40 211 lines, 4975 characters
%
```

Once stored on the router, go to a shell and rename the file to *juniper.conf*, as shown:

```
% ls -la
total 34
drwxr-xr-x    3 lab    staff    512 Nov 28 13:16 .
drwxr-xr-x  217 root   wheel   4096 Nov 28 12:21 ..
drwxr-xr-x    2 lab    staff    512 Nov 28 12:21 .ssh
-rw-r--r--    1 lab    staff   5032 Nov 28 12:46 old_junos_config
-rw-r--r--    1 lab    staff   5725 Nov 28 13:16 es_migrated.conf
% mv es_migrated.conf juniper.conf
% ls -la
total 34
drwxr-xr-x    3 lab    staff    512 Nov 28 13:16 .
drwxr-xr-x  217 root   wheel   4096 Nov 28 12:21 ..
drwxr-xr-x    2 lab    staff    512 Nov 28 12:21 .ssh
-rw-r--r--    1 lab    staff   5032 Nov 28 12:46 old_junos_config
-rw-r--r--    1 lab    staff   5725 Nov 28 13:16 juniper.conf
```

You must now su to root to execute commands that back up the existing *juniper.conf* to a new directory; this is done for safekeeping. You then copy the new *juniper.conf* into the location of the original *juniper.conf* file:

```
% su
Password:
```

After successfully switching to the root user, change to the */config* directory:

```
root@propane% cd /config
```

A new directory is created to store a copy of the current configuration:

```
root@propane% mkdir backup
```

And the current configuration environment is moved into the backup directory:

```
root@propane% mv /juniper.conf* backup/

root@PBR% ls backup/
juniper.conf.1.gz      juniper.conf.3.gz
juniper.conf.2.gz      juniper.conf.gz
```

With the original configuration safely backed up, the migration configuration file is copied to the */config* directory, where it will be evoked at the next boot:

```
root@propane% cp /var/home/lab/juniper.conf ./
```

The results are confirmed:

```
root@PBR% pwd
/config
root@PBR% ls
backup            juniper.conf
```

It is good to take one last look at the final *juniper.conf* file with vi or by dumping its contents to screen using the cat command in order to confirm that no corruption has occurred during the file transfer or editing and renaming processes, such as could happen with incorrect FTP transfer mode (ASCII should be used when working with the plain-text, uncompressed format file), or more likely because a Windows text editor inserted incompatible line breaks (also called end-of-line characters). In this example, things seem all right with the file:

```
root@PBR% cat juniper.conf | more
    system {
    host-name PBR;
    ports {
        console type vt100;
    }
    root-authentication {
        encrypted-password "$1$85xXcov4$fLHtgMlqxRSg24zO8Kbe81"; ## SECRET-DATA
    }
    login {
        user lab {
            uid 2003;
            class superuser;
            authentication {
                encrypted-password "$1$ocs3AXkS$JdlQW7z4ZIJblfFZD.fqH/"; ## SECRET-
DATA
            }
        }
    }
    services {
        ftp;
        ssh;
        telnet;
. . .
```

Note that a commit is not performed at this time because the new portions of the configuration file will not be understood by the JUNOS software now running. The new configuration is used later when you reboot as part of loading JUNOS software with enhanced services.

Step 4: Copy and install JUNOS software with enhanced services

With the original configuration migrated to be compatible with JUNOS software with enhanced services and now placed where it will take effect at the next reboot, it is time to obtain and load the desired JUNOS software with enhanced services package. Before attempting to load the new package, it is a good idea to first free up as much space as possible

Free up space. The limited compact flash storage space, combined with the lack of a hard drive for storing images that are being unpacked for installation, can create problems when you attempt to upgrade or downgrade JUNOS versions on any J-series router, regardless of whether they are JUNOS software with enhanced services packages or not. The following steps are general approaches to freeing up compact flash space. You will need root access to delete any files that are owned by root.

First, we use the CLI cleanup utility to rid ourselves of the easy, low-hanging fruit:

```
lab@propane> request system storage cleanup

List of files to delete:

        Size Date         Name
    449B Nov 26 23:03 /cf/var/log/install.0.gz
   7581B Nov 28 13:49 /cf/var/log/messages.0.gz
   6383B Nov 28 13:49 /cf/var/log/security.0.gz
Delete these files ? [yes,no] (no) yes
```

Next, delete the backup software package, if present. This package is used after an upgrade to revert back to the previous version using a request system software rollback command. The rollback image is no longer needed as the current software environment is being upgraded.

```
lab@propane> request system software delete-backup
Delete backup system software package [yes,no] (no) yes

lab@propane>
```

Confirm that you have enough compact flash space. The release notes for JUNOS software with enhanced services software Release 8.5R1 provide the following compact flash space guidelines:

> To copy the software image to the router and install using that image, you need at least 130 MB of available space on the compact flash.

> To install the software without copying the software image to the router you need at least 68 MB. You use the no-copy and unlink options with the request system software add command to prevent copying the package on the router during installation.

The show system storage command displays used and free space on the compact flash:

```
lab@propane> show system storage
Filesystem       Size     Used    Avail  Capacity  Mounted on
/dev/ad0s1a      213M     113M      98M     54%    /
devfs            1.0K     1.0K       0B    100%    /dev
devfs            1.0K     1.0K       0B    100%    /dev/
. . .
```

In this case, 98 MB of space is available on the flash, which is more than sufficient when the no-copy and unlink switches are added.

Install JUNOS software with enhanced services. You are now ready to upgrade the router to run JUNOS software with enhanced services. It is assumed that you have obtained the desired package from the Juniper support web site, and that the image is in place on the router being migrated. Good housekeeping says the package should be stored in the */var/tmp* directory, but this requires root access.

Tips for Freeing More Space

Large files left in user directories or in nonstandard places may consume so much space that you are not able to load a new software package. If you have shell access, try this handy command:

```
lab@propane> start shell
% find -x /cf -type f -exec du {} \; | sort -n
find: /cf/var/cron/tabs: Permission denied
. . .
0        /cf/etc/namedb/resolver.cache
. . .
448      /cf/var/log/dcd
1024     /cf/var/log/chassisd
1440     /cf/var/log/httpd
107776   /cf/var/tmp/junos-jsr-8.5R1.8-domestic.tgz
114512   /cf/packages/junos-8.5R1.8-domestic
```

The output is sorted from smallest to largest files found, so you want to focus on the entries near the end of the display. Once you know where the large files are, it is a simple matter to delete or move them off the router as desired. In this example, the largest files on the systems are the soon-to-be-installed JUNOS software with enhanced services in */var/tmp* and the currently installed JUNOS version in */var/cf*. Any other large files in user directories or in the */tmp* or */var/tmp* directory are good candidates for deletion. Note that symbolic links result in */var/home* being mapped to */cf/var/home*; therefore, you can use either path:

```
root@PBR% cd /var/home/
root@PBR% pwd
/cf/var/home
```

To perform the upgrade, issue the request system software add command followed by the path and name of the JUNOS software with enhanced services package to be installed—in this example, you must use include the no-copy and unlink switches because of space issues described previously, and you should *also* add the no-validate switch.

The no-validate option is used here to avoid validation of the active configuration, which is the previous, nonmigrated version, against the new software that is being installed. After installation, the migrated JUNOS software with enhanced services-compatible configuration file will be read by the new software, and all will be well.

```
lab@propane>request system software add jsr-8.5R1.8-domestic.tgz no-
copy unlink no-validate
WARNING: Unpacking package junos-8.5R1.8.tgz in /var/tmp/pkg_instmp
6287/junos-8.5R1.8
Installing package '/var/tmp/pkg_instmp6287/junos-8.5R1.8' ...
Verified junos-boot-jsr-8.5R1.8.tgz signed by PackageProduction_8_5_0
```

```
Verified junos-jsr-8.5R1.8-domestic signed by PackageProduction_8_5_0
Available space: 92264 require: 2405
WARNING: junos-8.5R1.8-domestic is already installed,
WARNING: moving it aside.
ls: junos.old: No such file or directory
JUNOS 8.5R1.8 will become active at next reboot
WARNING: A reboot is required to load this software correctly
WARNING:    Use the 'request system reboot' command
WARNING:        when software installation is complete
Saving state for rollback ...
Removing /var/tmp/pkg_instmp6287/junos-8.5R1.8
```

If desired, you can add the reboot switch to the request system software command to avoid having to reboot the router to complete installation. In this case, we can reboot at our leisure, but the suspense is getting heavy, so it's time to get it on, so to speak:

```
lab@propane> request system reboot
Reboot the system ? [yes,no] (no) yes
```

After a few minutes, the installation completes and your old router is back, except now it's capable of taking advantage of JUNOS software with enhanced services features:

```
Local package initialization:.
starting local daemons:.
kern.securelevel: -1 -> 1
Wed Nov 28 22:18:53 UTC 2007


PBR (ttyd0)

login: lab
Password:

--- JUNOS 8.5R1.8 built 2007-11-05 18:58:07 UTC
lab@PBR> show version
Hostname: PBR
Model: j4350
JUNOS Software Release [8.5R1.8] Enhanced Services
```

So, what changed?

The migrated configuration file—which as you may recall was based on the CoS configuration used at PBR in Chapter 9—is displayed. The only JUNOS software with enhanced services-specific addition is the new security stanza, displayed here:

```
regress@hay_PBR_r1> configure
Entering configuration mode

[edit]
regress@hay_PBR_r1# show services security {
    zones {
        security-zone Trust {
            host-inbound-traffic {
                system-services {
                    all;
```

```
                }
                protocols {
                    all;
                }
            }
            interfaces {
                all;
            }
        }
    }
    policies {
        default-policy {
            permit-all;
        }
    }
}
```

The effect of this stanza is to place JUNOS software with enhanced services into router context with resultant permissive connectivity for all interfaces and protocols. This is expected because the migrated configuration did not contain any security-related services. You can still use stateless filters to protect the router's control plane. This mode of operation is as close as you can get to having JUNOS software with enhanced services operate like standard JUNOS software.

Recall that router context is indicated by a default security policy that permits all communications. However, it's impossible to configure such a policy in a manner that will block communication of new interfaces or services/protocols unless you also update the security stanza to accommodate the additions. Consider this permissive security stanza:

```
[edit]
lab@PBR# show security
zones {
    security-zone Trust {
        host-inbound-traffic {
            system-services {
                ftp;
                http;
                https;
                ping;
                ssh;
                telnet;
                traceroute;
            }
        }
        interfaces {
            fe-0/0/0.1241 {
                host-inbound-traffic {
                    protocols {
                        ospf;
                    }
                }
            }
```

```
            fe-0/0/0.412 {
                host-inbound-traffic {
                    protocols {
                        ospf;
                    }
                }
            }
            loo.0;
        }
    }
}
policies {
    default-policy {
        permit-all;
    }
}
```

Even though there is a single trust zone and permissive accept-all policy, the lack of interface all, protocols all, or services all statements means that each new interface or service/protocol needs to be explicitly added. The point of all this is that there can be various levels of router context. A *true* router context uses the all keyword to accommodate future changes without the need for security modifications, just like regular JUNOS software.

A note on IPv6 and MPLS. IPv4 traffic is always handled as a flow in JUNOS software with enhanced services. In the initial release, flow-based forwarding for IPv6 and Multiprotocol Label Switching (MPLS) is not available. To prevent summary dropping of this traffic, you must add the following to the [edit security] stanza:

```
forwarding-options {
    family {
        inet6 {
            mode packet-based;
        }
        mpls {
            mode packet-based;
        }
    }
}
```

The set commands used to create router context are provided:

```
[edit]
lab@PBR# show security | display set
set security zones security-zone HOST host-inbound-traffic system-
services any-
service
set security zones security-zone HOST host-inbound-traffic protocols
all
set security zones security-zone HOST interfaces all
set security policies default-policy permit-all
set security forwarding-options family inet6 mode packet-based
set security forwarding-options family mpls mode packet-based
```

JUNOS Software with Enhanced Services Migration Summary

The migration from JUNOS software to JUNOS software with enhanced services is possible on many J-series and SSGm platforms. The migration steps are similar to performing a regular JUNOS upgrade, except there is a configuration conversion and a need to place the converted file in a location that is used when booting with the new software.

The web-based migration tool requires a support account, but it makes the ASP-based service's migration set to the ScreenOS service relatively straightforward. Before attempting to migrate, consult the web site for platform requirements, compact flash size, and available space. Having console access is always best when performing this type of process, but it is possible to perform the upgrade without losing network access.

Service Migration Case Study: JUNOS to JUNOS Software with Enhanced Services

This section focuses on a JUNOS configuration with ASP-based services that is migrated to JUNOS with JUNOS software with enhanced services, and therefore demonstrates much of the new configuration syntax for NAT and stateful-firewall services. The point of this exercise is to provide an example of the same set of services, in the same network context, along with the operational mode commands that are used to display and debug flow state.

Figure 11-6 shows the network topology for the services migration case study.

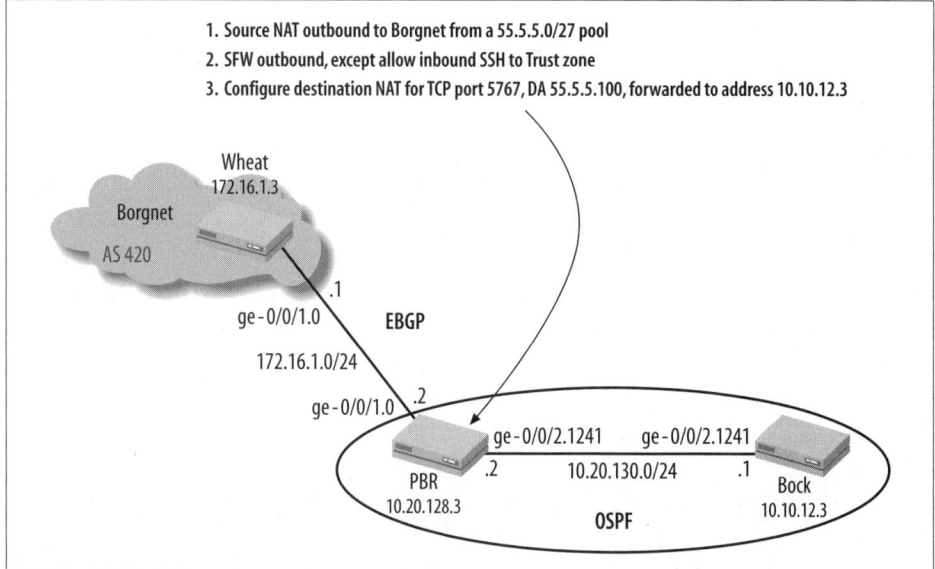

Figure 11-6. Services migration topology

As called out in the diagram, router PBR is the services-enabled router, and therefore the focus of the example. The particulars of this topology vary slightly from the example used in other chapters. These changes result from use of a different test bed with J-series routers that support JUNOS software with enhanced services. The primary change in the topology is the shift to J4350s that use GE interfaces. The link between Wheat and PBR no longer uses virtual LAN (VLAN) tagging, in order to accommodate a switch. Also, the routers are using their ge-0/0/0 interfaces for Out of Band (OoB) management purposes, providing Telnet, FTP, and other system services. The OoB network is not shown in Figure 11-6, but evidence of its presence can be noted in some of the captures that are provided. A represented set of services have been enabled on PBR. Specifically, it is configured to:

1. Perform stateful-firewall services on all outbound traffic, except traffic in rule 2.

2. Allow incoming SSH connections, but only to interfaces within the trust zone.

3. Perform source NAT (SNAT) on all traffic transiting PBR; locally originated BGP traffic is not subjected to NAT.

4. Perform destination NAT (DNAT) on TCP packets sent to destination address 55.5.5.100, port 5767; this traffic is forwarded to 10.10.12.3.

The Original JUNOS Software ASP-Based Service Set

The key aspects of PBR's configuration are shown, before the configuration is migrated to a JUNOS software with enhanced services-compatible configuration:

```
. . .
interfaces {
    sp-0/0/0 {
        unit 0 {
            family inet;
        }
    }
ge-0/0/0 {
        unit 0 {
            description out_of_Band_management;
            family inet {
                address 192.168.14.96/24;
            }
        }
    }

    ge-0/0/1 {
        unit 0 {
            description PBR-to-Wheat;
            family inet {
                service {
                    input {
                        service-set wan-services;
                    }
```

```
                    output {
                        service-set wan-services;
                    }
                }
                address 172.16.1.2/24;
            }
        }
    }
    ge-0/0/2 {
        vlan-tagging;
        unit 1241 {
            description PBR_to_Bock;
            vlan-id 1241;
            family inet {
                address 10.20.130.2/24;
            }
        }
    }
    lo0 {
        unit 0 {
            family inet {
                address 10.20.128.3/32;
                address 55.5.5.1/32;
            }
        }
    }
}
```

The interfaces stanza matches the topology shown in Figure 11-6. Note the definition of a services interface based on an ASP service set, as indicated by the sp-0/0/0 interface. The ge-0/0/0 interface provides OoB network management.

```
routing-options {
    aggregate {
        route 10.0.0.0/8;
        route 55.5.5.0/24;
    }
    autonomous-system 1282;
}
```

There is not much to note here, other than two aggregate routes that end up being advertised to BGP peering AS Borgnet. Because SNAT is in effect, the 10.0.0.0/8 is not technically needed. Note that the lo0 interface has a 55.5.5.1/32 address, which activates the aggregate for the 55.5.5.0/24 prefix, which represents the SNAT pool of addresses that are presented to the rest of the world.

```
protocols {
    bgp {
        export send-agg;
        group as_420 {
            type external;
            neighbor 172.16.1.1 {
                peer-as 420;
            }
```

```
        }
    }
    ospf {
        export send-borgnet;
        area 0.0.0.0 {
            interface ge-0/0/2.1241;
            interface ge-0/0/1.0;
            interface lo0.0 {
                passive;
            }
        }
    }
}
```

The protocol configuration sets up the External BGP (EBGP) peering to Borgnet and Open Shortest Path First (OSPF) area 0 operation to Bock. Note that export policies are in place for both protocols. And speaking of policies, here they are:

```
policy-options {
    policy-statement send-agg {
        from protocol aggregate;
        then accept;
    }
    policy-statement send-borgnet {
        from {
            route-filter 172.16.1.0/24 orlonger;
            route-filter 128.3.0.0/16 orlonger;
        }
        then accept;
    }
}
```

The two policies result in the advertisement of the 10.0.0.0/8 and 55.5.5.0/24 aggregates to Borgnet and the redistribution of the Borgnet BGP peering and loopback addresses through advertisement of the directly connected 172.16.1.0/24 route into OSPF:

```
services {
    stateful-firewall {
        rule all-algs {
            match-direction output;
            term 1 {
                from {
                    application-sets junos-algs-outbound;
                }
                then {
                    accept;
                }
            }
            term 2 {
                then {
                    accept;
                }
            }
```

```
        }
        rule all-ssh {
            match-direction input;
            term 1 {
                from {
                    applications [ junos-ssh junos-bgp ];
                }
                then {
                    accept;
                }
            }
            term 2 {
                from {
                    destination-address {
                        55.5.5.100/32;
                    }
                }
                then {
                    accept;
                }
            }
        }
    }
    nat {
        pool ext-block {
            address-range low 55.5.5.2 high 55.5.5.30;
            port automatic;
        }
        rule translate-all {
            match-direction output;
            term 1 {
                from {
                    source-address {
                        10.0.0.0/8;
                    }
                }
                then {
                    translated {
                        source-pool ext-block;
                        translation-type {
                            source dynamic;
                        }
                    }
                }
            }
        }
        rule pin-hole {
            match-direction input;
            term 1 {
                from {
                    destination-address {
                        55.5.5.100/32;
                    }
                    applications special-port-map;
```

```
            }
            then {
                translated {
                    destination-prefix 10.10.12.3/32;
                    translation-type {
                        destination static;
                    }
                }
            }
        }
    }
    service-set wan-services {
        stateful-firewall-rules all-algs;
        stateful-firewall-rules all-ssh;
        nat-rules translate-all;
        nat-rules pin-hole;
        interface-service {
            service-interface sp-0/0/0.0;
        }
    }
}
applications {
    application special-port-map {
        protocol tcp;
        destination-port 5767;
    }
}
```

The services configuration sets up a service set called wan-services, which provides a stateful firewall for all incoming traffic, except BGP, SSH, and a pinhole that is opened for TCP traffic sent to port 5767 and destination address 55.5.5.100. In the latter case, matching traffic has the destination address changed to 10.10.12.3, which is the loopback address of Bock. All traffic from the 10.0.0.0/8 space undergoes SNAT using a pool of addresses ranging from 55.5.5.2–55.5.5.30. Note that the 55.5.5.1 address assigned to the lo0 interface is left outside the NAT pool, as is the 55.5.5.100 destination address associated with pinhole traffic.

Original ASP-based service set: Operational analysis

Confirmation begins with the verification of BGP and OSPF at PBR:

```
[edit]
regress@hay_PBR_r1# run show bgp summary
Groups: 1 Peers: 1 Down peers: 0
Table      Tot Paths  Act Paths Suppressed  History Damp State  Pending
inet.0            1          1          0        0          0         0
Peer             AS    InPkt    OutPkt    OutQ   Flaps Last Up/Dwn State|#Active/
Received/Damped...
172.16.1.1      420       69        74       0       0
30:35 1/1/0              0/0/0
```

```
[edit]
regress@hay_PBR_r1# run show ospf neighbor
Address       Interface        State   ID          Pri  Dead
10.20.130.1   ge-0/0/2.1241    Full    10.255.14.97  128  33
```

To test the services, a Telnet session to 55.5.5.100, port 5767, is generated at Wheat, while pings are generated from Bock to Wheat's loopback address. The pings succeed (not shown), but the Telnet session that originated at Wheat to port 5767 is expected to fail. This is because there is no TCP process listening at port 5767 on Bock. Despite the connection failure, there are ways to confirm that DNAT is working.

The flow session table is displayed at PBR. Note that the current JUNOS ASP-based services are displayed using a show services command:

```
[edit]
regress@hay_PBR_r1# run show services stateful-firewall flows
Interface: sp-0/0/0, Service set: wan-services
Flow                                    State    Dir       Frm count
TCP       172.16.1.3:62162 -> 55.5.5.100:5767 Forward I        1
  NAT dest      55.5.5.100:5767       ->      10.10.12.3:5767
TCP       10.10.12.3:5767  -> 172.16.1.3:62162 Forward O        0
  NAT source    10.10.12.3:5767       ->      55.5.5.100:5767
```

The first pair of session entries reflects the DNAT pinhole traffic. Note the 5767 port number and TCP protocol, and that the destination address is translated to 10.10.12.3. The next entry is the return traffic that is the TCP reset that results because there is no process listening at Bock. The I and O flags indicate input versus output.

```
ICMP      172.16.1.3:1044   ->      55.5.5.2       Watch    I  2
  NAT dest      55.5.5.2:1044         ->      10.20.130.1:20783
ICMP      10.20.130.1:20783 ->      172.16.1.3     Watch    O  2
  NAT source    10.20.130.1:20783     ->      55.5.5.2:1044
```

This pair of entries represents the ping traffic generated at Bock. Note that the outgoing flow is undergoing SNAT, having the 10.20.13.1 address translated to a 55.5.5.5.2 address in this example.

```
TCP       172.16.1.2:64827  -> 172.16.1.1:179   Forward  O      146
TCP       172.16.1.1:179    -> 172.16.1.2:64827 Forward  I      144
```

The final pair of entries represents the BGP session (port 179), which is not subjected to SNAT due to the 172.16.1.2 address from which the BGP session originates. DNAT forwarding behavior (despite actual inability to form a Telnet connection) is confirmed by monitoring traffic at Bock's ge-0/0/2 interface:

```
21:01:38.368620  In IP 172.16.1.3.62269 > 10.10.12.3.5767: S 2699291864:2699291864(0)
win 65535 <mss 1460,nop,wscale 1,nop,nop,
timestamp 1790573405 0,sackOK,eol>
21:01:38.368639 Out IP 10.10.12.3.5767 > 172.16.1.3.62269: R 0:0(0)
ack 1 win 0
```

The traffic shows an incoming TCP connection request (SYN and ACK flags set) sent to destination port 5767, from 172.16.1.3. Note that Bock resets the connection, which is expected behavior here. DNAT port-forwarding success is not contingent on the device that receives the data actually *wanting* the traffic—the receipt alone is enough to confirm DNAT.

You can assume that an SSH session originated at Wheat to any of the 10.0.0.0/8 addresses within Beer-Co is successful (not shown). The same connection request using Telnet fails, due to the stateful firewall that is in effect.

The Migrated JUNOS Software with Enhanced Services Configuration

The original, ASP-based configuration shown earlier is run through the migration tool, for use with JUNOS software with enhanced services. The file is then copied and renamed on the router, and JUNOS software with enhanced services is loaded, as per the procedure detailed in "Migrating from JUNOS to JUNOS Software with Enhanced Services," earlier in this chapter. The altered portions of the migrated configuration are shown, and are commented on as appropriate. The first change to note is that the ASP-based sp-0/0/0 services interface has been removed. Note that a services interface is not present in the migrated configuration. In JUNOS software with enhanced services, a services interface is used to support route-based VPNs; it's called an st0 (secure tunnel) interface. This interface does not exist in the migrated configuration because no VPNs were defined.

The first section in the new stanza at the [edit security] hierarchy defines the NAT pool used in both DNAT and SNAT. The NAT pool names are the choice of the migration tool, and you can change them if desired.

```
[edit]
regress@hay_PBR_r1# show security
nat {
    destination-nat pool_10_10_12_3 address 10.10.12.3;
    interface ge-0/0/1.0 {
        source-nat {
            pool ext-block {
                address-range {
                    low 55.5.5.2 high 55.5.5.30;
                }
            }
        }
    }
}
. . .
```

The next section of the security stanza defines the security zones:

```
    . . .
zones {
        security-zone external_wan-services {
            host-inbound-traffic {
                system-services {
```

```
                    ftp;
                    ssh;
                    telnet;
                }
            }
            interfaces {
                ge-0/0/1.0;
            }
        }
        security-zone internal_wan-services {
            address-book {
                address address_55_5_5_100_32 55.5.5.100/32;
                address address_10_0_0_0_8 10.0.0.0/8;
            }
            host-inbound-traffic {
                system-services {
                    ftp;
                    ssh;
                    telnet;
                }
            }
            interfaces {
                ge-0/0/2.1241 {
                    host-inbound-traffic {
                        protocols {
                            ospf;
                        }
                    }
                }
                ge-0/0/0.0 {
                    host-inbound-traffic {
                        protocols {
                            ospf;
                        }
                    }
                }
                lo0.0 {
                    host-inbound-traffic {
                        protocols {
                            ospf;
                        }
                    }
                }
            }
        }
    }
. . .
```

The zones configuration defines two security zones: an external-wan-services zone that is associated with the EBGP peering interface and an internal-wan-services zone housing the internal and OoB interfaces. Figure 11-7 shows the resultant zone configuration.

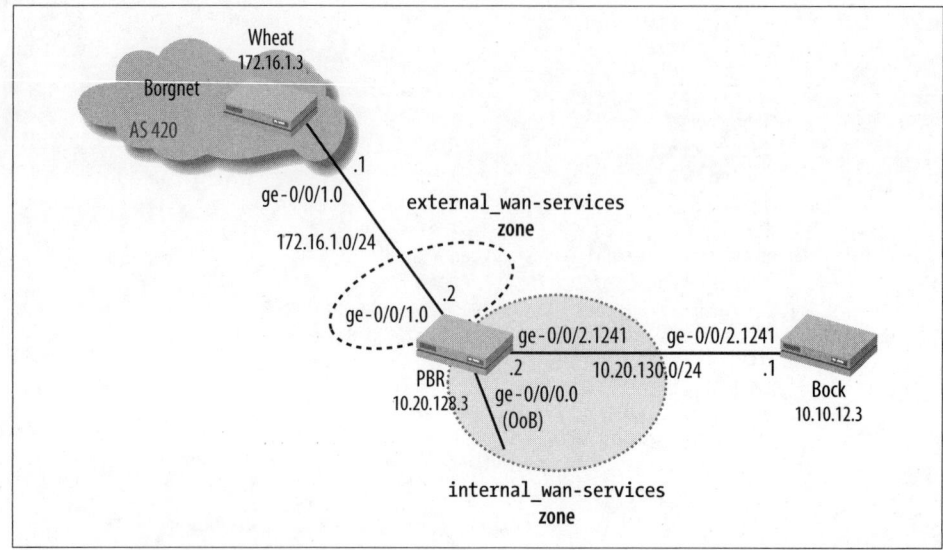

Figure 11-7. The migrated zone configuration

The external-wan-services zone is set to support a limited subset of host services. Note that some of these services were not reachable from external hosts in the original, ASP-based configuration. The presence of additional host services helps in fault isolation, and you can remove it later if desired—for example, to prevent Telnet access to the local router over the 172.16.1.0/24 subnet. BGP does not have to be explicitly allowed on the ge-0/0/1 interface because, as you will soon see, the stateful firewall is configured to allow incoming BGP (and SSH).

The internal-wan-services zone includes the router's lo0 interface, the ge-0/0/0 OoB interface, and the ge-0/0/2 interface that connects to Bock. This zone allows a wider range of system services, which is in keeping with the higher level of trust for this internal zone and which explicitly allows OSPF on the lo0 and ge-0/0/2 interfaces. It seems that ping was not added to the list of supported services during the migration, which means that internal ping testing is not possible until the list of supported host services is modified, a behavior that differs from the premigration environment. Also worth noting here is that the list of supported services or protocols always takes the *most specific* application. This means that when an interface has no explicit list of services, as in this example, the interface inherits the services specified under inbound host traffic. However, if you add a specific service to an interface, that interface no longer inherits the values of the inbound host services settings. The same is true for protocols. To provide an example, if you added BGP to inbound host traffic, you would expect to see that BGP traffic is *not* accepted by any of the interfaces. This is because as configured, each interface has its own protocol stanza and therefore ignores the protocols specified under inbound host traffic.

Adding a new interface, or adding a new protocol such as Internal BGP (IBGP) to the ge-0/0/2 interface, requires updates to the `internal-wan-services` zone to permit communications, given the secure context that resulted from migration of a configuration that used ASP-based stateful services.

The two address book entries create symbolic name-to-prefix mappings that are later used in NAT-related policy actions. The policy portion of the security stanza is examined:

```
    . . .
policies {
    from-zone internal_wan-services to-zone external_wan-services {
        policy all-algs_1 {
            match {
                source-address any;
                destination-address any;
                application cjunos-algs-outbound;
            }
            then {
                permit;
            }
        }
        policy translate-all_1 {
            match {
                source-address address_10_0_0_0_8;
                destination-address any;
                application any;
            }
            then {
                permit {
                    source-nat {
                        pool ext-block;
                    }
                }
            }
        }
    }
    from-zone external_wan-services to-zone internal_wan-services {
        policy all-ssh_1 {
            match {
                source-address any;
                destination-address any;
                application [ junos-ssh junos-bgp ];
            }
            then {
                permit;
            }
        }
        policy pin-hole_1 {
            match {
                source-address any;
                destination-address address_55_5_5_100_32;
                application special-port-map;
```

```
                }
            then {
                permit {
                    destination-nat {
                        pool_10_10_12_3;
                    }
                }
            }
        }
    }
}
```

The `internal_wan-services` to-zone `external_wan-services` policy chain controls communications from the internal to external WAN services zones. Therefore, it evokes ALGs, and then SNAT for source addresses that fall in the 10.0.0.0/8 range.

The `external_wan-services` to-zone `internal_wan-services` policy chain is used for flows that enter the external WAN services zone and egress on the internal WAN services zone. Here we see the explicit acceptance of both BGP and SSH via the `all-ssh_1` policy. The `pin-hole_1` policy then matches on an address book entry for 55.5.5.100, along with an application port map, to evoke DNAT based on the 10.10.12.3 address pool. All other incoming traffic must have matching state, or the stateful-firewall function discards the traffic, preventing it from entering the internal WAN services zone.

It's worth noting that the migration tool did not provide a policy to permit communications between interfaces belonging to the `internal-wan-services` zone. Recall that unlike ScreenOS, which has intrazone blocking disabled for the trust zone, the 8.5 version of JUNOS software with enhanced services has intrazone blocking enabled, for all zones—in effect, there is no differentiation between a zone named "trust" and one named "untrust" from a security policy perspective. As a result, you can expect that Bock will be able to ping the 10.20.130.2 interface address of PBR, which is accepted by the self-traffic policy (described shortly), whereas a ping or Telnet request to PBR's loopback address fails. The following policy can be added (but is not in this example) to allow unfettered communications among all interfaces in the internal zone:

```
from-zone internal_wan-services to-zone internal_wan-services {
    policy default-permit {
        match {
            source-address any;
            destination-address any;
            application any;
        }
        then {
            permit;
        }
    }
}
```

The remaining area of change in the migration is the [edit applications] stanza, as shown:

```
[edit]
regress@hay_PBR_r1# show applications
applications {
    application special-port-map {
        protocol tcp;
        destination-port 5767;
    }
    /* Applications not listed are not supported */
    application-set cjunos-algs-outbound {
        application junos-ftp;
        application junos-tftp;
        application junos-rpc-portmap-tcp;
        application junos-rpc-portmap-udp;
        application junos-rsh;
        application junos-rtsp;
        application junos-sqlnet-v1;
        application junos-sqlnet-v2;
        application junos-h323;
        application junos-realaudio;
        application junos-dce-rpc-portmap;
        application junos-sip;
    }
}
```

The applications group lists the custom port map used in the pinhole/DNAT and displays the currently supported ALGs.

Confirm JUNOS software with enhanced services operation

The confirmation of JUNOS software with enhanced services operation follows the same functional lines. However, now you use a show security command to monitor NAT, the stateful firewall, and other security-related services.

To ensure clean flow state, begin by clearing all flows. This is a disruptive operation and results in loss of management Telnet/SSH sessions, when used with the all keyword. Note that at this time, the OoB management session is cleared and console access is used to keep session state to a minimum.

```
regress@hay_PBR_r1> clear security flow session all
This command will terminate the current session too.
Continue? [yes,no] (no)yes
```

Once again, OSPF and BGP operation is confirmed:

```
regress@hay_PBR_r1> show ospf neighbor
Address      Interface        State  ID           Pri  Dead
10.20.130.1  ge-0/0/2.1241    Full   10.255.14.97 128   35

regress@hay_PBR_r1> show bgp summary
Groups: 1 Peers: 1 Down peers: 0
```

```
Table    Tot Paths  Act Paths Suppressed  History Damp State  Pending
inet.0          1          1          0        0        0        0
Peer           AS      InPkt     OutPkt     OutQ    Flaps Last Up/Dwn State|#Active/
Received/Damped...
172.16.1.1    420      2931      2966        0        6   6:33:21 1/1/0
0/0/0
```

The output confirms that both OSPF and BGP are operational: good. Once again, Bock generates pings toward Wheat, but this time rapid pings are used, and Wheat opens an SSH session to the loopback address of PBR. Both the pings and SSH connection are successful (not shown). The rapid pings are necessary because the stateful-firewall state ages out quickly for ICMP, so a higher volume of traffic ensures that the ICMP session state is present when the CLI command is executed.

The flow session state is displayed at PBR using the show security flow session command:

```
regress@hay_PBR_r1> show security flow session
Session ID: 1284, Policy name: self-traffic-policy/1, Timeout: 58
  In: 10.20.130.1/1 --> 224.0.0.5/1;ospf, If: ge-0/0/2.1241
  Out: 224.0.0.5/1 --> 10.20.130.1/1;ospf, If: .local..0
```

The first session represents OSPF traffic to and from the ge-0/0/2 interface, and is expected. Note that this traffic is accepted because OSPF is listed as a supported protocol under the ge-0/0/2.1241 interface. This results in acceptance of the traffic via a nonuser-configurable *self-traffic* policy. The self-traffic policy is evoked when traffic is addressed to the ingress interface itself, as opposed to being addressed to the loopback or other interface address.

```
Session ID: 1285, Policy name: self-traffic-policy/1, Timeout: 1788
  In: 172.16.1.2/59024 --> 172.16.1.1/179;tcp, If: .local..0
  Out: 172.16.1.1/179 --> 172.16.1.2/59024;tcp, If: ge-0/0/1.0
```

The next flow represents the EBGP session to Wheat, as indicated by the TCP protocol and 179 port values. As the EBGP peering session is interface-based, you again see acceptance via the self-traffic policy.

```
Session ID: 1539, Policy name: all-ssh_1/9, Timeout: 1780
  In: 172.16.1.1/58495 --> 10.10.12.3/22;tcp, If: ge-0/0/1.0
  Out: 10.10.12.3/22 --> 172.16.1.1/58495;tcp, If: ge-0/0/2.1241
```

The next flow is for the SSH test traffic originated at Wheat, which terminates at Bock's lo0 interface in this example. Note that SNAT is not performed for flows that are initiated from the untrust to internal-wan-services zone, as doing so would break the communications. Wheat in this case expects a response from the SSH session's target address, not from a SNAT pool address.

```
Session ID: 11748, Policy name: translate-all_1/8, Timeout: 60
  In: 10.20.130.1/10091 --> 172.16.1.3/14391;icmp, If: ge-0/0/2.1241
  Out: 172.16.1.3/14391 --> 55.5.5.26/1394;icmp, If: ge-0/0/1.0

4 sessions displayed
```

The final flow entry represents the ICMP test traffic from Bock to Wheat. Once again, SNAT operation is confirmed by the presence of a 55.5.5.x address in the outbound direction.

The destination and source NAT pools are also verified:

```
[edit security]
regress@hay_PBR_r1# run show security nat destination-nat summary
Pool name            Address range                    Port
pool_10_10_12_3       10.10.12.3
[edit security]
regress@hay_PBR_r1# run show security nat source-nat summary
Pool name     Address low     Address high    Interface     PAT
ext-block     55.5.5.2        55.5.5.30       ge-0/0/1.0    yes
```

The command output confirms that both DNAT and SNAT are correctly configured.

Though not shown, ping and Telnet traffic generated at Bock to PBR's 10.20.130.2 ge-0/0/2.1241 interface address succeeds, as expected. The same traffic fails when addressed to its 10.20.128.3 lo0 address due to lack of a policy that permits intrazone traffic in the internal-wan-services zone, as described previously.

Troubleshoot a flow problem

With the stateful-firewall and NAT aspects of the services configuration confirmed, it's time to move on to the DNAT function for TCP traffic sent to 55.5.5.100:5767. The connection is expected to fail again, but this time, rather than timing out as before, it is now observed to fail immediately:

```
regress@best_Wheat_r0> telnet 55.5.5.100 port 5767
Trying 55.5.5.100...
telnet: connect to address 55.5.5.100: Connection refused
telnet: Unable to connect to remote host
```

Also, a monitor interface traffic ge-0/0/2 command at Bock does not confirm the receipt of the DNAT traffic (not shown). In addition, upon examining the flow session table at PBR, there is no evidence of session state for the DNAT traffic.

Although complete coverage of the new services tracing and debug tools is outside the context of this chapter, the lack of DNAT operation affords a chance to demonstrate a typical flow-based troubleshooting scenario. You begin by configuring flow packet drop tracing. Note that most of the main hierarchies at the [edit security] stanza have their own tracing capability. For example, to trace and debug firewall authentication, configure tracing at the [edit security firewall-authentication] hierarchy.

A Word on Session Timeouts

The flow-based nature of JUNOS software with enhanced services results in a need to age out inactive flows to ensure that flow state does not grow without bounds. The default settings result in TCP-based session timeouts of 1,800 seconds, or 30 minutes. Additionally, the default settings do not reset (clear) TCP sessions upon age out. This can result in the sensation of a "hung terminal" session, where you find the terminal session unresponsive—as though the router had crashed. This behavior differs from that of JUNOS software, which has no such session timeouts given its packet-based forwarding paradigm.

There are a few ways to minimize these issues. First, you can add the tcp-rst option to the management traffic's ingress zone. This results in the TCP session clearing upon timeout, which leaves no doubt as to the connection status, thus minimizing the sensation of a hung terminal session. Another option is to configure longer session timeouts for local host management traffic, which is practical only when you have a specific policy for this management traffic; that is, you are not in router context with an accept-all policy. The code example shown matches on the junos-ssh ALG permitted by the all-ssh_1 policy and sets the TCP session timeout to a value of 3,600 seconds, or one hour (24 hours/86,400 seconds is the maximum). Note that a strict security policy favors the timely closing of idle management sessions, and that the following code also affects the timeout of transit SSH sessions, which can lead to excessive resource consumption should you encounter a large number of SSH sessions:

```
application junos-ssh {
    protocol tcp;
    inactivity-timeout 3600;
}

regress@hay_PBR_r1> show security flow session
. .
Session ID: 206256, Policy name: all-ssh_1/9, Timeout: 3590
  In: 172.16.1.1/50327 --> 10.20.128.3/22;tcp, If: ge-0/0/1.0
  Out: 10.20.128.3/22 --> 172.16.1.1/50327;tcp, If: .local..0
```

First, the list of security hierarchies is shown, and then the trace configuration for flows:

```
[edit security]
regress@hay_PBR_r1# set ?
Possible completions:
> alg                   Configure ALG security options
+ apply-groups          Groups from which to inherit configuration
data
+ apply-groups-except   Don't inherit configuration data from these
groups
> authentication-key-chains  Authentication key chain configuration
> certificates          X.509 certificate configuration
> firewall-authentication  Firewall authentication parameters
```

```
> flow                   FLOW configuration
> forwarding-options     Security-forwarding-options configuration
> ike                    IKE configuration
> ipsec                  IPSec configuration
> nat                    Configure Network Address Translation
> pki                    PKI service configuration
> policies               Configure Network Security Policies
> rtlog-options
> screen                 Configure screen feature
> ssh-known-hosts        SSH known host list
> traceoptions           Network security daemon tracing options
> zones                  Zone configuration

[edit security]
regress@hay_PBR_r1# show flow
traceoptions {
    file flow;
    flag packet-drops;
}
```

With the flow tracing configuration in effect, the DNAT traffic is again generated at Wheat. A flow trace can be rather chatty, so you can use the CLI match function to quickly find interesting data. In this example, the following trace output is observed:

```
*** flow ***
. . .
Dec  6 20:28:47 20:28:47.475440:CID-0:RT:55.5.5.100/5767,6
Dec  6 20:28:47 20:28:47.475446:CID-0:RT:<Root VSYS(I)>

Dec  6 20:28:47 20:28:47.475449:CID-0:RT:flow_first_routing: DEST
route-lookup failed, dropping pkt and not creating session nh:
4294967295
. . .
```

The trace output shows that a matching flow was in fact dropped by the root virtual system, with the cause being a lack of destination route. This behavior strikes a bell with regard to ScreenOS behavior for DNAT. When performing DNAT, ScreenOS requires a static route to the DNAT destination address—55.5.5.100 in this case—in order to determine the egress interface, and therefore the egress zone. This is needed because the security policy chain is a function of ingress zone to egress zone. This theory is confirmed with a show route at PBR:

```
[edit]
regress@hay_PBR_r1# run show route 55.5.5.100

inet.0: 31 destinations, 31 routes (30 active, 0 holddown, 1 hidden)
+ = Active Route, - = Last Active, * = Both

55.5.5.0/24        *[Aggregate/130] 23:07:08
                    Reject
```

It would appear that a reject next hop does not identify the egress zone, unless you consider /dev/null a zone. A quick static route hack is added:

```
[edit]
regress@hay_PBR_r1# show routing-options static
route 55.5.5.100/32 next-hop 10.20.130.1;
```

The DNAT test traffic is again generated. Note that the session is observed to time out, rather than being immediately closed:

```
regress@best_Wheat_r0> telnet 55.5.5.100 port 5767
Trying 55.5.5.100...
```

Matching flow state is now found in the session table:

```
[edit]
regress@hay_PBR_r1# run show security flow session
Session ID: 201676, Policy name: pin-hole_1/11, Timeout: 14
  In: 172.16.1.1/59547 --> 55.5.5.100/5767;tcp, If: ge-0/0/1.0
  Out: 10.10.12.3/5767 --> 172.16.1.1/59547;tcp, If: ge-0/0/2.1241
. . . .
```

Although not shown, a monitor traffic interface ge-0/0/2 command at Bock also confirms receipt of the DNAT forwarded traffic. This completes the verification of stateful services and confirms that the formally ASP-based services have been successfully migrated to operate in the JUNOS software with enhanced services environment.

Some other interesting commands

In this section, we will run a few interesting commands to demonstrate various commands that are useful when monitoring or troubleshooting JUNOS software with enhanced services. The show security zones command displays interface-to-zone mapping information. Recall that policy is not needed for communication among interfaces in the same zone:

```
[edit security]
regress@hay_PBR_r1# run show security zones

Security zone: Untrust
  Send reset for non-SYN session TCP packets: Off
  Policy configurable: Yes
  Interfaces bound: 1
  Interfaces:
    st0.0

Security zone: external_wan-services
  Send reset for non-SYN session TCP packets: Off
  Policy configurable: Yes
  Interfaces bound: 1
  Interfaces:
    ge-0/0/1.0

Security zone: internal_wan-services
  Send reset for non-SYN session TCP packets: Off
  Policy configurable: Yes
  Interfaces bound: 3
  Interfaces:
    ge-0/0/0.0
```

```
ge-0/0/2.1241
lo0.0

Security zone: junos-global
  Send reset for non-SYN session TCP packets: Off
  Policy configurable: Yes
  Interfaces bound: 0
Interfaces:
```

To display policy information, as needed for communication among zones, use the show security policies command:

```
[edit]
regress@hay_PBR_r1# run show security policies
Default policy: deny-all
From zone: Trust, To zone: Untrust
  Policy: allow-all, State: enabled, Index: 4, Sequence number: 1
    Source addresses: any
    Destination addresses: any
    Applications: any
    Action: permit, source nat
From zone: Untrust, To zone: Trust
  Policy: all-ssh, State: enabled, Index: 5, Sequence number: 1
    Source addresses: any
    Destination addresses: any
    Applications: junos-ssh
    Action: permit
  Policy: pin-hole, State: enabled, Index: 6, Sequence number: 2
    Source addresses: any
    Destination addresses: address_55_5_5_100_32
    Applications: special-port-map
    Action: permit, destination nat
```

The default deny-all policy confirms a secure context. For both interzone and intra-zone communications to succeed, the traffic must be explicitly accepted by a user policy.

JUNOS Software with Enhanced Services Summary

It's true, the services syntax has changed in JUNOS software with enhanced services. This is a change made necessary by the shift from ASP-based service sets to enhanced functionality made available by leveraging the world-class security features of ScreenOS.

Putting the functionality enhancements aside, many find the new syntax to be intuitive, especially if they have experience with ScreenOS and the associated NetScreen security devices.

Juniper Networks has made migration tools available to help ease the transition in services syntax, making the shift to JUNOS software with enhanced services something that should be considered, especially by enterprises that now deploy a two-box solution for their security and routing needs.

Conclusion

JUNOS software with enhanced services represents a significant increase in security, and in general services capabilities for supported platforms. With JUNOS software with enhanced services, users are no longer forced to compromise either services or routing when they opt for a single-box solution. Formerly, this required a multiple-chassis, best-of-breed approach, which added cost and complexity to the network.

In addition to the one-box benefits, that one box is found to run JUNOS software, albeit with enhanced services enabled. This means that all the benefits and advantages of JUNOS are still available, and the majority of operational experience carries directly over, allowing you to immediately feel at home when using JUNOS software with enhanced services.

It is expected that JUNOS software with enhanced services will continue to be expanded, meaning that new services and capabilities will be added. Consult the Juniper Networks web site for the latest information on JUNOS software with enhanced services features and capabilities.

Exam Topics

Currently, the Juniper Networks Certified Internet Expert (JNCIE-ER) examination is based on ASP service sets. As with all exam topics, this is subject to change. Candidates should consult the Juniper Networks web site for up-to-date information on certification examination tracks and topics.

Chapter Review Questions

1. What is the difference between secure and router context?
    a. There is no real difference; both modes support firewall and routing
    b. In secure context, you get the stateful firewall; in router context, you get routing
    c. Secure context has a default deny-all policy whereas router context has an accept-all policy
    d. Both modes have a default deny-all policy, but in router context, all interfaces are in the same zone
2. What is true regarding zones?
    a. You are limited to no more than five
    b. Each zone is restricted to a single interface
    c. Policy is needed to communicate between zones, unless in router context
    d. Policy is needed to communicate between zones

3. What is the result of loading a JUNOS software configuration into a JUNOS software with enhanced services router?

    a. Nothing, they are compatible

    b. You lose all connectivity, including console

    c. You retain console access, but all network connectivity is lost

    d. None of the above; the different hardware platforms make this impossible

4. What is the name of the services interface in JUNOS software with enhanced services?

    a. sp-0/0/0

    b. st-0/0/0

    c. es-0/0/0

    d. The zone-based nature means that a services interfaces is not required

5. Looking back at Figure 11-6, does the following session entry, as taken from PBR, indicate that NAT has been performed?

```
Session ID: 1285, Policy name: self-traffic-policy/1, Timeout: 1784
  In: 172.16.1.2/59024 --> 172.16.1.1/179;tcp, If: .local..0
  Out: 172.16.1.1/179 --> 172.16.1.2/59024;tcp, If: ge-0/0/1.0
```

    a. No, NAT is not being performed

    b. Yes, NAT is being performed

    c. Only SNAT is being performed

    d. Only DNAT is being performed

6. To the person who configures a J-series router, what has changed when running JUNOS software with enhanced services?

    a. ASP-based services such as IPSec, the stateful firewall, and NAT

    b. ASP services and routing protocol configuration

    c. The entire CLI has changed to accommodate new services

    d. Nothing; the new services are configured the same way as before

7. Which platform supports JUNOS software with enhanced services?

    a. M7i

    b. M10i and m7i

    c. Only J-series

    d. Certain J-series platforms and SSG 320m/350m platforms with a conversion kit

Chapter Review Answers

1. Answer: C. In secure mode, an implicit deny-all policy is in effect. In router context, an explicit accept-all policy is used. Even so, interfaces and their protocols have to be listed in a zone for communication to occur.

2. Answer: D. Policy is always needed to permit traffic between zones.

3. Answer: C. The lack of a security stanza in the original JUNOS configuration results in no interfaces, in any zones, preventing network connectivity.

4. Answer: B. A services interface is still required, to be placed in the untrust zone, for example. In this way, policy can evaluate traffic that is flowing across the services interface.

5. Answer: A. The use of 172.16.1.0/24 addressing indicates that no NAT has been performed. SNAT would involve 55.5.5.0/27, and DNAT was using 10.10.12.3 in this example. Note that self-generated traffic does not go through the NAT/policy engine.

6. Answer: A. Rest assured that the majority of JUNOS software and the CLI are the same. Only services configuration has changed.

7. Answer: D. ASIC-based platforms such as the M7i and M10i do not support enhanced services. Certain J-series and SSG platforms can be loaded/converted to operate with enhanced services.

Glossary

AAL

Asynchronous Transfer Mode (ATM) adaptation layer. A series of protocols enabling various types of traffic, including voice, data, image, and video, to run over an ATM network.

AAL5 mode

Asynchronous Transfer Mode (ATM) adaptation Layer 5. One of four ATM adaptation layers (AALs) recommended by the ITU-T. AAL5 is used predominantly for the transfer of classical IP over ATM. AAL5 is the least complex of the current AAL recommdations. It offers low-bandwidth overhead and simpler processing requirements in exchange for reduced bandwidth capacity and error-recovery capability. It is a Layer 2 circuit transport mode that allows you to send ATM cells between ATM2 intelligent queuing (IQ) interfaces across a Layer 2 circuit-enabled network. You use Layer 2 circuit AAL5 transport mode to tunnel a stream of AAL5-encoded ATM segmentation and reassembly protocol data units (SAR-PDUs) over a Multiprotocol Label Switching (MPLS) or IP backbone. *See also* cell-relay mode, Layer 2 circuits, standard AAL5 mode, trunk mode.

ABR

Area border router. Router that belongs to more than one area. Used in Open Shortest Path First (OSPF). *See also* OSPF.

access concentrator

Router that acts as a server in a Point-to-Point Protocol over Ethernet (PPPoE) session—for example, an E-series router.

accounting services

Method of collecting network data related to resource usage.

ACFC

Address and Control Field Compression. Enables routers to transmit packets without the two 1-byte address and control fields (0xff and 0x03) (which are normal for Point-to-Point Protocol [PPP]-encapsulated packets), thus transmitting less data and conserving bandwidth. ACFC is defined in RFC 1661, "The Point-to-Point Protocol (PPP)." *See also* PFC.

active route

Route chosen from all routes in the route table to reach a destination. Active routes are installed into the forwarding table.

adaptive services

Set of services or applications that you can configure on an Adaptive Services PIC (ASP). The services and applications include stateful firewall, Network Address Translation (NAT), intrusion detection services (IDSs), Internet Protocol Security (IPSec), Layer 2 Tunneling Protocol (L2TP), and voice services. *See also* tunneling protocol.

address match conditions

Use of an IP address as a match criterion in a routing policy or a firewall filter.

adjacency

Portion of the local routing information that pertains to the reachability of a single neighbor over a single circuit or interface.

Adjacency-RIB-In

Logical software table that contains Border Gateway Protocol (BGP) routes received from a specific neighbor.

Adjacency-RIB-Out

Logical software table that contains Border Gateway Protocol (BGP) routes to be sent to a specific neighbor.

ADM

Add/drop multiplexer. SONET functionality that allows lower-level signals to be dropped from a high-speed optical connection.

ADSL

Asymmetrical digital subscriber line. A technology that allows more data to be sent over existing copper telephone lines, using the public switched telephone network (PSTN). ADSL supports data rates from 1.5 Mbps to 9 Mbps when receiving data (downstream rate), and from 16 Kbps to 640 Kbps when sending data (upstream rate).

ADSL interface

Asymmetrical digital subscriber line interface. Physical WAN interface that connects a router to a digital subscriber line access multiplexer (DSLAM). An ADSL interface allocates line bandwidth asymmetrically. Downstream (provider-to-customer) data rates can be up to 8 Mbps for ADSL, 12 Mbps for ADSL2, and 25 Mbps for ADSL2+. Upstream (customer-to-provider) rates can be up to 800 Kbps for ADSL and 1 Mbps for ADSL2 and ADSL2+, depending on the implementation.

ADSL2 interface

ADSL interface that supports ITU-T Standard G.992.3 and ITU-T Standard G.992.4. ADSL2 allocates downstream (provider-to-customer) data rates of up to 12

Mbps and upstream (customer-to-provider) rates of up to 1 Mbps.

ADSL2+ interface

ADSL interface that supports ITU-T Standard G.992.5. ADSL2+ allocates downstream (provider-to-customer) data rates of up to 25 Mbps and upstream (customer-to-provider) rates of up to 1 Mbps.

AES

Advanced Encryption Standard. Defined in FIPS PUB 197. The AES algorithm uses keys of 128, 192, or 256 bits to encrypt and decrypt data in blocks of 128 bits.

aggregate route

Combination of groups of routes that have common addresses into a single entry in a route table.

aggregated interface

Logical bundle of physical interfaces. The aggregated interface is managed as a single interface with one IP address. Network traffic is dynamically distributed across ports, so administration of data flowing across a given port is done automatically within the aggregated link. Using multiple ports in parallel provides redundancy and increases the link speed beyond the limits of any single port.

AH

Authentication header. A component of the IPSec protocol used to verify that the contents of a packet have not changed, and to validate the identity of the sender.

ALI

ATM line interface. Interface between Asynchronous Transfer Mode (ATM) and 3G systems. *See also* ATM.

ANSI

American National Standards Institute. The U.S. representative to the ISO.

APN

Access point name. When mobile stations connect to IP networks over a wireless network, the GGSN uses the APN to distinguish among the connected IP networks (known as *APN networks*). In addition to identifying these connected networks, an APN is also a configured entity that hosts the wireless sessions, which are called Packet Data Protocol (PDP) contexts.

APQ

Alternate priority queuing. Dequeuing method that has a special queue, similar to strict-priority queuing (SPQ), which is visited only 50% of the time. The packets in the special queue still have a predictable latency, although the upper limit of the delay is higher than that with SPQ. Since the other configured queues share the remaining 50% of the service time, queue starvation is usually avoided. *See also* SPQ.

APS

Automatic Protection Switching. Technology used by SONET add/drop multiplexers (ADMs) to protect against circuit faults between the ADM and a router and to protect against failing routers.

area

1.Routing subdomain that maintains detailed routing information about its own internal composition as well as routing information that allows it to reach other routing subdomains. In Intermediate System-to-Intermediate System Level 1 (IS-IS), an area corresponds to a Level 1 subdomain. 2. In IS-IS and Open Shortest Path First (OSPF), a set of contiguous networks and hosts within an autonomous system (AS) that have been administratively grouped together.

ARP

Address Resolution Protocol. Protocol used for mapping IPv4 addresses to media access control (MAC) addresses. *See also* NDP.

AS

Autonomous system. Set of routers under a single technical administration. Each AS normally uses a single Interior Gateway Protocol (IGP) and metrics to propagate routing information within the set of routers. Also called a *routing domain*.

ASBR

Autonomous system boundary router. In Open Shortest Path First (OSPF), a router that exchanges routing information with routers in other autonomous systems (ASs).

ASBR Summary LSA

OSPF link-state advertisement (LSA) sent by an area border router (ABR) to advertise the router ID of an autonomous system boundary router (ASBR) across an area boundary. *See also* ASBR.

AS external link advertisement

OSPF link-state advertisement (LSA) sent by autonomous system boundary routers (ASBRs) to describe external routes that they have detected. These LSAs are flooded throughout the autonomous system (AS) (except for stub areas).

ASIC

Application-specific integrated circuit. Specialized processors that perform specific functions on the router.

ASM

1. Adaptive Services Module. On a Juniper Networks M7i router, provides the same functionality as the Adaptive Services PIC (ASP). 2. Any Source Multicast. A network that supports both one-to-many and many-to-many communication models. An ASM network must determine all the sources of a group and deliver all of them to interested subscribers.

ASP

Adaptive Services PIC. *See* adaptive services.

AS path

In the Border Gateway Protocol (BGP), the route to a destination. The path consists of the autonomous system (AS) numbers of all routers that a packet must go through to reach a destination.

ATM

Asynchronous Transfer Mode. A high-speed multiplexing and switching method utilizing fixed-length cells of 53 octets to support multiple types of traffic.

ATM-over-ADSL interface

Asynchronous Transfer Mode (ATM) interface used to send network traffic through a point-to-point connection to a DSL access multiplexer (DSLAM). ATM-over-ADSL interfaces are intended for asymmetrical digital subscriber line (ADSL) connections only, not for direct ATM connections.

atomic

Smallest possible operation. An atomic operation is performed either entirely or not at all. For example, if machine failure prevents a transaction from completing, the system is rolled back to the start of the transaction, with no changes taking place.

AUC

Authentication center. Part of the Home Location Register (HLR) in third-generation (3G) systems; performs computations to verify and authenticate a mobile phone user.

automatic policing

Policer that allows you to provide strict service guarantees for network traffic. Such guarantees are especially useful in the context of differentiated services for traffic-engineered label-switched paths (LSPs), providing better emulation for Asynchronous Transfer Mode (ATM) wires over a Multiprotocol Label Switching (MPLS) network.

auto-negotiation

Used by Ethernet devices to configure interfaces automatically. If interfaces support different speeds or different link modes (half duplex or full duplex), the devices attempt to settle on the lowest common denominator.

autonomous system external link advertisement

OSPF link-state advertisement (LSA) sent by autonomous system boundary routers (ASBRs) to describe external routes that they have detected. These LSAs are flooded throughout the autonomous system (AS) (except for stub areas).

autonomous system path

In the Border Gateway Protocol (BGP), the route to a destination. The path consists of the autonomous system (AS) numbers of all the routers a packet must pass through to reach a destination.

auto-RP

Method of electing and announcing the rendezvous point-to-group address mapping in a multicast network. JUNOS software supports this vendor-proprietary specification. *See also* RP.

backbone area

In Open Shortest Path First (OSPF), an area that consists of all networks in area ID 0.0.0.0, their attached routers, and all area border routers (ABRs).

backbone router

Open Shortest Path First (OSPF) router with all operational interfaces within area 0.0.0.0.

backplane

See midplane.

backup designated router

Open Shortest Path First (OSPF) router on a broadcast segment that monitors the operation of the designated router and takes over its functions if the designated router fails.

BA classifier

Behavior aggregate classifier. A method of classification that operates on a packet as it enters the router. The packet header contents are examined, and this single field determines the class-of-service (CoS) settings applied to the packet. *See also* multifield classifier.

bandwidth

Range of transmission frequencies that a network can use, expressed as the difference between the highest and lowest frequencies of a transmission channel. In computer networks, greater bandwidth indicates a faster data transfer rate capacity.

bandwidth model

In Differentiated-Services-aware traffic engineering, determines the value of the available bandwidth advertised by the Interior Gateway Protocols (IGPs).

bandwidth on demand

1. A technique to temporarily provide additional capacity on a link to handle

bursts in data, videoconferencing, or other variable bit rate applications. Also called *flexible bandwidth allocation*. 2. On a Services Router, an Integrated Services Digital Network (ISDN) cost-control feature defining the bandwidth threshold that must be reached on links before a Services Router initiates additional ISDN data connections to provide more bandwidth.

BBFD
Bidirectional Forwarding Detection. A simple hello mechanism that detects failures in a network. Used with routing protocols to speed up failure detection.

B-channel
Bearer channel. A 64 Kbps channel used for voice or data transfer on an Integrated Services Digital Network (ISDN) interface. *See also* D-channel.

BECN
Backward explicit congestion notification. In a Frame Relay network, a header bit transmitted by the destination device requesting that the source device send data more slowly. BECN minimizes the possibility that packets will be discarded when more packets arrive than can be handled. *See also* FECN.

Bellman-Ford algorithm
Algorithm used in distance-vector routing protocols to determine the best path to all routes in the network.

BERT
Bit error rate test. A test that can be run on the following interfaces to determine whether they are operating properly: E1, E3, T1, T3, and channelized (DS3, OC3, OC12, and STM1) interfaces.

BGP
Border Gateway Protocol. Exterior gateway protocol used to exchange routing information among routers in different autonomous systems (ASs).

bit field match conditions
Use of fields in the header of an IP packet as match criteria in a firewall filter.

bit rate
Number of bits transmitted per second.

BITS
Building Integrated Timing Source. Dedicated timing source that synchronizes all equipment in a particular building.

Blowfish
Unpatented, symmetric cryptographic method developed by Bruce Schneier and used in many commercial and freeware software applications. Blowfish uses variable-length keys of up to 448 bits.

BOOTP
Bootstrap protocol. A User Datagram Protocol (UDP)/IP-based protocol that allows a booting host to configure itself dynamically and without user supervision. BOOTP provides a means to notify a host of its assigned IP address, the IP address of a boot server host, and the name of a file to be loaded into memory and executed. Other configuration information, such as the local subnet mask, the local time offset, the addresses of default routers, and the addresses of various Internet servers, can also be communicated to a host using BOOTP.

bootstrap router
Single router in a multicast network responsible for distributing candidate rendezvous point (RP) information to all Physical Interface Module (PIM)-enabled routers.

BPDU
Bridge protocol data unit. A Spanning Tree Protocol hello packet that is sent out at intervals to exchange information across bridges and detect loops in a network topology.

BRI
Basic Rate Interface. Integrated Services Digital Network (ISDN) interface intended for home and small enterprise applications. BRI consists of two 64 Kbps B-channels to carry voice or data, and one 16 Kbps D-channel for control and signaling. *See also* B-channel; D-channel.

bridge

Device that uses the same communications protocol to connect and pass packets between two network segments. A bridge operates at Layer 2 of the Open Systems Interconnection (OSI) reference model.

broadcast

Operation of sending network traffic from one network node to all other network nodes.

BSC

Base station controller. Key network node in third-generation (3G) systems that supervises the functioning and control of multiple base transceiver stations.

BSS

Base station subsystem. Composed of the base transceiver station (BTS) and base station controller (BSC).

BSSGP

Base Station System GPRS Protocol. Processes routing and quality-of-service (QoS) information for the base station subsystem (BSS).

BTS

Base transceiver station. Mobile telephony equipment housed in cabinets and collocated with antennas. (Also known as a radio base station.)

buffers

Memory space for handling data in transit. Buffers compensate for differences in processing speed between network devices and handle bursts of data until they can be processed by slower devices.

bundle

1. Multiple physical links of the same type, such as multiple asynchronous lines, or physical links of different types, such as leased synchronous lines and dial-up asynchronous lines. 2. Collection of software that makes up a JUNOS software release.

bypass LSP

Carries traffic for a label-switched path (LSP) whose link-protected interface has failed. A bypass LSP uses a different interface and path to reach the same destination.

CA

Certificate authority. A trusted third-party organization that creates, enrolls, validates, and revokes digital certificates. The CA guarantees a user's identity and issues public and private keys for message encryption and decryption (coding and decoding).

CAC

Call admission control. In Differentiated-Services-aware traffic engineering, checks for adequate bandwidth on the path before the label-switched path (LSP) is established. If the bandwidth is insufficient, the LSP is not established and an error is reported.

CAIDA

Cooperative Association for Internet Data Analysis. An association that provides tools and analyses promoting the engineering and maintenance of a robust, scalable Internet infrastructure. One tool, cflowd, allows you to collect an aggregate of sampled flows and send the aggregate to a specified host that runs the cflowd application available from CAIDA.

callback

Alternative feature to dial-in that enables a J-series Services Router to call back the caller from the remote end of a backup Integrated Services Digital Network (ISDN) connection. Instead of accepting a call from the remote end of the connection, the router rejects the call, waits a configured period of time, and calls a number configured on the router's dialer interface. *See also* dial-in.

caller ID

Telephone number of the caller on the remote end of a backup Integrated Services Digital Network (ISDN) connection, used to dial in and to identify the caller. Multiple caller IDs can be configured on an ISDN dialer interface. During dial-in, the router matches the incoming call's caller ID against the caller IDs configured on its dialer interfaces. Each dialer interface accepts calls only from callers whose caller IDs are configured on it.

CAMEL

Customized Applications of Mobile Enhanced Logic. An ETSI standard for GSM networks that enhances the provision of Intelligent Network services.

candidate configuration

File maintained by the JUNOS software containing changes to the router's active configuration. This file becomes the active configuration when a user issues the commit command.

candidate RP advertisements

Information sent by routers in a multicast network when they are configured as a local rendezvous point (RP). This information is unicast to the bootstrap router (BSR) for the multicast domain.

carrier-of-carriers VPN

Virtual private network (VPN) service supplied to a network service provider that is supplying either Internet service or VPN service to an end customer. For a carrier-of-carriers VPN, the customer's sites are configured within the same autonomous system (AS).

CB

Control Board. On a T640 routing node, part of the host subsystem that provides control and monitoring functions for router components.

CBC

Cipher block chaining. A mode of encryption using 64 or 128 bits of fixed-length blocks in which each block of plain text is XORed with the previous cipher text block before being encrypted. *See also* XOR.

CBR

Constant bit rate. For ATM1 and ATM2 intelligent queuing (IQ) interfaces, data that is serviced at a constant, repetitive rate. CBR is used for traffic that does not need to periodically burst to a higher rate, such as nonpacketized voice and audio.

CCC

Circuit cross-connect. A JUNOS software feature that allows you to configure transparent connections between two circuits.

A circuit can be a Frame Relay data-link connection identifier (DLCI), an Asynchronous Transfer Mode (ATM) virtual channel (VC), a Point-to-Point Protocol (PPP) interface, a Cisco High-Level Data Link Control (HDLC) interface, or a Multiprotocol Label Switching (MPLS) label-switched path (LSP).

CDMA

Code Division Multiple Access. Technology for digital transmission of radio signals between, for example, a mobile telephone and a base transceiver station (BTS).

CDMA2000

Radio transmission and backbone technology for the evolution to third-generation (3G) mobile networks.

CDR

Call Detail Record. A record containing data (such as origination, termination, length, and time of day) unique to a specific call.

CE device

Customer edge device. Router or switch in the customer's network that is connected to a service provider's provider edge (PE) router and participates in a Layer 3 virtual private network (VPN).

cell relay

Data transmission technology based on the use of small, fixed-size packets (cells) that can be processed and switched in hardware at high speeds. Cell relay is the basis for many high-speed network protocols, including Asynchronous Transfer Mode (ATM) and IEEE 802.6.

cell-relay mode

Layer 2 circuit transport mode that sends Asynchronous Transfer Mode (ATM) cells between ATM2 intelligent queuing (IQ) interfaces over a Multiprotocol Label Switching (MPLS) core network. You use Layer 2 circuit cell-relay transport mode to tunnel a stream of ATM cells over an MPLS or IP backbone. *See also* AAL5 mode; Layer 2 circuits; standard AAL5 mode; trunk mode.

cell tax

Physical transmission capacity used by header information when sending data packets in an Asynchronous Transfer Mode (ATM) network. Each ATM cell uses a 5-byte header.

CFEB

Compact Forwarding Engine Board. In M7i and M10i routers, provides route lookup, filtering, and switching to the destination port.

cflowd

Application available from CAIDA that collects an aggregate of sampled flows and sends the aggregate to a specified host running the cflowd application.

CFM

Cubic feet per minute. Measure of air flow in volume per minute.

channel

Communication circuit linking two or more devices. A channel provides an input/output interface between a processor and a peripheral device, or between two systems. A single physical circuit can consist of one or many channels, or two systems carried on a physical wire or wireless medium. For example, the dedicated channel between a telephone and the central office (CO) is a twisted-pair copper wire. *See also* frequency-division multiplexed channel; time-division multiplexed channel.

channel group

Combination of DS0 interfaces partitioned from a channelized interface into a single logical bundle.

channelized E1

A 2.048 Mbps interface that can be configured as a single clear-channel E1 interface or channelized into as many as 31 discrete DS0 interfaces. On most channelized E1 interfaces, time slots are numbered from 1 through 32, and time slot 1 is reserved for framing. On some legacy channelized E1 interfaces, time slots are numbered from 0 through 31, and time slot 0 is reserved for framing.

channelized interface

Interface that is a subdivision of a larger interface, minimizing the number of Physical Interface Cards (PICs) or Physical Interface Modules (PIMs) that an installation requires. On a channelized PIC or PIM, each port can be configured as a single clear channel or partitioned into multiple discrete T3, T1, E1, and DS0 interfaces, depending on the size of the channelized PIC or PIM.

channelized T1

A 1.544 Mbps interface that can be configured as a single clear-channel T1 interface or channelized into as many as 24 discrete DS0 interfaces. Time slots are numbered from 1 through 24.

CHAP

Challenge Handshake Authentication Protocol. A protocol that authenticates remote users. CHAP is a server-driven, three-step authentication mechanism that depends on a shared secret password that resides on both the server and the client.

chassisd

Chassis daemon. A JUNOS software process responsible for managing the interaction of the router's physical components.

CIDR

Classless interdomain routing. A method of specifying Internet addresses in which you explicitly specify the bits of the address to represent the network address instead of determining this information from the first octet of the address.

CIP

Connector Interface Panel. On an M160 router, the panel that contains connectors for the Routing Engines (REs), BITS interfaces, and alarm relay contacts.

CIR

Committed information rate. The CIR specifies the average rate at which packets are admitted to the network. As each packet enters the network, it is counted. Packets that do not exceed the CIR are marked green, which corresponds to low-loss priority. Packets that exceed the CIR but are below the peak information rate (PIR) are marked yellow, which corresponds to medium loss priority. *See also* trTCM; PIR.

Cisco-RP-Announce

Message advertised into a multicast network by a router configured as a local rendezvous point (RP) in an auto-RP network. A Cisco-RP-Announce message is advertised in a dense-mode Physical Interface Module (PIM) to the 224.0.1.39 multicast group address.

Cisco-RP-Discovery

Message advertised by the mapping agent in an auto-RP network. A Cisco-RP-Discovery message contains the rendezvous point (RP) to multicast group address assignments for the domain. It is advertised in a dense-mode Physical Interface Module (PIM) to the 224.0.1.40 multicast group address.

classification

In class of service (CoS), the examination of an incoming packet that associates the packet with a particular CoS servicing level. There are two kinds of classifiers: behavior aggregate (BA) and multifield. *See also* BA classifier; multifield classifier.

classifier

Method of reading a sequence of bits in a packet header or label and determining how the packet should be forwarded internally and scheduled (queued) for output.

class type

In Differentiated-Services-aware traffic engineering, a collection of traffic flows which are treated equally in a Differentiated Services domain. A class type maps to a queue and is much like a class-of-service (CoS) forwarding class in concept. It is also known as a *traffic class*.

clear channel

Interface configured on a channelized Physical Interface Card (PIC) or Physical Interface Module (PIM) that operates as a single channel, does not carry signaling, and uses the entire port bandwidth.

CLEC

(Pronounced "see-lek".) Competitive local exchange carrier. Company that competes with the already established local telecommunications business by providing its own network and switching.

CLEI

Common Language Equipment Identifier. Inventory code used to identify and track telecommunications equipment.

CLI

Command-line interface. Interface provided for configuring and monitoring the routing protocol software.

client peer

In a Border Gateway Protocol (BGP) route reflection, a member of a cluster that is not the route reflector. *See also* nonclient peer.

CLNP

Connectionless Network Protocol. An ISO-developed protocol for an Open Systems Interconnection (OSI) connectionless network service. CLNP is the OSI equivalent of IP.

CLNS

Connectionless Network Service. A Layer 3 protocol, similar to Internet Protocol version 4 (IPv4). CLNS uses network service access points (NSAPs) instead of the prefix addresses found in IPv4 to specify end systems and intermediate systems.

cluster

In the Border Gateway Protocol (BGP), a set of routers that have been grouped together. A cluster consists of one system that acts as a route reflector, along with any number of client peers. The client peers receive their route information only from the route reflector system. Routers in a cluster do not need to be fully meshed.

CO

Central office. The local telephone company building that houses circuit-switching equipment used for subscriber lines in a given area.

code-point alias

Name assigned to a pattern of code-point bits. This name is used, instead of the bit pattern, in the configuration of other class-of-service (CoS) components such as classifiers, drop-profile maps, and rewrite rules.

command completion

Function of a router's command-line interface (CLI) that allows a user to enter only the first few characters in any command. Users access this function through the Space bar or Tab key.

commit

JUNOS software command-line interface (CLI) configuration-mode command that saves changes made to a router configuration, verifies the syntax, applies the changes to the configuration currently running on the router, and identifies the resultant file as the current operational configuration.

commit script

Script that enforces custom configuration rules. A script runs each time a new candidate configuration is committed and inspects the configuration. If a configuration breaks your custom rules, the script can generate actions for the JUNOS software.

commit script macro

Sequence of commands that allow you to create custom configuration syntax to simplify the task of configuring a routing platform. By itself, your custom syntax has no operational impact on the routing platform. A corresponding commit script macro uses your custom syntax as input data for generating standard JUNOS configuration statements that execute your intended operation.

community

1. In the Border Gateway Protocol (BGP), a group of destinations that share a common property. Community information is included as one of the path attributes in BGP update messages. 2. In the Simple Network Management Protocol (SNMP), an authentication scheme that authorizes SNMP clients based on the source IP address of incoming SNMP packets, defines which Management Information Base (MIB) objects are available, and specifies the operations (read-only or read-write) allowed on those objects.

confederation

In the Border Gateway Protocol (BGP), a group of systems that appears to external autonomous systems (ASs) as a single AS.

configuration mode

JUNOS software mode that allows a user to alter the router's current configuration.

Connect

Border Gateway Protocol (BGP) neighbor state in which the local router has initiated the Transmission Control Protocol (TCP) session and is waiting for the remote peer to complete the TCP connection.

constrained path

In traffic engineering, a path determined using the CSPF algorithm. The ERO carried in the Resource Reservation Protocol (RSVP) packets contains the constrained path information. *See also* ERO.

context node

Node that the Extensible Stylesheet Language for Transformations (XSLT) processor is currently examining. XSLT changes the context as it traverses the XML document's hierarchy. *See also* XSLT.

context-sensitive help

Function of the router's command-line interface (CLI) that allows a user to request information on the JUNOS software hierarchy. You can access context-sensitive help in both operational and configuration modes.

contributing routes

Active IP routes in the route table that share the same most-significant bits and are more specific than an aggregate or generated route.

control plane

Virtual network path used to set up, maintain, and terminate data plane connections. *See also* data plane.

core

Central backbone of the network.

CoS

Class of service. Method of classifying traffic on a packet-by-packet basis using information in the type-of-service (ToS) byte to provide different service levels to different traffic.

cosd

Class-of-service (CoS) process that enables the routing platform to provide different levels of service to applications based on packet classifications.

CPE

Customer premises equipment. Telephone, modem, router, or other service provider equipment located at a customer site.

craft interface

Mechanisms used by a Communication Workers of America craftsperson to operate, administer, and maintain equipment or provision data communications. On a Juniper Networks router, the craft interface allows you to view status and troubleshooting information and perform system control functions.

CRL

Certificate revocation list. A list of digital certificates that have been invalidated, including the reasons for revocation and the names of the entities that issued them. A CRL prevents usage of digital certificates and signatures that have been compromised.

CRTP

Compressed Real-Time Transport Protocol. Protocol that decreases the size of the IP, User Datagram Protocol (UDP), and Real-Time Transport Protocol (RTP) headers and works with reliable and fast point-to-point links for Voice over IP traffic. CRTP is defined in RFC 2508.

Crypto Accelerator Module

Processor card that speeds up certain cryptographic IP Security (IPSec) services on some J-series Services Routers. For the supported cryptographic algorithms, see the J-series documentation.

Crypto Officer

Superuser responsible for the proper operation of a router running JUNOS-FIPS software.

CSCP

Class Selector code point. Eight Differentiated-Services code point (DSCP) values of the form $xxx000$ (where x can be 0 or 1). Defined in RFC 2474.

CSNP

Complete sequence number PDU. Packet that contains a complete list of all the label-switched paths (LSPs) in the Intermediate System-to-Intermediate System Level 1 (IS-IS) database.

CSP

Critical Security Parameter. On routers running JUNOS-FIPS software, a collection of cryptographic keys and passwords that must be protected at all times.

CSPF

Constrained Shortest Path First. A Multiprotocol Label Switching (MPLS) algorithm that has been modified to take into account specific restrictions when calculating the shortest path across the network.

CSU/DSU

Channel service unit/data service unit. A channel service unit connects a digital phone line to a multiplexer or other digital signal device. A data service unit connects a data terminal equipment (DTE) device to a digital phone line.

CVS

Concurrent Versions System. A widely used version control system for software development or data archives.

daemon

Background process that performs operations for the system software and hardware. Daemons normally start when the system software is booted, and they run as long as the software is running. In JUNOS software, daemons are also referred to as *processes*.

damping

Method of reducing the number of update messages sent between Border Gateway Protocol (BGP) peers, thereby reducing the load on these peers without adversely affecting the route convergence time for stable routes.

database description packet

Open Shortest Path First (OSPF) packet type used in the formation of an adjacency. The packet sends summary information about the local router's database to the neighboring router.

data-MDT

Data-driven multicast distribution tree (MDT) tunnel. A multicast tunnel created and deleted based on defined traffic loads and designed to ease loading on the default MDT tunnel.

data packet

Chunk of data transiting the router from the source to a destination.

data plane

Virtual network path used to distribute data between nodes. *See also* control plane.

dcd

Device control process. A JUNOS software interface process (daemon).

DCE

Data circuit-terminating equipment. An RS-232-C device, typically used for a modem or printer, or a network access and packet switching node.

D-channel

Delta channel. A circuit-switched channel that carries signaling and control for B-channels. In Basic Rate Interface (BRI) applications, it can also support customer packet data traffic at speeds up to 9.6 Kbps. *See also* B-channel; BRI.

DCU

Destination class usage. A means of tracking traffic originating from specific prefixes on the customer edge router and destined for specific prefixes on the provider core router, based on the IP source and destination addresses.

DE

Discard-eligible bit. In a Frame Relay network, a header bit notifying devices on the network that traffic can be dropped during congestion to ensure the delivery of higher-priority traffic.

deactivate

Method of modifying the router's active configuration. Portions of the hierarchy marked as inactive using this command are ignored during the router's commit process as though they were not configured at all.

dead interval

Amount of time that an Open Shortest Path First (OSPF) router maintains a neighbor relationship before declaring that neighbor as no longer operational. The JUNOS software uses a default value of 40 seconds for this timer.

dead peer detection

See DPD.

default address

Router address that is used as the source address on unnumbered interfaces.

default route

Route used to forward IP packets when a more specific route is not present in the route table. Often represented as 0.0.0.0/0, the default route is sometimes referred to as the *route of last resort*.

demand circuit

Network segment whose cost varies with usage, according to a service level agreement (SLA) with a service provider. Demand circuits limit traffic based on either bandwidth (bits or packets transmitted) or access time. *See also* multicast.

dense mode

Method of forwarding multicast traffic to interested listeners. Dense mode forwarding assumes that most of the hosts on the network will receive the multicast data. Routers flood packets and prune unwanted traffic every three minutes.

DES

Data Encryption Standard. A method for encrypting information using a 56-bit key.

Considered to be a legacy method and insecure for many applications.

designated router

In Open Shortest Path First (OSPF), a router selected by other routers that is responsible for sending link-state advertisements (LSAs) that describe the network, thereby reducing the amount of network traffic and the size of the routers' topological databases.

destination prefix length

Number of bits of the network address used for the host portion of a classless interdomain routing (CIDR) IP address.

DFC

Dynamic flow capture. Process of collecting packet flows that match a particular filter list to one or more content destinations using an on-demand control protocol that relays requests from one or more control sources.

DHCP

Dynamic Host Configuration Protocol. Allocates IP addresses dynamically so that they can be reused when no longer needed.

dial backup

Feature that reestablishes network connectivity through one or more backup Integrated Services Digital Network (ISDN) dialer interfaces after a primary interface fails. When the primary interface is reestablished, the ISDN interface is disconnected.

dialer filter

Stateless firewall filter that enables dial-on-demand routing backup when applied to a physical Integrated Services Digital Network (ISDN) interface and its dialer interface configured as a passive static route. The passive static route has a lower priority than dynamic routes. If all dynamic routes to an address are lost from the route table and the router receives a packet for that address, the dialer interface initiates an ISDN backup connection and sends the packet over it. *See also* dial-on-demand routing (DDR) backup; floating static route.

dialer interface (dl)

Logical interface for configuring dialing properties and the control interface for a backup Integrated Services Digital Network (ISDN) connection.

dialer profile

Set of characteristics configured for the Integrated Services Digital Network (ISDN) dialer interface. Dialer profiles allow the configuration of physical interfaces to be separated from the logical configuration of dialer interfaces required for ISDN connectivity. This feature also allows physical and logical interfaces to be bound together dynamically on a per-connection basis.

dialer watch

Dial-on-demand routing (DDR) backup feature that provides reliable connectivity without relying on a dialer filter to activate the Integrated Services Digital Network (ISDN) interface. The ISDN dialer interface monitors the existence of each route on a watch list. If all routes on the watch list are lost from the route table, dialer watch initiates the ISDN interface for failover connectivity. *See also* dial-on-demand routing (DDR) backup.

dial-in

Feature that enables J-series Services Routers to receive calls from the remote end of a backup Integrated Services Digital Network (ISDN) connection. The remote end of the ISDN call might be a service provider, a corporate central location, or a customer premises equipment (CPE) branch office. All incoming calls can be verified against caller IDs configured on the router's dialer interface. *See also* callback.

dial-on-demand routing (DDR) backup

Feature that provides a J-series Services Router with full-time connectivity across an Integrated Services Digital Network (ISDN) line. When routes on a primary serial T1, E1, T3, E3, Fast Ethernet, or Point-to-Point Protocol over Ethernet (PPPoE) interface are lost, an ISDN dialer interface establishes a backup connection. To save connection time costs, the Services

Router drops the ISDN connection after a configured period of inactivity. Services Routers with ISDN interfaces support two types of DDR backup: on-demand routing with a dialer filter and with a dialer watch. *See also* dialer filter; dialer watch.

Differentiated-Services-aware traffic engineering

Type of constraint-based routing that can enforce different bandwidth constraints for different classes of traffic. It can also perform call admission control (CAC) on each traffic engineering class when a label-switched path (LSP) is established.

Differentiated Services domain

Routers in a network that have Differentiated Services enabled.

Diffie-Hellman

Method of key exchange across a nonsecure environment, such as the Internet. The Diffie-Hellman algorithm negotiates a session key without sending the key itself across the network by allowing each party to pick a partial key independently and send part of it to each other. Each side then calculates a common key value. This is a symmetrical method, and keys are typically used for only a short time, then discarded and regenerated.

DiffServ

Differentiated Services (based on RFC 2474). DiffServ uses the type-of-service (ToS) byte to identify different packet flows on a packet-by-packet basis. Diff-Serv adds a Class Selector code point (CSCP) and a Differentiated Services code point (DSCP).

DiffServ-aware

Paradigm that gives different treatment to traffic based on the experimental (EXP) bits in the Multiprotocol Label Switching (MPLS) label header and allows you to provide multiple classes of service (CoS).

digital certificate

Electronic file based on private and public key technology that verifies the identity of the certificate's holder to protect data exchanged online. Digital certificates are issued by a certificate authority (CA).

Dijkstra algorithm

See SPF.

DIMM

Dual inline memory module. A 168-pin memory module that supports 64-bit data transfer.

direct routes

See interface routes.

disable

Method of modifying the router's active configuration. When portions of the hierarchy are marked as disabled (mainly router interfaces), the router uses the configuration but ignores the disabled portions.

discard

JUNOS software syntax command used in a routing policy or a firewall filter. The command halts the logical processing of the policy or filter when a set of match conditions is met. The specific route or IP packet is dropped from the network silently. It can also be a next hop attribute assigned to a route in the route table.

distance-vector

Method used in Bellman-Ford routing protocols to determine the best path to all routers in the network. Each router determines the distance (metric) to the destination and the vector (next hop) to follow.

Distributed Buffer Manager ASIC

Juniper Networks ASIC responsible for managing the router's packet storage memory.

DLCI

Data-link connection identifier. Identifier for a Frame Relay virtual connection (also called a *logical interface*).

DLSw

Data link switching. Method of tunneling IBM System Network Architecture (SNA) and NetBIOS traffic over an IP network. (The JUNOS software does not support NetBIOS.) *See also* tunneling protocol.

DLSw circuit

Path formed by establishing data link control (DLC) connections between an end system and a local router configured for DLSw. Each DLSw circuit is identified by the circuit ID that includes the end system method authenticity check address, local service access point (LSAP), and DLC port ID. Multiple DLSw circuits can operate over the same DLSw connection.

DLSw connection

Set of Transmission Control Protocol (TCP) connections between two data link switching (DLSw) peers that is established after the initial handshake and successful capabilities exchange.

DNS

Domain Name System. A system that stores information about hostnames and domain names. DNS provides an IP address for each hostname and lists the email exchange servers accepting email addresses for each domain.

DoS

Denial of service. A system security breach in which network services become unavailable to users.

DPD

Dead peer detection. Protocol that recognizes the loss of the primary IPSec Internet Key Exchange (IKE) peer and establishes a secondary IPSec tunnel to a backup peer.

DRAM

Dynamic random access memory. Storage source on the router that can be accessed quickly by a process.

drop probability

Percentage value that expresses the likelihood that an individual packet will be dropped from the network. *See also* drop profile.

drop profile

Mechanism of random early detection (RED) that defines parameters that allow packets to be dropped from the network. When you configure drop profiles, there are two important values: the queue fullness and the drop probability. *See also* drop probability; queue fullness; RED.

DSAP

Destination service access point. Service access point (SAP) that identifies the

destination for which a logical link control protocol data unit (LPDU) is intended.

DS0

Digital signal level 0. In T-carrier systems, a basic digital signaling rate of 64 Kbps. The DS0 rate forms the basis for the North American digital multiplex transmission hierarchy.

DS1

Digital signal level 1. In T-carrier systems, a digital signaling rate of 1.544 Mbps. A standard used in telecommunications to transmit voice and data among devices. Also known as T1. *See also* T1.

DS3

Digital signal level 3. In T-carrier systems, a digital signaling rate of 44.736 Mbps. This level of carrier can transport 28 DS1-level signals and 672 DS0-level channels within its payload. Also known as T3. *See also* T3.

DSCP

Differentiated Services code point or Diff-Serv code point. Values for a 6-bit field defined for IPv4 and IPv6 packet headers that can be used to enforce class-of-service (CoS) distinctions in routers.

DSU

Data service unit. A device used to connect data terminal equipment (DTE) to a digital phone line. DSU converts digital data from a router to voltages and encoding required by the phone line. *See also* CSU/DSU.

DTCP

Dynamic Tasking Control Protocol. A means of communicating filter requests and acknowledgments between one or more clients and a monitoring platform, used in dynamic flow capture (DFC) and flow-tap configurations. The protocol is defined in Internet draft *draft-cavuto-dtcp-00.txt*.

DTD

Document type definition. Defines the elements and structure of an Extensible Markup Language (XML) document or data set.

DTE

Data terminal equipment. An RS-232-C interface that a computer uses to exchange information with a serial device.

DVMRP

Distance Vector Multicast Routing Protocol. Distributed multicast routing protocol that dynamically generates IP multicast delivery trees using a technique called reverse-path multicasting (RPM) to forward multicast traffic to downstream interfaces.

DWDM

Dense wavelength-division multiplexing. Technology that enables data from different sources to be carried together on an optical fiber, with each signal carried on its own separate wavelength.

dynamic label-switched path

Multiprotocol Label Switching (MPLS) network path established by signaling protocols such as the Resource Reservation Protocol (RSVP) and Label Distribution Protocol (LDP).

E1

High-speed WAN digital communications protocol that operates at a rate of 2.048 Mbps.

E3

High-speed WAN digital communications protocol that operates at a rate of 34.368 Mbps and uses time-division multiplexing to carry 16 E1 circuits.

EAL3

Common Criteria Evaluation Assurance Level 3. Evaluation Assurance Level is an assurance and compliance requirement defined by Common Criteria. Higher levels have more stringent requirements.

EBGP

External BGP. A Border Gateway Protocol (BGP) configuration in which sessions are established between routers in different autonomous systems (ASs).

E-carrier

E stands for *European*. Standards that form part of the Synchronous Digital Hierarchy (SDH), in which groups of E1 circuits are bundled onto higher-capacity E3 links between telephone exchanges or countries. E-carrier standards are used just about everywhere in the world except North America and Japan, and are incompatible with the T-carrier standards.

ECC

Error checking and correction. The process of detecting errors during the transmission or storage of digital data and correcting them automatically. This usually involves sending or storing extra bits of data according to specified algorithms.

ECSA

Exchange Carriers Standards Association. A standards organization created after the divestiture of the Bell System to represent the interests of interexchange carriers.

edge router

In Multiprotocol Label Switching (MPLS), a router located at the beginning or end of a label-switching tunnel. An edge router at the beginning of a tunnel applies labels to new packets entering the tunnel. An edge route at the end of a tunnel removes labels from packets exiting the tunnel. *See also* MPLS.

editor macros (Emacs)

Shortcut keystrokes used within the router's command-line interface (CLI). These macros move the cursor and delete characters based on the sequence you specify.

EGP

Exterior Gateway Protocol. An example is the Border Gateway Protocol (BGP).

egress router

In Multiprotocol Label Switching (MPLS), the last router in a label-switched path (LSP). *See also* ingress router.

EIA

Electronic Industries Association. A U.S. trade group that represents manufacturers of electronic devices and sets standards and specifications.

EIA-530

Serial interface that employs the EIA-530 standard for the interconnection of data terminal equipment (DTE) and data circuit-terminating equipment (DCE).

EIR

Equipment identity register. A mobile network database that contains information about devices using the network.

embedded OS software

Software used by a Juniper Networks router to operate the physical router components.

EMI

Electromagnetic interference. Any electromagnetic disturbance that interrupts, obstructs, or otherwise degrades or limits the effective performance of electronics or electrical equipment.

end system

In Intermediate System-to-Intermediate System Level 1 (IS-IS), a network entity that sends and receives packets.

EPD

Early packet discard. For ATM2 interfaces only, a limit on the number of transmit packets that can be queued. Packets that exceed the limit are dropped. *See also* queue length.

ERO

Explicit Route Object. An extension to the Resource Reservation Protocol (RSVP) that allows an RSVP PATH message to traverse an explicit sequence of routers that is independent of conventional shortest-path IP routing.

ESD

Electrostatic discharge. Stored static electricity that can damage electronic equipment and impair electrical circuitry when released.

ES-IS

End System-to-Intermediate System. Protocol that resolves Layer 3 ISO network service access points (NSAPs) to Layer 2 addresses. ES-IS resolution is similar to the way the Address Resolution Protocol (ARP) resolves Layer 2 addresses for IPv4.

ESP

Encapsulating Security Payload. A protocol for securing packet flows for IPSec using encryption, data integrity checks, and sender authentication, which are added as a header to an IP packet. If an ESP packet is successfully decrypted, and no other party knows the secret key the peers share, the packet was not wiretapped in transit. *See also* AH.

Established

Border Gateway Protocol (BGP) neighbor state that represents a fully functional BGP peering session.

Ethernet

Local area network (LAN) technology used for transporting information from one location to another, formalized in the IEEE standard 802.3. Ethernet uses either coaxial cable or twisted-pair cable. Transmission speeds for data transfer range from the original 10 Mbps, to Fast Ethernet at 100 Mbps, to Gigabit Ethernet at 1000 Mbps.

ETSI

European Telecommunications Standardization Institute. A nonprofit organization that produces voluntary telecommunications standards used throughout Europe.

eventd

Event policy process that performs configured actions in response to events on a routing platform that trigger system log messages.

exact

JUNOS software routing policy match type that represents only the route specified in a route filter.

exception packet

IP packet that is not processed by the normal packet flow through the Packet Forwarding Engine (PFE). Exception packets include local delivery information, expired Time to Live (TTL) packets, and packets with an IP option specified.

Exchange

Open Shortest Path First (OSPF) adjacency state in which two neighboring routers are actively sending database description packets to each other to exchange their database contents.

EXP bits

Experimental bits, also known as the class-of-service (CoS) bits, located in each Multiprotocol Label Switching (MPLS) label and used to encode the CoS value of a packet as it traverses a label-switched path (LSP).

export

Placing of routes from the route table into a routing protocol.

ExStart

Open Shortest Path First (OSPF) adjacency state in which the neighboring routers negotiate to determine which router is in charge of the synchronization process.

Extensible Markup Language

See XML.

external metric

Cost included in a route when Open Shortest Path First (OSPF) exports route information from external autonomous systems (ASs). There are two types of external metrics: Type 1 and Type 2. Type 1 external metrics are equivalent to the link-state metric; that is, the cost of the route, used in the internal AS. Type 2 external metrics are greater than the cost of any path internal to the AS.

FA

Forwarding adjacency. Resource Reservation Protocol (RSVP) label-switched path (LSP) tunnel through which one or more other RSVP LSPs can be tunneled.

fabric schedulers

Identify a packet as high or low priority based on its forwarding class, and associate schedulers with the fabric priorities.

failover

Process by which a standby or secondary system component automatically takes over the functions of an active or primary component when the primary component fails or is temporarily shut down or removed for servicing. During failover, the system continues to perform normal operations with little or no interruption in service. *See also* GRES.

Fast Ethernet

Term encompassing a number of Ethernet standards that carry traffic at the nominal rate of 100 Mbps, instead of the original Ethernet speed of 10 Mbps. *See also* Ethernet; Gigabit Ethernet.

fast port

Fast Ethernet port on a J4300 Services Router, and either a Fast Ethernet port or DS3 port on a J6300 Services Router. Only enabled ports are counted. A two-port Fast Ethernet Physical Interface Module (PIM) with one enabled port counts as one fast port. The same PIM with both ports enabled counts as two fast ports.

fast reroute

Mechanism for automatically rerouting traffic on a label-switched path (LSP) if a node or link in an LSP fails, thus reducing the loss of packets traveling over the LSP.

FBF

Filter-based forwarding. A filter that classifies packets to determine their forwarding path within a router. FBF is used to redirect traffic for analysis.

FCS

Frame check sequence. A calculation that is added to a frame for error control. FCS is used in High-Level Data Link Control (HDLC), Frame Relay, and other data-link layer protocols.

FDDI

Fiber Distributed Data Interface. A set of ANSI protocols for sending digital data over fiber-optic cable. FDDI networks are token-passing networks and support data rates of up to 100 Mbps (100 million bits). FDDI networks are typically used as backbones for WANs.

FEAC

Far-end alarm and control. A T3 signal used to send alarm or status information from the far-end terminal back to the near-end terminal, and to initiate T3 loopbacks at the far-end terminal from the near-end terminal.

FEB

Forwarding Engine Board. In M5 and M10 routers, provides route lookup, filtering, and switching to the destination port.

FEC

Forwarding equivalence class. Criterion used to forward a set of packets, with similar or identical characteristics, using the same Multiprotocol Label Switching (MPLS) label. Forwarding equivalence classes are defined in the base Label Distribution Protocol (LDP) specification and can be extended through the use of additional parameters. FECs are also represented in other LDPs.

FECN

Forward explicit congestion notification. In a Frame Relay network, a header bit transmitted by the source device requesting that the destination device slow down its requests for data. FECN and backward explicit congestion notification (BECN) minimize the possibility that packets will be discarded when more packets arrive than can be handled. *See also* BECN.

FIFO

First in, first out. Scheduling method in which the first data packet stored in the queue is the first data packet removed from the queue. All JUNOS software interface queues operate in this mode by default.

filter

Process or device that screens packets based on certain characteristics, such as source address, destination address, or protocol, and forwards or discards packets that match the filter. Filters are used to control data packets or local packets. *See also* packet.

FIPS

Federal Information Processing Standards. Defines, among other things, security levels for computer and networking equipment. FIPS is usually applied to military environments.

firewall

Security gateway positioned between two networks, usually between a trusted network

and the Internet. A firewall ensures that all traffic that crosses it conforms to the organization's security policy. Firewalls track and control communications, deciding whether to pass, reject, discard, encrypt, or log them. Firewalls also can be used to secure sensitive portions of a local network.

firewall filter

See stateful firewall filter; stateless firewall filter.

firmware

Instructions and data programmed directly into the circuitry of a hardware device for the purpose of controlling the device. Firmware is used for vital programs that must not be lost when the device is powered off.

first in, first out

See FIFO.

flap damping

See damping.

flapping

See route flapping.

flash drive

Nonvolatile memory card in Juniper Networks M-series and T-series routing platforms used for storing a copy of the JUNOS software and the current and most recent router configurations. It also typically acts as the primary boot device.

Flexible PIC Concentrator

See FPC.

floating static route

Route with an administrative distance greater than the administrative distance of the dynamically learned versions of the same route. The static route is used only when the dynamic routes are no longer available. When a floating static route is configured on an interface with a dialer filter, the interface can be used for backup.

flood and prune

Method of forwarding multicast data packets in a dense-mode network. Flooding and pruning occur every three minutes.

flow

flow

Stream of routing information and packets, which are handled by the Routing Engine (RE) and the Packet Forwarding Engine (PFE). The RE handles the flow of routing information between the routing protocols and the route tables and between the route tables and the forwarding tables, as well as the flow of local packets from the router physical interfaces to the RE. The PFE handles the flow of data packets into and out of the router's physical interfaces.

flow collection interface

Interface that combines multiple cflowd records into a compressed ASCII data file and exports the file to an FTP server for storage and analysis, allowing users to manipulate the output from traffic monitoring operations.

flow control action

JUNOS software syntax used in a routing policy or firewall filter. It alters the default logical processing of the policy or filter when a set of match conditions is met.

flow monitoring

Application that monitors the flow of traffic and enables lawful interception of packets transiting between two routers. Traffic flows can be passively monitored by an offline router or actively monitored by a router participating in the network.

flow-tap application

Application that uses Dynamic Tasking Control Protocol (DTCP) requests to intercept IPv4 packets in an active monitoring router and send a copy of packets that match filter criteria to one or more content destinations. Flow-tap configurations can be used in flexible trend analysis for detecting new security threats and lawfully intercepting data.

forwarding classes

Affect the forwarding, scheduling, and marking policies applied to packets as they transit a routing platform. The forwarding class plus the loss priority define the per-hop behavior. Also known as

ordered aggregates in the IETF Differentiated Services architecture.

forwarding table

JUNOS software forwarding information base. The JUNOS routing protocol process installs active routes from its route tables into the Routing Engine (RE) forwarding table. The kernel copies this forwarding table into the Packet Forwarding Engine (PFE), which determines which interface transmits the packets.

FPC

Flexible PIC Concentrator. An interface concentrator on which Physical Interface Cards (PICs) are mounted. An FPC is inserted into a slot in a Juniper Networks router. See also PIC.

fractional E1

Interface that contains one or more of the 32 DS0 time slots that can be reserved from an E1 interface. (The first time slot is reserved for framing.)

fractional interface

Interface that contains one or more DS0 time slots reserved from an E1 or T1 interface. Fractional interfaces allow service providers to provision part of one E1 or T1 interface to one customer and the other part to another customer. The individual fractional interfaces connect to different destinations, and customers pay for only the bandwidth fraction used and not for the entire E1 or T1 interface.

Fractional interfaces can be configured on both channelized Physical Interface Cards (PICs) and Physical Interface Modules (PIMs) and unchannelized, regular E1 and T1 PICs and PIMs.

fractional T1

Interface that contains one or more of the 24 DS0 time slots that can be reserved from a T1 interface.

fragmentation

In the Transmission Control Protocol/Internet Protocol (TCP/IP), the process of breaking packets into the smallest maximum size packet data unit (PDU) supported by any of the underlying networks. In the OSI reference model, this process is known as segmentation. For JUNOS applications, split Layer 3 packets can then be encapsulated in Multilink Frame Relay (MLFR) or the Multilink Point-to-Point Protocol (MLPPP) for transport.

Frame Relay

Efficient replacement for the older X.25 protocol that does not require explicit acknowledgment of each frame of data. Frame Relay allows private networks to reduce costs by using shared facilities between the endpoint switches of a network managed by a Frame Relay service provider. Individual data-link connection identifiers (DLCIs) are assigned to ensure that each customer receives only its own traffic.

frequency-division multiplexed channel

Signals carried at different frequencies and transmitted over a single wire or wireless medium.

FRF

Frame Relay Forum. A technical committee that promotes Frame Relay by negotiating agreements and developing standards.

FRF.15

End-to-end Frame Relay Implementation Agreement. An implementation of Multilink Frame Relay (MLFR) using multiple virtual connections to aggregate logical bandwidth for end-to-end Frame Relay. Released by the Frame Relay Forum.

FRF.16

Multilink Frame Relay Implementation Agreement. An implementation of Multilink Frame Relay (MLFR) in which a single logical connection is provided by multiplexing multiple physical interfaces for user-to-network interface and network-to-network interface (UNI/NNI) connections. Released by the Frame Relay Forum.

FRU

Field-replaceable unit. A router component that customers can replace onsite.

FTP

File Transfer Protocol. Application protocol that is part of the Transmission Control Protocol/Internet Protocol (TCP/IP) protocol stack. Used for transferring files among network nodes. FTP is defined in RFC 959.

Full

Open Shortest Path First (OSPF) adjacency state that represents a fully functional neighbor relationship.

fxp0

See management Ethernet interface.

fxp1

JUNOS software permanent interface used for communications between the Routing Engine (RE) and the Packet Forwarding Engine (PFE). This interface is not present in all routers.

fxp2

JUNOS software permanent interface used for communications between the Routing Engine (RE) and the Packet Forwarding Engine (PFE). This interface is not present in all routers.

Garbage Collection Timer

Timer used in a distance-vector network that represents the time remaining before a route is removed from the route table.

G-CDR

GGSN call detail record. Collection of charges in ASN.1 format that is eventually billed to a mobile station user.

generated route

Summary route that uses an IP address next hop to forward packets in an IP network. A generated route is functionally similar to an aggregated route.

GGSN

Gateway GPRS support node. A router that serves as a gateway between mobile networks and packet data networks.

Gigabit Ethernet

Term describing various technologies for implementing Ethernet networking at a nominal speed of one gigabit per second. Gigabit Ethernet is supported over both optical fiber and twisted-pair cable. Physical layer standards include 1000Base-T, 1Gbps over CAT-5e copper cabling, and 1000Base-SX for short to medium distances over fiber. *See also* Ethernet; Fast Ethernet.

GMPLS

Generalized Multiprotocol Label Switching. A protocol that extends the functionality of Multiprotocol Label Switching (MPLS) to include a wider range of label-switched path (LSP) options for a variety of network devices.

GPRS General Packet Radio System

A packet-switched service that allows full mobility and wide-area coverage as information is sent and received across a mobile network.

graceful restart

Process that allows a router whose control plane is undergoing a restart to continue to forward traffic while recovering its state from neighboring routers. Without graceful restart, a control plane restart disrupts services provided by the router.

graceful switchover

JUNOS software feature that allows a change from the primary device, such as a Routing Engine (RE), to the backup device without interruption of packet forwarding.

gratuitous

ARP broadcast request for a router's own IP address to check whether that address is being used by another node. Primarily used to detect IP address duplication.

GRE

Generic Routing Encapsulation. A general tunneling protocol that can encapsulate many types of packets to enable data transmission through a tunnel. GRE is used with IP to create a virtual point-to-point link to routers at remote points in a network. *See also* tunneling protocol.

GRES

Graceful Routing Engine switchover. In a router that contains a master and a backup Routing Engine (RE), allows the

backup RE to assume mastership automatically, with no disruption of packet forwarding.

group

Collection of related Border Gateway Protocol (BGP) peers.

group address

IP address used as the destination address in a multicast IP packet. The group address functionally represents the senders and interested receivers for a particular multicast data stream.

G.SHDSL

Symmetric high-speed digital subscriber line (SHDSL). Standard published in 2001 by the ITU-T with recommendation ITU G.991.2 G.SHDSL. G.SHDSL incorporates features of other DSL technologies such as asymmetrical DSL (ADSL). *See also* SHDSL; ADSL.

GSM

Global System for Mobile Communications. A second-generation (2G) mobile wireless networking standard defined by ETSI that uses TDMA technology and operates in the 900 MHz radio band. *See also* TDMA.

GTP

GPRS tunneling protocol. A protocol that transports IP packets between an SGSN and a GGSN. *See also* tunneling protocol.

GTP-C

GGSN tunneling protocol, control. A protocol that allows an SGSN to establish packet data network access for a mobile station. *See also* tunneling protocol.

GTP-U

GGSN tunneling protocol, user plane. A protocol that carries mobile station user data packets. *See also* tunneling protocol.

hashing

Cryptographic technique applied over and over (iteratively) to a message of arbitrary length to produce a hash "message digest" or "signature" of fixed length that is appended to the message when it is sent. In security, used to validate that the contents of a message have not been altered in transit. The Secure Hash Algorithm (SHA-1) and Message Digest 5 (MD5) are commonly used hashes. *See also* SHA-1; MD5.

HDLC

High-Level Data Link Control. An International Telecommunication Union (ITU) standard for a bit-oriented data-link layer protocol on which most other bit-oriented protocols are based.

health monitor

JUNOS software extension to the RMON alarm system that provides predefined monitoring for filesystem, CPU, and memory usage. The health monitor also supports unknown or dynamic object instances such as JUNOS processes.

hello interval

Amount of time an Open Shortest Path First (OSPF) router continues to send a hello packet to each adjacent neighbor.

hello mechanism

Process used by a Resource Reservation Protocol (RSVP) router to enhance the detection of network outages in a Multiprotocol Label Switching (MPLS) network.

HLR

Home Location Register. Database containing information about a subscriber and the current location of a subscriber's mobile station.

HMAC

Hashed Message Authentication Code. A mechanism for message authentication that uses cryptographic hash functions. HMAC can be used with any iterative cryptographic hash function—for example, Message Digest 5 (MD5) or Secure Hash Algorithm (SHA-1)—in combination with a secret shared key. The cryptographic strength of HMAC depends on the properties of the underlying hash function. Defined in RFC 2104, "HMAC: Keyed-Hashing for Message Authentication."

hold down

Timer used by distance-vector protocols to prevent the propagation of incorrect routing knowledge to other routers in the network.

hold time

Maximum number of seconds allowed to elapse between successive keepalive or update messages that a Border Gateway Protocol (BGP) system receives from a peer.

host membership query

Internet Group Management Protocol (IGMP) packet sent by a router to determine whether interested receivers exist on a broadcast network for multicast traffic.

host membership report

Internet Group Management Protocol (IGMP) packet sent by an interested receiver for a particular multicast group address. Hosts send report messages when they first join a group or in response to a query packet from the local router.

host module

On an M160 router, provides the routing and system management functions of the router. Consists of the Routing Engine (RE) and Miscellaneous Control Subsystem (MCS).

host subsystem

On a T640 routing node, provides the routing and system management functions of the router. Consists of a Routing Engine (RE) and an adjacent Control Board (CB).

hot standby

In JUNOS, method used with link services intelligent queuing interfaces (LSQs) to enable rapid switchover between primary and secondary (backup) Physical Interface Cards (PICs). *See also* warm standby.

HSCSD

High-Speed Circuit Switched Data. Circuit-switched wireless data transmission for mobile users, at data rates up to 38.4 Kbps.

HTTP

Hypertext Transfer Protocol. Method used to publish and receive information on the Web, such as text and graphics files.

HTTPS

Hypertext Transfer Protocol over Secure Sockets Layer. Similar to HTTP, with an added encryption layer that encrypts and decrypts user page requests and pages that are returned by a web server. Used for secure communication, such as payment transactions.

IANA

Internet Assigned Numbers Authority. A regulatory group that maintains all assigned and registered Internet numbers, such as IP and multicast addresses.

IBGP

Internal BGP. A Border Gateway Protocol (BGP) configuration in which sessions are established between routers in the same autonomous system (AS).

ICMP

Internet Control Message Protocol. Used in router discovery, ICMP allows router advertisements that enable a host to discover addresses of operating routers on the subnet.

IDE

Integrated Drive Electronics. Type of hard disk on a Routing Engine (RE).

IDEA

International Data Encryption Algorithm. An algorithm that uses a 128-bit key and is one of the methods at the heart of Pretty Good Privacy (PGP). IDEA is patented by Ascom Tech AG and is popular in Europe.

Idle

Initial Border Gateway Protocol (BGP) neighbor state in which the local router refuses all incoming session requests.

IDS

Intrusion detection service. A service that inspects all inbound and outbound network activity and identifies suspicious patterns that may indicate a network or system attack from someone attempting to break into or compromise a system.

IEC

International Electrotechnical Commission. *See* ISO.

IEEE

Institute of Electrical and Electronics Engineers. An international professional society for electrical engineers.

IETF

Internet Engineering Task Force. An international community of network designers, operators, vendors, and researchers concerned with the evolution of Internet architecture and the smooth operation of the Internet.

I-frame

Information frame used to transfer data in sequentially numbered logical link control protocol data units (LPDUs) between link stations.

IGMP

Internet Group Management Protocol. Used with multicast protocols to determine whether group members are present.

IGP

Interior Gateway Protocol, such as Intermediate System-to-Intermediate System Level 1 (IS-IS), Open Shortest Path First (OSPF), and the Routing Information Protocol (RIP).

IKE

Internet Key Exchange. Part of IPSec that provides ways to securely negotiate the shared private keys that the authentication header (AH) and Encapsulating Security Payload (ESP) portions of IPSec needed to function properly. IKE employs Diffie-Hellman methods and is optional in IPSec (the shared keys can be entered manually at the endpoints).

ILMI

Integrated Local Management Interface. A specification developed by the ATM Forum that incorporates network management capabilities into the Asynchronous Transfer Mode (ATM) user-to-network interface (UNI) and provides bidirectional exchange of management information between UNI management entities (UMEs).

IMEI

International Mobile Station Equipment Identity. A unique code used to identify an individual mobile station to a GSM network.

import

Installation of routes from the routing protocols into a route table.

IMSI

International Mobile Subscriber Identity. Information that identifies a particular subscriber to a GSM network.

IMT-2000

International Mobile Telecommunications 2000. Global standard for third-generation (3G) wireless communications, defined by a set of interdependent ITU recommendations. IMT-2000 provides a framework for worldwide wireless access by linking the diverse systems of terrestrial and satellite-based networks.

inet.0

Default JUNOS software route table for IPv4 unicast routers.

inet.1

Default JUNOS software route table for storing the multicast cache for active data streams in the network.

inet.2

Default JUNOS software route table for storing unicast IPv4 routes specifically used to prevent forwarding loops in a multicast network.

inet.3

Default JUNOS software route table for storing the egress IP address of a Multiprotocol Label Switching (MPLS) label-switched path.

inet.4

Default JUNOS software route table for storing information generated by the Multicast Source Discovery Protocol (MSDP).

inet6.0

Default JUNOS software route table for storing unicast IPv6 routes.

infinity metric

Metric value used in distance-vector protocols to represent an unusable route. For the Routing Information Protocol (RIP), the infinity metric is 16.

ingress router

In Multiprotocol Label Switching (MPLS), the first router in a label-switched path (LSP). *See also* egress router.

Init

Open Shortest Path First (OSPF) adjacency state in which the local router has received a hello packet but bidirectional communication is not yet established.

insert

JUNOS software command that allows a user to reorder terms in a routing policy or a firewall filter, or to change the order of a policy chain.

instance.inetflow.0

Route table that shows route flows through the Border Gateway Protocol (BGP).

inter-AS routing

Routing of packets among different autonomous systems (ASs). *See also* EBGP.

intercluster reflection

In a Border Gateway Protocol (BGP) route reflection, the redistribution of routing information by a route reflector system to all nonclient peers (BGP peers not in the cluster). *See also* route reflection.

interface cost

Value added to all received routes in a distance-vector network before they are placed into the route table. The JUNOS software uses a cost of 1 for this value.

interface preservation

See link state replication.

interface routes

Routes that are in the route table because an interface has been configured with an IP address. Also called *direct routes*.

intermediate system

In Intermediate System-to-Intermediate System Level 1 (IS-IS), the network entity that sends and receives packets and can also route packets.

Internet Processor ASIC

Juniper Networks ASIC responsible for using the forwarding table to make routing decisions within the Packet Forwarding Engine (PFE). The Internet Processor ASIC also implements firewall filters.

interprovider VPN

Virtual private network (VPN) that provides connectivity between separate autonomous systems (ASs) with separate border edge routers. It is used by VPN customers who have connections to several different Internet service providers (ISPs), or different connections to the same ISP in different geographic regions, each of which has a different AS.

intra-AS routing

Routing of packets within a single autonomous system (AS). *See also* IBGP.

I/O Manager ASIC

Juniper Networks ASIC responsible for segmenting data packets into 64-byte J-cells and for queuing resultant cells before transmission.

IP

Internet Protocol. The protocol used for sending data from one point to another on the Internet.

IPCP

IP Control Protocol. The protocol that establishes and configures IP over the Point-to-Point Protocol (PPP).

IPSec

IP Security. A standard way to add security to Internet communications. The secure aspects of IPSec are usually implemented in three parts: the authentication header (AH), the Encapsulating Security Payload (ESP), and the Internet Key Exchange (IKE).

IQ

Intelligent queuing. M-series and T-series routing platform interfaces that offer granular quality-of-service (QoS) capabilities; extensive statistics on packets and bytes

that are transmitted, received, or dropped; and embedded diagnostic tools.

IRDP

ICMP Router Discovery Protocol. A protocol that enables a host to determine the address of a router that it can use as a default gateway.

ISAKMP

Internet Security Association and Key Management Protocol. A protocol that allows the receiver of a message to obtain a public key and use digital certificates to authenticate the sender's identity. ISAKMP is key-exchange-independent; that is, it supports many different key exchanges. *See also* IKE; Oakley.

ISDN

Integrated Services Digital Network. A set of digital communications standards, which enable the transmission of information over existing twisted-pair telephone lines at higher speeds than standard analog telephone service. An ISDN interface provides multiple B-channels (bearer channels) for data and one D-channel for control and signaling information. *See also* B-channel; D-channel.

IS-IS

Intermediate System-to-Intermediate System. A link-state, interior gateway routing protocol for IP networks that also uses the Shortest Path First (SPF) algorithm to determine routes.

ISO

International Organization for Standardization. A worldwide federation of standards bodies that promotes international standardization and publishes international agreements as International Standards.

ISP

Internet service provider. A company that provides access to the Internet and related services.

ITU-T

International Telecommunication Union Telecommunication Standardization (formerly known as the CCITT). Group supported by the United Nations that makes recommendations and coordinates the development of telecommunications standards for the entire world.

ITU-T Rec. G.992.1

International standard that defines the asymmetrical digital subscriber line (ADSL). Annex A defines how ADSL works over twisted-pair copper (POTS) lines. Annex B defines how ADSL works over Integrated Services Digital Network (ISDN) lines.

jbase

JUNOS software package containing updates to the kernel.

jbundle

JUNOS software package containing all possible software package files.

J-cell

A 64-byte data unit used within the Packet Forwarding Engine (PFE). All IP packets processed by a Juniper Networks router are segmented into J-cells.

jdocs

JUNOS software package containing the documentation set.

jitter

Small random variation introduced into the value of a timer to prevent multiple timer expirations from becoming synchronized. In real-time applications such as Voice over IP and video, variation in the rate at which packets in a stream are received that can cause quality degradation.

jkernel

JUNOS software package containing the basic components of the software.

Join message

Physical Interface Module (PIM) message sent hop by hop upstream toward a multicast source or the rendezvous point (RP) of the domain. It requests that multicast traffic be sent downstream to the router originating the message.

jpfe

JUNOS software package containing the embedded OS software for operating the Packet Forwarding Engine (PFE).

jroute

JUNOS software package containing the software used by the Routing Engine (RE).

J-Web

Graphical web browser interface to the JUNOS Internet software on routing platforms. With the J-Web interface, you can monitor, configure, diagnose, and manage the routing platform from a PC or laptop that has Hypertext Transfer Protocol (HTTP) or HTTP over Secure Sockets Layer (HTTPS) enabled.

keepalive message

Message sent between network devices to inform each other that they are still active.

kernel

Basic software component of the JUNOS software. The kernel operates the various processes used to control the router's operations.

kernel forwarding table

See forwarding table.

kmd

Key management process that provides IPSec authentication services for encryption Physical Interface Cards (PICs).

L2TP

Layer 2 Tunneling Protocol. A procedure for secure communication of data across a Layer 2 network that enables users to establish Point-to-Point Protocol (PPP) sessions between tunnel endpoints. L2TP uses profiles for individual user and group access to ensure secure communication that is as transparent as possible to both end users and applications. *See also* tunneling protocol.

label

In Multiprotocol Label Switching (MPLS), a 20-bit unsigned integer from 0 through 1,048,575, used to identify a packet traveling along a label-switched path (LSP).

Label Distribution Protocol

See LDP.

label object

Resource Reservation Protocol (RSVP) message object that contains the label value allocated to the next downstream router.

label pop operation

Function performed by a Multiprotocol Label Switching (MPLS) router in which the top label in a label stack is removed from the data packet.

label push operation

Function performed by a Multiprotocol Label Switching (MPLS) router in which a new label is added to the top of the data packet.

label request object

Resource Reservation Protocol (RSVP) message object that requests each router along the path of a label-switched path (LSP) to allocate a label for forwarding.

label swap operation

Function performed by a Multiprotocol Label Switching (MPLS) router in which the top label in a label stack is replaced with a new label before the data packet is forwarded to the next hop router.

label values

A 20-bit field in a Multiprotocol Label Switching (MPLS) header used by routers to forward data traffic along an MPLS label-switched path (LSP).

LAN PHY

Local Area Network Physical Layer Device. A physical layer device that allows 10-Gigabit Ethernet wide area links to use existing Ethernet applications. *See also* PHY; WAN PHY.

Layer 2 circuits

Collection of transport modes that accept a stream of Asynchronous Transfer Mode (ATM) cells, convert them to an encapsulated Layer 2 format, and then tunnel them over a Multiprotocol Label Switching (MPLS) or IP backbone, where a similarly configured routing platform segments these packets back into a stream of ATM cells, to be forwarded to the virtual circuit configured for the far-end routing platform. Layer 2 circuits are designed to transport Layer 2 frames between provider edge (PE) routing plat-

forms across a Label Distribution Protocol (LDP)-signaled MPLS backbone. *See also* AAL5 mode; cell-relay mode; standard AAL5 mode; trunk mode.

Layer 2 VPN

Provides a private network service among a set of customer sites using a service provider's existing Multiprotocol Label Switching (MPLS) and IP network. A customer's data is separated from other data using software rather than hardware. In a Layer 2 VPN, the Layer 3 routing of customer traffic occurs within the customer's network.

Layer 3 VPN

Provides a private network service among a set of customer sites using a service provider's existing Multiprotocol Label Switching (MPLS) and IP network. A customer's routes and data are separated from other routes and data using software rather than hardware. In a Layer 3 VPN, the Layer 3 routing of customer traffic occurs within the service provider's network.

LCC

Line-card chassis. Term used by the JUNOS command-line interface (CLI) to refer to a T640 routing node in a routing matrix.

LCP

Link Control Protocol. A traffic controller used to establish, configure, and test data-link connections for the Point-to-Point Protocol (PPP).

LDAP

Lightweight Directory Access Protocol. Software protocol used for locating resources on a public or private network.

LDP

Label Distribution Protocol. A protocol for distributing labels in nontraffic-engineered applications. LDP allows routers to establish label-switched paths (LSPs) through a network by mapping network-layer routing information directly to data-link layer switched paths.

leaf node
Terminating node of a multicast distribution tree. A router that is a leaf node only has receivers and does not forward multicast packets to other routers.

LFI
Link fragmentation and interleaving. A method that reduces excessive delays by fragmenting long packets into smaller packets and interleaving them with real-time frames. For example, short delay-sensitive packets, such as packetized voice, can race ahead of larger delay-insensitive packets, such as common data packets.

liblicense
Library that includes messages generated for routines for software license management.

libpcap
Implementation of the pcap application programming interface. libpcap is used by a program to capture packets traveling over a network. *See also* pcap.

limited operational environment
Term used to describe the restrictions placed on FIPS-certified equipment. *See* FIPS.

line loopback
Method of troubleshooting a problem with physical transmission media in which a transmission device in the network sends the data signal back to the originating router.

link
Communication path between two neighbors. A link is up when communication is possible between the two endpoints.

link protection
Method of establishing bypass label-switched paths (LSPs) to ensure that traffic going over a specific interface to a neighboring router can continue to reach the router if that interface fails. The bypass LSP uses a different interface and path to reach the same destination.

link services intelligent queuing interfaces
See LSQ.

link-state acknowledgment
Open Shortest Path First (OSPF) data packet used to inform a neighbor that a link-state update packet has been successfully received.

link-state database
All routing knowledge in a link-state network is contained in this database. Each router runs the Shortest Path First (SPF) algorithm against this database to locate the best network path to each destination in the network.

link-state PDU
Packet that contains information about the state of adjacencies to neighboring systems.

link-state replication
Addition to the SONET Automatic Protection Switching (APS) functionality that helps to promote redundancy of the link Physical Interface Cards (PICs) used in LSQ configurations. If the active SONET PIC fails, links from the standby PIC are used without causing a link renegotiation. Also called *interface preservation*.

link-state request list
List generated by an Open Shortest Path First (OSPF) router during the exchange of database information while forming an adjacency. Advertised information by a neighbor that the local router does not contain is placed in this list.

link-state request packet
Open Shortest Path First (OSPF) data packet used by a router to request database information from a neighboring router.

link-state update
Open Shortest Path First (OSPF) data packet that contains one of multiple link-state advertisements (LSAs). It is used to advertise routing knowledge into the network.

LLC
Logical link control. Data-link layer protocol used on a LAN. LLC1 provides connectionless data transfer, and LLC2 provides connection-oriented data transfer.

LLC frame

Unit of data that contains specific information about the LLC layer and identifies line protocols associated with the layer. *See also* LLC.

LMI

Local management interface. Enhancements to the basic Frame Relay specifications provide support for the following:

- A keepalive mechanism that verifies the flow of data

- A multicast mechanism that provides a network server with a local data-link connection identifier (DLCI) and multicast DLCI

- In Frame Relay networks, global addressing that gives DLCIs global instead of local significance

- A status mechanism that provides a switch with ongoing status reports on known DLCIs

LMP

Link Management Protocol. Part of GMPLS, a protocol used to define a forwarding adjacency between peers and to maintain and allocate resources on the traffic engineering links.

load balancing

Process that installs all next hop destinations for an active route in the forwarding table. You can use load balancing across multiple paths between routers. The behavior of load balancing depends on the version of the Internet Processor ASIC in the router. Also called *per-packet load balancing*.

loading

Open Shortest Path First (OSPF) adjacency state in which the local router sends link-state request packets to its neighbor and waits for the appropriate link-state updates from that neighbor.

local packet

Chunk of data destined for or sent by the Routing Engine (RE).

local preference

Optional Border Gateway Protocol (BGP) path attribute carried in internal BGP update packets that indicate the degree of preference for an external route.

local RIB

Logical software table that contains Border Gateway Protocol (BGP) routes used by the local router to forward data packets.

local significance

Concept used in a Multiprotocol Label Switching (MPLS) network where the label values are unique only between two neighbor routers.

logical interface

On a physical interface, the configuration of one or more units that include all addressing, protocol information, and other logical interface properties that enable the physical interface to function.

logical operator

Characters used in a firewall filter to represent a Boolean AND or OR operation.

logical router

Logical routing device that is partitioned from an M-series or T-series routing platform. Each logical router independently performs a subset of the tasks performed by the main router and has a unique route table, interfaces, policies, and routing instances.

longer

JUNOS software routing policy match type that represents all routes more specific than the given subnet, but not the given subnet itself. It is similar to a mathematical greater-than operation.

loopback interface (lo0)

Interface that is always available because it is independent of any physical interfaces. When configured with an address, the loopback interface is the default address for the routing platform and any unnumbered interfaces. *See also* unnumbered interface.

loose hop

In the context of traffic engineering, a path that can use any router or any number of other intermediate (transit) points to reach the next address in the path. (Definition from RFC 791, modified to fit LSPs.)

loss-priority map
Maps the loss priority of incoming packets based on code point values.

lower-speed IQ interfaces
E1, NxDS0, and T1 interfaces configured on an intelligent queuing (IQ) Physical Interface Card (PIC).

LPDU
LLC protocol data unit. LLC frame on a data link switching (DLSw) network. *See* LLC frame.

LSA
Link-state advertisement. Open Shortest Path First (OSPF) data structure that is advertised in a link-state update packet. Each LSA uniquely describes a portion of the OSPF network.

LSI
Label-switched interface. A logical interface supported by the JUNOS software that provides virtual private network (VPN) services (such as VPLS and Layer 3 VPNs) normally provided by a Tunnel Services PIC.

LSP
1. Label-switched path. Sequence of routers that cooperatively perform Multiprotocol Label Switching (MPLS) operations for a packet stream. The first router in an LSP is called the ingress router, and the last router in the path is called the egress router. An LSP is a point-to-point, half-duplex connection from the ingress router to the egress router. (The ingress and egress routers cannot be the same router.) 2. *See* link-state PDU.

LSQ
Link services intelligent queuing interfaces. Interfaces configured on the Adaptive Services PIC (ASP) or Adaptive Services Module (ASM) that support Multilink Point-to-Point Protocol (MLPPP) and Multilink Frame Relay (MLFR) traffic and

also fully support JUNOS class-of-service (CoS) components.

LSR
Label-switching router. A router on which Multiprotocol Label Switching (MPLS) is enabled and that can process label-switched packets.

MAC
Media access control. In the OSI seven-layer networking model defined by the IEEE, MAC is the lower sublayer of the data link layer. The MAC sublayer governs protocol access to the physical network medium. By using the MAC addresses that are assigned to all ports on a router, multiple devices on the same physical link can uniquely identify one another at the data link layer. *See also* MAC address.

MAC address
Serial number permanently stored in a device adapter to uniquely identify the device. *See also* MAC.

MAM
Maximum allocation bandwidth constraints model. In Differentiated-Services-aware traffic engineering, a constraint model that divides the available bandwidth among the different classes. Sharing of bandwidth among the class types is not allowed.

management Ethernet interface
Permanent interface that provides an out-of-band method, such as Secure Shell (SSH) and Telnet, to connect to the routing platform. The Simple Network Management Protocol (SNMP) can use the management interface to gather statistics from the routing platform. Called *fxp0* on some routing platforms. *See also* permanent interface.

mapping agent
Router used in an auto-RP multicast network to select the rendezvous point (RP) for all multicast group addresses. The RP is then advertised to all other routers in the domain.

martian address

Network address about which all information is ignored.

martian route

Network routes about which all information is ignored. The JUNOS software does not allow martian routes in the inet.0 route table.

MAS

Mobile network access subsystem. A GSN application subsystem that contains the access server.

master

Router in control of the Open Shortest Path First (OSPF) database exchange during an adjacency formation.

match

Logical concept used in a routing policy or firewall filter. A match denotes the criteria used to find a route or IP packet before an action is performed.

match type

JUNOS software syntax used in a route filter to better describe the routes that should match the policy term.

MBGP

Multiprotocol Border Gateway Protocol. An extension to the Border Gateway Protocol (BGP) that allows you to connect multicast topologies within and between BGP autonomous systems (ASs).

MBone

Multicast Backbone. An interconnected set of subnetworks and routers that support the delivery of IP multicast traffic. The MBone is a virtual network that is layered on top of sections of the physical Internet.

MCS

Miscellaneous Control Subsystem. On the M40e and M160 routers, provides control and monitoring functions for router components and SONET clocking for the router.

MD5

Message Digest 5. A one-way hashing algorithm that produces a 128-bit hash used for generating message authentication signatures. MD5 is used in authentication header (AH) and Encapsulating Security Payload (ESP). *See also* hashing; SHA-1.

MDRR

Modified deficit round-robin. A method for selecting queues to be serviced. *See* queue.

MDT

Multicast distribution tree. The path between the sender (host) and the multicast group (receiver or listener).

mean time between failures

See MTBF.

MED

Multiple exit discriminator. An optional Border Gateway Protocol (BGP) path attribute consisting of a metric value that is used to determine the exit point to a destination when all other factors determining the exit point are equal.

mesh

Network topology in which devices are organized in a manageable, segmented manner with many, often redundant, interconnections between network nodes.

message aggregation

Extension to the Resource Reservation Protocol (RSVP) specification that allows neighboring routers to bundle up to 30 RSVP messages into a single protocol packet.

mgd

Management daemon. JUNOS software process responsible for managing all user access to the router.

MIB

Management Information Base. Definition of an object that can be managed by the Simple Network Management Protocol (SNMP).

midplane

Physically separates front and rear cavities inside the chassis, distributes power from the power supplies, and transfers packets and signals between router components, which plug into it.

MLD

Multicast listener discovery. A protocol that manages the membership of hosts and routers in multicast groups. IPv6 multicast routers use MLD to learn, for each of their attached physical networks, which groups have interested listeners.

MLFR

Multilink Frame Relay. Logically ties together individual circuits, creating a bundle. The logical equivalent of the Multilink Point-to-Point Protocol (MLPPP), MLFR is used for Frame Relay traffic instead of Point-to-Point Protocol (PPP) traffic. FRF.15 and FRF.16 are two implementations of MLFR.

MLPPP

Multilink Point-to-Point Protocol. Enables you to bundle multiple Point-to-Point Protocol (PPP) links into a single logical link between two network devices to provide an aggregate amount of bandwidth. The technique is often called *bonding* or *link aggregation*. Defined in RFC 1990. *See also* PPP.

MMF

Multimode fiber. Optical fiber supporting the propagation of multiple frequencies of light. MMF is used for relatively short distances because the modes tend to disperse over longer lengths (called *modal dispersion*). For longer distances, single-mode fiber (sometimes called *monomode*) is used. *See also* single-mode fiber.

mobile station

Mobile device, such as a cellular phone or a mobile personal digital assistant (PDA).

mobile transport subsystem

See MTS.

MPLS

Multiprotocol Label Switching. Mechanism for engineering network traffic patterns that functions by assigning to network packets short labels that describe how to forward them through the network. Also called *label switching*. *See also* traffic engineering.

MPLS EXP classifier

Class-of-service (CoS) behavior classifier for classifying packets based on the Multiprotocol Label Switching (MPLS) experimental bit. *See also* EXP bits.

MPS

Mobile point-to-point control subsystem. A GSN application subsystem that controls all functionality associated with a particular connection.

MRRU

Maximum received reconstructed unit. Similar to the maximum transmission unit (MTU), but is specific to link services interfaces. *See also* MTU.

MSA

Multisource Agreement. The definition of a fiber-optic transceiver module that conforms to the 10-Gigabit Ethernet standard. *See also* XENPAK module.

MSC

Mobile Switching Center. Provides origination and termination functions to calls from a mobile station user.

MSDP

Multicast Source Discovery Protocol. A protocol used to connect multicast routing domains to allow the domains to discover multicast sources from other domains. It typically runs on the same router as the Physical Interface Module (PIM) sparse mode rendezvous point (RP).

MSISDN

Mobile Station Integrated Services Digital Network Number. A number that callers use to reach a mobile services subscriber.

MTBF

Mean time between failures. Measure of hardware component reliability.

MTS

Mobile transport subsystem. A GSN application subsystem that implements all the protocols used by the GSN.

MTU

Maximum transmission unit. Limit on the data size for a network.

multicast

multicast
Operation of sending network traffic from one network node to multiple network nodes.

multicast-scope number
Number used for configuring the multicast scope. Configuring a scope number constrains the scope of a multicast session. The number value can be any hexadecimal number from 0 through F. The multicast-scope value is a number from 0 through 15, or a specified keyword with an associated prefix range. For example, link-local (value = 2), corresponding prefix 224.0.0.0/24.

multiclass LSP
In Differentiated-Services-aware traffic engineering, a multiclass label-switched path (LSP) functions like a standard LSP, but also allows you to reserve bandwidth for multiple class types. The experimental (EXP) bits of the Multiprotocol Label Switching (MPLS) header are used to distinguish among class types.

multiclass MLPPP
Enables multiple classes of service while using the Multilink Point-to-Point Protocol (MLPPP). Defined in RFC 2686, "The Multi-Class Extension to Multi-Link PPP."

multifield classifier
Method for classifying traffic flows. Unlike a behavior aggregate (BA) classifier, a multifield classifier examines multiple fields in the packet to apply class-of-service (CoS) settings. Examples of fields that a multifield classifier examines include the source and destination addresses of the packet, as well as the source and destination port numbers of the packet. See also BA classifier; classification.

multihoming
Network topology that uses multiple connections between customer and provider devices to provide redundancy.

MVS
Mobile visitor register subsystem.

named path
JUNOS software syntax that specifies a portion of or the entire network path that should be used as a constraint in signaling a Multiprotocol Label Switching (MPLS) label-switched path (LSP).

NAPT
Network Address Port Translation. A method that translates the addresses and transport identifiers of many private hosts into a few external addresses and transport identifiers to make efficient use of globally registered IP addresses. NAPT extends the level of translation beyond that of basic Network Address Translation (NAT). See also NAT.

NAT
Network Address Translation. A method of concealing a set of host addresses on a private network behind a pool of public addresses. It can be used as a security measure to protect the host addresses from direct targeting in network attacks.

NCP
Network Control Protocol. A traffic controller used to establish and configure different network layer protocols for the Point-to-Point Protocol (PPP).

NDP
Neighbor Discovery Protocol. A protocol used by IPv6 nodes on the same link to discover each other's presence, determine each other's link-layer addresses, find routers, and maintain reachability information about the paths to active neighbors. NDP is defined in RFC 2461 and is equivalent to the Address Resolution Protocol (ARP) used with IPv4. See also ARP.

neighbor
Adjacent system reachable by traversing a single subnetwork. An immediately adjacent router. Also called a peer.

NET
Network entity title. Network address defined by the ISO network architecture and used in CLNS-based networks.

NetBIOS

Network basic input/output system. An application programming interface used by programs on a LAN. NetBIOS provides a uniform set of commands for requesting the lower-level services required to manage names, conduct sessions, and send datagrams between nodes on a network.

network interface

Interface, such as an Ethernet or SONET/SDH interface, which primarily provides traffic connectivity. *See also* PIC; services interface.

network link advertisement

Open Shortest Path First (OSPF) link-state advertisement (LSA) flooded throughout a single area by designated routers to describe all routers attached to the network.

network LSA

Open Shortest Path First (OSPF) link-state advertisement (LSA) sent by the designated router on a broadcast or NBMA segment. It advertises the subnet associated with the designated router's segment.

network summary LSA

Open Shortest Path First (OSPF) link-state advertisement (LSA) sent by an area border router (ABR) to advertise internal OSPF routing knowledge across an area boundary. *See also* ABR.

NIC

Network Information Center. Internet authority responsible for assigning Internet-related numbers, such as IP addresses and autonomous system (AS) numbers. *See also* IANA.

NIST

National Institute of Standards and Technology. A nonregulatory U.S. federal agency whose mission is to develop and promote measurement, standards, and technology.

NLRI

Network layer reachability information. Information carried in Border Gateway Protocol (BGP) packets and used by the Multiprotocol Border Gateway Protocol (MBGP).

nonclient peer

In a Border Gateway Protocol (BGP) route reflection, a BGP peer that is not a member of a cluster. *See also* client peer.

notification cell

JUNOS software data structure generated by the Distribution Buffer Manager ASIC that represents the header contents of an IP packet. The Internet Processor ASIC uses the notification cell to perform a forwarding table lookup.

Notification message

A Border Gateway Protocol (BGP) message that informs a neighbor about an error condition, and then in some cases terminates the BGP peering session.

not-so-stubby area

See NSSA.

NSAP

Network service access point. Connection to a network that is identified by a network address.

n-selector

Last byte of a nonclient peer address.

NSR

Nonstop routing. A high-availability feature that allows a routing platform with redundant Routing Engines (REs) to preserve routing information on the backup RE and switch over from the primary RE to the backup RE without alerting peer nodes that a change has occurred. NSR uses the graceful RE switchover (GRES) infrastructure to preserve interface, kernel, and routing information.

NSSA

Not-so-stubby area. In Open Shortest Path First (OSPF), a type of stub area in which external routes can be flooded.

NTP

Network Time Protocol. A protocol used to synchronize computer clock times on a network.

Null Register message

Physical Interface Module (PIM) message sent by the first hop router to the rendezvous point (RP). The message informs the RP that the local source is still actively sending multicast packets into the network. *See also* RP.

numeric range match conditions

Use of numeric values (protocol and port numbers) in the header of an IP packet to match criteria in a firewall filter.

Oakley

Key determination protocol based on the Diffie-Hellman algorithm that provides added security, including authentication. Oakley was the key-exchange algorithm mandated for use with the initial version of ISAKMP, although other algorithms can be used. Oakley describes a series of key exchanges called *modes* and details the services provided by each; for example, Perfect Forward Secrecy for keys, identity protection, and authentication. *See also* ISAKMP.

OAM

Operation, Administration, and Maintenance. An ATM Forum specification for monitoring Asynchronous Transfer Mode (ATM) virtual connections. OAM performs standard loopback, fault detection and notification, and remote defect identification for each connection, verifying that the connection is up and the router is operational.

OC

Optical carrier. In SONET, the OC level indicates the transmission rate of digital signals on optical fiber.

OC3

SONET line with a transmission speed of 155.52 Mbps (payload of 150.336 Mbps) using fiber-optic cables. For SDH interfaces, OC3 is also known as STM1.

OC12

SONET line with a transmission speed of 622 Mbps using fiber-optic cables.

Open message

Border Gateway Protocol (BGP) message that allows two neighbors to negotiate the parameters of the peering session.

OpenConfirm

Border Gateway Protocol (BGP) neighbor state that shows that a valid Open message was received from the remote peer.

OpenSent

Border Gateway Protocol (BGP) neighbor state that shows that an Open message was sent to the remote peer and the local router is waiting for an Open message to be returned.

operational mode

JUNOS software mode that allows a user to view statistics and information about the router's current operating status.

op script

Operational script. Extensible Stylesheet Language for Transformations (XSLT) script written to automate network troubleshooting and network management. Op scripts can perform any function available through JUNOScript remote procedure calls (RPCs).

origin

In the Border Gateway Protocol (BGP), an attribute that describes the source of the route.

orlonger

JUNOS software routing policy match type that represents all routes more specific than the given subnet, including the given subnet itself. It is similar to a mathematical greater-than-or-equal-to operation.

OSI

Open Systems Interconnection. Standard reference model for how messages are transmitted between two points on a network.

OSPF

Open Shortest Path First. A link-state Interior Gateway Protocol (IGP) that makes routing decisions based on the Shortest Path First (SPF) algorithm (also referred to as the Dijkstra algorithm).

OSPF hello packet

Message sent by each Open Shortest Path First (OSPF) router to each adjacent router. It is used to establish and maintain the router's neighbor relationships.

overlay network

Network design in which a logical Layer 3 topology (IP subnets) is operating over a logical Layer 2 topology (Asynchronous Transfer Mode permanent virtual circuits [ATM PVCs]). Layers in the network do not have knowledge of each other, and each layer requires separate management and operation.

oversubscription

Method that allows provisioning of more bandwidth than the line rate of the physical interface.

P2MP LSP

See point-to-multipoint LSP.

package

Collection of files that make up a JUNOS software component.

packet

Fundamental unit of information (message or fragment of a message) carried in a packet-switched network; for example, the Internet. *See also* PSN.

packet aging

Occurs when packets in the output buffer are overwritten by newly arriving packets. This happens because the available buffer size is greater than the available transmission bandwidth.

packet capture

1. Packet sampling method, in which entire IPv4 packets flowing through a router are captured for analysis. Packets are captured in the Routing Engine (RE) and stored as libpcap-formatted files on the router. Packet capture files can be opened and analyzed offline with packet analyzers such as tcpdump and Ethereal. *See also* traffic sampling. 2. J-Web packet sampling method for quickly analyzing router control traffic destined for or originating from the RE. You can either decode and view the captured packets in the J-Web interface as they are captured, or save the packets to a file and analyze them offline with packet analyzers such as Ethereal. J-Web packet capture does not capture transient traffic.

Packet Forwarding Engine

Portion of the router that processes packets by forwarding them between input and output interfaces.

packet or cell switching

Transmission of packets from many sources over a switched network.

PADI

PPPoE Active Discovery Initiation packet. A Point-to-Point Protocol over Ethernet (PPPoE) initiation packet that is broadcast by the client to start the discovery process.

PADO

PPPoE Active Discovery Offer packet. A Point-to-Point Protocol over Ethernet (PPPoE) offer packet that is sent to the client by one or more access concentrators in reply to a PPPoE Active Discovery Initiation (PADI) packet.

PADR

PPPoE Active Discovery Request packet. A Point-to-Point Protocol over Ethernet (PPPoE) packet sent by the client to one selected access concentrator to request a session.

PADS

PPPoE Active Discovery Session Confirmation packet. A Point-to-Point Protocol over Ethernet (PPPoE) packet sent by the selected access concentrator to confirm the session.

PADT

PPPoE Active Discovery Termination packet. A Point-to-Point Protocol over Ethernet (PPPoE) packet sent by either the client or the access concentrator to terminate a session.

passive flow monitoring

Technique to intercept and observe specified data network traffic by using a routing platform such as a monitoring station that is not participating in the network.

path attribute

Information about a Border Gateway Protocol (BGP) route, such as the route origin, autonomous system (AS) path, and next hop router.

PathErr message

Resource Reservation Protocol (RSVP) message indicating that an error has occurred along an established path label-switched path (LSP). The message is advertised upstream toward the ingress router and does not remove any RSVP soft state from the network.

PathTear message

Resource Reservation Protocol (RSVP) message indicating that the established label-switched path (LSP) and its associated soft state should be removed by the network. The message is advertised downstream hop by hop toward the egress router.

pcap

Software library for packet capturing. *See also* libpcap.

PC Card

(Previously known as a PCMCIA Card.) The removable storage media that ships with each router that contains a copy of the JUNOS software. The PC Card is based on standards published by the Personal Computer Memory Card International Association (PCMCIA).

PCI

Peripheral Component Interconnect. Standard, high-speed bus for connecting computer peripherals. Used on the Routing Engine (RE).

PCI Express

Peripheral Component Interconnect Express. Next-generation, higher-bandwidth bus for connecting computer peripherals. A PCI Express bus uses point-to-point bus topology with a shared switch rather than the shared bus topology of a standard PCI bus. The shared switch on a PCI Express bus provides centralized traffic routing and management and can prioritize traffic. On some J-series Services Routers, PCI Express slots are backward-compatible with PCI and can accept Physical Interface Modules (PIMs) intended for either PCI Express or PCI slots.

PCMCIA

Personal Computer Memory Card International Association. Industry group that promotes standards for credit-card-size memory and I/O devices.

PDH

Plesiochronous Digital Hierarchy. Developed to carry digitized voice more efficiently. Evolved into the North American, European, and Japanese Digital Hierarchies, in which only a discrete set of fixed rates is available; namely, NxDS0 (DS0 is a 64 Kbps rate).

PDP

Packet data protocol. Network protocol, such as IP, used by packet data networks connected to a GPRS network.

PDU

Protocol data unit. A packet of data passed across a network. The term refers to a specific layer of the OSI seven-layer model and a specific protocol.

PEC

Policing equivalence classes. In traffic policing, a set of packets that are treated the same way by the packet classifier.

peer

Immediately adjacent router with which a protocol relationship has been established. Also called a *neighbor*.

peering

Practice of exchanging Internet traffic with directly connected peers according to commercial and contractual agreements.

PEM

1. Privacy Enhanced Mail. A technique for securely exchanging electronic mail over a public medium. 2. Power Entry Module. Distributes DC power within the router chassis. Supported on M40e, M160, M320, and T-series routing platforms.

penultimate router

Last transit router before the egress router in a Multiprotocol Label Switching (MPLS) label-switched path (LSP).

permanent interface

Interface that is always present in the routing platform. *See also* management Ethernet interface; transient interface.

persistent change

Commit script-generated configuration change that is copied to the candidate configuration. Persistent changes remain in the candidate configuration unless you explicitly delete them. *See also* transient change.

PE router

Provider edge router. A router in the service provider's network that is connected to a customer edge (CE) device and participates in a virtual private network (VPN).

PFC

Protocol Field Compression. Normally, Point-to-Point Protocol (PPP)-encapsulated packets are transmitted with a 2-byte protocol field. For example, IPv4 packets are transmitted with the protocol field set to 0×0021, and Multiprotocol Label Switching (MPLS) packets are transmitted with the protocol field set to 0×0281. For all protocols with identifiers from 0×0000 through 0×00ff, PFC enables routers to compress the protocol field to one byte, as defined in RFC 1661, "The Point-to-Point Protocol (PPP)." PFC allows you to conserve bandwidth by transmitting less data. *See also* ACFC.

PFS

Perfect Forward Secrecy protocol. A protocol derived from an encryption system that changes encryption keys often and ensures that no two sets of keys have any relationship to each other. If one set of keys is compromised, only communications using those keys are at risk. An example of a system that uses PFS is Diffie-Hellman.

PGM

Pragmatic General Multicast. A protocol layer that can be used between the IP layer and the multicast application on sources, receivers, and routers to add reliability, scalability, and efficiency to multicast networks.

PGP

Pretty Good Privacy. A strong cryptographic technique invented by Philip Zimmerman in 1991.

PHP

Penultimate hop popping. A mechanism used in a Multiprotocol Label Switching (MPLS) network that allows the transit router before the egress router to perform a label pop operation and forward the remaining data (often an IPv4 packet) to the egress router.

PHY

1. Special electronic integrated circuit or functional block of a circuit that performs encoding and decoding between a pure digital domain (on-off) and a modulation in the analog domain. *See also* LAN PHY; WAN PHY. 2. Open Systems Interconnection (OSI) physical layer. Layer 1 of the OSI model that defines the physical link between devices.

physical interface

Port on a Physical Interface Card (PIC) or Physical Interface Module (PIM).

Physical Interface Module

A network interface card installed in a J-series Services Router to provide physical connections to a LAN or WAN. PIMs can be fixed or removable and interchangeable. The PIM receives incoming packets from the network and transmits outgoing packets to the network. Each PIM is equipped with a dedicated network processor that forwards incoming data packets to and receives outgoing data packets from the Routing Engine (RE). During this process, the PIM performs framing and line-speed signaling for its medium type—for example, E1, serial, Fast Ethernet, or Integrated Services Digital Network (ISDN).

PIC

Physical Interface Card. A network interface-specific card that can be installed on a Flexible PIC Concentrator (FPC) in the router.

PIC I/O Manager

Juniper Networks ASIC responsible for receiving and transmitting information on the physical media. It performs media-specific tasks within the Packet Forwarding Engine (PFE).

PIR

Peak information rate. The PIR must be equal to or greater than the committed information rate (CIR), and both must be configured to be greater than 0. Packets that exceed the PIR are marked red, which corresponds to high loss priority. *See also* CIR; trTCM.

PKI

Public key infrastructure. A hierarchy of trust that enables users of a public network to securely and privately exchange data through the use of public and private cryptographic key pairs that are obtained and shared with peers through a trusted authority.

PLMN

Public Land Mobile Network. A telecommunications network for mobile stations.

PLP

Packet loss priority. Used to determine the random early detection (RED) drop profile when a packet is queued. You can set it by configuring a classifier or policer. The system supports two PLP designations: low and high.

PLP bit

Packet loss priority bit. Used to identify packets that have experienced congestion or are from a transmission that exceeded a service provider's customer service license agreement. This bit can be used as part of a router's congestion control mechanism and can be set by the interface or by a filter.

PLR

Point of local repair. The ingress router of a backup tunnel or a detour label-switched path (LSP).

point-to-multipoint connection

Unidirectional connection in which a single source system transmits data to multiple destination end systems. Point-to-multipoint is one of two fundamental connection types. *See also* point-to-point connection.

point-to-multipoint LSP

Resource Reservation Protocol (RSVP)-signaled label-switched path (LSP) with a single source and multiple destinations.

point-to-point connection

Unidirectional or bidirectional connection between two end systems. Point-to-point is one of two fundamental connection types. *See also* point-to-multipoint connection.

poison reverse

Method used in distance-vector networks to avoid routing loops. Each router advertises routes back to the neighbor it received them from with an infinity metric assigned.

policer

Filter that limits traffic of a certain class to a specified bandwidth or burst size. Packets exceeding the policer limits are discarded, or are assigned to a different forwarding class, a different loss priority, or both.

policing

Method of applying rate limits on bandwidth and burst size for traffic on a particular interface.

policy chain

Application of multiple routing policies in a single location. The policies are evaluated in a predefined manner and are always followed by the default policy for the specific application location.

pop

Removal of the last label, by a router, from a packet as it exits a Multiprotocol Label Switching (MPLS) domain.

port mirroring

Method in which a copy of an IPv4 packet is sent from the routing platform to an external host address or a packet analyzer for analysis.

PPP

Point-to-Point Protocol. A link-layer protocol that provides multiprotocol encapsulation. PPP is used for link-layer and network-layer configuration. Provides a standard method for transporting multiprotocol datagrams over point-to-point links. Defined in RFC 1661.

pppd
Point-to-Point Protocol daemon that processes packets that use the Point-to-Point Protocol (PPP).

PPPoE
Point-to-Point Protocol over Ethernet. Network protocol that encapsulates Point-to-Point Protocol (PPP) frames in Ethernet frames and connects multiple hosts over a simple bridging access device to a remote access concentrator.

PPPoE over ATM
Point-to-Point Protocol over Ethernet frames in Asynchronous Transfer Mode. Network protocol that encapsulates Point-to-Point Protocol over Ethernet (PPPoE) frames in Asynchronous Transfer Mode (ATM) frames for digital subscriber line (DSL) transmission, and connects multiple hosts over a simple bridging access device to a remote access concentrator.

precedence bits
First three bits in the type-of-service (ToS) byte. On a Juniper Networks router, these bits are used to sort or classify individual packets as they arrive at an interface. The classification determines the queue to which the packet is directed upon transmission.

preference
Desirability of a route to become the active route. A route with a lower preference value is more likely to become the active route. The preference is an arbitrary value from 0 through 255 that the routing protocol process uses to rank routes received from different protocols, interfaces, or remote systems.

preferred address
On an interface, the default local address used for packets sourced by the local router to destinations on the subnet.

prefix-length-range
JUNOS software routing policy match type representing all routes that share the same most-significant bits. The prefix length of the route must also lie between the two supplied lengths in the route filter.

primary address
On an interface, the address used by default as the local address for broadcast and multicast packets sourced locally and sent out the interface.

primary contributing route
Contributing route with the numerically smallest prefix and smallest JUNOS software preference value. This route is the default next hop used for a generated route.

primary interface
Router interface that packets go out on when no interface name is specified and when the destination address does not specify a particular outgoing interface.

promiscuous mode
Used with Asynchronous Transfer Mode (ATM) CCC Cell Relay encapsulation, enables mapping of all incoming cells from an interface port or from a virtual path (VP) to a single label-switched path (LSP) without restricting the VCI number.

protocol address
Logical Layer 3 address assigned to an interface within the JUNOS software.

protocol families
Grouping of logical properties within an interface configuration; for example, the inet, inet4, and Multiprotocol Label Switching (MPLS) families.

Protocol Independent Multicast
A protocol-independent multicast routing protocol. PIM dense mode is a flood-and-prune protocol. PIM sparse mode routes to multicast groups that use join messages to receive traffic. PIM sparse-dense mode allows some multicast groups to be dense groups (flood and prune) and some groups to be sparse groups (join and leave).

protocol preference
A 32-bit value assigned to all routes placed into the route table. The protocol preference is used as a tie breaker when multiple exact routes are placed into the table by different protocols.

provider router
Router in the service provider's network that is not connected to a customer edge (CE) device.

Prune message
Physical Interface Module (PIM) message sent upstream to a multicast source or the rendezvous point (RP) of the domain. The message requests that multicast traffic stop being transmitted to the router originating the message.

PSN
Packet-switched network. Network in which messages or fragments of messages (packets) are sent to their destinations through the most expedient route, as determined by a routing algorithm. Packet switching optimizes bandwidth in a network and minimizes latency.

PSNP
Partial sequence number PDU. A packet that contains only a partial list of the label-switched paths (LSPs) in the Intermediate System-to-Intermediate System Level 1 (IS-IS) link-state database.

public key infrastructure
See PKI.

push
Addition of a label or stack of labels, by a router, to a packet as it enters a Multiprotocol Label Switching (MPLS) domain.

PVC
Permanent virtual circuit. A software-defined logical connection in a network. *See also* SVC.

QoS
Quality of service. Performance, such as transmission rates and error rates, of a communications channel or system.

quad-wide
Type of Physical Interface Card (PIC) that combines the PIC and Flexible PIC Concentrator (FPC) within a single FPC slot.

qualified next hop
Next hop for a static route that allows a second next hop for the same static route to have different metric and preference properties from the original next hop.

querier router
Physical Interface Module (PIM) router on a broadcast subnet responsible for generating Internet Group Management Protocol (IGMP) query messages for the segment.

queue
First-in, first-out (FIFO) number of packets waiting to be forwarded over a router interface. You can configure the minimum and maximum sizes of the packet queue, queue admission policies, and other parameters to manage the flow of packets through the router.

queue fullness
For random early detection (RED), the memory used to store packets expressed as a percentage of the total memory allocated for that specific queue. *See also* drop profile.

queue length
For ATM1 interfaces only, a limit on the number of transmit packets that can be queued. Packets that exceed the limit are dropped. *See also* EPD.

queuing
In routing, the arrangement of packets waiting to be forwarded. Packets are organized into queues according to their priority, time of arrival, or other characteristics, and are processed one at a time. After a packet is sent to the outgoing interface on a router, it is queued for transmission on the physical media. The amount of time a packet is queued on the router is determined by the availability of the outgoing physical media, bandwidth, and amount of traffic using the interface.

RA

Registration authority. A trusted third-party organization that acts on behalf of a certificate authority (CA) to verify the identity of a digital certificate user.

radio frequency interference

See RFI.

RADIUS

Remote Authentication Dial-In User Service. An authentication method for validating users who attempt to access the router using Telnet.

RBOC

(Pronounced "are-bock".) Regional Bell operating company. Regional telephone companies formed as a result of the divestiture of the Bell System.

RC2, RC4, RC5

RSA codes. A family of proprietary (RSA Data Security, Inc.) encryption schemes often used in web browsers and servers. These codes use variable-length keys up to 2,048 bits.

RDBMS

Relational database management system. A system that presents data in a tabular form with a means of manipulating the tabular data with relational operators.

RDM

Russian-dolls bandwidth allocation model. An allocation model that makes efficient use of bandwidth by allowing the class types to share bandwidth. RDM is defined in the Internet draft *draft-ietf-tewg-diff-te-russian-03.txt*, "Russian Dolls Bandwidth Constraints Model for Diff-Serv-aware MPLS Traffic Engineering."

receive

Next hop for a static route that allows all matching packets to be sent to the Routing Engine (RE) for processing.

recursive lookup

Method of consulting the route table to locate the actual physical next hop for a route when the supplied next hop is not directly connected.

RED

Random early detection. Gradual drop profile for a given class that is used for congestion avoidance. RED tries to anticipate incipient congestion by dropping a small percentage of packets from the head of the queue to ensure that a queue never actually becomes congested.

refresh reduction

In the Resource Reservation Protocol (RSVP), an extension that addresses the problems of scaling, reliability, and latency when Refresh messages are used to cover message loss.

Register message

Physical Interface Module (PIM) message unicast by the first hop router to the rendezvous point (RP) that contains the multicast packets from the source encapsulated within its data field.

Register Stop message

Physical Interface Module (PIM) message sent by the rendezvous point (RP) to the first hop router to halt the sending of encapsulated multicast packets.

registration authority

See RA.

reject

Next hop for a configured route that drops all matching packets from the network and returns an Internet Control Message Protocol (ICMP) message to the source IP address. Also used as an action in a routing policy or firewall filter.

rename

JUNOS software command that allows a user to change the name of a routing policy, firewall filter, or any other variable character string defined in the router configuration.

Request message

Routing Information Protocol (RIP) message used by a router to ask for all or part of the route table from a neighbor.

resolve

Next hop for a static route that allows the router to perform a recursive lookup to locate the physical next hop for the route.

Response message

Routing Information Protocol (RIP) message used to advertise routing information into a network.

result cell

JUNOS software data structure generated by the Internet Processor ASIC after performing a forwarding table lookup.

ResvConf message

Resource Reservation Protocol (RSVP) message that allows the egress router to receive an explicit confirmation message from a neighbor that its Resv message was received.

ResvErr message

Resource Reservation Protocol (RSVP) message indicating that an error has occurred along an established label-switched path (LSP). The message is advertised downstream toward the egress router and it does not remove any RSVP soft state from the network.

ResvTear message

Resource Reservation Protocol (RSVP) message indicating that the established label-switched path (LSP) and its associated soft state should be removed by the network. The message is advertised upstream toward the ingress router.

revert timer

For SONET Automatic Protection Switching (APS), a timer that specifies the amount of time (in seconds) to wait after the working circuit has become functional before making the working circuit active again.

rewrite rules

Set the appropriate class-of-service (CoS) bits in an outgoing packet. This allows the next downstream router to classify the packet into the appropriate service group.

RFC

Request for Comments. Internet standard specifications published by the Internet Engineering Task Force (IETF).

RFI

Radio frequency interface. Interference from high-frequency electromagnetic waves emanating from electronic devices.

RIB

Routing information base. A logical data structure used by the Border Gateway Protocol (BGP) to store routing information. *See also* route table.

RID

Router ID. An IP address used by a router to uniquely identify itself to a routing protocol. This address may not be equal to a configured interface address.

RIP

Routing Information Protocol. Used in IPv4 networks, a distance-vector interior gateway protocol that makes routing decisions based on hop count.

RIPng

Routing Information Protocol next generation. Used in IPv6 networks, a distance-vector interior gateway protocol that makes routing decisions based on hop count.

RMON

Remote monitoring. A standard Management Information Base (MIB) that defines current and historical media access control (MAC)-layer statistics and control objects, allowing you to capture real-time information across the entire network. This allows you to detect, isolate, diagnose, and report potential and actual network problems.

RNC

Radio network controller. Manages the radio part of the network in UMTS.

route distinguisher

A 6-byte value identifying a virtual private network (VPN) that is prefixed to an IPv4 address to create a unique IPv4 address. The new address is part of the VPN IPv4 address family, which is a Border Gateway Protocol (BGP) address family added as an extension to BGP. It allows you to configure private addresses within the VPN by preventing overlap with the private addresses in other VPNs.

route filter

JUNOS software syntax used in a routing policy to match an individual route or a group of routes.

route flapping
Condition of network instability whereby a route is announced and withdrawn repeatedly, often as a result of an intermittently failing link.

route identifier
IP address of the router from which a Border Gateway Protocol (BGP), Interior Gateway Protocol (IGP), or Open Shortest Path First (OSPF) packet originated.

route redistribution
Method of placing learned routes from one protocol into another protocol operating on the same router. The JUNOS software accomplishes this with a routing policy.

route reflection
In the Border Gateway Protocol (BGP), the configuration of a group of routers into a cluster in which one system acts as a route reflector, redistributing routes from outside the cluster to all routers in the cluster. Routers in a cluster do not need to be fully meshed.

router ID
See RID.

router-link advertisement
Open Shortest Path First (OSPF) link-state advertisement (LSA) flooded throughout a single area by all routers to describe the state and cost of the router's links to the area.

router LSA
Open Shortest Path First (OSPF) link-state advertisement (LSA) sent by each router in the network. It describes the local router's connected subnets and their metric values.

router priority
Numerical value assigned to an Open Shortest Path First (OPSF) or Intermediate System-to-Intermediate System Level 1 (IS-IS) interface that is used as the first criterion in electing the designated router or designated intermediate system, respectively.

Routing Engine
Portion of the router that handles all routing protocol processes, as well as other software processes that control the router's interfaces, some of the chassis components, system management, and user access to the router.

routing instance
Collection of route tables, interfaces, and routing protocol parameters. The set of interfaces is contained in the route tables, and the routing protocol parameters control the information in the route tables.

routing matrix
Terabit routing system interconnecting up to four T640 routing nodes and a TX Matrix platform to deliver up to 2.56 terabits per second (Tbps) of subscriber switching capacity.

route table
Common database of routes learned from one or more routing protocols. All routes are maintained by the JUNOS routing protocol process.

RP
Rendezvous point. For Physical Interface Module (PIM) sparse mode, a core router acting as the root of the distribution tree in a shared tree.

RPC
Remote procedure call. A type of protocol that allows a computer program running on one computer to cause a function on another computer to be executed without explicitly coding the details for this interaction.

rpd
JUNOS software routing protocol process (daemon). A user-level background process responsible for starting, managing, and stopping the routing protocols on a Juniper Networks router.

RPF
Reverse path forwarding. An algorithm that checks the unicast route table to determine whether there is a shortest path back to the source address of the incoming multicast packet. Unicast RPF helps to determine the source of denial-of-service (DoS) attacks and rejects packets from unexpected source addresses.

RPM

1. Reverse-path multicasting. Routing algorithm used by the Distance Vector Multicast Routing Protocol (DVMRP) to forward multicast traffic. 2. Real-Time Performance Monitoring. A tool for creating active probes to track and monitor traffic.

RRO

Record route object. A Resource Reservation Protocol (RSVP) message object that notes the IP address of each router along the path of a label-switched path (LSP).

RSVP

Resource Reservation Protocol. A signaling protocol that establishes a session between two routers to transport a specific traffic flow.

RSVP Path message

Resource Reservation Protocol (RSVP) message sent by the ingress router downstream toward the egress router. It begins the establishment of a soft state database for a particular label-switched path (LSP).

RSVP Resv message

Resource Reservation Protocol (RSVP) message sent by the egress router upstream toward the ingress router. It completes the establishment of the soft state database for a particular label-switched path (LSP).

RSVP signaled LSP

Label-switched path (LSP) that is dynamically established using Resource Reservation Protocol (RSVP) Path and Resv messages.

RSVP-TE

RSVP-traffic engineering; Resource Reservation Protocol (RSVP) with traffic engineering extensions as defined by RFC 3209. These extensions allow RSVP to establish label-switched paths (LSPs) in Multiprotocol Label Switching (MPLS) networks. *See also* MPLS; RSVP.

RTP

Real-Time Transport Protocol. An Internet protocol that provides mechanisms for the transmission of real-time data, such as audio, video, or voice, over IP networks. Compressed RTP is used for Voice over IP traffic.

RTVBR

Real-time variable bit rate. For ATM2 intelligent queuing (IQ) interfaces, data that is serviced at a higher priority rate than other VBR data. RTVBR is suitable for carrying packetized video and audio. RTVBR provides better congestion control and latency guarantees than non-real-time VBR.

SA

Security association. An IPSec term that describes an agreement between two parties about what rules to use for authentication and encryption algorithms, key exchange mechanisms, and secure communications.

sampling

Method whereby the sampling key based on the IPv4 header is sent to the Routing Engine (RE). There, the key is placed in a file, or cflowd packets based on the key are sent to a cflowd server.

SAP

1. Session Announcement Protocol. Used with multicast protocols to handle session conference announcements. 2. Service access point. Device that identifies routing protocols and provides the connection between the network interface card and the rest of the network.

SAR

Segmentation and reassembly. Buffering used with Asynchronous Transfer Mode (ATM).

SCB

System Control Board. On an M40 router, the part of the Packet Forwarding Engine (PFE) that performs route lookups, monitors system components, and controls Flexible PIC Concentrator (FPC) resets.

SCC

Switch-card chassis. Term used by the JUNOS command-line interface (CLI) to refer to the TX Matrix platform in a routing matrix.

SCEP

Simple Certificate Enrollment Protocol. A protocol for digital certificates that supports certificate authority (CA) and registration authority (RA) public key distribution, certificate enrollment, certificate revocation, certificate queries, and certificate revocation list (CRL) queries.

SCG

SONET Clock Generator. On a T640 routing node, provides the Stratum 3 clock signal for the SONET/SDH interfaces. Also provides external clock inputs.

scheduler maps

In class of service (CoS), associate schedulers with forwarding classes. *See also* schedulers; forwarding classes.

schedulers

Define the priority, bandwidth, delay buffer size, rate control status, and random early detection (RED) drop profiles to be applied to a particular forwarding class for packet transmission. *See also* scheduler maps.

scheduling

Method of determining which type of packet or queue is transmitted before another. An individual router interface can have multiple queues assigned to store packets. The router then determines which queue to service based on a particular method of scheduling. This process often involves a determination of which type of packet should be transmitted before another; for example, first in, first out (FIFO). *See also* FIFO.

SCP

Secure copy. Means of securely transferring computer files between a local and remote host or between two remote hosts, using the Secure Shell (SSH) protocol.

SCU

Source class usage. A means of tracking traffic originating from specific prefixes on the provider core router and destined for specific prefixes on the customer edge router, based on the IP source and destination addresses.

SDH

Synchronous Digital Hierarchy. A CCITT variation of the SONET standard.

SDP

Session Description Protocol. Used with multicast protocols to handle session conference announcements.

SDRAM

Synchronous dynamic random access memory. An electronic standard in which the inputs and outputs of SDRAM data are synchronized to an externally supplied clock, allowing for extremely fast consecutive read and write capacity.

SDX software

Service Deployment System software. A customizable Juniper Networks product with which service providers can rapidly deploy IP services—such as video on demand (VoD), IP television, stateful firewalls, Layer 3 virtual private networks (VPNs), and bandwidth on demand (BoD)—to hundreds of thousands of subscribers over a variety of broadband access technologies.

services interface

Interface that provides specific capabilities for manipulating traffic before it is delivered to its destination; for example, the adaptive services interface and the tunnel services interface. *See also* network interface.

session attribute object

Resource Reservation Protocol (RSVP) message object used to control the priority, preemption, affinity class, and local rerouting of the label-switched path (LSP).

SFM

Switching and Forwarding Module. On an M160 router, a component of the Packet Forwarding Engine (PFE) that provides route lookup, filtering, and switching to Flexible PIC Concentrators (FPCs).

SFP

Small form-factor pluggable transceiver. A transceiver that provides support for optical or copper cables. SFPs are hot-insertable and hot-removable. *See also* XFP.

SGSN

Serving GPRS Support Node. Device in the mobile network that requests PDP contexts with a GGSN.

SHA-1

Secure Hash Algorithm 1. A secure hash algorithm standard defined in FIPS PUB 180-1 (SHA-1). Developed by the National Institute of Standards and Technology (NIST), SHA-1 (which effectively replaces SHA-0) produces a 160-bit hash for message authentication. Longer-hash variants include SHA-224, SHA-256, SHA-384, and SHA-512 (sometimes grouped under the name "SHA-2"). SHA-1 is more secure than Message Digest 5 (MD5). *See also* hashing; MD5.

sham link

Unnumbered point-to-point intra-area link advertised by a type 1 link-state advertisement (LSA).

shaping rate

In class of service (CoS), controls the maximum rate of traffic transmitted on an interface. *See also* traffic shaping.

shared scheduling and shaping

Allocation of separate pools of shared resources to subsets of logical interfaces belonging to the same physical port.

shared tree

Multicast forwarding tree established from the rendezvous point (RP) to the last hop router for a particular group address.

SHDSL

Symmetric high-speed digital subscriber line. A standardized multirate symmetric DSL that transports rate-adaptive symmetrical data across a single copper pair at data rates from 192 Kbps to 2.3 Mbps, or from 384 Kbps to 4.6 Mbps over two pairs, covering applications served by HDSL, SDSL, T1, E1, and services beyond E1. SHDSL conforms to the following recommendations: ITU G.991.2 G.SHDSL, ETSI TS 101-524 SDSL, and the T1E1.4/2001-174 G.SHDSL. *See also* G.SHDSL.

shim header

Location of the Multiprotocol Label Switching (MPLS) header in a data packet. The JUNOS software always places (shims) the header between the existing Layer 2 and Layer 3 headers.

Shortest Path First

See SPF.

shortest-path tree

See SPT.

SIB

Switch Interface Board. On a T640 routing node, provides the switching function to the destination Packet Forwarding Engine (PFE).

signaled path

In traffic engineering, an explicit path; that is, a path determined using Resource Reservation Protocol (RSVP) signaling. The ERO carried in the packets contains the explicit path information.

Simple Network Management Protocol

See SNMP.

simplex interface

Interface that treats packets it receives from itself as the result of a software loopback process. The interface does not consider these packets when determining whether the interface is functional.

single-mode fiber

Optical fiber designed for transmission of a single ray or mode of light as a carrier and used for long-distance signal transmission. For short distances, multimode fiber is used. *See also* MMF.

SIP

Session Initiation Protocol. An Adaptive Services application protocol option used for setting up sessions between endpoints on the Internet. Examples include telephony, fax, videoconferencing, file exchange, and person-to-person sessions.

SNA

System Network Architecture. IBM proprietary networking architecture consisting of a protocol stack that is used primarily in banks and other financial transaction networks.

SNMP

Simple Network Management Protocol. A protocol governing network management and the monitoring of network devices and their functions.

soft state

In Resource Reservation Protocol (RSVP), controls state in hosts and routers that expires if not refreshed within a specified amount of time.

SONET

Synchronous Optical Network. A high-speed (up to 2.5 Gbps) synchronous network specification developed by Bellcore and designed to run on optical fiber. STS1 is the basic building block of SONET. Approved as an international standard in 1988. *See also* SDH.

source-based tree

Multicast forwarding tree established from the source of traffic to all interested receivers for a particular group address. It is often used in a dense-mode forwarding environment.

sparse mode

Method of operating a multicast domain where sources of traffic and interested receivers meet at a central rendezvous point (RP). A sparse-mode network assumes that there are very few receivers for each group address.

SPF

Shortest Path First. An algorithm used by Intermediate System-to-Intermediate System Level 1 (IS-IS) and Open Shortest Path First (OSPF) to make routing decisions based on the state of network links. Also called the *Dijkstra algorithm*.

SPI

Security Parameter Index. In IPSec, a numeric identifier used with the destination address and security protocol to identify a security association (SA). When Internet Key Exchange (IKE) is used to establish an SA, the SPI is randomly derived. When manual configuration is used for an SA, the SPI must be entered as a parameter.

SPID

Service Profile Identifier. Used only in Basic Rate Interface (BRI) implementations of the Integrated Services Digital Network (ISDN). The SPID specifies the services available on the service provider switch and defines the feature set ordered when the ISDN service is provisioned.

split horizon

Method used in distance-vector networks to avoid routing loops. Each router does not advertise routes back to the neighbor from which it received them.

SPQ

Strict-priority queuing. A dequeuing method that provides a special queue that is serviced until it is empty. The traffic sent to this queue tends to maintain a lower latency and more consistent latency numbers than traffic sent to other queues. *See also* APQ.

SPT

Shortest-path tree. An algorithm that builds a network topology that attempts to minimize the path from one router (the root) to other routers in a routing area.

SQL

Structured Query Language. International standard language used to create, modify, and select data from relational databases.

src port

Transmission Control Protocol (TCP) or User Datagram Protocol (UDP) port for the source IP address in a packet.

SS7

Signaling System 7. A protocol used in telecommunications for delivering calls and services.

SSAP

Source service access point. Device that identifies the origin of an LPDU on a data link switching (DLSw) network.

SSB

System and Switch Board. On an M20 router, a Packet Forwarding Engine (PFE) component that performs route lookups and component monitoring and monitors Flexible PIC Concentrator (FPC) operation.

SSH

Secure Shell. A protocol that uses strong authentication and encryption for remote access across a nonsecure network. SSH provides remote login, remote program execution, file copy, and other functions. In a Unix environment, SSH is intended as a secure replacement for rlogin, rsh, and rcp.

SSH/TLS

Secure Shell with Transport Layer Security. A combination of two standard methods used to secure communications over the Internet. TLS is the name of a standard protocol based on SSL 3.0 and is defined in RFC 2246. In combination, SSH/TLS is also known as SSHv2 and uses FIPS-restricted cipher sets in a FIPS environment.

SSL

Secure Sockets Layer. A protocol that encrypts security information using public–private key technology, which requires a paired private key and authentication certificate, before transmitting data across a network.

SSM

Source-specific multicast. A service that allows a client to receive multicast traffic directly from the source. Typically, SSM uses a subset of the Physical Interface Module (PIM) sparse-mode functionality along with a subset of IGMPv3 to create a shortest-path tree (SPT) between the client and the source, but it builds the SPT without the help of a rendezvous point (RP).

SSP

Switch-to-Switch Protocol. Protocol implemented between two data link switching (DLSw) routers that establishes connections, locates resources, forwards data, and handles error recovery and flow control.

SSRAM

Synchronous static random access memory. Used for storing route tables, packet pointers, and other data such as route lookups, policer counters, and other statistics to which the microprocessor needs quick access.

standard AAL5 mode

Transport mode that allows multiple applications to tunnel the protocol data units of their Layer 2 protocols over an Asynchronous Transfer Mode (ATM) virtual circuit. You use this transport mode to tunnel IP packets over an ATM backbone. *See also* AAL5 mode; cell-relay mode; Layer 2 circuits; trunk mode.

starvation

Problem that occurs when lower-priority traffic, such as data and protocol packets, is locked out (starved) because a higher-priority queue uses all of the available transmission bandwidth.

stateful firewall filter

Type of firewall filter that evaluates the context of connections, permits or denies traffic based on the context, and updates this information dynamically. Context includes IP source and destination addresses, port numbers, Transmission Control Protocol (TCP) sequencing information, and TCP connection flags. The context established in the first packet of a TCP session must match the context contained in all subsequent packets if a session is to remain active. *See also* stateless firewall filter.

stateful firewall recovery

Recovery strategy that preserves parameters concerning the history of connections, sessions, or application status before failure. *See also* stateless firewall recovery.

stateless firewall filter

Type of firewall filter that statically evaluates the contents of packets transiting the router and packets originating from or destined for the Routing Engine (RE). Packets are accepted, rejected, forwarded, or discarded and collected, logged, sampled, or subjected to classification according to a wide variety of packet characteristics. Sometimes called access control lists (ACLs) or simply firewall filters, stateless firewall filters protect the processes and resources owned by the RE. A stateless firewall filter can evaluate every packet, including fragmented packets. In contrast to a stateful firewall filter, a stateless firewall filter does not maintain information about connection states. *See also* stateful firewall filter.

stateless firewall recovery
Recovery strategy that does not attempt to preserve the history of connections, sessions, or application status before failure. *See also* stateful firewall recovery.

static LSP
See static path.

static path
In the context of traffic engineering, a static route that requires hop-by-hop manual configuration. No signaling is used to create or maintain the path. Also called a *static LSP*.

static route
Explicitly configured route that is entered into the route table. Static routes have precedence over routes chosen by dynamic routing protocols.

static RP
One of three methods of learning the rendezvous point (RP) to group address mapping in a multicast network. Each router in the domain must be configured with the required RP information.

S/T interface
System reference point/terminal reference point interface. A four-pair connection between the Integrated Services Digital Network (ISDN) provider service and the customer terminal equipment.

STM
Synchronous transport module. CCITT specification for SONET at 155.52 Mbps.

strict
In the context of traffic engineering, a route that must go directly to the next address in the path. (Definition from RFC 791, modified to fit LSPs.)

strict hop
Routers in a Multiprotocol Label Switching (MPLS) named path that must be directly connected to the previous router in the configured path.

STS
Synchronous transport signal. Synchronous transport signal level 1 is the basic building block signal of SONET, operating at 51.84 Mbps. Faster SONET rates are defined as STS-*n*, where *n* is an integer by which the basic rate of 51.84 Mbps is multiplied. *See also* SONET.

stub area
In Open Shortest Path First (OSPF), an area through which, or into which, autonomous system (AS) external advertisements are not flooded.

STU-C
Symmetric high-speed digital subscriber line (SHDSL) transceiver unit–central office. Equipment at the telephone company central office that provides SHDSL connections to remote user terminals.

STU-R
Symmetric high-speed digital subscriber line (SHDSL) transceiver unit–remote. Equipment at the customer premises that provides SHDSL connections to remote user terminals.

sub-LSP
Part of a point-to-multipoint label-switched path (LSP). A sub-LSP carries traffic from the main LSP to one of the egress Provide Edge (PE) routers. Each point-to-multipoint LSP has multiple sub-LSPs. *See also* point-to-multipoint LSP.

subnet mask
Number of bits of the network address used for the host portion of a Class A, Class B, or Class C IP address.

subrate value
Value that reduces the maximum allowable peak rate by limiting the High-Level Data Link Control (HDLC)-encapsulated payload. The subrate value must exactly match that of the remote channel service unit (CSU).

summary link advertisement
Open Shortest Path First (OSPF) link-statement advertisement (LSA) flooded throughout the advertisement's associated areas by area border routers (ABRs) to describe the routes that they know about in other areas.

SVC

Switched virtual connection. A dynamically established, software-defined logical connection that stays up as long as data is being transmitted. When transmission is complete, the software tears down the SVC. *See also* PVC.

sysid

System identifier. Portion of the ISO nonclient peer. The system ID can be any six bytes that are unique throughout a domain.

syslog

System log. A method for storing messages to a file for troubleshooting or recordkeeping. It can also be used as an action within a firewall filter to store information to the *messages* file.

T1

Basic physical layer protocol used by the Digital Signal level 1 (DS1) multiplexing method in North America. A T1 interface operates at a bit rate of 1.544 Mbps and can support 24 DS0 channels.

T3

Physical layer protocol used by the Digital Signal level 3 (DS3) multiplexing method in North America. A T3 interface operates at a bit rate of 44.736 Mbps.

TACACS+

Terminal Access Controller Access Control System Plus. Authentication method for validating users who attempt to access the router using Telnet.

tail drop

Queue management algorithm for dropping packets from the input end (tail) of the queue when the length of the queue exceeds a configured threshold. *See also* RED.

T-carrier

Generic designator for any of several digitally multiplexed telecommunications carrier systems originally developed by Bell Labs and used in North America and Japan.

TCM

Tricolor marking. Traffic policing mechanism that extends the functionality of class-of-service (CoS) traffic policing by providing three levels of drop precedence (loss priority or PLP) instead of two. There are two types of TCM: single-rate and two-rate. The JUNOS software currently supports two-rate TCM only. *See also* trTCM.

TCP

Transmission Control Protocol. Works in conjunction with IP to send data over the Internet. Divides a message into packets and tracks the packets from point of origin to destination.

tcpdump

Unix packet monitoring utility used by the JUNOS software to view information about packets sent or received by the Routing Engine (RE).

TCP port 179

Well-known port number used by the Border Gateway Protocol (BGP) to establish a peering session with a neighbor.

TDMA

Time-Division Multiplex Access. A type of multiplexing in which two or more channels of information are transmitted over the same link, where the channels take turns to use the link. Each link is allocated a different time interval ("slot" or "slice") for the transmission of each channel. For the receiver to distinguish one channel from the other, some kind of periodic synchronizing signal or distinguishing identifier is required. *See also* GSM.

TEI

Terminal Endpoint Identifier. A terminal endpoint can be any Integrated Services Digital Network (ISDN)-capable device attached to an ISDN network. The TEI is a number between 0 and 127, where 0 through 63 are used for static TEI assignment, 64 through 126 are used for dynamic assignment, and 127 is used for group assignment.

terminating action

Action in a routing policy or firewall filter that halts the logical software processing of a policy or filter.

terms

Used in a routing policy or firewall filter to segment the policy or filter into small match and action pairs.

through

JUNOS software routing policy match type representing all routes that fall between the two supplied prefixes in the route filter.

Time-Division Multiplex Access

See TDMA.

time-division multiplexed channel

Channel derived from a given frequency and transmitted over a single wire or wireless medium. The channel is preassigned a time slot whether or not there is data to transmit.

timeout timer

Used in a distance-vector protocol to ensure that the current route is still usable for forwarding traffic.

TNP

Trivial Network Protocol. A Juniper Networks proprietary protocol automatically configured on an internal interface by the JUNOS software. TNP is used to communicate between the Routing Engine (RE) and components of the Packet Forwarding Engine (PFE), and is critical to the operation of the router.

token-bucket algorithm

Used in a rate-policing application to enforce an average bandwidth while allowing bursts of traffic up to a configured maximum value.

ToS

Type of service. The method of handling traffic using information extracted from the fields in the ToS byte to differentiate packet flows.

totally stubby area

Open Shortest Path First (OSPF) area type that prevents Type 3, 4, and 5 link-state

advertisements (LSAs) from entering the nonbackbone area.

traffic engineering

Process of selecting the paths chosen by data traffic to balance the traffic load on the various links, routers, and switches in the network. (Definition from *http://www.ietf.org/internet-drafts/draft-ietf -mpls-framework-04.txt*.) *See also* MPLS.

traffic engineering class

In Differentiated-Services-aware traffic engineering, a paired class type and priority.

traffic engineering class map

In Differentiated-Services-aware traffic engineering, a map among the class types, priorities, and traffic engineering classes. The traffic engineering class mapping must be consistent across the Differentiated Services domain.

traffic policing

Examines traffic flows and discards or marks packets that exceed service-level agreements (SLAs).

traffic sampling

Method used to capture individual packet information of traffic flow at a specified time period. The sampled traffic information is placed in a file and stored on a server for various types of analysis. *See also* packet capture.

traffic shaping

Reduces the potential for network congestion by placing packets in a queue with a shaper at the head of the queue. Traffic shaping tools regulate the rate and volume of traffic admitted to the network. *See also* shaping rate.

transient change

Commit script-generated configuration change that is loaded into the checkout configuration, but not into the candidate configuration. Transient changes are not saved in the configuration if the associated commit script is deleted or deactivated. *See also* persistent change.

transient interface

Interface that can be configured on a routing platform depending on your network needs. Unlike a permanent interface that is required for router operation, a transient interface can be disabled or removed without affecting the basic operation of the router. *See also* FPC; PIC; permanent interface.

transit area

In Open Shortest Path First (OSPF), an area used to pass traffic from one adjacent area to the backbone or to another area if the backbone is more than two hops away from an area.

transit router

In Multiprotocol Label Switching (MPLS), any intermediate router in the label-switched path (LSP) between the ingress router and the egress router.

transport mode

IPSec mode of operation in which the data payload is encrypted, but the original IP header is left untouched. The IP addresses of the source or destination can be modified if the packet is intercepted. Because of its construction, transport mode can be used only when the communication endpoint and cryptographic endpoint are the same. Virtual private network (VPN) gateways that provide encryption and decryption services for protected hosts cannot use transport mode for protected VPN communications. *See also* tunnel mode.

transport plane

See data plane.

TRAP

Reports significant events occurring on a network device, most often errors or failures. Simple Network Management Protocol (SNMP) TRAPs are defined in either standard or enterprise-specific Management Information Bases (MIBs).

triggered updates

Used in a distance-vector protocol to reduce the time for the network to converge. When a router has a topology change, it immediately sends the information to its neighbors instead of waiting for a timer to expire.

trTCM

Two-rate TCM polices traffic according to the color classification (loss priority) of each packet. Traffic policing is based on two rates: the committed information rate (CIR) and the peak information rate (PIR). Two-rate TCM is defined in RFC 2698, "A Two Rate Three Color Marker." *See also* CIR; PIR.

trunk mode

Layer 2 circuit cell-relay transport mode that allows you to send Asynchronous Transfer Mode (ATM) cells between ATM2 intelligent queuing (IQ) interfaces over a Multiprotocol Label Switching (MPLS) core network. You use Layer 2 circuit trunk mode (as opposed to standard Layer 2 circuit cell-relay mode) to transport ATM cells over an MPLS core network that is implemented between other vendors' switches or routers. The multiple connections associated with a trunk increase bandwidth and provide failover redundancy. *See also* AAL5 mode, cell-relay mode, Layer 2 circuits, standard AAL5 mode.

Tspec object

Resource Reservation Protocol (RSVP) message object that contains information such as the bandwidth request of the label-switched path (LSP) as well as the minimum and maximum packets supported.

tunnel

Private, secure path through an otherwise public network.

tunnel endpoint

Last node of a tunnel where the tunnel-related headers are removed from the packet, which is then passed on to the destination network.

tunneling protocol

Network protocol that encapsulates one protocol or session inside another. When protocol A is encapsulated within protocol B, A treats B as though it were a data-link layer. Tunneling can be used to transport a network protocol through a network that would not otherwise support it. Tunneling can also be used to provide various types of virtual private network (VPN) functionality such as private addressing.

tunnel mode

IPSec mode of operation in which the entire IP packet, including the header, is encrypted and authenticated and a new virtual private network (VPN) header is added, protecting the entire original packet. This mode can be used by both VPN clients and VPN gateways, and it protects communications that come from or go to non-IPSec systems. *See also* transport mode.

tunnel services interface

Provides the capability of a Tunnel Services PIC on an Adaptive Services PIC (ASP). *See* Tunnel Services PIC.

Tunnel Services PIC

Physical interface card (PIC) that allows the router to perform the encapsulation and de-encapsulation of IP datagrams. The Tunnel Services PIC supports IP-IP, Generic Routing Encapsulation (GRE), and Physical Interface Module (PIM) register encapsulation and de-encapsulation. When the Tunnel Services PIC is installed, the router can be a PIM rendezvous point (RP) or a PIM first hop router for a source that is directly connected to the router.

TX Matrix platform

Routing platform that provides the centralized switching fabric of the routing matrix.

UDP

User Datagram Protocol. In Transmission Control Protocol/Internet Protocol (TCP/IP), a connectionless transport layer protocol that exchanges datagrams without acknowledgments or guaranteed delivery, requiring that error processing and retransmission be handled by other protocols.

U interface

User reference point interface. A single-pair connection between the local Integrated Services Digital Network (ISDN) provider and the customer premises equipment.

UME

UNI management entity. The code residing in the Asynchronous Transfer Mode (ATM) devices at each end of a UNI (user-to-network interface) circuit that functions as a Simple Network Management Protocol (SNMP) agent, maintaining network and connection information specified in a Management Information Base (MIB).

UMTS

Universal mobile telecommunications system. Provides third-generation (3G), packet-based transmission of text, digitized voice, video, and multimedia, at data rates up to 2 Mbps.

UNI

User-to-network interface. ATM Forum specification that defines an interoperability standard for the interface between a router or an Asynchronous Transfer Mode (ATM) switch located in a private network and the ATM switches located within the public carrier networks. Also used to describe similar connections in Frame Relay networks.

unicast

Operation of sending network traffic from one network node to another individual network node.

unit

JUNOS software syntax that represents the logical properties of an interface.

unnumbered interface

Logical interface that is configured without an IP address.

Update message

Border Gateway Protocol (BGP) message that advertises path attributes and routing knowledge to an established neighbor.

update timer

Used in a distance-vector protocol to advertise routes to a neighbor on a regular basis.

UPS

Uninterruptible power supply. A device that sits between a power supply and a router or other device and prevents power-source events, such as outages and surges, from affecting or damaging the device.

upto

JUNOS software routing policy match type representing all routes that share the same most-significant bits and whose prefix length is smaller than the supplied subnet in the route filter.

UTC

Coordinated Universal Time. Historically referred to as Greenwich Mean Time (GMT), a high-precision atomic time standard that tracks Universal Time (UT) and is the basis for legal civil time all over the world. Time zones around the world are expressed as positive and negative offsets from UTC.

UTRAN

UMTS Terrestrial Radio Access Network. The WCDMA radio network in UMTS.

VBR

Variable bit rate. For ATM1 and ATM2 intelligent queuing (IQ) interfaces, data that is serviced at a varied rate within defined limits. VBR traffic adds the ability to statistically oversubscribe user traffic.

VC

Virtual circuit. A software-defined logical connection between two network devices that is not a dedicated connection but acts as though it is. It can be either permanent (PVC) or switched (SVC). VCs are used in Asynchronous Transfer Mode (ATM), Frame Relay, and X.25. *See also* VPI, VCI, PVC, SVC.

VCI

1. Vapor corrosion inhibitor. Small cylinder packed with the router that prevents corrosion of the chassis and components during shipment. 2. Virtual circuit identifier. A 16-bit field in the header of an Asynchronous Transfer Mode (ATM) cell that indicates the particular virtual circuit the cell takes through a virtual path. Also called a *logical interface*. *See also* VPI.

virtual channel

Enables queuing, packet scheduling, and accounting rules to be applied to one or more logical interfaces. *See also* virtual channel group.

virtual channel group

Combines virtual channels into a group and then applies the group to one or more logical interfaces. *See also* virtual channel.

virtual circuit

Represents a logical connection between two Layer 2 devices in a network.

virtual link

In Open Shortest Path First (OSPF), a link created between two routers that are part of the backbone but are not physically contiguous.

virtual loopback tunnel interface

See VT.

virtual path

Combination of multiple virtual circuits between two devices in an Asynchronous Transfer Mode (ATM) network.

VLAN

Virtual LAN. A logical group of network devices that appear to be on the same LAN, regardless of their physical location. VLANs are configured with management software, and are extremely flexible because they are based on logical, rather than physical, connections.

VLAN-tagged frame

Tagged frame whose tag header carries both virtual LAN (VLAN) identification and priority information.

VPI

Virtual path identifier. An 8-bit field in the header of an Asynchronous Transfer Mode (ATM) cell that indicates the virtual path the cell takes. *See also* VCI.

VPLS

Virtual private LAN service. An Ethernet-based multipoint-to-multipoint Layer 2 virtual private network (VPN) service used for interconnecting multiple Ethernet LANs across a Multiprotocol Label Switching (MPLS) backbone. VPLS is specified in the IETF draft "Virtual Private LAN Service."

VPN

Virtual private network. A private data network that uses a public Transmission Control Protocol/Internet Protocol (TCP/IP) network, typically the Internet, while maintaining privacy with a tunneling protocol, encryption, and security procedures. *See also* tunneling protocol.

VRF instance

Virtual private network (VPN) routing and forwarding instance. A Virtual Route and Forwarding (VRF) instance for a Layer 3 VPN implementation consists of one or more route tables, a derived forwarding table, a set of interfaces that use the forwarding table, and a set of policies and routing protocols that determine what goes into the forwarding table.

VRF table

Routing instance table that stores Virtual Route and Forwarding (VRF) routing information. *See also* VRF instance.

VRRP

Virtual Router Redundancy Protocol. On Fast Ethernet and Gigabit Ethernet interfaces, allows you to configure virtual default routers.

VT

Virtual loopback tunnel interface. A VT interface that loops packets back to the Packet Forwarding Engine (PFE) for further processing, such as looking up a route in a Virtual Route and Forwarding (VRF) route table or looking up an Ethernet media access control (MAC) address. A virtual loopback tunnel interface can be associated with a variety of Multiprotocol Label Switching (MPLS) and virtual private network (VPN)-related applications, including VRF routing instances, VPLS routing instances, and point-to-multipoint label-switched paths (LSPs).

warm standby

Method that enables one backup Adaptive Services PIC (ASP) to support multiple active ASPs, without providing guaranteed recovery times.

WAN PHY

Wide Area Network Physical Layer Device. A physical layer device that allows 10-Gigabit Ethernet wide-area links to use fiber-optic cables and other devices intended for SONET/SDH. *See also* LAN PHY; PHY.

WAP

Wireless Application Protocol. A standard protocol that enables mobile users to access the Internet in a limited fashion if WAP is supported and enabled on the mobile device, server, and wireless network. WAP users can send and receive email and access web sites in text format only (WAP does not support graphics).

WCDMA

Wideband Code Division Multiple Access. Radio interface technology used in most third-generation (3G) systems.

WDM

Wavelength-division multiplexing. Technique for transmitting a mix of voice, data, and video over various wavelengths (colors) of light.

WINS

Windows Internet Name Service. A Windows name resolution service for network basic input/output system (NetBIOS) names. WINS is used by hosts running NetBIOS over TCP/IP (NetBT) to register NetBIOS names and resolve NetBIOS names to IP addresses.

WRR

Weighted round-robin. Scheme used to decide the queue from which the next packet should be transmitted.

XENPAK

Standard that defines a type of pluggable fiber-optic transceiver module that is compatible with the 10-Gigabit Ethernet (10 GbE) standard.

XENPAK module

10-Gigabit Ethernet fiber-optic transceiver. XENPAK modules are hot-insertable and hot-removable. *See also* MSA.

XENPAK Multisource Agreement

See MSA.

XENPAK-SR 10BASE-SR XENPAK

Media type that supports a link length of 26 meters on standard Fiber Distributed Data Interface (FDDI) grade multimode fiber (MMF). Up to 300-meter link lengths are possible with 2000 MHz/km MMF (OM3).

XENPAK-ZR 10GBASE-ZR XENPAK

Media type used for long-reach, single-mode (80–120 km) 10-Gigabit Ethernet metro applications.

XFP

10-Gigabit small form-factor pluggable transceiver. A transceiver that provides support for fiber-optic cables. XFPs are hot-insertable and hot-removable. *See also* SFP.

XML

Extensible Markup Language. Language used for defining a set of markers, called tags, which define the function and hierarchical relationships of the parts of a document or data set.

XML schema

Definition of the elements and structure of one or more Extensible Markup Language (XML) documents. Similar to a document type definition (DTD), but with additional information and written in XML.

XOR

Exclusive or. A logical operator (exclusive disjunction) in which the operation yields the result of true when one, and only one, of its operands is true.

XPath

Standard used in Extensible Stylesheet Language for Transformations (XSLT) to specify and locate elements in the input document's Extensible Markup Language (XML) hierarchy. XPath is fully described in the World Wide Web Consortium (W3C) specification at *http://w3c.org/TR/xpath*.

XSLT

Extensible Stylesheet Language for Transformations. A standard for processing Extensible Markup Language (XML) data developed by the World Wide Web Consortium (W3C). XSLT performs XML-to-XML transformations, turning an input XML hierarchy into an output XML hierarchy. The XSLT specification is on the W3C web site at *http://www.w3c.org/TR/xslt*.

zeroize

Process of removing all sensitive information, such as cryptographic keys and user passwords, from a router running JUNOS-FIPS.

Index

We'd like to hear your suggestions for improving our indexes. Send email to *index@oreilly.com*.

B

BA (behavior aggregate) classification, 470, 698
   in ingress processing, 479, 491
   in rewrite marking, 497, 517, 524–527
   with DiffServ, 487, 544–546
backbone area, OSPF, 126, 698
backbone router, OSPF, 124, 698
backplane (see midplane)
backup designated router (see BDR)
backup tunnels, IPSec VPN, 417–425
backward explicit congestion notification
      (see BECN)
bandwidth, 698
   adding to IP networks, 465
   as QoS parameter, 469
bandwidth community support, BGP, 237
bandwidth model, 698
bandwidth on demand (on a link), 698
bandwidth on demand (on a Services
      Router), 699
base station controller (see BSC)
base station subsystem (see BSS)
Base Station System GPRS Protocol (see
      BSSGP)
base tranceiver station (BTS), 700
Basic Rate Interface (see BRI)
B-channel, 699
BDR (backup designated router), OSPF, 123,
      698
BE (Best Effort) forwarding class, 472
bearer channel (see B-channel)
BECN (backward explicit congestion
      notification), 699
behavior aggregate classification (see BA
      classification)
Bellman-Ford algorithm, 699
BERT (bit error rate test), 699
Best Effort (BE) forwarding class, 472
BFD (Bidirectional Forwarding
      Detection), 51, 130, 699
BGP (Border Gateway Protocol), 200–207,
      227, 699
   AS number for, 89, 212
   asymmetric link speeds with, 214–219
   asymmetric load balancing with
      baseline configuration, validating, 221
      configuring BGP peering for, 227–233
      configuring generated default route
         for, 223–226

export policy for, 227, 235
import policy for, 227, 234
multipath option for, 237, 238–242
per-packet load-balancing algorithm
   for, 237, 242–243
requirements for, 219
   bandwidth community support, 237
   compared to IGP, 201
   External (EBGP), 207–209, 215, 710
   for dual-homed network, 212, 213
   for enterprise
      requirements for, 219
      when to use, 212
   Internal (IBGP), 207–212, 215, 216,
      217–219, 718
   multihoming
      aggregate route for, 254–256
      attributes affecting, 271, 275–286
      EBGP peering for, 251–254
      IBGP peering for, 256–265
      inbound (export) policy for, 271–286
      outbound (import) policy for, 249,
         266–270
      requirements for, 247–249
      route reflection for, 261–262, 268
   path selection, 205–207
   route attributes, 203
   routing loops, preventing, 217–219
   routing policy for, 92, 93, 104
   transit services, not providing, 216
bgp.l2vpn.0 route table, 84
bgp.l3vpn.0 route table, 84
Bidirectional Forwarding Detection (see BFD)
bidirectional NAT, 366
binary trees, and route filters, 98–100
bit error rate test (see BERT)
bit field match conditions, firewall
      filters, 310, 311, 699
bit rate, 699
BITS (Building Integrated Timing
      Source), 699
Blowfish method, 699
books and documentation
   IPSec: The New Security Standard for the
      Internet, Intranets, and Virtual
      Private Networks (Doraswamy;
      Harkins), 367
   JUNOS Cookbook (Garrett), 24
   "JUNOS Enhanced Services Migration
      Guide", 652

context-sensitive help, 704
contributing routes, 704
Control Board (see CB)
control plane, 542, 704
    separation from forwarding plane, 1
    (see also RE)
conversation (session), with stateful
            firewall, 362
Cooperative Association for Internet Data
            Analysis (CAIDA)
Coordinated Universal Time (see UTC)
core, 704
CoS (Class of Service), IP (see IP CoS)
CoS bits (see EXP (experimental) bits)
cosd process, 705
count action, firewall filters, 312
count command, 8
CPE (customer premises equipment), 705
craft interface, 705
Critical Security Parameter (see CSP)
CRL (certificate revocation list), 705
CRTP (Compressed Real-Time Transport
            Protocol), 354–356, 705
Crypto Accelerator Module, 705
Crypto Officer, 705
CS PHB, 489
CSCP (Class Selector code point), 486, 705
CSNP (complete sequence number
            PDU), 705
CSP (Critical Security Parameter), 705
CSPF (Constrained Shortest Path First), 705
CSU/DSU (channel service unit/data service
            unit), 45, 705
ct1 media type, 33
Ctrl keystrokes (EMACs), 7
cubic feet per minute (see CFM)
customer edge device (see CE device)
customer premises equipment (see CPE)
Customized Applicationso of Mobile
            Enhanced Logic (see CAMEL)
CVS (Concurrent Versions System), 705

D

daemon, 705
damping, 706
data circuit-terminating equipment (see
            DCE)
Data Encryption Standard (see DES)
data integrity, 293, 368
Data Link Switching (see DLSw)
data packet, 706

data plane, 542, 706
data plane stimulation, for CoS, 519
data service unit (see DSU)
data terminal equipment (see DTE)
database description packet, 706
data-link connection identifier (see DLCI)
data-MDT, 706
dcd (device control process), 706
DCE (data circuit-terminating
            equipment), 45, 706
D-channel, 706
DCU (destination class usage), 706
DDR (dial-on-demand routing) backup, 707
DE (discard-eligible) bits, 471, 706
deactivate command, 706
dead interval, 706
dead peer detection (see DPD)
default address, 706
default route, 706
default-information originate command, 169
deficit counter, MDDR scheduler, 500
delay
    as QoS parameter, 469
    in IP networks, 465
delay buffer size, CoS, 502
delay variation (see jitter)
delete command, 14, 25
delta channel (see D-channel)
demand circuit, 706
demilitarized zone (see DMZ)
denial of service (see DoS)
dense mode, multicast, 571, 586, 588, 706
dense wavelength-division multiplexing (see
            DWDM)
deny command, 299
DES (Data Encryption Standard), 706
designated router (see DR)
destination class usage (see DCU)
destination NAT, 365, 434, 442–446
    preventing routing loops using, 400
    stateful firewall and, 444–446
destination prefix length, 707
destination service access point (see DSAP)
device control process (see dcd)
DFC (dynamic flow capture), 707
DHCP (Dynamic Host Configuration
            Protocol), 303, 707
dial backup, 707
dialer filter, 707
dialer interface, 707
dialer profile, 707
dialer watch, 707

liblicense library, 723
libpcap application, 723
Lightweight Directory Access Protocol (see LDAP)
limited operational environment, 723
line loopback, 723
line-card chassis (see LCC)
link, 723
Link Control Protocol (see LCP)
link fragmentation and interleaving (see LFI)
link layer, mapping IP multicast address to, 573–582
Link Management Protocol (see LMP)
link protection, 723
link services intelligent queuing interfaces (see LSQ)
Link Services PIC, 348
link state protocols (see LS protocols)
Link TRAPs, SNMP, 339
links, combining (see MLPPP)
link-state acknowledgment, 723
link-state advertisement (see LSA)
link-state database (see LSDB)
link-state PDU, 723
link-state replication, 723
link-state request list, 723
link-state request packet, 723
link-state update, 723
link-switching router (see LSR)
LLC (logical link control), 723
LLC frame, 724
LLC protocol data unit (see LPDU)
LMI (local management interface), 724
LMP (Link Management Protocol), 724
lo0 interface, 31
load balancing, 724
load command, 19–21
load factory-default command, 653
load override terminal command, 664
load set command, 21
loading, 724
load-sharing routing policy, 246
Local Area Network Physical Layer Device (see LAN PHY)
local loop, interface, 66
local management interface (see LMI)
local packet, 724
local preference attribute, BGP, 203, 724
local RIB, 724
local significance, 724
log action, firewall filters, 312
logging, Layer 3 services, 387–389

logical interface, 724
logical link control (see LLC)
logical operator, 724
logical properties, of interface, 39
logical router, 724
logical unit, for interfaces, 38, 39
login class, 297
longer match type, route filter, 101, 724
looking glass, 277
loopback filters, 317–319
loopback interface, 724
looped interfaces, 66
loops, preventing (see routing loops, preventing)
loose command, 331
loose hop, 724
loss pattern, as QoS parameter, 469
loss priority, CoS, 471
loss, as QoS parameter, 469
loss-priority map, 725
lower-speed IQ interfaces, 725
LPDU (LLC protocol data unit), 725
LS (link state) protocols, 92, 103
LSA (link-state advertisement), 122, 725
    areas and, 125–127
    filtering, 92
    flooding, 122, 125–126
    types of, 127
LSA messages, OSPF, 122
LSDB (link-state database), 122, 125, 723
LSI (label-switched interface), 725
LSP (label-switched path), 725
LSP (link-state PDU) (see link-state PDU)
LSQ (link services intelligent queuing interfaces), 725
LSR (label-switching router), 725
lt interface, 395

M

M7i routers
    CoS behavior for, 507–516
    queues, number of, 514
    services deployment on, 349
    WRED implementation, 513
MAC (media access control) layer, 725
MAC address, 573–582, 725
maintenance windows, 24
MAM (maximum allocation bandwidth constraints model), 725
management Ethernet interface, 31, 725
Management Information Base (see MIB)
management interface, 31

Colophon

The animal on the cover of *JUNOS Enterprise Routing* is Tengmalm's owl (*Aegolius funereus*), also known in North America as the Boreal owl. The owl's distinguishing features include pale or bright yellow eyes and a brown body spotted with white flecks (its belly is usually off-white).

This solitary, largely unsociable owl lives in thick forests throughout North America and in various mountain ranges throughout Eurasia. They often nest in the old homes of woodpeckers. Although the creatures are unfriendly, they may show loyalty to their families by raising their young generation after generation in the same home.

The bird's namesake is Swedish naturalist Peter Gustaf Tengmalm, who improved upon a previous classification system for the owl. Occasionally the bird's cry will sound like the peal of a funeral bell, hence the *funereus* in its species name. In North America, scientists named the owl after the Greek god of the north wind, Boreas, referring not to the owl's voice, but to its northern habitats.

While it is known for it funereal cries, the owl's voice does carry a range of notes. A commonly heard song from the owl is its territorial call, which sounds as if the bird is singing the word "poop" several times in rapid succession. When wooing a female, the male sings a series of stutters that eventually crescendos in a long trill of up to 350 notes.

The cover image is from *Dover's Animals*. The cover font is Adobe ITC Garamond. The text font is Linotype Birka; the heading font is Adobe Myriad Condensed; and the code font is LucasFont's TheSans Mono Condensed.

Related Titles from O'Reilly

Networking

802.11 Wireless Networks: The Definitive Guide, *2nd Edition*

Asterisk: The Future of Telephony, *2nd Edition*

Asterisk Cookbook

Cisco IOS Cookbook, *2nd Edition*

Cisco IOS Access Lists

Cisco IOS in a Nutshell, *2nd Edition*

DNS & BIND Cookbook

DNS and BIND, *5th Edition*

Essential SNMP, *2nd Edition*

Exchange Server Cookbook

IP Routing

IPv6 Essentials, *2nd Edition*

IPv6 Network Administration

Junos Cookbook

LDAP System Administration

Managing NFS and NIS, *2nd Edition*

Network Troubleshooting Tools

Network Warrior

RADIUS

ScreenOS Cookbook

sendmail, *4th Edition*

sendmail Cookbook

SpamAssassin

Switching to VoIP

TCP/IP Network Administration, *3rd Edition*

Time Management for System Administrators

Using Samba, *3rd Edition*

Using SANs and NAS

VoIP Hacks

Windows Server 2003 Network Administration

Wireless Hacks, *2nd Edition*

Zero Configuration Networking: The Definitive Guide

Arriving at the
maison de couture

THE MEC
SMILE

CAROLINE EVANS

HANICAL

MODERNISM AND
THE FIRST FASHION SHOWS
IN FRANCE AND AMERICA,
1900-1929

Yale University Press   New Haven and London

Design concept by Phil Baines
Layout by Gillian Malpass

Printed in China

Library of Congress Cataloging-in-Publication Data
Evans, Caroline, 1954-
  The mechanical smile : modernism and the first fashion shows in
France and America 1900–1929 / Caroline Evans.
     pages cm
  Includes bibliographical references and index.
  ISBN 978-0-300-18953-7 (alk. paper)
  1. Fashion shows–France–History.
  2. Fashion shows–United States–History.
  3. Modernism (Aesthetics)–France.
  4. Modernism (Aesthetics)–United States.
  I. Title.
  TT502.E824 2013
  746.9'20944–dc23
                2012028814

A catalogue record for this book is available from
The British Library

Endpapers: Stage costumes by Paul Iribe for *Rue de la Paix* at the
Théâtre Vaudeville illustrated in a fashion show line-up. Roger-Milès,
'Paquin, Canada et la drame', February or March 1912. Fashion Museum, Bath
and North East Somerset Council / The Bridgeman Art Library.

Page i: Illustration showing Baron de Meyer arriving at the *maison de couture*,
Harper's Bazar, April 1925.

Facing page: May Co buyer's card, closed and open. Paris, Bibliothèque
Forney.

Page vi: Bob Davis, New York buyer's card announcing the imminent arrival
of the new Paris fashions in New York in 1920. Paris, Bibliothèque Forney.

Greetings from Paris.

Am thinking of you as I attend the important Fall openings of the great couturiers

I am so eager to have you see the length of the new skirts & the new colors & the many interesting versions of the new silhouette.

Am about to return with many lovely original models & authentic copies of the successes. Will advise you soon of the exact date of our showing – Best wishes

Sincerely

Beatrice Oden

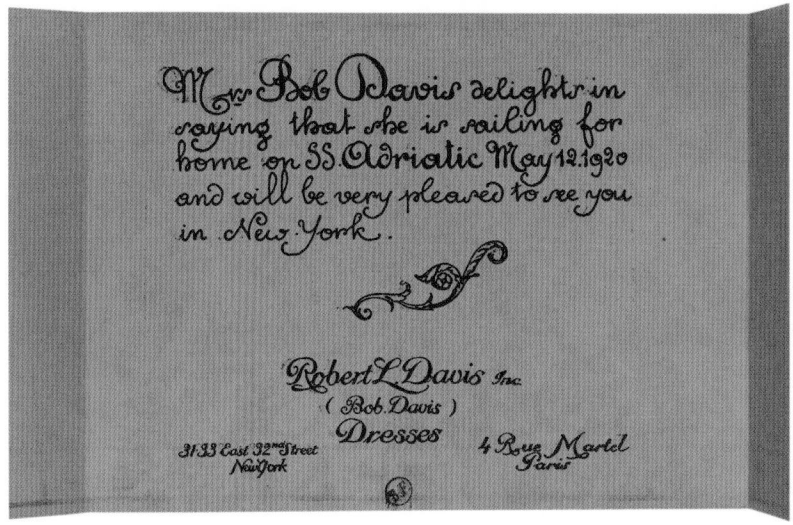

Mrs Bob Davis delights in
saying that she is sailing for
home on SS Adriatic May 12.1920
and will be very pleased to see you
in New York.

Robert L. Davis Inc.
(Bob Davis)
Dresses

31-33 East 32nd Street   4 Rue Martel
New York   Paris

CONTENTS

INTRODUCTION

1 Mannequins at Poiret
photographed for
L'Illustration in 1910.
(www.lillustration.com)

This history of the early fashion shows in the United States of America and France from about the 1880s to 1929 identifies their relationship to modernism. It argues that the Fordist aesthetics of the fashion show produced a modernist and rationalised body in which commerce and culture converged. By asserting that the show translated what one journalist called 'the arithmetic of fashion' into visual seduction, the book brings economic and design history together in a new formation. Indeed, the fashion show is a nodal point for the convergence of several different histories that are rarely written about together: those of business, international trade, consumption, women, work and fashion, as well as of cinema, revue theatre and visual art. The research for the book has led me to new sources, in particular film in the silent period, and new ways of thinking about theory as both historical and contingent. It has spurred me to think about new methods for writing the history of the body, and to investigate how its ephemeral and intangible t---s linger in fashionable ways of walking, moving and posing. As a result, the book makes the case for understanding fashion in a wider context than those of material culture and design history alone. It suggests that fashion is also an embodied, four-dimensional practice that exists in both space and time and, therefore, that it is an important, if often overlooked, part of the history of sensibilities as well as of commerce and culture.

The book falls into two parts consisting of six chapters each. Part I, a history of the first fashion shows from 1900, including a chapter on their nineteenth-century prehistory, introduces the key themes of the book: modernism, gender, class, the rationalisation of the body, and the commercial and cultural relations between America and France, both in the international garment trade and in the wider culture. It thus contains both synchronic and diachronic accounts, linking the history of the show to other aspects of visual culture in the period. Part II develops and explores some contradictions that emerged in Part I, by focusing on the contradictory figure of the mannequin, as the fashion model was called. These include: her ambiguous status as both object and subject; her physical malleability that mirrored the psychological malleability of the 'New Woman'; and her embodiment (highly disturbing to her contemporaries) of future sensibilities.

As a history of the first fashion shows, the book brings much new knowledge into the public domain and revises aspects of the existing literature that are either incomplete or erroneous. It shows how, from the nineteenth century, French haute couture was a global export industry, rather than a luxury trade catering only to rich individual clients, as is suggested in many older histories of couture.[1] It argues that this was the reason for the emergence of fashion shows, to sell the biannual collections to international buyers coming twice a year to Paris. The Paris trade was, however, an unusual one, in that it exported not goods but ideas, in the form of model dresses and the right to reproduce them. These were bought by overseas manufacturers to recreate them in simplified form on a mass scale for their domestic markets. Buyers from all over the world converged on Paris twice a year for the biannual collections but the most powerful were the North Americans, with their vast domestic markets and larger manufacturing capacity.[2] That is why the book focuses on France and America alone, as, respectively, the most important exporter and the most important importer in the international fashion trade. The coverage of the early twentieth-century fashion show foregrounds an aspect of fashion history rarely covered by historians, the crucial interface between the craft-based French fashion system and the mass production of the American garment industry.

Even so, this is not a complete history of fashion shows in both France and America over thirty years, as it leaves many gaps. Rather, it is the history of a relationship between the two countries, played out in the interaction of the fashion industries of each, a relationship which was therefore commercial, cultural and ideological at once. I have focused on the important periods of the Franco-American relationship as it developed over thirty years, rather than on the parallel developments of the fashion show in each country. That is why, for example, although all six chapters of Part I emphasise the importance of the idea of French fashion to Americans, only one, Chapter 4, is devoted to American fashion shows. Chapters 5 and 6 nevertheless show how the idea of 'American-ness' (américanisme) dominated French fashion in the 1920s, a shift due largely to economic factors, namely the impoverishment of France due to the First World War and changes in the relative values of the franc and the dollar in the post-war years.

Beyond the claims of individual designers, I looked to structures rather than narrative to think about this relationship. Certainly, there is no narrative to the fashion show: some women come into a room, they walk up and down and they exit. Other women, and a few men, look at them. This goes on for decades. The story of fashion modelling is far from exciting. On the contrary, it is stupefyingly monotonous. What gives it meaning are its commercial and cultural structures. These encompass the history of garment trade relations between France and America; the ideas of F. W. Taylor, published in 1911, on 'the scientific management of the workplace'; the development of mass production and the invention of Henry Ford's moving automobile assembly line in 1913; the emancipation of women; the development of cinema, variety theatre and the chorus line as modern forms of popular entertainment; and, in visual culture and art, the move towards abstraction, simultaneity and machine aesthetics.

More specific revisions to the early history of fashion shows concern the innovations of the designers Worth, Lucile and Poiret, and the contribution of other, less well known, designers. Charles Frederick Worth is credited as the first haute couturier to use living mannequins in the nineteenth century. Yet, as Chapter 1 shows, the house of Pinguat, which attracted a strong cohort of transatlantic buyers, also showed clothes on living mannequins in this period. The invention of the fashion show is usually attributed to the English designer Lucile (Lady Duff Gordon) in London around 1900 and she was undoubtedly innovative in this respect. Well before Lucile opened branches in Paris and New York, however, fashion shows were being staged in those cities by all sections of the industry, from American department stores to French couture houses. Furthermore, far from being initiated by Worth, Lucile and Poiret alone, as many fashion histories suggest (following the boastful claims of the designers themselves), early twentieth-century fashion shows were staged at all the major French houses between 1900 and 1910. Many are little known today, while others are better known but await their historians. They include Béchoff David, Beer, Boué Soeurs, Callot Soeurs, Doucet, Félix, Jenny, Margaine Lacroix, Paquin and Redfern, and there are many more.

Lucile was one of the early international designers, who opened first in London and then used her famous mannequins to open branches in New York (1910), Paris (1911) and Chicago (1914). Her work is rarely contextualised, however, with the industries of France and North America. By describing her relationship to both through the staging of her fashion shows in these cities, the book extends existing accounts. Similarly, the French couturier Paul Poiret is usually credited as the first to show his designs on uncorseted mannequins and the first to scandalise the public by taking his mannequins in skimpy dresses to the Paris races. Yet, as Chapters 3 and 10 show, both were achieved in 1908 by the firm of Margaine

Lacroix with its *robe Sylphide*, or 'sheath dress'. Finally, with regard to the pre-war period, Chapter 2 uncovers new material from the 1910s about the fashion shows and design stratagems of Jeanne Paquin and Jean Patou, the latter trading from 1912 as Parry, which reveal a proto-modernist design aesthetic a good ten years prior to the modernism that typifies 1920s styles.

Chapter 5 provides a rare account of how the Paris trade continued to operate throughout the First World War when the American garment industry became more important than ever to the French, who continued to stage fashion shows for American buyers, even under German bombardment. It reveals how the balance of power between buyers and sellers shifted subtly so that, by the 1920s, Americans were thought by the French, with some resentment, to be able to call the tune in fashion, due to the strength of the dollar against a weak franc. By the 1920s, most aspects of the modern fashion show were in place, as described in Chapter 6. Then, as today, couturiers understood its vital role in international marketing and promotion, not only sales. In 1911 Poiret had toured Europe with his French mannequins; in 1924 Patou visited America to recruit American mannequins to his Paris catwalk. Although the Great Crash of 1929 fundamentally shifted the trade relations of both countries, the book shows how the protocols and practices which are a central part of today's industry were established by 1929.

Beyond the specificities of early twentieth-century fashion history, the book takes a broader look at the question of modernism, both by inserting the fashion show into its history and by suggesting how that insertion might add to, or alter, the understanding of modernism itself. I scrutinise this issue in three respects throughout the book. Firstly, I assume that the body itself can be modernist, in its articulation and styling. Secondly, I argue that the fashion show not only reflected modernist sensibilities but also engendered them, which involves rethinking modernism through the agency of the body as both performative and gestural. Thirdly, I argue for the fashion mannequin's place in what I call a modernist flow of images, commodities, bodies and styles that circulated in the early twentieth-century city. All three approaches are deeply enmeshed in the history they interpret. They also overlap each other and, rather than discussing them as stand-alone topics, I thread them through the detailed and sometimes complex narratives of the fashion show and the mannequin. Drawing less on art historical accounts that focus on the relationship of modernism to the historical avant-gardes

and more on other cultural histories (literary, musical and theatrical), I situate modernism in the context of everyday life, leisure, popular culture and work. The book thus privileges modernist sensibilities, actions, performances, gestures and technologies over the images, texts, designs and artefacts of the modern movement.

The cultural theorist Peter Wollen has described 'the modernist body' as rational, hygienic and streamlined in his writing about Coco Chanel and Jean Patou's designs of the 1920s.[3] If the mannequin's body is 'modernist', however, hers is the modernism of what I call the 'rationalisation of the body' rather than of vanguard art and politics. I investigate this dominant theme throughout the book. Without a new relationship of time, motion and standardised bodies in the early twentieth century, French fashion would never have been able to promote itself so successfully on the world stage. I examine the gradual streamlining and rationalisation of the mannequin's body in the fashion show before and after the war, and compare this to the rationalisation of the body in adjacent fields. These include work (Taylorism and the early time and motion studies of the Gilbreths), leisure (cinema, popular dance crazes and the chorus line, including Kracauer's writing on the 'mass ornament') and art (the mechanical bodies and simultaneity of, for example, Marcel Duchamp and the Italian Futurists).[4] I look at the couture house interior as a lens that multiplied the image of the mannequin to infinity, so that she became an image of both backstage production and export sales. In all these ways, I argue, modernist production was 'pictured' in fashion marketing, as I link the first fashion shows to other economic and cultural arenas in which the body was similarly rationalised.

The fashion show was not only about the rationalisation of the body, however. It was also about movement and modernity in a period of the emancipation of women, at a time when modernity became particularly associated with speed and acceleration – that sense of the pace and dynamism of modern life that is apparent in the art of the Italian Futurists. These new iterations of modernity constructed a counter-narrative of the body, in which the mannequin is paradigmatically modern, not merely modernist. Through her styling and presentation, the early twentieth-century mannequin provides evidence that the conjunction of movement and modernity was not solely a feature of 1920s modernism but, rather, that a modernist articulation of the body was occurring in fashion before the First World War. Walter Benjamin described the advent of 'new velocities' that gave modern life an altered rhythm; from 1900 the desire to see women's fashion in motion flourished on both sides of the Atlantic, as mannequins tangoed, slithered, swaggered and undulated across the modelling stages of London, Berlin, Vienna, Paris and New York.[5] Before the war, Paris mannequins intrigued their public by appearing at the racetrack and on ocean liners, strolling amid the race-goers and the passengers. Back in the couture house, they were the object of the fascinated gaze, where their varied audiences, both male and female, comprised trade buyers, private clients and – a not insignificant category – fashion pirates. Wherever they went, their contemporaries regarded them as mobile clothes-horses but they were also modern subjects, women who popularised a new, slender ideal and professionalised the performance of walking and posing.

My analysis of these new body shapes, practices and performances is predicated on the notion that bodily styles – the walk, the pose and the gesture – can be modernist. Here I was inspired by the way in which the literary scholar Michael Levenson looks beyond art and literature to identify a series of early twentieth-century performative actions as constitutive of modernism: 'What once seemed the exclusive affairs of "modern masters", the "men of 1914" (as Wyndham Lewis called them), now stands revealed as a complex of inventive gestures, daring performances'.[6] Levenson differentiates what he calls textual and gestural modernism, finding evidence of the latter in the personal style of artists and their audiences:

> men in capes, women on bicycles, workers in the square, suffragettes in the street, audiences in the theatre. The increased visibility, not only of modernist art works but of modernist bodies, was central to the cultural milieu. Still more significantly, gestural Modernism appears in those ephemeral happenings staged by writers and artists – the spectacles engineered by Marinetti and the futurists and the riotous evenings at the Cabaret Voltaire among the Dadaists. We need to acknowledge the special character of gestural Modernism, a major lineage within the period constituted by unrepeatable spectacles. The performances were not offered as texts, nor were they made permanent in paint. If they survive at all, and this was not their aim, it is only in half-reliable newspaper reports or memoirs. But the unrepeatable event and the evanescent gesture that 'takes the place of poetry' [as T. S. Eliot suggested regarding the Parisian avant-garde] were crucial to the adversary culture.[7]

Levenson confines his argument to the oppositional artistic movements of Dada and Futurism, yet he is attentive both to audiences and to the effects of such 'cultural sensation' on turn-of-the-century everyday life, and argues that 'alongside the daily rituals of work and leisure were indelible signs of another way of life'.[8] He thereby finesses the canonical distinction between bourgeois conformity and avant-garde radicalism,

suggesting that in the late nineteenth century 'the dominant middle class culture was a culture of change, thrusting and ambitious in its industry, its technology, its empire', so that 'The agon of Modernism was not a collision between novelty and tradition but a *contest of novelties*, a struggle to find the trajectory of the new'.[9] It is in this sense that the emerging form of the fashion show can be understood as modernist, as a contest of novelties that were at once conservative and adventurous, allowing the fashion industry to imagine or, rather, to image-in, its immediate future. Although confined to the analysis of a certain type of artistic production, Levenson's concept of gestural modernism, and the attention he pays to audiences and popular media such as newspapers, suggest a new way to think about other forms of cultural encounter and urban spectacle, particularly those of fashion.

Such an approach runs counter to the distinction between modernism and mass culture made by Andreas Huyssen in *After the Great Divide* (1986), which was derived from the Frankfurt School's critique of mass culture.[10] From the mid-1990s, reacting against the idea of the autonomy of art, as well as to Huyssen's argument, a number of scholars began to identify a relationship between the literary avant-garde and the commercial cultures of modernism. In a series of materialist, socio-economic and philosophical readings of modernism, they traced links between avant-garde texts and the languages of advertising, marketing and celebrity.[11] John Xiros Cooper has even argued polemically that 'modernism . . . *is* . . . the culture of capitalism' and that capitalism 'emerges from the same gene pool as modernism' (although I disagree with much of his analysis and think it would be more accurate to say that modernism emerged in a particular phase of capitalism).[12] At the same time, the art historian Thomas Crow has despaired that radical art could ever avoid recuperation, lamenting that 'the avant-garde serves as a kind of research and development arm of the culture industry'.[13]

Be that as it may, as Lawrence Rainey has argued, 'Modernism's interchanges with the emerging world of consumerism, fashion and display were far more complicated and ambiguous than is often assumed'.[14] This is the junction box where fashion gets wired to other cultural and economic forms. In opening it up to see how they connect, the present volume foregrounds the role of fashion as a material, quotidian, cultural and commercial practice. By linking the fashion show to other such practices in work, leisure, consumption and art, I develop the idea of a modernism that is performative, gestural and corporeal. To the extent that modern fashion was embedded in movement, and therefore in time, I conceive of fashion as a situated, embodied and spatial practice –

even where it is impossible to revive its gestures from the amber of time – as much as a form of design or an item of commercial exchange.

Rainey's invocation of consumerism, fashion and display in relation to modernism brings to mind the dance historian Lynn Garafola's phrase 'lifestyle modernism', a term she uses to criticise a specific kind of consumerist chic which turned away from the revolutionary aspects of modernism to pander to wealthy conservatives and nationalists.[15] In common with those historians who have argued that phenomena as disparate as advertising and fascism may be modernist, I would make the case for a concept of modernism that stretches beyond art and literature to urban sensibilities and even to commercial exchange.[16] All the more reason, then, to situate the argument in the context of politics, albeit a more complex model than the binaries of vanguard and mainstream. Here the writing of David Harvey on the politics of modernism and space, Stephen Kern on the culture of time and space and Fredric Jameson on modernism and imperialism, all help to illuminate how macro-economic forces acted on the early twentieth-century spaces and bodies of modernism.[17] Fashion modelling was not only a new technology of the body in motion but also, and equally, of the image of the body in time, and Harvey and Kern's work helps to situate modernism politically and historically in relation to changes in technology, production, communications, and the ensuing changes in the measurement and perception of time, space and speed.

Jameson's essay is especially fruitful because of the way he connects the formal innovations of modernism to its political and material structures. Written in 1990, it set out to rethink the historical phenomenon of modernism in new ways. His argument that imperialism made its mark on the forms and structures of art and literature undoes the notions of 'the modern' as apolitical and of art as autonomous. In a lengthy analysis of the opening pages of E. M. Forster's *Howard's End*, Jameson discusses the spatial representation of the English countryside seen from a train window as it rushes by, and finds in it evidence of 'cinematographic perception'. He argues that two formal developments in the modernist period, movie technology and literary language, are congruent: both escape from notions of realism, empiricism, objectivity, psychology or subjectivity. Coming full circle, at the end of the essay he reconnects the cinematic spaces of the novel to imperialism and to the history of empire.

Jameson discusses clearly how, in a counter-intuitive way, modernism reflects changing notions of the physical landscape and, although he writes about the 'national' body in the landscape, his essay has real resonance for human bodies and, in particular, the modernist body. The 'new spatial language' that he identifies in Forster's writing is, in its own way, a part of what I call 'gestural modernism', captured in Jameson's description of a three-dimensional and bodily experience of space and time, one in which, by moving in and through it, bodies themselves create social, perceptual and even literary space.[18]

Nor can the politics of gender within the modern period be ignored. If the body was made modernist by the fashion show, which was a commercial enterprise, what were the implications for women as commodities, as tools of representation and as agents? Of course, one can partially answer that question with the extensive literature on gender and consumption in the period.[19] Clearly, Judith Butler's important work on performativity has influenced thinking about women and gender.[20] Both sets of ideas have informed my treatment of the 'doubleness' of the fashion model as both a subject and an object. Yet one can also take a sideways look at the question via Peggy Phelan's work on performance as 'unmarked'. Phelan intriguingly suggests that, in a culture in which images of women are still over-determined, a certain invisibility is in itself powerful.[21] Her ideas on the transient – hence 'unmarked' – nature of live performance have a direct relevance to early fashion modelling. Such an argument would seem tautological in the case of the spectacularly visible fashion mannequin were it not for her particular skill at turning herself into an abstraction.

In this, she embodied a central attribute of modernism. Another literary scholar whose work is particularly productive for thinking about encounters across high and low culture is Judith Brown, whose book on modernist glamour spans poetry and perfume. Brown finds the same ethereality in Chanel No. 5 as in Wallace Stevens, the same transparency in cellophane fashions as in Gertrude Stein's aesthetic of blankness.[22] Of central relevance to the performance of the first fashion models is Brown's argument that the aesthetic of blankness is a formal structure which was a significant component of modernist aesthetics; and that in the face of Garbo as much as in the poetry of T. S. Eliot, 'modernism defiantly took up the empty, the blank, or the transparent, projecting it as a historical condition and aesthetic ideal'.[23] In her claim that glamour was intrinsically modernist ('glamour in the period inheres in the very problem of modernist form') Brown describes many characteristics of the mannequin, namely impersonality, blankness, abstraction, surface, polish, the look of alienation, the eclipse of subjectivity, the effacement of personality and the lack of affect.[24] This is rich terrain from which to theorise the traditional affectlessness of fashion modelling as a significant cultural form, rather than as a simple failure to signify or to emote.

Can fashion be modernist, then? Undoubtedly yes and this book sets out to explore some of the ways in which it can be so. Few fashion historians, however, have explicitly situated fashion in the context of modernism. One of the rare books that has addressed the idea of fashion within modernism is by an architectural rather than a fashion historian. In *White Walls, Designer Dresses*, Mark Wigley argues that the ideas of contemporary dress reformers covertly pervaded modernist architectural writing; he posits fashion as a feminised 'other' that issued a challenge from within to the masculinist discourses of the modern movement.[25] In Wigley's illuminating account, fashion becomes a dark continent that reveals the anti-rational tectonics of the design discourses and manifestos of modernism.

The art historian Nancy Troy's *Couture Culture* looks at the tension between originality and reproduction in the art and fashion of modernism, focusing on the designer Paul Poiret and the artist Marcel Duchamp. Troy's understanding of how doubling lies at the heart of haute couture is fundamental to the premise of this book. Her account of modernism, too, spans elite and popular culture and draws on theatre history as much as art history to understand the hybrid nature of Poiret's fashion shows in the 1910s. Troy is also one of the few writers on the relationship between art and fashion who goes behind their superficial similarities to investigate the underlying structural differences between them; her book reminds one that although two phenomena look alike, it does not mean that they are the same thing.[26]

If few fashion scholars have considered fashion's relationship to modernism, many have written about its relationship to modernity.[27] Modernism and modernity are not antithetical, however. In her seminal work on fashion and modernity first published in 1985, Elizabeth Wilson argued for fashion as an engine of modernity, rather than a mere reflection of it. Her work has subtly informed much subsequent fashion scholarship, including this volume, in which the notoriously slippery distinction between modernism and modernity has proved hard to maintain at times, particularly in the attempt to situate modernist fashion in the context of everyday life rather than of art and design. More recently, Catherine Driscoll has argued that Coco Chanel's modernism lay not so much in her stylistic innovations as in the new image and idea of a fashion designer that she epitomised, as well as in the way her mannequins exemplified fashion in motion, in contrast to the static images of other designers. Driscoll differentiates between Modernism the movement and what she terms

modernism (with a small M) 'which names an attitude to modernity that has much less formal or temporal coherence'.[28] While such an approach can risk collapsing the categories of modernism and modernity into one, I too would argue strenuously for an expanded definition of modernism that can incorporate commerce, advertising and fashion – and not only the stylistic innovations of the last but also, for example, its bodily gestures, sensibilities and attitudes. In this respect, the focus of the present volume is not on modernist fashion design itself so much as on how the early twentieth-century fashion industry designed bodies as modernist.

Here dance and music scholarship has proved pivotal in formulating the idea of an embodied modernism, particularly books by Mark Franko, Rhonda Garelick, Mary Davis and Carrie J. Preston.[29] While Franko's study of Isadora Duncan, Martha Graham and Merce Cunningham puts the politics back into modernist dance, Garelick, Davis and Preston, in their different ways, put the popular back into modernism. Their treatments have implications for the study of fashion modelling in the period. Through the concept of 'bodily modernism', Preston highlights the practice of solo posing, while Garelick inscribes the turn-of-the-century dancer Loie Fuller in the modernist canon. Like the first fashion models, Fuller in her performances repudiated both the expression of emotion and the idea of the body as natural. Like them, Fuller produced herself as an object, introducing a 'modernist self-consciousness' to her performance by drawing attention to its own physicality.[30] Davis's treatment of the relationship of music, fashion and modernism explains the context in which the simplified tango of the popular dance craze of 1913 can be understood as a modernist dance, and the tango teas and tango fashion shows that it engendered a form of modernist spectacle. She shows how, particularly in the years leading up to the First World War, musical modernism, with its relationship to the rhythms of the body that fashion also enjoyed, combined avant-garde experimentation and popular melody without any contradiction.

The formal innovations of the Ballets Russes also provide suggestive evidence of a form of modernism rooted in the styling and choreography of the body in performance; they too helped me to think about how fashion used new ways of moving and posing on the modelling stage. Dance research prioritises human movement as a locus of social meaning, because 'social meanings are both enacted and produced through the body, and not merely inscribed upon it', as Jane C. Desmond argues; I found that the histories of dance, both popular and experimental, provided models from which to develop a concept of popular, performative and gestural modernism that 'worked' for the fashion show better than accounts of modernism in visual art and design.[31]

The final area in which I conceptualise the fashion show as modernist is with regard to cinematic time: Chapter 12 is devoted to the idea of the pose as a temporary halt in the flow of time. Fashion shows and film came into being at almost exactly the same moment and the history of the fashion shows covered in the book, from about 1900 to 1929, is almost the same period as silent film, from 1895 to 1929. Embracing modernist abstraction over psychological depth and realism, the mannequin in motion resembled a piece of film footage; the book concludes by positing the fashion show as a kind of film strip of modern sensibilities.

A principal contention of the book is that the fashion trade drew on the artistic language of modernism in the way it streamlined the body in the fashion show, both in the chorus-line formations of pre-war parades and in the modernist scenography of post-war shows that used colour and massed human bodies to create abstract moving patterns on stage. If, as Stuart Ewen argued, 'photogenic beauty rests its definition of perfection on a smooth, standardized, and lifeless modernism, a machine aesthetic in the guise of a human', in the mechanical smile of my title it reached its apotheosis.[32] Yet, against this rather stern view of the fashion show as modernist, and the fashion body as rationalised, reified, controlled and subject to the discursive regimes of early twentieth-century modernity, a counter-narrative emerged in the course of researching this book. It evoked the fleeting moments of lived experience that are barely recoverable nearly a hundred years later – the mannequin's walk, her pose, her smile, her gestures. These ephemeral traces of the past are etched by the modernist technologies of chronophotography and newsreel film or pictured in the banalities of fashion journalism and the surfaces of everyday life, including reflections long gone from the few remaining mirrored interiors of Parisian couture houses. Not so much a history as an archaeology of images, objects, spaces and gestures, for this aspect of the research I was inspired by Pierre Nora's work on 'realms of memory' to extrapolate from these fragments an idea of fashion as a situated, embodied and spatial practice as much as it is an image, object, design or artefact.[33]

The fashion show, despite its visual clarity and modernist idiom, revealed a set of paradoxes, or contradictions, which reflected those of modernity. Above all in the figure of the mannequin, these contradictions resolved themselves in images of ambivalence and alienation. New fashions required new ways of moving and the mannequins became technicians of the walk. The proleptic embodiment of future aspirations, pre-war mannequins spearheaded the new, slender body shape that is still the desired body ideal today. In all these respects the mannequin modelled modernism. Yet she modelled it in ways that were sometimes contrary. While Chapters 1 to 8 show how the mannequin's body was, first of all, a rationalised, abstracted body and, secondly, a gendered body in modern motion, Chapters 9 to 12 explore how hers was also a body that felt, gestured and thought, often invisibly, below the radar of historical investigation.

Here I was helped by the historian Daniel Wickberg's distinction between two impulses in cultural history. Wickberg differentiates the history of sensibilities from a more dominant trend that foregrounds categories of race, class and gender in social history.[34] Both draw on images as important visual sources but Wickberg distinguishes those historians for whom representations yield insights about discourse and cultural representation from those for whom images are powerful (and sometimes the only) sources of evidence of lived experience. Perhaps because of my interest in the former, I was all the more intrigued when the paucity of evidence of the latter piqued my curiosity. A sometimes disturbing figure, the mannequin was a new kind of working woman who embodied the idea of femininity as alterable and perfectible, an idea that escalated in the 1920s and was commensurate with the psychoanalyst Joan Rivière's articulation of 'womanliness as a masquerade' in 1929: a malleable, mobile, gendered, subject-in-process.[35] This idea of femininity as an unstable category challenged my simple classification of the modernist body as 'rationalised' and disrupted the neatness of my categories, as I began to find evidence of another body, revealing traces of subjectivities, of daily life and its vicissitudes, of gesture and of physicality. The walk, the pose, the smile and the disdainful attitude, those techniques of the body, were part of the professional repertoire of the mannequin. As much as they were discursive representations, they were also her daily bread and butter.

For this aspect of the research, I drew to some extent on the histories of labour, the body and sensibilities to think about a range of questions, spanning the working conditions and the more ephemeral, performative features of the mannequin's profession. Yet, while there is a store of rich and sometimes recondite literature on the histories of work and of the body, the mannequin herself proved curiously intransigent in this respect. If the mirrored interiors of the couture houses pictured her rationalisation

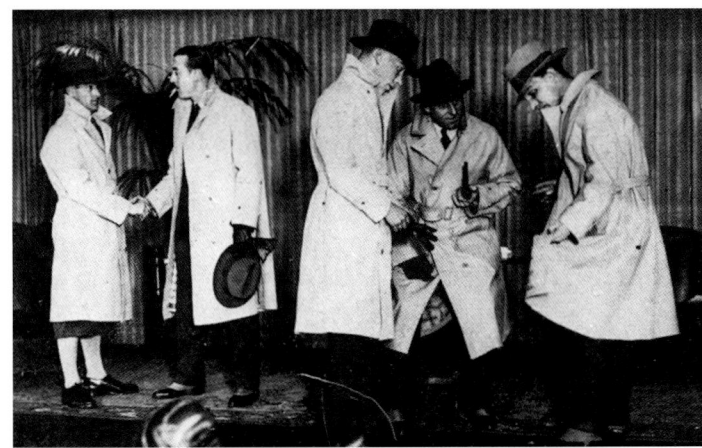

2 'England Has Dared' wrote the French magazine *Adam* in 1929, in its caption to this rare male fashion show at the Great Nottingham Co-operative in London. Courtesy Fashion Institute of Technology/ SUNY, FIT Library Department of Special Collections and FIT Archives.

within the fashion system by multiplying her to infinity, they also, simultaneously, bisected and refracted her image, camouflaging her in the very place of her employment, making her disappear from view as frequently as they revealed her.

So too did the real, embodied mannequin prove frustratingly hard to track. Her symbolic objectification was combined with a powerful historical invisibility. The latter was poignantly underscored by the few traces I found: occasional descriptions of salaries, strikes or employment practices; small legacies that actresses left to their favourite mannequins; descriptions of how hard it was for the mannequins to get in to work from the suburbs during the Paris floods of 1910; vivid photographs of a rare day out in Paris during the war; three surviving model dresses, no more, that can definitively be shown to have been worn by mannequins in fashion shows. To interpret these dislocated fragments, I drew on Nora's invocation of 'spaces, gestures, images and objects' and on his idea that traces of the past survive in modern bodies, languages and practices.[36] Here the valence of the sources sometimes proved surprising. Verbal accounts of the mannequin walk were often more evocative than visual images or film; the fashion press added a significant dimension to company records, when journalists impressionistically used the language of nineteenth-century fairy plays to show how fashion marketing occluded the show's commercial imperatives.

In a period when the social and economic emancipation of women were the urgent and pressing questions of the day, however, what kind of agency can be attributed to women whose performance was so fleeting, so ambiguous and so minimal? It would be easy to analyse the first mannequins solely as women who were objectified by the gender and economic inequalities of an advanced consumer society; yet, while they undoubtedly were

objectified by those processes, that would be to objectify them doubly. For they were also living women and women making a living, even if their working lives are not covered by labour historians of the garment trade. Like actresses, mannequins were barely respectable but, unlike them, they were not celebrities. Mute figures who never spoke except to utter the name or price of a dress, they were nevertheless forceful visual icons and, as such, issue a challenge to several gender and theatre historians' analyses of visual culture and female autonomy in the modernist period. The mannequins' image was powerfully suggestive to their contemporaries. They appear to have been a touchstone for concerns about femininity, nationhood, class, status and sexuality, judging by the many individual descriptions of them, which have to stand in for more solid, concrete evidence of their lives and work. Their objectification, as much as their professional capacity to dissimulate, troubled their contemporaries. It is above all in her staging of selfhood as a pose, her inauthenticity, her willed objectification and her reification of her own image that the mannequin's modernity still has currency today.

The fashion model is simply a more exaggerated version of everyone who has ever posed for a photograph or set themselves up as an object for the gaze. Modelling is about the relationship between reality and representation and the first mannequins foregrounded the way in which visual identity can be socially constructed through the power of self-representation.[37] Susan Sontag wrote that 'to live is also to pose'. In her study of the artist's model, Wendy Steiner discusses the implications of Sontag's claim and argues that, in contemporary image-driven media culture and social networking, we all constitute ourselves as models.[38] Reality itself is a constructed subject, mediated by modern technologies with which we image – and imagine – ourselves.[39] For this, the first fashion models provide a precedent in the way that, more than a hundred years ago, they struck attitudes and composed their own image for their audiences.

In researching their history, I found only a few descriptions of men's fashion shows in the 1910s and 1920s. Male modelling was largely a phenomenon of the late twentieth century. Even today, and despite the rise of men's fashion shows and men's magazines, fashion modelling continues to be associated with women in a particular way. Fashion modelling must be one of the few areas in which women are consistently better paid than men to do the same job. Tyra Banks's highly popular television series *America's Next Top Model*, and its global spin-offs, focuses only on aspiring women models. This gender imbalance alone suggests that some of the obsessive focus on women's public appearance that the first mannequins caused still exists today. Women continue to be associated with appearance and beauty in ways different from men so that, as the artist Marlene Dumas has written, 'to be a woman is to be a model de facto'.[40]

For all these reasons, the first fashion shows and models continue to be relevant to contemporary debates about the intersection of women, image, commerce and culture, despite the differences in the conditions of their production and reception then and now. The history of the mannequin is topical in today's 'size zero' debates; that of the fashion show is relevant to how people in the twenty-first century experience and understand the allure of consumer culture. The way that early fashion modelling was linked to parallel histories of the body in the spheres of work, leisure, consumption and art provides a model for thinking about how we continue to use our bodies to map both our dreams and our anxieties in the cultural imaginary. The history of the fashion show is part of women's history, of business history, of design history and even of intellectual history. It suggests a way to understand how these different histories are connected. It shows how the personal and the political come together in the lived experience of the body, through the way it highlights the intersection between subjectivity on the one hand and social and economic realities on the other.

THE FASHION SHOW

1
PRE-HISTORY
NINETEENTH-CENTURY FASHION MODELLING

3 Wax fashion doll of 1756–65. The doll wears a formal Court dress of striped and brocaded silk with a wired skirt. She has a solid wax head and limbs on a wire frame, with moulded and painted hair and glass eyes; a compass hangs at the waist. She stands on a wooden plinth; one of her wax feet is now missing. IT2212; 22797. © Museum of London.

The fashion show, being just over a hundred years old, is a relatively modern phenomenon in the seven hundred-year-old history of western fashion. Its origins lie in the development of the French haute couture system in the nineteenth century, with its global trade networks across Europe and the Americas. As well as making top-end clothing for individual clients, haute couture houses also dealt with manufacturers and wholesalers at all levels of the market. As an export trade the French garment trade was unusual: it sold not wholesale garments but designs, in the form of model dresses, and the rights to reproduce them.[1] Fashion shows were an essential part of this process and evolved as much for the convenience of trade buyers as for individual clients. They came into being at a time when the haute couture system was rapidly expanding. In 1850 there were 158 dressmakers in Paris; by 1863 there were 494 and, by 1870, 700.[2] Between 1872 and 1900, this figure increased to 1700.[3] By 1902, sixty-three per cent of haute couture sales were to overseas buyers and many ready-to-wear manufacturers only made for export.[4]

In structure and organisation the larger houses changed significantly in two periods, first in the 1850s and then again between 1880 and 1900.[5] It was as part of the second wave of bureaucratic reorganisation of couture firms in the 1890s that fashion modelling became established on a widespread basis for the benefit of the overseas trade buyers; its ubiquity can be measured by the number of living mannequins photographed at more than forty firms between 1897 and 1899 in a photographic album in the Musée Galliera in Paris (see **8**, **27** and **269**).[6] In this period, fashion modelling emerged and gradually came to be put on a more formal footing. Towards 1900 the fashion show as it is known today began to be staged, a far more theatrical event than simple fashion modelling. By 1910 it was well established. The first fashion shows were a hinge between commerce and culture, France and America, and production and consumption in the modernist period. Their underlying themes included the conjunction of movement and modernity, and the spectacle of women.

They were then, as they are now, an essential form of marketing and promotion and, although they have changed over the decades as the industry has changed, they also retain today many of the essential features that were established in the first decades of the twentieth century.

THE EARLIEST FASHION MODELS

In the eighteenth century, before fashion models existed, French dressmakers commonly promoted their work internationally by sending dolls, fashionably dressed in the latest modes, around Europe (**1**). The dolls, few of which survive today, made regular trips to foreign capitals.[7] They could be about 75 centimetres high (30 inches) and had miniature adult figures, rather than the childlike bodies of nineteenth-century toy dolls. They were known in England as 'babies' or 'jointed babies' and in France variously as *courriers de la mode*, *Grandes Pandores*, *Petites Pandores*, *poupées*, *grandes poupées*, *dolls à la mode* and *mannequins*. Julie Park identifies the eighteenth-century fascination with dolls as part of that century's burgeoning culture of consumption, in which the use of fashionable commodities cemented the construction of fashionable identities. She writes: 'Being a woman in the eighteenth century was an intensely mimetic and modern project, capturing not what women are, but what women are like'.[8] This mimetic relationship later underwrote the connection between the first fashion models and their audiences. In the fashion model of the late nineteenth and early twentieth centuries, contemporary observers, both writers and illustrators, saw the same 'charged encounters between the natural and the artificial, the original and the copy, and the human and the inhuman' that Park finds in the eighteenth-century fashion doll.[9]

Fashion dolls were female but, as Alison Matthews David has shown, the first living fashion models in Paris were not, in fact, women but men:

> Beginning in the 1820s, certain tailors hired handsome men known as 'mannequins', the ancestors of the fashion model, to display their latest creations in modish spots around Paris. The practice seems to have been current until the late 1840s. This live version of the mannequin appears repeatedly in written sources, suggesting it was an important trope in the period imagination.[10]

Indeed, there is some evidence that the practice persisted into the 1870s when a newspaper article described the promenade of male mannequins up the boulevards of the Champs-Élysées and into the Bois de Boulogne, to launch the spring modes, detailing how the mannequins were 'Obliged to promenade from the Mi-Carême magnificently dressed all day'.[11]

David describes a vaudeville performance of 1826 that featured a former artist's model, Hector, named after the ancient hero, who had become a 'mannequin, model for fashions'. Hector entered singing 'Brilliant model, faithful mirror, I sparkle with light and fire! I wander [*je vogue*] everywhere, setting the vogue, for the new looks in the catalogue'.[12] The play anticipated by a good eighty years the early twentieth-century stage plays depicting fashion modelling in couture houses.[13] These early male models, far from being glamorous figures, were described by their contemporaries as poor young men who were obliged to display modish clothing at the races and other fashionable venues. David notes the ambiguous class status of the male mannequin, 'a man whose profession was to rent out his body . . . he had to be elegant enough to appeal to dandies and poor enough to require a wage'.[14] He was paid either in money or in the clothes he modelled. Paid mannequins were required to return the clothes in the evening, which was considered pitiable, while those professional actors who worked as unpaid mannequins were more admired.[15]

The journalist and dandy Roger de Beauvoir observed that young actors were employed as mannequins to parade 'a risky suit, a dangerous waistcoat, or a contentious pair of trousers'[16] in the fashionable public spaces of Paris and David argues that when, many decades later, Worth and other couturiers sent their female mannequins to the races, 'Worth may simply have been feminizing an advertising practice long familiar to tailors'.[17] Perhaps men's greater freedom to parade unaccompanied in the early nineteenth-century city goes some way to explaining why it was they who were the first to model fashions in this way. For mid-century women, it was the 'roaring *lionne*' from the 'unrecognised but so-much studied world' of the *demi-monde*, parading in the Bois, who was a pattern-card for fashion.[18] The *lionne* was, however, as Anne Martin-Fugier argued, a *dandy au féminin*, an atypical woman who indulged in masculine sporting pursuits, took the occasional glass of Jenever or rum and smoked Havana cigars.[19]

It was only gradually, in the second half of the nineteenth century, that women began to be used as professional mannequins and then only in the privacy of the couture house. By the end of the century, most fashion models were female not male: the profession had become feminised. Before then, society women did not visit their dressmakers' premises, so there was no need for young women to model there. In the eighteenth century, a lady's dress might be made by a number of different individuals: the bodice and train by a lady's tailor, the underwear by a dressmaker (*couturière*) and the trimmings and fashionable decoration provided by a *marchand de modes*, or milliner. Until the end of the Second Empire (1852–70) these tradespeople would call on society women at their apartments or *hôtels particuliers* in the mornings to transact their business, and even to complete the work, for such clients rarely visited a milliner or a couturier.[20] Exceptionally, firms such as Worth, Virot and Laferrière received customers in their *maison*, rather than attending them at their homes.[21] By 1880, private clients had begun to visit the couture houses twice a year, in April and November, to see the new fashions modelled by living mannequins.[22] In the 1890s, it was common for fashionable society women to spend the afternoon looking in on the mannequins in the couture houses of Laferière, Rouff, Fred, Callot Soeurs, Worth, Doucet or Morin-Blossier.[23]

Although fashion modelling was relatively new, such visitors would already have been familiar with a different form of 'modelling' from the *tableau vivant* tradition. In both France and America, late nineteenth-century audiences were familiar with the public performance of 'living pictures' in many forms: mime, 'statue posing' or *poses plastiques*, 'attitudes', *tableaux vivants*, *tableaux mouvants* (which incorporated dance movements) and, from 1895, film. Lady Hamilton, in the eighteenth century, had performed 'attitudes' to her guests in her house in Naples – frozen poses based on classical reliefs, an early form of *tableau vivant*.[24] The first theatrical *tableaux vivants*, in which individuals posed in static attitudes based on paintings, date from the 1760s.[25] In the nineteenth century, *tableaux vivants* were often presented within scaled-up gilt picture frames, out of which the performers stepped to enact the coming to life of art, 'on the brink of animation', as Lynda Nead describes it.[26] For domestic drawing-rooms, *poses plastiques*, a variation of domestic *tableaux vivants*, became popular. Women simulated statuary, posing as if naked in white or flesh-coloured body stockings to represent mythical or classical subjects. *Poses plastiques* were practised in front of the mirror; Uzanne describes how the *cocodettes* of the Second Empire, women of the world whose ennui led to extremes of cosmetics, fashion and behaviour, 'took an almost fiendish delight' in arranging the draperies of such classical scenes.[27] He highlighted the scabrous nature of the event by describing society women in actresses' tights: 'the most doubtful stories in Greek mythology were represented on a mimic Olympus, by the fairest goddesses of society, clad in flesh-coloured tights'.[28] The idea of a 'living picture' continued to be mobilised in many early fashion shows and as late as the 1920s much of the newsreel film produced by the Manuel Frères studio in Paris used the format of turning the pages of a fashion

magazine in which the mannequin suddenly came to life.

MODELLING AT MAISON WORTH

One of the early firms to receive customers as if in a social setting, Worth was also among the first to promote fashion modelling to a mixed audience, reserving a brilliantly lighted mirrored salon so that ball gowns might be fitted under conditions closest to reality.[29] Palmer White wrote, although he did not cite his sources, that Worth chose his mannequins for their resemblance to his types of customers, 'as he conceived his clothes to dress certain women, not to represent an idealised standard, as became the practice later.'[30] Worth was not, however, as is usually claimed, the first couturier to use living mannequins in the nineteenth century, as they had already been used by mercers.[31] Rather, he adapted the practice for the dressmaker's establishment and was instrumental in the professionalisation of the fashion model as the industry grew. By the turn of the century, modelling had disappeared from the drapery establishments and was only to be seen at the high-class dressmakers.[32]

Charles Frederick Worth had arrived in Paris from London in the late 1840s and had gone to work at Gagelin et Opige, a silk mercer in the rue de Richelieu that was the first firm to handle cashmere shawls and ready-made coats (*confection*).[33] There he met Marie Vernet, his future wife, who was employed to model ready-to-wear clothing. In his memoir of 1928 their son Jean-Philippe wrote:

> The work my mother did at Gagelin's was similar to that of the modern mannequin. She wore the shawls and cloaks and dresses so that the prospective purchaser might judge them for himself. She was exceedingly successful in this, not only because she had grace and beauty, knew how to carry herself and to wear clothes, but because she had great charm and knew how to smile.[34]

Her education, recalled her son, 'had been summary' but she had been taught 'gracefulness and how to walk and how to dance', supplemented with some basic spelling, mathematics, geography, sewing, embroidery and tapestry (**2**).[35]

It was Charles's job to sell the models displayed by Marie and the couple worked closely together, both before and after their marriage. At Gagelin, Worth began to design simple muslin dresses for Marie to show the shawls off to advantage.[36] His early innovations in design were to fit bodices closer to the figure and to cut fabric so that the warp always lay in the direction taken by the principal movements of the body.[37] In other words, movement was a

4 Marie Worth in 1860. Anonymous photographer. From Jean Philippe Worth, *A Century of Fashion*, 1928.

consideration in the design, and movement – that is, having the clothes modelled by the living mannequin – also became the way to sell them. Early in the 1850s Worth was allowed to introduce a large dressmaking department at Gagelin, including a salesroom installed in 1856 so that overseas buyers could inspect and order from a collection of model gowns designed by him.[38] It is therefore probable that trade buyers were among the first audiences for fashion modelling at Gagelin.

In January 1858, when Marie was pregnant with the second of the couple's two sons, they left to set up in partnership with a third colleague under the name Worth & Bobergh. The firm was a *maison spéciale de confection*. The term *maison de couture* was not then current, as the Chambre Syndicale de la Couture et de la Confection pour Dames, which established it, was not to be created for another ten years, in 1868.[39] At Gagelin, even when pregnant, Marie had worked a twelve-hour day, modelling from eight in the morning to eight in the evening, 'her waist imprisoned in stays'.[40] At the new firm, she continued to model until the mid-1860s when she suffered a severe attack of bronchitis, after which she was permanently replaced by a series of *demoiselles de magasin* who were employed to model in her place and of whom she remained in charge.[41] Unlike them, Marie also acted as an unofficial model by wearing Worth gowns in society.[42] At Worth, the aristocracy mingled with kept women, in the salon that 'exhales some atmosphere of degraded aristocracy, some heady fragrance of elegance, wealth, and forbidden fruit', wrote the seventeen-year-old Count Primoli when he was taken there by his mother in the autumn of 1868.[43] It was in this louche atmosphere that the Worth mannequins paraded. However, such society accounts give no clue as

to the immense commercial scope and novelty of Worth's operation.[44]

The 1860s was the decade in which Worth probably made his first American exports in his own name and it seems likely that American buyers visiting the premises were shown the models on living mannequins, although there is no direct evidence of this.[45] In Emile Zola's *The Kill* (*La Curée*), published in 1872 and set in the 1860s, the protagonist Renée visits her dressmaker Worms (a portrait of Worth) for a fitting, although Zola does not mention any living mannequins.[46] Edith Saunders, however, claimed that in the 1860s his showrooms were filled with attractive young mannequins, many of them English, ready and waiting to model a dress for a client.[47] Le Petit Homme Rouge (Ernest A. Vizetelly) described a different phenomenon: 'passing hither and thither, there were young girls whose gowns, though black, represented the latest styles invented by the master, in such wise that by pointing to one or another of them a customer could at once indicate what kind of corsage, or sash, or "puff" she desired'.[48] If so, it was only the most fortunate clients who saw their dresses on these mannequins, as most had to choose their dresses from designs in an album. The idea of a black-clad army of living women as a walking catalogue of design details, as opposed to a mannequin who modelled directly to clients, suggests the quasi-industrial model of Worth's design production. More than a designer, Worth was a businessman.[49] His genius, long before the mass production of automobiles and other commodities, was to create a series of individualised products starting from a fairly simple and uniform module, the basic dress.[50]

MODELS

From the 1870s writers and journalists began to note the practice of fashion modelling in the couture houses and in this period the vocabulary of fashion modelling began to develop. In Europe, fashion models were known as mannequins, as they still are today in France; in the U.S.A. they were called models, except in the most aspirational and Europhile magazines. The French singer Yvette Guilbert, who had started out as a mannequin in 1883, differentiated the terms for an American audience in 1895: 'I became a mannequin, not a "model" in your sense of the word. We look upon mannequin and models as different things. The first means to try on dresses before customers, but a model in France is a girl who shows her figure before everybody, especially sculptors and painters'.[51]

In the dressmaking trade the word model had another meaning. It referred to the dress, not the living woman who wore it, and the term survived well into the second half of the twentieth century, as in the phrase 'model dresses from Paris'. Derived from the Latin word for measure or standard, *modulus*, the diminutive of which was *modellus*, from which came the old Italian *modello*, meaning the mould for producing things, the word drifted into French, *modèle*, in the sixteenth century, meaning a paradigm or archetype, and then into English shortly afterwards in the sense of a small representation of some object. In her discussion of 'the idea of the model', Wendy Steiner points out that 'modelling is a process in which an original is replicated in a copy or copies' and notes that the model can be identified both as the original and – less commonly – as the copy. The inherent doubleness of the model means that, whether the model is a person or a thing, they 'straddle an ontological divide'.[52]

The first usage of the term 'model' in the fashion trade was probably as a sample, specimen or industrial prototype.[53] Its usage as a mathematical model only developed in the twentieth century, as did the term 'fashion model', meaning the living woman rather than the model dress.[54] In 1907 the *New York Times* explained the difference: 'A saleswoman cries "Give me Mireille!" "Mireille" is not the name of a mannequin but that of a costume. Each dress has its name. It is more convenient than a number, also more aesthetic.'[55] When a client watching the fashion show in 1918 asked the mannequin, ' "Your name, Mademoiselle?" the mannequin would answer with the name of the dress: "Fantasy." "How are you called, mademoiselle?" "A perfect half hour." And so the list goes on as the clients see a dress they like and their vendeuses jot it down on the little card.'[56] The word model is thus ambiguous, and the potential for confusion between the

model dress and the living mannequin is rich: the fashion *modèle*, unlike the artist's model, was merely an inanimate garment, whereas the *mannequin*, who took her name from an inanimate dressmaker's dummy, was a living, breathing woman.

Models were all numbered but when the London dressmaker Lady Duff Gordon, trading as Lucile, initiated fashion shows at the turn of the century she also introduced the practice of naming rather than numbering gowns, inaugurating her 'gowns of emotion' at the same time as the new science of psychology was emerging.[57] In this, she followed corsetières who gave their creations suggestive names;[58] soon the majority of dressmakers gave their dresses names. At Paquin in 1913 the models were given numbers as well and the numbers were used to identify the garments in at least one newspaper report of the time.[59] Later in the decade Lucile changed back from names to numbers and her employee Edward Molyneux, who opened his own house after she sacked him in 1919, also used numbers, as did Chanel in the 1920s. In the early 1920s it became fashionable to give French dresses English names but the mannequins' French accents sometimes made it hard for foreign buyers to understand them.[60]

In the French dressmaking trade, the *modèle* was never sold.[61] It was a prototype whose sole purpose was to be copied and adapted for sale. Nancy Troy writes: 'Copying, it is important to keep in mind, is inherent in the very structure of haute couture' and 'All the major French couturiers recognised the double-edged sword of the American market place' as the source of both the most lucrative sales and the greatest piracy.[62] Models were all numbered for internal records and the couture houses kept careful track of them in their fight against copyright infringement. According to Mary Lynn Stewart, from the 1880s designers hired photographers to record their models for deposit at the Conseil des Prud'hommes (Industrial Relations Board) in order to document their ownership of the designs. Mannequins in these photographs were either live or inanimate and brightly lit to show detail.[63]

When the private client made her choice, the model dress was remade for her in all its luxury, perfectly adapted to her proportions. If the client was an overseas trade buyer, who might be either a retailer or a wholesaler, he or she bought the model with the rights to reproduce it *en série*, that is, to mass-produce it in several hundreds or even thousands of copies. There was no royalty on it and the right to reproduce might be for a limited period such as three months; limited or not, it was impossible for the French to enforce their rights in America and piracy was endemic.[64] The model garment sold to buyers was rarely the

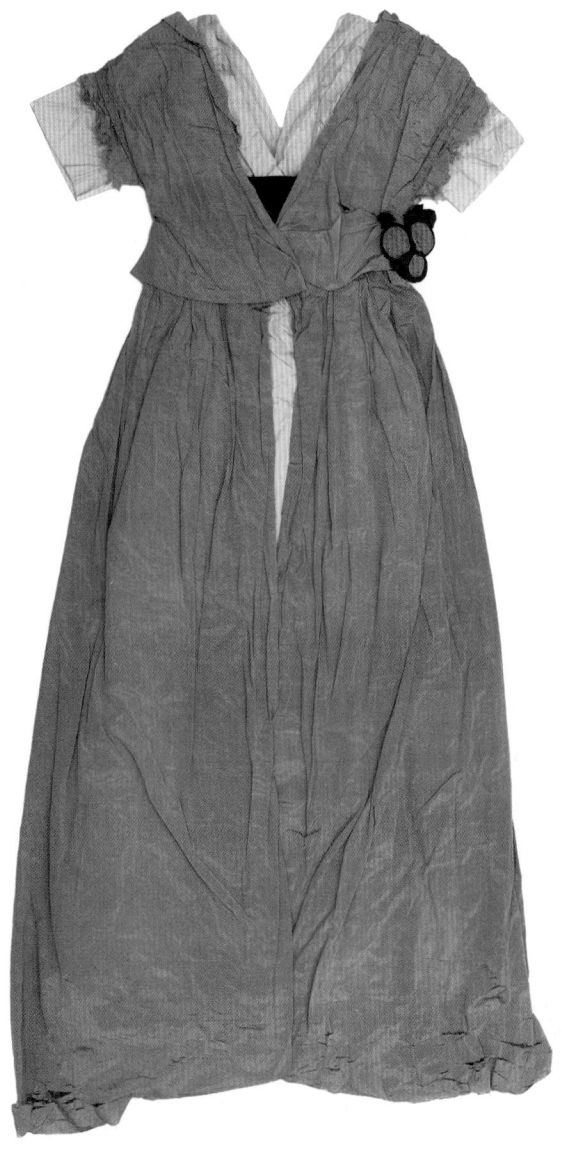

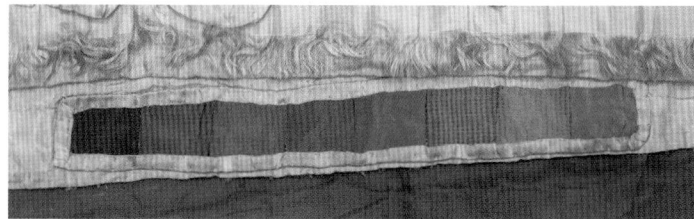

5 Paul Poiret, *Maintenon*, 1909. Model dress worn by the mannequin. Musée Galliera de la Mode de la Ville de Paris, GAL1986.122.1. Photograph Richard Hubert Smith.

a (left) Evening dress in mauve taffeta, a matching sash with two panels, stomacher and short sleeves in white taffeta, belt in black taffeta with three roses, flounced underskirt lined at the bottom with grey-blue muslin.

b (above) Colour swatch of silk taffetas stitched into hem showing alternative colourways for the dress.

c (left) Copyright registration protection label in white linen, stitched into the hem and stamped with the registration details: model name 'Maintenon', model number or price '800' and registration number '5272'.

elaborately finished garment that the private client received; it might be little more than a canvas toile, made up in inferior fabric, which came with sample fabrics and trimmings to show the materials it should be made up in by the buyer. In America, it was often further simplified before being put into production, so the final outcome was far removed from the original.

Models were made to fit individual mannequins who modelled them for an entire season.[65] As the mannequin had to put them on and take them off dozens of times in a single day, some concession to ease of dressing was made in simplified fastenings.[66] Model dresses might be displayed six times a day over two months, so with the constant changes they were more or less worn out by the end of the season; some were even remade.[67] At the end of the season they could only be sold secondhand, if at all.[68]

It appears that few survive; it is hard to identify, among the haute couture gowns in museum collections, those models worn by mannequins,[69] as opposed to the private customers' gowns which can generally be identified by their customised labels stitched behind the official label. (In the

case of a model dress, its name was written on a white band stitched into the hem.[70]) Yet, each of these couture gowns is a copy of the original *modèle* from which the customer would have made her choice by watching it being modelled in the salon by a mannequin. All couture gowns are thus something in the nature of a simulacrum that puts into question the status of the original. Baudrillard argued that reproduction always implies 'an anxiety, a disquieting strangeness' because it amounts to a kind of black magic in the way it detaches the copy from the original: 'reproduction is diabolical in its essence' because it effaces or negates the autonomy of the original.[71] In its spectral absence, the model gown resembles the photographic negative that Walter Benjamin described as the non-existent original engendering a multiplicity of copies in the form of the photographic print.[72] This is the clue to the industrial nature of the fashion model.

An extremely rare exception is a surviving model gown in the Musée Galliera in Paris, in mauve silk taffeta by Poiret from 1909 (**5a**). Sewn into the hem is a colour swatch of eight different colours which showed the other colours that

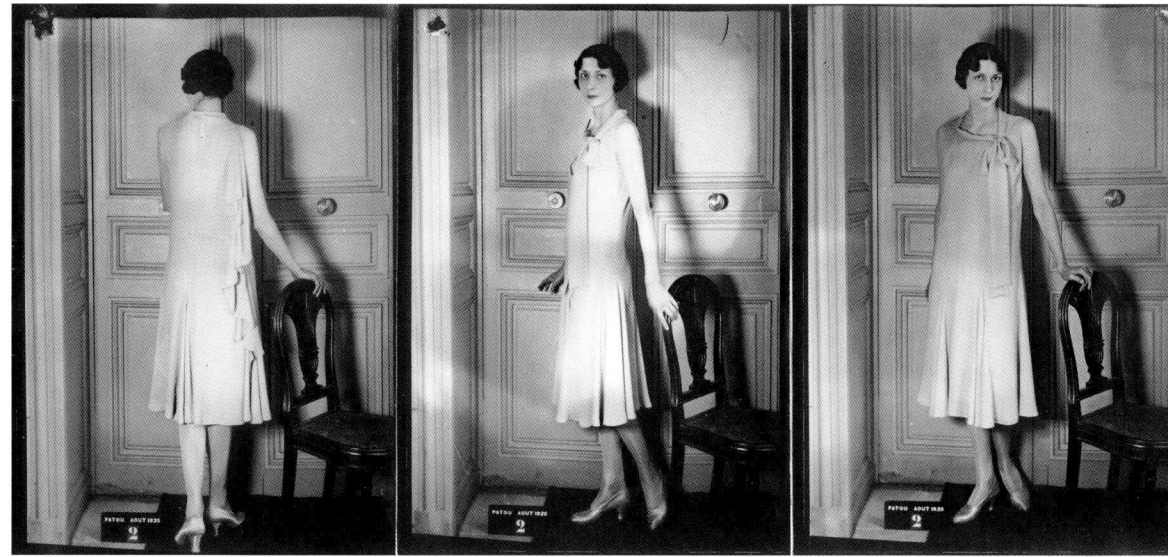

the dress could be made in (**5b**).[73] Next to it is a coarse linen label printed with the model name, its copyright registration number and either its price or the collection model number (**5c**).[74] The label proves that the design had been registered at the Conseil des Prud'hommes. The year 1909 was when French law changed to facilitate the registration of designs; Poiret may have been trying out a new system in this dress but there is no further information on its origins or on how it came into the Galliera's collection.

By and large, most such dresses have disappeared. However, many thousands of copyright photographs of them survive, especially from the 1920s, and are housed in the Paris archives and the Musée de l'Art de la Mode et du Textile (**6**). As well as recording the details of thousands of designs, they often provide the only material trace of the many anonymous mannequins who wore the model dresses. The photographs are both a haunting certificate of the mannequins' presence, to borrow Roland Barthes's phrase, and a testament to the more repetitive and unglamorous aspects of their daily work.[75]

MANNEQUINS

The word mannequin derives from the Dutch 'mainikin'. In French, it was used in the early seventeenth century to mean a wicker fruit-basket and also, by the end of the century, an articulated wooden doll used by artists.[76] Increasingly made of woven wicker from the eighteenth century, the articulated mannequin was known in English as a lay-figure. In the nineteenth century it became the

term to describe the French dressmakers' and tailors' dummies that came into production from the 1830s and 1840s.[77] Later in the century, the rue de la Paix in Paris became a centre of luxury and elegance and dressmakers with premises there would display their gowns in their salons on life-size wicker or wooden dummies known as *mannequins*.[78] These were the living fashion model's immediate predecessors, from which she acquired her name of living mannequin, *le mannequin vivant*. In 1863 Charles Dickens wrote an article entitled 'Dress in Paris' in which he fulminated against the way that the new 'man-milliners', in particular Worth, dressed and undressed the clients 'like the waxen figures in hair-dressers' shops'. He described Worth trying a dress 'on one of the living dolls of the chausée d'Antin' with meticulous care, occasionally standing back from his work to make his hand into the shape of an eye-glass through which he scrutinises the dress.[79] Whether the fitting which Dickens describes is on a client or a mannequin is unclear but his reference to hair dressers' mannequin busts (which had heads, unlike the full-length headless mannequins of the dressmakers) draws attention to a similarity between the inanimate and animate mannequin some years before the dummy gave her name to the living woman. The client he describes as 'the modern Eve, in process of formation, resigned and motionless, [who] silently allows her moulder to accomplish his creation'.[80]

Mannequin as a term for women who modelled was not, however, adopted before approximately 1870, despite its having been used since the 1820s to describe men who modelled. Instead, the women who modelled at Gagelin in the 1840s and at Worth in the 1860s were known as

7 'Un Voyage d'avril',
from J. J. Grandville, *Un
Autre Monde*, 1844.
Courtesy Carl Guderian.

demoiselles de magasin. Jean-Philippe Worth wrote: 'the word mannequin had not been coined at the time and, had it been, would have been considered an insult'.[81] Since the first mannequins' gowns were *prêtes à essayer* (ready to try on, unlike a couture model), these women were sometimes called *essayeuses*, which was also the word for a fitter. Another term for them was *sosies*, or doubles.[82] Perhaps this was because they were the double of the inanimate mannequin; or perhaps they were the double of the client, though never her equal.

Jean-Philippe claimed that the use of the word mannequin to describe the living model was launched by a journalist from *La Vie parisienne* who, having witnessed a dress being modelled for a client at Worth on a *vendeuse*, wrote an article about 'the *"Entrée de Mlle. Mannequin"*'. It was the first time that anyone had ever dared to call a *demoiselle de magasin* a mannequin. What would have happened had my mother been the saleswoman can well be imagined.'[83] The term was still not respectable by 1879 when Edmond de Goncourt referred contemptuously to *les demoiselles-mannequins* (the young girl-mannequins) who paraded in Worth's salon.[84] In 1880, a vaudeville play at the Théâtre Déjazet, *Le Mannequin*, was set in 'the boudoir of a man milliner, Simpson', as an American reviewer wrote, echoing some of Dickens's disdain for the ambience at Worth.[85]

Why did the word mannequin have these bad connotations? Since the late eighteenth century it had been used to mean an empty-headed, fashionable, man of straw.[86] Late in the nineteenth century its slang meaning remained that of an insignificant or contemptible person.[87] As soon as it also came to mean a tailor's dummy, that image too was used pejoratively. In 1844 Grandville (the pseudonym for the French caricaturist Jean-Ignace-Isidore Gérard) satirised the fashionable crowd at the Longchamp racecourse by representing them as no more than an assemblage of fashionable accessories (**7**), writing:

> It seems that in this country the fashion is to have oneself replaced in public promenades by body doubles made out of plaster, wood or wax. Elegance is created in effigy. Dresses, hairstyles, scarves,

diamonds, everything that epitomises the beauty, luxury or reputation of an individual, is on parade – only the individuals themselves are lacking. And indeed what good is the rest of the person? One only goes there to look at the clothes. The prophet was dreaming of the solemnities of fashion when he exclaimed: Mannequin of mannequins, and all is but mannequin![88]

When the term was applied to the female mannequins in the couture houses in the 1870s, its connotations shifted again to a darker register as it came to suggest the theme of femininity as a mechanical performance. In a century habituated to looking at women posing in the *tableaux vivants* and *poses plastiques* of both popular theatre and society drawing-rooms, the prurient disapproval and scorn evoked by the mannequin stands out. The Goncourt diaries of 1879 describe a pregnant mannequin modelling at Worth, seated motionless in the penumbra, recalling her predecessor Mme Worth who had modelled through both her pregnancies in the 1850s:

> A charming detail of elegant Parisian life. Among the young girl-mannequins who promenade in Worth's salons, showing the gowns of the illustrious couturier on their slender bodies, there is a young girl, or rather a lady-mannequin, whose speciality is to represent pregnancy in high society. Seated alone at a distance, in the half-light of a boudoir, in an interesting condition, she exhibits for the visitors' eyes a gown adapted with the utmost genius to the deformity of childbearing.[89]

At Pinguat, the 'famous couturier to courtesans', the Goncourt diaries take an even darker and more misogynist turn. They describe Pinguat's gloomy décor lit by gas lamps in 1883 where, 'In the midst of the lugubrious plants, brightened by funereal mantelpiece ornaments', there were

> women promenading their dresses, women who, because of this work as coat-hangers have lost a degree of life and gained a certain automatism. Most are young but nevertheless look old, and show, in their faded and crumpled features, something of the grimacing corruption of monkeys. It is amusing, when the clothes they show off to advantage are removed from their back, to see them parade in front of you, hopping and skipping, in the manner of undressed women who run wearing oriental slippers without heels.[90]

MOULAGE SUR NATURE

This diary entry stresses the mannequins' automatism and lack of life, an observation that continued to be made by other commentators well into the next century. The effect must have been compounded by the mannequins' black satin *fourreaux*, or sheaths, that they wore at all times.[91] This was a tight, enveloping dress-like undergarment that covered them from chin to wrists but remained visible beneath the colourful couture gowns they modelled (**8**). An article in 1880 from *L'Art de la mode* describes the *fourreau*-clad mannequins at work: 'Between the four mirrors of an immense salon . . . They come and go, thin and tall, neatly coiffed, with no jewellery, with the indifferent air of mannequins, removing and re-donning the same model ten times, and with a slow, rhythmic step they walk away and back again, to turn elegance to good account.'[92] This passage describes all the features that continued to fascinate observers of the new phenomenon of fashion modelling over the next forty years: the mirrored salons that multiply the mannequins' image, the repetitious nature of their task, modelling the same garment ten times a day and their indifferent manner. In this respect, the journalist writes, they are 'like' mannequins, that is, the lay-figure. All these features combine to make the fashion model something a little less than human: mechanical or doll-like in her smooth performance, her body is always svelte, her step rhythmic and her movement gliding; these too contribute to her slightly unnatural and even uncanny appearance.

In the 1890s, more than twenty years after the first descriptions of living mannequins, they continued to attract comment. An 1897 article on 'How Fashions are Made', in the French illustrated periodical *L'Illustration*, looked back at their history and described how the initial shock of the first mannequins at Worth had softened: 'little by little, the contemporary eye became accustomed to the eccentricity

and the boldness that had initially frightened it'.[93] In this sympathetic article, the sinister qualities of the living mannequin which had alarmed early commentators recede. Octave Uzanne, however, in 'The Parisian, as she is', the final chapter of his survey of a century of fashion published in 1898, felt that the modern woman herself had acquired something of the mechanical nature of the doll. This he attributed to women's education: 'Education has altered feeling, and scepticism has crept in unawares. Woman has been reduced to playing a doll's part in the contemporary puppet show./"Les petites marionnettes font, font, font,/Trois petits tours et puis s'en vont."/The doll is a lovely doll, no doubt. Her beauty is disturbing, but she is dangerous too'.[94] Changes to girls' secondary education from the 1880s may have provoked this melancholy comment that incorporates a well-known children's song; but Uzanne went on to argue that the introduction of 'foreign doctrines' to France 'stirred dreams of emancipation in the female breast'.[95] In Uzanne's passage some of the ambivalence expressed by earlier writers about the fashion mannequin is extended towards the woman of fashion, echoing Dickens's ambivalence from the 1860s. The writer focuses on the repetitive movements of the puppet ('font, font, font') who makes three turns and then is gone, like the living mannequin's appearance before her clients in the salon. In his 1900 book on the Paris mannequin trade, Léon Riotor described how the living mannequin came from the ranks of those 'female employees of regular size and proportions who took the name of the object which they replaced. It is from the girl-mannequins of fashionable couturieres that we nowadays copy the plaster busts'.[96] His illustration of 'moulding' the lay-figure from the living woman evokes the other meaning of *modèle* as a mould, rather than a prototype (**9**), and his text suggests that the dummies which served as the prototypes for the first living models had been superseded by the living women who, in turn, had become the pattern-cards for the lay-figures.

STRUCTURES OF DOUBLING: THE 'OPTICAL UNCONSCIOUS'

Nineteenth-century journalists' descriptions of the mannequin shared some concerns of those literary writers interested in ghost stories and the themes of the *Doppelgänger*, the doll and the automaton. The nineteenth-century literature on doubles and dolls is extensive, particularly, as Karl Miller has shown, in the romantic period when the *Doppelgänger* theme emerged.[97] Musset, Hoffmann, Nerval, Rank, Maupassant and Richard Strauss all wrote fiction about the threatening and sinister idea of the double.[98] Freud describes the double as the 'uncanny harbinger of death'[99] for, as Mladen Dolar succinctly put it, 'When the double appears, the time is up'.[100] Freud opened his essay 'The Uncanny', of 1919, with a discussion of E. T. A. Hoffmann's short story 'The Sandman', of 1817, in which its female protagonist, Olympia, the perfect fiancée, turns out to be an automaton.[101] Freud's essay dealt with dolls and doubling, looking back at the nineteenth-century literature of his youth from the far side of the Great War, at a moment when to look forward was to confront a different set of anxieties about women. Ambivalent responses to the emerging category of the fashion mannequin in this period were underwritten by fears of mechanisation and modernity in a period of increasing automation in industry.[102] The encroaching emancipation of women in both society and the workplace played a part in these anxieties too. Journalistic anxiety about the mannequin was linked not only to contemporary anxieties about her objectification but also to her troubling status as a new kind of working girl: a woman who wore fashion for money, rather than for the love of it.

The mannequin's status as a double (*sosie*) suggests both an uncanny doubling between the inanimate and the living mannequin, and a somewhat contradictory doubling with the woman for whom she modelled: close enough in appearance for the client to be able to identify with her, yet differentiated by her black satin *fourreau*, the mannequin was the very opposite of the client in terms of class, status and income. The client had her own body double too, lodged in the couture house, a lay-figure custom-made to replicate her own proportions, on which her dresses would be cut and fitted. In every house, usually near the attics, would be a room full of these ghostly dress forms, an army of headless clients of widely differing physiques and heights in unbleached canvas.

Thus a series of antimonies (alive–dead, animate–inanimate, object–subject, working girl–leisured client) lead ineluctably to their predicate: original and copy. The philosophical meanings of this opposition, as well as its powerful hold on fantasy, underpin both the ontological status of the fashion mannequin and the commercial organisation of haute couture as it developed in the second half of the nineteenth century. For, the *sosie*, or living mannequin, was a figurehead that brought larger structures of doubling in its wake. The image and idea of the double, in the form of its corollaries the copy, the reverse, the counterpart, the analogue, the multiple, the reflection and the mirror image, ran all the way through the culture and the commerce of the fashion house. Such doublings constituted the 'optical unconscious' of the industry, similar to the way in which Walter Benjamin identified photography as an 'optical unconscious' in 1931: as if it were a lens through which to glimpse a vision of modernity invisible to the naked eye in a rapidly changing world, too fractured and too fast-moving to be perceived as anything but an apparently disjointed series of still and moving images.

Indeed, it is with reference to walking, the definitive activity of the living mannequin herself, as opposed to photographs that break down the walk into stills, that Benjamin makes this point:

> Whereas it is a commonplace that, for example, we have some idea what is involved in the act of walking, if only in general terms, we have no idea at all what happens during the fraction of a second when a person *steps out*. Photography, with its devices of slow motion and enlargement, reveals the secret. It is through photography that we first discover the existence of this optical unconscious, just as we discover the instinctual unconscious through psychoanalysis.[103]

In the couture house, the multiplied images of the living mannequin provided a set of metaphorical 'stills' capable of constituting an optical unconscious that revealed, or pictured, a set of contradictions about the copy and original within the industry itself.[104]

The principal contradiction revolved round the model dress. Before Worth's innovations in the 1850s, a dress would be individually made for each client, in consultation with her; Worth not only instituted the idea of the pre-designed collection but he also sold it to the overseas buyers before the private clients even saw it. The private client, however, was never to know this; and, mimicking the aristocratic décor of the *hôtel particulier*, the modelling salon

10 (right) Living mannequin modelling *le jersey parisien* to a viscountess at Maison Le Roy. From *L'Art et la mode*, 1885. Musée Galliera de la Mode de la Ville de Paris. Photograph Richard Hubert Smith.

11 (far right) The seated viscountess watches three mannequins modelling *le jersey parisien* as the Le Roy sales-women look on. From *L'Art et la mode*, 1885. Musée Galliera de la Mode de la Ville de Paris. Photograph Richard Hubert Smith.

gave no clue to the hive of industry that lay behind it. In order to promote itself as a top-end, craft-based luxury trade, the French couture had to disguise its commercial links and, to some extent, its promotion was built on a lie. It claimed the high ground of French culture through its sale of luxurious one-offs but it depended for its lifeblood on selling toiles and patterns worldwide for mass production by foreign industries. This structure of doubling was disavowed in couture rhetoric yet built into the couture industry. The relationship between copy and original was replicated in the forms of doubling and differentiation of the image that shuttled from model to mannequin to client in the fashion show. Furthermore, the unique model worn by the Paris mannequin became serial in the mirrored walls of the couture house, as if to picture future sales and American production – *à la répétition*, as mass-produced clothing was called. This visualisation of knowledge was further replicated in the architecture and business organisation of the house, with the living mannequin in the fashion show functioning as the fulcrum between backstage production and front-of-house sales.[105]

WALKING MANNEQUINS: THE 1880S

In the 1880s mannequins began to be sent out of the couture house to model the latest fashions on foot in the Champs-Élysées and the Bois de Boulogne.[106] Here, for the first time, they acquired some public visibility, being taken out of the heady atmosphere of the elite couture houses and perhaps sparking public interest in fashion modelling. In July 1885 *L'Art et la mode* illustrated a mannequin at the house of Le Roy at 56 rue du Faubourg Poissonière, modelling an early form of sportswear to an aristocratic

client (**10**). Entitled 'study in Jersey', the feature illustrates the shopping trip of a viscountess to purchase garments in 'le jersey parisien' that will be suitable for the country-side. The caption relates that 'Madame asked for an all-purpose "jersey" [and] she was shown one, in a Turkish salon, in which one can move in every direction, and go and play croquet and lawn-tennis without tearing the garment which permits entirely flexible movement of the limbs'.[107]

This first visual illustration of a mannequin modelling differs markedly from the written descriptions cited so far, in which the mannequin, if she moves at all, is like an automaton. The 1885 mannequin, instead, wears sportswear, which requires active movement. She twists energetically in a tennis-playing pose to demonstrate the flexibility of the new Parisian jersey fabric that is also extolled in the text (playful putti even bounce on it in the pictures). The pose itself is unusual, in the repertoire of fashion illustration. It looks neither natural nor achievable, although its awkward quality may simply be due to the novelty of depicting a moving mannequin for an illustrator more used to showing static poses. A second image (**11**) shows three mannequins modelling in more naturalistic positions as the seated viscountess looks on, with the saleswoman in attendance. Although the tone of the article depicts Le Roy as an elite institution, a Bloomingdale's catalogue illustration of 1890 (**12**) shows how such fashions rapidly crossed the Atlantic and were promoted by American importers as Parisian specialities.[108] No images show buyers in this period, however; images like these only show mannequins modelling to aristocratic or royal clients. Unwilling to publicise their trade links, the French houses preferred instead to use the cachet of the individual clients to promote their reputation. The first visual image of

12 *La Parisienne* jersey suits from the American Bloomingdale's store catalogue, 1890. Collection of the New-York Historical Society, 82229d.

13 A mannequin at Redfern in Paris models a 'Scottish dress' to the Princess of Wales. The couturier and the kneeling saleswoman are pictured talking the client through the dress. Behind Redfern's head can be seen the life-size stuffed horse on which customers trying out their new riding habits could sit and see themselves in the mirrors. From *L'Art et la mode*, 1885. Musée Galliera de la Mode de la Ville de Paris. Photograph Richard Hubert Smith.

fashion buyers at a show is not until 1915 (see **108**) and even then only occurred as part of a wartime discourse of patriotism.

Four months later, *L'Art et la mode* showed another scene of mannequins modelling a tartan 'Scottish dress', this time to the Princess of Wales at Redfern in Paris (**13**).[109] Redfern was known for the *costume trotteur*, a walking suit in which the wearer could move comfortably, at a time when young women like the viscountess at Le Roy were beginning to want clothing in which they could move energetically for walking, tennis, cricket and even cycling.[110] It appears, then, that mannequins in the early 1880s, rather than posing in static *tableaux vivants*, may have been used to show fashion in motion, in a decade in which women were becoming interested in new sporting endeavours and in which an interest in human locomotion provoked a number of experiments in other fields.

THE THEORY OF THE WALK: VISUAL, AURAL AND WRITTEN ARTICULATIONS

In 1829 Honoré de Balzac wrote 'La Théorie de la démarche', or 'The Theory of the Walk', as an appendix to his 'Traité de la vie élégante'.[111] The first part of the 'Théorie' makes a plea for a science of human motion[112] but, although he claims he would like 'to codify the walk' (*codifier, faire le code de la démarche*), Balzac's text is largely aphoristic. He is in thrall to the allure of women in motion. Why, then, is the treatise called the 'theory' of the walk? The modern meaning of the word *théorie* is an explanation or a speculation; etymologically, the word comes from the

Greek *theorema*, meaning a spectacle, speculation, or theorem; *theorein* means to be a spectator, or to view.[113] Its first meaning was, thus, a vision rather than an intellectual enquiry: Balzac's 'Théorie de la démarche' might accordingly be understood less as an enquiry into the science of walking and more as a commentary on its spectacular nature, in particular when women walked in public. In 1835, however, the sixth edition of the dictionary of the Académie Française added two new definitions for the word *théorie*: a term signifying, firstly, the instruction of military manoeuvres and, secondly, the annual deputation of Athenians to Delphi and Delos in ancient Greece.[114] From this second definition the word rapidly came to be adapted to describe any procession of young women and early in the twentieth century was often applied to the mannequin parade or *défilé* as in, for example, *une souple théorie de mannequins*, which translates as 'a lithe procession of mannequins'.[115]

Three widely different 'theoretical' enquiries into walking were made in the 1880s, in science, literature and music, at exactly the same time that couturiers' mannequins were demonstrating the walk and fashion magazines were beginning to illustrate its poses. The physiologist Etienne-Jules Marey experimented with chronophotography to show the 'significant moments' of men walking, running and jumping.[116] The writer Auguste Villiers de l'Isle Adam published his novel *L'Ève future* (1886), or 'Eve of the Future', which detailed the construction and animation of a female android, devoting an entire chapter to her walk, 'La démarche'. Thirdly, the composer Eric Satie's three short piano pieces *Gymnopédies* (1888), based on classical Greek athletics (recalling the *théorie* or frieze effect), were an early experiment in the use of repetition and lack of development in musical form. They are short, repetitive pieces that prefigure modern ambient music, which evoke the patterns of couture house modelling in the same decade.[117] 'There is no development, no transition, only an instant prolonged', writes Alex Ross of Satie's *Gymnopédies*.[118] Fashion modelling, too, was based on repetition: endlessly walking and going nowhere, lacking in variety or theatrical narrative and using a limited repertoire of movements.

Villiers's novel is even more suggestive of the motifs and patterns of couture modelling. In it, a fictional Thomas Edison makes a copy of the ideal woman for his client Lord Ewald, not unlike a couturier who copies the ideal dress for the client. Edison shows Ewald a sample of the synthetic skin he has created for the android as if it were a fabric sample. 'And now, my Lord, would you like me to show you this ideal textile skin?'[119] The satiny quality of the android Hadaly's skin is such that, Edison claims, 'it completely overturns one's perceptions of Humanity. It becomes impossible to distinguish the prototype from the copy'.[120] Here, just as in the haute couture gowns bought by the foreign buyers that came to Paris in the 1880s, *le modèle* is used to mean a prototype (be it a model woman or a model gown) and *la copie* designates its reproduction: a dress or a woman cut to a pattern. Hadaly the android, 'Eve of the future', is one such pattern-card woman, as was the woman of fashion described by Dickens more than twenty years earlier on his visit to Worth as an 'Eve in the process of formation by her moulder'. In the novel, Edison muses on the infinite reproducibility of the mechanical woman, with her manufactured smile, gestures, walk and skin tones, much as later commentators were to ruminate on the reproducibility of the fashion mannequin's repetitive smiles, gestures and attitudes. Only the first android posed technical difficulties, says Edison. Having created the general formula, it is just a question of manufacturing: 'There is no doubt that soon millions of substrates just like her will be made', he jokes, 'and the first-comer industrialist will open a factory of ideals!'[121] In fashion, this science fiction had already come to pass. Alan Raitt points out that the plural *les idéals* is rare in French, though used by Hugo and Baudelaire, as well as by Villiers in an earlier draft of the novel, *Madame et son sosie* ('Madam and her Double'), where he wrote: 'My house is a factory of angels, I deal in ideals'.[122] So too did the couture houses, those factories of ideals in which the troubling relationship of original and copy was daily articulated in a modern commercial idiom.

Hadaly is animated by her maker who touches one of the rings on her silver-gloved hand, just as in the Redfern illustration of 1885 (**13**) the couturier guides the mannequin with his hand on her elbow as she moves for the client at his request. Villiers devotes many pages to the design and technical specification of Hadaly's walk. Her legs are 'a hermetic sheath of platinum', where the French word for sheath, *maillot*, recalls the black satin *maillot*, as the *fourreau* was also called, worn by fashion mannequins.[123] The effect is reinforced by the first sight of her up and walking, 'enveloped in long, full pleats of black satin'.[124] Her electrically controlled movements are calibrated 'according to the undulations of the living torso' so that the powerful electromagnets inside her create 'human movement itself'.[125] Delicate steel wires give her 'that gracious bend of the knee, that constant undulation, that billow in the walk that are so seductive in a mere woman'.[126]

These descriptions of the female android suggest uncanny parallels between doll and human, perfection and imperfection, the ideal and the real, parallels that the living mannequins of the couture houses also evoked in relation to the women who were their clients. Perhaps the most significant contribution to images of people running and walking, however, came from the scientist Etienne-Jules Marey and they were images ('chronophotographs') of men. Marey's goal was to split and freeze serial images of movement onto the same photographic plate, thus picturing time (**14**).[127] In 1881 he invented a photographic 'gun' that took twelve images per second, which was enough to synthesise the motion on a phenakistoscope; later he designed a new camera that created multiple exposures on a single plate. Marey staged his experiments in a specially constructed 'station' in the Bois de Boulogne, his *Station physiologique*, as he called it, just a short distance from the fashionable strolling grounds of the Longchamp racecourse and the avenue des Acacias where the *élégantes* and the newly professionalised mannequins practised one sort of *théorie de la démarche* while Marey articulated in images another type of theory of the walk.[128]

Marey's simultaneous images of men running, walking and jumping had their visual counterpart in several instances of popular ballet and revue theatre. In 1881, the internationally acclaimed ballet *Excelsior* illustrated the progress of science and civilisation in a series of massive set-pieces using choreographed human movement of up to five hundred actors to suggest mechanical action. Edmond de Goncourt saw it at the newly opened Éden-théâtre in Paris in 1883 and complained that it was 'a ballet you could call the St Vitus dance of the ballet. Nine hundred arms and nine hundred legs in the air'.[129] In the 1890s came the first chorus line-ups at the Folies Bergère. The five Barrington Sisters were not really sisters but five women of identical height and build who performed in identical make-up and strawberry-blonde wigs moving in formation, 'the five heads turning as one, the legs all raised to exactly the same height, the regimented gestures cued-in precisely to the music'.[130] If these images of the rationalised female body in the leisure sphere were the visual analogue of the way the rationalised body of the fashion mannequin was multiplied as a luxury ideal in the couture houses, they also pictured the ways in which working women's bodies were becoming increasingly regulated in the 1880s by the mechanisation of factory work.[131]

In America, Marey's contemporary, the photographer Eadweard Muybridge (who visited Marey in Paris in 1881) developed his own strand of simultaneous photography in the 1880s. His *Animal Locomotion* of 1887 was dedicated among other things to showing how galloping horses lifted all four hooves off the ground and was an important influence on French artists such as Degas in the late 1880s. It included images of both men and women in motion: running, jumping, dressing, dancing, washing. Lynda Williams has argued that Muybridge's use of new technology to record bodies in motion produced images that made the body appear mechanical and linked them to the first chorus lines.[132] As many commentators have pointed out, his images of women are far from scientific and betray a typically nineteenth-century taxonomy that places men before women and the nude above the clothed body. In particular, critics have noted how Muybridge's images of female dancers and artist's models in classical drapery engaged in pastoral activities bore no relation to the real lives and activities of women in 1885.[133] In one plate (**15**), however, he staged a social encounter between two fashionably dressed women who pass each other as if in

the street. They greet each other without stopping and the images are a filmic vignette of the fashionable footfall of the 1880s.[134] Here Muybridge acted as a scenographer of social walking, rather than a scientist or visual theoretician of movement in the manner of Marey.

THE PRACTICE OF THE WALK: *LA PASSANTE* AND THE WORKING WOMEN OF THE PARIS FASHION TRADE

This theory of the walk also had its counterpart in the practice of walking in the fashionable social spaces of the city. Fashionable strolling and fashionable looking were inextricably connected. 'In Paris, all is spectacle', wrote Balzac, 'no other people in the world have more voracious eyes'.[135] Social walking was no exception. In the nineteenth century the *défilé du Bois de Boulogne*, the Good Friday parade of fashionable people, went via the Champs-Élyssés which was lined with chairs that the 'common people' paid two sous to sit on and watch the carriages roll by.[136] In the Bois, where the aristocracy descended from its carriages, fashionable strolling legitimated, even solicited, staring in public. Walking and looking were co-dependant. Neither signified without the other in what the fashion historian Valerie Steele calls a 'ritualised fashion display'. She describes how the 'drama of seeing and being seen' was played out in a 'geography of fashion' that included the theatres, parks, racetracks, boulevards and department stores of Haussmann's Paris.[137]

Walter Benjamin cites Charles Blanc on the fashions of the Second Empire:

Everything that could keep women from remaining seated was encouraged; anything that could have impeded their walking was avoided. They wore their hair and their clothes as though they were to be viewed in profile. For the profile is the silhouette of someone . . . who passes, who is about to vanish from our sight. Dress became the image of the rapid movement that carries away the world.[138]

Blanche Lochmann argues that, following changing social practices, new literary and poetical motifs emerged in nineteenth-century French writing, so that the themes of the *passage* and the promenade progressively replaced that of the ball, providing a new focus on the erotic potential of the walk.[139] Although fashionable strolling was nothing new to the nineteenth century, an increasing emphasis on lives lived in the new public spaces of Haussmann's Paris, with its cafés, parks and boulevards, gave it a particular character in the second half of the century. The Goncourts wrote in 1860: 'Social life is going through a great evolution

. . . The interior is passing away. Life turns back to become public'.[140] This involved a sense of the accelerated speed of modernity. Lochmann argues that the late nineteenth century saw the birth of the railway, the automobile and the cinema as well as the fashion show and that 'this acceleration of men and things is the source of a modification of the look that is turned on the world'.[141]

Working women of Paris were as much the object of this new look as the fashionable *élégantes*. The idea of the anonymous female worker glimpsed from behind as she hurries through the city rapidly caught the literary imagination after the publication in 1860 of Charles Baudelaire's poem *À une passante*, as Claude Leroy has shown in his literary history of the female passer-by, *Le Mythe de la passante*.[142] Agnès Rocamora devotes a chapter of her book on Paris to the relationship between *la passante* and fashion in which she posits the *passante* as a more fruitful generic 'type' than the more commonly hypothesised *flâneuse*.[143] As Rebecca Solnit points out in

her history of walking, the *flâneuse* is a literary construction with no basis in social reality; whereas, as Rocamora shows, *la passante* was both a literary construction and a real working woman who hurried through the streets of Paris.[144] One example of a *passante* that is much indebted to the literary sources identified by Leroy was described in *L'Art et la mode* in 1884. An anonymous young woman, perhaps a worker in the garment trade, scurries through the streets of Paris. The journalist analyses her walk (she is alert, elegant and gentle) and comments on her tiny feet, using the verb *trottiner* twice to evoke the anonymous *trottin*.[145] Yet for all the particulars, the woman's age and beauty remain mysterious. The details of her fashionable dress give no clues about her class or respectability. Like Baudelaire's *passante*, she embodies the charm of the unknown.

So, too, does another *passante* of 1904, Paul Poiret's mannequin who is evocatively described walking through the streets of Paris (**16**) before she arrives at work and changes into the black *fourreau* (see **8**). After a day modelling luxury clothing, in the evening she reverted to being an anonymous *trottin*, part of the street life of the city, hurrying towards the metro that would take her to her suburban home.[146] 'Ghenya' describes her after work, surrounded by her admirers in the Café de Paris (**17**). The article situates her within the flux of urban femininity that makes up the modern city whose boulevards teem with women of all social classes. Side by side, the clients and the mannequins mingle in the city street: 'actresses and duchesses, *grisettes* and *trottins*, dowagers and *demi-vierges* flit about in this atmosphere heady with madness and unbridled pleasure where life is over-excited with such a

degree of nerves and excitation that death would barely get a hearing and the party would hardly stop for a matter of . . . national mourning'.[147] In this passage, not dissimilar to Simmel's description of the neurasthenia of city life from 1903, the mannequin becomes part of the feminine flow that characterises Paris as a city of leisure and pleasure.[148]

Georges d'Avenel's chapter on garment workers threading their way to work through the morning streets in 1905 described a moving panoply of women rather differently:

> In the morning between seven and nine o'clock, the streets of Paris present a spectacle without analogue anywhere else in the world, one made to charm the eye of the artist and attract the moving eye of the dreamer . . . Women descend, dressed sombrely, the majority with pale faces and serious expressions, from distant faubourgs towards the centre of the city . . . These women are . . . the workers of elegance. The apprentices, the 'arpettes', enter among the graver figures of the workers, mingling with these women's black dresses, which are almost uniforms, almost religious, some truly amazing dresses and costume inventions . . . The apprentices are . . . completely unique . . . thin little birds, with unclassifiable clothing . . . and the funniest hats . . . One could baptise this route . . . the Milliners' Way.[149]

At a time when mannequins and fashion shows were beginning to be widely written about in the press, this image of the black-clad workers filing through the streets also recalls the mannequins in their black satin *fourreaux*, while the extravagantly dressed *arpettes* suggest the lively invention of the couture fashions worn on top, so that the 'Milliners' Way' of women walking to work becomes a kind of fashion parade of the producers rather than the disseminators of fashion through the streets of Paris.

The descriptions of these women who raced through nineteenth-century Paris provide a moving backdrop to the dash and bustle of a city epitomised by fashionable and chic women. Leroy calls *la passante* a 'professional of transit' (*une professionelle du passage*) and she was also a professional of the Parisian *passages*.[150] He asks if, instead of an 'eternal' *passante*, we could not invent a *passante* for each moment (*pour tous les instants*, like Marey's chronophotographs) so that her movements would be unique yet serial: *l'unique à la répétition*.[151] Here Leroy's choice of language suggests a number of other images of reproduction in the nineteenth-century city: the mass-production of the ready-to-wear clothing trade, Marey's serial images of a single man walking (see **14**), the endlessly repeated gestures and poses of the mannequin in the couture house which echoed the structure of doubling at the heart of the haute couture and, finally, Villiers's Hadaly, a 'sublime creature of pure repetition'.[152]

Essentially, *la passante* is a pre-cinematic moving image. Like the mannequin, she exists to be seen and is part of the 'spectacularisation' of women in the late nineteenth-century city in which various urban spaces become a set for the staging of fashionable identities that legitimate the practice of social staring. The *passante*, however, is actually going somewhere, whereas the mannequin, once arrived at work, makes a profession of going nowhere. Paid simply to walk up and down, the mannequin's real affiliation is with two other, barely recognised, Parisian types, the *figurante* and the *marcheuse*.[153] The *figurante* was a mute extra of the Paris theatre, whose performance consisted simply of making gestures and who went uncredited on theatre bills.[154] The *marcheuse* (female walker) was a female supernumerary employed in the ballet and *café-concert* simply to walk onstage or between the tables 'in a provocative costume and a vast plumed hat', as the actress Mistinguett recalled in her memoirs.[155] This *marcheuse* was not even a *rat* (literally, rat), as the trainee members of the *corps de ballet* were called.[156] These spectral women were employed to come on stage but do almost nothing: merely to appear, to gesture and to walk. As described by Avenel, extras (*les figurants*) had much in common with mannequins: they were a 'mixed race' who had to be able to fit all sorts of shoes and wigs and to have 'ease of manner and some certainty in the walk' but also to be essentially passive and indifferent, in order to execute their regulated movements. The *corps de ballet* at the Opéra were considered especially adaptable to *la figuration*, being 'docile subjects, capable of wearing a garment with elegance'.[157]

Out of such humble, anonymous, almost invisible, performance prototypes emerged the fashion mannequin, a new professional for the new century. Like the ballet girls of the Opéra and the chorus girls and acrobats of the Châtelet Theatre, the first mannequins remained largely invisible outside the confines of the couture house. Over thirty years, most went unacknowledged by name in the press, where they continued to be referred to as *figurantes* until well into the 1920s: women who appear.[158] Something of the eeriness of fashion models is captured in this term that invokes Villiers's description of the first appearance of Hadaly, the female android and perfected woman. The android is copied from a real woman but is an improvement on her. As Hadaly comes to life, she quivers from head to foot: 'she became once more an apparition, the phantom re-animated itself'.[159]

2
1900-1914
THE RATIONALISATION
OF THE BODY

18 *Trottoir roulant* and
the Pavillon de l'Italie at
the 1900 Paris Exposition
Universelle. © Léon et
Lévy, Roger-Viollet/Getty
Images.

In the 1900 Exposition Universelle in Paris, visitors had the opportunity to circumnavigate part of the exhibition on the *trottoir roulant*, a moving pavement consisting of two parallel platforms that ran along the perimeter of the exhibition grounds at four and nine kilometres per hour (**18**). These were the respective speeds of slow strolling and fast walking, speeds that evoked the pace of two urban types, the leisurely *flâneur* (a male pedestrian) and the hurrying *passante*, or female passer-by. Unlike the *passante*, however, the travellers on the moving platforms, either fast or slow, looked as if they were gliding across the cityscape, thus reproducing the visual effect of the famous gliding walk of the Paris mannequins.

The moving pavement was one of several mechanical inventions in the period from 1870 to 1914 that included the escalator, the motion-picture camera and projector, Marey's photographic gun, the phonograph, the roller-coaster, the Ford assembly line and the zip fastener, all of which, Hillel Schwartz argued, 'made possible a significantly different sense of physical movement'.[1] Each smoothed the pattern of rhythm by creating a natural flow that eradicated the distinction between separate steps, movements, frames or images. Nurturing a new kinaesthetics that altered the ways in which people moved, exercised, acted and operated in the world, this equivalence between kinetics, bodies and machines existed equally in the moving pavement of the 1900 Exhibition and in the mechanical movements that were the specialty of the ideal – and idealised – mannequins of the couture houses.

This mannequin glide was not yet familiar to the public from the fashion show, which took place behind closed doors, but by 1900 mannequins could be seen strolling in the Bois de Boulogne and other fashionable venues where their employers sent them to test reactions to the new modes before the collections. On their return, sixty to eighty designs would be selected for the new season's collection that would then be shown in private fashion

19 Exhibition rooms at Maison Félix with clothing displayed on lay figures. From *Lady's Realm*, November 1900. London, Central Saint Martins College of Arts and Design Library.

20 The same *Lady's Realm* article of November 1900 also showed these living mannequins in *toilettes de visite* at Maison Félix, one of several couturiers who had 'a particularly good staff of living models, tall, graceful young ladies with perfect figures, who not only know how to wear a dress well but how to move about with ease and elegance', wrote the magazine. 'There are generally eight or ten of these, whose qualifications consist in possessing a graceful, supple figure of the average measurements adopted by the house', it went on, describing them as 'a certain class of women whose profession it is to be gowned conspicuously', and 'one of the most indispensable features' of Paris couture houses. London, Central Saint Martins College of Arts and Design Library.

shows to the overseas buyers.[2] One attempt to bring the fashion show to public attention was made in the Pavillon de la Mode at the 1900 Exhibition that displayed fashion in a series of elaborate tableaux on wax dummies. At first, the house of Worth chose to stage a tableau of a fashion show but the idea was vetoed by the other exhibitors as 'bizarre, a masquerade, undignified, not to be considered', mainly on the grounds that the wax mannequins were offensive.[3] Nevertheless, wax mannequins were used in the Exhibition's displays, including in a tableau of the fitting of a wedding dress at Worth. Such inanimate dress forms were used in the couture houses, too, but by 1900 they had been joined, in all but the most conservative Parisian houses, by a group of living mannequins employed to model the dresses (**19–21**).[4]

THE RISE OF THE PARIS FASHION SHOW

Fashion modelling became well established in the nineteenth century but it was not until the early twentieth that the fashion show, a distinctly theatrical phenomenon, came into being. The shows were pioneered by the houses with the biggest export business, such as Paquin which, in the late 1890s, began to organise shows in its salons at fixed times.[5] Other key designers in the development of the fashion show were Lucile, Poiret and, after the war, Patou. All four astutely developed this modern form of sales,

marketing and publicity and ensured that their innovations were widely publicised, so much so that their claims for their own innovations have entered both the mythology of the fashion business and several twentieth-century fashion histories, while little is known about the many other designers who also played a part in the development of the fashion show. Of these, Doucet and Worth are among the best known today, but of equal importance are Félix, Fred, Redfern, Wallès, Laferrière, Francis, Martial et Armand, Beer and Jenny, all houses that had large American sales.

Many of them demonstrated a degree of stagecraft from the start. At Redfern the mannequins modelled beguiling gowns to clients in vast salerooms with soft carpets, reported the new magazine *Femina* in 1901 (**22**).[6] Redfern, Paquin and Beer all had mirrored fitting rooms equipped with electricity for trying on stage costumes, a precedent set in the 1860s by Worth's *salon de lumière* brilliantly lit by hissing gas-jets with movable shades, in which customers could try out their ballgowns surrounded by mirrored walls on all sides.[7] Both Beer and Paquin had modelling stages, an innovation of Lucile's that became a feature of many Parisian and a few American firms (**24**). At Paquin's it was in 'a good-sized room, half of which was occupied by a platform with footlights; and powerful electric lights were thrown on this platform from the sides and above, precisely as in a theatre'.[8] Paquin is said to have concluded some of her shows with a ballet performance with the dancers all dressed in white.[9]

Maison LAFERRIÈRE
28, Rue Taitbout, PARIS

Un des Salons de vente

21 (above left) An early illustration from *Femina*, 15 November 1903, of mannequins modelling to clients in a French couture house. The caption reads: 'Here is a typical Parisian scene taken from life at a big couturier. The client has come to choose one of several toilettes, so some elegant young women who play the role of "living mannequins" are paraded before her. Dressed in the latest creations of the house, they come and go before the clients so they can better judge the general effect of the toilette.' Courtesy Fashion Institute of Technology/ SUNY, FIT Library Department of Special Collections and FIT Archives.

22 (above centre) A mannequin modelling to a client at Redfern in Paris. From *Femina*, 13 April 1901. The magazine explained: 'You may admire this robe that a *mannequin* is presenting for the admiration of a client. You know that, in dressmaking terminology, one calls *mannequins* those especially chosen young women with an extremely pretty physique from all points of view, who are responsible for wearing and showing off all the advantages of the new dresses.' Musée Galliera de la Mode de la Ville de Paris. Photograph Richard Hubert Smith.

23 (above right) Advertisement for the house of Laferrière showing a group of mannequins in the saleroom, first used in *Les Modes* in 1903. Courtesy Fashion Institute of Technology/ SUNY, FIT Library Department of Special Collections and FIT Archives.

The employment of mannequins was deemed 'a good trick, useful for sales' because even the most elephantine client imagined herself to be like the wasp-waisted mannequins.[10] Although fashion shows were not open to the public, living mannequins were part of a burgeoning publicity industry and soon couturiers began to use them in their advertising (**23**).[11] By 1907 Paris shows and mannequins, particularly at Paquin, Raudnitz, Beer and Félix, were regularly mentioned in the American newspapers.[12] By 1910, the same newspapers routinely referred to American fashion buyers' trips to Europe in their columns.[13] A *New York Times* journalist calculated in 1912 that in the two weeks after the shows approximately fifteen thousand gowns were manufactured for export and that the majority were bought for 'bait', that is, for advertising, rather than for copying.[14]

A French advertising guide published in 1912 and reprinted in 1922 cited psychological research to prove that viewers paid more attention to moving than static objects in its advocacy of the *homme-sandwich* (sandwich man) as a walking poster.[15] The fashion mannequin was an unwitting *femme-sandwich* but one who came wrapped in a fancy package, a set of styles and discourses that disguised her advertising role in a veneer of theatricality.[16] In the 1910s she came to prominence as a new form of working woman, much in the public eye as a modern Parisian type (**25**).[17]

During the first decade of the century, playing on their worldwide renown and secure in the patronage of a rich

24 (below) A stage at Maison Beer fitted with mirrors and electric lighting for trying on stage costumes and evening ball gowns. In the nineteenth century Worth had installed an entirely mirrored room fitted with adjustable gas lighting and, at the turn of the century, several couturiers had such mirrored fitting rooms equipped with electricity. Beer combined the mirrored fitting room with a modelling stage. *Illustrated London News*, 20 November 1903.

and leisured clientele, Parisian couturiers developed the spectacular side of their businesses. By 1910 shows were taking place at fixed hours in all the big couture houses. They evolved a set of protocols that mimicked an elite social occasion, fostering a sense of exclusivity, even though they were in reality commercial events. Entry was by invitation only, usually handwritten, though gradually couturiers began to have engraved cards made, as if to a private party at home. Anyone seeking entry without an introduction was regarded with great suspicion. In the shows, several mannequins modelled either together or one after another, either to private clients or to a group of buyers seated in the salon. The saleswoman or couturier acted as a guide, talking the customer through the dresses that were presented in a set order, from day to evening wear. Audience numbers ranged from a few to a score of people, both women and men. After 1911, following the innovation of the English dressmaker Lucile who served tea at her Paris fashion shows, French dressmakers also began to provide refreshments, and tea and cakes became champagne and canapés.[18]

By then, fashion modelling was deemed essential to sales. In the Paris floods of 1910, overseas buyers coming to the Paris salons in February were disappointed to see the clothes by candlelight, simply thrown over the backs of chairs, because the mannequins who lived in the suburbs could not get in to work. *Fantasio* announced that the floods had been disastrous for the couturiers, quoting the melancholy reflection of a disenchanted buyer: 'Mannequins without dresses just about pass! . . . But dresses without mannequins!'.[19] Mannequins had the

talent of seeming to bring clothes to life through movement. In 1911 one garment at Paquin 'was admirably shown on a tall, slim girl who seemed to know how to make the fur ripple on her figure as though it were on the body of a lissom animal'.[20] For the autumn of 1913, the short wired overskirts of the Paris mannequins, influenced by Poiret's lampshade tunics, were stiffened with 'supple featherbones', wrote the *Chicago Daily Tribune*, 'so supple indeed that, instead of standing away in an unbroken line these undulate in graceful curves, quiver with every motion of the body, and are fascinating to look upon'.[21] The feather boning at the edges of overskirts was covered with delicate trimmings such as lightweight ruching, velvet fringing or artificial flowers to add to the effect of bobbing and swaying when the wearer made the slightest move. In these ways, movement was incorporated into the designs of the dresses, highlighting the role mannequins could play in the design process as well as in publicity and sales.

From 1911 the role of modelling in the French industry was put on a more formal footing by the abolition of the nineteenth-century Chambre Syndicale de la Couture, des Confectionneurs et des Tailleurs pour Dames and its replacement by the Chambre Syndicale de la Couture Parisienne on 14 December 1910.[22] This in effect established haute couture as an autonomous trade and distinguished it from ready-to-wear (*confection*). Its status was defined by an *arrêté ministeriel* which decreed that haute couture houses had to make clothing to measure, to employ a minimum of twenty staff in the ateliers, to present collections twice a year, spring and autumn, consisting of a minimum of seventy-five models shown on living

mannequins and to offer these same collections at least
forty-five times a year to individual clients. This fiat
identified the buyers' shows as the important biannual ones
and put the slightly different procedure of private
modelling to individual clients on a more formal footing by
the requirement to repeat the collections to clients
individually many times a year.

Throughout the nineteenth century, American buyers
had gone to Paris biannually to acquire model dresses,[23]
which they then displayed in 'seasonal openings' at home
(**26**) but it was only in the twentieth century that fashion
journalists began to refer openly to the international
fashion calendar. In the couture houses, work started on
the design of the new season's collections in January and
July; they were shown in February and August, first to
buyers from the U.S.A. and then to those from Europe and
South America.[24] The autumn openings, as the fashion
shows were called, started on 15 August and, unlike today's
shows, were repeated daily over seven to ten days.[25] During
the 1910s and 1920s the dates of the openings gradually
moved forward a fortnight to 1 February and 1 August.[26]
From the early 1910s onwards, quite a few buyers coming
to the autumn openings would arrive in France as early as
May in order to observe the fashions worn by the
mannequins at the Paris races and on the boardwalks of the
fashionable resort towns of Trouville, Deauville and
Dieppe.[27] Those privileged few who routinely placed large
orders were given advanced previews by houses such as
Beer, Lanvin, Jenny and Mme Robert.[28] They were able to
ship home some early models for advanced sales in August,
claiming them as the first models from the new
collections.[29] In reality, these tended to be produced
expressly for the advanced openings and the buyers still
had to wait until 15 August when the real collections for the
autumn season were revealed for the first time to the full
cohort of overseas buyers. American buyers would then
exhibit their 'imports', both licensed and unlicensed copies,
in American fashion shows in October and November.
Then in the new year the American buyers would depart
again for Paris for the next round of biannual shows for the
spring collections.[30]

The pre-war years were profitable for French couture,
even though America's protectionist policies, in the form of
punitive import tariffs on foreign luxury goods such as
dress, often resulted in problems for the French industry.
New, and higher, import tariffs in 1909 put a temporary
brake on imports but inevitably these did not last and
American buyers remained integral to the Paris trade and
vice versa.[31] The American trade journal the *Dry Goods
Economist* maintained a Paris office in the fashionable
avenue d'Antin.[32] It habitually bought a number of

27 A mannequin wearing a flesh-coloured *fourreau* underneath the gown she models for Meyer et Morhange, September 1897. The image pre-dates written accounts of flesh-coloured as opposed to black *fourreaux* by several years. Anonymous photographer. From an album of photographs of model gowns from Parisian couture houses, 1897–8. Musée Galliera de la Mode de la Ville de Paris, 2004.658.1. Photograph Richard Hubert Smith.

28 In 1908 Lucile's London stage was interesting enough to contemporaries to be illustrated in both *Femina* in France and the *Illustrated London News* in the U.K. The caption to the French version reads: 'In London, for the presentation of the new models, it is now the fashion to give a sort of collective representation. Before a theatre pit of the queens of elegance, the mannequins gyrate on a stage, then approach the audience who is either enraptured or makes criticisms. This habit is in the process of becoming implanted in Paris, and this winter our great couturiers will stage performances of toilettes that will be no less sought after than our great opening nights at the theatre.' *Femina*, 1 September 1908. Musée Galliera de la Mode de la Ville de Paris. Photograph Richard Hubert Smith.

garments and accessories from the Paris shows in order to bring them to the attention of its readership and was at pains to point out that Paris fashions were relevant to the entire American garment industry, not only to the top end.[33] From the garments it purchased, the *Economist* produced full-page plates which it recommended retailers to exhibit in their shop windows. In this way, the Paris fashions that were modelled in the elite European houses were a vital part of the American industry at all levels, even if in reality they underwent such a change in the translation that the American copies bore almost no resemblance to the French originals.

Buyers at the Paris shows were carefully monitored. Only foreign buyers were allowed in; French retailers were banned, to prevent them from selling popularised versions of couture designs too close to home.[34] Nor did the French department stores (*grands magasins de nouveautés*) stage their own mannequin parades until the 1920s.[35] By contrast, those American, English, German and Austrian department stores that sent buyers to the French couture houses all staged domestic fashion shows of their Paris purchases. Despite the fact that Paris retailers did not hold fashion shows, one French source from 1902 suggests that the French ready-to-wear wholesalers did show clothes on live mannequins and that the modelling styles differed between wholesale houses and the elite rue de la Paix export establishments.[36]

LUCILE IN LONDON

The most significant contributor to the early development of the fashion show was not, however, a Parisian dress-maker but a London one, Lady Duff Gordon, trading as Lucile.[37] Around 1900 she staged her first London mannequin parades in her Hanover Square premises.[38] In the 1910s she took her mannequins onto the international stage, using their cachet and glamour to establish herself overseas, and she went on to become the first international designer to have branches in four cities at once (London, New York, Paris and Chicago).

Lucile did not invent the phenomenon of modelling, though nearly twenty years later she implied that she had.[39] Rather, she created the fashion show, or 'mannequin parade', a cross between an elite party and a theatrical event held in her luxurious salon or, in the summer, its garden.[40] Her second principal innovation was in the choice, styling and training of her mannequins. The first was a blonde girl in her early teens, Elsie Kings, who went to work for her in the late 1890s.[41] Elsie, who like many girls of her age and class, had never worn a corset, recalled that she was fitted with a corset 'cruelly lined with ribs of steel' and was assured that, if she tightened the laces each day, 'I would soon have less than my present enormous waistline of eighteen inches!'[42] Over the following weeks, Lucile trained her in 'charm of manner' and deportment, including walking with heavy books balanced on her head:

> daily I went through the gestures which would lead me to the proper manner of walking – quick, mincing, fashionable little steps or slow, languid, strolling ones. . . . I soon learned the angle at which my hands appeared whitest, long and slender; at what degree my head best displayed my slender neck. Over and over it was impressed upon me that I had the gift of beauty, and never, never, must I do anything but enhance it! The superficiality of it all, the constant posing and striving for effect, as compared to the naturalness of the present day life and model [in 1927] is almost unbelievable.[43]

Lucile trained all her mannequins in deportment, carriage and gesture, even going so far as to rename them with exotic stage names such as Corisande, Gamela and Hebe.[44] She also claimed that she was the first to take them out of the ugly black *fourreau*, although she did not acknowledge that other Paris and London dressmakers had used flesh-coloured *fourreaux* as early as 1897 (**27**) and many were abandoning it altogether by 1907.[45]

Her mannequins were widely admired by the English press which used them to proclaim a new kind of modern glamour. Trained to strike dramatic poses, during the parades they barely smiled and never spoke, their working-class origins as ambiguously veiled as the beautiful bodies they paraded to an audience of middle- and upper-class men and women, the men, Kaplan and Stowell argue, 'lured by the prospect of inspecting flesh as well as fabric.'[46] Elsie put it more decorously: 'romance came very often to our house. The beautiful girls attracted our customers' male friends, and down they would settle to the more secure if less exciting existence of marriage.'[47] The theme of working-class mannequins marrying rich or titled men later provided the plot for many fiction films such as Howard Hawkes's *Fig Leaves* of 1926.

In her autobiography of 1932, *Discretions and Indiscretions*, Lucile wrote

> The evolution of the mannequin was brought about in my grey salons in Hanover Square. . . . slowly the idea of a mannequin parade, which would be as entertaining to watch as a play, took shape in my mind. I would have glorious, Goddess-like girls, who would walk to and fro dressed in my models, displaying them to the best advantage to an audience of admiring women.[48]

Lucile had designed the stage costumes for the London production of *The Liars* in 1897 and understood how the couture house could function like a theatre in which women of all classes could see the latest styles being worn.[49] She was probably the first to build a modelling stage in her salon (Beer's Paris stage was first recorded in 1903; see **22**), wiring it for footlights in front and draping it in olive chiffon (**28**).[50] In 1904 it was described as

> a draped stage in soft French grey-green, on to which floated tall slender women with that sinuous walk which never fails to make its appeal to the warmer side of social life. They were dressed in elusive pale symbolic gowns, parables of beauty . . . the girl . . . walked towards me and away with that wonderful swaying step that Lucile teaches all her models.[51]

Randy Bigham writes that it took Lucile a few years to bring together all the elements of the fashion show.[52] They coalesced in her spring 1904 show at 23 Hanover Square: the stage, an orchestra, lights, tea, show invitations and show programmes, with a glittering mixture of guests from society and stage and even journalists to ensure the event was written up.[53] As each mannequin made her entrance, wearing a cloth band on her arm bearing the number of the dress, Lucile called out the name of the dress. Over the decade, she gave her gowns names with overtly sexual connotations, such as *Come to Me*, *The Captain with the Whiskers*, *The Sighing Sound of Lips Unsatisfied* and *When Passion's Thrall is O'er*. In 1905 she staged a 'Symposium of Dress'[54] and, in 1909, the 'Seven Ages of Woman', written by her sister the popular novelist Elinor Glyn. It included tableaux intended to appeal to 'the married woman who entertained, was entertained, and who could indulge in the luxury of a lover'.[55] The names and order of the gowns constituted a clear subtext of sexual pleasure and fulfilment: *The Desire of the Eyes*, *Persuasive Delight*, *Visible Harmony*, *A Frenzied Hour*, *Salut d'Amour*, *Afterwards* and *Contentment*.

The pace of early fashion shows was slow and the modern practice of ceaseless backstage quick-changes was anathema.[56] Shows often lasted an hour and a half or more and clients would wait while the mannequins' hair was rearranged to fit the style of each dress, with slippers and stockings changed to accessorise it correctly. Lucile was an innovator in co-ordinating and accessorising her mannequins, so a dress was always shown with matching boots, stockings, hat, gloves, handkerchief, veil and jewellery.[57] The garden shows even stretched to pedigree dogs with jewelled leashes co-ordinated to the mannequins' gowns.[58]

Lucile, like the French couturiers, publicised her fashion shows as elite, luxury spectacles for individual clients but

29a and b The mannequin seen walking to work in **16** is shown here modelling clothes later in the day. The journalist writes: 'And now, to work! We are going to see her again as an indefatigable mannequin dressed in turn in four models from Maison Poiret, each one prettier than the last. His models are not only delicious, they are presented in the most seductive and the newest way. M. Poiret is in this respect a veritable innovator. To present his models to his clients, he is of the opinion that they have to be seen in a complementary and appropriate environment . . . at his house, the mannequin only dons a new model after she has put on a different hat to suit the gown, so that the Parisienne can . . . judge the effect of the toilette under a large feathered hat or in conjunction with a flowered toque to make an indissoluble and delicious ensemble.' Here the mannequin models Paul Poiret gowns with hats by the well-known milliner Lewis. *Le Figaro-Modes*, February 1904. Courtesy Fashion Institute of Technology/SUNY, FIT Library Department of Special Collections and FIT Archives.

30 Louis Süe's design for Poiret's modelling stage, 1909. Fonds d'Archives Louis Süe, Centre d'Archives d'Architecture du XXième Siècle, DAF/Cité de l'Architecture et du Patrimoine.

she was also influential within the trade. Not long after her first shows, London department stores began to stage fashion shows, albeit less exclusive ones.[59] In 1908 *Femina* magazine in France illustrated her London stage (see **28**), and described the growing tendency to instal modelling stages in Paris as an innovation from London.[60] She visited America in 1907[61] and in both 1907 and 1908 she was included in fashion shows of French couturiers at Wanamaker's department store in Philadelphia, which suggests that she must have had some contact with department-store buyers. Although no details are known about Lucile's relations with French couture houses from the late 1890s to the 1900s, as a London dressmaker she would have been aware of the trade links between both cities.[62]

POIRET IN PARIS

While Lucile was developing her fashion shows in London, Paul Poiret opened his first maison de couture in Paris in 1903 at 5 rue Auber. In 1906 he moved to 37 rue Pasquier and in 1909 to a building at 9 avenue d'Antin which abutted 107 faubourg Saint-Honoré, where he remained until 1924 when he moved to the Rond-Point des Champs-Élysées.[63] From these premises Poiret made his own,

considerable, contribution to the history of fashion shows as a form of modern marketing and promotion. Like Lucile, Poiret was known for his seductive presentation and the way he carefully accessorised his mannequins: they too were considered singularly modern and intriguing (**29**).[64] In 1910 a journalist marvelled at the colours he put the mannequins in: Titian-haired, with pink and white skin, a mannequin dressed entirely in vibrant green was deemed 'extremely original'.[65] Also like Lucile, Poiret used his garden for fashion shows which were reported as far afield as New York and Chicago (**31**).[66] Unlike Lucile and Beer, however, Poiret did not build a stage for his mannequins until 1909 when he moved to an eighteenth-century *hôtel* in avenue d'Antin which he commissioned Louis Süe to renovate (**30**). There he installed a small proscenium stage, perhaps inspired by the *Femina* illustration of Lucile's stage the previous year (see **28**). Before as many as eighty women a day, from five to seven every afternoon (*de cinq à sept*), his mannequins, 'lissom as nymphs, file past in this living, colourful but wholly unpretentious scene', as he wrote in his memoirs.[67]

Poiret sold models to American buyers from the start but, like Lucile, did not publicise this fact, choosing instead to present himself as a couturier *de luxe*.[68] It was not until 1914 that he even referred to foreign buyers.[69] His extravagance was prodigious, often wasteful. Yet he clearly

had a sense of the requirements of international trade and maintained strong links with European and American department stores, travelling to Berlin in 1910, touring Europe in 1911, America in 1913 and both continents in the 1920s. He took pains to exclude unauthorised copyists from his shows and dealt with piracy by following a system 'which, so everyone assured him, would ruin him. Visitors to his establishment are asked to inscribe their names in a big book, also information as to who they are and where they come from. At the top of the page is a courteous announcement that a visitor is expected to buy at least one frock'.[70]

The mannequin parade was only one of the devices Poiret pioneered to promote his business as a form of what today is called 'lifestyle marketing'. In the years leading up to the First World War, besides running his couture house and staging fashion shows, he produced a perfume, he designed for the stage, he opened an interior design studio and school, he cultivated the press and he threw spectacular themed parties.[71] He went on overseas mannequin tours and commissioned illustrators to make luxury albums of his fashion designs. In 1911 he was the first to use both photography and film to promote his collections, modelled by his house mannequins.[72]

The fashion press of both America and France nearly always presented a benign, even adulatory, image of the

31 (top) Mannequin parade at Paul Poiret, illustrating an article entitled 'A lesson in elegance in a garden'. *L'Illustration*, 9 July 1910. (www.lillustration.com).

32 (above) 'Scenes of modern hysteria'. A caricature of a fashion show from Sem's album *Le Vrai et le faux chic*, 1914. Photograph Richard Hubert Smith.

33 Sem's fantasy of a black mannequin from *Le Vrai et le faux chic*, 1914. Photograph Richard Hubert Smith.

34 Poiret model imported and photographed by Wanamaker in April 1914. The mannequin wears a monocle and she thrusts her hands deep in her pockets in a masculine gesture. Washington, D.C., Library of Congress.

fashion shows of Poiret and Lucile. Only the left-wing press criticised couture employment practices.[73] In 1914, however, the caricaturist Sem (Georges Goursat) produced an illustrated album which viciously lampooned the new breed of modern couturiers. *Le Vrai et le faux chic* lambasts the excesses of modern fashion, reserving its most excoriating criticism for the new kind of fashion show which Sem called 'scenes of modern hysteria' (**32**).[74] He describes a vibrant atmosphere, over-saturated with exquisite perfumes and charged with waves of nervous feeling in an audience of deluded society women, actresses and courtesans who are all swept up in the 'delirium of dressing' by the mannequin parade: 'Around them, the mute mannequins with waxen smiles come, go and come again, brushing past them, enveloping them with the caress of their trailing garments, tirelessly repeated, intoxicating their imaginations with rhythmic and undulating movements, with seductive poses, with discreet and knowing contortions.'[75]

Sem attacks the new second-rate fashion houses that have spilled out from the rue de la Paix and were then opening all over Paris.[76] He does not name the designers he attacks and it is possible that the show illustrated here is a hybrid of Poiret and Lucile's shows, although the lampshade skirt suggests Poiret. Much of the rest of the album, particularly the section called 'Museum of Errors', is clearly an attack on Poiret, who responded vociferously in the press, threatening to retaliate with a book called *The True and False Talent*.[77] Another caricature of a fashion show depicts a room like Lucile's Paris salon, however, and Sem's textual references to tea, music and tangoing mannequins may also be a swipe at Lucile.[78] In the new houses, writes Sem,

There, there is no holding back. These shameless manufacturers have become veritable impresarios, staging a kind of gala each season and, under the pretext of launching the new fashions, organising the presentation of their new models like a music hall extravaganza. Between a tango by Mistinguett and a song by Fursy, on a stage garlanded by paper flowers and Chinese lanterns in the midst of the audience, they parade à la 'Sumurun'[79] to music, a strange corps de ballet which is more or less Russian, Persian or Romany, an entire procession of disjointed mannequins, of snake-women sheathed in venomous outfits who undulate, slowly convulse, stomachs forward like an offering, a foot trailing, miming a kind of purposeless tango before the eyes of the female audience – unhappy little snobs that these unprincipled managers over-excite with adulterated tea and mild drugs, while awaiting the next day when they will extend their cynicism so far as to drug them on cocaine and ether, the better to prepare them, to reduce them to a state of poor unconscious women, ready to submit to the most extravagant exploitation.[80]

Here, besides accusing the new wave of parvenu haute couturiers of drug-pushing, Sem was criticising them for vulgarising taste and reducing fashion to music hall. He was, as Nancy Troy has shown, virulently anti-Semitic and racist, even by the standards of his day.[81] Certainly, he attacked Poiret's orientalism in the pages that follow and added his own brand of primitivism in his description of the reptilian mannequins in the fashion show, while decrying the 'moral and material perversion in these scandalous exhibitions of a selection of mannequins from which only the negress is missing' (**33**).[82] This illustration of a black mannequin is perhaps an imagined one rather than a true depiction, since the first report of a black mannequin in Paris comes from 1928, but Sem's illustration is an oddity, not least because it is far different from his

35 Black and white newsreel footage from *Journal Gaumont* of Lucile mannequins modelling dresses and coats in 1914. These may be the Paris premises furnished and decorated by Liberty of London. Film still from Gaumont Pathé archives, Paris. 'La mode: robes et manteaux crées par Lucile', 1914. Ref 1403GJ 00025. © Gaumont.

virulently racist illustrations of African women in tribal dress in the pages that follow.[83] Although the tangoing mannequins of the fashion show, whom Sem excoriated, were always white, the dance itself was, as Alessandra Vaccari argues, a route whereby black culture came to Europe, creating an interface for cultural miscegenation.[84]

Poiret himself promoted both his orientalist fashions and a vision of himself as a pasha or head of a harem. From 1909 until 1924 when new backers took control of his company and put a brake on events, he staged a series of fashion shows, parties and fêtes in which his mannequins featured prominently. He also took them out and about with him in Paris, thus ensuring that they were publicised as his 'court', associated with his orientalism and, in particular, his representation of himself as a sultan at his famous Thousand and Second Night party on 24 June 1911.[85] Poiret's orientalism fascinated American journalists; one wrote that only a person 'who has eaten hashish, smoked opium, chewed the betel nut, or tasted the lotus leaf can imagine what they [his designs] are like'.[86] In this article, however, orientalism is conflated with masculinity: the writer describes a unisex couple at Poiret, where

> the man manikin accompanies the girl manikin in clothes which are likewise. Or approximately likewise. He wears trousers; so does she. He wears a prince Albert; so does she. He wears a top hat; she does the same. A cutaway; she beats him to it. He weareth hith thuthpenderth; she wears 'em also, or, rather, a pair of her own. Spats; she too.

In this way, Poiret's orientalism became conflated with a modern and transgressive gender masquerade (**34**); for, as Kenneth Silver argued, contemporary attacks on Poiret's orientalism were really attacks on his avant-gardism, in which his orientalism was conflated with a range of cultural 'others'.[87]

LUCILE ET CIE, PARIS

In 1910 Lucile opened the first of her international branches, in New York (see Chapter 4). The following year she did something considerably more audacious for an English dressmaker, establishing a branch in Paris, the cultural and economic capital of haute couture.[88] On 4 April 1911, at 11 rue de Penthièvre, Lucile et Cie opened to the public with an 'English tea' and a fashion show of two hundred models displayed by four London mannequins on a specially constructed modelling stage.[89] The *Dry Goods Economist* described how the strong overhead lighting above the sombre tones of the dark grey velvet drapery set off the model dresses to great advantage: 'This miniature theatre has created quite a sensation in Paris.'[90] Lucile's show drew so many visitors that it was repeated over five days.[91] For her second season, in August 2011, Lucile again held an afternoon tea with music and a guided tour round the new premises furnished and decorated by Liberty of London.[92] This became the pattern for Lucile's Paris shows, which might run over several days and feature 'music, tea and all the trimmings of a fashionable reception'.[93]

The distinctive style of her English mannequins was noted and Elsie Kings recalled 'the contrast between the sharp, almost staccato type of French girl who exhibited clothes, and our sinuous, dreamy, velvet-eyed models'.[94] Surviving newsreel footage from 1914 confirms how different Lucile's mannequins were from Paris mannequins, both in their longer, more slender physiques and in their languorously elegant modelling styles (**35**).

LE THÉATRE DU GRAND COUTURIER

A l'imitation de leurs confrères américains, la plupart des grands coutu-riers parisiens ont maintenant fait installer dans leurs hôtels un vérita-ble théâtre sur lequel les mannequins, revêtus des dernières créations de la mode, peuvent évoluer tout à leur aise pour montrer et mettre en valeur les mille et un détails de la robe à lancer... Des flots de lumière, artistement calculés, inondent la scène et se jouent dans les glaces qui ornent la salle ; assises à dis-tance convenable et dans le jour propice, les clientes peuvent, en toute con-naissance de cause, procéder au choix qui les attire. Clients, couturiers et mannequins, chacun se loue de cette innovation... Ajoutons que, pour cer-tains couturiers, le « théâtre » constitue en même temps une sorte de labora-toire où, dans le jeu des lumières et des ombres, il s'efforce à combiner har-monieusement les nuances et à draper artistement les étoffes... Le théâtre du grand couturier, à Paris, s'appelle le « salon des lumières » ; en voici un aspect croqué, par l'un de nos plus modernes artistes : M. Pierre Brissaud.

697

Les Robes de "Rue de la Paix", au Théâtre du Vaudeville

ROBES DESSINÉES PAR PAUL IRIBE, PUBLIÉES AVEC L'AUTORISATION DE Mme PAQUIN — CHAPEAUX LEWIS

36 (facing page) This Lucile fashion show in her Paris premises was illustrated in 'Le théâtre du grand couturier', *Femina*, 15 December 1911; **84** illustrates another fashion show there. The caption reads: 'In imitation of their American colleagues, the majority of the big Parisian couturiers have installed a veritable theatre in their salons in which mannequins, dressed in the latest fashionable creations, can glide entirely at their ease, showing and highlighting the thousand and one details of the dress they are launching

. . . the stage is flooded with artistically placed pools of lighting that play upon the mirrors decorating the room . . . Clients, couturiers and mannequins, all praise this innovation . . . here is a view of it sketched by one of our most modern artists, M. Pierre Brissaud'. Brissaud's illustration seems to have been copied from a set of photographs of modelling in the New York premises, prints of which survive in the Victoria and Albert Museum, London. Musée Galliera de la Mode de la Ville de Paris. Photograph Richard Hubert Smith.

37 (above) Stage costumes designed by Paul Iribe and executed by Paquin for the play *Rue de la Paix* at the Théâtre Vaudeville. The image is a composite photograph that uses the same actresses more than once: Maud Gipsy, Georgette Aman and Leprince each appear twice. *Comoedia illustré, Numéro exceptionnelle*, 1 February 1912. Fashion Museum, Bath and North East Somerset Council / the Bridgeman Art Library.

French press responses to Lucile's opening show were mixed. While *Excelsior* reviewed it in fulsome terms, *Fantasio* sneered at her 'gowns of emotion' and implied that she was both pretentious and vulgarly commercial. As for the sobbing violins accompanying the presentation, they were 'miaow-sic': caterwauling.[95] *Femina*, on the other hand, illustrated a Lucile fashion show in wholly flattering terms (**36**).[96] It even went so far as to suggest, unlike other French journalists who implied that the mannequin parade was quintessentially French, that the French were following an American precedent in fitting a modelling stage. Lucile had opened her New York house the previous year and, although she is not named in this article, it seems clear that the reference to American houses is to her. Two months after her first Paris opening, the Paris dressmaker Chary staged a fashion show in a rented theatre as a one-act playlet showing a day in the life of the mannequins, followed by music, tea and refreshments.[97] On the whole, however, while Lucile's contribution to fashion marketing and promotion is undeniable, it was far greater in America, where she was widely written about, than in France where she received considerably less press.[98]

Both Lucile and Poiret were satirised in a popular stage play, *Rue de la Paix* by Abel Hermant and Marc de Toledo, which opened at the Vaudeville Theatre in Paris in January 1912. The play was a glorified fashion show masquerading as a melodrama, with costumes designed by the fashion illustrator Paul Iribe and executed by Paquin (**37**). It concerned the rivalry between two couture houses whose directors, M. Baudry and Lady de Leeds, were thinly veiled portraits of Poiret and Lucile.[99] *The Boston Daily Globe* wrote that

> anyone familiar with the ways of the mannequins of the Rue de la Paix could not fail to recognise the faithful character studies. The Parisiennes, who are nothing if not a little malicious, are laughing in their sleeves at the veiled skit, in the last act, on the much advertised opening of a dressmaking atelier by a well-known society woman. It is not so very many months since we had, here in Paris, just such an opening day, and the skit at the Vaudeville is so lifelike that it might almost be said to be a little ill-natured.[100]

The play, which showcased Paquin's gowns for Iribe, opened just as the international buyers were arriving in Paris for the February 1912 openings. It was therefore avidly attended by Paquin's rival dressmakers, as well as by the buyers.[101] *Rue de la Paix* gives an insight into the commercial practices of elite fashion, opening with a scene of mannequins modelling not to luxury clients but to a woman buyer who is seated next to her commissionnaire, an important type of Parisian agent responsible for shepherding overseas buyers around the shows and

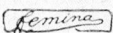

UNE HEURE D'ÉLÉGANCE AU THÉATRE FEMINA

UNE CONFÉRENCE DE Mlle JANE MARNAC ET DE M. ANDRÉ DE FOUQUIÈRES

LES DEUX ÉCOLES

(Felix.)

Mlle ALICE GUERRA LA DANSEUSE DES FOLIES-BERGÈRE QUI PRÊTA SON CONCOURS A LA FÊTE ORGANISÉE AU THÉATRE FEMINA. (in haut, en frise). QUELQUES-UNES DES TOILETTES QUI FURENT PRÉSENTÉES AUX SPECTATRICES DE LA FÊTE ORGANISÉE PAR LE COUTURIER PARRY.

Déteste et ne fais

Aime et fais

PARRY

Mlle MIREILLE CORBÉ FUT, PARMI LES ARTISTES QUI CONTRIBUÈRENT AU SUCCÈS DE LA MATINÉE, UNE DES PLUS APPLAUDIES DU PUBLIC. (A gau h). LE FRONTISPICE DU PROGRAMME DE LA MATINÉE : LES DEUX DESSINS DE DE LOSQUES SYMBOLISENT "LES DEUX ÉCOLES " DE LA MODE. D'APRÈS PARRY.

L'ÉTRANGE, la curieuse idée que vient de réaliser le Benjamin des couturiers, Parry! Il a organisé, au Théâtre Femina, une matinée, au cours de laquelle il a fait défiler les plus jolis et les plus pittoresques modèles de la saison, présentés par de ravissants mannequins, à propos desquels le fantaisiste réputé, Fernand Frey, conta de spirituels boniments.

Tout ce que Paris compte d'élégances dans l'aristocratie et dans le monde artiste, s'était rendu au Théâtre Femina. Dès trois heures et demie, une foule nombreuse s'était massée aux portes, et c'est à quatre heures, devant une salle ultra-bondée, où l'on remarquait notamment les personnalités suivantes :

Baronne Henri de Rothschild, Mme Cahen d'Anvers, marquise Yvanrey, Mme de Yturbe, Mme Soriano, duchesse de Guiche, princesse Murat, duchesse de Grammont, marquise de Noailles, princesse Yourkevitch, Mmes Mistinguett, Spinelly, Yane, M. Japy de Beaucourt, Mlle Maud

Gauthier, Jane Faber, Marthe Derminy, MM. Pierre Veber, Paul Strauss, Mlle Jane Aaron, M. et Mme Marcel Boulenger, Mlle Gaby Deslys, Mme Doyen, M. Gonzalès Moreno, Mme de Mouravieff, Mlle Geneviève Vix, marquise d'Anglesey, Mme Péquignot, Mme Tristan-Bernard, Mme Pierre

Mlle JEANNE MARNAC

QUI FIT AU " THÉATRE FEMINA " UNE CONFÉRENCE OU ELLE EXPOSA SES IDÉES SUR LA MODE. LA DÉLICIEUSE ARTISTE TRIOMPHE EN CE MOMENT A LA " BOITE A FURSY " OÙ ELLE PORTE UNE ROBE EXQUISE DE PARRY.

Lafitte, Mlle Mary de Buch, Mme Balletta, Ml'e Yvonne de Bray, M. et Mme Mühlbacher, M. et Mme Grebert, etc., que le rideau se leva sur une charmante causerie de Mlle Marnac et de M. de Fouquières.

L'exquise artiste exposa avec verve des idées modernes, audacieuses et imprévues sur la mode, sur ce qu'elle fut, sur ce qu'elle est, sur ce qu'elle sera. Puis M. André de Fouquières, émit sur l'élégance une opinion autorisée et d'une indiscutable maîtrise. Mais les deux conférenciers aboutirent à la même conclusion, qui est de renouveler le vêtement féminin.

Les auditions qui « illustraient » cette conférence, réunissaient les noms les plus aimés du public parisien : M. Francell et Mlle Lucy Vauthrin, de l'Opéra-Comique : Mlle Mireille Corbé, M. Gaston Secrétan, Mlle Alice Guerra et M. Brouett, Mlle Edmée Favart, MM. Pierre Juvenet et Vernaud.

Nous nous sommes rendus au rond point des Champs-Elysées où M. Parry nous a décrit en ces termes son impression :

« Je suis enchanté. Je ne me dissimule pas l'audace de mon geste, mais je n'ai qu'à m'en louer, si je dois m'en rapporter à la satisfaction de mes invités. Voyez-vous, j'ai une grande confiance en moi. C'est que j'essaie de défendre le goût français, la mode française. La ligne et la simplicité sont mon principal, mon unique souci, c'est en l'observant seulement que l'on peut vraiment créer, réaliser des modes gracieuses, artistiques et seyantes. Faire jeune et joli, tel est mon but. Je préfère mille fois un joli pied à une crinoline et une cheville gracieuse à un panier».

N'est-ce pas votre avis, mesdames ?

R. S.

organising their purchases and shipping for them. In the play the commissionnaire, with notebook in hand, writes down the names and prices of the dresses the American buyer selects.[102] The mannequins gossip backstage about the amorous intrigues of their clients and employers and the play paints a seamy picture of sexual laxity, commercial skulduggery and workplace exploitation at odds with the couturiers' own self-promotion.[103] Its tenor suggests, like Sem's caricatures, that fashion shows were a source of lively entertainment in the period.[104] Their satires reveal scenes of sexual and commercial lubricity absent from fashion journalism, which tended to endorse the system of which it was a part in flowery and hyperbolic language.

PARRY: THE FASHION LINE-UP AND MOTION CAPTURE

Early in 1912 Jean Patou opened his first couture house, Parry, at 4 Rond-point des Champs-Élysées, specialising in leather and fur. To launch the business, he organised an afternoon event at the Théâtre Femina which included a debate on fashion and a fashion show that were covered by *Femina* magazine (**38**). The page layout, like that of another collage (**39**), used a composite photograph to re-create a line of mannequins, an increasingly common type of layout in fashion and theatre magazines. Further examples (**42**) show the *Rue de la Paix* mannequins depicted like a chain of paper dolls; the composite photograph (see **37**) ranges them in a shallow V and re-uses three actresses twice as if they were modular; Doucet mannequins appear in a line (see **10**); and a 1912 spread on the latest fashions in sleeves uses the same format (**40**). Yet it also takes its imagery from the theatrical chorus line. A *Femina* cover of 1914 (**41**)

shows identical chorus girls styled like the New Woman, dressed in a modern and masculine working wardrobe: a dark blue and white uniform. Increasingly, after 1910, the gap narrowed between the fashion line-up and the chorus line, with its rows of anonymous and identical-looking girls. 'All Individuality Eliminated' reads the subtitle of an American article on the chorus line in 1913, describing how twenty-four girls, 'having at last been chosen and the contracts signed, the stage-manager at once starts to crush out any and all of the personal characteristics any of the twenty-four may possess and to develop them into mere reflections of each other.'[105] Each must move in perfect synchronicity with the others, down to the wink of an eye. Working in sets of eight, they are not even identified individually on show programmes – unlike model dresses, 'chorus girls haven't even got numbers'.[106]

Besides their link to the chorus line, these images of mannequin line-ups that picture the fashion show have a visual connection to another kind of *défilé*, the military parade, also intended to eradicate traces of individualism, which was captured in the techniques of chronophotography. Marey's assistant from 1881 to 1893 was Georges Demeny, one of the principal promoters of physical education in French schools and in the army.[107] Some of Marey's images of walking men (see **14**) were of Demeny himself while others were of soldiers filmed at the École militaire at Joinville, the training centre for military athletes and gymnasts outside Paris.[108] In 1913, 'the Marey apparatus for analysing movement' which could 'divide a given movement into half a dozen parts' was still being used to record military gymnastics at Joinville (**43**).[109] The image shows a single body in motion, using multiple pictures to map the movements of one individual in space and simultaneous time. Representations of fashion

41 (right) Chorus line from Massenet's *Panurge*, an opera first performed at the Théâtre de la Gaîté, Paris, on 25 April 1913. In French *un mouton de Panurge* is a person who unthinkingly follows others; it comes from the sheep that blindly follow each other in Rabelais's *Panurge*. Here identical chorus girls are styled as New Women in a modern and masculine working wardrobe: the caption announces that 'les jolis moutons de Panurge' have adopted a blue and white uniform. From the cover of *Femina*, 1 June 1914. Musée Galliera de la Mode de la Ville de Paris. Photograph Richard Hubert Smith.

42 (left) Stage costumes by Paul Iribe for *Rue de la Paix* at the Théâtre Vaudeville illustrated in a fashion show line-up. Roger–Milès, 'Paquin, Canada et la drame', February or March 1912. Fashion Museum, Bath and North East Somerset Council / the Bridgeman Art Library.

40 (above left) Illustration of sleeve details that used the fashion show format of a line of mannequins. *Femina*, 1 January 1912. Courtesy Fashion Institute of Technology/ SUNY, FIT Library Department of Special Collections and FIT Archives.

modelling in the same period (see **10** and **39–42**) were analogous to these images of military gymnastics. Both reveal common concerns about how to capture the image of the body in motion; in addition, they suggest commonalities between the ostensibly different bodily disciplines of fashion modelling and military parading that have nineteenth-century precedents, as the French historian Georges Vigarello suggested in his history of the pedagogy of bodily gesture and comportment, where he noted the similarities between the bodily stances required by early nineteenth-century military gymnastics and those of fashion.[110] These equivalent modes of regulation and display of the body bring the military parade and the fashion parade (both *défilés*) into proximity: they are two parallel manifestations of the standardised body in work and popular culture respectively.

A similar multiplication of body images was produced in the three-faced mirrors that became ubiquitous early in the twentieth century, giving women three simultaneous views of themselves from different angles. In an advertisement for a three-faced mirror from 1912 (**44**), the figure appears to have stepped out of the central panel and come alive,

43 (left) Military gymnastics in the École militaire at Joinville, photographed using the 'Marey apparatus' in 1913. *Illustrated London News*, 12 April 1913.

44 (below) Advertisement for a Brot three-faced mirror showing the actress Alice Nory in a Parry ensemble, also seen in **38**. *Femina*, 1 July 1912. Courtesy Fashion Institute of Technology/SUNY, FIT Library Department of Special Collections and FIT Archives..

Mlle Alice Nory, du Théâtre de l'Athénée, devant son Miroir-Brot
Le Catalogue illustré N° 5 est envoyé franco par
Charles BROT, Fabricant du Miroir-Brot, 89, Faubourg Saint-Denis, PARIS

turning from a representation into a real woman and gazing speculatively at the viewer with her finger on her chin. Although the styling of both the mirror and the fashion is modernist, the visual tradition of a woman who steps out of a picture frame (more usually carved gilt) comes from the nineteenth-century *tableau vivant* and was used again in more than one twentieth-century fashion show. This particular advertisement features Parry's design first shown in *Femina* six months earlier, where the dress was shown in motion on a mannequin who walks forward in a fluid modelling pose, one hand on her hip, the other gesturing in the air (see **38**). Her costume is ahead of its time: tubular, drop-waisted, loose and adaptable for walking, it anticipates the modernist, functionalist designs of the 1920s by a decade. It is used to illustrate the second of two schools of fashion, according to Parry, the first being an eighteenth-century one and the second a svelte, neo-classical one – Parry's choice – that prefigured Patou's streamlined modernism of the 1920s.[111]

In 1913 a Seventh Avenue buyer, Mr Lichtenstein, bought the entire Parry collection and in March 1914 Patou made the decision to open under his own name.[112] With an initial capital of 300,000 francs and a staff of three hundred, he planned to open his premises at 7 rue Saint-Florentin with a fashion show for the buyers on 1 August 1914. In the event, war was declared, Patou volunteered and had to report at Nancy, leaving the collection to be shown in his absence on 2 August. Although the firm remained open in his absence throughout the war,[113] it ran at a loss and it was only when he reopened on 1 March 1919 after the Armistice that he made a successful comeback.[114] From the start, Patou's modernist aesthetic appealed to American buyers; American business methods in turn appealed to Patou after the war. In the 1920s his

45 Marcel Duchamp, *Nude Descending a Staircase, No. 2*, 1912. Oil on canvas, 147 x 89.2 cm. Philadelphia Museum of Art, Philadelphia.

46 (below left) Robert Delaunay, *La Ville de Paris*, 1910–12. Oil on canvas, 267 x 406 cm. Musée National d'Art Moderne, Centre Georges Pompidou, Paris.

47 (below right) A generic illustration of a fashion-house mannequin showing her in front of a typical three-faced mirror that might either be free-standing or, as here, fitted to the wall. From L. Roger-Milès, *Les Créateurs de la mode*, Paris 1910. Musée Galliera de la Mode de la Ville de Paris. Photograph Richard Hubert Smith.

innovations in showing fashion brought movement, modernity and mechanisation together on the catwalk; his pre-war innovations at Parry suggest, however, that these had their origins in the 1910s.

THE BODY IN TIME AND SPACE

If the standardisation of the body in the pre-war fashion show echoed the serial imagery of the chorus line, it was also similar to imagery that explored the visualisation of movement in the fields of work, art and sport. The visual imagery of work was explored from 1912 onwards by the American production engineer Frank B. Gilbreth, whose diagrammatic studies visualised the work processes of labourers such as bricklayers; they were the predecessor of time and motion studies intended to effect economies of labour in the workplace. Gilbreth's interest in efficiency links him to the work of F. W. Taylor, whose *Scientific Management of the Workplace*, first published in 1911, investigated ways of rationalising the workplace by regulating the movements of the workers. Siegfried Gideon described Gilbreth as the inheritor of Marey because of the way that Gilbreth's images began 'to capture with full precision the complicated trajectory of human movement . . . that made visible the elements as well as the path of human motion'.[115]

In art, a number of artists began to picture time and motion in ways similar to the visual patterns of the fashion

48 Advertisement for a three-faced 'volte face' mirror by the firm of Postel & Olivier, showing the differing views it afforded: full face, three quarters, profile, back view, three quarters reversed. From the supplement to *Femina*, 15 October 1909. Courtesy Fashion Institute of Technology/ SUNY, FIT Library Department of Special Collections and FIT Archives.

show and chorus line, such as Marcel Duchamp's 'Cubo-Futurist' *Nude Descending a Staircase*, painted in 1912, influenced by Marey and exhibited in both Paris and New York at a time when images and descriptions of fashions shows were proliferating in illustrated magazines (**45**).[116] The same year, Robert Delaunay exhibited *La Ville de Paris* (**46**). His elongated women have the slenderness and poise of fashion mannequins; he layers tradition and novelty in his fractured and simultaneous portrait of the city of Paris, long associated with French fashion and its icons, the Eiffel Tower, the Seine and the alluring Parisienne.[117]

Delaunay's modernist Three Graces suggest the triple reflections of the period, created in the three-faced mirrors that were popular in both domestic homes and in couture houses (**47**; see **44**).[118] At Paquin's, each of the identical fitting rooms with glass and white wooden doors contained a large three-faced mirror in which the client could inspect herself from all points of view, in bright electric light.[119] The multiple viewpoints of the triple mirrors drew on the tradition of nineteenth-century fashion illustrations that showed three views of the same dress.[120] There had even briefly been a fashion periodical, *La Stéréoscope*, which supplied its readers with special glasses to read its double images three-dimensionally.[121] Yet, the novelty of the three-faced mirror was that it contained the possibility of multiple viewpoints, many more than three, as the two side-wings could be endlessly re-adjusted by the viewer to provide an all-round view of the figure. Popular at exactly the same time that Georges Braque and Pablo Picasso were producing their cubist paintings of objects seen from multiple viewpoints (1907–14), triple mirrors enabled a kind of interiorised cubist vision that put self-image centre

stage, a form of montage whereby the viewer could reconcile the three or more images in her or his head into a single, unified body image.

This capacity of the three-faced mirror to grant multiple images of the self is diagrammatically illustrated in an advertisement of 1909 (**48**). On the right is a realistic drawing of the woman in situ before the triple mirror: the left-hand drawing unspools the simultaneous views of her body in three-dimensional space and lays them out from left to right in consecutive two-dimensional viewpoints, captioned 'front', 'three quarters', 'profile', back' and so forth. The visual effect of the run of images is to suggest a cinematic flow of movement caught in a series of frozen poses of the kind recorded by Marey, Muybridge and Gilbreth. From 1910 onwards, representations of dynamic, simultaneous movement appeared not just in Duchamp's *Nude Descending a Staircase* (see **45**) and in the work of Robert Delaunay, but also in that of Sonia Delaunay and the Italian Futurists, particularly Gino Severini, who was in Paris at the same time. Images like this advertisement give a mainstream context to these artists' experiments with simultaneity. They show that cubist and 'simultaneous' ways of seeing were a feature of everyday bourgeois culture at the same time as, even prior to, the avant-garde's formal investigations of time, space and the image.

Further evidence of the popular taste for such effects is provided by an illustration of 'a curious photographic procedure' in a French fashion magazine of 1912 (**49**). The image shows one woman from the back and four reflections. These simultaneous views of the same woman are created by a mirrored 'corner' where two mirrors set at an angle to each other create the illusion of five identical

MIROIR - BROT
pour s'habiller et faire tous essayages

GALLERY ARRANGED FOR MULTIPHOTOGRAPHY.

individuals in conversation. This type of photograph, called a multiphotograph, was 'invented' in the 1890s and remained popular over several decades. Popular journals like *Scientific American* and, in France, *La Nature*, explained in diagrams how the effect was achieved (**52**). The angle between the mirrors determines the number of figures produced: a 90-degree angle produces three images, a 72-degree angle four images, a 60-degree angle five images, a 45-degree angle seven images 'and, if the mirrors are parallel [as they were in the mirrored dressing rooms and salons of the couture houses], theoretically, an infinite number of images will result'.[122] Multiphotographs were

enjoyed by such august and diverse figures as Condé Nast, the owner and publisher of *Vogue*, who had his picture taken in an Atlantic City photographic booth,[123] and Duchamp who had his taken in a Broadway booth in New York (**51**).[124]

Exactly the same visual games continued to be played in the fashion imagery of the 1920s, so a 1925 advertisement (**50**), for example, takes the multiple viewpoints of the triple mirror and rearranges them like a mannequin line-up of the pre-war years. Couture-house décor also produced the illusion of film strips of women in motion by installing mirrored fitting-room doors that reflected them as they

passed. At Maison Lenief the fitting rooms had concertina,
pull-out mirrored doorways that could be arranged to form
a line or a little box, with unbleached linen curtains
attached. At Drecoll the fitting-room doors were inset with
thin, vertical strips of mirror (**53a** and **53b**) so that people
walking down the corridor came in and out of vision like
pictures in a zoetrope, the nineteenth-century precursor of
cinema's moving images – yet more evidence that the
imagery and styling of the modernist body of the 1920s had
its origins in the pre-war years.

The early 1910s also saw the increasing participation of
women in sport and dance, which produced new
representations of the female body in motion. In 1913 Léon
Bakst designed the costumes for the Ballets Russes's ballet
Les Jeux, set in a future 1925, with music by Claude
Debussy.[125] Bakst claimed that he tried to express the idea
of the future in his costumes for the ballet's three tennis
players: ' "What is the characteristic of the age?" This
I asked myself before sitting down to evolve my costume.
I came to the conclusion that it was sportiveness . . . And
now the costume that I have imagined is based on woman's
desire for freedom of movement'.[126] The same year, in an
article on fashionable strolling in the Bois de Boulogne,
L'Illustration commented that the fashionable young ladies
who promenaded there were becoming more 'troubling'
not only because of their allure but also because now that
they were involved in sports they knew how to walk better:
'the young woman of today walks straight, with ease and
resolution, a young person who knows where she is going
and what she wants'.[127]

This image of modern femininity was played out in
Bakst's most startling costume for *Les Jeux*, knee-length
skirts for two female tennis players, executed by Paquin.[128]
Femina and *L'Illustration* routinely showed pictures of
sporting gestures alongside fashion ones, in which women
leapt, stretched and ran, such as that of August 1912 (**54**)
which breaks down the gestures of the tennis champion in

Au début de la partie, servant sa première balle. « Drivant » époussant la balle de tout le corps, la raquette basse. Venant de jouer un revers, la raquette ramenée. Près du filet gardé avec une autorité incontestée de championne. Rendant sa balle qu'elle voit la toucera. Coupant la balle avec précision. Jouant la volée de pied ferme. Un revers impressionnant à une terrible allure. Dans la frénésie du jeu, presque agenouillée pour toucher la balle.

« Lobbant » renvoyant la balle très haut. Attendant la balle de pied ferme. A la poursuite de la balle. Revers merveilleusement réussi. Se défendant devant le filet. Une marche sur une balle reçue. Une volée magistrale. Un « smash » (pour faire rebondir la balle très haut).

LES GESTES DE LA CHAMPIONNE

C'EST à Stockholm que se disputèrent cette année les Jeux Olympiques, ces grandes joutes de l'athlétisme moderne : peu de Français s'inscrivirent parmi les lauréats : seule Mlle Broquedis, et Femina est fière de l'enregistrer, remporta la couronne du tournoi de tennis. Nous avons prié la jeune triomphatrice de jouer à notre intention une partie de sport où elle remporta la victoire. Nous en reproduisons ici les principales attitudes. Nos lectrices admireront la sûreté de ce jeu tout à la fois précis, élégant et d'une grande allure.

54 'The champion's gestures' shows an interest in how to represent movement in a series of still images, similar to **43** and **45**. *Femina*, 15 August 1912. Courtesy Fashion Institute of Technology /SUNY, FIT Library Department of Special Collections and FIT Archives.

55 (facing page) Magazine article showing how to do the new fashionable dances the one-step and the Argentine tango. The steps are illustrated like a strip of film stills on either side of the page. *Femina*, 11 November 1911. Courtesy Fashion Institute of Technology/ SUNY, FIT Library Department of Special Collections and FIT Archives.

photographs that both borrow from Marey and parallel the visual experiments of artists at the time. A reader leafing through the magazine might, at the turn of a single page, move from the contemplation of Lucile's London stage to images from the 1912 Summer Olympics in Stockholm (the Games of the fifth Olympiad) and then on to an article on social dancing.[129]

In the early 1910s, the dance craze[130] gave rise to many articles in the same periodicals on how to do the new dances, such as one from *Femina* (**55**) that shows the movement and sequence of key steps in film-like images down the side of the page. The same curiosity was extended to modern dance such as the Ballets Russes's works by the stage magazine *Comœdia illustré*, which often showed sequences of movements from contemporary ballet performances, such as the dancer Natacha Trouhanova's 'dance of Salomé' represented by six frozen-motion poses.[131] In this period, writes Sarah Woodcock, 'Choreographers and designers began to cross boundaries. Choreographers studied art to learn the significance of gesture, pose and grouping, while designers learned to watch movement'.[132] The fashion images of the illustrated weeklies also showed the neo-classical poses of the dancer Isadora Duncan and her disciples and, although the dance costumes are frequently widely different from contemporary fashion plates, the poses can be strikingly similar.[133] Duncan deplored popular dance but her barefoot performance in 1907 may have been the inspiration for Madeleine Vionnet later that year when, employed at Doucet, she sent mannequins out to model in their bare feet.

TANGO TEAS AND FASHION SHOWS

The increasing popularity of sporting activities for women, the co-ordinated dance routines of the chorus line and the exhilaration of social dancing, from the tango to the *maxixe* (or *machiche*) and *très moutarde*, as well as many other popular dances, were the experiences of the body in motion that structured the viewing competences of pre-war fashion show audiences, and of the people who read about them in fashion magazines. As a stylised form of public intimacy, requiring contact not just of eye and hand but of the entire

DEUX NOUVELLES DANSES

LA LEÇON DE TANGO
Le boston, le double boston, le triple boston, furent longtemps les danses à la mode dans les salons *select*. Mais cette année la danse à la mode ce sera le *tango* argentin.

LE ONE STEP
Cette danse fera cet hiver concurrence au tango argentin. Les figurines qui bordent cette page à droite, et cette photographie en décrivent exactement les phases.

LE TANGO ARGENTIN
Le *tango* se compose de huit figures. Il importe de les exécuter rigoureusement en mesure, pour donner au *tango* son balancement caractéristique et charmant.

582

body, tango was a format perfectly suited for adaptation to the fashion show. At the beginning of the century, the syncopated patterns of American ragtime had arrived in Europe, chiming with the visual rhythms of chrono-photography, the chorus line and the fashion show. In 1903 *Les Modes* reported on the 'crazy, instantaneous, incredible vogue' for the new American dance *le cake-walk* that was replacing the passion for the *valse lente* (slow waltz).[134] For Jean Cocteau, it embodied the machine rhythms of modernity, brought from America to Paris in 1904 by the Elks, a husband and wife dance duo:

> They danced, they glided, they reared, they bent double, treble, quadruple, they stood straight again, they bowed. And behind them a whole town, the whole of Europe, began to dance. And at their example rhythm took hold of the new world and after the new world the old world, and rhythm passed into the machines and from the machines it returned to the men and could never stop again.[135]

By 1914 popular dance tended to generate a standardised set of bodily movements. In the tango craze, which had started in 1911, the sinuous Argentinian tango became a Parisian staple: as one American journalist in Paris wrote in 1914, the French tango 'is standardized, there are but five steps and of course everyone dances it alike. You can go anywhere in Paris and know that everyone will be dancing it alike and in a most exquisite manner.'[136] By 1913 the tango craze had spread to fashion. The dance craze motivated designers to make dance dresses that allowed for the requisite movement: it was logical, therefore, to show these dresses in dance movements rather than by the customary mannequin walk; Poiret declared the new dances such as the tango and *maxixe* 'the finest means of exhibiting women's gracefulness'.[137] In August 1913, Sem published the album *Tangoville sur mer*, in which he described 'the tango of Paris, perfumed, wavy, adorably chiffonned, a product of the rue de la Paix'.[138] That autumn, several couturiers incorporated dance demonstrations into their fashion shows. Also in 1913

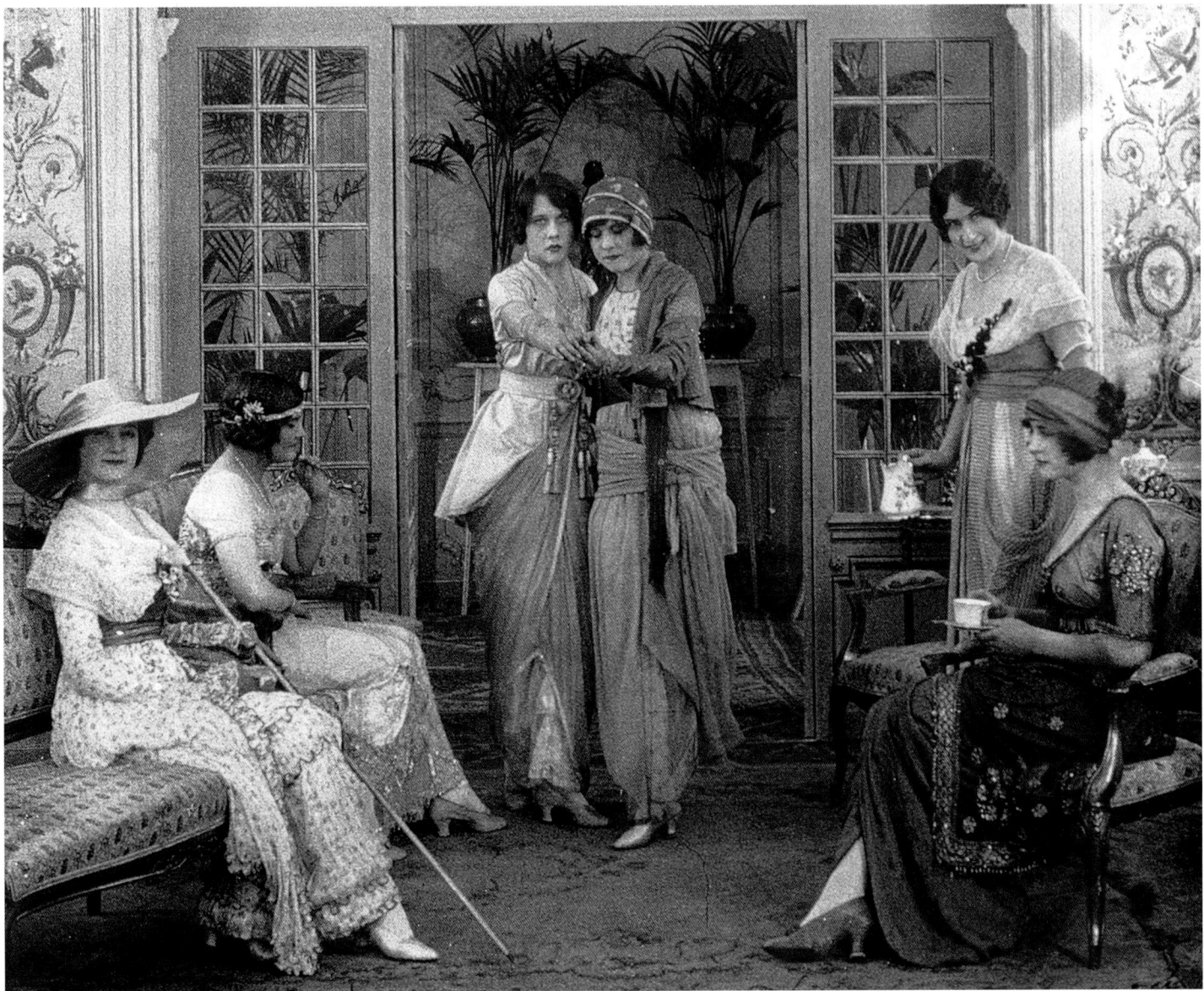

Poiret designed costumes for a play, *Le Tango*, at the Théâtre de l'Athénée,[139] and in September he invited the American dancers Irene and Vernon Castle (**56**) to dance at a tango dinner in the grounds of his house.

In New York, Lucile made Irene Castle's tango dresses,[140] while in Paris, Lucile's 1913 autumn opening on Tuesday, 14 October took the form of a *thé dansant*, with music, tea and tangoing on the little stage equipped with professional stage lighting.[141] The dancers were Lucile's pretty 'English manikins,' wrote American *Vogue*, 'who wore Lucile's smartest tango frocks and – most wonderful of all things! – tango hair!'[142] This consisted of coloured wigs in blue, green, violet or scarlet to match or contrast with the gowns they wore. Surviving newsreel shows her mannequins performing a tango modified by some social dance steps (**59**).[143]

Paquin, by contrast, launched her autumn 1913 tango fashions from her London branch. On Monday, 24 November, she inaugurated a series of tango teas at the Palace Theatre, modelled by London girls chosen more for

their looks than their dancing ability (**57**).[144] Her mannequins appeared on a white velvet-covered stage before descending on a narrow pathway into the auditorium to model four tango gowns, two for evening and two for day.[145] The fashion parade was preceded by professional dance demonstrations of the Argentine tango, the Brazilian *maxixe* and a 'Futurist Waltz (coquetterie)'. In the interval between the demonstrations and the fashion parade, tea was served in both the foyer and the auditorium, where the theatre seats had been removed and replaced with tea tables and chairs.[146]

Entry to Paquin's London Tango Teas was charged at five shillings and they ran every day of the week except Wednesdays.[147] They set a London vogue for combined fashion shows and tango teas, sometimes also shown with film, like a mixed variety programme.[148] In spring 1914 Paquin's mannequins modelled in New York in coloured tango wigs and tangoed in the intermission between shows, led by Irene and Vernon Castle.[149] Tango was a way to bring elite fashion to a wide audience. Its purpose was marketing and publicity, rather than direct sales. Not all the women at tango teas were potential customers but, by choosing to show her tango fashions in London and New York rather than Paris, Paquin guaranteed international press coverage.

Besides tango teas, popular dance could be seen on newsreels and practised in Parisian dance schools where fashionable people went slumming *de cinq à sept* and 'poets, . . . aristocrats and *élégantes*' took tea at side tables and learnt 'the new – and disreputable – dances.'[150] An American fashion journalist in Paris wrote: 'One goes to these spots [dance halls] for clothes as well as movement. . . The two are so closely connected over here, and elsewhere for that matter, that any discussion of one includes the other.'[151] The laxity of dance hall culture began to permeate couture presentations and in 1914 Redfern held a tea at the fashionable restaurant and dance hall in the Bois de Boulogne, the Pré Catalan, mixing theatrical turns and dance demonstrations with a fashion show.[152]

Jeanne Paquin's brother-in-law and one of her business partners, M. Joire, was an aficionado of popular dance hall culture and, in particular, of the tango. Mme Paquin said: 'He is a dancing enthusiast – not that he dances himself, but he loves to stand and watch the tango and other dances in vogue, for they are the mirror of modern life. He is intensely interested in the aesthetics of dancing.'[153] So too was Sonia Delaunay who designed the first 'simultaneous dress' in 1913, which she wore to the Bal Bullier dance hall, although only as a spectator.[154] By contrast, Gino Severini, passionately fond of dance halls, was himself an enthusiastic dancer who became interested in showing dancers in motion as opposed to what he saw as the static dance poses of Degas.[155] Severini's large dance hall painting, *La Danse du 'pan-pan' au Monico* (1909–11), with its suggestion of syncopation in the unexpected repetitions of the motif of the high-heeled shoe, was first shown in Paris in 1912.[156] However, it is his *Blue Dancer* of 1912 (**58**) that more effectively shows his intense interest in the movement of fabric and body together: the canvas is studded with real sequins stuck to the blue paint which is applied in translucent, faceted planes as thin as a layer of silk chiffon.

MOVING TO THE MUSIC: PAQUIN AND FASHION IN MOTION

The tango dress posed a particular challenge to designers: it had to allow movement without revealing too much leg. As the tango dancer leans her torso backwards beyond her centre of gravity, the back leg has to be extended and braced to take her weight. For this the fashionable skirts of the 1910s were too narrow and most couturiers solved the problem by introducing a slit up the back. Paquin, however, deplored the slit tango skirt.[157] Instead, M. Joire's idea for the new tango collection was to replace the slash by inserting godets below the knee, fishtails of fabric that flared out in movement over the calves but preserved a slim silhouette in repose.[158] In 1914 *Femina* described the Paquin mannequins tangoing in New York in the new designs: 'Their skirts which, following the line of the legs, were lightly pulled in by elastic at knee level, and then flared like the corollas of flowers, permitted a perfect freedom of movement.'[159] Mme Joire, Paquin's sister-in-law and other business partner, demonstrated it to the journalists: ' "You see," she went on, kicking her right foot backward, "when one raises one's foot in the dance, the skirt conforms perfectly to the motion, and there is nothing revealed" '.[160]

In designing the new skirts, Paquin adopted a new method. Rather than requiring the mannequin to stand immobile for hours in the traditional way while a dress was cut on her, Paquin asked her mannequins to move in the models as she designed them, dancing, walking around and sitting down, so that she could correct all the faults that movement revealed.[161] Paquin called this the quest for 'a very twentieth-century allure . . . with the minimum of fullness to give a woman entire freedom of movement', and for that 'we asked our mannequins to really live'.[162] The new skirt, 'conceived to accompany all the movements of the walk and the dance',[163] was launched in February 1914 on Paquin's mannequin tour of America. In France it was launched not by mannequins but by the actress Arlette Dorgière in Paul Gavault's *Ma Tante d'Honfleur* at the Théâtre des Variétés in Paris.[164] By April, it had been spotted at the Auteuil racetrack.[165] Paquin's incorporation of movement into the design process, and her design of clothes intended to be seen primarily in movement, anticipated by a decade Lucien Lelong's 'kinetic designs' of the 1920s. Like Patou at Parry, Paquin provides evidence that the conjunction of movement and modernity were not solely a feature of 1920s' modernism but, rather, that a modernist articulation of the body was occurring in the styling and showing of fashion before the First World War; the pre-war fashion show can, then, despite the Art Nouveau aesthetic of Paquin's dresses, be understood as modernist in its underlying structures and scenography.

It is, however, a complicated form of modernism, one that is imbricated with everyday life, leisure and work in more complex ways than many art historical accounts of modernism allow. On the one hand, the fashion mannequin inaugurated a new kind of female performance in the 1910s. In the early 1900s the living mannequin had remained haunted by her prehistory as a static object; in the pre-war years that ghost was laid as she transformed herself into a walking, dancing subject – indeed, one who often troubled those of her contemporaries who worried about the changing role of women in the modern world. In movement, the *mannequin vivant* comes properly alive: no longer a living doll but an animated woman, she follows Paquin's injunction to 'really live', *vivre réellement.* Yet, like her predecessor the *figurante*, it was as a silent woman performer that she really lived, one whose body was a speaking gesture, whose performance shared the characteristics of the new generation of actresses of the silent cinema such as Asta Nielsen, who turned their backs on nineteenth-century theatrical acting styles to create a new cinematic acting language of expressive movements of the entire body.

On the other hand, the scenography of the new mannequin performance situated it firmly in the realm of the rationalisation of the body. Paquin's skirt was 'the outcome of a modern necessity', according to its designer.[166] The dance crazes of the pre-war years linked the mannequin irrevocably to movement and modernity but, in severing the links with the idea of the mannequin as an essentially static dummy, this modernist aesthetic linked her firmly to another kind of standardised body, the mechanical, synchronised and occasionally robotic body of modernism, a body which was rationalised across the cultural and commercial fields of art, work and leisure.

It was also a visceral body, nevertheless, tuned to the rhythms of modernity. As fashion mannequins moved to the rhythm, the designers they worked for touched a nerve in their musical choices. In 1904 Lucile was the first to use music at a fashion show.[167] Then, in Paris in 1911, *Fantasio* mocked her 'miaow-sic'. By 1914 Sem was excoriating the mannequins parading to music, lambasting the tangos and music hall songs that accompanied them, but by then fashion show orchestras played popular dance tunes non-stop: 'tango, one-step, très moutarde, and furlana'.[168]

In 1913 the first performance of Stravinsky's *Rite of Spring* was received with outrage. Like much music of 1913–14, its tri-tonal harmonies were an exercise in simultaneity but that was not its only offence. Alex Ross argues that the ending of the first part of the *Rite of Spring*, the Dance of the Earth, 'prophesied a new type of popular art – low-down yet sophisticated, smartly savage, style and muscle intertwined. . . . For much of the nineteenth

century music had been a theatre of the mind; now composers would create a music of the body'.[169] Ross cites Virgil Thompson's explanation of how 'the body tends to move up and down in syncopated or polyrhythmic music because it wants to emphasis the main beat that the stray accents threaten to wipe out'.[170] The music of the body also provided a template for fashion modelling: physical, time-based and rhythmic, modelling can be organic and fluid or, equally, rule-bound and governed by conventions. At the same time that fashion began to absorb the rhythms of art and music, modernist music began to incorporate snatches of popular music like ragtime, jazz or tango, and to mimic the structures and patterns of fashion. Mary Davis argues that early twentieth-century fashion stood in an important relationship to 'French musical modernism'.[171] In one example, she describes how Erik Satie was commissioned in 1914 by the fashion publisher Lucien Vogel to produce a piece on the theme of fashion. Satie's score for *Sports et divertissements* incorporates the 'perpetual tango' and the racecourse, both associated with fashion modelling. Davis argues that it 'is nothing short of a musical adaptation of the fashion magazine, complete with up-to-date illustrations depicting the latest styles'.[172]

Ross identifies in Satie's work 'the germ of an alternative modernism' that would reach maturity in the 'machine-driven music of the twenties', a specifically Parisian modernism that was 'moving into the brightly lit world of daily life'.[173] In the 1920s this developed into what the dance historian Lynn Garafola calls 'lifestyle modernism' and 'the sophisticated commonplace', terms she uses to describe the compromised and conservative modernism of Cocteau in the 1920s: 'Piquant, amusing, replete with the accoutrements of modern living . . . lifestyle modernism identified the new consumerist chic of the upper class.'[174] Less judgementally, Ross recapitulates Garafola's account of lifestyle modernism as combining 'the spirit of high fashion, low culture and sexual play', an apt description but one which somewhat voids Garafola's thesis of its political critique.[175]

Before the 1920s, however, in the period leading up to the First World War, syncopation and rhythm produced a swing and looseness to the body; fluid tango dresses moved to the music and a sense of possibility was articulated not in things but in patterns, matrices and flows, moving between flesh and fabric, sound and vision, commerce and culture.

3
1900-1914
FRENCH FASHION
ON THE WORLD STAGE

60 Mannequins at the Auteuil races. *L'Illustration,* 6 June 1903. (www.lillustration.com).

On 1 July 1913 world time was first pipped from the top of the Eiffel Tower.[1] If the fashion show had links to the syncopated rhythms of the dance hall and Severini and Duchamp's images of simultaneity, so too was it linked to the standardisation of global time. Without that, French fashion could not have displayed itself on the world stage. Without its symbolic links to new forms of productivity, principally Henry Ford's moving assembly line of 1912, the automated mannequin parade could not have enjoyed the symbolic capital that it did. Jay Griffiths highlights the paradox that, while modernist innovations such as Stravinsky's *Rite of Spring*, first performed in May 1913, were giving time 'a fullness, a thickness and texture it had never had before', at the same time 'the global present thinned time to a radio beeeep, just when time had never been so public nor spread so thinly' due to the way that new technologies such as film and wireless radio brought simultaneity into daily life and consciousness more effectively than avant-garde music and literature.[2] David Harvey, too, noted the synchronicity between the first production line and the first radio signal that was beamed round the world from Paris, writing that the former 'fragmented tasks and distributed them in space' and 'used a certain form of spatial organisation to accelerate the turnover time of capitalist production' while the latter could 'collapse space into the simultaneity of an instant in universal public time'.[3]

First performed to a limited audience of professional buyers and private clients, the French fashion show quickly came to public attention via a rapidly expanding fashion press. Soon it was also taken on the road and across the world in different ways and media: many Paris couture houses sent mannequins to the races and to resorts; a few sent mannequin tours to European and American department stores, or on ocean liners; and some allowed the film companies Pathé and Gaumont into their couture house to film fashion modelling that was disseminated

internationally in newsreels after 1910. By 1915, as the *New York Times* reported, 'the exploiting of new ideas through mannequins at public places' was widespread.[4] Publicity and sales were facilitated by new media including the telegraph and film. In these ways, the couture houses harnessed the power of the international press to publicise their names and disseminate their designs through the new medium of the fashion show.

Just as the assembly line reduced the time it took to make a car from fourteen to two hours, so Poiret's and Paquin's international mannequin tours, with their vast amount of American press coverage, reduced the psychological distance between the fashion industries of each continent. The immediacy of fashion, and its ability to bridge continents, positioned it at the vanguard of future sensibilities as an engine of modernist change. Harvey argued that modernism was the consequence of changes in the perception of time and space – themselves linked to new technology and capitalist innovation – since the mid-nineteenth century, changes that peaked just before the First World War.[5] He cited Henri Lefebvre's argument for the early twentieth century as a moment of decisive change in sensibilities:

> Around 1910 a certain space was shattered. It was the space of commonsense, of knowledge, of social practice, of political power, a space hitherto enshrined in everyday discourse, just as in abstract thought as the environment of and channel for communication . . . Euclidian and perspectivist space have disappeared as a system of reference, along with other former 'common places' such as town, history, paternity, the tonal system in music, traditional morality, and so forth. This was a truly crucial moment.[6]

Griffiths describes how, after the distress signal sent by the Titanic on 14 April 1912 at midnight, the news flashed round the world by telegraph and argues that this use of time and simultaneity by newspapers put a new emphasis on temporality; once 'places of cultural *memory*', newspapers became focused on change.[7] Just as the news became fragmentary, episodic and brief, so fashion, with the advent of mass production and copying that were enabled by fashion shows, acquired the potential to become (as it indeed became) faster-changing, replaceable and disposable.

FASHION PLAYS

In both France and England 'fashion plays' had emerged in the 1890s, a new genre of light theatre in which leading ladies wore six to seven new dresses by a noted couturier or dressmaker in one production. A form of dramatised fashion plate, fashion plays were thin on plot and their dialogue was sparse. In the 1900s they were increasingly set in fashion houses as a thinly veiled excuse to stage a mannequin parade as part of the entertainment. Kaplan and Stowell describe the links between the commercial theatre and the dressmaking trade in London, based on exhaustive press research, in such a way as to make it clear that these stage plays were a logical predecessor of the fashion show; they did not, however, replace fashion shows once these came into existence but co-existed with them. It was the same in Paris. In the 1910s ninety per cent of the press coverage in Paquin's press albums consisted of theatre reviews, showing how important the stage press still was in fashion dissemination.[8] Both dressmakers and their clients attended these plays to observe fashion in motion;

the idea that a dressmaker would copy the latest fashions from the play only gradually became unacceptable: as the increasing use of photography and live modelling began to disseminate fashion in new ways, anxieties about copyright infringement and piracy came to the fore. At the same time, popular dance, too, played a role in the desire to see fashion in motion: Loie Fuller, who first arrived from America in Paris in 1892, was often cited as an inspiration for fashion, based on her dramatic manipulation of fabric on stage.[9]

THE RACETRACK

Since the early nineteenth century, the Easter *défilé de Longchamp* had been a kind of public fashion show in which the fashionable world, including dressmakers, drove through the Champs-Élysées watched by a paying public in cheap seats. After Longchamp was remodelled in the 1850s as part of the first stage of Haussmannisation, it became an even more important parading ground for fashion. So, too, did the horse-racing tracks at Auteuil and Chantilly where the public went to watch the new fashions as much as the horses.[10] In the 1860s, Worth first sent his wife to Longchamp to act as his unofficial mannequin. In 1890 the house of Pelletier-Vidal sent a group of mannequins to Longchamp where *L'Art et la mode* described them as a 'swarm of pretty women who seemed to have arranged to meet in the paddock like bees around a hive . . . who paraded without interruption from three to five o'clock under the stands'.[11] From 1900, journalists began to single out the appearance of the mannequins whose dress at the racetrack differentiated them from other women (**60**).[12] The public spaces of the races encouraged fashionable parading (**61**). In 1904 the Longchamp racetrack was again

remodelled and new stands designed by the architect Charles Girault. At 170 metres long (nearly 200 yards), they seated ten thousand spectators, twice as many as the nineteenth-century stands built in 1857 that they replaced, while the paddock below could accommodate another twenty thousand visitors on foot.[13] The new buildings, in iron and stone, incorporated arcades, stairways and porticos that created a venue for elegant posing, while the boardwalk on the paddock created vistas for fashionable strolling. On Palm Sunday, society women displayed the latest fashions there; towards five o'clock the race-goers proceeded to the buffet, resulting in a *revue des élégances*, or unofficial fashion show.[14] It remained an important place to both see and be seen in the latest fashions right up to the Second World War.

From 1900 professional women were regularly sent to the races. They might be actresses, mannequins or a semi-professional category, *les jockeys*, impoverished society women also known as 'amphibians', so called because they lived in two elements: they were customers in the salon, mannequins in the *cabine*. Young, beautiful and with mannequins' figures, they paid either a reduced price or none at all to wear the models they paraded at the races and other fashionable venues.[15] 'Is she a client?' asked Louis Roubaud in 1928. 'It is a privilege to be dressed for free. Is she a mannequin? It is an injustice to be paid only in vanity'.[16] All couture houses had their 'stable' of such *élégantes*, on average a dozen; Patou dressed about a hundred by 1934.[17] The *jockey* had to be recognisable by photographers and magazine readers as well as wearing the clothes well. Their popularity lasted on average five years, though several, such as Laure Jarney and Mlle Darteix, 'survived' nearly fifteen and twenty years respectively at the races.[18]

62 (right) Paquin's Empire line dress debuts at the racetrack in 1905. *Les Modes*, November 1905. Courtesy Fashion Institute of Technology/ SUNY, FIT Library Department of Special Collections and FIT Archives.

63 (far right) In this cartoon of 1914 two elegant young women watch the race while the other spectators watch them, the joke being on the equivalence between horseflesh and women. *Harper's Bazar*, September 1914.

64 (facing page) Three mannequins model Margaine Lacroix gowns at Longchamp in 1908. The clinging gowns, one blue, one white and one in Havannah brown, caused outrage because they were fitted tightly to the body and slit at the sides, so that the outlines of the mannequins' legs could be seen through their flimsy underskirts as they walked. *L'Illustration*, 16 May 1908. (www.lillustration.com).

Paquin carefully chose actresses such as Cécile Sorel and, some weeks before the Grand Prix race at Longchamp, the firm would 'permit it to be discreetly whispered' that she would wear a new Paquin gown, to ensure maximum press coverage when she did appear.[19] In 1905 Paquin chose the actress Paule Andral to launch her Empire line robe but sent a mannequin to the races to wear it (**62**).[20] The stern glare of the women in the background seems to erect an invisible pallisade between them and the mannequin who smiles for the camera. Such a critical gaze and keen scrutiny of the bystanders in racetrack photographs is often the most telling indication that the subject is a mannequin rather than a society woman.

From approximately 1911 the young amateur photographer Jacques-Henri Lartigue photographed mannequins and demi-mondaines at the races and the fashionable strolling grounds of the Bois de Boulogne. He described 'the "mannequins" who are more dressed up than the others' in 'especially beautiful dresses or prodigious hats made by the big couturiers or milliners' as the 'women to photograph' at the Auteuil racetrack. Lartigue noted too how the mannequins differed from other women: a ' "young lady mannequin" is someone special whom the other ladies do not greet, who smiles sweetly instead of getting cross when I point my camera at her, and who promenades everywhere without ever paying any attention to the horses'.[21] As in the salon, the

mannequin at the racetrack was mute. Nor, as Lartigue observed, would anyone talk to her. Her profession set her clearly outside the bounds of social intercourse.[22]

Three mannequins sent to Longchamp in May 1908, in gowns by the house of Margaine Lacroix, caused an immense scandal (**64**).[23] They strolled in the paddock, followed by vociferous comment on all sides. To a pair of admiring young men they appeared 'astonishing, and nearly naked, all three! No! Word of honour! Chic!' To two fat and painted old ladies, they seemed 'infamous, a monstrosity, and they have revolting busts that seem to outstare you'. A couple of elderly male aristocrats found their toilettes rather too showy but ogled them nevertheless. 'On all sides, from all corners of the race course . . . went up cries of joy, cries of distress and cries of revolt!' wrote *L'Illustration*. They were 'three young women who have come there not for pleasure but under orders, as one says in the regiment, and to launch a new fashion'. The magazine stressed the humiliation of the 'poor little mannequins' who were pushed, jostled and quite undressed by the crowd.

> You continued straight ahead, smiling, a little sad at heart. Only the couturier, who followed close by, seemed proud of your flesh which he promenaded.
>
> A fine horse trainer!
>
> And the crowd, the ugly crowd, piled up, rubbed shoulders, prevented you from going forward. Imagine, one could see your bodies beneath your clinging toilettes. . . .

Back at his firm, the couturier rubbed his hands and said:
– A successful day, my children! They'll be talking about you and about my toilettes. Here are the five louis that I promised you. And the three little mannequins began to cry.[24]

This description of the couturier as a horse trainer suggests an analogy between the working-class mannequins' bodies and horseflesh that was commonly made throughout the pre-war period when even well-bred mannequins were known as *jockeys*. An American journalist wrote in 1912: 'It is like a comedy to see the mannequins on the "pesage" [paddock] at Longchamp. They become the thoroughbreds of the rue de la Paix and they are coolly judged by the lorgnetted society dame or monocled swell whose only sportive manifestation is shown in giving "good points" or otherwise to these animated "clotheshorses"' (**63**).[25] In the post-war period, the comparison did not disappear but altered: the sleek bodies of mannequins were compared not to horses but to their replacement, the motor vehicle (see **143–5**).

Back in 1908, *L'Illustration* captured the prurience with which the mannequins' scant respectability and equally scant dress were met, revealing a salacious fascination with their voluptuous bodies at a time when the *robe d'intérieur* and *robe de soir* were strongly differentiated from tailor-made suits and coats for the street. Lartigue noted in his diary for 1911 how women wore different clothes at the Bois and at the races: 'at the races they're almost evening dresses'.[26] There the new mannequin fashions crossed the boundaries of respectability by revealing 'evening' and 'interior' bodies in outdoor and day-wear. What most disturbed their contemporaries, however, was not this sartorial inversion but that the mannequins paraded publicly for money, rather than from any natural feminine affinity with fashion: the mannequin appeared thus because she was paid to, and the association with prostitution was never far away.[27]

The press reports of the Margaine Lacroix mannequins at the races in 1908 rumbled on as far afield as London and America.[28] There was even a rumour that the mannequins had been arrested.[29] Thereafter, couturiers sent increasingly

provocative and suggestive gowns to the races, choosing mannequins who were themselves no less suggestive.[30] They appeared wearing all sorts of novelties, from wristwatches and American shoes to eighteenth-century powdered wigs.[31] These racetrack gimmicks were widely reported in the U.S.A., in the trade papers as well as in the upmarket magazines.[32] For most people, the racetrack was the only place they saw living mannequins.[33] In 1909 a British guide to Paris wrote that 'the most striking and audacious gowns are worn by "mannequins" or dressmakers' models who are paid to be stared at.'[34] Ridiculing the extreme fashions worn by the mannequins was par for the course; a jeering crowd would often follow them. At Longchamp in 1914, the crowd laughed outright at a mannequin who juxtaposed a black sheepskin parasol with a summer toilette of ivory lace and chiffon.[35] For a mannequin, being chosen among her colleagues to be sent to the races nevertheless provided welcome variety from the tedium of in-house modelling and Longchamp was considered the 'goal of bliss' (**65–7**).[36]

Twice a year in March and July, either side of the official trade shows in February and August, the rue de la Paix mannequins launched the new season's fashion at the racetrack, when society women were still out of town.[37] There they were immediately mobbed by a 'heterogenous racing crowd' of photographers, fashion writers, buyers, copyists and dressmakers.[38] 'The pencils scratch, the shutters click. It is the music of glory for the mannequins', declared *Femina* in 1910.[39] The *Gazette du Bon Ton* wrote:

> As soon as a young mannequin enters the stands or the paddock a swarm of parasites surrounds her. Twenty small dressmakers, one eye screwed up, lips pursed as if to hold a hundred pins, dissect the dress, scalp the hat. Sketchers descend on them . . . and produce anthropological, or more correctly gynemetrical, sketches. Film-makers and photographers jostle them and block their way with their tripods . . . [**68**].[40]

It was a mixed blessing, making the couturiers vulnerable to piracy as well as to publicity. A new gown trialled at the Auteuil races in July could be copied by an overseas buyer before the same dress was modelled in the August openings. In the spring of both 1912 and 1913 the major couturiers delayed sending their new fashions to the races in an attempt to prevent copying.[41] Despite their best efforts, in the summer of 1913 several savvy American dressmakers sketched the dresses when they finally appeared at the Paris races, sent them to New York on a fast steamer and had them made up and on sale in Newport in a fortnight flat.[42]

Photography added to the couturiers' vulnerability. From the late nineteenth century, society women seen at the races had been sketched for fashion magazines but, in the early twentieth century, they were increasingly photographed. The Seeberger Frères are the most famous racetrack photographers (**70**) but there were many others and between 1910 and 1920 several photographic agencies dealt in their work. For an annual subscription of 100–400 francs, they sent weekly pictures to overseas buyers and magazines in London, Berlin, Vienna, St Petersburg and New York. When these images of French socialites were published in American magazines, their clothes were immediately copied by American dressmakers so that, by the time the legitimately purchased imports arrived in New York for manufacture, they were valueless. In 1913 the French firm Béchoff David complained that it had no redress when a big American buyer returned his purchases and refused to pay for them on these grounds.[43] In Paris, couturiers could and did exclude photographers from their salons but they were powerless to exclude them from the races. Nevertheless, they tried. Petitioning the Prefect of Police, they argued that although the presence of photographers at the races might please society women, it jeopardised their own commercial interests. After due consideration, their petition was rejected and photographers continued to flood the racetrack: 'a small

LES MANNEQUINS A BORD

Les couturiers parisiens ont décidé dernièrement — à la suite des incidents que souleva l'apparition des jupes-pantalons à Auteuil — de ne plus envoyer leurs mannequins exhiber sur les champs de courses la mode nouvelle. Voici une amusante compensation à cette douloureuse proscription : les mannequins de la rue de la Paix ne paraissent plus sur nos hippodromes mondains, mais ils prennent passage sur les plus lointains paquebots où ils occupent, pour les riches passagères, les loisirs forcés de la traversée. Sur le pont, ce n'est, par les après-midi interminables, que défilés de mannequins et exhibitions de toilettes inédites. Les passagères séduites par ces nouveautés et impatientes de renouveler leur garde-robe démodée, font d'importantes commandes que le télégraphe a vite fait de transmettre à Paris ; quand les voyageuses sont parvenues au terme de leur déplacement, il leur suffit d'un ou deux essayages rapides pour pouvoir prendre livraison de leurs toilettes. C'est le dernier mot du progrès et du pratique...

69 (left) An open-air fashion show on deck. Illustration by Leon Fauret, *Femina*, 15 May 1911. Courtesy Fashion Institute of Technology/SUNY, FIT Library Department of Special Collections and FIT Archives.

70 (facing page) A fashionable woman at the races in 1909, photographed by Seeberger Frères. She appears indifferent to the intense scrutiny of the four onlookers, three men and one woman, perhaps because she is a professional mannequin. Bibliothèque Nationale de France.

army of artists and photographers were everywhere, catching the new models in the manner now censured by the dressmakers', wrote the *New York Times* in 1914.[44]

RESORTS AND OCEAN LINERS

The fashion season followed the social season. After the racing season ended in June, society left Paris in July and August and so too did the mannequins. By 1909 they were being sent to parade in the seaside resorts of Deauville, Trouville and Dieppe in the first fortnight of August, returning to Paris in time for the buyers' openings on 15 August.[45] Soon there were also spring and mid-season shows in the fashionable spring resorts of Nice and Monte Carlo and autumn fashion previews in June as part of Deauville's Grande Semaine.[46] Resort hotels staged combined fashion shows, tea dances and musical performances as part of what came to be called 'Riviera season' fashions.[47] They were also shown in February to buyers and in March to private clients at the fashionable resorts.[48]

In America, the *Boston Daily Globe* described the resort shows in 1914:

A number of beautiful mannequins, specially sent down from Paris for the purpose, stroll in and out between the tea tables, wearing the latest gowns and evening wraps. It is, of course, behind the scenes, a semi-business arrangement, and many important orders are the outcome of the 'parade', but the ordinary onlooker might well be excused for thinking it was merely an attractive 'show' got up to amuse the smart tea drinkers . . .[49]

At the resorts, buyers and private clients came closer to rubbing shoulders than they ever did in Paris. Observers also began to notice that, as the Parisiennes returned home, women were seen more and more in the same dresses from the big houses.[50] Resort fashions acquired the modernity of the multiple that was visualised in the fashion show line-ups (see **38–42**).

If the proximity of buyers and clients, and the increasing standardisation of couture, were implicit in the resort shows, the commercial backbone of the international fashion trade was clearly revealed in fashion shows on transatlantic ocean liners. In 1910 an enterprising Paris couturier sent a single mannequin across the Atlantic to mingle with potential private customers.[51] Then, in 1911, *Femina* illustrated a mannequin parade on board ship (**69**). The *Illustrated London News*, which also featured it, captioned the image 'The Liner as a Substitute for the Racecourse'.[52] As gusty winds blow, three mannequins hold their hats and cling to the ship's railings, while the customers smoke cigarettes in deckchairs. The *Femina* caption relates that the mannequins of the rue de la Paix

modelled endlessly on deck to the rich clients during the interminable afternoons of enforced leisure. Clients, in turn, could telegraph their orders to Paris so that, on arrival, only a couple of fittings were required before they could take delivery of their new toilette. 'It's the last word in progress and practicality', wrote *Femina*.[53] A number of couture houses went on to copy the practice, with mannequins parading round the ship in the costumes three or four times a day and clients ordering by wireless to Paris.[54]

The shipboard shows, however, like the resort ones, militated against customers obtaining exclusive designs and exacerbated an inherent contradiction of the mannequin parade: showing in new ways to new audiences also enabled new forms of piracy and copyright infringement, particularly in an age of wireless transmission. One American importer commented:

> Anything turned out by the great fashion makers is bound to be duplicated . . . in my opinion little or no attempt is made now to keep even the best imported models from the public eye. Some of these are paraded on shipboard coming over by mannequins hired for the purpose and orders are taken for duplicates before they ever reach New York. This is done by more than one of the most enterprising New York dressmakers . . .[55]

NEWSREEL FILM

From the 1910s, French fashion was widely disseminated overseas in newsreels, produced in a weekly format by Pathé-Frères from 1909 (*Pathé Revue*) and by Gaumont from 1910 (*Gaumont Journal*).[56] Early newsreels were short, with only two or three items on each reel, and the footage of Paris fashion was especially short. In 1911, however, Pathé expanded its fashion coverage by producing a series of short films entirely devoted to coming fashions for its *Pathé Animated Gazette*.[57] Many newsreels were in colour and in 1911 an American journalist observed that 'A growing feature of the imported films is the display in colors of the newest styles in gowns and hats in Paris. "Mannequins" of the smartest Paris shops glide up and down for the camera operators, and in a brief time the latest fashion hints are presented to the women of America'.[58] From 1912, Gaumont began using named actresses as well as professional mannequins to model clothes by couturiers such as Laferrière, Callot Soeurs and Drecoll.[59]

Distributed worldwide, French fashion newsreels promoted the idea of exclusive Paris fashion to a mass audience. The professional mannequins are shown modelling alone or in groups of up to three, usually in the intimate interiors of couture houses or film studios dressed with curtains or painted backdrops; less often they are in the open air, at the Bois de Boulogne or the Auteuil and Longchamp racetracks, and, occasionally, in specially constructed garden sets. Many of the surviving Gaumont newsreels from about 1912 to 1916 have English-language inter-titles and feature the Paris couturiers who were particularly successful with American buyers: Parry, Martial et Armand, Boué, Drecoll, Beer and Buzenet, as well as Lucile (who, as noted earlier, had her own American branches) and Paquin (who had a New York fur branch). Three of the highly innovative pioneers of the fashion show, Lucile, Paquin and Parry, opened their salons to the cameras and a fourth, Poiret, made his own films in the same period. Michelle Tolini-Finamore argues that Poiret played an important role in the development of the fashion show on film in the pre-war years. He was one of the early designers to embrace the film medium and was also the first to be credited with costume design for Sarah Bernhardt in *Queen Elizabeth* (1912; see **261** for the stage version).[60] These designers apart, however, fashion newsreels from the 1910s primarily showed the salons of middle-range rather than top-end French fashion, as well as the Paris department stores Trois Quartiers, Bon Marché and the Galeries Lafayette. The haute couturiers such as Poiret, Doucet and Redfern were featured not in newsreel but in elite magazines such as *Femina* and *Art et la mode* in France and *Vogue* and *Harper's Bazar* in America. By the 1920s, however, fashion newsreels also featured the mannequins of haute couturiers including Doucet, Patou, Lanvin and Poiret.

MANNEQUIN TOURS: POIRET IN EUROPE AND THE U.S.A.

Nineteenth-century French dressmakers regularly travelled abroad to sell paper patterns and model gowns that they exhibited in rented showrooms as far afield as London and even St Petersburg.[61] They showed the gowns on dolls until the 1890s, when living mannequins were substituted.[62] In the twentieth century Poiret conceived a spectacular form of travelling roadshow, the mannequin tour, or 'trunk show' as it was later called. Mannequin tours provided instant copy for the press and were an extremely effective way of promoting a designer's name overseas. Orchestrated and carefully planned, couturiers accompanied groups of mannequins on whistle-stop tours of foreign cities, staging fashion shows in department stores and holding press conferences. Poiret also lectured and showed films and slides on his tours. The three major tours in the pre-war

(Dessin inédit de Lepape.)

LA TOURNÉE DU GRAND COUTURIER

On sait qu'un grand couturier vient de promener à l'étranger ses modèles les plus sensationnels, présentés par de charmants mannequins. C'est une scène de ce voyage que Lepape interprète.

71 Poiret and his mannequins on their European tour. Illustration by Georges Lepape, *Femina*, 1 January 1912. The mannequin on the right wears *La Perse*, a cloak-like coat made from a woodblock-printed velvet designed by Raoul Dufy (now in the Costume Institute, The Metropolitan Museum of Art, New York). Lepape's drawing shows the textile print slightly smaller and less joined-up than the real one, but the shape and general idea are correct. The drawing may be based on the version of the coat made for the actress Ève Lavallière in 1911 in black on white with black fox-fur trim: see Harold Koda and Andrew Bolton, *Poiret*, 2007, pp. 66–9. Courtesy Fashion Institute of Technology/SUNY, FIT Library Department of Special Collections and FIT Archives.

period were Poiret's European tour of 1911, his American tour of 1913 and Paquin's American tour of 1914.

Perhaps Poiret got the idea in 1909, when he was invited to take his mannequins to London to model for Margot Asquith, the wife of the British Prime Minister.[63] Mrs Asquith, a patron and habituée of Lucile's shows, sent out invitation cards from her official residence at 10 Downing Street reading 'For Tea and Paris Fashions'.[64] Tea was taken, while Poiret's two French mannequins, Hortense and Josephine, assisted by a third, hired mannequin, modelled for two hours to social luminaries including the American-born countesses of Craven and Essex.[65] Since Poiret was a foreign dressmaker, and because he used the fashion show as a way to make sales from the Prime Minister's residence while avoiding the large import duties which he would otherwise have incurred, there was an enormous outcry in the British press. There were 285 articles written in 160 different papers, the most outraged headed 'Exhibition at Gowning Street'.[66]

In autumn 1910 Poiret travelled to Vienna, Brussels and Berlin, at the invitation of the owner of the Gerson department store, Philipp Freudenberg, where he presented his second hobble skirt collection on live mannequins on the store's modelling stage, equipped with stage lighting and accompanied by a Max Reinhardt production of *A Midsummer Night's Dream*.[67] Freudenberg

invited him back and in 1911 he included Berlin in a promotional tour of Central and Eastern Europe costing 60,000 francs.[68] He set out in October 1911 with his wife Denise, nine mannequins and a film of his fashions.[69] The tour secretary went ahead by rail with the dresses while the Poirets and the mannequins motored in two automobiles. Denise and Paul travelled in matching beige overcoats, co-ordinated with their beige Renault Torpedo and the chauffeur's livery: wholly a matching couple. The mannequins wore a travelling uniform of a blue serge tailor-made and a comfortable cloak in reversible beige plaid. On their heads they wore oil cloth hats with an embroidered P. 'It was extremely chic', wrote Poiret in his memoirs.[70] Over six weeks the party visited Frankfurt, Berlin, Potsdam, Warsaw, Moscow, St Petersburg, Bucharest, Budapest and Vienna, their penultimate stop, where they spent three days.[71] There Poiret lectured and the mannequins modelled in the Zedlitzhalle, a purpose-built structure designed by Joseph Urban, who later designed department-store fashion shows for Macy in the U.S.A.[72] One of the tour outfits that still survives is *La Perse*, a long cloak in a graphic navy and cream woodblock print designed by Raoul Dufy, with an electric-green silk lining and brown rabbit-fur collar and cuffs, which was illustrated, slightly inaccurately, in *Femina* in January 1912 (**71**).[73] Denise Poiret wore it over an ivory sack dress to the

72 Denise Poiret in an ivory silk sack dress in a suite at the Plaza Hotel, New York, in 1913, which Poiret had transformed with rugs, cushions and a screen from his interior décor firm La Martine. Photograph by Geisler & Baumann.

Berlin opening where she was a great success; after the tour, it remained in her collection.[74]

This European tour was a successful promotional and sales trip that was followed by licensing deals and in 1912 Poiret toured the French provinces with his mannequins.[75] However, the modelling costumes had incurred heavy import tariffs during his European tour. In 1909 Poiret had avoided paying import duty in London but in 1911 at the Polish–Russian border he was not so lucky: after fruitless argument with customs officials, he failed to persuade them that 'it was not a question of merchandise but of costumes intended to be shown as a spectacle'.[76] The clothes were impounded until Poiret paid the duty. This convinced him, on his 1913 tour of America, not to take living mannequins but, instead, a colour film of them.[77]

Poiret's 1911 film showed his mannequins modelling in his garden.[78] Now lost, it gave a full history of his designs.[79] In summer 1913 he showed a new film made for his forthcoming American tour at a 'cinematograph dinner' for thirty guests in the walled garden of his Paris house. One of the guests was the *New York Times* correspondent in Paris who described how 'the guests sat on the marble steps that run across half the front of the house, and suddenly, into their vision, came a dramatic parade of pictured mannequins who moved in and out of the garden trees, and sauntered on the graveled garden paths, wearing the very newest clothes that had been invented by Poiret that week'. Describing the filmed mannequins as 'Goddesses from the Machine', he felt that 'it was difficult to believe that these visions of lovely women and costly robes moving among the trees were produced by a machine'.[80] Poiret's film enabled him to take the dramatic modelling style of his mannequin Andrée from Paris to America: 'She does it in the cinematograph as she does it in the salon, and Americans will see it in the moving pictures with which Poiret will illustrate his lecture here', continued the *New York Times*.[81]

Sure enough, a few weeks later Poiret brought Paris to America on a four-reel film which he showed to large audiences of fashion professionals, press and public in New York and Chicago. He gave his own running commentary as the film, longer by far than fashion newsreels, showed 'gowns of original and startling color and cut' and mannequins who 'strutted across the cinematic screen', according to the American journalists. One wore the minaret or 'lampshade gown, whose "hoop" swayed with the motion of her body', while 'another model preened herself before a mirror and showed the basic principle of the trouser skirt'.[82] In addition, Poiret showed a few coloured slides to illustrate his orientalist colour combinations of blue and green, scarlet and black, purple and white. He even appears to have made a new film while in the U.S.A. using the Kinemacolor system.[83] The contemporary press coverage of his use of film in the U.S.A. seems to disprove later historians' accounts that Poiret's films were confiscated by the New York customs on grounds of obscenity.[84]

On 13 September 1913 Paul and Denise embarked on their three-week tour of America, taking with them the films and a portfolio of photographs of their mannequins modelling in their Paris premises. They travelled between the large American cities by train, wrote the *Chicago Daily Tribune*, with 'twenty trunks containing 100 gowns and 100 cushions. His wife, who accompanies him, dons the gowns and displays them from the cushions'.[85] On arrival, they successfully avoided paying duty on Denise's hundred gowns but were later obliged to pay import duty at thirty per cent on the embroidered silk cushions on which Denise lounged for the photographers (**72**).[86]

Denise Poiret fascinated the American press, even when it scoffed at her husband's designs.[87] She was, wrote American *Vogue*, 'slim, dark, young, uncorseted, untouched by paint or powder, "straight as a lance at rest",

untrammeled by high heels, pointed shoes or gloves'.[88] On the American tour, Poiret used her as his unofficial mannequin, stage-managing her appearances to dramatic effect.[89] In the middle of his New York press conference on 23 September 1913,

> the door at the side opened and a tall woman with a boyish figure appeared. She was Madame Poiret. She wore a robe of brocade crepe and turban of the same material, wrapped Turkish fashion about her head. Apparently the gown had no seam, but was on the order of a slip, with a round hole for the head to slip through.[90]

This was another version of Poiret's *robe de minute*, the sack dress that Poiret claimed could be run up in half an hour, which Denise had worn under *La Perse* on the 1911 tour and in which she lounged in New York's Plaza Hotel in 1913 (see **72**).

The Poirets' tour took them from New York to the major cities in the Northeast and Midwest, including Washington, Boston, Philadelphia, Baltimore, Toronto and Chicago. Everywhere they were hosted by the owners of the major department stores and Poiret lectured and gave press conferences indefatigably, always with Denise as his unofficial mannequin.[91] He claimed, however, that he was merely a tourist in America: 'Mme Poiret must wear clothes. That is the only purpose for which she has brought her costumes. She is not to act as my model'.[92] Nancy Troy has commented that 'Poiret's denial of a commercial interest, his disdain for advertising and publicity, were part and parcel of his self-construction as an artist and an aristocrat, an individualist who rejected fashion because it smacked of mass production', while, in fact, his real commercial concerns lay with the very things he disavowed so loudly.[93] She shows how in reality the tour was part of a co-ordinated and extensive public-relations campaign to promote to an American market those Poiret dresses inspired by his Minaret costumes designed for the Paris stage that year.[94]

Although American stores had initially refused to buy Poiret's Minaret gown, by autumn 1913 when he showed it on film in his U.S.A. tour, all the major New York importers bought it, including Gidding, Wanamaker and Gimbel.[95] They provide further evidence that, as Troy argues, Poiret's tour was highly effective in producing sales, even where the American market was initially resistant.[96] His efforts bore fruit in the autumn 1913 shows in three major New York department stores that adapted his orientalist imagery, Gimbels', Macy's and Wanamaker's (**73**).[97]

Troy argues that the spectacular nature of Poiret's marketing in this tour differed from his customary Parisian practice. There, his fashion presentations were elite, intimate and private.[98] She shows how his American marketing was devised in response to the particular conditions of merchandising French fashions in North America. French and American marketing methods differed, she concludes, in the way they mobilised the idea of art to sell consumer goods, so that 'Where Poiret sought to obfuscate the commercial aspect of his activities as a couturier and designer, the American department store magnate proudly proclaimed the union of art and commerce, and worked to make it visible in the physical environment and operating practices of his stores'.[99] This was the case but the two approaches – colossal American spectacles as opposed to intimate French displays – were two sides of the same coin. Lucile, too, staged her fashion shows along elite, Europhile lines in London, Paris and New York, yet also developed them as mass spectacles for Broadway and vaudeville.

On the European side, Nancy Green notes that in the fashion business 'French observers often had a double discourse', arguing internally for greater industrialisation and competitiveness but, to the outside world, asserting French elegance, taste and artistry.[100] Americans, too, felt ambivalent about French supremacy in fashion, from which they often felt unable to emancipate themselves, despite a burgeoning movement for American fashion. Both countries understood the different nature of each other's fashion industries and, despite their ambivalence, knew that they depended on the other. The fashion show was the pivot between them. In early twentieth-century fashion shows, commerce, culture and national ideologies converged and clashed. The language and tone in which fashion shows were reported and described in both French and American fashion marketing and journalism in the period is threaded with contradiction: they are mutually ambivalent, envious, admiring and fearful in different measures. Such reciprocal suspicion was not new, as Green points out: 'French garment manufacturers have been wary of growing American industrial strength since the nineteenth century, while American designers have been anxious about creating a distinctive American style since the early twentieth. Such comparisons, by manufacturers and industrial reporters, reveal transatlantic understandings of the garment "other" which fall into the realm of what I call reciprocal visions.'[101]

In October 1913 the Poirets sailed back to France. The tour had revealed to Poiret the extent of unauthorised copying in the U.S.A.[102] Back in Paris he and a number of other couturiers combined in late 1913 to create the Syndicat de Défense de la Grande Couture Française et des Industries Associés. Each responded somewhat differently to the perceived threat but nearly all went on to display an increasingly ferocious, and sometimes paranoid, antipathy to copyists and pirates, which set the terms of the fashion show in the post-war period. For, while the show was a vital international sales tool, it also leached designs and once the genie was out of the bottle it was impossible to contain it.

MANNEQUIN TOURS: PAQUIN IN THE U.S.A.

Maison Paquin sprang a surprise in February 1914 on its New York buyers who had just arrived in Paris for the spring collections, by announcing that it was about to leave on tour for America.[103] Knowing this, most of the buyers at Paquin's February openings were deterred from buying.[104] Expressly declaring that her aim was to overcome the threat posed to her business by foreign copyists, Jeanne Paquin subsequently went on the attack in the pages of *Femina* magazine against those buyers whose practices verged on piracy:

Those *overseas manufacturers* who do not hold back from any form of piracy have acquired the habit of very adroitly undercutting the models we launch, of removing their personality and their label, while retaining a slight Parisian cachet; of creating, in a word, exports which they launch as new fashions in both Americas, reinforced with much publicity and advertising. Since these products have, unfortunately, an entirely French allure and are mass-produced – as one says of cars – they sell at prices defying all competition, and we are excluded from the American market which, as everyone knows, is the most important in the world.[105]

Paquin's strategy to acquire her share of the market consisted of an aggressively extravagant marketing tour costing more than half a million francs.[106] Rather than a mannequin tour, it resembled a stage tour, with a hundred gigantic, identical trunks containing the costumes and accessories, a dismountable theatre and an entourage of fifteen to twenty people.[107] Led by Mme Joire (**74**), the tour and all its luggage departed from Paris's Gare Saint-Lazare in a flower-filled railway carriage on a foggy February morning. Besides Mme Joire herself, the entourage included a 'press agent', four to six mannequins, each with her own dresser to avoid any stage waits, a builder to erect and dismount the theatre in every town they visited and several electricians ('lightsmen') to light the stage.[108] The small theatre had a curtain, a proscenium stage and electric lighting. Its façade was painted as a temple with gold uprights and bore the name Paquin across the top; the set was decorated with scenes of the Paris boulevards and carpeted in velvet, recalling the white velvet carpets of Paquin's Tango Tea in London the year before (**75**). Once in America, Paquin's New York representative Charles Koenigswerther became responsible for the entire entourage and shepherded them everywhere.

They arrived in New York on 1 March 1914 (**76**) and were at once besieged by the press, which largely focused on the individual mannequins who were – unusually for 1914 – mentioned by name: the blonde Mlles Le Duc and Dupré (the latter carried a walking-stick and her skirt had 'the slightest perceptible slash'), Mlle Champoiseau and Mlle Roulet, a brunette, whose tasselled dress 'drew a chorus of Ohs! and Ahs!'. They wore tango gowns and matching tango wigs, Mlle Champoiseau's in 'brilliant rose mauve' and Mlle Roulet's in steel blue. At the end of the tour, *Femina* magazine itemised the number of proposals the mannequins had received: 47 for Fanny and 52 for Maud.[109] The American press paid great attention to their manner of posing and a dressmaker observed that French mannequins were required to show how the clothes should be worn, for 'it is so difficult to get American models who know how to show off a fine frock'.[110]

74 Mme Henri Joire, the sister of Jeanne Paquin's deceased husband. After his death, M. et Mme Joire ran the business with Jeanne Paquin. Photographed here on the American tour in 1914, Mme Joire was noted for her elegance. Washington, D.C., Library of Congress.

75 Paquin's travelling theatre made for her 1914 American tour, shown here in Chicago, the only venue in which the audience did not sit in groups at tables but in rows of theatre seats. *Femina*, 1 June 1914. Musée Galliera de la Mode de la Ville de Paris. Photograph Richard Hubert Smith.

Their first show, at New York's Ritz Carlton, was for wholesalers, buyers and press; admission was by invitation only. It was much over-subscribed, with crowds outside trying to get in, and opened nearly two hours late, at 4.45 pm, to an audience of nine hundred. After the show, Mme Joire escorted the journalists backstage to show them the rails of clothes. The shows were repeated in the afternoon and evening at the same venue on the next two days. *Femina* reported the show as if it were a society event, describing '*Le high-life new-yorkais*': certainly, Paquin's staging of the show replicated some of the characteristics of a Paris salon show but on a mass scale. Seated at little tea-tables, each member of the audience was given a show programme and while waiting for the show to commence a hidden orchestra played a range of popular dances: tangos, one-steps, très-moutardes and furlanas. Finally, the curtain rose and, as each mannequin came on, a uniformed page held up a card bearing the name of the model: Babette, Gladys, Pastorale. The music paused, the audience applauded the dress on stage, 'the projector beamed out an orange light and once again the orchestra took up its tune'. As the show progressed, 'noisy acclaim drowned out the orchestra; the tea cooled in its cups' and the fashion copyists were routed. It was followed by a tango tea-dance, led by Irene and Vernon Castle, while the mannequins showed the tango gowns in motion: 'their coloured wigs against masculine shoulders fanned the flames', wrote *Femina*, although the dialogue was of necessity kept to a bare minimum because the mannequins spoke not a word of American. 'But the audience used the international language of admiration, . . . in ohs! and ahs!, . . . as much in appreciation of the colored wigs as for the dresses conceived equally for the threnody of the tango and the vivacity of the très-moutarde'.[111]

In Boston, Paquin's show lasted an hour and a half, with an interval for tea and the famous coloured wigs making an appearance in the second half:

The lightsmen . . . followed the models with the spotlights as they sauntered down from the tiny stage, the length of the room, across the back, and so returned to the stage. . . . The management of the show was perfect. As each mannequin stepped on the stage, the lights in the hall grew or shrank to the "time of day" appropriate to the costume. For a walking suit, the auditorium lights come on full; for a tea gown, they dimmed one-half; for an evening gown, only the white glow of the spotlight remained. The girl would pose and turn gracefully for a moment on the stage; then, stepping down to the floor, she would come swaying along, slowly, stopping every few feet to allow an inspection of the gown she wore, but

never, so to speak, entirely losing headway. Each girl made the circuit of the hall, posed once more on the stage and disappeared. The next girl was invariably ready and waiting.[112]

By contrast, in Chicago, as a riposte to the French shows, an unnamed American firm organised an American fashion show, using both male and female mannequins (**77**). *Femina* commented on how different the physiques of American women were from Frenchwomen's and on their greater similarity to men:

> an admirable type of woman, these Americans, they are tall, well-developed, sporty, and they endow the dresses with a noble and characteristic appeal. To bring out the strange side of this exhibition, man mannequins alternated with their woman comrades, so that, between a silk dress and a golf skirt, mauve striped pyjamas or an overcoat with gray faille reveres was set off by slender and well-built young men.[113]

As well as New York, Boston and Chicago, the mannequins visited Pittsburgh, Washington and Philadelphia before returning to New York. Each city responded differently to the dresses; Philadelphians were first shocked but then delighted by the backless gowns, Pittsburgh loved the bright colours, Chicago took to the 'extreme' gowns. The *Washington Post* noted the high proportion of men in the audience. Everywhere the press reports were adulatory. In 1914, like today, fashion magazines were integral to an industry which is made up of not only designers but also – of equal weight – manu-facturers, buyers, journalists, publicity and sales departments working in tandem like a single organism. The breathless accounts of Paquin's tour make sense in that context, not as accurate reports of the trade relations between the French and American industries but as a necessary and logical type of fashion promotion – hence their picturesque tone. The society element of Paquin's first New York shows was important to promote the mystique of French fashions. It generated the social capital from which the economic benefits would flow from American buyers to French fashion houses.

Repeated several times over the following days, the subsequent shows were attended by out of town dressmakers who took careful notes. One Atlanta dress-maker consequently placed a display advertisement in the *Atlanta Constitution*, announcing that 'Paquin used her own mannequins from Paris to stage the performance . . . having attended these Paquin performances, having taken copious notes and purchased materials similar to these Paquin costumes, Mrs Davenport is now ready to reproduce or adapt them for Atlanta women'.[114] As a piece of shameless piracy, this example demonstrates both the benefits and the potential dangers that flowed from French mannequin tours. While the couturiers had created a highly productive form of marketing, promotion and sales in the U.S.A., they were also vulnerable to the very copying that they sought to combat.

Paquin made money along the way, charging from $2 to $5 entry to the shows in the American style.[115] Advertise-ments for the teatime shows to be held in large hotels were placed in local papers prior to their arrival in a new city.[116] Troy argues that Paquin's American tour was at once a success and a failure: 'Paquin, like Poiret, in fact embraced a vulgarised form of theatre – the fashion show – in order to stave off a parallel form of vulgarisation of haute couture'.[117] Yet, luxury French dressmakers had been doing this in other ways since the nineteenth century. There is no

LE DÉFILÉ DES MANNEQUINS HOMMES

Ce fut un spectacle plein d'imprévu que celui qu'organisa à Chicago une maison de couture américaine en conviant les mannequins parisiens à venir assister à un défilé de mannequins hommes lançant jaquette, veston ou pyjama. Les applaudissements des Françaises dominaient l'enthousiasme des Américaines.

76 (facing page)
Paquin's French mannequins arrive in New York. *Femina*, 1 June 1914. Musée Galliera de la Mode de la Ville de Paris. Photograph Richard Hubert Smith.

77 Male mannequins parade in a Chicago store, watched by Paquin's French mannequins. *Femina*, 1 June 1914, reported that the French mannequins sat in the first row of the audience, at first surprised and then appreciative of the boldness of the gesture. When a tall, dark-haired adolescent in a multi-coloured golf suit paused on stage, convinced of the importance of his mission, the French mannequins burst into applause. Musée Galliera de la Mode de la Ville de Paris. Photograph Richard Hubert Smith.

evidence that the new mannequin tours jeopardised the couturiers' status with their private clients. Poiret and Paquin's mannequin tours were no more than modern forms of promotion adapted for new communications and markets in the early twentieth century, in response to the anxieties about their place in world markets that, as noted earlier, Green discusses as a cause of the 'double discourse' of French couture.[118] They were, in fact, highly successful in the way they traded the symbolic and social capital of French haute couture for the economic capital of American buyers.

For this reason, there was always controversy about whether a mannequin tour was a performance or a sale, to which Paquin's was no exception. Despite American *Vogue*'s claim that Paquin's tour was a social not a commercial event, and that none of her clothes were to be sold to private patrons, the reality was that Paquin had already sold the entire collection before she left France, including the rights to reproduce it, to the New York importer B. Altman & Co. She was thus liable for U.S. import duty of the equivalent of 60,000 francs, which she paid on arrival, but she only handed over the collection on her departure. In late March, Altman's re-showed the entire collection in its large department store, using some of the same mannequins. The three shows held over three days

were collectively attended by 60,000 people and, according to Mme Joire, 'the exhibition rooms were crowded to over-flowing with most enthusiastic people'. On 24 March two of the French mannequins sailed home, followed by the other two the next day and by Mme Joire a few days later, who commented with some justification that the tour had been entirely successful.[119]

'It is a merry war to keep Paris dressmakers away from New York', pronounced the *New York Times*, reporting that the firms of Bernard and Doeuillet were shortly to follow Paquin and Poiret's initiative and stage American mannequin tours.[120] Meanwhile, Paquin's mannequins appeared in London in May, where they modelled the blue and mauve wigs that they had worn in New York.[121] Mannequin tours looked set to take off and, just like shipboard fashion shows, might have become an established genre had it not been for the outbreak of war in Europe in August 1914.

TIME, MOTION AND STANDARDISED BODIES

Following her U.S. tour, Mme Joire wrote an article for an American retail journal, 'My Impression of American Department Stores', in which she described their

78 Detail of a chorus line
from Massenet's *Panurge*,
an opera first performed
at the Théâtre de la Gaîté,
Paris, on 25 April 1913.
See **41**.

organisation and efficiency, from employees' rights to sales,
praised the enterprise and 'aggressive advertising' of their
managers and said how much the French could learn from
American retailing: 'The system seems highly perfected'.[122]
In common with many other French industrialists, she
displayed a keen appreciation of American efficiency in the
workplace. Increasingly, the more forward-looking French
couturiers like Paquin, Boué Soeurs and, after the war,
Patou and Lelong, recognised that they could learn from
American management systems. They admired the ideas of
F. W. Taylor whose book *The Scientific Management of the
Workplace* was first published in America in 1911. His
eponymous system, a precursor of time and motion studies,
aimed to increase efficiency in the workplace by a sort of
mechanical 'divide and rule' whereby each worker was
allocated a fixed task and a fixed way of performing it in a
fixed place. For example, an individual worker was no
longer allowed to use his judgement or to break off work to
sharpen a tool he was using: the former task was allocated
to a manager and the latter to a dedicated toolmaker. The
result was to 'deskill' workers and to make their daily work

mechanical, repetitive and boring. Between approximately
1910 and 1920 Taylorism became well established in
France, partly through its enthusiastic endorsement by the
tyre manufacturer Édouard Michelin. Taylor's book was
translated into French and applied during the First World
War to French government factories by the chemist Le
Chatelier.[123] Fashion journalists often cited it in their
descriptions of couture houses in the 1910s, and its
practices fed into aspects of French industry in the
1920s.[124] In fashion, Patou and Lelong adopted Taylorist
methods in the 1920s as part of their move towards more
up-to-date and 'American' ways of doing business.

During the pre-war period, both Taylorism and Fordism
were mirrored in the proto-industrial aesthetic of the
fashion show. The uniformity of the fashion show line-ups
(**78**, and see **38–42**) was invoked by Poiret's mannequins in
1911 when they motored across Europe in matching plaid
coats and monogrammed hats, styled as a *de luxe* version of
the rationalised body of modernism, perfectly co-ordinated
with their employers' beige car and travelling outfits. This
aesthetic rationalisation of the body evokes not only the

chorus line but also the mass production and uniform styling made possible by Henry Ford's automobile assembly line of 1913. Increasingly, as the imagery of the fashion show was disseminated internationally, its industrial aesthetic absorbed modern, American influences from both art and industry. Just as Duchamp's *Nude Descending a Staircase* of 1912 crossed the Atlantic in 1913 to be included in the Armory Show in New York, so too, as French couturiers travelled to the U.S., did the look of the production line feed into the aesthetics of modern European fashion through a particularly European idea of *américainisme*.[125]

Siegfried Giedion identified an inspiration and prototype for Ford's assembly line in the slaughterhouses of Cincinnati (1830–60) and Chicago (1860–85). There, a combination of automation and the division of human labour enabled the mechanisation of meat production in America on a mass scale.[126] One curious anecdote from the 1914 Paquin mannequin tour makes an unwitting connection between the automated slaughterhouse and the fashion show, both forms of mechanised meat market. Chicago had pioneered automated slaughterhouses and meat-packing plants in the 1870s, in which lines of pigs ready for slaughter were suspended by a hind leg from overhead mono-rails that transported them seamlessly through the various stages of slaughter, cleaning, dismem-berment, stamping and refrigeration.[127] In 1914 *Femina* recounted how,

> In Chicago, to amuse them [the mannequins], and to thank them for the unforgettable parade of their slenderness sheathed in precious materials, a gallant millionaire conducted them to a slaughterhouse and showed them the parade [*défilé*] of animals

under the knife of the slaughterer. Nothing is more striking than seeing a long procession [*théorie*] of unfortunate pigs descending on a slide, infernal toboggan, which, in an instant, are seized by a steel pincer and have their heads cut off in a single blow.[128]

What is striking in the original French is the use of modelling terms to describe the automated line: the parade of animals under the knife is a *défilé* and the long procession of pigs is a *théorie*. For, the mannequin parade too is a kind of production line of French glamour that turns bodies into cash. Like the chorus line, Paquin's slender, tall mannequins were almost identical in appearance.[129] The language of this article also implies a disturbing analogy between the production line of living women and slaughtered animals, of slender women and plump pigs that goes far beyond the jocular comparison of mannequins with horseflesh at the races. Rather, it evokes Walter Benjamin's claim that 'Fashion has opened the business of dialectical exchange between woman and ware – between carnal pleasure and the corpse'.[130] In his discussion of the Chicago slaughterhouses, Giedion argues that the 'mechanization of death' is a way of banishing the contact with death from everyday life.[131] So, too, may fashion banish the signs of change and decay in its insistence on youth, beauty and a perpetual present. Yet, fast behind the emphasis on individuality and youth that characterised the descriptions of early twentieth-century fashion parades came a fear of mass production, as contemporaries saw it, which threatened individualism and erased human values. In the St Vitus Dance of modernist production, be it an industrial assembly line, a theatrical chorus line or a fashion show, the business of dialectical exchange was at work.

4
1900-1917
AMERICA

79 Lucile's vaudeville version of *Fleurette's Dream at Peronne*, 1917. © Victoria and Albert Museum, London.

American fashion shows differed fundamentally from French ones from the start. Nancy Green has argued in her book on the garment industries of France and America that each country had a different definition of democracy in relation to fashion and taste; and that the French industry, being largely for export, focused more on self-promotion, whereas the American industry, producing largely for home consumption, tended to be more protectionist in its rhetoric.[1] The distinction helps to explain the continuing importance to both America and France of the Paris fashion show, as the locus where the former bought and the latter sold its national produce. In the U.S.A., by contrast, the American show rapidly became part of the American cultures of consumption and entertainment. It was a form of theatre and, while the elite French shows continued to be by invitation only for small audiences of well under a hundred, American shows were open to the public who came in their thousands, often paying for entry tickets. The commercial and dramatic possibilities of these shows inspired Broadway and vaudeville producers; soon both fashion promoters and theatre directors were devising elaborate shows as a form of mass spectacle. Meanwhile the American fashion manufacturers and buyers continued to visit the Paris 'openings' twice a year to purchase the new season's models that would then be recreated in simplified form and displayed again in American department store shows. The cachet of Paris was required to sell these American-manufactured designs right through the 1920s, despite a vigorous pro-American fashion movement that began before the First World War.[2]

THE MADISON SQUARE GARDEN FASHION SHOW 1903

In September 1903 New York's Madison Square Garden was the venue for a two-week event that ran from 31 August to 14 September called, simply, 'The Fashion Show'.[3] Set in a two-storey hall, it resembled a modern-day trade fair, with static displays of French and American fashions ranged in booths along opposite sides of the hall. American exhibitors included New York importers and retailers as well as designers, among them several department stores, including Wanamaker's which staged a silk-weaving demonstration. The French booths displayed all sorts of luxury goods, including 150 model gowns from Paris and a white silk corset of $300, studded with twenty-four diamonds and with solid-gold garter fastenings.

The great draw, however, was a series of live fashion shows held on a specially constructed modelling stage three and a half feet high and ten feet wide (about one by three metres), with a green curtain at the back through which the living mannequins entered. Only French fashions were modelled in the shows, not American ones. The first show was on 31 August at 8.30 pm. Eight mannequins came on stage in groups of three or four at a time and promenaded for approximately five minutes, accompanied by a string orchestra, before being replaced by the next group. All were American, mostly actresses from the New York stage. They displayed model gowns from Paris to an audience of buyers, manufacturers, importers and dressmakers, as well as the general public. The audience was predominantly, though not entirely, female; West Coast buyers constituted the masculine element. Their ogling of pretty girls did not escape the *Washington Post*, which published a satirical article on the proposed visit of a senator and a secretary of the Department of Commerce to address 'the burning question of garters' and 'the comparatively lame topic of corsets and petticoats'. During the shows, M. Otto Adler, a French 'delegate' sent by the Parisian dressmakers, acted as a lecturer to explain the European fashions to the audience, like the *bonimenteur*, or lecturer, in film and variety programmes of this period, an individual tasked with explaining the silent action as it unfolded to the audience.[4]

These 1903 shows ran twice daily and in the first three days attracted approximately five thousand people. They were so popular that the schedule was extended into a second week and entry was charged at 50 cents a head. A revolving programme of extra features on different evenings provided an additional draw. These included electrical displays, future fashions for 1934, corset demonstrations and guidance on age-appropriate dressing for women from eighteen to eighty. Only the plans to stage a 'French wedding reception' featuring both American and French gowns did not materialise. The event ended with a ball involving all the mannequins on 14 September and the model dresses were then sold off at half price.

When the show closed, one exhibitor, the store manager of Ehrich Brothers, a prominent New York importer of model gowns and hats from Paris, Berlin and Vienna, observed that it had been a triumph of advertising rather than sales. He was prescient; over the following decade fashion shows came increasingly to be used as a form of advertising, both in the retail and wholesale sectors, on an enormous scale and catering to popular taste.[5] Despite the immediate success of the Madison Square Garden Fashion Show, however, no individual department store appears to have attempted to stage another fashion show until the Francophile Wanamaker's in 1908.

THE FIRST DEPARTMENT STORE SHOWS

The Wanamaker store brought thousands of women and men into its vast shows. It and many other department stores had large theatres and lecture halls that, over the following years, were used for fashion shows. In Paris, entry to couture house fashion shows was strictly limited to those who bought, and 'just looking' was not encouraged, but in America the fashion show was part of a gigantic marketing system that created the desire for fashion and luxury goods by appealing across a wide spectrum of both trade and public, mixing sales with spectacle to varied audiences.

It began in the autumn of 1908, when both the New York and the Philadelphia branches of Wanamaker initiated live shows of Empire-line fashions from Paris.[6] The first Philadelphia show was spectacular. Its venue was Wanamaker's newly opened Egyptian Hall which seated nearly two thousand and was fitted with a stage, an orchestra pit for up to a hundred musicians and an enormous and splendid organ (see **82**). In keeping with the Empire styles, the theme of the fashion show was Napoleon and Josephine and fair mannequins were chosen 'as if they were in a Napoleonic court'. Napoleon had already been the subject of an exhibition in the store in 1905. In choosing this theme, the Wanamakers may have been influenced by two stage plays based on Napoleon's life that had been performed in Paris in 1899 and 1904 and by the highly popular history film produced by Pathé-Frères in France, *Épopée napoléonienne* (1903), which was shown both in France and in the U.S.A. between 1903 and 1905 and again, in a different version, in 1907. The film was in two parts, the first consisting of five tableaux subtitled *Napoléon Bonaparte* and the second of ten tableaux subtitled *L'Empire, grandeur et décadence*. Richard Abel has suggested that the film's tableaux were 'less a history or even a chronicle than a series of spectacular attractions, much like either wax museum tableaux or historical paintings'. He points out how film exhibitors in this period could, and frequently did, alter the order and number of tableaux they showed, which was possible given the short lengths of film reels; this emphasis on the set-piece or tableau also

80 (right) The opening scene of the Fête de Paris, at Wanamaker's store in Philadelphia in 1908, showing two mannequins posing in gilt picture frames from which they stepped out onto the stage to promenade in a setting showing the coronation of the Empress Josephine. *Wanamaker Originator*, 12 March 1909. John Wanamaker collection, Historical Society of Pennsylvania.

81 (below) The mannequins in the gilt frames wore the white satin and pink Empire style dresses shown in the centre of this page of the house newspaper, the *Wanamaker Originator*. As was the convention in 1908, the dresses' designers, Paquin and Margaine Lacroix, were not named. The 'Napoleonic coat' shown on the large figure was also modelled in the show. The article reproduced a number of press descriptions of the show from other newspapers. *Wanamaker Originator*, November 1908. John Wanamaker collection, Historical Society of Pennsylvania.

Coronation of Josephine—Fete de Paris, Wanamaker's, October 1, 1908

characterised the Wanamaker fashion show, which suggests a degree of familiarity with cinematic tableaux based on paintings from the Napoleonic period by Jacques-Louis David and Elisabeth Vigée-Lebrun.[7]

The softly lit stage was draped in red and gold, with two large gilt frames with red curtains placed on either side. Spotlights played on the gilt frames and, as the massive organ of the Egyptian Hall played softly, the curtains rose to reveal two mannequins in static poses in the frames. One wore a Margaine Lacroix sheath gown of the type that had caused outrage at the Paris races earlier that year; the other an Empire-line white broadcloth suit by Paquin, who had also launched her Empire line at the Paris races (**80** and **81**).[8] American audiences would have recognised this format from the *tableau vivant* tradition of 'statue posing' and 'living pictures'.[9] After posing, the Wanamaker mannequins stepped out of their frames and 'gracefully walked out upon the stage and paced up and down for the criticism and inspection of the audience'. The mannequins then froze again into *tableaux vivants* of eighteenth-century French paintings before flowing into motion once more as they descended into the audience, assisted by the page, and walked slowly up one aisle and down the other to give the spectators a final, close-up view. As in the 1903 Madison Square Garden show, a lecturer, here accompanied by 'a pretty child' dressed as a Napoleonic page, explained the 'lines of the costumes' as the mannequins emerged from their frames to model on stage.[10]

Every morning over three days the show was staged. Admittance on the first day was limited to high society by invitation only, as in a French show, but on the following two the general public was admitted, which was more typical of American shows. Wanamaker, which already had close links with the Paris fashion trade and from 1905 had sent its buyers to the biannual Paris shows, went to great lengths to stress its French associations.[11] It emphasised

the buyers' role as intermediaries between French and American tastes, and the store's function as the arbiter and interpreter of elite French fashion for American consumers.[12] Describing the 1908 Philadelphia show in its house journal, the *Wanamaker Originator*, the store asserted that the Napoleon and Josephine tableaux 'stamt [sic] Wanamaker's as the authorized interpreter of Paris.' It quoted from a press review of the show:

> Following the European custom, the gowns, wraps, suits, furs and millinery were shown on living models, beautiful young women, exquisite in form, feature and coloring . . . Every woman present felt that Paris was in the very heart of New York and that the very innermost secrets of fashion were being whispered to her in a living panorama of marvellous beauty.[13]

Wanamaker's added its own gloss, claiming that the show 'was the inspiration of Paris itself, caught up and elaborated on a scale that even Paris had never known. The Egyptian Hall was thronged for three days by the most fashionable audiences ever gathered under the roof of a great store'.[14]

It was Paris on an American scale, however. Wanamaker trumpeted that he had out-performed the French: 'The display far outshone anything the French have ever attempted in the showing of gowns' and 'Immense crowds, both at the morning and afternoon exhibition, found great

delight in this Wanamaker innovation'.[15] Europeans looked on these American shows with awe. When, a year later, Wanamaker staged a fashion show of its new European imports for autumn 1909, it was reported in the illustrated press of both London and Paris (**82**).[16] *Femina*'s illustration shows approximately twenty mannequins modelling on a long platform built at right angles to the stage and extending into the central aisle of the auditorium. It is draped in hangings, decorated with oriental rugs and ornamented by a number of potted palms. Its long, runway-like proportions are more like a modern catwalk than the little raised stage of Paris salons or of Lucile's London salon. *Femina* commented:

> Our transatlantic neighbours see everything on a grand scale; one could even say – and this photograph supports this – a colossal scale! Compare this immense 'field' of elegance, where the mannequins must travel not a few kilometres a day as they pass and re-pass before a crowd of buyers, to our modest salons where fifty women are squeezed in. The document we present today to our lady readers was taken at the 'shopping hour' in Wanamaker's establishment, a marvel of its kind, the department store that sells everything from fashion to kitchen ware, bootlaces to horses![17]

If Europeans were impressed by the grandeur and scale of American enterprise, they also disparaged its associations with mass production, mass consumption and

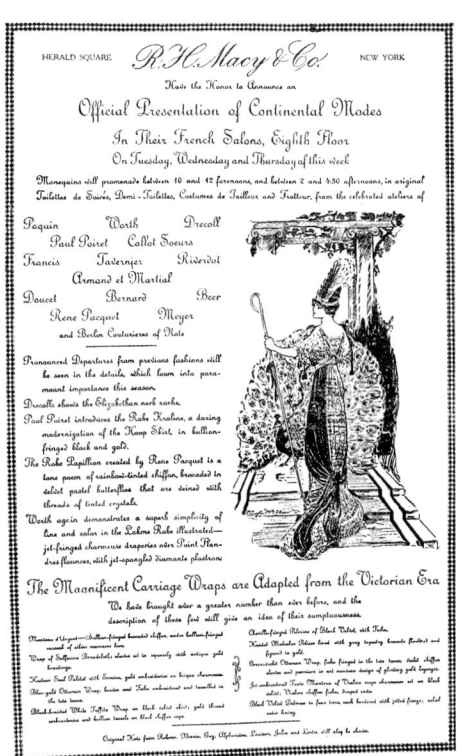

82 (facing page) Wanamaker fashion show of 1909 in the Egyptian Hall of the Philadelphia store, with its famous giant organ and Egyptian columns. *Femina*, 15 July 1910. Courtesy Fashion Institute of Technology/ SUNY, FIT Library Department of Special Collections and FIT Archives.

83 (right) This innovative newspaper advertisement for Macy's autumn 1911 fashion show used a new kind of typography and layout. Macy's also produced an invitation card on marbled paper and, for the show itself, a programme printed in violet on lavender-coloured paper with a cover depicting double doors that opened down the centre to reveal a picture of a proscenium arch and raised stage on which were printed details of fourteen of the gowns to be modelled in the show. The 5600 copies of this programme ran out after the first two days. Advertisement reproduced from the *Dry Goods Economist*, 30 September 1911.

uniformity. As early as the 1870s the Goncourt brothers had lamented 'the americanisation of women' and in 1910 E. Gomez Carrillo's *Psychologie de la mode* railed against the 'Yankee menace', arguing that American money was corrupting French taste.[18] When Paul Poiret toured American department stores in 1913 he said: 'You do everything on a gigantic scale. Everything is big . . . you have the largest stores in the world', but in the same breath he criticised the American woman for being 'mechanical' and having no soul: 'there is little individuality [in America]'.[19] Of the American girl, he pronounced 'even in her dress she is imitative'.[20] Her prototype could be seen in the large groups of mannequins that mingled on the Wanamaker runway in 1909 (see **3**). Marlis Schweitzer links the early twentieth-century American fashion model to Henry Ford's production line and to consumer culture in general; she describes the model 'walking in procession along a conveyor-belt-like runway' as a representative both of 'the loss of individuality within mass culture and the promise that with the appropriate consumption of goods one might find membership within a larger community and perhaps even win a moment in the spotlight'.[21] In the 1920s these pattern-cards of American modernity developed into a trans-continental ideal of universal chic, personified by rows of identical, streamlined, sleek women parading in monochrome dresses.

By the early 1910s fashion shows were common but not yet universal in American department stores.[22] Not even Wanamaker showed twice a year as a matter of course, as was established practice in Paris.[23] Fashion modelling was considered a French specialism well into the 1910s.[24] Nevertheless, William Leach has argued, by the early 1910s, the form of the American department store show had been

fixed.[25] When Rodman Wanamaker took over his father's New York branch in 1911, he 'immersed the entire store . . . in the glamor of Paris', as 'live models displayed gowns by Poiret, Worth and Paquin, with spotlights punctuating their comings and goings'.[26] Leach describes how mannequins 'paraded down ramps in store theatres or departments, spot-lighted by light engineers to a musical accompaniment, and often with theatrical effects or themes that might be Parisian, Persian, Chinese, Russian or Mexican, often with elaborate theatrical settings'.[27] Wanamaker staged its most spectacular orientalist extravaganza, the Garden of Allah fashion show, in both New York and Philadelphia in 1912–13, while Marshall Field in Chicago put on comparable extravaganzas.[28] In his comprehensive analysis of these shows, Leach reveals how the ubiquity of orientalist imagery was harnessed to business and sales.[29] This was the environment in which, as Nancy Troy shows, Poiret was able successfully to promote his own orientalist fashions on his American tour of 1913 and, in turn, to influence American department store shows at Macy's, Gimbel's and Wanamaker's.[30]

The scale and drama of these new department store shows was overwhelming. Macy's autumn 1911 fashion show, held twice a day over three days, was attended by roughly twelve thousand people (**83**).[31] Gimbel's initiated its biannual 'Promenade des Toilettes' fashion shows in 1910 (see **73**).[32] Typically, the store's auditorium would be dressed as an elaborate garden with abundant foliage, potted plants and palms, through which the mannequins wound their way between grassy banks with flowered borders, vine-draped pergolas, a fountain and formal flower beds.[33] As the decade progressed, mannequins routinely modelled twice daily for a fortnight, often on the large

raised runways that typified American shows.[34] In Paris, by contrast, modelling stages were smaller and squarer, often semi-circular and accessed by two or three steps, and were built into existing rooms (see **172**). Lucile's stages took this form too.[35] Today's long, raised runways are derived from early twentieth-century American shows that had to accommodate much bigger audiences (see **82**). In her book on the interface between fashion and popular theatre in the U.S.A., Schweitzer identifies the origins of the modern fashion runway in those designed for the New York stage by the Shuberts in their Winter Garden productions of the 1910s, including a runway that projected into the audience in *The Passing Show of 1914*.[36] The Viennese architect and theatre designer Joseph Urban's American stage designs of 1912–14 had incorporated innovative platforms raised two to three feet above the spotlights.[37] Urban designed a clear glass runway for the roof of Florenz Ziegfeld's New Amsterdam Theater in 1915. That year, Urban designed also, for Gimbel's, a fashion-show promenade stage that split in two, one half going stage left, the other stage right, and Schweitzer suggests that Ziegfeld's *Midnight Frolic* runway of 1915 may have been a 'sexed-up' version of the Gimbel's one.[38] The term 'catwalk' was not, however, used to describe these long modelling stages in this period; instead, as now, the term

designated a narrow, raised walkway, often along a bridge or above a theatre stage, that enabled workers to traverse the area below.

LUCILE IN NEW YORK

Meanwhile, in March 1910, the British-based Lucile opened her first overseas branch in New York.[39] There she installed a small stage in one room, as she had in London and Paris. For the opening parade, she brought from London four of her mannequins, Phyllis, Gamela, Corisande and Florence, and a hundred gowns: the chiffon curtains parted to reveal each mannequin posing on stage before parading slowly through the rooms to the melody of the 'Dream Waltz'. The London mannequins remained in New York for four months, to much acclaim, modelling alongside Josephine, an American mannequin, before returning home. *Harper's Bazar* showed the interiors of Lucile's branches in the U.S.A., France and England in 1914 (**84**). Lucile's New York studio, like the saleroom, was fitted out with a stage for her to judge the effects of her designs on her mannequins (**85**), suggesting yet again the new centrality of fashion modelling in the design process at this period. In 1915 she opened a fourth branch in

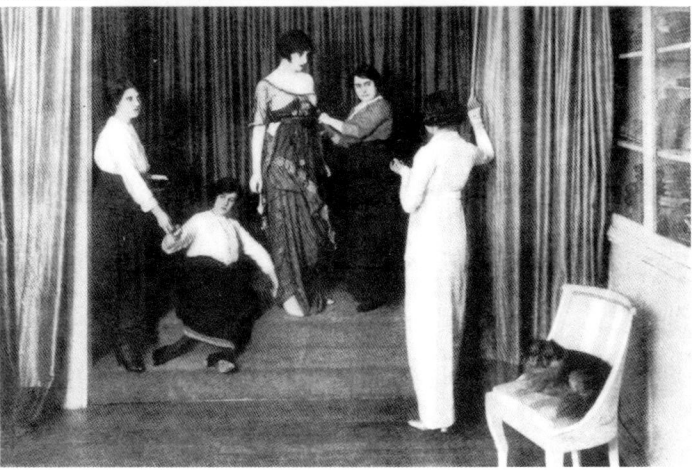

84 (facing page) An article from *Harper's Bazar*, August 1914, with photographs of a Lucile fashion show in her London garden, the London modelling stage, the New York premises, the Paris premises (see also **36**) and one of the two 'boudoir rooms' installed in Paris in 1911 for showing lingerie, one decorated and furnished in turquoise blue for a blonde, the other in deep rose for a brunette, with a dressing table covered in pink, veiled in white net and festooned with ropes of roses.

85 (right) Lady Duff Gordon at work in her New York studio at 160 Fifth Avenue. It was installed with a modelling stage and used primarily for photographic purposes. The biannual fashion shows took place in the salon proper at 37–39 West 57th Street. Courtesy Lewis Orchard: Lucile Ltd Collection.

Chicago at 1400 Lake Shore Drive. Already a successful international businesswoman, she also sold to department stores in other cities such as Blackstone's in Los Angeles. Her style of showing was European but she combined this with the large-scale ambition of America. While the French designers Poiret and Paquin toured the U.S.A. in 1913–14, Lucile simply moved between her established branches, crossing and re-crossing the Atlantic, sometimes taking her mannequins to and fro with her.[40]

The subtitles of a long article in the *New York Times* for 4 May 1913 convey the typical flavour of a Lucile show: 'Stage Hung with Velvet', 'Two Hours of Music', 'Elaborate Programmes', 'All Costumes Named' and 'Refreshments Served'. The article describes a series of interconnecting dark green rooms, professionally lit, that would have made a dramatic backdrop for Lucile's sometimes vibrantly coloured dresses in cerise and violet. Once admitted to the house, visitors exchanged their invitation cards for a 'very artistically done' show programme (**86**). Chairs filled each room, with the seats near the stage reserved for favoured clients. More than three hundred people were present and late-comers stood in the entrance hall. All the staff were dressed in varying shades of grey satin that denoted their status. The show lasted two hours and was accompanied by music played by 'a really excellent orchestra' stationed at the head of the stairs.[41] A hundred numbered and named gowns were shown on half a dozen mannequins, who wore a small piece of white muslin printed with the number of the model dress stitched onto their left sleeves. The dresses had the usual suggestive names. If asked by the customers, the mannequins gave the model number or name but otherwise remained silent. They modelled in twos and threes, so one group was always on stage while another changed backstage. Each group posed on the stage in the first salon before walking purposefully along the aisles between the chairs through all the rooms and back again. As always, they were particularly carefully accessorised and wore long, white gloves with the evening gowns. At the end of the parade, waiters appeared with tea, fois gras sandwiches and little cakes, after which some customers departed while others remained to inspect the dresses again, or to go upstairs to see the famous Rose Room.

Lucile created Rose Rooms for the display of lingerie in all her premises. Following her initiative, Gimbels' in New York initiated regular 'negligée shows' for women in 1913, displaying 'the intimate wardrobe' in scenarios including

86 (left) Cover of Lucile's spring 1917 show programme. These programmes typically opened to list all the models in order of showing. The autumn 1913 programme lists a hundred models by both name and number and states that the mannequins will also wear the number pinned to the left sleeve of the model gown. It advertises the new dresses as 'made in Paris by Lucile' and bears the legend 'Ho Girls, New Bare Knee Skirt is Here'. Fashion Institute of Technology/SUNY, FIT Library Department of Special Collections and FIT Archives.

87 Lucile's Rose Room in Chicago, showing Hebe modelling in 1915. The New York Rose Room was designed and furnished by Elsie de Wolfe. Its walls were decorated in pink silk veiled with white net, shirred top and bottom and finished with pink ruching. Doors and windows were hung with pink taffeta and the picture cords covered with ropes of pink and white satin rosebuds. Fashion Institute of Technology/SUNY, FIT Library Department of Special Collections and FIT Archives.

89 (facing page) Arjamand modelling *I Paid the Price* by Lucile, New York, 1917. Fashion Institute of Technology/ SUNY, FIT Library Department of Special Collections and FIT Archives.

88 Lady Duff Gordon's Six "Types"', *American Examiner*, Sunday, 13 March 1910, showing, from left to right, Florence (type 6), Corisande (type 2), Rossalba (type 5), Marion (type 3), Phyllis (type 4) and Gamela (type 1).

'La Parisienne Elégante In Her Boudoire'.[42] Lucile's Rose Rooms each had a small stage on which mannequins posed (**87**). These showrooms were orgies of cloth, as if one of Lucile's dresses had itself been transformed into a boudoir; the *New York Times* journalist found the effect 'beautiful, but rather overpowering'. They typify the connection between Lucile's décor and her designs, with floating chiffon curtains echoing the transparency of her dresses: as Susan Glenn observes, Lucile made abundantly clear the

relationship between 'clothes as eroticized commodities and women as sexualized objects'.[43]

In the early 1900s Lucile had been able to design for individual clients but, as the business grew, there were too many clients for her to design for each one individually. Instead, she began to hire mannequins who fitted into generic types and to design for them.[44] She clearly identified these types in a press article of 1910 (**88**).[45] Type No. 1 wore 'a dress that is effective at a distance . . .

designed to suit the particular style of Gamela who is a dark regal beauty with dark hair and inscrutable green eyes.' Type No. 2 was Corisande, 'a fair, blue-eyed, slight, gay little girl.' The dress was made short, 'suitable to her youth and her gayety . . . all the colors making for simplicity and youth.' Type No. 3, Marion, was 'a tall, slender, sad and dreamy girl . . . All the colors I take as meaning dreamy sadness. A dress fit only for a very quiet social occasion.' Type No. 4 was Phyllis, 'a brilliant little brown-eyed girl,' Type No. 5 Rossalba, 'an almond-eyed Eastern beauty, suggestive of the hareem' and Type No. 6 Florence, 'a fair-haired girl with blue eyes, and who, as her coloring suggests, has the sweetest nature in the world. Her type is of subtle softness'. Long descriptions of the fabrics and colours of the appropriate gowns accompany each description of the mannequin types. This rationalisation of design typologies suggests a modernist methodology even where Lucile's individual designs were not modernist in

style but floating, romantic and seductive. For all their differences, furthermore, there were also similarities between the scale of Lucile's business ambition and the massive scale of American department store shows. As with Paquin and Parry, Lucile's design methods invite a re-consideration of the nature of modernism in relation to fashion.

During the second decade of the century, Lucile took on her iconic (most photographed) mannequins: the Americans Arjamand and Dinarzade joined the English mannequins Dolores, Hebe and Phyllis (**89–93**).[46] Lucile gave them all exotic names and trained them in her dramatic and singular modelling style. Their heights varied, from the six-foot Dolores to the petite Phyllis. The latter tended to model the picture dresses and romantic gowns, while Dolores and Dinarzade wore the more modern, but also somewhat exotic, gowns.[47] Dinarzade, Arjamand and Hebe were also on the tall side. All the mannequins were

slender but nothing like as thin as today's models, apart from Arjamand, who was recruited specifically for her extreme thinness. Howard Greer remembered her as 'the first of the really emaciated mannequins ever to model fashionable clothes. She was so thin that we used to make cracks about stuffing cotton between her vertebrae so that people wouldn't think she was a skeleton'.[48]

Many of Lucile's mannequins went on to model elsewhere or to make careers on the stage, and several made spectacular marriages.[49] Dolores and Phyllis were discovered by Florenz Ziegfeld in about 1917 and went on to become Follies showgirls, often clad by Lucile, who also designed stage costumes and set pieces for Ziegfeld.[50] Their distinctive modelling styles provided the right 'fit' for Ziegfeld's showgirl taxonomy. After 1906, when Ziegfeld had produced *The Parisian Model*, his showgirls were selected along 'American' rather than 'European' lines, according to Linda Mizejewski: taller and longer-legged.[51]

After 1915 the Follies revues increasingly drew on this fashionable look and, as Mizejewski writes, the Follies showgirl became 'famous for her signature entrance on a staircase and her runway exhibition of the Ziegfeld Walk, a combination of pageantry strut and haute couture modelling'.[52] It was largely Lucile's mannequins, with their unique looks and mannerisms, who constituted this look in the Follies at a time when Lucile and several of her mannequins, alongside the set designer Joseph Urban and the dance director Ned Wayburn, were hired by Ziegfeld. Wayburn notoriously divided the chorus not by talent or gender but by height, proportions and dance type; he classified the types as A–E (just as Lucile had classified her mannequins, as noted earlier), training them with militaristic techniques.[53] Mizejewski describes Wayburn's 'A-team' as the tall, fashion mannequin-like performers who paraded slowly in elegant gowns, as opposed to the shorter 'ponies' or 'chickens' of the E-team who danced soft-shoe, acrobatics, tap and 'bucks' in chorus-girl style.[54]

Lucile's fashion mannequins' stage performance in the Ziegfeld Follies consisted of gliding and posing, as opposed to the chorus girls' high-kicking dance routines.[55] In 1917 Wayburn developed the distinctive Ziegfeld Walk for his A-team showgirls. It was, according to Robert Baral, 'a combination of Irene Castle's flair for accenting the pelvis in her stance, the lifted shoulder, and a slow, concentrated gait'.[56] The walk was designed for an entry down a staircase with steep rises, unlike the flat ramps of fashion shows: it required, argues Mizejewski, 'an unusually artificial thrust of hip and shoulder in order to keep one's balance'.[57] Schweitzer convincingly argues that Lucile's walk can be discerned as an element of the famous Ziegfeld Walk, a slow, stately, glide that typified the Ziegfeld Follies from 1915.[58] Her suggestion is based on a comparative analysis of photographs showing the bodily awareness and pose of Dolores modelling for Lucile and performing in the Ziegfeld Follies. Schweitzer writes that this evidence is not conclusive but suggestive. Her suggestion is given support by the fact that Lucile's mannequins, like Irene and Vernon Castle, moved between America and France in the 1910s, bridging the worlds of fashion, theatre and popular dance in two continents.[59] The Ziegfeld Walk also incorporated elements of Irene Castle's walk, a performer who was also dressed by Lucile.[60] Lucile's mannequins also acted as extras in the Castles' 1915 film *The Whirl of Life*, where the mannequins make up the audience for the Castles' dance demonstration at the end of the film.[61]

In the crossover from fashion to revue theatre, a set of connected fictions about race, class, gender and American national identity were thus consolidated in the fashion-mannequin performance. Mizejewski analyses how a racially white ideal was inscribed in the creation of the 'Ziegfeld Girl' through the adoption of what she calls an 'haute couture body' and 'the very designation of the fashionable "lady" as a white woman'.[62] While there were black theatre revues, there appear to have been no black fashion shows in this period or, if there were, no evidence of them survives.[63] The very exoticism of many of Lucile's mannequins, with their orientalist names, only reinforced their Anglo-Saxon ethnicity.

At the same time, the Follies Girl also had to be respectable, to which the class masquerade of the fashion mannequin contributed. Mizejewski shows how Ziegfeld drew on 'the mystifying practices of fashion and public relations' to imbue his Follies Girls with bourgeois respectability through the association with clothes modelling; their 'breeding' redeemed them from the chorus girl's association with prostitution and low life.[64] The reality

of fashion modelling, however, was that 'breeding' was a talented performance that privileged seeming over being. In 1914 a journalist described how Lucile trained her mannequins to behave like society women:

> She makes them ladies in the true sense of the word – teaches them how to walk, how to use their hands, how to speak, trains them in fact as carefully as though they were débutantes about to appear before royalty. 'My models must know how to wear clothes', she says. 'They must be as unconscious of them as a duchess. They must have grace and ease of manner. They must be ladies – else how ridiculous to expect them to demonstrate the dresses ladies are to wear.'[65]

Here white society women are clearly seen to have a stake in the visual appeal of the mannequin, with her capacity for class mimicry. However, as the decade progressed, society women became less clearly distinguishable from the actresses and mannequins for whose behaviour they provided the model. In her book on feminine 'types' in the 1920s, Liz Conor uses the term 'the modern appearing woman' as shorthand to describe the ways in which 'women were invited to articulate themselves as modern subjects by constituting themselves as spectacles'.[66] For the mannequin, this was a professional rather than a social requirement but she did so in the wider context of an increasing fluidity in female appearance across all classes, so that identification through dress and appearance, previously the markers of class and respectability, became progressively harder to make as the masquerade of ladylike behaviour and appearance approximated more and more the real thing. 'Masked with lipstick and rouge, all women were equally suspect'.[67]

WINDOW MODELLING AND THE POPULARISATION OF DEPARTMENT-STORE SHOWS

American department store shows began in the more upmarket and East Coast stores but rapidly spread across the entire U.S.A. In vain did the *Dry Goods Economist* urge retailers to show restraint and good taste in their staging of fashion shows.[68] The stores' wilder excesses were widely reported in the press. They cemented the concept of French fashion in the public mind so that, despite the movement to promote American fashion, French fashion retained its hold in the popular imagination. This may help to explain why the American industry continued to depend on the ideal of French fashion long after its most astute practitioners acknowledged publicly that they had no logical need of it. Consequently, and paradoxically, the

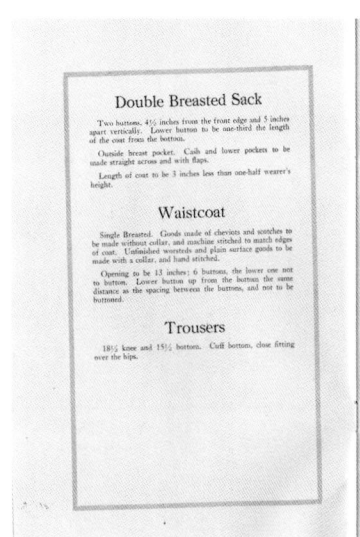 

dramatic potential of the mass-market American show perpetuated the need for the elite French show; thus American fashion buyers from all over the U.S.A. continued to travel to Paris twice a year to acquire the new season's imports.

From 1910 fashion shows began to be staged twice a year in Los Angeles and San Francisco, collectively organised by the major department stores and called the United Fashion Show.[69] Nevertheless, fashion modelling remained largely a New York phenomenon and West Coast stores usually sent away to New York for models (that is, living mannequins).[70] The stores' custom-built theatres facilitated theatrical shows, complete with programmes, characters and settings such as indoor gardens and 'Venetian' palazzi.[71] In addition, the stores staged promotional gimmicks. At Bullock's in Los Angeles in 1912, 'half a dozen beautiful living models' appeared and were helped into 'a really, truly, electric automobile' that drove up and down the wide aisles of the store, pausing only at the street entrances for the admiration of the huge crowd, before reversing back into the store. Finally, the car stopped indoors and 'the young ladies descended from the coupe and walked gracefully down to the street entrance and slowly turned and posed'.[72] At Blackstone's, also in Los Angeles, in 1914, where the fashion shows took place twice a day on the second floor, the publicity photograph advertising the show was meticulously recreated as a *tableau vivant* in the store window by a 'stately, posing girl in futurist attire'.[73]

Window modelling became a genre of its own.[74] It had its detractors as well as its supporters but was most popular with wholesalers and mass-market retailers.[75] In 1911, at L. Dimond & Sons in Providence, Rhode Island, four living mannequins promenaded through the various departments of the store, took the lift to the ground floor and assumed their positions in the shop window, one after another. For several hours mannequins continued to appear in the window, attracting a large crowd and causing so much congestion that the city had to order their removal.[76] In 1914 the *Los Angeles Times* reported that there were always crowds in front of the windows with living mannequins 'and frequently the assistance of police officers was needed to open the way for a long line.'[77] Perhaps such scenes were the basis for the window-modelling scene in the 1925 fiction film about a fashion model, *Irene*, in which the cheeky Irene humorously play-acts in the window, causing a near riot among the spectators.[78]

As Leach and Schweitzer both demonstrate, fashion shows featured in stores all over the U.S.A. by 1915 and were so popular that the crowds had to be dispersed by the police in small towns, where four to five thousand people might be attracted in a single afternoon. Spectators often had to stand on counters or tables to see the show: 'at the height of their popularity, fashion shows threatened to disrupt civic order to such an extent that police in New York and other cities required managers to take out licenses for all "live model" shows and even threatened to ban them altogether'.[79] This type of show had popular appeal distinct from the genteel presentations of the elite stores of the big cities but sharing the same theatrical impetus.

As public fashion shows became ubiquitous, they also came to be featured in wholesale and trade shows and by 1915 they were widespread.[80] They were seen as adding value to sales by showing clothes in motion 'with just the right amount of dash and style'.[81] Around 1915 male fashion shows began, predominantly in the wholesale sector.[82] A catalogue of 1916 from Kansas City lists the men modelling by name and city, including Bert Stanton from Chicago, Chas. M. Taylor from New York and Wm. G. Witkin from Philadelphia (**94**). The use of living mannequins in shows also encouraged fashion catalogues to switch from drawings to photographs.[83]

THEATRE, FASHION AND CONSUMPTION

The cultural historian Susan Glenn argues that theatre, fashion and sensual display converged in the early twentieth-century department store, which was instrumental in establishing the 'cultural circuitry' between

95 'Society Fashion Show and Garden Party at Hotel Maryland, Pasadena', *Los Angeles Sunday Times*, 23 March 1913.

theatre and fashion.[84] A typical department-store fashion show was described by a journalist in 1914:

> The orchestra played while specially trained mannequins displayed these gowns to their best advantage on the raised promenade. Mirrors were arranged at the entrance to the promenade, so that it appeared as if two models were entering, the reflection vanishing like an apparition as the living mannequin, carefully posed, stepped daintily down the steps, swaying from side to side in the music's rhythm.[85]

Department store shows were staged either in-house on specially built stages or in rented venues, such as theatres and opera houses, although, as Schweitzer argues, the latter option made them vulnerable to appropriation by vaudeville producers.[86] In her book *When Broadway Was the Runway*, Schweitzer shows in meticulous detail how the American fashion show developed in tandem in the department stores and revue theatres of New York. The fashion show was first adapted to Broadway in Ziegfeld's *Follies of 1912* and the Shuberts' *Passing Show of 1914*.[87] In 1915 the *Chicago Daily Tribune* noted the similarities between French mannequins and American showgirls: 'Paris has her mannequins, who are carefully trained to the profession of displaying fine frocks and finer feathers. New York has her show girls, whose profession is to show gowns and look bored and uninterested.'[88] Schweitzer, too, compares the mannequin to the showgirl. Unlike the chorus girl who had to sing and dance, the showgirl's role was simply to appear looking glorious; she was a 'finely crafted commodity as available and exchangeable as the clothes on her back'.[89]

To department stores, fashion shows were an attractive form of spectacle because they did not generally require a licence like other forms of theatrical display. To Broadway producers such as Ziegfeld and the Shuberts, the fashion show perfectly suited the speed, variety and continuous action of revue.[90] While pointing out the similarities between fashion and theatre, both Schweitzer and Glenn also highlight their differences, both in audiences and attitudes.[91] Revue theatre was far more irreverent and Schweitzer cites, for example, two shows that caricatured

Lucile: in the Shuberts' *Passing Show of 1912*, Lucile, whose own name was Lady Duff Gordon, figured as Lady Fluff Bored'Un, only months after she and her husband had notoriously escaped the Titanic on an empty lifeboat; and in their *Passing Show of 1916* she reappeared as Lady Bluff Gordon.[92]

The porosity between elite and mass markets was nowhere clearer than in the circular borrowings from the fashion shows staged on Broadway in vaudeville and in the department stores. This 'cultural circuitry' between Broadway and the department store was soon extended to include another kind of fashion show that developed in the period, the society charity fashion show, for which the outbreak of war in Europe in 1914 provided a fresh impetus. Far from being a simple trickle-down or 'trickle-up' effect, the interchange between them ran mercurially in every direction, as each greedily took new ideas from the other as soon as they appeared in newspaper accounts and lavishly illustrated fashion magazines. One of the early charity shows, in Pasadena in 1913, combined three elements that became typical: women on horseback, girls dressed for various sports and fashion mannequins.[93] It was staged in a hotel garden on a runway of oriental carpets laid out on the lawn, flanked by refreshment tables for the guests. At three o'clock in the afternoon, eight 'handsomely mounted' and 'stunning' horsewomen attended by liveried grooms suddenly appeared and thundered down the rugs before dismounting and promenading to and fro before the guests). After them came squads of 'tennis and golf girls' followed by professional American mannequins who for two hours recreated French modelling scenes from the Longchamp racetrack, wearing French imports from the I. Magnin department store (**95**). At night the show resumed inside the hotel, with spotlights trained on the grand staircase down which mannequins descended.

In 1914 the temporary closure of the Paris houses at the outbreak of war gave fresh impetus to the American fashion lobby.[94] Over 4–6 November 1914, the previously Europhile American *Vogue* turned tail and joined it, staging an elaborate Fashion Fête of American designs from prominent New York stores at the Ritz-Carlton Hotel.[95]

Although many of the fashions modelled were Francophile and luxurious, many others included American sportswear, such as the 'Polo Girl' and 'country costume' (**96**). They were modelled by no less than seventy-five mannequins who between them wore jewellery worth $300,000.[96] Both the element of 'bling' and the Nardi Polo costumes were soon copied in vaudeville.

The proceeds went to French war relief but the promotion of American fashions over French ones caused a fashion diplomatic incident. Several Paris couturiers subsequently refused entry to *Vogue*'s editors, seeing their sponsorship of the fashion fête as a challenge to the supremacy of French couture. *Vogue*'s owner, Condé Nast, had to send an emissary to Paris to mollify Poiret and the couture syndicate and suggest a 'French Fashion Fête' in New York, which indeed took place a year later.[97] Carolyn Seebohm argued that the New York fashion fête 'finally dethroned the French couture from its long dominion over the world of fashion. The dynastic succession of the great Paris houses endured . . . but their absolute hegemony was challenged'.[98] It was an important shift, if somewhat undermined by the return match a year later.

Meanwhile, the French worked hard to re-establish their cultural hegemony, exhibiting (unlike Germany and Britain) in the Panama-Pacific International Exposition from March to December 1915 in San Francisco. Staged to celebrate the opening of the Panama Canal, the world's fair had a different function for the French exhibitors, who were desperate to recoup lost ground and promote their national industry on a global stage. Their lavish fashion displays consisted of three dioramas: the Vichy spa, the Longchamp racetrack and the beach at the Côte d'Azur. They showed gowns by Beer, Callot, Chéruit, Doeuillet, Doucet, Jenny, Lanvin, Martial et Armand, Paquin, Premet and Worth.[99] Replicas of all the gowns were modelled in the U.S.A. at Wanamaker's in both New York and Philadelphia, in live mannequin parades set against backdrops of Monte Carlo, Nice and Longchamp, with changing lighting effects to recreate appropriate light for morning, afternoon and evening gowns.[100]

There the aura of exclusivity was maintained. It was in vaudeville, by contrast, that the barriers were breached between high and low culture, art and industry, theatre and fashion. In 1914 Paquin had toured 112 gowns worth more than $100,000 around America; her show, with its little paying theatre, may have inspired the Broadway theatre producer May Tully to stage the first vaudeville fashion show.[101] Twenty-six minutes long, Tully's *Fashion Show* opened at the Palace Theater, New York, in April 1915.[102] It was simple but effective, relying above all on dazzling costumes and a novel set consisting of an enlarged cover of

96 A 'country costume' representing 'athletic America' and a 'Polo Girl' costumed by Nardi shown at *Vogue*'s Fashion Fête featuring American fashion designs from prominent New York stores, held at the Ritz–Carlton Hotel in New York over three days in November 1914. *Vogue* (America) December 1914. Vogue; © Condé Nast.

Vogue magazine at the back of a garden with a lawn and pergola. Each time the cover was flipped back, a model stepped out of the pages of *Vogue*, sauntered round the garden and took up a pose.[103] Gradually the stage filled with twenty-five mannequins in picturesque groups (**97**). They were a mixture of professionals, society women and an artist's model, Audrey Munson, who had modelled for the Panama–Pacific Exposition and who started the poses as Eve 'in a garlanded robe of white' (**98** nos. 24 and 33). She was followed by a series of 'miladies': milady of the avenue, milady of the negligée, milady of the golf links, milady of the mountains, milady of the courts, milady of the campus, milady of the international cup, milady of the saddle, milady of the shops, milady of the hunt and milady of the yacht. The miladies were a cipher of the specifically American nature of the show, with its emphasis on college girls and sport, hunting and horse-riding, camaraderie and humour. As in the *Vogue* fashion fête, there was a Nardi-clad Polo Girl (see **98** nos. 3 and 6) and, as in the Pasadena show, two mannequins appeared on horseback. Two 'adorable' children were accompanied by their 'governess', whose chic hunting costume and rifle on her shoulder caused laughter in the audience (see **98** no. 16).

The show cost almost nothing to produce. Tully persuaded the Fifth Avenue stores to lend gowns and jewellery worth nearly $50,000 in exchange for free advertising. *Vogue*'s name came free too: Tully availed herself of it and the magazine obligingly promoted the show in an article entitled 'Vogue Plays a New Rôle'. *Variety* described it as 'an entertaining vaudeville speciality with a surrounding that fairly shrieks of style and expense'. The event typified the capacity of the American show to span high and low culture at once. Both aspirational and popular, its luxurious and costly commodities closed the programme, following variety acts such as 'Willard, "The Man Who Grows", one of the most puzzling human enigmas', a singing comedienne, a musical spectacle and a comedy skit. It was enormously popular both in New York and on the vaudeville circuit which it toured from East Coast to West. In Washington, its 'sports girls' demonstrated how to wear the clothes: 'with masculine insouciance slim white hands were thrust deep into front and side pockets as girl and gown models were paraded for approval'. In California, they were photographed lounging insouciantly on the bonnet of the latest Buick (**99**).

97 (facing page) May Tully's *Fashion Show* at the Palace Theater, New York, April 1915. *Vogue* (America), 1 June 1915. From left to right, the clothes are by Maison Bernard, O'Sullivan, Jenny import from Maison Maurice, Estelle Mershon, Bonwitt Teller, Harry Collins, Lucile, Lucile, Hickson, Bernard, Jean, Maison Maruice, unidentified. Photograph White Studio. Vogue; © Condé Nast.

98 (right) White Studio's contact sheets for Tully's *Fashion Show*. Alongside French fashions from New York importers, the images show Audrey Munson as Eve (24 and 33), Sadie Mullen as the Polo Girl (3 and 6), a Nardi riding costume (11), the governess in hunting costume with a rifle and a dog (16), the little girl in her charge (17), the bride (31 and 34) and bridesmaids (29). Billy Rose Theatre Division, New York Public Library for the Performing Arts, Astor, Lenox and Tilden Foundations.

Charity fashion shows were also staged in New York, Philadelphia and Saint Louis in 1915.[104] The most spectacular, in July 1915, was held at the Newport home of Mrs Hermann Oelrichs.[105] 'Fashion's Passing Show' combined pageantry and parties, professional mannequins and society women, American sportswear and French luxury. Twenty-two professional mannequins came from New York, six from Lucile, to wear the costumes made by their firms, modelling for the first time alongside society women. The parade was closed by Lucile's Hebe, in a bridal procession. All day long, society women paraded down the stairs (**100**) and mannequins posed on the terraces (**101**) or play-acted in the fountains (**102**). They rode in on polo ponies in Hickson costumes similar to Tully's Nardi-clad polo girl and staged tableaux in tennis skirts and blouses by Abercrombie and Fitch, and Nardi golfing costumes. In the evening, society women performed and professional mannequins paraded seventeen evening gowns in a play, 'Her ladyship's Wardrobe', written by Mrs Condé Nast, the wife of the publisher of *Vogue*.

Fashion shows were everywhere that year. Vaudeville took its ideas from the stores and the stores in turn competed with the theatres. Over 7–9 October 1915, the International Fashion Show, 'a fashion extravaganza' also entitled 'Yesterday or Tomorrow', was staged twice daily at Carnegie Hall in New York.[106] The four-act spectacle written by Pierre de Lanux featured fifty mannequins and four show girls, with scenery designed by Urban (who, as seen, had just begun to design for the Follies in 1915). Entry was charged at $3. Just days later, Gimbels' advertised its autumn 1915 *La Promenade des Toilettes* (also designed by Urban) as an exact, but free, copy of the Carnegie Hall show, staged twice a day in two shows of one and a half hours in the store's eighth-floor salons.[107] Gimbels' lavish shows then had to compete with those of the commercial theatre and began to incorporate some aspects of variety.[108] Unlike department stores, however,

the variety acts were not tied to the biannual timetables of the fashion industry; the Carnegie Hall International Fashion Show was restaged in December, featuring costumes by Callot, Bernard, Paquin, Cheruit, Poiret, Premet and Lanvin, with entry charged at a massive $8; the *Los Angeles Times* wrote: 'This swagger fashion show was staged like some bewitching musical review'.[109]

May Tully, meanwhile, had opened her second touring show, the 'Fall Fashion Show', at the Palace Theater in New York in October 1915, two weeks after the International Fashion Show at Carnegie Hall.[110] From New York, it went west and southwest via Texas, travelling for six months with great success, despite the complexities of touring such a large show. Consisting of about thirty-two people in all, the tour required six maids, two wardrobe women, a stage manager and four assistants. Like Tully's first show, its luxury contrasted incongruously with the variety acts it accompanied, which included acrobats, a musical duo, a comedy act and a 'feature photoplay', followed by a Ford Animated Pictorial film. At fifty-seven minutes, the 'Million Dollar Fashion Show', as it came to be known, was almost twice as long as the first and more than twice as opulent. Its management boasted that it was the most expensive vaudeville act in history: 'Luxury Run Mad', declared the show programme. More than a million dollars' worth of jewels and costumes were loaned by American stores at no cost to the producers; Tully even claimed that her idea was so successful that dressmakers and their clients in the audience were attempting to copy the costumes.

This 'Fall Fashion Show' was loosely based on a Cinderella theme and Tully claimed that the introduction of a theatrical story to a fashion show made it more appealing to a mixed audience, although the press response to a show that egged women on to such excessive consumption was ambivalent. It featured thirteen to nineteen showgirls (accounts differ), seventeen models and

100 (left) Society women in the 'Pageant of Nations' tableau in 'Fashion's Passing Show' held at the Newport home of Mrs Hermann Oelrichs in 1915. *Vogue* (America), 1 September 1915. Vogue; © Condé Nast.

101 (left) Two of Henri Bendel's professional mannequins at the Oelrichs' 'Fashion Passing Show'. *Vogue* described one as 'stately Josephine, his tall black-haired mannequin'. *Vogue* (America), 1 September 1915. Vogue; © Condé Nast.

102 (above) At 'Fashion's Passing Show' these three young women appeared as if from nowhere, ran through the gardens and jumped into the fountains, startling and delighting the guests. The Bonwitt Teller striped bathing costume on the left is similar to, though not the same as, the one in contact print 28 illustrated in **98**. *Vogue* (America), 1 September 1915. Vogue; © Condé Nast.

Panorama by White

Five fashion goddesses, photographed at the Palace Music Hall, in one of the scenes of the earliest of the Winter's Fashion Fêtes

A NEW THEATRICAL FAD

Why Study to Be an Emotional Actress When You Can So Easily Be an Emotionless Mannikin?

This miniature reveals Miss Lillian Mahoney—mannikin extraordinary—demonstrating how easy it is for a "perfect 34" to get into good habits

THE really popular thing nowadays in the way of a theatrical production is a Fashion Fête. The mannikins are having it all their own way. While the rage lasts, the actresses are nowhere.

Here are some pictures of the first of the season's Fashion Shows, the one so ably organized by Miss May Tully (who is some day surely going to be a producer on Broadway). This show ran for two crowded weeks at the Palace, with dozens of emotionless actresses wearing dozens of emotional gowns. Miss Tully's exhibition is now on the road and doing so well that even a little town like Fort Worth, Texas, had to have three days of it! You might think that these reviews would interest only the women. Oh, no! Not at all. At every performance strong men in the audience were entranced, hypnotised, immovable in their chairs.

And, as we go to press, here is *another* Fashion Fête, which ought to be the most remarkable of the year. It will open in the ballroom of the Ritz-Carlton on November 22, and will run for more than a week—afternoon and evening. We predict that this show at the Ritz—which will be wholly Parisian in character—will register the first notable success among the winter's charity entertainments.

Miss Sadie Mullen, mannikin, wearing—and how appropriately—"a royal charmeuse." Miss Mullen may not be royal, but charmeuse she indubitably is

© Portraits by Ira L. Hill

Miss Betty Brown, who was a body of biscuit colored crêpe and apricot colored satin, entirely surrounded by fur of nut colored beaver. A biscuit, an apricot, and a nut!—really, quite a little meal in itself

Here we see Miss Louise White, pretending that she is the "Vogue" girl. Vogue was the fashion magazine which, all through the show, was supposed to preside over the destinies of the fashions and the mannikins

Miss Emily Lee, the star of the occasion, who impersonated no less a heroine than Cinderella. In this fashion drama, she acquired her dresses—just as so many girls do in real life—merely by begging for them

two principals who were comedy actresses; one, Emilie Lea, played Jeanne, a poor working-class girl who received an invitation to a ball, fell asleep and dreamt that her fairy godmother had supplied her with marvellous clothes so that she became one of the world's best-dressed women. In reality it was more fashion show than stage play and consisted of fashion modelling interspersed with a few songs and high kicks. *Vanity Fair* noted this when it asked: 'Why Study to be an Emotional Actress When You Can So Easily Be an Emotionless Mannikin?' and its description of 'dozens of emotionless actresses wearing dozens of emotional gowns' is a reference to Lucile's 'gowns of emotion' (**103**). The magazine highlighted the professional indifference that distinguished the professional mannequin from the actress and – like the earliest observers of the fashion show – commented on the impassivity of the mannequins and that the fashion show was eclipsing the stage act: 'the really popular thing nowadays in the way of a theatrical production is a Fashion Fête. The mannikins are having it all their own way. While the rage lasts, the actresses are nowhere.'

The rage did not last long, however. Tully had many imitators but none so lavish.[111] Audiences could see larger and more opulent shows for free in the big department stores or at the picture houses where Pathé and Gaumont newsreels brought Parisian couture shows to American eyes. Even Tully's appeal palled after a while and early plans to create her fashion show as a biannual vaudeville feature languished alongside others.[112] Nevertheless, the phenomenon had tapped into the aspirations of American consumer culture and its entertainment industry in a way that would never have been possible in Europe, where fashion shows were firmly embedded in the fashion industry and its cultural production.

DREAM NARRATIVES

As fashion shows shared more and more characteristics with theatre, so they incorporated spindly narratives that gave them a certain dramatic structure and shape. After 1910 this frequently took the form of a reverie: a young woman falls asleep and dreams of a fantastical and splendid fashion show.[113] At the end, she wakes to find it was only a dream. This device gave narrative coherence to fantasy sequences of the display of gorgeous dresses in a form of entertainment that, like early cinema, relied on the mesmerising visual effects of movement and spectacle rather than story-telling for its appeal. Tom Gunning, in his analysis of the appeal of the first films to audiences, has characterised it as a form of 'attraction'.[114]

The show was a dream in another sense, too. What all early twentieth-century American fashion shows shared, be they in department stores, vaudeville or high society, was a specifically American form of collective dreaming: a dream of the good life. The fashion show allowed Americans to see France, and French fashion, as a place to dream. It exemplified two characteristics that William Leach has argued were essential to the emerging culture of consumption in America from the 1880s to the 1920s: the 'cult of the new' and the 'democratization of desire'.[115] Leach identifies this period as the moment in the development of American capitalism in which self-fulfilment, consumer pleasure, acquisition and consumption came to replace the ideals of community, civic well-being and hard work as forms of personal fulfilment and a route to happiness.[116] Fashion and style were, he argues, at the centre of the cult of the new, in the form of an endless supply of commodities that replaced earlier social and ethical values.[117] It is in this context that the 'bling' of the vogue for the fashion show in 1915 makes sense.

A month after Tully's show debuted in New York in October 1915, the Paris Fashion Fête that *Vogue* had promised the French couturiers a year earlier was staged at New York's Ritz-Carlton Hotel. Although a benefit for the widows and orphans of French soldiers, the principal function of the show was to mollify the French couturiers who had complained at the American bias of the *Vogue* Fashion Fête a year earlier. *Vanity Fair* mentioned the Fête in its coverage of May Tully and American *Vogue* devoted twenty pages to it, constituting a lavish catalogue of luxury French fashion available in New York that season.[118] By bringing Paris fashions to New York in this way, the couturiers cut out the middlemen, the American buyers and commissionaires who usually bought at the Paris fashion shows. Instead, the garments from the Fête were sold directly to the American stores. This notwithstanding, the 1915 French Fête was far less successful financially than the American Fête of 1914. It was, however, more spectacular. Running over several days, from 22 to 30 November 1915, approximately ninety models were shown, worth about $800 each, from prominent French couture houses including Worth, Poiret, Paquin, Callot, Doucet, Jenny, Chéruit, Lanvin and Premet (**104**). The forty-six mannequins, most of them American actresses, had been selected from six hundred applicants. They performed in a comedy playlet written by Roger Boutet de Monvel whose brief was to incorporate the showing of eighty models into a narrative. 'Don't forget the dialogue!' were Poiret's parting words to him.

104 Premet's cloak *Grande Fête* available from Franklin Simon in New York and modelled at the Paris Fashion Fête in New York's Ritz–Carlton Hotel in November 1915. *Vogue* (America), 15 December 1915. Vogue; © Condé Nast.

105 (facing page) Lucile's vaudeville version of *Fleurette's Dream at Peronne*, 1917. See **79**. © Victoria and Albert Museum, London.

By 1915 this typical high-society fashion show was deriving its form and content from vaudeville which had fused the fashion-show format with the showgirl one, so that the line between the fashion show and theatrical spectacle had become progressively eroded. It was, therefore, hardly surprising that Lucile, who designed both costumes and some numbers for the Follies from 1915 to 1921, should stage two fashion spectaculars of her own in 1916 and 1917: they were both charity and vaudeville shows, pitched respectively at an elite and a mass audience. The first, held at the Plaza in New York on the last two days of February 1916, was 'Chansons Vivantes', a charity event for the benefit of French soldiers' war orphans, the Orphelinat des Armées. *Vogue* described it: 'Weaving in and out among the misty green and blue draperies of the stage, the lovely manikins, clad in gowns for which no words have yet to be coined, posed and strolled and lured one lone, gorgeously clad, extremely level-headed young gentleman, who paid no attention to them whatever.'[119]

In the autumn of 1917, after America's joining the war on 6 April 1917, Lucile staged her next spectacle as a one-off charity fashion show at the Little Theatre in New York, a playlet entitled 'Fleurette's Dream at Peronne'.[120] It was based on a story devised by Lucile's sister Elinor Glyn,

which dramatised the life of a Parisian mannequin in war-torn France. The playlet opened with a vision of the refugee Fleurette asleep on a pile of dirty sacking while she dreamt of her former life in Paris:

> I showed Fleurette, a glorified Fleurette in my latest creations, having *petit déjeuner*; going for a walk with her friend Dolores; choosing new dresses at a *grande couturière's*; going to a dance, giving a party at her own house . . . and so on. The final scene showed the poor little girl back again in her cellar waking to realities, while the enemy shells screamed overhead.[121]

Lucile theatricalised these dreams, showing Fleurette dressing, breakfasting and going to a couturier.[122] Proceeds went to French war relief, the Secours Franco-Americain pour la France Dévastée, of which Glynn was vice-president, and the cast was recruited from Lucile's house mannequins, with Phyllis playing Fleurette and Dolores, who later appeared in the Follies.[123]

On 3 December 1917 the vaudeville version of *Fleurette's Dream* opened as part of a mixed programme at New York's Palace Theater reduced from two and a half hours to twenty-eight minutes (**79** and **105**).[124] There, sixty-eight dresses valued at approximately a million dollars were modelled by a dozen of Lucile's mannequins and Lady

Duff Gordon herself also made an appearance in her own name. It starred the mannequins Dolores, Dinarzade, Phyllis, Mauricette, Hildred, Clair, De Lys, Jill Wood, Virginia, Ruthair, Doris, Anangaraga, Sonia, Mona, Iseult, Majanah, Rosalys and Morgan de Fay. *Variety* described the mannequins as looking 'like tired showgirls, having a languid walk accomplished by crossing the feet at each step'. Nevertheless, the show was immensely successful with New York audiences, although reviewers commented on the luxury and inaccessibility of the clothing to ordinary people, one pointing out that 'the conspicuous points in the models [that is, model gowns] presented seemed to be fur-trimmed and even fur-lined negligées'. The pyjamas and robes were, wrote another, 'too ridiculous. . . . That they are clothes to be worn by ordinary mortals is unbelievable. The mannequins, nearly six feet tall, are draped and semi-draped in color after color' and there were 'only one or two models a human being might wear'.[125]

'Fleurette's Dream at Peronne' toured the Keith vaudeville circuit between December 1917 and May 1918. In Boston, where it played a week before Christmas 1917, the matinee show shared the bill, incongruously, with a film about Santa Claus and his reindeer, a large illuminated Christmas tree and 'a real jolly old Santa giving away real

presents to the little girls and boys who go upon the stage'. The *Boston Daily Globe* praised Lady Duff Gordon's 'musical fashion interlude' for its 'dazzling display by promenading mannequins' and for the costly and beautiful gowns, 'diaphanous, substantial, quaint and otherwise', adding that 'a lithe dancing girl appeared with the company in a wild, whirling feature'. For the evening the bill consisted of Pathé newsreels, a flying trapeze and head-balancing turn, a pretty girl violinist, a company of music-playing acrobats, a military skit with acrobatic dancing, two 'blackface comedians', other comic turns and a troupe of performing dogs.

Lucile's glamorised representation of war-torn Europe in 'Fleurette's Dream' was far removed from the commercial reality of the Paris trade, however, which was trying desperately to keep its head up in wartime. Her show had more in common with the social and commercial aspirations of American show business than the hard realities of European trade. Then more than ever France needed the American buyers to sustain its national industry and in Paris the fashion show continued throughout the war to be the portal between these two, apparently antithetical, worlds. Paradoxically, for the French, this required them to become more 'American' as the war drew on.

5

1914–1919
THE NATIONALISATION OF THE BODY

106 Bergdorf Goodman buyer's card sent from Paris to the Chicago branch customers to announce the imminent arrival of the latest imports. Paris, Bibliothèque Forney.

Throughout the First World War, despite an initial hiccough, the Paris fashion trade continued to go about its daily business as best it could. The American buyers were more important than ever. In a period when it was considered unpatriotic for Frenchwomen to dress fashionably, the French couture depended entirely on foreign income from the export trade. France had always relied on overseas buyers but in the absence of a home market during wartime, the power of American taste and money shifted subtly. As France emerged in the peace, there was a new sense that American taste was dictating. No longer were Americans expected to modify their purchases for the home market; the French began to see the need to produce for American tastes. That usually meant less outrageous and body-revealing fashions, which were more suited to an active, busy life and, above all, designs suitable for mass production. French attitudes to North America were ambivalent after the war. On the one hand, they admired its modernity – aggressive, progressive, rational – but on the other they feared and disapproved of its tendency to uniformity and conformity. Either way, the economic devastation of the First World War, followed by the currency fluctuations of the 1920s, meant that the French fashion trade could not afford to ignore the U.S.A.

THE AUTUMN 1914 SEASON

France declared war on Germany on 2 August 1914, a fortnight before the autumn openings, when fashionable women were still out of town. Much of the important work necessary to complete the new collections in the first fortnight of August was curtailed. Patou, Poiret and Jacques and Jean Worth volunteered immediately and left Paris for their regiments. Poiret described how he was called up on 2 August 1914 'at the very moment when I was preparing to have my mannikins parade as usual'.[1] Others volunteered or were called up soon after.[2] Some kept their houses open while they were at the front, others closed temporarily before reopening after a few months. Those foreign buyers who had arrived early in the city and who chose to remain after the outbreak of war had to apply for a *permis de séjour*.[3] As France mobilised in early August, however, the majority of the mid-August openings looked as if they were going to be cancelled. On 9 August the New York correspondent of the *Washington Post* wrote: 'Grim war has closed the citadel of fashion to all the world . . . the cables announce that the dressmaking establishments of Paris are all closed, and that the tailors have shouldered their guns and gone to the war.'[4] The newspaper reported that several enterprising American designers were already producing their own fashions to bridge the gap.[5] In fact, on 15 August, the traditional date for the openings, the majority of couturiers did show, although most re-used their winter 1913 dresses.[6] Some houses, though, opened simply to sell off what they had and then closed, while others did not open at all.[7]

The buyers were nearly all from North or South America (there were no Europeans) and about fifty of them did the rounds of the principal houses that remained open.[8] At Premet the first dress shown had such a short skirt that journalists thought it must be a mistake: 'Not at all. She [the mannequin] pirouetted around in the most pleased manner'.[9] Not all were able to show on live mannequins, however. In *Harper's Bazar* 'Mlle Chaquin' complained that 'The three or four openings which have occurred have been depressing past words. I saw Monsieur Worth just before he left for the front. All the suits and gowns were lying limp and lifeless over the tables and chairs in the large salon. Not a mannequin in sight, only two or three buyers'.[10] The *Chicago Daily Tribune* fashion correspondent, who had retreated to London 'owing to war conditions in France, and the uncertainty of receiving mail from there for some time to come', found that in London too 'over half the dressmakers were obliged to show their gowns over display chairs' due to the shortage of mannequins because so many had joined the Red Cross and 'the ranks of the great army of mannequins has thinned to an alarming extent.'[11] Later in November, for the mid-season Paris collections, several more houses failed to show on mannequins. The *New York Times* reported that, on account of the closing of the Paris shops, several mannequins, including 'two Belgian girls', had decamped to New York where they were modelling.[12]

Those couturiers who remained open in August instituted new payment terms, even for their oldest customers. On 2 August the French couture Syndicat met to agree that, due to the extraordinary financial stringencies caused by the outbreak of war, it could no longer afford to give credit to foreign buyers and would henceforth demand payment at the point of ordering.[13] Under difficult circumstances, the house of Premet defied this decree and continued to give its regular buyers the usual credit terms, much to the house's benefit.[14] Drecoll followed suit.[15] Callot and Chéruit required cash and would not accept cheques and Paquin required half the amount in cash.[16] Even in 1913, Callot had alienated the American buyers and was known for its high-handed treatment of them.[17] Private clients who were offended by the couturiers' new payment terms could take their custom to London where Worth, Paquin, Boué and Lucile had branches. By November, however, at the mid-season openings, an American buyer reported that those houses that sold to American buyers were keener than ever to do business with them and were no longer demanding cash in hand as they had in August.[18] Their biggest handicap was the difficulty of obtaining fabric and trimmings, as many of the French textile mills were closed.[19] American stores, however, frequently made up the new models in American fabrics.[20]

A dramatic account of an American buyer is given in *Harper's Bazar* for October 1914, just after the outbreak of war. Accompanying photographs of the latest imports from Worth and Béchoff David, the magazine recounts:

> Every war has its hero, but the business heroine of the Great War is Miss Mary J. Walls, the buyer of the imported models for the John Wanamaker stores. Through her achievement she has proved conclusively that business can be served by a woman with all her mind, all her soul and all her energies. When the mobilization order was posted in Paris and her friends were urging her to hasten to London, Miss Walls started on a round of the couturiers to find some fashion models to take back to the women in America.
>
> And she found them – the majority – at Béchoff David's. With seventy-one of these gowns, packed in osier baskets, Miss Walls drove in an automobile, in the dead of night, through seventeen pickets, men with guns, in order to reach Havre in time to sail on the *La France*, the first steamer from France after the declaration of war.
>
> It was a daring idea, born in the mind of a keen, clever business woman whose one aim was to serve to the best of her ability her chief, and she carried it to the finest conclusion with indomitable courage, without a thought of self, and with a perspicacity a man might envy. For this phase of the Message to Garcia, Mr. John Wanamaker decorated her with a diamond bar pin. This is the first time that a commercial establishment ever publicly decorated one of its members with a mark of merit and bravery – the Legion of Honor in the business world.[21]

The department store buyers had the highest status in the business; here the rhetoric of war is playfully co-opted in the description of the doughty female buyer as a fashion soldier who is decorated for her valour.

Three months later, another buyer visited Paris, George Heimerdinger of the George C. Heimerdinger Company at 137 Madison Avenue, New York. His account of the mid-season collections in November was less colourful but more detailed. He found the city deserted, with three out of five businesses closed and the rue de la Paix even worse. The department stores Bon Marché and Galeries Lafayette were empty. The male staff at many businesses was depleted, most Frenchmen under forty-six or forty-seven being at the front, and many women were in mourning, which gave the dressmakers little incentive to design novel fashions. Callot Soeurs was open for business as usual, even though both the sons of Mme Gerber, the Callot sister who was the chief designer, had been mobilised and one had been wounded twice. Mme Gerber had nevertheless managed to instal the firm in new premises in October 1914, where Mr Heimerdinger observed the mannequins 'going about showing the gowns in the same light-hearted way which marks their activities when there is no war, and the whole force seemed to be fairly busy.'[22] The show lasted three hours and featured a good 250 models; there were even a few private clients in evidence, as well as six to eight other buyers. At Paquin's things were less good. Few staff were present as most were working for the Red Cross and there were no mannequins at all. Twenty-five models were shown on wooden dummies which, said Mr Heimerdinger, 'naturally detracted a great deal from the effect'. At Agnès 'there were few signs of prosperity' but twenty-five models were shown on mannequins. At Chéruit confusion reigned and what clothes they had were displayed 'in the hand'. Little was for sale at Premet either. At Lanvin, things were slightly better and 'Drecoll was working full force, and there were few signs of war evident.' A hundred models were shown. Here, too, eight to ten buyers were present when Mr Heimerdinger visited and the sales staff were kept busy. Jenny's new premises near the Champs-Élysées was busy showing 'a great many models' to 'a good number of buyers' and several private clients; Doucet too was reasonably busy, as was Brandt and Martial et Armand, despite M. Armand being away on military service. On 18 and 19 November, Beer held a mid-season opening which Mr Heimerdinger attended, where he saw more than a hundred models. Doeuillet had closed on the outbreak of war but opened again on 18 November and Buzenet and Redfern were also open. Georgette, Poiret, Bulloz, Béchoff David, Lelong and Maurice Mayer were all closed; others were open but with nothing to show, such as Worth, whose establishment was given over to Red Cross activities.[23]

Against this description by an American buyer in Paris in the autumn of 1914 can be set another, the diary entries of an American woman living in Paris at the same time, which suggests that Mr Heimerdinger's presence there bucked the trend. H. Pearl Adam describes how empty Paris was of Americans in the autumn and winter of 1914:

> What an American would have thought of Paris if she arrived at the end of 1914 it is difficult to imagine. She would probably have thought she had come to another city by mistake – a city which had changed countries. Four months earlier Paris belonged to the Americans, North and South; her shops and her restaurants, her amusements and some of her society were for them alone, and American money was the dominating factor of external Parisian life. Without a word of warning she became French.[24]

Yet this was to change at collection times, as Paris worked hard to reassert its presence in foreign markets. In late December 1914 the Chambre Syndicale de la Couture issued a circular for distribution to buyers confirming its decision on 21 December to re-instate the pre-war pattern of seasonal openings at fixed dates.[25] Describing an unusually muted city on the first *réveillon* (Christmas Eve) of the war, the *New York Times*'s Paris correspondent cabled that, although the majority of the famous mannequins of the couture houses had disappeared from Paris life, the houses expected an upturn in time for the February fashion shows to overseas buyers.[26]

THE SPRING 1915 SEASON

The spring openings duly took place in February 1915. *Harper's Bazar* described the swagged flags of the allies that had replaced the colourful flowerboxes which in peacetime adorned the couture house façades. Indoors, it declared, it was business as usual: 'Mannikins parade in the salons, always with a smile on their faces though their hearts may be breaking, fitters, girded with pins, thread and scissors, pass swiftly through the rooms; the tingling of the telephones is pleasant music, and all the signs of a busy season are in evidence.'[27] Callot, Premet, Lanvin, Drecoll, Jeanne Hallée, Worth, Chéruit, Paquin, Doucet, Doeuillet, Bernard, Beer and Jenny were all open and the buyers expressed themselves contented with most, if not all, the new season's models.[28] The Fifth Avenue importer Gidding & Co bought from more than ten couture houses.[29]

Poiret and Patou did not show, Poiret being at the front at Lisieux and Patou on the Balkan front.[30] Worth, however, remained open, even though both Worth brothers were at the front. Drecoll, which was to play an important role in the 1920s in the development of the fashion show, still

107 Cover of *Harper's Bazar*, May 1915, showing names of French fashion designers whose goods were on sale in New York that season.

showed even though it had been excluded from the couture syndicate because of its Austro-Hungarian backing.[31] Callot Soeurs showed half the peacetime number of new models to an audience of half a dozen people, as opposed to the usual twenty-five. They were modelled by a third of the usual number of mannequins, wrote the *New York Times*, 'the famous mannequin Marion, one of the greatest beauties in Paris, being absent from the head of the procession', and the habitually remote Mme Gerber, the most austere of the three Callot sisters, unbent and 'superintended the opening and was conversational to customers for the first time in history'.[32] Nevertheless, the firm continued to be high-handed with the American buyers. It showed after all the other couturiers and then insisted on shipping directly to the U.S.A., ostensibly to avoid being pirated.[33] Although Callot subsequently brought forward its shipping date of 27 March by a week, its refusal to ship immediately was unpopular. 'As the maritime blockade was already established, the buyers left the room on the opening day, unwilling to buy', wrote the *New York Times*. 'The gowns from that house will arrive after the others, many of which were shipped by the buyers before they left.'[34]

Hard-headed business had to be transacted and sales made despite, indeed because of, the war. The goods were shipped and the May 1915 issue of *Harper's Bazar* showed Paris fashions from Callot, Chéruit, Doucet, Doeuillet, Lanvin, Jenny, Beer, Premet, Worth, Paquin, Redfern, Martial et Armand and the milliners and sportswear producers Maria Guy, Lewis, Caroline Reboux, Evelyne Varon, Suzanne Talbot and Georgette (**107**). American fashion magazines mobilised the war rhetoric of popular journalism, emphasising French patriotism and sacrifice. *Harper's Bazar* wrote: 'For the honour of France the couturiers held their spring openings as customary, believing that by bringing foreigners to Paris, making work for thousands who had families to support and securing coin of the realm of which everyone was in need, they were sharing with the man at the front the responsibilities of this perilous period.' It described how in momentary lulls behind the scenes in the couture houses, socks, mittens and hats were being knitted and consignments of underclothes made up for French soldiers at the front. Mmes Chéruit and Premet were reported to be working with the wounded in ambulance shelters, contributing to the Blue Cross Fund. Chéruit claimed that she was keeping her house open for her midinettes, her saleswomen working not for the customer but for wounded soldiers.[35]

American buyers did, undoubtedly, take a personal risk, both in crossing the Atlantic in person and in shipping their

108 Two English soldiers in uniform, peacetime buyers from Seymour in London, attending the Doucet spring 1915 openings. Illustration by Sabattier, *L'Illustration*, 1915. (www.lillustration. com).

goods home, risking 'interference by German submarines which would send thousands of dollars' worth of gowns to the whales.'[36] The rhetoric of American fashion journalism and publicity was also deployed to emphasise the bravery of the American buyers who travelled to Paris to select French fashions for the women of America. *Harper's Bazar* described them at the spring openings as 'this little group of brave, keen, alert Americans' who had been there for the last two or three weeks. The buyers admitted to some hardships – 'everyone admitted that the trip had been 'rotten' and would probably be worse on the return' – but they praised the collections and they too marvelled at how the usually haughty Mme Gerber of Callot Soeurs mingled with them.[37] A Gidding's advertisement proclaimed itself 'the Paris shop of America' and trumpeted that the new imports had been personally selected by Gidding's 'own representatives' in Paris.[38] Gimbel's advertised its spring 1915 imports by making a virtue of its buyer's fortitude:

> A Unique Triumph. And we are glad to announce that it was a woman – our Fashion Chief – who has carried this message of Paris to the American Women. She arrived on the S.S. 'Arabic' only on Saturday, and she brought the models with her as personal baggage. But back of her stood the power of our Paris branch – an organization unequalled in Europe.[39]

These imports were then demonstrated to American women in twice-daily fashion shows at Gimbel's on Broadway and 33rd Street.[40]

The French weekly *L'Illustration* deployed a similar patriotic rhetoric in its description of valiant British volunteer officers with important jobs in the *services de l'arrière*, who visited the spring 1915 openings at Doucet in Paris in their civilian role as buyers for the London house of Seymour (**108**): 'They had obtained leave to come and place their orders in Paris and, as attentively as if conducting a uniform inspection, they studied the costumes, of an elegant rectitude, presented by the mannequins with the gracious indolence which is traditional with them.'[41] This is one of the earliest visual illustrations of buyers as opposed to private clients at a fashion show and it is reasonable to suppose that it was only the jingoist rhetoric of war that enabled it. In peacetime conditions, couturiers would have been less likely to sanction an illustration of commercial buyers at work in their houses.

By the same token, an illustration of fashion modelling to private clients was less likely in wartime, as individual consumption of fashion was considered unseemly. Florence Brachet Champsaur has shown how the dominant fashion for French women during wartime became the tailor-made and that extreme simplicity prevailed.[42] Extravagant new fashions were not thought appropriate in the spring of 1915: 'Paris, far more than London, has been seared by the suffering of war', the *Harper's Bazar* fashion correspondent told her American readers.[43] The Paris diary of H. Pearl Adams reveals the dramatic change in women's clothing over the first six months of the war. 'A week before war broke out, I had spent an afternoon at Armenonville [the café and dancehall in the Bois de Boulogne] which was typical of those days', she writes. The young girls wore 'thin black frocks of satin, silk, chiffon, or all three, with shady hats . . . The black garbed girls were not in mourning; black and white were the fashionable colours that year. Their skirts were very narrow, their hats very wide, their sunshades very frilly.' They wore high-heeled shoes of velvet and suede which in those days were 'dearer than kid and consequently were fashionable'. They danced throughout a hot sunny afternoon, tea and refreshments could be bought, 'a wooden floor had been laid, and a tail-coated orchestra discoursed the latest negroid syncopations'. Towards evening they made their way back to central Paris.[44]

Six months later, all women wore black or navy tailor-mades and white or pink blouses were frowned on, Adam

109a and b Two Boué Soeurs interiors from 1926 showing the modelling stages in (a) New York and (b) Paris. From *Histoire de l'industrie et du commerce en France*, vol. ii, 1926. Les Arts Décoratifs, Paris, Centre de Documentation des Musées,

continued. A 'campaign for economy' developed which the couturiers tried to countermand by changing the silhouette from clinging skirts

> to the most abundant flutings, small hats to large, severe lines to complicated ones. . . . When the dressmakers decreed a change from narrow clothes to wide, they knew they were making sure of their turn-over for the spring of 1915. Later on, they would have been drummed out of town for such a manoeuvre; but we were new to war in those days, and had had no experience of profiteers. Many a Frenchwoman watched the troops come home in July 1919 in the garments she bought in March 1915.[45]

Despite the marked change in the fashionable line for spring 1915, many American buyers were disappointed by its simplicity. 'They had come to Paris in search of the sensational, the bizarre and the freakish; they wanted striking features which they could headline, as it were, copy and enlarge upon; styles that would at a glance throw into the discard all the costumes of the past season', wrote *Harper's Bazar*.[46] Instead, the couturiers showed them simple, wearable clothes that were usually reserved for the private clients.[47]

The Paris correspondent for *Harper's* had reported that there were about fifty American buyers in Paris for the February openings, both men and women, but in wartime they no longer entertained and were there strictly for business, eating modestly in restaurants where they chatted quietly together.[48] Neither could they scour the fashionable gathering places of the city for new modes, for 'on the eve of the openings . . . fashionable Paris has gone to ground.'[49] Although a few theatres were open, 'there are no side

shows of fashion where the buyers can glean hints of the developments they may expect to see on the morrow, as in other years. No races where the mannikins, wearing advance models from well-known establishments, may be inspected'.[50]

Even with these wartime austerities, the French initiative to restore its American trade links succeeded. In the U.S.A., where the closures of autumn 1914 had encouraged the view that American fashion would come to the fore, it was acknowledged by early 1915 that Paris had retained its significance. The *New York Tribune* put its finger on it when it declared that French dressmaking was not simply an art: 'To them now, it means bread. It is the big source of income for them and they must retain the patronage of Americans.'[51] Given that individual clients were less likely to travel to Paris for their spring 1915 wardrobes, the presence of American trade buyers in the city was all the more valued.[52] By April 1915, when French designers sent their costumes for display to the Panama Pacific Exhibition, its programme declared that, in France, 'Banks have begun to work again – workshops, mills and factories have been rapidly provided with capable hands . . . two thirds of the various industries have opened their doors anew.'[53]

The Paris firm of Boué Soeurs, founded in 1899, even opened an American branch in late 1915.[54] Its two directors, Sylvie and Jeanne Boué, worked under their married names of Mme Sylvie Montégut and Baronne d'Étreillis. Mme Montégut (known in the U.S.A. as Mme Montague) travelled frequently to New York throughout the war, despite its dangers, and recalled that 'the ships' captains appreciated our indifference to danger.'[55] Their seasonal migrations led to their being known as *hirondelles en dentelles* (swallows in lace) by the crews.[56] In spring 1915 Boué Soeurs had shown its new season's collection at a New York hotel, rather than in Paris, and immediately afterwards found and furnished premises for the new branch, bringing several French employees from Paris to work there. The newly furnished salons replicated the aura of the Paris house at number 9 rue de la Paix. It had 'dainty salons, with charming flower filled vases everywhere, glints of gold and rich materials, pretty mannequins gliding to and fro among the prospective buyers, [and] the odd cadence of the French language', which the *Washington Post* suggested was 'a bit of Paris' transposed to New York.[57] In fact, judging by two photographs from 1926 showing the Boué modelling stages in both Paris and New York (**109**), the Boué interiors seem to owe much to Lucile, another transatlantic success, whose Rose Rooms were also dressed with finely pleated and gathered fabric. After the war, Mme Montégut continued to travel to New York six to eight times a year, while her sister established branches in Egypt, Russia, Romania and Britain.[58] In 1920 Boué Soeurs advertised its daily mannequin parades at its New York premises at 13 West 56th Street, claiming, not quite accurately, to have established the only big French couture house in New York.[59]

Lucile remained in America for most of the war. In Paris, the rules of the newly constituted Chambre Syndicale de la Couture Parisienne limited membership to Parisian houses and it was unclear whether she could be accepted as a member or not, even though the rules were designed to exclude German and Austrian dressmakers rather than Allied ones.[60] Shortly after the outbreak of war she closed her Paris house and moved to New York. In one of her regular columns for *Harper's Bazar*, in 1915 she announced that after much thought she had concluded that 'it is likely that America can become a fashion centre.'[61] Schweitzer outlines Lucile's advocacy of American fashion from 1914 to 1915 in support of the 'Made in America' campaign launched in 1914.[62] Lucile produced a collection made entirely from American fabrics in February 1915.[63] However, in September 1916 she backtracked and explained to her American readers why she could no longer use American fabrics: the American textile manufacturers, rather than making exclusive designs for Lucile, also sold to the wholesalers who made cheap imitations of Lucile dresses by the thousand. As a result, her clients came back to complain when they found the fabrics in wide use; Lucile asked why the U.S. manufacturers would not produce exclusive designs for top-end designers like herself, as the French did.[64]

THE AMERICANISATION OF FRENCH FASHION

The 1915 autumn collections were larger than in previous wartime seasons. Callot, which showed its new winter styles on 12 August 1915, was back up to peacetime quantities and Chéruit too showed a collection of average size.[65] A popular Chéruit day costume for both home and travel was nicknamed 'the commuter's delight' by American buyers but, as the *New York Times* wrote,

> the original model for this costume has long been lost sight of in the various copies that have been made. Anything that has a knee-length coat of dark velvet, or velour, or broadcloth which exactly meets a deep hem on the skirt, this hem being made of the same material, while the entire upper part which reaches to the neck is made of something sheer and fine and of a different colour – anything in this style is now called by the name of 'commuter's delight'.[66]

In this way, a copy might be modified to such a degree in the U.S. that it was barely the same garment, yet still be marketed as Parisian, thus demonstrating how important the idea of French fashion remained to the American trade, despite both the stringencies of war in Europe and the best efforts of fashion promoters in America to encourage home-grown designers.

In October 1915 the latest Paris imports were shown in New York and other major American cities. Gimbel's featured Callot, Chéruit, Jenny, Lanvin, Paquin, Bernard, Doeuillet, Doucet, Martial et Armand, Weeks and Bulloz. The models had been brought to New York, announced the store, as 'the brilliantly successful results of our Fashion Expert's trip to Paris' and were shown in mannequin parades an hour and a half long, twice a day, at 10.30 am and 1.30 pm.[67] Throughout 1915 the French used further initiatives to promote couture in the U.S.A., from the Panama-Pacific International Exposition in San Francisco to the French Fashion Fête in New York. In an article translated for *Harper's Bazar* in February 1915, Poiret vehemently denied American fashion magazine reports that Paris couture had 'ground to a halt' and ridiculed the suggestion that 'a number of the New York dress-making houses have grouped themselves together (it seems incredible!) with the object of instituting what they call American styles!'[68] Poiret himself had not shown in Paris since the spring of 1914; but in autumn 1915 he exhibited a number of designs of eighteenth-century inspiration at the Panama-Pacific Exposition.[69]

The numbers of American buyers and journalists who made the journey to Paris for the August 1915 openings remained small.[70] Nevertheless, American taste was important and the couturiers were catering to it. Subtly, the

110 Jenny's spring 1916 collection: debutante dress imported by Wanamaker and photographed on an American mannequin, 20 March 1916. It was still typical for New York importers to buy Paris styles and re-photograph them on their own modelling stages. Courtesy Lewis Orchard: Lucile Ltd Collection.

balance was shifting from an idea of superior French taste into which Americans could buy, and then adapt for the home market, to an idea that the French had themselves to modify their fashions and adapt their own taste to appeal to the transatlantic market. Not everyone approved. The American dancer Isadora Duncan returned to Paris in August 1915 and lambasted the dressmakers in the newspaper *L'Intrinsigeant* for designing only for Americans, harmonising with the architecture of New York to satisfy 'Newport's vulgar snobbery'. 'Imagine my horror . . . on seeing a girl appear, flat-chested, her body cut short, in a species of upside down sunshade' and she added that 'even the mannequins showed signs of disgust as they stepped forth in the new fashions, as if they disapproved very strenuously of the ignoble modes they were displaying.'[71]

Duncan reproved the designers for not replicating French nursing uniforms or tricolor themes in patriotic French fashions, yet few French women wore high fashion in the summer of 1915, when even the 'fashionables' wore either black or the previous summer's clothes, as noted earlier. Before the war, 'at every opening you saw ten or fifteen of the noted demi-mondaines of Paris – beautiful, smart, soigné – showing with every gesture and step of their graceful walk the consciousness of their power, their beauty and sovereignty over a certain kingdom of Paris. Where are they all *gone?* For there isn't one left', wrote the *Chicago Daily Tribune* in 1918.[72] Nor could fashionable society be observed any longer in June and September at the races and in restaurants, another reason why fewer overseas buyers came to Paris during the war.[73] There was a sense that fashion was almost exclusively to be produced rather than consumed in wartime France. Even American *Vogue* highlighted the plight of Parisian garment workers with a photograph captioned 'Sewing girls gathered in disconsolate groups'.[74] The picturesque stereotype of the

cheerful midinette was hard to sustain in a war that made widows of women of all classes. Georges d'Avenel's account of the Milliners' Way of 1903 was reprised with a new melancholy in 1915 when the *New York Times* and the *Washington Post* described the women of the Paris dressmaking trades walking to work at seven o'clock in the morning in their widows' weeds:

> The ordinary sewing woman, with pricked and stained finger ends, comes first. A little later the smart class of milliners' models and seamstresses, the shop girls, stenographers, terminating with the mannequins and foreladies, the aristocracy of the great fur cloak and dressmaking establishments. War has reduced numbers and levelled conditions; the procession is still charming, but with new features. It is a long line of white and black. No crape here, for their mourning is democratic; rich bereavements alone may wear the aristocratic weeds. Those that work content themselves with black skirt and little jacket with white colarette. This little world that files past in the early hours is witness of the tribute Paris has paid to the 'patrie'.[75]

Keeping the focus on production, *Les Modes*'s Christmas 1915 issue described the continuing evolution of fashion since the outbreak of war as part of the industrial life of the country. 'Corinne' described the new silhouette of 'a diminutive woman with a short skirt and slender ankles imprisoned in high boots . . . the décolletages, the transparencies, the semi-nudity, have been left to the American clientele.'[76] Hers is a wartime reversal of the usual characterisation of the American woman's dress as sensible and practical, as opposed to the frivolities and coquetry of the Frenchwoman's dress.

Early 1916 saw the further consolidation of American influence. In 1914 an elite group of couturiers led by Poiret and Jacques Worth had formed a new syndicate, in addition to the existing couture syndicate that represented the entire trade. The new syndicate, called the Syndicat de Défense de la Grande Couture Française et des Industries s'y Rattachant, sought to impose stringent conditions on the sale of models to American buyers with a view to preventing piracy, and the buyers had protested strongly.[77] This 'defence' syndicate was split in January 1916 by a proposal to blacklist two American buyers with German names, one being the department-store owner Charles Kurzman. The house of Jenny resigned from the syndicate and, with Lelong, made successful overtures to the blacklisted buyers.[78] Such high-handedness of the old established firms such as Poiret, Paquin, Premet, Worth and Chéruit no longer stood them in good stead. The war had created opportunities for smaller houses such as Agnès that had 'rendered valuable service to American importers at the outbreak of hostilities'[79] and American buyers were happy to buy from newer, younger and more modern concerns. Arnold, Germaine, Bulloz, Patou, Chanel, Royant, Bernard and Nicole Groult all benefited from the syndicate's blacklisting by showing collections privately to American buyers before the syndicated houses' openings in the first week of February.

Jeanne Paquin observed at the August 1916 openings that 'French fashion is created today for Americans.'[80] So too did the American store-owner Henri Bendel, in an article for *Harper's Bazar* on 'The Adaptation of Fashions to the American Woman' in which he noted that the evening gowns shown at the Paris openings 'were created solely for the American buyer', for French women in wartime were wearing only *tailleurs*, or tailor-mades.[81] The French textile manufacturers, whose production sustained the couture trade, were also producing largely for the American market in wartime, reported one American textile buyer in September 1916.[82] From 1916 to 1917 Poiret adopted a new promotional strategy, offering his own reduced-price copies of dresses to the American market that, as Troy puts it, he described oxymoronically as 'genuine reproductions'.[83]

For the August 1916 openings, wrote *Harper's*, 'Paris put her best foot forward and during that month the aspect of the city seemed almost normal. The restaurants and the hotels were crowded with buyers, and the great dressmaking establishments throbbed with life. The openings as a whole were more satisfactory, more enlightening than any that have occurred during the last two years.'[84]

American buyers were intrigued to see the new premises of Callot Soeurs in the Champs-Élysées, in Louis XV style. The richness of both clothing and décor were in striking contrast to the austerity of the first wartime collections.[85] There was, however, a crisis in the production of textiles owing to the lack of raw materials and labour, which resulted in some surprising innovations, such as coats in heavy serge previously only used 'to stretch on office walls' and brocaded furnishing fabric for evening wear. The prices of Lyons silks were fifty to sixty per cent higher than before the war.[86] Nevertheless, the autumn modes made their way across the Atlantic and in September 1916 Wanamaker's in New York appealed to a Francophile customer by advertising in French 'les dernières créations de la mode française', '75 signed original models' by Callot, Lanvin, Bulloz, Doucet, Worth, Doeuillet, Jenny, Georgette, Paquin, Drecoll and Bernard (**110**).[87] Over at Best & Co on Fifth Avenue at 35th Street, daily mannequin parades showed French millinery imported from Suzanne Talbot, Georgette, Germaine, Caroline Reboux and others.[88]

This was the international picture but in Paris shortages were beginning to bite, with knock-on effects in the trade. A Czech newspaper article of 1916 describes a failed strike by mannequins about pay and benefits, as told by a mannequin called Josette. It is not clear if many workers were involved; Josette recounts that the brief strike was unsuccessful because the mannequins were badly organised. They were convinced that they were indispensable because the dresses were made specifically for them but, when they boycotted the house, the management simply replaced them with apprentices and apologised to the clients. 'So we suffer in silence, but we truly suffer, because our pay, which used to be very generous before the war, shrank during the war to the wage of a female primary school teacher. A hundred francs is what we get, and no more.' Josette suggests that it is no longer appropriate for a mannequin to supplement her income by taking a rich lover, as she would have done before the war. Parading and coquetry were acceptable in peacetime but now it would be shameful to act like a waxen doll. According to the fashion historian Marylène Delbourg-Delphis, in 1916 certain actresses, or *grues*, were disapproved of for parading their wealth in wartime; the nouvelles riches who copied them were just as poorly regarded.[89] The author of the Czech article ends by observing that Josette's humour and merriness are gone. She would like to change jobs but she cannot do anything else, she can only endure and wait.[90]

The charity Union des Femmes Françaises et Alliées had a Paris shop that sold the work of 'wives or relatives of officers in needy circumstances'; there one enterprising naval officer's widow created a range of fashionable garments displayed on 'pretty little doll-like manikins, who are in reality daughters of her needy friends.'[91] In view of the general poverty, perhaps it took some nerve – or indifference – to dress like Poiret's mannequin Pâquerette in 1916, as seen in one of a series of photographs (**111**)

taken by Jean Cocteau, whose ambulance unit had taken part in the Battle of the Somme from early July 1916 before he was recalled to Paris on 28 July. Everyday life was undoubtedly hard for Parisians, both economically and personally, especially during and after the big battles of the Somme and the Marne, but this series of a group of friends junketing around Paris over forty-eight hours shows them in high spirits. Emilienne Pâquerette Geslot, who was twenty in 1916 and at the time Picasso's companion, was an actress and mannequin. She worked for both Poiret and for his sister Germaine Bongard, who had a couture house on rue Penthièvre. André Salmon recalled seeing Cocteau 'in the congenial company of Pâquerette, the most precious of Paul Poiret's mannequins, green shoes, a rosewood-coloured dress, and an indescribable hat.'[92] This is the outfit she is wearing in Cocteau's photograph, taken just as the August openings were due.

Six months later, a general strike broke out in which the Paris tailors and seamstresses were involved. Nancy Green has given an account:

> The 1917 strike began on May 11 when two workers walked out at the Maison Jenny (*couture de luxe*) on the Champs-Elysées. By mid-June, 42,000 people were on strike, (30,000 women and 12,000 men) in a wide variety of sectors from banks to the food industry. The 25,000 *midinettes* from all clothing specialities (hats to corsets, women's wear to men's wear, dressmakers – often in the lead – to ready-made workers) were in the forefront on the streets and in the journalists' accounts as they demanded more money (a wartime cost of living raise), less work, and an end to the war, chanting: 'Our twenty *sous*! The English week! Give us back our 'boys'.'[93]

That September, the 'English week' was made law, giving the workers Saturday afternoons off and fifty-four hours'

pay for fifty hours of work. In the early twentieth century, both in the U.S.A. and in France, labour relations in the garment industries were bitter. As Green reveals, 'While New York garment industrial warfare peaked before World War 1 and then diminished under the combined impact of war, post-war prosperity and collective bargaining, Paris strike activity surged during the war'.[94] The first general strike of Paris tailors and seamstresses occurred in 1901 but the major strikes that Green argues 'made history' came in 1917 and 1919.

America had entered the war on 6 April, before the 1917 strike. In August 1917 the autumn openings were nevertheless reasonably large and well attended. Although not up to pre-war standards, the collections were bigger than at the start of the war, few falling below 120 models.[95] Nothing of the painful strike of May 1917 comes across in the French illustrator Drian's drypoint etching, for the Europhile American magazine *Harper's Bazar* in December that year, of elegant and languid mannequins in Chéruit's luxurious first-floor salon overlooking the place Vendôme; nor would a reader know that France was either at war or had been subject to serious industrial action from this depiction (**112**). Yet, for Parisians it was different. H. Pearl Adam wrote in her Paris diary for 1917:

> Dress came under restrictions . . . but these were not too severe and were heralded by the usual series of 'appeals' and 'recommendations' to the public. The difficulties first began to be felt in necessities. By the end of 1917 woollen fabrics had risen to fearsome prices; it was impossible to get durable serge or cloth for less than thirty shillings a yard. After the fall of Riga linen also became scarce, and sheets that cost 33 or 34 shillings before the war then cost six pounds – and have risen steadily ever since. Silk of course soon went up in price, thanks to Lyons having escaped the fate of the occupied northern textile districts. Paris

112 Mannequins at Chéruit, in the place Vendôme, 1917. Illustration by Etienne Drian, *Harper's Bazar*, December 1917.

dressmakers decided not to use more than four and half yards of any woollen material in one dress.[96]

Manufacturers put prices up anyway. Dyes were also difficult to obtain, many colours could not be had at all and none could be guaranteed, as placards proclaimed in all the dress shops. Black, which had been worn almost exclusively for two years, was far more expensive than other colours. Occasionally in summer a woman would wear pale fawn, or a girl white, but they were the objects of much attention and criticism.[97] 'Yet side by side with the sober clothing of the multitude, and the restrictions on their necessities, there was an orgy of luxury', wrote Adam. She describes scrambles in Paris shops for ready-to-wear clothing that came in dark colours but luxury fabrics, for accessories and for 'filmy, lacy, ribboned lingerie', much of it for the wives of profiteers' which, she writes, then resulted in the imposition of the luxury tax.[98]

In February 1918 the Paris mannequins were modelling the spring collections to buyers at Callot, Paquin, Chéruit, Doeuillet, Jenny, Martial et Armand, Worth, Chanel, Premet, Beer, Lanvin, Redfern and Poiret.[99] Despite shortages, there was no sign that the couture was flagging. Brachet Champsaur estimates that, despite galloping inflation, the French couture trade more or less sustained its usual level of exports during the war.[100] Established houses grew bigger and new ones opened. In May 1918 Redfern showed to his private clients, sending out printed invitations illustrated by Drian and containing the information that Redfern had made the lace dresses for two famous actresses, Cécile Sorel and Geneviève Vix, currently appearing in three Paris theatres.[101]

The fast-growing firm of Jenny was slowed down by the war but only in a way that was described in 1926 as 'sensible'.[102] Just before the war, Jenny (founded in 1911 by two women, Mme Jenny Sacerdote and Mme Le Corre) moved from the rue de Castiglione to a luxury *hôtel* on the Champs-Élysées, where it remained open throughout the war, not even closing in the first days of August 1914. Typical of many of the younger couture houses, rather than having a Parisienne clientele Jenny's was predominantly foreign, especially from North and South America.[103] In jingoistic language, Mme Sacerdote recalled how, over four years, 'braving the torpedoes, the buyers from New York and Chicago crossed the Atlantic and came to admire our models.'[104] Of the autumn 1918 openings in particular, she wrote:

At the beginning of the month of August 1918, we showed our collection. On the 5th and 7th the quarter was copiously shelled. The berthas sowed death in avenue Marceau, rue de Bassano and the place de l'Alma. As pieces of shrapnel tore through the air, the mannequins continued, without a murmur, to display (*mettre en valeur*) the line and style of the garments they had on. The seamstresses ran to the windows to see where the shells had landed and replied in proud street argot.[105]

AFTER THE WAR

New firms opened towards the end of the war and prospered. Lelong, despite being in the army, received his first clients in his uniform in September 1918.[106] Melnotte-Simonin (formerly of Poiret) also opened his new firm in September 1918.[107] The war ended with the armistice on 11 November 1918. The Treaty of Versailles was signed on 28 June 1919 at the Versailles Peace Conference and in Paris the armistice was finally celebrated on Bastille Day, 14 July 1919.[108] Poiret and Patou returned to Paris, where Poiret celebrated with parties[109] and Patou set up in business in his own name. American soldiers who had been demobilised in France created a ready-made American presence, with plans to construct a string of American bars along the road from the front at Château Thierry to Paris.[110] The *Chicago Daily Tribune* routed the idea of French individualism and distinguished French taste from American when it described the new house of Madeleine et Madeleine as American-influenced:

> On the edge of being a success, a sensation, and what do you think they are exploiting but the American figure and the late American styles! . . . in this French shop waistlines are long and skirts are straight. I don't believe there is a pannier in the place. . . . Mannequins tall and graceful sweep every afternoon through the vista of salons, dragging their spangled, velvet, and shot silk iridescent trains over the thick gray carpets. They reflect in the high wide mirrors; they stand before patrons, seated, breathless with the loveliness, in the deep divans and the beautiful gray chairs with their blue upholstery. One ventures a question to one's vendeuse – she does not dare suggest it to either of the Madeleines. But it is the crux of this story, and perhaps of a much longer story beyond.
>
> 'Haven't they – your designers – the house – it isn't possible I suppose, but just the same, haven't they been a very little bit influenced by America, and American styles?'
>
> 'O but madam, yes,' the vendeuse answered; 'infiniment!' [sic]
>
> You have the key to what may be an important situation. When I left America, America was insisting that it was going to create its own styles and perhaps the styles of others. Maybe America's dreams are going to come true.[111]

Here, the drop-waisted tubular form of a Madeleine et Madeleine evening gown with a wide belt at hip level was associated with the American figure. As is often the case, the figure of the mannequin embodies a national body type, or what is imagined to be one. The idealised American figure came to be represented in the 1920s by fashions – and mannequins – that were increasingly elongated and boyish, fashions that made their first appearance in Paris in the straight skirts and dropped waists worn by the

mannequins at Parry in 1912 (see **38**) and at Madeleine et Madeleine in 1919.

In her analysis of Poiret's fashions in this period, Troy argues that 'in the play between originality and reproduction, the logic of fashion emerges as a mechanism for understanding the cultural impact of the transformation from an artisanal to an industrial economy.'[112] This transformation permeated not only fashionable clothes and their mode of production but also fashionable bodies and their styling. Increasingly, the 'American' elements of French fashion came to be realised on the bodies of the mannequins who wore them and the way these bodies were styled in the couture salon. With the 1920s mannequin, an idealised, androgynous, modernist body became associated with both an industrial aesthetic and the economics of the international fashion trade, as France increasingly adopted what were considered to be American aesthetics and business practices. In 1923 American *Vogue* pointed out that while the French called its fashion industry *l'art de la couture*, the Americans called it the 'garment trade'.[113] That same year, however, the French illustrated weekly *L'Illustration* adopted the language of industry when it declared France to be a 'factory of elegance': 'In the same way that other countries export coal or agricultural machinery, we export elegance', it wrote, citing Worth, Paquin, Jenny and Poiret as ambassadors for French couture, all, as it happens, couturiers who were particularly assiduous at promotion via the fashion show.[114]

The war years produced an important change in the relations between the French couture and the American garment industry. Poiret and Paquin's American tours of 1913 and 1914 had shown the French couturiers how rapacious and productive the American industry was, from its entrepreneurial department-store owners to its rampant fashion pirates. More and more, the fashion journalism of both France and America constructed a fantasy of the other as a foil to its self-image. These images were both ideological and commercial; as Agnès Rocamora argues, the myth and the material reality of Paris fashion mesh in fashion discourse.[115] Indeed, as Green has argued, the 'transatlantic understandings of the garment "other" . . . fall into the realm of . . . reciprocal visions.'[116] The fashion industry of each country depended on an image of the other to make its sales and to bolster its sense of self through the creation of a cultural imaginary of 'French-ness' and 'American-ness'. Bridging these two realms, the fashion show was thus economic, cultural and ideological in equal measure in its reach.

Troy describes the relation between French and American fashion as one of original and copy that was also privileged in the discursive construction of modernism.[117]

She analyses the pre-war 'commercially staged fashion show' as a copy of the 'professionally mounted theatrical production.'[118] While pointing out that copying is 'inherent in the very structure of haute couture', Troy goes on to argue that the business, because it is poised between elite and mass culture, contains an intrinsic contradiction and that these 'supposed oppositions' are collapsed in haute couture when France and America encounter each other.[119] Another way, however, to analyse the mediation of the relationship of mass and elite culture in the Franco-American garment trades is not as a collapse, as Troy calls it, but as a continuing, dynamic, relationship of base and superstructure that can and does change according to circumstances, and did so throughout the war. Thus, couture could sustain its elite appeal on an ideological level while also appealing to a mass market on an economic level; it could do this even through periods of intense social, economic and political change. The harshest result of the First World War, beyond the hardships and losses it inflicted on French citizens, was economic: it almost bankrupted France.[120] During the war, therefore, the balance between these ideological representations shifted as violently as did the commercial relations both within and between couture and mass production in both countries.

The French desire for individualism, and a specifically French idea of good taste, may have led French women to patronise the artisanal and small scale rather than the mass-produced. Green argues, however, that to these 'cultural' reasons must be added two economic, political and juridical ones: copyright law, which differed substantially between both countries, and the effects of both world wars on each country. Before the First World War, France and America's industries developed in separate ways at different speeds; the war accelerated their development and crystallised their differences in ways that had long-term consequences in the 1920s.

These wartime shifts were a matter of life and death to the French. Green argues that the war was a disaster for the French economy and society and interfered with the dissemination of French fashion worldwide.[121] Up to 1914, half the private customers for haute couture were French. After the war, customers for French fashion were mainly North and South Americans, the French economy being significantly weakened.[122] In the 1920s the U.S.A., with the largest domestic market in the world for fashion, was the *deus ex machina* of French fashion, the backstage apparatus that propelled French shows into the international limelight. Underlying this is the near-bankruptcy of France

after the war, the resentment of America at France's refusal to repay its war debt and, in France, some resentment at the inequalities between a weak franc and a strong dollar, which led many in the French fashion business to feel that America could call the tune in matters of taste as well as money.[123]

In 1919, with silk stockings selling at $10 in Paris, recounted the *Los Angeles Times*, Paris mannequins were going bare-legged and the style 'is spreading to the elite. Perhaps soon only the poor will wear stockings.'[124] The war had changed not only the couture but its clientele. In July 1924 an article in *Harper's Bazar* entitled 'Beggars in Rolls Royces' described how the social protocols of the fashion world had changed since the war:

Labor now sups with royalty, working men rank with peers, and princes from the palace dance with midinettes in the Place. A pretty mannequin smartly clothed *à l'oeil* by her *maison* is envied by the cultured daughter of an impoverished ancient house, who, realizing the situation, grapples with it by becoming herself a mannequin. In short, the world, though not yet safe, has become a more pleasant place for democracy.[125]

In 1932, the American business magazine *Fortune* looked back:

Before 1914, only the extremely wealthy among American women looked to Paris for their fashions . . . After the war, the couturiers of Paris began to dress the whole Western world. Their ideas, much diluted, but still theirs, filtered down to the cheapest grades of dresses and flowed out over all Europe and both the Americas. Paris became, and has remained, the keystone of the whole arch of international fashion. Of late, this supremacy has been challenged by New York, where the American school of *couture*, long held in anonymous subjection by Paris, is fast becoming articulate. But Paris, for a while at least, is still Paris.[126]

This echoes a French thesis on haute couture written in 1931 that notes the mixture of classes and the triumph of the individual after the war.[127] The author includes a chapter on the 'Evolution of the Clientele', covering the instability of class divisions, the disappearance of European courts and their replacement with 'corned-beef princesses'. He writes that 'This new society is still in flux. He who was rich yesterday is today ruined, while another who was unknown yesterday makes his fortune.'[128] Perhaps only in this new, fluid, mobile society could the French fashion show have developed as it did in the 1920s when it became incorporated into balls, charity events and even car shows and society beauty contests.

6
1919–1929
FASHION IN MOTION

113 Fashion show on the French Riviera modelled by actresses. *Femina* 1928. Courtesy Fashion Institute of Technology/ SUNY, FIT Library Department of Special Collections and FIT Archives.

In the 1920s three themes dominated the French fashion show: showmanship, the rationalisation of the body and the association of movement and modernity. Fashion shows began to assume the far more public and spectacular character of American shows in the previous decade. No longer staged only for buyers and private clients behind closed doors, large society fashion shows modelled by glamorous mannequins, often on the Riviera resorts, were brought to an international audience through extensive coverage in fashion magazines and films (**113**). Gradually, as had always been the case with American fashion shows, the French show became a form of promotion rather than sales. As the shows moved into the public arena of spectacle and indirect advertising, the appearance of the mannequins became increasingly modernist. Industrial aesthetics – the look of the production line – began to permeate fashion-show styling and scenography, at the same time as American business methods were being adopted by younger houses such as Patou and Lelong. When Jean Patou returned to fashion design after the war, he claimed that his wartime experiences had taught him that the best way to run a business was 'along the lines of an army organisation', by which he meant not strict discipline but clear command and delegation.[1]

The streamlined, modernist bodies of the mannequins parading in the couture houses and resorts of the 1920s resembled the rationalised body that also figured in the realms of work, leisure and art. In the fashion show, commerce and culture meshed: economic values became cultural as they were grafted onto women's bodies which, in turn, acquired a value that was both economic and symbolic. Yet, for all the clarity of its modernist rhetoric, the ambiguous styling of the modernist mannequin in the decade's fashion show revealed an ambivalence about modernity, technology, Americanism, gender and the New Woman.

If such images of the modern woman could be chilling, however, they could also be alluring. On the mannequins, the fluid, beaded, dresses of the 1920s came alive as their weight swung against the movement of the body and the

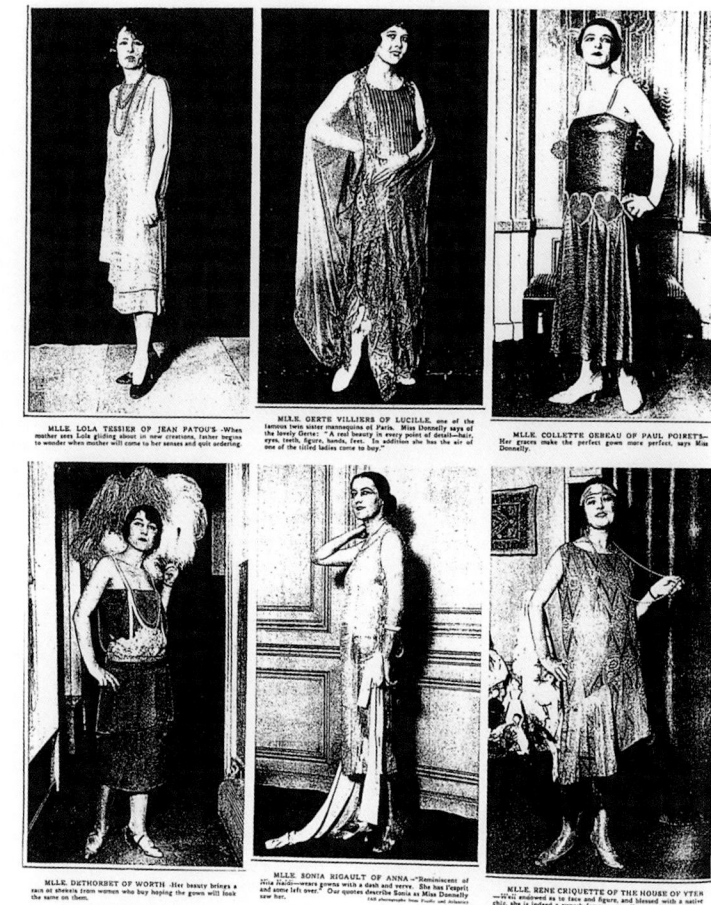

114 Dinarzade in Patou photographed by Baron Adolph de Meyer for *Harper's Bazar*, July 1925. Dinarzade, like Hebe, came to fame as a Lucile mannequin in the 1910s.

Hebe left Lucile with Molyneux in 1919 and Dinarzade became one of Patou's American mannequins in Paris in 1925.

115 'The Six Most Beautiful Mannequins of Paris', *Chicago Daily Tribune*, 25 January 1925.

light caught their reflective shimmer. In 1924 Lucien Lelong introduced his kinetic line, clothing designed in and for movement which, accordingly, had to be shown in movement, while the imperative to show fashion in motion found another analogue in two contemporaneous moving media: film and fast cars.

THE FASHION SHOW AS SPECTACLE

The American magazine *Harper's Bazar* played a significant role in reconceptualising the French fashion show as a social event in the 1920s, through its reports on the Paris collections by the photographer Baron Adolph de Meyer between 1922 and approximately 1929.[2] De Meyer's columns were the first regularly to describe individual mannequins, whose beauty and glamour he exalts: 'it hardly seems real; surely it is but fancy. And dreaming, my fancy decks them all in glittering brocades, in *diamanté*,

in endless ropes of pearls – Hebe, Sumurun, Ginette, Gaby – in fact, all the most famous Paris *mannequins*. They float before me, a whirl of beauty and a confused vision of magnificence' (**114**).[3] Such hyperbole was not limited to the Francophile upmarket *Harper's*; the *Chicago Daily Tribune* in 1925 showed 'The Six Most Beautiful Mannequins of Paris' (**115**), an example of how the vaunted exclusivity of elite French fashion modelling was easily adapted to the popular culture of showgirls and was disseminated to a mass market. In France, *L'Art et la mode* began a feature from 1923 on 'the prettiest mannequins of Paris' which, each issue, showed a full-page photograph of a named mannequin at a well-known couturier.[4]

Not only the mannequins but also the shows were eulogised. 'Chanel's opening was brilliant. There was a struggle for admittance and an atmosphere of expectancy', wrote *Harper's Bazar*, which, like American *Vogue*, began to describe the biannual trade openings as glamorous events

116 Opening at Jenny. Illustration for *Vogue* (America), 15 April 1923. Jenny usually showed on a Monday. The spring 1923 collection was delayed by several days and when it finally opened the salon was overwhelmed, wrote *Vogue*. 'A surging crowd, all trying to get in at once, and rooms so packed that even the entrance hall assumes the appearance of a crowded street-car, characterize the first shows at Jenny. Madame Jenny is always present, and if one is lucky she stations herself behind one's chair, calling attention to particular features of her immense collection and to models which are the favorite of her own perfect taste.' Vogue; © Condé Nast.

where hundreds of buyers clamoured for entry and many were turned away.[5] In April 1923 *Vogue* illustrated the crowded atmosphere of the spring opening at Jenny (**116**). The lofty yet confiding tone of de Meyer's articles, in which he converses with 'Mlle Chanel' and 'M. Worth' when he visits their fashion shows, brought his readers inside the exclusive world of haute couture. An illustration in *Harper's Bazar* of 1925 (**117** and **118**) shows his invitations tucked into the mirror, then his leaving home, driving across Paris, attending the shows, picking out the model to be photographed and, lastly, departing from the maison de couture into a starry night, driving home across the place Vendôme to sit up late at night at his desk 'recording impressions of collections' in his dressing gown.[6]

The transatlantic de Meyer admired these buyers' openings that resembled society events. Conservative French views of the post-war period were far different, however: social flux had led to a *déclassé* society. By 1927, wrote Paul Reboux, a journalist for the daily newspaper *L'Oeuvre*,

the foreign clientele [of the rue de la Paix] has substantially replaced the French clientele; the *nouveaux riches* have confidently taken the place of those nobles or *grands bourgeois* who previously enjoyed the grace of an inherited culture, thanks to a good fortune.

Money, recently acquired or resulting from a favourable change, has becomes the only master in this place where good sense used to reign supreme.[7]

It was in this evolving class context that, as the decade progressed, mannequin parades became progressively more integrated into social life and leisure. A fluidly constituted international social elite took to the French resorts for its pleasures. In the late summer, café society moved south from Paris to the Riviera, the Venice Lido or Biarritz, remaining there from August to mid-October.[8] As a result, a number of couturiers opened branches in Riviera resorts and staged gala fashion shows there, taking their mannequins south from Paris for the season. Meanwhile, at Deauville in Normandy throughout the 1920s, the mayor Henri Letellier organised endless events in the town's grandest hotels: polo, Rose Queen contests, *thés dansants*, and bathing beauty contests for society women that were, in fact, outdoor fashion shows of swimsuits and beachwear.[9] In resort fashion shows, couturiers supplied their clients with champagne and sandwiches 'while the mute mannequins parade, a jazz orchestra plays softly . . . and the soirée or "afternoon" concludes with dancing.'[10] Increasingly, couturiers had to be able to function like theatre producers, while also being both designers and

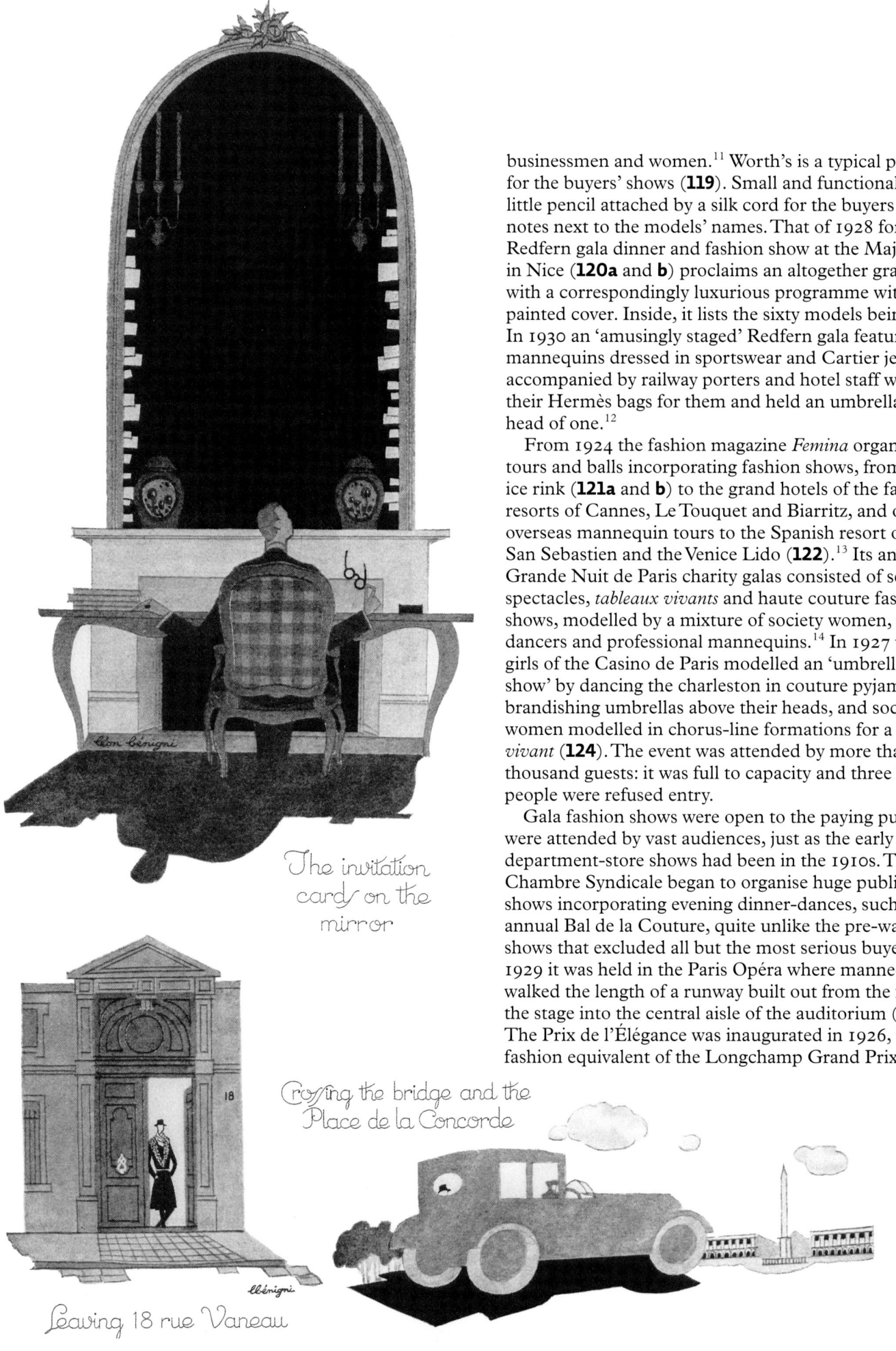

The invitation
cards on the
mirror

Crossing the bridge and the
Place de la Concorde

Leaving 18 rue Vaneau

businessmen and women.[11] Worth's is a typical programme for the buyers' shows (**119**). Small and functional, it has a little pencil attached by a silk cord for the buyers to scribble notes next to the models' names. That of 1928 for a Redfern gala dinner and fashion show at the Majestic Hotel in Nice (**120a** and **b**) proclaims an altogether grander event with a correspondingly luxurious programme with a hand-painted cover. Inside, it lists the sixty models being shown. In 1930 an 'amusingly staged' Redfern gala featured mannequins dressed in sportswear and Cartier jewellery, accompanied by railway porters and hotel staff who carried their Hermès bags for them and held an umbrella over the head of one.[12]

From 1924 the fashion magazine *Femina* organised galas, tours and balls incorporating fashion shows, from the Paris ice rink (**121a** and **b**) to the grand hotels of the fashionable resorts of Cannes, Le Touquet and Biarritz, and on overseas mannequin tours to the Spanish resort of San Sebastien and the Venice Lido (**122**).[13] Its annual Grande Nuit de Paris charity galas consisted of series of spectacles, *tableaux vivants* and haute couture fashion shows, modelled by a mixture of society women, actresses, dancers and professional mannequins.[14] In 1927 the chorus girls of the Casino de Paris modelled an 'umbrella fashion show' by dancing the charleston in couture pyjamas while brandishing umbrellas above their heads, and society women modelled in chorus-line formations for a *tableau vivant* (**124**). The event was attended by more than a thousand guests: it was full to capacity and three hundred people were refused entry.

Gala fashion shows were open to the paying public and were attended by vast audiences, just as the early American department-store shows had been in the 1910s. The Chambre Syndicale began to organise huge public fashion shows incorporating evening dinner-dances, such as the annual Bal de la Couture, quite unlike the pre-war couture shows that excluded all but the most serious buyers.[15] In 1929 it was held in the Paris Opéra where mannequins walked the length of a runway built out from the front of the stage into the central aisle of the auditorium (**125**).[16] The Prix de l'Élégance was inaugurated in 1926, the fashion equivalent of the Longchamp Grand Prix, where

Viewing the collection

117 and 118 (facing page and left) Baron de Meyer visits the shows. 'The invitation cards on the mirror', 'Leaving 18 rue Vaneau', 'Crossing the bridge and the Place de la Concorde' and 'Viewing the collection'. Illustrations for *Harper's Bazar*, April 1925.

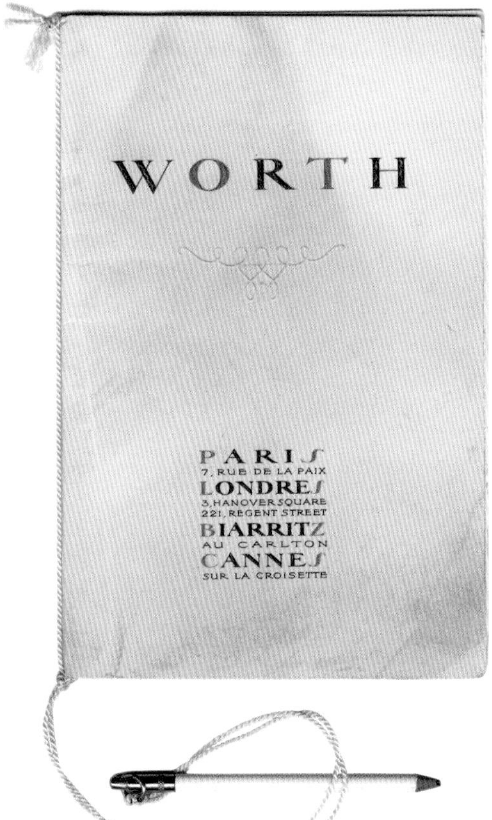

119 (below) Worth fashion show programme for autumn 1930: (left) closed and (right) open. The American buyer has jotted down details of models of particular interest. Courtesy Fashion Institute of Technology/ SUNY, FIT Library Department of Special Collections and FIT Archives.

WORTH

PARIS
7, RUE DE LA PAIX
LONDRES
3, HANOVER SQUARE
221, REGENT STREET
BIARRITZ
AU CARLTON
CANNES
SUR LA CROISETTE

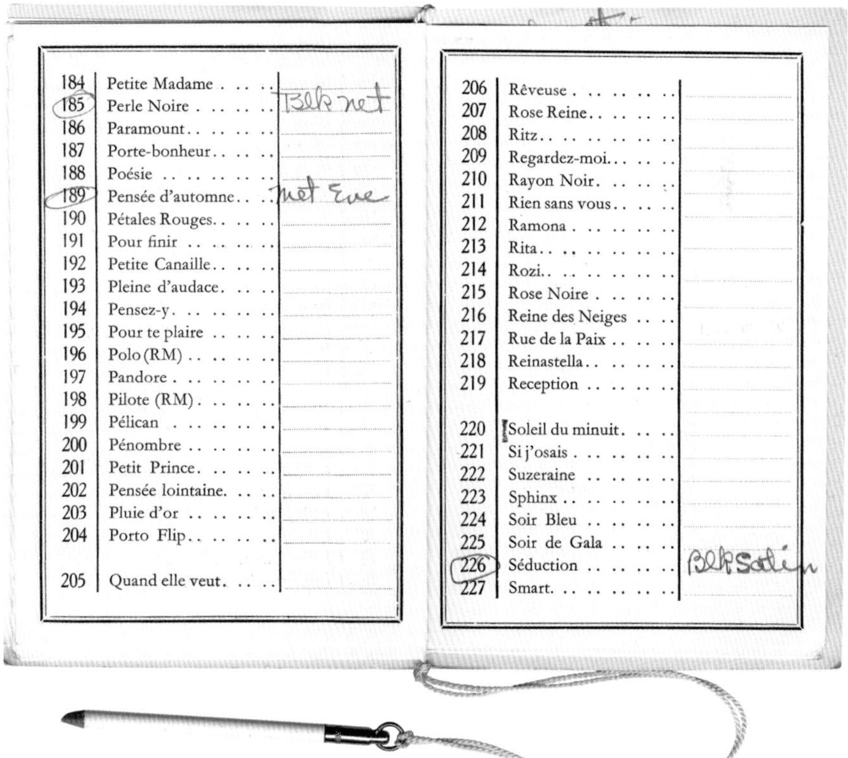

184	Petite Madame	
185	Perle Noire	Blk net
186	Paramount	
187	Porte-bonheur	
188	Poésie	
189	Pensée d'automne . . .	net Eve
190	Pétales Rouges	
191	Pour finir	
192	Petite Canaille	
193	Pleine d'audace	
194	Pensez-y	
195	Pour te plaire	
196	Polo (RM)	
197	Pandore	
198	Pilote (RM)	
199	Pélican	
200	Pénombre	
201	Petit Prince	
202	Pensée lointaine	
203	Pluie d'or	
204	Porto Flip	
205	Quand elle veut	

206	Rêveuse	
207	Rose Reine	
208	Ritz	
209	Regardez-moi	
210	Rayon Noir	
211	Rien sans vous	
212	Ramona	
213	Rita	
214	Rozi	
215	Rose Noire	
216	Reine des Neiges	
217	Rue de la Paix	
218	Reinastella	
219	Reception	
220	Soleil du minuit	
221	Si j'osais	
222	Suzeraine	
223	Sphinx	
224	Soir Bleu	
225	Soir de Gala	
226	Séduction	Blk satin
227	Smart	

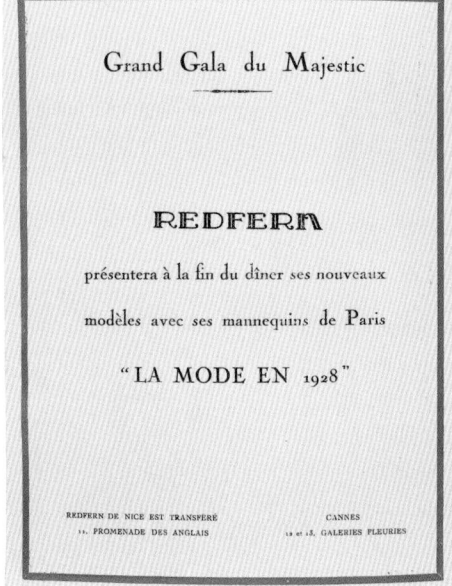

Grand Gala du Majestic

REDFERN

présentera à la fin du dîner ses nouveaux modèles avec ses mannequins de Paris

"LA MODE EN 1928"

REDFERN DE NICE EST TRANSFÉRÉ · · PROMENADE DES ANGLAIS   CANNES 13 et 15, GALERIES FLEURIES

1	SUR LE LAC	31	DANS LE PARC
2	FANDANGO	32	ISME
3	COLOMBINE	33	UN SOUFFLE
4	EAU PROFONDE	34	BILITIS
5	ENCHANTEMENT	35	NIOBÉ
6	RÉMINISCENCE	36	CAPTIVANTE
7	MUSCADIN	37	MON PLAID
8	EVENTAIL	38	DESSEIN
9	LOOK AT ME	39	NUIT DE PRINCE
10	POUR SORTIR	40	COQ D'OR
11	JEUNE HOMME	41	RISQUE
12	COUP DE FOUDRE	42	VILLA D'ESTE
13	MAURESQUE	43	TOSCANA
14	CHOU-CHOU	44	RITZ
15	POMPADOUR	45	TOUT OU RIEN
16	HOLLYWOOD	46	NADINE
17	MAGIE	47	DISCRÈTE
18	FLEUR BLEUE	48	MADRIGAL
19	TILLEUL	49	JANINE
20	BOUCHE EN CŒUR	50	LORENZACCIO
21	LES DISQUES	51	MARYLAND
22	TRIANON	52	NUIT
23	MONIQUE	53	BURLESQUE
24	FOOTING	54	MY LOVE
25	BOUTON D'OR	55	MADIANA
26	ESCLAVE	56	A TRAVERS PARIS
27	FÊTE GALANTE	57	AU BOIS
28	BONHEUR	58	CADET ROUSSEL
29	FOLLE PASSION	59	CASCADE
30	PERLE ROSE	60	PAGE D'AMOUR

couturiers rather than horses competed to take first prize. The 1928 prize went to the house of Jenny, at a fashion show modelled by fifty stage and screen stars.[17] Its winner was decided by public vote and half the 100,000 francs of prize money went to the anonymous workers of the winning house. In this way, the French couturiers began to solicit the involvement of a wider constituency of women than their usual customers. At the same time, Paris department stores also began to stage their own fashion shows.

Poiret, meanwhile, continued assiduously to stage fashion shows, parties and overseas tours. In 1921 his mannequins modelled in orientalist fashions in 'a glorified fashion show' and Egyptian Fête at the Cannes casino and

Mieux qu'une Fête... Une Idée...

Le MERCREDI 3 DÉCEMBRE à 4 heures et demie de l'après-midi

Sur la piste du "PALAIS de GLACE" (aux Champs-Élysées)

Grand défilé de Mannequins

ORGANISÉ PAR LE MAGAZINE

femina

Les Robes et Costumes pour les Sports d'Hiver.

LES PREMIÈRES MAISONS DE COUTURE DE PARIS PARTICIPERONT A CE DÉFILÉ ATTRACTIONS SENSATIONNELLES

PRIX D'ENTRÉE : **10 FRANCS**

122 (below) Summer fashion show at the Venice Lido, 1927. From left to right: Doucet, Chéruit, Lenief, Doucet, Nicole Groult, Philippe et Gaston, Max. *Femina*, September 1927. Courtesy Fashion Institute of Technology/ SUNY, FIT Library Department of Special Collections and FIT Archives.

123 (right) Poiret with five of his mannequins on tour in Copenhagen, 1925. The mannequins' touring uniform comprised yellow and green striped coats worn over dark blazers and houndstooth skirts. Newspaper cuttings from Poiret's press albums compare them both to music-hall chorus girls and to theatrical *figurantes*. Musée Galliera de la Mode de la Ville de Paris.

124 (right) 'La Grande Nuit de Paris' charity ball, 1927. Society women in chorus-line formation modelling white velvets. *Femina*, August 1927. Musée Galliera de la Mode de la Ville de Paris. Photograph Richard Hubert Smith

through most of the 1920s he sent mannequins to model at French resorts, from winter sports in St Moritz to beach parades at Le Touquet.[18] When he moved to new premises at the end of 1924, he staged a midnight procession of torch-bearing mannequins and midinettes who crossed the Champs-Élysées to the new house.[19] In the mid-1920s he toured with his mannequins in a uniform of double-breasted naval blazers, long wrap-around houndstooth skirts and distinctive loose coats with wide yellow and green stripes (**123**).[20] Poiret made several more European

125 (left) The Bal de la Couture at the Paris Opéra, 1929. The mannequins backstage wait to go on as other mannequins parade on stage, while two dinner-suited attendants hold up the names of the model and the designers on placards. © Photothèque des Musées de la Ville de Paris.

mannequin tours in the mid-1920s, to Bordeaux, Brussels,
Liège, Antwerp, Vienna, Prague, Budapest and in 1927 a
final lecture tour to the U.S.A.[21] His firm folded in 1929
and he was declared bankrupt in 1930.

In 1923 many of the larger houses transformed their
buyers' shows into social events, with little orchestras,
musical interludes, dancing and refreshments, treating the
buyers like the private clients (**126**).[22] That year, buyers'
shows became like evening parties (**127**). At Molyneux's
1923 Midseason Winter collections, 'tea and refreshments
were served to the strains of a distant and fairly discreet
band', wrote de Meyer.[23] An advertisement from 1924
shows another such opening at Lelong (**128**) where the

129a, b and c Two Vionnet fashion show invitations, c. 1923–4. The top two images show the back and front of a so-called 'personal invitation' numbered 1601 and in fact intended for buyers. The card invites them to visit three mornings a week to inspect the new premises to which Vionnet had moved in 1923, or to attend the regular afternoon shows from 2.30 pm from 4 September to see the new winter collection. At the bottom (c) is a different invitation card for a single fashion show of 'special designs' reserved for previous clients of the house. Rather than being numbered, this invitation is marked 'confidential'.

gesture of the woman in the foreground echoes the gesture of the mannequin seen modelling in the background through the door. By 1925 the practice had become extensive.[24] Fashion shows were accompanied by *thés dansants* or professional entertainers, the salons arranged like ballrooms or restaurants.[25] Night-time shows resembled formal parties, with all the buyers in evening dress.[26] At afternoon shows, refreshments and music were commonplace. In 1928 the journalist Marjorie Howard wrote in *Harper's*: 'I saw Yteb's collection at tea, where people stood about casually eating Russian cakes, while the mannequins passed among them. It is astonishing how a good buffet improves the look of the gowns!'[27]

For all the luxury of their shows, however, from 1925 onwards Parisian couture houses 'haemorrhaged sales', in Didier Grumbach's phrase, and in an attempt to curb their losses they intensified the sale of reproduction rights of couture models to sole buyers from overseas.[28] The most sought-after overseas buyers in Paris were the American commissionaires.[29] In 1922 Poiret had acknowledged that since the war many women could no longer afford haute couture and had designed some dresses *en série*, costing between 1200 and 1600 francs.[30] Even Vionnet, a virulent anti-copyist and defender of exclusive design, licensed some of her designs to a young French wholesaler, Eva Boex, in 1921, a contradictory position explored by Florence Brachet Champsaur in her paper on Vionnet's association with Galeries Lafayette.[31] Like all couturiers, Vionnet kept her private clients and her buyers apart, using different styles of showing to each (**129**). Twice a week, transatlantic liners disgorged the excited buyers at Le Havre where they clambered on board the trains for Paris.[32] There, in the big couturiers' salons, they would place numerous orders for different examples in varying sizes. These samples were destined to be made up for the large American stores who made their own design alterations for the American market. The system did not encourage originality or distinction. Grumbach argues that 'For America, haute couture represented no more than a luxury prêt à porter requiring the commissioners to choose according to the tastes of a traditional clientele little inclined to excess.'[33]

Patou, who was not himself a designer, did well in the 1920s because he wooed the American market.[34] In 1921 he expanded into adjoining premises, increasing his three large salons to a total of five or six.[35] By 1926, 1800 people a day were attending his shows in the first few days.[36] In 1923 he had initiated separate fashion shows for the press.[37] Known as *répétitions générales*, or full dress rehearsals, the press shows were held the evening before the buyers' shows and were, according to Meredith Etherington-Smith, a

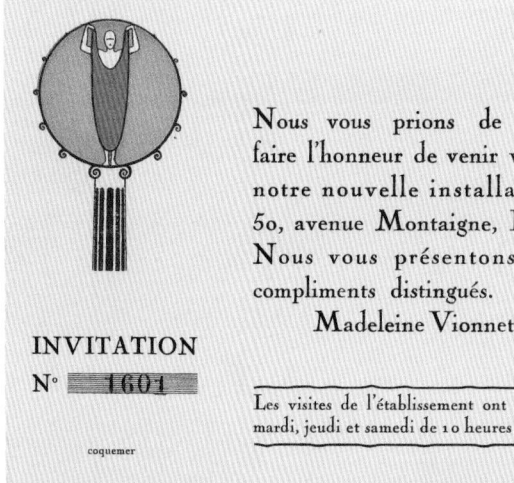

INVITATION N° 1601

coquemer

Nous vous prions de nous faire l'honneur de venir visiter notre nouvelle installation, 5o, avenue Montaigne, Paris. Nous vous présentons nos compliments distingués.
Madeleine Vionnet et Cⁱᵉ

Les visites de l'établissement ont lieu les mardi, jeudi et samedi de 10 heures à midi.

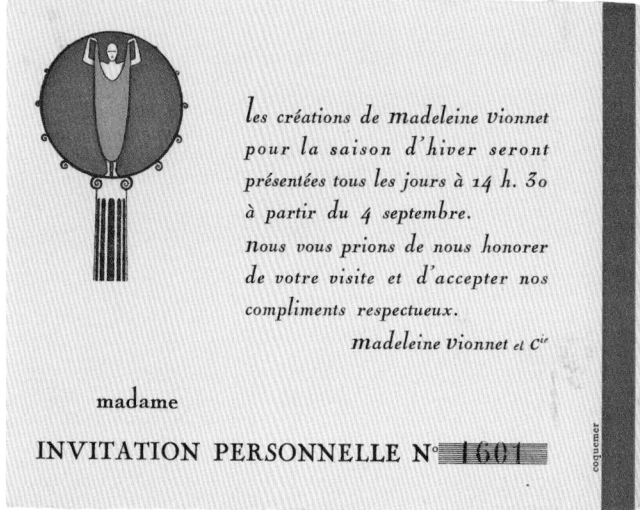

madame
INVITATION PERSONNELLE N° 1601

les créations de madeleine vionnet pour la saison d'hiver seront présentées tous les jours à 14 h. 3o à partir du 4 septembre.
nous vous prions de nous honorer de votre visite et d'accepter nos compliments respectueux.
madeleine vionnet et cⁱᵉ

le jeudi 20 septembre, à 14 h. 3o, nous présenterons un certain nombre de créations spéciales de madeleine vionnet. cette journée est spécialement réservée aux dames déjà clientes de la maison. nous espérons, madame, que vous nous honorerez de votre visite et nous vous prions d'accepter l'hommage de notre respect.

confidentielle

sté madeleine vionnet et cⁱᵉ

coquemer

'combination of grandeur, socializing and hard-headed business'.[38] They were organised like glamorous society parties in which journalists were deliberately seated amid celebrities, a form of flattery designed to encourage them to write favourable reviews. It seems to have worked. 'Thus is the journalistic profession raised from ignominy in the eyes of the mode to the glory of a critic of discrimination', wrote American *Vogue*, in its caption to a 1923 illustration (**130**). Patou made a point of inviting not only the fashion journalists but also male war correspondents who, *Vogue* wrote, 'succumbed in heaps to the attraction of white organdie.'[39] His innovation was shortly after copied by Doeuillet and a host of others (**131a** and **b**).[40]

The tenor of press shows was kept select and invitations were intentionally restricted. Lillian Farley, who modelled for Patou as Dinarzade from 1924 to 1925 (see **114** and **132**), recalled little tables arranged along the walls, with space for the mannequins to model in the centre of the room; on the tables stood champagne and cards with the guests' names. Footmen presented cigars and luxury cigarettes, uniformed *vendeuses* gave out bottles of perfume and finally the first models passed by a table where Patou was seated with his *première* and directors. Each dress had to be inspected and approved by him and even at this late stage several would be sent back. The collection was so big that it had to be split into two, sports and day clothes first, then an intermission during which a buffet supper was served, before the evening dresses were shown. In *Harper's* for April 1924 de Meyer described these gatherings:

> Turning the private view of a new collection into an evening party was inaugurated a year or two ago by this same genial and hospitable M. Patou. A lead which any number of houses have since followed. Supper tables for six were placed in the four great salons. There were ices, lemonades, and sandwiches, as well as a

great deal of champagne. The atmosphere was delightful, and a small booklet, laid out on each table, contained M. Patou's own views on fashions, as characteristically expressed by himself.[41]

Patou's press shows were a communication rather than a sales tool, like a modern-day fashion show. After the *répétition générale*, the first show to buyers was the most important. In a large house like Patou's, it was reserved for the American stores, with their huge spending power; the European buyers came the next day. The private shows took place two to three weeks later.[42] Lillian Farley describes modelling in a press show one evening followed by the buyers' show the next day:

> As I went through the door to show my first dress, I had the impression of stepping into a perfumed, silk-lined jewel casket, the atmosphere was so strongly charged. The men in their correct black tailcoats with the sleek pomaded hair; the women in gorgeous evening dresses, plastered with jewels. It was hot, so hot, and the air was stifling with the mixed odours of perfume and cigarettes.
>
> It was nearly one o'clock when the collection was over. The guests went off to spread the good word that Patou had rung the bell again and we went home to die. Twenty of us had shown five hundred models.
>
> The next afternoon was the opening for the American buyers. They came in droves. There was a totally different feeling from the party-like atmosphere which had prevailed the previous evening. These men and women were there on business. The European buyers came the next day and the salons sounded like the Tower of Babel.[43]

It was Patou's astute business sense and his sensitivity to American business methods, as much as his compelling stagecraft, which led him to recruit American mannequins to his Paris catwalk in 1924.

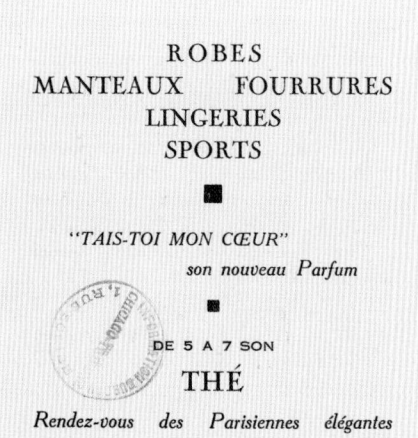

PATOU'S AMERICAN MANNEQUINS

Before he did so, he paved the way by hiring the Dolly Sisters as mannequins for a season. The Dollys, as they were known, were music-hall stars and good-time girls with expensive wardrobes; on stage they dressed identically and Patou made them a wardrobe of more than two hundred outfits for a promotional trip to the U.S.A. in spring 1924, which required two-hour fittings every day for two months prior to departure. Patou also designed their nightgowns, dressing-gowns and all their accessories, including handkerchiefs, hair-slides, colour-co-ordinated canes for each outfit and underwear. Their tour helped to promote Patou at a time when Chanel's American sales far outstripped his; the publicity stunt he conceived with the Dollys put him firmly on the 'fashionable American map'.[44] On tour, the Dollys embodied the doubling at the heart of couture. As twins, they confounded the idea of original and copy; as Patou's mannequins, they were *sosies*, or doubles, in the nineteenth-century terminology; as showgirls, they were harbingers of future fashions. They travelled as Patou's *mannequins de ville*, not unlike Poiret's wife Denise in 1913, except that he had travelled with her. Patou never travelled with any of his professional mannequins, even the Americans he went on to recruit later that year, unlike Poiret who had gone round Europe with his French mannequins in 1911.

On 14 November 1924, Patou placed an advertisement in the *New York Times*:

MANNEQUINS WANTED FOR PARIS

Jean Patou, the Parisian couturier, desires to secure three ideal types of beautiful young American women who seriously desire careers as mannequins in his Paris atelier. Must be smart, slender, with well-shaped feet and ankles and refined of manner. Sail within three weeks. Attractive salary proposition, one year's contract and travelling expenses paid both ways. Selection to be made by a jury at the offices of VOGUE, 14th floor, West 44th St. Apply Friday morning, 10 to 1.30.[45]

Five hundred applicants turned up and eventually six rather than three were chosen (**132**).[46] They arrived in Paris to much fanfare. Patou's 'importation' of American mannequins to the bastion of fashion was a calculated provocation in a city where the French woman was considered to be the personification of allure and chic and Paris the symbolic centre of fashion and the real centre of haute couture. The inflated rates paid to *les Nanas d'Amérique* was considered an affront to the French mannequins, *les belles filles Parisiennes*.[47] Patou, however, maintained that he needed American mannequins to model his clothes to his American clients because American women were leaner, longer and generally more slender than Frenchwomen. Nevertheless, he was careful to stress 'the exquisite desirability of both the rounded French Venus and the slender American Diana'.[48] In French *Vogue* for February 1925, the writer Colette contrasted Patou's American mannequins with their Parisienne counterparts, whom she characterised as 'sturdy French ponies'. She predicted that the American mannequins embodied the forward thrust of 1920s French fashion. They were 'a squad of archangels, in a chaste flight unimpeded by the Flesh, [who] will reorient fashion towards an increasingly slender line, cut with a single scissor slash from magnificent material.'[49]

This was not a new physical stereotype. Since the 1910s the American 'type' had been characterised as leaner, leggier and more athletic than the French. Marcel Prévost in 1910 had differentiated the American woman from the small, dark-skinned, plump Frenchwoman as 'a tall person,

rather slender, though vigorous looking' and declared that 'through hygiene and sports . . . a real American type has been formed, tall and strong.'[50] Sportswear was considered a specifically American contribution to fashion that perfectly showed off 'the greyhound silhouette' dear to American customers of the French haute couture.[51] Jenny had always promoted the 'American silhouette'; by the 1920s the idea of the active, sporting figure was popularly taken to be an American rather than a French one. Gradually, the French ideal of a twenty-five to thirty-year-old sophisticate ceded to an American ideal of youthful and slender girlishness, typified in 1924 by the extreme youth of Patou's two youngest American 'flapper' mannequins, aged sixteen and seventeen.[52]

On their arrival in Paris, the American mannequins debuted in the salon alongside their French colleagues on the evening of 5 February 1925. Patou staged their first appearance with typical showmanship: realising that his audience would expect distinct differences in the dresses designed for the French and American mannequins, he opened the show by sending them all out dressed identically in the thin cotton wraps they usually wore between fittings.[53] At a subsequent show, the mannequins emerged in identical dresses in two different colours.[54] No pictures of the first fashion show survive, if any were taken, but a French cutting shows eight American mannequins in

these wraps a month later (**133**). The same chorus-girl aesthetic appeared on another Paris stage on 16 June when the Fête du Théâtre et de la Parure (the Fashion and Theatre Fête) opened at the Exposition des Arts Décoratifs under the direction of Paul Poiret with a performance that linked fashion to music hall and other types of performance. It featured a fashion parade interspersed with dance and theatrical routines by, among others, Loie Fuller, Ida Rubenstein and the Tiller Girls (**134**).[55]

Comparing the image of Patou's mannequins with both the Tiller Girls in 1925 and the society women at the Grande Nuit de Paris in 1927 (see **124**), it is evident that the look of the chorus line which had first manifested itself in the fashion line-ups of the early 1910s had, by the second half of the 1920s, entered the lexicon of the fashion show at all levels of society. These line-ups evoke Siegfried Kracauer's description in 1927 of the chorus line as a symbolic representation of 'the capitalist production process'. Kracauer argued that, in the field of leisure, the chorus line and sporting parade were visual analogues of the modern industrial means of production and that the chorus line was thereby able to visualise 'significant components of reality [that have become] . . . invisible in our world'.[56] Similarly, Patou's line of mannequins made visible a relationship between Paris couture houses and the mass-produced fashions of New York's Seventh Avenue that

Les mannequins français se sont émus de voir le grand couturier parisien Jean Patou faire appel à des jeunes filles américaines pour présenter ses créations.
Voici, dans la tenue qu'elles revêtent entre deux présentations, les « concurrentes » d'outre-Atlantique, qui vont peut-être susciter une petite révolution au palais de la mode.

had to remain concealed from the individual couture clients.

As well as promoting his American mannequins, Patou enthusiastically endorsed both American business methods and leisure pursuits. He installed an American bar in his couture salon and played American music at his fashion shows.[57] This was not incompatible with a Parisian sense of modernity; despite the conservatism of some French critics, the late 1920s saw a French vogue for all things American. Elliot Paul, the Paris correspondent of the *Chicago Tribune* who lived in Paris from 1923, recalled that the 'younger French, some intellectual and others not, made a fetish of everything American and "modern"' and the French writer Paul Morand described the vogue for jazz, the charleston, dominoes, Mah-jong and cocktails as 'Americanophilia'.[58] Other French writers of the 1920s, such as André Siegfried and Georges Duhamel, were ambivalent about America and contrasted French individualism with American conformity.[59] They linked the latter to mass production and the production line and argued that American productivity had an effect not only in the economic realm but also on culture and subjectivity. Siegfried wrote: 'in the maximum efficiency of each worker . . . lies grave risk for the individual. His integrity is seriously threatened not only as a producer but as a consumer as well.'[60]

At the same time, however, these writers admired American productivity. The rabidly anti-American Duhamel remained impressed with the long legs of American women, just as the pro-American Patou had been in his selection of the American mannequins, even if Duhamel described the American woman at the wheel of her car as if she had come fresh off the production line: she is, he wrote, 'the modern goddess, published in an edition of two or three million copies'.[61] Here one might invoke both the Dollys, who came in an edition of two (with both of whom Patou reputedly had an affair) and Patou's American mannequins, who came in an edition of six.

In 1927 Paul Reboux worried that the internationalism of the rue de la Paix clientele might begin to influence the way the French dressed and complained that modernism was an Anglo-Saxon style composed of geometric cubes and planes.[62] The look of standardisation and an industrial aesthetic were commonly perceived to be typically American. An unnamed French dressmaker quoted in an American newspaper in 1922 decried the standardised dress of American women: 'It is absolutely unthinkable! Not until we have standardized women can we have standardized dress for them.' The same article commented that 'foreign women . . . are amazed at the sameness with which American women garb themselves all after the same pattern. They say our "mass fashions" are atrocious! . . . but in France . . . the significance of the word individuality is instinctive.'[63] The ideas that uniformity and standardisation were 'American' while individuality was 'French', and that these values could be grafted onto images of women, were important national stereotypes that lay behind Patou's marketing and promotional stratagems. As well as picturing American uniformity and mechanical production in his fashion show, Patou, like Lucien Lelong, ran his house according to the most up-to-date American business methods.[64] Patou's advertising budget was large, his salaries high and his prices relatively low.[65] He introduced daily staff meetings and profit shares for executives and extended the bonus system to mannequins, who were traditionally employed only on short-term seasonal contracts.[66] Instead of outsourcing specialisms like beadwork or embroidery, he installed specialist ateliers in-house. 'The organisation of his business is completely industrial', wrote a French source.[67] This rationalisation of the traditional couture atelier system was 'his chief business secret', argued the American writer Robert Forrest Wilson. It introduced 'some elements of the piecework and assembly plan of production': that is, some features of Ford's automated production line; Wilson noted that Lelong too was moving towards the 'scientific management of the dressmaking plant', a reference to the Taylor system that characterised many other houses in the mid-1920s.[68]

It was above all in his understanding of the role of the mannequin that Patou revealed a Taylorist analysis of his workforce as his best business asset. Patou, according to Wilson, replaced 'the trade's valuation of the mannequin as a piece of necessary furniture' with his own idea of 'her as an important factor in the sales organization'. Wilson wrote of Patou:

> He says his mannequin Lola is the best in the world. While she is a striking looking girl, in beauty she is overshadowed by golden-haired Gladys, a Scotch mannequin in Patou's establishment. But Lola sells twice as many gowns as Gladys, and Patou says she can outsell an ordinary mannequin six or seven to one. The reason is her great chic, a seemingly spiritual quality whose value in actual francs and centimes Patou's efficiency department shows to him in graphic business charts.[69]

Thus Lola's chic could be calculated actuarially.

The mannequin, tall and slender in reality, could also be represented as a tall and slender column in a bar chart, the taller the better, as Patou's 'efficiency department' made the translation from centimetres to centimes and francs. In America, John Powers opened the first model agency in New York in 1923. He described himself as 'a broker in beauty' and fashion models as 'commodities who must meet certain requirements'. In exchange, he converted

modelling into a lucrative profession in the 1920s.[70] Both Powers in New York and Patou in Paris identified their mannequins as commodities in the sense that their monetary value could be accurately calculated.

Lola was French (see **115**, top left) and was probably one of the house mannequins who modelled alongside the Americans in checkered wraps in February 1925 (see **133**). Comparing her figure with that of Dinarzade in a similar dress and body stance (see **114**), it seems that the Americans were not, in fact, noticeably thinner than the French mannequins. Patou's international *cabine* of mannequins stood, rather, for the symbolic and ideological differences between France and America that were predicated on the real differences not of anatomy but of currency – in particular the relative strength of the dollar against a weak franc. This was personified by the figures of the American and the French woman in the words of a business journalist who recalled how, in the 1920s,

> The fluctuations of Paris fashions . . . closely paralleled the fluctuations of the franc. It was essentially a struggle between the American woman and the *Parisienne* . . . the franc was falling, falling, falling all those years from 1919 to 1926. The American dictatorship flourished and Paris did not dare oust the tube dress and short skirt [previously identified as suiting the lean American figure better than the curvaceous French one] . . . In 1926 the franc sank to thirty-one to the dollar, and exportations (and with them the American influence) reached their height.[71]

In this way, the journalist mapped economic values (currency) onto cultural ones (images of woman), linking the two by association and reminding the readers of the economic base of these supposedly anatomical comparisons.

Nancy Green, in her analysis of 'reciprocal visions', has written: 'In what I would call a cultural language of production, national characteristics become an explanatory device for understanding the relative problems of French industry on the world market. . . . Furthermore, in this taste battle between nations, women have been assigned a particular role . . . as representatives of national character in a war of the wearers.'[72] She goes on to argue that 'French garment discourse has thus set up a certain dichotomy between art and industry paralleled by the difference between the French and American industries. . . . at the same time, the "modernization" fear has haunted the manufacturers. French analysts have combined both disdain and admiration for American ready-to-wear methods and style.'[73]

Crucial to the understanding of Patou's combination of superiority in asserting French taste, and his willingness to adapt to and flatter American taste, is Green's demonstration of how the American garment industry more or less agreed with the French 'imaginaire of the art–industry dichotomy', even if a vociferous rearguard zealously approved American ideals to the detriment of French fashion, which it disdained as unwearable and pretentious. In respect of this latter point, Patou was always careful to assert the simplicity of his designs, something which would have been understood as an American taste.[74] An article in American *Vogue* for April 1923 (**136**) illustrates Green's first point: 'the chiselled uniformity of the American type, and the lack of originality with which the type is dressed . . . is a purely American phenomenon'.[75] In fact, it was not. Uniformity itself became fashionable in the 1920s, when the aesthetics of modernism permeated all fashion shows, not just Patou's, as fashion itself played with the appearance of standardisation.[76]

THE MODERNIST BODY

In all but the most conservative of couture houses of the mid-1920s, the stage direction of the mannequins became increasingly modernist in its visual appeal as the fashion line-up lent itself to such stagecraft. Identical dresses began to be presented simultaneously in a range of colours: Patou showed identical dresses in different colours, under identical bronze lamé cloaks.[77] Vionnet's simple, anti-decorative dresses in black, white and brown would have made striking moving patterns in the salon,[78] while Patou's twenty or twenty-five mannequins filing through the salon in their checkered wraps (see **133**) must have looked like chronophotography in motion – Duchamp's *Nude Descending a Staircase* animated in geometric checks (see **45**). Bodies were styled identically, too: in 1926 all the Chanel mannequins wore their hair in a small chignon identical to Chanel's.[79] Patou showed his sportswear on uniformly sportive and bronzed mannequins. At Drecoll in 1927 a single sweater was shown in different colours on 'a bevy of mannequins appearing altogether'.[80] There were variations on the theme of replication too. In 1924 de Meyer described how 'Lelong shows some of his models in double; the two identical gowns are presented side by side, one on a slim silhouette, the other on a big and more mature mannequin. It is an unusual and rather extravagant innovation, but was much appreciated.'[81] In 1925 Lelong showed three different garments made from one model, haunting variations on the theme of doubling and multiplication in the couture business.[82]

The effects were increased when the mannequins were reflected in the tall mirrored walls of the salons; in *Vogue* for November 1924, a Redfern advertisement describes how

'innumerable mirrors reflect to infinity the elegant silhouettes adorned in tight, shimmering dresses and precious furs', as if the multiplication of capital could create luxury ad infinitum.[83] At Chanel in 1928, an entirely mirrored interior was installed that created the effect of a human kaleidoscope as the mannequins came down the circular staircase faceted with mirrors which splintered and refracted their image like a futurist painting of motion.

Sometimes the large number of mannequins massed on stage in the couture house shows were confusing. Van Campen Stewart complained in 1924 that he could not take in the four hundred models at Callot, 'for when half a dozen mannequins appear all at once for one's inspection, one gets bewildered, to put it mildly'.[84] At other times the mannequins' bodies could be organised to create abstract stage effects and de Meyer approved of Jenny's autumn 1926 staging:

> Her presentation, an artistic conception, has a beginning and a climax. Gowns of similar color and texture follow one another. . . . a series of black dresses is augmented with increasingly pink touches until the presentation becomes both black and pink. At one time I noticed some eight or ten of these moving about the showroom together. Soon it is all pink gowns, then a ravishing display of pink ostrich feathers in the form of scarves as well as pink fringed shawls designed by Madame Van Dongen, the great painter's wife. It is all perfectly well stage-managed.[85]

The following season Jenny, whose clientele was largely American, repeated the same effect of a chromatic shift but through a wider range of colours. Again, she showed her evening gowns *en série*, reported de Meyer, using the term for mass-produced clothing to describe the use of repetition on stage. 'First appear, in rapid succession, a number of black gowns, plain and jetted black. These are followed by black and pink ones, quite especially lovely, which gradually become entirely pink. Next we are shown a dazzling array of white and silver dresses leading on to gowns of various colours.'[86]

Traditionally, fashion shows had followed a strict order of display that obeyed the social logic and etiquette of fashionable dressing: day dress preceded evening wear, town clothes and sportswear were followed by tea dresses and opera cloaks.[87] This social logic imparted a narrative element to the fashion show, suggesting the evolution of a single day in the life of a fashionable woman.[88] In the mid-1920s the incorporation of a chromatic display, the proliferation of both mannequins and identical gowns in different colours, the installation of ever larger mirrors, all had the potential to disrupt the fashion narrative through doubling and repetition and to convert the body into an abstraction. In this, the staging of 1920s fashion shows is

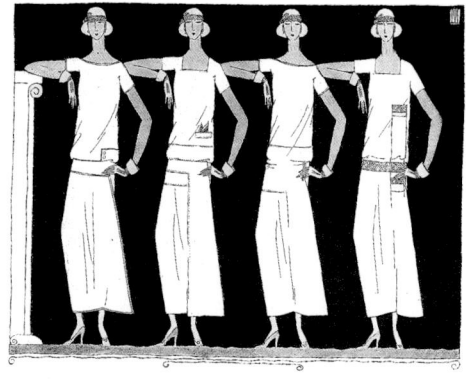

134 (below) The Tiller Girls of the Casino de Paris dancing 'The River of Diamonds' at the Fête du Théâtre et de la Parure in the 1925 Paris

Exposition des Arts Décoratifs. From *Encyclopédie*, vol. x, plate ix. British Library, wording TBC.

like the staging of chorus girls' acts in variety theatre: it turns them from individuals into one, autonomous moving mass.

These effects could be further played with by reversing them or juxtaposing them like the pieces of a modernist collage or cut-up, as Callot did in its spring 1925 show, mixing up the categories with 'a lovely bride first, an afternoon gown next, and a ball gown, a sports suit, and a pair of pajamas, passing all of them in rapid succession'. As a result, writes de Meyer, 'Watching a collection at Callot's is more diverting than elsewhere, more varied, more kaleidoscopic.'[89] This kaleidoscopic effect had already been created in the experiments in moving cloth by Sonia Delaunay who had exhibited her 'simultaneous textiles', on a system of turning rollers designed by her husband, next to Vionnet and Poiret's static displays at the 1924 Salon d'Automne.[90]

The doubling and replication of mannequins on stage in the couture houses was also found in fashion magazines' illustrations and society pages, where apparently identically dressed women were paired or multiplied in chorus-line formations (**135**). Patou's, Vionnet's, Jenny's, Chéruit's and their compatriots' innovations in fashion-show scenography have clear parallels in modernist art and design. In fashion illustration, for example, Ernesto Thayat's illustrations for the *Gazette du Bon Ton* adapted futurist 'lines of force' to evoke the swirling movements of fashion models on catwalks.[91] There is nothing to suggest, however, that these fashion designers were consciously using modernist art strategies; indeed, when they did collaborate it was with

decorative artists and illustrators rather than with avant-garde artists (Paul Poiret with Raoul Dufy, Jeanne Lanvin with Armand-Albert Rateau, Madeleine Vionnet with Ernesto Thayat, and Maisons Worth and Agnès with Jean Dunand).[92] Practices were different in New York where, for example, the Russian-American painter Louis Lozowick, influenced by Soviet constructivist art, painted a modernist background for a 1924 fashion show on a raised stage at Lord & Taylor department store (**137**); this rivalled Robert Mallet-Stevens's sets for the French film *L'Inhumaine* directed by Marcel l'Herbier with costumes by Poiret, also in 1924.[93]

While the French adapted the visual language of modernism and the clarity of its rhetoric, their fashion shows pictured modern commerce rather than futurist utopias. The fashion show was associated with individuated luxury consumption, yet it was also a symbolic representation of the processes of modern industrial production. That conceit found its way into fashion illustrations, for example in *Harper's Bazar*'s image of the new Paris fashions for autumn 1927 to New Yorkers (**138**), in which the massed mannequins hold hands like the linked arms of Patou's American mannequins on their arrival in France (see **132**). They are arranged not in a straight line but around a central hub to suggest a giant cog or industrial wheel, which is in fact a clockface, with fashions from all the major French houses pointing to the hour of the day. The image relies on the convention that there were different dresses for day, afternoon and evening wear, while also suggesting the inexorable passage of time in an

industry predicated on rapid changes of style. It combines time and motion in a single pictogram, a conjunction at the heart of Taylorism, and simultaneously invokes the Fordist aesthetic of 1920s fashion, reinventing the nineteenth-century 'wheel of fashion' illustrated by Grandville in the 1840s to suggest that production and consumption are not distinct but part of a single, indivisible process.

These designers' styling created an image of serial reproduction of both dresses and mannequins that drew on an industrial aesthetic. In their hands, the modernist body of the mannequin, despite its luxurious settings, graphically matched the aesthetics of automation, like Chanel's little black dress to which American *Vogue* on 1 October 1926 appended the caption: 'the Chanel "Ford" – the frock that all the world will wear – is Model 817 of black crêpe de chine'. Here *Vogue* referred to Henry Ford's dictum that the Model-T Ford came in 'any colour . . . so long as it is black', as he wrote in his autobiography, published in the U.S.A. in 1922 and in France in 1926.[94] In the fashion shows of the mid- to late 1920s, designers including Patou, Jenny and Chéruit grouped the mannequins' bodies into abstract machine-like formations on stage, grafting the imagery of the Fordist production line onto the body and subjectivity through modernist aesthetics.

Whether modelling individually to private clients or on giant stages to massed audiences of public, buyers and journalists, modelling was based on the repetition and standardisation of the individual mannequin's gestures and poses. From the early 1900s commentators had marvelled at the repetitive nature of her gestures and pondered the difficulties of modelling the same ten dresses ten times a day to ten different clients, each time as if it were the first. They worried that the mannequin was 'an object', the saleswoman had an 'industrial smile' and the couture house

was like a huge, well-oiled machine or Taylorist factory *de luxe*, with the mannequin as its front-of-house emblem.[95] As in the chorus line, individuality was renounced in favour of military precision. The mannequin's body, multiplied by mirrors and modes into a 'mass ornament', was a visual analogue of the Taylorist organisation of the couture house, with the movement of all the human parts rationalised in the interests of efficiency and economy. Just as the calibrated and standardised movements of the Taylorist worker made her or him a mere cog in the scientific management of the workplace, so the repetitive and stylised gestures of the fashion mannequin incorporated her as a living part of the machinery of the Parisian couture house, a huge, co-ordinated mansion of regulated and divided labour.

KINETICISM AND SPEED

Mannequins' moves were no less fluid for being stylised, however. The heavily beaded, embroidered and fringed dresses of the mid- to late 1920s relied on movement for their allure. At Chanel, de Meyer observed that 'When in motion this silver fringed gown looks like a dripping shimmering fountain on a moonlit night.'[96] The swing of Chanel's heavy ropes of pearls could be used by illustrators to show mannequins in motion, as chiffon panels floated free from tubular slips (**139**). In 1914 Paquin had designed tango dresses in movement and the dance craze continued after the war.[97] Sport was equally popular with fashionable women: 'The sports mode controls our sunlight mood as the dance mode directs our lamplight one', wrote *Harper's* in 1926.[98] The movement of both became incorporated in fashion design. 'Jenny is much given to introducing a

139 A fashion plate showing Chanel's clothing in motion. *Vogue* (France), 1 October 1925. Musée Galliera de la Mode de la Ville de Paris. Photograph Richard Hubert Smith

fluttering movement . . . achieved by boleros and circular flounces', wrote American *Vogue* in 1925 and four months later it reported that 'A new flattering, flowing silhouette which often slips back to the slim form when in repose, is the novelty of the collections.'[99]

In this climate, Lelong launched his 'kinetic design' ('clothes created for people on the move, and who step lively') with a show of three hundred models in August 1925.[100] He announced his new concept with a manifesto-like advertisement in French *Vogue* that evoked the cinema (**140**). Framed by a border depicting a film strip of a woman engaged in the fashionable pursuits of both sunlight and lamplight moods – motoring, horse-riding, walking, golfing, shooting and dancing – Lelong's advertisement read:

LUCIEN LELONG says:

In studying movement, the characteristic trait of our current existence, I have arrived at a new concept of Fashion.

Dressed in clothes which have not always been conceived with a view to the active life she leads, today's woman often has a frozen air.

I believe therefore that the first concern of a couturier must be to create clothes that are appropriate to this animated life.

A modern garment must be inspired by dynamism and conceived according to the varied movements with which it will be worn to which it has to lend itself.

And I think that this study of line and movement which I call cinematic design, comparing it to the development of a film in slow motion, is the only correct one for the logical creation of a dress suited to the gestures of modern life.

I have applied these principles in my new collection and have redoubled my efforts to imbue my models with the characteristic dynamism of the age.

The winter collection will be shown in the first week of August.[101]

Lelong opened the show as though it were a film, with mannequins seen moving behind a screen from which they emerged dressed in his 'kinetic clothes'.[102] He had apologised in the June issue of *Vogue* for showing his new designs on static mannequins at the 1925 Exposition des Arts Décoratifs.[103] In the late summer he began a full-scale promotion of his new ideas in the press. In *Harper's Bazar* in October, he abandoned the term 'cinematic design' in favour of 'kinetic design' in another double-page advertisement illustrating a fashion show (**141**):

Dresses inspired by the rhythm of movement

The incomparable Lucien Lelong has created kinetic design thus originating dresses which harmonize with the activities of modern life.

The fashionable woman of to-day must wear 'les robes en mouvement' 'Gowns in motion' – as their creator Lucien Lelong has called them. The most exclusive stores in the United States as well as the world over will show the – 'Gowns in motion' – signed LUCIEN LELONG couturier à Paris.[104]

In the advertisement, the mannequins have descended from Lelong's modelling stage and parade through the main salon where the perspective and shading of the image suggest a long runway, with the spectators gathered together at the curtained entrances in a long wall articulated by enormous plate-glass mirrors.

In November, Lelong inserted another declaration in French *Vogue*: 'My new concept of movement in the feminine line reported by the entire press has been followed by all the world./ But this new silhouette, sometimes interpreted without logic, has degenerated into exaggerations that kill rhythm and harmony./ I declare that the line "in movement" must be used in moderation in order to achieve its maximum grace.'[105] Lelong's vaunted designs employed common dressmaking features to allow ease of movement, as had Paquin's in 1914: little gathers,

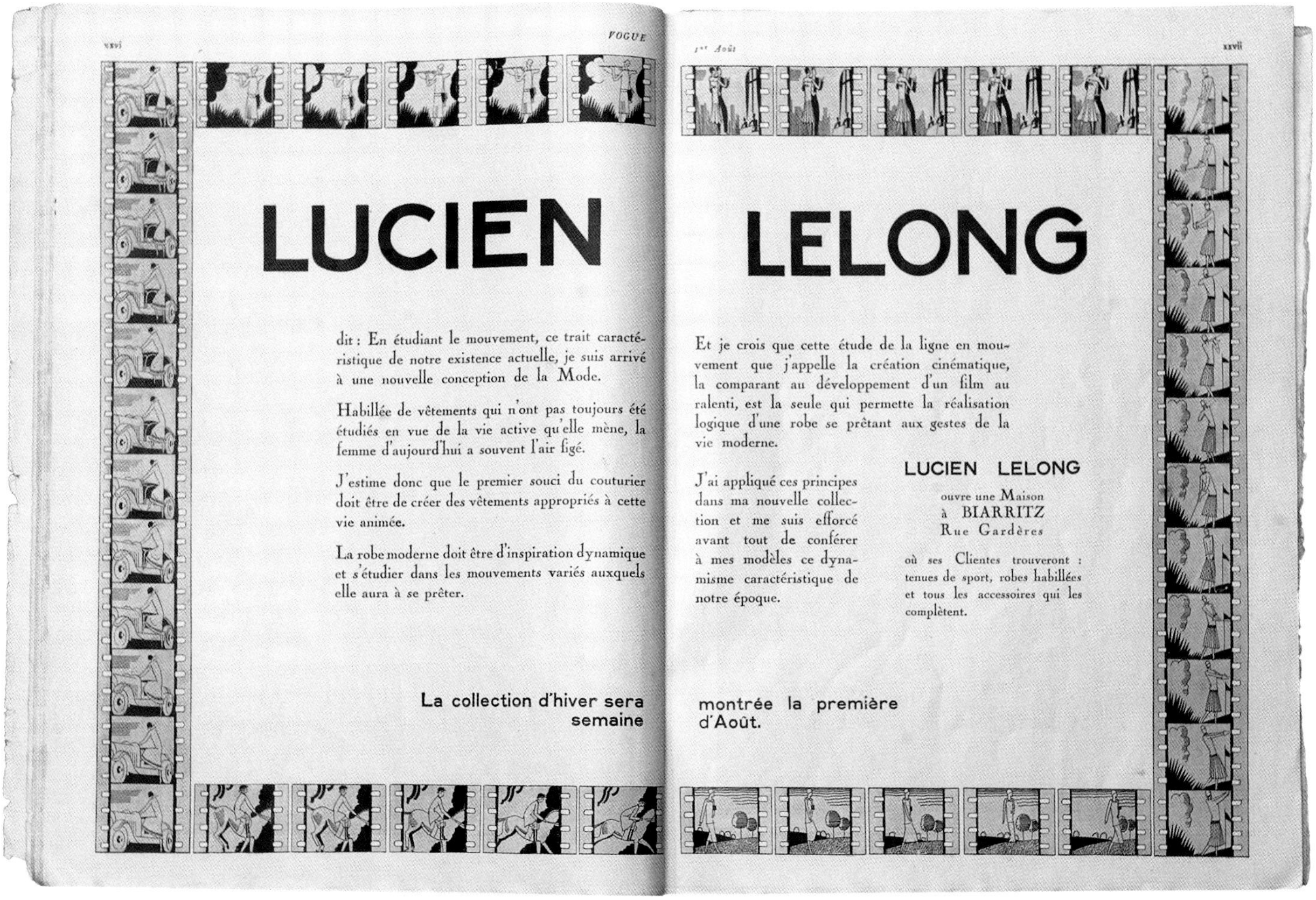

LUCIEN LELONG

dit : En étudiant le mouvement, ce trait caractéristique de notre existence actuelle, je suis arrivé
à une nouvelle conception de la Mode.

Habillée de vêtements qui n'ont pas toujours été
étudiés en vue de la vie active qu'elle mène, la
femme d'aujourd'hui a souvent l'air figé.

J'estime donc que le premier souci du couturier
doit être de créer des vêtements appropriés à cette
vie animée.

La robe moderne doit être d'inspiration dynamique
et s'étudier dans les mouvements variés auxquels
elle aura à se prêter.

Et je crois que cette étude de la ligne en mouvement que j'appelle la création cinématique,
la comparant au développement d'un film au
ralenti, est la seule qui permette la réalisation
logique d'une robe se prêtant aux gestes de la
vie moderne.

J'ai appliqué ces principes dans ma nouvelle collection et me suis efforcé avant tout de conférer
à mes modèles ce dyna-
misme caractéristique de
notre époque.

LUCIEN LELONG

ouvre une Maison
à BIARRITZ
Rue Gardères

où ses Clientes trouveront :
tenues de sport, robes habillées
et tous les accessoires qui les
complètent.

La collection d'hiver sera montrée la première
semaine d'Août.

140 (top) Lucien Lelong's announcement of his new winter collection for 1925, the 'kinetic line'. *Vogue* (France), August 1925. Musée Galliera de la Mode de la Ville de Paris. Photograph Richard Hubert Smith.

141 (above) Lucien Lelong double-page advertisement for his kinetic designs, showing a mannequin parade. *Harper's Bazar*, October 1925.

pleats and godets set into knee-length skirts intended to flare and swing in movement, which many other designers such as Doucet also used that season.[106] It is debatable whether a single designer can claim ownership of such a common dressmaking technique as a pleat or godet and Lelong's claims were inflated. Vionnet used the bias cut for similar reasons, to dress the 'supple, mobile, relaxed' body of the modern woman, with her 'free, active, emancipated movements' at work and play.[107] Furthermore, by the 1920s all designers who designed on living mannequins required the mannequin intermittently to move around during a fitting to see how the garment worked in motion.[108] Lelong's was, rather, a triumph of marketing, to boast of 'gowns in motion' just as Lucile a decade and half before had promoted 'gowns of emotion'. In 1929 Thérèse Bonney wrote:

> The modern spirit of Lelong is in evidence not so much in the interior itself which has kept its intrinsic effects as in the fine organization which shows a combination of executive ability and personal efficiency which would make Lelong a successful business man in any other field. He is the spirit of modern business. It was he who was the first to respond to the lure of advertising in the new spirit, the advertising which discounts dignity and tradition in favor of spectacular appeal and 'kinetic line'. He advertised his house in terms of movement instead of traditions.[109]

Lelong's 'campaign' is interesting precisely because it is 'spin', but spin based on an understanding of the important role of mannequins as embodiments of the abstract concepts of movement and modernity in the 1920s. Mannequins made the idea of fashion as a form of perpetual motion seem quintessentially modern. 'Vogue previews a moving silhouette of undulating lines for winter', wrote the French magazine in October 1925, 'the harmonious rhythm of the female body should henceforth no longer be ignored . . . waistlines should follow the slender flexibility of the female body. More than ever, slimness is de rigueur.'[110] So, too, were briskness and pep. *Harper's* in 1927 described the body styles of the slender mannequins that gave value to the new fashions in motion: 'a pale green sweater, striped with gray, is worn with a circular gray cape which when in motion is most effective, the brisk stride of the mannequin showing it off to advantage.'[111] Drecoll, too, wrote the magazine the year before, 'strikes a distinctly new note in sports clothes, admirably presented by a breezy looking young woman who not only presents the models but exemplifies how such clothes should be worn out of doors, and how one should move and carry oneself'.[112]

Continuing to promote his ideas for the spring 1926 collections, Lelong was interviewed by de Meyer.

> He [Lelong] says 'The spirit of the time reveals itself in the rate at which people move.' This sounds interesting, but, he admits, requires explanation. 'Assuming', he continues, 'that the pace of life changes constantly, fashion ought to follow suit, and express the spirit of such changes. To consciously capture this fleeting style is what I am striving for in my creations. The result should be what might be called "absolute style", at least momentarily absolute.'
>
> He further tells us that 'kinetic designing' is a method and not a fashion. The wearer's movement is taken into consideration, as

would be a texture, as part of a whole. Photographically speaking, kinetic creations are not designed for 'stills', but are meant for the motion-picture camera. Lelong claims that in merely trying to give expression to his theories and following kinetic principles, he has virtually given a name to present fashions and has coined the term 'kinetic styles'.[113]

An interest in the depiction of movement was by the 1920s a commonplace of visual art and had been so before the First World War.[114] What is more original, however, is Lelong's analogy between cinema and fashion that he had made in his first *Vogue* announcement (see **140**). In 1921 the film maker Jean Epstein compared the impermanence and 'momentary aesthetic' of the cinema with fashion. Beauty had speeded up, he wrote, as had fatigue, accelerating 'unstable metamorphoses'. Replacing the moribund fashion sketch, the conjunction of film and fashion created new affinities – both were moving forms with evanescent images that dated fast:

> An image cannot be durable. Scientifically, the reflex of beauty exhausts itself: the image becomes, in aging, a snapshot. . . . From autumn to spring, the aesthetic changes. One speaks of eternal canons of beauty when two consecutive Bon Marché catalogues concur in this drivel. Fashion in clothes is the most precise and best modulated appeal to voluptuousness. Film lends it certain charms, and is so faithful an image of our infatuations that, once it is five years old, seems no more agreeable to us than the magic lantern in a fair.[115]

Epstein's suggestion that film and fashion are both protean and never stand still, like Lelong's association of fashion and film, emphasised that both were time-based media. They led to the idea of speed and motion which, exemplified by the automobile with its sense of 'motoring fast' that Raymond Williams, in 1973, identified as intrinsic to twentieth-century modernity, found expression in fashion too in the 1920s.[116]

LE CONCOURS D'ÉLÉGANCE EN AUTOMOBILES

In tandem with fashion galas, the 1920s saw the development of the *concours d'élégance en automobiles*, society beauty contests in which women in luxury motor cars were awarded prizes for elegance (**142**).[117] At *Femina*'s fashion gala at La Baule in Brittany in October 1924, the fashion show was followed by a *concours d'élégance*. In the issue of *Femina* that reported it, the compelling image of a fashionable woman and her car is given a novel twist in the illustration of a car (a Torpédo sport 18 horse-power Voisin) painted to match the plaid of its driver, who has stopped to ask directions of a road-mender (**143**). The illustration accompanies an article that describes the symbiosis between woman and car when a woman is at the wheel: 'The Woman and the Automobile are made for one another . . . woman is like a privileged Centauress; she and her car are one body.'[118] The horse metaphor recalls the association of mannequins and horseflesh at the races in 1908, while the modernist grid of the plaid pattern suggests the streamlined body of modernism that Sonia Delaunay invoked when she painted a Citroën 5CV to match a coat she had designed (**144**).[119]

That these performances were watched by the American department stores is evidenced by Wanamaker's in Philadelphia, which, in 1926, temporarily installed a Packard in its fashion salon around which the store mannequins modelled (**145**). Its sign headed 'Milady's car' punned on the equivalence between a model car and a model woman: 'The Packard Improved Model – Beauty of the Boulevard – 1926.' In 1927 Lincoln cars were shown 'like Parisian modiste's parades' on a new kind of revolving stage named the 'Lincoln mannequin'. As in a fashion show, the clients reclined on a divan to watch the new colour combinations of the cars revolving in front of them like a mannequin on a stand.[120]

In their descriptions of the *concours d'élégance*, the magazines *Vogue* and *Femina* commandeered the vocabulary of fashion, so the parade of cars past the judges is a *défilé* and a car advertisement in *Vogue* in 1927 uses the term *la ligne* to equate female and mechanical elegance. *La ligne* literally means 'the line' but can also refer to the figure (as in *garder sa ligne*, to maintain one's figure). In the *Vogue* advertisement, a line drawing of a slender woman and a car is juxtaposed with the words 'a dress without lines is but a garment, a car without lines is but a vehicle, only the line creates elegance'.[121] It was this perceived equivalence that

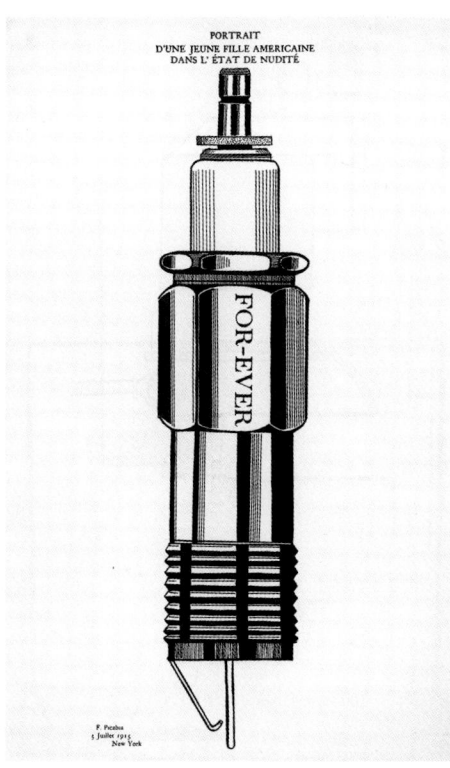

PORTRAIT
D'UNE JEUNE FILLE AMERICAINE
DANS L'ÉTAT DE NUDITÉ

FOR-EVER

146 Francis Picabia,
*Young American Woman
in a State of Nudity*, 1915.
From the magazine *291*,
nos. 5–6, July–August
1915.

underpinned the commodified sexuality of the *concours d'élégance* where mannequins, society women and motor vehicles competed in an erotic exchange between mass production and elite styling. Tag Gronberg has described the phenomenon as 'a mechanical beauty show', pointing out the elision between car bodies and women's bodies in these contests.[122] Just as, in the pre-war period, comparisons were drawn at the races between the mannequins' bodies and fine horseflesh, so in the 1920s at the *concours d'élégance* society women modelled bodies that were lean, stripped down and well maintained like a car.[123] This is what Peter Wollen has called the 'modernist body', exemplified in American *Vogue*'s comment from 1 October 1926 on the new fashions *en série*, that Chanel's little black dress was 'a Ford that all the world could wear'.[124]

Following the popularity of the Ford motor car that came off the fully automated assembly line in tens of thousands, the term 'Ford' entered the vocabulary of fashion in the 1920s to describe the dress in a collection that would sell in the millions in America.[125] From 1925 the American designer Elizabeth Hawes was employed by a Paris copy house to sketch illicitly (that is, to steal) as many designs as possible during the biannual collections. She recalled the collections at Patou:

> I was to sketch the Fords. A Ford is a dress which everyone buys. Patou decided what models were to be Fords. His showmanship was perfect and unique among the couturiers. He put Fords on six at a time . . . My job was to get all the Fords down cold . . . between Fords I surveyed the buyers . . . When a Ford appeared, all the minks and foxes [worn by the buyers] throbbed a little.[126]

The 'Ford' was a fashion business term and its industrial aesthetic connoted a particular look of serial repetition that

exemplifies how the mechanisms of fashion can 'think' to produce a mimetic body. In its capacity to visualise knowledge, the fashion body can replicate the industrial imagery of the chorus line or the streamlined and co-ordinated actions of the Taylorist body at work, as well as the mechanical female sexuality of, for example, Francis Picabia's *Young American Woman in a State of Nudity* (1915; **146**) or Duchamp's *Bride Stripped Bare by her Bachelors, Even* (1915–23). It was this look that came to dominate the scenography of fashion shows in the 1920s and that constituted a form of standardisation or rationalisation of the fashionable body.

The concept of the body as machine originated in the eighteenth century with La Mettrie's *l'homme machine* and was re-articulated in the emerging 'science' of behaviourism early in the twentieth century. Anthony Synott has argued that the modernist, mechanical body was intrinsic to behaviourism, citing John B. Watson, the founder of behaviourism, who in 1924 pointed out that 'the human body . . . is not a treasure house of mystery but a very commonsense kind of *organic* machine'. Watson referred to the individual as a body, the body as a machine and the machine as a car: 'Let us try to think of man as an assembled organic machine ready to run. We mean nothing very difficult by this. Take four wheels with tires, axles, differentials, gas engine, body; put them together and we have an automobile of sorts.' Synott argues that 'by the early twentieth century, biology, medicine, psychology and philosophy were largely agreed in their materialism: the body is all. This mechanistic construction of the body was congruent with the mechanization of society', and, after the first Model-T Fords were produced in 1908, the 'automobile transformed thinking about the body'.[127]

The commodified sexuality of the pre-war mannequins at the races whom spectators had compared to horseflesh in 1908 had morphed by the 1920s into an image of a fashionable body as stripped down, lean and polished as the bodywork of a motor vehicle. In 1931 this aesthetic appeared on stage at the Folies Bergère in *L'Usine à Folies* (the Follies Factory), a revue show inspired by Maurice Verne's 1929 book *Les Usines de plaisir* (The Pleasure Factories). Verne made the connection between revue theatre and the factory in his description of what Terri Gordon calls 'female factories engaged in the scientific fabrication of pleasure'.[128] On stage, *L'Usine à Folies* featured a modernist display called 'Chair et métal' (Flesh and Metal) that juxtaposed showgirls and futuristic wheel-works like a mid-1920s fashion illustration (see **138**).[129] When in 1926 *Harper's Bazar* wrote that 'we are only at ease in the midst of modern machinery', it demonstrated how fashion was ahead of other cultural forms in picturing the idea of the modernist body as a machine.[130]

Such a body was not, however, gender-neutral. Ideas about femininity, national identity and modernity were made visual in the early twentieth-century mannequin parade. Marlis Schweitzer argues that in the U.S.A. actresses were the vehicles that translated ideas about France to America. Unofficial fashion models and style arbiters, they demonstrated the appropriate way to wear and move in the new French styles that were generally considered freakish: 'Dressed in Paris fashion their bodies became public stages for dramatizing a series of collisions between foreign and domestic markets; between the private world of the home and the public world of the city street; and between nineteenth-century modernity and twentieth-century modernity.'[131] In France, mannequins embodied these contradictions. Up to the First World War, fashion show line-ups had rationalised the body even where the fashion designs remained Art Nouveau in style. Proto-modernist from its inception, even before it harnessed the modernist aesthetics of the 1920s, it standardised the female body through the visual devices of mirroring, uniforms, diet, modelling techniques, pose and scenography.

In the 1920s the fashion show drew on the artistic language of modernism to further these aims, mimicking the rational body of modernist art and design, from Duchamp to the Bauhaus. Its imagery was a visual analogue of contemporary management and business practices; it made these underlying structures intelligible in the cultural sphere, thus picturing the means of production in a representation geared ostensibly towards consumption. Yet, despite the visual clarity and modernist idiom of the mannequin parade, it revealed a set of paradoxes, or contradictions, which pictured those of modernity. These circulated above all round the image of the mannequin, both an objectified doll with an 'industrial smile' and a new type of independent career woman, distinct from the actress or chorus girl.

In the *concours d'élégance* the reified female body fused organic and mechanical elements. Business and poetry came together in the ambiguous figure of the fashion mannequin, as fears about increasing mechanisation and the changing role of women were projected onto her. While her languid poses suggested luxurious consumption, the mechanical exactitude of her gestures, repeated a hundred times a day, each as if for the first time, hinted at the industrial underpinnings of her business and provided a potent metaphor for the alienating quality of modern industrial processes. In the mannequin parade, two kinds of alienation converged: the alienation of the worker in the production line described by Karl Marx in the nineteenth century, with the alienated and alienating form of the early twentieth-century New Woman so feared by many of her contemporaries.

THE MANNE -QUIN

ARCHITECTURE
FACTORIES OF ELEGANCE

147 Scene from an album of fifty-one photographs of the firm of Worth in 1927. No. 14: a saleswoman and client in front of a large cheval mirror. See following pages for other examples from the album. © Victoria and Albert Museum, London.

The architectural spaces of the couture houses mirrored their commercial structure and in a few cases their interiors survive today as a reminder of the activities they witnessed in the past. At Chanel in the rue Cambon in Paris, the new collections are still made in the old ateliers on the upper storeys. The door to the third-floor design studio still bears the legend it bore when Coco Chanel worked there: 'Mademoiselle. Privé'. Unaltered too is the mirrored panel on the second-floor landing that opens into the apartment where, during the daytime, she ate, saw friends, met journalists and worked when not in the studio. There her décor, knick-knacks and Coromandel screens are preserved intact in the apartment that required neither bathroom nor bedroom because 'Mademoiselle' slept up the road at the Ritz Hotel. On the first floor, the grand modelling salon in which the early shows took place retains its architectural proportions if not its original décor. The staircase leading up to the second floor remains as it was, however, in the days when Chanel would sit on the landing looking down on the fashion shows in the salon below.

Chanel established her firm in these premises in 1921 and extensively refurbished them over three floors in 1928. The building is a quintessential 'place of memory' in the sense used by the French historian Pierre Nora in his magisterial survey of French culture and identity, *Lieux de mémoire* (1984–92), translated as *Realms of Memory: Rethinking the French Past*.[1] In his foreword to the first volume, Lawrence Kritzman observes that Nora's project is 'an attempt to read the signs of culture in places, objects and images that are marked by the past and remembered in the vicissitudes of contemporary consciousness.'[2] Nora himself, in his preface to the English-language edition, described his original motivation to study 'national feeling not in the traditional thematic or chronological manner but instead by analysing the places in which the collective heritage of France was crystallized, the principal *lieux*, in all senses of the word, in which collective memory was rooted, in order to create a vast topology of French symbolism'. The *lieux* are 'places, sites, causes [that are] material, symbolic, and functional'[3] – all the characteristics of a Parisian couture house. Far from grandiose, however, these *lieux*, or realms of memory, may also be marginal and fragmented. Nora found them where what he called the

milieux de mémoire were gone and little else remained. This approach is particularly fruitful for the fashion historian, who often finds that, despite the symbolic capital of French fashion, its material traces and business records are scant.

Nora's method was to excavate the remnants of national myths and symbols through an archaeology of fragments that consist of 'spaces, gestures, images and objects.'[4] If the surviving house of Chanel is one such site of memory, another is a photographic album documenting the house of Worth from 1927. Its images (more than fifty photographs) show both spaces and gestures: the interior arrangement and disposition of its rooms and their population by the entire workforce, from cooks to

mannequins, seamstresses to office workers, and from the director of the firm to the chauffeur (**147–62**). There are no records to suggest why or how the album came into being but it appears to have been made with the full consent of the house and constitutes an unusually thorough document of its activities. Its coverage of all aspects of a working couture firm, much at odds with the publicists' version of haute couture, suggests that it was probably made as an internal record and not for public dissemination. Furthermore, its photographs exemplify the way in which, as Nora suggested, images are important historical sources that a previous generation might have disregarded: 'ours is an intensely retinal and powerfully televisual memory. We can link the acclaimed "return of the narrative" evident in recent historical writing and the omnipotence of imagery and cinema in contemporary culture.'[5] Nora linked usage of the archival fragment, such as these images from the Worth archive that are unanchored by any written documentation, to the fragmented experience of life today. He argued that the fragment feels more 'real' as a mode of history-writing: the archive consists of fragments that are

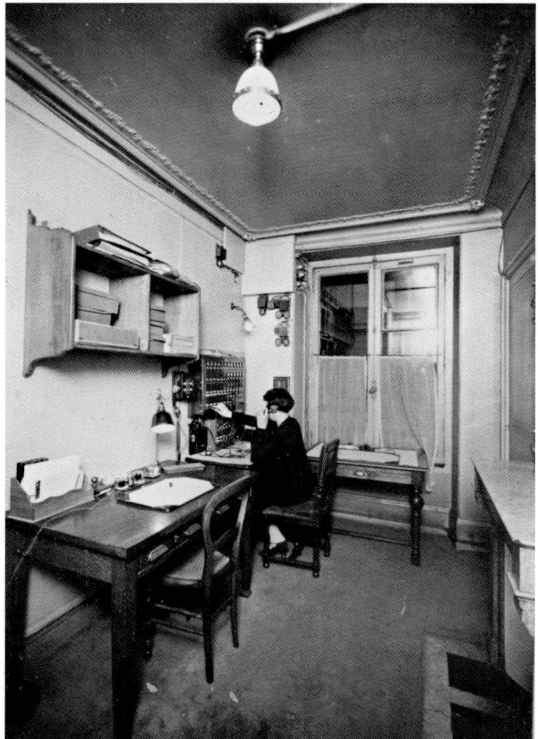

150 (top left) No. 35: staff arriving at the stockroom entrance (*la manutention*).

151 (above left) No. 16: office workers in *l'administration*.

152 (left) No. 27: telephonist.

153 (top right) No. 19: stockroom, with mannequin, designer and fitter in front of a three-faced mirror.

154 (above right) No. 34: wrapping atelier in the basement.

155 (facing page top left) No. 50: a sewing atelier.

156 (facing page centre left) No. 29: sketchers in top-floor atelier with good natural daylight.

157 (facing page bottom left) No. 53: preparing lunch in the kitchens.

158 (facing page top right) No. 30: furriers in fur atelier.

159 (facing page centre right) No. 37: a sewing atelier.

160 (facing page bottom left) No. 51: seamstresses' refectory at lunchtime.

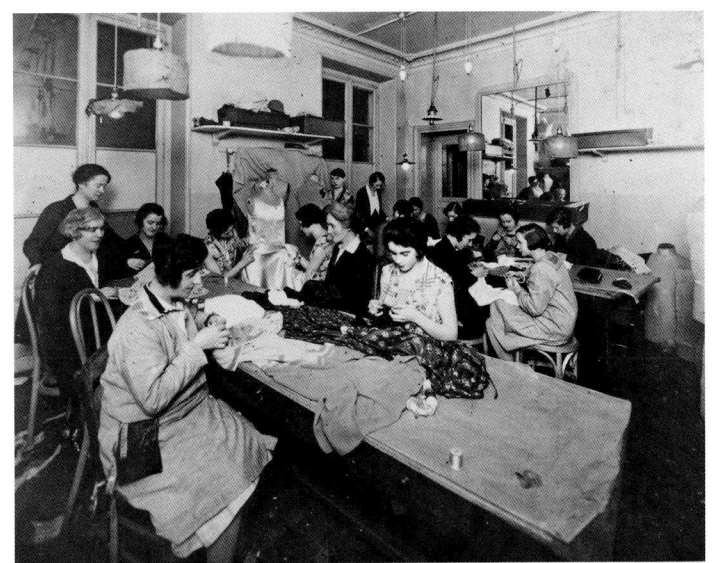

'shards of the past delivered to us by so many micro-histories'.[6]

The house of Worth closed in 1956 and its interior no longer survives but what the micro-history of the Worth album of 1927 reveals is the extensive backstage life of an industry that only ever promoted its front-of-house activities and was often extremely secretive about life behind the scenes. The difference between the two was immense. Worth's album starts with the salons and the boutique and gradually moves backstage to record the spaces and activities of the workrooms, studios, stores and offices. In was in these spaces that a dress began its life, moving over a period of a week from backstage production to front-of-house sales and dissemination. Through both parts of the house ran the leitmotifs of doubling, repetition and replication, yet each part was profoundly different from the other. The fashion show was the bridge between them and the mannequin one of the few privileged employees permitted to cross it.

BACKSTAGE: THE ATELIER SYSTEM

An illustration of 1902 (**163**) shows fashionable women and their carriages in the rue de la Paix from five to seven o'clock, the fashionable time for visiting one's couturier. Front of house, all was theatre: 'the curtain rises, the show begins'.[7] Backstage, there existed a vast and complex mechanism to support it, invisible to the clients. A typical large couture house might seem to consist of a small number of salons but in reality it occupied an entire building where nearly eight hundred women were in a perpetual foment of work, although the client was led to believe by her saleswoman that, behind the décor, there was but a tiny number of workers 'labouring exclusively for her'.[8] The suggestion of exclusivity was bolstered by handwritten invitations, ostensibly from the couturier himself to the private clients (**164**). Were the client miraculously permitted backstage, however, wrote the art

critic of *Le Figaro,* Arsène Alexandre, in his meticulously researched *Les Reines de l'aiguille* of 1902, 'she would be absolutely terrified, at first, by the formidable appearance of the place'.[9] After a backstage tour of all five floors of Redfern's entire organisation in 1901, another journalist wrote: 'I assure you that it is unbelievable how much there is in this factory, for it is a veritable factory of elegance'.[10]

It was in these 'factories of elegance' that the industrial aesthetic of the early fashion shows developed. The pattern-making tendency of the show can, in turn, be mapped back onto the industrial organisation of the fashion business. As a French magazine reported in 1924, it was above all an industrial business, a singular world of which some aspects touched on art and fantasy while others were confined to finance and industry: 'it is harshly practical and savagely industrious'.[11] Being a designer was far from the principal activity of a director of a couture house. Even in the nineteenth century Worth, the so-called 'father of haute couture', did not design himself but, over 1860–65, bought in designs from what Françoise Tétart-Vittu has called 'freelance industrial fashion illustrators' such as Charles Pilatte, Ernest Leduc, Robin, Leray and Paulin; in this respect Worth was a fairly typical couturier.[12] In the early twentieth century, many successful couturiers were not themselves designers, including Doucet, Patou and Lelong, though several had a strong sense of style. Others, such as Vionnet and Poiret, undoubtedly were designers. Vionnet was one of the few who had worked her way up through the apprenticeship system as a young girl and therefore understood cut and construction. She had worked for Kate Reilly in London and Doucet and Callot Soeurs in Paris before opening her own house in 1912. Poiret started out selling sketches freelance, including to Doucet, and then went to work as an employee at Worth and Doucet before opening his own house. At many houses, however, designs were either bought in from freelances or done in-house by the dressmakers (*premières d'atelier*) and designers (*modélistes*). Often the *premières* or *modélistes* were the real designers behind the house name. Yet in the 1920s

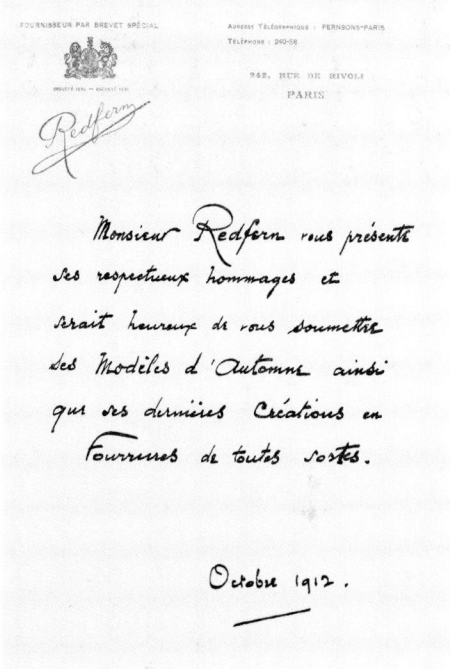

couturiers affected to ignore their own history and began
to lament the industrial nature of their business as if this
were a new phenomenon. In an interview of 1923 one
anonymous couturier complained that 'the haute couturier
(who is an artist) must also be a company director, a bank
manager, a factory owner'.[13] Another, in 1927, wrote:

> Formerly, the head of a great couture firm was a man used to
> handling fabrics and imagining garments. Today, he is much more
> of a *businessman* than a designer of frivolous slips. . . . That is why
> the grand couturier – instead of being an artist surrounded by
> samples creating beauty with fairytale ease – is no more than a
> slightly bald administrator in pince nez, installed in a commercial
> office surrounded by numbers, international tariffs and circulars.[14]

Indeed, one of the photographs from the Worth album (see
161) shows a slightly balding Jean-Charles Worth at his
desk rather than in the design studio.

The nameless couturier interviewed in 1923 says:
'*My* trade? It's in America that I learnt it best, from the
big automobile manufacturer Ford. I apply industrial
methods'.[15] He goes on to describe his working day which
starts at 8.30 am. All morning at fifteen-minute intervals he
is briefed by his departmental heads, with the assistance of
graphs, in a statement that recalls Patou's use of graphs:

My entire house is in graphs. I have my staff show them to me each
day: curves showing orders, deliveries, money out, money in,
proportion of day dresses, evening dresses, curves showing the
success of each model, curves showing sales in France and in the
different foreign countries, comparisons with the same month in
previous years, proportion of old and new clients, staffing
situation.

His afternoon is spent reading French, American and
English newspapers; the social columns give him
information about his clients, the financial pages about the
world economy. Luckily, he says, he has a good memory,
like his father. (This suggests that he may have been Worth,
or even Doucet, rather than Patou or Lelong, both of
whom were devoted to progressive American business
methods but neither of whom followed directly in their
father's footsteps.) There are also the files he keeps, not just
of the clients he already has but of future clients 'that we
must have'. In ten years, he has collected the names of
seventy thousand women from all over the world 'that have,
for us, their own physiognomy and personality'.[16] In this
interview, the couturier appears to feel the pressure of
modern commercial life keenly, as he struggles to keep tabs
on everyone and everything.

In 1927 Paul Reboux attributed the couturier's lapse from art into industry to the 'severity of our times' which compelled him to focus on debt recovery, customs officials and the treasury.[17] In reality it had been so since the nineteenth century.[18] Once dressmakers, principally Worth, began to present a series of models prepared in advance to suit the various circumstances of society life, as opposed to making dresses to order for clients, there followed a 'systemisation of dress'.[19] As the houses grew in size their organisation had to become more bureaucratic and labour more divided and specialised. Haute couture was called a luxury industry but it was no less an industry for that.[20]

By 1902, at least three of the rue de la Paix houses were visited by three thousand women at the height of the season.[21] Alexandre pursues the industrial metaphor by describing the house as a hive, full of industrious workers, and calls the ensemble a mechanism (*mécanisme*, which also means clockwork) that rested on 'a division of labour pushed to the extreme and admirably regulated'.[22] Similarly, in 1910, L. Roger-Milès, another art critic at *Le Figaro* who wrote an exhaustive book on Parisian haute couture, called it 'a very complex organism' and an 'industrial centre' with each of its parts strictly defined and regulated.[23]

These writers and interviewees were referring to the atelier system of haute couture production. The atelier (workroom) was a kind of organic, semi-autonomous cell, repeated ten to fifteen times throughout the house.[24] There were different ateliers, often several floors apart, for cutting out patterns, for sewing skirts, bodices and sleeves, for tailoring and drapery, for embroidery and trimmings, for sketching and photography (in the attics) and for wrapping and deliveries (in the basements).[25] Different aspects of the work were kept strictly segregated in different parts of the building. It was the job of the *arpètes*, or errand girls, many as young as twelve, to ferry dockets, samples, goods and pattern-pieces between rooms, like a human conveyor-belt or, as Alexandre wrote, like young bees in perpetual flight feeding the worker bees.[26] All around them were pools of electric light and the tinkling of the telephone.[27] There were also offices, stockrooms and refectories where meals were taken in two to five separate sittings, depending on the size of the house (see **151**, **153** and **160**).[28] From the formidably well-ordered stockrooms all fabrics taken out were carefully logged by a desk clerk (**165**); in the offices, the manu-facturing cost of every single dress, including materials and labour, was recorded in a ledger alongside all the client's personal details; Alexandre called the ledgers the houses' 'books of heraldry'.[29]

In the ateliers, each type of sewing had its especially trained seamstresses named after their function: *jupière*, *corsagière*, *manchière* (literally, skirt-maker, bodice-maker, sleeve-maker (**166**, and see **155** and **159**).[30] Other specialist workers made only buttonholes or trimmings. Each atelier had a strict internal hierarchy with a *première* who might be in charge of as many as thirty to forty women below her.[31] So specialised were couture apprenticeships that by the age of sixteen a girl could be a fully trained *jupière*, *corsagière* or even *manchière*.[32] No single worker had the knowledge or skills to create an entire dress nor did she ever do so, let alone move between the different ateliers, each of which had its *première* in charge of the *petites mains*, as the lowest rank of seamstresses above the apprentices were called.[33] Instead, the dress parts were moved from room to room and worked on separately. Only a few employees ever saw the completed dress.[34] This strict division of labour not only facilitated production but also militated against staff piracy.

Labour was seasonal: immediately the new collection had been made and shown, the majority of the workforce was laid off and the backstage frenzy of a busy couture house stilled as it moved into the 'dead season'. Hardly had the presentation of the biannual buyers' shows finished, when three quarters of the staff would be formally dismissed.[35] The fashion show thus represented the apotheosis of busy productivity in the annual rhythms of a couture house, after which it would effectively work at a quarter its capacity until about a month or more before the next collections. October and April–May were particularly busy months in which the seasonal staff were engaged and the houses hummed with activity. The autumn collections were the major ones and, after the houses closed for the summer season, work continued on these throughout August.[36] Mid-January to mid-March and mid-July to mid-September were the biannual 'dead seasons' for houses that only made for private clients but they were busy times in the houses that were preparing collections to show to the foreign buyers in August and February, where the mannequins would continue in employment in the period leading up to the collection.[37] Among the dressmaking staff, couturiers tended to retain the *premières mains* in their employ during the dead season but to lay off the *secondes mains* and *petites mains* who had to manage with these periods of unemployment.[38] At Patou, only 300 of the 1300 staff were permanent: the saleswomen, stockroom staff and heads of ateliers.[39] A house employing 3000 staff would be down to no more than 40 in the dead season; but the *petites mains* who worked for couture in the season might find employment in the wholesale trade at other times of year. The high seasons lasted one to three months, where three to four hours of overtime were common; in the low or dead season, under-employment prevailed. Three quarters of the

165 (above left) Stock-room in a couture house, 1902. Illustration by François Courboin, from Arsène Alexandre, *Les Reines de l'aiguille*, Paris, 1902. Spencer Collection, New York Public Library, Astor, Lenox and Tilden Foundations.

166 (above centre) Hand sewing in the corsages atelier, 1902. Illustration by François Courboin from Arsène Alexandre, *Les Reines de l'aiguille*, Paris, 1902. Spencer Collection, New York Public Library, Astor, Lenox and Tilden Foundations.

167 (above right) Modelling to private clients in a couture salon, 1902. Illustration by François Courboin, from Arsène Alexandre, *Les Reines de l'aiguille*, Paris, 1902. Spencer Collection, New York Public Library, Astor, Lenox and Tilden Foundations.

clothing workforce was female. Women who wanted to work in the low season had to work late into the night with no overtime pay. This situation prevailed in the 1890s when consumer demand came from both society women who wanted their ballgowns for the next day and foreign buyers who 'came twice yearly, placed large orders, and insisted on rapid delivery'.[40]

These biannual shows set the tempo for the alternating rhythms of employment and unemployment. The period leading up to the show was marked by frenzied activity and the show was also the moment when the model dress moved onto the next stage of its existence front of house. A buyer or client at the shows saw nothing of the backstage activity, however; she knew only her mannequin and her saleswoman.[41] Contemporaries perceived the backstage operation as a somewhat sinister organism, at once life-like and deathly. Mechanical, huge and trundling, the couture house seemed to have a life of its own yet to be composed of human parts, each person functioning as a tiny cog in an enormous machine. Alexandre describes how, were the private client allowed backstage at the moment when all the parts of the dress are magically assembled, like a dismembered enchanter in a fairy story putting himself back together, she would admire the mathematical way in which this great machine with fifteen hundred arms was regulated to complete as complex an operation as the execution of a costume.[42] In this image of production, the house is a human machine powered by arm movements, and the figure of a woman is dismembered and spread through its workrooms in the form of the garment pieces – sleeves, bodices, skirts. The body, in production, is fragmented as the parts are mapped onto the workspaces of the house. At the moment of potential consumption, it comes together; the body is made whole when the dress is ready to be modelled to the client (**167**). Alexandre's account suggests a form of commodity fetishism in which organic and mechanical movement have switched, so that the living mannequin resembles the inanimate mannequin

from which she takes her name, while the uncanny (*unheimlich*) *maison de couture* (a house but not a home) is a machine or an organism with between 1400 and 6000 human arms. The house is animated only because the human workers have become mechanical, with their divided and regulated labour dispersed through its rooms.

In this imagery the house is pictured as a body, in the sense discussed by the sociologist John O'Neill, who argues that the capacity of individuals and social groups to think anthropomorphically allows them to 'think bodies' through society and simultaneously to 'think society' through bodies.[43] For O'Neill, the body of consumer culture cannot be separated from the body politic and from the economy that both creates its appetites and, sometimes, feeds them, because 'commodities are good for thinking' as well as 'good for consuming'.[44] In the early twentieth-century couture house, a place of both production and sales, bodies and commodities appeared to exchange characteristics, as the body itself was mapped onto the house through its backstage production and that process replicated again on the bodies of the mannequins and their reflections in the mirrored walls of the modelling salons. For, once in the salons, the single figure of the mannequin was replicated in the mirrors like a series of 'repeated originals', as Vionnet was to call the dresses she licensed for U.S. sale in the 1920s,[45] invoking the *sosies* or multiples of the nineteenth century.

This typical form of haute couture production anticipated Henry Ford's first moving assembly line by some decades and it suggests an industrial model of production even though the individual skills required in each atelier were craft skills, often at a high level. Roubaud wrote that 'in this entire silent factory, there is no steel connecting rod, no fly-wheel, no conveyor belt . . . only hands'.[46] In fact, in France, hand-making was cheaper than machine-making in many instances.[47] The use of human cogs, however, in the form of the apprentices who moved between ateliers, and the strict division of labour between ateliers, suggest not only Fordism but also a kind of Taylorist efficiency even before Taylorism became popular in France. This backstage regulation extended to the mannequin's performance front of house, where her repetitive and stylised gestures in the parade incorporated her as a living part of the machinery of the couture house, a huge, co-ordinated mansion of regulated and divided labour, just as the calibrated and standardised movements of the Taylorist worker made him a mere cog in the scientific management of the workplace.

The architectural setting for the science of the smile and the calibration of desire was a kind of box of tricks, however. Madeleine Vionnet explained the preponderance of glass, white emulsion paint and light in her workrooms: 'I want my staff to work in transparency', she told Georges Le Fèvre for his 1929 book on the couture trade. To that end she employed two full-time painters whose job it was constantly to renew the walls with coats of emulsion. 'The walls here are not allowed to get old', commented Le Fèvre, 'Even the architecture of the building has a false front, like a secret box. You open a door, go through it, close it, and it is no longer the same door'. He meant the door between the ateliers where the dresses were made and the salon where they were modelled. Ornately panelled and carved on one side, plainly painted with Ripolin house-paint on the other, the door concealed backstage production from front-of-house sales. 'The eye is a little surprised, as in the theatre, at the brusque change of atmosphere. A large couture house is based on two principles, Fantasy and Profit. All problems are resolved according to these two elements', explained Le Fèvre.[48] There was no transparency at this juncture. The door was a material metaphor for the illusion and trickery on which haute couture depended to sustain itself. In its contrasting surfaces, one plain and one embellished, the back-to-back structures of manufacturing and sales were made literal. The mannequins negotiated this magic box as they crossed back and forth through the doorway leading to the hall of mirrors that was the salon.

From behind the scenes to the moment of revelation in the fashion show, the passage of the model – and the mannequin – was mirrored by the contrast between the functional, backstage working areas of the house and the salons. Erving Goffman's idea of the dramaturgy of everyday life provides a model of the relationship between the two halves. Goffman contrasted back and front regions: the former are spaces for 'the presentation of idealized performances' (such as the mannequins'), whereas in the backstage regions the 'dirty work' and 'long tedious hours of lonely labor' (the *petites mains*), on which the front region depends, take place.[49] The door between them marked the boundary, the corridor leading to it a liminal space of transition (see **148** and **149**).[50]

In 1929, Le Fèvre differentiated the two parts of the house as sales and fantasy. Nancy Troy has invoked David Chaney's phrase, 'the dramaturgy of interaction in buying and selling',[51] a concept that perfectly 'fits' the fashion show, with its theatrical nature that may either veil or disguise the commercial underpinnings and economic function of the theatrical event. The fashion house is built on profits and sells itself on dreams: in the fashion show they collided. Just as Siegfried Kracauer argued in 1927 that the chorus line of the same period symbolically pictured the industrial production line, so, in couture, the governing principles of the business were made visible through the structure and decoration of the building itself.

At every stage of the garment's progress through the house and beyond, economic values were rationalised and pictured through the body in the way its image was fragmented and distributed throughout the built space. The gestures of the living mannequin signalled the hours of the fashion calendar, from backstage modelling as the collections were being designed to front-of-house posing at the biannual openings. Such gestures both produced and enacted the space of the couture house, for it is in this way, as Henri Lefebvre argued, that the body has left its traces in built spaces.[52] He further argued that in its '*long history*' space became social space, not only predicated on a human measure but also imbued with human social relations so that space became produced as 'a set of relations and forms' and networks.[53] It is in this sense that the nineteenth- and twentieth-century couture house, with its strict divisions and classifications of labour, and of the realms of production and consumption, can be understood, marked by the industrial rhythms of the labouring body of fashion. For the couture house replicated what Lefebvre described as 'a fragmented body, represented by images, by words, and traded retail'.[54]

FROM THE ATELIERS TO THE SALONS

Lefebvre argued that social relationships are embedded in social space and his description of the operations of power on architectural space reads like a description of the spatial organisation of the French *maison de couture*, and in particular of the atelier system: 'The dominant tendency fragments space and cuts it up into pieces. It enumerates the things, the various objects, that space contains. Specialisations divide space among them and act upon its truncated parts, setting up mental barriers and practico-

168 The mannequins' *cabine* at Paquin in 1910. There is a three-faced mirror attached to the wall behind the mannequins. From L. Roger-Milès, *Les Créateurs de la mode*, 1910. Musée Galliera de la Mode de la Ville de Paris. Photograph Richard Hubert Smith.

social frontiers'.[55] In the couture house, the commercial structure of the backstage area was mirrored in the layout of its rooms. It required a strict division of labour that was mapped onto both the system of garment production and the bodies of the workers, as described earlier. The 'divide-and-rule' of dress production through the generation of numerous parts was made visible again front of house. There the fashion shows took place on modelling stages or in salons carpeted from wall to wall in velvet; in the bright electric lights and reflective mirrors, the mannequin's body was infinitely replicated, a reflection, too, of the way the dress itself – if successful – would be multiplied in the factories and workshops of America and Europe. And the reflection into infinity represented not only the future multiplication of the garment through space but also the multiplicaton of the mannequin through society as a femine ideal.

In cautioning against a semiotic reading of social space and the human traces left in it as a simple code that can be cracked, Lefebvre argued instead for the complexity and muddle of a social space produced as it is lived by its inhabitants. Such spaces cannot be read clearly and unequivocally, he wrote, unless they are 'a cheat, the most truculent of spaces', because the operation of social and economic powers that produce the space deliberately obfuscate its meanings.[56] Such obfuscation was to be found not only in the front-of-house theatrical effects and mirrored illusions but also in the backstage apparatus of professional modelling, where the mannequins occupied a dedicated room, the *cabine* (**168**), a space which later in the

century gave its name to the collective group of mannequins in a specific house. There they gossiped, read novels, chatted and played cards, painted their nails and sewed, surrounded by mirrors, make-up and discarded clothes, until they were called on to model.[57] From the *cabine* came 'the brouhaha of rapid voices, young, busy or gay, chattering like birds in an aviary'. Yet when they modelled in the salon they fell silent, except to enunciate the name and price of a dress when asked.[58] In the salon, only the client could ever be in a hurry, or have a *crise de nerfs* (a moment of hysteria). The mannequins, by contrast, remained supernaturally calm and measured in their pace and gestures. For the saleswomen, too, 'the smile is de rigueur, while the laugh is strictly prohibited'.[59] The mannequins' calm belied the frenzy backstage as *premières* and *vendeuses* screeched orders and junior staff ran here and there to produce the right garments for the clients in the salon.[60]

In the months before a collection, the mannequins were employed to work as what today are called 'fit models', standing for long hours while dresses were fitted on them. Louis Roubaud described how they gave life to the dresses: 'In the cabine, twenty living bodies multiplied in the mirrors will lend the inert dresses the movements of their hips, the breath in their chests, the beating of their hearts'.[61] There were twenty mannequins employed at Vionnet and in the month leading up to the collection they were used more and more in fittings in the ateliers before they showed the finished collection in the salon.[62] Le Fèvre describes how, towards the end of the month the first *toiles*

169 (above left) The main salon at Vionnet in 1924, with a line of mannequins waiting to emerge into the room. The salon has a Lalique glass ceiling and frieze. From *La Renaissance de l'art français et des industries de luxe*, June 1924. In October 1924 Adolphe de Meyer wrote in his *Harper's Bazar* column: 'It is only very recently that there have been any drawings or photographs of the interior of the Maison Vionnet. The house itself is remarkable for its atmosphere of new feeling and modern design. The walls, the floors and the simple modern furniture are in tones of gray that form a perfectly neutral background for the Vionnet collection. Madame Vionnet prefers modern interiors to the old French taste. The establishment that forms a background for the immensely modern and youthful clothes is not reminiscent of other days.' Musée Galliera de la Mode de la Ville de Paris. Photograph Richard Hubert Smith.

170 (above right) The Vionnet mannequin has come through the central arched doorway by Lalique and descends the shallow flight of steps into the large salon. *Harper's Bazar*, October 1927. Photograph Baron Adolphe de Meyer.

(prototypes in unbleached calico) start to come down from the ateliers. 'They are viewed on living mannequins . . . But these phantoms need animating'.[63] Next, he writes, the monochrome vision must be brought to life by choosing fabrics and trimmings for the dress. It was not only the costumes but also the mannequins who came to life over a month: from the endless hours of standing still as dummies in the ateliers while garments were pinned, cut and altered on them, they progressed to the fluid and professional modelling techniques they employed in the salons at showtime. This oscillation between stasis and movement characterised not only the mannequins' historical evolution from a fashion doll to a living doll, or *mannequin vivant*, but also their modelling styles of alternate walking and posing. Le Fèvre describes the moment before the show, with all the buyers waiting expectantly in the salon. The door to the mannequins' *cabine* remains closed; on one side the chatter and cigar smoke intensifies, on the other Ginette is looking for her lipstick and powder puff. Her colleagues push her gently by the shoulders, the door opens, the mannequin slowly descends the three marble steps (**169** and **170**). 'There is total, brusque silence. A big buyer from Cleveland takes his cigar out of his mouth and murmurs, "Lovely!" The dress is born.'[64]

The dress that started life dispersed through the ateliers in bits and pieces finally comes to life in the gaze of the buyer. Commentators including Alexandre, Roger-Milès and Le Fèvre use fairy-tale language and uncanny imagery to discuss the way the dress is called into existence: ghostly toiles require animation, dress parts are magically assembled and the final 'vision and kaleidoscopic sensation' eclipses the long, hard task of making the dress.[65] The dress was no sooner born than it began to multiply again. Roubaud described it as 'this dress which within a few weeks had had a thousand existences among a thousand distant young women in America'.[66] After the important buyer from Cleveland had placed his order, the dress became the foundation for the manufacture of hundreds, even thousands, of copies in American factories. For, as one French analyst in 1932 described the fashion show, it opened a floodgate to the world: 'The first mannequin advances: here is "la mode". It is an event. An event that sets in motion a thousand pencils, a thousand languages, it gives flight to a thousand cables and feeds a thousand headlines. Berlin, New York, London and Rome await what Paris has authorised.'[67]

DÉCORS, MIRRORS AND MULTIPLICATION

At showtime the gowns were modelled on the first floor, in a principal salon that in turn led off to a suite of four or five linked rooms through which the mannequins walked. Unlike the cramped, plain backstage areas, salons were usually decorated in the style of Louis XV or XVI or, less frequently, the Empire. Typically, the gold and white salons featured *boiseries* (wood panelling), inset mirrors and plate-glass windows; furniture consisted of the gilt chairs that are

171 Semi-circular modelling stage installed at Lucien Lelong at 16 avenue Matignon in 1923, inaugurated at a press show with a speech by Colette. The stage had up-to-the-minute stage lighting to replicate both sunlight and night-time effects. This illustration is an accurate representation of the room, except that the stage had three steps not two. It was positioned at the end of a long, rectangular salon with tall windows all along the right-hand wall alternating with large mirrors in the same size and shape (just seen, though slightly inaccurately represented, in **141**). The mirrors reflected the stage to the spectators seated on chairs facing it. From *Femina*, March 1924. Musée Galliera de la Mode de la Ville de Paris. Photograph Richard Hubert Smith.

still provided for fashion show audiences today, marquetry tables and velvet divans, but no ornaments and pictures to draw the eye away from the display of fashion. Draperies and carpets were in expensive fabrics in neutral colours such as dove grey so as not to interfere with the dress colours being modelled. The inner curtains might be of lace custom-made for the house.[68] These styles of décor remained unchanged after the First World War even when modernists such as Patou installed modern interiors in their own homes. Nearly all couture houses continued to be decorated in pre-war styles: 'lofty grey and gold rooms' at Doeuillet and 'cream and gold with great brocaded armchairs for the buyers' at Martial et Armand, both in the place Vendôme.[69] The modernist interiors of Vionnet, Louiseboulanger and Chanel were in the minority.

Couturiers used theatrical devices, as described earlier, including professional stage lighting, artfully positioned mirrors and, often, actual stages. The use of dazzling lighting to show clothes in the setting in which they were designed to be worn had been pioneered by Worth in the nineteenth century who, when displaying ballgowns on his mannequins, showed them in a blaze of lighting, far in excess of the usual salon lighting, to recreate the effects of ballroom lighting.[70] Lucile's Paris stage was fitted with stage lighting and, during shows, would suddenly be

transformed by warm and dazzling coloured lights, emerald greens and amethyst purples, shortly followed by a mannequin, as if produced by a magician, wrote a journalist.[71] To describe these fairy-tale worlds, journalists often had recourse to fairy-tale language and used the metaphors of magic, ghosts and the popular theatre tradition of *féeries*, a genre of stage play that had been updated for film by the film-maker Georges Méliès, who specialised in magical transformations on film.[72] Like stage magic or film, fashion presentations had the power to reverse the seasons and swap day for night. In 1918 Melnotte-Simonin, previously of Maison Poiret, opened in Paris, with 'a remarkable initiative: he installed a little stage with a little park so that he could present his collections in an appropriate décor: it was thus that in January he presented his collections in a summer décor and in July his winter gowns in a winter décor'.[73] In 1923 Lelong installed a semi-circular modelling stage with up-to-the-minute stage lighting that replicated both sunshine and night-time effects and received wide press coverage.[74] An illlustration in *Femina* (**171**) depicts its inauguration at a press show, with speeches by Lelong, Colette and members of the American press.[75]

By the late 1920s stages equipped with powerful stage lights that had been pioneered by Beer and Lucile in the

8
AUDIENCES
THE COMMERCE
OF THE LOOK

JE FAIS
DES TAILLEURS ANGLAIS
RUE DE LA PAIX..
QUOI DE PLUS CHIC
ET DE PLUS
PARISIEN

ELLIS REED
13, RUE DE LA PAIX

186 Buyer's card from
Ellis Reed, Toronto,
announcing the arrival
of the new Paris
fashions in Toronto.
Paris, Bibliothèque
Forney.

If the fashion show was a form of theatre, the mannequin
was its spectacular star. Why, then, move the scrutiny to her
various audiences, as this chapter does? Why turn the gaze
180 degrees back on itself, to think about spectatorship in
1900 or 1914, and then again in the 1920s? Why consider
the act of looking? The answer is that looking at the
onlookers reveals something that cannot be seen in an
analysis of the show alone: the economy of the gaze, and
the commerce of the look, which form the underlying
structure of the spectacle.

Not only this. Fashion shows were unique in having a
high proportion of women in their audiences. The first
private clients were women, even in the mid-nineteenth
century. Trade buyers were of both sexes and, as the show
developed for their benefit between 1900 and 1930, the
proportion of female to male buyers greatly increased. The
existence of these largely female audiences for fashion
shows at the beginning of the twentieth century issues a
challenge to John Berger's claim in the 1970s, in his analysis
of western art and advertising, that men look and women
are looked at, and that women are the 'to be looked-at' sex.[1]
In addition, it adds a further level of complexity to ideas
developed in feminist film theory from the 1970s on the
'male gaze'; these sought to elucidate how women look at
images of women in mainstream Hollywood cinema and
were subsequently extended to many other fields of visual
culture by cultural historians and theorists.[2] If, as Mary
Ann Doane and other writers argued, the gaze of women
who look at other women is narcissistic and identificatory,
in the fashion show it was also, and simultaneously,
mercantile and calculating, particularly when the spectator
was a professional buyer rather than a private client: then
she, like the mannequin, was a woman working the look.[3]

Fashion-show audiences were varied and their viewing
competences differed. There is a class dimension to the
gaze of the rich, and frequently aristocratic, women, often
accompanied by their husbands or male protectors, who
watched the working-class mannequins modelling for
them. If the woman's was a shopping gaze perhaps the

man's was a lascivious one; or perhaps the two are not so
easily distinguished, and here one might invoke Gamman
and Makinen's term 'consumer fetishism of the erotic' to
describe both male and female viewing positions of
privilege.[4] The international buyers who went to the shows
were at work, by contrast: their livelihoods, and their
employers', rested on the business decisions they made.
Theirs was a commercial gaze, predicated on a working
calculation of income and expenditure. A third category,
the illicit copyists and pirates who, with considerable
ingenuity, also attended the shows, had to develop a strong
visual memory and to cultivate an invisible gaze that did
not appear to be absorbing anything, in order to avoid
being forcibly thrown out.

No single theory of 'the gaze' can be attributed to such
varied spectators. Instead, one can posit several gazes in
relation to the first fashion shows, gazes that were fluid and
mobile, because class, gender and professional status, far
from being mutually exclusive terms, are intersecting
categories that change in time and space. There is more
than one subject-position for each individual at a given
time and the gaze itself is not transcendent: rather, it is
performative and hence historically situated and specific.
Jonathan Crary's *Techniques of the Observer* (1992) shows
that vision has a history which changes over time as a
consequence not only of technological changes but also of
developing bodies of knowledge and emerging discourses.
Further, as Abigail Solomon-Godeau has argued, 'the
emergence of new iconographies of the feminine –
iconographies that are effectively *about* the feminine as
spectacle – needs to be historicized as well as
psychoanalyzed.'[5]

TYPES OF SHOW

The heterogeneous audiences for early fashion shows
included private clients, trade buyers and
commissionnaires, journalists, copyists and pirates. Private
clients and trade buyers were kept strictly separate and
never attended the same shows.[6] As noted earlier, the
buyers' shows took place twice a year, in August and
February. Gradually, from the 1910s, mid-season shows
were introduced, so there came to be four collections a
year, of which the autumn shows were particularly
important.[7] The private clients' shows took place a month
or so later, in September and March, fitting with the social
season.[8] In the hot days of August the mannequins would
model winter furs and velvets in Paris while the private
clients holidayed on the Riviera.[9] Likewise in winter, the
clients went south to the resorts in February when the
trade buyers were in Paris. The atmosphere between private
and trade shows differed. Two illustrations from *Fantasio* in
1912 and 1913 (**187** and **188**) give a flavour of their
different presentational styles, with the spectators using
lorgnettes and even binoculars to suggest different ways of
looking: the client's genteel way of holding her lorgnette
differentiates her from the aggressive mode of spectatorship
of the unappealing buyers who peer short-sightedly
through their devices.

Contemporary descriptions confirm that there were
widely different modelling styles in each type of show. The
private clients' shows were slower in pace, wrote Simon in
1931, because private clients took longer to make up their
minds and were harder to please, so the mannequins
worked harder.[10] This, he argued, reflected the way that
'The division of the clientele into two categories, buyers
and clients, whose interests are in some ways opposite,
places the couturier in a dilemma. The buyer acquires the
model to reproduce it as rapidly as possible and to vulgarise
it. The client wants the exclusivity of her dress or coat'.[11]
This flavour of exclusivity was preserved in the style of

LA CARICOUTURE

188 Caricature of a group of fashion buyers scrutinising three mannequins, whose near-nudity in this trade show contrasts with their more decorous appearance in the private clients' show illustrated in 187. The costumes are based on the Paquin-made and Iribe-designed costumes for the *Rue de la Paix* play described in Chapter 2. 'Petits contes au Khalife sur les harems de la couture', *Fantasio*, 15 August 1913. Paris, Bibliothèque Forney.

showing: two 1920s illustrations (**189** and **190**) depict the social element of any show, whether it was to trade or private buyers. In the first, the white-clad saleswomen talk the customers through the collection; in the second, Adolph de Meyer discusses the collection with a French actress who is choosing her wardrobe for an American tour. To the far right of this image, a client appears to be speaking to a mannequin. As in many images of fashion show audiences, the gaze is always mediated by conversation or by explanation.

Press shows were initiated in 1923 at Jean Patou. Before the First World War, journalists were poorly treated by the houses, where they were often suspected of being pirates. In 1913 the *New York Times* Paris correspondent wrote:

> In getting news of the fashions, one feels like a war correspondent. One has to go under the shot and shell of the enemy and is even in terror of being mortally wounded by those in one's own camp. At any moment you may be arrested and hanged for a spy. You can imagine how one's nerves and temper are frayed at the end of two weeks.[12]

It was no better after the war, as American *Vogue* complained, with the journalist 'seated on an uncomfortable stool, in the darkest or the most glaring corner, pencil and paper prohibited and confiscated if produced, feeling like a worm and looking guilty and uncomfortable'.[13] In 1923, however, everything changed for the better, with the inauguration of specially staged press shows. *Harper's Bazar* concurred: 'our standing has entirely changed, you know, since the armistice. Instead of creeping into corners like the humble worms we were once considered, we come ostentatiously, in evening dress, to have our ears soothed by sweet strains of Hawaiian music, our palates tickled by *fois gras* sandwiches and champagne.'[14] The job of the journalists was to produce fashion rhetoric, not hard sales, and this type of presentation was geared to the production of dreams.[15]

THE COMMERCIAL GAZE

The overseas buyers had to be harder-headed. They represented three categories of enterprise: ready-to-wear manufacturers with their own distribution networks, dressmakers working for individual clients and department stores which made to measure for individual clients, or made small batches of licensed copies.[16] Twice a year they converged on Paris from all over the world and filled the fashion salons. American illustrations (**191** and **192**) show the crowd of buyers at a Worth show, their bustle and presence a marked contrast to the discreet elegance and airy interiors that illustrators depict in their representations of private clients' shows (see **189** and **190**). Foreign buyers in Paris often used the services of a commissionnaire, an influential figure (**193**) who might represent as many as fifty to a hundred buyers, looking after every aspect of their trip from itineraries, sales, passports to customs.[17] A Gimbels' store buyer's directory to the Paris shows in spring 1928 (**194**) gives an indication of the volume of shows a regular Paris buyer from a big New York department store had to cover over a ten-day period and through which the commissionnaire would shepherd them.

Professionals of the gaze, the buyers had to evaluate and make rapid commercial decisions on the basis of what they saw. The *Washington Post* claimed that the gaze defined them: 'men and women whose keen glances and crisp valuations mark the profession they adorn'.[18] In 1910 they were described by Roger-Milès: 'the professionals . . . are seated all around the salons – for they occupy the sides of several salons – chatting little, very attentive, rapidly analysing the model gown as it passes before them, and calculating the likely chance of success with their clients of the model before them'.[19] They had to think fast. Not for them the luxury of prevarication. In 1911, the *New York Times* described watching the mannequins parade all day from 10 in the morning until 5 in the afternoon.

As we sit and watch this kaleidoscopic change of color and form there is little time to philosophise; no moment in which one can permit a reverie as to the fictitious glory which surrounds this exhibition of great gowns, and the diplomacy and intrigue and heart ache that it is causing. If one begins to think of other things one would lose sight of a gown that might be famous over two continents in the next two weeks. . . . If one had been philosophising, as one wants to do, one would have lost the moment. At these private exhibitions one cannot think about anything but the subject in hand, and if one is a dressmaker or a buyer the brain goes like a whirligig.[20]

Although illustrators tended to show only male buyers, in fact buyers were both male and female and the job gave many women on both sides of the Atlantic opportunities and status, although they were not paid as much as men.[21]

Magazines such as *Fantasio* parodied female buyers as harridans and frumps (see **188**), women who dress in any and all styles, who are not shocked by eccentricity and who

demand novelty above all. Seated round the edge of the large salon, they watch the *défilé* like hawks with their list of purchases in their hands, wrote the magazine.[22] They have a 'frank nature' and are not above cutting their own deals with the saleswomen or bribing the house illustrators for unauthorised toiles and sketches. After the morning show, the buyers negotiate sales with the saleswomen; the models are feverishly stripped from the mannequins and find their way into the expert hands of the buyers, who handle them ruthlessly as they criticise and dissect the fragile chiffons, calculating their commercial value and estimating their future return. The magic of the show has disappeared and the originality and the cachet of a Paris gown is gone, writes *Fantasio*: the dress will be reproduced with variations and will please no one.[23] Thus the ethereal vision of the mannequin gives way to a limp piece of cloth in the hand representing the cost of materials, labour and export duties.

Leaving aside its undoubted misogyny, the *Fantasio* article reveals the appraising and frankly acquisitive gaze of

A PARIS PREMIER FASHION OPENING

THE GREAT AMERICAN CHECKBOOK

191 a and b (right)
An important American
buyer at the Paris shows
in 1912, depicted with (a)
a show programme or
notes, and (b) a cheque-
book. *Washington Post,*
19 September 1909.

the female buyer at the fashion show. This type of female
spectatorship calls for a different analysis from the late
twentieth-century psychoanalytic model of the gendered
gaze of cinema that limits the opposition of male and
female to one between active and passive, looking and
being looked at. In her essay 'Modernity and the Spaces
of Femininity' Griselda Pollock finesses this binarism by
historicising the different types of knowledge and
experience which individuals bring to bear on the act of
looking; and she situates this in an evaluation of space as at
once social, imagined and represented.[24] In her analysis of
the female Impressionist painters in the nineteenth century,
Pollock looks in particular at how the space inhabited and

painted by her subjects is both material and ideological,
describing how the look of the artist at the point of
production will to some extent determine the look of the
spectator at the point of consumption.[25]

The spaces of femininity operated not only at the level of what is
represented, the drawing-room or sewing-room. The spaces of
femininity are those from which femininity is lived as a
positionality in discourse and social practice. They are the product
of a lived sense of social locatedness, mobility and visibility, in the
social relations of seeing and being seen. Shaped within the sexual
politics of looking they demarcate a particular social organization
of the gaze which itself works back to secure a particular social

192 (left) American
buyers at Worth in 1923,
sketching, taking notes
and deciding what to buy.
Vogue (America), 15 April
1923. Vogue; © Condé
Nast.

193 (above)
Commissionnaire at
Drecoll in 1923.
The caption describes
the dress which 'a stately
mannequin gracefully
exhibited to a critical,

but impressed
commissionnaire'.
Illustration by Woodruff,
Vogue (America), 15 April
1923. Vogue; © Condé
Nast.

ordering of sexual difference. Femininity is both the condition and the effect.[26]

Pollock's focus on space as a locus of power relations of the gaze has some relevance to the position of American women fashion buyers early in the twentieth century. There were, however, considerable differences in the material and visual economies of the couture house and the woman artist's studio in the nineteenth century: in the fashion house, the female buyer had the power; a fashion buyer is, paradoxically, a sort of producer – of capital, through the stock she buys to transpose and disseminate to her domestic market – rather than a consumer. She capitalises femininity for new markets.

It is thus perhaps misleading to suggest the couture house as a space of femininity in the sense that Pollock uses it to designate the 'separate spheres' occupied by men and women in the nineteenth century. Couture house buyers were highly unusual in that they were of either sex and, although most roles in the fashion industry were gender-specific, buyers' were not. Pollock goes on to argue that 'The spaces of modernity are where class and gender interface in critical ways, in that they are the spaces of sexual exchange'.[27] Certainly, in the French couture houses, class and gender interfaced as Pollock describes; but they were spaces of commercial exchange. That is not, of course, to say that the commercial excluded the sexual –

far from it: the two were often imbricated. In the increasingly visual consumer cultures of the nineteenth century, the image of woman was reified across many fields. Sexual and commodity fetishism converged in images of woman that were, as Abigail Solomon-Godeau has put it, 'the erotic spectacle of a reified femininity itself produced in commodity form'.[28] The fashion show developed as part of this visual culture and, to borrow a phrase from Walter Benjamin, the fashion mannequin was a part of the 'libidinal life' of the couture business.[29]

Indeed, it was a business. So when in the 1910s an American buyer watched mannequins modelling, she would do so with dollar signs in her eyes, as she translated the visual economy of the couture house into the money economy of American mass production. If there was a significant difference between particular individuals in this scenario, it might be between buyers and mannequins, rather than between men and women. The pure visuality of the mannequins, their 'to-be-looked-at-ness' was the counterpoint of the pure visionality of the buyers, their unwavering business gaze. In the modelling salon, 'femininity', in the ideological sense used by Pollock, lost some of its coherence as a concept. For if women buyers were the subjects and women mannequins the objects of the gaze, the social, economic and ideological differences among them might be greater than any biological, psychic or even cultural similarities.

OPENINGS NOW READY

A LA REINE D'ANGLETERRE		249, Rue Saint-Honoré
LUCILE		11, Rue de Penthièvre
O'ROSSEN		12, Place Vendôme
GORIN		22, Rue Bayard
GOUPY		10, Rue de Castiglione
NATHALIE DAVIDOFF		23, Rue de la Ville-l'Evêque
MADELEINE MONTJARET		14, Rue Duphot
MAGDELEINE DESHAYES		6, Rue de la Paix

Monday 23rd January 1928

A.M.	P.M		
10. »	2. »	JANE	10, Rue de la Paix
	3. »	GERLINE	16, Place Vendôme
	3. »	Madeleine HENRIETTE	20, Rue Godot-de-Mauroy

Tuesday 24th January 1928

10.30	3. »	MARTHE & RENÉ	2, Rue Volnay
10.30	3. »	CHAMPCOMMUNAL	5, Rue de Penthièvre

Wednesday 25th January 1928

		TAO	32, Avenue de l'Opéra
	3. »	IRFE	19, Rue Duphot
11. »	2.45	LONDON TRADES	92, Av. des Champs-Elysées
	3. »	JANE REGNY	11, Rue La Boëtie
10.30	3. »	CLAIR SŒURS	100, Faubourg Saint-Honoré
10.30	3. »	JEAN MAGNIN	22, Rue d'Aguesseau
10.30	3. »	MARGAINE LACROIX	29, Avenue Marigny
10.30	2.30	Charlotte APPERT	259, Rue Saint-Honoré
	2.30	TOLLMANN	35, Rue Miromesnil
10. »	2. »	SHALL & WILL	26, Place Vendôme

Thursday 26th January 1928

A.M.	P.M.		
10. »	3. »	MILER SŒURS	75, Faubourg Saint-Honoré
	3. »	WELLY SŒURS	21, Faubourg Saint-Honoré
	4. »	ARDANSE	37, Rue de la Bienfaisance
	3. »	YTEB	14, Rue Royale
10. »		HENRI VERGNE	3, Rue du 29 Juillet
		YVONNE CARETTE	46, Avenue Montaigne
	3. »	Germaine LECOMTE	23, Rue Royale
	2.30	GERMAINE	24, Rue Pasquier

Friday 27th January 1928

10.30	2.30	JEAN LATOUR	46, Rue de Douai
	2.45	Lucién LELONG	16, Avenue Matignon
	3. »	MARY NOWITZKY	82, Rue des Petits-Champs
10.30		BERTHE	124, Faubourg Saint-Honoré
10. »	3. »	Paul CARET	222, Rue de Rivoli
	2.45	Yvonne DAVIDSON	24, Rue Marignan
	3. »	GEORGETTE	144, Av. des Champs-Elysées
10.30		BRANDT	16, Rue de la Paix
	5. »	BISHOP	3, Rue Vernet
		JACQUET	40, Rue Marbeuf

Saturday 28th January 1928

	2.30	AGNÈS	7, Rue Auber
	4. »	MARCEL ROCHAS	100, Faubourg Saint-Honoré
	3. »	GEORGES & JANIN	25, Rue La Boëtie
	3. »	REDFERN	242, Rue de Rivoli

Monday 30th January 1928

10. »	3. »	MARTIAL & ARMAND	10, Place Vendôme
	3. »	LIPSKA	146, Av. des Champs-Elysées
	3. »	CYBER	4, Place de l'Opéra

A.M.	P.M.		
	2.30	ROLANDE	127, Av. des Champs-Elysées
	3. »	JOSEPH PAQUIN	10, Rue de Castiglione
	2.30	NICOLE GROULT	29, Rue d'Anjou
	3. »	Juliette COURTISIEN	9, Rue Richepanse

Tuesday 31st January 1928

	2.30	BLANCHE LEBOUVIER	3, Rue Boudreau
10. »		CLAIRE ANY	5, Rue du Mont-Thabor
	3. »	JANE DUVERNE	11, Rue Richepanse
	5. »	MELNOTTE SIMONIN	4, Rue de la Paix
10. »	3. »	LENIEF	374, Rue Saint-Honoré
	2.30	DRECOLL	136, Av. des Champs-Elysées
10. »	2.30	HEIM	48, Rue Laffitte

Wednesday 1st February 1928

10.30	3. »	PHILIPPE & GASTON (all day)	120, Av. des Champs-Elysées
	3. »	SUZANNE TALBOT	10, Rue Royale
10.30	3. »	BECHOFF	9, Faubourg Saint-Honoré
11. »		ALICE BERNARD	40, Rue François 1er
	3. »	CHANTAL	65, Av. des Champs-Elysées

Thursday 2nd February 1928

11. »	3. »	PAUL POIRET	43, Av. Victor-Emmanuel III
		Madeleine VIONNET	50, Avenue Montaigne
	2.30	LOUISEBOULANGER	3, Rue de Berri
	3. »	PREMET	8, Place Vendôme
	3. »	JENNY	70, Av. des Champs-Elysées

Friday 3rd February 1928

	3. »	RENÉE	50, Av. des Champs-Elysées
10. »		DŒUILLET	24, Place Vendôme
	3.30	CHARLOTTE	55, Av. des Champs-Elysées
	2.30	BEER	7, Place Vendôme

Saturday 4th February 1928

A.M.	P.M.		
10. »	3. »	JEAN PATOU (all day)	7, Rue Saint-Florentin

Monday 6th February 1928

	3. »	CHANEL	31, Rue Cambon
10. »		Jeanne LANVIN	22, Faubourg Saint-Honoré

Tuesday 7th February 1928

	2.30	CALLOT Sœurs	9, Av. Matignon

Wednesday 8th February 1928

		WORTH	7, Rue de la Paix

Friday 10th February 1928

	3. »	DUVIL	26, Av. des Champs-Elysées

NOT KNOWN

MOLYNEUX (between Feb. 1 and 3rd)		5, Rue Royale
DOUCET		21, Rue de la Paix
BERNARD & Cie		33, Avenue de l'Opéra

194a–c (this and facing page) A New York store buyers' guide to Paris fashion shows for the spring 1928 collections (a), held from late January onwards. The first open page (b) gives some idea of the number of shows the buyers would attend each day, as well as the great number of firms, many unknown today, showing to overseas buyers. The second page (c) shows how the most important firms like Chanel and Patou showed towards the end of the collections in early February. Courtesy Fashion Institute of Technology/ SUNY, FIT Library Department of Special Collections and FIT Archives.

I've Even Sketched Models While Peeking Through Curtains.

195 A rare illustration of a 'fashion pirate' at work. Illustration by John La Gatta, *Liberty*, 21 June 1924. The byline to this article on 'stealing styles' in a mass-market American magazine describes the 'pirate' as a democratic American bringing fashion to the masses: 'She is smart, she is dainty and charming. The twinkle in her eye hides a native shrewdness. She talks entertainingly of Paris, London – the capitals of the world. She is a blessing to America's Main Street and a curse to the Parisian modiste. She is a fashion pirate! Her identity, she insists, must be left hidden in this confessional, but here is her story. Her startlingly frank revelations will amaze most women.' Collection of the New-York Historical Society.

VISUAL MEMORY AND THE PIRATES' GAZE

For obvious reasons, although there are copious descriptions of fashion pirates, there are no images of them, except fictional ones. One from 1924 is unusual (**195**). Yet piracy was rife. The houses had no choice but to put themselves at risk twice a year.[30] The private clients remained oblivious but the dressmakers, buyers, journalists and illustrators all knew of 'the spying, the police system, the closed doors, the ejected outsiders, the lies, the intrigues and the dishonesty that are going on all the time behind those closed doors and draped windows'.[31] It was to no avail. Edna Woolman Chase, the managing editor of American *Vogue*, recalled in her memoirs that 'the instant the collections have taken place, and days before the buyers' purchases can reach the United States by ship or even plane, an admirably drawn, accurately documented portfolio of all the best French models is on the desk of almost every Seventh Avenue manufacturer. It is an international spy system to turn the military green with envy.'[32]

The houses vigilantly policed entry at show time. Far from welcoming visitors, they made it as hard as possible to gain access to the shows; well-known journalists and illustrators might be summarily ejected.[33] Prospective private clients were as carefully vetted as professional buyers and entry was not guaranteed. Any new visitor to the house, however elegant and affluent she appeared, however many letters of recommendation she bore, was only admitted after careful enquiries and investigations.[34] Each house had 'a cordon of spies' employed to ascertain the precise identity and purpose of everyone trying to get in.[35] By 1909, wrote one journalist, 'the easily swinging doors of the houses of several years ago are . . . unknown today.'[36] Extreme precautions were taken to exclude undesirable people. In 1912 Paquin put seven detectives throughout her house who allowed no one in except bona fide buyers.[37] Some couturiers resorted to employing private detectives to follow buyers in the street if they were suspected of taking their legitimately purchased models to copy houses in order to sell them on; if it was proved that they were copying them illegally, they would be excluded from the shows. Despite this, buyers who had not been expelled continued to sell on to buyers who had.[38] A good visual memory was vital. 'It is the down-stairs manager's business to remember the faces of the fashion pirates', wrote *Harper's Bazar* in 1924.[39] In the 1920s Jean Patou was reputed to employ a 'physiognomist' who could remember copyists' faces from previous seasons.[40]

Saleswomen acted as guardians at the gates during the collections; they decided who to turn away and appraised the worth of aspiring customers.[41] If the houses were initially unwelcoming, suspicion went both ways, with many American buyers fearful that they were being tricked.[42] One American journalist complained that the saleswomen had the 'indescribable knowing manner of the Parisian business woman who, with cold level glances, appraises your exact financial value, and with courteous words and smiling lips that belie the glance compliments you for your residence on the planet while she permits you to see the absolute inutility of attempting to get the best of her trained judgement in any particular'.[43] To bona fide customers, by contrast, saleswomen were assiduous in their attentions. Each customer was assigned her or his own saleswoman who spoke English, a prerequisite for dealing with American and English clients and buyers.[44]

Who were the pirates? Anyone and everyone: local copyists, overseas buyers, private customers after a bargain, or the *premières* of rival houses who might even disguise themselves as ancient English countesses with fake accents.[45] In 1912 the *Washington Post* described 'fashion thieves' as well educated with plenty of savoir faire: 'they have nothing in common with the regular criminal classes'.[46] *Harper's* in 1924 wrote:

> Some of these pirates come in the interest of certain American manufacturers who bootleg on a large scale – manufacturers who keep down their 'overhead' by stealing designs in lieu of buying model gowns. Yet others of the pirates are the less highly organized pick-pockets, who do business with the bootleg dress-makers in Paris itself. Three dollars a sketch by the way, is the market price for this particular brand of local business. Low overhead, indeed.[47]

There was a fine line between pirates and bona fide buyers. American manufacturers would buy the requisite three to five models to ensure their re-admittance the following season and then memorise the remainder. Although sketching was not permitted, they devised a shorthand of minimal dots and dashes to record details of the dresses on their programmes.[48] The injunction on sketching at the shows made the role of the look, and visual memory, a special feature of this aspect of the dress trade which was traversed by a complex relay of looks, of both the pirates trying to steal the designs and the house employees trying to prevent them, followed by the look of the customer at the mannequins. 'The most valuable pirate is the one with a good, retentive memory', wrote one self-confessed pirate.[49]

German buyers had a particular reputation for piracy, perhaps due to French prejudice during and after the war.[50] The Germans also had the 'photographic eye', according to Georges Le Fèvre who described how they came in carefully picked teams comprising specialists in coats, dresses, day dresses and evening dresses; each member of the team watched the models that were their specialism in the mannequin parade, remembering detail, and then went to order them at a nearby copy house.[51] Patou's mannequin Dinarzade recalled that

> The Germans were the *bêtes noirs* of the sales people. They bought little, and would ask to see a model over and over again; always in groups of four or five. It was well known that each one would memorise a certain part of the dress, one studying the sleeve details, another the skirt, and still another the trimmings. Back at their hotel they could make an accurate sketch of the model, to be copied at home.[52]

Even piracy, it seemed, could be Taylorist, in the divide-and-rule of human memory whereby individual copyists working in teams were assigned a particular part of a dress to memorise, uncannily replicating the cellular atelier system backstage.

Local copy houses provided another threat.[53] There were 200–500 in Paris in the 1920s, of which several grossed more than five million francs a year.[54] They acquired models by various devious means. After graduating from college in the U.S.A., Elizabeth Hawes arrived in Paris in 1925 and went to work for a high-class copyist.[55] Copying was, she wrote, 'a fancy name for stealing' and the copyists obtained most of their models from customers, mistresses and foreign buyers.[56] When they could get them no other way they bought them but that too required some subterfuge: Hawes, posing as an *ingénue* American, would be dispatched to buy the model, either having it fitted on herself or, if it was an older woman's model, ordering it for her 'mother' whose measurements she provided. After three seasons, she left and went to work for Mme Ellis, an American buyer based in Paris and employed by a New York manufacturer:

> The situation among American buyers in Paris during the year I worked there was very simple. As a buyer of expensive French models for American mass production, you stole what you could and bought what you had to. Almost every important buyer took to the first showing of every couturier a sketcher. The sketcher was ostensibly an assistant buyer. Her real job was to remember as many of the models as possible and subsequently sketch them for the buyer to copy in New York later.[57]

All the couture houses, she observed, 'knew perfectly well that one in every eight people at an opening was a sketcher', which gives some idea of the scale of fashion piracy at the shows.[58]

Sketchers were not permitted to sketch during the collections but had to watch and memorise, assisted by whatever notes they could take without being thrown out, and then rush home to draw the dresses. Hawes observed that 'A sketcher has a special photographic way of looking at a dress, engraving its image on her mind, marking her

program a little too freely'.[59] It was particularly hard at Chanel's shows, where very tall saleswomen with 'icy stares' were posted in every corner overlooking the crowd.[60] The models 'flew in and out' so there was very little time to look at them. Hawes came to see her theft as a game she developed not with the saleswomen, however, but between herself and the mannequin:

> Her part was to try and get the dress out of the room before I could master the cut of it. My part was to digest its intricacies without missing a seam or a button. I was good. By the time I'd finished my second season of sketching I could have designed you as pretty a Chanel as the master herself. But swiping her designs accurately was violent mental exercise. If you made any more moves with your pencil than enough to write the equivalent of a number, someone suddenly leaned over your shoulder and grabbed your paper out of your hand. And these were the sketches the buyers wanted most.[61]

Hawes's account reveals the crucial role of visual memory in copyright theft that transports intangible capital through a strategic relay of glances. The calculating look of the buyer, the saleswomen's icy stares, the blank gaze of the mannequins, the photographic memory of the sketchers, together constitute a visual economy of the gaze networked to the real economy of the international garment industry. It was predicated on close observation of detail, on speed and on subterfuge: it was far different from the lingering, pleasurable, indulgent gaze of the private client or her male companion.

OBJECTIFICATION: PRIVATE CLIENTS AND MALE SPECTATORS

Since Worth's day, the private clients had been a mixture of the *faubourg* and the *demi-monde* and this mixture continued to characterise fashion show audiences in the early twentieth century.[62] They included artists and writers as well as society women; at the opening matinée in 1907 of the Salle de Théâtre Femina in the seven-storey Femina building on the Champs-Élysées, both Henry James and Edith Wharton were seated in the audience of six hundred (**196**).[63] After the war, fashion show audiences became even more heterogeneous and varied. The fashion writer Roger Boutet de Monvel described the louche and *déclassé* atmosphere of the post-war fashion show as 'a promiscuous indulgence' of journalists, financiers, men of letters and painters, politicians, actresses in fashion and others who aspired to be so, women of the world and women of the demi-monde.[64]

Although women were the customers for haute couture, a minority of men formed part of the audience at the first fashion shows. Some were professional buyers but others were not and various commentators criticised their ogling of the mannequins.[65] At Lucile in London, the novelist Marie Corelli described 'the quaint peacock-like vanity of the girl "mannequins" who strutted up and down, moving their arms about to exhibit their sleeves and swaying their hips to accentuate the fall and flow of flounces and draperies' but she excoriated the behaviour of so-called 'gentlemen' (Bond Street *flâneurs*, Carlton-lounge loafers and Picadilly-trotters) who 'formed nearly one half of the audience and stared with easy insolence at the "Red Mouth of a Venomous Flower" or smiled suggestively at the "Incessant Soft Desire". They were invited to stare and smile, and they did it. But there was something remarkably offensive in their way of doing it'.[66]

196 (facing page) The opening of the Théâtre Femina on the Champs-Élysées in 1907, with many famous artists, writers, actors and society figures in the audience, including Henry

James and Edith Wharton. The room had a moving floor that could be inclined from the stage to the floor. *Femina*, 15 April 1907. Courtesy Fashion Institute of Technology/SUNY, FIT

Library Department of Special Collections and FIT Archives.

197 (below left) A difficult client at Doucet in 1913. 'Figures parisiennes, le mannequin', *L'Illustration*, 27 December 1913. (www.lillustration.com)

198 (below right) An American customer at Doucet in 1913 scrutinises the model dress close up. 'Figures parisiennes, le mannequin', *L'Illustration*, 27 December 1913. (www.lillustration.com).

Sous l'œil de la cliente difficile.

L'examen du modèle par des clientes d'Amérique.

Well into the 1920s, mannequins continued to be described as an attractive spectacle for male spectators, including husbands.[67] Men were still in the minority at the collections, however, and not all were at their ease in the hyper-feminine environment. Roubaud described 'Here and there, a man bewildered by his isolation, paradoxical as a wolf intimidated by sheep.'[68] This description chimes with two illustrations from 1913, each of a mannequin modelling to a couple (**197** and **198**). In both, the woman's gaze is the determining one and her male companion appears passive or indifferent by contrast. The first shows the imperious manner of the difficult client, as opposed to the downcast gaze of her mousy husband; the second depicts the keen scrutiny of two American women customers (note the monocle used by one, to designate looking), in contrast both with the seated man's indifference and the mannequin's compliant, doll-like stance. Such female clients were considered the terror of the mannequins, while other clients dithered and had to see everything twice.[69] One French author reported that American women were more rapacious customers, buying more, making faster decisions and bargaining harder.[70] By contrast, an American journalist characterised the Frenchwoman as the more authoritative and careful shopper.[71] Whichever was the case, these pictures suggest that the fashion show was a forum for women to stare at other women with authority and composure, as a preliminary to buying what they saw.

In this respect, the American experience of popular theatre provides a comparable model of female spectatorship. Linda Mizejewski argues in her study of the Ziegfeld Follies that female glamour made a powerful appeal to American women as both consumers and spectators, particularly after 1915 when the long-legged Ziegfeld girl with her gliding walk and high-end fashions came increasingly to resemble a fashion mannequin (and,

indeed, sometimes was one). Mizejewski discusses Laura Mulvey's description of the female film actress's 'to-be-looked-at-ness' in her psychoanalytic analysis of visual pleasure in Hollywood narrative cinema, arguing that Mulvey's 'psycho-sexual' model of spectatorship provides a compelling explanation of male fantasy but not of women's engagement with glamour and commodification.[72] In Mizejewski's account, female audiences had a particular stake in the issues of glamour, commodification, race and nationalism embodied by the Follies, and in how these ideas circulated. So too did the female spectator of the Paris fashion show, who brought a range of social, psychic and economic competences to bear on her contemplation of the fashion mannequin beyond the binarism of the gendered gaze.

The money and class privilege of the private client gave her authority, which might suggest an objectifying gaze. What Gamman and Makinen have called 'consumer fetishism of the erotic' need not be limited to male spectators but can extend to the women buyer, be she a professional or an amateur of the look.[73] If the buyer's gaze was frankly commercial, the private client was not outside the circuitry of sales either but, for her, shopping was a social rather than a professional activity. As was the case with the female buyers, the differences between the private client and the mannequin were greater than their similarities. The activity of looking, or staring, was underwritten by the class dynamic of rich and privileged women looking at working girls: this symbolic form of doubling and differentiation between client and mannequin was cruelly seized on by caricaturists like Sem, whose images of fashion shows often satirised the delusions of rich, fat and old clients watching beautiful young mannequins modelling (see **32**).

An account of mannequins modelling to private clients at Paquin in 1913 reports that the clients never look at the

199a and b A modelling scene from the 1915 fiction film *The Spendthrift* set in Lucile's New York salon in which Lucile's mannequins Hebe (a) and, perhaps, Yaha (b), model to the characters in the film, a Follies showgirl and her male protector, on the left. The frontal modelling style that addresses the client uniquely is unusual, even for Lucile. Washington, D.C., Library of Congress.

200a and b An unidentified mannequin modelling a Lucile gown to the dancer Irene Castle in the Castles' film *The Whirl of Life*, 1915. Billy Rose Theatre Division, New York Public Library for the Performing Arts, Astor, Lenox and Tilden Foundations.

mannequins' faces.[74] Here the gaze of the observer, described by Jonathan Crary as a new form of essentially abstract, multiple vision that had developed early in the nineteenth century, was turned with absolute indifference onto the mannequin.[75] The client's penetrating look cut through the mannequin to render her culturally transparent and socially non-existent: it was, in Crary's words, 'the petrifying gaze of a new consumer-observer' which, he argues, developed late in the nineteenth century.[76] This is nowhere better exemplified than in an anecdote told by Louis Roubaud in his book on haute couture of 1928. In a chapter called 'Your Dress is Not Yours!' he tells the poignant story of two Ginettes: Mlle Ginette Demail, a client, and Ginette the mannequin who models to her.[77] Although the two women cross paths in the salon, there is no encounter, for each completely ignores the other. To the client, the mannequin is nameless, simply uttering the name of a different dress each time she enters the salon. One day Ginette the mannequin becomes engaged and tells her colleagues that she plans to leave the firm and retire from modelling once married; but in March, only a few days before the wedding, her fiancé breaks off the engagement. Ginette Demail is also engaged and is shopping for her wedding dress. For the next month Ginette the mannequin has the bitter task of closing the fashion show in the traditional bridal gown (followed by two maids of honour carrying her train) in which Ginette Demail will be married.

These contemporary sources suggest that the mannequin's individuality was not so much objectified as completely erased in the look of the female client. There is, however, one unusual instance where the mannequin turned the gaze on the client. The 1915 American fiction film *The Spendthrift* contains a modelling scene set in the New York house of Lucile and using her mannequins to model to the fictional characters (**199**). It illustrates the type of louche narrative on which Lucile capitalised in her marketing and promotion. The mannequin Hebe models directly and exclusively to the showgirl customer, ignoring her male companion, while the saleswoman stands back and takes a passive role (**199a**). In the background another mannequin, Yaha, enters through the curtain. Next, Yaha models to the customer in an even more intense solo performance (**199b**). After twirling on the modelling stage she descends to stand directly in front of the showgirl, looking down at her from her superior height, and stares deeply into her eyes as she raises her arms and performs for her alone. She executes two turns and after each she fixes the client again with a relentless and unswerving look. Although the client with her superior purchasing power might usually be assumed to have the dominant gaze, here the mannequin's is the powerful one, as if she were making eyes at her, and the showgirl and her protector are the objects of the mannequin's gaze. This scene is atypical, however, and other films of Lucile's mannequins modelling (see **35** and **57**) confirm that their more usual style was one of haughty indifference, matching that of the clients themselves. In the film *The Whirl of Life* (1915) Lucile's mannequin models for the dancer Irene Castle less intrusively: while she smiles graciously at the client, she keeps her physical distance from her, combining a graceful walk with a smooth 360-degree turn on the spot (**200**).

In the event that husbands or other men went to the opposite extreme of their wives and paid too much, inappropriate, attention to the mannequins, mannequins simply turned a gorgon gaze onto the man in question. One of their attributes was to appear not to know that they were being looked at, and to cultivate an automaton-like

201a and b Film of a fashion show at an unnamed couture house in the late 1920s, possibly Worth, showing (a) cuturier and mannequin, and (b) clients and saleswoman. Lobster Films, Paris.

impassivity, so that the very blankness of their behaviour could induce discomfort. As the *Washington Post* described in 1909:

> The girls walk about the room slowly and without apparent knowledge that they are scanned admiringly, curiously, pitilessly, as the case may be. Sometimes they walk close to you and stand for a full minute with wide-open eyes, absolutely devoid of expression, looking into yours, and then turn slowly and walk away. It is noted that some of the Frenchmen, blasé as they are, look a little embarrassed by this unexpected attention.[78]

Crary argues that late nineteenth-century fashion and consumer culture engendered a new, impassive mastery of the self that was virtually somnambulistic: 'we are shown a body with eyes open but which do not see'.[79] He cites T. J. Clark's discussion of fashion and class in the 1880s: 'Fashion and reserve would keep one's face from *any* identity, from identity in general. The look which results is a special one: public, outward, "blasé" in Simmel's sense, impassive, not bored, not tired, not disdainful, not quite focused on anything.'[80] Crary posits that from the late 1870s 'within the emerging commodity world of fashion, the ephemerality of attentiveness comes into play as a productive component of modernization, and the display here [in a fashion plate], the body an armature for the commodity, is a momentary congealing of vision, a temporary immobilization within a permanently installed economy of attraction/distraction'.[81] In the early twentieth-century fashion show, the mannequins' deployment of what Crary calls 'fashion's congealed vision', that is, the mannequins' refusal to look back at the men who ogle them insultingly, could itself be strategic and independent.

As Uzanne wrote in 1912, 'They are attractive to the eye, but haughty and cold, and very inaccessible to admiration'.[82]

If the face was a façade, behind the scenes the mannequins could be merciless. In 1910 *Fantasio* described how

> The foreign buyers have the air of 'appraising' – if I dare say it – the mannequins. On the pretext of looking close-up at the latest puffed sleeve or the low-necked collar, they look covetously at the pretty girls who display these fashions. Between themselves, the mannequins, who do not much care for them, dub them with charming and prettily evocative names: *Rosbif* or *Choucroute*. The gentlemen are served![83]

The mannequins may be objectified by the spectators but their resilient wit raises the question of who is for consumption. Women's looks may be served up for their visual appeal, and their bodies ogled, but they retaliate with scornful food metaphors turning the tables linguistically, if nothing else. The text accompanying *Fantasio*'s illustration of 1913 (see **188**) describes how the male buyers stand behind the female ones, their faces flushed at the sight of half-naked mannequins with whom some exchange knowing looks, some, who kept horses in their youth, whistling with complete impropriety, others insolently staring at the mannequins who despise them. 'It's a charming assembly'.[84] The description in *Fantasio* of the frankly commercial gaze and proprietorial manners of the male buyers is biting. Yet it also describes how the mannequins held their own. A particularly well-oiled commissionnaire may finger the material of a skirt, or rearrange the drapery of a bodice on the pretence that it is too revealing, but the flexible mannequin does not get upset over something so small: she simply smiles and does not linger longer than it suits her.

One semi-documentary fashion film from about 1926 shows a couture house fashion show, alternating scenes of a real couturier (who may be Jean-Charles Worth[85]) talking a journalist or buyer through the collection (**201a**) with scenes of a glamorous fictional client whose older male companion exhibits a roving eye for the mannequins, to add comedy to the scene (**201b**). The client's roving eye is juxtaposed with the professional's roving hands in this admixture of fiction and factual film; it exemplifies Judith Mayne's argument that the mode of address in early cinema was inevitably gendered in that it employed 'human figures to embody both the visual fascination and the rudimentary narrative structures of early film'.[86] All eyes are on the mannequins. The look of the female client's male companion forms a counterpoint to the touch of the male couturier who, in talking the female buyer or journalist through the collection, seems unable to take his hands off the mannequin whom he manipulates and revolves like a living doll on a turntable. This short film shows the visual seduction of modelling luxury clothing in an elite setting; it also reveals, as the camera follows the mannequins through the salons in alternating close-ups and long shots, a complex set of gender, economic and class relations among the couturier, his mannequins, his saleswoman and his two types of female customer, the private client and the professional buyer or journalist. These scenes, be they actualities or fictional reconstructions, highlighted the class and gender masquerade that was a structural part of fashion as both industry and image.

VISUAL IDENTIFICATION AND THE HAPTIC GAZE

The mannequin was not only objectified by the protocols of modelling; indeed, the designers who pioneered early fashion shows claimed that their women customers identified with the mannequins. In 1918 Mme Renée at Premet, herself a former mannequin, 'looks so beautifully' in the model dress, wrote one journalist, 'that everyone in the room is ordering it regardless of whether they'll look like Renée'.[87] Ten years before, another wrote: 'Every facility is afforded [the client] to "see herself as others see her" and this too is the function of the mannequin: the saleswoman endorses this by telling the client who watches the mannequin modelling a dress "Ah madame, now you see yourself as others will see you." '[88] Women were encouraged to construct themselves as an image in the

Femina photographic studio, too, a commercial space where the *ateliers de pose*, or posing studios, on the seventh floor of the Hôtel Femina were presided over by the fashion photographer Henri Manuel.[89]

Thus the fashion show was intended to grant women an image of themselves as they would be. For, as Arsène Alexandre observed of the mannequin in 1902,

> her talent is not so much to assume the allure and the expression which suits all the models she shows as to give the buyer the illusion that she too could wear the model just as well. As in the theatre, when we modestly think, as an actor pronounces a lovely phrase or makes a sublime gesture: 'That's how I would have done it in her place', so, fascinated by the suppleness of the young woman who turns and twists before her, playing the role of her dress of the moment, the client must suddenly say to herself: 'That's exactly what would suit my type of beauty'.[90]

Lucile, who claimed that she doubled her sales within six months of introducing mannequin parades in London in the late 1890s, also highlighted the spectators' identification with the mannequin. Looking back on her earliest shows from the turn of the century, she recalled in her memoirs:

> You see, I knew the value of a picture to women, the subtle allure of atmosphere. Women who would gaze unmoved at my loveliest model when it was offered for their inspection in the cold, gray light of a winter morning would come back in the afternoon, when a parade was in progress, see it worn by Gamela or Hebe, and buy it immediately. All women make pictures for themselves, they go to the theatre and see themselves as the heroine of the play, they watch Marlene Dietrich or Greta Garbo acting for them at the cinema, but it is themselves that they are watching really, and when the lights are lowered to a rosy glow, and soft music is played and the mannequins parade, there is not a woman in the audience, though she may be fat and middle-aged, who is not seeing herself looking as those slim, beautiful girls look in the clothes they are offering her. And that is the inevitable prelude to buying the clothes.[91]

Writing in 1932, Lucile invokes the narcissistic identification of the cinema spectator in exactly the same way that Alexandre had invoked that of the theatre spectator in 1902 to explain the audience's identification with the mannequins.

Both accounts suggest that the fashion show operates as a mirror to the client's desires, with the mannequin as a double of the self that is both idealised and other. For, while the client risks losing herself in an undifferentiated narcissistic identification with the ideal, the double nature of the gaze rescues the self from annihilation in the mirror, by objectifying and differentiating the image as other. In her history of the mirror, Sabine Melchior-Bonnet writes:

'Examining the self in the mirror of "know Thyself" allows the individual to understand himself through the mastering of his consciousness, whereas by creating his image in the mirror of others, he becomes a spectacle for himself under exterior gazes'.[92] Drew Leder has argued that a degree of alienation from the body is a necessary part of identity and that it is provided by vision, the sense most separate from the body because it is turned outwards; Leder posits that the lived body combines both first- and third-person perspectives in order to have the distance necessary for functioning.[93] Thus, the mirror may solicit both first-person identification and third-person objectification at once, which Melchior-Bonnet characterises as 'the doubled gaze . . . both introspective and mimetic' through which an individual can define him or herself as a subject.[94]

Other accounts, however, stressed the gullibility of the woman of fashion. The blank façade and impervious manner of the mannequin then becomes a mirror for the customer's false desires and identifications that are encouraged by the salesman's flattery. In the illustration from 1912 (see **187**) the couturier stands behind the client, bending down to just above her vantage point, aligning his gaze with hers. He is, writes the magazine, a man who understands women: 'Woman finds in him not only a mirror that returns her image embellished, but an accomplice who encourages her taste for coquetry, inconstancy and prodigality.'[95] In this account, women, the mirror and the man are all fickle. Having established the idea that women identified with the mannequins, journalists frequently used this as an image of female cupidity and delusion, in which women are dupes of the look. In 1907 a *New York Times* report wrote:

> From the time she enters, the 'cliente' loses her free will. Her surrender is complete when, in front of her, on a tiny stage hung with soft-tinted silks, she watches the slow promenade of the 'mannequin', a pretty girl with an unlimited quantity of Parisian chic. Here is where the hypnotism comes in. Old and angular the client may be, but in her mind's eye she sees herself wearing that lovely dress in the same lovely way. She buys.[96]

Whether they are sympathetic or critical, all such accounts of the visual allure of the fashion show prioritise visual identification through the look. They ignore the haptic competence of audiences. Yet early twentieth-century female audiences had a highly developed knowledge and tactile experience of fabric and garment construction, far more so than today's women. Stella Bruzzi has challenged the idea that the female gaze is an internalised male gaze by arguing that the act of looking might be based on attraction to the garment, not the women wearing it.[97] Bruzzi does not discuss haptics but her point suggests a look that anticipates touch. Such a 'muscle memory' or image triggers a sensation which, in fashion, would be based on an intimate knowledge of the tactile experiences of fabric. As Susan Stewart has written, 'We may apprehend the world by means of our senses, but the senses themselves are shaped and modified by experience and the body bears a somatic memory of its encounters with what is outside of it.'[98] Such a form of 'sight-knowledge' might be activated for a seventeenth-century audience, for example, by the drapery in a van Dyck painting, or for an eighteenth-century one by the Lyons silk in a Boucher.[99] Laura Marks writes about it as 'tactile epistemology' and argues that it is essentially mimetic rather than symbolic, triggering material, specific and textured areas of corporeal knowledge.[100]

Thus a tactile memory of silk, velvet or skin can be evoked by a fashion image or performance; and the viewer, depending on their specific historical moment, will bring their own 'sensorium' to bear on the image: 'spectatorship is thus an act of sensory translation of cultural knowledge', writes Marks.[101] This is what Iris Marion Young suggests in her essay 'Women Recovering Our Clothes' when she argues that the pleasures of touch, bonding and fantasy exceed the restrictions of the internalised male gaze that writers such as Anne Kaplan and Sandra Bartky, as well as Mulvey and Doane, have argued constitutes women's way of looking at images of other women:

> Thus we might conceive a mode of vision, for example, that is less a gaze, distanced from and mastering its object, but an immersion in light and colour. Sensing as touching is within, experiencing what touches it as ambiguous, continuous, but nevertheless differentiated. When I 'see' myself in wool it's partly the wool itself that attracts me, its heavy warmth and textured depth. Some of the pleasure of clothes is the pleasure of fabric . . . History documents the measure of nobility and grace through fabric. Women have been imprisoned by this history, have been used as mannequins to display the trappings of wealth. But feminine experience also affords many of us a tactile imagination, the simple pleasure of losing ourselves in cloth.[102]

In the early twentieth-century fashion show, it is not hard to imagine the ways in which a haptic, material, 'fashion gaze' might be determined by the cultural competence of both buyers and clients, women to whom the scrutiny of textile and garment came easily, women accustomed to choosing a fabric first and a design second, women who recognised the different weaves of velvet, crepe and satin, wool broadcloth and silk faille, saw the decorative possibilities of lace, feathers and ribbons, understood which fabrics were stiff and sculptural and which would flow with the body, which would rustle in motion and which remain silent, which catch the electric lighting of a ballroom and which absorb it in inky blackness. The trade buyer, by contrast to the private client, also had an eye for, and a memory of, how these effects might be translated into cheaper fabrics and simplified patterns for mass production.

Fashion in motion catches the glint of light off a beaded dress, a waterfall of sequins, the swing of a heavy skirt, the ethereal float of chiffon; in the fashion show, movement brings textile and body into a dynamic relationship, making the space around the body haptic too.[103] At the end of the nineteenth century, the Austrian art historian Alois Riegl formulated two, contradictory, modes of vision, the optic and the haptic.[104] Riegl was a textile curator; his model of optical visuality was predominantly one of long-distance vision, while he identified haptic visuality as a type of looking that moves over the surface of its object rather than plunging into illusionistic depth, 'not to distinguish form so much as to discern texture. It is more inclined to move than to focus, more inclined to graze than to gaze', as Marks writes.[105] Marks has developed Riegl's ideas in relation to embodiment in contemporary film in ways that are illuminating for the early twentieth-century image of the body in moving forms such as the fashion show. She argues that all the senses are involved 'in the audiovisual act of cinematic viewing' and that 'in haptic *visuality* the eyes themselves function like organs of touch'.[106] (Here the French term for window-shopping comes to mind: *lèche-vitrines*, or licking the windows.[107]) While few fashion historians have focused on the question of how women appreciated, used and enjoyed clothes, and there is not the equivalent of reception studies in film to gauge how contemporary audiences would have understood early

202 Colette and her husband, Willy, riding in the Bois de Boulogne in 1905. Colette, who was to write perspicaciously about fashion mannequins and speak at fashion show openings, in later life opened a beauty parlour. *Figaro-Modes*, 1 July 1905. Courtesy Fashion Institute of Technology/SUNY, FIT Library Department of Special Collections and FIT Archives.

203 Composite photograph of fashionable promenaders on the sentier de la Vertu in the Bois de Boulogne. *Femina*, 1 July 1914. In his diary entry for 29 May 1910, the sixteen-year-old Jacques-Henri Lartigue described the avenue des Acacias where people promenaded up and down, looked at and greeted each other, 'some remaining in their vehicle or on horseback, the others, particularly if they had a pretty dress to show off, descending to walk along the "sentier de la Vertu"'. For, 'in the Acacias, there are three pathways: that of the vehicles, that of the horse-riders and the little pedestrians' path under the trees called the "sentier de la Vertu"'. Musée Galliera de la Mode de la Ville de Paris. Photograph Richard Hubert Smith.

fashion shows, a knowledge of the properties of fabric, and the complexities of cut, suggest one type of muscle memory that might be triggered for contemporaries in the early fashion shows.

Young goes beyond the idea of a haptic gaze predicated on expert knowledge alone, however, and suggests that it is allied to a 'tactile imagination, the simple pleasure of losing ourselves in cloth . . . Women take pleasure in clothes, not just in wearing clothes, but also in looking at clothes and looking at images of women in clothes, because they encourage fantasies of transport and transformation.'[108] Thus the fashion show has the capacity to satisfy complex modalities of looking, from the imaginative pleasure of the individual shopping for herself to the professional imagination of the buyer who envisions the garment remade for the mass market in another continent.

THE SENTIER DE LA VERTU

If the formal shows were held behind closed doors in the couture houses, their unofficial public displays occurred in the Bois de Boulogne and at the racetrack. There, 'social life was a perpetual podium', wrote Marylène Delbourg-Delphis.[109] Agnès Rocamora argues that 'the street is to the *passantes* what the catwalk is to models: a space where their beauty and allure is offered to the scrutinising gaze of others'.[110] Nineteenth-century Paris provided the spaces for both men and women of fashion to display themselves publicly. In that activity, both sexes could, and did, play the observer too: such self-scrutiny was a practice of everyday life. Paul Poiret was appalled at the lack of mirrors in public spaces when he visited America in 1913: 'For me, who lives in a land where there are mirrors even in the street and between the shops, this seems extraordinary; where then can one analyse oneself, and control one's deportment and bearing, if one has not the aid of these constant witnesses?'[111]

For every woman who walked through the city, whether she strolled or hurried, were she working class or upper class, there was a potential onlooker; and where she went, as much as how she walked, determined the judgements that her audience made about her. Yet, although women walking in public spaces were always the potential objects of the gaze, it would be a mistake to categorise that gaze as exclusively male. Particularly when the ambulatory woman was a fashionable one, the onlookers in the Bois and the Champs-Élysées were just as likely to be female as male. If they were dressmakers out scouting for the latest fashions, they were exclusively female. Fashion plates, too, and from the 1890s the increasing use of photographs in French

fashion magazines, encouraged women to scrutinise the image of other women. In the case of fashionable strolling in the nineteenth century, as in the fashion show in the twentieth, both surveyor and surveyed were just as likely to be women, this being a social and spatial practice in which the close scrutiny of one woman by another, albeit varied and complicated by the dynamics of class, was legitimated and even naturalised.

A photograph from 1905 shows Colette and her husband, Willy, riding in the Bois, one of the principal sites of fashionable Parisian display (**202**). The social ritual of walking and driving in the Bois remained fashionable from the middle of the nineteenth century up to the First World War. In the twentieth century, it formed a direct parallel to the fashion show which by then was taking place in couture houses and department stores. The central avenue that bisected the Bois, the avenue des Acacias, was its most fashionable promenade (**203**).[112] With its adjacent footpath that came informally to be known as the 'sentier de la Vertu' (Path of Virtue), 'Les Acacias' was a prominent social space that constituted a stage for the display of fashionable identities where people went both to see and be seen. A fashionable woman in the Bois was caught mid-stride by the young Jacques-Henri Lartigue who would sit on the metal chairs waiting to snap a passing *élégante* (**204**). His photograph of 1913 shows the similarity to the layout of the modern catwalk, with its lines of empty chairs awaiting an audience, which highlights the activity of looking, recalling the nineteenth-century 'two-sous chairs' that lined the Champs-Élysées. Captioned 'Those who watch' (*ceux qui regardent*), the illustration from *Femina* in 1914 highlights the importance of the audience to this social ritual (**206**). Its pair, captioned 'Those one watches' (*ceux qu'on regarde*), shows the fashionable line of passers-by who are the object of the gaze (**208**). Social life is conceived as a fashion show in this image. Together both images highlight the co-dependence of audience and spectators, conjoined by the social gaze that meshes a sense of fashionable identity as one of simultaneously seeing and being seen. Walking and looking – the principal activities of the fashion show – were also constituents of social life and subjectivity in this period, not only part of couture house display and professional modelling but also informing it, especially when mannequins were sent to the races and the Bois to show off the latest fashions.

The article in *Femina* is devoted to the sentier de la Vertu and focuses almost exclusively on the spectators. It gives a rare picture of the audiences for fashionable display, including fashion shows in public.[113] It is also important for its date, July 1914, just weeks before the outbreak of war. Among the fashionable paraders (those one watches; see

208) are designers (*premières* and *couturières*) in *lingeries*, jewellery and perfumes from the elite couture houses in the place Vendôme, as well as aspiring actresses. Together they form 'a heterogeneous multitude, a compact crowd of men, women, *amazones*, dogs, horses and vehicles which seems to have sprung from the ground by a miracle. One sees fabulous hats and extravagant skirts, all the eccentricities and fantasies of fashion, above all the most audacious: it is the most curious, gaudy and unexpected spectacle.'[114]

There were also photographers, both amateur and professional, described by an American journalist in 1914 as 'shabby old men in dingy frock coats and greasy tall hats' who stop fashionable women 'now and then to beg for a pose, keenly appreciative of the difference between mannequin, *demi-mondaine* and *dame du monde*, but always procuring the pictures – the lady of fashion is ever gracious on these morning promenades'.[115] Yet, as the sixteen-year-old Lartigue experienced it, the social gaze was trammelled

LE SENTIER DE LA VERTU

PAR

ROGER BOUTET DE MONVEL

CEUX QUI REGARDENT. — MIDI MOINS LE QUART, LA FÊTE BAT SON PLEIN : ALLEMANDS, ANGLAIS, ARGENTINS, ET QUELQUES FRANÇAIS PRENNENT PLACE, COMME AU SPECTACLE.

by class relations, when, as was more common at the races than in the Bois, the woman under observation was a mannequin, a woman to whom nobody spoke, who simply smiled gently and did not object to being photographed, who had no male protector to chase away unwelcome photographers.[116] Then the glare of the onlookers could be terrible, be they male or female (205).

The magazine *Fantasio*, devoted to popular theatre and showgirls rather than fashion and with a more scabrous and irreverent approach, described the male stare at the sentier in the same period. Commenting that its name (the Path of Virtue) was a Parisian irony, since it was frequented above all by free spirits (*les esprits larges*), it identifies the sentier as a place for strolling (both *déambulation* and *flânerie*) for rich, fashionable and aristocratic people from midday to one o'clock.[117] There the expert and speculative gaze of connoisseurs could observe 'a skirt in flight, the departure of the best chosen legs, perhaps wishing for the strong wind to lift the light fabrics'.[118] The focus on legs in motion in a

periodical that often featured the chorus girl reflects a contemporary sense of movement and modernity in the acts of walking and of making synchronised leg movements that are as much a feature of fashionable display as of professional modelling in the pre-war years. When Lartigue described in his diaries the excitement of photographing fashionable women in the Bois, he wanted above all to capture the woman in the very act of walking, her leg extended:[119]

There I am, lying in wait, seated on a metal chair, with my camera all set up. Distance: 4 to 5 metres; shutter speed: 4 mm; diaphragm stop: that depends on which side *she* arrives. I'm good at judging the distance by eye. What is less easy, is that *she* should have just one foot ahead at the correct moment to press the shutter (which is the most entertaining thing to calculate).[120]

As she approaches, he is shy and trembling a little: 'twenty metres . . . ten . . . eight . . . six . . . *click*!' and he takes the picture.[121] His shutter makes so much noise that the

207 'L'Allée des Acacias before dinner'. The low viewpoint shows the legs of the spectators watching the fashionable *défilé* in the Bois. *Femina*, August 1924. Musée Galliera de la Mode de la Ville de Paris. Photograph Richard Hubert Smith.

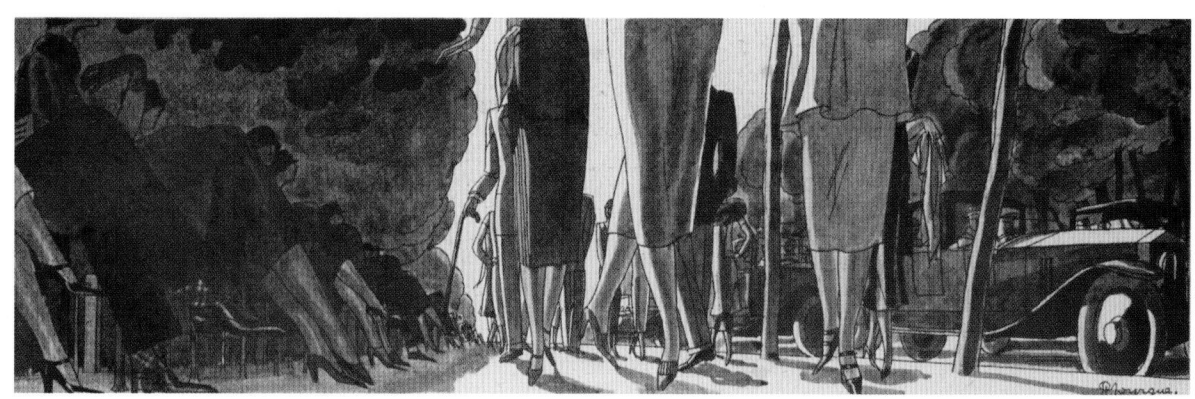

206 (facing page top)
'Those who watch – a quarter past twelve, the spectacle is in full swing: Germans, English, Argentinians, and some French people are seated, as at the theatre'.

Illustration by Bernard Boutet de Monvel, *Femina*, 1 July 1914. Musée Galliera de la Mode de la Ville de Paris. Photograph Richard Hubert Smith.

208 (below) 'Those one watches – the usual types: very young people, distinguished foreign ladies, exotic princesses, actresses en route to fame and female designers from the place Vendôme, are found here every morning.' Illustration by Bernard Boutet de Monvel, *Femina*, 1 July 1914. Musée Galliera de la Mode de la Ville de Paris.

Photograph Richard Hubert Smith.

CEUX QU'ON REGARDE. — LES HABITUÉS-TYPE : TOUT PETITS JEUNES GENS, ÉTRANGÈRES DE MARQUE, PRINCESSES EXOTIQUES, ACTRICES EN VOIE D'ÊTRE CÉLÈBRES PREMIÈRES DE LA PLACE VENDOME S'Y RETROUVENT CHAQUE MATIN.

woman jumps as much as he does. Anne Hollander has argued that fashion photographs, although static, captured the passion to see clothing in motion through 'the blur of chic – the dash, the vivid, abstract shapes, a face, a body and clothes all perceived as a mysterious, not quite personally identifiable mobile unit. . . . The quick impression, the captured instant, was the new test of elegance'.[122]

By the 1920s the Bois had lost its pre-eminence as a fashion site.[123] *Femina*, however, still showed it in pre-war terms but in 1924 emphasising the repetition of the leg (chorus-line like) created by the diminishing single-point perspective and low viewpoint, as if the essence of the parade of walkers to the right, and line of sitters to the left, could best be captured by their legs alone (**207**). By contrast, the high viewpoint of Drian's elegiac evocation of the pre-war sentier, produced in 1915 when the park and the racetrack were empty of fashionable strollers, frames the pathway with empty chairs and fashionable figures as if they were mannequins modelling in the salon (**209**). In 1914, just before the outbreak of war, its modernity had been highlighted in a *Fantasio* article that compared it to 'a cinema, a couture salon, a boulevard, a corner of M. Bergson's lecture theatre, a counter at the Galeries Lafayette; a little faubourg Saint-Germain, a little the other faubourgs'. Describing the social scene of elegant men and women coming and going, *Fantasio* called it 'an admirable cinema'.[124] Here the sentier is seen to share the cinematic quality that is inherent in the fashion show too, its walkers equipped with a restless, mobile gaze of the kind that Anne Friedberg has identified with the coming of the cinema.[125]

209 (below) 'L'Avenue du Bois' in wartime. Illustration by Etienne Drian, *Gazette du Bon Ton*, summer 1915. Courtesy Fashion Institute of Technology/ SUNY, FIT Library

Department of Special Collections and FIT Archives.

9

OBJECTS
INDUSTRIAL
SMILES

210 Mannequins in a couture house in 1905. Max Rivière, 'La Journée d'un mannequin', *Femina*, 15 October 1905. Courtesy Fashion Institute of Technology/ SUNY, FIT Library Department of Special Collections and FIT Archives.

The varied gazes of fashion show audiences converged on a single figure, the mannequin. Reified, she seemed hardly human. She never spoke except when requested to by the client and appeared passive and robotic to her contemporaries. The repetitive nature of her performance was described as early as 1880, endlessly appearing, disappearing and re-appearing in the mirrored salons, donning and re-donning the same model time after time over her black *fourreau*.[1] In many ways she was objectified by the working processes and protocols of her industry. Yet, more than an object of the gaze alone, she was also an effect, a screen onto which the viewer might project an idea or fantasy. The mannequin had the capacity to turn herself into an image by pretending to be an object. Then she became an abstraction rather than a living woman.

In order for her to fulfil this function, it helped that little was known about her social reality or individual life; glimpses of her lived experience are all the more vivid for their scarcity. Her real name was replaced by a pseudonym on entry to the couture house, occasionally prefaced by a respectful 'Mademoiselle'.[2] An anomaly among the staff, she was one of 'a little unclassified brood' poised between 'the aristocracy of the workforce and the proletariat', wrote a commentator in 1925.[3] The mannequin protagonist of a novel of 1937 admits: 'We are hardly popular in the ateliers. They consider us to be luxury dolls, kept women, hussies who insult the work of the proletariat'.[4] Nor have they proved popular with subsequent labour historians of the garment trade who have focused instead on the workers who made the clothes. Nevertheless, the mannequin was much written about in the press and, as she emerged into public consciousness around 1900, the process of mythologising her was already under way. Contemporary fiction and popular journalism contain lurid and colourful accounts of mannequins who murder their lovers or marry millionaires. Middle-market illustrated papers and magazines, by contrast, described mannequins as a new

211 (right) A mannequin at Maison Marion Soeurs in 1904 in the black *fourreau* worn under the couture gowns she modelled. *Figaro-Modes*, February 1904. With the advent of electric light, the mannequins' black torsos looked increasingly odd to contemporaries and gradually fell from grace; in 1910, L. Roger-Milès described the *fourreau* as 'their uniform, their servitude, their hindrance'. Courtesy Fashion Institute of Technology/SUNY, FIT Library Department of Special Collections and FIT Archives.

212 (facing page left) 'Seizing a new idea', *Lady's Realm*, June 1900. The photograph shows a mannequin in the *fourreau* over which the couturier Monsieur Wallès is 'sketching in charcoal on white muslin an idea for the embroidered vest of his newest model'. Wallès sketches literally on the body of the living mannequin, using her torso as a form of drawing board. London, Courtesy of Central Saint Martins College of Art and Design Library.

213 (facing page right) Similarly, a mannequin was often required to stand still for hours while the couturier fitted a dress on her. Here Redfern and his *première* fit a model on the mannequin. From L. Roger-Milès, *Les Créateurs de la mode*, 1910. In 1923 *L'Illustration* described how 'The living mannequin stands immobile. Around her, one drapes pieces of fabric. One cuts, one tries a movement, one pins, one creases, one destroys precious silks. Sometimes success is rapid and the work emerges, easy and joyous, from inspired hands. But often the work is unrewarding. One undoes, and remakes, a fold that falls badly twenty times, hours pass, the mannequin faints with fatigue.' Musée Galliera de la Mode de la Ville de Paris. Photograph Richard Hubert Smith.

kind of working woman, another picturesque Parisian type to join the *grisettes*, *petites mains* and *trottins* of the garment trade. Yet, with the exception of Lucile's mannequins in America, few became celebrities and French mannequins rarely attained the glamour and status of actresses.[5] Little is known of the material conditions of their daily life and work; the historical invisibility of these women whose job it was to be visible is paradoxical.

THE MANNEQUIN AS A LIVING OBJECT

A new kind of professional, in the first years of the century the figure of the mannequin gradually emerged into French public consciousness, largely through coverage in a lively and vibrant French fashion press that developed from about 1900. Fashion writers were particularly troubled by what to call her.[6] Derived from the word for an inanimate dummy, the trade term *le mannequin* seemed brutal and shocking when applied to the living woman, *le mannequin vivant*. It suggested an unwarranted passivity and implied

that she was an object, yet it was also accurate and practical. It was considered slangy and disrespectful but what else would do? 'Walker' (*marcheuse*) was hardly respectful either, 'model' (*modèle*) was already in use for the dresses she displayed and *essayeuse*, which had been used in the nineteenth century, was really the name for a fitter, rather than someone who tried on gowns. Journalists nevertheless fretted at inflicting such a mechanical, automatic term on charming young women. Over fifty years, the word continued to provoke anxiety, as did the mannequins themselves, being peculiarly modern emblems of emerging femininities.

Part of the difficulty came from the fact that the mannequin was both a woman and a commercial object. Journalists did not shy away from describing her physical charms as business assets: her commercial qualifications were 'an elegant figure, a graceful carriage, lady-like manners, and angelic patience', wrote one.[7] She was 'a necessary part of the furniture' wrote another.[8] Her objecthood was thus linked both to her commercial role in sales and to her prototype, the nineteenth-century wicker or wax mannequin. She was often compared to the elegant wax dolls of the period or to shop-window dummies.[9] All femininity on the surface, she nevertheless appeared void of femininity as a core value, like Villiers's hollow metal android who simulates femininity more effectively than the flesh and blood woman.

The doll-like effect was augmented by the *fourreau* (**211**).[10] Made either as a one-piece in black satin or as a two-piece consisting of a close-fitting satin skirt and a silk jersey top, the *fourreau* was worn over a corset and under the gowns the mannequins modelled. Its contradictions troubled commentators almost as much as the term *mannequin*. It was practical, allowing the wearer to slither rapidly in and out of the large number of gowns she

modelled in a day. It was hygienic, protecting the dresses from soiling. Yet it was also a uniform and 'a mark of subjection', wrote Alexandre, and it made the mannequin look like a culverin with a woman's head. As Morgan Jan argues, 'this denial of the body is also a way of reifying the mannequin – long despised, living off her body, like a prostitute'.[11]

From the start of the century, the *fourreau* had its critics and soon after it began to disappear. In 1905 *Femina* bemoaned its 'vulgar' presence beneath the sumptuous and costly mannequins' gowns but the accompanying illustration shows no sign of the *fourreau* it denigrates (**210**). In 1907 Madeleine Vionnet claimed to have presented uncorseted, barefoot mannequins without the *fourreau* at Doucet, where she designed from 1907 to 1914.[12] At other houses it was worn only in the winter. In London, Lucile was the first designer to abandon it, around the turn of the century, followed by others such as Kate Reilly where Vionnet had worked before returning to Paris to work for Doucet.[13] By 1910 it had disappeared in all but the most conservative French houses, perhaps because its peculiar black silhouette beneath pastel evening gowns suddenly looked wrong in the bright glare of electric lighting that had replaced the sombre gloom of gaslight.[14] Before it was abandoned altogether it was briefly replaced by a pink or white jersey version, which was deemed even worse because it evoked the female wrestlers of fairground booths (see **27**).[15] When, finally, mannequins began to model gowns against their bare flesh, the initial outrage they provoked soon diminished and the practice became accepted.

The dehumanising effect of the *fourreau* was matched by the way both couturiers and clients treated the mannequins.[16] A mannequin might be pushed and pulled hither and thither to model for the client or made to stand for hours while the couturier designed on her motionless body (**212** and **213**).[17] She was required to be almost totally lacking in initiative and will, moving like an automaton and modelling with 'indifferent docility, without nerves and without thoughts'.[18] Roger-Milès described how the saleswoman had an 'industrial smile' and the mannequins walked 'with measured steps'.[19] Modelling was repetitive, monotonous and tiring but, he wrote, the mannequins never let it show:

> Smiling, gracious, very feminine, diverse and chameleon-like, they promenade each costume through the salons in an ordered fashion, modelling individually to each client. They pass, advance, stop, turn, continue. Twenty or thirty times they make the same gesture, step and turn, only to disappear and then reappear some minutes later, dressed in a new toilette that the backstage dressers have hastily put on them.[20]

Uniform in their mechanical modelling styles, their resemblance to each other was augmented by the uniforms they wore on foreign tours outside the houses (see **123** and **133**); by the scrupulous care their employers took to regulate their diets so they neither put on nor lost too much weight; and by the mirrored interiors of the houses in which they appeared as fantasmagoric doubles, gliding silently through these enormous palaces of consumption.[21]

Mannequins were only permitted to speak when spoken to and not always then. Paquin's mannequin Dicka recalled in 1906 that she was promoted to 'talking mannequin' because she spoke English. This meant that she was allowed to answer customers when they spoke to her, to assist in sales and to sit with the saleswomen at lunch. It was both better paid and brought the added benefit that the *secondes* in charge of the ateliers no longer screamed at her from morning to midnight in the full season.[22] Generally, however, the mannequin was mute, unlike the talking vendeuse. When the journalist Alison Settle interviewed Paul Poiret for the London *Daily Mirror* in 1920, the couturier arrived with four of his mannequins, splendidly dressed in green and gold uniforms with peaked caps. All six lunched together but when the writer attempted to speak to them, she recalled, 'Poiret put a hand on my arm, warningly. "No, mademoiselle," he said, "do not speak to the girls, they are not there." Quite definitely they were, but not socially, he was indicating.'[23]

Settle was right to suggest that mannequins were not yet socially respectable but she was wrong in another way: by the 1920s mannequins had a powerful symbolic presence. They were eloquent icons of modernity, even in their silence. Yet they remained largely anonymous in the fashion press. Apart from Lucile's mannequins who, particularly in America, acquired the aura of celebrity through her

214 Inspired by the play *Le Mannequin* at the Théâtre Marigny in 1914, *Fantasio* magazine decided for the first time to name and show Paris mannequins in their own right, just like actresses. In the first of three articles, it identifies mannequins at Margaine Lacroix, Paquin and Redfern. Altogether, the articles identified forty mannequins from twenty-one couture houses, including Paquin, Redfern, Drecoll, Laferrière, Boué, Martial et Armand, Agnès and Lanvin, but none from the more elite houses such as Poiret and Worth. Whereas the first two articles referred to the mannequins by their first name prefixed by 'Mlle', the final one simply called them by their first names. The text makes it clear that their job is to model to rich buyers and makes no mention of the private clients. *Fantasio*, 1 March 1914. Paris, Bibliothèque Forney.

promotion of them, no Paris mannequins were written about as individuals. Nor were they named, although in 1914, after the success in Paris of the stage play *Le Mannequin, Fantasio* magazine came up with the novel idea of publishing a feature on the mannequins of Paris. It asked why they too should not be written up like actresses and its three articles on 'the prettiest mannequins of Paris' for the first time named these previously anonymous women of the French couture (**214**).[24] By the 1920s *L'Art et la mode* had a regular feature on the most beautiful mannequins of Paris but, despite being named and photographed, the mannequin remained a generic type rather than a celebrity personality. Being recognisably individual was not desired. Thérèse Bonney wrote: 'Their greatest asset is a well-proportioned body and a sense of this particular kind of drama which lies perhaps in an abstraction approaching art. Symbols of beauty, not flesh-and-blood beauty; mannequins, not individuals!'[25]

It was an abstraction that approached money rather than art, however. In 1902 Alexandre explicitly noted that the mannequin's professional allure, like the actress's, was connected to monetary value: 'The mannequin assumes the value of the dresses that she wears, exactly as the actress does with the innumerable costumes that she dons'.[26] An act of modern magic, the mannequin's body was trammelled by money once she put on the dress. Then she became a figure of capital in motion. In the 1920s American *Vogue* explicitly linked the mannequin's smiling demeanour to sales, in its description of the 'voice with the smile' with which she gave details of the gown on request.[27] Here the smiling mannequin evokes Walter Benjamin's description of the erotic potential of saleability when it takes the form of the chorus girl or prostitute, two figures with whom the fashion mannequin had much in common. Benjamin wrote:

> In the form taken by prostitution in the big cities, the woman appears not only as commodity but, in a precise sense, as mass-produced article. This is indicated by the masking of individual expression in favour of a professional appearance, such as makeup provides. The point is made still more emphatically, later on, by the uniformed girls of the music-hall review.[28]

So too was it made by the professional fashion mannequin's performance of impassivity in which her value became subsumed into the dress she was modelling for the buyers.

In this, however, the mannequin embodied money itself rather than the commodity, demonstrating its draining effect on the individual as described by Georg Simmel in *The Philosophy of Money* (1900, expanded 1907).[29] Simmel went beyond a purely economic study of money to analyse its profound impact on social and emotional values. As Mathieu Deflem explains:

> Simmel debates how money also determines culture and the whole rhythm of life. Modern life becomes an intellectual endeavour excluding emotional considerations in favour of calculability. The culture of things replaces the culture of persons, and the creativity of mind is subject to a process of reification (*Vergegenständlichung*) in terms of calculable matter. . . . Money thus manages to reify all that social life – including the economy but also culture – entails as content, transforming qualitative worth into quantifiable functionality. Through the formal qualities of its operation, money enables exchange at a distance and an extreme abstractness that fragments people into formal properties, each of which carries a price-tag.[30]

The mannequin did not carry a price tag but she spoke it on request and she wore the number of the model dress on her arm. Barred from displays of individual temperament in the salon, her reified figure substituted what Deflem calls 'quantifiable functionality' for 'qualitative worth'. Her capacity to turn herself into an abstraction made her impermeable by everyday life: as the hermetic *fourreau* contained her body, so too did the mirrored salons circumscribe her performance, giving only the illusion of depth. As her image ricocheted soundlessly between the mirrored walls of the couture houses and into modern subjectivities, nothing spilled over. Tim Armstrong argues that whereas the body was increasingly technologised and fragmented by nineteenth-century medicine and science, commodity culture promised a unified or whole body: 'In the modern period, the body is re-energised, re-formed, subject to new modes of production, representations and commodification'. Such representations of the body in advertising, cosmetics, cosmetic surgery and cinema are 'prosthetic in the sense that they promise the perfection of the body'.[31] Heading this parade of bodies in the representations of fashion is the figure of the mannequin.

WORKING CONDITIONS, PAY AND TRAINING

In 1913 Jacques Doucet told a journalist that a great couturier looked on his mannequins as a race-horse proprietor regarded his stable of stallions.[32] After the war, images of Poiret and Patou surrounded by their mannequins suggest a proprietorial relationship; indeed, Poiret assiduously cultivated the oriental metaphor of himself as a pasha, with the mannequins acting as his court or slave girls.[33] Every couture house had its *cabine* of between twelve and twenty mannequins; after the war they numbered between fourteen and thirty.[34] Many pre-war mannequins were young girls who lived in the suburbs and came from respectable lower middle-class families. Their working lives were fairly restricted by modern standards. They were not allowed to leave the premises during business hours, the *chef de cabine* kept a strict eye on them and was often in touch with their parents, and the couturier might dictate their diets as well as their deportment. At Patou, the head of personnel was Maurice Le Bolzer who had been Patou's *aide de camp* during the war and who transferred his experience of command and control to *les affaires des femmes*. Responsible for the mannequins, he banned tea and coffee from the *cabine* – unthinkable in other houses – so as not to dirty the dresses.[35]

Few hard facts are known about the mannequins but amid the hypostasised descriptions are rare, partial, accounts of their daily lives and working conditions.[36] They would walk to work across Paris in the mornings, arriving at 9 am when they changed out of their street clothes and boots into fine shoes and the *fourreau*, in those houses where it was still worn. A timekeeper was employed to clock them in; there were fines for late arrivals and, less often, bonuses for punctuality.[37] A wartime novel describes the scene in the morning in the *cabine* of 1913, 'waiting for the first clients who rarely arrived before eleven o'clock, the mannequins, in corsets and silk drawers, some armed with powder puffs and rice powder, others with lipstick cases or brown, blue or black eye pencils, mingling and chattering in the little pale green room where they dress and undress at speed'.[38] Several houses employed a hairdresser to dress the mannequins' hair 'to harmonise with all the shades and tones of the gowns' which they were to wear that day.[39]

During the ten to fourteen days of the biannual shows, mannequins modelled from approximately 10 am to 8 pm, with an hour off for lunch which was taken in-house.[40] August was particularly wearisome because they had to trail heavy winter furs through the hot, deserted salons for the buyers. During the shows, they had to change between forty to a hundred times a day, showing some gowns up to a dozen times; together they modelled about five hundred gowns in a single show.[41] The daily grind was repetitive but the mannequin had to display each gown as if it were the first time, remaining sweet-tempered, smiling and 'to seem to take as much pleasure from this slow waltz the tenth time as the first'.[42]

Mannequins were seasonally employed and would be laid off in the dead season, as noted earlier.[43] Their salaries are particularly hard to determine: few contracts of employment survive and it is unlikely that many ever existed.[44] Newspaper accounts of their pay are largely anecdotal and do not give their sources; all suggest,

however, that mannequins were paid considerably less per annum than the top salespeople and designers but a fair amount more than the seamstresses in the ateliers, who were also seasonally employed.[45] In the 1880s the young Yvette Guilbert was paid 250 francs ($30 at pre-war rates of exchange) a month as a mannequin and designer combined. Between 1905 and 1914, mannequins' salaries ranged from 150 to 200 francs a month ($30–38). When, in 1914, there was a drop of more than fifteen per cent in the number of mannequins in Paris, the couturiers reluctantly acknowledged that this might be due to low salaries. By contrast, American mannequins in 1913 were paid twice as much as French mannequins, receiving on average $20–25 a week in New York and occasionally much more. Ten years later, John Powers opened the first American model agency and made modelling a lucrative profession. In 1923 his models earned on average $35 a week, rising to $500 a week in 1930.

After the war, French mannequins' salaries rose steadily throughout the early to mid-1920s, reflecting post-war inflation.[46] So, for example, the pay at Chanel rose from 150 to 300 francs ($27–54) in 1918 to 2000 francs ($93) in 1925.[47] Most mannequins in the early 1920s received between 300 and 350 francs a month, though some were paid as little as 250 and a few as much as 800 francs per month; by 1928, 500 francs was considered a disgracefully low starting salary, particularly if the mannequin was tall. In addition to their salaries, some houses supplied mannequins with one or two pairs of silk stockings a month (only to be worn at work), likewise shoes and, very occasionally, a suit. Luncheon was provided but it was considered so meagre that the mannequins had to supplement it from their own pockets.

It is hard to generalise, however, as salaries were not standardised in the industry, varying widely both between and within each house where no mannequin was paid the same and one or two achieved startlingly higher pay than the rest. At Chanel, for example, it was common for one mannequin to be paid twice or even three times more than another: rates of pay varied in 1920 from 500 to 900 francs ($36–63) and in 1925 from 750 to 2000 francs ($36–93). It was a similar tale at Jean Patou, who in 1924 paid only 20 francs a day to his Parisian mannequins but an astounding, if perhaps apocryphal, 75,000 francs a year to the American ones. At Lanvin in 1927–8 the seventeen-year-old Russian mannequin Thea Bobrikova received an enormous monthly salary of 1100 francs.

Nor was there any standardised professional training for the job which depended largely on stamina and physical grace. Mannequins were taught to walk and to pose in the couture houses, although they had also to have some natural ability.[48] The smallest of gestures were practised. Dicka recalled modelling for Paquin at the turn of the century: 'We were constantly posing – acting our part! We had our audience – critical and appreciative. We had to learn confidence, poise, self-control and a stage presence. Indeed, I found the music hall stage easy after all that!'[49] Mannequins might be instructed either by various *chefs d'atelier* or by the couturier himself.[50] The training was informal and varied from house to house. In 1922 Poiret told a French journalist that it took six months for him to train a Paris mannequin to study gesture and the walk.[51] Yet in 1925 he contradicted himself, telling the English press: 'I do not teach her to walk or to twirl; the other mannequins teach a new one all that is necessary to know about that. It is easy to learn for there is little to learn.'[52] As well as copying others in the house, mannequins also studied the stage performances and press photographs of actresses; they practised by striking poses in front of the *cabine* mirrors, something which ordinary women were instructed to do in their domestic mirrors.[53]

Such informal ways of acquiring bodily skills and competences were characterised as a form of social memory by the sociologist Paul Connerton.[54] The skills of fashion modelling, walking and posing that are learned and mobilised through being repeatedly enacted can be argued to be performative in the sense used by Judith Butler.[55] However, Connerton's work suggests that such actions are also memory traces materialised and his analysis proposes how fashion modelling styles might be passed on as part of a house tradition, so that modern poses survive as a trace of past ones.[56] Indeed, the survival of these early twentieth-century poses today suggests that this is the case and that fashion poses are what both Pierre Nora and Michel de Certeau wrote about as a form of embodied memory.[57] Like the dancer, the mannequin had to have a particular sensitivity to body memory, cultivated through her transfer of the weight of the body in time and space.[58] Roubaud describes how each mannequin in a couture house developed a slightly different style: Charlotte was regal, Arlette rolled on her heels, smiling happily, Lydia flexed on each leg, accompanying each flexion with an arm gesture. Marinette played the butterfly, which always succeeded, spreading out her chiffon skirt then letting it fall with a flick. Jeannie alternately raised and lowered her belt with a natural gesture, showing the little pockets that were the most original feature of the dress by negligently putting the tips of her fingers in them. Marguerite displayed such suppleness of her lower back that in the cabine she was sometimes dubbed a snake-woman act.[59] Such modelling styles constituted the individual body signature of a mannequin.[60]

The informal methods of training mannequins in-house are shown in two fictional films set in real modelling locations, the couture house of Drecoll and the Galeries Lafayette department store. In Tony Lekain's *On demande un mannequin* (1923) a young girl from a poor background becomes a mannequin and enters a new world (**215a and b**). Early scenes show her transformation through hair, make-up, styling and informal modelling lessons. In a late silent film, *Au Bonheur des dames* (directed by Julien Duvivier, 1930), Dito Parlo plays Clara, a young girl who is taken on as a mannequin and, as part of her training, is taught a modelling technique that had remained unchanged over nearly twenty years: she turns on the spot as if revolving on a mechanical turntable, using exactly the same technique that is shown at Boué Soeurs in 1913 in an early newsreel.[61]

In 1925 the American press jeered at French plans to set up a modelling school and teach a course of about twenty lessons in 'pausing and posing, strutting and gliding', as well as 'instruction in the art of "wearing furs" and initiation into the secret of "showing off" a gown'.[62] They came to nothing. Modelling was not put on an official footing in France until the 1950s when the first model agencies opened. In New York, by contrast, the Powers Model Agency opened in 1923 and in London the Lucy Clayton school for models opened in 1928.

THE STANDARDISED BODY

Couturiers loftily pronounced on the perfect feminine proportions required of a good mannequin. In 1903 M. Joire of Paquin described his ideal as if it were an engineering specification: a long figure, a small head on a not over-thin neck, broad shoulders, a 36-inch bust, 21-inch waist and 37-inch hips, the ideal height overall being 5 foot 2 inches, waist to foot 41 inches, shoulder to elbow 14 inches, elbow to wrist 11 inches, circumference of wrists 6 inches. Admitting that these proportions were extraordinarily rarely found, he went on to say that he employed mannequins of different sizes, chosen nevertheless for the perfection of their figures.[63] In 1913 Doucet's formula was of bland uniformity: 'She must be a beautiful model, well proportioned with an established format – neither fat nor thin, with legs, shoulders and a waist'.[64] In this passage, Doucet uses the term *modèle* instead of *mannequin* to suggest a prototype woman. Other designers also specified a generic woman, neither too plump nor too slender, with well-formed limbs and graceful carriage and posture. Opinions varied as to whether her face had to be beautiful but all agreed that a perfect figure was essential.[65]

As fashions became slimmer, however, the mannequin was forced to follow suit. In 1912 the *Boston Daily Globe* published a hard-hitting article on the French mannequin, critical of the requirements of the newly fashionable slender figure. Only those applicants who meet the precise physical requirements for the job are taken on: 'Here the tape measure becomes the judge' and only if the applicants' height, hips, waist and bust are approved does she stand a chance of employment. Once engaged,

> Her apprenticeship is hard and her reign, once she has reached the top of her calling, is as brief as the life of the butterfly which she typifies. The bugbear of her existence is the fear of getting fat. To qualify her for the state of exaltation, neither beauty nor intellect is essential. Lines, weight and measurement represent the trinity that

make her eligible for the position. . . . The sword hangs daily over her head, menacing her very life. She has become the slave of measurements. She is haunted by the fear of fat. She has recourse to diets. Pastries and sweets are ruthlessly expelled from her menu and hunger is never allowed satisfaction. If in spite of a Spartan regime the scales show added weight she rushes frantically to a Turkish bath after her work at night, while Sunday's recreation time will have to be spent under reducing heat or thinning vapours. The physical fatigue of her profession aids her, however, in keeping the wolf, Flesh, from the door. The constant changing of gowns and the strain of always standing are good assistants in driving away fat.

Being too thin, however, was not an insuperable problem, went on the paper. 'If her lines are good and she has grace and suppleness she will not meet with defeat. The art of the fitter will cover this deficiency with pads.'[66]

The requirement for a standard body size in living mannequins corresponded with the increasing standardisation of mass-produced clothing sizes, as well as with the standardisation of the body in art and design.[67] In America, mannequins were required to have an average bust measurement of 36–38 inches and standard-sized arms, necks and all other measurements, set as a ratio to correspond with the bust measurements.[68] The standardised body size was considered desirable in a saleswoman, too, but not as important as the capacity to sell, even in the department stores that sold clothing in standard sizes. Several French houses employed mannequins of different 'types' to represent both different clients and different dresses: some would be put in debutante gowns, others in tea gowns.[69] In the U.S.A. in the 1920s, there were slender mannequins in the uptown retail stores and fuller-figured mannequins employed to model to wholesalers, including fashions for 'stouts'.[70]

MANNEQUINS, MYTHS AND REALITY

In France, mannequins could continue to work after marriage if they wished.[71] Many mannequins started work at the age of fifteen or sixteen and some continued to work until about thirty, although other sources suggested four to five years was the limit for a modelling career in a large house. 'All ideal states come to an end. . . . If beauty is not a necessity, youthfulness is. One morning comes a little note of dismissal', wrote the hyper-critical *Boston Daily Globe* in 1912.[72] The press liked to suggest that a mannequin would get her come-uppance once her beauty had faded and there is a slightly spiteful tone to much of its coverage. For example, the *New York Times* wrote:

There are among these mannequins some whose beauty will prove their fortune, and some who will soon leave the Rue de la Paix. But the others, when their beauty is on the wane, when they become stouter and older, finish their careers in the workrooms, thus passing from a position which flattered their feminine instincts of coquetry and luxury, when they were in the limelight and much admired, to an obscure position, where they are not only ignored, but forgotten.[73]

In reality, many went on to enjoy successful second careers. Those who went on the stage or into films included Yvette Guilbert, Dicka and Arletty, who had modelled for Poiret.[74] Those who stayed in fashion moved into either design or sales; the latter required them to take an evening course in English at Berlitz.[75] Mme Paquin, Mme Chéruit, Mme Marguerite Wagner (the chief designer for Drecoll) and Jenny Sacerdote of Jenny all started as mannequins and ended as directors of their own couture houses.[76] Others made successful marriages.[77] Yet others found male protectors, as many salacious accounts reported.[78] The memoir of the Paris correspondent for the *Chicago Tribune* who lived in Paris from 1923 describes one such relationship between Nadia Visnovska, a Polish mannequin at Maggy Rouff, and her French suitor M. de Malancourt, a '*bon vivant* of uncertain age'. Having been taken by an American millionaire to drop in at a fashion show at Maggy Rouff one afternoon, the Frenchman first saw her in the mid-1920s: 'standing hands on hips, in front of a triple mirror, naked as a goddess and many times as beautiful. She had ivory skin and blue-black hair, a body that could be young and strong without muscles or bulges, tapering hands and feet and a rich mezzo voice that made her Polish-French electric'.[79] He paid court to her, she liked him, they started an affair but she insisted on continuing to work as a mannequin so he was tortured by the idea 'of her peeling off her clothes in the presence of all and sundry in the couturier's establishment'.[80] He rented the room below her attic apartment and fitted it up for her in extravagant style. They were still together fifteen years later when the Germans occupied Paris in 1939 and Nadia, 'as lovely at thirty-six as she had been at twenty-one', was incarcerated for three days in 'the dread stadium'. On her release, Malancourt took her directly to his home on the Right Bank, married her in both a civil and a religious ceremony, took her through Vichy, where 'he signed over enough assets to her to keep her almost anywhere any length of time', and on to the Swiss border where, using her new French passport, she went safely through the gate. Having given her absolutely all his money, Malancourt, turning his back on Vichy France, went south to Lyons where he remained throughout the war.[81]

Only in such extreme circumstances would a respectable man marry a mannequin. Socially, mannequins were a race apart, with 'the lips heavily crimsoned, the eyes blackened, the brows delicately penciled'.[82] Throughout the nineteenth century, make-up had been associated with actresses who were thought to be promiscuous.[83] Popular accounts picture mannequins as amoral and sexually depraved. As late as 1921 a particularly harsh French commentator wrote: 'She is aware that she would do just as well in the place of the rich parvenue, in the luxury whose pleasures she enjoys, which she cannot not enjoy. For her trade is close to female prostitution due to its customs, its way of life and its resemblance to a meat-rack.'[84]

A novel of 1907, *Yette, mannequin*, painted a picture of the mannequin as a racy and barely respectable figure.[85] Yette is a sixteen-year-old seamstress who dreams of becoming a mannequin. She has a fiancé, Emile, a clerk, who wishes to marry her but she becomes embroiled with a sleazy older man employed by the couture house, M. Dupéril (a pun on the French for danger), and allows herself to be seduced by him in exchange for an emerald ring. Later, she is taken on as a mannequin by Dupéril's employer, M. Magnet, who also falls for her and invites her to become his mistress for 500 francs over and above her earnings as a mannequin. Although she subsequently leaves her job to marry a rich man, she is bored and wishes to resume her old life as a mannequin. She despises men and she begins a relationship with another former mannequin, Yvonne Laclos. (Lesbianism was often associated with fashion mannequins and was the theme of a popular song of 1908.[86]) The novel ends on a note of melodrama as her previous fiancé, now an impoverished flower-seller, dies in the middle of the place de la Concorde as he tries to sell flowers to the two women who are riding in an automobile. As the weeping Yette kneels in the road, cradling the dying man in her arms, a passing cab driver exclaims 'Ah! Mince! On se croirait à l'Ambigu!', referring to the Théâtre de l'Ambigu, a popular melodrama theatre.

Melodrama also coloured press reports of mannequins as far afield as America where the French mannequin was a figure of fascination. In one report, the Marquise de Villevert had been 'at different times, a mannikin, a domestic servant, and a barefoot dancer' in both Paris and London before she met and married her marquis.[87] Most came to sticky ends, however. A Beer mannequin was reported to have drowned tragically while boating in the Seine with the man she was to marry.[88] In a lurid account from 1912, Angèle de Mehaute, a young mannequin from a poor but honest middle-class family in Quimper in Brittany, arrived in Paris aged eighteen, met and fell in love with a young man from a higher social class, Maurice

Roussat. They lived together for three years before he confessed his desire to marry Angèle to his mother who vehemently objected on the grounds that 'no son of hers, she said, should ever marry a girl whose business was to show off her figure'. Subsequently Angèle, abandoned by her lover, dismissed from her job and with a baby due, killed first Maurice and then herself.[89] Another, Gaby Dufour, died from a drug overdose in 1926.[90] Yet many of these stories, which abounded, were 'the result of strenuous press-agenting'.[91] The mundane realities of the mannequins' lives were as likely to include long hours, varicose veins and flat feet.

The Parisian mannequin was not necessarily French. To some extent she was a fiction perpetuated within the business and in reality the couturiers' *cabines* were surprisingly international, full of mannequins from several European countries and, after the mid-1920s, from North America. Both Chanel and Irfé, a Russian house in Paris, employed a number of White Russians who had fled to Paris after the Revolution; about a hundred emigré Russian mannequins worked in all the big Paris houses in the 1920s.[92] The employment ledgers at Chanel suggest an international *cabine* in the 1920s: surnames are French, Anglo-Saxon, German, Polish, Russian and, perhaps, North African in the case of Louise Ali Akbat Khan Valide who was employed in April 1927 at 1000 francs a month.[93] Patou's *cabine* too was international, not only American and French.

As in New York, however, French fashion modelling remained resolutely white, despite the popularity of jazz and the runaway success of Josephine Baker in *La Revue Nègre*, which opened at the Théâtre des Champs-Élysées in October 1925. Baker modelled a Chéruit dress alongside other revue stars at *Femina*'s 'Grande Nuit de Paris' in July 1927; in February of that year a black mannequin had modelled in a fashion show for the first time, according to an American fashion journalist who described 'the present excitement of Paris artists over African Negro art, *l'art nègre*, as they call it. Evidence of this is found in several collections, notably at Chéruit's, where a colored mannequin wears an astonishing frock of brown and white printed triangles, going "every which way"!'[94] While there were black stars in revue theatre, there was none in Paris fashion. Patou showed on suntanned mannequins and had introduced his sun oil, Chaldée, in 1927 but the mannequins were always white.

THE MANNEQUIN AND CLASS MASQUERADE

In 1904 'Ghenya' described a mannequin in the street (see **16**): 'You would take her for a woman of the world, except that it is the wrong time of day for visits or promenades, and this pretty woman is walking to work. She is a mannequin! Eh! What! So elegant? But why not?'[95] To Ghenya, mannequins were figures of modern glamour who confounded class expectations: 'Tall women with the air of little marquesses with small, gracious gestures', they combined 'the piquancy of the *trottin* [with] the charm of the elegant lady'.[96] For Max Rivière only Parisiennes 'of very humble extraction' were possessed of the innate elegance to wear a gown so far beyond their means in the salon.[97] This belief that only working-class Parisiennes had the requisite elegance and talent to pass themselves off as something that they were not suggests that the talent for imitation was valued above the real thing.[98]

When, in the post-war period, educated middle-class and aristocratic women sought work as mannequins, the couturiers were highly mistrustful of them.[99] Some complained that society women looking for easy work would find modelling harder than they expected. One, who did not want to be named, said 'This profession requires only allure and stamina. It rapidly rejects women who have never worked. We prefer them to be professionals or very young girls, for whom this trade is an advancement.'[100] Poiret claimed that even though the profession was tempting many women who would have previously despised it, society women were unemployable because they neither enjoyed the milieu nor had 'the "mannequin" style'.[101]

Roger-Milès was keenly aware of the contrast between the appearance of these beautiful, admired and opulent women in their elaborate model gowns at work (**216**) and the harsh reality of their social situation. Seen in the street, he writes, they are suddenly 'no more than anonymous *trottins* who, with tarnished elegance, parsimonious stylishness, return home to a humble interior, where virtue has a singularly harsh aspect, and where duty offers by way of recompense an excessively tedious fatigue and lassitude'.[102] Emile Henriot took a different view in his five-page article devoted to the mannequin in 1913.[103] There she was represented as having the capacity for successful class masquerade in an illustration of two mannequins at Doucet, 'as distinguished as society women', who emerge from the house into the street (**217**). The article opens with a description of all the female workers flowing out of the couture house at the end of the day, differentiating the mannequins as particularly slender, supple and beautiful. Henriot describes them as

216 (left) Line drawing of a mannequin from L. Roger-Milès, *Les Créateurs de la mode*, 1910. Musée Galliera de la Mode de la Ville de Paris. Photograph Richard Hubert Smith.

217 (right) Mannequins leaving work at Doucet in 1913, 'as distinguished as society women'. *L'Illustration*, 27 December 1913. (www.lillustration.com).

'ravishingly dressed, whose noble walk and harmonious carriage cause the passing workman to turn and, in his imaginative language, to characterise this Venus of the faubourgs: "nice body, that bird",' as nice a body as the Venus de Milo's, adds Henriot.[104]

The mannequin's 'every air and grace' is not, however, the result of 'generations of nobility' but of a rigorous training in behaviour and deportment, wrote the *Chicago Daily Tribune*. 'She must try to imitate to the life the smiles, the pouts, the lifted eyebrows and the distinguished gestures of the women of the realm of society'.[105] Modelling styles imitated the body styles of what the newspaper called 'la grande dame'.[106] The deceptive similarities between the working-class mannequin and the higher-class client on whose appearance her performance was modelled disturbed American commentators. In 1909 the women's magazine the *Delineator* praised 'Those wonderful professional peacocks whose raiment advertises the designer in whose employ they are' yet questioned the sagacity of using 'this comparatively new form of advertising' because, even though women of fashion refused to compete with them, they risked being mistaken for them.[107] The magazine declared: 'On the whole . . . we are rather to be congratulated that the mannequin has not made her appearance as yet in America.'[108]

As such accounts makes plain, the mannequin was not well born, she only appeared so and, Henriot argues, was keenly aware of the differences between her own situation and the client's.[109] Dicka recalled how painful it was not being allowed to wear the clothes out of the house. 'We put all our money on our backs. It was too terrible to go out

into the world dressed badly, after being beautifully dressed all day!' Despite their youth, beauty, energy and talent, at the end of the day they had to change out of 'gorgeous evening cloaks and furs' back into their 'simple little black suits, cheap stockings and cheap shoes', a fact which struck many commentators as bitter.[110] Worst of all, the mannequins had to cede to the clients' rank and money and do their bidding by bending, turning, standing, sitting, walking and posing on command (see **198**).[111] As American *Vogue* wrote in 1923,

> It is trying, no doubt, having to repeat the name of a model hundreds of times in succession to foreign ears which won't understand it, trying to be pulled and jerked back and dragged in every direction at once, and called 'maddermoiselle'; to having one's laces pinched and one's ribbons patted, and being treated like a mechanical figure with no human feelings whatever. But all that is an essential part of the metier, and a girl who submits with good grace is invaluable to her house.[112]

The social flux of the 1920s added a layer of complexity to the mannequins' class masquerade. By then, not only were mannequins marrying into higher social classes (some of Lucile's and Patou's mannequins made spectacular marriages[113]) but also a few society women were becoming mannequins. Stories were told of a princess, formerly a Poiret client who then modelled at Lenieff, and a Russian baroness at Chanel.[114] At Irfé in 1927, a visitor expressed surprise to find that the mannequins wore their clothes like ladies. 'They no doubt *are* in private life', replied the journalist.[115] The indolent attitudes of Chanel's mannequins, photographed by de Meyer in 1927 (**218**),

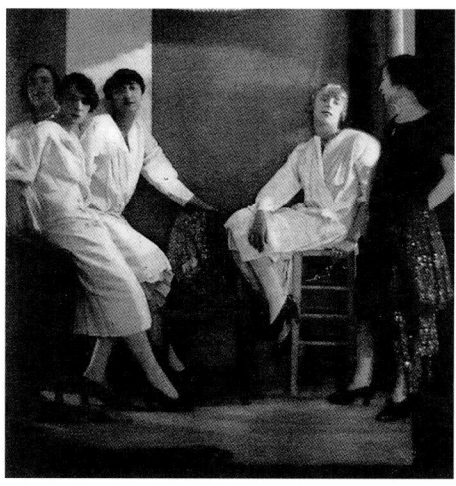

218 Russian mannequins at Chanel. Photograph by Adolph de Meyer, *Harper's Bazar*, October 1927.

suggested a languid grace, a fashionable pose and a nonchalance that de Meyer's journalism had focused on too, in his articles for *Harper's Bazar* of the 1920s. 'The many good-looking mannequins at Chanel's impress me as looking like well-dressed society women. All of them are smart, wear youthful clothes, and convey the impression of being well bred'.[116] De Meyer also noted that at Patou the mannequins did not look like mannequins: 'On the contrary, they give the impression of being smart society women of the kind one might meet at Cannes and Biarritz – come across from the Ritz to walk through one of Patou's salons.'[117]

An index not so much of social mobility as of class instability, mannequins both before and after the war exemplified how style and fashion could be markers of emerging social identities, a way both to differentiate and identify the self in new urban landscapes. Noting a craze for cheap luxury in Paris in 1911, an American newspaper observed how even mannequins were now pursuing luxury looks in imitation of the clients. 'Cheap luxury is at the bottom of it': as the rich run after every new fashion, lower-class women follow the same pattern. 'The streets are full of people in smart clothes. Styles are constantly changing. And everyone is in style.'[118] As expensive dressmakers use cheaper materials for increasingly chic clothes, ' "I'll have one like this myself!" thinks the mannequin girl who shows the gown. . . . handmaking is dying out . . . and the same machine-made lace of beautiful perfection is worn alike by the working girl and the rich society leader. All is novelty and change.'[119] The mannequin resembles a machine-made woman, robotic and perfect. Her evolution follows that of fashion in which the handmade loses its value in a period of change from craft to mass production. The early twentieth-century fashion show strung the mannequins together like the long ropes of cultured pearls that Chanel popularised in the 1920s: too lustrous, too uniform and too perfect for plausibility, they incarnated the treacherous and uncanny instability of appearances in a changing world.[120]

ENVISIONING THE SELF, ANIMATING THE DRESS

'Self has become her [the mannequin's] sole thought', lambasted the *Boston Daily Globe* in 1912. She has over-polished, over-tinted nails, powdered and painted cheeks, 'trained' eyebrows and eyelashes. 'Mirrors at back of her, mirrors in front of her, she never ceases in her long drawn gaze of complete satisfaction.'[121] Yet professional narcissism was part of the job for mannequins, who studied their own attitudes and appearances as critically as if they were a stranger's in the three-faced mirrors of the *cabine*. Such reflexivity and self-scrutiny can produce a degree of objectivity about the self amounting to objectification – the 'third-person' as opposed to the 'first-person' view of the self.[122] In her discussion of Colette and fashion, Anne Freadman discusses Anne Hollander's claim that the rise of abstract art and decorative design in this period allowed Western Europeans 'to accustom their eyes to visions of themselves as shapes' in support of her argument that the sleek, flat, 'flapper' body of the 1920s made femininity into 'an entirely visual affair'.[123] Similarly, Alison Matthews David describes how, in the sale catalogues from the 1860s of the mannequin-maker Pierre Lavigne advertising bespoke mannequins in the form of the customer, women were encouraged 'to identify their own bodies with their busts and to imagine themselves judging the visual effect of their dresses as a third party would, by seeing themselves in the round. Lavigne encourages the potential consumer of a bespoke female mannequin to engage in self-inspection with the aid of her body double.'[124]

Fifty years later, the living mannequin was similarly enabled by the three-faced mirrors to see herself in the round, as a lay-figure. The degree of distance from her activity – she is not a mannequin but is playing the role of one – is noticed by several commentators and contributes to the idea that fashion modelling is an activity that dislocates and alienates women from their natural femininity through the requirement to perform it in many 'versions' and ways: publicly, for money, and as a form of work rather than leisure. However, Freadman adds a corrective to Hollander's analysis by bringing the mannequin's performance back to considerations of materiality and temporality that prevent her from becoming pure image:

> the narrative embodied by an individual model as she disappears backstage then reappears is a story of multiple transformations achieved by changes of costume. The capacity for such transformation was exactly what the narratives of fashion were promising. A mannequin's job is not merely to display the clothes, but to abstract her body to the point where a woman in the audience, a potential client, dreams the dream of transfiguration, her body in those clothes, her very self become insubstantial. . . . What is at stake is the relation between the body and the clothes.[125]

Freadman goes on to discuss Colette's writing on fashion that investigates its relation to 'the redesign of the body, its stylized postures and gestures, its physical competences' which, as Freadman explicitly notes, cannot be separated from the economics of the fashion trade. Thus the mannequin's closeness to the commodity form that she models – the ambiguity of her status between subject and object – echoes the ambiguity of her appearance between working-class girl and leisured middle-class lady client. The uncanny effect of her double nature was augmented by her silence.[126] Gabriele Brandstetter argues that the impassivity of the fashion model is, paradoxically, how she gets the dress to come to life.[127] The mannequin's uninterested performance is part of 'a cult of expressionlessness' required by the industry whereby a model's face must never compete with her dress, so that a degree of inscrutability, even a robotic quality ('the self-management rhetoric of the model'), is part of the job.[128]

Both her silence and her objecthood, however, were a performance, but of a peculiar kind. Freadman argues that the mannequin must be capable of turning her own image into an abstraction.[129] Only then can the client see herself in the clothes the mannequin wears. The mannequin's cultivation of indifference is one of her 'techniques of the body' that contribute to that process – part of her professional portfolio of movement, pose and gesture. If she is objectified, it is as much the result of her own performance of objecthood as of the look of the spectator. She constitutes herself as an object through pose, gesture, attitude and her own glassy gaze. One could argue that the mannequin was reified by the processes of industrial capitalism, which at the turn of the century produced images of women that fused sexuality and commerce, but that would be to deny any agency to the mannequins themselves, as professionals of the pose. The 'paradox of the pose', as Brandstetter calls it, is that the mannequin presents herself as an object: she actively models impassivity.[130] This pose is a hieroglyph of her professional

inscrutability. If it is perceived as cold, that may be due to her identity as a new kind of working woman at the start of the century, whose chilly allure was far different from the warm and reassuring 'parasexuality' of the cosy Edwardian actress and barmaid that Peter Bailey described.[131] Instead, the living mannequin was a professional enigma of a particularly modern sort: she was adept at wilfully turning herself into an object.

As Henriot pointed out in 1913, rather than acting the role of someone else, mannequins mimed their own role in the act of bringing the dress to life.[132] Agents of transformation, they functioned as tricksters whose role was to animate the dress while effacing their own personality in the performance of a dress: to become a dress. The act requires a degree of magical thinking. One journalist described them as *princesses éphémères*, ephemeral princesses with exotic names who took on the qualities of the dress they modelled. So accustomed were they to answering to the name of the dress that, when mannequins from different couturiers who did not know each others' names fell into conversation at the annual Bal de la Couture, they addressed each other by the name of the dress they wore.[133] Paul Reboux, a journalist on *L'Oeuvre* newspaper, describes how the mannequin could suppress her individual personality in the salon and transform herself into 'a sort of harmonious construction':

> She is no longer a living person. Above all, she is no longer a woman aware of the pleasure of wearing new clothes. Her face is inexpressive. Her lips smile mechanically. When asked 'What is your name?' she replies . . .
>
> She replies, yes, but in the most unexpected way. What is her name? It is *Plaisir d'amour . . . Chartreuse . . . Rien qu'un moment . . . Le premier oui . . . Fauvette . . . Feuille de rose . . . Kamtchatka . . . Cinq à sept . . . Apollon . . .*[134]

There is a flavour of the literature of the uncanny in this account of a woman who seems to have transformed herself into a living, speaking garment. She is further rendered inhuman and alien in the French original by the fact that, because *mannequin* is a masculine noun, the paragraph opens not with 'elle s'avance' to describe her coming into the room but with the masculine *il*. Only when the term 'woman' is introduced ('no longer a woman') does the gender shift in the pronoun: *she* replies but it is as a talking dress. 'Her' name is *Pleasures of Love* or *The First Yes*.

On stage, the mannequin's model dress, like the actor's costume, constitutes what the Renaissance historians Ann Rosalind Jones and Peter Stallybrass have called a 'material mnemonics' in their description of the magical power of the object, when they argue that 'clothes have a life of their own; they both *are* material presences and they *absorb* other material and immaterial presences. In the transfer of clothes, identities are transferred from an aristocrat to an actor, from an actor to a master, from a master to an apprentice.'[135] Thus Jones and Stallybrass identify the shifting values of the dress as part of what Arjun Appadurai called 'the social life of things'.[136] The model dress is an object with an exceptional degree of agency but it is the mannequin who endows it with agency, creating the vital relationship between human and thing. As such it has the ability to 'absorb so many different narratives', as Jones and Stallybrass write, that it is both 'a semiotic device and . . . a trifling piece of cloth', one that stages 'the evacuation of the real' in the interests of a powerful representation.[137]

To achieve this, the mannequin required a certain basic talent for chameleonism.[138] Here props and accessories were helpful to create the impression of naturalness in what was in fact a highly artful performance. Parasols and walking sticks helped to hold the arms away from the body.[139] Waist-length strings of pearls could be threaded through the fingers and toyed with; handbags, purses and fans facilitated a range of arm and hand gestures. The feet must never be kept side by side, whether standing or sitting, to avoid creating the visual effect of a solid block. Instead, one foot had to be placed in front of the other at all times to show off the line of the instep; 'In standing, the heel on one foot is raised and the weight carried on the sole, a bit coquettishly, therefore French', wrote an American journalist in 1925.[140] Even the most seemingly natural attitudes were cultivated: a journalist of 1923 described the mannequins in the couture house

219 A modelling gesture at Paquin. *Les Modes,* 1916. Courtesy Fashion Institute of Technology/ SUNY, FIT Library Department of Special Collections and FIT Archives.

> Strolling, sauntering, pausing to reef in a curl or shift a buckle, apparently more carefree than butterflies. . . . Through the rooms they stroll one after another, perhaps every four minutes passing by in a different gown. Usually the walk is one of rather affected grace, little artificial gestures, a carefully cultivated swing of the hips or slouch of the shoulders. And the curl that is always being pushed back into place is one that has been trained to fall, permitting just that gesture.[141]

These mannerisms were an artful version of what Rudolf Laban later called 'shadow moves', the tiny and apparently meaningless gestures that shadow more purposive movements.[142]

Such styles of the body taught the customer how to wear the clothes too. A typical modelling gesture at Paquin (**219**) was described in *Harper's Bazar*: 'The Paquin manikin still glances coquettishly out at the world across a high collar of fur. She is denied pockets this season . . . but her pretty fingers are so employed in fastening the high collar and in drawing it even higher about her pretty chin that she really has no use for pockets. And this little habit of tucking up

the collar, with all sorts of pretty gestures of the hands, is in effect a part of the Paquin silhouette.'[143] Here, the mannequin's function is akin to the eighteenth-century dancing master or deportment coach who teaches movement, gesture and grace.

In her treatment of American fashion and theatre in this period, Marlis Schweitzer distinguishes 'the semiotically rich actress' from the 'semiotic indeterminacy' of the showgirl who, she argues, is a blank slate, with no public identity apart from the one bestowed on her by designers, choreographers and producers.[144] At face value, the fashion mannequin appears to embody these values. Despite learning her gestures from actresses, her real antecedents were not famous performers or artists' models but two invisible figures of the nineteenth-century stage who really were semiotically indeterminate, the *figurante* and the *marcheuse*. Like them, and like *les filles* of the chorus line, mannequins were silent performers whose individual names were never credited in fashion programmes or theatre showbills. Schweitzer describes the showgirl as 'a visually appealing alternative to wax or wooden mannequins without a past or a future, the ideal antidote to the highly vocal, politically motivated New Woman'.[145] Living mannequins, by contrast, were not so much a pleasing alternative to their inanimate counterparts as a disturbing animation of them. They had the capacity to animate a dress while effacing their own personality, magically deflecting the look to convert their own 'semiotic indeterminacy' into a semiotically busy dress, a dress capable of bearing both social meaning and the freight of desire, in the sense suggested by Jones and Stallybrass. Further, in their similarity to the clients, mannequins enacted a kind of class masquerade; and their status as professionals rather than amateurs of fashion marked them out as a new kind of working woman whose very silence and professionalism could freeze their audience. A modern Medusa, the mannequin combined the apparently contradictory attributes of the animate and inanimate and it was her oscillation between both, as well as her capacity to endow the dress she modelled with an agency of its own, that made her uncanny.

Her otherworldly appearance made her the target of much scrutiny. As much as the mannequin was admired and idolised, she was also criticised and anathematised. She represented both a 'self' with which to identify and an 'other' to vilify. She was often singled out for her 'freakishness'. By May 1913, Paris mannequins were seen as outré by the American press, where they begin to be cited as exemplars of extreme fashion: a masculine jacket lacks only a watch-chain 'but some progressive mannequin will soon provide that detail also'.[146] Mannequins wearing extreme fashions at the races attracted mockery: 'Whether they were members of a new cult or followers of a novel fashionable cure could not be ascertained, for the laughter of the onlookers soon convinced the daring exponents of the freakish mode that their attempt met only ridicule, and they left immediately'.[147] An American newspaper in 1918 described the Paris mannequins as 'the summit, the peak, the nth power of ugliness, all but one dreamy olive skinned Jewess who is really beautiful but is annoyingly conscious of it'. Asking why the fashion houses cannot instead employ some of the many pretty girls on the streets, it goes on to describe another: 'There is one [mannequin] who looks like a blessé de la guerre with a black patch over her eye held in place by an ugly string around her blond hair'. Another is '40 if she's a day' with such black circles round her eyes that they might be painted on.[148]

At the same time, the mannequin intrigued and entertained her contemporaries. Her role was to wear the clothes that other women were not yet wearing; when she wore the showpiece, a garment never intended to be worn but simply to attract publicity, she was most herself – the woman whose only essence was malleability, mirroring the instability of fashion. The showpiece was first described as such in 1913.[149] Wigs in vivid blues, greens and reds, trick dresses that were transformed on the catwalk, a luminous skirt with miniscule electric light-bulbs inside, a Poiret dress made entirely of straw, bright green moleskin fur coats, miniature Victorians muffs, bare feet in gold sandals, were all intended to cause shock and laughter and to make everyone talk.[150] So was excessive undress. In 1922 mannequins paraded at Longchamp with one bare shoulder painted in orchid-coloured zebra stripes to match the fabric of their dresses.[151] In 1928 Patou's latest American mannequins 'scored a big hit' in backless gowns cut so low that the fabric had to be stuck to their bodies with adhesive tape.[152]

It was the mannequin's job to be able to carry all these off. Chameleon-like, she had to be able to switch rapidly, to show herself by turns 'simple, alert, essentially Parisienne in a day dress, virginal in a young girl's dress, haughty and provocative in a ball gown'.[153] The mannequin could 'pass'; that was her modernity, that she was both an object and a subject. As she oscillated easily between the two, in a period of monetary instability she destabilised the currency of social class and undercut any essentialist model of identity and appearance. She was an impresario of the self in a paradoxical world in which surface assumed the importance of depth, yet class and money still mattered. In 1925, writing for French *Vogue*, Colette described the mannequin's essential ambiguity:

> The mannequin slides between groups like a long, glittering shuttle, and throws out threads. A disturbing collaborator, it is on the mannequin that a bundle of efforts converge, the importance of which no one recognises. The public appreciates the value of the tasks done by others in couture, such as the weaver, the designer, the cutter, the saleswoman, the couturier who is in charge of them: when it comes to the mannequin, it holds back, dreams, admires or suspects. Among the modernised forms of the most luxurious industry, the mannequin, vestige of a voluptuous barbarity, is like a plunder-laden prey. She is the conquest of the look without rupture, a living bait, the passive realisation of an idea. Her ambiguous profession confers ambiguity upon her. Her gender is uncertain, linguistically. One says 'this mannequin is charming' [*ce mannequin est charmante*], and her work consists of simulating idleness. A demoralising mission holds her at an equal distance from her employer and from the ordinary workers. Is it a laughing matter, to excuse the strange humour and caprice of the mannequin? No other female profession contains such powerful elements of moral disintegration as hers, which imposes the exterior signs of wealth on a poor and beautiful girl.[154]

10
PROLEPSIS
FUTURE BODIES

220 Detail from a magazine page (see **227**) showing one of twenty close-up photographs of trouser skirts. *Femina*, 1 April 1911. Courtesy Fashion Institute of Technology/SUNY, FIT Library Department of Special Collections and FIT Archives.

'All the fashions of which we scribblers write are not worn by the people at large, but by mannequins. . . . And so when the people ask you what others are wearing in Paris early in the season the only available answer is that the mannequins are projecting what others will wear when the season begins', wrote the *New York Times* in 1911.[1] Just as Villiers described his metal android in the 1880s as a 'future Eve', so Colette identified Patou's slender mannequins in 1925 as 'a squad of archangels' of the future. French mannequins wore future fashions and embodied future aspirations and ideals.[2] For fashion, as Georg Simmel observed in 1904, 'leads the individual on the road which all travel'.[3] The cultural historian Susan Glenn has written that actresses whose bodies were staged self-reflexively were 'presumptive avatars of fashion' and could be admired for their opulence and beauty; but their association with goods for consumption through fashion and adornment 'reduced female identity to the status of an erotically charged object'.[4] Yet, in the way that they highlighted the relationship of dress and body in motion, particularly how they appeared to bring a dress to life, French mannequins seemed not so much 'reduced' to objecthood as fantasmagorically projected – still a fantasy but a fantasy of immanence in what they promised the women who watched them. Clad in 'the dress which others will only don after tomorrow, the coat of the next moment, the train of the next season, the invention which will be all the rage', they were, as Emile Henriot wrote in 1913, 'a fashion show of ambassadresses' who modelled modern disguises and new body shapes.[5]

THE UNCORSETED BODY

Among the first women to go uncorseted in the twentieth century, mannequins played a significant role in the corset's decline. As they modelled new and extreme fashions in minimal underwear, they shifted attention from the torso to the legs and developed new ways of walking and holding the body. While no ordinary woman, however fashionable, would have worn such extreme fashions, mannequins made

them desirable and paved the way for modified versions to be adopted by all women of fashion. With these changes came a slenderising of the fashionable ideal that further set mannequins apart from other women; mannequins came to be seen, for the first time, as impossibly and unrealistically thin. In this they were, as the predominantly slender fashionable body shape of the twenty-first century has confirmed, proleptic avatars of future fashions.

The redesign of the female body began with the introduction of two new dress shapes: Paquin's Empire line in 1905 (see **62**) and Margaine Lacroix's Sylphide dress in 1904 (**221**), sometimes also called a Directoire dress when it had a slit skirt (see **64**). The Empire line was a flowing neo-classical dress, with a high waist just below the bust line; the Sylphide a figure-hugging Princess line dress, cut in long pattern-pieces running from the bust to the hips or upper thigh without a seam at the natural waist. Always difficult to wear due to its narrowness, the Princess line had been pioneered by Worth in the 1880s. Margaine Lacroix's Sylphide was a neo-classical interpretation made in flimsy fabrics that clung to the torso and legs. It was also known as the Sylphide sheath (*fourreau Sylphide*) or simply, as it evolved in America, the 'sheath dress'.[6] Both the Empire line and the Sylphide remained in fashion for several years and were instrumental in changing body ideals before the First World War. Both emphasised different aspects of the body in motion from the popular S-shaped silhouette, which accentuated the natural waist and remained stiff and static as the wearer moved. The flowing fabric of the new dresses moved with the body, revealing the legs, ankles and feet in motion in new ways that disturbed some commentators.[7] Most designers continued to produce both the new styles and the older, waisted ones simultaneously but, due to its novelty, the Empire line, with its many variations in cut and construction, received more publicity.

Poiret, despite the claims of several fashion historians, was neither the first nor the only designer to promote the new styles. Nor was he the most influential in the U.S.A. It was Paquin and Margaine Lacroix's innovations that

opened the 1908 show at Wanamaker's Philadelphia store in 1908 (see **80** and **81**). Further, in Wanamaker's New York show that autumn, it was Worth's black Directoire dress that made an impression: 'One should have seen it on the slender blonde mannequin who wore it at the opening in order to realise where its charm lay, to understand into what lovely lines it fell with every movement of the wearer, how it clung to the lithe figure without immodesty or eccentricity'.[8] The comment suggests that without the mannequin the gown had little 'hanger' appeal, needing to be seen in motion for its full effect.

While the Empire line did not require a tightly-laced waist, it was a demanding fashion. It required a slimmer and more flexible figure, created by completely different corsetry which changed both the silhouette and the style of movement of the body. The mannequins who wore it were heralds of future fashion. They looked like a race apart, they wore extreme fashions that other women would not then wear and the new styles gave them a new public visibility. Mannequins played an even more important role in promoting the Sylphide gown, because it revealed the body in new ways. This was the notorious dress that caused outrage when three mannequins appeared in it at the Longchamp races in 1908 (see **64**). Their visibility was not only in the field of style change but also in the overlapping, and far more potent, areas of public morality and gender ideals. The mannequins' semi-nude appearance at a social site of fashion lit a fuse connecting ideas about propriety, sexuality, class and women in urban leisure spaces.

At first no one knew the identity of the designer of the Sylphide dresses at the races but the next day an enterprising American journalist tracked the dresses to Margaine Lacroix where he found a fair, willowy mannequin modelling one:

> It was beautifully molded to her body, from the breast down. One could almost believe that the dress was the sole garment that adorned her shapely person. There was certainly no room for frills or frou-frou, for lingerie of any kind. Her tread was as silent and lithe as a panther's. She paused in front of us, then slowly turned.

On the right side the skirt was split to the waist line, caught together loosely with ornamental buttons down as far as the knee. From the knee down the skirt was open. Beneath could be seen a silken underskirt, absolutely plain and clinging as tightly to the person of the wearer as, say, paper does to the wall. I asked for plans and specifications.[9]

Worn without additional foundation garments, the Sylphide dress consisted of a tight, elastic, silk jersey undergarment to which the underskirt was attached. The stockings were attached to the inside of the underskirt, which obviated the need for garters and held the underskirt in place. Knitted 'strong and tight', the jersey undergarment extended from the bust to the knee and served as a 'surrogate corset'. The outer garment was 'made to serve as its own corset', the bodice strengthened with a little whalebone but not so much as to destroy its suppleness.[10]

Intended by Mme Lacroix to 'achieve a supreme degree of slenderness while retaining a powerfully suggestive, undulating and supple walk', the Sylphide required a punishingly slim figure and the effect of the dress in motion suggests why mannequins were particularly suited to model it.[11] Its precedent, Mme Lacroix's neo-classical Tanagra dress that had been launched in 1889, continued to sell well into the new century (**222**).[12] Although it looks conventional to modern eyes, the Tanagra was innovative too because it came with its own specially adapted corset, which was the concept that Mme Lacroix took forward into the Sylphide dress of 1904. The Sylphide was cut longer and narrower than the Tanagra and fitted the torso more tightly; the earlier dress was promoted as especially flattering to the fuller figure and continued to be sold with a corset, albeit a modified and soft one.[13] For customers who preferred the youthful lines of the Sylphide but did not have a mannequin figure, there was a range of additional undergarments: the 'sylphide brassiere' in silk mesh, the silk jersey 'sylphide sheath', tight as a glove, and for the stouter woman a robust sheath made entirely of kid-skin, *la Gaine*.[14] By 1910 the firm was producing corsets specially

223 The Margaine Lacroix 'sylphide sheath' corset. *Les Modes*, March 1910. Courtesy Fashion Institute of Technology/ SUNY, FIT Library Department of Special Collections and FIT Archives.

designed for both Tanagra and Sylphide dresses (**223**) and the advertisement's claim that the Margaine Lacroix 'sylphide-sheath corset' was 'indispensable under clinging gowns' gave the lie to the claim that *robes Sylphides* were being worn without corsets at all.

The mannequins continued to spearhead new, corset-less fashions but for customers the corset had simply been replaced in the name of liberty with equally elaborate but slightly differently shaped and constructed foundation garments. This may be assumed to have been the case with Poiret's vaunted elimination of the corset. His biographer Palmer White claimed that Denise Poiret first wore a gown without a corset in October 1906; her corset was replaced with a thin lightweight rubber garment and, soon after, Poiret may have instructed his mannequins to go corset-less. White described the ensuing difficulties which the mannequins had in holding up their stockings without a corset: at first Poiret told them just to roll their stocking tops over garters to keep their stockings up but then he added suspenders to the girdle. For stockings, he replaced black with 'champagne-colour' ones and, later, coloured stockings.[15]

In 1907 Madeleine Vionnet designed her first collection for Doucet where she sent the mannequins out barefoot and uncorseted. Her biographer Betty Kirke describes the impact it caused:

> That made some noise . . . it was almost a scandal,' Vionnet said. The first noise came from the dressing room. The day before Vionnet's collection was shown, the models were briefed about a daily bath, which was not one of their habits. With bare feet exposed, there was the additional problem of cleaning under the toenails. The usual chatting in the models' dressing room became verbal rebellion. A few things were thrown around, but Vionnet's strong will prevailed and the models showed the collection 'in their skins,' clean skins at that.[16]

Kirke goes on to recount that the powerful saleswomen at Doucet were so outraged by Vionnet having shown this collection on uncorseted mannequins that they refused to market it to the clients, so that it never saw the light of day. Vionnet later complained that when Poiret shortly afterwards introduced uncorseted mannequins in his own house, he received the credit that should have been hers for eliminating the corset at fashion shows.[17]

Several years before both Vionnet's and Poiret's claim to have eradicated the corset, however, actresses such as Eve Lavallière boasted that they neither needed nor wore a corset.[18] Among mannequins, it was common for working-class girls who started modelling at an early age never to have worn one, though they might be put in one by their employers.[19] In 1913 an American newspaper reported: 'Most of them are exceedingly thin and graceful. Only a few have ever worn a corset.'[20] Most women, however, continued to wear some form of corset up to the First World War, although popular dance and sport demanded more flexible foundations. In 1914 the dancer Irene Castle argued that it was the dance craze, not designers, that had forced a change in fashion design away from 'long cruel corsets' and 'the tight snakiness of the hobble skirt': 'Paris began to dance, and of course once Paris began to dance all the world began to tap its feet.'[21] As a result, modern clothes, shoes and underwear had become light and easy to wear, she wrote. Dancing abolished trains, introduced slit skirts and influenced the fabrics in fashion, creating a vogue for crêpe de chine, chiffon velvet and soft taffetas. 'The modern dances are the reformers of fashion', she concluded.[22]

LEGS

The principal outrage caused by the Sylphide dress was its clinging and tight fit over the legs that often necessitated a slit skirt in order to walk. A slit at the front or side rather than the back foregrounded the extended leg as the wearer stepped out. *Fantasio* described Margaine Lacroix's dresses seen at the Longchamp races in 1908 as 'shamelessly slit to the hip' (see **64**).[23] The diaphanous underskirts revealed by the slits were 'so clinging that the whole outlines of the figures were visible and in each case the material was so thin that it might almost have been called transparent', reported an American newspaper. 'One of these extraordinary young persons had her tight skirt cut up at one side – in true Directoire style – and as the tiny folds of material swayed in the wind it became evident that underneath she was wearing tights.' Tights on show suggested actresses and dancers and the same journalist doubted that the scandalously dressed young women could be mannequins. Even though 'it is a well-known fact that many of the big dressmakers do dress up their best "mannequins" in new and startling costumes for the race meetings', she suspected that they were 'young actresses from one of the boulevard music halls. It is not possible that any first-rate firm would permit their "mannequins" to appear in such sensational costumes.'[24] Margaine Lacroix did, however; the far racier *Fantasio* sympathised that the 'three poor young girls, on this provocative mission, had to show these dresses without any connections to the commercial stage.'[25]

The American buyers bought them, nevertheless, and they appeared in the autumn 1908 openings in New York, where sheath dresses from two unnamed Paris firms were displayed.[26] Such fashions demanded slender mannequins who knew how to walk. These 'willowy wand girls'[27] wore only 'a scant allowance of petticoat' in modelling these clinging gowns, which gave them a particular allure.[28] Their fabrics were described as 'limp and clinging' and mannequins wore a *monlage* or 'sheathblocker' under them, consisting of a corset-waist with layers of fabric attached to prevent the slim skirts from becoming entangled with their legs.

> As in all these French frocks the skirt hung quite limp and very long. How a woman can walk gracefully in these clinging skirts falling closely about the feet and spreading on the floor all around is a mystery, but the young women who wore the frocks at the opening [at Wanamaker] demonstrated the fact that it could be done. Rumor had it that they had gone through a severe course of training before they mastered the art, but they certainly handled the difficult problem with an easy nonchalance which was encouraging to the novice.[29]

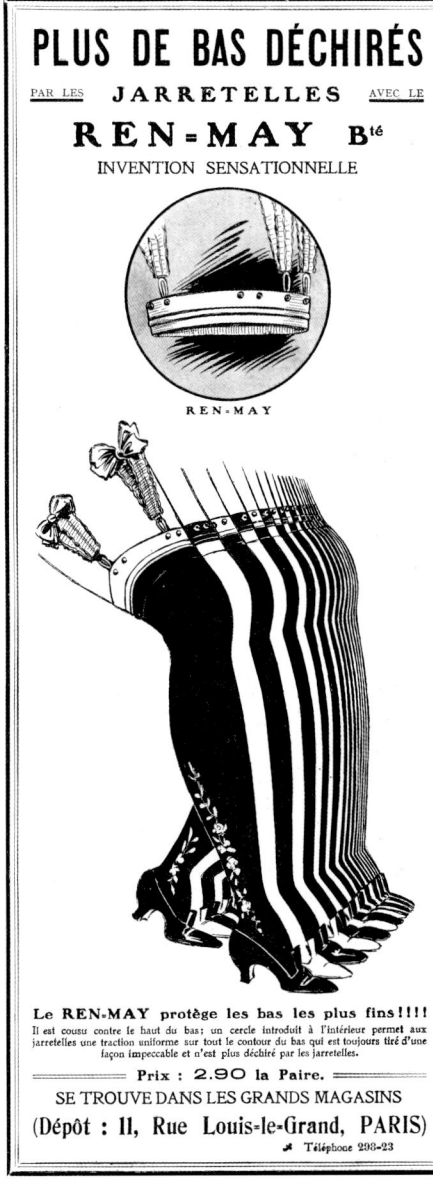

PLUS DE BAS DÉCHIRÉS

PAR LES **JARRETELLES** AVEC LE

REN=MAY B^té

INVENTION SENSATIONNELLE

REN-MAY

Le **REN-MAY** protège les bas les plus fins !!!!

Il est cousu contre le haut du bas; un cercle introduit à l'intérieur permet aux jarretelles une traction uniforme sur tout le contour du bas qui est toujours tiré d'une façon impeccable et n'est plus déchiré par les jarretelles.

══ Prix : 2.90 la Paire. ══

SE TROUVE DANS LES GRANDS MAGASINS

(Dépôt : 11, Rue Louis-le-Grand, PARIS)

Téléphone 293-23

224 'No more torn stockings'. Advertisement for suspenders using a 'chorus line' of legs. *Femina* supplement, 1 November 1910.

Like their French counterparts, the American mannequins wore the slit skirts over contrasting coloured tights, causing journalists to comment both on the amount of leg on show and on how every movement of the body was visible through the thin fabric of the dresses.[30] Worn with scant underwear, or slit to reveal coloured stockings, the style was only for mannequins. 'This way of dressing would, of course, be extreme for the average woman, even though she were appropriately slim', wrote the *New York Sun* in 1908, and a woman 'will follow the fashion only so far as her figure allows . . . yet on those slender mannequins, who exhibited the scores of French gowns in the lower Broadway house (Wanamaker's), the most clinging of the models was not indecent.'[31]

The new designs required all women who wore them, however, to be slim. In 1908 a *Chicago Daily Tribune* article was headed 'No hips. Women use all sorts of means to reduce their hips'. The article suggested a range of methods, from elongated, tighter corsets, fewer voluminous petticoats and the substitution of skin-tight knee-length silk

225 A slit skirt at the Paris races in summer 1909. Photograph Seeberger Frères. Paris, Bibliothèque Nationale de France.

226 Davidow 'Quatre-Quartier' divided skirt. *Dry Goods Economist*, 24 June 1911.

knickerbockers, to exercise and consultations with doctors and 'the physical culture people'. It described the near-nude effect of the new French Directoire gown in transparent, unlined fabric layered over a flesh-coloured chiffon undergarment. 'Flesh colored tights, flesh colored undergarments, flesh colored stockings, even flesh colored silk jerseys to wear under lingerie waists abound in the wardrobe of the French woman of fashion just now.' The article went on to explain that the new gown was 'drawn tightly in at the ankle and sometimes even tied in tightly inside the skirt which makes locomotion somewhat difficult.' Transparent and slit at one side, it was worn at the races only by mannequins but could be adapted for customers by the addition of 'sumptuous cloaks'.[32] Thus was the body of the mannequin differentiated from that of other women.

The fashion magazine *Harper's Bazar* too recoiled at this degree of French nudity, describing the sheath dresses seen in Paris as billboard images of 'burlesque Amazons', far different from the toned-down versions it showed in its pages.[33] It declared that the 'undress effect' of these new fashions was 'bewildering', as was the new undergarment they required, a strapless, boned, elongated corset combined at mid-thigh with a petticoat, the entire garment being cut in a Princess line for a smooth fit under the flimsy fabric of the dress.[34] 'They and the other experiments in gossamer underwear are the pivots on which all the extremes of fashions turn.'[35] They are only worn by mannequins, the magazine explained nine months later in 1909, when the vogue for extremely narrow skirts was replaced by wide skirts that flared from the thigh below a Princess-line bodice 'made with a jersey tightness . . . from the bust to below the hips'. The new skirts used between 3 and 5.5 metres of fabric (about 3–6 yards); one was said to be 12 metres (nearly 13 yards) wide; 'However, none but the professional model as yet is wearing even the four yard garment'.[36]

Wide or narrow, the new skirts' hems drew the eye inexorably to the mannequins' legs. More and more would women's legs be on view, wrote *Fantasio* in 1908, and there would be few women who could say that they were not showing the colour of their stockings.[37] In the following issue *Fantasio* reported that sheath skirts caused outrage but were attractive if slit so that women could walk.[38] During the 1909 racing season a few mannequins appeared in tailor-mades with side-slit skirts (**225**). Also in 1909, Pathé produced *Le Language des pieds*, a fiction film told entirely in shots of a couple's legs and feet.[39] In 1910 Martial et Armand revealed the calves in a skirt hem that was short in front and behind, only long at the sides.[40] The next year saw the anonymous film comedy *Polycarpe, inspecteur de la mode* (Polycarpe, Fashion Inspector) in which Polycarpe, armed with a measuring stick, pursues women in the streets of Paris to control their skirt length, provoking a series of comical catastrophes.[41] Again in 1911 *Fantasio* described a bare-legged variety dancer, 'Timmy, mischievous *gamine* of .the café-concert who "sings with her legs" If we have bare-breasted dancers why not bare-legged ones?' asked the magazine.[42] The image of the chorus girl informed the suspender advertisement of 1910 in *Femina* (**224**) featuring the stockings that women were wearing under their newly revealing skirts. In 1912 Pathé's publicity film for shoes at Galeries Lafayette focused exclusively on the mannequins' ankles and calves, at a time when skirt lengths were rising faster than ever before.[43] Then, on 23 March 1913, at the Auteuil racecourse, three mannequins appeared without shoes and stockings, in Directoire dresses slit to the knee at the back. 'The young women, apparently not in the least disturbed by the early Spring wind, walked calmly over the green lawns of the paddock with their feet protected only by thin sandals, daintily tied at the ankle with silk ribbons.'[44]

THE BODY ON SHOW: JUPE-CULOTTES, SLIT SKIRTS AND LAMPSHADE DRESSES

The sheath dress was difficult to walk in and during the years leading up to the war designers produced a range of other skirt types, from Poiret's infamous hobble skirt (also hard to walk in) to Béchoff David and Poiret's trouser skirt, or *jupe-culotte*, also known as the *robe pantalon* and the *jupe-pantalon*.[45] Later came the minaret or lampshade gown and, meanwhile, the slit skirt continued to be made. At the races, mannequins appeared in dresses and skirts that focused to a seemingly obsessive degree on the lower leg. Elaborately looped, draped and caught-up textiles and trimmings, revealed, progressively, first the ankle and then the calf, or the suggestion of them, through thin, sometimes unlined, underskirts.

Béchoff's *jupe-culotte* was scandalously masculine and Poiret's scandalously oriental. As ever, it was the mannequins who were sent out as an advance guard to wear it in open-air venues that required a longer stride than the couture house salon. In September 1910 mannequins parading *jupe-culottes* were treated with scant ceremony on a Parisian racecourse.[46] Increasingly popular by 1911, the *jupe-culotte* replaced the narrow skirt of the sheath dress, giving women greater mobility but arousing even greater public opprobrium (**227**).[47] That summer *Fantasio* wrote that skirts were rising so fast that not only the ankle but also the calf was on show.[48] Particularly at the races, calves and ankles were revealed in motion under slit, bifurcated and looped-up skirts as women stepped out. *Les Modes* in 1911 showed three women who may be either mannequins or women of fashion (**228**): the point is their determined walk, and consciousness of being looked at, as they sweep along the boardwalk as if the races were the venue for a public fashion show – which indeed they were.

American responses varied. *Harper's Bazar* reported that 'So far only professional models, employed by the dressmakers who are trying to introduce this absurd fashion, have been seen wearing the trouser-skirt or *jupe-culotte*' but the daily papers endorsed it: 'The harem skirt is no longer a freak of the Paris mannequins but a fashionable reality'.[49] Filene's department store in Boston cited Poiret's mannequins at the races as an endorsement in an advertisement for a dress it appeared to have copied illicitly at the Paris racetrack.[50] In April 1911 all the big French designers successfully trialled a new hybrid gown on mannequins at the races. Its asymmetrical knee-high split only showed when the wearer moved and the gown was favourably reviewed in the U.S.A. where it was rapidly copied.[51] Then in June, the American importer Davidow promoted its own divided skirt to the American trade,

illustrating it not as French orientalism but as American sportswear, with an energetic young woman playing baseball in her 'Quatre-Quartier' skirt (**226**).

As the slit skirt came to be accepted, the Paris dressmakers increased the competition and put their mannequins in more extreme fashions to attract the American press and buyers. Over 1911 and 1912 the previously conventional Callot Soeurs began to show scandalously revealing gowns: diaphanous, short and narrow, with a low décolletage both back and front, their high Directoire-style waists tapered to uneven hems, while their tight skirts were slashed high at either the side or the front to expose the ankles, or draped over the hips in such a way as to expose every curve and angle of the figure.[52] As a result, Callot's autumn 1911 opening was packed with buyers anticipating a show combining the near-nudity of the Ballets Russes with the dancing girls of the Bal Tabarin nightclub. One New York dressmaker reputedly paid someone to sit in a chair from 9 o'clock in the morning to save her place until she could get there for the show. She reported that while the skirts of the new gowns were exaggeratedly draped and tightly fitted at the hips and ankles, the bodices were not nearly so transparent and low-cut as at Poiret and she repeated a joke going round that a woman dressed by Callot and Poiret would wear only a belt, for Poiret put nothing above the waist and Callot put nothing below it.[53]

While Callot's extreme fashions were criticised by some American journalists, they also revelled in their descriptions of such extreme, body-revealing styles which they announced would be modified for American consumers. By 1912 Paris mannequins were routinely displaying costumes that created a gulf between French and American ideals.[54] Following Callot's lead, Worth showed the new, scandalous gowns in 1912:

Paris, Aug 21. Worth, the most conservative dressmaker in Europe among the great houses, has just given a private opening of Winter costumes for the benefit of hundreds of American buyers. For the first time in the career of this celebrated house there were sensational gowns. No one in that world has talked of much else since.

That Worth of all men should join the procession of sensationalists has caused not only anxiety but deep thought in all those who are interested in fashions as a part of the world's serious movements. . . . His skirts are excessively narrow . . . Some of his evening gowns are less than a yard wide and are slashed in front for at least six inches so that one may move along somehow. Added to that, he shows one or two models that are transparent to the knees. Callot introduced this idea last year and everyone thought it was decidedly cheap and tawdry to attract attention by

227 (right) Magazine page showing seven line drawings and twenty close-up photographs of trouser skirts. *Femina*, 1 April 1911. Courtesy Fashion Institute of Technology/SUNY, FIT Library Department of Special Collections and FIT Archives.

228 (facing page) 'Jupe culotte at the races'. *Les Modes,* March 1911. Courtesy Fashion Institute of Technology/ SUNY, FIT Library Department of Special Collections and FIT Archives.

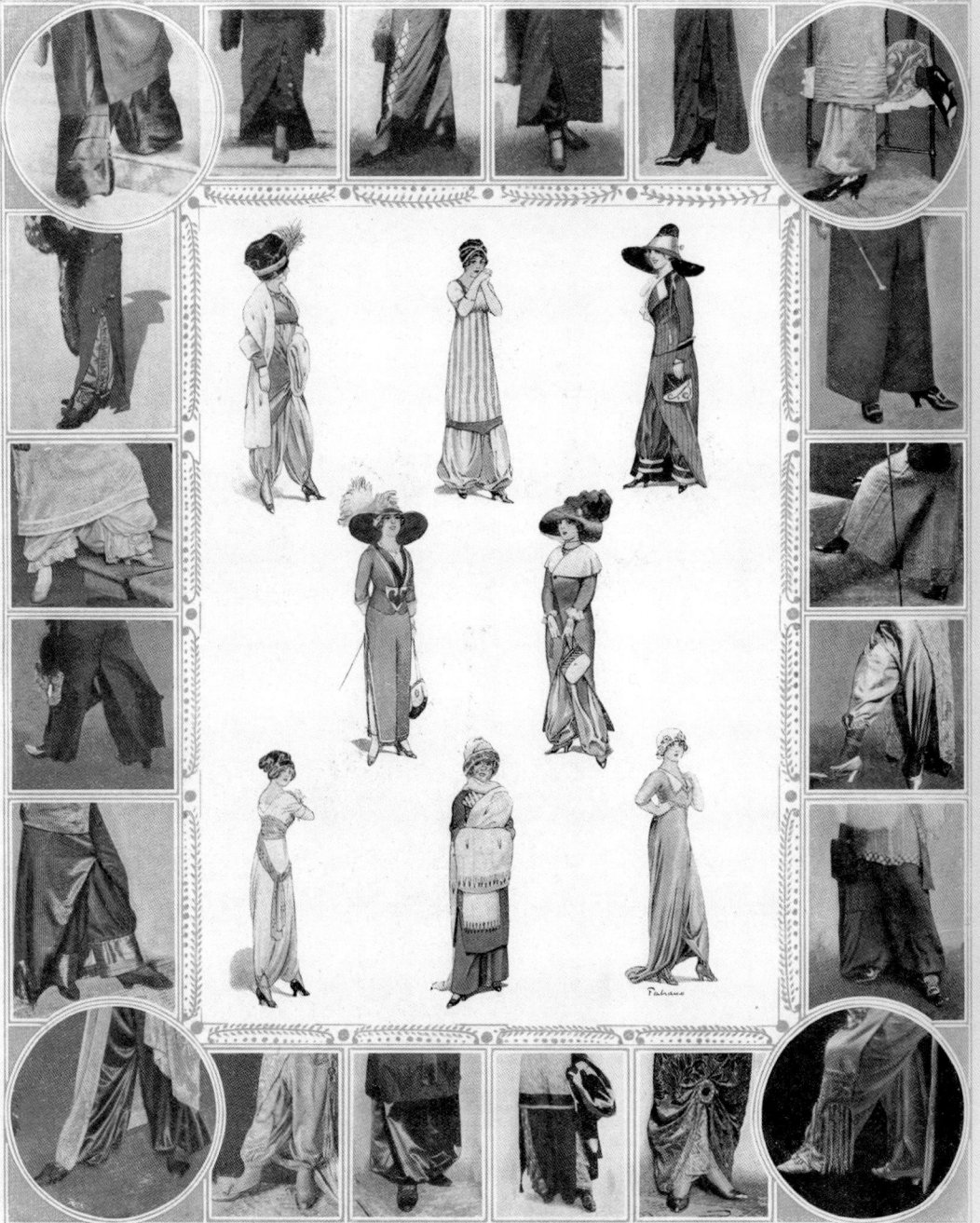

LES "DERNIERES" DE LA ROBE-PANTALON

MALGRÉ la « mauvaise presse » qui l'a accueillie, la robe-pantalon a encore tenté de s'imposer et de nouveaux modèles en sont sortis ici et là. Ces nouveaux essais ne semblent pas devoir rencontrer plus de succès que les premiers et nous assistons vraisemblablement aux « dernières » de la robe-pantalon. Nous avons cru utile de montrer ici une suite à peu près complète des différents modèles qui se sont produits de cette mode éphémère et désormais historique : les photographies et les dessins que nous reproduisons ci-dessus auront un jour une incomparable valeur documentaire et anecdotique... Maintenant, il est permis de rechercher si la tentative malheureuse à laquelle nous venons d'assister n'influencera pas quelque peu la mode réelle de la saison d'été : d'aucuns le pensent et d'ores et déjà il est probable que la principale conséquence de cette tentative sera de prolonger le règne des robes étroites — du moins pour les tailleurs. Nos lectrices savent cependant que la mort de « l'étroit » avait été naguère décidée et que l'on avait inventé la robe-pantalon pour lui succéder.

172

Orientalising a gown in this method. . . . the American buyers who gathered from every part of our continent certainly opened their eyes and gasped as the parade of mannequins began in the white and silver rooms on the Rue de la Paix at the house of Worth. . . . skirts are narrow at the hem and cling to the body like a sweet potato vine. . . .[55]

Only mannequins could model such extreme and body-revealing fashions. At Premet a mannequin in a tea gown of white lace over flesh-pink tulle revealed white satin tights down to the knee, where they were met by flesh-pink stockings worn with gold gladiator sandals.[56] As skirts rose, heels became higher and 'the mannequins paraded in American shoes, or rather shoes made on American lasts' with a shorter vamp, higher arch and straighter heels, most of them supplied by Charley, on the rue Clichy.[57] In 1913 skimpy hemlines on uncorseted gowns combined with a whisper of tulle over bare shoulders made for extra-light costumes.[58] Transparency characterised that season's designs, outdoing Directoire fashions and approvingly reported by the *New York Times* when modelled by 'a tall mannikin' whose skirt was 'slightly open on the left side, allowing the stockings to be seen'.[59]

By 1913 wired lampshade overskirts were common, following the trend set the previous season by Poiret's costumes for the play *Le Minaret* (see **73**). Conservative houses like Worth and Redfern decorously filled the knee-length slits in their underskirts with chiffon, lace or embroidery. The back of the neckline, however, was cut increasingly low, sometimes as low as the waistline, to reveal a naked back, uncovered by lace or chiffon; this caused a Paquin mannequin, 'little Martha', to wear her pendant at the back.[60] Legs were still on show at Poiret, Callot and Drecoll in the spring 1914 collections, with high slits at the back and sides of narrow silk and brocade skirts that revealed the mannequins' legs as they made their entry or exit on the modelling stage.[61] In what were to be the final shows before the outbreak of war, a 'rage for transparency' and 'extreme sheerness' predominated, similar to the effect that Lucile's mannequins had demonstrated from the beginning of the century in the flesh-coloured undergarments they wore below her diaphanous gowns. The new flesh-coloured corsets of 1914 were 'made from the sheerest possible material . . . and the effect produced under a transparent bodice is decidedly X-rayish', pronounced the *Chicago Daily Tribune*, which declared them

but another attempt on the part of fashion to reduce all garments to a state of utter transparency. . . . Flesh colored brassieres are carrying out the same nude fashion effects. This style originated with the French Couturiers using the flesh colored linings for the

229 A fashionable woman photographed at the Chantilly races with sunlight shining through her unlined skirt. *L'Illustration*, 21 June 1913. (www.lillustration.com).

transparent bodices. Mousseline de soie and other materials correspondingly sheer are used for these brassieres, which mold and support the body and which blend in perfectly with the color of the body . . . Corset cover brassieres are an idea which Premet has spent much time in elaborating, and they are both pretty and decidedly useful. They are worn under the sheer blouses, which are growing more daring all the time.[62]

American *Vogue* described these last collections before the First World War, the spring 1914 openings, with 'frocks so abbreviated, so transparent and so décolleté' worn by the mannequins with 'their exquisitely modelled chests . . . their beautiful shoulders and backs, their long sinuous arms, their shapely limbs, and their neat ankles'.[63] The young Erté, who went to work for Poiret in 1913, recalled these extremely décolleté dresses worn with tulle scarves over bare shoulders so that their wearers 'seemed to rise, nude, out of fluffy clouds'.[64]

For all that the fashions and corsets were softer and more comfortable, such revealing styles brought their own difficulties. In a photograph from 1913 (**229**) a fashionable woman stands at the Chantilly races in an unlined skirt through which the late afternoon sunlight shines to reveal her legs silhouetted beneath the flimsy fabric. As Anne Hollander wrote, comfort in dress is psychological as much as it is physical:

> Old sartorial difficulties – trains and whalebones – were exchanged for new ones: the psychologically taxing problems of looking comfortable and dressing simply while being rather exposed. Bad legs or a bad figure had no hiding place, and the need for a good one was never more obvious. Comfort . . . in clothing is a mental rather than a physical condition.[65]

The move to a more revealing body silhouette brought further changes: as the outer discipline of the corset receded, the inner disciplines of diet and exercise came to the fore.[66] Increasingly, the couturiers began to choose more slender mannequins, whose physique made them appear a race apart from other women.

THE SLENDER BODY

In the years leading up to the First World War, mannequins were sent into public places to model the newly fashionable slender, active body. The shift in the fashionable female shape from a full figure to today's slim ideal is often erroneously thought to be a 1920s development but the American historian Peter Stearns suggests that in the U.S.A. it originated in the 1890s.[67] The French fashion historian Marylène Delbourg-Delphis wrote that in France the desire to be thinner began around 1900; she argued that fashionable women were not, however, as slender as fashion illustrations after 1912 might suggest and women did not really become much thinner before 1914.[68] Mannequins, however, often were. Their slimmer silhouette placed a new emphasis on the legs, on the nude body beneath the clothes and on the body in motion. These continue to characterise the fashionable female figure today, which is slender, active and, compared with earlier periods, revealingly dressed. When the mannequin 'modelled' the new, slender body shape, she turned her back on the stiff body forms of the nineteenth-century wicker mannequin and towards the differently articulated body of the future, one whose flexions were conditioned by popular dance and sport: as she walked, her form assimilated the rhythms of modernity.

Paquin's mannequin Dicka recalled in 1906 that a mannequin had to have a 'fashionable' rather than a 'good' figure:

> '[A]s I am now, I am too plump to be an ideal mannequin, although ideals are changing of late. The very important American trade long ago brought in the American type mannequin – wearing the costumes of a robust girl. You understand, the mannequin

ought really to have the ideal figure of this or that type of customer. Because what is she there for? Why, simply to wear and show off the models of the season! There are skinny, bony mannequins, and very badly made; but being properly corseted and wearing the mannequin's "sheath" instead of underclothes, the costume molds itself to the girl and the girl to the costume.'
> 'Must she be skinny to be an ideal mannequin?'
> 'No!' cried Dicka, 'I was never skinny! I was a mannequin for Americans!'[69]

Here Dicka reveals a typically contemporary idea of the American woman as being more strapping than the dainty Frenchwoman (**230**). This notion was modified over the following decade so that by the 1920s the Frenchwoman had come to be seen as the sturdier and more curvaceous, while the American woman was perceived as leaner and more athletic.

In the 1900s the statuesque ideal still prevailed. In 1908 an article in the American *Harper's Bazar* on 'How to Get Plump' recommended the ideal weight for a woman of 5′1″ as 120 lbs (8 stone 8 lbs or 54.5 kg) and for 5′9″ as 162 lbs (11 stone 8 lbs or 73.5 kg).[70] At that time, to be thin (that is, thin by today's standards) was still considered unattractive, although, as Stearns points out, by 1900 a more slender aesthetic prevailed among East Coast women, in contrast to the voluptuous image of the actress.[71] Yet in 1912, *Harper's Bazar* carried an article on weight loss called 'How To Reduce Flesh'.[72] Over only four years, approximately 1910–14, the fashionable female shape changed radically in fashion imagery, becoming slenderer, taller and with more emphasis on the appearance of the body in motion.[73] Just as the styling and scenography of Paquin's and Patou's shows before the war were proto-modernist, so too were the body types of the mannequins they selected; the modernist body of Chanel and Patou in the 1920s had their precedents in those at Paquin and Parry before the war. Indeed, Hillel Schwartz has argued that the 'new kinaesthetic' of early twentieth-century physical culture attuned human bodies and sensibilities to the rhythm of machines in ways that are still here today: 'Our bodies themselves have been configured into machinehood: they run smoothly or break down, compute or go haywire. We lead monotonic lives punctuated by obsessions with an impossible perfection (mechanization) of the body in sport, in sexual congress and in childrearing. We are uncomfortable with anything less than a streamlined figure, flawless, odourless, detached and detachable.'[74]

It was mannequins who largely spearheaded the streamlining of the fashionably taller body shape in the pre-war years but the fashion industry that masterminded it. In 1909 Lucile announced herself a supporter of the move

230 The Frenchwoman and the American in 1913. 'A friendly personification of the *entente cordiale*: "Mademoiselle" and "Miss"'. *L'Illustration*, 14 June 1913. (www.lillustration.com).

231 Mannequins at Poiret posing in front of the parterre of his garden in 1910. Poiret's mannequins were slender and petite in this period.

The day of the tall mannequin was still to come. *Femina*, 1 August 1910.

from an Edwardian wasp-waist to a larger, 26-inch one. She decreed that all her mannequins

> must have a uniform waist measurement of 24½ inches. There was an outcry from the mannequins, some of whom had been brought up under the old regime, where the fashionable modiste's model was required to lace in to 18 inches. 'Pad your corsets out', was Lucile's reply to this protest, and that is how the mannequins at this celebrated establishment are able to show the correct waist.[75]

In 1910 mannequins were still petite. One newspaper cited the ideal mannequin measurements as a 40-centimetre (15¾-in) waist and 165-centimetre (5′5″) height: 'it was the small woman who controlled the market. She was made supreme by the eccentric Poiret, Poiret the Bold' (**231**).[76] By 1912, however, the same source declared, 'The golden age of the little woman is ended. One unspecified couture house with a large English and American clientele is showing this season on mannequins who are 1.75 to 1.77 tall' (about 5′9″ to 5′10″).[77] The quest for taller manne-quins was epitomised in the U.S.A. by Lucile's Dinarzade at over 1.80 (nearly 5′11″) and Dolores, almost as tall. By the late 1920s this was the norm and the minimum height for a fashion mannequin was 1.70 metres (about 5′7″).[78]

If the mannequins were taller, they were also more slender. The 'narrow line' (*la ligne étroite*) of the early 1910s required a slim figure and different underwear. In June 1912 the regular fashion column of *Fantasio* announced: 'It's done! The reign of the narrow line has won . . . the female toilette is completely reinvented'. It went on to describe how the new line required women to be thin; larger women were trying to slim down and 'massage, diet and electricity are, in this noble aim, conscientiously employed'.[79] The mannequins in the couture houses, meanwhile, were ahead of the game. Their employers had been selecting and moulding their appearance for years through diet and styling. The *New York Times* fashion correspondent complained at the August 1912 Paris openings that the new draped silhouette with bulky fabric at the hips might not suit the fuller figure:

> One cannot tell at these openings what any fashion will look like on our American figures. I wish someone would confess how these mannequins are kept thin! House after house presents dozens of girls who do not weigh over 120 pounds, many of them not that much, and yet they are live wires, as far as health and alertness go. They have been parading up and down the salons now for fourteen days, from 10 A.M. until 5 P.M. – a veritable treadmill for them – and they look as happy and vigorous today as they did when they started. So they are not weakened by being there. Our Anglo-Saxon figures look Amazonic beside theirs.[80]

232 'As with fashion, so with the mannequin'. *Femina*, 1 November 1911 (photographs by Art Femina and Reutlinger). The magazine shows how dramatically the desired mannequin figure had changed between 1908 and 1911. Musée Galliera de la Mode de la Ville de Paris. Photograph Richard Hubert Smith.

There had always been a gap between the client and mannequin, in terms of income, class and youth; in the 1910s it widened to included body type, thus further separating the mannequin's appearance from the rest of womankind. In 1910 Roger-Milès differentiated the mannequin from the client as a woman with 'obliterated hips, a scant bust, a thin figure, an elegant carriage'.[81] As the fashionable shape became slimmer, another American journalist complained in 1911, in terms remarkably similar to objections today to the body ideal promoted by the use of extremely thin models, that

> only slight curves are endurable to those who create styles. The ultimatum that went forth in the great dressmaking houses that no mannequin should weigh over 140 pounds tells a tale that is too pathetic to emphasise or elaborate. It simply means that three-fourths of the women of the world are not formed right, or rather not covered with the exact proportion of flesh that the law of fashion lays down.[82]

In 1912, in an article on the 'Folly of Slenderness', Colette excoriated the modern craze for dieting brought on by the Tanagra dress.[83] She describes her friend Valentine in her new Tanagra corset that stretches from her armpits to just above her knees, with a rigid bust and long whalebones like armour-plating. The corset's advertisement claims that it completely flattens the stomach, the hips and any posterior projection. Colette pours scorn on this: 'completely', she repeats, witheringly. She thinks it makes her friend, who is already slender, look like a pink sausage and asks her 'Vous souffrez beaucoup?' Valentine looks very

surprised and says that all corsets are like that nowadays 'because of the Tanagra dress . . . it is indispensable; it is the fashion. Everyone is thin. Don't you find it attractive? It is the triumph of the slender figure.' On the contrary, Colette declares her friend to be both mad and ugly, with no breasts, bottom or stomach. *La ligne droite* is a cretinous fashion (*une vogue imbécile*) she writes, in which a woman can neither sit nor bend but only stand upright. It is the death of beauty and the impoverishment of the female race.[84]

Colette vigorously attacks both the Tanagra corset and the newly slender body ideal that it heralded. The new thin ideal cannot be construed solely as a detrimental imposition on women, however, but as a complex dialectic of constriction and liberation, in which the imperative to be thin was inseparable from the freedom to be active and mobile. This was the rhetoric that Colette attacked in her article and, in this sense, the regulation of the body may always be marked by contradiction.[85] What became apparent in the fashion industry was the malleability of the professional mannequin's image, not to be confused with the malleability of her body through diet and exercise. In 1911 *Femina* showed two similarly clad mannequins three years apart to demonstrate how the fashionable figure had changed in that short time (**232**). The caption asks rhetorically 'Are women's bodies infinitely malleable?' and goes on to answer that while 'fashion would seem to prove it', in fact 'we hasten to say that fashion is not the only cause: the couturiers are expert at choosing "mannequins" whose bodies best adapt themselves to the character of new fashions, hence the antithesis that our photographs bring to light.'[86] So if one mannequin will no longer do, another can be found to replace her. It is precisely this malleability that was required to produce the chorus-line appearance of fashion line-ups in 1912. In *Femina*'s description of Paquin's mannequins in 1914 as 'tall, thin, elegant and almost identical', the mannequin's image was becoming as standardised as the rationalised bodies of art, leisure and work.[87] By 1923 Colette was complaining that fashion planed the body to the bone, minimising its flesh and its tempting curves. 'Where are the beautiful women of some fifteen years ago who wore the fortunes of the couturiers on their noble shoulders?' she asked. 'What has become of that splendid Louisa, winner of a beauty prize, who trailed velvets and brocades barely pinned to her faultless body through the *quartier Vendôme*? The mannequin of today puts her seventeen years on show while she is still growing, her pointed elbows and her collarbone saltcellars as hollow as a schoolgirl's.'[88]

Lucile, too, required her mannequins to be slender, despite having installed a kitchen in the basement of her New York house to provide food and drink for them at work.[89] At some time during her New York period from 1910 to 1922, probably during the war, while at work in her New York studio she contemplated the revival of heavy brocade as a fashion fabric. Her employee, Elsie, a former mannequin, recalled her announcing 'Elsie, I have it! I know what I want! I would like to find a girl I can drape brocades on, a girl so thin that one could count every bone in her body! In fact, what I want is the thinnest girl in all the world!'[90] Accordingly, she advertised for 'the thinnest girl in the world', heading it 'Urgent', and found Arjamand, as she renamed her (see **89**).[91] Elsie described Arjamand as 'tall, dark, thin, graceful and exotic . . . she was in type a slender, swaying reed, so thin, I often feared, as I later watched her pace the long rooms in the divinely draped brocaded gowns, she would bend, then break, and dissolve into a graceful, luxurious heap upon the floor'.[92] Until she went to work for Lucile, however, Arjamand, whose real name is not given by Elsie, had 'seemed unaware of her graces', had loathed being thin and had been preoccupied with a diet intended to help her gain weight.

While this example is extreme and perhaps singular, the general trend for slenderness persisted into 1913, requiring tall, slim mannequins about whom journalists endlessly complained: fashionable women were seen 'by the score', wrote one, who was 'sadly watching the slender mannequins parading about in costumes which would make a woman with a forty six inch hip measure look like an animated barrel'.[93] The new coats are decreed 'really charming when the hipless mannequin had displayed them'

at a fashionable tailor's but produced the opposite effect on the client. Lucile herself pointed out, in her column for *Harper's Bazar* in 1913, that that season's fashions were

> only for the young and slim. I cannot yet give a word of comfort or hope to the fat or the middle-aged that they may be in the height of fashion and yet not be ridiculous. But I am going to invent some dresses with flowing dignified lines and with ample stuff in them, and no 'hitches' up in unexpected places.[94]

By 1914 the boyish silhouette had won. That year the majority of the mannequins at the annual Bal des Couturiers appeared without corsets, a few in body-skimming girdles in the thinnest elastic, boned just enough to keep them smooth.[95] That season's ultra-narrow skirts even outlawed petticoats, which were replaced with fine silk crêpe de chine bloomers for afternoon dress and even finer silk chiffon ones for evening dress.[96] The new season's fashions are pre-eminently for the slender woman, wrote the *Chicago Daily Tribune*, and the couturiers' shift of interest to slender women 'will be gratifying for all women inclined to slimness, for it is a well known fact that for years the stout woman has been the one considered, and the thin woman neglected'. Now 'the slender woman has achieved a distinction and wrested for herself the right to be considered'.[97]

It was as mixed a blessing as the earlier requirement for the statuesque figure. In the 1920s the slender ideal was consolidated. Colette bemoaned the geometry of modern fashions that banished smooth curves, 'arrogant' breasts and shapely hips.[98] Chanel chose mannequins in her own, slender image, even fitting the fuller-figured ones with a whaleboned brassiere to flatten their more ample bosoms.[99] While some couturiers only dressed thin women, others like Vionnet would also dress the fuller figure.[100] The increasing emphasis not only on slenderness but also on youth and activity produced an image of women as uniform: 'short hair destroys diversity', wrote the comtesse de Noailles in 1926, 'and gives us a repeated image of identical napes. . . . Certainly our epoch favours their appearance of permanent youth'.[101] Through such simple forms of body styling as make-up and hair-cuts, the malleability of the mannequin could be extended to all women. It came, however, with more punishing regimes for older women. On her return to Paris in 1928 after four years' absence, another commentator in *Vogue* noted that women appeared not to age between forty and fifty-five or sixty but only due to exercise, to violent showers and to an abstemious diet composed almost exclusively of vegetables and fruit.[102]

In 1924–5, Patou's American mannequins had been promoted as more slender and taller than their French counterparts. Over the following years, Patou recruited several more groups of American mannequins and in 1928 approached Florenz Ziegfeld for help in finding a new type of 'girl'.[103] The years in which mannequins were required to be at their thinnest were 1924–8.[104] After then, the 'Boyish form is passé', announced the papers; 'Jean Patou will have none of the cropped and skinny type which in Paris is known as "La Garçonne".'[105] Although she was fuller-figured, the 'new' mannequin's body was no less rationalised, recalling Ned Wrayburn's draconian specifications for the Ziegfeld Follies: 'The perfect woman, as outlined under the new rules, should measure up to the standards tabulated on this page', at the top of the article:

THE NEW "NATURAL WOMAN,"
According to Jean Patou and Florenz Ziegfeld
WEIGHT . . . . 128 lbs.
HEIGHT . . . . 5 ft. 7 in.
BUST.. . . . . 34 in.
WAIST. . . . . 27 in.
HIPS. . . . . 35 in.
CALF.. . . . . 14 in.
ANKLE .. . . .7 in.[106]

From Ziegfeld, Patou took the idea of a precise specification of the body proportions required for the chorus line and applied it to the mannequin line-up, much as he had tabulated his mannequins' chic in terms of profitability in the mid-1920s.[107]

In 1929 the fashionable shape, while still slender, shifted from the stick-thin flapper. In Paris, two hundred mannequins were reported to have lost their jobs because they were too thin; a hundred of them appealed to the Parisian Tribune of Commerce, asserting that they could not be expected to modify their figures to suit the fashions. Fifteen 'whose forte had always been "the famine line" plead that they ruined their health keeping thin and now are unable to recoup the lost poundage'.[108] While this account must be taken with a pinch of salt, it indicates that the tyranny of fashion may have lain more in the constantly changing ideal of the female figure rather than in the requirement to be thin.

Peter Stearns has discussed a range of possible causes for the shift to a thin ideal from the early 1900s in France, including the hypothesis that slimmer fashions expressed a decline in maternity.[109] Susan Bordo has argued that the late nineteenth-century interest in diet was a precursor to the twentieth-century culture of slimness.[110] Mary Louise Roberts has also analysed women's faith in the malleability of the body in 1920s France and their belief that they could alter the body through the self-imposed regimes of diet,

exercise and beauty products.[111] She argues that, although these requirements were harsh, which might suggest that fashion was no more than a marketing ploy on the part of its producers, fashion nevertheless offered a complex form of liberation to its consumers, the women who wore it: 'by conceiving of fashion as a language of movement and change, even when it was not, designers like Paul Poiret and Coco Chanel created a visual fantasy of liberation [which] . . . then became a cultural reality in itself that was not without political importance'.[112] She remarks that the quick-change of appearances 'represented a visual declaration of sudden change in women's lives as well as in fashion' and that this was political in ways that were 'strange and contradictory': a fantasy of social liberation which was nevertheless purely individualistic, fashion privileged the appearance of emancipation over its reality. However, as she points out, the look scandalised and infuriated its critics; in that respect alone, it was effective and political, because of how it became part of the cultural imaginary.[113]

At the same time that fashions changed towards a more slender, body-revealing ideal, doctors increasingly identified eating disorders. Elizabeth A. Williams describes a growing focus in medical practice from the late nineteenth century to 1914 on psycho-gastric disorders such as obesity, diabetes, gastropathy, 'nervous vomiting', bulimia and anorexia, which resulted from changing medical perceptions of the central nervous system but which was also a response to cultural anxieties about gender, especially about women, in the period. Doctors at the *fin de siècle* for the first time identified 'a distinct disease entity characterised by repugnance for or refusal of food and labelled as some kind of "anorexia".'[114] Yet the first calls for a slender body came not from fashion designers but from doctors: Stearns shows how the fashionable ideal of *embonpoint* was at odds with medical demands for dieting before the First World War.[115] Only after the war did fashion writers begin to advocate a slimmer figure. What is not clear, however, in the early twentieth century any more than in the early twenty-first, is whether there was any causal connection between the slender figures of mannequins and the female vogue for extreme dieting and physical exercise in pursuit of a slim, toned and youthful-looking body.

GENDER MASQUERADE

Roberts argues that the regulatory aspects of fashion could, and did, co-exist with its imaginative and self-creative aspects. Her arguments are not far removed from the consideration of the social role and importance of the way that the pre-war mannequin entered the cultural imaginary.[116] In her malleability, her quicksilver appearance and sudden transformations, the mannequin spoke the quick-change theatricality of the early twentieth century, including its gender masquerade. Erté masqueraded in 1913 at the society first night of a play at the Théâtre de Vaudeville as one of Poiret's mannequins, dressed in an ermine and red velvet coat and turban, but afterwards declined Poiret's invitation to model for him professionally.[117] Elizabeth de Gramont described how, when the vogue for boyish-looking mannequins was at its peak in 1927–8, one firm slipped an adolescent boy to model into its fashion show and no one noticed.[118] The mannequin's performance, be s/he female or male, modelled the indeterminacy of gender as something that could be as effectively conveyed by walk, gesture and pose as by biological sex. An early example of womanliness as a masquerade, the mannequin is living proof that femininity can be studied, learnt, imitated and perfected.

In the 1926 American comedy film *Irene*, the 'couturière' 'Mme Lucie' – who is a man – teaches three novices to model. Despairing at their failure to walk properly, he minces across the room making appropriate arm gestures and executes a swift sashay as the three young women look on and learn (**233**). The comedy, not unsympathetic, resides in the teaching of femininity by a biological man to young women. Mme Lucie's masquerade, like the mannequins' high heels, divorces femininity from nature and articulates it as something that can be learnt, modelled and updated to suit that year's styles. To French audiences in the 1920s, the masquerade of femininity was not unfamiliar through the music-hall performer Barbette, a man whose act involved transforming himself into a women on the high wire through gesture, pose and attitude.[119] Generally, however, male effeminacy was a subject for comedy. In the 1924 film *Les Ombres qui passent*, the buffoonish hero smartens himself up by going to a tailor, buying smart shoes and, in one comical scene, putting on lashings of pomades and perfumes from a set of feminine bottles ranged in front of a three-faced mirror (**234**). Patou's press book for 1924 contains a cutting of Charlie Chaplin 'guying' the three tall mannequins from Patou, Lelong and Drecoll (**235**). Then, as a gimmick, in 1925, Lanvin briefly introduced fashion shows for bored husbands waiting during their wives' fittings (**236**).[120] Male fashion shows still remained the exception, however, and in 1929 the French magazine *Adam* illustrated a British one under the heading 'England Has Dared: Male Mannequins' (see **2**).[121]

233 (above) Modelling scene from the 1926 comedy film *Irene* directed by Alfred E. Green. A young Irish girl, Irene O'Dare, gets a job modelling for the couturière 'Madame Lucie' who turns out to be an exquisite young man with white gloves and a cane. He is initially displeased with Irene's technique: 'I've seen sausages with more style than you. A little nonchalance – diablerie – esprit du corps' he urges her. Here he teaches her and her two friends how to do it in an exemplary performance of femininity. 'The most important thing is the carriage. You mustn't walk – you must ooze along.' Madame Lucie leads the way, sashaying briskly with his hands on his hips, followed by the three girls with books on their heads. Irene stumbles. 'You're impossible – you walk almost like a man!' is his verdict. 'So do you!' she replies, quick as a flash. Washington, D.C., Library of Congress.

234 (below) In this scene from the 1924 film *Les Ombres qui passent* directed by Alexandre Volkoff, the male protagonist who has been led astray by city ways primps before a three-faced mirror arrayed with a range of women's toiletries and perfume bottles. © Cinémathèque Française.

235 (above) Charlie Chaplin posing with fashion mannequins at New York's Sax & Company in 1925. The mannequin in the centre is one of Patou's house mannequins. 'This is the way I would pose', says Chaplin in the caption, 'were I to appear in these creations from Patou, Lelong and Drecoll'. *Theatre Magazine*, November 1925.

236 (below) Male mannequin at Lanvin. *Harper's Bazar*, July 1925, wrote tongue in cheek: 'Lanvin has a tailoring establishment for men with manikins and everything. . . . the prettiest man gives you a jack-knife bow in the doorway. (that's the salesman) . . . He claps his hands and into the room comes a male manikin. . . . He is built to wear clothes. His sleek black hair is vaselined to the polish of a brand new door-knob. . . . His socks are superb. He stands before you, walks away, and then sits down so you can get the idea of a reclining pose. He disappears and returns in a Norfolk suit and then his brother manikin enters in a gorgeous silk house robe.'

Gender masquerade in the 1920s signified entirely differently for men and for women. In her discussion of Victor Margueritte's 1922 novel *La Garçonne*, Mary Louise Roberts has argued that its themes of gender instability and inversion are the result of a post-war crisis of masculinity as much as they are an articulation of what it meant to be a modern woman in the period. Monique, the androgynous heroine, figures both as a new woman and as a 'no-man', the man who had been made frail or feminine by the war.[122] Something of the androgyny of the *garçonne* had always characterised the mannequin, not necessarily in her bodily styling but in her alienated appeal as a pure abstraction. The noun is masculine, *le mannequin*, and thus also neuter in French; in 1896, an article in *L'Art et la mode* suggested that the earliest mannequins might have been of either sex: 'She or He has beautiful gestures, always the same, a supremely bored manner, an affected grace. It's French elegance that moves in long processions before the dazzled eyes of foreigners.'[123] Here the mannequin is both idealised as French and conceived of as being outside gender norms, the artifice of her performance distancing her from everyday banality.

The mannequin's adaptability was progressively more necessary as skirt shapes and corsetry changed in the early years of the century, from the hobble, Polonaise, Directoire and Sylphide dress to the *jupe-culotte* and *robe-pantalon* and the almost transparent fashions of 1912–13. In all of them the mannequin offered a perpetual promise of becoming, in which appearance acted as a holding station for a fantasy of immanence, her body a stage for debates about morality, gender and class. If mannequins were tricksters, specialists in magical thinking with the ability to bring a dress to life, they were also time-travellers, bringing future visions into the present to show women what they could become. Like Hadaly, the mechanical woman of Villiers's nineteenth-century *L'Ève future*, the early twentieth-century mannequin epitomised the idealised female body in what Annette Michelson calls a 'fantasmic mode of representation.'[124]

11
MOVEMENT
THE MANNEQUIN WALK

237 Detail from Enrico Sacchetti's fashionable poses, from Gabriel Mourey, 'Les Caprices de la ligne', *Gazette du Bon Ton*, May 1913. See **241**.

'She had the gift of imitation. Raised on the tiptoes of her worn ankle boots, puffing herself up like a peacock spreading its tail, she advanced and withdrew on the parquet with a harmonious step, assumed coquettish poses, and slid, light and undulating.'[1] In the 1907 novel *Yette, mannequin*, René Maizeroy describes a young girl's first attempt to replicate the singular walk of the Paris mannequins, with raised head and upright posture. French mannequins were known for their particular, gliding walk, even in clothes in which other women found it hard to walk at all. As fashions and social expectations changed, so too did the mannequin walk, sometimes with surprising speed and variety. In the 1910s, mannequins produced, in turn, a hunched walk determined by narrow fashions, a rolling walk influenced by popular dance crazes and a high-heeled strut produced by higher shoes. After the First World War, in the 1920s, a bored slouching walk distinguished them, with the hips and stomach pushed well forward. In all these changes, the mannequins proved themselves as malleable as the fashionable body shape and as protean as fashion itself.

Over thirty years, the mannequin walk went from a comparatively fixed way of holding the body upright within its own centre of gravity, to a far more fluid and expansive kind of movement as mannequins gestured with their arms and flexed their torsos, creating a mobile silhouette through the shifting relationship of shoulders to hips. It is possible to chart some of the changes as well as the constancies in the early twentieth-century mannequin walk, and to relate them to the history of social walking and to both popular dance crazes and avant-garde dance performance. In the same period, for example, through the contribution of choreographers such as Michel Fokine, classical ballet techniques evolved, similarly to the mannequin walk, from a fixed, predominantly vertical torso with activity concentrated in the legs, to a pliant torso extended further into space by fluid arm movements.[2] Hillel Schwartz identified a trend across all forms of physical culture from a calm, upright and corseted body to one whose 'chief pattern was the spiral; its deepest resource was torsion'.[3]

GESTURE AS HABITUS

Gestures are social and, as Keith Thomas has argued in his introduction to Bremmer and Roodenburg's history of the gesture, such studies are important because they reveal 'an indispensable element in the social interaction of the past' and are 'a key to some of the fundamental values and assumptions underlying any particular society; as the French historians would say, it illuminates *mentalité*'.[4] Thomas's reference to *mentalités* aligns the history of gesture, deportment and movement with the history of sensibilities. Daniel Wickberg differentiates the 'old' history of sensibilities from the 'new' cultural history, arguing that whereas recent cultural historians have tended to view images and objects from the past as constitutive of categories such as race, class and gender rather than as evidence of lived experience, historians of sensibilities focused on 'the primacy of the various modes of perception and feeling, the terms and forms in which objects were conceived, experienced, and represented in the past'.[5]

In the early twentieth century deportment was considered amenable to study and improvement through teaching; this brought with it an awareness of posture as a form of distinction.[6] French gymnastic teaching gave girls a sense of poise while in the U.S.A. gestural posing was used well into the century in a new form of elocution training that had been developed from the 1880s.[7] Jean Patou declared that the essence of *chic* was to be found in bodily style and stance, rather than a way of wearing clothes. 'Some of it is in the way a woman holds her head, carries her shoulders, uses her hands – but most of all it is how she puts her foot on the floor. When I engage mannequins, that is what I first look at – how the girl puts her foot on the floor.'[8] Coco Chanel taught her mannequins a posture based on her own, as Bettina Ballard recalled: 'She has invented that famous Chanel stance that looks relaxed as a cat, and has an impertinent chic; one foot forward, hips forward, shoulders down, one hand in a pocket and the other gesticulating.'[9]

The idea that posture could be studied and hence modified was not limited to professional mannequins; deportment was part of a fashionable bearing. In 1914 American *Vogue* commented that every time the Parisienne changed couturier 'she is compelled to change her pose and her way of looking at life'.[10] The article described how fashions affected bodily stance and posture, so that

> When we wear one of the new short skirts we must stand with our feet squarely under us, and not with one foot thrust out in the foreground, as has been our custom for the last three seasons. That pose came in with the skirt that was slit in front and which hung in slanting folds . . . but the short skirt, which is already fairly well launched, is not slit, and so demands a different pose.[11]

'New fashions teach new gestures', decreed French *Vogue* in 1921, in an article devoted to fashionable posing.[12] Announcing that modern life was producing simpler gestures, it argued that the weight of a bead-encrusted evening dress would affect how women sat at the opera, while long and fluid scarves would teach women the art of manipulating fabric around them. Why not study the art of walking, eating or sitting for an hour a day, it asked, for the science of expressions and gestures is most important in modern life, when the angle of a head or a walk becomes decisive.[13]

Tracing the history of something as ephemeral as the walk poses a challenge, however, in terms of both method and interpretation.[14] Karlheinz Stierle has argued that in the nineteenth century Balzac 'carnivalised' the language of science in his 'Théorie de la démarche' in order to describe the walk, venturing into a marginal terrain of knowledge and urban experience that had no official discourse.[15] This method was, as Balzac himself observed, poised between science and madness, amenable only to 'people who find wisdom in a fallen leaf, gigantic problems in evanescent smoke, theories in the vibrations of light, thought embedded in marble statues, and horrible movement in immobility.'[16] Indeed, such are the types of modern trace in which the physical gestures and bodily attitudes of the past can be discerned: 'slight' sources such as fashion journalism or popular fiction yield more than supposedly weightier ones such as company records or government archives. Fragmentary images of the walk can be found in the vestiges of material culture that Pierre Nora relied on: 'spaces, gestures, images and objects'.[17] Photographs, fashion plates, journalism and memoirs provide evocative vignettes of the first mannequins in motion but do not actually show the walk; early film, by contrast, shows ways of walking and posing but is not entirely reliable due to its variable filming and projecting speeds. To the historian, finding and then making sense of these fragments can feel more archaeological than historical and reading 'sensibilities' off them is especially complex.

A number of historians have done so, nevertheless. Michael Braddick argues for the historian's need to analyse and understand the whole cultural and social context of a gesture, not only its meaning in relation to speech and the mind.[18] This is similar to the social theorist Pierre Bourdieu's concept of 'habitus', a set of dispositions that generate practices and perceptions, including bodily practices such as stance, gait and gesture. In his *Outline of a Theory of Practice* (1977) Bourdieu used the term 'bodily hexis' to describe how discourses and ideologies are embedded in sensibilities and bodies: 'Bodily hexis is political mythology realised, *em-bodied*, turned into a permanent disposition, a durable manner of standing, speaking and thereby of *feeling* and thinking.'[19] Much in this vein, Georges Vigarello's history of how posture, the walk and other bodily styles were inculcated over several centuries shows how movement is not natural but socially and culturally constructed. His history of the pedagogy of the body draws on sources ranging from etiquette books, corsets, gymnastic routines and fashion plates.[20]

Other historians have suggested combining traditional historical methods with those of cultural anthropology and ethnography.[21] Angela Latham has argued that the 1920s flapper's look 'was as much a pose as it was a particular style of clothing women wore' and that, therefore, to re-experience the 'socially bequeathed sparks of lives now biologically extinguished', the historian looking for sensory clues about the performance of female identity in the 1920s should seek out the 'sensory experiences represented in the archives of history'. Latham has described her methodology as 'historical performance ethnography' and argued for 'a virtual kinaesthetic understanding of the cultural world', because 'the performative aspects of a historical culture – or any culture for that matter – are highly saturated with sensory clues'.[22] Similarly, the dance historian and theorist Susan Leigh Foster has discussed how the historian of bodies experiences through his or her own body a longing to find the vanished bodies of history, arguing that the historian always has a stake in her findings and thus develops a kind of 'kinesthetic empathy' with the bodies of the past, an unofficial type of identification not sanctioned by the methods of the discipline of history.[23]

Thinking about kinaesthetics involves thinking about bodies, practices, spaces and subjectivities. This, in turn, suggests that elements of early twentieth-century fashion were embedded in movement as well as time; and that fashion is a situated, embodied and spatial practice as much as it is a form of design or an item of commercial exchange.[24] Here Joanne Entwistle's definition of fashion as 'a situated bodily practice' comes into play. Drawing on a combination of structuralism and phenomenology, Entwistle argues that the former treats the body as 'a socially constituted and situated object' and the latter as an 'embodied experience'.[25] Their combination suggests a way to understand the performance and visual appeal of the early fashion mannequin as both culturally constructed and subjectively experienced; furthermore, there was a feedback between the two in the production of what Liz Conor has called the 'woman-object', when women in the early twentieth century were invited to articulate themselves as modern subjects by constituting themselves as spectacles.[26]

If early twentieth-century modernist identities were increasingly constructed and maintained in the visual register, looking and vision were also bodily practices. The idea of fashion as a situated, embodied and spatial practice is useful not only to sociologists but also to cultural, literary and art historians. The literary scholar Michael Levenson has argued that modernism is not just 'soft culture' but also consists of 'hard, causal powers of modern action' that include habits and routines: 'the pace of walking, a style of gazing, a tensing of the muscles. Our bodies become modernized, and there we dwell, in those modernized bodies, in technologies, and also in concepts and images as products of modernization'.[27] Levenson shifted his attention from the study of literary texts alone to 'a complex of inventive gestures, daring performances', a kind of postural avant-garde that existed beyond the artistic production of the modern movement.[28]

For Levenson, the early twentieth-century walk is part of a modernist sense of time speeded up, and he has invoked Koselleck's philosophy of historical time – a sense of time accelerating as constitutive of modernity.[29] The ascendency of novelty as a category of experience that Levenson connects to avant-garde literature is also related to fashion in the early twentieth century, with its new forms of dissemination, in moving media (the fashion show and fashion newsreel) and in a new 'slapdash' style of fashion illustration that mimicked motion in the many new fashion publications of the century.[30] Levenson argues that the concept of the new is itself a technology, not merely an effect of technology; in the walking fashion mannequins of the new century, it was a technology of the body. The fashion mannequin's gliding walk mimicked the gliding motion of the *trottoir roulant* at the 1900 Exposition. Her smooth revolutions on the spot imitated the mechanical turntables used in nineteenth-century theatres for *poses plastiques*.[31] Her fashion line-ups of the pre-war years resembled the working bodies of the chorus line and the regulated bodies of Taylor's system of scientific management of the workplace. The replication of the mannequin's image through diet, exercise, uniforms and mirrors suggested the productivity and speed of Henry Ford's moving assembly line. In these ways, although hers was a modernised body in the sense identified by Levenson, it was not a product of the avant-garde but of new technology, work and popular entertainment. It was materialised between production and consumption, commerce and culture, and disseminated world-wide through fashion magazines and newsreel film.

SOCIAL WALKING

City strolling has an impressive roster of proponents, from John Gay's *Trivia* in the eighteenth century, with its chapter on what to wear to walk in the London rain, to the unstructured strolling of Baudelaire's nineteenth-century *flâneur*, 'botanising on the asphalt', as Benjamin described him.[32] In the twentieth century, it spans the urban 'drifting' or *dérive* of Guy Debord and Michel de Certeau's 'rhetoric of walking' in the modern city.[33] The differences between male and female strollers in public spaces have been described by a number of writers, from Janet Wolff's feminisation of Baudelaire's stroller, *la flâneuse*, to Agnès Rocamora's mobilisation of Claude Leroy's book on *la passante* in her discussion of fashion.[34] Beyond the drawing room and the stage, female movement and gesture were not as value-free in the nineteenth century as Balzac's 'Théorie de la démarche' of 1833 suggests but were, rather, important indicators of social status. Pose was gendered and, in public spaces, women's bodily gestures were highly coded. Valerie Steele has described how the prostitutes of the Second Empire were identifiable in Constantin Guys's sketches not from their clothing but from their sartorial gestures and mannerisms: their way of raising a skirt excessively high, or prolonging the sight of the lower legs, was different from the way an ordinary woman raised her skirts to cross a muddy street.[35] Rocamora describes how the *passante*, a respectable working girl, had to vary her walk in different zones of the city, speeding up in the street and slowing down in the park, in order not to appear disreputable.[36]

While fashionable strolling is a kind of catwalk, as exemplified by the appearance of women at the races and in the Bois de Boulogne, the origins of the bodily styles of couture house fashion modelling lie elsewhere. Their history resides not in open metropolitan spaces but in domestic interiors and in the theatre. The mannequin walk can be tracked back to its eighteenth- and nineteenth-century origins in the deportment and dancing master's lessons. In the early nineteenth century, the Parisienne was known for her appealing and unique walk.[37] In 'La Théorie de la démarche' Balzac argued that walking should be taught as part of '*l'air noble*', a reference perhaps to the deportment lessons of the period.[38] A woman in the nineteenth century was expected, like the mannequin who came after her, to be accomplished and graceful in her movements and gestures. During the Second Empire it fell first to the dancing master and later to the deportment coach to instruct ladies on the social etiquette of bowing, curtseying, waving gracefully to passing acquaintances and making introductions.[39] Graceful attitudes and finely nuanced bodily stances were an intrinsic part of these social niceties and were clearly understood to be teachable rather than innate.

In the late nineteenth century, physical education for all girls was introduced in the French education system. From the 1860s, private schools had taught deportment, including 'a rigidly straight posture and a graceful (smooth) way of walking'.[40] Then, from 1891, the state system of gymnastics for girls in elementary school incorporated some dance.[41] In the early twentieth, supporters of Swedish gymnastics for girls believed that 'the system promised an elegant carriage, graceful gait, and decisive demeanour'.[42] Gymnastic training was held to inculcate gender-appropriate qualities: in girls these were 'good posture, firm breasts, supple movement and self-mastery' that equipped women not for work but for marriage and motherhood.[43] All these forms had the potential to create a 'muscle memory' in the eye, that is, an experience of embodiment that could inform viewing competences of future audiences at fashion shows, for, as Mary Lynn Stewart has argued, 'girls and women acquire bodily awareness through their physical activities, which act directly upon and through the body'.[44]

They learnt from film and magazines too. By 1900, popular magazines served a similar function to the deportment coach. A set of photographs taken by Jessie Tarbox Beales, a professional photographer in New York at the turn of the century, shows how the task of the deportment coach was being taken over by magazines (**238**). These magazine images were produced in a period when journalism (and, from the 1910s, newsreel) was democratising many aspects of elite fashion for a mass audience. Mannequins, too, were role models through these new media. In 1935 Pascal Pia suggested that mannequins were the new deportment teachers: 'if we no longer know any teachers of attitudes, we still possess some veritable technicians of deportment: couture mannequins.'[45]

The evolution of the walk was not limited to fashion and theatre. In their article on the history of posture in the U.S.A., David Yosifon and Peter Stearns describe how a new, lounging stance and a 'graceful slouch' developed in the early twentieth century in tandem with new dance crazes, particularly, though not exclusively, among fashionable people, for ideas about posture crossed all social groups. They argue that 'in the early decades of the twentieth century, posture became a significant issue in middle class socialization, far more widely discussed than in the nineteenth-century', while the advent of full-length mirrors in middle-class homes created a new body consciousness, as for the first time people became

accustomed to scrutiny of the entire body, not just the head and shoulders.[46] In France, too, the three-way mirrors of the early twentieth century encouraged a mobile, fluid view of the body.[47]

THE MANNEQUIN WALK 1900–1910

'A dress is a thing that walks', declared an anonymous couturier in 1902, 'we make moving sculpture.'[48] Motion came to seem the best way to show fashion.[49] To her contemporaries, the mannequin was a walking dress, a Galatea of the ateliers.[50] Her style of walking set her aside from other women and so too did the fact that she walked for a living. She was a walking machine, a new kind of professional who schooled her face to fit the dress and her walk to fit the job.[51]

That walk was both distinctive and recognisable, similar to the way of placing the ball of the foot on the ground before the heel which produces the distinctive walk of ballet dancers. In 1913 Doucet said:

> The first virtue one requires of a mannequin is that she knows how to walk, to walk with ease, nobility and grace. And it is not given to all the world to be able to walk in this way, with the entire body, the foot placed flat, at once solidly and lightly – not like a hen sitting on its eggs. The mannequin who knows that has won the game. She has 'arrived'.[52]

Above all, the French mannequin walk was distinguished by its gliding quality.[53] In 1902 Alexandre described how the mannequins walked 'with a rhythmic step as if dancing, gliding, undulating and arching their backs'.[54] Others described how they undulate, sail, saunter or trail.[55] The artifice of the Parisian mannequins' walk was recognised to be a necessary function of showing clothes off to advantage.[56]

The walk evolved with underwear and dress fashions and, from 1905 to 1910, the Sylphide, hobble and Polonaise skirts each produced a different kind of walk. The Sylphide dress required a new body posture that realigned the torso so that the shoulders were directly above the hips, the bust thrown forward and the spine maintained straight in a natural S-shape.[57] If worn without a foundation garment, the dress was practically impossible to walk in decorously, except when demonstrated by a mannequin.[58] *Fantasio* suggested that the style encouraged languishing and reserved attitudes among fashionable women precisely because dresses were so straight and clinging that they inhibited spontaneous movement. 'Melancholy is being widely worn this season', it reported.[59]

In 1910 the *Atlanta Constitution* declared that 'most changes of modes necessitate a new manner of walking'. It wondered how the gliding walk produced by the Directoire gown would be modified for the Polonaise gown – loose at the ankles but tied tight at the knee – that would inevitably 'necessitate some kind of eccentricity of walk' and asked 'will the new feminine limp become fashionable?'[60] The *New York Times* wrote that, to wear the Polonaise skirt well, a woman 'must have acquired a peculiar pose of the figure which is distinctly Parisian – the shoulder forward, the chin well in the air, the arms hanging loose! The general effect is peculiar, but undoubtedly attractive when seen at its best.'[61]

The brief vogue for the hobble skirt produced another distinctive walk in 1910: Lucile claimed that her Directoire skirts of that year produced a 'hobbled, little-girl walk'.[62] In 1910 Poiret introduced his hobble skirt, of which he notoriously boasted 'I freed the bust but I shackled the legs.'[63] *Fantasio* showed the 'hobble bands' worn underneath the hobble skirt to prevent the wearer taking too large steps (**239**) and which turned simple walking into a skill, converting unconscious action into self-conscious technique. A French journalist commented on the deleterious effect on fashionable women's gait: 'Dressed in restricting skirts, narrowed in the middle and caught up by a *martingale* . . . Parisiennes all have the air of engaging in the joyful sport of sack racing . . . nowadays it takes a real science to know how to walk.'[64]

Enter the mannequins, technicians of the walk. As skirts became more difficult to walk in, for reasons of both practicality and decorum, the mannequins' expertise gave them a new function and a different visibility. They showed not only new fashions but also new ways of standing and

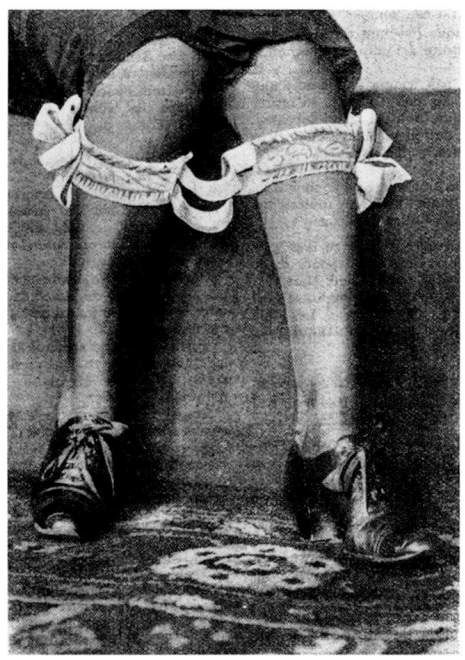

239 Hobble-skirt bands worn underneath narrow dresses to prevent the wearer taking big steps that would tear the material. *Fantasio*, 15 November 1910. Paris, Bibliothèque Forney.

moving. Only trained French mannequins were considered competent to carry off the new, extreme fashions in tied-in skirts; the athletic swinging walk of the American girl strained the hem (see **230**), wrote one journalist.[65] At Poiret's, the mannequins mastered the hobble skirt, walking with tiny steps in a 'sliding, undulating walk'.[66] This undulating walk was described by Poiret in his autobiography where he recalled his favourite mannequin Andrée expanding like a sea anemone in a benign current as she walked.[67]

While nineteenth-century aristocratic women had practised the walk in the drawing room, actresses performed it on stage. Their performance in the theatre and ballet provided the templates for the walking mannequins of the future. The mannequin walk was what Marcel Mauss identified as a 'technique of the body' in his 1934 essay of that name. For Mauss, ways of walking were always acquired, not inherent. He wrote that people learn by copying: 'the individual borrows the series of movements of which he is composed from the action executed in front of him, or with him, by others.'[68] This suggestion that a person is 'composed' of movements evokes the imagery of Marey and Muybridge (see **14** and **15**). While ill in a New York hospital, Mauss noticed that the nurses were walking like the actresses in films; 'returning to France, I noticed how common this gait was, especially in Paris. The girls were French and they too were walking this way. In fact American walking fashions had begun to arrive over here, thanks to the movies'.[69] He argued that walking was only one of many aspects of daily life that were 'techniques' including 'those fundamental fashions that can be called the "modes of life", the *modes*, the *tonus*, the matter, the manners, the way'.[70]

Out of such minutiae is meaning made, in mundane acts and everyday gestures. Thus, for example, the speed of the mannequins' walk varied according to whether they modelled in retail or wholesale houses. Different modelling styles suited different parts of the trade. Alexandre described how at wholesale houses the modelling style was more 'abstract' and 'focused' and the mannequins' beauty 'more regular; it would not do for them to put on a voluptuous display'.[71] Thirty years later, the same custom persisted in New York where wholesale mannequins modelled to fast foxtrots and those in retail shops to slow waltzes, on the grounds that the wholesale buyers could judge faster. In 1933 *Fortune* magazine described a recognisable modelling style as a technique in exactly Mauss's sense:

> There's a regular technique to modelling clothes. This is the procedure for modelling a dress: walk in with hands on hips and a coy look for the buyer. Turn around, cross arms in front so that the lines of the back can be seen, walk away. Turn again and walk forward to show the fall of the drapery. Then exit, with a nice smile over the shoulder. This smile, too, is for the buyer – and it is important. Coats are more involved because the lining has to be shown. Fur pieces have to be wrapped along the shoulders, then around the hips, held out in front the way a butler holds a big platter, and then laid on the floor. All very fast, like a scarf dance.[72]

Mauss's ideas help to explain how all ways of walking are not natural but learnt. 'The position of the arms and hands while walking . . . are not simply the product of some purely individual, almost completely psychic, arrangements and mechanisms . . . There exists an education in walking too', he wrote.[73] He argued that techniques of the body are learnt through a combination of education and copying which he calls 'prestigious imitation', whereby one person imitates the actions of another who he has perceived as successful or desirable.[74] Thus, for example, mannequins could incorporate the walking elements of popular dance performances, such as the Gaby Glide and the Castle Walk, named after the French Gaby Deslys and the American

Irene Castle, both of whom enjoyed success in both Paris and New York.[75] In these ways the walk, a technology of the new that criss-crossed the Atlantic, moved in fluid, continually evolving and hybrid forms, much as popular music did.[76]

The walking styles and influence of the actresses whom the mannequins copied were described by the press; Cécile Sorel's famous 'pantheresque' walk, with its 'springing step with hips well forward and head thrown back' was imitated by women of fashion and mannequins all over the world.[77] Colette wrote about the 'eloquent legs' of the actress Mistinguett, with her walk like the actress Réjane's.[78] Mannequins copied each other too and their modelling styles were in turn disseminated to many more women via the cinema. These are typical ways that fashion mannequins acquired 'techniques of the walk', as described by Mauss. Their instruction was rarely explicitly verbal or literal but depended on a kind of tacit recognition of bodily styles, the kind of pedagogy of the body that Vigarello described in the ways that children are taught to sit up, sit still, sit straight or run in an approved manner:

> Suggested images and sketched gestures induce positions and comportment in silence, anodyne phrases or unintentional-seeming words designate a posture which masks an elaboration that is at once both half-conscious and laborious; phrases heavier than orders fix appearances and deportment with analytical or solemn precision. The body is the first place where the hand of the adult marks the child, it is the first space in which the social and psychological limits of its conduct are imposed, it is the emblem where culture inscribes its signs like so many blazons.[79]

However, he went on to say that the language of such 'instruction' is oblique: 'The body is spoken in a lateral, allusive language, simultaneously veiling and signalling the pedagogical importance of posture and the correction of physical attitudes in the course of relations between adults and children.'[80] Vigarello thus argued that the physical training of the body is always below the radar of official discourse and is determined by relations of power between adult and child. The relationship between the couturier and mannequin was no less determined by an unequal balance of power and the ultimate sanction was the sack. The Russian Kisa Kuprina, who worked for Poiret in 1925, described being taught 'to walk slowly with a haughty air, to turn, to change with the speed of light'. She recalled that Poiret was imperious and would line the mannequins up and examine each one 'with a long, heavy stare. Then, fixing on one, he would suddenly flap his hand as if chasing away a fly. That meant the girl was fired.'[81]

THE EVOLUTION OF THE MANNEQUIN WALK, 1911–1920

The 'Poiret walk' was famous and an intrinsic aspect of his Empire-line gowns of autumn 1911. They were, however, just as hard to walk in as the hobble, observed the *New York Times*:

> Unless one has the Poiret walk, I should think it would be quite useless to wear one of his extreme gowns. One can imagine nothing more hideous than such a frock on the swinging, athletic figure of a certain type of Anglo-Saxon woman.
>
> Not all the Frenchwomen can wear his gowns, but his mannequins are chosen so carefully and walk so well in their peculiar manner that the gowns and hats they exhibit gain a new beauty. One model who shows the wraps should receive a large salary for walking across the stage if she never opened her mouth; there is nothing in Paris to equal her mannerisms and affectations of gait. She is the most striking figure that any dressmaker has secured.[82]

Poiret's distinctive modelling style of 1911 was considered oriental, along with his designs. Between 1910 and 1914 his mannequins launched the so-called 'Russian stance' or *pose à la Russe*: stomach forward, feet at right angles, hand on hips. It lent itself to Poiret's Directoire-inspired designs with narrow skirts, high waists, enormous aigrettes and huge wrap-around fur collars. Towards the end of the war a new and different modelling style evolved. Cocteau described mannequins 'pushing out the stomach, walking like a crab and a praying mantis, putting one hand on the hip and making the jaw-line cruel and disdainful'.[83]

The mannequins at Poiret went uncorseted, like several other couturiers', which gave their walk an extra suppleness.[84] A corset might slim down the figure but it also produced an unfashionable rigidity and stiffness of movement. The undulating walk of the mannequins required a flexible, pliant torso. Erté described how Poiret's uncorseted fashions facilitated a new way of walking exemplified by the chic actress Jacqueline Forzane in 1913, whose carriage was typical of that period: 'head held high, torso tilted backwards and stomach thrust forward'.[85] However, modified corsets were made for women who bought the new styles and they, too, changed the walk. In 1911 the American trade journal the *Dry Goods Economist* explained how:

> This means a new poise for the body, a poise which brings the shoulder on a line with the hip bones, which naturally through the action of the muscles lifts the abdomen, expands the diaphragm and restores the body to its natural, beautiful lines. The fashionable woman now, instead of leaning forward and stumbling

over her toes, walks erect with back flat, the chest out and curving gently, the diaphragm fully expanded, the abdomen high, but receding in line with the curve of the hips. . . . It is incredibly beautiful, and graceful as well, because it expresses action and life always and never rigidity.[86]

Through such detailed coverage in American newspapers and trade journals, French ways of walking and dressing were used to promote imported fashions in America.[87]

One American journalist compared the effect of the dresses modelled in Paris in 1912 by French mannequins with that of the same dresses worn by the customers in New York:

> one now begins to see the clothes on Americans and a few Frenchwomen, instead of on the mannequins, and the exhibition is decidedly interesting. . . . you know it is one thing to see a series of gowns exploited by professionals, and quite another to see them worn by women who do not make a profession in clothes. The former are trained to walk, to pose, to exhibit to its best advantage every line that the designer intends to make fashionable, whereas the average woman has no such training.[88]

Thus the mannequin is seen to import a new area of expertise or fashion know-how that the ordinary woman must acquire – not only the skill of dressing well but also of moving gracefully in her clothes. As skirt shapes changed seasonally, mannequins had to be able to demonstrate how to manipulate the drapery of fuller waists and narrower hems in high-heeled, buckled shoes; they were sufficiently accomplished to carry off these and other new styles with drama and panache.[89]

What was at stake was the relationship between bodies and clothes and the way the latter could redesign the former, as Anne Freadman has it, when clothing and sensibility mesh.[90] As a result, not only the dress but also the bodily style might become popular. In 1912 in Chicago, the latest fashionable walk inspired by Paris mannequins was designated the 'Ingenue Crouch' (**240**):

> Now comes the 'ingénue crouch' to test the adaptability of the woman of fashion who would conform not only to the modes of the moment but to the 'manner of going' as prescribed by the Paris dressmakers.
>
> This newest form of locomotion is a complete reversal of the 'athletic stride' which for so long a time was one of the distinguishing characteristics of the American girl; neither does it resemble the 'Parisian glide,' the 'hobble trip,' nor the 'turkey trot walk.' It has been described by its followers as a languorous motion suggestive of Nazimova [the stage and silent film actress] and Ethel Barrymore – but more so. To the unprejudiced observer it looks as if the 'ingénue croucher' were suffering from an acute attack of indigestion and locomotor ataxia, and that the doctor's

office was miles away. Nothing else can explain the manner in which the adept of the 'crouch' pursues her languorous, slouching way along the street. . . .

> Doubtless, after all, the new walk is the result of the narrow skirt. The blame for it can be laid at the door of the Paris couturieres who have for so many moons now kept their patrons within the restricting confines of the narrow skirt that the said patrons and the thousands of their imitators have forgotten what freedom of movement is. Thus the new walk is really not a 'freak', but the result of the mincing steps made necessary by the 'hobble'.
>
> The first exponents of the latest form of pedestrianism were naturally the Paris mannequins. So upon their heads be the blame! As they slouched along the Champs Elysées and at the races even their lovely draperies were forgotten by milady of fashion. 'Ha,' said she, making the great discovery: ''tis a new walk I see; it's horribly ugly, but what is a poor woman to do? For it's fashionable, else the mannequins would not be doing it.' And immediately she, too, began to slouch.
>
> From Paris the new walk was exported to New York, where 'everybody's doin' it now', and where incidentally it was given its name. Miss Fanny Brice of 'The Whirl of Society' company brought it with her to Chicago and, braving the caustic remarks of her friends . . . 'it is the fashion, so what are we poor women to do?'
>
> What, indeed! There seems nothing to do if you would be in style except to forget that you have a backbone and crouch 'ingenuely'.[91]

The picture breaks the walk down into three Muybridge-like images resembling the how-to articles on dance of the period (see **55**) and the passage makes a number of significant points. It differentiates the athletic American woman's walk from the smaller steps of the Parisienne. It attributes a specific, and singular, walk to the Paris mannequins and describes how this influenced both social walking and theatrical performance (Fanny Brice's) in the U.S.A. It identifies three or four specific types of walk: the gliding walk, the tripping or mincing walk produced by the hobble skirt, the languorous, slouching walk and, in the second paragraph, the Turkey Trot walk. The latter was a fashionable dance, thought by many to be disreputable, and its inclusion in the article shows that popular dance influenced walking styles too.

'The 1913 stoop' did not take off. At the Chantilly races the 'curiously crumpled up figure launched earlier in the season' was deemed a failure: 'women are once more carrying themselves erect'.[92] Paquin, Redfern and Doeuillet decried the hobble skirt and produced narrow, draped dresses that left the feet free so that, according to the London *Daily News*, 'a more or less graceful walk will therefore become a possibility, if the art has not been

240 'Walk Like this if You Would Be Up-To-Date', *Chicago Daily Tribune*, 3 November 1912.

Walk Like THIS If You Would Be Up-To-Date

Broadway Has "Fallen For It"—Hard—It's the "Ingenue Crouch," a Wiggly, Wobbly, Ambling Stride, Brought Down on Us by the Tight Skirt and the Problem Play.

NOW comes the "ingénue crouch" to test the adaptability of the woman of fashion who would conform not only to the mode of the moment but to the "manner of going" as prescribed by the Paris pacemakers.

This newest form of locomotion is a complete reversal of the "athletic stride" which for so long a time was one of the distinguishing characteristics of the American girl; neither does it resemble the "Parisian glide," the "bobble trip," nor the "turkey trot walk." It has been described by its followers as a languorous motion suggestive of Nazimova and Ethel Barrymore—but more so.

To the unprejudiced observer it looks as if the "ingénue croucher" were suffering from an acute attack of indigestion and locomotor ataxia, and that the doctor's office was miles away. Nothing else can explain the manner in which the adept of the "crouch" pursues her languorous, shuffling way along the street.

But the health culturists, who so vehemently denounced the "yard wide" skirt now sit back with folded arms and gloat their "I told you so's," for their predictions seem to have been fulfilled in the "ingénue crouch."

But what will milady of fashion care for these calamity howlers? When that imperious dame, fashion, decreed that "lines" should be the thing did not all her loyal followers roll miles up and down the sacred precincts of their boudoirs and go on diets that would try the soul of a Hindu fakir in order to obey the decree?

The idea, after all, the new walk is a result of the narrow skirt. The blame for it can be laid at the doors of the Paris couturiers who have for so many seasons now kept their patrons within the restricting confines of the narrow skirt that the said patrons and the thousands of their imitators have forgotten what freedom of movement is. Thus the new walk is really not a "freak," but the result of the mincing steps made necessary by the "bobble."

The first exponents of the latest form of pedestrianism were naturally the Paris mannequins. So upon their heads be the blame! As they slouched along the Champs Elysées and at the races even their lovely draperies were forgotten by milady of fashion. "Ha!" said she, making the great discovery; "'tis a new walk I see; it's horribly ugly, but what is a poor woman to do? For it's fashionable, else the mannequins would not be doing it." And immediately she, too, began to slouch.

From Paris the new walk was exported to New York, where "everybody's doin' it now," and where incidentally it was given its name. Miss Fanny Brice of "The Whirl of Society" company brought it with her to Chicago and, braving the caustic remarks of her friends, who persistently advised her to "brace up—the worst is yet to come," introduced it to the curious throngs along Michigan avenue. Now the prediction is that before the snow flies the "ingénue crouch" will be the only method of locomotion allowable in "polite society."

"It's the fashion," said Miss Brice, as if that settled the whole thing. "It may be injurious to the health; it may be the height—or depth—of ugliness and the despair of the stout woman; but it is the fashion, so what are we poor women to do?"

What indeed? There seems nothing to do if you would be in style except to forget that you have a backbone and crouch "ingénuely."

The First Picture Shows the Step Forward.

The Second One Shows the Poise, and the Third the Stride.

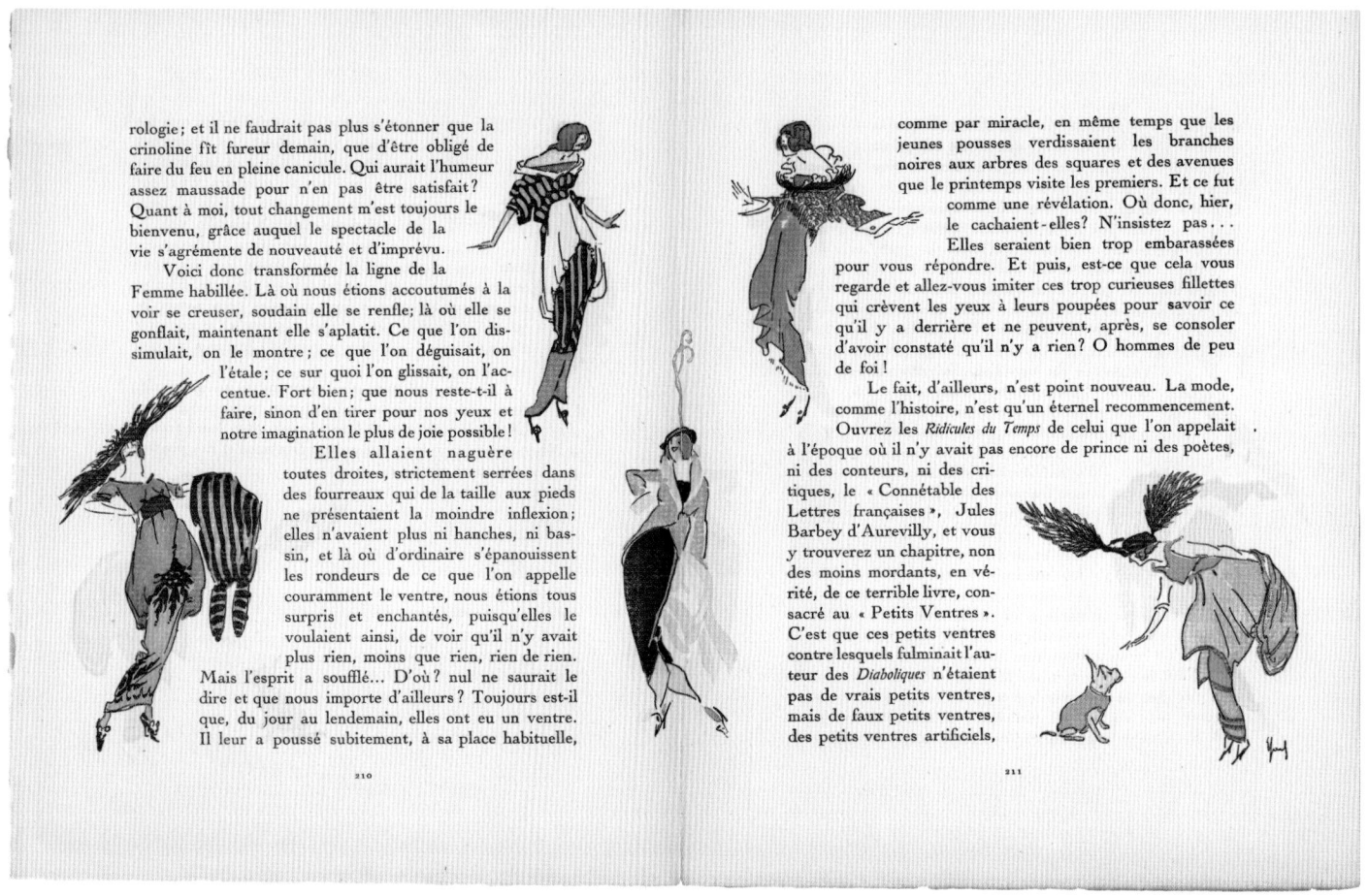

lost'.[93] Their narrow skirts encouraged a *contrapposto* posture, illustrated in the *Gazette du Bon Ton*'s vignettes of bodies in motion, some with shoulders far forward, others with shoulders back and hips forward and the majority with the shoulders forward and the stomach concave (**241**). The article describes how female posture and walking have dramatically changed the appearance of the body:

> where she used to arch, she bulges; where she used to swell, now she flattens herself; what she used to hide she now reveals; what she used to disguise she now flaunts; what she underplayed she now accentuates . . . They [women] used to be upright, tightly squeezed into sheath dresses from top to toe which inhibited the slightest inclination of the body; they no longer had hips or a pelvis, and where the curves of what we commonly call the stomach used to flourish we were surprised and delighted, since they desired it thus, to see nothing there, less than nothing, absolutely nothing . . . suddenly, miraculously, the stomach is back in its usual place . . . where were they hiding it yesterday? . . . Formerly she walked with tiny steps, a neat trot; now she is more relaxed, and freer; where she hid her stomach, she now exaggerates it . . . And with the stomach, the nape of the neck is also on show for the first time . . . but how hard it is to describe the overall allure of the female body. Instead these Sachetti drawings so full of movement, so relaxed, sometimes a little excessive but always truthful, can describe the new seductions, charms and unexpected new graces of the women of spring 1913 better than I.[94]

This journalist sees bodily styles and ways of posing, moving and holding the body, as a kind of fashion that women can assume with the new season. If the illustrations, which are stylised and exaggerated, cannot be relied on to tell the 'truth' about pose, gesture, movement, the text nevertheless suggests a belief that bodily stance and movement are self-conscious choices which place the individual in a particular social world: part of the cultivation of a civilised self. It is a kind of *sprezzatura*, as the performance and dance scholar Gabriele Brandstetter points out in her comparison of the contemporary fashion model's relaxed stance with the *sprezzatura* of Castiglione's *Book of the Courtier*: a style of the body that can be cultivated and enacted publicly.[95]

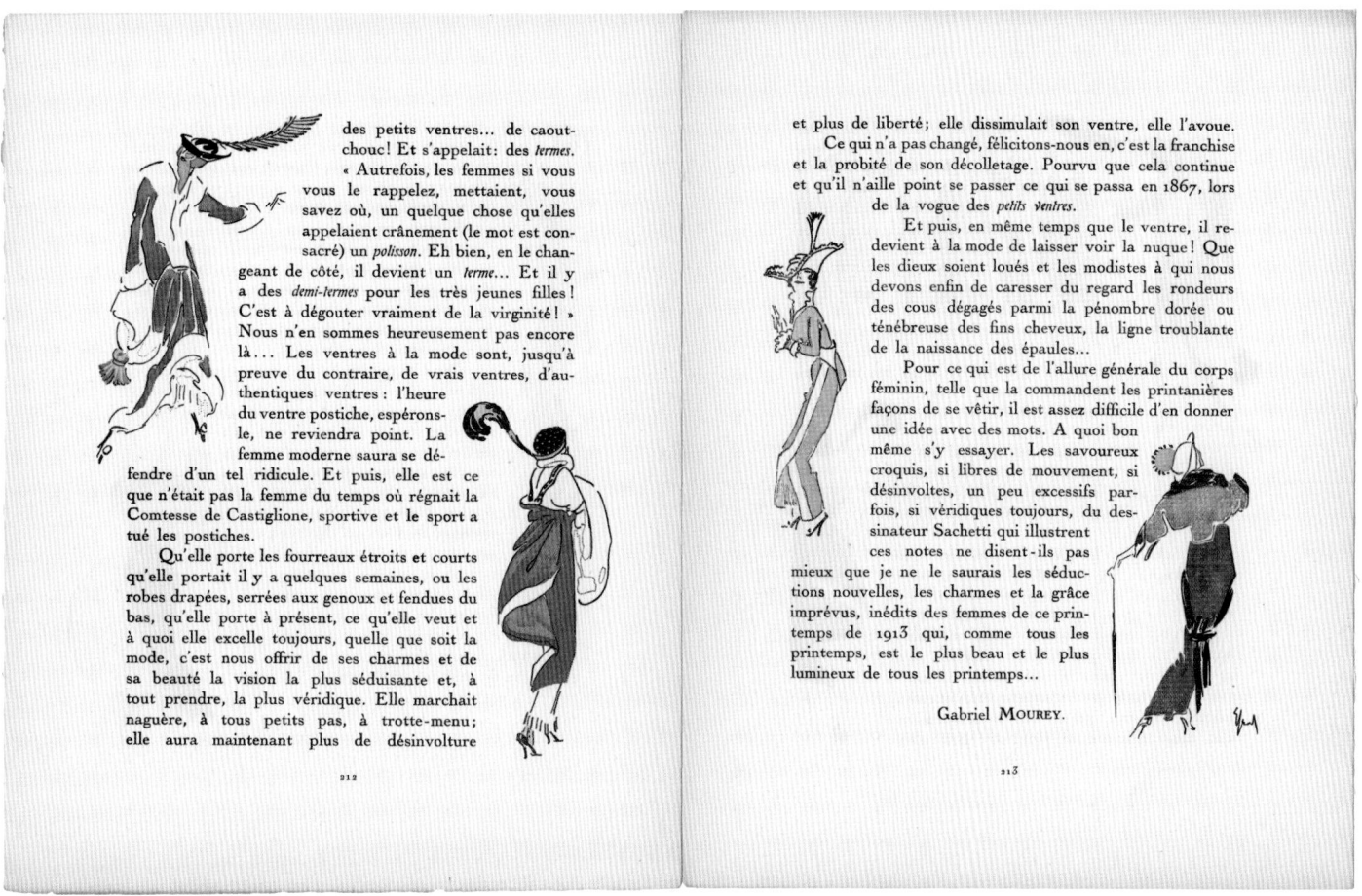

'Such is the power of fashion, which dictates not only the colour of hair and complexion but also the shape of the body. The feminine body is, to the designer, essentially a malleable entity which fashion moulds in its own way', commented Erté in his description of the 1913–14 vogue of walking slinkily *à la léopard*. This was inspired by the actress Ida Rubenstein's 1913 stage walk that she performed with a leopard on a long chain in Gabriele D'Annunzio's *La Pisanelle ou la mort*.[96] Throughout the 1910s Lucile's mannequins continued to demonstrate the typical Lucile 'slithering' walk.[97] Cecil Beaton wrote: 'The fame she [Lucile] brought to the outstanding Hebe and Dolores is legendary. Drian, the painter, has described these tall women mincing about in their turbans and trailing trains as looking like impertinent lobsters.'[98]

Modelling styles differed between couture houses. From 1910 newsreels brought these styles to a mass audience. There is, however, no research to date on the reception of fashion newsreel, so it is not known how audiences viewed them. Nor can many conclusions be drawn about the history of the walk from early film. Most cameras were hand-cranked and films were shot at variable speeds from 19 to 24 frames per second and projected slightly faster at between 22 and 24 frames per second.[99] There was enormous variation between them and there is now some doubt in many cases about the correct projection speed. Nevertheless, these early newsreels indicate several clear differences in both modelling and directing styles. For example, the mannequins at Boué in 1913 (**242**) were lively and flirtatious, compared to the haughty elegance of those at Lucile in 1914 (see **35**).

The modern eye is not impartial, however. Modern filming techniques as well as modern spectatorship inevitably become 'naturalised' so that the films of an earlier period appear quaint to later eyes. So, for instance, contemporaneous descriptions of the mannequins' walk in the 1910s are infused with a sense of their lithe modernity, yet only a decade later they appeared anachronistic to eyes used to the relaxed style of 1920s modelling (**243**). Joseph Roth described the pre-war newsreel footage of fashion, dances and five o'clock teas that he watched in a Paris cinema in 1926:

from neck to hips the models are panelled in satin, from their hips down to the fake Persian rug, they are curtains from provincial stages. . . . when they sit down, they pluck up a skirt with two fingers, flash us an ankle, and we die! . . . All the women, when they smile, lay their heads on one shoulder. And when are they ever not smiling, the flirts? They bat their eyelids open and shut like precious cabinets, full of promises.[100]

Yet contemporaries described these same mannequins in vivid motion: twirling in billowing taffeta at Paquin, mincing in extremely short and narrow evening skirts at Drecoll, swaying between the buyers like delicate canoes navigating the rocks at Poiret and walking with a snake-like gait at Redfern.[101] At the autumn 1915 openings, 'Paris was . . . a stage across which hundreds of pretty mannequins, coiffed, scented, and dressed as no lily of the field ever dreamed of being dressed, have minced, and pattered, and swayed, and turned, and scampered off – all on heels absurdly and scandalously high.'[102]

Mauss wrote that shoes transform the walk and certainly the high heels of 1914–15 would have produced a different way of walking.[103] The shoes caused particular interest in the 1915 collections, perhaps because of the new above-ankle hemlines that season: 'One of Jenny's pretty mannequins is shod in ribbon-laced shoes . . . Paquin's mannequins wear strapped sandals of bronze kid, and Beer's tailored suits are shown above extremely high black leather boots with extremely high heels.'[104] Laura Mulvey has observed of the flapper in the 1920s that her boyish figure erased the maternal while 'her high heels and "posed" stance evoked a mechanical movement that took femininity away from nature into culture. The flapper had an emblematic relationship to modernity and the robotic world of mechanisation.' Mulvey invokes Kracauer in her description of the seductive and genderless grace of technology invoked by the flapper as 'Her heels clicked down the street, her fingers tapped on typewriter keys.'[105] If the flapper used her fingers at work in the 1920s, the mannequin used her feet to comparable effect in the 1910s and earlier. Professional mannequins served as an advance guard of fashionable women, walking into the future in their high heels, narrowed skirts and increasingly body-revealing fashions, particularly during wartime, when no other Parisian woman could wear such clothes without censure.

SOCIAL DANCING AND THE RHYTHMS OF MODERNITY

During 1912–13 the tango craze in Europe and America began to influence both fashion and modelling styles. The dance required a flexible torso and produced a concave silhouette described by Cocteau: 'Couples knotted together, their shoulders motionless, executed the slow Argentinian promenade'. Other new dances also affected the walk and the stance. Cocteau observed: 'And here is the fox-trot and the Très moutarde and those elegant women with aggressive elbows who bound up and down to Sambre-et-Meuse.'[106] Lucile's mannequins tangoed in 1913 (see 59) and Paquin's in 1914, on their arrival in New York, where Femina described 'the supple gestures and lively poses of the mannequins, and the tangos and bostons played by the orchestra'.[107] In 1913 Henriot described the Paris mannequin's walk as if she were dancing:

she rolls her hips, she advances as if tangoing, relaxed, supple and feline . . . she is 'well-proportioned' I'm telling you. She knows how to walk, and her whole body participates in her walk. There is dance in her, and it is of her, without doubt, that the poet wrote: *Even when she walks, one would say she is dancing* . . . Now it is only in Paris that one walks thus. And, in Paris, it is only the mannequins who know how to walk this well. And it's as well, for it's their profession.[108]

There was clearly a close connection between social dancing and fashion modelling. The new dances required a new relaxed stance (244), epitomised by Irene and Vernon Castle who had great success in both Paris and America before the war. Their acrobatic style of dancing was particularly popular in France where they performed at the Café de Paris. Returning to America, they found that the modernity of their style chimed with an emerging new vogue for 'cabarets and the modern dances, so called'.[109] Irene Castle was a fashion icon and shared some of the 'body techniques' of the mannequins of the period. 'Mrs Castle has youth, grace and a perfect mastery of all the new ballroom and cabaret dances. She also has a bored expression, a blasé walk and a wardrobe of extreme styles', commented one journalist in 1916.[110] Cecil Beaton wrote of her:

THE CASTLE WALK

She invented a whole balance of movement, with the pelvis thrust forward and the body leaning backwards, giving her torso the admirable lines and flat look of Cretan sculpture. This stance necessitated, if she were standing still, the placing of one leg behind her as a balance. Within the compass of these basic axes she turned her body to the four winds, raising a shoulder against the direction in which she was going. The 'trademark' of the raised shoulder became a sort of fetish that many women were to copy. Such movements seemed only possible with an extraordinary sense of balance and an innate sense of design. It was as if a gyroscope were inside her, always stabilising the body's framework no matter which tangent it moved off.[111]

Indeed, the raised shoulder later became a staple of fashion modelling.

The couple invented their own dance, the Castle Walk, which they taught in their dance school and illustrated in

their 1914 dance manual (**245**). The dance, in its most basic form, consisted simply of walking, but walking in a self-conscious and mannered way, not unlike fashion modelling. It was a reversal of the usual technique of throwing the weight down on the foot. Instead, the weight was thrown upwards, producing an irreverent, energetic, high-spirited form of locomotion based on the one-step, an easy dance performed to rag-time music. In *Modern Dancing* the Castles tell readers how to do it, starting by walking as in a one-step: 'Now, raise yourself up slightly on your toes at each step, with the legs a trifle stiff, and breeze along happily and easily, and you know all there is to know about the Castle Walk.' Turning corners involved simply leaning the body slightly 'a little like riding a bicycle round a corner.' Rather than continuing in a straight line, dancers could continue the curve, walking in smaller and smaller circles in the same slanting position until they were walking almost in one spot, from where they could straighten up and start off down the room again. 'It sounds silly and it is silly. That is the explanation of its popularity!'[112] Yet it was not intended to be bumptious. The Castles themselves described it as 'the sliding and poetical Castle Walk'.[113]

Simplicity was the key to the success of the Castle Walk and a gliding walk was the essence of many other dances that also did not require complicated footwork or strict choreography.[114] The one-step, the Hesitation waltz, the tango, the maxixe and the Half and Half, were all based on a simple, stylised and mannered walk.[115] In them, the gliding mannequin walk which all women could recognise from newsreels could become the basis of the action; in their dance school the Castles taught walking to the music before the dance steps.[116] Only once a student had mastered a basic dancing walk for the tango, the maxixe and the foxtrot, could they improvise additional moves according to their talent and taste. 'Walking to Tango time', as Vernon writes in *Modern Dancing*, must be smooth, gliding and slow: 'it is not as easy as it may seem; it should be practised frequently so as to make it smooth. The shoulders must not go up and down, the body must glide along without any stops.'[117] This description is identical to the mannequin glide that can be seen in newsreels of the time. As in a mannequin walk, smoothness was all. The Castles' book contains a one-page injunction against certain bodily attitudes:

> Do not wriggle the shoulders. Do not shake the hips. Do not twist the body. Do not flounce the elbows. Do not pump the arms. Do not hop – glide instead. Avoid low, fantastic and acrobatic dips. Stand far enough away from each other to allow free movement of the body in order to dance gracefully and comfortably . . . Drop the Turkey trot, the Grizzly Bear, the Bunny Hug, etc. These dances are ugly, ungraceful and out of fashion.[118]

The experience of social dancing in the dance crazes of Europe and America had the capacity to give fashion show audiences a corporeal understanding of fashion modelling triggered by a subjective 'body knowledge' or memory of wearing fashion in motion that today's audiences have lost. It suggests that, to go back to the questions of identification discussed in an earlier chapter in relation to audiences, contemporary viewing competences would have been structured by the embodied experience of wearing the new fashions on the dance floor, by what Iris Marion Young calls the 'tactile imagination' afforded by female experience, 'the simple pleasure of losing ourselves in cloth'.[119] To that one could add another simple pleasure of the period, that of losing oneself in the rhythms of modernity.

In his essay on the artist and designer Sonia Delaunay, Chris Townsend describes a body that was, along with Italian futurist painting and the choreography of the dancer Valentine de Saint Point in 1912, 'intercalated into the modern world' through rhythm.[120] This world included the 'rhythmic gymnastics' of the new Dalcroze dance and exercise system (the mannequin walk was even described as a kind of Dalcroze), as well as the visual rhythms of artists.[121] Townsend proposes that, in Delaunay's simultaneous designs, fashion enabled a specific representation of the modernist body 'both as a body moving in space and time, and as a surface'.[122] He argues that the simultaneous dress that she designed and wore to the Montmartre dance hall, the Bal Bullier, in 1913 was not a critique or an internalisation of rhythm but a 'repetition and extension of its surface effects: rather than seeking to find itself, the subject is lost in the play of modernity on corporeality'.[123]

By contrast, the living mannequins who modelled in the couture houses mimicked the mechanical glide of the modern escalator and film dolly whose smooth operation were the very opposite of dance-hall rhythms. Townsend remarks that Delaunay's 'surrender of consciousness in favour of sensation, her enslavement to the superficial, unifying effects of rhythm, mimes modernity's subordination of individual reflectivity'.[124] Perhaps, but the smooth, mechanical glide of the mannequins could be said to subordinate reflexivity even more effectively, to the point of effacing it, in fact. Townsend's assertion that Delaunay's dress mimicked the visual and aural patterns of both jazz and film does, nevertheless, suggest another prototype for fashion modelling, and for fashion as both a visual field and a haptic object endowed with temporality through the body.[125] In modelling, the body moves in four dimensions, in both time and space simultaneously. The visual patterns and discipline of the mannequin walk may have unconsciously mimicked those of Taylorism and Fordism, its smoothness may have imitated inorganic mechanical motion, but in its simultaneity (which is exactly what makes it hard to describe) it also mimicked the visual experiments of artists such as the Delaunays and the Italian futurists.

THE MANNEQUIN WALK IN THE 1920S

After the war, the mannequin walk continued to be described as swaying, gliding, undulating, majestic and rhythmic.[126] Yet something had changed. Colette nostalgically recalled the rolling, swaying, undulating walk

Copyrighted by Ella Jane Hardcastle.

"PROPER AND IMPROPER."

This picture, under the title "Proper and Improper Way to Dress," has been widely circulated by the Y. W. C. A. in its educational campaign against certain modern tendencies.

FAITES-MOI CELLE-CI
ROBE DU SOIR, DE DOEUILLET

of pre-war mannequins when she reviewed the new season's collections for *Vogue* in the mid-1920s:

> I have already seen two hundred dresses modelled in one month. At the dawn of the season, it is a fashion show that instructs while it amuses one. I learnt how stomachs are being worn this year: flat, with the arrogance of a shield, balanced from front to rear, from rear to front. Where are the rolling hips, Spanish or Martiniquais, of the mannequins of 1914? It is a matter of hips! We no longer have anything lateral.[127]

Here Colette intriguingly refers to the seductive walk as coming from the French colony of Martinique, suggesting a black walk, long before there were black mannequins in Paris. She also suggests that a fuller-figured mannequin will have a different walk from a slim, boyish one: with no back and forth motion of the stomach, the abdomen becomes, as Anne Freadman has observed, a 'simple hinge' to which the legs are attached.[128] A modernist walk, perhaps.

The principal change, however, was in the stance, which became slouching, with the hips well forward. Drooping was the fashionable posture – rounded back, dropped shoulders, neck extended, knees flexed.[129] Colette described how a famous tennis champion (perhaps Suzanne Lenglen) adopted two entirely different stances for work and leisure. On court she held herself upright and balanced, with an elegant S-shaped curve to her spine; photographed for a fashion magazine in 1923 in her evening dress, she slouched, revealing an unforeseen curvature of the spine that inverted the arch of her lower back and pushed her drooping shoulders forward.[130] In 1925, when Patou imported young Americans to his Paris catwalk, he said: 'I am enchanted with them. I made them keep their flapper slouch, instead of assuming the traditional French mannequin walk.'[131] One such ex-flapper, from a generation of affluent, privileged New York

girls born about 1905, in 1934 recalled her fourteen-year-old self:

> Our gait was necessarily slow, because of galoshes and the 'college walk': we marched arm in arm, Leona and I, when we weren't at the movies, with a drawling slow-motion, sliding as near to the side-walk as we could manage, our flat bellies thrust out before us, our backs arched as for a swan-dive; we almost broke our necks with the effort to hang our felt-lidded heads like blasé flowers.[132]

'The "flapper look"', writes the historian Angela Latham, 'comprised a pose, a posturing, a contrived demeanor – in short, a performance.'[133] Their walk was lop-sided, round-shouldered and slouching, pushing the stomach and hips forward and sideways, allowing the torso to sag and slouch (**246**).

In fashion, this slouch was translated into the hips-forward modelling posture typifying the 1920s that is still familiar today (**252**). The *Vogue* editor Bettina Ballard observed the 'tall Russian mannequins moving around in a bored, slouched way' at Chanel in the late 1920s.[134] Beaton described how Chanel 'trained her mannequins with all the loving discipline of a Petipa or a Balanchine, teaching them to walk on their toes, with their pelvis thrust well forward' and he recalled Cocteau's account of Chéruit's mannequins, who were similarly trained at that time: 'Chéruit could be heard crying the whole length of the red and gold salons: "Mesdames, throw out your stomachs! Don't draw in! Bulge! Bulge! Throw out your stomachs!"'[135]

Each mannequin had to have her own modelling style to differentiate her from the others (regal, smiling, negligent, supple and so forth) but by the 1920s any mannequin worth her salt had also to have at least two or three different walks: she needed different styles and speeds for sportswear, daywear, tea gowns and evening dresses.[136] In

248 (left) Film still of two mannequins walking through a park, c. 1927–8. Lobster Films, Paris.

249 facing page) Professional mannequins simulate aristocratic poise in the salon of Maison Agnès, c. 1925. Photograph Henri Manuel. Musée Galliera de la Mode de la Ville de Paris, GALK 2889.2. Photograph Richard Hubert Smith.

1925 Suzanne, a mannequin at one of the three largest houses in Paris, explained how the mannequins were taught three different walks, for morning, afternoon and evening dress. The morning gait was brisk and businesslike, the afternoon one a leisure walk for promenading (the Spanish Walk) and the evening one was, if not wholly seductive, at least designed to please:

> When one marches for street dress she is taught to put heel and toe down practically at the same time, with feet somewhat apart, to take some fairly long steps and swing the legs from the hips. A brusque, sharp air of going on some important business errand is the idea . . . With the afternoon dress, the toe is put down first with a marked toe plant. No long steps are taken. Steps about the length of the foot itself and the feet are placed in front of each other. An easy, relaxed, informal lilt to the body, and it is implied madame has time for informal guests this afternoon. This is sometimes called the Spanish Walk. The evening costume calls for a walk of quite another mood. It is delicate, gracious, with a bit of sophistry thrown in. A trifle more spring to the step. You walk as though you were walking on eggshells or as though your feet were going to come down on something fragile and easily breakable. The head is held on a neck arched forward slightly. The body is permitted a bit of a slouch with the stomach slightly protuberant. Nothing of the haughty or grande dame about this walk. Kind of an 'out-to-capture-or-at-least-to-please' air is prescribed for the evening dress.[137]

Suzanne's description tallies with Mauss's ethnographic descriptions of culturally diverse ways of moving the body in the performance of daily tasks. He thinks he can recognise a girl who has been raised in a convent by the way she walks with her fists closed and recalls his third-form teacher shouting at him for walking with his hands flapping wide open.[138]

Descriptions of the mannequin walk may reveal more about the subjectivity of the writer than the actual walk but they nevertheless suggest that the idea of the walk as something that could be cultivated, studied, varied and performed was part of the cultural construction of femininity. In the 1920s fashion journalists began to write about the walk as if it were a style of the body that could be altered, just as the figure could be altered through diet and exercise. Differences were national as well as gendered. In 1923 French *Vogue* described a typical young American woman who arrives in Paris with 'her dresses, her colouring

and her Fifth Avenue walk' and immediately realises that she is in a foreign country and must adapt.[139] In the Bois,

> the Frenchwomen's walk . . . will be a considerable surprise. This suppleness that has nothing to do with a sporting suppleness, these mannerisms and discreet gestures will be a great source of surprise to her. She will attempt to adjust her step to those of her new friends. She will understand that long strides may have plenty of allure but that the little French step possesses a pretty distinction.[140]

Vogue implies that another woman's walk can be assimilated, like Mauss's Frenchwomen with their American film-star walk, or the way that in 1926 a brief vogue for clear crystal heels caused American women to copy the Paris mannequins' gliding walk, according to one newspaper.[141] In the 1920s Nancy Cunard's unique gait resembled that of the mannequins of her day. It was described by Aldous Huxley in his word-portrait of her as Myra Viveash in *Antic Hay* (1923): 'He watched her as she crossed the dirty street, placing her feet with a meticulous precision one after the other in the same straight line, as though she were treading a knife edge between goodness only knew what invisible gulfs.'[142]

Many films of fashion modelling have survived from the 1920s, not only newsreel but also fiction films that began to feature mannequin parades. They show a range of more fluid modelling styles that are augmented by the more fluid camera angles and movement, so that mannequins and camera move together in a seductive duet (**248**). These mannequins modelling in a public park are constantly 'acting' for the camera in the sense of turning , chatting and shooting the occasional sly glance at the spectator as if to check that they are still watching, while the camera, too, is in constant movement, circling them, coming in close, withdrawing.[143]

Lekain's *On Demande un mannequin* of 1923 is a fiction film, set and filmed in the real house of Drecoll.[144] It shows two sequences of fashion modelling, one in the main salon and one on a modelling stage built into a little salon accessed by a long corridor.[145] In the main salon (see **53c**), the camera remains static but the mannequins are always in motion, their movements fluid and unbroken. There are always three in frame at any one time and as they pass through the salon they strike 'moving poses' while walking, turning and gesturing with their hands, often holding up

their long ropes of pearls with one hand while extending the other arm out and downwards as they move. Sometimes they sashay their hips. They come and go at an even and rapid pace so that the whole sequence is smooth. The clients interact with them, pointing at the dresses and asking them to show details. One mannequin holds her skirts out to the side but the majority simply display them through more naturalistic, yet mannered, walking styles. Only on the modelling stage in the little salon (see **172a–c**) do they model on the spot and when they rotate it is done remarkably smoothly with no movement of the upper body to indicate that they are moving their feet. They could be on a revolving turntable, all the while making gracious arm gestures. Descending the steps of the stage, one mannequin crosses her legs as she walks, much like modern models, although another is less accomplished and even loses her balance and wobbles slightly on the bottom two steps.

The professional mannequin walk remained a Parisian speciality.[146] Yet the modelling styles of the 1920s suggest a conception of fashionable womanhood that encapsulated the idea of malleability and change for all women, whereby bodies could be elongated, slimmed and even given a new look through ways of moving: thus a drooping shoulder, a concave stomach or a gliding walk became just one of so many styles of the body. These bodily styles might appear to be innately aristocratic, as the snobbish de Meyer suggested when he noted 'one of those typically smart Lelong mannequins – slender and distinguished, with slightly raised shoulders, wearing their clothes like those "to the manner born"', but they were part of the professional repertoire of all fashion mannequins (**249**).[147] Appearing to be ladylike was crucial, as was actually being working class, at least until the 1920s. Whatever her class background, however, a mannequin who could not learn the walk would never be successful, as Roubaud makes clear in his chapter devoted to the subject, 'Do you know how to walk?'[148] There, the French mannequin Ginette mocks Armande, a Belgian who has just lost her job precisely because she cannot learn the walk. 'You know how to walk in Brussels; you'll never know how to walk in Paris!'[149]

12

FLOW
THE MANNEQUIN POSE

250 Four mannequins modelling in the sales room at Doucet, showing the typically restrained modelling style and upright stance of 1910. From L. Roger-Milès, *Les Créateurs de la mode*, 1910. Musée Galliera de la Mode de la Ville de Paris. Photograph Richard Hubert Smith.

Into the new century walked the mannequin, striking a series of 'signature' modelling poses that continue to be recognised as fashion poses today. Her performance created a dialectic between stasis and motion that was replicated in, and even anticipated by, both still and moving images. In film, the mannequin would pause to strike a dramatic static pose, as if to halt time. By contrast, the frozen poses of fashion photographs often tried to evoke or capture a sense of motion. The live performance of fashion modelling also consisted of a perpetual oscillation between stasis and motion, from the walk to the pose and back again. Both in her live performance, and in film and fashion plates that themselves oscillated between images of motion and stasis, the mannequin embodied many contradictions and ambiguities that fascinated her contemporaries in other fields. Firstly, the pose in the photograph was often a reflection on movement and how to show it. Secondly, the pose played a role within the mannequin walk, both as a way to picture time and as a device to stage a formal, modernist kind of abstraction. Thirdly, the pose in the fashion show was itself inherently cinematic, in that it operated like the single frame within the moving images of film.

FASHION AND MODERNIST FLOW

The mannequin's performance was one of many fragmented narratives of the early twentieth century. During the fashion show, it was impossible to differentiate images as commodities from commodities as images. In this respect the mannequin's image joined a rhythmic flow of other images, signs and commodities that circulated within and between the metropolitan centres of the new century. The flow was one of literal movement but also in the sense of traffic. Within it steered the image of the moving mannequin in fashion magazines and film and in this way she played her role in modernism. This was a traffic which mingled commerce and culture, so that money and commodities rubbed up against modernist sensibilities and artefacts.[1] These interchanges generated new modes of exchange and circulation that might be commercial, sexual or artistic – or a combination. With them went a certain metaphysical and epistemological destabilisation of daily life that was noted by writers from Oskar Bie to Georg Simmel.[2] In their accounts, fashionable gestures and styles jostled with the deepest aspirations of contemporary society, which were staged on the elegant surfaces of everyday events.[3] Stepping into this traffic, the mannequin was immediately stylised herself, as well as contributing her own style to the spectacle of modern life.[4] As she entered its slipstream, her gestures and walk marked the time of modernity like a metronome. For the fashion show staged not only modernist bodies but also modernist time, in which the flow of motion was punctuated by the pose.

Louis Roubaud describes one such typical modelling scene in Copenhagen in the 1920s, where a group of French mannequins, probably Poiret's, are on tour (see **123**):

> The thirty instruments of the orchestra burst into the *Marseillaise*. Raphaëlle appeared – delicate, smiling, slender – Raph who had been so soundly asleep on the chaise longue in the *cabine*. At every obstacle encountered – table or chair – she made a stop, a hesitation that animated the chiffon and crepe. With a gesture of apology or impatience she side-stepped a spectator to show off a fold, some braid or an embroidery that was worth the surprise revelation.[5]

Her fluid walk was interrupted by frequent pauses when she froze for a split-second, sketching a vivid hieroglyph of the garment in space, before flowing gracefully into another shape. As the mannequin struck her pose, the gesture seemed to isolate her momentarily from the flow of time, like a plate from Muybridge's *Animal Locomotion* (see **15**). Raph's infinitesimal pauses that make her chiffons tremble are part of the mannequin performance no less than the walk and Roubaud's description of her stop-start modelling style highlights the oscillation between stasis and motion that typified fashion modelling in the period.[6] In her tiny, artful hesitations, Raph marks the pose as a pause in a flow of movement. The moment of stillness does not signal a lack of energy, however, but is charged with latency that will tip Raph into motion a second later.[7] In her article on fashion modelling, Gabriele Brandstetter argues that the pose is no more than a brief point of stillness that 'carves definition for a figure out of a flowing and undefined state of blended motions'. What she calls 'the paradox of the pose' is that it is both a still and 'the figuration of movement'.[8]

The paradox of a still image that suggests movement was not limited to fashion: the problem of how to represent movement in still images was being explored in a number of disparate areas at the turn of the century, including art history, philosophy, science and dance. Within this wider context, the fashion pose takes its place in a gallery of visual images of movement. These included what were called 'positions of visibility', 'significant moments' and 'privileged moments' by the scientists, philosophers and artists who theorised them. Their experiments produced hieratic and gestural representations of the human figure in frozen movement that share many characteristics with fashion posing and its representation in magazines and on screen. All were concerned with the paradox of how to represent motion in still images at a time when film enabled, or was about to enable, the representation of moving images of the body.[9] The pose is thus related to a 'problem' of representation being investigated in a number of parallel fields which can be characterised as a 'modernist' enquiry, albeit one with nineteenth-century antecedents.

In 'La Théorie de la démarche' (1833) Balzac stressed the natural harmony of the human walk, but in his eighth aphorism declared that 'Human movement breaks down into distinct MOMENTS; if you interfere with it, you end up with the rigidity of the mechanical.'[10] He anticipated many subsequent efforts to analyse and even regulate human movement by breaking it down into its constituent parts over the following hundred years. The 'science of motion' was developed in the 1870s in the new discipline of kinematics, a branch of mechanical engineering concerned with movement in machines and, particularly, the development of a visual syntax for the representation of mechanical movement. Both kinematics and, later, film were an important part of the cultural history of movement that included concerns about how to convey its effects in still images.

Marey's scientific photographs from the 1880s shattered the temporal and spatial unity of the image, something that later preoccupied several artists early in the twentieth century. The problems of representation interested Marey and Chapter 10 of his 1884 book *Le Mouvement* was devoted to showing how chronophotography could help artists to represent movement as it really was. He had found that a surfeit of split-second photographs was actually hampering the 'clear expression of movement' and accordingly the images required selection and editing to give a truer picture.[11] Marey called the relatively static poses of particular gestures 'positions of visibility' and wrote that chronophotography could show which they were; in fencing they would be images of the fencer firstly

preparing for his thrust and then with his arm outstretched having completed the lunge. Thus the frozen pose 'solves' the problem of how to describe actions in images. The 'decisive moment', as it was later called, represents the missing whole and a narrative of time can be read into the still fragment.[12] Marey's 'positions of visibility' were also a way of visualising what the naked eye cannot catch, so the staging of the 'position of visibility' is always a fiction in the sense that the 'invisible' portion that we cannot see, or do not read as a definitive gesture, is omitted.

The first illustration of a mannequin from 1885 (see **10**) suggests a 'position of visibility' similar to Marey's fencer's lunge, as the mannequin demonstrates a tennis-playing gesture to show off the elasticity of the jersey as she models her own flexibility. Most illustrations of fashion poses, however, were more decorative and less linked to functionality; the 'positions of visibility' adopted by fashion mannequins might lend themselves to a systematic taxonomy of different poses as they developed in the twentieth century, if such a thing could be plotted, but it would be an abstract, even languorous and serpentine, language of the body, rather than a representational one.[13] Unlike the walk, the pose developed slowly over the decades, as the upright and restrained posing styles of the 1900s gave way to more fluid, expansive gestures in the 1920s (**250**, **251** and **252**). However, it is hard to find any significance in either beyond the evolution of a fashionable appearance.

If the pose is a frozen moment, the idea of the flow of time from which it is extracted was made visible in the dance performances of Loie Fuller, who was often cited as an inspiration for fashion from the 1890s to the 1900s.[14] The spiralling undulation of Fuller's serpentine dance linked her individual dance movements in a perpetual loop, unlike other kinds of dance based on achieving key 'figures' linked by transitions from one movement to another. This continuity in Fuller's dance, often achieved by swirling fabrics, visualised the trajectory of gestures in space as continuous, so as to make movement itself visible as a flow, divorced from the body.[15] The philosopher Henri Bergson, too, hypothesised the flow of existence as consisting of 'uninterrupted change' which we disregard until it 'becomes sufficient to impress a new attitude on the body'.[16] In *Creative Evolution*, first published in France in 1907, he referred to 'the absurd proposition that movement is made of immobilities'.[17] He developed the concept of 'significant moments' to describe the episodes of time that stand out from its duration (*la durée*). Human movement thus marks the passage of time. For Bergson, however, movement is distinct from the space covered and hence the space covered can be divided up infinitely into 'immobile sections'; but it cannot thereby be reconstituted.

This kind of visual patterning began to be used particularly by the French fashion magazine *Femina* in its fashion page layouts (**253**). Here the same mannequin models four different, if similar, outfits that are photographed separately but reassembled on the page to suggest a sequence of time where none really exists. These types of fashion image in turn take their visual patterns

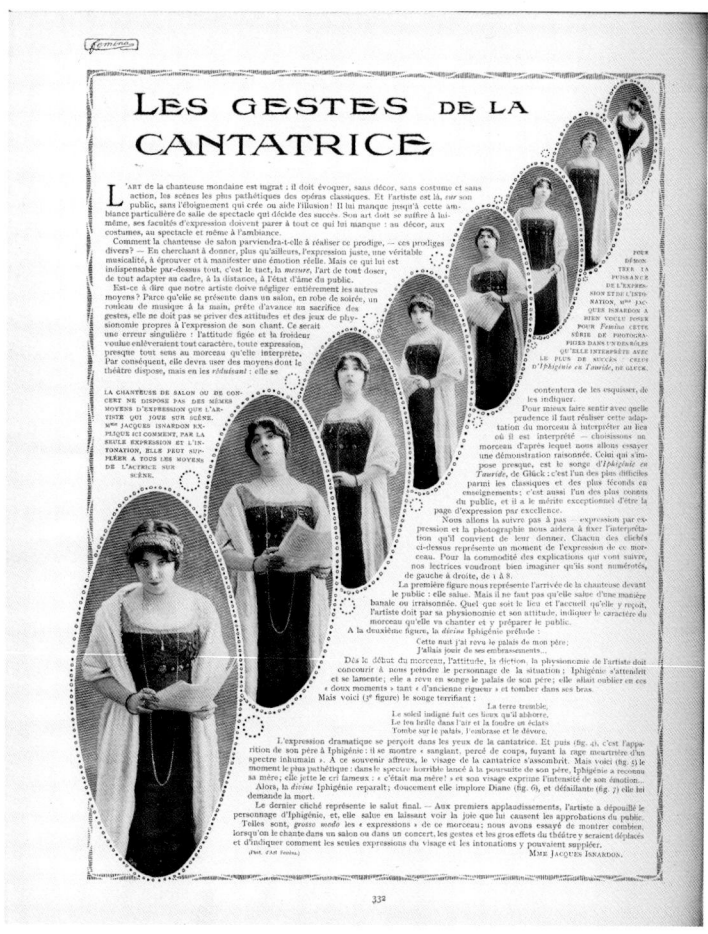

from the multiple images of chronophotography as it was simplified and reinterpreted in new types of fashion magazine layouts of tennis players and popular dancers (see **54** and **55**). These static images in the pages of *Femina* suggest Bergson's 'significant moments' for, as Erin Brannigan has summarised this, 'our "psychical life" becomes a series of discontinuous "separate steps", new attitudes or directions cut out of the "endless flow" of life'.[18] Bergson likened them to beads on a string, where the beads represent the poses or 'privileged moments' through which we make sense of the formless flow of existence represented by the string.[19] Here the structural similarities with the fashion show are striking, as the flow of the fashion show was interrupted by the poses that ruptured the *durée* of the performance and punctuated it with 'significant moments'.

On a page from 1911, *Femina* showed 'the singer's gestures' (**254**) and the accompanying text linked the narrative of the opera to every singing gesture. The singer has no props, writes the author, only her voice and the attitude she strikes. The photographs show her singing a section of Iphigenia's dream from Gluck's *Iphigenia in Tauris*, 'step by step, expression by expression and photography will help us to fix the interpretation that we make of them. Each of the photographs represents a moment in the section'.[20] The writer then describes the images from left to right, correlating the singer's expressions and demeanour to the words she is singing at the given moment. More relevant for fashion posing is the fact that this article appeared in a fashion magazine alongside its images of posing mannequins and of young women demonstrating the poses of the newly fashionable dances and sports. Again, the image is typical of *Femina*'s graphic layouts which often had recourse to the visual language of chronophotography and the film still. By contrast, a series of photographs by Arnold Genthe published in *Vanity Fair* in 1919 (**255**) try impressionistically to capture fabric in motion, the magazine's text describing how hard it is for the photographer 'to catch the fugitive charm of rhythmic motion'.[21]

This type of imagery and ideas traversed art, film and popular culture, as well as fashion in the period. Similar experiments within the avant-garde include Vsevolod Meyerhold's invention of 'static' or 'motionless' theatre from 1905,[22] Duchamp's *Nude Descending a Staircase* (see **45**) and the Italian futurists' exploration of simultaneity and representation. Within popular culture, the late nineteenth and early twentieth century had seen the rise of film editing and of comics, both of which used a selection of 'significant' or 'privileged' moments to tell a story.[23] Film editing can be used to pause the story too. Charles Musser makes the point that the function of the film close-up (something like the pose in the fashion show) is not to forward the film narrative so much as to pause it in order to give the audience the chance to look at the stars.[24] Film-strip imagery also permeated fashion magazines in 'how to'

Catching Drapery in Motion

Is the Prime Essential in the Difficult Art of Photographing a Dancer

253 (facing page left) 'Blanc et noir'. Four of the autumn 1910 season's black and white ensembles are shown on the same mannequin in a composite page layout similar to the fashion show line-ups shown in **39** and **40**. *Femina*, 1 November 1910. Courtesy Fashion Institute of Technology/ SUNY, FIT Library Department of Special Collections and FIT Archives.

254 (facing page right 'Les Gestes de la cantatrice', *Femina*, 11 June 1911. Courtesy Fashion Institute of Technology/SUNY, FIT Library Department of Special Collections and FIT Archives.

255 (right) 'Catching Drapery in Motion'. Photographs by Arnold Genthe, *Vanity Fair*, May 1919. General Research Division, New York Public Library, Astor, Lenox and Tilden Foundations.

instructional articles on popular dances, usually showing four or more photographs of the various moves (see **55, 240** and **245**).[25]

In the workplace, Frank and Lillian Gilbreth's 'Space-Time Studies in Scientific Management' sought to visualise motion scientifically in order to measure how long it took to achieve certain tasks.[26] In the fashion workplace, perhaps the most banal and certainly the most boring form of fashion posing was the biannual task of sitting for the copyright photographs that consisted of three consecutive images in space and time: side, front, back (**256**). Several times a year, the mannequins sat for these fixed-format photographs that the fashion houses produced by the thousand every season. Unseen by public or buyers, the photographs were used to register the designers' copyright. The legal requirement was simply to freeze time so that a designer might be able to prove by a photograph that he or she had designed the dress prior to the date of copyright infringement. Consequently, the mannequins barely bother to model in these photographs. The limited economy of their gestures suggests a self-imposed Taylorist economy: why put more effort into it than necessary, when hundreds of such photographs were taken that no one would look at, simply to be lodged at the Conseil des Prud'hommes? In them, the monotonous *durée* of fashion modelling is patterned by the rhythmic beat of the same three monotonous poses that mark time in the fashion season.

These fashion 'mug shots' were based on a simple triad of hieratic poses that mirrored Alphonse Bertillon's famous system of police records, in use from 1883. Employed by the Paris Prefecture of Police to rationalise its vast quantity of photographs into a working system of identification, Bertillon developed what he termed a 'signalectic' system of identification consisting of a *portrait parlé*. This was a standard identification card inscribed with anthropomorphic details of the subject and one full-face and one profile photograph (**257**). The Bertillon system remained in use throughout the period in which these fashion copyright photographs were used by the majority of the large couture houses.[27] Recalling Allan Sekula's description of nineteenth-century photography as an archive of the criminal and of the social body, the thousands of surviving fashion copyright images constitute a record of the working body of the early twentieth-century fashion mannequin: rationalised, multiplied, subject to clock time and fashion time, they are an index of monotonous seasonality, images not of criminals but as a counter to criminality.[28]

Finally, at the same time that the mannequins were striking their poses in the fashion houses, the German art historian Aby Warburg was working on his 'mnemosyne atlas' (1923–9).[29] In a series of large panels stretched with black cloth, Warburg arranged images of the human figure in motion gleaned from different sources: classical statuary, art reproductions, modern advertisements, maps and

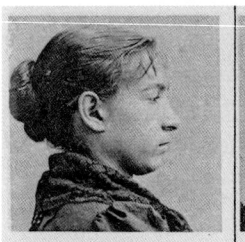
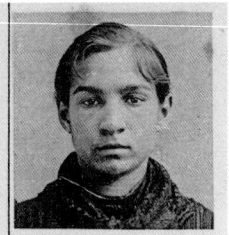
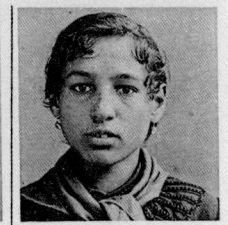

257 (left) Two physiognomic 'portraits' of gypsy women illustrating the Bertillon system that was used in police photography from the 1880s onwards. From Alphonse Bertillon, *Identification anthropométrique: instructions signalétiques*, 1893. Courtesy Wellcome Library, London.

256 (above) Suzanne Talbot, 1925. Copyright registration photograph. Les Arts Décoratifs, Paris, Centre de Documentation des Musées,

personal photographs. Warburg's idea suggested an afterlife for temporal gestures that resurfaced over different periods from classical antiquity to the Renaissance and the present day.[30] Thus modern fashionable poses, themselves sometimes based on classical paintings, found their way into an art historical enquiry, as Warburg juxtaposed a Renaissance painting of Judith holding the head of Holofernes with a 1920s advertisement showing a female golfer wielding her club.[31] Warburg's arrangements montaged different images of movement together in an inherently cinematic and ahistorical way based on a typology of poses rather than on historical connections.[32]

Like Warburg's mnemosynes, early twentieth-century fashion poses created a typology of forms divorced from sequential logic or historical connection, in a visual scheme of human gestures that might echo those of the past but signified little more than decoration to their audiences. At the turn of the century, neo-classical poses were part of the vocabulary of *tableaux vivants* and *poses plastiques* and, as such, part of the everyday body language of theatre and social life (**258**). The fascination of the *tableau vivant*, as Lynda Nead has argued, lies in the juxtaposition of 'arrested motion and the animation of apparently lifeless forms'.[33] Nead describes this as a 'constant and provocative

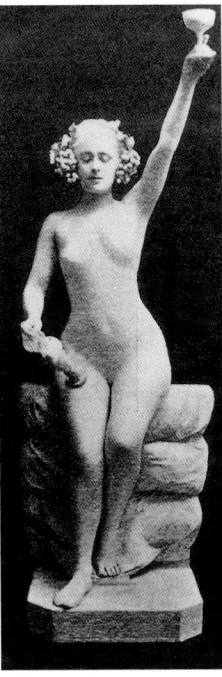

THE POSE: MODERNIST ABSTRACTION

At the heart of the mannequin performance was a staged performance of impassivity in all its forms. The mannequin was inaccessible, disdainful and indifferent. In itself this was a pose, even when it was enacted in motion. A journalist described the mannequins' languid disengagement in 1900, 'trailing in their perplexingly suggestive novelties . . . affected, nonchalant, and a trifle weary'.[37] Backstage it was different. There bad temper could manifest itself in the changing rooms; the *Atlanta Constitution* describes the grunts, scratches, wriggles, slaps and insults which the mannequins hurled at the dressers as they peeled the clothes off them and slid others on. Yet then, wrote the newspaper, 'out into the first salon, slowly, gracefully, like a ghost lily drifts our beauty, smiling reflectively as if meditating on the inferior lot of all the rest of humanity.'[38]

This public staging of hauteur was observed time and time again by contemporaries. A journalist of 1901 described a mannequin who is 'strikingly handsome, but her mouth droops at the corners, which gives her a slightly bored expression . . . At each new appearance the bored expression on her countenance deepens'.[39] At Poiret, Andrée was known for her loftiness. She would 'enter a room in a gorgeous wrap. This she unfastens at the throat and lifts from the shoulders, letting it slip carelessly to the floor as she walks on without a backward look. The one principle which Poiret instils is disdain and contempt of the clothes which are being exhibited.'[40] At Vionnet in 1922 the scornful mannequins 'are slender women with impeccable figures, with simple gestures which habit or boredom prevents them from completing. They have the cold nonchalance of oriental princesses who know they are destined for a futile radiance in the mysterious shadow of the seraglio, and every step betrays their disillusioned haughtiness.'[41] The journalist, the only man in the audience, calls the modelling salon 'a charming morgue', *une morgue charmante*, a phrase that evokes the formaldehyde of fashion posing, where the mannequin is reified through the cultivation of indifference.

The pose of indifference, boredom or disdain was a synecdoche of the entire mannequin performance. It was the specialism of Hebe and Dolores, both trained by Lucile (for Hebe see **92**; for Dolores see **91**). An illustration of 1921 (**260**) shows the mannequins at Molyneux for whom Hebe worked at the time. A year after this image appeared in *Harper's Bazar*, the *New York Times* described Hebe's 'fascination of unapproachability'. She even refused interviews and job offers in order to keep this fascination intact, wrote the newspaper, going on to describe how

oscillation between stasis and movement' and it also characterised fashion modelling.[34] The fashion show reversed the oscillation, however; its flowing movement would seem to pause for a split second before resuming, whereas the *tableau vivant* consisted of lengthy, immobile poses that would periodically be interrupted by movement as the performer either assumed or abandoned the pose.

The fashion show was an animated *tableau vivant* for the age of cinema. *Tableaux vivants* gradually died out after 1900 and at least one newspaper suggested that their role had been replaced by fashion modelling. Hundreds flocked to see the fashion mannequin, wrote the *New York Times* in 1922, 'with orchestra and bouquets and stage setting and jealously guarded tickets of admission'. With the 'art of pose' the mannequin had replaced both the society woman and the actress as a professional beauty and, indeed, 'has the advantage over them both, since she has to be neither social, nor stagey, but merely beautiful.'[35] The final sentence refers to the tradition of the *tableau vivant* which was performed in both the theatre and society drawing rooms. It is precisely in this quality of being 'merely' beautiful, however ('neither social nor stagey') that the modernism of the mannequin resides. As Andrea Cote and Joelle Jensen argue, 'the rhetoric of the pose is both visual and performative'.[36] A *poseuse plastique* for the modern period, the mannequin's was a gestural and performative type of modernism that promised everything but gave nothing away.

259 A manneqin in a
gold tissue and lace gown
at Drecoll, photographed
in 1924 by Adolph de
Meyer. *Harpers Bazar*,
October 1924.

260 The modelling style
at Molyneux in 1921. 'The
mannequin moves slowly
from one end of the room
to the other, passing
before the long mirrors
with her head poised like
that of some long-
plumed bird. There is a
murmur of delight – little
exclamations of wonder;
jewelled women
straighten their slender
backs with interest. The
mannequin walks slowly
to each group; her head is
a marvel of indolence and
grace. She pauses a
moment between parted
curtains. The gown is a
success', wrote *Harper's
Bazar*, November 1921.

> Hebe has a slow, gliding walk. . . . has a turn of the head which
> sends artists mad . . . a capacity for wearing clothes as though they
> grew on her. . . . she is, curiously, rather shy, and it is this little
> reservation which completes her . . . she has to perfection the air of
> not seeing you. When she walks though the gray salons she conveys
> the impression that she is quite alone and by not so much as a
> flicker of an eyelash does she acknowledge the presence of a crowd
> of interested and admiring spectators.[42]

As for Dolores, who modelled for Lucile, Elspeth Brown
describes her 'supreme affectlessness' and 'blank
expression' in the photographs by Adolph de Meyer for
American *Vogue* in 1919, arguing that 'this lack of
expression was, in fact, one of Dolores's defining
performances'. Brown characterises Dolores's 'facial
expressions, gestures and movement vocabulary' as a
'subdued style . . . marked by fluidity and unhurried grace
. . . studied movements, characterized by an elite hauteur
signified by an uplifted chin and unsmiling countenance'.[43]
Drecoll's mannequin is shown similarly posed in
1924 (**259**) in the splendid isolation of the gilded
salons.

These mannequins embodied Georg Simmel's
description from 1903 of the blasé attitude that modern
urban life engendered.[44] Simmel argued that reserve was a
typically urban mental attitude and noted the 'specifically
metropolitan extravagances of self-distanciation, of caprice,
of fastidiousness, the meaning of which is no longer to be
found in the content of such activity itself but rather in its
being a form of "being different" – of making oneself
noticeable' or, as he also puts it, 'striving for individual
forms', and it is in this way that fashion comes to be central
to metropolitan life.[45] The mannequin simply
professionalised this cultivation of affectlessness. In this
respect, her performance pre-empted the postmodern
concept of the waning of affect by many decades, for the
modernist mannequin was 'affectless' from the outset, even
in the nineteenth century when her resemblance to the
inanimate doll and automaton first troubled her
observers.[46]

If ever the mannequin smiled – and it was rarely –
nobody thought it was genuine.[47] Again and again,
journalists from the beginning of the century commented
on the repetitive nature of the mannequin's smile as if to

acknowledge the hollowness at its heart. Her mechanical smile has a precedent in Villiers's *L'Ève future* of 1886, in which the android Hadaly is fitted with six stock smiles described by her inventor, based on those of a real woman, Miss Alicia Clary:

> I . . . devoted myself to chiselling on the android's central cylinder none but perfectly co-ordinated movements, none but the most subtle glances and joyous or serious expressions . . . Would you like to see the several dozen photochromatic pictures on which are marked the points (precise to several thousandths of a millimetre) where the grains of metallic powder had to be placed in the flesh for the exact magnetic implementation of Miss Alicia Clary's five or six basic smiles? I have them right here in these boxes.[48]

The simulacrum of the nineteenth-century literary android's smile anticipated the fashion model's smooth performance in the 1920s. 'How much mystery is there in their look, their impersonal idol's smile!' wrote a French journalist in 1923.[49]

That fascination also underlay the first descriptions of nineteenth-century fashion models, with their links to the doll and the dressmaker's dummy, as well as subsequent descriptions in which they seemed to come alive and be animated in early twentieth-century word-pictures. However, such animation brings with it a certain estrangement. Like the moving toy and the *tableau vivant*, the fashion show privileged the optical allure of movement and stasis. In the fashion show they became stand-alone qualities, disengaged from any narrative or psychological

identification with the human form. This element of 'making strange' alienates the image of the body from the idea of individual personality or sentiment, and privileges motion over emotion. Its pure motility put it at the boundaries of the organic and the inorganic, of the human and the mechanical, and of the lifelike and the deathly.

It was the very emptiness of her performance that constituted the mannequin as a paradigm of modernist glamour in the early twentieth century and connected her to multiple modes of representation spanning cinema, literature, visual art and popular culture, advertising and commodity culture. The literary scholar Judith Brown argues that glamour is a form of abstraction that binds high modernism with, for example, the film vamp and the Eton crop hairstyle. Her analysis is suggestive for the impassive mannequin performance in its move 'away from insistent subjectivity towards the impersonal style that modernism promoted', be it in the cinema or in literature.[50] In her chapter on celebrity, Brown links this type of modernist dislocation to popular notions of 'personality' that emerged in the early twentieth century, as well as to literary concerns with 'changes in human character', and she connects both to the emergence of media 'stars' in the same period.[51] The emptiness that Brown identifies equally in the face of Greta Garbo and in modernist poetry is also to be found in the mannequin's glassy stare and impersonal mien. Indeed, Brown's description of Garbo who 'seems to specialize in doing, expressing, emoting *nothing*' could have been written expressly about the fashion model. If the extinction of personality was one of literary modernism's central principles, which Garbo enacted on screen, the point can equally be made of those earlier practitioners of the genre of impersonality, the living mannequins whose behaviour was characterised by an unyielding silence and an impassive façade long before the advent of cinema.[52]

This voiding of personality was not limited to the blank facial expression but extended to all the physical gestures of the mannequin. Part of her performance involved striking graphic, linear poses to make shapes with her body in space. These were often copied from stage actors' gestures and, like the actors of early film, the mannequin offered up a reservoir of gestures and poses for the modern age.[53] The singer Yvette Guilbert in particular, who had been a mannequin in her youth, was known for her mesmerising arm gestures.[54] Sarah Bernhardt, the 'Princess of Gesture', created increasingly simplified large gestures and struck grand bodily attitudes for her American tours in order to communicate with audiences seated at a great distance in huge theatres, who anyway might not understand French (**261**).[55] Mannequins copied them both (**262**), as well as the stage gestures of the actresses Gabrielle Réjane and Cécile Sorel.[56] They copied only the forms, however, of these actresses' pantomimic gestures and dramatic poses, not their signifying power. Instead, mannequins emptied their poses and gestures of their stage meaning, performing them all with the same disdainful and blasé attitude.

The big gestures of theatrical mime, too, provided an analogue for fashion modelling, once stripped of their melodrama. A part of the nineteenth-century pantomime tradition, mime continued to be an important form of theatrical posing and remained popular in the period of the first fashion shows.[57] There were two kinds of mime, corresponding to the static and moving elements of fashion modelling. The first, *mime de poses*, or posing mime, consisted of static posing and featured in the *tableaux vivants* of the Paris Théâtre de Variétés.[58] (Known in English as 'statue posing', it was also a popular drawing-room pastime.) The second, *mime de gestes*, or moving mime, was used in the *pantomimes blanches* of the Paris theatre. These were dramatic narratives of love and passion in which emotions such as anguish, love, jealousy, terror, hatred and affection were expressed in stagey gestures.[59]

Both types of mime could provide blueprints for fashion walking and posing, as could the emerging genre of silent film acting that used the whole body expressively, exemplified by the Danish film actress Asta Nielsen. The mannequin, like the film actress, had to work with her body to develop a silent repertoire of movements, gestures and poses. In 1911 the French actress and fashion icon

Mistinguett described two, apparently contradictory, styles required by cinema acting: vivid movement for long shots and relative immobility for close-ups.[60] Like mime artists, Mistinguett evoked the contrast between the moving image and the still, the very elements that alternated in the fashion show when the mannequins periodically froze and unfroze in their passage through the modelling salons and on to the dressing rooms backstage (see **53**). Mistinguett's description of two types of cinema acting corresponded to two types of modelling: first, showing the garment in motion and, second, showing its detail in temporary slow motion, achieved by striking a pose.

Unlike the theatrical and film poses, however, fashion posing was not a communicative language of the body. Indeed, it was the opposite of acting which required characterisation, impersonation and narrative. Paradoxically, this made fashion modelling particularly modern. Despite nineteenth-century attempts to codify the theatrical gesture, by the 1900s there were no longer socially agreed meanings in or out of the theatre that could be ascribed to particular gestures.[61] Nor was there much sense that gesture could communicate an inner state of mind or an intention.[62] The historian Michael Braddick argues that this resulted from changing notions of identity, so that the idea of an inner self which could be expressed by outer gesture was replaced by an idea of the self as constituted on the surface of appearances.[63] Here was a new paradox of the pose: that meaning lay on the surface but was indecipherable.

It was in precisely this environment that the first mannequins came to public attention at the turn of the century: as the embodiment of pure 'outer performance'. How much meaning can a fashion pose bear, after all? At most it might amount to the body signature of the mannequin, a flourish of graceful but meaningless gestures, like a nineteenth-century writing master's flourishes.[64] Yet the proliferation of gestures in the modelling and acting styles of this period seems to support Giorgio Agamben's claim, in his 'Notes on Gesture', that 'an era that has lost its gestures is, for that very reason, obsessed with them; for people who are bereft of all that is natural to them, every gesture becomes a fate. And the more the ease of these gestures was lost under the influence of invisible powers, the more life became indecipherable.'[65] Agamben locates the beginning of this loss in the bourgeois consumer culture of the 1880s, the decade in which fashion mannequins were coming into public consciousness for the first time. In particular, he sees the acting styles of early cinema as a desperate attempt to recover or record what had been lost, which leads him to assert that 'gesture rather than image is the cinematic element'.[66] Agamben endorses

Deleuze's concept of the 'movement-image' of cinema but takes it further to argue that once the integrity of all images is fragmented in modernity there remain only gestures: 'this means that the mythical fixity of the image has been broken, and we should not really speak of images here but of gestures . . . Cinema leads images back into the realm of gesture'.[67]

In his discussion of dance gestures Agamben postulates that gestures are part of the medium that produces them. Rather than having any extrinsic meaning, they are pure 'mediality'. So too is the fashion pose. This is both what makes it incapable of signifying and what makes it, paradoxically, significant. A part of what the literary scholar Susan McCabe has called 'the modernist obsession with nonteleological movement', the fragmented, repetitive poses and bodily styles of the first mannequins shared the kind of 'cinematic modernism' that McCabe finds in the dislocated bodily attitudes of Gertrude Stein, Man Ray and Charlie Chaplin.[68] While Agamben's concerns in 'Notes on Gesture' are primarily with the politics and ethics of gesture, as opposed to its aesthetics, his ideas suggest a way to think about the empty gestures and hollow poses of the fashion mannequin as both an aesthetic and a particularly modernist ethic of alienated impersonality and emptiness.

All unencumbered motility without psychology, the mannequin's poses leave no trace, in the sense described by Henri Lefevbre, who conceptualised living bodies in space as a current or flow without consciousness. Pose creates what Lefevbre calls a 'gestural system' with its own internal and spatial logic, so that a 'gestural action' might consist simply of turning round, a gesture like the revolution on the spot of the professional mannequin which merely marks space for its duration, rather than leaving a trace or vestige such as a footprint.[69] Part of the visual culture of modernism, the mannequin played a role in the breaking up of the image and its reconceptualisation through new technologies and sensibilities. Her performance was, in Agamben's sense, cinematic and she is, furthermore, the figuration of what he elsewhere calls '*mute* experience', 'anterior both to subjectivity and to an alleged psychological reality'.[70]

THE FASHION SHOW AS A FILM STRIP OF MODERNIST SENSIBILITIES

The fashion mannequin was not a prime mover in the history of modernism. She simply played a minor part in the proliferation of a range of images of surface, alienation, flow and decoration, as against those of narrative coherence, inner life and meaningful gesture. There was,

nevertheless, something inherently cinematic about the fashion show itself which made the form modernist, not only in the way it regulated and rationalised the human body. Partly, this lay in the simple fact that both fashion shows and film revealed the human body in motion; it is no accident that they developed in almost exactly the same period. As Christopher Breward writes, the 'material, temporal and symbolic properties' of film echoed modern fashion itself.[71] Cinema, the 'Seventh Art', was the new medium of the modern age.[72] In this context, the mannequin played her role in shaping modern ideas about continuity and discontinuity in ways similar to film. The fashion show, like early film, was intermedial in being connected to other media and different cultural spaces.[73] It is the way in which the dramaturgy of the mannequin intersects with many other types of episodic, fragmentary and anti-linear narratives and images across the fields of popular culture and technology that establishes her performance as part of a modernist flow of images and commodities at the turn of the century.

Early fashion shows, like early film, privileged surface appearance and the visual flow of bodies in motion. In particular, the visual appeal of the fashion show resembled that of 'actualities', the earliest form of short, single-shot films that reproduced everyday movement, actions and scenes. Compare, for example, the mannequin modelling in the fashion salon, as she enters, glides, turns, pauses for a split second to pose, then resumes her walk and exits the salon in a single flowing move, to the film *La Sortie de l'usine* (shown for the first time in Paris in December 1895): a tide of workers surges out of the Lumière film factory in Lyons at the end of a working day in June 1894, the women in respectable hats and laundered blouses. Both scenes simply show human motion as it unfolds in front of the eye or camera, rather than an event or a decisive moment; both privilege the visual fascination of movement over psychological depth, narrative or truth, in a beguiling flow of effects and surfaces; both compress and flatten any putative story or personality into a form of abstraction by showing moving bodies as a visual pattern rather than a narrative device. In *Cinema 1*, Deleuze linked film's temporality to movements in ballet and mime; so too film is linked to fashion modelling in the period.[74] Like the first film, fashion shows were 'attractions', to use the term adopted by the film historians André Gaudreault and Tom Gunning to describe the way that early film privileged showing over telling. Gaudreault and Gunning relate early film to forces such as the changing experience of time and modernity to explain how the beguiling effects of motion, rather than storytelling, might be the defining feature of the experience of watching early film.[75]

263 (right)
A scene from the 1907
film *Transformation*
(*Métempsychose* [*sic*]),
directed by Segundo de
Chomón, Pathé Frères)
that recreates a famous
stage illusion in which
one object or person
metamorphoses into
another. Here a statue
bust turns into a butterfly
fairy who performs a
number of dazzling
costume transformations.
AFF/CNC.

264 (facing page)
The modelling gesture of
holding open a coat, in a
catwalk parade held
aboard the Cunard liner
Franconia during
Liverpool's Civic Week in
1925. Photograph
Brooke/Getty Images.

Soon cinema became more complex as film-makers began to use stop-motion and other techniques that turned actions into events, and to develop the techniques of film editing that eventually enabled more sophisticated narratives. The fashion show, meanwhile, continued relatively unchanged over decades.[76] In this sense it remained an attractions-based format, as Mila Ganeva argues in her discussion of Weimar popular films that incorporated fashion shows. In these films, the fashion shows provided a contrast between firstly, a 'paradigmatic cinematic moment' that focused in close-up on the spectacular body of the mannequin and, secondly, a significant break in the narrative flow, offering spectators 'glimpses of the earlier cinema of attraction. This disruption associated with the fashion show in early Weimar cinema reflected – even in the most straightforward and trivial narratives – the experience of modernity, which was in essence the experience of an environment becoming increasingly distracting, disjunctive and fragmented'.[77] Ganeva thus neatly pinpoints the sense of a flow of images, objects and practices which caught up both fashion and film in its eddies, carrying some along with the main current while others broke away and drifted into side pools.

The mannequin's blankness also had a close relationship to film, at least in the way that film was perceived by contemporaries. Brigitte Peucker has argued that in the relatively new medium of cinema whose essence was understood to be movement, 'cinematic bodies – the human figures subjected to motion in films – were generally perceived as attenuated, as 'merely' the sum of their actions and movements, and were often contrasted negatively with so-called theatrical bodies', which were understood to be imbued with soul and sensibility, as opposed to the one-dimensional 'pure surface' of the cinematic body.[78] By the 1920s, as the film historian Angela Dalle Vacche writes, invoking the contemporary film theorist Béla Balázs, 'in the silent film melodramas of the twenties, the power of bodies, faces and objects could speak more eloquently than literary or theatrical language'.[79] In 1921, the film-maker Jean Epstein described cinema in ways that suggest that silent film was closely similar to fashion modelling. Cinema is a 'theatre of the skin', he wrote; with no stage between the spectacle and the spectator, it is 'an aesthetic of proximity' and 'an aesthetic of suggestion. One no longer narrates, one indicates . . . on screen, the essential quality of a gesture is never to realise itself. The face is not expressive like a mime's but, better, it is suggestive.'[80]

It was in fashion modelling that the 'gesture that never realises itself' and the 'suggestive face' reached their apotheosis. In the way that the pose was both a still and a figuration of movement, the mannequin's stop-start modelling style shared the nature of film. The paradox of the fashion pose was also the paradox of film, identified by many early twentieth-century commentators when they observed that film consisted of a great number of still images that only gave the illusion of continuous movement once projected.[81] The mannequin's performance underlined the relationship between continuity and discontinuity that was also at the heart of film. When she paused, she even evoked the early camera operator's capacity to halt time by temporarily stopping filming to create stop-frame effects by making adjustments to the set or the actors before resuming filming.

As well as being formally similar, fashion and film were also distinct forms that interacted. The relationship was two-way and both forms interacted with other media in a process of 'vernacular modernism' – that is, as Ganeva describes it, 'a modernist aesthetic that articulates and mediates a wide array of quotidian visual practices' in relation to both film and fashion, including advertising and merchandising.[82] Here different kinds of modernist flow converged: the flow consisting of the literal movement of the fashion model, the visual flow of film and the commercial flow, or traffic, of images and commodities.

Beyond that, the relationship between film and fashion also impacted on sensibilities. By 1910 the visual language of film had begun to percolate into fashion journalism, suggesting that the viewing competences of fashion writers were structured at least partly by cinema. The sense that cinema was introducing new ways of seeing and thinking about the world was articulated in 1900 by Bergson in a lecture at the Collège de France on the 'Cinematographic

Mechanism of Thought'.[83] He developed the theme in *Creative Evolution*, using the example of soldiers walking to explain his ideas about visual perception and consciousness: 'we take snapshots, as it were, of the passing reality, we have only to string them on a becoming . . . we hardly do anything else than set going a kind of cinematograph inside us'.[84] As noted earlier, the French word for a military parade, *défilé*, also meant mannequin parade or fashion show, and Bergson's cinematic description of watching soldiers marching preceded fashion journalists' descriptions of fashion models at work by only a few years. In 1910 *Femina* magazine called the forthcoming autumn fashions 'a veritable cinematograph of tomorrow's fashion'.[85] The *Chicago Daily Tribune*, also in 1910, described French fashion as a 'rapid film rush', epitomised by the photographs in American department stores of Parisian mannequins 'striding along a wind blown walk' on the boulevards or at the races.[86] In July 1910, in a long article on Paul Poiret's couture house, *L'Illustration* wrote about the couturier's mannequin parades in the formal gardens of the house. Poiret's command of the parade is described in filmic terms, highlighting how he stops, starts and even reverses it on command, as if he were himself a film operator. The action also resembles the stop-action effects, dissolves and superimpositions typical of

Méliès, who cut and re-joined his own films to produce the trick effects and transformations that made women appear, multiply and disappear on screen as if by magic.

> With a word, a gesture . . . [Poiret] directs the cortege . . . a sign from him, a syllable, throws them forward, halts them, then makes them start again, go, come back on themselves, cross over, mix, according to his fantasy, as if it were a ballet with lazy movements . . . and return, suddenly, to show off for a moment the curve of their hips.[87]

In 1914 a journalist in *Fantasio* magazine described the parade of fashionable people in the Bois de Boulogne as 'an admirable cinema'.[88] The very first film-makers had, in their turn, understood the appeal to audiences of costume in motion, even if it took a few years for film of actual fashion modelling to appear, as it increasingly did from the 1910s.[89] Sometimes fashion posing even created the visual effects of moving fabrics that were popular in the early films, especially the genre of skirt-dancing.[90] The effect of opening the arms to display a cloak or coat while modelling became a standard and enduring pose. It was first described in 1912, when a mannequin at Callot in a nasturtium-yellow dress made of satin and tulle under a draped coat of nasturtium-red panne velvet dramatically 'swung back the fronts of the coat, which she held out by means of a strap through which her hands were passed. The effect was exactly like that of a flower suddenly bursting into bloom as you looked'.[91] It also recalled the use of fabrics by actresses in transformation films who mimicked butterflies by repeatedly opening and closing their arms to unveil a new pair of wings each time, as in Segundo de Chomón's *Transformation* (*Metempsychose* [*sic*], 1907) (**263**).[92] In fashion modelling, it became a staple gesture, persisting well into the 1920s (**264** and see **172**),[93] when it can again be found in film, such as the nightclub scene in Fritz Lang's *Metropolis* in which, as Ganeva has shown, the robot Maria's nightclub dance owes its gestures and stance to fashion poses.[94]

FASHION TIME, MODERNIST TIME

The final kind of flow in which the fashion show partakes is the flow of time. In *The Emergence of Cinematic Time*, Mary Ann Doane argues for the important role played by early film in the restructuring of time in capitalist modernity in the late nineteenth and early twentieth centuries.[95] She posits that 'movement is often represented as the embodiment of time, and it is difficult to conceive of an access to time which is not mediated by movement or change (which in itself seems ineluctably wedded to movement).'[96] At the turn of the century, film was a new technology that enabled the reconceptualisation of the image as 'the permanent record of fleeting moments', as Doane describes it.[97] Fashion modelling was also a new technology, not only a technology of the body in motion, as previous chapters have explored, but also, and equally, of the image of the body in time.

Both film and fashion modelling were preceded by chronophotography, an important precursor. Marey and Muybridge's images from the 1880s of running, jumping and strolling men and women constructed a rationalised hybrid of time and motion that was proto-modernist.[98] As Doane argues, 'the manifest project of modernity – and of the cinema in the wake of Marey and Muybridge – is to make time visible, representable'.[99] The moving fashion show created not only a modernist body but also a modernist representation of time. Doane characterises the rapid diffusion of the pocket watch in the late nineteenth century as an 'impulse to *wear* time' and she describes how 'time was indeed *felt* – as weight, as a source of anxiety and as an acutely pressing part of representation'.[100] In the fashion show, time was not represented, however, so much as modelled and embodied by the mannequin at work. It is the complexities of the pose, as the pause in the flow of

time, that form the links between early fashion shows, early film and modernist time.

In the same period, a number of writers were concerned with the idea of the fleeting moment which emerged as a modernist concern in the work of Benjamin and Martin Heidegger, as well as in modernist fiction where it offered a non-narrative model to illustrate what Judith Brown calls the 'multiple voices, random images and encounters, sensations and fragmentary meanings of the period'. Indeed, she asserts that the momentary was 'the defining trope of the modern' and it is in this way that the pose is inherently modernist, be it in Virginia Woolf's pose as a writer or the real-time fashion mannequin's pose on the modelling stage.[101]

The fashion show plays with time, speeding it up, halting it and slowing it down through the visual patterning of the mannequin performance. Walking on, off, on, off, for up to one and a half hours at a time, sometimes even longer, replaying her poses like variations on a theme, and always multiplied in the mirrored walls, the mannequin offered the possibility of ceaseless repetition and re-vision, her poses the 'visual adjectives' of the fashion show, as Seymour Chatman described the detail that saturates the cinematic frame.[102] Indeed, audiences had no choice but to witness her continual appearance and disappearance, which shared some of the repetition and pulsing visual rhythms of nineteenth-century optical toys such as the praxinoscope and zoetrope. That perhaps explains the charm of Poiret's mannequin Raph, whose hesitations at the evening fashion show in 1925 seemed to pause the action in real time. The domestic technology of the twenty-first century makes it easy to repeat, rewind, and restore the image; to pause, freeze-frame, slow down and re-run motion. Early twentieth-century fashion show audiences had no such means but the mannequin did the job for them, through her endless appearance, disappearance and re-appearance, like a walking *Fort-Da* game.

The successful international dissemination of French fashion via the mannequin tour and the international press depended on the restructuring of time through technologies such as the telegraph, as well as its standardisation in international accords. Doane argues that the technology of early film embodied, or materialised, this sense of time itself as rationalised in the way its divided and static frames are 'instants of time', so that 'cinema participates in the rationalization of time characterizing the industrial age'.[103] In the couture house, the mannequin was the metronome of fashion time. The movements of her standardised body in both pre- and post-war shows, like the simplified steps of modern social dancing, were related to how, in the late nineteenth and early twentieth centuries, as Doane argues, 'time became increasingly reified, standardized, stabilized, and rationalized' in ways that were closely linked to new technologies, processes and changing patterns of work.[104] So it was in fashion, too, both in the calibrated rhythms of the fashion mannequin and in the individual stop-start time of the fashion worker, seasonally laid off to fit the regular and regulating cycles of fashion time and business time.

Part of the flow of modernist images and practices, the fashion mannequin eddied in and out of the field of vision, a perpetual present without meaning or content, her rhythmic abstraction like the rolling textiles in motion of Sonia Delaunay's simultaneous fashions, or the pulsating rhythms of early film that mesmerised its audiences with the sight of motion rather than through narrative. All malleable femininity, the mannequin epitomised surface as essence, in its full contradiction: a woman with no diction, who did not speak but who eloquently appeared, gifted above all in striking a fleeting pose and then flowing back into fluid motion. Through gestural performativity, an emphasis on body as surface and the staging of vacancy as formal values that were also techniques of the body, the mannequin swam with the tide of early twentieth-century modernism, alongside Loie Fuller's fluid moving dances, Bergson's *durée* and the cinema of attractions.[105]

AFTERWORD

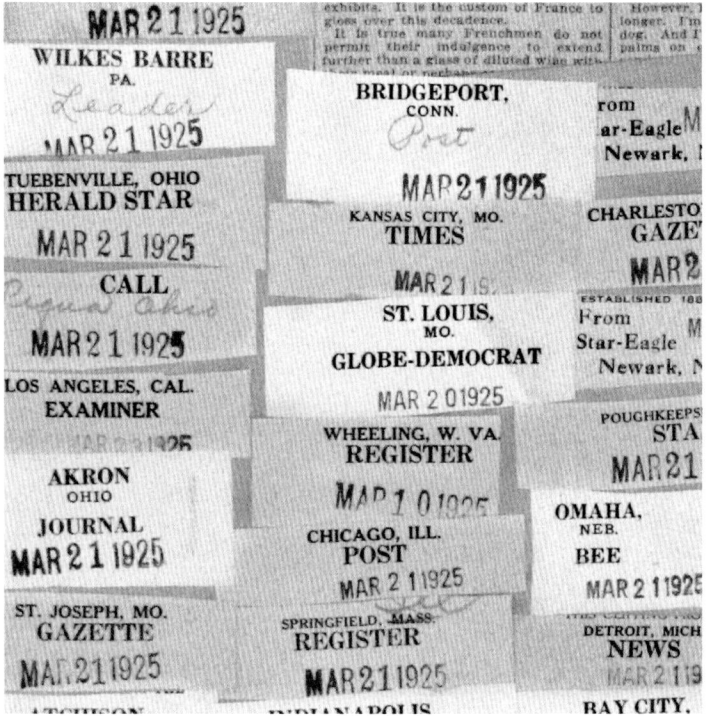

265 Detail from newspaper cuttings of March 1925 from the Jean Patou press album. See **266**.

How, finally, to balance the books? Is it possible to reconcile the legacy of the fashion show with the inheritance of the mannequin?

AFTER 'LE KRACH': WALKING INTO THE FUTURE

Fashion shows went from strength to strength in the twentieth century and continue today to be a central part of the promotional strategies of the fashion industry, despite their huge cost. Many of the characteristics of today's shows have their origins in the developments of the first shows more than a hundred years ago. There were, however, several effects of the Crash of 1929, all economic, that accelerated changes in fashion shows and their attendant transactions: fashion buying, copying and piracy. In 1931 the author of a doctoral thesis on haute couture as a luxury industry, Philippe Simon, wrote:

> The agricultural crisis that has afflicted the United States since 1926, the New York stock market crash in November 1929, have modified the composition of the couturiers' salons. Other women, newly come to elegance, have replaced the clients who, over the previous ten years had, little by little, become refined by prolonged contact with luxury and good taste.[1]

With it, he continued, came a series of problems which the couturier had never before encountered. The couturier had profoundly to remodel his house and learn to design for a new kind of client who led a new kind of life and whose tastes in fashion were extremely variable. Instead of waiting for the clients to come to him, he had to follow new markets.[2] Some, like Chanel, Patou and Lelong, had already done so. Others, however, were not so adaptable. The conservative Charles Creed was one of the last houses in Paris to begin to hold mannequin parades, preferring instead to show twice a year on a dozen or so miniature dummies, no more than two feet high, dressed in perfect replicas of the collection. It was only the third generation of Creeds, in the form of the young Charles Creed who had been apprenticed to Bergdorf-Goodman in New York in 1929 (where he had observed how all the saleswomen were chosen for their looks and manners), who persuaded his

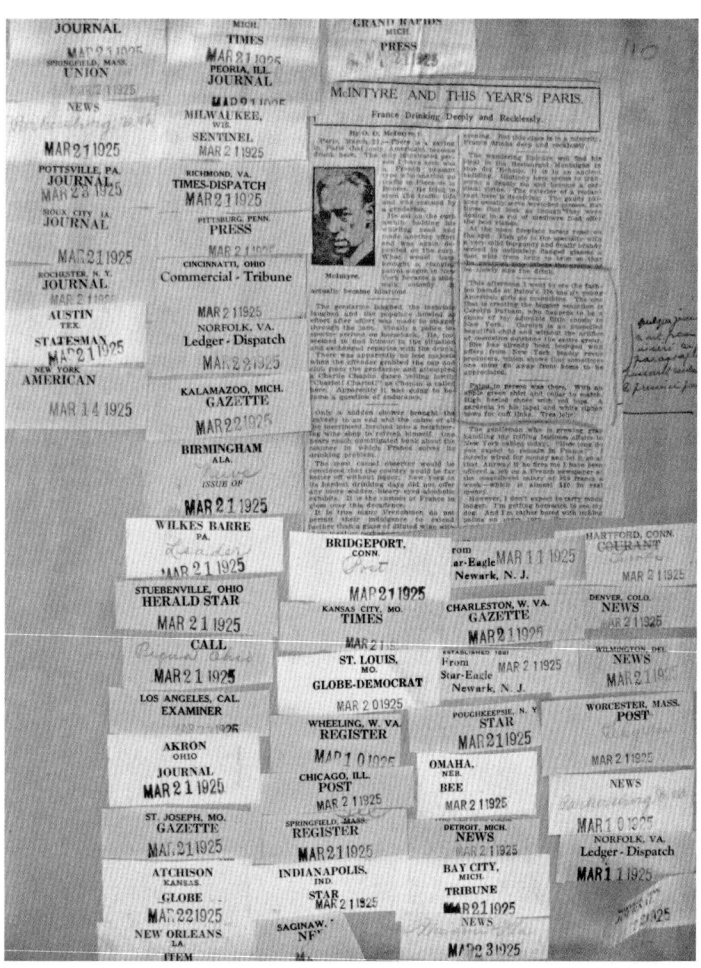

266 Newspaper cutting from the Jean Patou press album showing an article from March 1925 on Patou's American mannequins and forty-nine different U.S. newspapers in which it was syndicated. Patou employed an American press agency to syndicate his publicity across the U.S.A. and meticulously recorded it in his press albums.' Patou Archive.

father to initiate the 'new-fangled notion' of mannequin parades.[3]

The more progressive Paris houses all recognised how important it was to promote their firms through international press reports of their fashion shows. In the mid-1920s Patou had used an American cuttings agency; nine tenths of the cuttings in his press books were from English-language newspapers (**266**). By 1930 *Women's Wear Daily* and the *Daily News Record*, the two most important publications in the American garment industry, both owned by E. W. Fairchild, had permanent representatives in Paris whose job it was to visit the fashion show previews ('advance showings') 'so that complete reports may be carried in his publications on the day of the openings'.[4] Fairchild's organisation was immense, only exceeded in size by the four great news-gathering agencies of the world, Associated Press, United Press, Reuters and International. As well as feeding his own newspapers with new fashion information, Fairchild's agency fed information to five other periodicals in New York, Chicago, Paris and London 'and in many series of analyses and charts he provides all the knowledge and forecasts that the trade requires', wrote *Fortune*, the American business magazine.[5]

American influences in French fashion were multifarious. In the 1920s many independent Paris couture houses were subject to mergers (Doeuillet and Doucet) and takeovers (Poiret, Drecoll, Beer and Agnès), as one-man or one-woman businesses sold majority shareholdings and became joint stock companies. 'Just as Ford has been imitated by Citroën, the tendency to merge smaller units into large ones, which is associated with American business methods, has left its mark upon the hitherto highly individualistic trade of the Parisian dress designer', wrote the *New York Times* in 1928.[6]

In 1932 *Fortune* outlined the relationship between the French and American industries in a candid analysis of the fashion show. It reported in precise detail all the features of the Paris shows: the salons were 'nerve centers of an industry', and 'the scene of The Opening. To the various salons four times a year (August and February for the major openings, April and November for the mid-season openings) throng the smart set and the press to see what may be worn the next season.'[7] As, too, did the buyers, commissionaires, pirates, copyists, the whole commercial panoply for whom the shows existed, as *Fortune* had described in an earlier article in 1930 with frank clarity:

Today hundreds of buyers . . . and many, many jobbers go to Paris for the openings each season. Each man brings back with him models, for which he has paid $300 or more. This model no American woman would wear. Nor would any French woman. It is to the purchaser what shorthand notes are to the stenographer. It may be made from any kind of material, the cheaper the better. If the original had fur anywhere upon it, the model will indicate it with white muslin or sleazy crepe. Each model is a trade secret for its owner. He hides it carefully. When he is home again, his designer will *adapt* it, rarely *copy* it. The inexperienced eye is often unable to detect any similarity between the model and the copy. But no matter. The dress qualifies as a Lanvin or a Patou or a Worth because the American designers (drawing, likely $10,000 to $25,000 a year in salary) had a twist and fold of cloth for which his boss paid $500 hanging in front of him as he worked. The similarity may not extend beyond the general arrangement of buttons or the flare of a cuff.

The birth of a 'copy' is attended with great secrecy. The manufacturer or jobber knows that if his new number is particularly 'hot', it will be recopied (actually copied this time) and on the market at $10 less than his price in a few days. The theft, manufacture, and retail sale of a style idea has been accomplished in three hours.[8]

Some buyers did not even buy models from the Paris shows, just paper patterns, sketches and references.[9] Even the author of this article described the American fashion industry as 'this berserk industry'.[10] The French industry, by contrast, was pronounced obscure: 'Indeed, the industry exists by virtue of obscurity. For the industry is an industry of ideas . . . Only the *haute couture* rests its millions of francs of profit . . . upon the artistic fecundity of some thirty to fifty designers . . . only the *haute couture* could succeed in the manipulation of such a crazy structure.'[11]

In fact, it did not always succeed and frequently failed to control its own 'crazy structure'. It was a relatively new kind of business, less than half a century old in 1900, and one that, as Levasseur argued in 1912, and Simon again in 1931, had insufficient experience of international trade in a rapidly expanding global market.[12] If the Paris industry maintained its symbolic capital, so that the idea of French fashion still dominated the American 'imaginary', it is hard to see how that really impacted productively on its economic capital. The gap between the two could be immense. In 1922, Premet named a black satin slip dress with white collar and cuffs *La Garçonne* at the time of the success of the novel of the same name; Premet sold a thousand 'original copies' but another million pirated copies changed hands.[13] In 1931 a record price of 3500 francs was reached for a single French couture dress that was reproduced 50,000 times by an American manufacturer. Despite the sale being legitimate, the couture house received no pecuniary benefit from 'this extraordinary success'.[14] Even in 1938, Elizabeth Hawes noticed that the cracks were showing.[15] An American working in Paris fashion in the 1920s, alert to the rapid developments in mass production in the U.S.A., she felt

that the French system was anachronistic. 'It creaked', she wrote.[16] She observed that couture was not steadily profitable; a couturier could earn good money in prosperous times but could not survive a long recession.[17]

At the 1925 Paris 'Exposition des Arts Décoratifs', seventy-five couture houses had been represented. That year, couture and ready-to-wear together constituted fifteen per cent of French exports. Garment exports dropped slightly in the late 1920s but only tailed off sharply after the Crash. Before that, America was France's second major importer of clothing, after Great Britain, as opposed to its pre-First World War position in sixth place. Throughout the 1920s, the price of a French custom-made dress that took fifty hours to produce remained competitive, compared to its American and British equivalents, being approximately seventy per cent cheaper than in Britain and a good thirty per cent cheaper than in the U.S.A. After the Crash, however, the ratios shifted and gradually, as the 1930s drew on, French dresses began to cost slightly more than their British equivalents and, while they remained cheaper than American ones, it was by considerably less, about fifty-five per cent.[18] These figures, however, relate to custom-made dresses and take no account of America's far superior mass-manufacturing capacity. In 1930 the U.S. garment industry in its entirety consisted of eight thousand small manufacturers, a hundred million garments a year, and employed two thirds of the Russian-Jewish population of the U.S.A.[19] The more exclusive Fifth Avenue stores continued to purchase part of their stock from Paris, and part of it was locally manufactured on Ninth Avenue, but already stores like Hattie Carnegie on 49th Street had their own garment factories and the more downmarket stores mass-produced dresses at affordable prices starting as low as $1 to $6.[20]

As Didier Grumbach, the current head of the Fédération de la Couture, points out, the Crash of 1929 sounded the end of 'this opulent trade' of sales to U.S. buyers.[21] The Crash produced the 1930 Hawley-Smooth law in the U.S.A., which imposed a massive ninety per cent duty on imported clothes, and, in many other countries, similarly prohibitive customs duties and import quotas.[22] To avoid the new ninety per cent import tax, American buyers in Paris increasingly purchased toiles instead of models. Toiles were design prototypes made up in unbleached canvas, an essential early stage of the design process that the houses previously barely sold. After the 1930 tax, buyers bought the toile with the right to make it up in large numbers. A new system of temporarily importing 'bonded models' to the United States evolved; these models were only temporarily admitted to the country and held in customs bond for no longer than six months to avoid 'exorbitant

267a and b Two pages from the Lucien Lelong booklet for *La Robe Édition*, 1934: (a) 'Against the false luxury of ready-to-wear and mass production, La Robe Édition expresses feminine elegance through class and personality'; (b) prices (left) and pubic invitation (right) to the fashion show for the spring 1932 collection. Les Arts Décoratifs, Paris, Centre de Documentation des Musées, all rights reserved.

import duties'.[23] As Alexandra Palmer notes, 'the actual bonded material was a disposable commodity from its conception' because, although it was technically a loan, in reality the bonded model would not be returned to Paris after use but sold on to third-party buyers in Canada or South America.[24]

This, in conjunction with the continuing activities of foreign copyists, pushed couture further towards decline. In 1929 three fifths of couture sales were export sales but over the next six years these shrank by over seventy per cent, as garments dropped from eighth to twenty-seventh place in the French export tables. Whereas in 1925 they had topped 2 billion francs, in 1931 they fell to 483,479,000 francs and in 1936 to 51,224,000 francs.[25]

The Crash caused significant unemployment in the Paris fashion houses. Grumbach cites Paul Poiret who, in 1932, was interviewed by *Heim* magazine:

Couture is dying precisely through being built up on too broad a base. Gone are the braided flunkies at the door. Gone the carpets everywhere, the tapestries on the walls, the sumptuous shop windows. Gone the numerous staff. Gone the collections of 400 models with showy furs. Gone the little suit that is reproduced 1500 times. Gone the shops with huge rents on the Champs-Élysées.[26]

Poiret himself was really gone by the time he made this statement, having gone into liquidation in 1930, though he valiantly ploughed on and in 1933 struck deals with both Liberty of London and Le Printemps in Paris.[27] Although he was in ruins financially, Poiret was still an innovator in his willingness to move from couture to ready-to-wear. Not unexpectedly, his flamboyant style and rampant individualism were not transferred successfully to the department store setting.[28]

In 1934 Lucien Lelong made a more significant move to bridge the gap between couture and mechanised mass production with his 'Lucien Lelong Editions'. The collection comprised sixty models priced from 350 to 900 francs, far less than the cost of a couture gown from Lelong. They were ready-to-wear, although could be made to measure for a supplement of 100 francs, and were manufactured in the Lelong ateliers in avenue Matignon in small runs, using luxury fabrics and a certain amount of hand-stitching. To explain and publicise his new concept of *la robe éditon*, Lelong published a little booklet, *La Robe et l'époque*, which included an open invitation to the regular showing of his spring 'Collection Edition' every day, on mannequins, from 10 am to 12.30 pm and again from 2 to 6.30 pm (**267**).[29]

Over the decade, the French Chambre Syndicale de la Couture Parisienne made great efforts to regularise trade practices and to protect its industry in a rapidly changing world market. The private clientele continued to change in later decades too: from 1943 to 1970, the number of individual haute couture clients shrank from 20,000 to 2000. By 1990, they were 200.[30] Overseas buyers were still important, however. From 1930 to the 1970s, America remained French couture's biggest market.[31] So much was haute couture an export industry that French manufacturers were refused entry to the salons of the big couturiers who wished to preserve their national market, until 1945 when French manufacturers were admitted to couture collections on payment of a fee, for which they received no more than 'visual rights' (*un droit de vision*) which allowed them to draw inspiration from the models but not to copy them literally.[32] That year the Chambre Syndicale decreed that couture houses must hold regular, twice-yearly fashion shows in Paris, on dates fixed by the Chambre, of a collection of at least seventy-five original models created by the firm. Collections had to be shown on a minimum of three living mannequins and the presentations to individual clients had to take place at least

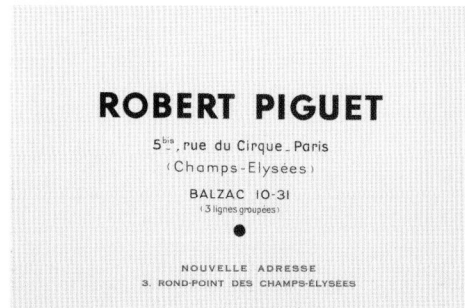

ROBERT PIGUET

5ᵇⁱˢ, rue du Cirque - Paris
(Champs-Elysées)

BALZAC 10-31
(3 lignes groupées)

●

NOUVELLE ADRESSE
3, ROND-POINT DES CHAMPS-ÉLYSÉES

PRÉSENTATION pour *Collection d'hiver*

à partir du *2 août* 193*9* à *10.30* heures

jours suivants 10¹⁄₄-15ʰ et 17 heures

Commissionnaire *Roditti*

Cque   Maison *Mr Michel Weill*
                                San Francisco

Vendeuse *M.ᵉ Téioraume*

CETTE CARTE EST STRICTEMENT PERSONNELLE ET DOIT
ÊTRE PRÉSENTÉE A L'ENTRÉE MUNIE DE SES TALONS

TALON A REMETTRE
A VOTRE VENDEUSE

Mois *8 août* 1939
Cᵐᵉ *Roditti*
Cque
Maison *Mr Michel Weill*
Ville *San Francisco*
Vendeuse *Téioraume*

TALON D'ENTRÉE

Mois *8 août* 19 *39*
Cᵐᵉ *Roditti*
Cque
Maison *Mr Michel Weill*
Ville *San Francisco*
Vendeuse *Téioraume*

268 Buyer's card for Robert Piguet's winter collection, 1939. The card is for Mr Michael Weill of San Francisco and gives the names of both his commissionnaire, Roditti, and his saleswoman at Piguet, Mme Téioraume [illegible]. It specifies that he must present the card to gain entry and gives the dates and show times that he can attend. Courtesy Fashion Institute of Technology/ SUNY, FIT Library Department of Special Collections and FIT Archives.

forty-five times a year in the couture house's own premises.[33]

The trade magazine *L'Exportateur française* published schedules of fashion shows for trade buyers throughout the 1920s but it was only in the early 1930s that the Chambre Syndicale established an official calendar of members' fashion shows and reduced the official size of a collection from approximately four hundred to one hundred. Only houses listed on the official calendar could claim to belong to 'haute couture'. Those who did not stage fashion shows, but still sold to professional buyers as well as to private clients, were designated 'moyenne couture'. These houses often took their inspiration from haute couture but simplified the designs in such a way that they appealed to overseas buyers, particularly English ones.[34] The third category, 'petite couture', designated those dressmakers who only made one-offs for private clients.

Once the Chambre Syndicale assumed the monopoly of informing the buyers of the fashion show calendar in the 1930s, it could control the earliest date for delivery of models to buyers and the authorised date for press publication of the model. It also introduced the formal requirement that buyers had first to register for a buyer's card in order to gain access to fashion shows in the houses (**268**). In exchange for the buyer's card, the buyer would undertake not to swap models with other buyers (a common form of copying) and not to buy from copyists. It enabled buyers to see the shows a month before the private clients. They were charged forty per cent more than the private clients for models without fittings. For this they acquired exclusive reproduction rights limiting them to making the dress in fabric, excluding sketches, paper patterns of the dress, hiring out, transfer or returns. Up to 1960, sales to buyers constituted approximately a fifth of a couture house's business.[35]

This regulation was a rearguard attempt to staunch the flow of export losses suffered by haute couture since 1925, augmented by the increasing strength of the franc in the late 1920s and finally put paid to by the Crash of 1929. Until that time, Grumbach argues, French couture had been extremely competitive in world markets.[36] Green has written that while 'the shock waves of the New York stock market crash of 1929 took a few years to reach Depression levels in France (hardest hit from April 1932 to 1937) they had an immediate effect on the Parisian garment industry. *Les riches américaines* left Paris at once, cancelling orders and leaving garments unpaid at their dressmakers.' The crisis, she argues, then spiralled down to other sectors of the industry, while 'the 1920s became remembered as a golden age of exports.'[37]

Fashion piracy, in contrast and despite the best endeavours of the houses, only increased as a result of the Crash. Exorbitant American import duties encouraged American buyers to purchase fewer models and, wherever they could, to acquire them by other means. Buyers frequently worked together to form a vast international resource to share models among themselves. Some store buyers even sold on to ready-to-wear manufacturers or to buyers in other countries. The couture houses' willingness to sell toiles, rather than models, encouraged copying, simply because it was much easier to copy a paper pattern than a model gown. As a result, many American buyers no longer attended the Paris openings and, instead, their stores maintained local offices with 'resident buyers' in Paris, which Grumbach describes as 'veritable centres of industrial espionage'.[38] No longer was espionage limited to the shows, as advance information about new design trends could be gleaned ahead of schedule. Prestigious American stores including Macy's and Saks openly advertised copies of model dresses that had not been legitimately obtained. In 1929, for example, a Macy's advertisement for half-price copies of Jane Regny sweaters was revealed by a Paris newspaper to have been produced from illegally obtained models which the store had had copied in Vienna by the hundred.[39]

From 1933, Elsie Cobin, the most redoubtable of American fashion pirates, habitually bought twenty or so models from each of the large Paris houses at the twice-yearly collections. She imported them to the U.S.A. where she arranged trade fashion shows modelled by live mannequins. Her New York shows were only for copyists; each client could either sketch at her show (forbidden in Paris shows) or hire the dress for a limited time, sufficient to copy it.[40] It was only on one of her Paris buying trips in 1949 that the Paris police put a stop to her activities.[41] Cobin, however, was merely a particularly assiduous practitioner of a custom that was already well established when Philippe Simon described it in 1931.[42]

Fashion piracy was perceived as a problem in French haute couture for most of the twentieth century. The French fought a losing battle against it through a range of stratagems: blacklisting copyists, forbidding photography and sketching during fashion shows, only admitting buyers who bought a minimum number of models per season and, when they caught them at it, pursuing copyists through the courts. The embargo on photographing or sketching at shows lasted until the 1970s when couture declined in importance as ready-to-wear gained. Grumbach elegantly articulates the insoluble nature of the problem that copyists and pirates posed to the system of haute couture:

> The perversion of the system is simply a function of its character: how not to be copied, if the goal of the sale is to be copied? It was an illusion, given these circumstances, to imagine that one could control the use of models that had already arrived at their destination. The best defence would have been simply to refuse to sell paper patterns, but the loss would have been even greater.[43]

Nevertheless, the fashion show survived these vicissitudes and remains important today, when it displays little sign of losing its allure. In the first thirty years of its inception it evolved from Lucile's 'gowns of emotion' to Lelong's 'gowns in motion', from Poiret's exoticism to Patou's streamlined modernism. Increasingly it served both wholesale and retail sectors and was represented in films, plays and novels. It adapted to the changing patterns of the industry throughout the twentieth century, including new modes of production and marketing in ready-to-wear after the 1960s and, more recently, in fast fashion in an age of globalisation.[44] Fashion designers have recently used moving image as opposed to live presentation in the latest evolution of the fashion show or 'streamed' their live shows over the internet to reach larger audiences. Websites such as SHOWstudio have expanded the creative possibilities of digital fashion film and the large fashion houses now produce viral promos that circulate on the internet. If the first couturiers were 'ideas merchants' (marchands d'idées[45]), it was in the fashion show that their ideas took concrete form. Today the show continues to visualise the modern cultural imaginary across the spectrum of fashion production and sales, from small independent designers to global brands, combining new visual technologies with what are now old traditions, the conventions and customs first developed in the early 1900s fashion industry.

THE MANNEQUIN IN THE VOID

Yet, against the realities of business lies the seduction of the image. If this book falls into two halves, it is because they cannot be reconciled in one, even by double-entry book-keeping. The legacy of the first fashion shows was a new sales and publicity mechanism that was in its own right progressive, modernist and productive, but the mannequin, its principal protagonist, inherited something of an entirely different order. A modernist caryatid, she was both decorative and structural – an ornament that bore the weight of capital. A new kind of working woman, she was a figure freighted with ambiguity and contradiction. She wore fashionable clothes for money rather than love and thereby brought the oldest profession and the newest into uncomfortable proximity. Wedged between business and poetry, she embodied both human gain and the perceived loss of humanity that high finance implies.

Giorgio Agamben, in his essay 'Infancy and History', identifies a 'void of experience' in the foundational texts of literary modernism that he sees as a kind of alienation created by commodity culture and its objects. In Proust he finds 'No longer really any subject but only – with singular materialism – an infinite drifting and a casual colliding of objects and sensations', in Baudelaire a 'fascination with commodities and maquillage – the supremely inexperiencible'. He describes Rilke's excoriation of the false experience of 'the "appearance of things" which "bear down from America" and have now transposed their existence "within the vibration of money".' All these fears and fantasies characterised not only 'high' but also 'low' modernism at the turn of the twentieth century: in the latter, the mannequin was a figuration of money, inauthenticity, Americanism and modernity, a figure poised between two contradictory worlds. Indeed, Agamben suggests that Rilke's work is neither esoteric nor mystical 'but concerns the daily life of a citizen of the twentieth century.' From Rilke's differentiation of pure, unencumbered experience (Dasein) from the human need to accumulate objects that make life 'liveable' (erlebbaren) and 'sayable' (säglichen) Agamben identifies 'the fact of being suspended between these two worlds like one of the "disinherited".'[46]

The mannequin too was suspended, interjacent and disinherited, between these two worlds. A chasm between the two, vast and uncharted, went unexplored in the emerging femininities of the twentieth century – a no-man's land peopled by women. The mannequin, gendered neuter (or, rather, both male and female: linguistically male yet corporeally female), inhabited this interstitial space, breathing the rarified air of the high-ceilinged rooms in which she modelled, lived, gossiped, talked and walked. Figuring capital, she was at once a hinge, a pivot and an enigma: she was the optical unconscious of the new century. Hers was a regimented body, synchronised to the regimes of the rationalised body of art, work and leisure; but it was also a body in motion, one which came alive, walked and worked, as part of the new life of the twentieth century, but in an ambiguous and unique way. A subject who reified herself as part of her professional performance, chilly and distant, she fitted none of the existing typologies of the new woman.

Lucy Clairin's novel of 1937, *Journal d'un mannequin*, is a first-person narrative set in a fictional Paris couture house called Boris.[47] There are seven mannequins in the *cabine*, all in their mid-twenties. One is virginal and reads the poetry of Paul Valéry between modelling, another has a right-wing senator for a boyfriend who first met her when he accompanied his wife to a fashion show and a third, Gisèle, has a double life as a nude dancer called Floralie in the evenings. One day the narrator, Alice, who is about to be sent to model in the Cannes branch, is taken upstairs to the ateliers by the *première* Mané to be fitted for the clothes she will take with her to Cannes. Standing patiently for an hour while the dresses are fitted on her, she notices a door labelled 'Musée Grévin', the name of the Paris waxworks museum. Afterwards, she asks the *première* about it and is invited to open it and explore. Inside, a staircase leads up to a long room filled with dressmakers' dummies in all sizes and shapes ranged along its four walls:

There are big ones, little ones, fat ones, thin ones, grotesque ones and hideous ones.

From all the bodies, the head is missing.

'Here is my Musée Grevin', Mané said to me with a big gesture. 'Do you realise? . . . Each of them has her name on a label. These are the mannequins of our clients . . . No more measurements to take from them . . . can you believe I collect them, what horrors!'[48]

A similar scene is described by Roubaud in 1928, who is taken by a couturier to a room filled with mannequins, each one a precise copy of the client. Roubaud describes a row of 'dead women in cotton canvas' hanging in a line in the basement cupboards like Bluebeard's wives, their names written on the doors: 'Mme A . . ., Mlle B . . ., Mme de M . . .'. He and his companion discover the mannequin of a young actress who has recently died and throw it out.[49]

Haute couture and fashion modelling are threaded through with the theme of the double, with its deathly connotations, which runs back to nineteenth-century business protocols and forward to the modern woman and her image. Where there is a double, as opposed to a copy, there is no original. In haute couture, because it is an industry, everything is a double of something else. The client's dress is a copy of the model dress, the lay figure is a copy of the client, the living mannequin and the client are copies of each other that do not quite match and so on, ad infinitum. The only original is the model dress, worn for a season by the mannequin and then sold off or given away. The absence of the model dress from museum collections replicates the absence of the living mannequin from history. For this is a story of absences as well as doubles, of a series of disappeared mannequins, gestures, poses and traces, barely a history, simply the tale of a few women walking up and down and striking poses.

In Clairin's novel, as the two women stand in the room surrounded by the body doubles of all their clients, the *première* seizes an enormous mannequin whose bust and stomach are one. ' "This", she said to me, putting her hand on the mannequin's shoulder, "is the richest woman in the world. It is the difficult American client that the mannequins all call 'Mistress Fear' ".' The two identify various other clients from their dummies and Alice exclaims 'But there are only monsters here!' They search fruitlessly for some pleasanter examples and finally the *première* says to the mannequin: 'When I have the blues, when life disgusts me, I leave the atelier for a moment . . . and I come up here. Then I feel the rare pleasure of not being bad looking, in front of all these rich women, most of them hideous and all of them decapitated!'[50] Her expression of resentment points violently to what happens when an exclusionary nexus of women, beauty and money is created, like the image of commodity fetishism in *The Ladies Paradise* where Zola describes a row of headless figures arranged on a staircase, sumptuously dressed dummies in the latest fashions, each, where the head should be, with a big hatpin impaled in its red cloth-covered neck, bearing a large card with the price of the dress.[51]

Yet there is a counter-narrative to this violence. The mannequin herself is a living, breathing woman, with aspirations, hopes and fears. In *Journal d'un mannequin* Alice goes south to the Riviera to model for her employer. She is due to appear in a big fashion show at 'Le Sporting' in Monte Carlo, 'in perhaps the most beautiful room in the world', certainly the most elegant one, where the richest people in the universe congregate.[52] All the most important Paris houses will show their dresses on their own mannequins. The fashion show is scheduled for 11 pm and the mannequins dine at 8.30 at the Hôtel de Paris,

where their presence in the dining room causes a sensation among the English and American clientele. After dinner, the women smoke an English cigarette and drink a Benedictine.[53] Later, the show takes place. Clairin describes the applause, the lights, the size of the venue, the length of the immense runway that Alice walks, with her heart in her mouth, traversing the vast room to cross a specially constructed little bridge. When she comes back to the dressing room after showing her first dress, she feels such exhilaration that she wants nothing more than to change into the second dress and go straight out again to the same applause and adulation.

The novel describes the working life of a mannequin over a year. It includes female friendships, difficult clients, mannequins who moonlight, sexual encounters and, in its descriptions of modelling at large galas, an effulgent, fly-by-night spectacle that, like the circus big top, packs up every morning, moves on and is gone, lost to history. The book is unusual in its exploration of the mannequin's subjectivity and her daily life; most commentators seem to have taken their cue from her professional inscrutability and described only the façade. Yet it is hard not to be intrigued by the historical invisibility of women whose job it was to be visible. If little detail survives of their real lives, they remain as image, part of the visual flow of the early twentieth century, beginning with one of the early photographs of a

fashion mannequin from 1898 (**269**) in which the image of the anonymous photographer appears like a palimpsest in the background. It is from an album in the Musée Galliera of photographs of mannequins in several Paris houses in 1897–8. The album, in which the photographer endearingly cuts off the mannequins' heads and over-exposes half his pictures, is a monument to incompetence. In this one, he has failed to notice his own mirror-image in the background and inadvertently put himself in the picture for posterity. As a companion piece, a professional triple copyright image (see **256**) shows an anonymous mannequin modelling hats for the French sportswear designer Suzanne Talbot in 1925. For the central, full-face, shot the woman, who is seated sideways, turns to face the camera without moving her body (**270**). In most of these copyright photographs the mannequin barely bothers to model; perhaps there was little time to do so, in the rush to photograph all the different models in the same repetitive format. Yet here the mannequin breaks into a smile as she turns towards the camera, so that in its very hastiness the image shows her vibrant, alive and in the moment, her smile banishing the deathliness of the double, despite the repetitive nature of her task.

One of many types of female worker in the Parisian garment trade, the mannequin's experience has gone unexamined by historians and cultural theorists alike. Like

the *passante*, she always seems to be departing, on her way out of the frame towards Agamben's modernist elsewhere. In this respect the mannequin resembles Molly Nesbit's description of the fashionable and sexualised female Parisienne who disappeared from Atget's photographs of the city with which she was associated.[54] Towards the end of his book on the *passante*, Claude Leroy writes that she is a figure of Baudelairean modernity and that, with the passing of the historical avant-gardes, the link that the *passante* guaranteed has been broken, a link that was forged under the sign of rupture, between writing and absence. The list of authors he has covered brings its mirror games, he writes. He describes the literary *passantes* he has discussed in their final parade: 'the obscure and the famous, the apparitions and the revenants, the long queue of strangely worrying women. Melancholy and modernity, muses and mutes, the woman in mourning, the Mother and Death.'[55] Like the *passante*, the mannequin is a gesture of figural absence, not a real woman but a literary trope – the sign of appearing and the sign of disappearing. 'Comment faire revenir la survenante? Survenir la revenante?' asks Leroy. 'How to bring back the apparition? Make the revenant appear?'

This literary conundrum seems simple to solve in the industrial world: invent the concept of the fashion show and people it with living mannequins. Mix up the mannequin and the model, already linguistically confused. Substitute the woman for the dress and vice versa. Roubaud does this in his account of the cabine: 'A mannequins' *cabine*: it consists of two hundred dead dresses, like pressed flowers flattened in a book and twenty, little, moving, living slips. If I knock on the door and make my male voice heard, the twenty slips will come back in twenty uniform sheaths. They are red satin at Mounet' (**271**).[56] They were red at Boris, too, Clairin reports.

Roubaud writes: 'Everywhere, the dress is made for the woman. Here, the woman for the dress. The dress says: "Do not be overweight, or you will be fired like a bad servant; learn to walk according to my rhythm; you are no more than my wearer; you and I are not of the same world; do not flatter yourself that you will ever have my life".'[57] Later he observes how the mannequins barter clothes in the *cabine*. 'Luckily, in their wardrobe, the dresses sleep! They are "from on high". If they could hear and see them, they would despise the children of the people!'[58] The dresses are asleep in the cupboards of the *cabine*, the clients' dummies are asleep in the basement cupboards; but the mannequins, like the toys in Ravel's *Les Enfants et les sortilèges*, are wide awake and at play, doing deals, conducting business, while the world of things sleeps.

Animated dolls, the mannequins are also real women, however, and, in the dialectic between the client and the mannequin, the double (or the inversion) becomes an image of class inequality that provokes righteous indignation about the unequal distribution of money in a class-based society. How could it not be when, as Colette observed, the exterior signs of wealth are imposed on a poor but beautiful girl and she is obliged to parade them before her richer, and less beautiful, social superiors? Yet, the mannequins were hardly working class and within the couture house hierarchy they were a group apart. In their liminality, early twentieth-century mannequins were at their most modern. As they crossed from backstage to front-of-house, they passed literally in the sense of passing before the clients and metaphorically in the sense of passing as clients, or at least as their image. Like the literary *passante*, their passage was both ephemeral and elusive. 'Semiotically indeterminate' perhaps, a *figurante* certainly, the mannequin modelled the contradictions of modernity.

NOTES

INTRODUCTION

1 There are signs that this trend is being revised. Among books and articles on haute couture, there are some honourable exceptions that acknowledge its commercial nature, such as Palmer 2001, Stewart 2005, Stewart 2008 and Grumbach 2008, and there are a few labour histories of the French garment trade, notably Green 1997. More recent business histories of French haute couture and its international links include Pouillard 2011, Brachet Champsaur 2012, Font 2012, Polese and Blaszczyk 2012.

2 In the 1920s, New York was 'the up-and-coming, competing fashion centre' with Paris. Pouillard 2011, 320.

3 Wollen 1993, 20–21 and 44.

4 Kracauer 1995, 75–86. On fashion, Taylorism and the mass ornament, see Evans 2008.

5 On 'new velocities', see Walter Benjamin, 'Konvolut B (Fashion)', in Benjamin 1999, 65.

6 Levenson 1999, 2.

7 Levenson 2011, 247.

8 Ibid., 6.

9 Ibid., 5.

10 Huyssen argued that 'modernism constituted itself through a conscious strategy of exclusion, an anxiety of contamination by its other: an increasingly consuming and engulfing mass culture'. He added that modernism's insistence on the autonomy of art, 'its radical separation from the culture of everyday life', were challenged as soon as it arose but the implication is that the challenge came from everyday life not artists. Huyssen 1986, vii. For a critique of Huyssen's valorisation of modernism's autonomy, see Jameson 1992, 14–16. Jameson argues instead that modernism was a reactive symptom of cultural crises, rather than a new 'solution' in its own right.

11 Lawrence Rainey looked at how writers used 'new strategies for reputation building' from other spheres. Kevin Dettmar and Stephen Watts argued that marketing and modernism were compatible. Douglas Mao argued for philosophical and socio-economic readings of modernism by looking at the ontology of the object within modernism as both a concrete commodity and an auratic symbol. Michael North analysed the proximity of art and commerce in the modern period and argued that avant-garde art had close ties with the 'culture industries'. Aaron Jaffe argued that although modernist authors rejected mass culture in favour of elite cultural forms, they reflected the economy of celebrity culture in their strategies for creating a market for their work. All five explicitly take issue with Huyssen's account. Jaffe's idea of 'ordinary modernism' leads him to investigate the material production and consumption of texts. Like Rainey, he argues that modernism's forms and structures are those of the world around it and by looking at the everyday he reaches the conclusion that 'modernist culture is ordinary', citing Raymond Williams's polemical essay 'Culture Is Ordinary'. Rainey 1998, 4; Dettmar and Watts 1996; Mao 1998, 6 and 11; North 1999, 206; Jaffe 2005, 7.

12 Cooper also seeks to analyse modernism in the context of its material and socio-economic history rather than seeing it as primarily a literary phenomenon. Cooper 2004, 23 and 28.

13 Crow, 'Modernism and Mass Culture in the Visual Arts', in Buchloh, Guilbaut and Sorkin 2004, 215–64. See also Abigail Solomon-Godeau and Peter Hailey, 'Modern Style: Dressing Down', *Artforum*, 42, 9, May 2004, 192–4.

14 Rainey 1998, 7.

15 Garafola 1998, 98ff.

16 So, for example, Jessica Burstein argues that 'Chanel was a cold modernist who triumphed on the market'. Burstein ascribes a central role to fashion in the construction of what she terms 'cold modernism'. Burstein 2012, 12–13, 19 and 130. On advertising as modernist, see Wicke 1993, cited in Driscoll 2010, 149, and Beale 1999, 11–47: in 'Advertising as Modernism', the opening chapter of her book on inter-war France, Marjorie Beale argues that the fragmented language of French post-war advertising was shared by high modernist literary texts of the period. On fascism as modernist, see Griffin 2007, who argues that fascism, rather than being anti-modern as is often argued, was a 'total form' of modernism in its own right.

17 Harvey 1989; Kern 2003; Jameson, 'Modernism and Imperialism', 152–69; Jameson 2007. See also Armstrong 1998 and Danius 2002, esp. 1–54.

18 Jameson 2007, 63. See also Lefebvre 1991, 170. Silverman 1996, 203, argues that the pose exerts a representational force so great that it radiates outwards and transforms the space around the body and everything that comes into contact with it into an imaginary photograph.

19 Among the great many texts on women as both the objects of consumption and as consumers from the nineteenth to the twentieth centuries, too numerous to cite, the essays by Abigail Solomon-Godeau and Kathy Peiss in Grazia and Furlough 1996 are pertinent to these questions.

20 Butler 1990.

21 Phelan 1993, 6–7, 31 and 146–8.

22 J. Brown 2009, 20–43 and 145–72.

23 Ibid., 5, 34–5, 110, 159 (citing Jeremy Gilbert-Rolfe, *Beauty and the Contemporary Sublime*, New York: Allworth Press, 1999, 112–13), 161.

24 J. Brown 2009, 8 and 42.

25 Wigley 2001. See also Sparke 1995.

26 Troy 2003, 3.

27 Vinken 1997; Lehmann 2000; Evans 2003; Wilson 2003; Breward and Evans 2005.

28 Driscoll 2010, esp. 136 on modernism and 145–6 on Chanel and motion; Wilson 2003. For a discussion of Chanel and modernism in relation to ideas about the copy, the original and the human body as mechanised and reproducible. See Burstein 2012, 127–50.

29 Franko 1995; Davis 2006; Garelick 2007; Preston 2011.

30 Garelick 2007, 16, 156–8 and 161.

31 Jane C. Desmond, 'Embodying Difference: Issues in Dance and Cultural Studies', in Carter 1998, 158.

32 Ewen 1988, 89. Jennifer Craik argues that 'The model constitutes the technical body of Western consumer culture.' Craik 1994, 70.

33 Nora 1996, 1997 and 1998.

34 Wickberg 2007.

35 Joan Rivière, 'Womanliness as a Masquerade' (1929), reprinted in Burgin, Donald and Kaplan 1986.

36 Nora 1989, 9 and 13.

37 Steiner 2010, 4.

38 Susan Sontag, 'The Photographs *Are* Us', *New York Times Magazine*, 23 May 2004, 28, cited in ibid., 192 n. 5. See also Steiner's discussion, ibid., 2–5.

39 As Cote and Jensen write: 'We share, spy and self-reflect while posting on Flickr and broadcasting over Youtube, Myspace and Facebook. Digital technologies offer new control as we continue to photograph ourselves until we've perfected the appearance we want to project. Our images become avatars, personifying ideals as they stand-in for the corporeal self. The act of posing emphasizes an awareness of being observed. Culled from the collective image bank, a pose portrays the desire for self-realization and display. From labor-intensive portrait painting to assembled digital imagery the impulse is the same – to extend our likeness into the public realm, to challenge the passing of time, to create a record of ourselves as flawed, shallow or vulnerable as we may be. "In front of the lens, I am at the same time: the one I think I am, the one

others want to think I am, the one he makes use of to exhibit his art" (Roland Barthes).' Cote and Jensen 2007, 7–8, citing Roland Barthes, *Camera Lucida*, New York: Hill and Wang, 1981, 13.

40 Marlene Dumas cited by Steiner who writes that in Dumas's work 'the image is presented as depth, and pose as revelation'. Steiner 2001, 222–30.

CHAPTER 1

1 This was the designer Paul Poiret's analysis in 1921. He felt that the foreign buyer should pay a different price from the private client buying a dress because the buyer bought an idea. He stated that when haute couturiers sold to commissionnaires (trade buyers' agents) they aided the diffusion of the dress, hence the foreign buyer should be seen as its editor (because they would alter it in the course of reproduction). Paul Poiret, 'De la contrefaçon dans la couture', *Excelsior*, 16 December 1921. All translations are mine unless otherwise stated.

2 White, 'Mesdames', n.d., 31.

3 Avenel 1902, 71.

4 Ibid., 83 and 103. In 1912 Uzanne put couture exports at 50% and listed three distinct types of buyer: various overseas middlemen; the English, American and German dressmakers who visited Paris twice a year for the shows; and private clients from overseas. Uzanne 1912, 38. See also Worth 1895, 71–89, for detailed figures on the expansion of the French dressmaking trade in the second half of the nineteenth century.

5 Alexandre 1902, 54.

6 Anonymous photographer. Album of photographs of model gowns from Parisian couture houses, 1897/1898. Collection of Musée Galliera de la Mode de la Ville de Paris, 2004.658.1.

7 Bachmann 1973; Peers 2004, 15–19.

8 Park 2010, 103.

9 Ibid., 104.

10 David 2002, 80.

11 Newspaper article of 1872 cited in Françoise, 'Carnet de Notes de Françoise', *Femina*, 15 April 1912, 230.

12 Rochefort and Georges Duval, *Le Tailleur des bossus, où l'Orthopédie, contrefaçon en 1 acte et en vaudeville*, Paris: J. N. Barba, 1826, 6, cited in David 2002, 82.

13 On British fashion plays from this period, see Kaplan and Stowell 1994. French plays included *Le Mannequin* (1880) satirising Worth; *La Rue de la Paix* (1912) satirising Lucile and Poiret; *Le Mannequin* (1914).

14 David 2002, 83.

15 Newspaper article of 1872 cited in Françoise, 'Carnet de Notes', 230. David 2002, 81.

16 Roger de Beauvoir, 'Le tailleur', in *Les Français vus/peints par eux-mêmes*, Paris: L. Curmer, 1841, 246, cited in David 2002, 81.

17 Ibid.

18 Entry for Sunday, 16 July 1865 from Whitehurst 1873, vol. I, 100–01.

19 Martin-Fugier 1990, 360.

20 Avenel 1902, 73; Richardson 1987, 63; Jones 2004, 151 ff. Octave Uzanne writes that a fine lady of the First Empire would receive her tradespeople in the morning followed by her deportment coach. Uzanne 1898, 56.

21 Le Petit Homme Rouge 1907, 311.

22 Karl Steen, 'Les Emplettes', *L'Art et la mode*, September 1880, 37.

23 Uzanne 1898, 174.

24 Nead 2007, 70.

25 Gabriele Brandstetter, 'Pose–Posa–Posing – Between Image and Movement', in Bippus and Mink 2007, 258; Hillel Schwartz, 'Torque: The New Kinaesthetic of the Twentieth Century', in Crary and Kwinter 1992, 97–8.

26 Nead 2007, 74–5.

27 Uzanne 1898, 128 and 139.

28 Ibid., 138–9. See also Jeanne Baron, 'Arts et chiffons', *L'art et la mode*, June 1881, 13 and 98–100.

29 Saunders 1954, 110; White, 'Mesdames', 27.

30 White, 'Mesdames', 27.

31 Marley 1980, 103.

32 Uzanne 1912, 110.

33 Worth 1928, 10.

34 Ibid., 13–14.

35 Ibid., 36.

36 Avenel 1902, 73–4.

37 Worth 1928, 17–18.

38 Saunders 1954, 46.

39 Grumbach 2008, 434. Coleman analyses the shift in production in the 1860s from *couture à façon*, made for the individual client, to *haute couture*, the presentation of a collection of models. Coleman 1990, 33–4.

40 Worth 1928, 22.

41 Ibid., 56 and 69.

42 Marley 1990, 103.

43 Richardson 1987, 38–9.

44 On Worth's innovations see Marley 1990, 98–102, 140–42 and 209.

45 Coleman 1990, 33–4.

46 Zola 1981, 138–9.

47 Saunders 1954, 110.

48 Le Petit Homme Rouge 1907, 312.

49 Tétart-Vittu argued that Worth, far from being copied by the *confectionneurs* (ready-to-wear dressmakers) was himself a copyist, with lucrative overseas sales and well-orchestrated publicity. She described him as a specialist in sales (*un commis*, an exalted sales assistant) rather than a tailor or dressmaker. The secret of his success resided in his choice of a foreign clientele, both American and Russian; his export garments bore his label authenticating them as genuine Paris gowns. Similarly, Pinguat, with his Anglo-Saxon partner Hudson, initiated a successful American career with his overseas sales, despite being humbly described as a *confectionneur*. Françoise Tétart-Vittu, 'Naissance du couturier et du modéliste', in Musée de la Mode et du Costume 1992, 36.

50 Montagné-Villette 1990, 15.

51 'Yvette Guilbert Comes', *Chicago Daily*, 8 December 1895. The word had been used to signify an artist's model since the seventeenth century. See entry number 3 under 'modèle'

in *Le Grand Dictionnaire Robert*, vol. VI, 1985, 500. On the role and nature of the artist's model in nineteenth-century France, see Corbin, Courtine and Vigarello 2005, vol. II, 97–9.

52 Steiner 2010, 12.

53 See the entries under 'modèle', especially '4. Un, le modèle de' and '5. Objet' in *Le Grand Dictionnaire Robert*, vol. VI, 1985, 501–2.

54 For an extended discussion of the meaning and etymology of the term *modèle*, see Evans 2011.

55 'The Paris Mannequin, How She Helps to Beguile Women in the Dressmaker's Shop', *New York Times*, 10 November 1907.

56 Carolyn Wilson, 'Spring Fashion Openings Draw Paris Crowds', *Chicago Daily Tribune*, 31 March 1918.

57 Duff Gordon 1932, 72–3; O'Neill 2007, 61; Bigham 2012, 55. Lucile is always credited as having invented the naming of dresses but in 1910 L. Roger-Milès described how Paris couturiers were naming their dresses according to current affairs and he located the origin of naming rather than numbering dresses in the eighteenth century, when trimmings, colours and textiles as well as garments were given highly suggestive names, such as *les plaintes indiscrètes*, *la grande réputation*, *l'insensible* and *le désir marqué*. Lucile's use of sexually suggestive names thus seems to have had earlier precedents; Bigham argues that she copied the eighteenth-century court dress-maker Rose Bertin's habit of naming gowns. Ibid. Roger-Milès cited a text from 1779 describing a woman seen at the Opéra wearing a dress *soupir étouffé*, decorated with *regrets superflus*, with lace in the centre *de candour parfait*, a trimming of *attention marquée*, shoes *cheveux de la reine*, embroidered with diamonds in *coups perfides* and emeralds *venez-y-voir*, hair dressed with *sentiments soutenus*, a bonnet of *conquête amusée*, garnished with *plumes volages*, with ribbons of *oeil abattu*, having *un chat* on her shoulders, the colour of *gens nouvellement arrivés*, and so on. Roger-Milès 1910, 88–90.

58 Steele 2001, 133.

59 *Chiffons*, 13 October 1913. 'Paris Makers to Hold Show Here', *New York Times*, 7 November 1915.

60 'A Seat at the Paris Openings,' *Vogue* (America), 15 April 1923, 39–49 and 42.

61 Le Fèvre 1929, 143.

62 Troy 2003, 239 and 248.

63 Stewart 2005, 117.

64 'De la contrefaçon dans la couture', *Excelsior*, 16 December 1921. Pouillard 2011.

65 'Rising Star of the Paris Mannequin', *New York Times*, 23 July 1922.

66 'Paris Couturiers: How the World's Fashions are Determined – Fitting the Costumes to Buyers by Aid of Mannequins', *Los Angeles Times*, 6 January 1901.

67 'Paris Preparing the New Modes', *Christian Science Monitor*, 6 August 1912.

68 'Paris Couturiers', *Los Angeles Times*, 6 January 1901.

69 A few Poiret model dresses are listed in the Poiret auction catalogue (see *La Création en liberté* 2005) but I have not been able to trace their purchasers. There are two Lucile dresses donated by the designer to the Museum of London which were made for the actresses Lily Elsie and Gertie Miller in 1910 and 1911 and worn by her models Hebe and Gamela when she opened in Paris in 1911. Lucy Duff Gordon, letter to the Curator of the London Museum dated 22 May 1928, collection of the Museum of London, 28.125/1-2. The letter is legibly reproduced in O'Neill 2007, 58. Both dresses are well worn and stained under the armpits, suggesting that they were worn for a full season at the very least. Their accession numbers and catalogue details are: 28.125/1, 1910–11, pale blue silk satin, associated with Gertie Miller, inscribed 'Paris Model no.134'; and 28.125/2, 1910-11, green georgette, associated with Lily Elsie, inscribed 'Paris Model no.178'.

70 'Spring Fashions Not Yet Decreed by Paris Arbiters,' *New York Times*, 18 January 1914.

71 Baudrillard 1993, 84 n. 1.

72 Walter Benjamin, 'The Work of Art in the Age of Mechanical Reproduction', in Benjamin 1973, 226.

73 Guillaume Garnier assisted by Françoise Tétart-Vittu, 'Catalogue of Exhibits', in Musée de la Mode et du Costume 1986, 218.

74 The collection model number was different from the copyright registration number and hence each dress might have two numbers. Poiret (and several other couturiers) would put a canvas tape behind the label with the model number, often accompanied by the name of the client, the title of the model and the name of the atelier worker responsible for the gown's fabrication. It was done for purely practical reasons, as when, for example, a client wanted to be sure that her dress conformed in every detail with the model dress she had seen on the mannequin. Ibid., 242.

75 Barthes 1999, 87.

76 See Jean Nicot, *Le Thresor de la langue françoyse* (1606) and *Dictionnaire de l'Académie française*, 1st edition 1694.

77 I have drawn extensively on David 2002 for the material in this chapter concerning the etymology and origins of the term mannequin and the development of the lay-figure in the nineteenth century.

78 Reboux 1927, 8.

79 Charles Dickens, 'Dress in Paris', *All the Year Round*, vol. IX, 28 February 1863, 7–12.

80 Ibid., 9.

81 Worth 1928, 13–14.

82 Grumbach 2008, 14; White, 'Mesdames', 27.

83 Worth 1928, 69–70. *La Vie parisienne* for 26 February 1870 described a mannequin parade in thinly veiled terms. Tétart-Vittu in Musée de la Mode et du Costume 1992, 37.

84 'Les demoiselles-mannequins', entry for Friday 9 May 1879, vol. III, Goncourt 1956, 19. The Goncourt diary's usage of the term is

described as contemptuous (*avec mépris*) in Musée Galliera 2006, 144.

85 'The Decline of the Drama, Third Rate Plays at the Paris Theatres', *New York Times*, 29 November 1880.

86 *Dictionnaire de l'Académie française*, 5th edition, 1798. 'On dit figurément d'un homme, *C'est un vrai mannequin*, presque au même sens qu'on dit, *C'est un homme de paille*, pour dire, que c'est une fausse apparence d'homme, un homme nul et sans caractère, que l'on fait mouvoir comme on veut.' An abbreviated version of this disparaging definition survives in the 6th edition of 1835. The definition of a mannequin as both a shop dummy and a fashion model occurs only in the 8th edition of 1932–5.

87 Barrière 1889, 224.

88 'Il paraît que dans ce pays la mode est de se faire représenter dans les promenades publiques par des sosies en plâtre, en bois ou en cire. On fait de l'élégance en effigie. Robes, coiffures, écharpes, diamants, tout ce qui résume la beauté, le luxe ou la réputation de la personne, est au rendez-vous; elle seule est absente. A quoi bon du reste la personne? On ne va là que pour voir des habits. C'est en songeant aux solennités de la mode, que le prophète s'est écrié: Mannequin des mannequins, et tout n'est que mannequin!' J. J. Grandville, *Un autre monde*, Paris: H. Fournier, 1844, 70, cited in David 2002, 65.

89 'Un joli détail de la vie élégante parisienne. Parmi les demoiselles-mannequins qui, dans les salons de Worth, montrent et promènent sur leurs sveltes corps, les robes de l'illustre couturier, il est une demoiselle ou plutôt une dame-mannequin, dont la spécialité est de représenter la grossesse de la *high life*. Assise, seule à l'écart, en le clair-obscur d'un boudoir, elle exhibe aux yeux des visiteuses, dans un état intéressant, la toilette appropriée avec le plus de génie à la déformation de l'enfantement.' Entry for Friday 9 May 1879, vol. III, Goncourt 1956, 19.

90 Pinguat is described as 'le fameux couturier des lorettes' and the diary goes on to describe how 'Entre ces lugubres verdures, égayées par cette garniture de cheminée *pompe funèbre*, des femmes promenant sur elles des robes, des femmes qui, à ce métier de porte-manteaux, ont perdu quelque chose de vivant et ont gagné d'automatisme. La plupart sont jeunes et toutefois paraissent vieillottes et laissent voir, dans leurs traits fanés et fripés, de la corruption grimaçante des singes. C'est amusant, le moment où on leur prend, sur le dos, le vêtement qu'elles étalent et font valoir, de les apercevoir défiler devant vous sautillantes, à la façon des femmes dévêtues et qui couraient avec des babouches sans talon.' Entry for Thursday 22 March 1883, ibid., 242.

91 A *fourreau* was a tight, figure-revealing 'dress', according to Barrière 1889, 162.

92 'Entre les quatre glaces d'un salon immense . . . Elles vont, viennent, minces et longues,

nettement coiffées, sans un bijou, de l'air indifférent de mannequins, ôtant et remettant dix fois le même modèle, et d'un pas lent, cadencé, s'éloignant, se rapprochant pour en faire valoir l'élégance.' Steen, 'Les Emplettes', 36–7.

93 '[L]'oeil des contemporaines s'accoutumait peu à peu à l'excentricité et à la hardiesse qui l'avaient effrayé tout d'abord.' Saint-Léger, 'Comment se créent les modes', *L'Illustration*, 11 December 1897, reprinted in *L'Illustration: Journal Universel* 1987, 62–3.

94 Uzanne 1898, 166.

95 Ibid.

96 '[E]mployées de taille et de proportions régulières qui prirent le nom de l'objet qu'elles remplaçaient. C'est sur les filles-mannequins de couturières en vogue qu'on copie actuellement les bustes en plâtre.' Riotor 1900, 86. Like the Goncourt diary before him, Riotor's terminology for mannequins is disparaging and the term *filles-mannequins* implies that they were not respectable.

97 Rank 1989; Miller 1985. On the enduring fascination about what it means for a woman to be represented as machine and on her demonic sexuality as a threat to male authority, see 'The Vamp and the Machine: Fritz Lang's *Metropolis*', in Huyssen 1986, 65–81.

98 See Melchior-Bonnet 2001, 'The Competition of the Double', 255–8.

99 Freud, 'The Uncanny' (1919), 1953–73, 235.

100 Dolar 1991, 14.

101 Freud, 'The Uncanny', 234–5.

102 For the argument that in the late nineteenth century, literary representations of the automaton became gendered as female in response to industrialisation, see Huyssen 1986, 70, and Wollen 1993, 35–71.

103 Walter Benjamin, 'A Small History of Photography' (1931), in Benjamin 1985, 242. See also 'The Work of Art in the Age of Mechanical Reproduction' (1936), in Benjamin 1973, 219–53. For a short discussion of Benjamin's concept of the optical unconscious as expressed in both these essays, see Terry E. Smith, 'Review. Rosalind Krauss, *The Optical Unconscious*', *Modernism/modernity*, vol. 2, no. 1, January 1995, 193–6.

104 On the complexities and contradictions of the idea of the original and the copy in fashion, see Troy 2003, 7–10, 193–6 and 239–41.

105 Avenel 1902, 79.

106 Musée Galliera 2006, 144.

107 'Madame a demandé un jersey à tout faire, on lui en montre un, dans un salon turc, avec lequel on peut s'agiter de toute façon et aller jouer au crockett et au lawn-tennis sans faire craquer le vêtement et en laissant toute la souplesse aux membres', *L'Art et la mode*, 25 July 1885, 402.

108 From 1879, e.g., Wanamaker staff were sent to live in Paris in order to purchase new fashions for the U.S. store and, from 1893, the store, like many others in the U.S.A., held regular

spring and autumn exhibitions of its French imports, with particular emphasis on Paris fashion. Wanamaker 1911, 196, 198, 209 and 271.

109 *L'Art et la mode*, 14 November 1885, 594–5.

110 White, 'Mesdames', 33–4.

111 Balzac 1922. 'La Théorie de la démarche' was first published in *L'Europe litéraire*, August–September 1833. The 'Traité de la vie élégante' is discussed in Steele 1998, 57ff.

112 Balzac 1922, 140–42.

113 Chambers Twentieth Century Dictionary, new edition 1959.

114 *Dictionnaire de l'Académie française*, 6th edition, 1835. Both definitions reappear in the *Émile Littré Dictionnaire de la langue française* of 1872–7 and the *Dictionnaire de l'Académie française*, 8th edition, 1932–5, which adds to the definition of a classical procession: 'Il se dit, par extension, dans le langage courant, d'un Ensemble de personnes s'avançant en procession, en rangs. *Une théorie de jeunes filles.*'

115 Emile Henriot, 'Le Mannequin', *L'Illustration*, 27 December 1913, reprinted in *L'Illustration: Journal Universel* 1987, 112–16. There are many other examples, including, 'Tandis que défilait devant moi une théorie de jeunes femmes . . . je pus admirer à mon aise le sens inné du goût et de l'esthétique.' Untitled cutting in the Poiret Press Albums from *Homme libre*, 5 November 1923; 'Une gracieuse théorie de jeunes filles . . . au départ d'une course de bicyclettes', *Femina*, October 1924, 32; 'La lente théorie des deux cent modèles d'une collection', René Vincent, 'Silhouettes et modes d'aujourd'hui', *L'Illustration*, 12 March 1927, 149.

116 Braun 1992, 93–100.

117 For a discussion of Satie in relation to fashion, esp. the *Gymnopédies*, see Davis 2006, 106–7, 112–13 and 115–16.

118 Ross 2008, 45.

119 'Maintenant, milord, ajouta Edison en regardant Lord Ewald, tenez-vous à ce que je vous montre ce textile derme idéal?' Villiers 1993, 265.

120 '— et ceci au point de bouleverser complètement les sens de l'Humanité. Il devient tout à fait impossible de distinguer le modèle de la copie.' Ibid., 264–5.

121 Edison's speech in full is 'La première Andréide seule était difficile. Ayant écrit la formule générale, ce n'est plus désormais, laissez-moi vous le redire, qu'une question d'ouvrier: nul doute qu'il ne se fabrique bientôt des milliers de substrats comme celui-ci — et que le premier industriel venu n'ouvre une manufacture d'idéals!' Ibid., 241.

122 'Ma maison est une manufacture d'anges, je tiens commerce d'idéals.' Alan Raitt in Villiers 1993, 425 n. 2. In fact, Villiers's 'creation' of the fictional android precedes by some years the real Thomas Alva Edison's 'talking dolls' produced in 1889, a year after Villiers's death, which were fitted with Edison's phonograph invented in 1877. See 'Edison's Eve' in Wood

2002, 137–8. Wood discusses alternative hypotheses: either Villiers's prescience gave Edison the idea or Edison's early ideas and inventions had been sufficiently in the public domain for Villiers to have known about them.

123 'Cet hermétique maillot de platine'. Villiers 1993, 228.

124 'Enveloppée en d'amples et longs plis de satin noir'. Ibid., 253.

125 '[S]elon les ondulations du torse vivant', 'c'est le mouvement humain lui-même'. Ibid., 229 and 233.

126 '[C]e plié gracieux, cette ondulation ferme, ce vague dans la démarche, qui sont si séduisants chez une simple femme'. Ibid., 229.

127 Braun 1992, 64.

128 On Marey's *Station physiologique*, see ibid., 70–76.

129 'Excelsior à l'Éden, un ballet qu'on pourrait appeler le ballet de la danse de Saint-Guy. Neuf cent bras et neuf cent jambes perpétuellement dans l'air.' Entry for 19 February 1883, Goncourt, vol. III, 1956, 236.

130 Castle 1984, 35.

131 On women, gender and the mechanisation of factory work in mid-nineteenth-century France, see Joan W. Scott, ' "L'ouvrière! Mot impire, sordide . . .": Women workers in the Discourse of French Political Economy, 1840–1860', in Joyce 1987, 119–42. On women and work in France from 1879 to 1919, see Stewart 1989. For a succinct statement of the impact on European sensibilities of the speed of technological change over 1875–1900, see Tickner 2000, 190–92. For a more general survey of representations of women and technology, focusing on the nineteenth and twentieth centuries, see Wosk 2001.

132 Lynda Williams, *Hardcore*, Berkeley and Los Angeles: University of California Press, 1989, cited in Brookman 2010, 95.

133 Brookman 2010, 95.

134 Both Muybridge and Marey's inventions prefigured cinema and Marey himself even made films as part of his pursuit of the representation of movement. Braun 1992, 150–99 and 228–62 (chs 4 'Animating Images: The Cinematographic Method' and 6 'Marey, Muybridge and the Cinematographic Method'). The first films shown to a paying public were in 1895 in Paris; the period of silent cinema and the rise of the fashion show coincided almost exactly (see Ch. 12 here).

135 'À Paris, tout fait spectacle . . . Aucun peuple du monde n'a eu des yeux plus voraces.' Balzac 1988, 188 (first published in the *Revue de Paris*, March–April 1833).

136 Entry for Monday 22 May 1865 in Whitehurst 1873, vol. I, 81–2. Entry for Monday 10 February 1868 in Whitehurst 1873, vol. II, 73. For a description of the 1830s, see Uzanne 1898, 101–2. For a description of the parade of fashionable carriages to and from the Bois in the late 1860s, see Zola 1981, 39–51 and

330–36. For the 1890s, see Paul Bonhomme, 'Chronique mondain', *L'Art et la mode*, 21 June 1890, 300. See also Martin-Fugier 1990, 331, and Rocamora 2009, 41–3.

137 Steele 1998, 8 and 135.

138 Charles Blanc, 'Considérations sur le vêtement des femmes', Institut de France, 25 October 1872, 12–13, cited in Benjamin 1999, 74. With thanks to Olga Vainstein for suggesting this quotation here.

139 Lochmann cites Balzac's *Autre étude de femme*: 'cette façon d'avancer le pied en moulant la robe avec une si grande précision qu'elle excite chez le passant une admiration mêlée de désir, mais comprimé par un profond respect'. Blanche Lochmann, 'L'Art de lever le pied: de la Théorie de la démarche au défilé', Musée Galliera 2006, 148.

140 'La vie sociale y fait une grande évolution . . . L'intérieur s'en va. La vie retourne à devenir publique.' Entry for Sunday 18 November 1860, Goncourt, vol. I, 1956, 835.

141 'Cette accélération des hommes et des choses est à l'origine d'une modification du regard porté sur le monde'. Lochmann, 'L'Art de lever', 146.

142 Leroy 1999. Leroy traced this literary myth as it developed through a web of French writers from Gérard de Nerval and Barbey d'Aurevilly to André Breton and Philippe Soupault and beyond.

143 Rocamora 2009, 126–55.

144 Solnit 2002, 200. On the the eighteenth-century *grisette*, the nineteenth-century *midinette* and the *trottin*, so called because, as an errand girl, she 'trotted' (*trottiner*) for a living, see Rocamora 2009, 97 and 143; Steele 1998, 68–73.

145 Frivoline, 'Art et chiffon', *L'Art et la mode*, 18 October 1884, 553. Uzanne described the *trottins* as 'fourteen to seventeen years of age . . . light and graceful creatures with an elastic, dawdling gait . . . They walk in their shocking boots on the asphalt or wood of the streets either to the wholesale houses, or to carry to fashionable customers the latest hat in feathers or flowers. Almost all are real Paris slum children . . . full of fun, drollery, and slyness, these street urchins in petticoats are the monkeys of the workroom'. Uzanne 1912, 76–7.

146 Guy Hickok, 'The Girls Who Change Their Dresses 7,000 Times a Year,' *Atlanta Constitution*, 1 April 1923. In 1928 Ginette, a mannequin, recounted that she wore sportswear away from work; Roubaud 1928, 157.

147 'Théâtreuses ou duchesses, grisettes ou trottins, douairières ou demi-vierges papillonnent dans cette atmosphère grisante de folie et d'effrénée jouissance où la vie se trouve surexcitée à un degré si grand de nervosité et d'éréthisme que c'est à peine si la mort s'y entend et que c'est à peine à la fête un instant s'interrompt lorsqu'il s'agit . . . d'un deuil national.' Ghenya, 'La Journée d'un mannequin', *Le Figaro-Modes*, February 1904, 15.

148 Georg Simmel, 'The Metropolis and Mental Life' (1903), in Simmel 1971, 324–39.

149 Georges d'Avenel, *Le Mécanisme de la vie moderne*, Armand Colin, Paris, 1900–05, vol. IV, 1–2, 4 and 12, quoted in Steele 1998, 139. There are also descriptions of the *midinettes* streaming to work in the mornings like a flock of birds across Paris and of the dress of needlewomen, dressmakers and milliners in the streets in Uzanne's 'map of feminine Paris'. Uzanne 1912, 43, 46–8 and 74–5.

150 Leroy 1999, 256.

151 Ibid., 255.

152 'Hadaly, sublime créature de pure répétition'. Ibid.

153 'Celles-là [les mannequins] ne sont en effet que des *figurantes* . . . Les grands rôles sont tenus par les "premières vendeuses".' Avenel 1902, 79–80.

154 Writing about the *figurante* in the theatre, Avenel refers to 'the mute "minor roles" of women's theatre" which demand no more than a sufficiently attractive appearance and face': les "petites rôles" muets des théâtres "à femmes". De celles-là on n'exige qu'une apparance et un visage suffisamment attrayant'. Ibid., 278.

155 Mistinguett 1954, 19.

156 Barrière 1889, 244. Uzanne uses *rat* to designate only the child ballet pupils aged seven to nine. Uzanne 1912, 153.

157 'Ils exécutent ponctuellement les mouvements réglés . . . Dans cette race mixte des figurants, à moitié acteurs, à moitié décors, tour à tour héros, bêtes et machines, dont le pied doit être fait à toutes les chaussures et la tête à toutes les perruques . . . [they have certain skills] tout ce qui exige de l'aisance dans les manières et quelque sûreté dans la démarche. . . . le figurant est en général assez passif, fort indifférent.' At the Opéra, M. Gailard succeeded 'en faisant figurer . . . le corps de ballet où se rencontrent des sujets dociles, capables de porter un costume avec élégance.' Avenel 1902, 279–81.

158 E.g., Robert de Beauplan, 'Après la grève des cousettes: dans les coulisses de la grande couture', *L'Illustration*, 19 May 1923, reprinted in *L'Illustration: Journal Universel* 1987, 139.

159 '[E]lle redevenait apparition: le fantôme se réanimait.' Villiers 1993, 242.

CHAPTER 2

1 Hillel Schwartz, 'Torque: The New Kinaesthetic of the Twentieth Century', in Crary and Kwinter 1992, 88–9.

2 These early fashion shows were known in English as 'openings'. See 'Paris Couturiers: How the World's Fashions are Determined – Fitting the Costumes to Buyers by Aid of Mannequins', *Los Angeles Times*, 6 January 1901.

3 Jean-Philippe Worth recalled in 1928 that the firm of Worth et Cie planned four tableaux to represent the four seasons: the Longchamp racecourse for autumn, an aristocratic mansion for winter, a seaside resort for summer and a *défilé*, or fashion show, for spring. Worth 1928, 187.

4 For press coverage of mannequins at specific houses, see Kathleen Schlesinger, 'The Growth of a Paris Costume', *The Lady's Realm*, June 1900, 210–16; 'Intime', 'A Parisian Prince of Dress', *The Lady's Realm*, November 1900, 21–6; Marquise de Bal, 'Une journée chez un grand couturier (Redfern)', *Femina*, 13 April 1901, 125–8; 'Paris Couturiers', *Los Angeles Times*, 6 January 1901; Avenel 1902, 72–4; Evelyn M. Lang, 'Great Parisian Dressmakers: Paquin and Laferrière', *The Lady's Realm*, February 1902, 620–25; ' "Launchers of Fashion": How Paris Modes are Started on their Victorious Careers', *The Tatler*, 31 January 1906, 172; 'Chez un grand couturier Parisien – les mannequins', *Femina*, 15 November 1903, 735.

5 Musée Galliera 2006, 145; Reeder 1990, 11.

6 Marquise de Bal, 'Une journée', 125–8.

7 Saunders 1954, 110. Saunders cites the source for her description of the mirrored *salon de lumière* as Le Petit Homme Rouge, 1907, 311–13.

8 Evelyn M. Lang, 'Great Parisian Dressmakers', *The Ladies' Realm*, February 1902, 620–25.

9 Reeder 1990, 25, citing Garland 1970, 96.

10 'Ce petit truc est utile à la vente'. Avenel 1902, 79.

11 In 1902 illustrated magazines like *L'Illustration* generated a significant portion of the French advertising business. Fashion magazines constituted an important category within illustrated magazines; more than two million examples per week emanated from Paris alone. Avenel 1902, 132–3. For press that describes fashion modelling as a form of advertising, see Ghenya, 'La Journée d'un mannequin', *Le Figaro-Modes*, February 1904, 14–19; 'Very Pretty Work: Women Now Receive Compensation Simply Wearing the Costliest and Most Exquisite of Dresses', *Boston Daily Globe*, 29 September 1907; E. M. Newman, 'Nothing to do but Wear Fine Clothes!' *Chicago Daily Tribune*, 16 November 1913.

12 'Paris Has the Scotch Craze', *Washington Post*, 7 October 1906; 'Short Sleeves and Long Gloves Win Out in the Battle for Supremacy', *Washington Post*, 6 October 1907; 'Smaller Waists Are Demanded', *Atlanta Constitution*, 6 October 1907; 'Very Pretty Work', 1907; 'Models that Exhibit Season's Startling Innovations', *Washington Post*, 22 September 1907; 'Gifts for Dogs', *Los Angeles Times*, 31 March 1907.

13 'Glimpses of Paris Fashions Show Favorite Materials', *Washington Post*, 11 September 1910; 'Exclusive Gowns Shown to the Visiting Dressmakers', *Chicago Daily Tribune*, 25 September 1910. For French descriptions of the overseas buyers, see Roger-Milès 1910, 59; Giafar, 'Petits Contes au Khalife sur les harems de la couture', *Fantasio*, 15 August 1913, 56–7.

14 Anne Rittenhouse, 'What the Well-Dressed Woman is Wearing', *New York Times*, 29 September 1912. Appearing unobtrusively from the wings, the fashion mannequin 'marches before your vision as obtrusively as an advertisement', wrote an American commentator in 1915. Lynd 1915, 24–6. With thanks to Alessandra Vaccari for bringing my attention to this source.

15 Louis Angé, *Traité pratique de publicité commerciale et industrielle*, 2 vols, Éditions Pratique de Publicité Commerciale et Industrielle, 1922, cited in Gronberg 1998, 88 and 108 n. 18. In contrast, in his coverage of French advertising in 1902 Avenel claimed that the sandwich man, 'walking with a dejected step' (*marchant d'un pas morne*), had already fallen into disuse. Avenel 1902, 168.

16 Ghenya, 'Journée d'un mannequin'; 'Very Pretty Work', 1907: the mannequin is 'economically related to the humblest wage earners, the sandwich man, for she is a walking advertisement'. Mannequins were 'just animated billboards' who were 'employed . . . to act as walking advertisements', wrote the *Chicago Daily Tribune* in 1913. Newman, 'Nothing To Do!'. In March 1911 a journalist even commented with heavy sarcasm on the pushiness of mannequins promoting *jupe-pantalons* in a fashionable tea salon: 'all that is needed now is to disguise the *homme-sandwich* as a *femme-pantalon*'. 'Ces jeunes personnes poussèrent l'amabilité jusqu'à murmurer, sans qu'on les en prie, le nom du couturier dont elles exhibaient les modèles. Ce fut gai. Il ne reste plus qu'a déguiser les hommes-sandwichs en femmes-pantalon!' Le Mannequin d'Hozier, 'Modanités', *Fantasio*, 15 March 1911, 574.

17 See Emile Henriot, 'Figures parisiennes: le mannequin', *L'Illustration*, 27 December 1913, reprinted in *L'Illustration: Journal Universel* 1987, 112–16.

18 'Free Lunches for Women Who View Fashions', *Chicago Daily Tribune*, 3 May 1914. After the war, this hospitality was extended to the press too.

19 'C'est ce qui inspira à un acheteur désabusé cette réflexion mélancolique: "Les mannequins sans les robes . . . passe encore! . . . Mais les robes sans les mannequins! . . ." ' Le Mannequin d'Hozier, 'Modanités', *Fantasio*, 15 February 1910, 502.

20 'Belted Coats Continued by the House of Paquin. Also Immense Reveres and Collars', *New York Times*, 15 October 1911.

21 Mary Buel, 'Radical Changes in Paris Fashion', *Chicago Daily Tribune*, 24 August 1913.

22 Grumbach 2008, 434.

23 Tétart-Vittu describes the nineteenth-century American buyers' spring and autumn visits to Paris to buy 'reproduction models' (*modèles reproducteurs*) of the cloaks and gowns on sale in the rue Vivienne which Parisian newspapers described pejoratively as export

products (*produits d'exportation*). Françoise Tétart-Vittu, 'Couture et nouveautés confectionnées', in Musée de la Mode et du Costume, 1992, 35. Georges d'Avenel recounted how, during the 6–7 months of the siege of Paris and the Commune in 1870, foreign buyers went instead to Berlin to buy *confection* (ready-to-wear models) and in this way the Paris trade lost the U.K. and U.S. buyers to Germany until c. 1883, when French standards were raised and the foreign buyers returned. Avenel 1902, 93–4.

24 The division between North American and other foreign buyers was more formal in the larger houses due to the greater number of buyers they received. There, the first two or three days were usually reserved for the North American buyers and the following days allocated to the South American, British, German and Russian buyers. European buyers came from many cities, including London, Berlin, Vienna, St Petersburg. 'Paris Couturiers', *Los Angeles Times*, 6 January 1901; Roger-Milès 1910, 59; 'Predictions Confirmed: New Season Tendencies Made Clear by Style Creators Showings', *Dry Goods Economist*, 9 September 1911, 41; 'Paris Fashions for the Autumn', *New York Times*, 8 October 1911; Anne Rittenhouse, 'What the Well-Dressed Woman is Wearing', *New York Times*, 29 September 1912.

25 'Facts, Features and Fancies for Women', *Los Angeles Times*, 14 August 1909; 'A Paris Show of Fashions', *Washington Post*, 19 September 1909; Rittenhouse, 'What the Well-Dressed Woman is Wearing', *New York Times*, 18 February 1912.

26 Occasionally it slipped even further forward to the last weeks of January and July respectively. Bonney 1929, 2.

27 'Facts, Features', 1909; Anne Rittenhouse, 'Clothes Worn at the French Races Again Eccentric – New Turban the Highest Hat in Decades', *New York Times*, 7 August 1910; 'Paris Preparing the New Modes', *Christian Science Monitor*, 6 August 1912; 'Paquin Inaugurates the Most Radical Change of the Season: The Flare Skirt', *Harper's Bazar*, July 1914, 51.

28 A large order consisted of twenty-five or more models. 'New Season Models: Features of Advance Showings Made by Paris Dressmakers', *Dry Goods Economist*, 19 August 1911, 65.

29 These were later to become formalised as mid-season collections. 'Au Revoir, Paris Garb', *Washington Post*, 9 August 1914; 'To Know the Fashions which Are to Be Is the Prime Wisdom', *Harper's Bazar*, August 1914, 44–5.

30 Rittenhouse, 'What the Well-Dressed Woman is Wearing', *New York Times*, 29 September 1912.

31 On the imposition of import tariffs in 1909, see 'A Paris Show of Fashions', *Washington Post*, 19 September 1909.

32 'At Fall Race-Meet: Toilettes of Fashionables at Longchamps Offer Many Good

Suggestions', *Dry Goods Economist*, 2 October 1909, n.p.

33 'Features of the "Economist" Models', *Dry Goods Economist*, 24 June 1911, 39.

34 Pouillard 2011, 323.

35 Brachet Champsaur 2012, 50. There is a suggestion that by 1914 some Paris department stores had begun to copy the showing techniques of the couturiers. Sem 1914, n.p. [3–4].

36 In the retail stores in 1902, 'The mannequin only exists as a real one [meaning an inanimate one] . . . The dresses are without heads and without movement; they do not walk, alive, before the buyer [NB: the buyer is female]' ('le mannequin n'existe qu'à l'état de vrai mannequin . . . Les robes sont sans têtes et sans mouvement; elles ne passent pas, vivantes, devant l'acheteuse'). Alexandre 1902, 174–5.

37 On Lucile, see Steele 2000; Matheson and Sorkin 2005; O'Neill 2007, 51–72; Safer 2007; Mendes and Haye 2009; Schweitzer 2009; Bigham 2012; Tolini-Finamore 2013.

38 Bigham 2012.

39 'The Story of the Greatest Fashion Expert in the World', *Portfolio of Lady Duff-Gordon's Original Designs*, catalogue for Sears Roebuck and Co, Chicago, Fall & Winter 1916–17, 6. See also Avery Strakosch, 'Fashions for the Famous: Dressmaking Days With Lady Duff-Gordon, as Told by Her First Model, Miss Elsie', *Saturday Evening Post*, 29 January 1927, 12–13 and continued on 91, 94. In her memoir Lucile was clear about what her contribution was, claiming credit only for the 'evolution of the mannequin parade' and that 'some resourceful soul conceived the idea in Paris of having living models'. Duff Gordon 1932, 67 and 68. Lucile's contribution was to theatricalise the fashion show. Bigham 2012, 37–8.

40 Avery Strakosch, 'Fashions for the Famous: Dressmaking Days With Lady Duff-Gordon, as Told by Her First Model, Miss Elsie', *Saturday Evening Post*, 19 February 1927, 35–6 and continued on 98, 101–2, 104. This is the second of three long articles that constitute a rich source, bearing in mind Bigham's caveat that Miss Elsie's dates are frequently incorrect by about two years.

41 Strakosch, 29 January 1927, 12.

42 Ibid.

43 Ibid.

44 Ibid., 91. Howard Greer described Hebe as 'a divinely beautiful brunette from London'. Greer 1952, 40.

45 In 1932 Lucile recalled 'the mannequin show with which I opened the Paris branch of Lucile Limited [in 1911] – an occasion when an English designer working with English work people caused something of a sensation by presenting the dresses on lovely English model girls with suitable gloves, shoes, jewels, etc, to complete the costume, whereas up to that time the French dressmakers had always shown their dresses on mannequins wearing fitted long sleeved black satin slips, giving

them the exact appearance of dummies.' Her claim that the French were still using the black *fourreau* in 1911 is wrong, however (see Chs 1 and 9 for when it fell out of use in Paris). Lucy Duff Gordon, letter to the Curator of the London Museum dated 22 May 1928, collection of the Museum of London, 28.125/1-2. The letter is legibly reproduced in O'Neill 2007, 58. On Lucile and the *maillot*, or *fourreau*, see also Bigham 2012, 48–54.

46 Kaplan and Stowell 1994, 119.

47 Strakosch, 'Fashions for the Famous', 19 February 1927, 98.

48 Duff Gordon 1932, 67–8.

49 Kaplan and Stowell 1994, 8–14.

50 Duff Gordon 1932, 70; Strakosch, 29 January 1927, 23. These accounts are inconsistent but press sources suggest that Lucile's early interiors in Hanover Square were grey and the curtains of the stage green: *London Daily Express*, 29 April 1904; *Washington Times*, 22 May 1904; *Los Angeles Herald*, 3 December 1905; *Bystander*, 16 May 1906; *London Daily Express*, 26 February 1909. In 1912 there was a change to a mauve and white scheme: *Home Notes*, 25 April 1912; *London Daily Express*, 20 March 1912. With thanks to Randy Bigham for these references. See too Bigham 2012, 64.

51 The Saunterer, 'The New Art of Woman: Being the Expression of Personality in Curves and Colours', reprinted by Lucile Limited, 25 Hanover Square, from *The Smart Set*, May 1904 (Pamphlet, London, AAD/2008/6/43).

52 Bigham also correctly points out that Duff Gordon's autobiography telescopes some historical events into a single event. Bigham 2012, 37. The precise dates for events is often hard to establish due to inconsistencies in the surviving primary sources.

53 Ibid., 37–8. See also Strakosch, 29 January 1927, 91; Duff Gordon 1932, 72–5; Kaplan and Stowell 1994, 68–9.

54 This was a fashion show with an elaborate printed programme explaining her gowns of emotion, with flashes of limelight in the wings of the stage and a Hungarian band. Marie Corelli, 'Marie Corelli, Novelist, on the Madness of Clothes', *Washington Post*, 30 July 1905.

55 The 'Seven Ages of Woman' traced in seven acts from birth to death the dress-cycle of a society woman: the school girl, the debutante, the fiancée, the bride, the wife, the hostess and the dowager. Etherington-Smith and Pilcher 1986, 90.

56 Strakosch, 19 February 1927, 102. Gabriele Brandstetter discusses the specific historical temporality of the pre-twentieth-century pose. While posing in the eighteenth and nineteenth centuries had its fixed rules so that, after three minutes of a tableau, the curtain would fall, in the twenty-first century, Brandstetter argues, posing and the moves between poses have been speeded up, citing the living tableaux of the artist Vanessa Beecroft. Her assertion that there was a more

leisurely pace of posing is borne out by the timing of the first fashion shows, which not only lasted much longer than contemporary ones – anything from an hour and a quarter to three hours – but proceeded at a slower pace and were staged repeatedly over several days. The modern fashion show lasting only twenty minutes and staged once is far different. All the points raised by Brandstetter are indeed confirmed by descriptions of the first mannequins modelling in the early part of the twentieth century. Gabriele Brandstetter, 'Pose-Posa-Posing: Between Image and Movement', in Bippus and Mink 2007, 250. On the temporality of the pose, Brandstetter cites Craig Owens, 'Posieren', in Herta Wolf (ed. in collaboration with Susanne Holschbach et al., *Diskurse der Fotografie: Fotokritik am Ende des fotografischen Zeitalters*, Frankfurt-am-Main: Suhrkamp Verlag, 2003, vol. II, esp. 107ff). On nineteenth-century posing for fashion photography she cites Holschbach 2006.

57 'Mid-Channel in Paris Fashions', *Vogue* (America), 1 December 1913, 35–7; Strakosch, 19 February 1927, 102.

58 Bigham 2012, 39.

59 *Sketch*, 4 April 1904, cited in Kaplan and Stowell 1994, 119.

60 In 1911 an American journalist complained that Beer was not using its stage that season, 'the stage being surely the most dramatic way of showing off splendid gowns that has ever been invented'. 'Paris Fashions for the Autumn,' *New York Times*, 8 October 1911. The image of Lucile's stage also appeared in the *Illustrated London News*.

61 There are numerous references to Lucile's 1907–8 trip to New York to join her sister on her bookselling tour for *Three Weeks*. These include the *New York Herald* (21 December 1907), the *New York Times* (23 December 1907), the *Washington Times* (15 January 1908), the *Oakland Tribune* (4 January 1908) and the *Los Angeles Times* (19 January 1908). With thanks to Randy Bigham for these references.

62 *Wanamaker Originator* 1908. Wanamaker 1911, 273. On English buyers in Paris houses, see e.g. Taylor 1983. English buyers regularly visited the Paris houses where they would have seen the mannequins modelling, while French firms like Worth and Paquin had London branches; French dressmakers such as Madeleine Vionnet routinely came to work in the London trade for a few years to learn English.

63 For a detailed chronology by Tétart-Vittu, see Musée de la Mode et du Costume 1986.

64 Ghenya, 'La Journée d'un mannequin', February 1904. See also 'Waistless Gowns Are Again Exploited by Poiret and the Best Wraps in Paris Are Made by Him', *New York Times*, 15 October 1911, which describes how the Poiret mannequins wore small velvet hats co-ordinated with their coat suits.

65 Gustave Babin, 'Une leçon d'élégance dans un parc', *L'Illustration*, 9 July 1910, 21–2.

66 In the evening, the mannequins modelled for an entire hour both indoors and out, whichever was felt appropriate to the colours and shapes. Babin, 'Une leçon', 21–2. See also Troy 2003, 88–9. Poiret's idea of open-air fashions in motion caught the American imagination. In August 1910 the *Boston Daily Globe* reported that Poiret had decided that 'dresses that are to be worn in the street, at race courses, at garden parties or at the seaside should be seen in the open air. It seems obvious enough, but no-one had thought of it before.' 'Dresses shown out of doors', *Boston Daily Globe*, 21 August 1910. George Barclay, 'Journey with Mere Man', *Chicago Daily Tribune*, 11 September 1910.

67 Poiret 1931, 113.

68 Troy 2003.

69 'M. Poiret on His Imports of American-made Silks', *New York Times*, 15 March 1914.

70 'Great Dressmaking Artist: Rise and Phenomenal Success of M. Poiret', *Christian Science Monitor*, 3 November 1911. In his memoir Poiret recalled that he only permitted entry to his first shows to clients who agreed to place a definite order. Poiret 1931, 113.

71 On Poiret's life and work, see White 1973; Musée de la Mode et du Costume 1986; Deslandres 1987; Mackrell 1990; Troy 2003; Baudot 1997; Koda and Bolton 2007.

72 On Poiret's film, see Babin, 'Une leçon', 21; 'Poiret's Elaborate Reception' and 'Lucile's New Paris House', *Dry Goods Economist*, 9 September 1911, 44. On the presence of the mannequins at the 1002nd Night Party, see Montoison, 'La fête chez Paul', *Fantasio*, 15 July 1911, 829. For the thirteen Steichen photographs of Poiret's mannequins in his couture house, see Paul Cornu, 'The Art of the Dress', *Art et décoration*, April 1911, with drawings by Georges Lepape. In the 1920s Poiret went on to act with Colette in a touring play, *La Vagabonde*, to design costumes for several French films and, while on a promotional tour with his mannequins in 1923, to star with them in a Czech comedy film, *The Kidnapping of Fux Banker*, in which Poiret played himself, credited as 'Leon' Poiret, presenting his collection to a young debutante. See Marketa Uhlirova, 'Scandal, Satire and Vampirism: *The Kidnapping of Fux Banker*', in Uhlirova 2008, 107–17.

73 For a selection, see Poiret's press albums, Centre de Documentation, Musée de l'Art de la Mode et du Textile, Paris.

74 '[C]es scènes d'hystérie moderne'. Sem 1914, n.p. [2]. Carolyn Wilson, 'M. Poiret Versus M. Sem', *Chicago Daily Tribune*, 5 July 1914.

75 'Autour d'elles passent, virent et repassent des mannequins muets, au sourire de cire, les frôlant, les enveloppant de la caresse de leurs robes traînantes, inlassablement renouvelées, grisant leur imagination de mouvements onduleux et rythmés, de poses séduisantes, de contorsions discrètes et savants.' Sem 1914, n.p. [2].

76 Poiret had moved in 1909 to the avenue d'Antin, further west than the majority of rue de la Paix couturiers, who only followed him west after the war.

77 Wilson, 'M. Poiret Versus M. Sem'.

78 I am grateful to Randy Bigham for his pointers about Lucile which indicate that it could have been she who was being parodied in this image and elsewhere in the album. In my own view, the evidence remains equivocal. Although Lucile's Paris shows featured tangoing mannequins, so did many others, including Paquin's. Also, as Nancy Troy points out, Poiret designed the costumes for Richepin's play *Le Tango* in December 1913. Troy 2003, 179. Little can be concluded from the dress styles caricatured in Sem's album of 1914 because by then all the major houses were showing adaptations of Poiret's lampshade tunic including, among many, Boué, Lucile and Redfern. One of Sem's grounds for attack on *le faux chic* is that these fashions are 'not truly French' and he deplores the foreign influence on French fashion and of the Rights for Women movement; Lucile was clearly both a woman and a foreigner (though not a Suffragist) but Poiret's orientalism and his commercial links with Vienna and Berlin also laid him open to accusations of having foreign tastes and affiliations. From a close reading of Sem's text it is impossible to conclude definitively that any particular designer was being caricatured in the illustration reproduced here and, although I think it is marginally more likely to be Poiret than Lucile, it is not even clear that the image is a portrait of any specific designer, especially since Sem's attack is always on 'designers' in the plural. Certainly, both Poiret and Lucile exemplified Sem's idea of *le faux chic*. Sem wrote that he could not name the designers for fear of legal action and that he had changed a few details in his illustrations to avoid a charge of plagiarism. The designers he names as having *le vrai chic* are Paquin, Chéruit, Doeuillet, Worth and the milliners Mmes Georgette and Demay. The album also carries advertisements for Doucet (couture), O'Rossen (riding costumes), Carette (tailors) and Gélot (hats), so one can safely assume that it is none of these.

79 *Sumurun* was an orientalist pantomime based on a story from the Arabian Nights containing a dancing scene of scantily clad slave girls; directed by Max Reinhardt in Berlin in 1911, it travelled to London and New York in 1912. Parisian audiences had already seen slave girls in barefoot dances and the dance of the frenzied orgies culminating in their massacre by the Shah's eunuchs in the Ballets Russes's *Schéhérezade* in 1910. Garafola 1998, 35. In 1920 *Sumurun* was made into a film by Ernst Lubitsch starring Pola Negri. See Peter Madsen, 'A Short Material History of a World Classic: *The Arabian Nights' Entertainments*', Islam in European Literature project, University of Copenhagen, http://complit.ku.dk/islamineuropeanliteratur e/workingpapers/dokument6/ accessed

12 August 2011. Sumurun was also the modelling name of Vera Ashby, a Lucile mannequin who followed Molyneux when he set up in his own name in 1919 after he had been fired by Lucile. See also Keenan 1977, 111–13.

80 'Là, plus de retenue. Ces faiseurs sans vergogne, devenus de véritables impresarii, montent des espèces de gala à chaque changement de saison et, sous prétexte de lancer la mode nouvelle, organisent la présentation de leurs modèles inédits comme une féerie de music-hall. Entre un tango de Mistinguett et une chanson de Fursy, ils font parader en musique, sur une scène enguirlandée de fleurs en papier et de lampions jusqu'au milieu du public, à la "Sumurun", un étrange corps de ballet plus ou moins russe, persan ou valaque, toute une théorie de mannequins désarticulés, de femmes serpents enduites de toilettes venimeuses qui ondulent, se convulsent lentement, le ventre en offrande et un pied traînant, mimant une sorte de tango à vide sous les yeux des spectatrices, – malheureuses snobinettes que ces managers sans scrupules énervent de thé frelaté et de vague dopings, en attendant le jour prochain où ils pousseront le synécisme jusqu'à les enivrer de cocaïne et d'éther pour les mieux mettre au point, les réduire à l'état de pauvres inconscientes prêtes à subir la plus extravagante exploitation.' Sem 1914, n.p. [3–4].

81 Troy 2003, 181–4.

82 'C'est une oeuvre de perversion morale et matérielle . . . dans ces exhibitions scandaleuses de mannequins au choix où il ne manque que la négresse'. Sem 1914, n.p. [4].

83 Reproduced in Troy 2003, 183–4, pls 2.64 and 2.65.

84 Alessandra Vaccari, 'Fashion and Tango', paper given at the United Kingdom Association of Art Historians annual conference, 29 March 2012.

85 Wollen 1993, 1–2; Troy 2003, 15, 101–4, 109–10, 113–16, 202–3, 208–9, 211 and 278.

86 'Paris Mode Mannish', *Washington Post*, 24 March 1914.

87 Silver 1989, 174–81.

88 La Raconteuse, 'Lady Duff Gordon Enters Business: Her Dressmaking Establishment Causes Sensation', unattributed article from Lucile Press Books, 1911, FIT, New York.

89 Raconteuse, 'Lady Duff Gordon'.

90 'Poiret's Elaborate Reception' and 'Lucile's New Paris House', *Dry Goods Economist*, 9 September 1911, 44.

91 'Une grande dame créatrice de la mode', *Excelsior*, 8 April 1911, 9.

92 'Poiret's Elaborate Reception' and 'Lucile's New Paris House', ibid.

93 Mary Buel, 'Paris Dressmakers Coming to America', *Chicago Daily Tribune*, 18 May 1913.

94 Strakosch, 19 February 1927, 102. An American paper wrote that 'The "mannequins" . . . were beauties, and . . . although they were English, every one of

them, they looked quite different from the general French idea of what English girls look like'. Raconteuse, 'Lady Duff Gordon'.

95 'Une grande dame créatrice', 9. 'Une lady-couturière – en son hôtel – a entrepris de révéler ses créations aux Parisiennes en les faisant accompagner . . . d'une musique approprié . . . petite flute, violon langoureux, ou tremolo. Chaque robe – ô ma tête, ô esthète – a une signification. Espérons que, grâce à un phonographe invisible gracieusement offert, elles seront vendues avec le petit air adéquat.' Le Mannequin d'Hozier, 'Modanités', *Fantasio*, 15 April 1911, 646.

96 'Le théâtre du grand couturier', illustrated by Pierre Brissaud, *Femina*, 15 December 1911, 697. The caption to this illustration does not identify Lucile by name but it is clear from several contemporary photographs that it shows her Paris salon. The photographs are in the Lucile album called 'Memento' in the Archive of Art and Design, London, AAD/2008/6/28. One is also reproduced in 'Lady Duff Gordon – "Lucile" ', *Harper's Bazar*, August 1914, 39. Brissaud's illustration bears some similarities to this photograph in the disposition and posing of the mannequins, suggesting that he may have used it as the basis for his drawing.

97 Mary Buel, 'Novelties Seen in Midsummer Openings of Paris Shops', *Chicago Daily Tribune*, 4 June 1911. Chary's play may possibly have been inspired by Lucile and her London 'Seven Ages' show in 1909; it in turn may have inspired Lucile to stage further plays in New York over the following years.

98 For an alternative view on Lucile's impact on Paris, see Bigham 2012, 36 and 40.

99 For an analysis of the Poiret character, and a description of the critical reception of Paquin's costumes, see Troy 2003, 133 and 137–46.

100 Idalia de Villiers, 'Sensational Gowns Arouse Paris', *Boston Daily Globe*, 18 February 1912.

101 'Rue de la Paix is a National Asset', *The New York Herald* (Paris), 18 February 1912, 11.

102 Ibid.

103 The play was light entertainment but for more serious treatments of the iniquities of dressmakers' establishments and the maltreatment of mannequins, such as Granville Barker's *The Madras House* of 1910 and Edward Knoblock's *My Lady's Dress* of 1913, see Kaplan and Stowell 1994, 122–50. These London plays offered critiques of Lucile and Poiret respectively.

104 'Dress on the Stage: A Disappointing Play in Paris', *Daily Mail* (London), 23 January 1912; 'La Mode au théâtre: la "Rue de la Paix" au Vaudeville', *Le Gaulois*, January 1912; Théodore Massiac, 'Courrier des théâtres: au Vaudeville', *Petite république*, 23 February 1912.

105 Charles Belmont Davis, 'Ladies of the Chorus', *Harper's Bazar*, November 1913, 26–7 and 70.

106 Ibid.

107 Braun 1992, 70.

108 Ibid., 71 and 81.

109 *Illustrated London News*, 12 April 1913, 478–80.

110 Vigarello 1978, 10.

111 R.S., 'Une heure d'élégance au Théâtre Femina: une conférence de Mlle Jane Marnac et de M. André de Fouquières', *Femina*, 15 March 1912, 157. 'Line and simplicity is my principal, my only concern . . . to make women young and pretty is my goal. I prefer a thousand times a pretty foot to a crinoline, and an ankle to a pannier', 'M. Parry' is quoted as saying in the text. Patou expressed the same sentiment about the foot and ankle in 1924 in his choice of American mannequins.

112 Etherington-Smith 1983, 23 and 25.

113 An American department store advertisement in 1916 reports on designs by Patou, Doeuillet and Georgette seen on the Côte d'Azur. 'Fashion Notes from Nice and Monte Carlo', Display Ad 13, no title, Marshall Field and Company, *Chicago Daily Tribune*, 1 February 1916.

114 *Histoire de l'industrie* 1926, 123.

115 Giedion 1969, 25 and 79.

116 Duchamp's painting was first shown on 10–30 October 1912 in the Salon de la Section d'Or at the Galérie la Boétie, alongside other images of movement. In 1913 it was shown in the Armory Show in New York at a time when fashion shows loomed as large in the public consciousness as they did in Paris. Ottinger 2009, 194.

117 For a discussion of this painting, see Tag Gronberg, 'Deco Venus', in Arscott and Scott 2000, 142–55. In relation to fashion and the *Parisienne*, see Rocamora 2009, 167–8.

118 See also Gronberg's discussion of a Sonia Delaunay fashion photograph in 1925 that uses a mirror and three views of female figures, drawing on the language of fashion photography. Ibid.

119 Evelyn M. Lang, 'Great Parisian Dressmakers: Paquin and La Ferrière', *The Lady's Realm*, February 1902, 620–25.

120 On nineteenth-century French fashion journalism, see Françoise Tétart-Vittu, 'Le chic parisien: image et modèles dans la presse illustré', and Anne Barbera, 'Des journaux et des modes', in Musée de la Mode et du Costume 1990, 93–102 and 103–17; *Glossy* 2004.

121 Michelle Tolini-Finamore argues that the link between fashion illustration and film dates back to the short-lived fashion periodical *La Stéréoscope* in 1857. Tolini-Finamore 2013. See also Davis 2006, 10; Pauline Gay-Fragneaud and Patricia Vallet, 'Répertoire et notices historiques des revues de mode', in *Glossy* 2004, 65–79.

122 See entry on 'Multiphotography' in Hopkins (1898) 1976, 451–3.

123 Five multiphotographs of Condé Nast are reproduced in Seebohm 1982, 145.

124 There is also an example by Umberto Boccioni of 1905–7 entitled *I-We* (in Italian, *Io-noi*). Lista 2001, 18.

125 On the origins of the ballet in the London garden of Lady Ottoline Morrell in July 1912, see Buckle 1975, 341 and Garafola 1998, 58–9.

126 *Illustrated London News*, 14 May 1913. Garafola also recounts that, in an interview for *Le Figaro* on the eve of the ballet's première, the dancer Nijinsky said: 'The man that I see foremost on the stage is a contemporary man. I imagine the costume, the plastic poses, the movement that would be representative of our time'. He observed that the modern gestures of strolling, newspaper-reading and tango-dancing had nothing to do with those of previous centuries and hoped that the gestures of modern sports, 'the creators of plastic beauty', would last into the future as the expression of the early twentieth century. Garafola 1998, 58–9.

127 E.B., 'Le Matin au Bois', *L'Illustration*, 14 June 1913, 559–62.

128 Buckle 1975, 341. John E. Bowlt assesses Bakst's 'monochrome, functional sportswear' for the tennis players in *Jeux* as being 'not so very far' from the Soviet constructivist designs of Liubov Popova and Vavara Stepanova. He describes the knee-length tennis skirt as 'an audacious development in fashion, at once enhancing her sexuality and, at the same time, symbolizing women's freedom from the strictures of her nineteenth-century social round', adding that in all his Paris stage productions between 1909 and 1914 'Bakst exposed the mobility of the human body'. John E. Bowlt, 'Léon Bakst, Natalia Goncharova and Pablo Picasso', in Pritchard 2010, 104–5.

129 See Pierre Brissaud, 'Le théâtre du grand couturier', *Femina*, 15 December 1911, 697, for the Lucile picture. The next page shows 'les Femmes aux Jeux Olympiques' in which the female athletes' sporty bodies engaged in gymnastics, swimming and archery contrast with Lucile's decorative aesthetic. For further images of sporting events and of French physical education, see *Femina*, 13 April 1912 (French physical education, eight natural exercises, all men); *L'Illustration*, 15 June 1912 (the French female tennis team at play); *L'Illustration*, 29 June 1912 (coverage of the gymnastic 'Olympics'); *L'Illustration*, 8 March 1913 (line drawings of discus-throwing in antiquity); and *L'Illustration*, 14 June 1913 (the world tennis championships at Saint-Cloud showing women tennis players, accompanied by a text arguing that tennis is a game equally accessible to both sexes).

130 Popular magazines and newspapers in both France and America endlessly discussed the dance craze. See e.g. 'La Leçon de tango', *L'Illustration*, 29 March 1913; 'Le vrai tango', *Femina*, 1 May 1913, 689; 'Tango', *Fantasio*, 15 May 1913, 702; 'Tangoville', *L'Illustration*, 16 August 1913, 134–5; Christiana, 'Un Tango chez Lucile', *Sim*,

November 1913; Robert Voucher, 'Tango et Furlana', *L'Illustration*, 7 February 1914, 106–7; 'New Dances Influence Paris Fashions for Spring Wear', *New York Times*, 12 April 1914; Margaret Hawkesworth, 'In Honour of the Dance: The Lulu Fado, and Other New Dances', *Harper's Bazar*, September 1914, 40–41; 'Spring Weather Delights Paris', *New York Times*, 5 April 1914.

131 'Encore les Ballets Russes', *Comoedia illustré*, 1 June 1909, 459ff, reproduced in Davis 2010, 38–9. There is another such double-page spread from *Comoedia illustré*, 15 June 1912, reproduced in Pritchard 2010, 130.

132 Woodcock, 'Wardrobe', in Pritchard 2010, 131.

133 Duncan strongly dissociated herself from modern dance which she decreed 'but a weird acrobatic performance and those who "trot", "tango" or "hesitate" are but contortionists'. 'When Greek meets Greek then comes the Duncan dance', *Harper's Bazar*, July 1914, 36–7. Mary Davis analyses the importance of 'the Paris fashion enterprise', including magazines and publishers, to the Ballets Russes. Davis 2010, 25–59.

134 '[L]a vogue folle, instantanée, incroyable' and 'Le cake-walk à la ville', *Les Modes*, April 1903, 267 and inside back cover.

135 Cocteau 1987, 568.

136 Hawkesworth, 'In Honour of the Dance', 41. By July 1914 the tango had spread like a disease over Europe, wrote an American woman in Paris: up to the outbreak of war on 1 August, 'everybody tangoed and bunny-hugged and matchiched.' *Adam* 1919, 3, 319. See also Davis 2006, 138–42, 'French Fashion and the Tango Teas'.

137 Poiret quoted in 'To Bring 100 Gowns,' *New York Times*, 7 September 1913.

138 Sem quoted in Troy 2003, 177–8.

139 See ibid., 179.

140 One example from 1914, accession number C.I.47.571, Costume Institute of the Metropolitan Museum of Art, New York, can be seen on their website.

141 Christiana, 'Un Tango chez Lucile'.

142 E.G., 'Mid-Channel in Paris fashions,' *Vogue* (America), 1 December 1913, 35–7.

143 With thanks to Lewis Orchard for identifying this as a 'tango lite' or hybrid dance.

144 On Tuesday 25 October 1913 the *Daily Mirror* carried an advertisement for a new, taller kind of show girl required to perform at tango teas: 'fortune awaits tall pretty girls who can dance the tango and wear dresses well. It is often more important for a girl to be able to wear a dress well than to be able to dance.' For coverage of Lucile's London tango teas, see *Daily Mail*, 19 November 1913; *Daily Telegraph*, 20 November 1913; *The Stage*, 20 November 1913; *Sporting Life*, 21 November 1913; *Daily Chronicle*, 22 November 1913; *Illustrated London News*, 22 November 1913; *Daily Express*, 23 November 1913; *Observer*, 23 November 1913; *Daily Graphic*, 24 November 1913; *Daily Telegraph*, 25 November 1913; *Sunday Times*,

25 November 1913. See also Reeder 1990, 23–4.

145 *Daily Express*, 22 November 1913; *Illustrated London News*, 25 October 1913.

146 *Daily Telegraph*, 25 November 1913.

147 *Winning Post*, 22 November 1913.

148 'Super-Tango Tea Enthralls London', *New York Times*, 26 April 1914. At the London Opera House a tango tea was staged in conjunction with a colour fashion film showing a fortnight before Paquin's tango teas at the Palace; it is not known if this too was by Paquin, as Reeder suggests. *Daily Mail*, 19 November 1913; Reeder 1990, 9–10.

149 The tall, blonde, mannequin Mlle Lianette Le Duc demonstrated the tango skirt, dancing the one-step, the hesitation waltz and the *maxixe* with an amateur volunteer, in the absence of the professional dancer, and followed up with a solo demonstration of the *maxixe*. 'Dances in Tango Gown', *New York Times*, 7 March 1914; 'Fads and Fancies for Milady', *Washington Post*, 9 March 1914.

150 On tango footage in cinemas, see Claude Cherys, 'The Sunday Post Women's Page', *Washington Post*, 5 April 1914. On the louche atmosphere of Parisian dance schools, see Le Frotteur, 'Maison de danse', *Fantasio*, 1 June 1912, 767.

151 'New Dances Influence Paris Fashions for Spring Wear', *New York Times*, 12 April 1914.

152 'Wonders of Paris Frocks Shown Amid Picturesque Settings', *Washington Post*, 30 August 1914.

153 *New Orleans Times*, 5 April 1914. See also Gaston Davenay, 'La Vie de Paris: la naissance de la Mode', *Le Figaro*, 9 March 1914; 'The Paquin Gown of 1914: A Revolution in Woman's Silhouette', *Westminster Gazette*, 2 February 1914; 'Feminine Fashion will show Revolution in the Silhouette'; 'The Paquin Gown of 1914', *New York City Press*, 12 April 1914; *Le Monde illustré*, undated and untitled article by 'Countess Maud' from 1914.

154 My account of Delaunay's involvement in fashion is drawn largely from the following: Sherry Buckberrough, 'Sonia Delaunay entre le Paris des émigrés russes et la clientèle bourgeoisie éclairée', in Palais Galliera 1997, 100–05; Gronberg 1998; Tag Gronberg, 'Deco Venus' in Arscott and Scott 2000, 142–55; Gronberg 2002; Tag Gronberg, 'Sonia Delaunay's Simultaneous Fashions and the Modern Woman', in Chadwick and Latimer 2003, 109–23; Chris Townsend, 'Slave to the Rhythm: Sonia Delaunay's Fashion Project and the Fragmentary, Mobile Modernist Body', in Brand and Teunissen 2006, 360–81; Leeuw-de Monti and Timmer 2011.

155 Severini 1995, 53–4. Severini had moved to Paris in 1906 from where he kept Italian artists informed of Paris developments by correspondence. Boccioni, Carrà and Russolo visited Paris in October 1911.

156 The Italian Futurists' first Paris exhibition was at Galerie Bernheim-Jeune on 5–24 February 1912. It featured eleven paintings,

including Severini's *La Danse du 'pan-pan' au Monico*. The painting was destroyed, probably during the Second World War, but repainted by the artist from a postcard in Rome in 1959–60. Ottinger 2009, 166.

157 Davenay, 'La Vie de Paris', *Le Figaro*, 9 March 1914.

158 'Show Paris Gowns to an Eager Crowd', *New York Times*, 5 March 1914. 'Paquin inaugurates the most radical change of the season: the flare skirt', *Harper's Bazar*, July 1914, 52–3.

159 J. Laporte, 'La tournée du grand couturier', *Femina*, 1 June 1914, 341.

160 'Show Paris Gowns to an Eager Crowd', *New York Times*, 5 March 1914.

161 'The Paquin Gown of 1914', *New York City Press*, 12 April 1914; Davenay, 'Vie de Paris'.

162 '[U]ne allure très vingtième siècle . . . avec un minimum d'ampleur, de donner à la femme toute la liberté de ses mouvements . . . nous avons demandé à nos mannequins de vivre réellement'. Javotte, 'Chez ceux qui lancent la mode: chez Paquin', *Le Matin*, 21 March 1914.

163 '[C]onçue pour accompagner tous les mouvements de la marche et de la danse'. 'Une jupe nouvelle', *France commerce*, 1 April 1914.

164 'At the maison Paquin', *Sunday Times*, 22 March 1914.

165 'Paquin', *Le Figaro*, 14 April 1914.

166 'Paquin Gown of 1914', *Westminster Gazette*, 2 February 1914.

167 Steele 2000, 10, cited in Lisa Seantier, 'Les Archives sonores du défilé', in Musée Galliera 2006, 235.

168 Laporte, 'La tournée', 341.

169 Ross 2008, 76.

170 Ibid., 91.

171 Davis 2006, 2.

172 Ibid., 65. See also Davis 1999.

173 Ross 2008, 45.

174 Garafola 1998, 95, 100 and 115. With thanks to Alistair O'Neill who first brought my attention to Garafola's concept of lifestyle modernism.

175 Ross 2008, 106.

CHAPTER 3

1 Global time was fixed in 1884 when Greenwich, England, was made the zero meridian and the global day of 24 hours agreed. It was, however, opposed by the French until 1912 when, at the International Conference on Time in Paris, they accepted that the meridian would be English. Harvey 1989, 266; Griffiths 1999, 15.

2 Griffiths 1999, 17, 18–19 and 25–6.

3 Harvey 1989, 266.

4 'Fashion Departs from Straight and Narrow Path', *New York Times*, 10 October 1915.

5 Harvey 1989, 265–76. For an expanded discussion of changing perceptions of time and space from the mid-nineteenth century and the early twentieth, and their relation to modernism in the context of economic, technological and cultural change in the period, see Harvey 1989, 260–83, 'Time-Space Compression and the Rise of Modernism as a Cultural Force'.

6 Henri Lefebvre, *La Production de l'éspace*, Paris 1974, trans. and cited in Harvey 1989, 266.

7 Griffiths 1999, 16.

8 It is clear from the descriptions of the costumes in stage reviews that the theatre press was producing meticulously detailed fashion writing, sufficiently detailed for readers to be able to use it as a guide in copying or adapting stage costumes to their private wardrobes. There are many examples of this phenomenon in the Paquin Press Albums held in the Bath Fashion Museum. For the links among fashion, theatre and the emerging genre of the fashion show in England, see Kaplan and and Stowell 1994. For a searing French critique of the practice, see *La Poilue* 1916, a novel that includes pre-war scenes of launching new fashions in theatrical productions.

9 E.g. Saint-Léger, 'Comment se créent les modes', *L'Illustration*, 11 December 1897. The author describes the movement in Fuller's performance, achieved through the play of light and colour on fabric, which textile manufacturers and couturiers seek to reproduce.

10 Maxime du Camp cited in Richardson 1987, 113; Delbourg-Delphis 1981, 76. In 1913 a typical American report ran: 'Most of the ladies go to Longchamp or Auteuil not so much to look at the horses as at the mannequins and the dresses'. 'Tourists Swarm in Paris', *Washington Post*, 15 June 1913.

11 '[C]et essaim de jolies femmes qui semblaient s'être donné rendez-vous au pesage, comme des abeilles autour d'une ruche . . . ont défilé sans interruption de trois heures à cinq heures, au pied des tribunes.' Baronne de Spare, 'Art et chiffons', *L'Art et la mode*, 21 June 1890, 289.

12 Odette, 'Au Grand Steeple-chase d'Auteuil: mousselines et dentelles', *L'Illustration*, 6 June 1903, 379.

13 Ghenya, 'À Longchamp', *Le Figaro-Modes*, April 1904, 12–13.

14 Ibid.

15 'Jockeys' could receive substantial discounts of up to 75% for wearing new models; if the model had already been worn by the professional mannequin in the house and required some mending and cleaning, then the jockey paid nothing for it. Roubaud 1928, 170.

16 'Est-elle cliente? C'est un privilège d'être habillée gratuitement. Est-elle mannequin? C'est une injustice de n'être payée qu'en vanité.' Ibid.

17 Since the late nineteenth century, women such as the Marquise Hervey de St Denis, known as *lanceuses*, *jockeys* or *mannequins nobles*, had been given clothing and jewellery by the 'man milliners' Poole and Redfern and the jeweller Boucheron to promote in society circles. Marquise de Fontenoy, 'Penniless but Aristocratic', *Washington Post*, 16 March 1898; 'Marquise de Fontenoy's Letter', *Chicago Daily Tribune*, 16 March 1898. For twentieth-century accounts, see ' "Launchers of Fashion": How Paris Modes are Started on their Victorious Careers', *The Tatler*, 31 January 1906, 172; 'Pose at Modiste's Show', *Boston Daily Globe*, 22 December 1912; 'A Merry Holiday Prank of London Society Set', *Los Angeles Times*, 23 December 1912.

18 Xavier Demange, 'Mondanités', in Aubenas and Demange 2006, 33–4.

19 Fitz-Gerald, 'How Paris Fashions are Created and Launched', *Woman's Home Companion*, October 1905, 14–15, quoted in Reeder 1990, 11.

20 'Muff was Made Just Like Small Rug', *Boston Daily Globe*, 13 January 1907.

21 'Aux courses, ce n'est pas comme au Bois: "les femmes à photographier", les plus jolies et les plus excentriques, sont pour la plupart celles qu'on appelle les "mannequins", c'est à dire des femmes plus pomponnées encore que les autres, choisies pour venir montrer, au milieu de la foule du "pesage", des robes spécialement belles ou des chapeaux mirobolants fait par les grands couturiers ou les modistes. Une "jeune fille mannequin", c'est quelqu'un de spécial à qui les autres dames ne disent pas bonjour, qui sourit gentiment au lieu de se fâcher quand je la vise dans mon appareil, et se promène partout sans jamais s'occuper des chevaux.' Entry for 30 March 1911, Lartigue 1975, 97; see also entry for 29 May 1910, ibid., 80.

22 Even as late as 1937, the mannequin protagonist of a popular novel gets into trouble with her employer for masquerading as a woman of the world and flirting with a client's husband at the races where she has been sent to model. She is chatted up by a viscount and she implies she is a *femme du monde* by talking about the couture customers as if they were her friends. The viscount is fooled and then astounded when the couturier comes back and says genially 'ah! Caught you out, Robert, paying court to my mannequin!' Nevertheless, she reports, her ensemble was a success, and she was photographed three times. Clairin 1937, 75–6.

23 The fullest description of the three mannequins is in Pierre Wolff, 'Les "Merveilleuses" de la troisième république', *L'Illustration*, 16 May 1908, reprinted in *L'Illustration: Journal Universel* 1987, 84–5. See also Georges Grappe, 'La commerce des revues' and 'Le Jolie Mensonge des merveilleuses', *Fantasio*, 15 June 1908, 990–93; Idalia de Villiers, 'Dangers of the Directoire Style', *Boston Daily Globe*, 14 June 1908 (reporting four not three mannequins). Although the event was widely reported in the French and foreign press, none named the couturier, giving rise to much speculation as to who it was. Only one journalist who did the rounds of the couture houses the next day,

including Worth, Paquin, Drecoll and Doucet, identified the designer as Margaine Lacroix. 'More Light on the Spring Gown that Scandalized the Parisians', *Washington Post*, 24 May 1908; 'French Modistes Differ on the Directoire Gowns', *New York Times*, 24 May 1908. Later sources which substantiate the identification of Margaine Lacroix are Le Mannequin d'Hozier, 'Modanités', *Fantasio*, 15 November 1908, 283 (which also describes their being accompanied to the races by a *couturière*, also suggesting Mme Lacroix); *La Ville Lumière* 1909, 535 (although identifying the racecourse as Auteuil not Longchamp); Delbourg-Delphis 1981, 35 (who cites the Tanagra dresses but not the designer); Woon 1926, 75. These primary sources combine to outweigh the claims of both Poiret himself and of later historians. Poiret 1931; White 1973, 41; White, 'Mesdames' and 'Text of a lecture on Paul Poiret', n.d., 55 and 24; Deslandres 1987; Mackrell 1990.

24 Wolff, 'Les "Merveilleuses" '.

25 'Poor Girls Wear Gorgeous Gowns', *Boston Daily Globe*, 22 December 1912.

26 Lartigue 1975, 97.

27 It had some basis in truth, because mannequins were poorly paid and many were also kept women. As an old lady, Vera Ashby, who had modelled as Sumurun for Lucile and Molyneux in the 1910s–20s, recalled: 'I hated the position of the women like us. Most of the models were kept, or as we used to say then, "looked after" by men'. Keenan 1977, 111–13.

28 *L'Opinion*, 23 May 1908. A week after *L'Illustration*'s report on 16 May, a Chicago chorus girl was sighted in a sheath gown which Schweitzer suggests must have been a copy based on photographs of Paris mannequins. Schweitzer 2009, 147 n. 28.

29 'More Light on the Spring Gown', *Washington Post*, 24 May 1908; 'French Modistes Differ', *New York Times*, 24 May 1908.

30 Le Mannequin d'Hozier, 'Modanités', *Fantasio*, 15 June 1910, 786.

31 Mary Buel, 'Clothes Worn at the Grand Prix', *Chicago Daily Tribune*, 11 August 1912; Mary Buel, 'Radical Changes in Paris Fashions', *Chicago Daily Tribune*, 24 August 1913.

32 'Beautiful Waistcoats of Duvetyn Among Recent Imported Novelties', *New York Times*, 3 August 1913; 'Fleecy Gowns of Hand-Painted Gauze', *Boston Daily Globe*, 26 October 1913.

33 When the seventeen-year-old Lartigue saw his first fashion show in the rue de la Paix, he described the Paquin and Poiret dresses in his diary for 15 December 1911 as being 'worn by mannequins like those at the races, that's to say tall, young, living women'. Lartigue 1975, 112.

34 Alice Ivimy, *A Woman's Guide to Paris*, London: James Nesbitt, 1909, 92, cited in Steele 1998, 170.

35 'Exquisite Gowns of Costly Simplicity Displayed at Garden Parties by French Fashion Leaders', *Washington Post*, 14 June 1914. With thanks to Martina Grünewald for identifying Breitschwanz, the sheepskin from which the parasol was made.

36 'Poor Girls Wear Gorgeous Gowns', *Boston Daily Globe*, 22 December 1912.

37 'At Fall Race-Meet: Toilettes of Fashionables at Longchamps Offer Many Good Suggestions', *Dry Goods Economist*, 2 October 1909; 'Spring Weather Delights Paris', *New York Times*, 5 April 1914; 'Ideas that Promise to Survive and Some of Those Now Doomed', *New York Times*, 5 April 1914.

38 'La grande journée des mannequins', *Femina*, 15 June 1910, 310–11; 'Snapshots taken on the Bois de Boulogne', *Dry Goods Economist*, 12 August 1911, 27; 'Hold Back the New Styles', *New York Times*, 25 February 1912. For further descriptions of the crowds of professionals at the races, see 'Fashion's Fads and Fancies', *Washington Post*, 28 February 1912; Bessie Ascough, 'Fashions Direct from Paris', *Chicago Daily Tribune*, 31 July 1914.

39 'Grande journée', *Femina*, 15 June 1910, 312.

40 'Dès que l'une d'elles [les mannequins] pénétrait aux tribunes, au pesage, un essaim de parasites l'entourait de mille supplices. Vingt petites couturières, l'oeil cligné, les lèvres pincées, comme pour retenir encore un cent d'épingles, disséquaient la robe, scalpent le chapeau. Des dessinatrices se penchaient, avec un sourire, un aire de demander l'aumône et traîtreusement esquissaient une fiche d'anthropométrie, plus exactement de gynémétrie. Les cinématographistes et les photographes bousculeurs tiraient leur mitraille à images et bloquaient avec leurs trépieds des Pythies de la mode qui faisait pitié.' Régis Gignoux, 'Aux courses', *Gazette du Bon Ton*, June 1914, 193–6.

41 'Hold Back the New Styles', *New York Times*, 25 February 1912; 'Fashion's Fads', *Washington Post*, 28 February 1912; 'Paris Dressmakers Withhold Models', *New York Times*, 9 April 1912; 'Hues of Rainbow in Spring Gowns', *New York Times*, 17 February 1913; 'Costumers Angry', *New York Times*, 8 December 1913.

42 'Americans Lose No Time', *New York Times*, 24 August 1913.

43 'Une Croisade: les couturiers déclarent la guerre aux photographes', *Excelsior*, 6 December 1913; 'Fashions Filched by the Camera', *Daily News* (London), 8 December 1913.

44 'Ideas that Promise', *New York Times*, 5 April 1914.

45 'Facts, Features and Fancies for Women', *Los Angeles Times*, 14 August 1909.

46 'La Grande Semaine', *Harper's Bazar*, October 1913, 40.

47 The Hotel Ruhl in Nice inaugurated tea dances in January 1913 and even more successful dress parades from March 1913. Idalia de Villiers, 'Bunchy Draperies the New Fad', *Boston Daily Globe*, 22 March 1914. By 1914 hotel competition was so stiff in Nice that one advertised regular afternoon entertainments including ragtime dances, singers from La Scala Opera and a mannequin parade of the latest Paris gowns. 'Princess Quits Retirement', *Washington Post*, 23 February 1914.

48 Sometimes the Riviera fashions were shown to the buyers in the resorts in February, sometimes they saw them in Paris before the same fashions were shipped to the resorts to be shown to the private clients in March. 'Spring Fashions Not Yet Decreed by Paris Arbiters', *New York Times*, 18 January 1914.

49 Villiers, 'Bunchy Draperies'.

50 'Grande Semaine', *Harper's Bazar*, October 1913, 40, 59–60 and 79.

51 Le Mannequin d'Hozier, 'Modanités', *Fantasio*, 1 September 1910, 108.

52 Leon Fauret's 'The Liner as a Substitute for the Racecourse: "Models" Aboard Ship', *Illustrated London News*, 27 May 1911, 785; also 'Les Mannequins à Bord', *Femina*, 15 May 1911, 261.

53 '[C]'est le dernier mot du progrès et du pratique', *Femina*, 15 May 1911, 261.

54 'Ocean-Going Mannequins', *Boston Daily Globe*, 29 November 1914.

55 'Fashions Not Exclusive Even With Paris Gowns', *Washington Post*, 19 March 1911. For a thorough and meticulous treatment of newsreel film and fashion shows, see Tolini-Finamore 2013, ch. 4, 'Goddesses from the Machine: The Fashion Show on Film'.

56 Many examples from 1909 onwards can be seen on the French Gaumont-Pathé website, some under *défilé* and many more simply under *mode*. See www.gaumontpathearchives.com.

57 Leese 1976, 9.

58 Reel Observer, 'In the Moving Picture World', *Chicago Daily Tribune*, 26 November 1911; see also Hanssen 2009.

59 The earliest in the Gaumont-Pathé archives is *Paris: l'actrice Lucie Hamard presente la mode Laferrière dans un salon* (1912, Journal Gaumont), GP ref. 1214GJ 00009, followed by *Arlette Dorgère, chez Drecoll* (1913, Gaumont), GP ref. 1309GJ 00003.

60 Tolini-Finamore 2013, ch. 4.

61 Tétart-Vittu in Musée de la Mode et du Costume 1992, 35 nn. 13 and 14.

62 P.V., 'Notes de Carnet', *L'Art et la mode*, 5 December 1896, 924.

63 Poiret 1931, 80.

64 'Snap Shots at Social Leaders', *Washington Post*, 15 May 1909.

65 *Evening News* (London), 5 July 1920 (Poiret was reported as describing the 1909 date).

66 The number of press articles was counted in 1920 and given as evidence in the English courts when Poiret successfully sued the London-based theatrical costumier trading as 'Jules Poiret, Ltd' in a passing off action. *Evening Standard*, 5 July 1920; *Glasgow Daily Record*, 6 July 1920.

67 Poiret 1931, 153.

68 Ganeva 2008, 121; Mila Ganeva, 'Elegance and Spectacle in Berlin: The *Gerson* Fashion Store and the Rise of the Modern Fashion Show', in Potvin 2009, 121–38. Heather Hess,

'The Wiener Werkstätte and the Reform Impulse', in Blaszczyk 2008, 123. On the cost of the tour, see Robert, 'Tagesneuigkeiten: Poiret in Wien. Die gestrige Generalprobe', *Wiener Sonn- und Montagszeitung*, 27 November 1911, 6. On the tour in general, see Le Mannequin d'Hozier, 'Modanités', *Fantasio*, 15 December 1911, 373–4.

69 Only six mannequins, each a different height and size, from a 'small medium' to a 'slender majestic' one, are described in a Viennese newspaper: Robert, 'Tagesneuigkeiten', 6.

70 Poiret 1931, 117.

71 Heather Hess, 'The Lure of Vienna: Poiret and the Wiener Werkstätte', in Koda and Bolton 2007, 39–40. On Poiret's sojourn in Vienna, on 25–7 and possibly also 28–9 November 1911, see Claire Batek, 'Die neuesten Poiret-Modell', *Neues Wiener Journal*, 26 November 1911, 11; 'Die Abendkleider in Paris', *Prager tagblatt*, 26 November 1911, 30; Robert, 'Tagesneuigkeiten', 2; C. P., 'Was Monsieur Poiret über die Mode denkt: Eine Unterredung mit dem Modekünstler', *Neues Wiener Journal*, 26 November 1911, 5; 'Tagesneuigkeiten', *Montagszeitung*, 27 November 1911, n.p.; 'Poiret in Wien', *Wiener Zeitung*, 27 November 1911, 3; Robert, 'Tagesneuigkeiten. Poiret in Wien', 6; 'Tagesneuigkeiten: Generalprobe Poiret', *Neues Wiener Journal*, 27 November 1911, 1; 'Die erste Poiret-Confèrence in der Urania: Zugunsten der Vereine Lupusheilstätte, Wiener Wärmestuben und erstes öffentliches Krankenhaus', *Neues Wiener Journal*, 28 November 1911, 3; 'Das Schönheitsideal in der Frauentoilette: Conference Paul Poiret', *Unterhaltungs-Beilage des "Prager Tagblatt"*, 3 December 1911, 17; Fritz Huber, 'Der Wiener Modeclub gegen Poiret', *Neues Wiener Journal*, 3 December 1911, 3. With thanks to Marketa Uhlirova for finding these references and many thanks to Martina Grünewald for translating them and for researching a detailed chronology of Poiret's Vienna stay.

72 Robert, 'Tagesneuigkeiten: Poiret in Wien', 6. Poiret's lecture at the Urania department-store theatre on 27 November 1911, accompanied by a film, was attended by Josef Hoffmann, Gustav Klimt and Kolo Moser. 'Die erste Poiret-Confèrence', 3.

73 The surviving garment is illustrated in Koda and Bolton 2007, 66–9 and can also be seen on the website of the Costume Institute, Metropolitan Museum of Art, New York.

74 White 1973, 37 and 62.

75 See colour illustration of Poiret and his mannequins at a restaurant table in Lyon on the cover of *Art, goût, beauté*, June 1912.

76 Poiret 1931, 117.

77 'To Bring 100 Gowns', *New York Times*, 7 September 1913.

78 The film also contained scenes of him cutting and creating a dress on the living mannequin. No footage survives. In Vienna in 1911, it was screened before the live fashion show. 'Die erste Poiret-Confèrence in der Urania', 3; see

also Troy 2003, 212; White, 'Text of a lecture', 2003, 20.

79 'Poiret's Elaborate Reception', *Dry Goods Economist*, 23 September 1911, 42; 'Man Better Dressmaker', *Washington Post*, 24 December 1911.

80 'Poiret, Creator of Fashion Here', *New York Times*, 21 September 1913; see also Tolini-Finamore 2013.

81 'Poiret, Creator of Fashion Here', *New York Times*, 21 September 1913; *Sketch* supplement, 1 April 1914, 8–9.

82 'Wants Women to be Audacious in Dress', *New York Times*, 26 September 1913; 'Poiret and the Fashions', ibid., 27 September 1913; 'Poiret Startles Chicago Women', *Chicago Daily Tribune*, 7 October 1913.

83 'Kinemacolor is taking natural pictures of the latest creations of Paul Poiret, the Parisian designer, including a number of radiant and diaphanous garments . . . M. Poiret is in this country at present, lecturing on women's styles, and is personally watching the production.' 'Poiret Creations Pictured', *Motography*, vol. x, no. 8, 18 October 1913, 296.

84 Leese 1976, 10. On Roman Catholic criticism, see Tolini-Finamore 2013 [ch. 4, n. 82] and White, unpublished lecture, 2003, 20–21.

85 'Some Striking New Styles – French Dressmakers Now Visit North America', *New York Times*, 31 August 1913; 'King of Gowns Due Tomorrow', *Chicago Daily Tribune*, 5 October 1913.

86 'Paul Poiret in a Custom Dispute', *New York Times*, 27 January 1914. The cushions, which were judged to be worth double the value that he had declared them at, incurred an additional 30% aggregated penalty. Poiret sold them to a New York retailer before his departure from the U.S.A.

87 At the Blackstone Hotel in Chicago, 'Mme Poiret wore several of her husband's inventions during the day, and red Russian leather boots,' reported the *Chicago Daily Tribune* which described Poiret's designs as 'oddities' and quoted several prominent Chicago dressmakers who scoffed at his color combinations, his extreme designs and his dresses 'like Christmas trees'. 'Poiret Startles Chicago Women,' *Chicago Daily Tribune*, 7 October 1913.

88 'The Prophet of Simplicity', *Vogue* (America), 1 November 1913, 42–3 and 142.

89 On Poiret's use of Denise as his mannequin, see Caroline Evans, 'Denise Poiret: Muse or Mannequin?', in Koda and Bolton 2007, 27–8.

90 'House Gowns Minus Corsets', *Los Angeles Times*, 24 September 1913.

91 In New York alone, where his host was John Wanamaker (the son of the founder of the department store), Poiret lectured at the Horace Mann School, the Pratt Institute in Brooklyn, Columbia University and the department stores of J. F. Gidding, Gimbel Brothers, R. H. Macy and Wanamaker's. On his various lecture venues and Denise's

appearance at his side, see 'Wants Women to be Audacious', *New York Times*, 26 September 1913; 'Brings Latest Style', *Washington Post*, 1 October 1913; ' "No Immodesty in Dress-Art" ', Says Designer', *Christian Science Monitor*, 2 October 1913; 'M Paul Poiret in Boston', *Boston Daily Globe*, 3 October 1913; 'King of Gowns Due Tomorrow', *Chicago Daily Tribune*, 5 October 1913; 'Trouser Skirts Predicted', *Washington Post*, 7 October 1913; 'Trouser Skirt is Sure to Come', *Boston Daily Globe*, 7 October 1913. See Troy 2003, 212.

92 'Costumes: Paul Poiret Criticises the Commercialization and Capitalization of his Visit to the Country', *Women's Wear*, 22 September 1913, 1, cited in Troy 2003, 215.

93 Troy 2003, 215. ' "No Immodesty in Dress-Art" ', *Christian Science Monitor*, 2 October 1913.

94 Troy 2003, 212.

95 In both 1911 and 1912 the *Dry Goods Economist* had reported that Poiret's orientalist, wire-hemmed Minaret gowns were insufficiently commercial to warrant any coverage. One described 'the so-called "crinoline" dresses, introduced in Paris by the harem skirt man, Poiret – which, by the way, are not crinoline dresses at all, but Oriental gowns having a light boning in the hem of the tunic. Since they possess no merchandising value, these productions have no interest for the trade.' 'Fashions in Your Town', *Dry Goods Economist*, 23 September 1911, 3. See also 'Fall Fashions Displayed in New York Stores', ibid., 5 October 1912, 117. In October 1913, however, both Gidding and Wanamaker imported the minaret-style tunic and Gimbel claimed to have imported it in 1912, according to Troy 2003, 217. See 'The Style Influence of "Le Minaret" ', *Women's Wear*, October 1913, 4–5. In Paris, the milliner Mme Georgette had been the first to wear the Minaret tunic in public after Poiret had invented it for the stage; she wore it at The Drags, where it was immediately copied, according to American *Vogue*, though it is not clear by whom. Anne Rittenhouse, 'The Women Who Create the Mode in Paris', *Vogue* (America), November 1914, 52–3 and 100. Wanamaker's version of Poiret's Sorbet model was illustrated in *Harper's Bazar* alongside two other Poiret models imported by Gidding & Co, next to a short article describing Poiret's Persian Fête in Paris. 'Exclusive Poiret Costumes', *Harper's Bazar*, November 1913, 37.

96 Troy 2003, 232.

97 Ibid., 227 and 223; 'Poiret Belittles Our Women', *Los Angeles Times*, 2 November 1913.

98 Troy 2003, 227.

99 Ibid., 229.

100 Green 1997, 107–8.

101 Ibid., 106.

102 For Poiret's response to the situation see Troy 2003, 232–6.

103 'Paquin to Exhibit Here', *New York Times*, 13 February 1914.

104 Ibid. 'Paris Openings Show No Gowns Radically New in Style', *New York Times*, 1 March 1914.

105 'Certains couturiers méritent-il le nom de couturiers? Plutôt des *fabricants étrangers* ne reculent devant aucune contrefaçon ont pris l'habitude de démarquer très adroitement les modèles que nous lancions, de supprimer leur personnalité, leur marque d'origine, de leur laisser toutefois un demi-cachet parisien, d'en faire en un mot des articles d'exportation et de les lancer dans les deux Amériques, à grand renfort de réclame et de publicité. Comme ces productions avaient malgré tout une allure française et que fabriquées par séries – comme on dit pour les automobiles – elles pouvaient se vendre à des prix défiant toute concurrence, nous étions distancés sur le marché américain qui, comme chacun sait, est le plus important du monde.' Jean Laporte, 'La Tournée du grand couturier', *Femina*, 1 June 1914, 339, and see Troy 2003, 249, for her translation and discussion of this passage.

106 'La dépense engage à cette époque pour une tell'entreprise dépassa 500,000 francs.' *Histoire de l'industrie* 1926, 112.

107 This account is derived from the following press sources: 'Foll'modes', *Fantasio*, 1 February 1914, 469; 'Paquin to Exhibit Here', *New York Times*, 13 February 1914; 'Latest Paris Fashion News by Cable to the Times: Merry War on to Keep Paris Dressmakers from New York', *New York Times*, 22 February 1914; 'Says We Don't See many Good Styles', *New York Times*, 26 February 1914; 'New Dances Inspire a Style in Skirts', *New York Times*, 2 March 1914; 'Show Paris Gowns to an Eager Crowd', *New York Times*, 5 March 1914; 'Display Ad 6', *New York Times*, 4 March 1914; 'Dances in Tango Gown', *New York Times*, 7 March 1914; 'Fads and Fancies for Milady', *Washington Post*, 9 March 1914; 'The Models Shown at Maison Paquin', *Vogue* (America), 15 March 1914; 'So Say the Paris Openings,' ibid.; 'Gowns from Paris', *Boston Daily Globe*, 18 March 1914; 'Boston Goes to See the Latest Paquin Gowns', *Boston Daily Globe*, 21 March 1914; 'French Mannequins Finish Their Tour', *New York Times*, 25 March 1914; 'Paquin Mannequins to Show Gowns', *New York Times*, 26 March 1914; '60,000 Went to See Paquin Gowns', *New York Times*, 29 March 1914; Laporte, 'Tournée', 339–42; Suzanne Joire, 'My Impressions of American Department Stores', *Dry Goods Guide*, June 1914, 16–17; *Histoire de l'industrie* 1926, 112; see also Steele 1998, 236; Troy 2003, 223; Font 2012, 36.

108 The sources vary from four, six to even a dozen mannequins. The *Femina* illustration in Laporte's article shows seven. Most American press reports of the Paquin fashion shows on the tour describe a combination of three to four French mannequins who modelled alongside two American mannequins employed locally.

109 Laporte, 'Tournée', 342.

110 'Show Paris Gowns to an Eager Crowd', *New York Times*, 5 March 1914.

111 'Le projecteur fuse une clarté orange derechef [sic] l'orchestre repart'; 'Les acclamations imposent silence à l'orchestre: le thé se refroidit dans les tasses'; 'Les perruques de couleur attisent des flammes contre les épaules masculines' and 'Mais l'admiration se traduit par les mêmes gestes sous toutes les latitudes . . . des oh! Des ah! . . . s'adressent tant aux "coloured wigs" qu'aux robes conçues également pour la lente mélopée du tango et la vivacité de la très-moutarde.' Laporte, 'Tournée', 341.

112 'Boston Goes to See', *Boston Daily Globe*, 21 March 1914.

113 'D'admirables types de femmes ces Américaines, grandes, étoffées, sportives, qui donnaient une allure noble et caractéristique aux robes dont elles se revêtaient. Pour faire ressortir le côté étranger de cette exhibition, des mannequins hommes alternaient avec leurs camarades femme et entre une robe de soirée et une jupe de golf, un pyjama à rayures mauves ou un pardessus à revers de faille grise était mise en valeur par de jeunes hommes minces et bien découplés.' Laporte, 'Tournée', 342.

114 Display Ad 19, *Atlanta Constitution*, 11 March 1914.

115 In New York, entry was charged at $3 rising to $5 when the shows were over-subscribed; in other cities entry was $2. Display Ad, *Chicago Daily Tribune*, 15 March 1914; Display Ad 36, *Boston Daily Globe*, 19 March 1914; Laporte, 'Tournée', 341.

116 Display Ad, *Chicago Daily Tribune*, 15 March 1914; 'Gowns from Paris', *Boston Daily Globe*, 18 March 1914; Display Ad 36, *Boston Daily Globe*, 19 March 1914. Exceptionally, the Chicago show was held in a theatre and the audience sat in theatre seats.

117 Troy 2003, 251 and preceding discussion 248–51.

118 See nn. 100 and 101 above.

119 'French Mannequins Finish Their Tour', *New York Times*, 25 March 1914.

120 'Latest Paris Fashion News', *New York Times*, 22 February 1914.

121 Louise Lederer, 'An interesting interview with Madame Paquin – Yesterday, To-day and To-morrow', *Lady's Mode*, May 1913, 924–7.

122 Joire, 'My Impressions', 16–17.

123 Books on Taylorism appeared in France in 1913 and 1917. Goldberg 1991, 67.

124 For the integration of Taylorist ideas into French fashion production, see Stewart 2001, 191–2. On Taylorism in France, see Meuleau 1992; Kanigel 1997; Moutet 1997. For an account of how Taylorism affected women workers in France in the inter-war years, see Reynolds 1996, 99–105, who describes how during the war the American system was pioneered in French munitions factories and was known in France, interchangeably, as Taylorism, *la rationalisation* or Fordism and as *OST*, or *l'organisation scientifique du travail*. For a summary of the way the French responded to Taylorism after approximately 1925, see Roberts 1994, 187. By way of contrast, see Roubaud who, in 1928, argued in romantic terms that haute couture had resisted American rationalisation and that 'M. Taylor, in imagining his system, could not have imagined the imponderable or foreseen a formula to restrain "the air of Paris", or to mechanise the little fingers of our working girls' ('M. Taylor, en imaginant son système n'avait pu penser l'impondérable ni prévoir une formule pour comprimer "l'air de Paris" ou pour mécaniser les petits doigts des filles de nos faubourgs'). Roubaud 1928, 216.

125 On European artists' and couturiers' ideas about *américanisme*, that is, 'the myth and the reality of American industry, consumerism and the "new" American woman', in the mid-1910s, see Troy 2003, 267.

126 Giedion 1969, 213 ff.

127 Ibid., 228–40.

128 'Enfin, c'est Chicago: pour les divertir et les remercier du défilé inoubliable de leurs minceurs engainées d'étoffes précieuses, un milliardaire galant conduit les mannequins aux abattoirs et leur offre le défilé des animaux sous le couteau du sacrificateur. Rien n'est plus saisissant que de voir descendre sur une glissière, toboggan infernal, une longue théorie de malheureux cochons qui, en un instant, sont happés par une pince d'acier et ont la tête tranchée d'un seul coup.' Laporte, 'Tournée', 341–2.

129 Ibid., 339.

130 Walter Benjamin, 'Konvolut B (Fashion)', in Benjamin 1999, 62.

131 Giedion 1969, 240 and 242.

CHAPTER 4

1 Green 1997, 116–18.

2 'American Women Responsible for Sensational French Styles', *New York Times*, 5 July 1914; 'The Dressmakers of the US', *Fortune*, December 1933, 37–8. On the appeal of French fashion to American women in the years before the First World War, see Kristin Hoganson, 'The Fashionable World: Imagined Communities of Dress', in Burton 2003, 260–78. On the emergence of the American fashion movement in the 1910s, see Green 1997, 113–14; Marlis Schweitzer, 'American Fashions for American Women: The Rise and Fall of Fashion Nationalism', in Blaszczyk 2008, 130–49; Sandra Stansbery Buckland, 'Promoting American Designers, 1910–44: Building Our Own House', in Welters and Cunningham 2005, 99–121; Pouillard 2011, 336–7. For the development of American fashion in the 1930s, see Arnold 2009. On the American garment trade's continuing reliance on the idea of French taste, see Naether 1928, 79 and Hawes 1938, 94.

3 My account is derived from the following: 'New York Fashion Show', *Washington Post*, 31 August 1903; 'Fashion Show', *Hartford*

Courant, 31 August 1903; 'Fashion Show Opens at Garden', *New York Tribune*, 1 September 1903; 'Fashion Show Opening', *New York Times*, 1 September 1903; 'New York Fashion Show Opens', *Washington Post*, 1 September 1903; 'Conjunction of Depew and Cortelyou', ibid; 'Women Rush to See Fashion Show', *Chicago Daily Tribune*, 1 September 1903; 'Acres of Latest Modes', *Boston Daily Globe*, 1 September 1903; 'Fashion Show Opens at Garden', *New York Tribune*, 1 September 1903; 'New Dress Models for Fashion Show', *New York Times*, 2 September 1903; 'Wedding Reception at Fashion Show', *New York Tribune*, 4 September 1903; 'Bridegroom's Clothes Did Not Fit', *New York Tribune*, 5 September 1903; 'Fashion Show's Prize Gowns', *New York Times*, 8 September 1903; 'Devery to Attend Fashion Show', *New York Tribune*, 8 September 1903; 'To Give Instruction in Dressing,' *New York Daily Tribune*, 9 September 1903; 'Asks Receiver for Fashion Show', *New York Tribune*, 9 September 1903; 'New York City', *New York Tribune*, 12 September 1903; 'Vaudeville', *New York Times*, 13 September 1903; 'Plan Fashion Show for Next Year', *New York Tribune*, 13 September 1903; 'Shown on Living Models: Ehrich Bros' Innovation in Display of Imported Garments and Hats', *Dry Goods Economist*, 10 October 1903, 14.

4 Germain Lacasse, 'The Lecturer and the Attraction', in Strauven 2006, 181–91.

5 Leach 1994, 101.

6 My account is derived from the following: *Wanamaker Herald*, Philadelphia, March 1905; *Wanamaker Anniversary Herald*, 11 April 1908, 1; *Wanamaker Originator*, November 1908 (this issue of the house newspaper reprinted four American press articles that provide much of the information about the 1908 show: 'Living Pictures of Empire Fashion', *The Philadelphia North American*, 2 October 1908; 'Gowns at Wanamaker's, Exquisite Paris Creations Exhibited on Living Models', *The Philadelphia Enquirer*, 2 October 1908; Harriet Hubbard Ayer, *The New York World*, n.d.; 'Fête de Paris a Glance at Past', n.d.). See also Wanamaker 1911, 201.

7 Abel 1998, 94–5 and 492. On the film's American distribution in 1903–4, Abel cites Charles Musser, *High-Class Moving Pictures: Lyman H. Howe and the Forgotten Era of Travelling Exhibition, 1880-1920*, Princeton University Press, 1991, 137–8. They suggest that the tableaux enacted by the mannequins in the show were recreations of earlier French paintings of scenes from the lives of Napoleon and Josephine and David's *Madame Récamier*, Elisabeth Vigée-Lebrun's *Self-Portrait with her Child* and, as a finale, David's *Coronation of Napoleon and Josephine*. Furthermore, in fashion imagery of the early 1900s, Josephine, Empress of France, was often represented, as here, as 'Empress of Fashion' and many fashion mannequins were renamed Josephine.

8 The balance of evidence suggests that the sheath dress modelled here was by Margaine Lacroix and not, as many historians have suggested, Poiret. In New York, mannequins wore coloured tights under their slit Sylphide dresses at several of the autumn 1908 shows. The colour combinations suggest Poiret as a possible designer: 'Napoleon blue' tights and slippers with a buff dress, green tights under a champagne-coloured dress and cherry tights under a mole-coloured dress. However, the off-centre front slit, sometimes with buttons holding the slit together, make it far more likely, in conjunction with the information in Ch. 3 n. 23 above, that Margaine Lacroix was the designer. Marie Olivier, 'Latest Hints from Paris', *Harper's Bazar*, September 1908, 855–7; 'Famous Author and Fashion Writer of the New York Sun Proclaims Wanamaker's Exhibition of Fashions the Greatest in America', *Wanamaker Originator*, 1908 (Historical Society of Pennsylvania, Wanamaker Papers, Box 75, folder *Wanamaker's Originator*, 1908, 1909).

9 McCullough 1986; Chapman 1996; Hillel Schwartz, 'Torque: The New Kinaesthetic of the Twentieth Century', in Crary and Kwinter 1992, 97–8; Schwartz 1996, 66–7.

10 This practice, common to some film shows of the period, had already featured in film shows held in Wanamaker's Egyptian Hall in New York. 'Paul Revere's Ride as shown in the motion pictures in Egyptian Hall', *Wanamaker Anniversary Herald*, 7 April 1908, 3.

11 John Wanamaker's son Rodman ran the Wanamaker Paris Bureau from 1890 to 1898 and was largely responsible for introducing French ideals of taste to the American stores. On his return to the U.S.A., he worked first with his father in Philadelphia and then took command of the New York store in 1911. 'Gowns at Wanamaker's', *Philadelphia Enquirer*, 2 October 1908, from *Wanamaker Originator*, November 1908. See also Coleman 1990, 34 and Leach 1994, 100.

12 On fashion intermediaries, see Blaszczyk 2002, esp. the intro; Entwistle 2009; Polese and Blaszczyk 2012, 6.

13 'Fête de Paris a Glance at Past', *Wanamaker Originator*, November 1908.

14 *Wanamaker Originator*, 12 March 1909.

15 'Gowns at Wanamaker's', *Philadelphia Enquirer*, 2 October 1908.

16 *Illustrated London News*, 1 January 1910, 30; *Femina*, 15 July 1910, 385. The *Femina* caption wrongly stated that the show took place in New York, but the *Illustrated London News* correctly identified the venue as the Philadelphia store.

17 'Nos voisins d'outre-Atlantique voient tout en grand; on pourrait même dire – et cette photographie vient à l'appui – en colossal! Comparez cette immense "champ" d'élégance où, devant une foule d'acheteuses, passent et repassent des mannequins qui doivent faire ainsi pas mal de kilomètres dans la journée, à nos modestes salons, où

cinquante dames réunies étoufferaient. Le document que nous présentons aujourd'hui à nos lectrices a été pris a l'heure du "shopping", dans les établissements Wanamaker, la merveille du genre, le magasin de nouveautés où l'on vend de tout, des modes et de la cuisine, des lacets de bottes et des chevaux!' *Femina*, 15 July 1910, 385.

18 'L'américanisation de la femme', entry for 16 January 1877, Goncourt, vol. II, 1956, and E. Gomez Carrillo, *Psychologie de la mode*, 1910, cited in Delbourg-Delphis 1981, 86.

19 'New York Has No Laughter and Young Girls', *New York Times*, 19 October 1913.

20 'Our Girls Puritans, Is M. Poiret's Idea', *New York Times*, 14 October 1913.

21 Schweitzer 2009, 180.

22 Ibid., 179, citing the *Merchants Record and Show Window*, November 1909, 39.

23 'Events in Society Circles', *Chicago Daily Tribune*, 17 March 1912.

24 'Very Pretty Work: Women Now Receive Compensation Simply Wearing the Costliest and Most Exquisite of Dresses', *Boston Daily Globe*, 29 September 1907; 'Style Manikins. Important Factor in Selling Clothes. Well Known in Paris, but an Innovation in America', *Boston Sunday Globe*, 6 December 1914.

25 Leach 1994, 103.

26 Ibid.

27 Ibid., 101–2.

28 Ibid., 110–11.

29 Ibid., 105–7 and 110–11.

30 Troy 2003, 212–28.

31 'French Gowns at Macy's: Elaborate Display of latest Creation', *Dry Goods Economist*, 23 September 1911, 27; 'Highly Distinctive Ad: Attractive Publicity in Connection with Macy's Imported Gown Display', *Dry Goods Economist*, 30 September 1911, 41.

32 Leach 1994, 102 and Schweitzer 2009, 182. Gimbel's Promenade des Toilettes became a regular, twice-yearly fixture over the following years. For subsequent 'promenades des toilette', see 'Importance of Detail in Afternoon Gowns', *New York Times*, 30 March 1913; 'Poiret Belittles Our Women', *Los Angeles Times*, 2 November 1913; Display Ad 20 – No Title, *New York Times*, 15 March 1914; Display Ad 5 – No Title, ibid., 17 March 1914; Display Ad 7 – No Title, ibid., 25 March 1914; Display Ad 20 – No Title, ibid., 4 October 1914. For a photograph of three models from the Gimbel's Promenade des Toilettes, see 'Button-in-Front Dresses at Last, at Last!' *Washington Post*, 1 April 1914.

33 My account is derived from the following: 'Fall Fashions Displayed in New York Stores', *Dry Goods Economist*, 5 October 1912, 117; 'Paris Fashions on Parade in Autumn Bower', unidentified New York newspaper cutting, Paquin press albums, 9 October 1912.

34 'The Paris Fashion Fête', *Vogue* (America), 15 December 1915, 33–52, esp. 35. The use of raised runways was recommended as early as 1911: 'Use of Living Models: Should Be Done

Right, If at All – How to Obtain Models', *Dry Goods Economist*, 19 August 1911, 41–2. A 700-foot long raised runway is described in 'Even Standing Room a Premium During Gimbel's Promenade', *Dry Goods Economist*, 31 March 1917, 7. See also 'In the Social World', *New York Times*, 28 March 1920; 'Society Women in a Fashion Review', ibid., 13 April 1920.

35 Following Lucile's precedent, in 1913 Schneider-Anderson, a New York dressmaker that designed for fashion and the stage, installed a semi-circular raised and canopied modelling stage fitted with curtains and stage lights. 'The Drawing Room', *Vogue* (America), 1 June 1913, 56.

36 Schweitzer 2009, 187.

37 Carter 1974, 41.

38 Mizejewski 1999, 91 and Leach 1994, 145, cited in Schweitzer 2009, 187.

39 I am grateful to Randy Bigham for his help in clarifying many of the details. My account is derived from the following: 'Fashion's Fads and Fancies', *Washington Post*, 28 February 1910; 'How She Dresses the "400"', *Chicago Examiner*, 8 May 1910; 'The Conquest of New York: four mannequins take the town by storm', unattributed article in Lucile press album, 1910; untitled article in Lucile press album, *Daily Mirror* (London), 21 February 1910; 'Lady Duff-Gordon Imports 4 Beauties: English Models Arrive to Display Titled Dressmaker's Creations', unattributed article in Lucile press album, 1910; 'Americans Enthusiastic Over the New Gowns Shown by Beer: Doeuillet Strikes a Happy Medium in His Costumes', *New York Times*, 15 October 1911; 'Lucile's New Paris House', *Dry Goods Economist*, 9 September 1911, 44; 'Of Interest to Women: The Story of Just What Happens At One of the Fashionable Dress-maker's Openings', *New York Times*, 4 May 1913; E.G., 'Mid-Channel in Paris Fashions', *Vogue* (America), 1 December 1913, 35–7; Olive Gray, 'Fashions in Daylight Before Admiring Eyes', *Los Angeles Times*, 6 March 1914. For the account of Lucile's New York house and studio by Howard Greer, the Hollywood costume designer who worked for her in the 1910s, see Greer 1952, 40–43.

40 According to Bigham, Dolores, Hebe and Phyllis, who were all English by birth, travelled most frequently between all four salons, being the mannequins most in demand by Lucile's customers. None of her American mannequins, who included Dinarzade, Arjamand, Bonita and Josephine, went abroad while employed by Lucile Ltd, although Dinarzade did so when she joined Patou in 1925. See also Bigham 2012, 49–52.

41 That same season, at Lucile's London premises 'draped with green damask and decorated with ferns and hydrangeas in gold baskets with orange satin bows, a hidden orchestra played ragtime while the visitors took tea and admired the gowns worn by mannequins.' 'People in the Passing Show', *Washington Post*, 17 April 1913.

42 Display Ad 15 – No Title, *New York Times*, 4 May 1913; Display Ad 20 – No Title, *New York Times*, 4 October 1914.

43 Glenn 2000, 163.

44 With thanks to Molly Sorkin for this point.

45 'Lady Duff Gordon's Six "Types"', *American Examiner*, 13 March 1910.

46 There were many other American mannequins, many of whom can no longer be identified, such as Thelma and Yaha. Avery Strakosch, 'Fashions for the Famous: Dressmaking Days With Lady Duff-Gordon, as Told by Her First Model, Miss Elsie', *Saturday Evening Post*, 29 January 1927, 12–13, 91 and 94; ibid., 26 February, 23; Greer 1952, 40; Keenan 1977, 111.

47 With thanks to Molly Sorkin for these observations.

48 Greer 1952, 40.

49 See e.g. Keenan 1977, 111.

50 Schweitzer lists Phyllis, Mauricette, Dinarzade and Dolores as appearing in the 1917 Ziegfeld/Dillingham production *Miss 1917*, and in subsequent years Gamela, Clairie, Anangaraga, Sovia-Moria, Boneta, Iseult, Majanah, Corisande, Delys and Hildred. Carter, *The World of Flo Ziegfeld*, 60, cited in Schweitzer 2009, 194–202 and 286–7 n. 80. See also Duff Gordon 1932, 215; Mizejewski 1999, 91 and 95; Glenn 2000, 163; Matheson and Sorkin 2005, 32.

51 Mizejewski 1999, 65. On Ziegfeld's idea of the 'American Girl', see also 76–7 and 115–17.

52 Mizejewski's use of the term 'haute couture' suggests that she means 'high fashion', rather than its specific usage within the French fashion trade. Ibid., 21.

53 Schweitzer 2009, 199–200, who cites Wayburn's own description in *Theater Magazine* in 1913 of four, not five types, A–D, the A types being tall and graceful, the D types shorter and more accomplished dancers. *Theater Magazine* wrote: 'The "D" girl is a dancer. She is small, healthy and trained for vigorous dancing.' The E dancer cited by Mizejewski was either a later addition or was less important. According to Susan Glenn, 'A separate category of the very shortest E girls did only precision dancing'. Glenn 2000, 182 (citing Barbara Cohen Stratyner's *Ned Wayburn and the Dance Routine*).

54 Mizejewski 1999, 94–5. On Wayburn, see also Glenn 2000, 182.

55 Mizejewski 1999, 21.

56 Robert Baral, *Revue: A Nostalgic Reprise of the Great Broadway Period*, New York: Fleet, 1962, 61, cited in Mizejewski 1999, 97, and Schweitzer 2009, 200.

57 Mizejewski 1999, 97.

58 Schweitzer 2009, 199–202.

59 On the Castles' crossover appeal, see Wallace 1986, 40.

60 Among many examples, Lucile designed Irene Castle's costumes for *Watch Your Step* at the New Amsterdam Theater in New York. There are illustrations in *Harper's Bazar*, February 1915, 41, and a surviving dance

dress from the show, called 'Love in the Mist', is in the Costume Collection of the Metropolitan Museum of Art, New York (accession number C.I.47.57.1) and can be seen on its website where it is dated 1914.

61 My thanks to Molly Sorkin for identifying them in the film.

62 Mizejewski 1999, 129; for the full discussion, see her ch. 4, 'Racialized, Glorified American Girls', 109–35.

63 I found no evidence of black fashion mannequins in the U.S.A. in the Schomberg division of the New York Public Library before the 1950s. However, there is a short piece of surviving sound film from 1929 of fashion modelling for African Americans in the University of South Carolina's Newsfilm Library. It is classified as 'MVTN 4 167 (B) Harlem's Latest Fashions RC2515, 7 November 1929, B&W, sound, 7.52 minutes' and is described as showing 'several scenes from "Annual Fashion Review" display latest fashion for evening gowns in Harlem.' The same library has a 1929 Chinese fashion parade from Shanghai: 'MVTN 2 249. Chinese fashion show RC 2023, 4 March 1929, B&W, sound, 8.89 minutes'. On the absence of models and actresses of colour in early twentieth-century American theatre, Schweitzer writes that on the American stage in the period before the First World War the new thin ideal required by the fashionable sheath gown was predominantly a white one. Schweitzer 2009, 109–10. However, the histories of early twentieth-century fashion and theatre vary considerably regarding racial difference and representation. Glenn 2000, 49–56. For ways in which African American performance traditions were incorporated into white chorus routines 'producing a racial mimicry on stage that rendered invisible the contributions and bodies of black performers' see Brown forthcoming. Brown also discussed the orientalism of Lucile's staging of her mannequins.

64 Mizejewski 1999, 89.

65 'Lady Duff Gordon: "Lucile"', *Harper's Bazar*, August 1914, 38–41.

66 Conor 2004, xv.

67 Laurie J. Monahan, 'Radical Transformations: Claude Cahun and the Masquerade of Womanliness', in Zegher 1995, 130. See also Dean 1992, 70.

68 'Use of Living Models', *Dry Goods Economist*, 19 August 1911, 41–2. On this article, see Schweitzer 2009, 183 and 186.

69 'The Fashion Fête', *Los Angeles Times*, 25 September 1910. The United Fashion Show became a biannual fixture by 1911 and spread to San Francisco: see e.g. Olive Gray, 'Chic Styles in the Show', *Los Angeles Times*, 16 March 1911; 'Dame Fashion is Shown in Brilliant Role, Raiment Show Delights Femininity', *San Francisco Chronicle*, 6 September 1912; 'Fashion Show Opens Tomorrow', *San Francisco Chronicle*, 13 September 1911; 'Beautiful Fashion Show to Begin Wednesday Evening', *Los Angeles*

Times, 17 September 1911; 'Beautiful Living Models Unveiled', ibid., 25 September 1913; 'Fashion Show Closes Today', ibid., 27 September 1913.

70 'The Fashion Show Beautiful', *Los Angeles Times*, 15 September 1912; 'Girl Models Make Showing Clothes an Art', *Christian Science Monitor*, 11 October 1913.

71 'Dame Fashion', *San Francisco Chronicle*, 6 September 1912; 'Real Garden, Living Models', *Los Angeles Times*, 23 September 1913.

72 'Real Novelty: Living Fashion Bullock's Idea', *Los Angeles Times*, 15 March 1912.

73 Olive Gray, 'Art and Beauty in Los Angeles Stores', *Los Angeles Times*, 24 September 1914.

74 According to Schweitzer, the first store to use living models in its windows was Bonwitt Teller and Co. in Cincinnati in the early 1890s. Schweitzer 2009, 282 n. 21. See also 'Beautiful Fashion Show to Begin Wednesday Evening', *Los Angeles Times*, 17 September 1911; 'New Seasons's Newest in Stores of Los Angeles', ibid., 19 September 1912; 'A Man Behind the Scenes of Merry Fashion Fête', ibid., 20 September 1911; 'In Exquisite Array Before the Mirror', ibid., 5 March 1914.

75 Window-modelling was endorsed by the trade in 1911 when two hundred members of the National Association of Window Trimmers voted at their annual convention to replace papier-mâché dummies in windows with live models. 'Favor Living Window Model, National Trimmers Condemn Papier Mache Displays, Girls Displace Old Form', *Chicago Daily Tribune*, 2 August 1911. See also Mme X, 'Comment', *Chicago Daily Tribune*, 7 November 1915; Olive Gray, 'Among the Stores and Amidst the Shops', *Los Angeles Times*, 31 May 1916.

76 'Held "Style Parade," Living Models Successfully Employed by L. Dimond & Sons, Providence, R.I.', *Dry Goods Economist*, 29 April 1911, 35; 'Girl Models', *Christian Science Monitor*, 11 October 1913; Schweitzer 2009, 183.

77 'In Exquisite Array Before the Mirror', *Los Angeles Times*, 5 March 1914.

78 The German film *Asphalt* (1929), directed by Joe May, and Paul Fejos's *Sonnenstrahl* (1933) also contain window-modelling scenes. With thanks to Marketa Uhlirova for bringing these films to my attention.

79 Schweitzer 2009, 183; Leach 1994, 103. See also Berry 2000, 54.

80 Among the early trade bodies to begin to use fashion shows were the American Ladies Tailors Association in 1910 and, in 1911, the 14th Annual Convention of the National Association of Window Trimmers of America, the National Association of Merchant Traders of America and the National Association of Clothing Designers' semi-annual convention. The last featured the Men's Living Models Fashion Show, from whose audience women were barred. *New York Times*, 10 October

1910; *Washington Post*, 15 February 1911; 'Men's Fashion Creators Meet Today', *Boston Daily Globe*, 30 June 1911; 'Clothing Designers See Boston Attractions', ibid., 1 July 1911; *Dry Goods Economist*, 12 August 1911, 37.

81 'Girl Models', *Christian Science Monitor*, 11 October 1913.

82 'Tailors Plan Special Show', *Los Angeles Times*, 29 September 1915; 'Handsome Watch for C. M. Cusk. Brewster Tells of Coming Styles. Subject Illustrated by Living Model in Latest Garments', *Hartford Courant*, 9 September 1915; Olive Gray, 'Among the Stores and Amidst the Shops', *Los Angeles Times*, 31 March 1916.

83 Fashion Camera Company (New York) advertisement for 'Merchandise Photography' inviting clients to choose between '*fanciful* drawings or *factful* photographs . . . posed on *living models*'. *Dry Goods Economist*, 5 August 1911, 22.

84 Glenn 2000, 164.

85 'Directoire Gowns Rival the Early Victorian Crinoline', *Atlanta Constitution*, 5 April 1914. On the theatrical staging of the department store show, see 'Girl Models', *Christian Science Monitor*, 11 October 1913.

86 Schweitzer 2009, 181–2.

87 Schweitzer 2009, 186–7.

88 'Chicago Beauties Show Off Chicago Creations', *Chicago Daily Tribune*, 20 September 1915. On the show girl, see Glenn 2000, 158 and 188–215; Schweitzer 2009, 186–91.

89 Schweitzer 2009, 191.

90 Ibid., 186.

91 Glenn 2000, 165; Schweitzer 2009, 179 and 191.

92 Schweitzer 2009, 192 and 285 n. 52.

93 'Society Fashion Show and Garden Party at Hotel Maryland, Pasadena', *Los Angeles Times*, 23 March 1913. For a precursor, see 'Society Meetings and Entertainments', *Chicago Daily Tribune*, 29 September 1911. At Redfern in Paris there was even a life-sized leather horse which either the mannequins or the client would mount to gauge the effect of the riding habits in which Redfern specialised. 'Living Models in the Shops of Paris Dressmakers Lure Women to Purchase Gowns so Attractively Displayed', *Chicago Daily Tribune*, 10 May 1908.

94 John Corrigan, Jr., 'Cotton Dresses for the Women', *Atlanta Constitution*, 21 September 1914: 'This patriotic movement originated with Miss Genevieve Clark, daughter of speaker Champ Clark' and was intended to boost the American cotton industry at a time when war had curtailed both French fashions and the American cotton market. Lucile, who remained in America for the duration of the war, continued to promote American fashion in her fashion journalism for *Harper's Bazar*, although by 1916 she had gone back to using French silk rather than the American fabrics she had endorsed up to 1915.

95 'New York Fashions Are Adjudged Smart', *Vogue* (America), December 1914, 38–48. For a description of the fête based on this account in *Vogue*, see Seebohm 1982, 96.

96 'Society's Stamp on Fashion Fête Wins Artistic Center from Paris', *Washington Post*, 8 November 1914.

97 'Paris Makers to Hold Show Here', *New York Times*, 7 November 1915.

98 Seebohm 1982, 101. See also Troy 2003, 275–7.

99 Chase and Chase 1954, 118–27; Steele 1998, 238.

100 Doris E. Fleischman, 'A Description of Some of the Best Gowns in the Replica Exhibit at Wanamaker's', *New York Tribune*, 18 April 1915. See also *Harper's Bazar*, May 1915, 42–3; Troy 2003, 244–8.

101 A description of Paquin's Boston show foregrounds both its theatrical expertise and the extravagant number of costly gowns. 'Boston Goes to See the Latest Paquin Gowns', *Boston Daily Globe*, 21 March 1914. On Tully's Fashion Show, see 'Theatrical Notes', *New York Times*, 5 April 1915; 'Fashion Plate Novelty Act Something New for Palace', *Variety*, 9 April 1915, 5.

102 My account of the show and its vaudeville tour is based on the following, the majority of which are in the May Tully cuttings file in the ephemera collection of the Billy Rose Theatre Division of the New York Public Library for the Performing Arts: Wynn, 'Palace Fashion Show', *Variety*, 14 April 1915; 'Two Vaudeville Headliners Furnish Peculiar Contrast', *Variety*, 16 April 1915, 6; unattributed cutting dated 20 April 1915; *Dramatic Mirror*, 21 April 1915; 'Faces Which Will Fascinate from the Footlights This Week', *Washington Post*, 9 May 1915; 'Keith's Only Rival of Stock Companies', ibid; 'Peggy Hopkins, in Stage Debut Here, Proves That American Gowns Can Vie With Best That Paris Produces', ibid., 11 May 1915; 'Vogue Plays a New Rôle', *Vogue* (America), 1 June 1915, 33–4; Grace Kingsley, 'At the Stage Door', *Los Angeles Times*, 28 June 1915; 'At the Stage Door', *Los Angeles Times*, 6 July 1915; *Dramatic Mirror*, 23 October 1915; 'Stage Has Real Fashion Parade', *New York Telegraph*, [1915]; 'Dame Fashion Leads Orpheum Parade', *Brooklyn Eagle*, [n.d.].

103 Tully's staging may have been influenced by a charity benefit held at New York's Waldorf Astoria in 1914 that featured socialites posing in *tableaux vivants* inspired by covers of *Vogue* and *Vanity Fair* created by the illustrators Helen Dryden and George Plank. Seebohm 1982, 165. Both Dryden and Plank were Condé Nast illustrators. Blackman 2009, 10.

104 'The Fashion Fête in Philadelphia', *Harper's Bazar*, February 1915, 34–7; 'Sixty Society Women Became Manikins to Their Own Dressmakers at the Carnival and Fashion Show Held for Charity in the St Louis Coliseum', *Vogue* (America), May 1915, 55. See also 'Style Show Aids Victims of War', *New York Tribune*, 27 October 1914; Helen

Bullitt Lowry, 'Rude Intrusion of Facts into Fashion', *New York Times*, 1 August 1920.

105 'Pageant of Nations at Newport Fêtes', *New York Times*, 25 July 1915; 'Fashions for Next Autumn Are Still Unsettled', *New York Times*, 22 August 1915; ' "Fashion's Passing Show" at Newport', *Vogue* (America), 1 September 1915, 28–39, 116 and 120.

106 On this show, see Display Ad 16 – No Title, *New York Times*, 26 September 1915; 'Actresses in Fashion Extravaganza', ibid., 29 September 1915; 'Written on the Screen,' ibid., 3 October 1915; Katherine T. Von Blon, 'New York Sees Finest Modes', *Los Angeles Times*, 5 December 1915.

107 Display Ad 5 – No Title, *New York Times*, 14 October 1915.

108 One Gimbel's advertisement that season promised a new feature, 'an autumn bridal procession', alongside sports, evening and day-wear and audiences of up to 20,000; another announced: 'Of course the tiny Gnome will precede the appearance of the mannequins, and represent *The Spirit of All Fashions*, past and present.' Display Ad 5 – No Title, *New York Times*, 12 October 1915; Display Ad 5 – No Title, ibid., 14 October 1915.

109 'New York Sees Finest Modes', *Los Angeles Times*, 5 December 1915.

110 My account of Tully's second touring fashion show is based on the following, the majority of which are in the May Tully cuttings file, ephemera collection of the Billy Rose Theatre Division of the New York Public Library for the Performing Arts: 'Gems and Gowns Star at Palace', *New York Tribune*, 12 October 1915; Sime, 'New Acts Next Week "Fall Fashion Show",' *Variety*, 15 October 1915, 14; Display Ad 21 – No title, *New York Times*, 23 October 1915; *Dramatic Mirror*, 23 October 1915; 'Current Attractions', *Washington Post*, 21 November 1915; 'May Tully Will Appear in Big Fashion Show', *Pittsburgh Leader*, 3 December 1915; 'A New Theatrical Fad: Why Study to be an Emotional Actress When You Can So Easily Be an Emotionless Mannikin?' *Vanity Fair*, December 1915, 70; *Des Moines Register and Reader*, 10 January 1916; 'Palace Theater', *Hartford Courant*, 10 April 1916; 'Real Fashion Show at Palace Theater', *Hartford Courant*, 11 April 1916. See also Schweitzer 2009, 206–8.

111 Schweitzer 2009, 207.

112 'Two Vaudeville Headliners Furnish Peculiar Contrast', *Variety*, 16 April 1915, 6.

113 The device of the dream was used in a serious stage play, Edward Knoblauch's *My Lady's Dress*, which transferred from London's Royalty Theatre (where it had premiered in winter 1913) to the New York City Playhouse in October 1914. ' "My Lady's Dress" Most Interesting', *New York Times*, 12 October 1914; see also Kaplan and Stowell 1994, 140–50; Hoganson, 'Fasionable World', 260–61. Subsequent fashion shows using the dream were 'Her Ladyship's Wardrobe' by Mrs Condé Nast, at the 1915 Oelrichs' charity

show, May Tully's 'Million Dollar Fashion Show' of 1915–16 and Lucile's 'Fleurette's Dream at Peronne' of 1917 (see below).

114 For the foundational articles on, and subsequent debates and modifications of, the theory of the cinema of attractions, see Strauven 2006.

115 Leach 1994, 3.

116 Ibid., 3–12.

117 Ibid., 5.

118 For these and other accounts of the fête, see 'Fashion Fête for War Fund', *New York Times*, 12 November 1915; 'The Paris Fashion Show Has Brought a New Epoch', ibid., 28 November 1915; 'New Theatrical Fad', *Vanity Fair*, December 1915, 70; 'The Paris Fashion Fête', *Vogue* (America), 15 December 1915, 33–52; 'The Paris Fashion Fête in New York', *Vanity Fair*, January 1916, 66. See also Troy 2003, 282–4.

119 *Vogue* (America), 1 April 1916, 54–5.

120 Schweitzer, however, is adamant that it was not a fashion show. Schweitzer 2009, 202–9.

121 Duff Gordon 1932, 267–8.

122 Ibid., 234.

123 See Schweitzer 2009, 'Fashioning the Ziegfeld Girl', 194–203. Ziegfeld subsequently bought the opening scenes of 'Fleurette's Dream' and reworked it for the Ziegfeld Follies, poaching Dolores from Lucile.

124 For the vaudeville version of 'Fleurette's Dream', see 'Fashion Display at the Palace', *New York Times*, 4 December 1917; 'Patsy' Smith, 'Among the Women', *Variety*, 7 December 1917, 10; Sime, 'Lady Duff Gordon: Fashion Show', ibid., 20; The Skirt, 'Among the Women', ibid., 14 December 1917, 18; 'Attraction at the Theaters: Brilliant Fashion Show at Keith's', *Boston Daily Globe*, 18 December 1917. See also Schweitzer 2009, 208–9.

125 The Skirt, 'Among the Women', *Variety*, 14 December 1917, 18.

CHAPTER 5

1 'From the Trenches. Paul Poiret, the famous Paris couturier, writes exclusively for Harper's Bazar', *Harper's Bazar*, February 1915, 11. Patou, whose show was due to take place on 2 August, was mobilised as an infantry officer on 3 August. Leaving his house open during his absence, he returned briefly to Paris on convalescent leave in 1916 and then spent the rest of the war as an officer in the Zouaves on the Eastern front. *Histoire de l'industrie* 1926, 123.

2 Doeuillet, M. Wagner of Drecoll, M. Winter of Premet and M. Armand of Martial et Armand all fought in the war. Anne Rittenhouse, 'Couturiers Under Arms', *Vogue* (America), 15 October 1914, 44–5 and 118; 'Paris Will Give Spring Styles', *New York Times*, 6 December 1914.

3 Mlle Chaquin, 'The War Notwithstanding', *Harper's Bazar*, October 1914, 46–7 and 86.

4 'Au Revoir, Paris Garb, War Cuts Off Fall Creations: Americans Set Styles', *Washington Post*, 9 August 1914.

5 Ibid.

6 Brachet Champsaur 2004a, 12.

7 'Fashion Show Opens', *Washington Post*, 17 August 1914. Poiret, Doucet and Beer did not open at all. Worth sold what it had and then closed the shop. Rittenhouse, 'Couturiers Under Arms', 44–5 and 118. Callot, Chéruit, Premet, Drecoll, Bernard and Redfern all had openings, either in their houses or as 'little fashion shows' in various hotels. 'Paris Holds Fashion Openings Thanks to Patriotic Women', *New York Times*, 6 September 1914. Jenny and Béchoff David both showed. Jenny, '*La Mode* as I See It', *Harper's Bazar*, December 1914, 36–7 and 86. 'First gowns from the firing line brought by "The Lady of the Decoration"', *Harper's Bazar*, October 1914, 42.

8 'Fashion Show Opens', *Washington Post*, 17 August 1914. 'Paris Holds Fashion Openings', *New York Times*, 6 September 1914.

9 'Paris Will Give Spring Styles', *New York Times*, 6 December 1914.

10 Chaquin, 'War Notwithstanding', 46–7 and 86.

11 Bessie Ascough, 'Fashions from London', *Chicago Daily Tribune*, 8 September 1914.

12 'Blacksmiths in Horse Show Ring', *New York Times*, 15 November 1914.

13 *New York Times*, 4 October 1914. The article is headed 'Paris, 21 September'.

14 Ibid. See also Rittenhouse, 'Couturiers Under Arms', 44–5 and 118.

15 A relatively young house, opened in 1904, Drecoll had always marketed its designs to overseas exporters. *Histoire de l'industrie* 1926, 117.

16 'Fashion Show Opens', *Washington Post*, 17 August 1914.

17 In February 1914 Callot Soeurs had excluded from its spring opening several large New York buyers who had not bought directly from the firm the previous summer, and announced that it was keeping its best collection for the French opening to private clients in April. Despite this hostility towards American buyers, the firm was rumoured to have taken $600,000 in orders from Americans in 1913. 'Latest Paris Fashion News by Cable to the Times: Merry War on to Keep Paris Dressmakers from New York', *New York Times*, 22 February 1914.

18 'Paris Will Give Spring Styles', *New York Times*, 6 December 1914.

19 Ibid; Jenny, '*La Mode* as I See It', 36–7 and 86.

20 'Smart Designs Inexpensively Developed in American Fabrics', *Harper's Bazar*, December 1914, 38–9.

21 'First Gowns from the Firing Line', *Harper's Bazar*, October 1914, 42.

22 'Paris Will Give Spring Styles', *New York Times*, 6 December 1914.

23 'Paris Will Give Spring Styles', *New York Times*.

24 Adam 1919, 36–7.

25 Brachet Champsaur 2004a, 12.

26 'Paris Gaiety's Gone: Even Restaurants Not Allowed to Keep Open Longer Than Usual', *New York Times*, 25 December 1914.

27 Nita Norris, 'Paris – Before the Spring Openings', *Harper's Bazar*, February 1915, 50–51 and 92.

28 Nita Norris, 'Paris – The Dictator', *Harper's Bazar*, January 1915, 15–16; 'Fashion Vs. the War Zone', *New York Times*, 14 March 1915.

29 *Harper's Bazar*, March 1915, 86.

30 On Poiret, see 'Paris Holds Fashion Openings Despite the War', *New York Times*, 28 February 1915. On Patou, see *Histoire de l'industrie* 1926, 123.

31 'Fashion Vs. the War Zone', *New York Times*, 14 March 1915. E. Aine, the president of the renamed Chambre Syndicale de la Couture Parisienne, explained in an article in *Harper's Bazar* that the French dressmakers were 'trying to rid themselves of the pernicious outside influences that for the last few years have invaded the Parisian market and foisted upon the public models called "Parisian"'. Clearly implying that he meant houses of German or Austrian origin, he described how, soon after war broke out, in order to exclude them the syndicate had dissolved itself and formed 'a Syndicate of "Parisian Dressmaking Houses", which accepts as members only houses of really French origin and inspiration.' E. Aine, 'French Models at the San Francisco Exposition', *Harper's Bazar*, May 1915, 42–3.

32 'Show Paris Gowns Despite the War', *New York Times*, 12 February 1915.

33 'Fashion Vs. the War Zone', *New York Times*, 14 March 1915.

34 'Paris Holds Fashion Openings Despite the War', *New York Times*, 28 February 1915.

35 Norris, 'Paris – Before the Spring Openings', 50–51 and 92.

36 'Fashion Vs. the War Zone', *New York Times*, 14 March 1915. In 1929 Le Fèvre recalled how American buyers had braved enemy submarines and crossed the Atlantic to buy French models during the war: 'n'oublions pas qu'ils traversaient l'Atlantique pendant la guerre pour nous acheter nos modèles, et en dépit des sous-marins.' Le Fèvre 1929, 81. See also Font 2012, 36.

37 Nita Norris, 'Paris Demonstrates Supremacy at the Spring Openings', *Harper's Bazar*, April 1915, 34–5 and 67.

38 Advertisement for H. Gidding & Co, *Harper's Bazar*, March 1915, 86.

39 Display Ad 7 – No Title, *New York Times*, 17 March 1915.

40 Ibid.

41 'Ils avaient obtenu un congé pour venir faire leurs commandes à Paris, et c'est aussi attentivement que s'ils avaient passé à une revue de détail qu'ils étudièrent les costumes, d'une élégante correction, présentés par les mannequins avec cette gracieuses indolence qui chez eux est traditionnelle.' 'Rue de la Paix – Dans les Salons d'un grand couturier parisien: présentation des nouveaux modèles du printemps 1915 aux acheteurs d'une maison de Londres', *L'Illustration*, February 1915, reproduced in *Journal Universel* 130–31.

42 Brachet Champsaur 2004b, 208–10 and 221–2.

43 Nita Norris, 'Paris: The Court of Final Resort', *Harper's Bazar*, May 1915, 36–7 and 96.

44 Adam 1919, 3–5.

45 Ibid., 43 and 47–8.

46 Norris, 'Paris: Court of Final Resort', 36–7 and 96.

47 Ibid.

48 Nita Norris, 'Paris: On the Eve of the Openings', *Harper's Bazar*, March 1915, 42–3 and 100.

49 Ibid.

50 Ibid.

51 Doris E. Fleischman, 'A Description of Some of the Best Gowns in the Replica Exhibit at Wanamaker's', *New York Tribune*, 18 April 1915.

52 'The Merchant's Point of View', *New York Times*, 21 February 1915.

53 Paul Adam, 'La Costume de Paris', Panama-Pacific International Exposition, *The 1915 Mode as Shown by Paris*, Paris edition, English text, New York: Condé Nast, 1915, 16.

54 Font 2012, 39–40.

55 'Les commandants des bateaux se plaisent à rappeler notre indifférence au danger.' Mme Montégut quoted in *Histoire de l'industrie* 1926, 114–15.

56 Roubaud 1928, 198.

57 'Youthful Air of Paris Gowns', *Washington Post*, 2 May 1915.

58 *Histoire de l'industrie* 1926, 114–15.

59 'C'est un des fiertés de notre vie d'avoir établi sur de telles bases l'unique grande maison de couture française à New-York', *Histoire de l'industrie* 1926, 114–15. In fact, as Lourdes Font has shown, Redfern was the first to open a New York branch, in the 1890s. From 1912 Paquin had a fur branch there although Font argues that it was not strictly a branch. Font 2012, 34–5. Boué Soeurs also claimed to be 'the only rue de la Paix house in America' in an advertisement on p. 49 of the 1920 programme for the Ziegfeld production of *Sally* at the New Amsterdam Theater, New York, a production that featured Lucile's former mannequin Dolores, dressed on stage both by Lucile and, in her famous butterfly and bat costumes, by Pascaud of Paris.

60 At the first meeting of the Chambre Syndicale members on 15 February 1911 Poiret questioned whether 'Lucile of London' could be admitted. The eligibility of foreign members was finally decided by the syndicate in 1928, when only those firms with Austrian or German directors or backers were excluded from membership. An exception was made for those Austrians or Germans who were naturalised French of twenty or more years' standing. The restriction remained in force until in 1937. Grumbach 2008, 30 and 104 n. 23.

61 Lady Duff Gordon (Lucile), 'The Last Word in Fashions', *Harper's Bazar*, February 1915, 42–3.

62 Schweitzer 2009, 209–11.

63 'The Spring Openings at Lady Duff Gordon's (Lucile)', *Harper's Bazar*, February 1915, 44–5.

64 Lady Duff Gordon (Lucile), 'The Last Word in Fashions', *Harper's Bazar*, September 1916, 72–3. Lucile had reiterated her praise for the new French fabrics in *Harper's Bazar*, December 1915, 70–71.

65 'New Winter Styles in Paris Show Long "Russian" Coats and the Lavish Use of Furs', *Washington Post*, 14 August 1915.

66 'Paris Makers to Hold Show Here', *New York Times*, 7 November 1915.

67 Display Ad 4 – No Title, *New York Times*, 5 October 1915.

68 Poiret was nevertheless clearly worried about the success of the movement to promote American dress and the threat it posed to the French couture. 'From the Trenches', *Harper's Bazar*, February 1915, 11.

69 'The Paris Fashion Show Has Brought a New Epoch', *New York Times*, 28 November 1915. This was at a time, despite his activity in promoting French fashion overseas, when in Paris Poiret was the victim of what appear to have been entirely unjustified accusations of 'boche taste' and 'goût munichois'. Kenneth Silver argues convincingly that it was Poiret's cosmopolitanism and orientalism that drew the attack, which lasted for two years, from August 1915 to September 1917. Silver both investigated and contextualised what he called 'the Poiret affair' that was instigated by the editor of the magazine *La Renaissance politique, littéraire et artistique*. Silver cited as major factors underlying the accusations against Poiret not only Poiret's successful pre-war trade links with Berlin and Vienna but also the fact that before the war Germany had proved an increasingly successful competitor to France in the export of decorative arts. Silver 1989, 167–85. In further support of the tendency to see orientalism as anti-French, in 1915 Aine, the president of the French couture syndicate (see n. 31 above), claimed that before the war 'under cover of a Parisian establishment, many houses of foreign inspiration launched so-called Paris fashions which had nothing of the Parisian about them, and which, by their exaggeration, caused the association of the adjectives "exotic" and "Parisian"'. Aine's words were written to promote the fifty French models that had just gone on show at the Panama-Pacific International Exposition in San Francisco. In light of this statement, and in the wider context of the Poiret affair, it is unsurprising that Poiret chose to mark his return in 1915 to couture production at the

San Francisco exhibition with eighteenth-century inspired dress, rather than with his orientalist designs of 1913. Aine, 'French Models', 42–3.

70 'Fashions for Next Autumn Are Still Unsettled', *New York Times*, 22 August 1915.

71 Isadora Duncan reported in 'Paris Modes Shocking', *Washington Post*, 29 August 1915.

72 Carolyn Wilson, 'Spring Fashion Openings Draw Paris Crowds', *Chicago Daily Tribune*, 31 March 1918.

73 'Fashions for Next Autumn', *New York Times*, 22 August 1915.

74 *Vogue* (America), 1 June 1915, 31.

75 'Men from the Front Find Paris Changed, Even the Shopgirls More Serious Than of Old – Flashy Dress is Seen No More', *New York Times*, 8 August 1915; 'Paris Vastly Changed, Reservist Home from the Front Has Curiosity Excited', *Washington Post*, 15 August 1915.

76 '[D]e petites femmes à jupe courte et fines chevilles emprisonnées dans de hautes bottes . . . des décolletages, des transparences, des demi-nudités, c'eût été renoncer à la clientèle américaine'. Corinne, 'Opinions sur nos grands couturiers: sur la mode pendant la guerre', *Les Modes*, December 1915, 14–16.

77 On the establishment and activities of the new syndicate, see Troy 2003, 269–82.

78 'Predict Failure of Poiret's Plan', *New York Times*, 15 January 1916.

79 Emilie de Joncaire, 'From Paris', *Harper's Bazar*, March 1916, 58–61.

80 Jeanne Paquin quoted in ibid., August 1916, 45–51.

81 Henri Bendel, 'The Adaptation of Fashions to the American Woman', *Harper's Bazar*, June 1916, 64–5.

82 Emilie de Joncaire, 'From Paris', *Harper's Bazar*, September 1916, 60–67.

83 Nancy J. Troy, 'Introduction: Poiret's Modernism and the Logic of Fashion', in Koda and Bolton 2007, 17 and 23. These were promoted in a glossy brochure containing 14 black and white photographs of the dresses on mannequins, with descriptions, prices and illustrations to identify the genuine Poiret label, as opposed to imitations.

84 'The Autumn Openings in Paris', *Harper's Bazar*, October 1916, 70–71.

85 Emilie de Joncaire, 'From Paris', *Harper's Bazar*, August 1916, 45–51.

86 Joncaire, 'From Paris', *Harper's Bazar*, September 1916, 60–67. On textile shortages during the latter half of the war, see also Brachet Champsaur 2004b.

87 Display Ad 36 – No Title, *Christian Science Monitor*, 20 September 1916.

88 Display Ad 8, *New York Times*, 24 September 1916.

89 Delbourg-Delphis 1981, 97.

90 'The Destiny of Parisian Mannequins' ('Osud pařížských manekýnek'), *Národní Listy*, 25 June 1916, 6. I am grateful to Marketa Uhlirova for bringing this article to my attention and for translating it for me.

91 Joncaire, 'From Paris', *Harper's Bazar*, September 1916, 60–67.

92 '[D]ans la compagnie favorable de Pâquerette, le plus précieux mannequin de Paul Poiret, bottines vertes, robe bois de rose, indescriptible bibi, Pâquerette exposant à Montparnasse le chef-d'oeuvre de l'avenue d'Antin'. Salmon 1950, 207, cited in Klüver 1997, 12. In July 1916 Salmon had organised a major exhibition of 166 works by 52 international artists including Picasso's *Les Demoiselles d'Avignon* at the Salon d'Antin, a space made available by Poiret at his business, consisting of a complex of buildings he owned at 26 rue d'Antin and where his mannequins had paraded daily before the war. Klüver 1997, 61–5.

93 Green 1997, 86–7.

94 Ibid., 86.

95 'From the Great Paris Couturiers', *Harper's Bazar*, October 1917, 60–61.

96 Adam 1919, 126–7.

97 Ibid., 127.

98 Ibid., 128–9.

99 J.F., 'En regardant les collections', *Femina*, March 1918, 12–15.

100 Brachet Champsaur 2004b, 213.

101 Redfern invitation to see summer models from 3 pm on 6 May 1918. Centre de Documentation, Musée de l'Art de la Mode et du Textile, Les Arts Décoratifs, Paris.

102 *Histoire de l'industrie* 1926, 121.

103 Ibid.

104 'Jenny', *La Renaissance de l'art français et des industries de luxe*, special number, June 1924, 347.

105 Ibid.

106 *Histoire de l'industrie* 1926, 126.

107 Ibid.

108 For a summary of the postwar devastation of France, see Silver 1989, 187.

109 Ibid., 226.

110 'Paris Women Bar Stockings', *Los Angeles Times*, 2 July 1919.

111 'The Last Word in Paris Fashions', *Chicago Daily Tribune*, 21 September 1919.

112 Troy 2003, 'Introduction', 17–24. See also Koda and Bolton 2007, 24.

113 'A Seat at the Paris Openings', *Vogue* (America), 15 April 1923, 39–49.

114 Robert de Beauplan, 'Après la grève des cousettes: dans les coulisses de la grande couture', *L'Illustration*, 19 May 1923, reprinted in *L'Illustration: Journal Universel* 1987, 137–40.

115 Rocamora 2009.

116 Green 1997, 106.

117 Troy 2003, 193 and 196.

118 Ibid., 196–7.

119 E.g., through the legal discourses that Nancy Troy examines: Troy 2003, 239, 251 and 260–65.

120 Dupeux 1976, 203–5.

121 Green 1997, 119–20.

122 Grumbach 2008, 87.

123 For an American account of the fluctuation of the value of the French franc in relation to the American dollar after the First World War, see Dulles 1933.

124 'Paris Women Bar Stockings', *Los Angeles Times*, 2 July 1919; Mary Brush Williams, 'The Last Word in Paris Fashions', *Chicago Daily Tribune*, 14 September 1919. Earlier in the year the mannequins at the races wore bare legs over 'high-heeled slippers cut away at the instep and the side, leaving only a sort of network of leather thongs'. 'Col. House Sees Fair Bare Legs at the Races', *Los Angeles Times*, 15 May 1915. See also 'French Launch Stockingless Fad at Longchamps', *Chicago Daily Tribune*, 14 May 1919; 'Paris Girls Show How to Economize', *Boston Daily Globe*, 13 May 1919.

125 Van Campen Stewart, 'Beggars in Rolls Royces', *Harper's Bazar*, July 1924, 59.

126 'The Dressmakers of France', *Fortune*, vol. VI, no. 2, August 1932, 72.

127 Simon 1931, 20.

128 'Cette nouvelle société est encore mouvante. Tel qui était riche la veille est aujourd'hui ruiné, un autre au contraire hier encore inconnu parvint à la fortune.' Ibid., 97.

CHAPTER 6

1 'Jean Patou: A Modern Couturier', *Harper's Bazar*, December 1924, 55–9; Etherington-Smith 1983, 27.

2 'This and That', *Harper's Bazar*, May 1922, 84, announced that the Baron and Baroness had sailed from New York to resume permanent residence in their native Paris.

3 Baron de Mayer, 'There Really Is a New Mode in Paris', *Harper's Bazar*, January 1923, 31–4. For similar examples, see de Meyer's regular columns in *Harper's Bazar* for November 1922, 39–43 and 132; October 1924, 188; January 1923, 32; February 1923, 34, which includes photographs of the mannequins Sumurum and 'the incomparable Hebe'.

4 The first was Hebe at Molyneux, in 1922. 'Les Plus Jolis Mannequins de Paris', *L'Art et la mode*, 16 December 1922, n.p. There followed a gap of several months until the series started to run, irregularly, from 21 July 1923 to 2 July 1927. The mannequins featured were from a variety of houses including Premet, Beer, Worth, Lucile, Philippe et Gaston, Drecoll, Cyber, Margaine Lacroix, Charlotte, Jean Magnin, Béchoff David and Lelong.

5 Marjorie Howard, 'Paris Letter', *Harper's Bazar*, February 1926, 118. See also de Meyer's column in *Harper's Bazar* for April 1926, 121–2; October 1926, 76–9 and 170; February 1926, 75.

6 'Baron de Meyer views the Mode', *Harper's Bazar*, April 1925, 98–101 and 103.

7 'La clientèle étrangère s'est abondamment substituée à la clientèle française; les nouveaux enrichis ont pris avec assurance le rang de ceux qui, nobles ou grands bourgeois, avaient reçu, avec la fortune, les grâces d'une

culture héréditaire. L'argent, récemment acquis ou résultant d'un change favorable, est devenu seul maître en ce lieu où la bienséance régnait jadis souverainement.' Reboux 1927, 10.

8 Etherington-Smith 1983, 69.

9 Letellier's aide-de-camp, the American millionaire Erskine Gwynn, later married Josephine Armstrong, one of Patou's American mannequins. Etherington-Smith 1983, 65.

10 'Tandis que défilent les mannequins muets, un orchestre ou un jazz joue en sourdine. Les maîtres de céans qui savent le mieux recevoir font circuler, parmi leurs invités, coupes de champagne et sandwiches, et la soirée or *l'afternoon* s'achève en dansant.' R. de B., 'Silhouettes et modes d'aujourd'hui', *L'Illustration*, 12 March 1927, reprinted in *L'Illustration: Journal Universel* 1987, 149.

11 On the similarities in stagecraft between fashion shows and stage plays, see ibid., 148.

12 Marjorie Howard 'Paris Letter', *Harper's Bazar*, March 1930, 30.

13 The first *Femina* fashion show was reported in *Femina*, August 1924, 14.

14 The first Grande Nuit de Paris was held in 1926 in conjunction with the newspaper *Le Figaro* at the Hôtel Claridge and was reported in three issues of *Femina* that year, May, June and August. The Claridge was often used for fashion events and was the location for the *thé dansant* scene in Tony Lekain's 1923 fashion film *On Demande un mannequin*. The 1927 Grande Nuit de Paris featured extravagant fashion shows modelled by chorus girls, society women and actresses, reported, again, in three issues of *Femina* for 1927, May, June and August.

15 For 60 pictures over 5 pages of mannequins modelling at the Bal de la Couture on Saturday 14 February 1925 at the Théâtre des Champs-Élysées, see 'Le Bal de la Couture', *L'Art et la mode*, 14 February 1925, n.p. See also P. St G. Perrot, 'Impressions of the Bal de la Couture', *The 'Liberty' Lamp*, April 1926, 34–5.

16 'Le Bal de la Couture à l'Opéra: présentation des mannequins', *L'Illustration*, 2 March 1929, reprinted in *L'Illustration: Journal Universel* 1987, 153.

17 'La Grande Saison de Paris: le Prix de l'Élégance aux portiques des Champs-Élysées', *L'Illustration*, 30 June 1928, reprinted in ibid., 226.

18 Van Campen Stewart, 'Poiret's Egyptian Fête Delights Cannes', *Harper's Bazar*, March 1921, 39. 'A Poiret Parade at St Moritz', *Glasgow Bulletin*, 18 January 1992; 'Last Night's Fête at Le Touquet–Paris Plage', *Daily Mail*, 22 August 1926.

19 'Whom Do the Ladies Dress to Please?', *Washington Post*, 12 April 1925.

20 They wore these on visits to London in October 1924, Copenhagen, Stockholm and Berlin in November 1925 and again in Berlin in May or June 1926. Poiret took his mannequins to London twice in 1924, in June and October. 'Veterans at Attention', *Los Angeles Times*, 15 June 1924. They are photographed in their uniforms on their return from London in October 1924. 'Le Retour sensationnel de M. Paul Poiret', *Excelsior*, 4 October 1924. 'Cameragraphs', *Atlanta Constitution*, 26 October 1924. They were seen in Stockholm a week later; *Stockholms-Tidningen*, 12 October 1925. In November they were reported in Copenhagen in six Danish press cuttings over 12–14 November; *B.T.*, 12 November 1925; *Politik*, 12 November 1925; *Fyns Stifstidende*, 13 November 1925; *Ekstrabladet*, 13 November 1925; *B.T.*, 14 November 1925; *Kobenhavn*, 14 November 1925; *Politiken*, 14 November 1925. There was also a magazine feature in *Vore Damen*, 19 November 1925. The Musée Galliera, Paris, has an album of photographs from this tour containing many that appear in the Danish press cuttings. The mannequins had been in Berlin in June and November 1925 and returned in May 1926; *Berlingske Tiden*, 14 November 1925; *Vore Damer*, 19 November 1925; 'Poiret in der Komödie', *Vossische Zeitung*, 18 May 1926; *Uhu*, 4 January 1933, 89. Thanks to Mila Ganeva for the last two references. One of the twelve Poiret mannequins selected to show his designs at the Komödie theatre was the Russian Kisa Kuprina who recalled the green- and-yellow striped coats; Vassiliev 2000, 410–11.

21 In March 1924 they modelled in Vienna. 'Tailors Riot as Paris Gowns Win Elite of Vienna', *Chicago Daily Tribune*, 1 March 1924.

22 'Les Élégances d'hiver, au mois d'août, à Paris: une présentation de mannequins chez un grand couturier des Champs-Élysées', *L'Illustration*, 18 August 1923, reprinted in L'Illustration 1987, 148.

23 De Meyer, *Harper's Bazar*, January 1923, 32.

24 'Baron de Meyer views the Mode', *Harper's Bazar*, April 1925, 100–01 and 103. Marjorie Howard, 'Paris Draws a New Colour Line', *Harper's Bazar*, April 1927, 85.

25 'Paris Openings Forecast Mode', *New York Times*, 22 August 1926.

26 'A Seat at the Paris Openings', *Vogue* (America), 15 April 1923, 39–49; Howard, 'Paris Draws a New Colour Line', 88 and 91; R. de B., 'Silhouettes et Modes', 148–9.

27 Marjorie Howard, 'Paris Sounds a New Note', *Harper's Bazar*, April 1928, 201.

28 'Pour endiguer, par example, l'hémorragie des ventes dont elle souffre à partir de 1925'. Grumbach 2008, 7.

29 On the role of the commissionnaire-exporter (*commissionnaire-exportateur*) in the Paris dressmaking trade, see Albert Tronc, 'Paris, capitale du commerce', *L'Exportateur française*, 22 May 1923, 'Le rôle du commissionnaire', 440–41.

30 Poiret's rationale was that 'les moments sont difficiles pour quantités de femmes cocottes dont la situation a dû changer depuis la guerre'. His efforts to produce an early version of off-the-peg clothes as an haute couturier are illustrated in *Vogue* (France), 1 October 1922, 11.

31 On Vionnet's attitude to, and experience of, copyright infringement, see Christine Senailles, 'Lutter contre la copie', in *Madeleine Vionnet* 1994, 18–21; Kirke 1998, 129–32; Grumbach 2008, 225; Brachet Champsaur 2012, 57–8. Brachet Champsaur perceptively surveys the contradictions of Vionnet's position and her research in the Galeries Lafayette archive reveals what no previous research has shown, that Madeleine Vionnet in effect owned the Eva Boex company.

32 Poiret 1931, 43.

33 'Pour l'Amérique, l'haute couture ne représente alors qu'un prêt-à-porter de luxe qui exige des commissionnaires un choix susceptible de satisfaire une clientèle traditionelle peu inclinée à l'excès'. Grumbach 2008, 90.

34 For Patou's account of the degree to which, and the ways in which, he managed the design process at his house, see 'Jean Patou, a Modern Couturier', *Harper's Bazar*, December 1924, 55–9.

35 Baron de Meyer, 'Paris Collections Seen by a Connoisseur', *Harper's Bazar*, November 1922, 39–43 and 132.

36 Over 1919–20 Patou's business expanded fivefold, in 1921 by 10 times, in 1922 by 14 times, in 1923 by 25 times, in 1924 by 30 times. *Histoire de l'industrie* 1926, 123.

37 Etherington-Smith 1983, 44–7, wrote that Elsa Maxwell, who had opened a nightclub for Molyneux in 1922, claimed the credit for the invention of the *répétition générale*, or gala couture opening, for Patou.

38 Ibid., 45. See also 'Baron de Meyer Attends the Paris Fall Openings', *Harper's Bazar*, October 1928, 71.

39 'A Seat at the Paris Openings', *Vogue* (America), 15 April 1923, 41.

40 Ibid.

41 'Baron de Meyer Attends the Openings', *Harper's Bazar*, April 1924, 79. See also his account of the previous season, subtitled 'Patou's Clever Opening', in Baron de Meyer, 'Paris Opens Another Season', *Harper's Bazar*, October 1923, 47.

42 Simon 1931, 85.

43 Chase and Chase 1954, 166–7.

44 Etherington-Smith 1983, 79.

45 *New York Times*, 14 November, 1924. The advertisement is reproduced as a facsimile in 'Vogue Chooses Six Mannequins for Jean Patou', *Vogue* (America), 1 February 1925, 50–51.

46 Different sources show that initially a higher number was chosen, between seven and nine, and different photographs show different numbers; by the time they arrived in Paris most sources suggest they were six. A small minority of the photographs show more than six but it is not clear whether the additional mannequins are American or not. For a fuller account of the event, see Evans 2008, 243–63.

47 '20 francs par jour aux belles filles Parisiennes dont il solicite l'engagement, il offre 75,000 francs par an aux Nanas d'Amérique.' Alfred Varella, 'L'homme aux six belles girls', *Journal du peuple*, 13 December 1924; Maîtrepierre, 'Les six belles de New-York jugées par trois petits mannequins qui ne sont de Paris', *Paris-Midi*, 29 December 1924.

48 Chase and Chase 1954, 163.

49 The French mannequins were 'doubles ponettes françaises' according to Colette. Of the Americans, she wrote 'Cette escouade d'archanges va, d'un vol chaste que nulle chair ne retarde, entraîner la mode vers une ligne toujours plus svelte, vers un vêtement encore simplifié dans sa construction, taillé d'un seul coup de ciseaux dans une matière magnifique,' Colette, 'Printemps de demain', *Vogue* (France), 1 February 1925, 31.

50 Marcel Prévost, 'American Women I Have Met', *Harper's Bazar*, January 1910, 23. On American views of the differences between French and American women's bodies before the First World War, see Schweitzer, in Blaszczyk 2008, 144. Schweitzer cites articles from the *New York Times* in 1909 and 1912 describing the French woman as 'short and thick', the American as tall, thin, broad-shouldered, athletic and 'republican in every essence of her being'. They suggest that the views of the mannequin 'Dicka', which I cite in Ch. 10 below, on the larger size of American women in 1906 may already have been on the way out.

51 O. C. Lawson, 'Overselling Paris', *Saturday Evening Post*, 16 October 1925.

52 On the French ideal age, as opposed to the American ideal, see 'For First Time French Subordinate Themselves in Bidding for Trade', *Washington Post*, 29 April 1923.

53 Chase and Chase 1954, 166.

54 *Les Échos*, 11 February 1925.

55 Gronberg 1998, 9–10.

56 Kracauer 1995, 75–6.

57 *New York Times*, 31 July 1926.

58 Paul 2001, 97; Paul Morand, *New York*, 1929, cited in Brooks 1987, 840. See also *Evening World*, New York, 28 November 1925, and *Comoedia*, 14 September 1928, on the vogue for *américanisme*.

59 Siegfried 1927. André Siegfried's book, a bestseller in France in 1927, had been researched in New York in 1925. Duhamel 1974 was titled *Scènes de la vie future* in French.

60 Siegfried 1927, 348–9 (U.S. edition). These points were made again in the 1930s by György Lukács, whose description of commodity fetishism emphasised the way that the commodity form dominates all social relations, and by Antonio Gramsci in his writing on America, in his *Prison Diaries*.

61 On American women's 'delectable' legs, 'uniform like those of the chorus girl', see: Duhamel 1974, 64, and Brooks 1987, 1851, n22. On the 'edition' of the modern Goddess ('even her charming laughter simulates that of Hollywood actresses') see Duhamel 1974, 66.

62 Reboux 1927, 23.

63 'Fewer Typewriters and More Sewing Machines the Salvation of the Modern Girl, says French Modiste', *Atlanta Constitution*, 25 June 1922. See also Basil Woon, 'For the First Time French Subordinate Themselves in Bidding for Trade', *Washington Post*, 29 April 1923.

64 On Patou, see Baron de Meyer, 'Paris Collections Seen by a Connoisseur', *Harper's Bazar*, November 1922, 39–43 and 132. On Lelong, see *Fortune* 1932, 74 (month missing).

65 Wilson 1925, 71–2.

66 Ibid., 72.

67 'L'organisation de son affaire est complètement industrielle'. *Histoire de l'industrie* 1926, 123. It extended to the conduct permitted in the workrooms. An article on working conditions in the dressmaking trade in 1922 stated that whereas a degree of personal vivacity was permitted in the workrooms before the war, by 1922 the couture houses had taken to regulating the duration of individual tasks. These times were set without consulting the workers who made the items and were always to the advantage of the *première d'atelier* who received a percentage of all profits and so, in effect, had an interest in all work being completed as fast as possible. 'The reader would be shocked to know how much profit some houses make, compared to how little they pay their staff,' wrote Suzanne Lion, 'Le sans-gêne des maisons de couture', *Peuple*, 8 August 1922. In the early 1920s Madeleine Vionnet's manager Louis Dangel introduced time and motion studies. Brachet Champsaur 2012, 55.

68 Wilson 1925, 72–3. On the industrial organisation of the Paris couture house, see also the catalogue of the 1925 Paris Exposition, *Encyclopédie des arts décoratifs*, vol. IX, 1978, 13, 14 and 22.

69 Wilson 1925, 72 and 73.

70 Leach 1994, 309.

71 *Fortune*, 2 August 1932, 79–81. See also Woon, 'For the first time', *Washington Post*, 29 April 1923.

72 Green 1997, 110.

73 Ibid., 111, 106.

74 *History de l'industrie* 1926, 123.

75 *Vogue* (America), 15 April 1923, 37.

76 Delbourg-Delphis 1981, 106.

77 *Vogue* (America), 15 May 1925; 'Two Shades in Modernistic Treatment', ibid., 1 May 1927, 66.

78 On Vionnet, see *Vogue* (France), 1 February 1924, 16. On Patou, see Hawes 1938, 59. More generally, see Marjorie Howard's column in *Harper's Bazar* for October 1925, 200, and Marjorie Howard 'Paris Draws a New Colour Line', ibid., April 1927, 85.

79 'And One More Striking', *Vogue* (America), 15 February 1926, 81.

80 Baron de Meyer, 'The Paris Openings Number; Baron de Meyer Analyses the Mode', *Harper's Bazar*, April 1927, 77.

81 'Baron de Meyer reports the New Mode from each opening of the great houses', *Harper's Bazar*, October 1924, 186. See also 'Sheath Gown a Novelty', *The Washington Post*, 10 August 1924; Howard, 'Paris Draws a New Colour Line', 85 and 90.

82 *Vogue* (France), 4 April 1925, 23.

83 At Redfern 'les glaces innombrables reflètent à l'infini des silhouettes élégantes parées de fourreaux châtoyantes, drapées dans les fourrures précieuses.' *Vogue* (France), November 1924, 118–19. See also Bonney 1929, 14, who describes the mirrors at Louiseboulanger.

84 Van Campen Stewart, 'The Paris Openings: Spring 1924', *Harper's Bazar*, April 1924, 58.

85 'The Paris Openings described by Baron de Meyer', *Harper's Bazar*, October 1926, 78.

86 'Baron de Meyer analyses the Mode', 80. The following season de Meyer explicitly referred to 'the fashionable aspect of the woman dressed *en série*'; de Meyer, *Harper's Bazar*, October 1927, 85.

87 See e.g. Wilson 1925, 50.

88 Such a day is commonly mapped out in fashion magazines. E.g., in 1924 French *Vogue* described the day of a fashionable *New-Yorkaise* in Paris: 9am a walk in the Bois de Boulogne, 11am attend a fashion show, 1pm lunch at the Ritz, 5pm tea at home, 7.30pm dinner in a restaurant, 9.15pm arrival at the theatre. 'Un voyage autour du Cadran en compagnie d'une élégante New-Yorkaise', *Vogue* (France), 1 January 1924, 12–13.

89 'Baron de Meyer views the Mode', *Harper's Bazar*, April 1925, 98 and 170.

90 Sherry Buckberrough, 'Sonia Delaunay entre le Paris des émigrés russes et la clientèle bourgeoise éclairée', in Palais Galliera 1997, 100.

91 Benton, Benton and Wood 2003, 107 n. 78. With thanks to Marketa Uhlirova for bringing this to my attention.

92 Catherine Join-Diéterle, 'Mode des Années folles, entre modernité et modernisme', in Musée Galliera 2007, 23. For a nuanced discussion of an instance in which art was 'put at the service of *la couture*', see the discussion of a photograph of mannequins posing in Sonia Delaunay coats in 1925 in Tag Gronberg, 'Deco Venus', in Arscott and Scott 2000, 142–55.

93 Lozowick had visited Moscow in 1924 and wrote several articles on the constructivists and encouraged their exhibition in New York. He enlarged his constructivist-inspired drawings for both the Lord & Taylor fashion show and his stage sets for the production *Gas* in 1926. In 1927 he designed a dress containing cubist machine patterns for Gilda

Gray, a Ziegfeld Follies 'shimmy girl' that was included in Macy's *Art in Trade* exhibition held 2–6 May 1927. Wilson, Pilgrim and Tashjian 1986, 65–6 and 229.

94 Ford and Crowther 1926, 72.

95 Alexandre 1902, 13; Roger-Milès 1910, 134.

96 'The Paris Openings: Baron de Meyer Reports the New Mode From Each Opening of the Great Houses', *Harper's Bazar*, October 1924, 64–79, 89 and 90.

97 On the dance craze, see 'Letter from Paris', *Harper's Bazar*, March 1921, 37 and 41.

98 'Marjorie Howard's Paris Letter', *Harper's Bazar*, February 1926, 80–87 and 158.

99 'The Mid-Season Collections', *Vogue* (America), 15 January 1925, 70; ibid., 15 April 1925, 39.

100 Bettina Bedwell, 'The Last Word in Paris Fashions', *Chicago Daily Tribune*, 20 September 1925. There is, however, an earlier photograph of the kinetic line in *Vogue* (America), 15 July 1925, 7.

101 Lucien Lelong double-page advertisement, *Vogue* (France), 1 August 1925, xxvi–xxvii.

102 Bedwell, 'Last Word'.

103 *Vogue* (France), 6 June 25, 45.

104 Double-page advertisement, *Harper's Bazar*, October 1925, 56–7. See also *Vogue* (America), 15 October 1925, 25.

105 *Vogue* (France), 11 November 1925, xxxi.

106 Ibid., 13.

107 'Les mouvements d'une femme moderne sont libres, émancipés, actifs. . . . Pour ces corps souples, remuants, aisés, j'ai utilisé la diagonale, le plein biais, qui donne toute l'élasticité de l'étoffe.' Roubaud 1928, 34. The couturier in this book is given the name 'Jeanne Mounet' but so many of the features of her couture house that are described throughout the book correspond to the house of Madeleine Vionnet that the quotation, with its reference to the bias cut for which she was well known, can be inferred to be Vionnet's.

108 Ibid., 25.

109 Bonney 1929, 16–17.

110 'La mode qui vient', subtitled 'Vogue prévoit pour l'hiver une silhouette mouvante aux lignes onduleuses', *Vogue* (France), 10 October 1925, 3.

111 'The Paris Openings Number: Baron de Meyer Analyses the Mode', *Harper's Bazar*, April 1927, 77.

112 'Baron de Meyer Attends the Openings', ibid., April 1926, 122.

113 Ibid., 115–22 and 202.

114 For an expanded cultural history covering, among other things, ideas about speed and the representation of movement in time in the still imagery of the period, see Kern 2003, 21–4, 84, 109–30.

115 'Une image ne peut pas être durable. Scientifiquement, le réflexe de beauté se fatigue: l'image devient, en vieillissant, cliché. . . . De l'automne au printemps, l'esthétique change. On parle des canons éternels de la beauté quand deux catalogues successifs du BON MARCHÉ confondent ces radotages. La mode des costumes est l'appel à la volupté

le plus exacte, le mieux modulé. Le film y emprunte certains charmes, et il est la si fidèle image de nos engouements que, vieux de cinq ans, il ne convient plus qu'à la lanterne du forain.' Epstein 1921, 177 and 179–80.

116 Raymond Williams, *The Country and the City* (1973), Hogarth Press, London, 1993, 242, cited in Marcus 2007, 142. On the association with motoring and fashionability in the 1920s, see Mary Louise Roberts, 'Samson and Delilah Revisited: The Politics of Fashion in Nineteenth-Century France', in Chadwick and Latimer 2003, 78. On 'the modern experience of vertiginous speed' produced by the automobile and the cinema in the early twentieth century, see Sara Danius, 'Modernist Fictions of Speed', in Classen 2005, 412–19.

117 In association with *L'Intransigeant* newspaper, Femina's *concours d'élégance féminine en automobile* began to be staged annually at beach resorts from 1927. For the 1928 one, held in Nice on 22 June, the competitors, who were all fashionable women, had a cocktail with the jury on arrival, before participating in a parade (*défilé*) of more than 200 automobiles that passed before the jury seated on the terrace of the Cascade restaurant. *Femina*, July 1928, 38–9, and ibid., August 1929, 4–5, 7, 8, 23–7. For further descriptions of *concours d'élégance*, see Marjorie Howard in *Harper's Bazar*, March 1930, 30 and 180, and ibid., June 1930, 68. For film footage of a Parisian *concours d'élégance* in 1928, see 'Actualités', 1928, ref.no.46232, Archives Françaises du Film, Paris.

118 'La Femme et l'Auto sont faites l'une pour l'autre. . . . la femme est-elle comme une Centauresse privilégiée; elle fait corps avec sa voiture.' *Femina*, October 1924, 32. On the relationship of the female body and motor vehicle both in the *concours d'élégance* and in the 1925 Paris exhibition, in the form of Sonia Delaunay's co-ordinated ensemble and decorated car, see Gronberg 1998, 124–30.

119 Gronberg 2002. On the modernist body see Wollen 1993, 20; Levenson 2011, 247.

120 'Paris Mode Used to Show New Machines', *Los Angeles Times*, 7 August 1927. As early as 1922, *Harper's Bazar* summed up an emerging trend combining French chic and American modernism in 'New French Sports Clothes and American Cars', *Harper's Bazar*, September 1922. In 1916 Lucile had designed a car interior in the U.S.A. for the Chalmers 1917 Touring Sedan. See e.g. Chalmers advertisement in *Colliers*, 16 September 1916. In 1927 the French couturiers Madeleine Vionnet, Philippe & Gaston, Lucien Lelong, Callot Soeurs, Lanvin, Premet, Drecoll, Poiret, Patou and Jenny all produced colour schemes for automobiles and their fittings for the Paris firm of E.I. du Pont & Nemours & Co that sold them in America. 'Bright Colours to Distinguish New Machines', *Los Angeles Times*, 30 January 1927.

121 'Une robe sans ligne n'est qu'un vêtement. Une voiture sans ligne n'est qu'un vehicule. La ligne seule crée l'élégance'. Advertisement for Galle coachbuilders. *Vogue* (France), 1 July 1927.

122 Gronberg 1998, 125.

123 For a feature in a fashion magazine on cars at the races that highlights the transition from horse racing to car racing as a fashionable pursuit in the mid-1920s, see James de Coquet, 'Quarante chevaux contre un', *Gazette du Bon Genre*, June 1924, 377–9. Its October 1924 issue was a special edition devoted to the automobile.

124 Wollen 1993, 20. See also Burstein 2012, 143–50.

125 Trade buyers were on the lookout for Fords but private buyers were counselled to avoid them. See e.g. 'The Way Round Paris', *Vogue* (U.K.), late March 1927, 70.

126 Hawes 1938, 59.

127 John B. Watson, *Behaviorism* (1924), University of Chicago Press, 1966, 49 and 269, quoted in Synott 1993, 28.

128 Cited in Terri J. Gordon, 'GIRLS, GIRLS, GIRLS: Re-Membering the Body', in Brueggemann and Schulman 2005, 92. Gordon's chapter contains a detailed treatment of the image of the 'femme-machine' in revue theatre and its links to technology and militarism in the inter-war years. On the mirroring, multiplying and machine aesthetics of the chorus line, see esp. 91–3 which include a description from 1929 of the similarity between chorus girls and cars.

129 Castle 1984, 205.

130 *Harper's Bazar*, February 1926, 64.

131 Schweitzer 2009, 145.

CHAPTER 7

1 Nora (3 vols) 1996, 1997 and 1998.

2 Nora 1996, xiii.

3 Ibid., xv and 14.

4 Nora 1989, 9.

5 Nora 1989, 17. This translation of Nora's introduction from the 1984 French edition succinctly summarised his project, which had not yet been translated into English. The phrase reappeared in slightly different words in the English 1996 translation: 'our memory is intensely retinal, powerfully televisual. The much touted "return of the narrative" in recent historical writing has to be linked to the ubiquity of visual images and film in contemporary culture.' Nora 1996, 13.

6 Nora 1989, 17.

7 'Le rideau s'entr'ouvre. Le défilé commence.' Reboux 1927, 15. See also Roubaud 1928, 20. Le Fèvre described 'the stage where the troop of saleswomen and mannequins successfully act the scenes of a play' (*les tableaux*, also used to describe scenes in a film) for the hundredth time before the clients: 'It falls to them to rehearse the next spectacle' ('la scène où la troupe des vendeuses et des mannequins joue pour la centième fois devant les clients, les tableaux de la pièce à succès.

À elles de préparer le prochain spectacle'). He pointed out that couture uses some of the same terms as theatre such as *répétition générale*, or dress rehearsal, which in fashion is the final presentation before the buyers' one. Le Fèvre 1929, 36, and 65–6.

8 'Elle éprouve cette illusion qu'il n'y a, derrière le décor, qu'un très petit nombre d'ouvrières travaillant exclusivement pour elle.' Alexandre 1902, 80. Uzanne made the same point: 'The important clients as a rule only see the attractive surface of these great businesses, and have no knowledge of the prodigious amount of work done behind the scenes. They see a score of pretty girls called *mannequins* who try on the costumes and a few skilful fitters. But, employed in carrying out their orders, there are eight hundred girls working in feverish haste, in small, gloomy, badly lighted rooms, carefully concealed out of sight.' Uzanne 1912, 40–41.

9 '[E]lle serait absolument terrifiée, d'abord, de l'aspect formidable que présente la maison de travail.' Alexandre 1902, 80.

10 'Je vous assure que c'est incroyable, tout ce qu'il y a dans cette usine, car c'est une véritable usine d'élégance.' Marquise de Bal, 'Une Journée chez un grand couturier (Redfern)', *Femina*, 13 April 1901, 125.

11 'Une maison de couture est, avant tout, une affaire industrielle . . . Bref, tout un monde, un monde spécial, turbulent, affairé, nerveux, passionné, vit autour de cette ruche industrielle qu'est une grande maison de couture, et ce monde, par certains côtés, touché à l'art et à la fantaisie . . . mais par d'autres, il confine à la finance et à l'industrie et il est âprement pratique, sauvagement travailleur'. 'La Couture parisienne', *Europe Nouvelle*, 20 December 1924.

12 'Dessinateurs industriels en modes'. Françoise Tétart-Vittu, 'Naissance du couturier et du modèliste', in Musée de la Mode et du Costume 1992, 39.

13 'Le grand couturier, qui est un artiste, doit être aussi un chef de maison de commerce, un directeur de banque, un patron d'usine.' Robert de Beauplan, 'Après la grève des cousettes: dans les coulisses de la grande couture', *L'Illustration*, 19 May 1923, reprinted in *L'Illustration, Journal Universel* 1987, 137–40. See also Roubaud 1928, 78, who writes that couturiers must be 'heads of industry, artists and financiers' ('Des chefs de l'Industrie, des artistes, des financiers'), and the fashion volume of the 1925 Paris 'Art Déco' exhibition catalogue which describes how modern business has forced the couture houses to practise a form of Taylorism more usual in ready-to-wear: 'l'industrialisation des maisons de couture a déterminé une organisation méthodique des services. On y saurait pratiquer la taylorisation propre aux ouvrages en série'. *Encyclopédie des arts décoratifs*, vol. IX, 1977, 22–3.

14 'Autrefois, le chef d'une grande maison de couture était un homme habitué à manier des étoffées et à imaginer des modèles.

Aujourd'hui, il est beaucoup plus *businessman* que créateur de combinaisons frivoles. . . . C'est pourquoi le grand couturier – au lieu d'être un artiste environné d'échantillons et créant de la beauté avec une aisance féerique – n'est plus qu'un administrateur un peu chauve, le nez chaussé d'un lorgnon, installé à un bureau commercial, environné de cotes, de tarifs internationaux, de circulaires.' Reboux 1927, 12.

15 Beauplan, 'Après la grève', 137–40.

16 Ibid. Uzanne described how the couture houses kept colour-coded books of their customers' financial viability: 'there is the *white* list of those who have an assured income and pay cash; a *yellow* list of those whose means are moderate, and who only pay after frequent requests; and finally a *black* list for those whose resources are most uncertain, and who never pay for anything.' Uzanne 1912, 39. In her book on haute couture in the 1950s, Alexandra Palmer describes the 'refined and complex record-keeping system' at the house of Christian Dior which opened in 1947: each private client had her own file recording not only personal details, such as passport number, measurements and credit rating, but also her personality ('hard or easy to handle'). Likewise files were kept on professional buyers, with full details of their every purchase, and of the model dresses, including which mannequins had worn them, their show number, and full details of every client who bought each dress. Palmer quotes the house on this but goes on to say: 'Tantalizing as this is for researchers, I have not been able to get access to any of this type of record and was repeatedly told they did not exist. Either they have been disposed of or, more likely, are considered either an infringement of the client's privacy or too commercial to support the myth of couture as an art.' Palmer 2001, 44–5.

17 Reboux 1927, 12.

18 Alexandre 1902, 54; Shonfield 1982, 57–9; Coleman 1990, 34; Tétart-Vittu in Musée de la Mode et du Costume 1992, 36–9.

19 '[U]ne systématisation dans la parure.' Simon 1931, 13.

20 Levasseur 1912, 30; Willoughby 1926, 35; Roubaud 1928, 22, calling the ateliers 'une usine silencieuse', a silent factory. Gerber 1932, 236 describes haute couture as 'a barracks, a factory'. Maggy Rouff, who worked in Paris in the 1920s, fancifully describes the couturier as 'an extremely sensitive and delicate machine', one which cannot be repaired if it goes wrong. Rouff 1942, 224.

21 Alexandre 1902, 81. These three would probably have been Paquin at number 3, Worth at number 7 and Doucet at number 21.

22 'Le mécanisme générale repose sur une division de travail poussée à l'extrême et admirablement réglée.' Alexandre 1902, 50–51, 83. On the organisation of the couture house, see also Kathleen Schlesinger, 'The

Growth of a Paris Costume', *The Lady's Realm*, June 1900, 210–16; Elizabeth Dryden, 'The Secret of the Paris Hat', *Harper's Bazar*, July 1909, 700–02; Marie Monceau, 'Dressmaking Openings Will Shortly Be Held by Noted Paris Firms', *Philadelphia Enquirer*, 18 February 1912.

23 Roger-Milès 1910, 127.

24 Beauplan, 'Après la grève', 139.

25 Worth 1895, 90–91; Alexandre 1902, 50–51. Roger-Milès 1910 contains photographs of several specialist ateliers in 1910, including sketchers, embroiderers, fur-seamstresses, bodice-makers, skirt-makers, milliners and tailors. The last were nearly all male workers, whereas all the other categories were exclusively female workers. It also shows the silk store, the stockroom, the wrapping atelier and the refectory.

26 Alexandre 1902, 49. On the age, training and hierarchy of *arpètes* and apprentices, see Levasseur 1912, 24–5.

27 '[D]es flots de lumière électrique, des tintements du téléphone', Alexandre 1902, 50–51.

28 For an early reference to a refectory in a couture house, see Bal, 'Une Journée', *Femina*, 13 April 1901, 126–7, who describes how, at Redfern, two hundred employees of both sexes ate lunch in two sittings, an hour apart. For an early photograph of a couture house refectory at lunchtime, see Roger-Milès 1910, 160.

29 Alexandre 1902, 43–5; Roger-Milès 1910, 132. Stock control was strict. Almost 30,000 dockets were issued a month for the release of lengths of cloth. It was carefully measured: 20 cm over or under in the manufacture of a single dress mattered little but an error in the 8–10,000 dresses, the typical annual production figure in a large house by 1923, could affect the balance by many hundred thousand francs. Beauplan, 'Après la grève', 137–40.

30 Worth 1895, 90–91; Alexandre 1902, 83; Roger-Milès 1910, 127; Reboux 1927, 12.

31 Roger-Milès 1910, 128; Levasseur 1912, 23.

32 Levasseur 1912, 27.

33 On the problems associated with apprentices specialising by the age of sixteen so that workers had no proper understanding of the entire garment, see ibid., 30. On the *petites mains*, see ibid., 24.

34 Monceau, 'Dressmaking Openings', *Philadelphia Enquirer*, 18 February 1912.

35 Grumbach 2008, 48.

36 Roger-Milès 1910, 126.

37 Levasseur, 1912, 82.

38 Alexandre 1902, 85.

39 Jean de Mouy, interview with the author, Paris, 28 July 2007.

40 Stewart 2001, 176–7.

41 Alexandre 1902, 79–80. Twenty years later, the same arguments were made in the same descriptions, of an army of female workers over eight floors in an enormous building of which the client remained in total ignorance. Beauplan, 'Après la grève', 137–40.

42 '[E]lle verrait, un beau matin, toutes les pièces dispersés de son vêtement se donner rendez-vous, se rejoindre et s'adapter parfaitement les unes aux autres, comme on voit, dans les contes de fée, des enchanteurs, coupés en morceaux, se recoller d'eux-mêmes et courir à la bataille!' 'Elle admirerait alors, pour peu qu'elle eût le don de l'admiration, la façon mathématique dont est réglée cette grande machine à quinze cents bras, pour pouvoir ainsi mener à bien une opération aussi complexe que l'exécution d'une costume.' Alexandre 1902, 80–81. In similar vein, twenty-seven years later Le Fèvre observed the process of designing a dress at Vionnet as a collaboration required between fifteen brains and thirty hands ('quinze cerveaux . . . trente mains'), suggesting that the workforce operates like a single organism or machine. Le Fèvre 1929, 41–2.

43 O'Neill 2004, xi.

44 O'Neill 2004, 57. A number of anthropologists and sociologists have conceptualised the body as plural, e.g. Mary Douglas's two bodies and Scheper-Hughes and Lock's three bodies, all summarised by Synott 1993, 229 and 236.

45 'Repeated Original' was Vionnet's trademark name for the ready-to-wear designs she made in 1926 for the Wanamaker store. Kirke 1998, 133. Brachet Champsaur 2012, 55.

46 '[D]ans toute l'usine silencieuse, il n'y a ni bielle d'acier, ni volant, ni courroies . . . Mais mains.' Roubaud 1928, 22.

47 Hawes 1938, 17.

48 'L'oeil s'étonne un peu, comme au théâtre, du changement brusque d'atmosphère. Une grande maison de couture s'appuie sur deux principes: La Fantaisie et le Rendement. Tous les problèmes y sont résolus sous ces deux aspects. L'architecture même du bâtiment est à double fond comme un coffre à secret. On ouvre une porte, on entre, on la renferme sur soi, et ce n'est plus la même porte. D'un côté, elle était ciselée comme une chasse; de l'autre, elle est nue et peinte au ripolin.' Le Fèvre 1929, 36–7.

49 Goffman 1990, cited in Rocamora 2009, 52.

50 Douglas 2002. For an outline of the relevance of the concept of liminality to cultural studies, see the discussion of the ideas of the anthropologists Victor Turner and Mary Douglas in Smith and Riley 2009, 76–8.

51 Troy 2003, 231, citing David Chaney, 'The Department Store as a Cultural Form', *Theory, Culture & Society*, 1, no. 3, 1983, 24.

52 Henri Lefebvre described how bodies produce spaces: 'There is an immediate relationship between the body and its space, between the body's deployment in space and its occupation of space. . . . each living body *is* space and *has* its space: it produces itself in space and it also produces that space. This is a truly remarkable relationship: the body with the energies at its disposal, the living body, creates or produces its own space.' Lefebvre 1991, 170.

53 'In the history of space as such . . . the historical and diachronic realms and the generative past are forever leaving their inscriptions upon the writing-tablet, so to speak, of space. The uncertain traces left by events are not the only marks on (or in) space: society in its actuality also deposits its script, the result and product of social activities. Time has more than one writing-system.' Lefebvre went on to argue that the measure for first buildings was the human body ('thumb's breadths, feet, palms, and so on') so that built space, 'along with the way it was measured and spoken of, still held up to all the members of a society an image and a living reflection of their own bodies.' Ibid., 110–11 and 116ff.

54 Ibid., 195. In the same passage he goes further, describing the 'social body' as 'a body battered and broken by a devastating practice, namely the division of labour, and by the weight of society's demands'.

55 Ibid., 89–90.

56 Ibid., 140ff, esp. 142 and Fr. edition, 167–70. See also Shields 1988, 14.

57 The *cabine* was also referred to as the *confortable* (Ghenya, 'La Journée d'un mannequin', *Le Figaro-Modes*, February 1904, 14–17) and the *cagibi* (Max Rivière, 'La Journée d'un mannequin', *Femina*, 15 October 1905, 491–2). For further references to the *cabine*, see 'The Paris Mannequin, How She Helps to Beguile Women in the Dressmaker's Shop', *New York Times*, 10 November 1907; Emile Henriot, 'Figures parisiennes: le mannequin', *L'Illustration*, 27 December 1913, reprinted in *L'Illustration, Journal Universel* 1987, 112–16; Beauplan, 'Après la grève', 137–40; Reboux 1927, 18; Roubaud 1928, 185–6.

58 'De temps en temps, sur un appel, le mannequin dit le nom dont on a baptisé le costume qu'elle présente, et, comme les spectateurs ne sont pas ici des esthètes ni des contemplatifs, le prix; puis, le silence renaît et ce n'est qu'à côté, dans les pièces voisines, où les mannequins se métamorphosent, que l'on perçoit le brouhaha de voix rapides, jeunes, affairées ou gaies, qui bavardent comme des oiseaux dans une volière.' Roger-Milès 1910, 67–8.

59 'Chez les vendeuses, le sourire est de rigueur, mais le rire est strictement prohibé.' Roubaud 1928, 166.

60 Roger-Milès 1910, 134.

61 'Et dans la cabine, vingt corps vivants multipliés par les glaces, allaient prêter aux robes inertes les mouvements de leurs hanches, le soufflé de leur poitrine, les battements de leur coeur.' Roubaud 1928, 6.

62 Le Fèvre 1929, 53.

63 'On les revoit sur mannequins vivants . . . Mais il faut animer ces fantômes'. Ibid., 50.

64 '[S]ilence brusque et total. Un gros acheteur de Cleveland a retiré son cigare de sa bouche et murmure: "Lovely!" La robe est née.' Ibid., 70–71. The mannequin at 'Jeanne Mounet', a

fictional couture house that combines the features of several real ones, especially Madeleine Vionnet, is also called Ginette. Roubaud 1928, 153 ff.

65 'Je ne parle pas de la conception technique des costumes: je m'en tiens au seul point de vue de la vision et de la sensation kaléidoscopique qu'elle doit imprimer sur la rétine de ces commissionnaires à qui l'on fait la faveur de cette représentation unique et rare, longue comme trois tragédies.' Roger-Milès 1910, 60.

66 'Cette robe qui, déjà, en quelques semaines, avait eu mille existences animées par mille filles lointaines d'Amérique'. Roubaud 1928, 49.

67 'Le premier mannequin s'avance: voici "la mode". C'est un événement. Un événement qui déclenche mille crayons, mille stylos, mille langues, qui donne le vol à mille câbles: mille rubriques en sont alimentées. Berlin, New-York, Londres, Rome attendant ce que Paris a consacré.' Gerber 1932, 235.

68 'A Paris Show of Fashions', *Washington Post*, 19 September 1909.

69 'A Seat at the Paris Openings', *Vogue* (America), 15 April 1923, 39–49.

70 Saunders 1954, 110; Grumbach 2008, 17.

71 Maud, 'La Mode,' *La Rampe*, 16 November 1916, 12–13.

72 Roubaud describes the fashion show as 'une féerie en 300 robes' (a *féerie* in 300 dresses). Roubaud 1928, 163.

73 '[I]l fit aménager une petite scène et un petit parc qui lui permirent de pouvoir présenter ses collections dans un décor approprie: c'est ainsi qu'il présente au mois de janvier ses collections dans un décor d'été et en juillet ses robes d'hiver dans un décor d'hiver.' Melnotte-Simonin also used innovative lighting techniques in his display for the 1925 Paris 'Arts Décoratifs' exhibition that involved models painted with a phosphorescent process ('sur procédé phosphorescent qu'il a été le seul à exposer'). *Histoire de l'industrie* 1926, 127. There is colour film footage of Melnotte-Simonin's *peintures phosphorescentes*, dresses decorated with painted phosphorescent flowers, in 'La Mode: création Melnotte-Simonin', 1927, ref. no. 128150, Archives Françaises du Film, Paris.

74 At Lelong 'a special, invisible device can be operated at will to produce either the lighting of chandeliers for evening dresses, or the brightness of real sunlight for day wear' ('un dispositif spécial invisible peut faire briller à volonté soit la lumière des lustres pour les robes de soirée, soit l'éclat véritable du soleil pour les toilettes de ville'). *Histoire de l'industrie* 1926, 126. See also *Vogue* (France), 1 February 1924, and 'Lucien Lelong', *La Renaissance de l'art français et des industries de luxe*, June 1924, 4. Lelong also used a similar installation for a fashion show in an exhibition of French taste in New York that year. *Vogue* (France), June 1924, 112–13.

75 *Femina*, March 1924, 32; 'Baron de Meyer Attends the Openings', *Harper's Bazar*, April 1924, 76–8, 170, 172 and 174.

76 'A Seat at the Paris Openings', *Vogue* (America), 15 April 1923, 42.

77 Roubaud 1928, 204. See Ch. 4, p. 82.

78 Charles-Roux 1993, 160.

79 The idea of a 'web of mirrors' comes from Georges Didi-Huberman's discussion of representation both as a net or mesh of mirrors and as a mirrored 'box of representation'. He writes: 'Kant, pertinently, spoke to us of limits. He drew, as from within, the contours of a net – a strange, opaque net whose mesh is made only of mirrors. It is a device of enclosure, extendable as nets sometimes are, certainly, but as closed as a box: the *box of representation* within which every subject will throw himself at the walls as at reflections of himself. Here, then, is the subject of knowledge: it is speculative and specular at the same time, and the recovering of the speculative by the specular – of intellectual reflection by imaginary self-captation – is precisely wherein lies this *magical* character of the box, its character as resolvent closure, as self-satisfying suture. How then to get out of this magic circle, this box of mirrors, this circle defines our own limits as knowing subjects?' Didi-Huberman goes on to discuss how the image plays with the world of logic, which suggests an intriguing parallel with the perplexing visual logic of the mirrored boxes and interiors of the couture houses. Didi-Huberman 2005, 139.

80 Joan Rivière, 'Womanliness as a Masquerade' (1929), reprinted in Burgin, Donald and Kaplan 1986.

81 The manufacture of mirrored glass quadrupled in France in the second half of the nineteenth century: 'Mirrors were now placed everywhere, in luxury hotels, restaurants, cafés, building entryways, theatres, casinos and at the opera'. Melchior-Bonnet 2001, 97.

82 '[U]ne coquette sale carrée, toute en glaces, et qui, en un coup de bouton, s'allume merveilleusement grâce aux véritables "feux de rampe" disposés au ras du sol'. 'Une journée chez un grand couturier (Redfern)', *Femina*, 13 April 1901, 126. Pinguat too had a *salon de lumière* fitted out with mirrors and gas lighting. See Coleman 1990, 16, and Marley 1980, 104.

83 See entry on the 'Mystic Maze' in Hopkins 1976, 84–5.

84 Colette 1963, 99.

85 '[D]e façon à donner tous les effets du théâtre et à *répéter* une robe, comme on étudie et met on scène une pièce toute entière'. Alexandre 1902, 99.

86 There is a photograph of another example at Chéruit, where the mirror was fitted with six large directional lights at the top. Roger-Milès 1910, 16. There is film footage of a mannequin modelling in front of a three-way mirror from the early 1920s entitled 'Parisienne en robe de soirée drapée', at time code 980 of 'Les Arts du vêtement', 1928, ref. no. 4028, Archives Françaises du Film, Paris.

87 The *psyché* began life as a full-length free-standing mirror which might be flanked with sconces and side mirrors. The central panel could pivot round the horizontal axis to modify the angle of vision. On the history and nineteenth-century origins of the *psyché*, see Melchior-Bonnet 2001, 85. The 'three-faced mirror' or *miroir à trois faces* that became popular early in the twentieth century was a development of the same idea, with same-size side mirrors and, the crucial difference, with hinged side mirrors that made it possible to manipulate the image in a vertical plane, thus producing three simultaneous but different views of the body in the round. See also Tietjens Meyers 2002; Doy 2005.

88 There are four Brot advertisements from *Figaro-Modes* for February, April, May and June 1905 with endorsements from the actresses Arlette Dorgière, Mlle Dieterle, Ellen Therval and Georgette Sandry. Arlette Dorgière announces 'if truth still existed she'd want no other mirror than Mr Brot's'; Georgette Sandry asserts that 'for all fashionable women, your three-faced mirrors are without contest the agents of grace', while Mlle Dieterle says 'Dear Mr Brot, Thanks to your ravishing three-faced Psyche one can be judge and judged at the same time'.

89 There are images of internal mirrored casements at Callot Soeurs, Redfern, Paquin, Madame Georgette (milliner), in Roger-Milès 1910, 14, 26, 39, 65, 68. These show casement windows fitted with mirrors, juxtaposed with identical casements fitted with clear glass, creating spatial complexity in an interior. Less frequently, entirely mirrored walls were fitted, consisting either of single, enormous pieces of mirrored glass or of a grid of smaller rectangles bolted to the wall with chrome fixings. In 1867 there was a mirrored wall in the main salon at Worth with garments displayed on wooden forms in front of it; Coleman 1990, 16. There is an image of the actress Réjane at a fitting at Doucet in front of a mirrored wall in *Femina*, 1 December 1903, reproduced in Coleman 1990, 163. There are photographs of mirrored walls or large mirrored wall panels at Worth, Chéruit, Doucet and Béchoff David in Roger-Milès 1910, 27, 33, 38, 48. These large mirrored walls are sometimes set at a right angle to, and are the same size and shape as, the shop window and sometimes are simply juxtaposed with the other windows, as at Worth. At Louiseboulanger 'The mirrors set in modernistic screens . . . gain their effectiveness from showing vistas of the salons at strange angles, and in affording glimpses of the mannequins in diverting poses.' Bonney 1929, 14.

90 Madame de Graffigny, *L'Art de se mettre en ménage*, Paris 1910, cited in Melchior-Bonnet 2001, 95.

91 Flora McDonald Thompson, 'Autumn Days in Paris', *Harper's Bazar*, October 1905, 931–2.

92 Lelong's new premises of 1924 alternated mirrors and windows in identical frames, a common feature of couture interiors, as was the juxtaposition of door frames and mirror frames that could be seen at Worth.

93 Jean-Luis Borgès, 'Les Miroirs', *L'Auteur et autres textes*, Paris: Gallimard 1953, 121, cited in Melchior-Bonnet 2001, 268.

94 Lefebvre 1991, 181; Shields 1988, 20, citing Fr. edition, 216 (Shields's paraphrasing is found in the Eng. edition: Lefebvre 1991, 185–86).

95 'Ainsi inattendues et surgissantes, elles étonnent et frappent d'avantage. Arrivant de loin, d'un pas cadence et comme dansant, évoluant, ondulant, se cambrant, on craint qu'elles ne disparaissent comme elles sont venues, et il faut reconnoître que, dans ce milieu un peu solonnel, les robes paraissent plus fleuries et plus rares par l'isolement, et les femmes quasi plus surnaturelles.' Alexandre 1902, 109.

96 White 1973, 50. Guillaume Garnier described how, in the main salon of the avenue d'Antin, furnished in the Directoire style, the mannequins entered one by one via the oeil-de-boeuf doorway. Guillaume Garnier assisted by Françoise Tétart-Vittu, 'Catalogue of Exhibits', in Musée de la Mode et du Costume 1986, 221.

97 'A Paris Show of Fashions', *Washington Post*, 19 September 1909.

98 Wilson 1925, 38. Peacock Alley was the name for the regular parade of fashionable people in the 300-foot long lobby-floor corridor of the Waldorf-Astoria Hotel at the junction of Fifth Avenue and 34th Street, New York, now the site of the Empire State Building. Allen 1993, 123. Wilson may also have been referring to Robert Z. Leonard's 1922 film of the same name that starred the ex-Follies girl Mae Murray as 'Cleo of Paris'.

99 Maud, 'La Mode', *La Rampe*, 16 November 1916, 12–13.

100 Double-page advertisement, *Harper's Bazar*, October 1925, 56–7.

101 'Paris Yields to None in Fashion World', *New York Times*, 2 December 1928.

102 *Harper's Bazar*, April 1929, 190.

103 O'Neill 2004, 60.

104 'King of Gowns Due Tomorrow', *Chicago Daily Tribune*, 5 October 1913; 'Paris Fall Openings', ibid., 12 October 1913.

105 In 1920 Patou claimed to make about 1000 models per annum, of which only about 10% were successful, meaning that he made his entire profits from 100 models per annum. He would sell the remaining 900 off at relatively low prices, in fact at a considerable loss (a dress that cost 1200 francs to make would be sold off at 400 francs) so that to make his profit he had to sell the remaining dresses at 2000 francs. He claimed that were it not for being so copied he would be able to sell cheaper. *Moniteur de l'exportation*,

October 1920, n.p. Roubaud 1928, 12;
Le Fèvre 1929, 59; Poiret 1931, 43,
all substantiate that the proportion of
successful dresses in a collection was 10%,
and an American reporter put it even lower,
at 7%. 'Paris Yields to None', *New York Times*,
2 December 1928. See also Stewart 1989,
110.

106 Anne Rittenhouse, 'Dress', *Atlanta Constitution*, 21 September 1922.
107 Kracauer 1995, 75–6.
108 Anne Rittenhouse, 'What the Well-Dressed Woman is Wearing', *New York Times*, 29 September 1912.
109 '[N]ous sommes au royaume du nouveau. Créer, créer'. Beauplan, 'Après la grève', 139.
110 French Ministry of Commerce figures published in 1919, cited in Grumbach 2008, 40.
111 'Shall American Woman Follow Paris Styles?' *New York Times*, 6 October 1912.
112 'Paris Openings Show No Gowns Radically New in Style', *New York Times*, 1 March 1914.
113 For a discussion of the original and copy in art (Duchamp) and in fashion (Poiret), see Troy 2003, ch. 4, 'The Readymade and the Genuine Reproduction', 266–326.

CHAPTER 8

1 Berger 1972.
2 Laura Mulvey's influential essay from 1975, 'Visual Pleasure and Narrative Cinema', reprinted in Mulvey 1989, generated debates on the 'male gaze' and on female spectatorship throughout the 1980s in which many scholars extended Mulvey's arguments from film to art, advertising and popular culture. For a discussion of the gendered gaze in relation to fashion in particular, see Rocamora 2009, 145–55. Mulvey herself has modified her original analysis to take account of subsequent historical research on female audiences for film, arguing that 'the constitution of the audience in the 1920s, for example, complicates the "male gaze" that I discussed in "Visual Pleasure and Narrative Cinema" '. Laura Mulvey, 'Unmasking the Gaze: Feminist Film Theory, History and Film Studies', in Callahan 2010, 17.
3 Doane 1982; Doane 1988–9.
4 Gamman and Makinen 1994, 182.
5 Crary 1992. Abigail Solomon-Godeau, 'The Other Side of Venus: The Visual Economy of Feminine Display', in Grazia and Furlough 1996, 128.
6 Roger-Milès 1910, 59; Roubaud 1927, 1. Only one contradictory account reports that buyers mixed with American millionaires and European aristocrats. 'A Paris Show of Fashions', *Washington Post*, 19 September 1909.
7 On trade shows and trade buyers in general, see 'Paris Couturiers: How the World's Fashions are Determined – Fitting the Costumes to Buyers by Aid of Mannequins', *Los Angeles Times*, 6 January 1901; 'Paris Show of Fashions', *Washington Post*, 19 September

1909; Marie Monceau, 'Dressmaking Openings Will Shortly Be Held by Noted Paris Firms', *Philadelphia Enquirer*, 18 February 1912; Anne Rittenhouse, 'What the Well-Dressed Woman is Wearing', *New York Times*, 18 February 1912; 'Interior Views of Paquin's', *New York Herald*, Paris, 3 March 1912; Anne Rittenhouse, 'What the Well-Dressed Woman is Wearing', *New York Times*, 8 September 1912; 'Fashions of Paris for America', *Chicago Daily Tribune*, 22 February 1913; 'New Things Shown by the Big French Dressmakers', *New York Times*, 28 September 1913; 'Paris Openings Show No Gowns Radically New in Style,' ibid., 1 March 1914; 'Paul Poiret's Spring Opening', *Harper's Bazar*, April 1914, 24–5; 'American Women Responsible for Sensational French Styles', *New York Times*, 5 July 1914; Corinne Lowe, 'At the Paris Openings', *Chicago Daily Tribune*, 7 October 1917; 'A Seat at the Paris Openings', *Vogue* (America), 15 April 1923, 40; Le Fèvre 1929, 77–80; Hawes 1938, 58–63.
8 Although the majority of houses showed to overseas buyers first, and were reluctant to let private clients in during that period because of the risk of piracy, at Doucet the mannequins modelled in the morning to overseas buyers and commissionaires and in the afternoon for the private clients and, backstage, for the couturier's alterations. Emile Henriot, 'Figures parisiennes: le mannequin', *L'Illustration*, 27 December 1913, reprinted in *L'Illustration: Journal Universel* 1987, 112–16.
9 'The dressmakers' openings have ceased as far as the buyers are concerned, and the individuals who are buying for their personal needs are hard at work. How the mannequins stand the strain from 10 A.M. until 5 P.M. every day in Winter clothes and furs is a wonder for all who look on.' 'Paris Fashions for the Autumn', *New York Times*, 8 October 1911.
10 'La cliente, installée dans un fauteuil, fait virevolter à son gré le mannequin.' Simon 1931, 88. See also Max Rivière, 'La Journée d'un mannequin', *Femina*, 15 October 1905, 491–2.
11 'La répartition de la clientèle en deux catégories, acheteurs et clients, dont les intérêts sont en quelque sort opposés, place le couturier dans un dilemme. En effet, l'acheteur acquiert le modèle pour le reproduire le plus rapidement possible et le vulgariser. La cliente désire l'exclusivité de sa robe ou de son manteau.' Simon 1931, 78.
12 'New Things Shown by the Big French Dressmakers', *New York Times*, 28 September 1913. See also Rittenhouse, 'What the Well-Dressed Woman is Wearing', 8 September 1912.
13 'Seat at the Paris Openings', 40.
14 Marjorie Howard, 'Paris Draws a New Colour Line', *Harper's Bazar*, April 1927, 85.
15 See also Ch. 6, p. 124.
16 This classification is from Grumbach 2008, 91.

17 Le Fèvre 1929, 81–6. On commissionnaires in general, see Simon 1931, 72–4; Rittenhouse, 'What the Well-Dressed Woman is Wearing', 8 September 1912.
18 'Paris Show of Fashions', *Washington Post*, 19 September 1909.
19 '[L]es professionnels et les professionnelles qui sont tour à tour Américains, Anglais, Argentins, Brésiliens, Allemands, Autrichiens, Italiens, etc. Ceux-ci sont assis autour des salons – car ils occupent les côtés de plusieurs salons – causant peu, très attentifs, faisant au passage l'analyse rapide du modèle qui leur est montré, et supputant la chance de succès possible de ce modèle dans leur clientèle.' Roger-Milès 1910, 59. For an account of the mannequins' working day, see Rittenhouse, 'What the Well-Dressed Woman is Wearing', 8 September 1912.
20 'Paris Fashions for the Autumn', *New York Times*, 8 October 1911.
21 '[D]es professionnels et des professionelles' was how the professional buyers were described in Roger-Milès 1910, 59. Unusually for this period, the job appears to have been done interchangeably by both men and women and there is nothing to indicate any differentiation of rank or status between male and female buyers. In 1902 John Wanamaker employed a seasoned female buyer of forty-nine who had 'crossed the ocean seventy times' and by 1915 a third of American retail fashion buyers were women. Fashion buyers who attended the Paris collections had the highest status of all in the industry; they were feted and filmed in both Paris and New York. Leach 1994, 95–7. See also Hamburger 1940, 100–01. In the early 1920s six of the female buyers at the New York store Bonwit Teller & Co. earned over $20,000 a year. Ibid. On the opportunities for travel and career advancement that the job gave female fashion buyers in the U.S., see Leach 1994, 91, 95–9.
22 Giafar, 'Petits contes au Khalife sur les harems de la couture', *Fantasio*, 15 August 1913, 56–7.
23 Ibid.
24 In her introduction to the 2nd edition of *Vision and Difference* in which this important essay appears, Pollock invokes a psycho-analytic model of looking to describe a 'psycho-linguistic position within the structuring of sexual difference. "Femininity" does not invoke any empirically experienced notion of women.' Yet her essay does combine empirical and theoretical analyses of gender relations in social spaces in the nineteenth century. Pollock 2003, xvii and xxxv. With regard to the gendered space of the fashion show, in her discussion of American and Canadian fashion shows in the 1950s Alexandra Palmer writes: 'Fashion shows were an essentially gendered construction for women, featuring women, and usually produced by women, in the feminine space of the shop.' Palmer 2001, 124. Earlier in the twentieth century they were not exclusively feminine but frequently predominantly so.

25 Pollock 2003, 92–3.
26 Ibid., 93.
27 Ibid., 99.
28 Solomon-Godeau, 'Other Side of Venus', 129.
29 Walter Benjamin, 'Konvolut J: Baudelaire', in Benjamin 1999, 339.
30 Robert de Beauplan, 'Après la grève des cousettes: dans les coulisses de la grande couture', *L'Illustration*, 19 May 1923, reprinted in *L'Illustration, Journal Universel* 1987, 139.
31 Rittenhouse, 'What the Well-Dressed Woman is Wearing', 18 February 1912.
32 Chase and Chase 1954, 167.
33 Anne Rittenhouse, 'Paquin Makes Skirts Wider', *Public Ledger*, Philadelphia, 14 September 1912.
34 'Paris Show of Fashions', *Washington Post*, 19 September 1909.
35 Flora McDonald Thompson, 'Our Paris Letter', *Harper's Bazar*, January 1904, 49–51.
36 'Paris Show of Fashions', *Washington Post*, 19 September 1909.
37 Rittenhouse, 'Paquin Makes Skirts Wider'.
38 'Fake Paris Gown Dealers Receive Their Death Blow', *New York Herald*, 19 February 1913.
39 Helen Bullitt Lowry, 'Beware of the "Clever Little Copyist" ', *Harper's Bazar*, October 1924, 87.
40 On the role of memory in the fashion industry, see a long article in the American trade journal the *Dry Goods Economist* codifying the business practices of the fashion trade, from buying to selling and advertising, including the good organisation of a business. It extols the virtues of 'training the memory' which is deemed 'a matter of considerable moment in retailing and one that seldom receives the careful attention it deserves'. It stresses the importance of remembering names, faces, prices and terms, as well as style developments. It argues that 'good memory can be acquired' and it recommends positive forward thinking and concentration as a means of memory-training. However, it does not mention visual memory, which was more often associated with fashion piracy. *Dry Goods Economist*, Fashion Number, 24 June 1911, 3–4.
41 McDonald Thompson, 'Our Paris Letter', 49–51.
42 Rittenhouse, 'What the Well-Dressed Woman is Wearing', 18 February 1912.
43 'Paris Show of Fashions', *Washington Post*, 19 September 1909.
44 Flora McDonald Thompson, 'Autumn Days in Paris', *Harper's Bazar*, October 1905, 931–3; dated 'Paris, September 1905', this article describes a visit to a *grand couturier* in detail.
45 Gabrielle Cavellier, untitled news cutting (Paquin press album, Bath), *Progrès de la Somme*, Amiens, 28 January 1914.
46 'Facts and Fancies in a Woman's World', *Washington Post*, 18 April 1912.
47 Lowry, 'Beware'. The three-dollar sketch was indeed cheap when at 1924 exchange rates an inexpensive couture day dress from Vionnet

or Callot might cost around $135 for a private client.
48 'Stealing Styles! The True Story of a Fashion Pirate', *Liberty*, vol. 1, no. 7, 21 June 1924, 7.
49 Ibid., 5.
50 Prejudice against German copyists went back to the nineteenth century, perhaps as early as the time of the Franco-Prussian War of 1870–71. For an elaborate late nineteenth-century disquisition on the German proclivity for piracy as well as their commercial acuity, see Worth 1895, 95–100.
51 '[L]'oeil photographique'. Le Fèvre 1929, 81–2.
52 Chase and Chase 1954, 166–7.
53 For a lengthy description of a copy house, see Roubaud 1928, 79–87. The copy house had its own *cabine* of four mannequins. See also Hawes 1938, 52–3, 62 and 88, cited in Stewart 2005, 111.
54 Stewart 2005, 111.
55 Hawes 1938, 38–47, 52–63.
56 Ibid., 38.
57 Ibid., 52–3.
58 Ibid., 56.
59 Ibid.
60 Ibid., 60.
61 Ibid., 61.
62 Carolyn Wilson, 'Spring Fashion Openings Draw Paris Crowds', *Chicago Daily Tribune*, 31 March 1918.
63 Max Rivière, 'La Maison des magazines', *Femina*, 15 April 1907, 174–5 and 184–5.
64 R. de B., 'Silhouettes et modes d'aujourd'hui', *L'Illustration*, 12 March 1927, reprinted in *L'Illustration: Journal Universel* 1987, 148–9.
65 'Women are in the majority, but a fair sprinkling of men separate the mass. They are mostly of the commercial class, buyers, representatives of celebrated houses in Europe and America.' ' Paris Show of Fashions', *Washington Post*, 19 September 1909. For the criticism of male behaviour at the shows, see Marie Corelli cited in Kaplan and Stowell 1994, 6 and 121.
66 Marie Corelli, 'Marie Corelli, Novelist, on the Madness of Clothes', *Washington Post*, 30 July 1905.
67 R. de B., 'Silhouettes et modes', 148–9; Reboux 1927, 15. Roubaud, however, felt that husbands were an annoyance because they put their wives off buying. Roubaud 1928, 164–5.
68 'Çà et là, un homme ahuri de son isolement, paradoxal comme un loup intimidé par des brebis.' Roubaud 1928, 164.
69 Rivière, 'Journée d'un mannequin', 491–2.
70 Louis Roubaud wrote: 'Both North and South Americans decide boldly and faster so they buy six, ten or fifteen dresses at one time. But they haggle as if at the market. It is not a question of money; their *amour propre* is at stake. They do not wish, as one of them said to another, to catch the "smile of exploitation" on the saleswoman's face. They are certainly the only clients to whom one could not offer American prices.' The final

comment is ironic: 'American prices' refers to American trade buyers who traditionally paid more for models because they reproduced on a larger scale than other buyers. 'Du Nord ou du Sud, les Américaines se décident hardiment et d'autant plus vite qu'elles achètent à la fois six, dix, quinze robes. Mais elles marchandent comme à la foire. Ce n'est pas une question d'argent; leur amour-propre est en jeu. Elles ne veulent pas surprendre, comme disait l'une d'elles, sur les lèvres de la vendeuse, le "sourire d'exploitation". Ce sont bien les seules clients à qui l'on ne puisse jamais faire des prix Américaines.' Roubaud 1928, 165.
71 One article says that a typical Frenchwoman will go with a friend and take at least two hours; she is more methodical and businesslike in placing her order than her American equivalent 'who, with one eye on the clock, casts a nervous and preoccupied glance at the mannequins as they pass in ceaseless review'. 'Shopping in Paris', *New York Times*, 28 April 1912.
72 Mizejewski 1999, 31–2. Mulvey concurred, when she wrote, 'In retrospect, it seems that the textual focus characteristic of "Visual Pleasure and Narrative Cinema" may have overinvested in the psychic structures of cinematic pleasure, especially the specificity of the male gaze. However this theoretical perspective "unmasks" the central place of sex and sexuality, however censored, at the heart of the Hollywood star system.' Mulvey, 'Unmasking the Gaze', in Callahan 2010, 29.
73 Gamman and Makinen 1994, 182.
74 Michel Georges-Michel, 'Pall-Mall-Paris', *Gil Blas*, 22 October 1913.
75 Crary 1992, 1–24.
76 Crary 2001, 117. He discusses its depiction in two paintings by Manet of 1879, *In the Conservatory* and *Chez le Père Lathuille*; 90–108.
77 'Ta robe n'est pas à toi!' Roubaud 1928, 153–60.
78 'Paris Show of Fashions', *Washington Post*, 19 September 1909.
79 Crary 2001, 99 and 100.
80 The passage occurs in the discussion of Manet's *Bar at the Folies-Bergère*, 1882. Clark 1984, 253–4, cited in Crary 2001, 99.
81 Crary 2001, 115–17.
82 Uzanne 1912, 110.
83 'Les acheteurs étrangers ont surtout l'air de "priser" – si j'ose le dire – les mannequins. Sous prétexte de regarder de près la bouffette de la manche dernier cri ou le décolleté de la collerette, ils ont, pour les jolies filles qui exhibent ces modèles, des regards convoiteurs. Celles-ci, qui ne les apprécient que fort peu, les affublent entre elles de ces noms charmants et si joliment évocateurs: *Rosbif* où *Choucroute*. Ces messieurs sont servis!' Le Mannequin d'Hozier, 'Modanités', *Fantasio*, 1 March 1910, 538.
84 Giafar, 'Petits contes', 56.
85 With thanks to Molly Sorkin for this identification.

86 Mayne 1990, 166.
87 Wilson, 'Spring Fashion Openings'.
88 'Living Models in the Shops of Paris Dressmakers Lure Women to Purchase Gowns so Attractively Displayed', *Chicago Daily Tribune*, 10 May 1908.
89 *Femina*, 1 March 1907, 109. The posing studios were illustrated in Rivière, 'Maison des magazines', 178–81.
90 'Son talent est encore moins de prendre l'allure et l'expression qui conviennent à tous les modèles qu'elle montre que de donner à celle qui vient acheter l'illusion qu'elle pourrait elle-même les porter aussi bien. De même qu'au théâtre nous pensons modestement, lorsque l'un de ce personnages prononce une belle parole ou accomplit une action sublime: "C'est comme cela que j'aurais fait à sa place", de même, fascinée par la souplesse de la jeune femme qui tourne et vire devant elle et joue le rôle de sa robe du moment, la cliente doit se dire soudain: "Voilà tout à fait ce qui convient à mon genre de beauté".' Alexandre 1902, 105–6.
91 Duff Gordon 1932, 78.
92 Melchior-Bonnet 2001, 156; see also 182.
93 Leder 1992, 92–9.
94 Melchior-Bonnet 2001, 156. In the early twentieth century, several practitioners in the developing fields of psychiatry, psychology and psychoanalysis explored ideas about body-image in ways that highlighted the importance of appearance and identification in identity construction. These include Gabriel Tarde's *Les Lois de l'imitation* (1890) translated as *Laws of Imitation* (1903) and the American James Mark Baldwin's writing from the 1890s. Subsequent writing on the relationship of body, self-image and identity includes Joan Rivière on masquerade, Jacques Lacan on the mirror stage, Charles Horton Cooley on the 'looking glass self' and Paul Schilder on how individuals build up body-images of themselves through an aggregate of images and events. See Joan Rivière, 'Womanliness as a Masquerade' (1929), reprinted in Burgin, Donald and Kaplan 1986, 35–44; Cooley 1964; Schilder 1970 and, for a nuanced discussion of Schilder in relation to fashion, see Arnold 2009, 39–40, 44–5, 53 and 69. For a discussion of Lacan's early thinking on the mirror stage in relation to fashion, see Evans 1999, 28 nn. 1 and 2. For a discussion of early cinema and 'vizualizing self-consciousness' that also reviews the ideas of Tarde, Cooley and Baldwin, see Auerbach 2007, 42–50.
95 '[L]a femme trouve en lui non seulement un miroir qui lui renvoie son image embellie, mais un complice qui provoque son goût de coquetterie, d'inconstance et de prodigalité.' Mad Apolam, 'La Mode qui vient', *Fantasio*, 1 October 1912, 154.
96 'The Paris Mannequin, How She Helps to Beguile Women in the Dressmaker's Shop', *New York Times*, 10 November 1907. See also 'Paris Couturiers: How the World's Fashions are Determined', *Los Angeles Times*, 6 January 1901.
97 Bruzzi 1997, 24.
98 Stewart 1999, 19.
99 On the look that anticipates touch, see Paterson 2007, esp. chs 5 and 6, 'How the World Touches Us: Haptic Aesthetics' and 'Tangible Play, Prosthetic Performance', 79–126.
100 Marks 2000, 138–45. Marks makes a nuanced plea for the importance of a form of tactile epistemology that avoids lapsing into an essentialised idea of the body and of experience.
101 Ibid., 153. For a suggestion that historians might remember the importance of the feel as well as the look of clothing, see Smith 2007, 107 and 109. Smith also highlights the tactile nature peculiar to nineteenth-century 'ladies' work' such as sewing and invokes what Constance Classen calls a 'tactually oriented aesthetic based on traditional women's work' that consisted of handcrafts such as lace, sewing, beadwork and scissorwork to produce objects that were not only handmade but also made to be touched. Constance Classen, 'Feminine Tactics: Crafting an Alternative Aesthetic in the Eighteenth and Nineteenth Centuries', in Classen 2005, 228–39.
102 Young 2005, 69–70.
103 Giuliana Bruno discusses the relationship of film, fashion, materiality and space, arguing that space is haptic and the visual has a 'texture'. She argues that 'architectural space is akin to fashion as something we come into contact with epidermically . . . as beings moving into space we apprehend space haptically . . . it is the entire being that is in touch with space. Everything, even our eyes, have skin on them. So the skin is our first coating, our first dress, and then fashion becomes our second skin. Fashion is the way we decorate our epidermic selves . . . and then architecture becomes the third skin. Architecture is the third fold of space we come into contact with.' She goes on to argue that film, too, is a material object that fashions space: 'Hence it all folds together in this kind of architexture, for fashion, architecture, and film are able to refashion in visual folds and permeable textures the way we look at the world.' 'Cultural Cartography, Materiality and the Fashioning of Emotion: Interview with Giuliana Bruno', in Smith 2008, 147 and 148.
104 Discussed in Nead 2007, 196. See also Iversen 1993.
105 For her discussion of several art historians who have 'suggested alternative economies of looking that are more appropriate to tactile images' including Svetlana Alpers (1983) and Naomi Schor (1987), see Marks 2000, 162–9.
106 Ibid., 130 and 162. See also Lant 1995, 65.
107 On the association of sex and shopping evoked by the term *lèche vitrines*, see Garb 1998, 108.
108 Young 2005, 70 and 71.
109 'La vie sociale était un podium perpétuel.' Delbourg-Delphis 1981, 76.
110 Rocamora 2009, 12.
111 Poiret 1931, 262. Earlier, he had described the mirrored fitting rooms he installed in the rue d'Antin. Ibid., 110.
112 Steele 1998, 171.
113 Roger Boutet de Monvel, 'Le Sentier de la Vertu', *Femina*, 1 July 1914, 395–8. A similar illustration from 1913 in another illustrated journal, captioned 'On the edge of the sentier de la Vertu', shows a row of spectators watching the passers-by, and the disappearing foot of the *élégante* who is already on her way: 'une élégante vient de passer', recounts the journalist. E.B., 'Le Matin au Bois', *L'Illustration*, 14 June 1913, 559–62; illustration on 562.
114 The sentier is suddenly peopled 'd'une multitude hétéroclite, d'une foule compacte d'hommes, de femmes, d'amazones, de chiens, de chevaux et de véhicules qui semblent comme par miracle surgir du sol. On y voit des chapeaux fabuleux et des jupes extravagantes, toutes les excentricités de la mode, toutes les fantaisies surtout les plus audacieuses: c'est le spectacle le plus curieux, le plus bariolé et le plus inattendu.' Boutet de Monvel, 'Le Sentier', 397.
115 'Wonders of Paris Frocks Shown Amid Picturesque Settings', *Washington Post*, 30 August 1914.
116 Entry for 29 May 1910, Lartigue 1975, 80. See Ch. 3 n. 21 above.
117 'L'ironie parisienne a dénommé sentier de la Vertu cette allée étroite fréquentée surtout par les esprits larges.' Jehan Montoison, 'Têtes de bois', *Fantasio*, 15 June 1911, 769.
118 '[L]'envol d'une jupe, le départ des jolies jambes triées sur le mollet, désirant peut-être le vent puissant qui soulèverait les voiles légers.' Ibid., 770.
119 Goldberg argues that Lartigue never wanted to let the moment go and that he relished 'the magic fleeting moment when the photo puts the laws of gravity on hold'. Goldberg 1991, viii.
120 'C'est là que je suis à l'affût, assis sur une chaise en fer, mon appareil bien réglé. Distance: de 4 à cinq mètres; vitesse: fente de rideau 4 mm; diaphragme: cela dépendra de quel coté *elle* arrivera. Je sais très bien juger la distance à vue de nez. Ce qui est moins facile, c'est *qu'elle* ait juste un pied en avant, au moment de la mise au point correcte (c'est ce qu'il y a de plus amusant à calculer).' Diary entry for 29 May 1910, Lartigue 1975, 80.
121 '[V]ingt mètres . . . dix mètres . . . huit . . . six . . . *clac!*'. Ibid., 81.
122 Hollander 1993, 331 and 332.
123 The sentier de la Vertu seems to have fallen out of fashion after the war. 'Le matin, vers midi, des Parisiennes de qualité font du "footing" avenue du Bois et ne s'aventurent que rarement dans le sentier de la Vertu, comme il était d'usage en 1914.' A. de Fouquières, 'Sous les lustres', *Almanach du marque d'or*, 1921, 23. An American

guidebook devoted a chapter to it in 1926 for the benefit of Americans in Paris but admitted that the Bois was fast becoming passé to the French. Woon 1926, 125.

124 '[U]n cinéma, un salon de couture, un boulevard, un coin de la salle de conférence de M. Bergson, un comptoir aux galeries Lafayette; un peu faubourg Saint-Germain, un peu les autres faubourgs'. Montozon, 'Le Bois sacré', *Fantasio*, 15 June 1914, 772. The same article goes on to call the sentier 'un admirable cinéma'. Ibid., 775.

125 Anne Friedberg has used the metaphor of 'window shopping' to describe the roaming gaze of a mobile modern subject that anticipates the cinema. She has identified two types of gaze: the virtual and the mobile, or mobilised: 'The *virtual gaze* is not a direct perception but a *received* perception mediated through representation . . . [It] travels through an imaginary *flânerie* through an imaginary elsewhere and an imaginary elsewhen. The *mobilized gaze* has a history, which begins well before the cinema and is rooted in other cultural activities that involve walking and travel. The virtual gaze has a history rooted in all forms of visual representation (back to cave painting), but produced most dramatically by photography. The cinema developed as an apparatus that combined the "mobile" with the "virtual." Hence cinematic spectatorship changed, in unprecedented ways, concepts of the present and the real.' Friedberg 1993, 2–3.

CHAPTER 9

1 Karl Steen, 'Les Emplettes', *L'Art de la mode*, September 1880, 36–7. For the French original, see ch. 1 n. 92 above.

2 In the film *On Demande un mannequin* (1923, dir. Tony Lekain) the working-class protagonist is renamed Nicole on becoming a mannequin. Further examples of mannequins' names can be found in the *Fantasio* articles cited in n. 24 below.

3 Wilson 1925, 43. Alternatively, they were described as set apart from the other because they formed part of the 'mannequin class'. 'Francis, Tailor to Royalty, Is Making Some Very Quiet Gowns', *New York Times*, 13 October 1911; Clairin 1937, 56.

4 'Nous ne sommes guère aimées, dans les ateliers. On nous considère comme des poupées de luxe, des filles entretenues, des noceuses qui insultent au travail des prolétariennes.' Clairin 1937, 56.

5 A 1914 newspaper observed that the actress Cecile Sorel, always an extravagant dresser, 'never, at any time, looks like a smart mannequin! She has adopted the grande dame style of dress and she never turns aside from it.' Claude Cherys, 'The Sunday Post Women's Page', *Washington Post*, 5 April 1914.

6 My discussion of early twentieth-century attitudes to the use of the term *mannequin* to designate a living fashion model is derived from the following: Steen, 'Les Emplettes';

Alexandre 1902, 104–5; 'Chez un grand couturier parisien: les mannequins', *Femina*, 15 November 1903, 735; Max Rivière, 'La Journée d'un mannequin', *Femina*, 15 October 1905, 491–2; 'Les Mannequins au Salon d'automne', *L'Art et la mode*, 26 July 1924. In America, by contrast, the mannequin was usually known as a 'model' and in the British press mannequins were referred to by a range of terms, including 'living lay-figures', 'living models', 'manikins' and *porteuses*, e.g. Kathleen Schlesinger, 'The Growth of a Paris Costume', *Ladies Realm*, June 1900, 210–16.

7 'More Light on the Spring Gown that Scandalized the Parisians', *Washington Post*, 24 May 1908. See also 'How Paris Leads in the Fashions', *Chicago Daily Tribune*, 22 September 1901.

8 Wilson 1925, 72.

9 Maizeroy 1907, 156; Reboux 1927, 15–16.

10 My discussion of the *fourreau* is derived from the following: Steen, 'Les Emplettes', 1880, 37; Alexandre 1902, 107–8; Rivière, 'Journée d'un mannequin'; 'The Paris Mannequin, How She Helps to Beguile Women in the Dressmaker's Shop', *New York Times*, 10 November 1907; Le Mannequin d'Hozier, 'Modanites', *Fantasio*, 15 February 1909, 477; Roger-Milès 1910, 138–9. See also Guillaume Garnier assisted by Françoise Tétart-Vittu, 'Catalogue des pièces exposées', in Musée de la Mode et du Costume 1986, cat. no. 18, 215–16.

11 'Cette négation du corps est aussi une forme de réification du mannequin – longtemps méprisé, vivant de son corps, comme les prostituées.' Morgan Jan, 'Le Mannequin: du portmanteau au top model', in Musée Galliera 2006, 213.

12 Bertin 1956, 172; Bruce Chatwin, interview with Madeleine Vionnet, *Sunday Times Colour Supplement*, 4 March 1973; Coleman 1990, 148; Kirke 1998, 35. Golbin 2009.

13 Duff Gordon 1932, 67; Avery Strakosch, 'Fashions for the Famous: Dressmaking Days With Lady Duff-Gordon, as Told by Her First Model, Miss Elsie', *Saturday Evening Post*, 29 January 1927, 12–13, 91 and 94; Marley 1980, 176; Taylor 1983; Matheson and Sorkin 2005, 32.

14 Roger-Milès 1910, 138.

15 Castle 1984, 97–8. In the late nineteenth century, ballet dancers, burlesque performers and actresses wore flesh-coloured tights to preserve their modesty on stage; from 1894 actresses at the Folies Bergère performed in *tableaux vivants* in flesh-coloured body stockings. In *poses plastiques* white body stockings simulated the marble of classical statuary. Nead 2007, 75. See also Hillel Schwartz, 'Torque: The New Kinaesthetic of the Twentieth Century', in Crary and Kwinter 1992, 71–126, esp. 'Attitudes', 97–102. The flesh-coloured body stocking provided a contrast to the black *fourreau* of the first mannequins, which was sometimes also worn by actresses on stage. Rémy 1964, 93. In her description of the silk and cotton

'fleshings' worn by the Ballets Russes onstage in the early twentieth century, Sarah Woodcock argues that in spite of the creases and wrinkles that they created at the elbows and knees, contemporary audiences 'saw' bare flesh on stage and in movement. It may simply be that they saw the shape of the body beneath the clinging knitted fabrics in silk or cotton. Either way, such visions of the body created unprecedented visual associations of actresses, society women and mannequins. Sarah Woodcock 'Wardrobe', in Pritchard 2010, 143.

16 Jan, 'Le Mannequin', 213.

17 Schlesinger, 'Growth of a Paris Costume', 210–16; Robert de Beauplan, 'Après la grève des cousettes: dans les coulisses de la grande couture', *L'Illustration*, 19 May 1923, reprinted in *L'Illustration: Journal Universel* 1987, 137–40.

18 Rivière, 'Journée d'un mannequin', 491; 'Living Models in the Shops of Paris Dressmakers Lure Women to Purchase Gowns so Attractively Displayed', *Chicago Daily Tribune*, 10 May 1908; Reboux 1927, 54; Beauplan, 'Après la grève', 137.

19 Roger-Milès 1910, 134. The book was also summarised in an article in *Illustration* that described how the mannequins come and go at a measured pace: 'les mannequins vont et viennent à pas comptés.' 'Les Créateurs de la mode', *L'Illustration*, 19 November 1910, reprinted in *L'Illustration: Journal Universel* 1987, 94–100.

20 'Souriantes, gracieuses, très femmes, très diverse en leurs apparitions caméléonesques, elles promènent à travers les salons, en ordre réglé, et un à un, chaque costume; elles passent, s'avancent, s'arrêtent, tournent, continuent, font vingt fois, trente fois, le même geste, le même pas, la même volte, pour disparaître, puis reparaître quelques minutes après, vêtues d'une autre toilette, dont les équipes d'ouvrières les ont parées avec hâte.' Roger-Milès 1910, 59.

21 Two accounts from 1913 describe the extreme lengths to which couturiers went to supervise their mannequins. In the first, they are trained as strictly as athletes: 'They eat only certain things, they walk and exercise, they throw heavy weights above their heads, they practise sitting and rising, standing and bending.' E. M. Newman, 'Nothing to Do but Wear Fine Clothes!', *Chicago Daily Tribune*, 16 November 1913. In the second, the couturier strictly controls their diets: 'The mannequins of the Grand Couturier are like the stallions of the race horse proprietor. He watches over them, he takes care of them, he does not suffer them to get fatter or thinner. Their lives, outside the workshops, are not entirely . . . regular? In his own house, he attempts to remedy these disorders. He "drugs" them, dare I say it, to keep them on form. And, from the beginning of February, he visits the kitchens of his refectory to ensure that red meat is omitted from the midday meal. He submits them to

an exclusively vegetarian diet because of their complexions, and to keep intact the freshness of their skin, so that they do not put on any weight. Not everything is rosy in the life of a Grand Couturier, nor is it in the mannequin's.' ('Les mannequins du Grand Couturier sont comme les étalons du propriétaire de chevaux de courses. Il les surveille, il en prend soin, il ne souffre pas qu'ils engraissent ou qu'ils maigrissent. Leur vie, en dehors de l'atelier, n'est-elle pas très . . . régulière? – Il s'efforce de remédier, chez lui, à ces désordres; il les "dope", si je l'ose dire, il les tient en forme. Et, dès les premiers jours de février, il passe aux cuisines de son réfectoire, et leur fait supprimer les viandes rouges au repas de midi. Il les soumet à une alimentation exclusivement végétarienne – à cause du teint, pour leur conserver intact la fraîcheur de la peau, afin qu'ils n'épaississent point. Tout n'est pas rose dans la vie du Grand Couturier, dans celle du mannequin non plus.') Emile Henriot, 'Figures parisiennes: le mannequin', L'Illustration, 27 December 1913, reprinted in L'Illustration: Journal Universel 1987, 112–16. An orange diet for mannequins is described in Roubaud 1928, 27 and 181.

22 'Yvette Guilbert Comes', Chicago Daily, 8 December 1895; Sterling Heilig, 'Janitor's Daughter Found She Had a Figure and Soon Became a Professional Beauty', Atlanta Constitution, 16 September 1906.

23 Unpublished account of an interview with Paul Poiret, c. early 1920s, accession number B.10.3, Alison Settle Archive, University of Brighton Design Archives, East Sussex.

24 'La Corbeille des plus jolis mannequins de Paris', Fantasio, 1 March 1914, 521; 'La Corbeille des plus jolis mannequins de Paris', ibid., 15 March 1914, 554–5; 'La Corbeille des plus jolis mannequins de Paris', ibid., 1 April 1914, 581.

25 Bonney 1929, 5. For the coverage in the 1920s by L'Art et la mode of individual mannequins, see ch. 6, n. 4.

26 Alexandre 1902, 105.

27 'A Seat at the Paris Openings', Vogue (America), 15 April 1923, 42. On 'the voice with the smile', Susan Strasser cites a piece of doggerel published for American travelling salesmen in 1911: 'I smile because I know it pays, It means dollars and cents in many ways.' The couplet is from a poem by W. E. Hooker, 'The Smile That Pays', The Sample Case, August 1911, 82, cited in Strasser 1993, 168.

28 Walter Benjamin, 'Konvolut J: Baudelaire', in Benjamin 1999, 339 and 346.

29 Simmel 1990.

30 Deflem 2003, 67–96.

31 Armstrong 1998, 2–3.

32 Henriot, 'Figures parisiennes', 112. For the full text see n. 21 above.

33 Wollen 1993, 1–11.

34 Schlesinger, 'Growth of a Paris Costume', 1900, 215; 'Living Models in the Shops of Paris Dressmakers Lure Women to Purchase Gowns so Attractively Displayed', Chicago Daily Tribune, 10 May 1908; 'Many Women Needed to Produce Fashions', Christian Science Monitor, 1 February 1916; untitled cutting in Poiret press albums; Homme libre, 5 November 1923; Wilson 1925, 43, 50; L'Officiel, August 1925.

35 Jean de Mouy recalling the house of Patou, interview with the author, Paris, 28 February 2007.

36 The information about mannequins' working lives and salaries is derived from the following: 'Yvette Guilbert Comes', Chicago Daily, 8 December 1895; Schlesinger, 'Growth of a Paris Costume', 215; Ghenya, 'La Journée d'un mannequin', Figaro-Modes, February 1904, 14–19; Rivière, 'Journée d'un mannequin', 49–92; 'The Paris Mannequin, How She Helps to Beguile Women in the Dressmaker's Shop', New York Times, 10 November 1907; Roger-Milès 1910, 148; Henriot, 'Figures parisiennes', 112–16; Guilbert 1927, 8; Reboux 1927, 19; Roubaud 1928, 177.

37 Even after the war, late arrival in the morning could result in the deduction of half an hour or a full hour's pay. Nor was the legal requirement of a maximum eight-hour day adhered to in the couture houses: Suzanne Lion, 'Le sans-gêne des maisons de couture', Peuple, 8 August 1922. In 1922, a left-wing paper named Boué and Worth as the most iniquitous, docking salaries for a single day's absence due to ill health. Sibyl, 'Pauvres mannequins! Malheureuses petites couturières!' Guignol enchaîné, 10 September 1922.

38 'En attendant les premières clientes qui n'arrivent guère avant onze heures, les mannequins en corset et culottes de soie, les unes armées de houppettes à poudre de riz, les autres, d'étuis de rouge pour les lèvres ou de crayons bruns, bleus ou noirs pour les yeux, évoluant en jacassant dans le petit salon vert pâle où elles s'habillent et se déshabillent au galop.' La Poilue 1916, 262. On mannequins and make-up, see also Flora Macdonald Thompson, 'Autumn Days in Paris', Harper's Bazar, October 1905, 931–3; Henriot, 'Figures parisiennes', 112.

39 'Living Models in the Shops', Chicago Daily Tribune, 10 May 1908.

40 Rivière, 'Journée d'un mannequin', 491–2. The law of 2 November 1892, modified by the law of 30 March 1900, had for the first time limited the legal working day for women in factories and ateliers, initially to eleven and then to ten hours. Willoughby 1926, 21–2. The male working day was not subject to any legal limit and in other trades the law of 1900 divided the workforce; the predominance of female labour in the dressmaking trade, however, meant that the law benefited the majority and did not cause ructions within the workforce. Levasseur, 1912, 33.

41 Alexandre 1902, 105. See also Rivière, 'Journée d'un mannequin', 491–2; 'Paris Show of Fashions', Washington Post, 19 September 1909; 'La Grande Journée des mannequins: le revers de la médaille', Femina, 15 June 1910, 312.

42 Alexandre 1902, 105; 'Reports on Wages and Conditions', Los Angeles Times, 9 July 1911; Paris correspondent of the Dry Goods Economist cited as source.

43 Heilig, 'Janitor's Daughter'; 'New Gowns Worn at Paris Races', New York Times, 28 July 1912; Wilson 1925, 43.

44 By 1912 contracts of apprenticeship had fallen out of favour. Levasseur 1912, 35. I have found no mention of mannequins' contracts until the 1920s. Some are reproduced in Vassiliev 2000, 402.

45 On French seamstresses and milliners pay, see Flora Macdonald Thompson, 'Our Paris Letter', Harper's Bazar, February 1907, 136–8; Elizabeth Dryden, 'The Secret of the Paris Hat', Harper's Bazar, July 1909, 700–02; Uzanne 1912, 42, 82–3 and 86–7, citing research on the industry by the deputy and ex-journalist Charles Benoist. The information on mannequins' pay is derived from the following: 'Yvette Guilbert Comes', Chicago Daily Tribune, 8 December 1895; 'How Paris Leads in the Fashions', Chicago Daily Tribune, 22 September 1901; Alexandre 1902, 89; Rivière, 'Journée d'un mannequin', 491–2; 'Living Models in the Shops', Chicago Daily Tribune, 10 May 1908; 'Reports on Wages and Conditions', Los Angeles Times, 9 July 1911; 'Poor Girls Wear Gorgeous Gowns', Boston Daily Globe, 22 December 1912, reprinted abridged in ibid., 29 December 1912; 'Girl Models Make Showing Clothes an Art', Christian Science Monitor, 11 October 1913; 'Shortage of Mannequins', New York Times, 19 April 1914; 'Paris Mannequins in Demand as Wives for Wealthy Suitors', Washington Post, 10 May 1914; 'Famine in Mannequins', Boston Daily Globe, 17 May 1914; Guilbert 1927, 8; Leach, 1994, 309. All sums in French francs in this chapter are cited in old French francs. For 1913 and earlier years, the dollar sums cited have been converted to francs at the 1913 rate, this being the earliest available year. For 1914 and subsequent years, francs have been calculated at the rate current for those years. All calculations based on Officer 2009.

46 The information on mannequins' pay in the post-war period is based on the following: Clair Fanny, 'Mannequin d'hier et mannequin d'aujourd'hui', Le Populaire, 28 April 1921; Sibyl, 'Pauvres mannequins!', 10 September 1922; Guy Hickok, 'The Girls Who Change Their Dresses 7,000 Times a Year', Atlanta Constitution, 1 April 1923; Alfred Varella, 'L'homme aux six belles girls', Journal du Peuple, 13 December 1924; Maîtrepierre, 'Les six belles de New-York jugées par trois petits mannequins qui ne sont de Paris', Paris-Midi, 29 December 1924; Wilson 1925, 44; Roubaud 1928, 177–8; Vassiliev 2000, 402 and 408.

47 The surviving ledgers at Chanel reveal that the only two Chanel mannequins employed in

1914 and 1915 received 90 francs a month ($17 at the 1915 exchange rate). In 1923 thirteen mannequins were employed at Chanel on salaries ranging from 500 to 1500 francs a month. At the lower end of the scale, six received salaries between 500 and 800 francs. The average salary of 900 francs was paid to five mannequins. The two highest paid were Raymonde Rumplo de Lowenhalt (sic; probably Rompler von Löwenhalt; 1000 francs) and Tatania Korenoff (1500 francs). Salaries for other employees that year were *première d'atelier* 1250 francs, *coupeur* (cutter) 1100 francs, *tailleur* (tailor) 1000 francs, *comptabilité* (accounts) 650 francs, *habilleuse* (dresser) 400 francs, *dactylo* (typist) 400 francs. It is impossible to say whether these sums were typical of Paris couture or not. In this period, Chanel employed a number of Russian émigrés in Paris. Figures from the register of seasonally employed staff for the period 1 January 1913 to 12 December 1927, courtesy of the Chanel Archive, Paris. Eleanor Lansing Dulles gives the various post-war rates in this inflationary period: from 5.5 francs to the dollar throughout the war, the rate rose in 1919 to over 10 francs to the dollar and in 1920 to 17 francs. Dulles 1933, 24.

48 'Living Models in the Shops', *Chicago Daily Tribune*, 10 May 1908; Newman, 'Nothing to Do'.
49 Heilig, 'Janitor's Daughter'.
50 Newman, 'Nothing to Do'.
51 Huguette Garnier, 'Eut-on être mannequin sans aucun apprentissage? Les couturiers interrogés répondent tous "non" ', *Excelsior*, 22 November 1922.
52 Untitled cutting from Poiret press albums: *Tit-Bits* (London), 23 May 1925.
53 Melchior-Bonnet 2001, 96.
54 Connerton 1989, 13–14. Connerton described how learned skills are a form of 'fluid performance' that are incorporated into the body, having been 'acquired in such a way as not to require explicit reflection on their performance'. He called these skills 'habit memories' and described a fluid piano performance as 'a remembrance in the hands'. Ibid., 93 and 102.
55 Butler 1990.
56 Gradually, wrote Connerton, an individual's bodily skills come to seem to 'belong' to them so that 'postures and movements which are habit memories become sedimented into bodily conformations'. Drawing on Maurice Merleau-Ponty, he argued that when our fingers find the keyboard letters of the alphabet without our having to look for them, then 'habit is a knowledge and a remembering in the hands and in the body; and in the cultivation of habit, it is our body which "understands".' Such 'incorporated bodily practices' are also, he argued, mnemonic, even though they leave no trace: 'the past can be kept in mind by a habitual memory sedimented in the body . . . memory, or tradition, gets passed on in non-textual and

non-cognitive ways'. Thus he argued that the body is socially constituted in a double sense, both as 'an object of knowledge or discourse' and because 'it is culturally shaped in its actual practices and behaviour'. Connerton 1989, 95 and 102–4.
57 Nora argued that 'true memory . . . has taken refuge in gestures and habits, in skills passed down by unspoken traditions, in the body's inherent self-knowledge, in unstudied reflexes and ingrained memories'. Nora 1989, 13. Michel de Certeau examined the 'practice of everyday life' to find traces of the past in modern bodies, languages and practices: he tracked the 'auditory space' of the voice from Verdi's operas to Marguerite Duras's films and correlated changes in the gestures of the domestic cook with changes in the food industry. 'These are the reminiscences of bodies lodged in ordinary language', he wrote. 'The poetic sounds of quoted fragments remain.' Certeau 1988, 154 and 163; Certeau et al. 1994, 199–213. While it may be intriguing to attempt to read signs of the past off present-day fashion poses, the approach risks essentialising the body, however. Like Certeau, Nora dehistoricised the body in his evocation of a corporeal truth running below the radar of cultural life; Marianne Hirsch has taken him to task for his reification of materialised memory in his concept of 'the unstudied reflexes of the body'. Hirsch 1997, 22. As Marcel Mauss argued in 1934, and Michel Foucault after him, in his introduction to the *History of Sexuality*, the body is nowhere more cultural than where it appears to be most natural. Mauss 1995; Foucault 1990. Nevertheless, Certeau and Nora's approaches highlight some difficulties in writing the history of sensibilities, particularly when considering movement, feeling and vision as analytical categories; the idea of the pose as a trace may have some currency in understanding how poses are transmitted. Nora 1996, 13. On feeling as an analytical category see Brown 2009, 270 n. 1.
58 It is due to 'la facture cinématique de ses gestes' and 'Parce qu'elle travaille avec le poids, la danse est un puissant activateur des états de corps passés', as expressed by the dance historian Annie Suquet, 'Scènes: le corps dansant – un laboratoire de la perception', in Corbin, Courtine and Vigarello 2005, vol. III, 405.
59 Roubaud 1928, 178–9.
60 Suquet invokes Rudolf Laban's description of an individual's gestures, and their way of transferring weight, as their body signature. Suquet in Corbin, Courtine and Vigarello 2005, vol. III, 406. She cites Laban's *The Mastery of Movement* (1950). See also Lefebvre 1991, 206, on dance, gesture and rhythm.
61 Journal Gaumont (newsreel film), 'Présentation de la mode du soir dans un salon parisien', 1913. Archives Françaises du Film.

62 'Mannequins Taught To Strut, Glide, Pose', *Washington Post*, 8 November 1925. See also 'Mannequin School Planned for Paris', *Los Angeles Times*, 6 October 1923, although such accounts typically describe mannequin schools as planned rather than established.
63 'Paquin Leading Dressmaker of Paris Tells What is the Ideal Figure', *Chicago Daily Tribune*, 30 August 1903. M. Paquin was in fact dead by 1903 and the firm was a partnership consisting of his widow Jeanne and his brother and sister-in-law M. and Mme Joire. The 'M. Paquin' cited in this article was M. Joire. The deceased 'M. Paquin' was originally called Joseph Jacob who had opened the couture house in his own name, later changing it to a 'less Jewish' one, so the firm became Paquin. There he ('Feu Paquin') was primarily responsible for the mannequins during his lifetime and reportedly took a real interest in them while keeping a bizarre distance, such as not permitting a mannequin to eat in the same restaurant as him. Bing, 'Madame Paquin', *Fantasio*, 1 March 1913, 534.
64 Henriot, 'Figures parisiennes', 112.
65 'Living Models in the Shops', *Chicago Daily Tribune*, 10 May 1908; 'How Fashions Are Created: Paris Loots the World to Set the Styles', *Chicago Daily Tribune*, 14 December 1913.
66 'Poor Girls', *Boston Daily Globe*, 22 December 1912, and abridged in ibid., 29 December 1912.
67 Jeacle 2003.
68 'Girl Models Make Showing Clothes an Art', *Christian Science Monitor*, 11 October 1913.
69 'Paris Show of Fashions', *Washington Post*, 19 September 1909.
70 Helen Bullitt, 'Rude Intrusion of Facts into Fashion', *New York Times*, 1 August 1920. In 1924 the classified advertisements section of the same newspaper contained three advertisements for size 16 models in wholesale houses, whereas size 12 was required by the retail houses. Classified Ad 6 – no title, *New York Times*, 12 November 1924.
71 In France, four tenths of married women remained in the workforce, as opposed to one tenth in Britain. Stewart 2001, 148.
72 'Poor Girls', *Boston Daily Globe*, 22 December 1912, and abridged in ibid., 29 December 1912; 'How Fashions Are Created', *Chicago Daily Tribune*, 14 December 1913.
73 'The Creators of New Fashion Seen at Close Range', *New York Times*, 25 December 1910.
74 Heilig, 'Janitor's Daughter'; Reboux 1927, 20; Arletty 1971, 52 and 67–8.
75 'Creators of New Fashion', *New York Times*, 25 December 1910; Henriot, 'Figures parisiennes', 112–16.
76 Mme Paquin had been a mannequin first at Rouff and then at the new firm opened by her future husband, Joseph Jacob, that subsequently became Maison Paquin. Bing, 'Madame Paquin', 534. Mme Chéruit began as a mannequin at Raudnitz before she married M. Chéruit and became the

principal designer at the house of which he was the business manager. 'Cheruit Features the Full Skirt', *New York Times*, 15 March 1914. After she ceased modelling, Mme Marguerite Wagner became the chief designer for Drecoll and the wife of its manager, M. Wagner. Anne Rittenhouse, 'The Women Who Create the Mode in Paris', *Vogue* (America), November 1914, 52–3 and 100. Jenny Sacerdote started her career as a mannequin and then a saleswoman at Béchoff David before founding Jenny in 1911. While heading her own firm, she retained her slim figure and buyers often requested the gown she herself wore. 'Jenny, Who Is One of the Chief Mainstays of Well-Dressed American Women, Shows Clothes with Moderate Panniers', *New York Times*, 19 March 1916.

77 'Mannequin Mart is Target Range for World Sheiks', *Atlanta Constitution*, 25 October 1923; 'Paris Women Seek Jobs as Mannequins', *New York Times*, 23 November 1923.

78 E.g. *Fantasio*, 1 June 1913, contains a passing reference to a mannequin who recognised a former Paquin mannequin in a mistress who had become a client.

79 Paul 2001, 54.

80 Ibid., 55.

81 Ibid., 319.

82 'Paris Show of Fashions', *Washington Post*, 19 September 1909.

83 Stewart 2001, 11.

84 'Elle n'ignore pas qu'elle serait aussi bien à sa place que la riche parvenue, dans le luxe dont elle aime, dont elle ne peut pas ne pas aimer les jouissances. Car son métier tient à la prostitution féminine par ses habitudes, son mode de vie, son apparence d'étal.' Fanny, 'Mannequin d'hier'.

85 Maizeroy 1907. With thanks to Alison Matthews David for bringing this novel to my attention.

86 The popular waltz from 1908 in which an attractive young mannequin declines a male suitor because she has a female partner is 'Mam'zelle Mannequin' by Charles Quinel and Henri Bachmann. On the association of mannequins with lesbianism, see Uzanne 1912, 110; Clairin 1937, 38 and 104.

87 'Mannikin Now a Countess', *New York Times*, 5 February 1914.

88 'Paris Fashions for the Autumn', *New York Times*, 8 October 1911; 'Slashed Skirts, Short and Narrow, Were Shown in Greater Numbers by Callot Sisters Than Elsewhere', *New York Times*, 15 October 1911.

89 'Unable to Wed Her Lover, Girl Kills Him and Herself', *Atlanta Constitution*, 21 January 1912.

90 'Deaths in Drug Orgies Start Paris Crusade', *Chicago Daily Tribune*, 12 April 1926.

91 Hickok, 'Girls Who Change Their Dresses'.

92 'Paris', *Washington Post*, 21 December 1924. There were Russian mannequins at Chanel, Jenny, Chantal, Molyneux, Poiret, Patou, Worth, Lanvin, Vionnet and Drecoll. In 1927

four out of Lanvin's twenty-four mannequins were Russian. Vassiliev 2000, 387–418.

93 From the register of seasonally employed staff for the period 1 January 1913 to 12 December 1927, Chanel Archive.

94 Marjorie Howard, 'Paris Draws a New Colour Line', *Harper's Bazar*, April 1927, 85–7. In 1929 the French magazine *Adam* featured a black Moulin Rouge star modelling a swimming costume alongside pictures of beauty-parade contestants. *Adam*, 15 July 1929. On the absence of black fashion mannequins in the U.S.A. before the 1920s, see ch. 4, n. 63. On negritude, fashion and Man Ray's work in the 1930s, see Grossman 2010, 126–45.

95 Ghenya, 'Journée d'un mannequin', 14–19.

96 'Grandes dames avec des airs de petites marquises aux gestes menus et gracieux . . . Les mannequins ont, avec le piquant du trottin, le charme de la femme élégante.' Ibid.

97 'Pour être mannequin, il faut être grande et bien faite, posséder cette élégance innée qui fait certaines petites parisiennes, d'extraction bien humble, qui adoptent ce métier.' Rivière, 'Journée d'un mannequin', 491–2.

98 'Elle a le don de l'imitation'. Alexandre 1902, 109. 'Le mannequin vient du peuple. Elle était ce qu'on désigne de l'expression imagée, un beau brin de fille.' Fanny, 'Mannequin d'hier', 1921.

99 Garnier, 'Eut-on être mannequin'.

100 'Cette profession n'exige que des qualités physiques et de l'allure. Elle rebute rapidement les femmes qui n'ont jamais travaillé. Nous les préférons des professionnelles ou de très jeunes filles, pour qui ce métier est plutôt un avancement.' Ibid.

101 'Il y a "le style 'mannequin' ".' Ibid.

102 They are 'de belles dames qui, à la fin de la journée, ne seront plus que d'anonymes trottins, à l'élégance lustrée, à la coquetterie parcimonieuse, lesquels trottins rentreront dans un intérieur humble, où la vertu a une mine singulièrement revêche, et où le devoir offre pour récompense un surcroît de fatigue rebutante et de lassitude.' Roger-Milès 1910, 138–9.

103 Henriot, 'Figures parisiennes', 112–16.

104 'Elle est bien "balancée", la môme . . . La Vénus de Milo est balancée, elle aussi'. Ibid., 112.

105 Newman, 'Nothing to Do'.

106 Ibid.

107 *Delineator* cited in 'Facts, Features and Fancies for Women', *Los Angeles Times*, 14 August 1909.

108 Ibid.

109 Henriot, 'Figures parisiennes', 112. On the class ramifications of her job, see also 'Poor Girls Wear Gorgeous Gowns', *Boston Daily Globe*, 22 December 1912, and abridged in ibid., 29 December 1912.

110 Roger-Milès 1910, 137; Hickok, 'Girls Who Change'. In 1928 Ginette, a mannequin, recounts that she wears sportswear when not at work. Roubaud 1928, 157.

111 Uzanne 1912, 41.

112 'Seat at the Paris Openings', *Vogue* (America), 15 April 1923, 42.

113 Dolores married the American millionaire William Tudor Wilkinson in 1923, Hebe married the wealthy Harold L. Kingsland. 'Rich Mr Harriman Wants a Model Wife', *Atlanta Constitution*, 23 March 1924. Patou's American mannequin Josephine Armstrong married a Vanderbilt nephew, Erskine Gwynne. 'Marriage Announcement – No Title', *Atlanta Constitution*, 30 May 1926; 'Article 2 – No Title, *Los Angeles Times*, 16 June 1926. Dorothy Smart married Lyman Bill, a millionaire publisher. 'E. L. Bill to Marry Beautiful Manikin', *Washington Post*, 27 February 1928. June Dibble married Fred Almy, the 'cowboy millionaire'. 'Patou Cables for Models', *New York Times*, 27 June 1928; 'Wanted – Six "Natural Girls" for Manikins', *Chicago Daily Tribune*, 19 August 1928.

114 'For First Time French Subordinate Themselves in Bidding for Trade', *Washington Post*, 29 April 1923.

115 There were also descriptions of Russian princesses modelling at Chantal. Marjorie Howard, 'Paris Draws a New Colour Line', *Harper's Bazar*, April 1927, 80–85 and 93. The Chantal mannequins were described by de Meyer as 'all of them ladies of aristocratic birth'. Baron de Meyer, 'Individuality in Dress', *Harper's Bazar*, September 1928, 118.

116 *Harper's Bazar*, October 1925, 99 and 190.

117 'Baron de Meyer Describes the Collections', ibid., October 1927, 78.

118 'So All Paris Loses Thrift', *Los Angeles Times*, 20 September 1911.

119 'American Women Shocked by Parisian Extravagance', *Washington Post*, 3 September 1911. The same quotation appears in 'So All Paris Loses Thrift', *Los Angeles Times*, 20 September 1911. Although these two articles are not identical they contain several identical phrases and paragraphs.

120 Schwartz 1998, 195.

121 'Poor Girls Wear Gorgeous Gowns', *Boston Daily Globe*, 22 December 1912, abridged in ibid., 29 December 1912.

122 See Ch. 8 nn. 94 and 95 above. Leder 1992, 92–9; Melchior-Bonnet 2001, 156.

123 Hollander 1993, 336, cited in Freadman 2006, 341. Also Freadman 2006, 340.

124 David 2002, 88.

125 Freadman 2006, 342.

126 On the double nature of the model, see Steiner 2010, 1–2.

127 Here I have slightly condensed Brandstetter's argument, leaving out her formulation of this impassivity as 'nude', a quality which she suggests is, in fashion models, not about being naked but about skin being 'the empty canvas, like in painting, which becomes the carrier for form and colour.' See Gabriele Brandstetter, 'Pose-Posa-Posing – Between Image and Movement', in Bippus and Mink 2007, 248 and 250.

128 Brandstetter relates the late twentieth-century fashion model's 'cult of expressionlessness' to

Freud's discussion of the doll and automaton in 'The Uncanny'. Ibid., 250–52.

129 Freadman 2006.

130 Wendy Steiner makes exactly this point about the artist's model. 'Being both an art object and a human subject, a model inhabits two worlds and muddles the distinction between them.' Steiner 2010, 1–2.

131 Bailey 1990, 148–72.

132 'On dirait qu'elles vont réciter des vers et de jouer un rôle. Elles se contentent de mimer le leur' ('They make do with miming their own'). Henriot, 'Figures parisiennes', 112.

133 Jean Ravennes, 'Aux sanctuaires mystérieux de l'élégance et de la mode', Revue Française, 9 April 1922, 84.

134 'C'est n'est plus une personne vivante. Surtout, ce n'est plus une femme sensible au plaisir de porter un costume nouveau. Son visage est inexpressif. Ses lèvres sourient mécaniquement. Quand on lui demande: "Comment vous appelez-vous?" elle répond . . ./Elle répond, oui, mais de la manière la plus inattendue. /Quel est son nom? C'est Plaisir d'amour . . . Chartreuse . . . Rien qu'un moment . . . Le premier oui . . . Fauvette . . . Feuille de rose . . . Kamtchatka . . . Cinq à sept . . . Apollon . . .' As far as suppressing the mannequin's individual personality, Reboux writes, 'à force d'être assimilés à un support, à force de n'être qu'une sorte de construction harmonieuses servant à tender l'étoffe d'une robe, beaucoup de mannequins perdent leur personnalités comme pour mieux s'assimiler les personnalités successives qu'on leur impose.' Reboux 1927, 16 and 17.

135 Jones and Stallybrass 2000, 14, 204.

136 Appadurai 1988.

137 Jones and Stallybrass 2000, 14, 206.

138 Soley-Beltran 2004.

139 Mildred Holland, 'Making the Most of Personality', Washington Post, 4 October 1924.

140 Antoinette Dowerthy, 'Walks for Everyday Costume', Washington Post, 12 April 1925; Chicago Daily Tribune, 12 April 1925.

141 Guy Hickok, 'The Girls Who Change Their Dresses 7,000 Times a Year', Atlanta Constitution, 1 April 1923.

142 See Marian North, 'Shadow Moves', in McCaw 2011, 257–64.

143 Harper's Bazar, November 1917, 70–71.

144 Schweitzer 2009, 188.

145 Ibid. In this discussion, Schweitzer also cites Glenn 2000, 162, and Mizejewski 1999, 90–100.

146 'New Varieties of Waistcoats Continue to be Invented', New York Times, 25 May 1913.

147 'Fashion Freaks Astonish Auteuil: "Three Graces," Stockingless and Sandaled, Excite Merriment of Paris Racegoers', New York Times, 24 March 1913.

148 Carolyn Wilson, 'Spring Fashion Openings Draw Paris Crowds', Chicago Daily Tribune, 31 March 1918.

149 The concept of the showpiece existed from the early 1910s; this first instance from 1913 comes in a description of a pink taffeta skirt draped like Turkish trousers with gold lace pantalettes that 'would make a charming little dancing dress, although it was meant for a show piece'. 'Fashions of Paris for America', Chicago Daily Tribune, 22 February 1913.

150 Anne Rittenhouse, 'What the Well-Dressed Woman is Wearing', New York Times, 6 October 1912; Mary Buel, 'Paris Evening Gowns', Chicago Daily Tribune, 26 January 1913; 'Fashion Freaks Astonish Auteuil', New York Times, 24 March 1913; 'New Things Shown by the Big French Dressmakers', New York Times, 28 September 1913; Christiana, 'Un Tango chez Lucile', Sim, 1 November 1913; E. G., 'Mid-Channel in Paris Fashions', Vogue (America), 1 December 1913, 35–7; 'To Popularize Colored Wigs', New York Times, 29 January 1914; 'The Higher the Better', Boston Daily Globe, 30 January 1914; 'New Dances Inspire a Style in Skirts', New York Times, 2 March 1914; 'So Say the Paris Openings', Vogue (America), 15 March 1914, 36; 'Boston Goes to See the Latest Paquin Gowns', Boston Daily Globe, 21 March 1914; Idalia de Viliers, 'Bunchy Draperies the New Fad', Boston Daily Globe, 22 March 1914; Claude Chrys, 'Bunchy Effects and Frills Are Two Features of Advanced Fashions Shown in Beautiful Gowns Now being Exhibited on the Riviera', Washington Post, 22 March 1914; 'Callot and Turkish Trousers', New York Times, 29 March 1914; 'Paris Racing Gown is Made of Straw', Washington Post, 8 May 1922. See also Musée de la Mode et du Costume 1986, 232, cat. no. 185 bis.

151 'Painted Shoulder Newest Paris Fad', Washington Post, 26 June 1922.

152 'Knees Are Covered in New Paris Mode Revealed by Patou', Washington Post, 5 August 1928.

153 '[S]imple, alerte, essentiellement parisienne dans une robe de ville, virginale dans une robe de jeune fille, altière et provocante dans une robe de bal.' Alexandre 1902, 105.

154 'De l'un à l'autre groupe, le mannequin glisse comme une longue navette étincelante, et jette les rets. Collaboratrice inquiétante, c'est au mannequin qu'aboutit un faisceau d'efforts dont personne ne méconnaît plus l'importance. Le public estime à sa valeur la tâche du tisseur, du modéliste, du coupeur, de la vendeuse, du couturier qui les dirige: arrivé au mannequin, il se réserve, rêve, admire ou suspecte. Parmi les formes modernisées de la plus luxueuse industrie, le mannequin, vestige d'une barbarie voluptueuse, est comme une proie chargée de butin. Elle est la conquête des regards sans frein, le vivant appât, la passive réalisation d'une idée. Sa profession ambiguë lui confère l'ambiguïté. Déjà son sexe, verbalement, est incertain. On dit: "Ce mannequin est charmante", et son travail consiste à simuler l'oisiveté. Une mission démoralisante la tient à égale distance du patron et des ouvrières normales. N'y a-t-il pas là de quoi justifier, excuser l'étrange humeur et le caprice du mannequin? Aucun autre métier féminin ne contient d'aussi puissants facteurs de désagrégation morale que celui-là, qui impose à une fille pauvre et belle les signes extérieurs de la richesse.' Colette, 'Mannequins', Vogue (France), 1 April 1925, 33.

CHAPTER 10

1 'Paris Fashions for the Autumn', New York Times, 8 October 1911.

2 Villiers 1993. Colette, 'Printemps de Demain', Vogue (France), 1 February 1925, 31. Rebecca Arnold has argued that dancers, actresses and fashion models are avatars of future subjectivities. Arnold 2009, 57.

3 From 'Fashion' (1904) in Simmel 1971, 302. Simmel goes on to add, apocalyptically, that 'The more nervous the age, the more rapidly its fashions change . . . as fashion spreads, it gradually goes to its doom.'

4 Glenn 2000, 169.

5 Emile Henriot, 'Figures Parisiennes: Le Mannequin', L'Illustration, 27 December 1913, reprinted in L'Illustration: Journal Universel 1987, 112–16.

6 For a treatment of the sheath dress in 1908 in the U.S.A. see Schweitzer 2009, 143–54.

7 Paquin's 1905 Empire line is described as fluxeuse by Delbourg-Delphis 1981, 32. See also Schweitzer 2009, 145.

8 'Famous Author . . .', Wanamaker Originator 1908. Reprinted in the same issue, see also 'Gowns that Charm', New York Sun, 1908. 'Living Pictures of Empire Fashion', Philadelphia North American, 2 October 1908.

9 'More Light on the Spring Gown . . .', Washington Post, 24 May 1908. 'French Modistes Differ on the Directoire Gowns', New York Times, 24 May 1908. It was this split skirt that Mme Lacroix called directoire, after the early nineteenth-century French period, differentiating it from fashions that she described as simply 'neo-classical' or 'Greek'.

10 'More Light on the Spring Gown', Washington Post, 24 May 1908. 'French Modistes Differ', New York Times, 24 May 1908.

11 A number of sources discussed the sinuous body-image created by the Sylphide dress and the complex question of the underwear it required. The dream of the refined Parisienne, according to Mme Lacroix, was 'atteindre au suprême degré de sveltesse tout en gardant la démarche onduleuse et souple d'une puissante suggestion'. La Comtesse Lise, 'La "silhouette sylphide"', Figaro-Modes, June 1904, 17. In the next issue of the magazine, the 'Robe Sylphide' was described as a 'vraie trouvaille de l'esthétique moderne, supplée au corset au moyen d'une ingénieuse combinaison de dentellure. Elle amincit indéfiniment tout en gardant à la silhouette une onduleuse souplesse. C'est un peu le secret d'irrésistible grâce des Parisiennes connues par leur impeccable élégance, qui, toutes, se rencontrent 19, boulevard Haussmann, dans les salons de Mme Margaine Lacroix, l'artistique créatrice.' 'Robe Sylphide', ibid., July 1904, 20. Another

source wrote that Mme Margaine Lacroix had created 'the famous Sylphide dresses, which are worn without corsets, and the Sylphide brassieres, so well known, which leave women with freedom and suppleness of movement' ('les fameux robes *sylphides*, qui se portent sans corset, et les brassières *sylphides*, si réputés, qui laissent à la femme toute la liberté et toute la souplesse des mouvements'). *La Ville lumière*, 1909, 535. More generally, on the corset in this period, see Stewart 2001, 72–4, and Steele 2001, 143–55.

12 'More Light on the Spring Gown that Scandalized the Parisians', *Washington Post*, 24 May 1908. 'French Modistes Differ on the Directoire Gowns', *New York Times*, 24 May 1908. The *robe Tanagréenne* was 'a model created along antique lines'. *La Ville Lumière*, 1909, 535; 534 shows a photograph of the interior of Maison Margaine Lacroix showing two Tanagra dresses on dress forms. See also Ghenya, 'L'Après-Midi d'une Parisienne (En Mars)', *Figaro-Modes*, March 1904, 10–11.

13 'More Light on the Spring Gown', *Washington Post*, 24 May 1908. 'French Modistes Differ', *New York Times*, 24 May 1908.

14 The two types of sheath described are 'la *Gaine*, toute en peau de chevreau, est venue combler les desiderata des femmes très fortes voulant quand même l'allure juvénile de la svelte jeunesse. . . . le *fourreau-sylphide* tout en tricot de soie, gantant les formes avec une douce fermeté et supprimant à l'oeil toute trace de corset. Cette sorte de maillot idéal corrige les défauts du buste et met en valeur les lignes heureuses avec un art parfait.' La Comtesse Lise, 'La "silhouette sylphide" ', *Figaro-Modes*, June 1904, 17.

15 Palmer White, text of a lecture on Paul Poiret, n.d., p. 14, in Palmer White Papers, Bibliothèque Forney, Paris.

16 Kirke 1998, 35.

17 Ibid. For Poiret's claim to have been the first to eliminate the corset, see Poiret 1931, 72–3.

18 'Les Arbitres d'élégance', *Le Figaro-Modes*, 15 April 1903, 13–14.

19 E.g. Avery Strakosch, 'Fashions for the Famous: Dressmaking Days With Lady Duff-Gordon, as Told by Her First Model, Miss Elsie', *Saturday Evening Post*, 29 January 1927, 12–13 and 91, 94.

20 'How Fashions Are Created – Paris Loots the World to Set the Styles', *Chicago Daily Tribune*, 14 December 1913. Strakosch, 'Fashions for the Famous', 12.

21 Castle and Castle 1980, 144–5.

22 Ibid., 145–8.

23 The full text describes 'la robe effrontément ouverte jusqu'à la hanche, parce que il plût à une couturière et à trois mannequins de risquer la métamorphose d'une légende en une réalité.' Georges Grappe, 'Le Jolie Mensonge des merveilleuses', *Fantasio*, 15 June 1908, 990–93. For an image that shows the slit clearly, see Mary Evans Picture Library, no. 10133560.

24 Idalia de Villiers, 'Dangers of the Directoire Style', *Boston Daily*, 14 June 1908.

25 The full text is: 'Nous l'avons échappé belle! Récemment, au pesage de Longchamp, trois mannequins se promenaient en robes qui avaient la prétention de renouveler à l'usage de "nos divines Samothraces" – ce joli nom donne à nos élégantes fut inventé par notre spirituelle confrère Albert Flamant – les modes du Directoire. Ah! Ma chère! Fut un prodigieux hourvari. Encore les trois pauvres filles, chargées de cette mission provocante, eussent révélé uniquement des robes sans histoire de commerces de revue, le Tout-Paris du turf déclara avec indignation que ces modes, qui pouvaient s'adapter à une réaction thermidorienne, ne convenaient nullement à une époque où l'on crée des ligues contre le Nu.' Georges Grappe, 'Le Jolie Mensonge', *Fantasio*, 15 June 1908, 990.

26 Marie Olivier, 'Latest Hints from Paris', *Harper's Bazar*, September 1908, 855–7.

27 Unattributed article from *Wanamaker Originator* 1908.

28 'Living Models in the Shops of Paris Dressmakers Lure Women to Purchase Gowns so Attractively Displayed', *Chicago Daily Tribune*, 10 May 1908.

29 'Gowns that Charm', *New York Sun*, 1908, reprinted in *Wanamaker Originator* 1908.

30 Olivier, 'Latest Hints from Paris'.

31 'Gowns that Charm', 1908.

32 'American Women Probably Will Adopt a Modified Form of the Audacious New Directoire Gown', *Chicago Daily Tribune*, 31 May 1908.

33 Olivier, 'Latest Hints from Paris', 857.

34 Pictured in Marie Olivier, 'Advance Fashions for 1909', *Harper's Bazar*, October 1908, 921.

35 Ibid., 919.

36 Marie Oliver, 'Midsummer Fashions', *Harper's Bazar*, July 1909, 667–71.

37 Le Mannequin d'Hozier, 'Modanités', *Fantasio*, 1 November 1908, 247.

38 Le Mannequin d'Hozier, 'Modanites', *Fantasio*, 15 November 1908, 283. Such narrow skirts without slits were shown in-house at Martial et Armand in spring 1914 but, since they were extremely narrow at the knee before flaring out again at the hem, an American *Vogue* journalist worried that 'at the knee the skirt is so ridiculously narrow that I could not help wondering if it would split if the manikin attempted to sit down'. 'So Say the Paris Openings', *Vogue* (America), 15 March 1914, 36.

39 Abel 1998, 220. Legs had been a feature of early films, e.g. *Four Beautiful Pairs* and *Shocking Stockings*, both by American Mutascope & Biograph Co., 1904.

40 Le Mannequin d'Hozier, 'Modanités', *Fantasio*, 15 September 1910, 144.

41 The film can be viewed in the Forum des Images in Paris.

42 Timmy was identified as 'la danseuse aux jambes nues' in 'Timmy, gamine-espiègle du café-concert qui "chante avec ses jambes"', *Fantasio*, 1 October 1911, 171.

43 'Paris, chaussures, femmes aux Galeries Lafayette', ref. 1912, 18, Pathé, at www.gaumontpathearchives.com.

44 'Fashion Freaks Astonish Auteuil: "Three Graces", Stockingless and Sandaled, Excite Merriment of Paris Racegoers', *New York Times*, 24 March 1913. The *New York Times* described in much detail the French shoes designed to coordinate with the gowns at the November 1915 Paris Fashion Fête in New York (see Ch. 4 above), including a pair of sandals worn over bare feet 'but these might be put down as accessories'. 'The Paris Fashion Show Has Brought a New Epoch', ibid., 28 November 1915.

45 In 1908 *Fantasio* reported an early instance of the *jupe-culotte*, saying that this winter women will be wearing tight, revealing and inconvenient satin culottes ('cette culotte de satin, collante, moulante, et inconvenante'), albeit covered by a skirt. 'Le Mannequin d'Hozier, 'Modanités', *Fantasio*, 1 November 1908, 247.

46 Le Mannequin d'Hozier, 'Modanités', *Fantasio*, 1 September 1910, 108. These mannequins may have been from Béchoff David. See Michel Psichari, 'Les essais d'une mode nouvelle', *L'Illustration*, 18 February 1911, 103–4 and the cover image. In March 1911 *Femina* showed trouser skirts by Parry, Béchoff David and Martial et Armand, and reported sighting young girls wearing the 'neo-oriental' trouser skirt in the Bois and even 'risking the boulevards' ('et même se risquer sur les boulevards'). There, it was reported, two young women were followed by a crowd hurling mostly rude cries at them so that the two trembling young women sought refuge with the *sergents de ville* who hid them in a cellar near the Madeleine for two hours until they procured a car to carry them rapidly to safety: H. A., 'La robe pantalon', *Femina*, 1 March 1911. For further accounts of the *jupe-culotte* see *Fantasio*, 1 February 1911, 466, and ibid., 1 March 1911, 520.

47 Flossie, 'La robe pantalon', *Femina*, 15 February 1911, 82. For a discussion of the controversy and of the implications of the *jupe-culotte* for women, including its association with masculinity, racial otherness, female emancipation and sexual inversion, see Troy 2003, 116–28, and Davis 2010, 132–5.

48 Le Mannequin d'Hozier, 'Modanités', *Fantasio*, 1 June 1911, 754.

49 'Advance Frocks for Summer', *Harper's Bazar*, May, 1911, 221. 'Edna May Quits Stage for Ever', *Washington Post*, 19 February 1911.

50 'Russian Knicker Dress – Silk Knickers, ending in chiffon and lace ruffles – disclosed by side openings in the skirt. Poiret's mannequins displayed similar models in Paris very recently'. Display Ad 56 – No Title, *Boston Daily Globe*, 5 February 1911. Indeed, it was so recent that the designs must either have been pirated or their details telegraphed from Paris to Boston on the day they

appeared at the races. 'Pasha Petticoat Next', *Washington Post*, 5 March 1911.

51 'Spring Gowns at Longchamp', *New York Times*, 23 April 1911. These events were reported by telegraph to Ireland and thence by wireless to New York. By June 1911, the American trade journal the *Dry Goods Economist* was reporting that 'the real slashed skirt is already in evidence on the streets of our large cities, but the cut is decidedly CONSERVATIVE. EVEN this so-called modest adaptation is a little too startling for the general trade. The simulated slash effect, however, produced by the arrangement of pleats or facings, is well liked and promises to be a familiar style a little later in the season'. 'Slashed Skirt Effects', *Dry Goods Economist*, 24 June 1911, 99.

52 Anne Rittenhouse, 'What the Well-Dressed Woman is Wearing', *New York Times*, 6 October 1912; 'Slashed Skirts, Short and Narrow, Were Shown in Greater Numbers by Callot Sisters Than Elsewhere', ibid., 15 October 1911.

53 'Slashed Skirts, Short and Narrow'.

54 'The woman who is well-dressed on this side of the ocean is the one who allows the modistes of Paris to offer the new styles and who selects the conservative, refined exploitations of the modes. American women do not wish to place themselves in the class of the mannequins, who show the extreme in fashion; and the successful women are they who modify a feature and who never forget the very important personal equation.' Anne Rittenhouse, 'What the Well-Dressed Woman is Wearing', *New York Times*, 29 September 1912. See also 'French dresses that Americans will wear', *Los Angeles Times*, 1 September 1912. Rittenhouse, 'What the Well-Dressed Woman is Wearing', 6 October 1912. Like Americans, French women, supposedly 'tired of finding their perfect legs on show above the knee', also inserted underskirts: 'Lasses, un peu, de découvrir, par l'ouverture des jupes, leurs jambes parfaites, un peu pus haut que les genoux, les élégantes ont imaginé de faire placer, dans cet interstice malencontreux, un délicieux volant de tulle plissé et transparent'. Le Mannequin d'Hozier, 'Modanités', *Fantasio*, 1 December 1912, 324. See also Lucile Duff Gordon, 'Paris Fashions in Transit', *Harper's Bazar*, September 1913, 38 and 44.

55 Anne Rittenhouse, 'What the Well-Dressed Woman is Wearing', *New York Times*, 1 September 1912.

56 Anne Rittenhouse, 'What the Well-Dressed Woman is Wearing', *New York Times*, 13 October 1912.

57 'What Every Woman Should Know', *New York Times*, 20 October 1912.

58 Le Mannequin d'Hozier, 'Modanités', *Fantasio*, 15 March 1913, 590.

59 'Diaphanous Waists the Rage in Paris', *New York Times*, 19 May 1913.

60 'Paris Fall Openings', *Chicago Daily Tribune*, 12 October 1913; Michel Georges-Michel, 'Pall-Mall-Paris', *Gil Blas*, 22 October 1913.

61 'So Say the Paris Openings', *Vogue* (America), 15 March 1914, 36; 'Drecoll Retains the Modified Slash in Skirts', *New York Times*, 15 March 1914; 'Fashion Freaks Astonish Auteuil', ibid., 24 March 1913; 'Callot and Turkish Trousers', ibid., 29 March 1914.

62 Louise Morely, 'Flesh Colored Corsets Under X-Ray Gowns', *Chicago Daily Tribune*, 29 March 1914.

63 'So Say the Paris Openings', *Vogue* (America), 15 March 1914, 34.

64 Erté 1975, 22.

65 Hollander 1993, 339.

66 Wollen 1993, 20–21.

67 Stearns 2002, although, as Stearns points out, the origins and evolution of the slender body ideal were uneven; preface, viii. For an account of changes in the fashionable female shape between 1910 and 1929 see Thesander 1997, 107–30. For a general cultural history of obesity, see Gilman 2008.

68 Delbourg-Delphis 1981, 32–3. Georges Vigarello puts it a little later, from 1910–20. Vigarello 2004, 191. See also Stewart and Janovicek 2001, who point out important discrepancies between the representation and the reality of the slender body in the period 1890s to 1930.

69 Sterling Heilig, 'Janitor's Daughter Found She Had a Figure and Soon Became a Professional Beauty', *Atlanta Constitution*, 16 September 1906.

70 'How to Get Plump', *Harper's Bazar*, August 1908, 787–9.

71 Stearns 2002, 11–12.

72 *Harper's Bazar*, March 1912, 144.

73 On early twentieth-century interest in representations of fashion in motion, especially through photography, sport and film, see Hollander 1993, 330–32 and 338–40.

74 Hillel Schwartz, 'Torque: The New Kinaesthetic of the Twentieth Century', in Crary and Kwinter 1992, 105. On the mechanical and streamlined body of modernism, see Burstein 2012, 13 and 125ff.

75 'Society Outside the Capital', *Washington Post*, 22 September 1909.

76 'Poor Girls Wear Gorgeous Gowns', *Boston Daily Globe*, 22 December 1912, repr. abridged in ibid., 29 December 1912.

77 Ibid. Another journalist wrote that 'the houses this season are looking for taller mannequins, from 1m 68 cm to 1m 72cm'. 'Importance of the Silhouette', *New York Times*, 30 March 1913.

78 Roubaud 1928, 193.

79 'C'en est fait! le règne de la ligne droite a vécu. . . . La toilette féminine est complètement rénovée. . . . massage, régime, électricité, sont, dans ce noble but, consciencieusement employés.' Le Mannequin d'Hozier, 'Modanités', *Fantasio*, 15 June 1912, 818.

80 Anne Rittenhouse, 'Panniers come back into Favor in Paris', *New York Times*, 16 September, 1912.

81 'Un mannequin aux hanches éffacés, au corsage avare, à la taille mince, au port élancée.' Roger-Milès 1910, 54.

82 'Ruffles Are Popular', *New York Times*, 24 December 1911. The same article refers to 'the Oriental slimness of the moment', probably a reference to Denise Poiret who successfully wore her husband's oriental fashions on his mannequin tour of Europe at this date.

83 Colette Willy, 'La Folie des minceurs', *Fantasio*, 1 March 1912, 521–2.

84 Colette describes Valentine in 'un tuyau, gaine, gouttier, en jersey de soie rose, qui commence au pli de l'aisselle et fini un peu au dessus du genou'. It has 'un buste rigide, de longues baleines assurent le blindage de l'appareil, et quatre amarres de ruban le relient aux bas de soie hanneton'. According to the advertisement, 'il supprime totalement le ventre, les hanches et toute saillie postérieure'. Valentine explains the corsets are made thus 'à cause des robes Tanagra . . . Il faut bien: c'est la mode. Tout le monde est mince. Vous ne trouvez pas ça jolie? C'est le triomphe de la ligne.' Ibid. The Tanagra continued to be a signifier of thinness in the early 1920s when 'Tanagra dragées' were a brand of slimming pills. Mary Louise Roberts, 'Samson and Delilah Revisited: The Politics of Fashion in Nineteenth-Century France', in Chadwick and Latimer 2003, 82.

85 Georges Vigarello argued that the pedagogy of bodily stance and gesture is similarly marked by contradiction so that, for example, the hand an adult leaves on a child may be as much a mark of elegance as one of domination and constraint. Vigarello 1978, 10–11.

86 '[L]e corps de la femme serait-il donc malléable à merci? . . . la mode semblerait le prouver . . . hâtons-nous de dire que la mode n'est pas la seule cause: les couturiers sont experts à choisir des "mannequins" dont le corps s'adapte le mieux au caractère des modes nouvelles et de là surtout vient l'antithèse que nos photographies mettent en lumière.' 'Telle mode tel mannequin', *Femina*, 1 November 1911, 601.

87 Jean Laporte, 'La tournée du grand couturier', *Femina*, 1 June 1914, 339.

88 'Où sont les belles filles qui portaient, il y a quelques quinze ans, la fortune des couturiers sur leurs nobles épaules? Qu'est devenue cette splendide Louisa, titulaire d'un prix de beauté, qui traînait, dans le quartier Vendôme, velours et brocarts à peine épinglés à son torse sans défaut? Le mannequin d'aujourd'hui offert ses dix-sept ans en train de grandir, ses coudes pointus et ses salières de candidate au brevet simple.' Colette, 'Almanach des Modes présentes, passées et futures pour 1923', repr. in *Colette et la mode* 1991, 145.

89 Avery Strakosch, 'Fashions for the Famous: Dressmaking Days With Lady Duff-Gordon, as Told by Her First Model, Miss Elsie', *Saturday Evening Post*, 19 February 1927, 35–6.

90 Avery Strakosch, 'Fashions for the Famous: Dressmaking Days With Lady Duff-Gordon, as Told by Her First Model, Miss Elsie', ibid., 26 February 1927, 99.

91 Arjamand 'came of simple American heritage' but was informed by Lady Duff Gordon 'You are the beautiful Indian princess Arjmonde [sic] come to life again, after having been laid to rest in the Taj Mahal, that most beautiful tomb in the world.' Ibid. See also Greer 1952, 50.

92 Strakosch, 'Fashions for the Famous', 26 February 1927, 99. On the necrophyliac associations of extreme thinness in fashion models, see Jobling 1998 and De Perthuis 2003.

93 'Importance of the Silhouette', *New York Times*, 30 March 1913.

94 Lucile Duff Gordon, 'Paris Fashions in Transit', *Harper's Bazar*, September 1913, 44. In fact Lucile did go on to design for the fuller figure in her designs for Sears Roebuck.

95 Mary Buel, 'Early Spring Styles Delight Parisian Women', *Chicago Daily Tribune*, 1 February 1914.

96 Louise Morely, 'Flesh Colored Corsets Under X-Ray Gowns', *Chicago Daily Tribune*, 29 March 1914.

97 Ibid.

98 'Court, plat, géométrique, quadrangulaire, l e vêtement féminin s'établit sur des gabarits qui dépendent du parallélogramme, et 1925 ne saluera pas le retour de la mode à courbes suaves, du sein arrogant, de la savoureuse hanche.' Colette, 'Printemps de demain', *Vogue* (France), 1 February 1925, 31, repr. in *Colette et la mode* 1991, 66. See also Freadman 2006 for a nuanced reading of Colette's writing on fashion, esp. on the 1920s vogue for slenderness.

99 'Quelquefois, les mannequins vivants choisis par Mademoiselle avaient des poitrines rebondies. Mademoiselle souhaitant effacer la poitrine (elle voulait retrouver sa silhouette personnelle), elle faisait faire un bustier en tulle de coton doublé. Ce bustier était baleiné et de couleur chair. Le mannequin à qui le bustier était destiné devait le porter chaque fois pour une présentation devant Mademoiselle.' White, 'Mademoiselle Chanel', n.d., 6.

100 Madeleine Vionnet, *La Renaissance de l'art français et des industries de luxe*, numéro spéciale, 7th year, no. 6, June 1924.

101 La Comtesse de Noailles, 'Jeunesse des Femmes', *Vogue* (France), 1 April 26, 33. She writes: 'Il me faut à présent constater que si les femmes ont, par leurs courts cheveux, détruit la diversité, et nous imposent une vision répétée de nuques semblables, qui font songer à ces fruits en espalier que la chaleur des serres développent également, il est certain que notre époque est favorable à leur aspect de permanente jeunesse. On ne voit plus des femmes vieilles. Un sort de confiance, de gaîté intérieure est répandue en elles et vient fleurir à leur surface. Cheveux taillés, cheveux colorés, robes alertes, chapeaux désinvoltes communiquent aux gestes, au coeur même, l'heureuse vigueur. L'âme reflète l'apparence. Les femmes ont l'âge de leur habillement.'

102 'Paris 1927–1928 vu par la princesse Jane San Faustino', *Vogue* (France), March 1928, 35. See also Stearns 2002 and Comiskey 2005.

103 'Patou Cables for Models', *New York Times*, 27 June 1928.

104 Pascal Pia, 'Code de Mannequin', *Voila*, 9 March 1935, 6.

105 'Wanted: Six "Natural Girls" for Manikins', *Chicago Daily Tribune*, 19 August 1928.

106 Ibid.

107 On Ziegfeld's chorus-girl specifications, which consisted of a militaristic way of classifying girls into four types, from A to D (later expanded to five, from A to E), see Ch. 4 n. 53.

108 'Dressmakers Turn Shylocks', *Los Angeles Times*, 14 March 1929; 'Lacking Curves, Parisian Models Lack Jobs, Too', *Chicago Daily Tribune*, 14 March 1929.

109 Stearns 2002, 160. See also Gilman 2008.

110 Bordo 1993, 185.

111 Roberts 1994, 82.

112 Ibid., 84. Roberts outlines the paradoxes and complexities of 1920s fashion that support her argument in 'The Illusion of Being Free', 81–7.

113 Ibid., 84 and 86.

114 Elizabeth A. Williams, 'Gastronomy and the Diagnosis of Anorexia in Fin-de-Siècle France', in Forth and Accampo 2010, 92.

115 Stearns 2002, 165–7.

116 Roberts 1994, 81–7. Elizabeth Wilson discusses how cultural fantasy and economic reality mesh in fashion, so that 'It [fashion] manufactures dreams and images as well as things, and fashion is as much a part of the dream world of capitalism as its economy'. Wilson 2003, 14. Similarly, Agnès Rocamora highlights the fusion of the real and the imaginary in fashion discourse when she describes Parisian fashion spaces as 'a geography at the junction of the lived and the imagined'. Rocamora 2009, 35ff.

117 Erté 1975, 32.

118 'Their type changes often. Two or three years ago, these young ladies had to resemble young boys, to the point where Maison X . . . slipped an adolescent boy in the midst of the nymphs, and no-one noticed' ('Le type de ceci change souvent. Il y a deux ou trois ans, ces demoiselles devraient ressembler à des garçonnets, au point que la maison X . . . glissa un adolescent au milieu des nymphes, et nul ne s'en aperçut'). Elizabeth de Gramont, 'La Mode en 1930', *Le Correspondent*, 25 December 1925, 870.

119 Amy Lyford, '"Le Numéro Barbette": Photography and the Politics of Embodiment in Interwar Paris', in Chadwick and Latimer 2003, 223–35. Similarly, Linda Mizejewski has compared the performance of femininity by Ziegfeld's Follies showgirls to that of 'illusionists' in the same period, that is, male to female cross-dressing performers such as Julian Eltinge. Mizejewski 1999, 103–6.

120 O. O. McIntyre, 'Something for Monsieur: Jeanne Lanvin Opens a Department for the Diversion of Shopping Husbands', *Harper's Bazar*, July 1925, 87 and 108.

121 'L'Angleterre a osé: mannequins masculins', *Adam*, 15 December 1929, 67. It featured photographs of two separate male mannequin parades staged in London under the auspices of the Great Nottingham Cooperative; one photograph showed raincoats modelled by five men and the other a wedding parade.

122 Roberts 1994, 60.

123 'Chez le grand couturier évoloue le mannequin vivant. Elle ou Il a de beaux gestes, toujours les mêmes, un air suprêmement ennuyé, une grâce apprêtée. C'est l'élégance française qui se meut en longue théorie devant les yeux éblouis de l'étranger.' P. V. 'Notes de carnet', *L'art et la mode*, 5 December 1896, 924.

124 Michelson 1984, cited in Mulvey 2006, 49.

CHAPTER 11

1 'Elle avait le don de l'imitation. Haussée sur les pointes de ses bottines usées, se gonflant de même qu'un paon qui fait la roue, elle a avancé et reculé sur le parquet d'un pas harmonieux, pris des poses coquettes, glissé légère, ondoyante.' Maizeroy 1907, 61.

2 Garafola 1998, 37–8; Hillel Schwartz, 'Torque: The New Kinaesthetic of the Twentieth Century', in Crary and Kwinter 1992, 75.

3 Schwartz, 'Torque', 77.

4 Keith Thomas, 'Introduction', in Bremmer and Roodenburg 1993, 5–6.

5 Wickberg 2007.

6 On the desired posture from the late nineteenth and early twentieth centuries see Vigarello 2004, esp. 166–72.

7 Nancy Lee Chalfa Ruyter, 'Antique Longings: Genevieve Stebbins and American Delsartean Performance', in Foster 1996, 70–89.

8 'As Told by Jean Patou', *Washington Post*, 7 December 1924.

9 Ballard 1960, 55.

10 'From Paris to Monte Carlo and Return', *Vogue* (America), 15 April 1914, 27.

11 Ibid.

12 'La mode nouvelle fait maître de nouveaux gestes', *Vogue* (France), 1 December 1921, 3–7.

13 Even Suzanne Lenglen, the tennis champion and fashion icon who was frequently dressed by Patou, claimed, perhaps disingenuously, that instead of trying to set new records on the tennis court she sought instead 'to create an elegant movement, a general equilibrium in a gesture'. From Janet Flanner, *Paris Was Yesterday*, cited in Stewart 2001, 169.

14 Keith Thomas discusses the difficulties of the endeavour and outlines the range of methods and sources on which a historian of gesture might draw. Thomas, 'Introduction', 4–8.

15 'Ainsi fait-il entrer à nouveau dans un discours scientifique 'carnavalisé' ce qui a été exclu du savoir social officiel et de son discours.' Stierle 2001, 203.

16 'Je parle pour les gens habitués à trouver de la sagesse dans la feuille qui tombe, des problèmes gigantesques dans la fume qui s'élève, des théories dans les vibrations de la lumières, de la pensée dans les marbres, et le plus horrible des mouvements dans l'immobilité.' Honoré de Balzac quoted in ibid., 204–5.

17 Nora 1989, 9.

18 Michael Braddick, 'Introduction: The Politics of Gesture', in Braddick 2009, 1. He describes the history of gesture as a 'relatively new historical terrain' that is better established in the social and behavioural sciences (see esp. Kendon 2004) but outlines some key texts in this emerging area of historical research. He suggests that historical scholarship on gesture 'represents a kind of linguistic analysis, or an approach to the mind–body problem, rather than a sociology of non-verbal communication as Goffman, Bourdieu, Foucault or Elias might have considered it. But it is this latter approach which is most likely to appeal to historians.' Ibid., 11–12.

19 Bourdieu 1977, 93–4. For Bourdieu's concept of *habitus* as a form of 'embodied history', see Bourdieu 1990, 56.

20 For an expanded historical analysis of several centuries of training the body in deportment, including posture, movement and bearing, see Vigarello 1978. He argued that fencing, horse-riding, dancing, medical discourses and corsets all schooled the body to an upright posture between the sixteenth and eighteenth centuries; in the early nineteenth, gymnastics, etiquette books and fashion plates played a role in determining posture. On nineteenth-century posture in relation to fashion, see ibid., 128–33. On the female walk in the nineteenth century, see Vigarello 2004, 143–4. On the Parisienne's undulating walk see Taxile Delord (1841) cited in Rocamora 2009, 144 n. 100. On schooling the body in the first half of the twentieth century, see Vigarello 1978, 269–97. For a polemical treatment of how the female body is culturally and socially 'trained', see Lefebvre 2004, 'Dressage', 38–45. He asserts that the rhythms which determine all forms of bodily training in Western imperialist society are derived from military training since Roman times. He argues that this 'virile model' was imposed above all on women in 'the *dressage* of girls and women' who nevertheless resisted in various forms: 'It [femininity] occasionally fainted, in order subsequently to *rebel*.' Ibid., 41–2.

21 See Braddick 2009, 1. Robert Muchembled, 'The Order of Gestures: A Social History of Sensibilities under the Ancien Régime in France', in Bremmer and Roodenburg 1993, 130–31. Muchembled invokes both the anthropologist Clifford Gertz's 'thick description' of the 'gestures and attitudes of spectators of Balinese cock-fights' and the ethnologists Erving Goffman and Edward T. Hall, suggesting that the historian can borrow the methods of cultural anthropology to help to 'reconstruct worlds which he can no longer experience physically'.

22 Latham 2000, 13–14.

23 Foster 1995, 6–7. In contrast, Heidi Gilpin cautions against kinaesthetic empathy insofar as it constitutes a sentimental attachment to the lost bodies of the past. Heidi Gilpin, 'Lifelessness in Movement, or How Do the Dead Move? Tracing Displacement and Disappearance for Movement Performance', in Foster 1996, 106.

24 On fashion as a spatial practice, see Breward 2004, 11. On fashion and space in general, see Potvin 2009. On fashion and place in general, see Breward and Gilbert 2006.

25 Entwistle 2000, 12.

26 Conor 2004, 15 and 15–39.

27 Michael Levenson, '1913 and 1914: Two Years in the History of Modernism', the London Modernism Seminar, Senate House, University of London, 2 June 2007.

28 Levenson 1999, 2.

29 All references to Levenson in this paragraph are to the London Modernism Seminar, 2007.

30 'The quick impression, the captured instant, was the new text of elegance'. Hollander 1993, 332.

31 The apparatus for displaying revolving *tableaux vivants* in the nineteenth century are described by Nead 2007, 73. See also Vardac 1949 on how such nineteenth-century stage mechanisms were replicated in twentieth-century cinematic illusion. On the fashion modelling technique of revolving on the spot, see the Gaumont Journal film footage of Boué in 1913 and Drecoll in 1920, where the camera focuses on the mannequins' way of moving their feet to effect a smooth revolution of the body on the spot without creating any movement in the shoulders, to give the effect of a mechanical turntable or a revolving ballerina in a music box. 'La Mode à Paris: Créations Boué Soeurs', 1913, Gaumont Pathé Archives, ref. 1319GJ 00014, and 'Paris Fashion Film: Créations Drecoll', 1920, Gaumont Pathé Archives, ref 2000GD 00657.

32 Benjamin 1997, 36.

33 Debord 1994; de Certeau 1988, 100. For a history of walking, see Solnit 2002.

34 Leroy 1999; Wolff 1990; D'Souza and McDonough 2006; Rocamora 2009, 126–55.

35 Steele 1998, 170.

36 Rocamora 2009, 135.

37 Vigarello 2004, 149–50. He cites a range of nineteenth-century sources that remark on the 'génie de la démarche' of the Parisienne, which is fluid, undulating, animated. She is proud of her feet and legs, and Vigarello comments that she has a 'manière remuante et industrieuse d'exhiber la beauté'.

38 Balzac 1922, 152–3; Steele 1998, 57 ff, discusses Balzac's 'Traité de la vie élégante' in some detail, although not 'La Théorie de la démarche'.

39 Richardson 1987, 63; Uzanne 1898, 56.

40 Stewart 2001, 152.

41 Ibid., 159.

42 Ibid., 154.

43 Ibid., 158.

44 Ibid., 147.

45 'Si nous ne connaissons plus de professeurs d'attitude, nous possédons encore de véritables techniciennes du maintien: les mannequins de couture.' Pascal Pia, 'Code de mannequin', *Voilà*, 9 March 1935, 6. He goes on to say that the mannequin is not a spontaneous production of nature, a woman is not born a mannequin ('Le mannequin n'est pas une production spontanée de la nature . . . une femme ne nait pas mannequin'), suggesting that she can, however, become one, in the manner of Simone de Beauvoir's assertion in *The Second Sex* a few years later: 'one is not born but, rather, becomes a woman'.

46 Yosifon and Stearns 1998, 1064–6, 1068, 1085. They describe a range of body practices that inculcated moral ideals about posture and show how not only schools but also colleges used a range of devices to make students of both sexes aware of posture in the 1920s and 30s, including shadowgraphs, schematographs and posture tracings (1076). These were systems of dots traced on images of the body not dissimilar to Marey's and the Gilbreths' methods for measuring human movement.

47 Delbourg-Delphis 1981, 41; Vigarello 2004, 177–9.

48 'Une robe est une chose qui marche'; 'nous faisons de la sculpture qui bouge'. Alexandre 1902, 61 and 72.

49 'The only really satisfactory way to judge of how a dress will look is, of course, upon the human figure, as every dressmaker knows.' 'Intime', 'A Parisian Prince of Dress', *Lady's Realm*, November 1900, 23 and 25.

50 Nead 2007, 60–68, discusses the cultural significance of Galatea in this period.

51 Laurence, 'Paris Couturiers: How the World's Fashions are Determined – Fitting the Costumes to Buyers by Aid of Mannequins', *Los Angeles Times*, 6 January 1901. 'Their moral situation is entirely particular', wrote Roger-Milès of mannequins in 1910; 'one only asks of them that they be beautiful, slender, shapely and stylish, that they know how to walk, to move and position their arms, to kick aside the train of a dress, to adapt their young faces to an expression which is that of the costume they are clothed in' ('Leur situation morale est tout à fait spéciale: on ne leur demande que d'être belles, d'avoir de la ligne, du galbe, 'de la branche', de savoir marcher, remuer et placer les bras, écarter du

pied la traîne d'une robe, adapter leur visage de jeunesse à une expression qui soit celle du costume dont on les revêt'). Roger-Milès 1910, 137. The book was profiled and this passage paraphrased in 'The Creators of New Fashion Seen at Close Range', *New York Times*, 25 December 1910.

52 'La première vertu que l'on demande à un mannequin, c'est de savoir marcher, de marcher avec aisance, avec noblesse et grâce. Et cela n'est pas donné à tout le monde de savoir marcher, comme il faut marcher, de tout le corps, le pied bien à plat, solidement et avec légèreté en même temps, – non pas comme une poule sur ses oeufs. Le mannequin qui sait cela a partie gagnée. C'est le mannequin "arrivé".' Emile Henriot, 'Figures parisiennes: le mannequin', *L'Illustration*, 27 December 1913, reprinted in *L'Illustration: Journal Universel* 1987, 112.

53 'The mannequins enter the room with the peculiar gliding walk that is learned in the showrooms. . . . It is as distinct in its way as the walk of the spear girl in a musical comedy, and once learned is never afterward forgotten.' 'A Paris Show of Fashions', *Washington Post*, 19 September 1909.

54 '[D]'un pas cadencé et comme dansant, évoluant, ondulant, se cambrant.' Alexandre 1902, 109.

55 On the mannequin's 'undulating slenderness' ('sa sveltesse onduleuse'), see Max Rivière, 'La Journée d'un mannequin', *Femina*, 15 October 1905, 491–2. The mannequin 'sails' in 'Paris Couturiers: How the World's Fashions are Determined – Fitting the Costumes to Buyers by Aid of Mannequins', *Los Angeles Times*, 6 January 1901. She 'saunters' in 'The Paris Mannequin: How She Helps to Beguile Women in the Dressmaker's Shop', *New York Times*, 10 November 1907. She 'trails' in Katharine de Forest, 'Autumn Days in Paris', *Harper's Bazar*, 10 November 1900, 178.

56 'They have a way of walking, holding themselves and turning which is in no way that of real life', for they must be able 'to pass to and fro, to turn, to tilt their heads, to smile; to trot, or to assume an attitude that is either majestic, nonchalant, or cheerful.' Alexandre, 1902, 105.

57 'The poise of the figure will be of the utmost importance. The line down the front of the dress must be perfectly straight, and this necessitates throwing the shoulders and bust well forward, while the back, at the same time, must show a graceful curve, elegantly continued by the long skirt as it sweeps following behind the wearer.' 'Smaller Waists Are Demanded', *Atlanta Constitution*, 6 October 1907.

58 The *Washington Post* deemed Paquin's version, worn without petticoats, suitable only for paying social calls in a carriage, 'walking, save of a leisurely and studied sort, being practically impossible in connection with the trailing, clinging fold.' Yet, 'when we saw the costume on a tall, slender girl who filled the role of mannequin we were conscious only of the exceeding grace of the skirt.' 'Models that Exhibit Season's Startling Innovations', *Washington Post*, 22 September 1907.

59 The full quotation is 'La mélancolie se porte beaucoup cette saison. Il est de bon ton de s'essayer aux attitudes languissantes et, comme la chasse, réservées. Les robes actuelles si étroitement collantes en sont cause, il a beau 'y avoir place pour tout', il y en a si peu que tous les mouvements spontanés sont défendus: ces robes interdisent toute expansion: d'où les attitudes des élégantes.' Le Mannequin d'Hozier, 'Modanités', *Fantasio*, 15 August 1909, 71.

60 'It Is Style for Women to Limp', *Atlanta Constitution*, 23 January 1910. With its high skirt at the front revealing the feet and ankles, 'the wearer of this gown would cause as much sensation as did the mannequins who first donned the slashed Directoire gown in Paris'.

61 Anne Rittenhouse, 'Clothes Worn at the French Races Again Eccentric – New Turban the Highest Hat in Decades', *New York Times*, 7 August 1910.

62 The description is embedded in an account by Lucile in which she recalled designing Directoire-style dresses for the chorus line of a London play produced by George Edwards in 1910 and, finding a few left over, adding them to a fashion show in Paris, which in fact she could not have done since she did not open in Paris until 1911. 'The Story of the Greatest Fashion Expert in the World', in 'Portfolio of Lady Duff-Gordon's Original Designs', Sears Roebuck and Co., Chicago, Fall and Winter 1916–17, f. 6.

63 Poiret 1931, 73. A disapproving American journalist criticised Poiret for the extreme narrowness of his skirts this season: 'he is first, last and always an extremist and has achieved his reputation by audacity of idea rather than by the beauty of his creations'. 'The Hobble in Disfavor; Skirts are Still Narrow', *Washington Post*, 25 September 1910.

64 'Vêtues de jupes étriques, resserrées au milieu et rattrapées par une *martingale* . . . les parisiennes ont toutes l'air de se livrer au joyeux sport de la course en sac. . . . Il faut maintenant une vraie science pour savoir marcher.' Le Mannequin d'Hozier, 'Modanités', 644.

65 The tied-in skirt 'requires a trained mannequin to carry it off with perfect grace!' and mannequins 'are trained to wear novel and eccentric toilets gracefully . . . to walk, and to stand still and to sit!' Mme de Villiers, 'Dispute Over the Tied-in Skirt', *Boston Daily*, 18 September 1910.

66 Gustave Babin, 'Une leçon d'élégance dans un parc', *L'Illustration*, 9 July 1910, 21. Poiret's mannequins are also described as a 'parade of undulating mannequins' ('un défilé de mannequins onduleux') in Roger-Milès 1910, 94.

67 Poiret 1931, 146.

68 Mauss 1995, 459. Foucault took many of his ideas on 'technologies of the body' from Mauss.

69 Ibid., 458.

70 Ibid., 465.

71 At the wholesalers, 'les mannequins y sont un rien plus abstraits, de manières plus concentrées et de beautés plus régulières; il ne conviendrait pas qu'elles déployassent ici les froufrous voluptueux'. Alexandre 1902, 167.

72 *Fortune*, January 1933, 12.

73 Mauss 1995, 458, 459, 460.

74 Ibid., 459.

75 On the Gaby Glide, see Gardiner 1986, 62, 64 and 66; and Davis 2006, 281 n. 45; on the Castle Walk, see Castle 1984, 81–2. Davis describes how the Gaby Glide, a dance based on an 'Apache' dance known as the *valse chaloupée*, became an overnight craze in France after the French actress Gaby Deslys and her dance partner the Hungarian-American Harry Pilcer brought jazz rhythms from New York to Paris in 1917.

76 On how jazz criss-crossed between France and America see Gillroy 1993.

77 Described as an 'arch-mannequin also of modes', Sorel was known for 'her gowns, her jewels, gestures, gait', that were imitated world-wide. H. I. Brock, 'America, We are Here!' *New York Times*, 17 December 1922. Sorel was described in another article as having the bearing of royalty, although 'no longer young . . . she is slender and of medium height, and the famous walk is of the essence of youth. It is a gait of pantheresque grace before which a world has bowed – to which critics have given too small space. There is a challenge in the springing step, hips well forward and head thrown back, a challenge as when a wild thing padding through African jungles suddenly pauses and looks about.' Diana Rice, 'French Art's Ambassadress Extraordinary', *New York Times*, 3 December 1922.

78 Colette, *Le Matin*, cited in Castle 1984, 167.

79 'Images suggérées, gestes esquissés induisant dans le silence positions et comportements, phrases anodines où les mots sans y paraître dessinent un maintien qui masquera une élaboration à demi consciente en même temps que laborieuse; phrases plus lourdes d'ordres donnés fixant avec une précision analytique ou solennelle les apparences et la tenue. Le corps est le premier lieu où le main de l'adulte marque l'enfant, il est le premier espace où s'imposent les limites sociales et psychologiques données à sa conduite, il est l'emblème où la culture vient inscrire ses signes comme autant des blasons.' Vigarello 1978, 9.

80 'Le corps s'est parlé dans une langue latérale, allusive, voilant et signalant à la fois l'importance pédagogique de la tenue et la correction des attitudes physiques dans le procès des rapports entre adultes et enfants.' Ibid., 9.

81 Kisa Kuprina quoted in Vassiliev 2000, 410.

82 'Waistless Gowns Are Again Exploited by Poiret and the Best Wraps in Paris Are Made by Him', *New York Times*, 15 October 1911.

83 Cocteau 1987, 173.

84 The mannequins at Poiret and 'half a dozen others' were corsetless, 'or if there is anything worn, it is simply a ceinture, just sufficient to keep the girdle of the gown in place' because, 'to be fashionable, one must be supple'. 'Draped tailored Skirts and Contrasting Coats', *Chicago Daily Tribune*, 1 June 1913.

85 Erté 1975, 26.

86 'New Corset Features', *Dry Goods Economist*, 24 July 1911, 31.

87 E.g., 'A few mannequins imported from Paris also added the inimitable walk that the rue de la Paix made famous.' 'The Paris Fashion Show Has Brought a New Epoch', *New York Times*, 28 November 1915.

88 Americans in particular were considered by this journalist to be less accomplished at walking in the new fashions than French women. Anne Rittenhouse, 'Drapery Richness in New Fashions', *New York Times*, 23 September, 1912.

89 At Doucet a striking model in black and white chiffon, tulle and lace was worn by a mannequin 'who carried it off in a dramatic manner. She knew full well how to make every point tell.' 'Doucet's Gowns Indicate Persian and Russian Influence', *New York Times*, 15 March 1914. Rittenhouse, 'Drapery Richness'.

90 Freadman argues that this is one of the strengths of Colette's writing on fashion, to understand the interface of body and garment as one. Freadman 2006, 342.

91 'Walk Like THIS if You Would Be Up-To-Date', *Chicago Daily Tribune*, 3 November 1912.

92 'Slim Figure Wins in Paris Mode', *New York Times*, 16 June 1913.

93 'Woman Walks Again', *Daily News* (London), 10 March 1913.

94 'Là où nous étions accoutumés à la voir se creuser, soudain elle se renfle; là où elle se gonflait, maintenant elle s'aplatit. Ce que l'on dissimulait, on le montre; ce que l'on déguisait, on l'étale; ce sur quoi l'on glissait, on l'accentue . . . Elles allaient naguère toutes droites, strictement serrées dans des fourreaux qui de la taille aux pieds ne présentaient la moindre inflexion; elles n'avaient plus ni hanches, ni bassin, et là où d'ordinaire s'épanouissent les rondeurs de ce que l'on appelle couramment le ventre, nous étions tous surpris et enchantés, puisqu'elles le voulait ainsi, de voir qu'il n'y avait plus rien, moins que rien, rien de rien . . . Toujours est-il que, du jour au lendemain, elles ont eu un ventre. Il leur a poussé subitement, à sa place habituelle, comme par miracle . . . Où donc, hier, le cachaient-elles? . . . Elle marchait naguère, à tous petits pas, à trotte-menu; elle aura maintenant plus de désinvolture et plus de liberté; elle dissimulait son ventre, elle l'avoue . . . Et puis, en même temps que le ventre, il redevient à la mode

de laisser voir la nuque! . . . Pour qui est de l'allure générale du corps féminin . . . si libres de mouvement, si désinvoltes, un peu excessifs parfois, si véridiques toujours . . . il est assez difficile d'en donner une idée avec des mots . . . Les savoureux croquis, si libres de mouvement, si désinvoltes, un peu excessifs parfois, si véridiques toujours, du dessinateur Sachetti . . . ne disent-ils pas mieux que je ne le saurais les séductions nouvelles, les charmes et la grâce imprévus, inédits des femmes de ce printemps de 1913.' Gabriel Mourey, 'Les caprices de la ligne', *Gazette du Bon Ton*, May 1913, 210–13.

95 Gabriele Brandstetter, 'Pose–Posa–Posing – Between Images and Movement', in Bippus and Mink 2007, 250–51.

96 Erté 1975, 26 and 31.

97 Matheson and Sorkin 2005, 32.

98 Beaton 1954, 33–4.

99 Kevin Brownlow, 'Silent Films – What Was the Right Speed?' in Elsaesser 1990, 282–90; Hayward 1993, 71.

100 From an article in the *Frankfurter Zeitung*, 11 June 1926, reprinted in Roth 2004, 175–7.

101 At Paquin in 1912 a mannequin modelled a Polonaise-style dress in rose-pink taffeta with a wide skirt caught in below the knee and loose sleeves that billowed out when the mannequin swirled. 'When the mannequin came in wearing it, a man of fashion who was looking at the gowns with his wife broke into such enthusiasm about it that the mannequin was so delighted that she swirled and swayed before him as though she were posing for living pictures.' Anne Rittenhouse, 'Paquin Shows Wider Skirts Than Usual and Long Coats Gathered at the Waist-line – She Also Shows large Panniers', *New York Times*, 6 October 1912; 'Gown That a Man Admired', *Christian Science Monitor*, 15 October 1912. At Drecoll, 'The manner in which the mannequins mince in and out of a salon is enough to show a client how she ought not to have her skirt cut.' 'Drecoll Retains the Modified Slash in Skirts', *New York Times*, 15 March 1914. Poiret in 1914 described his mannequins 'moving with infinite grace, lightly swaying they advance through the *salons* like delicate canoes balancing between dangerous rocks.' 'Paul Poiret's Spring Opening', *Harper's Bazar*, April 1914, 24–5. In 1914 at Redfern, by contrast, the indifferent mannequins had a 'snake-like walk'. 'Wonders of Paris Frocks Shown Amid Picturesque Settings', *Washington Post*, 30 August 1914. At Lanvin, 'Madame Lanvin's manikins do not . . . walk with the debutante slouch.' 'So Say the Paris Openings', *Vogue* (America), 15 March 1914, 36. These texts vividly convey the excitement, movement and up-to-date modernity of the fashion show as it was perceived in the 1910s, whereas film, for all its novelty as a medium in the 1910s, can appear anachronistic to modern eyes. The differences between types of source suggest that a 'problem' of interpretation for historians, since written

descriptions from, say, 1910 are no more 'truthful' or value-free than filmed ones.

102 'A Little of Everything at the French Openings', *Vanity Fair*, October 1915, 85–6 and 108.

103 Marcel Mauss, 'Techniques of the Body' (1934), in Crary and Kwinter 1995, 460.

104 'Little of Everything', *Vanity Fair*, October 1915, 85–6 and 108.

105 Mulvey 2006, 50.

106 Cocteau 1987, 173–4.

107 Jean Laporte, 'La tournée du grand couturier', *Femina*, 1 June 1914, 339–41.

108 'Elle roule sur ses hanches, elle avancé comme en tanguant, découplée, souple et féline . . . Elle est "balancée" vous dis-je. Elle sait marcher, et tout son corps participe à sa démarche. Il y a de la danse en elle, et c'est d'elle, sans aucun doute, que le poète a dit: *Même quand elle marche, on dirait qu'elle danse* . . . Or, il n'y a qu'à Paris que l'on marche ainsi. Et, à Paris, il n'y a que les mannequins qui sachent aussi bien marcher. Et aussi bien, c'est tout leur métier.' Henriot, 'Figures parisiennes', 112–16. In 1928, Roubaud, too, described the fashion show in abstract terms as if it were pure, disembodied, formal movement: 'The presentation is a dance without music. A dress arrives, passes, stops, turns. The bust swells, the skirt moves, the flounces float' ('La présentation est une danse sans musique. Une robe survient, passe, s'arrête, se tourne. Le corsage se gonfle, la jupe s'anime, les volants volent'). Roubaud 1928, 163. Reboux, similarly, writes: 'She advances with a balanced step, her hips rolling. Her head oscillates. There is nonchalance and suppleness in this walk that seems to be in rhythm with some imperceptible music' ('Il s'avance d'un pas balancé. Ses hanches roulant. Sa tête oscille. Il y a de la nonchalance et de la souplesse dans cette démarche que semble rythmer une imperceptible musique'). Reboux 1927, 16. Both describe the mannequin's walk in terms not so different from Villiers de l'Isle-Adam's android Hadaly from *L'Ève future* (1886), with rolling ball-bearings in her hips; see Ch. 1 above.

109 Irene Castle, 'My Memories of Vernon Castle', part 3, *Everybody's Magazine*, January 1919, 38.

110 Aronson, ' "Watch Your Step" a Hit', *Gainsville Times*, 8 February 1916.

111 Beaton 1954, 92. This description correlates with Irene Castle's dancing performance in the film *The Whirl of Life* (1915) in which Irene is lithe and athletic; she not only dances but also swims, dives and rides a horse astride. When she dances, her movements are fluid and continuous; she moves in several directions at once, so that often the weight of her garments carries the fabric in one direction while her body has already moved in another. In this way, the weight and fluidity of the clothes are displayed to advantage. She also does little back and side kicks in a different direction from her torso, producing

further rippling effects in the cloth. The film can be seen in the Billy Rose Theatre Division of the New York Public Library.

112 Castle and Castle 1980, 46.

113 Ibid., 20.

114 A popular dance manual describes 'the Walking Boston' or 'One Step Waltz' as being 'about balancing the weight of the body successively on one foot after the other with one foot ahead in a walking pose'. The author exhorts the reader to 'get plenty of swing into your action' but to keep both feet on the floor. Walker 1914, 37–9.

115 The walk was slightly different for each dance. The simplest, the one-step, consisted merely of walking in time to the music, the man walking forwards and the woman backwards, which could be modified by the addition of dance steps. In the tango, the introduction of the eight-step 'gives a slight up-and-down motion to the walk very similar to a modified Cake Walk'. The two-step introduced 'a perceptible swaying motion' to the maxixe. Castle and Castle 1980, 47, 102, 108 and 112.

116 Ibid., 126.

117 Ibid., 80 and 89.

118 Ibid., n.p.

119 Young 2005, 70. See also ch. 8 and nn. 99–102 above.

120 Chris Townsend, 'Slave to the Rhythm: Sonia Delaunay's fashion Project and the Fragmentary, Mobile Modernist Body', in Brand and Teunissen 2006, 252 and 373.

121 Schwartz, 'Torque', 75.

122 Townsend 2006, 361.

123 Ibid., 377.

124 Ibid., 379.

125 Ibid., 374 and 369. Tag Gronberg has analysed Sonia Delaunay's window display of her Boutique Simultanée at the 1925 'Art Déco' exhibition as a 'particularly vivid evocation' of both cinema and dance, in the form of Delaunay's simultaneous textiles displayed in motion, both on a system of moving rollers and manipulated by living mannequins. Gronberg 2002, 272–88.

126 E.g. Robert de Beauplan, 'Après la grève des cousettes: dans les coulisses de la grande couture', *L'Illustration*, 19 May 1923, reprinted in *L'Illustration, Journal Universel* 1987, 137–40. One singular account describes 'a sort of swaying of the hips or very slow belly dance, a dawdling form of undulation, a seal's waltz' ('une espèce de déhanchement ou de très lente danse du ventre, une manière de se traîner onduleusement, une valse de phoque'), *La Vie parisienne*, 23 March 1918, quoted in Aubenas and Demange 2006, 218. For more generic descriptions, see Andrée Viollis, 'Comment on prépare la mode', *Petit Parisien*, 14 March 1923. At Vionnet, 'there is genius in these majestic and rhythmic walks'('il y a, en effet, du génie dans ces démarches majestueuses et rythmiques'). Jean Ravennes, 'Aux sanctuaires mystérieux de l'élégance et de la mode', *La Revue française*, 9 April 1922, 84. At Yteb the

Russian mannequin Nina Von Hoyer was instructed to walk 'without any fuss, and no undulating or unnecessary movement which so many French models have'. Vassiliev 2000, 255.

127 '[J]'ai déjà vu, en un mois, défiler deux cent robes. C'est, à l'aube d'une saison, un défilé qui instruit, en amusant. J'y appris comment on porte cette année le ventre, qui conserve, bien que plat, une arrogance de bouclier et se balance d'avant en arrière, d'arrière en avant. Où est le roulis de hanches, espagnol or martiniquais, des mannequins de 1914? Il s'agit bien de hanches! nous n'avons plus rien de latéral.' Colette, 'Trop court', reprinted in Colette 1991, 78–9.

128 Freadman quotes this passage in full and discusses it in relation to the fashionable boyish figure of the 1920s. Freadman, 2006, 340.

129 Aubenas and Demange 2006, 34.

130 Colette, 'Almanach des modes présentes, passées et futures pour 1923', reprinted in Colette 1991, 145.

131 *New York Herald Tribune*, 6 February 1925; *New York Telegram*, 6 February 1925.

132 Tess Slesinger, 'Memoirs of an ex-flapper', *Vanity Fair*, 1934, 26, 27 and 70.

133 Latham 2000, 18–21.

134 Ballard 1960, 15.

135 Beaton 1954, 164, cited in Aubenas and Demange 2006, 218.

136 E.g., wrote Louis Roubaud, 'Ginette' wore sportswear and tailored suits with 'unconcerned allure' ('allure dégagée'); she modelled her daywear casually ('avec désinvolture'), leaving her coat to trail a little to show off the matching coat-lining and dress; and she accelerated her pace for the vaporous and light tea-gowns that required many tiny and gracious movements. She regulated the slowness of her steps and her gestures to suit the richness of her evening dresses. Roubaud 1928, 178–80.

137 Antoinette Dowerthy, 'Walks for Everyday Costume', *Washington Post*, 12 April 1925 and *Chicago Daily Tribune*, 12 April 1925. At Poiret, too, the mannequins had a range of walks, starting with a 'natural, unaffected walk; graceful but not exaggerated. It is quite different from the mincing saunter of mannequins in most other parts of the world. And surely you have observed the dash with which a Poiret mannequin displays some gay sports model; the brisk air with which she enters the salon in a trim tailor-made trotteur; the leisurely, sliding grace with which she trails across the carpet some gorgeous evening gown suave and alluring as moonlight. That dash, that briskness, that leisurely grace embodies Poiret's idea of a mannequin who is also an artist.' 'Whom Do the Ladies Dress to Please?' *Washington Post*, 12 April 1925.

138 Mauss 'Techniques of the Body', 458.

139 'La journée d'une Américaine à Paris', *Vogue* (France), 1 July 1923, 3–5; see 4 for the Fifth Avenue walk.

140 'La démarche des Françaises . . . étonnera beaucoup: cette souplesse, qui ne ressemble en rien à la souplesse sportive, ces manières, ces gestes discrets lui seront un grand sujet d'étonnement. Elle essayera de régler son pas sur celui de ses nouvelles amies. Elle comprendra que la grande enjambée peut avoir beaucoup d'allure mais que le petit piétinement français possède une jolie distinction.' Ibid., 5.

141 'Fashions from London and Paris', *Atlanta Constitution*, 11 July 1926.

142 Quoted in Teitelbaum 2010, 89. With thanks to Peter McNeil for bringing this to my attention.

143 There was also, however, another, far different, formulaic and static style of fashion film produced by the Manuel Frères studios in the 1920s. The modelling style in these films is static too, perhaps reflecting the fact that Manuel Frères was an established fashion photography studio specialising in still imagery from the beginning of the century.

144 *On Demande un mannequin*, 1923, black and white silent, directed by Tony Lekain, costumes and locations by Drecoll, starring Monique Chrysès and André Luguet, 30 minutes. It has been restored by the Cinémathèque Française, Paris, where it can be viewed, cat. no. DVD 2322.

145 In *Au Bonheur des dames* (1930, directed by Julien Duvivier), Dito Parlo plays a mannequin who also models both in a spacious salon and on a specially constructed raised octagonal stage in a little room at the Galeries Lafayette department store.

146 Henriot, 'Figures parisiennes', 112–16; Reboux 1927, 16; Roubaud 1928, 163.

147 Baron de Meyer, 'Individuality in Dress', *Harper's Bazar*, September 1928, 63.

148 'Savez-vous marcher?' Roubaud 1928, 173–82.

149 'Tu sais marcher à Bruxelles; tu ne sauras jamais marcher à Paris!' Ibid., 174. Roubaud relates that Armande could strike *poses plastiques* like a sculpture but could not walk. Ginette recalled that she herself could not walk at the beginning but had learnt by observing her colleagues, while Marie-Jeanne, who hopped like a bird in the beginning, taught herself by posing in the *cabine* mirrors. These are typical ways of acquiring 'techniques of the walk' as described by Mauss.

CHAPTER 12

1 See Intro. nn. 11–14 above.

2 See Oskar Bie's essay 'Social Intercourse' (1905) as discussed in Anderson 1992, 99. Georg Simmel, 'The Metropolis and Mental Life' (1903) and 'Fashion' (1904), in Simmel 1971. See also Siegfried Kracauer, 'Cult of Distraction' (1926), in Kracauer 1995, 323–8, as discussed by Ganeva 2008, 116–17.

3 Anderson 1992, 44.

4 Ibid., 42.

5 'Par les trente instruments de l'orchestre, la *Marseillaise* éclate. Fine, souriante, élancée, apparaît Raphaëlle – Raph qui dormait d'un si grand coeur sur la chaise longue de la cabine. De toute obstacle rencontré – table ou chaise – elle fait un arrêt, une hésitation qui anime la mousseline et le crêpe. D'un geste d'excuse ou d'impatience pour écarter un spectateur elle met en valeur un froncé, un galon ou une broderie qui méritait d'être découvert comme une surprise.' Roubaud 1928, 196. Roubaud identifies the city, Copenhagen, and this, combined with the fact that the house of the fictional Jeanne Mounet is described as being in the same place as Poiret's, at the Rond-point du Champs-Élysées, suggest that the fashion show being described is Poiret's.

6 For some descriptions of the stop-start style of modelling, or of mannequins periodically pausing, see 'Paris Fashions for the Autumn', *New York Times*, 8 October 1911; 'Show Paris Gowns to an Eager Crowd', *New York Times*, 5 March 1914; 'Mannequins Depart', *Boston Daily Globe*, 22 March 1914; 'Paris Yields to None in Fashion World', *New York Times*, 2 December 1928. At Melnotte-Simonin the mannequins did not walk but turned on the spot, making expansive arm gestures. See film footage in 'La Mode: création Melnotte-Simonin', 1927, ref. no. 128150, Archives Françaises du Film, Paris. The same smooth revolution on the spot can be seen in the section entitled 'ces tissus ont la souplesse et la vie des plis antiques' in 'Les Arts du vêtement', 1928, ref. no. 4028, Archives Françaises du Film. See also ch. 11 n. 31.

7 'La qualité, la charge expressive du mouvement trouvent leur source dans cette latence.' Annie Suquet, 'Scènes: le corps dansant – un laboratoire de la perception', in Corbin, Courtine and Vigarello 2005, vol. III, 401.

8 Brandstetter argues that the fashion pose functions as a hiatus in the flow of action, rather than an action in itself. Like the dancer's pose that she also describes, it creates a point of stillness that gives the observer time to collect his or her vision and thoughts, and provides a contemplative form of 'attraction for the imagination'. Gabriele Brandstetter, 'Pose-Posa-Posing – Between Image and Movement', in Bippus and Mink 2007, 256 and 258. On posing, see also Owens 1992.

9 Doane 2002, 3–4.

10 'Le mouvement humain se décompose en TEMPS bien distinctes; si vous le confondez, vous arrivez à la roideur de la mécanique.' Balzac 1922, 167.

11 Braun 1992, 79. Braun writes that Marey's work came to the attention of a new generation of artists in 1895 when Paul Richer's two treatises using chronophotography for artists were published: *Physiologie artistique de l'homme en mouvement* and *Atlas d'anatomie artistique*.

12 Reasons 2006, 137. With thanks to Marco Pecorari for this reference. The term 'decisive moment' was coined in a later period than that covered here, when the English edition of Henri Cartier-Bresson's 1952 book *Images à la sauvette* was titled *The Decisive Moment*.

13 Brandstetter argues that the modern fashion model's capacity for endless motion and pose are stereotypical codes that are repetitive and yet 'unendingly rich in variation' and suggests that, with some research, an atlas of fashion poses could be assembled. Whether there would be any point to such an atlas is moot, however: and it seems more important to look, as Brandstetter does, at the idea of gesture and pose in fashion modelling, than statistically to log their infinite yet minute variations. Brandstetter, 'Pose-Posa-Posing', 248–50.

14 Worth 1895, 35–6; Saint-Léger, 'Comment se créent les modes', *L'Illustration*, 11 December 1897, repr. in *L'Illustration: Journal Universel* 1987, 62–3.

15 Brannigan 2003; Uhlirova 2013.

16 Bergson 1911, 2, quoted in Brannigan 2003, 4.

17 Bergson 1911, 324–5.

18 Ibid., 4; Brannigan 2003, 4.

19 Bergson 1911, 323, also discussed in Marcus 2007, 139.

20 'Pas à pas – expression par expression et la photographie nous aidera à fixer l'Interprétation qu'il convient de leur donner. Chacun des clichés ci-dessus représente un moment de l'expression de ce morceau.' Mme Jacques Isnardon, 'Les Gestes de la cantatrice', *Femina*, 11 June 1911.

21 'Catching Drapery in Motion', *Vanity Fair*, May 1919.

22 Garafola 1998, 53.

23 See André Gaudreault, 'Editing: Early Practices and Techniques', in Abel 2005, 204–6, and 'Editing: Tableau Style', in ibid., 209–10; Donald Crafton, 'Comic Strips', in ibid., 148–50.

24 Charles Musser, 'Rethinking Early Cinema: Cinema of Attractions and Narrativity' (1994), in Strauven 2006, 389–416, esp. 411–12.

25 An early example are the instructions for a popular dance, *la chaloupée*, created by Mistinguett and Max Dearly in a Moulin Rouge revue. *Fantasio*, 15 August 1908, 48.

26 Giedion 1969, 104.

27 The Bertillon system was officially accepted for use by the Paris police in the same decade in which the first fashion models were recorded in images and rapidly adopted across Europe, Canada and the U.S.A. Despite its efficacy being frequently called into question from the late 1890s, it remained in use well into the 1920s. Finn 2009, 6, 23–6, 28 and 32.

28 Sekula connects images of criminals to everyday sentimental portraits in his analysis of a range of nineteenth-century institutional practices that constitute what he calls 'archives'. These were bureaucratic but also social collections of photographs, i.e. police records and domestic albums or *cartes de visite*, which ordered and classified both 'normal' and 'deviant' bodies into hierarchical categories. Sekula 1986, 3–64.

29 Michaud 2004.

30 Warburg called his collection 'a ghost story for adults'; quoted in ibid., 260.

31 Ibid., 262.

32 On the cinematic and pre-cinematic nature of the atlas, see 'Appendix 2. Crossing Frontiers: Mnemosyne Between Art History and Cinema', ibid., 277–91. See also 'New York: The Movie Set' and 'Etienne-Jules Marey and the Man with the Silver Button', ibid., 41–66, 86–90, 98–102 and 261–2.

33 Nead 2007, 77.

34 Ibid., 72.

35 'Rising Star of the Paris Mannequin', *New York Times*, 23 July 1922.

36 Andrea Cote and Joelle Jensen, 'Identifiable Gestures', in *Posing*, Abrons Art Center at Henry Street Settlement, New York, 2007, 3–9.

37 Katharine de Forest, 'Autumn Days in Paris', *Harper's Bazar*, 10 November 1900, 1787.

38 Guy Hickok, 'The Girls Who Change Their Dresses 7,000 Times a Year', *Atlanta Constitution*, 1 April 1923.

39 'Paris Couturiers: How the World's Fashions are Determined – Fitting the Costumes to Buyers by Aid of Mannequins', *Los Angeles Times*, 6 January 1901.

40 E. M. Newman, 'Nothing To Do but Wear Fine Clothes!' *Chicago Daily Tribune*, 16 November 1913. See also 'Poiret, Creator of Fashion Here', *New York Times*, 21 September 1913.

41 'Ce sont de sveltes femmes, impeccables de ligne, avec des gestes simples que l'habitude ou l'ennui les empêchent d'achever. Elles ont le nonchaloir des princesses orientales qui se savant destinées à n'avoir qu'un inutile éclat dans l'ombre mystérieuse du sérail, et chacun de leurs pas traduit leurs fiertés désabusées.' Jean Ravennes, 'Aux sanctuaires mystérieux de l'élégance et de la mode', *La Revue Française*, 9 April 1922, 84. For nonchalance, see also Alix Marius, 'Mesdames, voici la mode', *La vie*, 6 April 1923: 'Des mannequins . . . filent en des poses souples, nonchalantes, hiératiques'.

42 'Rising Star of the Paris Mannequin', *New York Times*, 23 July 1922.

43 The images are from *Vogue* (America) for 15 April 1919. E. H. Brown 2009, 267. Brown writes: 'her style of blank hauteur . . . I would argue became the template for fashion models more generally' (264–5) but she does not adduce any evidence for this claim, which I do not think is sustainable; the descriptions of mannequins since 1900 that I have unearthed suggest that Lucile's mannequins did not have the monopoly on hauteur.

44 On the blasé attitude, see Simmel, 'Metropolis and Mental Life', 329–30. Simmel argues that we cultivate the blasé attitude partly as a defence against the complex stimuli of city life, partly through an

inability to distinguish between categories of things in a society dominated by a money economy. See also Harvey 1989, 26.

45 See Georg Simmel, 'Fashion' (1904), in Simmel 1971, 294–323, 331–2 and 336.

46 On the 'waning of affect', see Jameson 1991, 10. See also Fredric Jameson, 'Postmodernism and Consumer Society', in Kaplan 1988, 13–29.

47 Exceptionally, the mannequins at Jenny did smile. 'Jenny, Who Is One of the Chief Mainstays of Well-Dressed American Women, Shows Clothes with Moderate Panniers', New York Times, 19 March 1916.

48 'Je ne ciselais . . . sur les aspérités du cylindre-moteur de l'Andréide, les seules ensembles parfaits des mouvements, unis aux regards ainsi qu'aux expressions radieuses ou graves . . . Voulez-vous voir les quelques douzaines de spéciales épreuves photochromiques sur lesquelles sont piqués les points (précis à des millièmes de millimètre près), où les grains de poudre métalliques ont été disséminés, en la carnation, pour l'exacte aimantalisation des cinq ou six sourires fondamenteux de Miss Alicia Clary? Je les ai là, dans ces cartons.' Villiers 1993, 341–2.

49 Andrée Viollis, 'Comment on prépare la mode' Petit parisien, 14 March 1923.

50 While acknowledging the history of glamour in earlier centuries, Brown argues convincingly that 'it is not until the modern period that these [attributes] combine into an ideal form, a form that demands the pervasiveness of technology in everyday lives, the draining of life into black and white images, stylized form, and a literature that so frequently – and lyrically – circulates around abstraction, loss, and a central structuring emptiness.' J. Brown 2009, 1, 5 and 7. See also Burstein on 'cold modernism'. Burstein 2012.

51 Ibid., 97–120.

52 Ibid., 103, 116 and 117. In her discussion of Garbo, Brown also discusses Roland Barthes's famous two-page essay on Garbo, first published in English in 1972 in Mythologies.

53 Tesse 2004, 82. On the influence of stage mannerisms on fashion modelling in early twentieth-century German fashion photographs, see Holschbach 2006.

54 'Those arms, long and awkward by themselves, can yet execute a series of remarkable gestures that are capable of bringing a house to its feet. These gestures are pure art, and in them lies the fascination of Guilbert. She never rants with her arms; the gestures are queer yet graceful movements, simple withal, and somehow in their naturalness they tell the whole story of the song she is singing.' 'Yvette Guilbert Comes', Chicago Daily, 8 December 1895.

55 Paul Morand wrote that 'Rostand always called her 'the princess of gesture'.' Morand 1931, 167. See also Glenn 2000, 17–18, 25.

56 'Poor Girls Wear Gorgeous Gowns', Boston Daily Globe, 22 December 1912, reprinted abridged in ibid., 29 December 1912; Helen Bullitt Lowry, 'Rude Intrusion of Facts into Fashion', New York Times, 1 August 1920.

57 Hillel Schwartz, 'Torque: The New Kinaesthetic of the Twentieth Century', in Crary and Kwinter 1992, 98–9.

58 Rémy 1964, 10. On static posing more generally, see Preston 2011.

59 Mime de gestes required spare, expressive gestures, in the view of Georges Wague, the mime artist who taught Colette and later became a teacher at the conservatoire. He had a sign on his studio wall proclaiming: 'the minimum of gestures corresponds to the maximum of expression.' Ibid., 34 and 49.

60 'Mistinguett fait du ciné', Fantasio, 15 December 1911, 356–8. As Georges Méliès put it, film acting required 'few gestures, but gestures that are clean and clear . . . exact poses are indispensable . . . gesture is everything'. Georges Méliès, 'Les Vues cinématographiques', Annuaire général et international de la photographie, Paris, 1907, cited in Robinson 1993, 33. For the full text, see Appendix B: 'Kinematographic Views' (1907) by Georges Méliès, edited with an introduction and annotations by Jacques Malthête', in Gaudreault 2011, 133–52. See also Schwartz, 'Torque', 101. On cinema acting, see Pearson 1992 and Tesse 2004.

61 For histories of gesture and its meaning from classical antiquity to the eighteenth century, see Vigarello 1978; Muchembled 1988, 437–8; Jean-Claude Schmitt, 'The Ethics of Gesture', trans. Ian Patterson, in Feher 1989, part 2, 128–47; Georges Vigarello, 'The Upward Training of the Body from the Age of Chivalry to Courtly Civility', trans. Ughetta Lubin, in ibid., 149–99; Bremmer and Roodenburg 1993; Kendon 2004, 4 and 17–22; Dillon 2007; Braddick 2009, 18. On the meaningfulness of gesture, see Keith Thomas, 'Introduction', and Joaneath Spicer, 'The Renaissance Elbow', in Bremmer and Roodenburg 1993, 4 and 85; Vigarello 1978, 11. For a discussion of 'the complexity of the gestural realm' and the relationship of gestures to space, see Lefebvre 1991, 212–18. On the attempts of the nineteenth-century actor François Delsarte to codify theatrical gesture as a 'science', ascribing particular meanings to specific poses, see Genevieve Stebbins (ed.), Delsarte System of Expression (1885), New York: E. S. Werner, 1902, and Angélique Arnaud, François Del Sarte, Paris, 1882, both cited in Schwartz, 'Torque'. Delsarte had no long-term success, despite the best efforts of his American disciple Steele Mackay. Dancers in the early twentieth century such as Isadora Duncan and Ruth St. Denis ignored Delsarte's attempts to codify gesture and instead focused on his ideas of free movement and the expressive power of the torso. For the relevance of Delsarte's theories on early twentieth-century theatre, film and dance performance, see Preston 2011, 58–9.

62 Kendon 2004, 4 and 63–4.

63 Braddick 2009, 32–3. Warren Susman made a similar argument about American society in the same period, i.e. that from the 1900s ideas about selfhood and identity became flashier and more concerned with surface, as a result of changing social structures. Susman 1984, esp. 278–81.

64 This was the criticism of Delsarte's language of gestures made by the Boston Courier, 16 December 1888, cited in Vardac 1949, 144.

65 Agamben 1993, 137. Agamben's thesis is argued on scanty historical evidence: see Dillon 2007. It is not dissimilar from Richard Sennett's in The Fall of Public Man (1977, 1993) where he discusses the essential dignity of nineteenth-century bourgeois life as he describes the schooling of appearance and behaviour in the public realm.

66 Agamben 1993, 138. See also Noys 2004.

67 Georgio Agamben, 'Notes on Gesture', in Agamben 1993, 138–9.

68 McCabe connects the fragmented, repetitive bodies of all three and describes the 'avant-garde plotlessness' of Chaplin's performance in his early gestural films such as The Tramp (1916) where he is repeatedly knocked down by a car, every time standing up and dusting himself off again, so that it seems as if he will never progress across the road. There are formal similarities between this kind of repetition and the repetitive and beguiling poses and gestures of the first mannequins, too, especially their repeated appearances and disappearances in the fashion show. McCabe 2001, 435–7. On this aspect of Chaplin's performance McCabe cites Walter Benjamin and Deleuze's Cinema 1, 169–70.

69 Lefebvre 1991, 174; Shields 1988, 17.

70 Georgio Agamben, 'Infancy and History: An Essay on the Destruction of Experience', in Agamben 1993, 36.

71 Breward 2003, 131. See also Giuliana Bruno, who has suggested resemblances in the materiality of film and fashion, 'Cultural Cartography, Materiality and the Fashioning of Emotion', interview with Giuliana Bruno in Marquard Smith 2008, 148.

72 The term was coined by Ricciotto Canudo in 1912, after the 1911 publication of his book La Naissance du sixième art (Birth of the Sixth Art), in which he argued that cinema was a synthesis of the six arts (architecture, sculpture, painting, music, dance, poetry) proposed by Hegel in his lectures on aesthetics. Canudo wrote Le Manifeste des sept arts the following year (1912) but the article was not published until 1923 in La Gazette des sept arts. Jean Cocteau called cinema the 'Tenth Muse' to much less success. On writing about cinema in the modernist period see Marcus 2007; see also Donald, Friedberg and Marcus 1998.

73 On the intermediality of the first film, see Gaudreault 2011, 62–71 and 101–5.

74 Deleuze 1985, 5–7. See also Doane 2002, 180.

75 Tom Gunning and André Gaudreault, 'Early Cinema as a Challenge to Film History' (1986), in Strauven 2006, 365–80. Strauven

usefully reprints not only this first article but also four other early papers in which the definition of the 'cinema of attractions' was challenged, amended and revised both by its authors and by other scholars; these are by Donald Crafton (1987, revised 1994), André Gaudreault and Tom Gunning (Japanese version 1986, French version 1989), Tom Gunning (1986, revised 1990) and Charles Musser (1994). The anthology also includes a retrospective review of his own theory by Gunning, 'Attractions: How They Came into the World', 31–9.

76 Hanssen 2009; Caroline Evans, 'The Walkies: Early Fashion Shows and Silent Cinema', in Munich 2011, 110–34.

77 Ganeva 2008, 141. See also Michelle Tolini-Finamore's chapter on the cinema of attractions in Tolini-Finamore 2013.

78 Peucker 1995, 8–9.

79 Dalle Vacche, 2008, 151.

80 He describes cinema as 'un théâtre de la peau', 'une esthétique de proximité' and 'une esthétique de suggestion. On ne raconte plus, on indique. . . . A l'écran la qualité essentielle du geste est de ne point s'achever. Le visage n'exprime pas comme celui du mime, mais, mieux, suggère.' Epstein 1921, 171 and 172.

81 Both Henri Bergson and the film-maker Jean Epstein compared it to Zeno's paradox. For a nuanced discussion of these points see Doane 2002, ch. 6, 'Zeno's Paradox: The Emergence of Cinematic Time', 172–205. Doane also notes the 'multiple temporalities' of film disentangling 'the temporality of the apparatus itself – linear, irreversible, "mechanical"', which is what I refer to here, from 'the temporality of the diegesis, the way in which time is represented by the image' as in flashbacks, for example, and 'the temporality of reception' which encompasses viewing conditions as well as spectator responses (ibid., 30).

82 Ganeva cites Miriam Hansen who used the term 'vernacular modernism' to describe how early cinema interacted with the commercial culture of the period; Ganeva extends the term to describe a similar interface between film and fashion in the modernist period, ranging from tie-ins to visual codes. Ganeva 2008, 117 and 142 n. 12, citing Miriam Bratu Hansen, 'The Mass Production of the Senses: Classical Cinema as Vernacular Modernism', in Gledhill and Williams 2000, 332–50.

83 Cited in Giedion 1969, 28.

84 Bergson 1911, 323.

85 '[U]n véritable cinématographe de la mode de demain'. Marie-Anne L'Heureux, 'Nouveautés d'automne', Femina, 1 October 1910, 514.

86 Gene Morgan, 'Revue de la Ville: Picture of Models Good Drawing Card', Chicago Daily Tribune, 25 September, 1910.

87 Gustave Babin, 'Une leçon d'élégance dans un parc', L'Illustration, July 1910, 21–2.

88 'Un admirable cinéma'. Montozon, 'Le bois sacré', Fantasio, 15 June 1914, 772.

89 Evans, 'Walkies', in Munich 2011, 110–34.

90 In both France and the U.S.A., dance (usually women dancing, and incorporating fabric in motion) was a category of early film. See Laurent Guido, 'Rhythmic Bodies/Movies: Dance as Attraction in Early Film Culture', in Strauven 2006, 139–56. In France in 1900–02, more than half Gaumont's production consisted of dance films, many of which used dancers from Paris theatres. Abel 1998, 78.

91 Anne Rittenhouse, 'What the Well-Dressed Woman is Wearing', New York Times, 6 October 1912. The article has two line drawings to illustrate this.

92 Marketa Uhlirova, 'Costume in Early Cinema, the Aesthetic of Opulence, and the Living Screen', in Birds of Paradise, Fashion in Film Festival, New York, 2011.

93 E.g. at the 1926 Bal de la Couture held at the Paris Opéra in April 1926, 'One ingenious looking young debutante held her evening cape of white satin drawn demurely together, and then with a sudden movement of her arms, flung it wide apart, revealing the lining – one solid mass of shimmering paillettes [sequins], like some medieval coat of mail.' P. St G. Perrot, 'Impressions of the Bal de la Couture', The 'Liberty' Lamp, April 1926, 34. In July 1927, at the Hôtel Excelsior at the Lido in Dinard, Femina presented a beauty and automobile contest at which a mannequin from Chéruit, draped in a cape of gold, opened it like the wings of a scarab beetle revealing a dress of gold tulle sparkling over a grey ground. Femina, September 1927, 33.

94 Ganeva 2008, 127–41.

95 Doane 2002, 3–4.

96 Ibid., 178.

97 Ibid.

98 On Marey's influence on artistic modernism, see Braun 1992, 264–316. On the relation of his work to Taylorism and to the Gilbreths' time and motion studies, see 320–48. While Doane also discusses the visualisation of time in film and other media as a product of rationalisation, she does not relate it to modernism. Instead she mobilises the important concept of contingency to argue that both cinematic time and contingency are a function of modernity. Doane 2002, 190. My argument is slightly different to the extent that I suggest that the concepts of modernist bodies and modernist time can contribute to an expanded but historically specific definition of modernism, as opposed to the more generic term 'modernity' as applied to this period.

99 Doane 2002, 190.

100 Ibid., 4.

101 Leo Charney, 'In a Moment: Film and the Philosophy of Modernity', in Charney and Schwartz 1995, 279 and 283; also cited in J. Brown 2009, 79–80.

102 Chatman 1990, 40.

103 Doane 2002, 162. See also n. 98 above; I may have misrepresented her argument by omitting any reference to contingency and chance in my discussion of modernist time.

104 Ibid., 4–11.

105 Brannigan describes Fuller's manipulations of metres of silk panels stiffened by the insertion of wooden battens as creating a dramatic, swirling image of a moving body that is abstracted: 'the resulting spectacle is a figure in constant transformation; an unstable signifier sourced in, yet moving beyond, the efforts and intentions of the dancer. . . . This was a dance of transformation through motion . . . marked by instability as a signifier and a quality of constant flux . . . Fuller's dance was all "in-betweeness", a flowing image of Bergson's idea of duration.' Brannigan 2003, 6–7.

AFTERWORD

1 'La crise agricole que s'est abattue sur les États-Unis depuis 1926, le krach de la bourse de New-York en novembre 1929, ont modifié la composition des salons du couturier. D'autres femmes, nouvelles venues à l'élégance, ont replacé des clientes qui, depuis dix ans, s'étaient peu à peu affinées par un contact prolongé avec le luxe et le bon goût.' Simon 1931, 97.

2 Ibid., 97–8.

3 Creed 1961, 70 and 197.

4 'Cloak and Suit', Fortune, June 1930, 94.

5 Ibid.

6 'Paris Yields to None in Fashion World', New York Times, 2 December 1928.

7 'The Dressmakers of France', Fortune, August 1932, 21.

8 'Cloak and Suit', 99.

9 Simon 1931, 109; Pouillard 2011, 323.

10 'Cloak and Suit', 99.

11 'Dressmakers of France', 17.

12 It was, as Levasseur pointed out, only fifty years old in 1912. Levasseur 1912, 9. In 1931 Simon attributed many of its problems to its relative newness, writing that it was only three quarters of a century old, which was not long enough to accumulate sufficient experience of international commerce. Simon 1931, 10.

13 Wilson 1925, 53.

14 '[C]ette réussite extraordinaire.' Simon 1931, 111.

15 Hawes 1938, 111.

16 Ibid., 113.

17 Ibid., 107.

18 Roughly calculated from annual figures for 1920–37 tabulated in Grumbach 2008, 42.

19 'Cloak and Suit', 100.

20 Ibid., 96.

21 Grumbach 2008, 90.

22 These exacerbated the already heavy Fordney-MacCumber tariffs introduced in 1921–2. See Simon 1931, 125–6.

23 For an account of the little-known bonded model system, see Palmer 2001, 135–68.

24 Ibid., 139 and 147.

25 Grumbach 2008, 43.

26 'La couture se meurt précisément d'être montée sur un trop grand pied. Finis les larbins galonnés à la porte. Finis les tapis partout, les tapisseries sur les murs, les

vitrines somptueuses. Fini le nombreux personnel. Finies les collections de 400 modèles avec des fourrures catapulteuses. Fini le petit ensemble que l'on répète 1,500 fois. Finis les magasins à gros loyers aux Champs-Élysées.' Grumbach 2008, 48. Jean Patou, too, decreed that 'the years of abundance being over' ('les années d'abondances étant passées'), he must produce a stringently edited collection. Jean Patou, *Du Changement et des nouveautés dans la mode féminine, été 1931*, fashion show programme and promotional booklet for summer 1931, collection Bibliothèque Forney, Paris, CC2404.

27 In London Poiret's opening dress parade took place over three days from Monday 3 to Thursday 5 October 1933 at 2.45 pm in the Tudor Building of Liberty's department store. The invitations were personally addressed, attendees were only permitted to see one show and a meal was served free of charge with each show. At Le Printemps, Pierre Laguionie invited Poiret to create a ready-to-wear line for the shop. In order to launch it as a fashion show, the 'Pont d'Argent' was constructed for Poiret to present the four annual collections that he was contracted to produce for a monthly salary of 20,000 francs. The information about Poiret's Liberty shows is based on ephemera in the Liberty archive including the house journal *The Liberty Lamp* and a surviving Liberty invitation card to a Paul Poiret Dress Parade on 3–4 October 1933 (Westminster Archive Centre, London). For the Printemps shows, including images of them, see Musée Galliera 2006, 56 and Grumbach 2008, 176–7.

28 Grumbach 2008, 225–6.

29 Film of the collection is at the Gaumont Pathé archive, Paris, refs 3447EJ 23328 and 3447EJ 23254.

30 Grumbach 2008, 89.

31 Ibid., 90.

32 Ibid., 87 and 91.

33 Musée Galliera 2006, 157.

34 Grumbach 2008, 31.

35 Ibid., 89.

36 Ibid., 42, citing Germaine Deschamps, *La Crise dans les industries du vêtement et de la mode à Paris pendant la période de 1930 à 1937*, Paris: Librairie Technique et Économique, 1938, 65.

37 Green 1997, 86.

38 '[V]eritables centres d'espionnage industriel'. Grumbach 2008, 97.

39 *Les Échos*, 16 June 1929, cited in Grumbach 2008, 97.

40 Ibid., 98.

41 Grumbach 2008, 98, citing Carlier 1956.

42 Simon 1931, 109.

43 'La perversion du système n'est que la conséquence directe de son propre fonctionnement: comment ne pas être copié si le but de la vente est justement d'être copié? Il était illusoire, à partir de cet état de fait, d'imaginer pouvoir contrôler l'utilisation des modèles parvenus à destination. La

meilleure des défenses aurait pu être l'interdiction pure et simple des patrons, mais la perte aurait été encore plus important.' Grumbach 2008, 98–9.

44 There is a growing body of critical writing on fast fashion, ethics and globalisation, much of it on the internet. Early treatments of the topic include: Ross 1997; Neissen, Leshkowich and Jones 2003; Goodrum 2005; Segre Reinach 2005.

45 Paul Poiret, 'De la contrefaçon dans la couture', *Excelsior*, 16 December 1921.

46 Giorgio Agamben, 'Infancy and History: An Essay on the Destruction of Experience' [1978] in Agamben 1993, 41–3.

47 Clairin 1937.

48 'Il y en a de grands, de petits, de gros, de maigres, de grotesques, de hideux. A tous ces corps, la tête manque. "Voila mon Musée Grévin", me dit Mané, avec une grande geste. "Tu te rends compte? . . . Chacun d'eux, sur une étiquette, porte son nom. Ce sont les mannequins de nos clientes . . . Avec eux, plus de mesures à prendre . . . crois-tu que j'en collectionne, des horreurs!" ' Clairin 1937, 57.

49 Roubaud 1928, 28–9.

50 ' "Ça", me dit-elle, en posant la main sur l'épaule du mannequin, "c'est la femme la plus riche du monde. C'est la cliente difficile d'Amérique que tous les mannequins appellent 'Madame Peur' " . . . "Mais il n'y a que des monstres, ici" . . . "Lorsque j'ai le cafard, lorsque la vie me dégoûte, je lâche un instant l'atelier . . . et je monte ici. J'éprouve alors le plaisir rare d'être pas mal faite, devant toutes ces femmes riches, pour la plupart hideuses et, toutes, décapitées!" ' Clairin 1937, 57.

51 Zola 1995, 6.

52 'au Sporting de Monte-Carlo, dans la plus belle salle peut-être du monde'. Ibid., 151.

53 Ibid., 168–9 and 182–4.

54 Molly Nesbit, 'In the absence of the parisienne' in Colomina 1992, 307–25.

55 Leroy 1999, 257. '[L]es inconnues et les reconnues, les survenantes et les revenantes, la longue file des étrangement inquiétantes, Mélancholie et Modernité, les muses et les muselées, la femme en deuil, la Mère et la Mort.' Ibid.

56 'Une cabine de mannequin: c'est encore deux cent robes mortes, aplaties comme des fleurs dans un livre et vingt petites chemises vivantes, remuantes. Si nous frappons à la porte et que je fasse entendre ma voix d'homme, les vingt chemises rentreront dans vingt fourreaux uniformes. Ils sont en satinette rouge chez Mounet.' Roubaud 1928, 184.

57 'Partout la robe est faite pour la femme. Ici, la femme est faite pour la robe. La robe dit: "N'ayez pas trop de chair, ou vous serez chassée comme une mauvaise servante; apprenez à marcher selon mon rythme; vous n'êtes rien que ma porteuse; vous et moi nous ne sommes pas du même monde; ne vous

flattez pas d'avoir jamais mon destin." ' Ibid. 184–5.

58 'Heureusement, dans leur penderie, les robes dorment! Elles sont "de la haute". Si elles pouvaient les entendre et les voir, elles mépriseraient les enfants du peuple!' Ibid., 186–7.

BIBLIOGRAPHY

NOTE ON CITATION OF NEWSPAPER AND MAGAZINE ARTICLES

In many instances, no page numbers are cited because none remains in the form in which the press cuttings were consulted by the present author – either electronic databases or couturiers' press books. These articles can be traced through the following sources.

The American newspapers listed below are accessible in the Proquest Historical Newspapers digital archive where citations can be searched by title or keyword:

Atlanta Constitution
Boston Daily Globe
Chicago Daily Tribune
Christian Science Monitor
Hartford Courant
Los Angeles Times
New York Times
New York Tribune
Washington Post

Of the cuttings from Lucile's, Poiret's, Paquin's and Patou's press albums, all but the last are in public archives. The Poiret albums are in the Centre de Documentation, Musée de l'Art de la Mode et du Textile, Paris. The Paquin ones are in the Bath Fashion Museum and research centre. The majority of the Lucile cuttings are in the Fashion Institute of Technology, New York, and the minority in the National Art Library, London.

Where a citation includes a page number, the papers and periodicals can be consulted in libraries and archives. These include fashion magazines such as *Vogue* (British, American and French), *Harper's Bazar* (America) and *Femina* (France) and illustrated weeklies such as *L'Illustration* (France) and the *Illustrated London News* (Britain).

A

ABEL, Richard. 1998. *The Ciné Goes to Town: French Cinema 1896–1914*. Updated and expanded edition. Berkeley and Los Angeles: University of California Press.
—. (ed.) 2005. *Encyclopaedia of Early Cinema*. New York and London: Routledge.
ADAM, H. Pearl. 1919. *Paris Sees It Through: A Diary. 1914–1919*. London, New York and Toronto: Hodder and Stoughton.
AGAMBEN, Giorgio. 1993. *Infancy and History: Essays on the Destruction of Experience* (1978). Trans. Liz Heron. London: Verso.

ALEXANDRE, Arsène. 1902. *Les Reines de l'aiguille: modistes et couturières (Étude parisienne)*. Paris: Théophile Belin.
ALLART, André, and Paul CARTERON. 1914. *La Mode devant les tribunaux: législation et jurisprudence*. Paris: L. Tenin.
ALLEN, Irving Lewis. 1993. *The City in Slang: New York Life and Popular Speech*. Oxford and New York: Oxford University Press.
Almanach du Marque d'or. 1921. Première année, à l'enseigne du Marque d'Or chez Derambez, 25 rue Lavoisier, Paris.
ANDERSON, Mark. 1992. *Kafka's Clothes*. Oxford: Clarendon Press.
APPADURAI, Arjun (ed). 1988. *The Social Life of Things: Commodities in Cultural Perspective*. Cambridge University Press.
ARLETTY. *La défense*. 1971. Paris: Editions de la Table Ronde.
ARMSTRONG, Tim. 1998. *Modernism, Technology and the Body*. Cambridge University Press.
ARNOLD, Rebecca. 2009. *The American Look: Fashion, Sportswear and the Image of Women in 1930s and 1940s New York*. London and New York: I. B. Tauris.
ARSCOTT, Caroline, and Katie SCOTT (eds). 2000. *Manifestations of Venus: Art and Sexuality*. Manchester and New York: Manchester University Press.
AUBENAS, Sylvie, and Xavier DEMANGE, with Virginie CHARDIN. 2006. *Les Seebergers: photographes de l'élégance 1909–1939*. Paris: Seuil and Bibliothèque Nationale de France.
AUERBACH, Jonathan. 2007. *Early Cinema's Incarnations*. Berkeley, Los Angeles and London: University of California Press.
AVENEL, Le Vicomte Georges d'. 1902. *Le Mécanisme de la vie moderne*. Part 4. Paris: Librairie Armand Colin.

B

BACHMANN, Manfred. 1973. *Dolls the Wide World Over: An Historical Account by Manfred Bachmann and Claus Hansmann*. Trans. Ruth Michaelis-Jena with Patrick Murray. London: Harrap.
BAILEY, Peter. 1990. 'Parasexuality and Glamour: The Victorian Barmaid as Cultural Prototype'. *Gender and History*, II, 2, 148–72.
BALIDES, Constance. 1998. 'Scenarios of Exposure in the Practice of Everyday Life: Women in the Cinema of Attractions' (1993). In Annette Kuhn and Jackie Stacey (eds), *Screen Histories: An Introduction*. Oxford University Press, 63–80.
BALLARD, Bettina. 1960. *In My Fashion*. New York: David McKay Co. Inc.

BALZAC, Honoré de. 1922. *Traité de la vie élégante* (1829), *suivi de la Théorie de la démarche* (1830). Paris: Éditions Bossard.
—. 1988. *Ferragus* (1833). Paris: Flammarion.
BARD, Christine. 1998. *Les Garçonnes*. Paris: Flammarion.
BARRIÈRE, Albert. 1889. *Argot and Slang: A New French and English Dictionary*. London: Whittaker and Co.
BARTHES, Roland. 1981. *Camera Lucida*. New York: Hill and Wang.
BAUDOT, François. 1997. *Poiret*. London: Thames and Hudson.
BAUDRILLARD, Jean. 1983. *Simulations*. Trans. Paul Foss, Paul Patton and Philip Beitchman. New York: Semiotext(e).
—. 1993. *Symbolic Exchange and Death* (1976). Trans. Iain Hamilton Grant, intro. Mike Gane. Los Angeles, London, New Delhi, Singapore: Sage Publications.
BEALE, Marjorie A. 1999. *The Modernist Enterprise: French Elites and the Threat of Modernity, 1900–1940*. Stanford University Press.
BEATON, Cecil. 1954. *The Glass of Fashion*. London: Cassell.
BELLO, Patrizia di. 2005. 'Vision and Touch: Women, Photography and Visual Culture in the 19th Century'. In Vanessa Toulmin and Simon Popple (eds). *Visual Delights – 2: Exhibition and Reception*. Eastleigh: John Libbey Publishing.
—. 2003. 'The "Eyes of Affection" and Fashionable Femininity: Representations of Photography in 19th Century Magazines and Society Albums'. In A. Hughes and A. Noble (eds). *Phototextualities: Intersections of Photography and Narrative*. Albuquerque: University of New Mexico Press.
BENJAMIN, Walter. 1973. *Illuminations*. Trans. Harry Zohn. Glasgow: Fontana Collins.
—. 1985. *One Way Street and Other Writings*, 240–57. Trans. Edmond Jephcott and Kingsley Shorter, intro. Susan Sontag. London: Verso.
—. 1997. *Charles Baudelaire: A Lyric Poet in the Era of High Capitalism*. Trans. Harry Zohn. London: Verso.
—. 1999. *The Arcades Project* (1972–89). Trans. Howard Eiland and Kevin McLaughlin. Cambridge, Mass., and London: Harvard University Press.
BENSON, Susan Porter. 1986. *Counter Cultures: Saleswomen, Managers and Consumers in American Department Stores 1890–1940*. Urbana: University of Illinois Press.
BENTON, Charlotte, Tim BENTON and Ghislaine WOOD (eds). 2003. *Art Deco 1910–1939*. London: V&A Publications.
BERGER, John. 1972. *Ways of Seeing*. London: BBC and Penguin Books.

BERGSON, Henri. 1911. *Creative Evolution* (1907). Trans. Arthur Mitchell. London: Macmillan.

BERRY, Sarah. 2000. *Screen Style: Fashion and Femininity in 1930s Hollywood*. Minneapolis and London: University of Minnesota Press.

BERTIN, Célia. 1956. *Paris à la Mode*. London: Victor Gollancz.

BIBESCO, Princesse. 1928. *Noblesse de robe*. Paris: Bernard Grasset.

BIGHAM, Randy Bryan. 2012. *Lucile - Her Life by Design: Sex, Style, and the Fusion of Theater and Couture*. Raleigh, N.C.: Lulu Press Inc.

BINN, N. T. 2005. With Franck Garbarz. *Paris au cinéma*. Paris: Éditions Parigramme.

BIPPUS, Elke, and Dorothea MINK (eds). 2007. *Fashion Body Cult*. Stuttgart: Arnoldsche Art Publishers.

BLACKMAN, Cally. 2009. *100 Years of Fashion Illustration*. London: Lawrence King.

BLASZCZYK, Regina Lee. 2002. *Imagining Consumers: Design and Innovation from Wedgwood to Corning*. Baltimore: Johns Hopkins University Press.

— (ed). 2008. *Producing Fashion: Commerce, Culture, and Consumers*. Philadelphia: University of Pennsylvania Press.

BONNEY, Thérèse and Louise. 1929. *A Shopping Guide to Paris*. New York: Robert McBride and Co.

BONY, Anne. 1911. *Les Années 10*. Paris: Éditions du Regard.

BOON, Marcus. 2010. *In Praise of Copying*. Harvard University Press, 2010.

BORDO, Susan. 1993. *Unbearable Weight: Feminism, Western Culture and the Body*. Berkeley and London: University of California Press.

BORGÉ, Jacques, and Nicolas VIASNOFF. 1998. *Archives de la mode*. Paris: Éditions Michèle Trinckvel.

BOURDIEU, Pierre. 1977. *Outline of a Theory of Practice*. Trans. Richard Nice. Cambridge University Press.

—. 1990. *The Logic of Practice*. Trans. Richard Nice. Cambridge: Polity Press.

BRACHET CHAMPSAUR, Florence. 2004a. 'French Fashion During World War I'. *Business and Economic History On-Line*, II. See http://www.thebhc.org/publications/BEHonline/2004/Champsaur.pdf

—. 2004b. 'De l'odalisque de Poiret à la femme nouvelle de Chanel: une victoire de la femme?'. In Évelyne Morin-Rotureau (ed.). *Combats de femmes 1914–1918*, 200–26. Also at http://www.cairn.info/combats-de-femmes-1914–1918—page-200.htm

—. 2012. 'Madeleine Vionnet and Galeries Lafayette: The Unlikely Marriage of a Parisian Couture House and a French Department Store, 1922–40'. *Business History*, LIV, I, 48–66.

BRADDICK, Michael J. (ed.) 2009. *The Politics of Gesture: Historical Perspectives*. Oxford University Press.

BRAND, Jan, and José TEUNISSEN (eds). 2006. *The Power of Fashion: About Design and Meaning*. Arnhem: Uitgeverij Terra Lannoo BV and ArtEZPress.

BRANNIGAN, Erin. 2003. ' "La Loïe" as Pre-Cinematic Performance – Descriptive of

Continuity of Movement'. *Senses of Cinema*. http://www.archive.sensesofcinema.com/contents/03/28/la_loie.html

BRAUN, Marta. 1992. *Picturing Time: The Work of Etienne-Jules Marey (1830–1904)*. Chicago and London: University of Chicago Press.

BREMMER, Jan, and Herman ROODENBURG (eds). 1993. *A Cultural History of Gesture: From Antiquity to the Present Day*. London: Polity Press.

BREWARD, Christopher. 2003. *Fashion*. Oxford University Press.

—. 2004. *Fashioning London: Clothing and the Modern Metropolis*. Oxford and New York: Berg.

— and Caroline EVANS (eds). 2005. *Fashion and Modernity*. Oxford and New York: Berg.

— and David GILBERT (eds). 2006. *Fashion's World Cities*. Oxford and New York: Berg.

BROOKMAN, Philip. 2010. *Edweard Muybridge*. London, Washington, D.C., and Göttingen: Tate Publishing in association with the Corcoran Gallery of Art and Steidl Publishers.

BROOKS, Charles W. 1987. *America in France's Hopes and Fears, 1890–1920*. New York and London: Garland.

BROWN, Elspeth H. 2005. *The Corporate Eye: Photography and the Rationalization of American Commercial Culture 1884–1929*. Baltimore and London: Johns Hopkins University Press.

—. 2009. 'De Meyer at *Vogue*: Commercializing Queer Affect in First World War-Era Fashion Photography'. *Photography & Culture*, II, 3, 253–74.

—. Forthcoming. 'The Commodification of Aesthetic Feeling: Race, Sexuality and the 1920s Stage Model', *Feminist Studies*, XL, I, spring.

BROWN, Judith. 2009. *Glamour in Six Dimensions: Modernism and the Radiance of Form*. Ithaca and London: Cornell University Press.

BRUEGGEMANN, Amina M., and Peter SCHULMAN (eds). 2005. *Rhine Crossings: France and Germany in Love and War*. Albany: State University of New York.

BRUZZI, Stella. 1997. *Undressing Cinema: Clothing and Identity in the Movies*. London: Routledge.

BUCHLOH, Benjamin H. D., Serge GUILBAUT and David SORKIN (eds). 2004. *Modernism and Modernity: The Vancouver Conference Papers*. Halifax: Press of Nova Scotia College of Art and Design.

BUCKLE, Richard. 1975. *Nijinsky* (1971). Harmondsworth: Penguin.

BURGIN, Victor, James DONALD and Cora KAPLAN (eds). 1986. *Formations of Fantasy*. London and New York: Methuen.

BURKE, Billy, with Cameron SHIPP. 1950. *With a Feather on My Nose*. Foreword by Ivor Novello. London: Peter Davis.

BURMAN, Barbara, and Carole TURBIN (eds). 2003. *Material Strategies: Dress and Gender in Historical Perspective*. Oxford: Blackwell.

BURSTEIN, Jessica. 2012. *Cold Modernism: Literature, Fashion, Art*. University Park, Pa.: Pennsylvania University Press.

BURTON, Antoinette M. (ed). 2003. *After the Imperial Turn: Thinking With and Through the Nation*. Durham, N.C.: Duke University Press.

BUTLER, Judith. 1990. *Gender Trouble: Feminism and the Subversion of Identity*. London and New York: Routledge.

C

CALLAHAN, Vikki (ed.). 2010. *Reclaiming the Archive: Feminism and Film History*. Detroit: Wayne State University Press.

CARLIER, Jean. 1956. *Freddy – Souvenir d'un mannequin vedette: dans la coulisse de la haute couture parisienne*. Paris: Flammarion.

CARLSON, Hannah. 2008–9. 'Idle Hands and Empty Pockets: Postures of Leisure'. *Dress*, XXXV, 7–27.

CARTER, Alexandra (ed.). 1998. *The Routledge Dance Studies Reader*. London and New York: Routledge.

CARTER, Randolph. 1974. *The World of Flo Ziegfeld*. London: Paul Elek.

CASTLE, Charles. 1984. *The Folies Bergère*. London: Methuen.

CASTLE and CASTLE, Mr and Mrs Vernon. 1980. *Modern Dancing* (New York: Harper, 1914). New York: Da Capo Press (facsimile edition).

CERTEAU, Michel de. 1988. *The Practice of Everyday Life* (1984). Trans. Steven Rendell. Berkeley, Los Angeles and London: University of California Press.

—, Luce GIARD and Pierre MAYOL. 1998. *The Practice of Everyday Life*. Volume 2: *Living and Cooking* (1994). Trans. Timothy J. Tomasik. Minneapolis and London: University of Minnesota Press, new revised and augmented edition.

CHADWICK, Whitney, and Tirza True LATIMER (eds). 2003. *The Modern Woman Revisited: Paris Between the Wars*. New Brunswick, N.J., and London: Rutgers University Press.

CHAPMAN, Mary. 1996. ' "Living Pictures": Women and *Tableaux Vivants* in Nineteenth-Century American Fiction and Culture'. *Wide Angle*, XVIII, 3, July, 22–52.

CHARLES-ROUX, Edmonde. 1993. *Le Temps Chanel*. Paris: Édition du Chêne.

CHARNEY, Leo, and Vanessa R. SCHWARTZ (eds). 1995. *Cinema and the Invention of Modern Life*. Berkeley: University of California Press.

CHASE, Edna Woolman, and Ilka CHASE. 1954. *Always in Vogue*. London: Victor Gollancz.

CHATMAN, Seymour. 1990. *Coming to Terms: The Rhetoric of Narrative in Fiction and Film*. Ithaca and London: Cornell University Press.

CLAIRE, Jean (ed.). 1991. *The 1920s: Age of the Metropolis*. Montreal Museum of Fine Arts.

CLAIRIN, Lucy. 1937. *Journal d'un mannequin: feuillets d'une année*. Paris: Fasquelle Éditeurs.

CLARK, T. J. 1984. *The Painting of Modern Life: Paris in the Art of Manet and His Followers*. Princeton University Press.

CLASSEN, Constance (ed). 2005. *The Book of Touch*. Oxford and New York: Berg.

CLÉMENT, Catherine. 1994. *Syncope: The Philosophy of Rapture*. Trans. Sally O'Driscoll with Deidre M. Mahoney. Foreword by Verena Andermatt Conley. Minneapolis and London: University of Minnesota Press.

COCTEAU, Jean. 1987. *Paris Album 1900–1914* (first published in *Le Figaro*, then as *Portraits-Souvenir*, Paris: Éditions Bernard-Grasset, 1956). Trans. Margaret Crosland. London: Comet/W. H. Allen.

COFFMAN, Elizabeth. 2002. 'Women in Motion: Loie Fuller and the "Interpenetration" of Art and Science'. *Camera Obscura*, XVII, 1, 1–104.

COHEN-STRATYNER, Barbara Naomi. 1989. 'Fashion Fillers in Silent Film Periodicals'. In Barbara Naomi Cohen-Stratyner (ed.). *Performing Arts Resources, Vol. 14: Performances in Periodicals*, 127–42. New York: Theatre Library Assoc.

COLEMAN, Elizabeth Ann. 1990. *The Opulent Era: Fashions of Worth, Doucet and Pinguat*. London and New York: Thames & Hudson and the Brooklyn Museum.

COLETTE. 1963. *Claudine in Paris* (1901). Trans. Antonia White. Harmondsworth: Penguin Books.

—. 1991. *Colette et la mode*. Drawings by Sonia Rykiel. Paris: Éditions Plume and Calmann-Levy.

COLOMINA, Beatriz (ed). 1992. *Sexuality and Space*. New York: Princeton Architectural Press.

COMISKEY, Carolyn. 2005. 'Cosmetic Surgery in Paris in 1926: The Case of the Amputated Leg'. *Journal of Women's History*, XVI, 3, 2004, 30–54. Reprinted as '"I Will Kill Myself … If I Have to Keep My Fat Calves!": Legs and Cosmetic Surgery in Paris in 1926'. In Christopher E. Forth and Ivan Crozier (eds). *Body Parts: Critical Explorations in Corporeality*, 247–63. Lanham, Boulder, New York, Toronto, Oxford: Lexington Books.

CONNERTON, Paul. 1989. *How Societies Remember*. Cambridge University Press.

CONOR, Liz. 2004. *The Spectacular Modern Woman: Feminine Visibility in the 1920s*. Bloomington and Indianapolis: Indiana University Press.

COOLEY, Charles Horton. 1964. *Human Nature and the Social Order*. New York: Schocken.

COOPER, John Xiros. 2004. *Modernism and the Culture of Market Society*. Cambridge University Press.

COPLEY, F. B. 1923. *Frederick W. Taylor: Father of Scientific Management*. New York and London: Harper & Brothers.

CORBIN, Alain, Jean-Jaques COURTINE and Georges VIGARELLO (eds). 2005. *Histoire du corps*. Vol. 2: *De la révolution à la grande guerre*. Ed. Alain Corbin. Vol. 3: *Les Mutations du regard: le XXe siècle*. Ed. Jean-Jacques Courtine. Paris: Seuil.

COTE, Andrea and Joelle JENSEN. 2007. 'Identifiable Gestures'. In Andrea Cote and Joelle Jensen (eds), *Posing*. New York, Abrons Art Centre and Lulu Publications. See also http://www.readbag.com/valerielamontagne - pdf-catalogue-posing, accessed 1 April 2013

COURTOIS-L'HEUREUX, Fleur. 2009. *Arts de la ruse: un tango philosophique avec Michel de Certeau*. Bordeaux: É.M.E./FNRS.

CRAIK, Jennifer. 1994. *The Face of Fashion: Cultural Studies in Fashion*. London: Routledge.

CRARY, Jonathan. 1992. *Techniques of the Observer: On Vision and Modernity in the Nineteenth Century*. Cambridge, Mass., and London: MIT Press.

—. 2001. *Suspensions of Perception: Attention, Spectacle, and Modern Culture*. Cambridge, Mass., and London: MIT Press.

— and Sanford KWINTER (eds). 1995. *Incorporations*. New York: Zone Books.

La Création en liberté: univers de Paul et Denise Poiret 1905–1928. 2005. Sale catalogue, Drouet-Richelieu, Paris, 10 and 11 May 2005. 2 vols. Paris: PIASA.

CREED, Charles Southey. 1961. *Maid to Measure*. London: Jarrolds.

D

DALLE VACCHE, Angela. 2008. *Diva: Defiance and Passion in Early Italian Cinema*. Foreword by Guy Maddin. Austin: University of Texas Press.

DANIUS, Sara. 2002. *The Senses of Modernism: Technology, Perception, and Aesthetics*. Ithaca and London: Cornell University Press.

DARMON, Pierre. 2002. *Vivre à Paris pendant la grande guerre*. Paris: Fayard.

DAVID, Alison Matthews. 2002. 'Cutting a Figure: Tailoring, Technology and Social Identity in Nineteenth-century Paris'. PhD diss., Stanford University.

DAVIS, Mary E. 1999. 'Modernity à la mode: Popular Culture and Avant-Gardism in Erik Satie's "Sports et Divertissements"'. *Musical Quarterly*, LXXXIII, 3, autumn, 430–73.

—. 2006. *Classic Chic: Music, Fashion, and Modernism*. Berkeley, Los Angeles and London: University of California Press.

—. 2010. *Ballets Russes Style: Diaghilev's Dancers and Paris Fashion*. London: Reaktion.

DEAN, Carolyn. 1992. *The Self and Its Pleasures: Bataille, Lacan and the History of the Decentred Subject*. Ithaca and London: Cornell University Press.

DEBORD, Guy. 1994. *Society of the Spectacle* (1967). Trans. Donald Nicholson-Smith. London: Zone Books.

DEFLEM, Mathieu. 2003. 'The Sociology of the Sociology of Money: Simmel and the Contemporary Battle of the Classics'. *Journal of Classical Sociology*, III, 1, 67–96.

DELBOURG-DELPHIS, Marylène. 1981. *Le Chic et le Look: histoire de la mode féminine et des moeurs de 1850 à nos jours*. Paris: Hachette.

DELEUZE, Gilles. 1985. *Cinema 1: The Movement-Image*. Trans. Hugh Tomlinson and Barbara Habberjam. Minneapolis: University of Minnesota Press.

—. 1995. *Negotiations 1972–1990*. New York: Columbia University Press.

DE PERTHUIS, Karen. 2003. 'Dying to be Born Again: Mortality, Immortality and the Fashion Model'. PhD diss, University of Sydney.

DESLANDRES, Yvonne. 1987. *Poiret: Paul Poiret 1879–1944*. London: Thames and Hudson.

— and Florence MÜLLER. 1990. *Le Costume: de la restauration à la Belle Epoque*. Paris: Flammarion.

DETTMAR, Kevin J. H., and Stephen WATTS (eds). 1996. *Marketing Modernisms: Self-Promotion, Canonization, Rereading*. Ann Arbor: University of Michigan Press.

DIDI-HUBERMAN, Georges. 2005. *Confronting Images*. Trans. John Goddman. University Park, Pa.: Pennsylvania State University Press.

DILLON, Brian. 2007. 'Inventory/Talk to the Hand'. *Cabinet*, issue 26, Magic, summer. http://www.cabinetmagazine.org/issues/26/dillon. php, accessed 12 August 2012.

DOANE, Mary Ann. 1982. 'Film and the Masquerade: Theorizing the Female Spectator'. *Screen*, XXIII, 3–4, September–October, 74–87.

—. 1988–9. 'Masquerade Reconsidered: Further Thoughts on the Female Spectator'. *Discourse*, XI, fall/winter, 42–54.

—. 2002. *The Emergence of Cinematic Time: Modernity, Contingency, the Archive*. Cambridge, Mass., and London: Harvard University Press.

DOLAR, Mladen. 1991. '"I shall be with you on your wedding night": Lacan and the Uncanny'. *October*, LVIII, 'Rendering the Real: A Special Issue', ed. Parveen Adams, 5–23.

DONALD, James, Anne FRIEDBERG and Laura MARCUS (eds). 1998. *Close Up, 1927–1933: Cinema and Modernism*. Princeton University Press.

DÖRIG, James. 1925. *La Mode et la couture: vocabulaire franco-anglais*. Paris: private press.

DOUGLAS, Mary. 2002. *Purity and Danger: An Analysis of the Concepts of Pollution and Taboo* (1966). London: Routledge.

DOY, Gen. 2005. *Picturing the Self: Changing Views of the Subject in Visual Culture*. London: I. B. Tauris.

DRISCOLL, Catherine. 2010. 'Chanel: The Order of Things'. *Fashion Theory*, XIV, 2, June, 135–58.

D'SOUZA, Aruna, and Tom McDONOUGH (eds). 2006. *The Invisible Flâneuse? Gender, Public Space and Visual Culture in Nineteenth-century Paris*. Manchester University Press.

DUFF GORDON, Lady (Lucile). 1932. *Discretions and Indiscretions*. New York: Frederick A. Stokes Co.

DUHAMEL, Georges. 1974. *America the Menace: Scenes from the Life of the Future* (1930). Trans. Charles Miner Thompson. Boston: Houghton Mifflin, c. 1931; reprinted New York: Arno Press.

DULLES, Eleanor Lansing. 1933. *The Dollar, the Franc and Inflation*. New York: Macmillan Co.

DUPEUX, Georges. 1976. *French Society, 1789–1970* (1972). Trans. Peter Wait. London: Methuen; New York: Barnes & Noble.

E

ELSAESSER, Thomas (ed) with Adam BARKER. 1990. *Early Cinema: Space, Frame, Narrative*. London: BFI Publishing.

Encyclopédie des arts décoratifs et industriels modernes au XXème siècle. 1977. 12 vols. Paris: Imprimerie Nationale, Office Centrale d'Éditions et de la Librairie, n.d. [c. 1925]. Reprinted New York and London: Garland Publishing Inc. Vol. 9.

ENTWISTLE, Joanne. 2000. *The Fashioned Body: Fashion, Dress and Modern Social Theory*. Cambridge: Polity Press in association with Blackwell.

—. 2009. *The Aesthetic Economy of Fashion Markets and Values in Clothing and Modelling*. Oxford and New York: Berg.

— and Agnès ROCAMORA. 2006. 'The Field of Fashion Materialized: A Study of London Fashion Week'. *Sociology*, XL, 4, August, 735–51.

— and Elizabeth WISSINGER (eds). 2012. *Fashioning Models: Image, Text and Industry*. Oxford and New York: Berg.

EPSTEIN, Jean. 1921. *La Poésie d'aujourd'hui: un nouvel état d'intelligence. Lettre de Blaise Cendrars*. Paris: Éditions de la Sirène.

ERTÉ [Romain de Tirtoff]. 1975. *Things I Remember: An Autobiography*. London: Peter Owen.

ETHERINGTON-SMITH, Meredith. 1983. *Patou*. London: Hutchinson.

— and Jeremy PILCHER. 1986. *The 'It' Girls: Lady Duff Gordon, the Couturiere 'Lucile', and Elinor Glyn, Romantic Novelist*. London: Hamish Hamilton.

EVANS, Caroline. 1999. 'Masks, Mirrors and Mannequins: Elsa Schiaparelli and the Decentred Subject'. *Fashion Theory*, III, 1, 3–32.

—. 2003. *Fashion at the Edge: Spectacle, Modernity and Deathliness*. New Haven and London: Yale University Press.

—. 2008. 'Jean Patou's American Mannequins: Early Fashion Shows and Modernism'. *Modernism/Modernity*, XV, 2, April, 243–63.

—. 2011. 'The Ontology of the Fashion Model'. *AA Files*, 63, autumn, 56–69.

EWEN, Stuart. 1988. *All Consuming Images: The Politics of Style in Contemporary Culture*. New York: Basic Books.

F

FEHER, Michael, with Ramona NADDAFF and Nadia TAZI (eds). 1989. *Fragments for a History of the Human Body. Part Two*. New York: Zone Books.

FELSKI, Rita. 1995. *The Gender of Modernity*. Cambridge, Mass.: Harvard University Press.

FINN, Jonathan. 2009. *Capturing the Criminal Image: From Mugshot to Surveillance Society*. Minneapolis and London: University of Minnesota Press.

FISCHER, Lucy. 1979. 'The Lady Vanishes: Women, Magic and the Movies'. *Film Quarterly*, XXII, fall, 30–40.

—. 1981. 'The Image of Woman as Other: The Optical Politics of Dames'. *Film Quarterly*, XXX, 1, fall 1976, 2–11. Reprinted in Rick Altman (ed). *Genre: The Musical*, 70–84. London: Routledge & Kegan Paul and British Film Institute.

FLANNER, Janet. 1972. *Paris Was Yesterday, 1925–1939*. Ed. Irving Drutman. New York: Popular Library.

FONT, Lourdes M. 2012. 'International Couture: The Opportunities and Challenges of Expansion, 1880–1920'. *Business History*, special issue on fashion, ed. John Wilson and Steven Toms, LIV, 1, 30–47.

FORD, Henry, and Samuel CROWTHER. 1926. *My Life and Work* (1922). New York: Doubleday.

First translated into French as *Ma Vie et mon oeuvre*. Paris: Payot, 1926.

FORTH, Christopher E., and Elinor ACCAMPO (eds). 2010. *Confronting Modernity in Fin-de-Siècle France*. Basingstoke and New York: Palgrave Macmillan.

FOSTER, Susan Leigh (ed). 1995. *Choreographing History*. Bloomington and Indianapolis: Indiana University Press.

—. 1996. *Corporealities: Dancing Knowledge, Culture and Power*. New York: Routledge.

—. 2011. *Choreographing Empathy: Kinaesthesia in Performance*. Abingdon and New York: Routledge.

FOUCAULT, Michel. 1990. *The History of Sexuality, Vol. 1: An Introduction*. Trans. Robert Hurley. Harmondsworth: Penguin.

FOURNIER, Suzanne. 1953. *Cousu Main*. Paris: S.S.P.

FRANKO, Mark. 1995. *Dancing Modernism/Performing Politics*. Bloomington and Indianapolis: Indiana University Press.

FREADMAN, Anne. 2006. 'Breasts are Back! Colette's Critique of Flapper Fashion'. *French Studies*, LX, 3, 335–46.

FREUD, Sigmund. 1953–73. 'The Uncanny' (1919), *Standard Edition of the Complete Psychological Works of Sigmund Freud*. Trans. James Strachey. Vol. 17, 217–56. London: Hogarth Press and the Institute of Psychoanalysis.

FRIEDBERG, Anne. 1993. *Window Shopping: Cinema and the Postmodern*. Berkeley, Los Angeles and London: University of California Press.

G

GAINES, Jane, and Charlotte HERZOG (eds). 1990. *Fabrications: Costume and the Female Body*. New York: Routledge.

GAMMAN, Lorraine, and Merja MAKINEN. 1994. *Female Fetishism: A New Look*. London: Lawrence & Wishart.

GANEVA, Mila. 2008. *Women in Weimar Fashion: Discourses and Displays in German Culture, 1918–1933*. Rochester, N.Y: Camden House.

—. 2009. 'Elegance and Spectacle in Berlin: The Gerson Fashion Store and the Rise of the Modern Fashion Show in the Early Twentieth Century'. In John Potvin (ed.). *The Places and Spaces of Fashion: 1800–2007*. New York: Routledge.

GARAFOLA, Lynn. 1998. *Diaghilev's Ballets Russes*. New York: Da Capo Press.

GARB, Tamar. 1998. *Bodies of Modernity: Figure and Flesh in Fin-de-Siècle France*. London: Thames & Hudson.

GARDINER, James. 1986. *Gaby Deslys: A Fatal Attraction*. London: Sidgwick & Jackson.

GARELICK, Rhonda K. 2007. *Electric Salome: Loie Fuller's Performance of Modernism*. Princeton and Oxford: Princeton University Press.

GARLAND, Madge. 1970. *The Changing Form of Fashion*. New York: Praeger.

GAUDREAULT, André. 2011. *Film and Attraction: From Kinematography to Cinema*. Trans. Timothy

Bernard. Urbana, Chicago and Springfield: University of Illinois Press.

GAVAULT, Paul. 1914. *Le Mannequin*. Paris: *La petite Illustration*, no. 36, 18 April.

GERBER, Pierre. 1932. *La France travaille: coutures et modes*. Vol. 2. Paris: Horizons de France.

GIEDION, Siegfried. 1969. *Mechanization Takes Command* (1948). New York and London: W.W. Norton & Co.

GILBERT, James, Amy GILMAN, Donald M. SCOTT and Joan W. SCOTT (eds). *The Mythmaking Frame of Mind: Social Imagination and American Culture*. Belmont, Cal: Wadsworth.

GILLROY, Paul. 1993. *The Black Atlantic: Modernity and Double Consciousness*. London: Verso.

GILMAN, Sander L. 2008. *Fat: A Cultural History of Obesity*. Cambridge: Polity.

GLEDHILL, Christine, and Linda WILLIAMS (eds). 2000. *Reinventing Film Studies*. London: Edward Arnold.

GLENN, Susan A. 2000. *Female Spectacle: The Theatrical Roots of Modern Feminism*. Cambridge, Mass., and London: Harvard University Press.

Glossy. 2004. Musée de la Mode de Marseille: Images et Manoeuvres Éditions.

GOFFMAN, Erving. 1990. *The Presentation of Self in Everyday Life* (1959). London: Penguin.

GOLBIN, Pamela (ed). 2009. *Madeleine Vionnet*. New York : Rizzoli.

GOLDBERG, Vicki. 1991. *The Power of Photography*. New York, London and Paris: Abbeville.

GONCOURT, Edmond and Jules de. 1956. *Journal: mémoires de la vie littéraire*. Ed. Robert Ricatte. 4 vols. Paris: Fasquelle and Flammarion.

GOODRUM, Alison. 2005. *The National Fabric: Fashion, Britishness, Globalization*. Oxford: Berg.

GRAMONT, Elizabeth de. 1966. *Souvenirs du monde*. Paris: Grasset.

Le Grand Dictionnaire Robert de la langue française. 1985. 2nd edition updated by Alain Rey. Paris: Le Robert.

GRANDVILLE, J. J., and Taxile DELORD. 1844. *Un autre monde*. Paris: Fournier.

GRAZIA, Victoria de, and Ellen FURLOUGH (eds). 1996. *The Sex of Things: Gender and Consumption in Historical Perspective*. Berkeley, Los Angeles and London: University of California Press.

GREEN, Nancy L. 1994. 'Art and Industry: The Language of Modernization in the Production of Fashion'. *French Historical Studies*, XVIII, 3, spring, 722–48.

—. 1997. *Ready-to-wear and Ready-to-work: A Century of Industry and Immigrants in Paris and New York*. Durham, N.C., and London: Duke University Press.

GREER, Howard. 1952. *Designing Male*. London: Robert Hale.

GRIFFIN, Roger. 2007. *Modernism and Fascism: The Sense of a Beginning under Mussolini and Hitler*. Basingstoke and New York: Palgrave.

GRIFFITHS, Jay. 1999. *Pip Pip: A Sideways Look at Time*. London: Flamingo.

GRONBERG, Tag. 1977. 'Beware Beautiful Women: The 1920s Shop-window Mannequin and a Physiognomy of Effacement'. *Art History*, XX, 3, September, 375–96.

—. 1998. *Designs on Modernity: Exhibiting the City in 1920s Paris*. Manchester University Press.

—. 2002. 'Sonia Delaunay: Fashioning the Modern Woman'. *Women: A Cultural Review*, XIII, 3, November, 272–88.

GROSSMAN, Wendy A. 2010. *Man Ray, African Art, and the Modernist Lens*. Washington, D.C.: International Art and Artists.

GRUMBACH, Didier. 2008. *Histoires de la mode* (1993), Paris: Éditions du Regard.

GUILBERT, Yvette. 1927. *La Chanson de ma vie (mes mémoires)*. 20th edition. Paris: Bernard Grasset.

H

HAMBURGER, Estelle. 1940. *It's a Woman's Business*. London: Victor Gollancz.

HAMMERTON, Jenny. 2001. *For Ladies Only? Eve's Film Review, Pathé Cinemagazine 1921–33*. Hastings: Projection Box.

HANSSEN, Eirik Frisvold. 2009. 'Symptoms of Desire: Colour, Costume, and Commodities in Fashion Newsreels of the 1910s and 1920s'. *Film History*, XXI, 107–21.

HART, Avril. 1993. 'Court Dress for a French Fashion Doll 1765–75: Haute Couture in Miniature'. *National Art Collections Fund Review*, 31 December, 2–5.

HARVEY, David. 1989. *The Condition of Postmodernity: An Inquiry into the Origins of Cultural Change*. Oxford: Basil Blackwell.

HAWES, Elizabeth. 1938. *Fashion is Spinach*. New York: Random House.

HAYWARD, Maria, and Elizabeth KRAMER (eds). 2007. *Textiles and Text: Re-establishing the Links between Archival and Object-based Research*. London: Archetype Publications.

HAYWARD, Susan. 1993. *French National Cinema*. London and New York: Routledge.

HERZOG, Charlotte. 1990. 'Powder Puff Promotion: The Fashion Show-in-the-Film'. In Jane Gaines and Charlotte Herzog (eds). *Fabrications: Costume and the Female Body*, 134–59. New York: Routledge.

HIGASHI, Sumiko. 1994. *Cecil B. DeMille and American Culture: The Silent Era*. Berkeley: University of California Press.

HIRSCH, Marianne. 1997. *Family Frames, Photography, Narrative and Postmemory*. Cambridge, Mass.: Harvard University Press.

Histoire de l'industrie et du commerce en France: l'effort économique français contemporain. 1926. 4 vols. Paris: Éditions d'Art et d'Histoire.

HOGANSON, Kristin L. 2007. *Consumers' Imperium: The Global Production of American Domesticity, 1865–1920*. Chapel Hill: University of North Carolina Press.

HOLLANDER, Anne. 1993. *Seeing Through Clothes* (1975). Berkeley: University of California Press.

HOLSCHBACH, Susanne. 2006. *Vom Ausdruck zur Pose: Theatralität und Weiblichkeit in der Fotografie des 19. Jahrhunderts*. Berlin: Reimer.

HOPKINS, Albert A. 1976. *Magic: Stage Illusions, Special Effects and Trick Photography* (first published as *Magic: Stage Illusions and Scientific Diversions, Including Trick Photography*, 1898). New York: Dover Publications.

HOWES, D. 2005. *The Empire of the Senses: The Sensual Cultural Reader*. Oxford and New York: Berg.

HUMM, Maggie. 2003. *Modernist Women and Visual Cultures: Virginia Wolf, Vanessa Bell, Photography and Cinema*. New Brunswick, N.J.: Rutgers University Press.

HUYSSEN, Andreas. 1986. *After the Great Divide: Modernism, Mass Culture, Postmodernism*. London: Macmillan.

I

IVERSEN, Margaret. 1993. *Alöis Riegl: Art History and Theory*. Cambridge, Mass., and London: MIT Press.

L'Illustration: Journal Universel. 1987. *Les Grands Dossiers de l'Illustration: la mode: histoire d'un siècle, 1843–1944*. Paris: Livre de Paris.

J

JAFFE, Aaron. 2005. *Modernism and the Culture of Celebrity*. Cambridge University Press.

JAMESON, Fredric. 1991. *Postmodernism, or, the Cultural Logic of Late Capitalism*. Durham, N.C.: Duke University Press.

—. 1992. *Signatures of the Visible*. New York and London: Routledge.

—. 2007. *The Modernist Papers*. London: Verso.

JEACLE, Ingrid. 2003. 'Accounting and the Construction of the Standard Body'. *Accounting, Organizations and Society*, XXVIII, 4, May, 357–77.

JOBLING, Paul. 1998. 'Who's That Girl? "Alex Eats", A Case Study in Abjection and Identity in Contemporary Fashion Photography'. *Fashion Theory*, II, 3, 209–24.

JOHNSON, Donald Clay, and Helen Brady FOSTER (eds). 2007. *Dress Sense: Emotional and Sensory Experiences of the Body and Clothes*. Oxford and New York: Berg.

JONES, Ann Rosalind, and Peter STALLYBRASS. 2000. *Renaissance Clothing and the Materials of Memory*. Cambridge University Press.

JONES, Jennifer M. 2004. *Sexing La Mode: Gender, Fashion and Commercial Culture in Old Regime France*. Oxford and New York: Berg.

JOWITT, Deborah. 1988. *Time and the Dancing Image*. New York: William Morrow.

JOYCE, Patrick (ed). 1987. *The Historical Meanings of Work*. Cambridge University Press.

K

KANIGEL, Robert. 1997. *The One Best Way: Frederick Winslow Taylor and the Enigma of Efficiency*. New York: Viking.

KAPLAN, E. Ann (ed). 1988. *Postmodernism and its Discontents*. London: Verso.

KAPLAN, Joel H., and Sheila STOWELL. 1994. *Theatre and Fashion: Oscar Wilde to the Suffragettes*. Cambridge University Press.

KEENAN, Brigid. 1977. *The Women We Wanted to Look Like*. London: Macmillan.

KENDON, Adam. 2004. *Gesture: Visible Action as Utterance*. Cambridge University Press.

KERN, Stephen. 2003. *The Culture of Time and Space: 1880–1918* (1983). With a new preface. Cambridge, Mass., and London: Harvard University Press.

KIRKE, Betty. 1998. *Madeleine Vionnet*. With a foreword by Issey Miyake. San Francisco: Chronicle Books.

KLÜVER, Billy. 1997. *A Day with Picasso: Twenty-four Photographs by Jean Cocteau*. Cambridge, Mass.: MIT Press.

KODA, Harold, and Andrew BOLTON (eds). 2007. *Poiret*. New York, New Haven and London: Metropolitan Museum of Art and Yale University Press.

KRACAUER, Siegfried. 1969. *History: The Last Things before the Last*. Oxford University Press.

—. 1995. *The Mass Ornament* (1927). Trans., ed. and intro. Thomas Y. Levin. Cambridge, Mass., and London: Harvard Unvirsity Press.

KUISEL, Richard F. 1993. *Seducing the French: The Dilemma of Americanization*. Berkeley, Los Angeles and London: University of California Press.

L

LAKOFF, George, and Mark JOHNSON. 1999. *Philosophy in the Flesh: The Embodied Mind and Its Challenge to Western Thought*. New York: Basic Books.

LANT, Antonia. 1995. 'Haptic Cinema', *October*, LXXIV, fall, 45–73.

LARTIGUE, J.-H. 1975. *Mémoires sans mémoire*. Paris: Éditions Robert Laffont.

LATHAM, Angela J. 2000. *Posing a Threat: Flappers, Chorus Girls and Other Brazen Performers of the American 1920s*. Hanover, N.H., and London: Wesleyan University Press published by University Press of New England.

LEACH, William. 1994. *Land of Desire: Merchants, Power and the Rise of a New American Culture*. New York: Vintage Books.

LEDER, Drew. 1992. *The Absent Body*. Chicago University Press.

LEESE, Elizabeth. 1976. *Costume Design in the Movies*. Bembridge, Isle of Wight: BCW Publishing.

LEEUW-DE MONTI, Matteo de, and Petra TIMMER. 2011. *Colour Moves: Art and Fashion by Sonia Delaunay*. Ed. Matilda McQuaid and Susan Brown. London: Thames & Hudson.

LEFEBVRE, Henri. 1991. *The Production of Space* (1974). Trans. Donald Nicholson-Smith. Oxford and Cambridge, Mass.: Blackwell.

—. 2004. *rhythmanalysis: space, time and everyday life* (1992). Trans. Stuart Elden and Gerald Moore, intro. Stuart Elden. London and New York: Continuum.

LE FÈVRE, Georges. 1929. *Au secours de la couture (industrie française)*. Paris: Éditions Baudinière.

LEHMANN, Ulrich. 2000. *Tigersprung: Fashion in Modernity*. Cambridge, Mass., and London: Harvard University Press.

LEROY, Claude. 1999. *Le Mythe de la passante: de Baudelaire à Mandiargues*. Paris: Presses Universitaires de France.

LEVASSEUR, J. 1912. *La Question de l'apprentissage dans la couture*. Paris: Librairie A. Rousseau.

LEVENSON, Michael. 2011. *Modernism*. New Haven and London: Yale University Press.

— (ed). 1999. *The Cambridge Companion to Modernism*. Cambridge University Press.

LISTA, Giovanni. 2001. *Futurism and Photography*. London: Merrell with the Estorick Collection.

LUPANO, Mario, and Alessandra VACCARI (eds). 2009. *Fashion at the Time of Fascism: Italian Modernist Lifestyle 1922–1943*. Bologna: Damiani Editore.

LYND, Robert. 1915. 'Thoughts at a Tango Tea'. *The Book of This and That*, 24–6. http://www.readbookonline.net/readOnLine/53568/ accessed 12 December 2011.

M

MACKRELL, Alice. 1990. *Paul Poiret*. London: Batsford.

Madeleine Vionnet: les années d'innovation 1919–1939. 1994. Lyons: Musée des Tissus.

MAIZEROY, René. 1907. *Yette, mannequin*, Les Parisiennes series. Paris: Felix Juven.

MAO, Douglas. 1998. *Solid Objects: Modernism and the Test of Production*. Princeton University Press.

MARCUS, Laura. 2007. *The Tenth Muse: Writing about Cinema in the Modernist Period*. Oxford University Press.

MAREY, E. J. 1895. *Movement*. Trans. Eric Pritchard. London: William Heinemann.

MARINETTI, Filippo Tomasso. 1909. *Poupées électriques*. Paris: Bibliothèque Internationale d'Éditions E. Sansot et Cie.

MARKS, Laura U. 2000. *The Skin of the Film: Intercultural Cinema, Embodiment, and the Senses*. Durham, N.C., and London: Duke University Press.

MARLEY, Diana de. 1980. *History of Haute Couture 1850–1950*. London: Batsford.

—. 1990. *Worth: Father of Haute Couture*. 2nd edition. New York: Holmes & Meier.

MARTIN-FUGIER, Anne. 1990. *La Vie élégante ou la formation du Tout-Paris: 1815–1848*. Paris: Points.

MATHESON, Rebecca Jumper, and Molly Frances SORKIN. 2005. *Designing the It Girl: Lucile and Her Style*. New York: Museum at Fashion Institute of Technology.

MAUSS, Marcel. 1995. 'Techniques of the Body' (1934). In Crary and Kwinter 1995, 454–77.

MAYNARD, Margaret. 1999. 'Living Dolls: The Fashion Model in Australia'. *Journal of Popular Culture*, XXXI, 2, summer, 191–205.

MAYNE, Judith. 1990. *The Woman at the Keyhole: Feminism and Women's Cinema*. Bloomington and Indianapolis: Indiana University Press.

McCABE, Susan. 2001. '"Delight in Dislocation": The Cinematic Modernism of Stein, Chaplin and Man Ray'. *Modernism/Modernity*, VIII, 3, September, 429–52.

McCARTHY, James Remington, and John RUTHERFORD. 1931. *Peacock Alley: The Romance of the Waldorf-Astoria*. New York: Harpers and Bros.

McCAW, Dick (ed). 2011. *The Laban Sourcebook*. London and New York: Routledge.

McCULLOUGH, Jack W. 1986. *Living Pictures on the New York Stage*. New York: Columbia University Press.

McMANUS, Blanche. 1911. *The American Woman Abroad*. New York: Dodd, Mead and Co.

McMANUS, James. 2008. 'Mirrors, TRANS/formation and Slippage in the Five-way Portrait of Marcel Duchamp'. *The Space Between*, IV, 1, 125–48.

MELCHIOR-BONNET, Sabine. 2001. *The Mirror: A History*. Trans. Katharine H. Jewett. New York and London: Routledge.

La mémoire de Paris, 1919–1939. 1993. Paris: Mairie de Paris.

MENDES, Valerie D., and Amy DE LA HAYE. 2009. *Lucile Ltd: London, Paris, New York and Chicago, 1890s–1930s*. London: V&A Publishing.

MEULEAU, Marc. 1992. 'Les HEC et l'évolution du management en France, 1881–années 1980'. Thèse du doctorat, Université de Paris X.

MICHAUD, Philippe-Alain. 2004. *Aby Warburg and the Image in Motion*. Trans. Sophie Hawkes, foreword Georges Didi-Huberman. New York: Zone Books.

MICHELSON, Annette. 1984. 'On the Eve of the Future: The Reasonable Facsimile and the Philosophical Toy'. *October*, XXIX, summer, 3–20.

MILLER, Karl. 1985. *Doubles*. Oxford University Press.

MISTINGUETT. 1954. *Mistinguett: Queen of the Paris Night*. Trans. Lucienne Hill. London: Elek Books.

MIZEJEWSKI, Linda. 1999. *Ziegfeld Girl: Image and Icon in Culture and Cinema*. Durham, N.C., and London: Duke University Press.

MONTAGNÉ-VILLETTE, Solange. 1990. *Le Sentier: un espace ambiguë*. Paris: Masson.

MORAND, Paul. 1931. *1900*. Paris: Éditions de France.

MOUTET, Aimé. 1997. *Les Logiques de l'entreprise: la rationalisation dans l'entreprise française de l'entre-deux-guerres*. Paris: Éditions de l'EHESS.

MUCHEMBLED, Robert. 1988. *L'Invention de l'homme moderne: Culture et sensibilités en France du XV ͤ au XVII ͤ siècle*. Paris: Librairie Arthème Fayard.

MULVEY, Laura. 1989. *Visual and Other Pleasures*. London: Macmillan.

—. 2006. *Death 24x a Second*. London: Reaktion.

MUNICH, Adrienne (ed). 2011. *Fashion in Film*. Bloomington and Indianapolis: Indiana University Press.

MUSÉE de la Mode et du Costume. 1986. *Paul Poiret et Nicole Groult: maîtres de la mode Art Déco*. Paris: Palais Galliera.

—. 1990. *Femmes fin de siècle, 1885–1895*. Paris: Palais Galliera.

—. 1992. *Au paradis des dames: nouveautés, modes et confections 1810–1870*. Éditions Paris-Musées.

MUSÉE Galliera. 2006. *Showtime: le défilé de mode*. Éditions Paris-Musées.

—. 2007. *Les Années folles 1919–1929*. Éditions Paris-Musées.

N

NAETHER, Carl A. 1928. *Advertising to Women*. New York: Prentice-Hall Inc.

NEAD, Lynda. 2007. *The Haunted Gallery: Painting, Photography, Film c. 1900*. London and New Haven: Yale University Press.

NEISSEN, Sandra, Ann Marie LESHKOWICH and Carla JONES (eds). 2003. *Re-orienting Fashion: The Globalization of Asian Dress*. Oxford: Berg.

NESBITT, Molly. 1987. 'What Was an Author?' *Yale French Studies*, 73, Everyday Life, winter, 229–57.

NORA, Pierre. 1989. 'Between Memory and History: *Les Lieux de Mémoire*'. *Representations*, 26, spring, 7–25.

—. 1996, 1997 and 1998. *Realms of Memory: Rethinking the French Past (Lieux de mémoire, Paris: Gallimard, 7 vols, 1984–92)*. Trans. Arthur Goldhammer, ed. and foreword Lawrence D. Kritzman. 3 vols. New York: Columbia University Press.

NORTH, Michael. 1999. *Reading 1922: A Return to the Scene of the Modern*. New York: Oxford University Press.

NOYS, Benjamin. 2004. 'Gestural Cinema? Giorgio Agamben on Film'. *Film-Philosophy*, VIII, 22, July. http://www.film-philosophy.com/vol8-2004/n22noys, accessed 12 August 2012.

O

OFFICER, Lawrence H. 2009. 'Exchange Rates Between the United States Dollar and Forty-one Currencies'. Measuring Worth. http://www.measuringworth.org/exchangeglobal/, accessed 12 August 2012.

O'NEILL, Alistair. 2007. *London – After a Fashion*. London: Reaktion.

O'NEILL, John. 2004. *Five Bodies: Re-Figuring Relationships*. London, Thousand Oaks and New Delhi: Sage Publications.

OTTINGER, Didier (ed). 2009. *Futurism*. Paris: 5 Continents Editions/Éditions du Centre Pompidou.

OWENS, Craig. 1992. *Beyond Recognition: Representation, Power, and Culture*. Berkeley, Los Angeles and Oxford: University of California Press.

P

PALAIS Galliera. 1995. *Le dessin sous toutes les coutures: croquis, illustrations, modèles, 1760–1994*. Éditions Paris-Musées.

—. 1997. *Europe 1910–1939: quand l'art habillait le vêtement*. Éditions Paris-Musées.

PALMER, Alexandra. 2001. *Couture and Commerce: The Transatlantic Fashion Trade in the 1950s*. Vancouver: UBC Press with Royal Ontario Museum.

PARK, Julie. 2010. *The Self and It: Novel Objects and Mimetic Subjects in Eighteenth-century England*. Stanford University Press.

PARKER, Derek and Julia. 1975. *The Natural History of the Chorus Girl*. Newton Abbott, London and Vancouver: David & Charles.

PATERSON, Mark. 2007. *The Senses of Touch: Haptics, Affects and Technologies*. Oxford and New York: Berg.

PAUL, Elliot. 2001. *The Last Time I Saw Paris* (1942). London: Sickle Moon Books.

PEARSON, Roberta E. 1992. *Eloquent Gestures: The Transformation of Performance Style in the Griffiths Biograph Films*. Berkeley: University of California Press.

PEERS, Juliette. 2004. *The Fashion Doll: From Bébé Jumeau to Barbie*. Oxford and New York: Berg.

PENDERGRAST, Mark. 2003. *Mirror Mirror: A History of the Human Love Affair with Reflection*. New York: Basic Books.

PERNIOLA, Mario. 1995. *Enigmas: The Egyptian Moment in Society and Art* (1990). Trans. Christopher Woodall. London: Verso.

PERRY, Gill. 1995. *Women Artists and the Parisian Avant-Garde*. Manchester and New York: Manchester University Press.

Le Petit Homme Rouge [Ernest A. Vizetelly]. 1907. *The Court of the Tuileries 1852–1870: Its Organization, Chief Personages, Splendour, Frivolity and Downfall*. London: Chatto & Windus.

PEUCKER, Brigitte. 1995. *Incorporating Images: Film and the Rival Arts*. Princeton University Press.

PHELAN, Peggy. 1993. *Unmarked: The Politics of Performance*. London and New York: Routledge.

La Poilue, par une première de la rue de la Paix. 1916. Paris: Albin Michel.

POIRET, Paul. 1931. *My First Fifty Years* (*En habillant l'époque*). Trans. Stephen Haden Guest. London: Victor Gollancz, 1931.

POLESE, Francesca, and Regina Lee BLASZCZYK. 2012. 'Fashion Forward: The Business History of Fashion'. *Business History Review*, LIV, 1, 6–9.

POLLOCK, Griselda. 2003. *Vision and Difference: Feminism, Femininity and the Histories of Art* (1988). New intro. by the author. London and New York: Routledge.

POTVIN, John (ed). 2009. *The Places and Spaces of Fashion, 1800–2007*. London and New York: Routledge.

POUILLARD, Véronique. 2011. 'Design Piracy in the Fashion Industries of Paris and New York in the Interwar Years'. *Business History Review*, LXXXV, 2, summer, 319–44.

POWERS, John. 1941. *The Powers Girls: The Story of Models and Modeling and the Natural Steps by Which Attractive Girls Are Created*. New York: E. P. Dutton.

PRESTON, Carrie J. 2011. *Modernism's Mythic Pose: Gender, Genre, Solo Performance*. Oxford University Press.

PRITCHARD, Jane (ed). 2010. *Diaghilev and the Golden Age of the Ballets Russes*. London: V&A Publications.

R

RAINEY, Lawrence. 1998. *Institutions of Modernism: Literary Elites and Public Culture*. New Haven and London: Yale University Press.

RANK, Otto. 1989. *The Double: A Psychoanalytic Study* (1914). London: Karnak-Maresfield.

REASONS, Matthew. 2006. *Documentation, Disappearance and the Representation of Live Performance*. London: Palgrave Macmillan.

REBOUX, Paul. 1927. *La Rue de la Paix*. Paris: Éditions Pierre Lafitte.

REEDER, Jan Glier. 1990. 'The Touch of Paquin 1891–1920'. MA diss., State University of New York, Fashion Institute of Technology.

RÉMY, Tristan. 1964. *Georges Wague: le mime de la belle époque*. Paris: Georges Girard.

REYNOLDS, Siân. 1996. *France Between the Wars: Gender and Politics*. London and New York: Routledge.

RHYS, Jean. 1987. *The Collected Short Stories*. Intro. Diana Athill. New York and London: W. W. Norton.

RICE, Shelley. 1997. *Parisian Views*. Cambridge, Mass., and London: MIT Press.

RICHARDSON, Joanna. 1987. *Portrait of a Bonaparte: The Life and Times of Joseph-Napoleon Primoli 1851–1927*. London: Quartet Books.

RIOTOR, Léon. 1900. *Le Mannequin*. Paris: Bibliothèque Artistique et Littéraire.

ROBERTS, Mary Louise. 1994. *Civilization Without Sexes: Reconstructing Gender in Postwar France, 1917–1927*. Chicago and London: University of Chicago Press.

—. 2002. *Disruptive Acts: The New Woman in Fin-de-Siècle France*. Chicago and London: University of Chicago Press.

ROBINSON, David. 1993. *Georges Méliès: Father of Film Fantasy*. London: British Film Institute.

ROCAMORA, Agnès. 2009. *Fashioning the City: Paris, Fashion and the Media*. London and New York: I. B. Tauris.

ROGER-MILÈS, L. 1910. *Les Créateurs de la mode*. Paris: Éditions du Figaro.

ROSENSTONE, Robert A. 1995. *Visions of the Past: The Challenge of Film to Our Idea of History*. Cambridge, Mass., and London: Harvard University Press.

ROSS, Alex. 2008. *The Rest is Noise: Listening to the Twentieth Century*. London: Fourth Estate.

ROSS, Andrew (ed). 1997. *No Sweat: Fashion, Free Trade and the Rights of Garment Workers*. New York and London: Verso.

ROTH, Joseph. 2004. *The White Cities: Reports from France 1925–39*. Trans. and intro. Michael Hofmann, based on an original German selection by Katharina Osche. London: Granta Books.

ROUBAUD, Louis. 1928. *Au pays des mannequins: le roman de la robe*. Paris: Éditions de France.

ROUFF, Maggy. 1942. *La Philosophie de l'élégance*. Paris: Éditions Littéraires de France.

S

SAFER, Samantha Erin. 2007. 'Promotion Queen: Lucile, Lady Duff Gordon'. MA diss., Victoria and Albert Museum/Royal College of Arts.

SALMON, André. 1950. *Montparnasse*. Paris: Éditions André Bonne.

SAUNDERS, Edith. 1954. *The Age of Worth: Couturier to the Empress Eugénie*. London, New York and Toronto: Longmans, Green and Co.

SAYRE, Henry M. 1989. *The Object of Performance: The American Avant-Garde since 1970*. Chicago and London: University of Chicago Press.

SCHILDER, Paul. 1970. *The Image and Appearance of the Human Body: Studies in Constructive Energies of the Psyche*. New York: International Universities Press Inc.

SCHWARTZ, Hillel. 1996. *The Culture of the Copy: Striking Likenesses, Unreasonable Facsimiles*. New York: Zone Books.

SCHWARTZ, Vanessa R. 1998. *Spectacular Realities: Early Mass Culture in Fin-de-Siècle Paris*. Berkeley and Los Angeles: University of California Press.

SCHWEITZER, Marlis. 2009. *When Broadway Was the Runway: Theater, Fashion, and American Culture*. Philadelphia: University of Pennsylvania Press.

SEEBOHM, Caroline. 1982. *The Man Who Was Vogue: The Life and Times of Condé Nast*. London: Weidenfeld and Nicolson.

SEGRE REINACH, Simona. 2005. 'China and Italy: Fast Fashion versus Prêt à Porter. Towards a New Culture of Fashion', *Fashion Theory*, IX, 1, March.

SEKULA, Allan. 1986. 'The Body and the Archive'. *October*, XXXIX, winter, 3–64.

SEM. 1914. *Le Vrai et le faux chic*. Paris: Succès.

SEVERINI, Gino. 1995. *The Life of a Painter: The Autobiography of Gino Severini*. Trans. Jennifer Franchina. Princeton University Press.

SHATTUCK, Roger. 1968. *The Banquet Years: The Origins of the Avant Garde in France 1885 to World War I* (1955). Rev. edition. New York: Vintage Books.

SHIELDS, Rob. 1988. 'An English Précis of Henri Lefebvre's "La Production de l'éspace"'. Working paper. Urban and Regional Studies, Sussex University.

SHONFIELD, Zuzanna. 'The Great Mr Worth'. *Costume: The Journal of the Costume Society* (U.K.), XVI, 1982, 57–9.

SIEGFRIED, André. 1927. *America Comes of Age, a French Analysis* (*Les États-unis d'aujourd'hui*). New York: Harcourt, Brace and Co.

SILVERMAN, Kaja. 1996. *The Threshold of the Visible World*. London and New York: Routledge.

SILVER, Kenneth E. 1989. *Esprit de Corps: The Art of the Parisian Avant Garde and the First World War, 1914–1925*. Princeton University Press; London: Thames & Hudson.

SIMMEL, Georg. 1971. *On Individuality and Social Forms: Selected Writings*. Ed. and intro. Donald N. Levine. Chicago and London: University of Chicago Press.

—. 1990. *The Philosophy of Money* (1900, 1907). Ed. D. P. Frisby. London and New York: Routledge.

SIMON, Philippe. 1931. 'Monographie d'une industrie de luxe: la haute couture'. Thèse pour le doctorat, Université de Paris.

SIROP, Dominique. 1989. *Paquin*. Paris: Adam Biro.

SMITH, Mark M. 2007. *Sensory History*. Oxford and New York: Berg.

SMITH, Marquard (ed.). 2008. *Visual Culture Studies*. Los Angeles, London, New Delhi, Singapore: Sage Publications.

SMITH, Philip, and Alexander RILEY. 2009. *Cultural Theory: An Introduction* 2nd edition. Malden, Mass., and Oxford: Blackwell.

SOLEY-BELTRAN, Patricia. 2004. 'Modelling Femininity'. *European Journal of Women's Studies*, XI, 3, August, 309–26.

SOLNIT, Rebecca. 2002. *Wanderlust: A History of Walking*. London: Verso.

SPARKE, Penny. 1995. *As Long as It's Pink: The Sexual Politics of Taste*. London: Pandora Press.

—. 2008. 'International Design and Haute Couture'. *Journal of Design History*, XXI, 1, spring, 101–7.

STALLABRASS, Julian. 2002. *Paris Pictured: Street Photography 1900–1968*. London: Royal Academy Publications.

—. 2007. 'What's in a Face? Blankness and Significance in Contemporary Art Photography'. *October*, CXXII, fall, 71–90.

STEARNS, Peter. 2002. *Fat History: Bodies and Beauty in the Modern West*. New York and London: New York University Press.

STEELE, Valerie. 1998. *Paris Fashion: A Cultural History*. 2nd edition. Oxford and New York: Berg.

—. 2001. *The Corset: A Cultural History*. London and New Haven, Yale University Press.

STEELE, Victoria. 2000. 'The Fashion Stages of Lucile, Lady Duff Gordon'. PhD diss., University of Southern California.

STEINER, Wendy. 2001. *Venus in Exile: The Rejection of Beauty in Twentieth-century Art*. University of Chicago Press.

—. 2010. *The Real Real Thing: The Model in the Mirror of Art*. Chicago and London: Chicago University Press.

STEWART, Mary Lynn. 1989. *Women, Work and the French State: Labour Protection and Social Patriarchy, 1879–1919*. Kingston, Montreal, London: McGill-Queens University Press.

—. 2001. *For Health and Beauty: Physical Culture for Frenchwomen 1880s–1930s*. Baltimore and London: Johns Hopkins University Press.

—. 2005. 'Copying and Copyrighting Haute Couture: Democratizing Fashion, 1900–1930s'. *French Historical Studies*, XXVIII, 1, winter, 103–30.

—. 2008. *Dressing Modern Frenchwomen: Marketing Haute Couture, 1919–1939*. Baltimore: Johns Hopkins University Press.

— and Nancy JANOVICEK. 2001. 'Slimming the Female Body? Re-evaluating Dress, Corsets, and Physical Culture in France, 1890s–1930s'. *Fashion Theory*, V, 2, 173–94.

STEWART, Susan. 1999. 'Prologue: From the Museum of Touch', 17–38. In Marius Kwint, Christopher Breward and Jeremy Aynsley (eds). *Material Memories: Design and Evocation*. Oxford and New York: Berg.

STIERLE, Karlheinz. 2001. *La Capitale des signes: Paris et son discours*. Preface Jean Starobinski. Trans. from German Marianne Rocher-Jacquin. Paris: Éditions de la Maison des Sciences de l'Homme.

STRASSER, Susan. 1993. 'The Smile That Pays: The Culture of Traveling Salesmen, 1880–1920', in James B. Gilbert, et al., eds, *The Mythmaking*

Frame of Mind: Social Imagination and American Culture. Belmont, Ca.: Wadsworth.

STRAUVEN, Wanda (ed). 2006. *The Cinema of Attractions Reloaded*. Amsterdam University Press.

SUSMAN, Warren. 1984. *Culture as History: The Transformation of American Society in the Twentieth Century*. New York: Pantheon.

SWINNEY, John B. 1942. *Merchandising of Fashions: Policies and Methods of Successful Speciality Stores*. New York: Ronald Press.

SYNOTT, Anthony. 1993. *The Body Social: Symbolism, Self and Society*. London and New York: Routledge.

T

TAYLOR, Frederick Winslow. 1911. *The Principles of Scientific Management*. New York and London: Harpers and Brothers Publishers.

TAYLOR, Lou. 1983. 'Marguerite Shoobert, London Fashion Model 1906–1917'. *Costume* (U.K.), XVII, 105–10.

TEITELBAUM, Mo Amelia. 2010. *The Stylemakers: Minimalism and Classic Modernism 1915–1945*. London: Philip Wilson Publishers.

TESSE, Jean-Philippe. 2004. 'Les gestes qui sauvent'. *Cahiers du cinéma*, no. 587, February, 82.

THESANDER, Marianne. 1997. *The Feminine Ideal*. London: Reaktion.

TICKNER, Lisa. 2000. *Modern Life and Modern Subjects: British Art in the Early 20th Century*. London and New Haven: Yale University Press.

TIERSTEN, Lisa. 2001. *Marianne in the Market: Envisioning Consumer Society in Fin-de-Siècle France*. Berkeley and Los Angeles: University of California Press.

TIETJENS MEYERS, Diana. 2002. *Gender in the Mirror: Cultural Imagery and Women's Agency*. Oxford University Press.

TOLINI-FINAMORE, Michelle. 2013. *Hollywood Before Glamour: Fashion in American Silent Film*. New York: Palgrave Macmillan.

TOUSSAINT-SAMAT, Maguelonne. 1990. *Histoire technique et morale du vêtement*. Paris: Bordas.

TOWNSEND, Chris. 2006. 'Slave to the Rhythm: Sonia Delaunay's Fashion Project and the Fragmentary, Mobile, Modernist Body'. In Brand and Teunissen 2006.

TROY, Nancy. 1991. *Modernism and the Decorative Arts in France: Art Nouveau to Le Corbusier*. New Haven and London: Yale University Press.

—. 2003. *Couture Culture: A Study in Art and Fashion*. Cambridge, Mass., and London: MIT Press.

U

UHLIROVA, Marketa (ed). 2008. *If Looks Could Kill: Cinema's Image of Fashion, Crime and Violence*. London: Koenig Books.

—. 2013. *Birds of Paradise: Costume as Cinematic Spectacle*. London: Koenig Books and Fashion in Film.

UZANNE, Octave. 1898. *Fashion in Paris: The Various Phases of Feminine Taste and Aesthetics from 1797 to 1897*. Trans. Lady Mary Lloyd. London: William Heinemann.

—. 1912. *The Modern Parisienne*. With an introduction by the Baroness von Hutten. London: William Heinemann.

V

VARDAC, A. Nicholas. 1949. *Stage to Screen: Theatrical Method from Garrick to Griffith*. Cambridge, Mass., Harvard University Press.

VARGISH, Thomas, and Delo E. MOOK. 1999. *Inside Modernism: Relativity Theory, Cubism, Narrative*. New Haven and London: Yale University Press.

VASSILIEV, Alexandre. 2000. *Beauty in Exile: The Artists, Models, and Nobility Who Fled the Russian Revolution and Influenced the World of Fashion*. Trans. Antonina W. Bouis and Anya Kucharev. New York: Harry N. Abrams.

VIGARELLO, Georges. 1978. *Le Corps redressé: histoire d'un pouvoir pédagogique*. Paris: Jean-Pierre Delarge, Éditions universitaires.

—. 2004. *Histoire de la beauté: le corps et l'art d'embellir de la renaissance à nos jours*. Paris: Éditions du Seuil.

La Ville lumière: anecdotes et documents historiques, ethnographiques, littéraires, artistiques, commerciaux et encyclopédiques. 1909. Paris: Direction et Administration.

VILLIERS DE L'ISLE-ADAM, Auguste. 1993. *L'Ève future* (1886). Intro. Alan Raitt. Paris: Gallimard.

VINKEN, Barbara. 1997. 'Eternity: A Frill on the Dress'. *Fashion Theory*, I, 1, 59–67.

W

WALKER, Caroline. 1914. *Modern Dances and How to Dance Them*. Chicago: Saul Brothers.

WALLACE, Carole, et al. 1986. *Dance: A Very Social History*. New York: Metropolitan Museum of Art with Rizzoli.

WANAMAKER, John. 1911. *Golden Book of the Wanamaker Stores, Jubilee Year, 1861–1911*. Philadelphia, Penn: Wanamaker.

WELTERS, Linda, and Patricia CUNNINGHAM (eds). 2005. *Twentieth-Century American Fashion*. Oxford: Berg.

WHITE, Palmer. [n.d.]. 'Mesdames', Palmer White Papers, Bibliothèque Forney, Paris.

—. 1973. *Poiret*. London: Studio Vista.

—. [n.d.]. 'Mademoiselle Chanel', drawing on interviews with Chanel employees in the 1980s–90s. Palmer White Papers, Bibliothèque Forney, Paris.

—. [n.d.]. Text of a lecture on Paul Poiret. Palmer White Papers, Bibliothèque Forney, Paris.

WHITEHURST, Felix M. 1873. *Court and Social Life in France under Napoleon the Third*. Vols 1 and 2. London: Tinsley Brothers.

WICKBERG, Daniel. 2007. 'What is the History of Sensibilities? On Cultural Histories, Old and New'. *American Historical Review*, June, 661–84.

WICKE, Jennifer. 1993. 'Modernity Must Advertise: Aura, Desire and Decolonization in Joyce'. *James Joyce Quarterly*, XXX–XXXI, 1, no. 4, 593–613.

WIGLEY, Mark. 2001. *White Walls, Designer Dresses: The Fashioning of Modern Architecture*. Cambridge, Mass.: MIT Press.

WILLOUGHBY, Gertrude. 1926. *La Situation des ouvrières du vêtement en France et en Angleterre*. Paris: Presses Universitaires.

WILSON, Deborah S., and Christine Moneera LAENNEC (eds). 1997. *Bodily Discursions: Genders, Representations, Technologies*. Albany: State University of New York Press.

WILSON, Elizabeth. 2003. *Adorned in Dreams: Fashion and Modernity*. Rev. and updated edition. London: I. B. Tauris.

WILSON, Richard Guy, Dianne H. PILGRIM and Dickran TASHJIAN. 1986. *The Machine Age in America 1918–1941*. New York: Brooklyn Museum with Harry N. Abrams.

WILSON, Robert Forrest. 1925. *Paris on Parade*. Indianapolis: Bobs-Merrill Company.

WISSINGER, Elizabeth. 2007. 'Modeling a Way of Life: Immaterial and Affective Labor in the Fashion Industry'. *Ephemera*, VII, 1, 250–69.

—. 2009. 'Modeling Consumption: Fashion Modeling Work in Contemporary Society'. *Journal of Consumer Culture*, IX, 2, July, 273–96.

WODEHOUSE, P. G. (Pelham Grenville). 1954. *Bring on the Girls: The Improbable Story of Our Life in Musical Comedy*. London: Herbert Jenkins.

WOLFF, Janet. 1990. *Feminine Sentences: Essays on Women and Culture*. Cambridge: Polity Press.

WOLLEN, Peter. 1993. *Raiding the Icebox: Reflections on Twentieth-century Culture*. London and New York: Verso.

WOOD, Gaby. 2002. *Living Dolls: A Magical History of the Quest for Mechanical Life*. London: Faber and Faber.

WOON, Basil. 1926. *The Paris that's not in the Guide Books*. New York: Bretano's.

WORTH, Gaston. 1895. *La Couture et la confection*. Paris: Imprimerie Chaix.

WORTH, Jean Philippe. 1928. *A Century of Fashion*. Trans. Ruth Scott Miller. Boston: Little Brown and Co.

WOSK, Julie. 2001. *Women and the Machine: Representations from the Spinning Wheel to the Electronic Age*. Baltimore and London: Johns Hopkins University Press.

Y

YOSIFON, David, and Peter N. STEARNS. 1998. 'The Rise and Fall of American Posture'. *American Historical Review*, issue 103, 4, October, 1057–95.

YOUNG, Iris Marion. 2005. *On Female Body Experience: 'Throwing Like a Girl' and Other Essays*. Oxford University Press.

YOXALL, Harry. 1966. *A Fashion of Life*, London: Heinemann.

Z

ZEGHER, M. Catherine de. 1995. *Inside the Visible: An Elliptical Traverse of Twentieth-Century Art*. Cambridge, Mass., and London: MIT Press.

ZOLA, Emile. 1981. *La Curée* (1872). Preface Jean Borie, ed. Henri Mitterand. Paris: Gallimard.

—. 1995. *The Ladies Paradise* (1883). Trans., intro. and notes by Brian Nelson. Oxford and New York: Oxford University Press.

INDEX

NOTE

Page numbers in *italics* refer to an illustration or information in a caption; the caption may appear on a facing page.

and modernist abstraction 243–7
and modernist flow 237–43, 248
paradox of 197, 238
and photographs 237
and self-representation 8
stasis and motion 237, 238, 242–3, 246, 248
tableaux vivants and *poses plastiques* 13, 18, 242–3, 246, 301*n*.149
training and practice in 191
poses plastiques 13, 18, 221, 242, 243, *243*
'positions of visibility' 238–9
posture
and body shape 228
full-length mirrors and awareness of 222–3
gesture and habitus 220–21
of military and fashion bodies 43–4
physical education training 222
training of mannequins 35, 220
see also walking
Powers, John and model agency 128, 190, 192
pregnant mannequins and maternity designs 18
prehistory of fashion shows 11–27
Premet (fashion house) 91, 97, *98*, 102, 103, 104, 109, 176, 210
La Garçonne dress 255
premières d'atelier (dressmakers) 144, 146
press coverage of fashion industry
American coverage of buyers' trips to Europe 31, 32, 102
deportment lessons 222, *223*
on mannequins 192–3, 194–5, 199
interest in individual mannequins 116, *116*, 188–9, *188*
melodramatic stories 193–4
mockery of extreme fashions 63, 199, 226, *227*
and modernist sensibilities 58
Paris seasons in wartime 102
plight of French garment workers in wartime 108
Poiret's filmed shows 68
postwar American-influenced designs 112
working conditions 38, 109
see also fashion journalism *and individual titles*
press shows in 1920s 123–4, *124–5*, 165
Preston, Carrie J. 6
previews for privileged clients 33
Prévost, Marcel 125–6
Primoli, Count 14
Prix de l'Elégance 118, 120
production methods
and automated systems 75, 115
atelier system as machine 147–8
and eradication of individuality 127, 131
in fashion magazine imagery 130–31, *131*
modernist imagery and mannequins 135–7
chorus line and capitalist production methods 126, 160, 189
division of labour in ateliers 146, 147–8, 149
Patou's embrace of modernist methods 115, 124, 128
and rationalisation of the body in fashion and industry 3, 7, 24, 74–5, 81, 115
see also mass production
productive bodies: mannequins as 160
productivity and profitability 160–61
prostitution 189, 222
association of mannequins with 62, 88, 187, 193
Proust, Marcel 258

Pru, Edwina (Patou mannequin) *127*
public fashion shows in 1920s 118, *120*
public spaces
fashion for strolling 24–6, 49, 179, 222
mannequins' appearances in 21–2, 29, 57–8, 182
and piracy risk 63, 66, 70, 72, 207
resorts and ocean liners 64, *64*, 66, *249*
la passante and workers on streets of Paris 25–7, *32*, 222, 261
'le sentier de la Vertu' *178*, 179–83, *180–83*
see also races: mannequins at
publicity *see* advertising and promotion
Puttnam, Carolyn (Patou mannequin) *127*

R

races
fashionable display at Eastertime 59
mannequins at 12, 18, 33, 54, 57, *57–62*, 59–64, *65*, 66
controversial fashions *61*, 206, *206*, 207, *209*, 210–11, *210*
recreation in American charity show 90
racial prejudice and Sem's satire 38–9, *38*
radio: first transmission in France 57
Rainey, Lawrence 4, 5, 262*n*.11
Raitt, Alan 23
Raph (Raphaëlle, Poiret mannequin) 238, 250
Rateau, Armand-Albert 130
rationalisation of the body 29–55
and chorus line 3, 7, 24, 43, *43–4*, 75
and capitalist production methods 126, 160, 189
categorisation of Ziegfeld showgirls 87–8
and fashion show line-ups *121*, 126, *127*, 129–30, *130*
and leisure 3, 24
dance and dance crazes 52–5
and mannequins 3, 7, 24, *41–5*, *43*, 55
loss of individuality in America 81
Lucile's categorisation into types 84, *84–7*, 86
mechanical movement of mannequin glide 29, 221, 232
need for standardised body 192, 211–12, 214
Patou's choice of American mannequins 125–9, *126–7*
modernist body 115, 129–31
modernist fashions in America and standardised body 127–8, 129
and production methods in fashion industry 3, 7, 24, 115
and work 3, 24, 46, 74, 155
see also machine aesthetic and body
Raudnitz (fashion house): introduction of fashion shows and live mannequins 31
ready-to-wear manufacturers (*confectionneurs*) 27
buyers for 165
dilution of French designs 123
exports from France 11, 255
French responses to American method 128
introduction of fashion shows and live mannequins 34
Lucien Lelong Editions collection 256, *256*
visual rights at fashion shows 256
see also garment industry; tailor-made clothes in wartime France
'realms of memory' 7, 8, 139–40, 144

Reboux, Caroline (milliner) 109
Reboux, Paul 117, 127, 146, 197
Redfern (fashion house) 2, 66, 103, *187*, 260
costumes for actresses 111
and introduction of fashion shows 30
invitations 144, *145*
living mannequins modelling to clients *31*
mannequins in *Fantasio* feature *188*
mirrors in salon and fitting rooms 129, 155, *155*
resort fashion shows as spectacle 118, *120*
and revealing styles 210
runway stage 152
'Scottish dress' and *costume trotteur* 22, *22*, 23
tango tea fashion show 54
walking and designs 226
refreshments at fashion shows 32, 39, 83, 122, 123
tango tea fashion shows 53, *53*, 71
regulation of haute couture fashion 32–3, 256–7
Reilly, Kate (fashion house) 187
Réjane, Gabrielle (actress) 246, 286*n*.89
repeated images
layouts in fashion magazines *41–5*, 43, 130, *130*, *153*, 239–40, *240*
of mannequins and reproduction of models 149, 152, 157, 159, 221
and mirrors *44–5*, *45*, *46*, 47–8, *47*, *48*, 147, *154*, 155
modernist abstraction in fashion shows 129–31, *130–31*
répétitions générales as press shows 123–4, *124–5*
reproduction and fashion 2, 6
ambivalence of couture houses over commercial sales 32, 35–6, 73
dichotomy of originals and copies 12, 15, 16, 21
model dresses for reproduction 15–17, *16*, 20–21, 23, 150, 160, 254–5
'bonded models' 255–6
conditions of purchase 257
organised piracy in America 257–8
repeated images of mannequins and reproduction of models 149, 152, 157, 159, 221
rights to reproduce haute couture designs 2, 11, 15–16, *16–17*, 17, 21, 123, 257
see also mass production; piracy in fashion; repeated images
resorts
fashion shows as spectacle in 1920s 115, *115*, 116–21, *120*, *121*
mannequins in public spaces 64, 66
rhythm and modernity 232
Riegl, Alois 178
Rilke, Rainer Maria 258
Riotor, Léon 19–20, *19*
Rittenhouse, Anne 160
Riviera: fashion shows as spectacle in 1920s *115*, 117–18, *119*
'Riviera season' fashions and events 64
Rivière, Joan 7, 155
Rivière, Max 194
robe pantalon see trouser skirts
Robert, Mme (fashion house) 33
Roberts, Mary Louise 215, 216–17
Robin (freelance designer) 144
Rocamora, Agnès 25, 26, 112, 179, 222
Roger-Milès, L. 146, 150, 165, *186–7*, 188, 194, 213, 263*n*.57, 298*n*.51
Roodenburg, Herman 220
Ross, Alex 23, 55

ACKNOWLEDGEMENTS

I would like to thank the Leverhulme Trust of Great Britain for the generous award of a three-year Major Research Fellowship in 2007–10 which enabled the laborious work of archival research in two continents. It is impossible to overstate the value of the uninterrupted thinking time it afforded, as well as the practical opportunities it gave me, and its impact has been lasting.

The genesis of this book has been long, and for support at the early stages of my thinking I am grateful to the AHRC-funded Fashion and Modernity project at the University of the Arts London from 2001 to 2004. At Central Saint Martins College of Arts and Design, I have enjoyed the support of Professor Jane Rapley, head of college until her retirement in 2012, Professor Janet McDonnell and her former colleagues in the research department, and Anne Smith, Dean of Fashion and Textiles. I owe a further debt of gratitude to Dr Louise Wallenberg and the Centre for Fashion Studies at Stockholm University for generous support with the illustrations, without which this book would have looked very different.

I am grateful to the many museum and archive staff, several of whom have since moved on to other institutions, for sharing their resources, time and specialist knowledge. At the Musée Galliera de la mode de la ville de Paris, Anne Zazzo, curator of Showtime: Le défilé de mode, shared her research and gave me access to material, including images, on an unprecedented scale. It was a privilege to work with her, and I thank her profoundly, as well as her colleagues Lisa Seantier, Sylvie Lécallier in the *photothèque* and Dominique Revellino in the library. At the Musée de l'art de la mode et du textile (Musées de l'union centrale des arts décoratifs) I am grateful to Caroline Pinon and Marie-Hélène Poix. Thanks, too, to the staff at the Bibliothèque Forney, the Bibliothèque Historique de la ville de Paris and the various divisions of the Bibliothèque nationale de France; to Marika Genty, Cécile Goddet-Dirles and their colleagues at the Chanel archive in Paris; and to Jean de Mouy, great nephew of Jean Patou and former president of the house of Patou. At the Fashion Institute of Technology in New York, I thank Valerie Steele, Patricia Mears, John Corrins, Claire Sauro and Molly Sorkin. Special thanks go to Karen Cannell, Keeper of the Special Collections at FIT, for her generous help with images without which this book would be considerably the poorer. At the Costume Institute of the Metropolitan Museum of Art in New York, I thank Harold Koda, Andrew Bolton, Shannon Bell Price and Stéphane Houy-Towner; at the Billy Rose Theatre Division of the New York Public Library for the Performing Arts, Jeremy Megraw; at the Chicago History Museum, Timothy Long and Debbie Vaughan; at the Philadelphia Museum of Art, Dylis Blum. Thanks also to the staff at the Historical Society of Philadelphia, the New York Historical Society, the Museum of the City of New York, Parsons Library, and the many divisions of the New York Public Library and the Library of Congress, Washington. In London, I was generously helped by Edwina Ehrman and Oriole Cullen at the Museum of London and later at the Victoria and Albert Museum. As always, I am grateful to all the staff in the Central Saint Martins library, especially to Laura Grant for her help with images. Thanks, too, to everyone at the Bath Fashion Museum, the History of Advertising Trust, Brighton University archives, the British Film Institute library and archives, the British Library, Guildhall Library and the National Art Library.

My heartfelt thanks go also to all the individuals who contributed in so many ways, more than I can mention here. They include Anja Aronowsky Cronberg, Beatrice Behlen, Cally Blackman, Reggie Blaszczyk, Franziska Bork Petersen, Florence Brachet Champsaur, Christopher Breward, Claire Browne, Randy Bigham, Judith Clark, Amy de la Haye, Phyllis Dillon, Zoe Evans, Noemi Fábry, Anne Freadman, Lorraine Gamman, Mila Ganeva, Francesca Granata, Alison Matthews David, Lewis Orchard, Roger Sabin, Molly Sorkin, Michelle Speitz, Andrew Stephenson and Caitlin Evans Storrie. Rebecca Arnold, Jane Gibb, Joanne Morra and Teal Triggs read and critically commented on my proposal in its early stages. Marketa Uhlirova and Agnès Rocamora painstakingly read the first complete draft of the manuscript, as well as later revisions. Rhonda Garelick, Alistair O'Neill, Véronique Pouillard, Marlis Schweitzer, Ivo Evans Storrie, Calum Storrie, Michelle Tolini Finamore and Olga Vainstein read and commented on individual chapters at key stages. I thank them all for their insight and wisdom.

For help with translations from German, Flemish, French, Czech and Swedish sources I am grateful to Martina Grünewald, Annaflor Oostinjen, Renate Stauss,

Agnès Rocamora, Paula von Wachenfeldt, Philip Warkander and Marketa Uhlirova. For their unstinting work at different stages of the picture research, I thank Cat Smith and Hannah Durham in London, and Kenia Cabral and Marlène van de Casteele in Paris. At Yale University Press I would like to thank my editor, Gillian Malpass, for her encouragement throughout the project and for seeing it through to completion; Katharine Ridler who edited the book and rescued my *faux amis* at the last minute; the two anonymous reviewers who commented on the initial proposal; and the third anonymous reviewer for reading the completed manuscript and making such perspicacious and constructive suggestions in the final stages.

For their hospitality on my overseas trips, I thank Jane and Jim Griffin, and Amanda and Corentin de Tregomain. Thanks is too small a word to extend to those at home. Nevertheless, for their hilarity and high spirits, I am grateful to my extended household: Caitlin, Ivo, Phoebe and Rae. And for more than I can ever describe, I thank my partner Calum Storrie.

Lastly, I would like to thank Corinne Hamak who, as a student in 1998, asked the first question that set in train this project; and to acknowledge the incalculable contribution of all the students before and since who helped me to develop the body of thinking and research behind this book.